MW01039396

# MEMOIRS OF NIKITA KHRUSHCHEV

*Memoirs of*

# Nikita Khrushchev

VOLUME 1

# COMMISSAR

〔 1918–1945 〕

*Edited by*

## Sergei Khrushchev

*Memoirs translated by* George Shriver
*Supplementary material translated by* Stephen Shenfield

*The Thomas J. Watson Jr. Institute for International Studies*
BROWN UNIVERSITY • PROVIDENCE • RHODE ISLAND

THE PENNSYLVANIA STATE UNIVERSITY PRESS • UNIVERSITY PARK • PENNSYLVANIA

*The translation and publication of the memoirs in this edition have been made possible through funding provided by the Martha and Artemis Joukowsky Family Foundation, David Rockefeller Sr., David Rockefeller Jr., Timothy Forbes and the Forbes Foundation, the Kairis family, the Donald R. Sohn Foundation, the Carnegie Corporation of New York, Harry Orbelian of San Francisco, Edward H. Ladd of Boston, and the Thomas J. Watson Jr. Institute for International Studies of Brown University. The donors do not take responsibility for any statements or views expressed in this work.*

Library of Congress Cataloging-in-Publication Data

Khrushchev, Nikita Sergeevich, 1894–1971.
[Vremia, liudi, vlast'. English]
Memoirs of Nikita Khrushchev / editor, Sergei Khrushchev ; main translator, George Shriver.
p.      cm.
Includes bibliographical references and index.
Contents: v. 1. Commissar, 1918–1945
ISBN 0-271-02332-5 (alk. paper)
1. Khrushchev, Nikita Sergeevich, 1894–1971. 2. Heads of state—Soviet Union—
Biography. 3. Soviet Union—Politics and government—1953–1985.
I. Khrushchev, Sergei.  II. Title.

DK275.K5 A3 2004
947.085'2'092—dc21
2003007060

The complete memoirs on which this translation is based were originally published in Russian in four volumes as *N. S. Khrushchev: Vremia, liudi, vlast'*, by Moskovskiye Novosti. Copyright 1999 by Moskovskiye Novosti.

It is the policy of THE PENNSYLVANIA STATE UNIVERSITY PRESS to use acid-free paper. Publications on uncoated stock satisfy the minimum requirements of American National Standard for Information Sciences—Permanence of Paper for Printed Library Material, ANSI Z39.48–1992.

# Contents

**APPENDIXES**

# Translator's Preface

THIS IS A translation of Volume 1 of the four-volume complete edition of the memoirs (*Vospominaniia*) of Nikita Khrushchev (Moscow: Moskovskiye Novosti [Moscow News] Publishing Company, 1999, 848 pp.). The title in Russian, *Vremia, liudi, vlast'* (literally, "Time, people, power"), rendered more freely, suggests "The Times and People I Have Known, and My Years in Power."

Dr. Sergei Khrushchev of Brown University, son of Nikita Khrushchev, has been the editor of this English edition. I have translated the main text, and Stephen Shenfield has translated the supplementary material, as well as the notes from the Russian edition and the photo captions. For American readers—or more broadly, for readers in the English-speaking world—explanatory notes have been added that were not in the Russian edition. Some of these notes were written by Sergei Khrushchev (SK), and some by Stephen Shenfield (SS), or by me (GS)—in consultation with Dr. Khrushchev.

Certain materials in this English edition did not appear in the Russian version, while some parts of the Russian edition were omitted. In the Editor's Foreword, Dr. Khrushchev specifies what was added or left out.

This first volume, I think, will be of interest to the general reader, not just the specialist. It tells far more about the author's life during the 1920s and 1930s, and through World War II, than did *Khrushchev Remembers,* a selection from these memoirs that was published in 1970. I make this point, not to derogate *Khrushchev Remembers,* but to stress the much fuller picture of the author's life that is presented in this edition.

Although times have changed, many readers in the English-speaking world will find this more complete version of the Soviet leader's memoirs still of interest. After all, Nikita Khrushchev is remembered by many as America's "main enemy" in the first post-Stalin decade of the Cold War (roughly 1954–1964), especially in a number of Cold War crises. Many recall the incident when he reportedly pounded his shoe at the United Nations. (An Appendix in a later volume explains this incident.) Also frequently remembered is the notorious quotation, "We will bury you" (Khrushchev discusses this unfortunate phrase in his account of his 1959 visit to the United States, which will appear in Volume 3 of the present edition).

More important, Nikita Khrushchev is remembered as the Soviet leader who denounced Stalin in 1956 and began a process of "de-Stalinization," which ultimately led to Gorbachev and perestroika. The many readers curious about what the Soviet Union was and what went on in its internal life, what Stalinism was, how it arose and operated, and what contributed to "de-Stalinization" will find much material to ponder in this first volume of the memoirs.

Despite the truism about translation—"If it's faithful, it isn't beautiful"—our policy has been to stay very close to the Russian original. And we have sought to retain the informal, "storytelling" tone generally used by N. S. Khrushchev when he taped these memoirs, often in the presence of friends or family to whom he was recounting what he remembered (and what he did not), usually without references to published sources or archival documents, and with frequent digressions, as might occur with anyone retelling "the story of my life."

Nikita Khrushchev had a very good memory (as described in Sergei Khrushchev's "The History of the Creation and Publication of the Khrushchev Memoirs [1967–1999]" elsewhere in this volume), and his account of events generally seems to be accurate. Here we are speaking not of his interpretations, but of the chronology of events, what happened and when. Notes have been added where his recollection or understanding of facts is clearly in error.

Researchers consulting the four-volume Russian edition or the original tape recordings archived at several locations can easily see instances in which we may have departed a little from the original for the purpose of making the text more readable or clearer for English-language readers.

Although the responsibility for the final wording of the translation is mine, I wish to acknowledge several individuals who helped in various aspects of producing the final translation. In addition to indispensable input by Sergei Khrushchev, I wish to thank Stephen Shenfield and Ann Farkas, the copy editor, for many helpful suggestions (although I did not always take them). Also I wish to thank Dara Noyes, Todd Miller, Alice Whittenburg, and Alicja Mann.

### Spelling of Russian Names

In Volume 1 we have used, and propose to use in all volumes, the more familiar and readable forms of Russian names (rather than employing across the board the Library of Congress system of transliteration). This way of spelling Russian names is more accessible to the general reader.

For example, most newspapers, magazines, and books in English that are aimed at the general reader will speak of the notorious Beria (which the Library of Congress system would spell as "Beriia").

Another example is a family name of some prominence in Soviet history, the Alliluyevs. Stalin married Nadezhda Alliluyeva, and in these memoirs Nikita Khrushchev tells about her tragic death. Svetlana Alliluyeva, the daughter of Nadezhda and Stalin, attracted considerable attention in the late 1960s when she left the Soviet Union and eventually became an American citizen. The name is generally recognized in English in the form given above—Alliluyev for male members of the family, Alliluyeva for female members. But the Library of Congress system would inadequately represent the name as "Alliluev." This is like spelling "Hallelujah" without the *j*.

We have generally used -*y*- rather than -*ii*, -*yi*, or other variants, and generally have not used diacritical marks to indicate the "soft sound" or "hard sound" in Russian. The Russian letter called "ee kratkoye" has usually been transliterated as *i*.

Thus, we have Vyshinsky, Tukhachevsky, Rokossovsky, and Malinovsky (not "Vyshinskii," "Tukhachevskii," "Rokossovskii," or "Malinovskii"), Yagoda, Yezhov, and Mikoyan (not "Iagoda," "Ezhov," or "Mikoian"), Biryuzov and Blyukher (not "Biriuzov" or "Bliukher"), Penkovsky, Rozengolts, and Vasilkovsky (not "Pen'kovskii," "Rozengol'ts," or "Vasil'kovskii"), Sergei (not "Sergey"), Demyan Bedny (not "Dem'ian Bednyi"), Yuzovka (not "Iuzovka"), and so on.

On the other hand, in a few cases the title of a publication in Russian may be given according to the Library of Congress system as an aid to readers seeking that publication in a library catalogue. Note, however, that the spelling *Izvestia* is used for the main Soviet government newspaper, rather than *Izvestiya* or *Izvestiia*.

Also, in some cases, we have used -*yo*- rather than -*e*- or -*ë*- to render a letter of the Russian alphabet that is spelled like an *e* but pronounced like "yoh." For example, Budyonny (rather than "Budennyi") and the river Psyol (rather than Psel). Also the spelling Oryol is used (rather than "Orel") for the city whose name in Russian means "eagle" and which is pronounced "or-YOL" (with the stress on the second syllable). Of course, Khrushchev's name itself contains this letter *e* that is pronounced "yoh" (or "oh"), but to render his name, as some do, with the spelling Khrushchov is not advisable. The familiar form of the spelling is the one used.

As an exception to our general transliteration style, the names of tsars are Anglicized—for example, Tsar Alexander, Nicholas II, Peter the Great. (We use the spelling *tsar* rather than *czar*.) Similar exceptions to our transliteration style occur in the case of well-known individuals, the spellings of whose names have become established in English—for instance, Leo Tolstoy (rather than "Lev Tolstoi"). Maxim Gorky (rather than "Maksim Gor'kii"), and Joseph (not "Iosif") Stalin and Leon Trotsky (not "Lev Trotskii").

In general, we have tried to give English equivalents rather than use unfamiliar Russian terms in our text. One exception, "Stavka," is discussed below under "Military Terms." Sometimes after giving an English equivalent we have included the Russian word or phrase in parentheses, for example, "we will bury" (*zakopaem*), and "Moscow City Archives Association" (Obyedinenie Moskovskikh Gorodskikh Arkhivov). We do this to inform those readers who might want to know the wording in the Russian original for a particularly interesting, unusual, or difficult term or phrase. Thus, when N. S. Khrushchev lists the tools of his trade as a machinist, explaining that he set aside his toolbox to become a professional party official (around 1935), we give the Russian names of those tools (although some of these terms now, in all likelihood, are obsolete).

When the titles of Russian periodicals or books have more than one word, the main words are capitalized, and usually an English version of the title is given in parentheses, with initial capitalization of the key words—for example, *Novy mir* (New world), *Voprosy istorii* (Problems of history), *Argumenty i fakty* (Arguments and facts), and *Vremia, liudi, vlast'* (Time, people, power).

## Chinese Names

For Chinese names in the memoirs, we have generally used the pinyin spelling, the official romanization system of the People's Republic of China. (Thus, we have Zhou Enlai, rather than "Chou En-lai," and Mao Zedong, rather than "Mao Tse-tung.") The older (Wade-Giles) spelling is retained for Chiang Kai-shek and the political party he headed, the Kuomintang, because those spellings have been used in English since the 1920s, if not earlier, and therefore are the most familiar in that case.

## Administrative Terms

We have used the terms *gubernia* and *uyezd* for the few cases where the prerevolutionary territorial-administrative structure of Russia is mentioned.

In prerevolutionary Russia the usual term for a province was *gubernia*. The author refers, for example, to Kursk *gubernia* (his native province) and Yekaterinoslav *gubernia* (a neighboring province).

Each *gubernia* was subdivided into many "counties," the Russian term for this smaller territorial-administrative subdivision being *uyezd*.

After the Soviet revolution, the *gubernia* was replaced by the *oblast* as the larger administrative division in the Russian and other republics generally. We have used the word "province" for *oblast*. And we have used "district" for the Russian term *raion,* designating the smaller subdivisions constituting the *oblast*.

Some territorial-administrative divisions in outlying areas or along Russia's historical borders have a different name. The term is not *gubernia* or *oblast,* but *krai*. We have translated *krai* as "territory"—for example, the Maritime Territory (*primorsky krai*) or Stavropol Territory (*stavropolsky krai*). A separate territorial-administrative structure was used for military purposes. We have translated the Russian term *voyenny okrug* as "military district."

The Union of Soviet Socialist Republics (USSR; officially established in 1922–24, in the wake of the Bolshevik revolution and the Russian Civil War) consisted of a number of republics, fifteen for most of the period after World War II. Each republic had its own territorial-administrative structure. The terms "province" (*oblast*) and "district" (*raion*) are also used to refer to such divisions even when speaking of the non-Russian republics.

The republics were supposed to be independent governmental structures for major non-Russian nationalities in a voluntary union with the Russian Socialist Federated Soviet Republic, or RSFSR. Thus, the Ukrainians, Belorussians, Moldavians, Latvians, Lithuanians, Estonians, Georgians, Armenians, Azerbaijanis, Kazakhs, Kirghiz, Turkmen (or Turcomans), Tajiks, and Uzbeks each had their own Soviet Socialist Republic, or SSR.

(When referring to the historical region that is now an independent country, Ukraine, we do not precede the name with the definite article. Ukrainians living in the English-speaking world object to the phrase "the Ukraine," which suggests it is an outlying part of Great Russia. We do not speak of "the Russia," "the Belorussia," the Lithuania," and so forth. Ukraine, being a nation in its own right, does not need a "the" in front of it.)

Within the various republics, especially the RSFSR, there were autonomous republics (for example, the Karelian Autonomous Soviet Socialist Republic, or Karelian ASSR; in Russian, the term was *avtonomnaya respublika*). There were also autonomous oblasts (*avtonomnye oblasti*) and autonomous districts (*avtonomnye okrugi*) for other non-Russian minority nationalities and ethnic groups. The Karelian ASSR is a special case. It was upgraded to become the Karelo-Finnish SSR after the Soviet-Finnish war of 1939–40, but its status as an autonomous republic, or ASSR, within the RSFSR was restored in 1956.

## Military Terms

As mentioned, much of this first volume deals with World War II, particularly that part of the war that in the Soviet Union was called the Great Patriotic War. The Great Patriotic War began with the invasion of the USSR by the armies of Nazi Germany and its allies on June 22, 1941, and ended with the fall of Berlin, Hitler's death, the unconditional surrender of Germany, and the final routing of all Nazi armies on May 9, 1945. May 9 is still celebrated in Russia as Victory Day.

Some of the military terms used in this first volume require explanation.

STAVKA: This Russian proper name is often translated as General Headquarters, or GHQ for short. But we have simply used the Russian word in transliterated form, especially to avoid confusion with General Staff (in Russian, *generalny shtab* or *genshtab* for short).

The Stavka was the directing body of a larger entity called the Supreme High Command (in Russian, *verkhovnoye glavnokomandovanie*), consisting of a number of top military and party officials and chaired by Stalin.

FRONT: In Soviet military terminology, a "Front" is roughly the equivalent of an "Army Group" in Western military terms; that is, a military force of two or more armies and associated units. But we have used the same word in English as is used in Russian, "Front." We have used terms such as "battlefront" or "the frontlines"—without capitalization—in cases where the Russian word has a more general meaning and does not refer to a specific military force responsible for a particular geographic area.

NAPRAVLENIE: For the Russian term *Napravlenie* we have used "Area" or "Area Command," rather than "Direction," "Sector," or "Axis." We have generally used "sector" for the Russian term *uchastok*. (There is no exact equivalent in English for the special military-administrative entity designated by the term *Napravlenie*; plural *Napravleniya*.)

A helpful explanation regarding the term *Napravlenie* is found in a Soviet source:

To improve control of the Fronts, the State Defense Committee formed three High Commands of Directions [*Napravleniya*] on July 10, 1941:

The North-Western Direction (Commander-in-Chief Marshal K. Ye. Voroshilov, Member of Military Council A. A. Zhdanov, Chief of Staff General M. V. Zakharov);

the Western Direction (Commander-in-Chief Marshal S. K. Timoshenko, Member of Military Council N. A. Bulganin, Chief of Staff General G. K. Malinin);

the South-Western Direction (Commander-in-Chief Marshal S. M. Budenny [Semyon Budyonny], Member of Military Council N. S. Khrushchev [from August 5, 1941], Chief of Staff A. P. Pokrovsky.

When forming these High Commands, the State Defense Committee expected that they would help the Supreme Command to improve troop control, and coordinate the operations of Fronts, the Air Force and the Navy....

But the first few months showed that the High Commands did not live up to what was expected of them.... The High Commands of Directions had neither reserve troops nor material resources at their disposal to influence the course of operations. Nor could they enforce any fundamental decision without the consent of the Supreme Command, and were thus reduced to the role of intermediary instances [bodies]. In 1942, they were abolished. (From the official English translation of Zhukov's memoirs: Georgy K. Zhukov, *Reminiscences and Reflections*, 2 vols. [Moscow: Progress Publishers, 1985], 1:342–43)*

Some translators use the term "axis" for *Napravlenie*. But in the case of the military command organizations established in 1941–42 it does not seem appropriate to use that translation. The Soviet armed forces were fighting the troops of the Axis (Hitler's Germany, Mussolini's Italy, and their allies such as Hungary and Romania). They would hardly have used the term "axis" (in Russian, *os*) for military formations on the Soviet side of the war against the Axis powers. The term *Napravlenie*, which literally means "Direction," may have been chosen for purposes of encouragement at a time of defeat and retreat, suggesting that Soviet forces would soon be advancing in "the Western Direction," the "Southwestern Direction," and so forth.

Ordinal numbers in the names of armies have been spelled out in the cases of "First" through "Twentieth." For numbers higher than "Twentieth," figures have been used: for example, 21st, 58th.

### NEP, War Communism, Five-Year Plans

The New Economic Policy, or NEP (1921–28), was instituted by the Soviet government to replace War Communism (1918–21), the policy followed during the Civil War, when virtually all economic enterprises were nationalized, rationing and government control were imposed on most economic activity,

---

*These memoirs of Zhukov were published in book form in Russian as *Vospominaniia i razmyshleniia*, in 1969. In the last chapter of this volume of Khrushchev's memoirs, he rightly casts doubt on Zhukov's war memoirs, stating that they were heavily edited by top military officials who had a stake in rewriting history to suit their own purposes. The dissident Soviet historian, Anton Antonov-Ovseyenko, son of one of the leaders of the Bolshevik revolution, reports Zhukov's own comment about the published version: "Those memoirs—they're not mine."

Nevertheless, the quotation above dealing with the fairly narrow question of the "High Commands of Directions" in 1941–42 can be assumed to be accurate. It is consistent with Nikita Khrushchev's account of the formation of the "High Command" of the Southwestern Area (*Napravlenie*); see the part of this first volume entitled "People and Events of Summer and Fall 1941," Russian pp. 326 ff.

and—particularly galling to the peasant majority of the population—free trade in grain and other agricultural products was banned, while enforced contributions of farm products were taken by the state.

Under the NEP, free trade was permitted again; most peasants paid a tax in kind, but could freely sell the remainder of their produce; wealthier peasants (the so-called kulaks, or "fists") were allowed to rent land and hire labor on a limited basis; in the cities, many private businesses, including some with foreign investors, were also allowed.

The NEP was followed in 1929 by the First Five-Year Plan, which ushered in the era of all-out industrialization, forced collectivization, and in general the highly centralized Soviet planned economy. The First Five-Year Plan was completed in four years (1929–32). The subsequent Five-Year Plans up to the end of the Soviet era in 1991 were as follows:

Second Five-Year Plan, 1933–37
Third Five-Year Plan, projected for 1938–42, but interrupted by the war, 1941–45
Fourth Five-Year Plan, 1946–50
Fifth Five-Year Plan, 1951–55
Sixth Five-Year Plan, projected for 1956–60, but many planning targets were changed, and a new plan was introduced—the Seven-Year Plan
Seven-Year Plan, 1959–65 (end of the Khrushchev era)
Eighth Five-Year Plan, 1966–70 (beginning of the Brezhnev era)
Ninth Five-Year Plan, 1971–75
Tenth Five-Year Plan, 1976–80
Eleventh Five-Year Plan, 1981–85
Twelfth Five-Year Plan, 1986–90 (the Gorbachev era: the role of central planning is reduced; fragmentation of the planned economy)
Soviet era ends in 1991

### Soviet Governmental Institutions

The Soviets were originally councils of workers', peasants', and soldiers' deputies that arose during 1917, a year of widespread revolt in Russian society against the tsarist order and its disastrous involvement in World War I. (During the 1905 revolution in Russia, the same types of councils, or Soviets, made their first appearance.)

In September and October (Old Style), the Bolsheviks won a majority in most of the Soviets, and at the Second All-Russia Congress of Soviets

(October 25–27, 1917, Old Style), the Bolshevik-led Military Revolutionary Committee of the Petrograd Soviet carried out an insurrection in the capital city, deposed the Provisional Government, and turned all governmental power over to the Soviets.

The All-Russia Congress of Soviets elected a Central Executive Committee (CEC) to serve as the ruling governmental body between congresses of Soviets (local and regional councils). The CEC established a Council of People's Commissars (Russian acronym, Sovnarkom) as a kind of cabinet to handle the day-to-day affairs of government. Lenin was the first chairman of the Sovnarkom, the equivalent of prime minister. The president of the CEC was the titular head of state, a post held for much of the Soviet era by Mikhail Kalinin.

Most of the people's commissars in the first Soviet government were Bolsheviks, but two were members of the Left Socialist Revolutionary Party (Left SRs, for short). After the summer of 1918, when the Left SRs rebelled against the Bolshevik majority, virtually all top posts in the Soviet government were held by Bolsheviks. By 1922 all other parties besides the Communist Party (Bolshevik) were banned, and as the sole ruling party the Communist Party filled all major posts in the Soviet government from then until the late Gorbachev era (1989 and after).

The formal institutions and offices of Soviet government were maintained, although the real decision-making power resided in the leadership bodies of the Communist Party (the Politburo, or Presidum, of the party's Central Committee). Thus every province and district had its Soviet (with its Executive Committee), and each republic, like the USSR as a whole, had its CEC (or later, its Supreme Soviet). Communist officials (and pro-Communist "non-party people") were regularly elected to all Soviet posts, local, regional, and national, by huge majorities.

After a new Soviet constitution was adopted in 1936, a Supreme Soviet was elected by universal suffrage. As indicated, the central body (whether CEC or Supreme Soviet), chose the Council of People's Commissars (based on decisions by following Communist leaders' orders in the Politburo or Presidium). In 1946 the name of this top government body was changed to Council of Ministers, and the People's Commissariats, which carried out most of the work of government, became Ministries. Thus, for example, the People's Commissariat of Foreign Affairs (Russian acronym, Narkomindel) became the Ministry of Foreign Affairs. Also, for example, in 1958, Nikita Khrushchev became chairman of the Council of Ministers, the equivalent of prime minister—although his real source of power was his position as "first secretary" of the Communist Party of the Soviet Union.

### State Security Organizations (Secret Police)

The Cheka was the first Soviet state security organization. This acronym was taken from the Russian initials of the first two words in the name, Chrezvychainaya Komissiya (Extraordinary Commission), of an organization established by the new Soviet government in December 1917 to combat sabotage and counterrevolution. A Chekist was originally a member of the Cheka, but by extension the term continued in use to designate any operative of the security police agencies that succeeded the Cheka.

After the Civil War, the Cheka (1917–22) was succeeded by the GPU (State Political Administration). In 1923, this became the OGPU (Unified State Political Administration, which in turn was reorganized in 1934 as the NKVD (People's Commissariat of Internal Affairs). In 1941 a separate NKGB (People's Commissariat of State Security) was established, while police duties not directly involving "state security" were left to the NKVD. In 1946 the NKVD was changed to the MVD (Ministry of Internal Affairs). In 1954, after Stalin's death and the removal of Beria, a new body was established, the KGB (Committee of State Security) under the Council of Ministers; that is, the security police organization was reduced in status from a ministry to a "committee" of the Soviet government's highest body, but still remained very powerful.

### Communist Party and Russian Social Democratic Labor Party (RSDLP)

The terms "Communist," "Socialist," and "Social Democratic" are capitalized when they refer to a particular organization, political party, government, or the like, or membership in one of these. They are not capitalized when the reference is to the general ideas, doctrines, theories, and so on, of these movements or to a society organized on the principle "from each according to ability, to each according to need."

The Russian Social Democratic Labor Party (Rossiyskaya Sotsial-Demokraticheskaya Rabochaya Partiya) was officially founded in 1898 at a conference in Minsk, but it was almost immediately broken up by repressive action of the tsarist authorities; at the Second Congress of the RSDLP, held in exile (in Brussels and London, 1903), two factions emerged—the Bolsheviks, or members of the majority (*bolshinstvo*); and the Mensheviks, member of the minority (*menshinstvo*).

The RSDLP continued as a more or less united party, with other factions besides the two main ones; in 1912, the two main factions ran different slates in the Duma elections and were functioning de facto as separate parties; the disagreements between the two wings became so severe after the outbreak of revolution in Russia in February 1917 that the Bolshevik faction held a separate conference and congress and officially adopted the name RSDLP (Bolshevik).

In April 1918 the name was changed to Russian Communist Party (Bolshevik), or RCP(B) (in Russian, Rossiyskaya Kommunisticheskaya Partiya [Bolshevikov]). In 1925, after the formation of the Union of Soviet Socialist Republics, the party was renamed All-Union Communist Party (Bolshevik), or AUCP(B) (in Russian, Vsesoyuznaya Kommunisticheskaya Partiya [Bolshevikov], or VKP[B]). In 1952, at the Nineteenth Party Congress, the name Communist Party of the Soviet Union (CPSU) (in Russian, Kommunisticheskaya Partiya Sovetskogo Soyuza) was adopted, and the word "Bolshevik" was dropped from the official title.

In these memoirs the phrase "the party," unless otherwise indicated, refers to the CPSU or one of its predecessor or subordinate organizations, since from the early 1920s until 1989 this was the ruling party with a monopoly on power, the only legal political party in the Soviet Union. Generally we do not capitalize such phrases as "the Party," "the revolution," and so on.

Nominally the highest body of the party was its congress, with delegates from local and regional party organizations deciding on policy and electing a Central Committee, or CC. Central Committee plenums, or plenary sessions of the CC, were usually important policy-making events. The Central Committee in turn elected a Political Bureau, or Politburo, responsible for running the party between congresses and CC plenums. Stalin's first major base of power was his control of the Secretariat of the Central Committee, of which he became general secretary in 1922. Later he came to dominate the Politburo. In the last year of Stalin's life and the immediate post-Stalin era, the term "Politburo" was changed to "Presidium," and instead of "general secretary" Khrushchev bore the title "first secretary." Under Brezhnev, the terms "Politburo" and "general secretary" were restored.

The party had committees in each administrative unit of the USSR. We have translated the names of such committees as follows:

"district committee" for *raionny komitet* (*raikom* for short)
"city committee" for *gorodskoi komitet* (*gorkom* for short)
"province committee" for *oblastnoi komitet* (*obkom* for short)
"territory committee" for *krayevoi komitet* (*kraikom* for short)

### "Reds" and "Whites" in the Russian Civil War

N. S. Khrushchev frequently refers to events of the Russian Civil War, and to certain structures of the Soviet armed forces, without much explanation, because such matters would be familiar to readers in Russia. But since Western readers may not know who or what the main contending forces were in the Russian Civil War and may not be familiar with the institution of political officers in the Soviet armed forces, I have added some explanatory paragraphs on these points.

During the year 1917, amid the many revolutionary upheavals in Russian society, there occurred the formation of Red Guards, irregular units of industrial workers, sometimes merely factory guards, at other times a form of workers' militia.

In October 1917 (November according to the Western calendar), directed by the Bolshevik-led Petrograd Soviet, Red Guard units assisted revolutionary-minded army units in carrying out insurrections in Petrograd and Moscow. As a result, full political power was vested in the Soviets (councils of workers', soldiers', and peasants' deputies of a kind that had first arisen during the 1905 revolution; these institutions of popular rebellion against the tsarist system revived and spread all over Russia during 1917 and after).

The Soviet government established in October 1917 (November in the West) did not at first have a regular army, although many Red Guard units were active. Similarly, the counterrevolutionary forces, especially those who wished to restore the tsarist order, formed units called White Guards. In February 1918 the Soviet government established the Red Army and soon brought the numerous irregular Red Guards or Red guerrilla detachments under a central command. Thus, the forces fighting to defend and assert the authority of the Soviet government were commonly called "the Reds" in the Civil War. And the counterrevolutionary forces were called the White Guards (later reorganized as White armies) or, more simply, "the Whites."

*Military Commanders and Political Officers*

In the Soviet armed forces there was special concern about political supervision over military commanders.

In the Russian Civil War the Red Army made use of many former tsarist officers as commanders of military units, but political commissars from the Communist Party were assigned to oversee and ensure the loyalty of these potentially traitorous ex-tsarist military men. Thus, each major military unit had its commander, for military decision making, and its commissar, for political supervision.

By the time of World War II, all the military leaders in the Soviet armed forces were Communists, but still a political officer was assigned to each major military command, as before, to oversee the military decisions of the commanders and presumably to ensure their loyalty as well. According to N. S. Khrushchev, a Military Council—which had responsibility for an Army, a Front (Army Group), or an "Area Command" (*Napravlenie*)—consisted of the commander, the "first member" of the Military Council (a political officer), and a "second member," whose responsibilities lay more in the realm of logistics. Khrushchev himself was a "first member," a political officer, although during World War II, in 1943, he was given the military rank of lieutenant general.

*Congresses and Conferences of the RSDLP and Communist Party, 1898–1991* (Dates before 1918 are given according to the Old Style of the Russian calendar, which was 12 or 13 days earlier than the Western European calendar. The ordinal numbers for congresses and conferences have been spelled out in all cases, First through Twenty-Eighth.)

First Congress of the RSDLP, held in Minsk, March 1–3, 1898.

Second Congress of the RSDLP, held in Brussels and London, July 17–August 10, 1903; majority (Bolshevik) and minority (Menshevik) caucuses formed, although the Bolsheviks did not always remain a majority in the RSDLP.

Third Congress of the RSDLP, London, April 12–27, 1905; adopted the program and organizational structure of the Bolsheviks.

First Conference of the RSDLP, Tammerfors, December 12–17, 1905.

Fourth (Unity) Congress of the RSDLP, Stockholm, April 10–25, 1906; formally reunited Bolsheviks and Mensheviks, but in fact the two groups maintained separate programs and organizations.

Second Conference of the RSDLP, Tammerfors, November 3–7, 1906.

Fifth Congress of the RSDLP, London, April 30–May 19, 1907; had a Bolshevik majority.

Third Conference of the RSDLP, Kotka, Finland, July 21–23, 1907.

Fourth Conference of the RSDLP, Helsinki, November 5–12, 1907.

Fifth Conference of the RSDLP, Paris, December 21–27, 1908.

Sixth All-Russia Conference of the RSDLP, Prague, January 5–17, 1912; at this conference the "Menshevik liquidators" were expelled from the party, and a purely Bolshevik leadership was elected, headed by Lenin.

Seventh All-Russia Conference of the RSDLP, Petrograd, April 24–29, 1917; took the name RSDLP (Bolshevik) and adopted Lenin's "April Theses" calling for socialist revolution in Russia.

Sixth Congress of the RSDLP (Bolshevik), Petrograd, July 26–August 3, 1917; adopted the policy of armed insurrection to transfer "All Power to the Soviets," leading to the Bolshevik revolution of October 23–24, 1917.

Seventh (Emergency) Congress of the Russian Communist Party (Bolshevik), or RCP(B), March 6–8, 1918; adopted new name of the party, now the ruling party of Soviet Russia; approved the Brest-Litovsk treaty with Germany, taking Russia out of World War I.

Eighth Congress of the RCP(B), Moscow, March 18–23, 1919.

(From this time on, all party congresses and conferences were held in Moscow.)

Eighth All-Russia Conference of the RCP(B), December 2–4, 1919.

Ninth Congress of the RCP(B), March 29–April 5, 1920.

Ninth All-Russia Conference of the RCP(B), September 22–25, 1920.

Tenth Congress of the RCP(B), March 8–16, 1921; adopted the New Economic Policy (NEP).

Tenth All-Russia Conference of the RCP(B), May 26–28, 1921.

Eleventh All-Russia Conference of the RCP(B), December 19–22, 1921.

Eleventh Congress of the RCP(B), March 27–April 2, 1922; Stalin made "general secretary," head of the Secretariat of the party's Central Committee.

Twelfth All-Russia Conference of the RCP(B), August 4–7, 1922.

Twelfth Congress of the RCP(B), April 17–23, 1923; because of illness Lenin did not participate; the first party congress without him since the Bolsheviks came to power.

Thirteenth Conference of the RCP(B), January 16–18, 1924; condemned the Left Opposition formed around Trotsky in fall 1923.

Thirteenth Congress of the RCP(B), May 23–31, 1924; first congress after Lenin's death; Zinoviev, Kamenev, Bukharin, Rykov, and Stalin take the leadership.

Fourteenth Conference of the RCP(B), April 27–29, 1925; first party conference attended by Nikita Khrushchev.

Fourteenth Congress, December 18–31, 1925; clash between the "Leningrad opposition," headed by Zinoviev and Kamenev, and the party majority, headed by Stalin, Rykov, and Bukharin; party's name changed to All-Union Communist Party (Bolshevik), or AUCP(B).

Fifteenth Conference of the AUCP(B), October 26–November 3, 1926; sharp debate between the party majority, headed by Bukharin, Rykov, and Stalin, and the United Left Opposition, headed by Trotsky, Zinoviev, and Kamenev.

Fifteenth Congress of the AUCP(B), December 2–19, 1927; all leaders of the United Left Opposition expelled from the party, including Trotsky, Zinoviev, and Kamenev (the latter two being readmitted later after renouncing their views).

Sixteenth Conference of the AUCP(B), April 23–29, 1929; the First Five-Year Plan and "all-round collectivization" have begun.

Sixteenth Congress of the AUCP(B), June 26–July 1, 1930, the "right deviation," headed by Bukharin and Rykov, was condemned.

Seventeenth Conference of the AUCP(B), January 30–February 4, 1932.

Seventeenth Congress of the AUCP(B) (the "Congress of Victors"), June 26–July 13, 1934; all opposition groups had been expelled or renounced their views and capitulated; the whole party was "united around Stalin"; meanwhile, Hitler had come to power in Germany.

Eighteenth Congress of the AUCP(B), March 10–21, 1939; first party congress after the Kirov assassination and the mass purges, arrests, and executions of "enemies of the people"; World War II was imminent.

Eighteenth Conference of the AUCP(B), February 15–20, 1941; World War II had begun; despite the Soviet-Nazi "friendship" treaty of September 1939, Hitler was about to invade the Soviet Union.

Nineteenth Party Congress, October 5–14, 1952; party's name changed to Communist Party of the Soviet Union (CPSU) without the tag "Bolshevik." This was the first party congress to be held after six years of World War II and seven postwar years; it was also the last party congress dominated by Stalin, who died shortly after this congress, in March 1953.

Twentieth Party Congress, February 14–25, 1956; "de-Stalinization" was begun with Khrushchev's "secret speech" denouncing Stalin's crimes.

Twenty-First (Extraordinary) Party Congress, January 27–February 5, 1959.

Twenty-Second Party Congress, October 17–31, 1961; more revelations about the crimes of Stalin.

Twenty-Third Party Congress, March 29–April 8, 1966; the first party congress after the ouster of Khrushchev, marking the beginning of consolidation of power by Brezhnev.

Twenty-Fourth Party Congress, March 30–April 9, 1971.

Twenty-Fifth Party Congress, February 25–March 5, 1976.

Twenty-Sixth Party Congress, February 23–March 3, 1981.

Twenty-Seventh Party Congress, February 25–March 6, 1986; first party congress of the Gorbachev era.

Twenty-Eighth Party Congress, July 1990; last congress of the CPSU.

The Twenty-Ninth Party Congress, scheduled for fall 1991, was never held. In the wake of the failed coup by party conservatives in August 1991, the activities of the CPSU were suspended, and by the end of that year it was dissolved together with the Soviet Union.

*George Shriver*

# Editor's Foreword

[ DR. SERGEI KHRUSHCHEV ]

*Senior Fellow, Thomas J. Watson Jr. Institute for International Studies*
*Brown University, Providence, Rhode Island*

## *The First Complete Russian Edition*

The four-volume Russian edition of my father's memoirs (*Vremia, liudi, vlast'*, by Nikita Sergeyevich Khrushchev) produced by the Moscow News publishing company in 1999 has a total of 2,448 pages (approximately 1.5 million words). It is the first, and thus far the only, complete edition of the memoirs and is based on transcripts of all the tape recordings dictated by N. S. Khrushchev from 1966 to 1971.* Moscow News has graciously granted a license for preparation of this translation based on its edition.

## *Other Russian Editions*

During the years 1990–95, the Russian journal *Voprosy istorii* (Problems of history) published the most complete version of the memoirs up to that time. However, only the basic version of the transcribed tape recordings was used; variants were omitted, which of course made that edition less informative.

In 1997 the Moscow publishing house VAGRIUS brought out a one-volume, 508-page edition of this work by N. S. Khrushchev under the title *Vospominaniia: Izbrannye fragmenty* (Memoirs: Selected fragments). It was based entirely on the *Voprosy istorii* edition.

## *The Tape Recordings in Russian*

Copies of the tape recordings dictated by my father may be found in a number of different archives, but working with them is extremely difficult because, as a result of technical difficulties when the tapes were copied, the "chapters" (or sections treating particular topics) became fragmented and dispersed among different tapes and parts of tapes. In order to bring them together, it was necessary in every case to work out a puzzle by matching up separated parts.

The archive at Brown University accomplished this arduous and challenging task, reestablishing the logical continuity of the original recordings,

---

*For information on the process by which Nikita Khrushchev tape-recorded his memoirs, how the tapes were transcribed and edited, how the Soviet authorities tried to confiscate this material, and how it all came to be published, see Sergei Khrushchev, "The History of the Creation and Publication of the Khrushchev Memoirs, 1967–1999," in the Appendixes to this volume.

and restoring my father's voice to a more or less normal quality of sound reproduction. (Because of speed fluctuations during the dubbing of the original tapes his voice was distorted, sometimes to the point where it became unrecognizable.) Now that the recordings have been digitalized and catalogued, researchers can compare published texts against the tape recordings. However, it must be kept in mind that dictated material on a particular topic is found not only in the main "chapter," or section dealing with that topic. In one or another context dictated passages on the same subject exist on various tapes and parts of tapes.

The tape recordings served as a draft for my father's memoirs, and he returned more than once to a topic that interested him, sometimes in different "chapters" that had little to do with one another. Sometimes my father, from forgetfulness, dictated a passage on a particular topic more than once.

In editing the text, I placed passages united by a common theme in one chapter or section, and repetitions were relegated to the Appendixes of the Russian edition. (These repetitions have been omitted from the present English-language edition.) Thus, in order to compare a particular sentence or paragraph of the printed Russian text with the tape-recorded version it may be necessary not only to listen to the corresponding part of the dictated material but also, in some cases, to search through the entire text of the Russian edition.

During his life, N. S. Khrushchev was able to review and correct transcripts of the texts in Volume 1 of the Russian edition and, partially, the beginning of Volume 2. He made some additions to the text, and these of course do not appear in the tape-recorded version. These changes can be found in the original transcripts (on the front and back sides of the sheets containing the relevant texts), which are preserved in Moscow in the Unified Moscow City Archives (Obyedinenie Moskovskikh Gorodskikh Arkhivov). Copies of these transcripts may also be found in the archives of Brown University in the United States.

As indicated above, I have given, in a separate chapter, a detailed account entitled "The History of the Creation and Publication of the Khrushchev Memoirs, 1967–1999," The chapter appears in the Appendixes to Volume 1 of the present edition.

### Previous American Editions

Let me say a few words about earlier editions of the memoirs of Nikita Khrushchev in English.

These first appeared in the United States. In 1970 Little, Brown published a 525-page volume, *Khrushchev Remembers* (translated and edited by Strobe Talbott, with introduction, commentary, and notes by Edward Crankshaw). Then in 1974 the same publisher issued a 542-page volume, *Khrushchev Remembers: The Last Testament* (translated and edited by Strobe Talbott, with introductions by Edward Crankshaw and Jerrold Schecter); and finally, in 1990, a 203-page volume entitled *Khrushchev Remembers: The Glasnost Tapes* (translated and edited by Jerrold Schecter with Vyacheslav Luchkov; foreword by Strobe Talbott). All three volumes are now out of print.

In the West, these books were collectively referred to as the Khrushchev memoirs. Unfortunately, the editors prepared these texts as they saw fit and drastically abridged them. Thus, what my father had to say about World War II takes up more than 400 pages in the Russian edition of his memoirs, but in the American edition, no more than 50 pages are devoted to this subject. Sections dealing with agriculture, housing construction in the USSR, and some other subjects drastically were abridged in the American volumes.

In the Brezhnev era it was impossible for the American publisher to contact my father or me, and because of the difficulties the translators encountered in dealing with the dictated material in Russian, a certain number of mistakes of meaning appeared in the Little, Brown editions. Sometimes the original idea was turned into its opposite. All it took for this to happen was the omission of a "no" or a "not" by mistake.

Besides that, the American editors sometimes added their own material to what the author had said. For example, they "wrote in" a section—based on their own level of competence—about N. S. Khrushchev's early years. Not knowing the name of my father's first wife, they came up with "Galina," instead of her actual name, Yefrosinya. This made it look as though my father had failed to remember his first wife's name.

For all their shortcomings, the American editions had a tremendous impact. Until 1990 no other published version of my father's memoirs existed. Meanwhile, the dictated tapes and the transcripts—or decodings of the recordings, edited by me—ended up "under confinement," lying for a long time in the safes of the CPSU Central Committee in its building on Staraya Ploshchad (Old Square) near the Kremlin in Moscow.

### The Present Edition

The present edition, as indicated above, is based on the four-volume complete Russian edition (Moscow News Publishers, 1999). The main difference between that Russian edition and this English one lies in what is included in the Appendixes (as well as the short biographies, explanatory notes, and maps especially prepared for this edition, as described below).

The alternate versions or repetitions dictated by my father have been omitted from this English edition. They are nearly as great in size as the main text, but they add practically nothing in content. They are of interest mainly to those researchers who are particularly fastidious and who like to dig up nuances of difference in published materials and other such details of lesser importance. Researchers of that kind usually know Russian and may consult the complete four-volume Russian edition or, better yet, the tape recordings themselves.

Besides the above-mentioned alternate versions of the memoirs, Appendixes in the four-volume Russian edition include quite a few documents of interest. Thus, out of the total of 847 pages in Volume 1 of the Russian edition, its Appendix has 110 pages of "Documents" in small type (pp. 719–828). Volume 2 has 102 pages of such "Documents" (pp. 725–826) out of a total of 847. Volume 3 has 74 (pp. 611–84) out of a total of 703. And Volume 4, out of a total of 727 pages, has 204 pages of "Documents" and other materials in small type (pp. 487–690).

Sometimes these "Documents" and other materials in the Russian-language Appendixes do not relate directly or personally to N. S. Khrushchev. More important, the cost of translating and publishing all of them would have exceeded our budget. Therefore, only the most interesting (from our point of view, of course) were selected for inclusion in the present English-language edition.

We have included two documents in the Appendixes to the present edition that did not appear in the Russian edition—first, the memoirs of my mother, Nina Petrovna Khrushchev (maiden name, Kukharchuk); second, an excerpt from the memoirs of Nikolai Zakharov (first published in 2000), along with notes by two other key eyewitnesses, concerning the "shoe-banging" incident at the United Nations in 1960. Zakharov was head of the KGB's Ninth Directorate, responsible for guarding top officials of the Soviet Union.

We have included the recollections by Zakharov (and others) because my father, in his memoirs, did not recall very clearly the incident that occurred at the United Nations.

As for my mother's reminiscences, they are an organic, highly personal, and indispensable supplement to my father's memoirs. My mother and father shared a long and happy life from 1924 to 1971. Together they raised five children and survived the repression of the Stalin era, World War II, the joyous time of renewal after Stalin's death, and the sorrows of political disfavor after 1964.

The indicated divergences from the four-volume Russian edition, which do not affect the main text of the memoirs, have made it possible for us to produce a three-volume English edition without losing anything fundamental. Undoubtedly, to have three volumes rather than four will also be a greater convenience to the reader.

Volume 1 of the present edition is essentially the same as Volume 1 of the Russian edition. In Volume 2 of the present edition we have combined material having mainly to do with domestic policy and events in the Soviet Union—including "Part I" of the memoirs from Volume 2 of the Russian edition and the full text of the memoirs from Volume 4 of the Russian edition.

In Volume 3 of the present edition we include those parts of the memoirs that deal mainly with post-Stalin foreign policy, world affairs, and international issues—materials found in "Part II" of Volume 2 and all of Volume 3 of the Russian edition. Material from the Appendixes of the Russian edition relating to domestic matters has been placed in Volume 2 of the present edition, while that concerned with international relations has been placed in Volume 3 of the present edition.

### Andrei Bitov's Introductory Essay

It is traditional for any substantial publication of historically controversial material to be preceded by an "Introduction." Usually this gives the reader a bit of instruction on what is good or bad in the author's work, which of the author's opinions are correct and which are wrong. Evidently the assumption is that readers are not well enough informed to figure out such things for themselves. However, there is no guarantee that the writer of the "Introduction" understands the subject better than the author. It may simply be that the author and the "Introducer" have different views of the world, and that the latter wishes to impose his view on the reader.

That is why I never read "Introductions," and advise others not to. What I usually say is: "Use your own head. Trust your own judgment."

I make an exception, however, in the case of the introductory essay in the present edition. This essay by Andrei Bitov, an outstanding contemporary Russian writer, is a remarkably rich, vivid, and concise piece of writing, which gives a striking picture of who Nikita Khrushchev was, against the background of the epoch he lived in. I urge you to read it. You won't regret it.

I wish to express my gratitude personally to Andrei Bitov for permission to reprint his essay in the present edition, and I thank Susan Brownsberger for her excellent translation.

### Acknowledgments

My thanks to George Shriver for his splendid translation of the main text, the memoirs themselves. He is a professional writer who has translated or edited dozens of books on Soviet history and politics, including the auto-biographical novel by Nikolai Bukharin, *How It All Began* (Columbia University Press, 1998), and *Conversations with Gorbachev* (Columbia University Press, 2002)—the latter consisting of edited transcripts of conversations between Mikhail Gorbachev and his Czech friend Zdenek Mlynar, a leader of the Prague Spring of 1968.

In consultation with the editor, the present translation has been carefully checked for accuracy; at the same time it seeks to retain the author's vividness of expression and the nuances of meaning in the Russian original. The translator has added commentaries and notes in cases where a literal rendering alone might not enable the English-language reader to fully grasp the author's intended message.

Stephen Shenfield, Ph.D., translated the supplementary material in the Appendixes to the present edition, the notes from the Russian edition, and the photo captions. He also compiled short biographies on most of the persons mentioned in the memoirs. And he has written (in collaboration with George Shriver and myself) additional notes for the benefit of readers who may be unfamiliar with the background to the events described. Dr. Shenfield, one of today's best specialists on Russia, is the author of *Russian Fascism: Traditions, Tendencies, and Movements* (New York: M. E. Sharpe, 2001).

Ann Helgeson, Ph.D, has provided an excellent selection of maps for this edition. Without these it would be impossible for readers to orient themselves amid the welter of retreats and advances by Soviet troops in the shifting fortunes of the war with Germany from 1941 to 1945. Dr. Helgeson (AH) has also contributed some of the notes about places.

Yuri Shapoval, a professor of Ukrainian history, has provided invaluable assistance in preparing some of the notes and biographies pertaining to the period when N. S. Khrushchev was in Ukraine.

My son Nikita, who lives in Moscow, has helped to clarify and verify questions of fact and to obtain archival information not available in the United States.

The present edition would not have been possible without financial support from both individuals and institutions. They have demonstrated their awareness that without an accurate understanding of the past no successful advance into the future is possible. I wish to thank above all my good friends Martha and Artemis of the Martha and Artemis Joukowsky Family Foundation, David Rockefeller Sr. (with whom my father met many times), David Rockefeller Jr., Timothy Forbes and the Forbes Foundation, the Kairis family, the Donald R. Sohn Foundation, the Carnegie Corporation of New York, Harry Orbelian of San Francisco, and Edward H. Ladd of Boston.

This edition is, above all, the product of fruitful collaboration between The Pennsylvania State University Press and the Thomas J. Watson Jr. Institute for International Studies of Brown University. These institutions have shown that they understand full well the truth expressed in the following observations by Professor Abbott (Tom) Gleason, an authority on Russian history:

> Nikita Khrushchev's memoirs are a priceless addition to the archival materials being studied by historians, which usually contain an official version of events, but lack breadth and do not reflect the clash of opinions when decisions were made. The memoirs are unique and highly valuable: they relate events as they happened, providing details not found in any other source.
>
> These are the only memoirs of a Soviet leader at the highest level of government that have not been censored. Khrushchev was subjected to pressures from the Brezhnev leadership because of the frankness of his memoirs, and they demanded that he stop working on them. Nevertheless, he continued. Without this source of information our knowledge of the history of Russia, particularly of the Cold War period, [would] remain imperfect.

Not only has the Watson Institute taken a direct and active part in the implementation of this joint project; it has also contributed generously toward the costs of publication.

Professor Thomas Biersteker, director of the Watson Institute, and Sanford G. Thatcher, director of The Pennsylvania State University Press, have in fact been the driving forces behind this project. I want to express my profound gratitude to both of them, as well as to Professor Abbott Gleason and all members of the staff at the Watson Institute and at The Pennsylvania State University Press for the efforts they have contributed toward making this edition of my father's memoirs a reality.

# The Baldest and the Boldest

[ ANDREI BITOV ]

*Translated by Susan Brownsberger*

THAT'S A START for a portrait of Khrushchev: he was *the baldest and the boldest.*

Which means that my portrait of him must start with a portrait: bald, rotund, a bulbous nose, ears that stuck out, a belly, and a peasant shirt. People laughed at him. No one ever noticed that this laughter was already freedom, that it was a holiday from *Stalin's* portrait. His boldness, after all, was masked by his appearance. He had concealed himself behind it in Stalin's time. The peasant shirt, the belly—they were for when he entertained the Mustache with watermelon and a heel-tapping *hopak*. He long remembered his abasement: he internalized Stalin's lesson.

Nature had helped him when she made his face. She patched it together carelessly from little wads of dough, the way children make their own little pie when given scraps of the real one. And she left it to Nikita to learn everything. When people talk about his lack of culture, they are forgetting how much he did learn. Accepting what he had received from Nature—the most open, the most ingenuous of faces, a face one might have called foolish—he made use of it to lock away his treasure: not only his boldness but also his pride, his strength, his will, his intellect. That is, he became a whole man, a man of character. And wholeness is exactly what makes a political figure great.

Keep that point in mind: it helps us to refine our everyday concepts of "the people" and the national character. Stalinist art put a lot of work into this, with the stage and screen begetting their own People's Artistes. These all seemed to be workers promoted "from the masses" and therefore enjoyed a broad-based popularity that has never, I must say, been equaled. It may have had little to do with art, but it was reason enough for Stalin to love movies. He was fond of directors. In a way, he was one himself, on a movie set that covered one-sixth of the world. Look at his collection of Politburo members: one in a pince-nez, another wearing a saber at his side, a third with a mustache wider than his shoulders, a fourth—enough that he be an Armenian or a Jew. They all laughed on cue at the same Stalinist comedy film in Stalin's viewing room: *Volga-Volga,* or, yet again, *Volga-Volga.* Khrushchev was the last to take his seat in that room. An assistant manager with a canvas briefcase, he was straight out of *Volga-Volga,* as if he'd stepped down from the screen in the role of People's Artiste Igor Ilyinsky.[1] But Khrushchev was so thoroughly the People's that he was *not* an Artiste. Too much the people's, too much from the masses, he got no respect.

Such was the man who pushed aside Stalin's falcons and appeared before us. We laughed in relief. At the way he made toasts at cocktail parties in England. At the way, in the newsreel, he rolled along like a ball ahead of Marshal Tito and his beautiful wife. At the way he kept trying to catch up with America in meat and milk, and made everyone taste a bite of corn-on-the-cob instead of shaking hands.

And we failed to notice that all this was happening for the first time in history. For the first time our general secretary had gone to England and been received with honor. For the first time he had met with the "hangman cur" Tito in Yugoslavia. For the first time our premier had been to America, where he was enthusiastically received and from which he returned with corn-on-the-cob. And it was the first time we'd been threatened with a corncob instead of the muzzle of a gun.

All this had been preceded by an act of unparalleled historical boldness—the boldness of his report on Stalin at the Twentieth Congress. In this matter of denouncing the cult of personality, people most often mention Khrushchev's service to his country. But that dizzying boldness! After all, it was a moment when he was alone! Not alone like a tyrant, but alone as an agent of history. A statesman acting for us all. At the risk of his life, not merely his career. Truly, the easy thing would have been to shoot him down right then. . . . All this has been described many times, and I can't reconstruct it in sufficient detail. Though I should try. It was, in the first place, a superb, many-move chess problem, conspiracy vs. conspiracy. Marshal Zhukov helped him with it. These sleepy Central Committee members, still practically in their long johns, practically guarded by submachine guns, brought in on military airplanes from all over the Soviet Union, and probably thinking, out of habit, that they're about to be shot and should never, *never* have executed Beria—lo and behold, here they are, *not* shot but in a conference room, ready to support any change at the top, any turnabout, if only. . . . And here's Nikita Sergeyevich (so, for the moment, he's still "one of us"), he lays aside the sheets of the "agreed-on" report and for the first time in the experience of the Party reads out the pages of a report agreed to by no one.

Stamped "Secret," his "closed-door" report was read aloud to everyone at party and Komsomol meetings. This first instance of *glasnost* was garbed in a uniform of secrecy for all. A peculiar instance of *samizdat*—which got its start under Khrushchev.

When it came to music, he loved the song "Rushnichok," about Mother and motherland. Although he gave the go-ahead for Solzhenitsyn's *One Day in the Life of Ivan Denisovich,* he labeled the artists at the Manezh Exhibition pederasts. But what fame his vituperation engendered! Worldwide! Poets, novelists, sculptors, filmmakers . . . Yevtushenko, Voznesensky, Neizvestny, Khutsiev, Aksyonov, Akhmadulina . . . all these names and more. After Khrushchev, the regime stopped criticizing unknowns and dealt with them in private—beat them through cotton padding (no black-and-blue marks).

What did Khrushchev himself do, and what was done under Khrushchev?

Did he provoke the Cuban missile crisis, or did he and Kennedy together avert it?

East Germany. Poland. Hungary, 1956. . . .

The Berlin Wall!

Pounding his shoe at the UN—that he did do himself.

Who, then, was this blacksmith forging metal with a shoe, who was this shoemaker trying to drive shoe nails with a blacksmith's hammer?

A man who wanted to leap the abyss in two bounds, Churchill said.

All of this is *History.* Not just our unexpected joy in freedom. *All* of it is History, because Nikita, for the first time, allowed her to take a step on her own. He set *History* free.

She's been rambling around Russia like a drunk ever since.

And it felt as if we'd been launched into outer space.

The Rehabilitation. How quickly we had thawed! In our still-feeble liberalism, we could already snicker at the quality of it: at the bureaucratic absurdity of slips of paper granting liberty to people who had been murdered; at the miserliness of compensation payments to families and pensions to survivors; at the shoddiness of the apartments sometimes allotted to them. But people forget that these vile little papers—*and* the apartments, *and* the compensation payments—had to be given out in the *many, many millions!* Then too he had corn to plant, sputniks to launch, congresses to convene, and America to catch up with in meat and milk. Decorations to award and receive, dams to build in Africa. Dogs to send into orbit, and then Gagarin. . . . What is hard to remember now, and was hard to understand then, is this: he was working among those same people, in that same Stalinist milieu where doubt was unthinkable, where they did not doubt the system and still counted any kind of doubt a crime. They believed religiously. Suslov the ideologist was always right there. Khrushchev was working with *them* and had come from them himself. There could be no criticism, only isolated "mistakes." Yet the very possibility of admitting a mistake had been made real for the first time by Khrushchev. But what a mistake he had chosen for starters! *The* mistake, the biggest of all. Stalin himself.

Khrushchev's role could not be minimized, because it was impossible to minimize Stalin, at least as a villain. Stalin wasn't a mistake—Khrushchev was. The mistake had been to let someone fully human come to power.

"Mikoyan's grabbing the receiver," he said, excitedly congratulating the first woman in orbit. How sincerely glad he was to speak with Kennedy one day, outer space the next. . . . They grabbed the receiver away. They deposed the mistake. It was simpler to deal with someone not fully human.

The story goes that when this happened Khrushchev couldn't believe it, but even so, he instantly *understood.* He knew all about these things, and here he'd been carried away by daydreams, he had rested on his laurels, lost his vigilance. . . . When he found himself locked up at his dacha, where the same agents who had been his own guards now guarded against him, he kept running up and down the garden paths with his swift, light step, every so often clutching his head. Yes, his step was actually light and swift, as is sometimes true of very stout people. This, too, we had failed to notice when we laughed at his stoutness. . . . He rushed up and down the garden and beat his brow, exclaiming, "Fool! I didn't succeed!" But what hadn't he succeeded in? Averting the plot? . . . Seeing him rush up and down as rhythmically and steadily as a caged animal, his distressed womenfolk tried to comfort him. With the thought that he had nevertheless succeeded in doing a lot. . . . "Fools! I didn't succeed in rehabilitating Bukharin!"

We are left to guess why Bukharin in particular. This is for the historian and the political scientist. I don't think it was because he felt any kind of pity or esteem for him. I think he may have needed Bukharin so that he could avoid making outward changes in the communist idea and yet kill off Leninist-Stalinist dogma concerning the farmlands.

That would have been the next-biggest *mistake.* But two such big mistakes are too many for one historical figure. So he had tackled another mistake as a test: he had abolished some perks, the special foods and services for high officials. This was not merely a mistake, it was *unforgivable.* This—though they had been tolerating him, hypnotized by the Stalinist power he still held as general secretary—*this* the apparatchiks did not forgive him.

Nevertheless, and this was supreme justice, Khrushchev remained alive. Only because he himself had prepared the way, by denouncing the cult of personality and rehabilitating its victims, was he not declared an enemy of the people and shot. Such a thing was no longer possible.

He was left to raise tomatoes.

We can all remember how Khrushchev complicated matters with agriculture.[2] But you can't take away his talent. He had the talent of the peasant, and his vegetable patch grew the biggest tomatoes in the neighborhood. He was so proud of them that he kept being unable to pick them, kept trying to catch the fall sunshine, kept running out every morning to see whether they hadn't become even bigger and redder. All right, I'll pick them tomorrow, he would think each time. Let them hang a little longer. . . . One bright morning the old man came out and they were black—there had been a frost in the night. The story is that he took this sad event much harder than his own dismissal. He just about had a heart attack, just about died.

Not long after, he did die.

I have seen his last photograph. He looks very much thinner. He is oddly, I would say elegantly, dressed. He wears a soft Borsalino hat and an overcoat with a cape. He leans on a cane. All this suits him perfectly. His ears hardly stick out. His features are strong. And he looks at you with a human gaze. Such a clear, bitter gaze, so understanding of you, and so forgiving.

And again supreme justice triumphed: they gave him a human burial. He was not embalmed and entombed in a wall, not cremated. He was buried in the ground. At Novo-Devichy Monastery.

Moscow–Berlin, April 1994

1. *Volga-Volga* was a popular Soviet musical comedy film of the 1930s. Stalin loved to watch it himself and showed it to his guests dozens of times. In the film the actor Igor Ilyinsky plays the part of a manager in a small Volga town, a man who looks rather like Khrushchev—short, plump, simple, and lively. [SK]

2. During the years when Khrushchev was in power, the output of Soviet agriculture practically doubled. However, as a result of the sharp rise in wages, there were intermittent shortages of various food products, especially meat, in the stores. These shortages created the popular impression that the performance of agriculture was deteriorating. [SK]

# Abbreviations and Acronyms

| | |
|---|---|
| ASSR | Autonomous Soviet Socialist Republic |
| AUCP(B) | All-Union Communist Party (Bolshevik) |
| CC | Central Committee |
| CEC | Central Executive Committee [of the USSR] |
| Cheka | Extraordinary Commission for Combating Sabotage and Counterrevolution [secret police] |
| Comintern | Communist International |
| CP(B)U | Communist Party (Bolshevik) of Ukraine |
| CPSU | Communist Party of the Soviet Union |
| Gosplan | State Planning Commission |
| GPU | State Political Administration [secret police] |
| KGB | Committee for State Security [secret police] |
| Komsomol | Young Communist League |
| MGB | Ministry of State Security [secret police] |
| MVD | Ministry of Internal Affairs |
| NKVD | People's Commissariat of Internal Affairs [secret police] |
| OGPU | Unified State Political Administration [secret police] |
| Osoaviakhim | Society for Assistance to Defense, Aviation, and Chemistry |
| RCP(B) | Russian Communist Party (Bolshevik) |
| RSDLP | Russian Social Democratic Labor Party |
| RSFSR | Russian Soviet Federated Socialist Republic |
| Sovnarkom | Council of People's Commissars |
| SRs | Socialist Revolutionaries [members of the Socialist Revolutionary Party] |
| SSR | Soviet Socialist Republic |
| Stavka | General Headquarters of the Supreme High Command |
| TASS | Telegraph Agency of the Soviet Union |
| USSR | Union of Soviet Socialist Republics |

# Prologue

FOR A LONG time now my comrades have been asking me whether I was going to write my memoirs (and not just asking, but urging me to).* Because I, and my generation in general, lived in very interesting times: the revolution, the Civil War, and everything connected with the transition from capitalism to socialism, as well as the developing and strengthening of socialism. It was an entire epoch. It fell to my lot to take an active part in the political struggle from the very first days after I joined the party [in 1918]. The whole time I held elected positions of one kind or another. The Civil War and the Great Patriotic War, and domestic developments in our country, have been treated extensively in the press. But there are "blank spots" that are incomprehensible to many. For a long time they were incomprehensible to me as well. After Stalin's death, when we had the opportunity to acquaint ourselves with archival material that had previously been unknown to us, we began to see many things in a different light. Previously there had been only the blind confidence that we had in Stalin, and therefore everything that was done under his leadership was treated as necessary, as the only correct thing that could have been done. But when we ourselves began thinking in a somewhat critical way, we began checking the facts, to the extent possible, against archival data.

Many people who meet and talk with me ask if I am going to write my memoirs about the period in which I lived. They all argue, and I myself understand this, that it was a time filled with great responsibilities, a very important period in history, and that therefore people would want to know about it from a man who was right there, who lived in those times and held a high position, as happened with me. I would like future generations to have the opportunity to judge for themselves the things that transpired in the period when I was alive. This period was indeed one of great significance. It was a magnificent time because of the grandeur of the actions carried out by the party in reconstructing industry, agriculture, culture, and public administration. At the same time, many things were done that hindered our forward development, and if these things had not been done, our achievements would have been even grander.

---

*When he was starting to record his memoirs, N. S. Khrushchev made these preliminary remarks, describing what he planned to dictate; hence, his use of the future tense. [SK]

I understand the concern of these friends who have insistently urged me to take up the pen. A time will come when literally every word of people who lived in our era will become "worth its weight in gold." This will be especially true of people whose fate it was to be near the helm of power, from which the entire enormous ship of our state was steered in restructuring the sociopolitical life of our country, in the process exerting an enormous influence on developments worldwide. However, I must work without actually having access to archival materials. It is too complicated [to try to use such materials], and in my situation now it is probably impossible.

I want to be very truthful [*ochen pravdivym*—that is, very accurate about the facts], and I will refer to facts so that future generations (and it is for them that I am writing) can verify them. I will indicate sources that may be referred to in order to find out about things in more detail, to verify and understand the facts. On many questions that I consider especially interesting for future generations the facts were recorded in minutes. People can acquaint themselves with these in detail. These archival materials are not accessible today, but some day they will become available to everyone. Even today I don't think the bulk of this material is closed to the public.

I would like to express my opinion on a number of questions, knowing from experience that future generations will eagerly grasp at every word dealing with this extremely important period of history, one filled with great responsibilities, the one in which we lived, worked, and built a powerful state. This was done by our efforts, by the efforts of the people, the party, and the leaders of that time, who were the organizers of the masses. It was my good luck to be one of that number, on various rungs of the ladder at various times, from base-level party organizations all the way up to the top leadership bodies—the Central Committee of the CPSU, its Politburo and Presidium—and the top posts of chairman of the Council of Ministers and first secretary of the Central Committee of the CPSU. It fell to my lot to be present when many important questions were decided, and I took part in putting those decisions into effect. I was a participant in the events of this crucial time. I therefore consider it my duty to express my opinion.

I know in advance that no opinion will satisfy everyone, and it is not my intention to try to do that. My only wish is that, among the opinions that will be recorded in one form or another and that will remain as a legacy for future generations, my opinion too will become known. There were commonly held opinions and there were differences on many particular questions. This is only natural. There is nothing contradictory in this. In fact, that's how it will be in the future as well. The truth is born out of debate.

Even in a single party, standing on the basis of a single, highly principled Marxist-Leninist viewpoint, people can have different conceptions, different shades of opinion, in trying to decide one or another question. Living in a time when a flexible approach is required for solving problems, I know that differing points of view arise, views that may even be sharply opposed to one another, but that doesn't bother me.

I place my reliance on those people who in the future will, as it were, act as judges. It will be the people themselves who will judge, who will acquaint themselves with this material and draw their own conclusions. I don't think that what I say is necessarily the truth. No, each person will find the truth for himself or herself, comparing different points of view on one or another question at one or another time. That is all I wish for. Only a foolish person wants to "cut everyone's hair to the same length," to reduce everything to one and the same level, to denounce as heresy or stupidity or even a crime anything that doesn't fit a certain viewpoint. Let history itself be the judge. Let the people judge.

For that reason I ask in advance that I be forgiven for any inaccuracies the reader may find in my memoirs. I am presenting my own personal view. This is how I see things now, how I understand them and write about them. I don't want to adapt myself to what others want, to be a timeserver. I don't want to hold my tongue or suppress the truth. I don't want to gloss things over or varnish our reality. Our reality doesn't need varnishing because in itself it is grand and immense enough. It was my good fortune, certainly, to have lived at such a critical, transitional time, a time when we broke up the old way of life, based on capitalist-landowner foundations, tossed it aside, and built a new life on the basis of new theories and a new practice.

Theory without practice is dead. What happened with us was that on the basis of the most advanced theory, Marxist-Leninist theory, we laid the groundwork for achievements in practice. This is a very complicated matter, because during this period [of transition from capitalism to socialism] mistakes and miscalculations, whether intended or not, cannot be excluded. As the saying goes, may our descendants forgive us. May they consider the fact that this was the first experience [in trying to build socialism]. That's why it was unique, and as for subsequent attempts, they were a kind of repetition of the first. May we be judged in such a way that allowances are made for the conditions in which we lived and worked. We did our work first, and only afterward did we start to write memoirs, so that the good things created in our history by us, by the party, the working class, and the toiling peasantry, would not be lost sight of, and so that the mistakes—and I would also say, the crimes committed in the name of the party and for the party, supposedly—would not be repeated.

Today it is clear that there was abuse of power. The reports at the Twentieth Party Congress, and again, to some degree, at the Twenty-Second Party Congress, shed light on the causes giving rise to this abuse. I think that everything was correct that was said on this subject [by those two party congresses]. Even today I take my stand on the positions adopted then, and it is precisely from that standpoint that I will tell about the times of heavy responsibility on the eve of the Great Patriotic War and during the war, and then I will continue to lay out the course of events as long as I have the strength to do so, relating how I saw and understood events then and how I evaluate them now.

Where to begin? I think it's necessary to begin with the figure of Stalin. Why? That will become clear (if I succeed in carrying this project through to the end). If I were to try, to some degree, to give an explanation at this point, I could say that before Stalin's death we considered everything done under him to have been irreproachably correct, the only thing possible for the revolution to survive, and for it to develop and grow stronger. It's true that in the final period of Stalin's life, the time leading up to the Nineteenth Party Congress [1952] and especially just after it, some doubts began to arise in our minds. I am speaking of those who were in his immediate circle (myself, Bulganin, Malenkov, and to some extent, Beria). We had no opportunity to test those doubts then. Only after Stalin's death, and not all at once, did we find enough party and civic courage to lift the curtain and look behind the scenes of history. It was then that I learned some facts I want to shed light on now.

**THE MEMOIRS**

# The Beginning of the Road

## A LITTLE ABOUT MYSELF

In my childhood[1] at first I lived in a village and came to love the peasant way of life. But for the most part I spent my childhood years in mining towns with my father, who worked in the coal pits. I have an especially distinct memory of his work at the Uspenskaya mine, four versts[2] south of Yuzovka (now Donetsk).[3] As for myself, I worked in my youth at a machine-building plant, then at a mine, then I served in the Red Army.

In our village of Kalinovka, in Kursk *gubernia*,[4] the farms were not large; in fact, they were small. The peasants had no machinery, only the wooden plow and the small metal plow, *pluzhok*—although it's true that by then the wooden plow was something you rarely encountered. The *pluzhok*, a light-weight one-horse plow, was intended for the weak peasant horse. A large or heavy metal plow, which allowed you to plow deep, would have been too much for the little peasant horse to pull. As a rule, the peasant plowed the earth with a *pluzhok* harnessed to just one horse, so he was working with barely one horsepower. There were absolutely no mineral fertilizers; people had no notion of such a thing.

In my home village people raised mainly wheat for the market and oats for a nearby horse farm. It was a splendid horse farm. Farming operations there were conducted at a very high level, although the landowners had no tractors at that time. They plowed deep and used a lot of manure. Apparently they practiced seed selection, resulting in really good-quality, choice seed, so that the harvest they got was something quite unimaginable for the peasants at that time: 30 to 35 centners of wheat per *desyatina*.[5]

In 1908 my father and mother were hired to work on the wealthy estate of the landowner Vasilchenko. By then I was a teenager, fourteen years old, and I worked there, too, during the plowing season as a driver of oxen. It was heavy work for someone of my age; you had to lift the yoke onto the oxen's necks to harness them to the plow. That was one of the duties of the driver, not the plowman.

After that there began my years of work at coal mines and factories, experience with strikes, then the revolution, then the Civil War. I'm not going to talk about all that, or maybe I will just mention it here or there in the course of my narrative.

In early 1922 I returned to the Donets Basin (Donbas)[6] from the Red Army. As a member of a Communist Party mobilization team I traveled out to the rural areas, to the villages, to help carry out a spring sowing campaign. We went to the villages of the Maryinsky district. People had lived quite well there earlier, but in the famine of 1921 many died and instances of cannibalism occurred.[7] Our entire work consisted of this: we gathered the peasants together and appealed to them to sow their crops well and on time, and better yet, to do the sowing much earlier than usual. We ourselves didn't understand very well what we were saying. My speech was fairly primitive, as were the speeches of the other comrades. After all, I had never really done agricultural work, and my whole knowledge was based on what I had seen as a child living with my grandfather in Kursk *gubernia*.

That same year, 1922, I went to study at a workers' school *(rabfak)*.[8] The secretary of the county *(uyezd)* party committee was Zavenyagin.[9] When I finished my studies at the *rabfak*, Moiseyenko[10] had already become secretary of the district party committee. (By then they had switched over from *uyezd*s to *okrug*s, districts.)[11]

After finishing the *rabfak* in 1925, I didn't get the chance to attend an institution of higher education. I wanted to study and acquire a profession. I had an aptitude for engineering, and I dreamed of going to mechanical engineering school. As a machinist I loved the technical aspects of my profession, and I loved machinery. But in Yuzovka they said to me: "No! You have to take up party work because that's the most important thing right now."

So I became secretary of the party committee in Petrovo-Maryinsky county *(uyezd)*, whose character was rather mixed. This was expressed in the fact that Maryinsky county, properly speaking, was an agricultural region, but there were coal pits in the area. They were called the Petrovsky pits. (Previously they had been the Karpovsky pits.) The new name was in honor of Grigory Ivanovich Petrovsky,[12] a prominent Communist Party figure. Back when he had been a deputy in the Fourth State Duma[13] he had come to this region once. I cannot say for sure whether he had given a speech, but he had been ready to speak. I was invited to that workers' meeting, which was being held illegally [Social Democratic organizing being banned by the tsarist authorities]. Then they canceled the meeting. I don't know the details because I was not one of the organizers. I was simply told that the police had gotten wind of the location of the meeting, and Grigory Ivanovich had said that since that was the case, the meeting should not be held. I had already gone to the location designated for the meeting, but people who had been specially posted there warned me that the meeting was off. Petrovsky had come there because he had been elected to the Duma from Yekaterinoslav *gubernia,*[14] in which those coal pits were located.

When I took over the job of first secretary of the party's *uyezd* committee I had to deal with everything, including agriculture. The committee offices were located in a workers' settlement at a coal mine called Trudovskaya No. 5. That coal mine is still in operation now.[15] Back then it was a small mine with a little miners' settlement located in the steppes near the large and well-to-do village of Maryinka.[16] The village of Grigoryevka was situated not far away, and even closer to the coal pits was the large village of Kremennaya. If you call yourself a mushroom, then get in the mushroom basket![17] Since I had been elected secretary of the *uyezd* committee, I had the obligation to give instructions and directions that applied to all areas. So I became a person who had been dragged into a position of responsibility. I was responsible not only for the state of agriculture in the county but also for the amount of coal produced, and for the functioning of the Krasnogorovsky ceramics factory. This was the only factory in the Donbas that produced the firebrick used for lining the insides of blast furnaces and open-hearth furnaces. What my functions came down to were not so much to ensure the production of agricultural goods as to extract such goods from the peasant households.

In 1926 at a party conference for the district I was elected to head the organizational department of the district party committee. The organizational structure was as follows: the person in charge of the organizational department was the deputy first secretary. Moiscyenko was then the only secretary in the district committee. Later he and I went our separate ways; we didn't get along. His life had a tragic end; he was shot as a result of the arbitrary events that occurred in the 1930s [i.e., the Stalin-era repression]. I am convinced that he was an honorable person.

In the district committee we were also concerned with agriculture. At that time agriculture was rising like yeast-filled dough. Lenin's New Economic Policy (NEP)[18] served as the stimulus for this growth and became a powerful engine driving private initiative. As a result agriculture quickly revived to the prerevolutionary level and in some respects exceeded that level. In 1925 we had as great a quantity of food products as you could wish, and they were cheap. After 1922, with the famine and cannibalism of that year, there now came a time when food was abundant. You could see agriculture growing before your eyes. It was simply a miracle. In the village of Maryinka at the beginning of the spring sowing campaign in 1922 I had held various public meetings and seen what state the peasants were in then. They were literally swaying in the breeze; they didn't walk to the meeting; they crawled there. But when I came back to that same village as secretary of the *uyezd* committee it was hard to recognize them. It was simply miraculous the way people had come up in the world. Well-to-do peasants were given the possibility of hiring labor. Kulaks took advantage of this and they would rent agricultural enterprises and flour mills.

In short, private economic initiative, on a rather far-reaching basis, was permitted, and agriculture very quickly revived and fully supplied all the demands of the market. Our main challenge at that time was competition with private producers. We had to provide the Maryinka cooperative with goods and make sure it served the population better and sold more products.

1. N. S. Khrushchev was born in 1894. [GS]

2. A verst is an old Russian measure of length, equal to 3,500 feet—that is, about two thirds of a mile or just over 1 kilometer. [SS]

3. Yuzovka was established as a coal-mining settlement in 1870. It was named after the British capitalist Hughes, who invested in the first coal mines. In 1924 the town was renamed Stalino, and in 1961 it became Donetsk. The districts mentioned in the text encompassed mainly the western part of the Donbas, an acronym for the Donets Basin, the basin of the Donets River, in southeastern Ukraine. These district organizations of the RCP(B) consisted predominantly of miners, although there were also quite a few metalworkers. The mines of the Petrovo-Maryinsky district were mainly in the basin of the Volchya River.

4. Kalinovka is situated in the far west of Kursk province. [SS]

5. In Russia, a centner is 100 kilograms; a *desyatina* is the equivalent of 2.7 acres. [GS]

6. The Donbas was one of the main industrialized regions of tsarist Russia and the Soviet Union, centered on coal mining, metallurgy, and the chemical industry. Mining of the rich coal deposits along the lower reaches of the Donets River (also known as the Seversky Donets River) and the development of metallurgical and other industries began in the 1870s. [GS]

7. In 1921–22, Ukraine and southern Russia were swept by a famine in which at least 5 million people starved to death. [SS]

8. A *rabfak* (an acronym for "workers' faculty") was a special school at which students from working-class backgrounds received preparatory training to compensate for their inadequate schooling, with a view to their subsequent attendance at a higher educational institution. [SS]

9. A. P. Zavenyagin. See Biographies.

10. Moiseyenko was one of the leading party officials in Ukraine. See Biographies.

11. An *okrug* consisted of several rural *uyezdy*. [SK]

12. G. I. Petrovsky. See Biographies.

13. Petrovsky was a deputy in the Fourth State Duma for the Russian Social Democratic Labor Party (Bolshevik) (RSDLP). The Gosudarstvennaya Duma (State Duma) was a parliamentary body permitted by the government of Tsar Nicholas II in the wake of the 1905 revolution, when absolutist rule was modified. The First Duma, elected in February–March 1906, was boycotted by the RSDLP. (For more on the RSDLP, see the Translator's Note at the beginning of this volume.) The First Duma was dissolved by the tsar in July 1906; the Second Duma, which convened in March 1907, was also dissolved by the tsar after three months. The Third Duma was elected according to a new and highly restrictive electoral law of June 1907; for the most part the Third Duma and its successor, the Fourth, were quite conservative; in cases where these Dumas opposed the policies of the tsarist government, they had little, if any, power. In the Fourth Duma, elected in 1912, the Social Democrats won fourteen seats; eight of their representatives were Mensheviks and six were Bolsheviks, one of the latter being Grigory Petrovsky. Sessions of the Fourth Duma were

discontinued by the tsar as one of his last acts during the five days of the February revolution of 1917, which put an end to the monarchy. [GS]

14. Yekaterinoslav *gubernia* was situated in what was then southern Russia. The city of Yekaterinoslav was founded in 1776 and named in honor of Empress Catherine II. It was renamed Dnepropetrovsk in 1926. [SS]

15. That is, in 1967, when this passage was dictated. [GS]

16. Maryinka was a coal-mining settlement just to the southwest of Donetsk. It is now virtually a suburb of Donetsk and is the center of the Maryinsky district. [SS]

17. This proverb means something like: "If you hold a title, you have to do everything that goes with the job." [GS]

18. The NEP was the New Economic Policy, introduced by Lenin in March 1921 at the Tenth Party Congress. [SS]

## THE FOURTEENTH PARTY CONFERENCE

In April 1925 the Fourteenth Party Conference opened. I was elected a delegate to that conference from the Yuzovka party organization. The head of the party organization was Moiseyenko (or Kostyan, as we called him). I have already mentioned him. He had been a student at a medical institute but had not graduated; he was an excellent orator and a good organizer. He was distinguished by a rather strong petty bourgeois inclination, and he had connections with and was surrounded by people who were virtually Nepmen.[1] That's why, later on, we removed him as secretary. This scandalous affair reached the ears of the Central Committee of the Communist Party (Bolshevik) of Ukraine, or CP(B)U.[2] A commission came to visit us. It looked into our disputes and recognized that the conclusions we had come to were well founded, so that indeed he was relieved of his duties as secretary.

Then when a conference was held Moiseyenko literally won over the Communists of the Yuzovka district, persuading them to change their minds. Because of his training and education he stood a full head above all the other members of our active party group. I forget how many delegates we elected from our Yuzovka organization then. It was about eight people with a full vote, if I remember right, and four people with only a consultative vote, including myself. Delegates were elected democratically then. I headed the Petrovo-Maryinsky district party organization, and it held sixth or seventh place as far as the number of party members went. Yuzovka held first place, then came the Makeyevka district, and then, it seems to me, the Budyonny district, the Rutchenkovo mines, and so on, with the Petrovo-Maryinsky district coming last. That's why I was elected with only a consultative vote.

Still, it was a great joy for me. The main thing was a chance to visit Moscow, have a look at the capital city of the Soviet Union, attend a union-wide conference, and see and hear the party leaders. At the party conference, the Ukrainian organization was assigned a central place in the large meeting hall. (Today the USSR Supreme Soviet holds its sessions there. At that time, it seems, it was called Saint Vladimir's Hall;[3] it had not yet been rebuilt; the columns on the inside of the hall made it awkward for such large sessions. But there was no other appropriate meeting place in the Kremlin, and that was the location where party conferences and congresses were held.) To the left of us was the Moscow delegation, and to the right the Leningrad delegation. We occupied the center of the space, and in that center the Yuzovka delegation had first place. The militant proletarian Donbas organization held a place of honor in general within the Ukrainian party organization. Kaganovich[4] was then secretary of the Central Committee of the CP(B)U; Chubar[5] was president of the Council of People's Commissars; Grigory Ivanovich Petrovsky was chairman of the All-Ukraine Central Executive Committee of Soviets; and Skrypnik[6] was a member of the CP(B)U Politburo; Shlikhter[7] also held a prominent position in the Ukrainian party organization.

The work of that party conference made an especially powerful impression on me. I saw the leaders of our government and party. They were right there, close up. We were living in the House of Soviets on Carriage Row.[8] (I think it was called the House of Soviets.) We lived rather simply. There were bunks, and as the saying goes, we simply threw ourselves on them when we wanted to sleep. I remember that Postyshev,[9] who it seems to me was secretary of the Kharkov party organization,[10] came there with his wife, and they slept there right alongside us, both his wife and himself. This led to jokes being made at Postyshev's expense. We were all young then. Despite the jokes Postyshev enjoyed respect in the party organization, and he had my respect too.

I would get up early and go on foot to the Kremlin in order to arrive before the other delegates and find a good seat. Each delegation had an area assigned to it, but within that space each delegate could take whatever place was free. We wanted to reserve for ourselves the front rows closest to the speakers' platform; so we had to get up early and hurry there without breakfast. One day I left and took a streetcar without knowing the route numbers, and it turned out the streetcar didn't go where I wanted; instead it took me off to no one knows where. After that I dispensed with the services of the transportation system and went on foot. I had to get up early and run, but on the other hand, the route I took brought me to the Kremlin without fail, and I was able to take a seat in the meeting hall close to the front.

Later on they began taking photographs of the delegation. Stalin already stood out at that conference. He was recognized as the person of first importance not only by us, the rank and file leaders of party organizations. The head of the party organization of our province, Moiseyenko, asked Stalin, in the name of the Yuzovka delegation, to have his photograph taken with us. We were told that Stalin had agreed and that he would let us know later when he would have the time to do it. We waited. Finally during one of the breaks we were told to gather at Catherine's Hall,[11] where our entire delegation would be photographed as a unit. Of course we all gathered there, and then Stalin arrived. We all began to take our seats and Stalin sat right in the middle of us, as we had asked.

Why am I reminiscing about this photography session? The photographer kept fussing around his camera. His name was Petrov, a major specialist in his field who had worked at the Kremlin for many years.[12] All the party officials who had been at conferences and congresses knew him. As the photographer Petrov began giving instructions to one or another person, which way to turn the head, which way to look, Stalin suddenly made a remark: "Comrade Petrov loves to give orders, but among us you can't go issuing orders like that. You can't order us around!" This incident made a good impression on my friends and me. (We later compared views on the subject.) It seemed to us that Stalin really was a democratic-minded person, that a remark like that was not accidental, that this joke was an organic expression of Stalin's nature. Later during the work of the conference Stalin's speech and his other remarks seemed to us also to speak in his favor. I was filled more and more with a profound respect for this individual.

1. *Nepmen* were successful private businessmen of the NEP era. [GS]

2. The Communist Party (Bolshevik) of Ukraine was the Ukrainian organization of the All-Union Communist Party (Bolshevik). [SS]

3. Saint Vladimir's Hall was a hall in the Great Kremlin Palace in Moscow, named in honor of Saint Vladimir and also in honor of those who had been decorated with the Order of Saint Vladimir. [SK]

4. L. M. Kaganovich. See Biographies.

5. V. Ya. Chubar. See Biographies.

6. N. A. Skrypnik. See Biographies.

7. A. G. Shlikhter. See Biographies.

8. Karetnyi riad (Carriage Row) was a fashionable street in downtown Moscow, near the Kremlin. [SK]

9. P. P. Postyshev. See Biographies.

10. Kharkov was at that time the capital of Soviet Ukraine. [SS]

11. Catherine's (Yekaterininsky) Hall, named after Empress Catherine II of Russia, was another hall on the same level of the Great Kremlin Palace as Saint Vladimir's Hall. [SK]

12. G. G. Petrov was at that time one of the most popular government photographers.

## A FEW WORDS ABOUT THE NEP

I will say a few words at this point about the New Economic Policy (NEP). I remember that time well when destruction and hunger were suddenly followed by the revival of the towns, when food products appeared and prices began to fall. The NEP was of course a retreat. But it allowed us to cope with the consequences of the Civil War and to regain our strength. Lenin's wisdom became apparent in this policy. In 1921 he adopted this dangerous but necessary and unavoidable, courageous, decisive, and far-seeing measure—the transition to the NEP. You could say that it was a rather general term, but in essence what this policy did was to give private property a chance to revive, and it allowed the kulaks to take on a new life, not to mention the middle peasants.[1] Merchant and trader elements also raised their heads and got back on their feet pretty solidly.

In 1925 I encountered Nepmen. There were such persons who had control of the flour mills and rented them out. The following anecdote is typical: One man who rented out time at his flour mill proved to be a former Red Army soldier who had distinguished himself during the Civil War and had been awarded the Order of the Red Banner.

We had frequent debates and arguments, I remember, on the subject of the NEP among the leading cadres of the party, both on the county level and the district level. In the district we were often called in and invariably given a talking-to, as they said then (and still say now), for the fact that we weren't selling enough bread through the cooperative system—also not enough meat and other food products. As secretary of the district committee, I went almost every day to the bazaar (or free market area) and had a good look. The party slogans then were "Learn How to Trade!" and "Who Will Defeat Whom?"[2] Through the cooperatives we were supposed to defeat the merchants and the system of private commerce, thus taking control of commerce into our hands, not through administrative measures, but rather by doing better work in commercial operations through the system of cooperatives. Our aim was to sell goods cheaper, serve customers better, and deliver a higher-quality product. Those were the levers we were supposed to use to win out in this competition.

When I went to the bazaar, I would see our cooperative stands selling their goods, and alongside them would be the owner of a private shop. It was always painful for me to observe this situation because there would be more people crowding around the privately owned stores; yet these were blue-collar and white-collar workers; that's the only kind of people there were in the mining towns. Why were things turning out this way? The meat we had for sale was just as good, but the private owner did a better job of packaging and paid more attention to the customers. Besides that, the housewife wanted a chance to choose, she wanted to fuss around a little, to look at this and that and feel it with her own hands, and the private merchant accommodated her. The private traders also had their steady customers to whom they gave credit, and that was very important. The cooperatives did not give credit.

Some days, after walking around at the bazaar, I directed my steps to the main store of the cooperative system, and there I met with my friend Vanya Kosvinsky. He was chairman of the workers' cooperative. He was a very good comrade, a Communist who had distinguished himself during the Civil War. He fought behind the lines of the White Army and also commanded an armored train.[3] (The armored train was a primitive contraption that the workers themselves had manufactured in their workshops.) I remember as soon as I would open the door, he would say right off: "Well, Comrade, have you come here to cuss me out again?"

I would reply: "Yes, Comrade, I've come to cuss you out."

He said: "I've already been there and seen it myself. But what can I do? We're doing everything that it seems we need to, do but still the private merchants attract more customers."

In the autumn there was a flood of agricultural goods and other products—vegetables, melons, poultry. The Petrovo-Maryinsky district at that time was the district farthest to the southeast in the Yuzovka industrial area; it was, as they say, the edge of the world for the coal-mining region. There were no more mines after that. (Nowadays the mining has been extended farther, all the way to Dnepropetrovsk.)[4] That's why peasants lived in that area; it was no longer a mining region. The villages were well off and had good land in the black earth regions of the steppes.[5] Some villages in the area had populations of Greek origin, sometimes very large villages. These Greeks were herders. They loved to raise sheep and had a lot of them. Therefore they had a lot of mutton and sheep's milk cheese for sale, and the peasants brought geese, ducks, and turkeys to the market, and all of it was cheap. The prewar standard for prices still prevailed then. Before the war a pound of meat in Yuzovka and the surrounding regions cost about fifteen kopeks.[6] In 1925 and 1926 meat still cost fifteen kopeks. Up until 1928 there was an abundance of meat.

I've strayed from the subject a little at this point, but the digression is still relevant. In the Petrovo-Maryinsky district there were two communes back then.[7] The commune in Maksimilianovka, a large, beautiful village, worked especially well. There was a party organization there, too. Back then it was called a party cell. The chairman of the board of the commune was a man named Kolos, a man of enormous size, a real titan, whose build seemed to corresponded to his name.[8] He died long ago. Even in the 1920s he was well on in years. He was a very decent man and a good Communist, originally a tailor by profession. His deputy was a remarkable peasant activist by the name of Yemelyan Gomlya, or as the Ukrainians called him, Yemelka Gomlya. He was an intelligent man with a terrific sense of humor. When he would give a speech criticizing the bureaucratic practices in Soviet government institutions people would, as the saying goes, split their sides laughing. He was often present at party conferences and district congresses. I remember a speech he gave once, criticizing the leaders of the district for the fact that they rarely visited the villages: "What's the matter with all of you? Here we beg you and beg you to come visit us from the district center, but apparently it's hard to see the villages from where you are, because here in the center there's so much smoke [from the mines and the metallurgical works] that beyond all this smoke you just can't see us." And he brought up other, similar instances [of official shortcomings].

Their commune was doing well, and that was not so common at that time among the communes. Most were called consumer communes; that is, they didn't produce enough to cover their costs, and so they lived off subsidies from the government. But this commune got along on its own resources. Good people and good organizers had come together there. They cultivated the land successfully, and they were good honest workers. They had no tractors. I myself had only heard about tractors at the time; I had heard that they existed but had never, as they say, set eyes on one. Mainly they used oxen and horses then. The political situation was good then. The workers understood the party's slogans and took them to heart. After all it was painful to carry through that policy, the NEP, but they understood it correctly.

Stalin didn't "gain recognition by the broad public," to use philistine language, until the time when a sharp internal struggle broke out in the party, the struggle with the Trotskyist opposition in 1923–24.[9] Stalin rose to the top as an organizer, as general secretary of the Central Committee. At that time Stalin's special role was perceived only dimly in wider party circles; I'm not even talking here about non-party people. Zinoviev[10] especially distinguished himself in the party struggle at that time. He was then chairman of the Executive Committee of the Communist International (Comintern). The Comintern had won great authority: It was an international Communist organization, steering a course toward world revolution.[11] As the head of it, Zinoviev, consequently seemed to be the chief figure in this movement. Bukharin[12] was also very popular at that time and highly respected. As I recall, his book entitled *The ABC of Communism* was already published by then.[13] Every young Communist studied the Communist world outlook above all on the basis of "his" book, and Bukharin's popularity partly arose from that.

I personally saw and heard Bukharin speak when I was still serving in the Red Army in 1919. Our unit was stationed in Kursk, and for some reason Bukharin and a large group of Communists came to visit Kursk at that time. Bukharin spoke before the active party membership of the province. I was also invited as the secretary of the party cell in my military unit. That's where I saw Bukharin and heard him speak. Everybody liked Bukharin a lot because of his pleasant personality and his democratic nature, which had great importance then (and it's still of importance today). Yes, everyone liked him a lot, and I myself was literally enchanted with him. Later I met comrades who were part of his group. They were ordinary rank-and-file Communists from Moscow who were on the same level of political development as me. They also spoke about Bukharin's democratic qualities, and that was especially attractive then. They said that they lived together with him in the same dormitory and ate from the same soup kettle in the dining room, and so on. Of course that was something of great importance.

A similar incident concerning Stalin comes to mind. I had a friend named Lev Abramovich Rimsky. He and I worked together in the Donbas region for many years, and later I met him again in Moscow. He was a friend of Tevosyan.[14] They had been together at the Mining Academy; they had both graduated from there and kept their friendship alive afterward. Rimsky worked in the personnel department at the People's Commissariat of Ferrous Metallurgy, and had begun his political activity as a member of the Young Communist League[15] in Odessa.[16] Later he worked in the Kiev province committee and in Stalino.[17] I worked with Rimsky—it seems to me this was in 1926—when I was elected to head the organizational department of the district party committee after I had left the Petrovo-Maryinsky district. As I have said, the second secretary of the district committee, then Moiseyenko, served as the person in charge of the organizational department in those days; secretary was ; there was only one secretary, and the other person was in charge of the organizational department and was considered the deputy secretary of the district committee. After him came the person in charge of the agitation and propaganda department. Sergeyev[18] was in charge of the agitation and propaganda department then. I forget his real name; he was Jewish. He was a remarkable Communist, devoted to the party cause, and a good worker. Unfortunately, like many thousands of others, he perished during the years of terror that Stalin imposed on the party. As for Rimsky, he was head of the district party school.[19] I don't remember the exact year, 1926 or perhaps 1927, but those attending that party school made a trip to Moscow in order to expand their horizons, to have a look at the capital city and see its sights. It was a natural desire of everyone in the Soviet Union, and not just in the Soviet Union, to visit Moscow.

Rimsky, as he related later, decided to call Stalin and ask him to receive the delegation. I don't think it's likely that the entire complement of students from the party school made that trip, but quite a large group did, probably about sixty people. Besides, that's not so important for the subject at hand. As Rimsky related: "I made a telephone call and they connected me with Stalin (that impressed me—Stalin's accessibility), and I asked him to receive me along with the other students from the party school." Stalin agreed and said that he would let Rimsky know (he wrote down his address) when he would be able to do it. Then a telephone call came, and the group went to the Kremlin (back then, before 1937, the Kremlin was still open to ordinary citizens), and they went in through the Nikolsky Gates.[20] I forget now what questions Stalin expressed an interest in. I am recalling this episode because I remember a characteristic statement made by Stalin, which made a big impression on me. As Rimsky told the story, when he first spoke with Stalin he said: "Comrade Stalin, we are from the former town of Yuzovka. Today it has been renamed and bears your name. That's why we wanted you to write a letter to the workers of the former Yuzovka, to the workers of Stalino. That would make a good impression on the population of the Stalino district."

Stalin answered him as follows: "I'm not some big landowner, and the workers in the factories there are not my serfs. I will not write to them, and I don't like it when others do such things." Lev Abramovich Rimsky was a strict party person, a man of exceptional purity and honesty. He was extremely punctilious and correct as a Communist, down to the tiniest details, and this scrupulousness and meticulousness suffused his entire consciousness, all of his activity, the way he conducted himself his entire life. Therefore he was pleasantly surprised by what had happened. When he came home, he told everyone; he told about all this at the party district committee, and it became common knowledge throughout the district. This remark of Stalin's made a very big impression. The incident testified to Stalin's democratic qualities, his accessibility, and his correct understanding of his position and place.

I recall another incident from the same time, when the sharp conflict with the Trotskyists had broken out, and then later with the supporters of Zinoviev. I was engaged in party work the whole time. I was the head of the organizational department in the district committee and took part in the work of the Fourteenth Party Conference and the Fourteenth Party Congress as well as the Fifteenth Party Conference and the Fifteenth Party Congress. I haven't tried to sort out the exact years just now, and it's not so essential: After all, that's not what I'm talking about, but about Stalin's personality. Back then the practice was to make a stenographic record of the proceedings of Politburo meetings. Everything was taken down by stenographers, and the stenographic record was distributed to party organizations. These records reached even the district party offices, and the active party membership would be summoned and would gather there to read these stenographic records. I recall one particular stenographic record that we read. We read it with painstaking care because we wanted to get to the essence of the differences in the debates, to determine our own attitudes toward them. It seems to me that Stalin was arguing either with Trotsky[21] or with Zinoviev, and I remember an expression he used that pleased me. Stalin was trying to make some point, and the others disagreed with him and would not yield on this question; the dispute became very sharp, and when they refused to agree with him Stalin expressed himself as follows: "Well, what's the matter with you? I am doing everything I can to maintain the unity of the party, to ensure its monolithic character. This is necessary for victory. But if you are going to conduct yourselves this way, then God be with you." I paid special attention to this phrase of Stalin's. Of course I was not a religious person then, and even earlier in my life I had not been, and of course this expression did not identify Stalin as a religious man, even though he had been a seminary student. What it meant was this: What am I to do with you people? I don't wish you harm, and may God be with you, so that you will rethink your position, so that you yourself will come to understand how mistaken your position is. This kind of patience, as I understood it then, was pleasing to me. It spoke in Stalin's favor.

Later, when I really got to know Stalin, I remembered this and understood that there was subtlety and a jesuitical element here. He was playing on people's feelings, trying to show how patient he was, to demonstrate his desire for party unity, and to show, if not respect, at least patience toward the views of other members of the collective in which he worked as a part.

This was deception and trickery. It was cold calculation. He wanted—to put it crudely—to throw out a baited hook and catch people who sincerely wanted to understand him favorably, and I was one of those who fell for Stalin's baited hook.

1. *Kulaks* were relatively well-to-do peasants. Their status was contrasted with that of the *bednyak* (impoverished poor peasants) and *batrak* (landless laborers). The term *serednyak* ("middle peasant") was used for the bulk of the peasantry, who were neither as well off as the kulaks nor as poor as the poor peasants and landless laborers. [GS/SS]

2. This refers to the competition in the Soviet economy between socialist or cooperative economic institutions, on the one hand, and privately owned capitalist ones, on the other. [GS]

3. Armored trains, used by the Bolsheviks as mobile command posts and centers of agitation, played an important role in the Civil War. [SS]

4. Dnepropetrovsk is a large city on the Dnieper River in east central Ukraine. [SS]

5. The steppe is a wide belt of flat land in southern Russia, originally open grassland, similar to the American prairie. [SS]

6. One ruble consists of 100 kopeks. [SS]

7. These communes were collective farms formed on a voluntary basis in the 1920s before the onset of forcible collectivization. On the communes all property, including housing and livestock, was held in common, and all work was organized on a collective basis. [GS/SS]

8. The Russian word for "colossus" is *koloss.* [GS] G. A. Kolos was an active participant in the peasant movement in Ukraine.

9. Here and henceforth, N. S. Khrushchev uses terms that were current at the time and that still remained in use when he dictated his memoirs.

10. G. Ye. Zinoviev. See Biographies.

11. The Comintern was the directing center for Communist parties in different countries. It was disbanded in 1943. [SS]

12. N. I. Bukharin. See Biographies.

13. *Azbuka kommunizma* (The ABC of Communism) was in fact co-authored by Bukharin and Ye. A. Preobrazhensky, a prominent party economist. It set out Communist doctrine in a simple popular style and included the party program as an appendix. The book was first published in 1919. An English translation was published in 1966 by the University of Michigan Press, Ann Arbor. [SS]

14. I. F. Tevosyan. See Biographies.

15. This organization was known in Russian as the Komsomol, an acronym for Kommunisticheskii Soyuz Molodezhi (Communist Union of Youth). It was the youth adjunct to the Communist Party. [SS]

16. Odessa is a large port on Ukraine's Black Sea coast. [SS]

17. Kiev, a large city in central Ukraine, is the current capital of Ukraine. Stalino was the new name given to Yuzovka (now Donetsk) in 1924. [SS]

18. K. M. Sergeyev occupied a number of party posts.

19. The party schools were one element in the system of party education designed to improve the educational level, theoretical training, and work qualifications of members of the AUCP(B) within the framework of compulsory political study. In the 1920s this system included a series of rungs from the primary schools of political literacy up to the Communist universities. The district party school was an intermediate rung in the system.

20. The Nikolsky Gates in the Kremlin are also known as Saint Nicholas's Gates.

21. L. D. Trotsky. See Biographies.

## THE FOURTEENTH PARTY CONGRESS

A sharp struggle with Zinoviev's supporters unfolded at the Fifteenth Party Congress. [Actually, it was the Fourteenth Party Congress] The Leningrad delegation presented a letter to the presiding committee of the congress, demanding on the basis of the party rules that a counterreport be presented by its delegation. The delegation proposed Zinoviev and wanted him to give a counterreport to the main report by Stalin. Right now I can't remember exactly, but it seems to me that at the Fourteenth Party Congress [actually the Thirteenth] Zinoviev was still giving the main report,[1] and that Stalin gave an accompanying, or second, report on the organizational question. By the time of the Fifteenth [Fourteenth] Congress Stalin himself was giving the main report.

For us delegates to the congress this demand was entirely understandable. Different points of view and different policies had appeared in the Politburo, where a majority and a minority now existed. That's why the report was now to be given—not by Zinoviev, as had happened right after Lenin's death—but by Stalin. I remember that even as we arrived at the congress, "the sparrows were twittering about everything," as the saying goes. Among ordinary people you could hear the view being expressed rather openly that a deep split in the party had occurred.

During this Congress we were housed as before, on Carriage Row in the Third House of Soviets. We were told that Yakov Arkadyevich Yakovlev[2] would be coming to visit us, and he would inform us about the disputed questions that had arisen in the party and that would be aired at the congress. Yakovlev arrived. He was then an official of the Workers' and Peasants' Inspection.[3] As I recall, Sergo[4] was chairman of the Workers' and Peasants' Inspection and Yakovlev was one of Sergo's deputies. No one but members of the Ukrainian delegation was admitted to the gathering. Kaganovich was the head of the Ukrainian delegation then, and its leadership included Petrovsky, Chubar, Shlikhter, and Skrypnik, the chief members of the Politburo of the Central Committee of the Communist Party (Bolshevik) of Ukraine. Yakovlev told us about the main questions on which there were disagreements with Zinoviev's supporters and said the problem was very acute. In this way we were more or less being primed. In that sense this was a factional meeting, but it was held with Stalin's consent and, I think, on his instructions. I don't know who else among the leaders of the Politburo of the AUCP(B) knew about the meeting.

When the congress began, and when its leading bodies were being formed, Zinoviev's supporters immediately proposed him as co-reporter, to give an alternate report from the Central Committee. That was the usual way. So Stalin gave his report, and then Zinoviev gave his counterreport. Once again we occupied a position in the center of the meeting hall, with the Leningrad delegation to our right and the Moscow delegation to our left. We kept in contact with the Moscow delegation on all questions and "took up arms" against the Leningrad opposition, as it was called then. At that point I happened to encounter an old comrade [Abramson], who I respected greatly, but I encountered him now as an enemy, not a friend.

When I had returned from the Red Army in 1922, the editor of the newspaper *Diktatura Truda* (Dictatorship of Labor)[5] in Yuzovka had been Abramson. I don't remember his first name. Now he was in Leningrad working as a secretary of one of the party's district committees. He was a very good Communist, yet here he was a Zinoviev supporter, as all the Leningraders were. Among the well-known figures in the party who supported Zinoviev, one in particular was Badayev.[6] The Zinovievites had also drawn in Nikolayeva[7] to add weight to their delegation. She was also a good, active party member and spoke with great passion; she really was a fine orator. The debates continued after the congress sessions, individually and in small groups, with personal clashes taking place during breaks between sessions of the congress, in Saint George's Hall[8] and in the corridors. In short, wherever two people belonging to opposing camps encountered each other a debate flared up.

Stalin, Bukharin, and Rykov[9] spoke for the line of the Central Committee, that is, Stalin's line. That's putting it crudely, but that's how people talked—the line of the Central Committee was one thing, and the line of the opposition was another. One delegation—I forget which party organization it was from—presented the presiding committee of the congress with a steel broom.[10] Rykov took the broom and said: "I am handing this broom to Comrade Stalin. May he use it to sweep away all our enemies." This was received with friendly applause and laughter, and even Rykov smiled on that occasion. A little while later Rykov himself became a victim of this broom, and I remember his words and how they were spoken then. Evidently Rykov trusted Stalin and never thought the broom might be turned against the party to do it harm; he thought it would be used only against the anti-party renegades, the opposition, which had deviated from the general line.

We had no doubts then that Stalin, and those who had gathered around Stalin and were supporting him, were correct. Even today I think that our ideological struggle then was fundamentally correct. If Stalin's personality had been different, these disagreements, which reached such a white-hot pitch of intensity, might not have become so tragic and fatal. I am speaking this way now, but back then such questions did not arise for us. Back then, the saying was: "When you chop wood, chips fly." In other words, a merciless struggle was being waged against the opposition.

If we look back over the path traveled by our party and people and evaluate Stalin's role at that time in the light of the path we have traveled, viewing his role against the background of those events and the balance of forces at the time, it comes out to be essentially positive. I have in mind his role in fighting against such opposition groups as the Trotskyists, the supporters of Zinoviev, and the Right-Left Bloc of Syrtsov and Lominadze.[11] If we are to evaluate Stalin's personal role, we can say that he really distinguished himself. His role and activity in rallying the party, mobilizing its forces to overcome difficulties, restore industry and agriculture, and move toward industrialization and the building up of the Red Army—these were decisive things. And so it is not accidental that Stalin occupied the leading place in the party and that the party supported him. It must be kept in mind also that in the early years of the revolution his name was not widely known among the broad masses or even within the party itself. Zinoviev, Kamenev, and especially Bukharin were much more popular. Lenin was right when he said: "Bukharchik is the favorite of all the party."[12] Our cadres learned Marxism-Leninism from the *ABC of Communism* written by Bukharin. Bukharin's popularity among the broad masses was great. Nevertheless, preference went to Stalin as an organizer, while Bukharin held a prominent place in the party as a propagandist and agitator. He was the editor of *Pravda,* and he really was the kind of editor *Pravda* needed. He organized the dissemination of Marxist doctrine to a very wide audience. Although, as Lenin said, Bukharin also made mistakes.

1. That is, the main report to the congress on behalf of the Central Committee. [GS]

2. Ya. A. Yakovlev. See Biographies.

3. The Workers' and Peasants' Inspection was an agency tasked with checking up on the work of government departments. [SS]

4. "Sergo" was the nickname of G. K. Ordzhonikidze (see Biographies).

5. This newspaper made its first appearance in 1918. In 1922 it was the publication of the Yuzovka district committee of the RCP(B) and of the district executive committee.

6. A. Ye. Badayev. See Biographies.

7. K. I. Nikolayeva. See Biographies.

8. Saint George's (Georgiyevsky) Hall was a hall in the Great Kremlin Palace in the Kremlin, named after Saint George the Dragon Slayer. The

name also honored all those who had been decorated with the Order of Saint George. [SK/SS]

9. A. I. Rykov. See Biographies.

10. It was a delegation representing 6,000 Stalingrad metalworkers.

11. S. I. Syrtsov and V. V. Lominadze. See Biographies.

12. This statement appeared in a document written by Lenin in December 1922 and January 1923, shortly before a stroke removed him from political activity; his death followed a year later, in January 1924. The document, together with several other letters and articles of the same time, represented his last political action, which became known as Lenin's "Testament." "Bukharchik" was an affectionate nickname for Bukharin. For more on Lenin's "Testament," see below, p. 637 n. 49. [GS/SS]

## THE MOVE TO KHARKOV

In 1928 I was transferred to work in Kharkov. The government of Ukraine and the Central Committee of the CP(B)U had their offices there at that time. I was confirmed as deputy head of the organizational department of the Central Committee, a department headed by Nikolai Nestorovich Demchenko,[1] who I respected greatly. And he deserved it. He also died before his time, perishing at the hands of Stalin, even though he was completely devoted to the party's general line, to the Central Committee, and to Stalin personally.

Why was I transferred to Kharkov? After Moiseyenko, at our request, was relieved of his duties as secretary of the Yuzovka party organization, a man named Stroganov[2] came to us to serve as the secretary of our district committee. He himself was from the Nizhny Novgorod[3] party organization and had been a member of the party since 1905. He wasn't a bad person, but somewhat limited. He didn't meet the needs being placed on Stalino, which was large, militant, and diverse, a major industrial region. We had not only the coal industry and metallurgy and chemistry there but also the construction industry and agriculture. In short, Stalino was a major center, above all an industrial center but also an agricultural one to no small degree. Stroganov turned out to be too minor a figure. We received him very politely and, so to speak, tested and probed him from all sides and sniffed out how he would be, considering he was an Old Bolshevik. Later people spoke cuttingly about him, saying that although he was an Old Bolshevik, he was also an old worn-out shoe—even though he was actually not that old. He loved to drink, and he drank pretty heavily. Then he began to get involved in intrigues. In short, he didn't fit in right, and a situation arose in which the active party members began ignoring him, which thereby placed me in a rather difficult position: I was merely his deputy, but on all major questions people came to see me and not him.

I understood why, but this was difficult for me and humiliating for him. People came to see me because I had grown up in the region; my father had worked at the Uspenskaya mine, four versts south of Yuzovka. I had spent my childhood and my youth there, and I had learned the machinist's trade there at the Bosse[4] factory. I had a very large circle of friends. We had spent our childhood and youth together and worked together in the mines. By that time I knew my way around pretty well on questions of production—in the coal industry, chemical industry, metallurgical industry, and construction. Such things were our main concern then. In those days a leader who didn't know his way around on matters of coal production, metallurgy, the chemical industry, and construction was considered, to put it crudely, an idiot. That was precisely the position Stroganov found himself in, although as a man he was not stupid. He too later perished, poor fellow, and I felt sorry for him then, and I still feel sorry for him. He didn't deserve to be arrested and shot, as he was.

Kaganovich, who was first secretary of the Central Committee of the CP(B)U, asked me to come to the offices of the Central Committee, and there he proposed that I transfer to work in Kharkov in the organizational department of the Central Committee. The motivation he gave for this proposal was that there were very few working-class people in the Central Committee apparatus. He was right about that. There were a great many people of highly varied backgrounds with not much of a record as workers. And at that time a lot of importance was placed on the social origin of officials who held party and government posts. "We need to proletarianize our apparatus," he said.

I said: "I consider that to be correct, but I would like to see it proletarianized without me. I'm very reluctant to leave Stalino. I'm well rooted in the general situation and circumstances, and very attached to Stalino and the people there. So leaving would be very difficult for me. I wouldn't know the new situation, and I wouldn't be able, it seems to me, to accustom myself to the organizational department of the Central Committee and get along well there."

But I did know the situation [in the CC organizational department]. After all I was the head of the organizational department of the district committee and consequently had attended many meetings of the organizational department of the CP(B)U Central Committee; and organizational-department officials from the Central Committee had come to visit us to investigate certain cases or for other purposes. I knew many of them, and I agreed with Kaganovich that some of these people deserved little confidence; many of them didn't even deserve respect, even if there were no grounds for lack of confidence in them. And so I felt that I would be unwelcome in Kharkov. In the Central Committee of the CP(B)U, there was an envious attitude toward Stalino, and indeed the Stalino party organization had a strong sense of its place in the party and therefore perhaps gave some grounds for this envy. After all, the way we felt was this—we were proletarians; we were miners, metalworkers, chemical industry workers, the salt of the earth and the salt of the party.

I requested that if I had to leave Stalino (to give Stroganov an opportunity to develop and not interfere with his becoming the central figure, so that people would recognize him and go to him first, as the primary leader of the district party organization), I should be sent to Lugansk.[5] I don't remember now the last name of the secretary of the Lugansk district committee of the party, but I liked him a lot. He and I were on very good terms, and so I would have been happy to go there. That's why I requested that I be sent to Lugansk. I would have liked working as secretary of another district party committee. Evidently such work was available there. Kaganovich said to me: "If you put the question that way, then there's no need for us and the Central Committee to have you leave Yuzovka. So stay where you are."

I said goodbye and left. Then I began thinking, and I came to the conclusion that if the Central Committee had made me a proposal like this—to work as deputy head of the organizational department of the CP(B)U Central Committee, quite a high position, all in all—then evidently there were some weighty considerations that had prompted Kaganovich to make this proposal.

Kaganovich had a very good attitude toward me. He and I had become acquainted in the first days of the February revolution. He was also working in Yuzovka then, and he spoke at the first mass rally that was held in Yuzovka, and I was there, too. [Earlier,] as a representative of the workers' deputies of the Rutchenkovo mines, I had taken part in a rally at the first district conference [of workers' Soviets], held in Bakhmut (our district's capital city). Then for a second time, a week or two later, we gathered in Yuzovka, and that's where I met Kaganovich. He was there as a representative from the Yuzovka party organization and conducted himself fairly energetically at those meetings and conferences. He was using the name Kosherovich then.[6] I didn't even know that his real name was Kaganovich; I knew him only as Kosherovich. Not only did I have a lot of confidence in Kaganovich, but, as we used to say, I supported him 100 percent.

Kaganovich was not yet a generally recognized party leader then (let alone one of the top chiefs of the party). His relations with the collective membership of the CP(B)U Central Committee were very complicated. The so-called oldsters [the veteran party members] were waging a struggle against him—that is, Petrovsky, Chubar, and others. The Yekaterinoslav group, where Grigory Ivanovich Petrovsky's influence was strong, did not recognize Kaganovich's authority. Actually the Donbas was the base of Kaganovich's support, primarily Stalino, Lugansk, and Artyomovsk (formerly Bakhmut). In Bakhmut it was not so much that confidence was placed directly in Kaganovich, but in Radchenko,[7] who in turn supported Kaganovich. The party secretary in Bakhmut was Nikitenko, and he was very close to Radchenko. As for Radchenko, he was chairman of the Council of Trade Unions of Ukraine. He himself was a worker, a man with a lot of authority, a member of the party, it seems, since 1912, and he too died before his time. Although Radchenko was a leader who sometimes engaged in intrigue, he was an honest man, and there could be no doubt about his devotion to the cause of the party. The intrigues he engaged in had to do with particular individuals, not with the party as a whole or its general line.

So then after my conversation with Kaganovich, after weighing everything carefully, I no longer wanted to remain in Stalino, because I saw that bad relations could develop between Stroganov and me, and I didn't want any conflict with him. He had just been sent to Stalino, and he didn't yet know industry there, but he could get to know it. That was no reason to withhold respect from him. I concluded that it would be better for me to leave and let him put down roots there. So I told Kaganovich that I was agreeable to being transferred to the organizational department of the CP(B)U CC, but on the condition that they send me to work at the first opportunity out in some district, and it didn't matter to me which one, except that I'd prefer an industrial district. As I saw it I didn't know much about agriculture and had never worked in agricultural regions; rather, I had continually been linked with industry and I felt at home in that sphere.

I began work at the new location. As I had anticipated, I didn't like the work very much in Kharkov. It was office work. What with all the piles of paper, you never got to see real life. That's a specialized kind of work, but I'm a man of the soil; I like concrete practical activity, coal, metal, the chemical industry, and to some extent agriculture. In Stalino agriculture was not the main thing; the main thing for us there was coal. Coal is the bread and butter of industry, and that's where we focused our main attention. I was on good terms with the leadership in the coal industry. Rukhimovich[8] was in charge of it then. I had a lot of respect for him. (He too died before his time; he was shot.) I was also on good terms with the leader of Yugostal[9] (officially that was the Ministry of Ferrous Metallurgy of the South), which was located in Kharkov. It seems that Ivanov[10] was in charge of it then. I didn't know him as well as I knew Rukhimovich because Rukhimovich never held a conference of coal industry workers or economic management officials without my participation. He always invited me, and I attended as a representative of the party's district committee. And suddenly all of this was interrupted, and I found myself occupied with paperwork. And that was a kind of food I didn't like. It immediately repelled me. I went to see Kaganovich on this matter once or twice and began to remind him that he had promised to help me get away from that kind of work.

1. N. N. Demchenko. See Biographies.
2. V. A. Stroganov. See Biographies.
3. Nizhny Novgorod is a city about 300 kilometers due east of Moscow. [SS]
4. A metal factory built initially with French capital.
5. Lugansk is a city in eastern Ukraine, situated north of the Donbas. [SS]
6. Under the pseudonym of Boris Kosherovich he worked at the footwear factory of the New-

Russia Society and took part in the activity of the local Bolshevik organization.
7. A. F. Radchenko. See Biographies.
8. M. L. Rukhimovich, See Biographies.
9. The combine Yugostal (South Steel) was created in 1921 as the leading state organization for management of metallurgical factories and coal mines in the south of the country.
10. S. N. Ivanov was an engineering, economic, and party official.

## THE MOVE TO KIEV

One day Kaganovich called me up and said: "You've been asking me to transfer you to party work in some other district. If you're not opposed, I would suggest Kiev to you. A decision has been made that Comrade Demchenko will go to Kiev as secretary of the district committee there, and Demchenko is asking that you be allowed to go there, too, to head the organizational department of the Kiev district committee under him. If you agree, you can get a ticket literally this very day (it was a Sunday) and make the trip to Kiev. All of this is already known there; Demchencko knows, and he'll be happy to welcome you."

I agreed without even stopping to think. Among us at that time the Kiev organization was not considered a militant proletarian organization. Kiev was reputed to have a strong Ukrainian nationalist tendency, and that really was the case. The proletariat was weak there, and the intelligentsia was grouped around the Ukrainian Academy of Sciences. Hrushevsky[1] headed the intelligentsia then. The Trotskyist organization was also strong there. It was considered that it would be difficult to work there, especially for a Russian. People's attitudes toward Russians were not especially good then. And so I presumed the nationalists would consider me a hopeless "Rusak."[2] Things would be difficult there for me.

Nevertheless I immediately bought a ticket and made the trip to Kiev that very evening. By morning I was already there. This was the first time in my life I had been in Kiev, a very large city. Before that, strictly speaking, and not counting Moscow, I had seen only Kharkov, Yekaterinoslav, and Mariupol.[3] I'm not mentioning Bakhmut here, and as for Yuzovka, it was not yet considered a city, just a town. Kiev made a strong impression on me. As soon as I arrived I went to the shores of the Dnieper River[4] with my suitcase still in my hand, because I had heard so much about it and read a fair amount about it. I wanted to see this mighty river.

Together with Demchenko I began my party work in Kiev. The chairman of the Executive Committee of the Soviets of Kiev province was Voitse-khovsky. He also died before his time; he too was shot. He was a man with a considerable residue of Ukrainian nationalism about him. Earlier he had belonged to the Social Democratic organization in Ukraine, but he was an honorable and respectable person. A soft and easygoing man, he was a pol-ished intellectual, but quite a pleasant individual and a very diligent worker. In Kiev he was very much at home. Demchenko had studied at a medical school but had not graduated. He had been a member of the party since 1916, and his leanings were not especially toward the workers; he was much more inclined toward the intellectuals and occupied himself with the affairs of the Academy of Sciences. Later he was assigned by the CP(B)U CC to work with the Communist Party of Western Ukraine (or as the Ukrainians called it, Zakhidna Ukraina), that is, the Lvov[5] region, Ternopol[6] region, and so forth. That was a big political job and I thought he handled it well.

That's how I ended up in Kiev. A huge amount of ongoing local internal work—both with industrial workers and with the rural regions—was piled on me. I must confess that it's very pleasant for me to recall those times now. The work went easily and well for me. The Kievans' attitude toward me was one of great confidence and, I would even say, respect. There were also difficulties; there were a lot of unemployed people, something we didn't encounter in the Donbas region. The year was 1928, and in Kiev unemployed workers demonstrated, marching down the streets carrying the red banner. We brought them together in an old building of the Kiev City Duma,[7] where there was a meeting hall that would fit four or five hundred people, and there they held a rally. Mensheviks and Socialist Revolutionaries were still active, and there were many Ukrainian nationalists. Trotskyist influence was also strong, and the Trotskyists were taking advantage of the difficulties that existed in Kiev.

These unemployed people were fairly characteristic [of Kiev], because unemployment in Ukraine in general didn't exist then; in fact there was a shortage of workers; but in Kiev there were a lot of unemployed people, even Communists. They had gone without work for years. When I would propose to them: "Please, I can find work for you right away," they would seem to be overjoyed.

They would ask: "Where?"

I would say: "In the Donbas."

"No," they would say, "we'll keep looking." And so for an entire year they
would hunt for work, and it seemed they were ready to keep at it for another
year or two. But they didn't want to go to the Donbas. That would be going
out into the provinces. That's where the mine workers were, and they
weren't inclined toward that kind of labor. I felt indignant over this because
I had spent my childhood there. For me the Donbas and Yuzovka were my
native element and I longed to be among the miners; I had grown attached
to them.

I spent the whole of 1928 working in Kiev. In 1929 my thirty-fifth year was
already knocking at the door. That was the last year in which I could still
even think about entering an institution of higher education. Meanwhile I
had graduated only from a workers' school and I kept feeling a great yearning
to obtain a higher education. Therefore I began trying to arrange to be sent
away to study.

1. Mikhailo S. Hrushevsky was a Ukrainian
historian, literary critic, and statesman who played
a central role in the rise of the Ukrainian national
movement. See Biographies.

2. A pejorative Ukrainian term for a Russian.
[GS]

3. Mariupol is situated on the Sea of Azov in
eastern Ukraine, south of Donetsk. [SS]

4. The Dnieper River is the main river of
Ukraine. It flows south through Kiev, then south-
east to Dnipropetrovsk, and empties into the
Black Sea. [SS]

5. Lvov is the main city of western Ukraine.
Lvov is the Russian form. The Ukrainian form is
Lviv, the Polish form Lwow, and the German form
Lemberg. [SS]

6. This town was known as Tarnopol until
1944, when it was renamed Ternopol. The Ukrainian form is Ternopil. The town is situated east of
Lvov in western Ukraine.

7. Later this building was to house the Kiev
City Teacher's House.

## AT THE INDUSTRIAL ACADEMY

I ran into opposition about going to study. By then Kaganovich had already
gone to Moscow to work at the Central Committee, and Kosior[1] had been
sent to take his place in Ukraine. The opinion in Kiev was that I was someone close to Kaganovich (and that actually was the case) and that therefore I
was leaving because I didn't want to deal with Kosior, among other things—
that I didn't want to work with him and give him support. That wasn't so. I
didn't know Kosior very well, but I respected him. In his character Kosior
was rather mild and easygoing, a pleasant person and an intelligent one. I
would say that in his relations with people, he was superior to Kaganovich,
but as an organizer he was not as good. Kaganovich was a more precise and

more energetic person. He was a real whirlwind. He might even chop wood, as the saying went, but he would carry out the task set by the Central Committee. He was more of a go-getter than Kosior.

I thought it was necessary to go to Kharkov and explain myself to Kosior. I told him: "I am already thirty-five years old. I want to study. Please try to grasp what I am saying. I am asking the Central Committee of the CP(B)U to understand and support me, and I am asking that the Central Committee recommend me for admission to the Industrial Academy. I want to be a metallurgist." Kosior took an understanding attitude toward my request and agreed. When the question of my leaving was raised, Demchenko was very hurt and upset, and for a long time he tried to persuade me not to go, although he too took an understanding attitude toward the fact that a person wanted to get a higher education. That's when I saw and felt what attitude people really had toward me.

When I raised the question of going away to study and asked that I be relieved the decision was not made all at once. After a session of the Central Committee Bureau several comrades came to see me and said: "Do you really want to go study or is it perhaps that things aren't working out between Demchenko and you? Tell us frankly." They said this in a way that hinted they would support me if things weren't working out between Demchenko and me and that our relations were turning out badly.

I replied: "No, I would like you to understand me correctly. The relations between Demchenko and me are of the best. With a man like Demchenko I would be willing to work on and on indefinitely, but I want to get a higher education."

They said: "Well, that's different. In that case we'll support you." And at the next session the appropriate resolution was adopted.

I left for Moscow. There too, I ran into difficulties, because I didn't have a long enough record of working in leading positions in economic management. The comrades at the Industrial Academy said that I didn't meet their criteria, and they recommended that I go take courses in Marxism-Leninism sponsored by the party's Central Committee. They said: "This educational institution has been established for people who are going to be managers and directors." I had no option but to trouble Kaganovich (who was then a secretary of the Central Committee) and ask that the CC support me. I fought to achieve what I wanted. Kaganovich supported me, and thus in the end I did become a student at the Industrial Academy.

I found a place then in a dormitory on Pokrovka Street, building No. 40. That building is still standing, though I don't know what it's used for now.

For those days it was a good dormitory with a system of corridors and individual rooms. In short, the conditions were ideal. The classroom building of the Industrial Academy was located on Novo-Basmannaya Street, which was not far away. I didn't need to take a streetcar, but went by foot across the Zemlyanoi Wall and then straight through an alley where, as I recall, the House of Old Bolsheviks was located, then I turned left onto Novo-Basmannaya. This route took only a few minutes, so that I got a little exercise every day.

I began my studies at the Academy. The people there were very diverse, both in their commitment to the party and their general level of preparedness. Many had completed nothing more than rural elementary school and knew only the four operations of arithmetic; on the other hand there were people who had secondary education. I had come there, having completed studies at a workers' school, which was considered secondary education. Our group of students—as it had been selected—was fairly strong, but we had one or two comrades who lagged behind in mathematics, and they held us back. These were adults, and they were persistent; a teacher didn't have to insist that they study harder; instead, the students themselves demanded that the teacher do his job. But everything takes time. A student might not have been called up to the blackboard, but he would go up there on his own initiative and torment the teacher because he couldn't understand this or that mathematical formula. The rest of us would be sitting there and getting angry because this was holding us up; the student was struggling over something that for us was already a bygone stage.

That's the way it was in 1929. But when I came back to the Academy in fall 1930 I encountered a different situation: a great many people had shown up at the Academy who didn't especially want to learn, but because of the political conditions that had arisen they felt forced to leave their party or trade union work or their activity in economic management. And so they were crawling all over the higher educational institutions. The Industrial Academy became a place where people could find refuge, where they could sit things out for a while, because the stipend received by the students was excellent, the food at the dining hall wasn't bad, and the dormitory was all right. Everyone had a room, and some people who had been big shots in economic management even had the possibility of obtaining two rooms and setting themselves up there with their families.

Kuibyshev,[2] chairman of the State Planning Commission,[3] was acting as patron of the Industrial Academy. Well, what could be higher than that? He was a respected and influential person who really gave support to the Industrial Academy. That was a period of sharp struggle against the "Rights."[4] The

"Rights" were seriously spreading and intensifying their activity. They included Rykov, Bukharin, and Uglanov [who were top party leaders].[5] They were waging a battle and a very strong one. The leadership of the party cell at the Academy was controlled by the "Rights." Khakharev[6] was secretary of the party cell, a fairly influential person with a prerevolutionary record in the party going back, it seems to me, to 1906 or 1907. He was from Nizhny Novgorod and was well known as a person who had worked in the underground. Grouped around him was what you might call the Old Guard. But it had been defeated. After all, it had come out against the party's general line. It grouped itself around Bukharin and supported him, Uglanov, and Rykov against Stalin and against the party's Central Committee.

We had come there from the south. There was a fairly large group of us from the same home region [in the south] (people from the Donbas, Dnepropetrovsk, Lugansk, Artyomovsk, and Kharkov). We took our stand in support of the positions of the Central Committee. A fight broke out, and I too was drawn into that fight on a fairly active basis. I was supported mainly at that time by Tabakov. (Later he too perished, although he was innocent; he too was shot.) By nationality he was Jewish, and a very good Communist. I got to know him when he was director of a trust and later an association of enterprises for the production of ceramic goods for the metallurgy industry. The Krasnogorovsky factory for the production of firebrick for lining blast furnaces and open-hearth furnaces was located in the Donbas, and Tabakov was engaged in that work. I had established good contacts with him, he had relied on the Yuzovka organization, and here we were at the Academy very much bound together. We had the same point of view on party matters, and other comrades supported us, for example, Alliluyev from the Far East. It seems that he is still alive today, retired and on a pension. (This Alliluyev is no relation to the Alliluyev who was Stalin's father-in-law, despite the same last name.) We had other comrades there, and it was a fairly large group, but still we were in the minority. It might seem that I am digressing. People might wonder what this has to do with the main subject of my memoirs. After all my intention was to talk about Stalin and his role. But this does have direct bearing on that subject.

At the Industrial Academy a fierce battle was being fought for the general line of the Central Committee against the "Rights," the Zinoviev supporters, and then the Right-Left bloc of Syrtsov and Lominadze.[7] In this struggle my role in the collective stood out sharply, and all of this could be seen by the Central Committee. So my name came to the fore as an active party member heading a group of Communists who were waging a struggle against the supporters of Uglanov, Rykov, and Zinoviev and against the Trotskyists at the Industrial Academy. The political battle that went on was very sharp and intense. After all, most of those at the Academy were party members with prerevolutionary records, and it must be said it was a very solid group, with influential people in it. For example, I remember a Comrade Makarov[8] from the Donbas. He had been the director of the Yuzovka [metallurgical] works. He himself was from Nizhny Novgorod and had been a member of the party since 1905. He was an intelligent and highly respected comrade. He didn't officially state that he agreed with the "Rights," but he supported them and never uttered a peep against them. Evidently he had come to some sort of agreement or arrangement with the "Rights" that he would conduct himself in a rather concealed manner, not reveal himself as a supporter of the opposition. He was usually thought to support the "general line" of the party, but in fact by his actions he helped to strengthen the Uglanov-Bukharin-Rykov group.

The ferocity of the struggle can be shown by the following example. It took us an entire session one day to elect the presiding committee for the general meeting of our party organization, and the meeting itself could not be started until the following day. I remember how my comrades kept proposing my candidacy for the presiding committee, but two or three times I lost the vote and never was elected. During this voting for the presiding committee, all the candidates had to go to the rostrum and give an account of their political biographies. Anyone whose record as a party member began after the revolution was, in effect, already doomed. That's the kind of struggle that took place. There was a special way of electing the bureau that ran the affairs of the party cell. I was nominated several times, but we were unable to carry my candidacy through in any way. Finally I was elected to the inspection commission, but the truth is that later I lost the vote there again. In general at that time there was very frequent voting to reelect the bureau of the party cell; because such a fierce fight was under way, the people kept changing.

The newspaper *Pravda* frequently spoke out against the "Rights," and as a rule, after each such article in *Pravda* another general party meeting would be called and it would elect a new bureau. But the "Rights" adjusted themselves in such a way that when Khakharev was no longer able to remain secretary of the party organization at the Industrial Academy, Levochkin was nominated. He was from Bryansk.[9] He was a less notable figure, but in essence he too was a "Right" and so the line of the bureau directing the party cell continued in support of the "Rights" even after these new elections. Once again an article appeared in *Pravda*. Another stormy meeting was held, and it took a long time to elect a presiding committee, but finally I was elected to it. I became chairman of the general meeting of the party organization at the Industrial Academy, which in effect was the general meeting for the Academy as a whole, because all the people at the Academy were party members. The meeting proceeded in a very stormy atmosphere. The impetus for this election came from certain events that I will now describe.

This was in 1930. The party was getting ready for its Sixteenth Congress. Meetings to hear official reports from the leadership were being held in the local areas. Once again a wide-ranging, deep-going debate began. The "Rights," in order to remove me from participation in the debate before the election of delegates to the district party conference, thought up the following maneuver. We were sponsoring a collective farm named after Stalin in Samara[10] province and were raising funds so that the collective farm could buy agricultural equipment. The bureau of the party cell decided to send delegates to deliver the equipment to the collective farmers. Of course this "delivery of equipment" was purely symbolic because we didn't actually take machines there with us. We simply knew the price of these machines and were going to announce that we had raised such-and-such an amount of money so that this or that piece of agricultural equipment (a sower, a combine, and so forth) could be purchased, and we were delivering this amount to the party organization of the collective farm named after Stalin. A delegation was chosen to make this trip. It consisted of two people, Sasha Zdobnov[11] and me. Zdobnov was also a student at the Industrial Academy. He was from the Urals and a good comrade. (It seems that he, too, perished in the mass slaughter, the "meat grinder" of 1937.)

Along the way I read a pamphlet explaining what a combine was. We arrived, held a meeting, and stayed there several days. That's when I found out about the real situation in the countryside. Previously in practical terms I simply couldn't imagine the situation, because we were living in isolation at the Industrial Academy, and we had no idea what the real life experience was then in the villages, what they were going through. We went there and encountered a situation of literal starvation. People were moving around slowly, like flies in the autumn, because of malnourishment. I remember [we attended] a general meeting of the collective farmers. We spoke through a translator the whole time, because the ethnic composition of the population at that collective farm turned out to be Chuvash,[12] and all of them with one voice were begging us to give them bread. The machinery didn't make much of an impression on them. These people were starving. This was the first time I had seen such a thing. They put us up in the home of some widow. She was so poor she didn't even have bread. What we had brought along with us for the trip was the only thing we had to eat, and we shared that with the widow.

We finished up our job there and returned to Moscow, and at that time party conferences of the Moscow districts were already under way. Our party organization elected about ten people or more; I don't remember exactly how many. The number of students at the Industrial Academy was large, and the number of people per elected delegate was small at that time, because the Moscow party organization, compared with its present-day numbers, was also relatively small. Among those elected from the Industrial Academy to the district conference were Stalin, Rykov, and Bukharin. I don't remember whether Uglanov was elected. It seems to me he was not, because his candidacy was the most odious [to the Stalin leadership]. As for Bukharin and Rykov, they were elected because they were members of the Politburo. As we saw it, the "Rights" had carried out a well thought-out and clever move, getting Rykov and Bukharin elected at the conference specifically by our organization without of course declaring that they were acting in behalf of the "Rights." People had proposed that leaders of the party should be elected to the district conference in the name of our party organization, and they specified the three candidates: Stalin, Rykov, and Bukharin. At that time Bukharin and Rykov still had such high status that their candidacies could not have been bluntly rejected. After all, they were members of the Politburo. And so it wasn't possible to speak in support of Stalin while rejecting Rykov and Bukharin. That evidently would not have found support within the Politburo at that time. Some Academy students who supported the "Rights" were also elected.

Tabakov, my closest comrade, told me about this, and we candidly exchanged opinions, he and I, on all political questions. He was a fairly well developed person and well trained in political respects. Late one night the phone rang, and I was called to the phone. This was unusual because I had no acquaintances in Moscow. When I went to the phone, a voice said: "This is Mekhlis,[13] the editor of *Pravda,* speaking. Can you come to see me at the editorial offices?"

I said I could.

He said: "Then get ready now and I'll send a car for you. Come right away. I have some business to take up with you."

I answered: "All right."

Within a few minutes a car was outside the dormitory of the Industrial Academy. I got in and we went to the *Pravda* offices. This was my first acquaintance with Mekhlis. He read me a short letter from the Industrial Academy, which told about the political machinations that had been arranged to elect a delegation of "Rights" from the party organization at the Academy. Everyone knew that the absolute majority of those studying at the Industrial Academy in Moscow were Old Bolsheviks,[14] former directors of factories, plants, and industrial associations. They were receiving training and retraining there to raise their technical qualifications. Mekhlis read the text of this letter and asked: "Do you agree with the content of this correspondence?"

I said: "I was not there then."

He said: "I know that you weren't there, but is this memo accurate?"

I said: "I agree completely that it reflects reality."

He said: "Could you sign it?"

I said: "How do you mean, Could I sign it? I'm not the one who wrote it, and I don't know the author."

He said: "No, no, your name wouldn't figure in the matter, and there won't even be an author indicated. I have confidence in you. I've heard about you and the positions you've taken. If you sign it, that means the situation really is reflected truthfully in this note, the situation that has developed in the Industrial Academy party organization."

I said, "All right," and I signed it. He immediately took me back in his own car to the dormitory at the Industrial Academy.

The next day *Pravda* came out with this correspondence. It was a bolt from the blue. The whole Academy began to boil and bubble, classes were called off, and all the organizers of party groups at the Academy demanded a meeting. Levochkin, the secretary of the party organization, was forced to hold a meeting.

The party cell split. Most of the managerial types[15] who were studying at the Academy were apolitical, and some of them were simply dubious elements. I knew some of them; they were our own people from Donetsk. They came over to me and said: "Why are you starting a squabble? What do you need this for?"

I answered: "Listen, you don't understand a thing. We're dealing with the 'Rights' here. What direction do you think they're taking you in?" And they really didn't understand what the devil it was all about, who the so-called "Rights" were and who was on the "Left."

This was the stormiest meeting of all. I was elected to the presiding committee, and I became the chairman of the meeting. The group that supported the positions of the Central Committee and was waging a battle against the "Rights" really became activated at this point. That meant we were fighting against the leadership of our organization, because for the most part they were "Rights." I don't remember how long that session went on. It ended with all the delegates being recalled except for Stalin. This included Rykov and Bukharin and representatives of our party organization. After that we elected new delegates, including myself, to the district party conference.

I was elected to the bureau of the party organization (I don't remember by how large a majority) and I also became secretary of the party organization. We then developed a very energetic campaign of struggle against the "Rights." The word spread around Moscow that a big fight was going on at the Industrial Academy. Yes, it was a fight, a very intense battle, but we "restored order." Our party cell ended up taking a strong position in support of the Central Committee, and that meant in support of Stalin, the general secretary of the Central Committee and the main leader of the country.

It was through this activity of mine at the Industrial Academy evidently that I got to know Stalin. Stalin was of course impressed that our party organization supported him. Actually we didn't talk that way then; we merely spoke in defense of the general line of the party. And even today I think it was correct to support the line whose main proponent then was Stalin.

As I have already indicated, Stalin heard about me precisely when I was a student at the Industrial Academy. It was precisely then that the "Rights" of Moscow and Gorky[16] had been routed, and they had all come to the Industrial Academy. And so it was a kind of incubator for the "Rights," a breeding ground for microbes of right-wing orientation. They held fairly strong positions there. For example, there was Pakharov from Nizhny Novgorod, a party member since 1903, as I recall. He was a very decent person. I had known him as a factory director, because he was the head of the Yuzovka metallurgical works when I returned from the Red Army. Then there was Korshunov, who among other things was a good friend of Molotov[17] and used to get together with him on their days off. But this venture undertaken by the right-wing bureau of the party organization fell flat on its face. They had sent me off as a representative of the party organization of the Academy to the collective farm to eliminate the possibility of my being elected to the district party conference and to avoid the possibility of my speaking at the conference. Instead this group suffered a catastrophe. All of its representatives were recalled, and supporters of the general line of the Central Committee of the AUCP(B) were elected to the party conference of the Bauman district.

This all happened so fast that the documents authorizing us to attend the district conference that were received and distributed among the newly elected delegates had been made out to the previous delegates. I also went to that conference with a document belonging to someone else. When they began to check documents, they said that my document belonged to someone else. I answered: "Yes, it was written out in his name, but I am the one it was for." Things worked out all right, because the party organization of the Bauman district already knew about everything. But the incident involving this document with which I arrived at the conference ended up being the cause of a joke.

In the Bauman district committee of the party, not everyone had taken a sufficiently clear-cut position. The secretary there was a man named Shirin.[18] It's hard for me to say whether he was actually a "Right" or simply a passive person who was not politically mature enough and not politically active enough. When he came to visit us at the Academy he met with no respect; people wouldn't even let him speak. Then a man named Tsikhon[19] came, an authoritative individual, people's commissar of labor, who had previously been secretary of the Bauman district committee (later he too perished; they shot him too), and we wouldn't let him speak either. He said: "Listen, I've had dealings with construction workers, and even among them there was less disorder than there is here among you, and after all you are Academy students."

In short, the Bauman district organization was not particularly militant, but I didn't consider it an opposition organization that supported the "Rights." We came to an agreement among the delegates that I would speak at the conference and present our position so that no one would think that we had elected any "Rights." I should add that when I spoke I was greeted rather coldly by the conference. I had already been elected secretary of the party organization of the Academy by then. That's why I was the one to speak, so that the district party conference would know that the Industrial Academy party organization was taking a firm stand for the general line of the party and that the election of "Rights" had been a trap laid by the former party leadership at the Academy, which sympathized with the "Rights" and which now had lost the confidence of the party membership and been voted out of office.

During my speech, disapproving voices could be heard, saying things like, "Yeah, we know what the Industrial Academy is." It had developed a bad reputation in the sense of its line within the party. So I had to demonstrate that the delegates who had made these negative remarks did of course have grounds for withholding their confidence, but I asserted that the delegation now present at the district party conference reflected a different point of view from the delegates who had been elected earlier and that we now stood firmly on party positions (in support of the party's general line, the usual way of stating it in those days). Then the party conference began to trust us.

After that my name began to be better known in the Moscow party organization and the Central Committee. Strictly speaking, that is what determined my subsequent fate as a party official. As I learned later, my fate was also predetermined by the fact that Nadya Alliluyeva, Stalin's wife, was studying at the Industrial Academy at the same time I was. Until I was elected secretary, I had not known that she was also a student there with us. But she observed this whole struggle firsthand, and when she went home she probably informed Stalin about it. Of course she also told him about other people. There was Vorobyov,[20] a gallant young fellow from the Komsomol. He stopped just short of calling Stalin "Nicholas the Bludgeon."[21] In general Vorobyov cursed Stalin in every possible way. In our understanding at the time, this was a crime. We considered this kind of talk a direct attack on the party. It was only later, after many decades, that we understood that this characterization was accurate and that this nickname actually fit Stalin very well.

In general the Bauman conference proceeded amid great tumult. I didn't attend the first several sessions. I didn't yet have my credentials then, but I was told about this later. Lenin's widow, Nadezhda Konstantinovna Krupskaya,[22] spoke at that conference, and her speech was not well received. Her speeches then didn't fit in properly with the party's general line, and many people said, especially in discussions in the corridors, that they condemned what she had said. Of course I too supported that kind of position back then. I and others had an ambivalent feeling: on the one hand, we had respect for Nadezhda Konstantinovna as Lenin's companion in arms and the person closest to him; on the other hand, when she spoke she didn't support Stalin. Much later I began to evaluate this quite differently. That was mainly after Stalin's death when I began to view Stalin's activity differently and to make a different assessment of him as a leader and as an individual. It seems that Nadezhda Konstantinovna in her own way at that time had been absolutely correct. But the party conference didn't understand her. It didn't receive her speech warmly, but rather condemned it.

That's how my activity as a party official began. Shortly after [the conference], I was elected to the party's Bauman district committee. That happened in January 1931, but the conference had been held, it seems to me, in July 1930. It was then that I got to know Bulganin.[23] (He was the director of Elektrozavod [the Electric Works], a famous electric plant located in the Bauman district. [The plant produced light bulbs and other electrical items.]) A party conference was going on in Moscow, and I was placed on the commission whose task was to check up on the party organization at Elektrozavod. In those days people who had long records as party members (in my case it was since 1918) were brought in to carry out these verification procedures, and there were not enough such people for all of Moscow. We were not especially eager to do that kind of thing, because it took us away from our studies. Bulganin himself didn't go through this checking-up process. He was out of the country at the time, and only after he returned did we [of the commission] have a talk with him. He made a very good impression on me then. Because of his excellent work, he later received a very distinguished award—the Order of Lenin.

Let me return to the subject of Alliluyeva. She was the party organizer of a group at the Academy. She came to see me once and said: "I would like to consult with you on our understanding of the party line. Our party group is now discussing this question: 'How are we to correctly state the political characteristics of the present moment?'" This discussion was connected with the struggle against the "Rights." I gave her an answer, but later, after she had left, I began thinking to myself: "When she goes home she's going to tell Stalin, and what's he going to say?" But on the next day she didn't say anything, and I didn't ask. Apparently my assessment turned out to be correct. When I began to meet with Stalin [after becoming party secretary of the Bauman district] I didn't understand at first why he kept referring to certain details about my activity at the Industrial Academy. I held my tongue and didn't reply. I didn't know whether to be happy or to shrink into a little ball. I thought to myself: "Where does he know this from?" Then I saw that he seemed to be smiling, and it dawned on me that evidently Nadezhda Sergeyevna [Alliluyeva] had informed him in detail about the life of our party organization and my role as its secretary and had presented me in a positive light.

It was probably after this that Stalin told Kaganovich: "Take Khrushchev to work for the Moscow Committee."[24] The prospect of working with Kaganovich impressed me because I had a lot of confidence in him and respect for him. (It was only later that I got to know his true character; as soon as I became aware of his coarseness, it aroused my antipathy.) Meanwhile, I was brought into the work of the citywide Moscow party organization, which was a great honor. After all, this was the party organization of the capital city. I will never forget how uneasy I felt there.

Kaganovich asked me once: "How do you feel?"

I said: "Very bad."

He was surprised: "Why?"

I answered: "I don't know anything about city management, and all such questions have to be decided here."

He asked: "What are your relations with Bulganin?" (Bulganin had by then become chairman of the Moscow Soviet.)

I said: "Speaking formally, we're on very good terms, but I think that he won't accept me as a real leader in the field of city management, and after all for the city that is the number one thing."

He said: "You are overestimating him and underestimating yourself. Does he come to see you?"

I said: "Well, he does come sometimes to coordinate things. But it seems to me that he knows his business better, and if he comes to see me, it's simply because I'm a secretary of the Moscow Committee. But in general we're on very good terms, and I have a lot of respect for him."

Later, after we had worked together for a while, I saw that Bulganin was actually rather superficial and a lightweight. He didn't go deeply into problems of the economy, and on political questions he might even be considered apolitical. He never lived a very intense political life. I didn't know the story of his life, although I knew that he had worked with the Cheka on the railroads as part of the struggle against "bagmen."[25] Later he had been promoted to be director of Elektrozavod. Evidently he had not been a bad director for those days. After all he did have a secondary education, which was a rare thing back then. As a rule it was working-class people who became directors. Kaganovich used to call him a bookkeeper. And it's true that in his style of work Bulganin was like a bookkeeper.

At that time I thought that I had been brought in simply to give support to Bulganin. As it happened, Stalin always summoned the two of us together or invited us to family dinners at his home and he would always jokingly say: "Hey, you two City Fathers, come on over for dinner." Kaganovich didn't go there with us. Although he remained a secretary of the Moscow Committee, Stalin evidently didn't acknowledge him in that role any longer, but considered him a secretary of the Central Committee. And we two "City Fathers" represented Moscow. In essence that was the case, because Kaganovich simply didn't have the physical capacity to involve himself in municipal affairs. He was up to his ears in the work of the Central Committee. He was a very diligent worker, and as the saying goes, he never knew if it was day or night outside.

1. S. V. Kosior. See Biographies.
2. V. V. Kuibyshev. See Biographies.
3. The State Planning Commission was the agency responsible for making plans for the Soviet economy. The Russian acronym Gosplan stands for Gosudarstvennaya Planovaya Komissiya. [SS]

4. The "Rights" were members of a so-called right-wing opposition in the Communist Party, who argued in favor of prolonging and expanding the New Economic Policy. The followers of Zinoviev and Trotsky were usually called the Left Opposition. Between the "right" and the "left"

wings stood Stalin's "center" faction, whose policies won out as the party's "general line." [SS/ES]

5. N. A. Uglanov. See Biographies.

6. K. G. Khakharev occupied a number of leading party posts.

7. S. I. Syrtsov (1893–1937) was chairman of the RSFSR Council of Ministers and a member of the Politburo in 1929. He was supposedly the central figure in a right-wing opposition group in the party. V. V. Lominadze (1897–1935) was a former supporter of Stalin who created a left-wing opposition group in the party in 1928–29. The two men were accused of cooperating to form the Right-Left bloc of Syrtsov and Lominadze. Syrtsov was expelled from the Central Committee and lost his leading positions in 1930. He was arrested during the purges and died in detention. Lominadze committed suicide in 1935, apparently to avoid arrest. [SS]

8. I. G. Makarov was director of the Yuzovka (Stalino) metallurgical works from 1922 to 1924 and again from 1932 to 1936.

9. A. Levochkin, party secretary at the Industrial Academy, was replaced by Khrushchev. [GS] Bryansk is situated in the southwestern corner of Russia near the border with Ukraine, about halfway between Moscow and Kiev. [SS]

10. Samara is situated west of the Ural Mountains on the Volga River, in southeastern European Russia. [SS]

11. A. Z. Zdobnov occupied various party posts.

12. The Chuvash are an ethnic minority who speak a Turkic language and live mainly in the Middle Volga region. [SS]

13. L. Z. Mekhlis. See Biographies.

14. Old Bolsheviks were those who joined the party before the revolution of October 1917. [SS]

15. That is, people involved in economic management and planning rather than in purely political leadership. The Russian term is *khozyaistvenniki.* [GS]

16. In 1932 the city of Nizhny Novgorod was renamed Gorky in honor of the famous writer Maxim Gorky, who came from that city. [GS]

17. V. M. Molotov. See Biographies.

18. A. P. Shirin occupied a number of party posts.

19. A. M. Tsikhon. See Biographies.

20. V. N. Vorobyov was an organizer in the Young Communist League and in the general youth movement.

21. Nikolai Palkin (Nicholas the Club) was a derogatory nickname given to Tsar Nicholas I, son of Tsar Paul I, because of the harsh repression that characterized his rule. The sobriquet Palkin comes from *palka,* "stick," "club," or "cane." It also suggests "Little Paul" (Pavelkin), a reference to the father of Nicholas I. [GS]

22. Besides being Lenin's wife, N. K. Krupskaya was a prominent official and writer in the field of education and an activist in the women's movement. See Biographies.

23. N. A. Bulganin. See Biographies.

24. The Moscow committee of the party was formed from the Moscow city committee together with the Moscow province committee. [SK]

25. "Bagmen" were people, especially peasants, who smuggled bags of wheat or other food products into the cities to engage in private trade, which was banned under so-called War Communism during the Civil War. [GS]

## PERSONAL ACQUAINTANCE WITH STALIN

Visiting Stalin for meals at his home was especially pleasant as long as Nadezhda Sergeyevna was alive. She was a principled, party-minded person and, at the same time, a considerate hostess who in the Russian tradition offered her guests bread and salt. I felt very bad when she died. The celebration of the October revolution was going on just before her death.[1] Demonstrators were marching, and as part of the group of active party members I was standing alongside the Lenin Mausoleum. Alliluyeva was standing next to me and we were talking. It was chilly. Stalin was on top of the mausoleum in an overcoat. (In those days he always went around in an overcoat.) The buttons were unbuttoned, and the overcoat was hanging open. The wind was blowing. Alliluyeva looked up at him and said: "My husband didn't bring his scarf. He's going to catch cold and get sick again." This was all very motherly and so full of domestic concern. It didn't fit in at all with the concept that had become part of our consciousness—of Stalin as the great leader.

The demonstration ended and everyone went home. The next day Kaganovich gathered together the secretaries of the Moscow district committees of the party and told us that Nadezhda Sergeyevna had died suddenly. I thought to myself: "How could this be? I was just talking with her yesterday. Such a beautiful woman, in the full bloom of life." I sincerely grieved for her, but I thought: "Well, what can you do? All sorts of things happen in this life, and people die."

A day or two later Kaganovich gathered us together again, this same group of party officials, and said: "I am passing along Stalin's instructions. Stalin has ordered me to tell you that Alliluyeva did not just die; she shot herself." That was all. We were given no reason. She shot herself and that was it. When she was buried, Stalin accompanied her coffin to the cemetery. You could see from the look on his face that he was suffering greatly and grieving over her.

It was only after Stalin's death that I found out the reasons for the death of Nadezhda Sergeyevna. There are documents pertaining to this matter. We asked Vlasik,[2] the head of Stalin's personal guard, "What were the reasons that caused Nadezhda Sergeyevna to commit suicide?"

This is what he told us: "After the parade everyone went, as always, to Voroshilov's[3] house for dinner. (He had a large apartment in the Kremlin. I myself had dined there several times.) A rather narrow circle of people gathered there for dinner that day, the commander of the parade being included on that occasion. As I recall it was Kork.[4] People's Commissar of War Voroshilov had been the official reviewer of the parade, and several members of the Politburo, those closest to Stalin, were also present. They went there directly from Red Square. (Demonstrations lasted a long time back in those days.) They had dinner there, as was the custom, and they ate and drank a great amount, as was also customary on such occasions. Nadezhda Sergeyevna was not there. When it was over they all went their separate ways, including Stalin. He left but didn't go home. It was already late by then. And Nadezhda Sergeyevna began to worry—Where in the world was Stalin? She began searching for him by telephone. First she called the dacha."

They were living then in Zubalovo—not where Mikoyan[5] has been living recently, but on the other side of the gully.[6] The duty officer answered the phone. Nadezhda Sergeyevna asked: "Where is Comrade Stalin?"

"Comrade Stalin is here."

"Is someone with him?"

The man on duty answered: "Gusev's wife is with him." The next morning when Stalin arrived home, his wife was already dead. Gusev was a military man who had also been present at the dinner at Voroshilov's place. When Stalin had left he had taken Gusev's wife with him. I myself never met Gusev's wife, but Mikoyan says she was a very beautiful woman.

When Vlasik told this story, he made the following comment: "The devil only knows. That duty officer who answered the phone was an inexperienced fool. She asked, and he came right out and told her."

At the time there were vague rumors that Stalin himself had killed her. I myself heard such rumors. Evidently Stalin also knew about them. When rumors circulated the Chekists recorded them and reported them. Later, people said that when Stalin went into the bedroom where he found his dead wife, Nadezhda Sergeyevna, he didn't go in alone, but took Voroshilov with him. It's hard to say if that's really so. Why would it be necessary to go into the bedroom with Voroshilov? If he wanted to have a witness, it means he already knew she was dead. In short, this aspect of the matter remains murky to this very day.

In general I knew very little about Stalin's family life. I can judge it only on the basis of the meals we had there and from isolated remarks. Sometimes when Stalin had had a few drinks, he would start to reminisce. He told us once: "Sometimes I'd lock myself up in my bedroom and she would bang on the door and shout, 'You're an impossible person. It's impossible to live with you.'" He told us that when little Svetlanka[7] got angry she would repeat her mother's words: "You're an impossible person." And she would add: "I'm going to complain about you."

Stalin would ask her: "Who are you going to complain to?"

"To the cook!" For her, the cook was the highest authority.

After Nadezhda Sergeyevna's death, at Stalin's home I sometimes encountered a beautiful young woman with the typical features of people from the Caucasus. She tried to avoid meeting us coming or going. You saw only the flash of her eyes, and she immediately disappeared. Later I was told that this woman was Svetlanka's governess. But before long she disappeared. From some remarks by Beria,[8] I understood that this woman was his protégée. Well, I can only say that Beria was a person who knew how to pick "governesses."

I felt sorry about Alliluyeva purely on a human basis. She was a remarkable individual. When she was a student at the Industrial Academy in the textiles department, specializing in the chemistry of synthetic fabrics, she was elected as a leader by her party group and used to come see me to coordinate various political formulations. In that situation I was always kind of looking over my shoulder, thinking: "She'll go home and tell Stalin what I said."

The Ukrainian writer Vinnichenko[9] wrote a short story entitled "Pinya."[10] Pinya was elected to be the "elder" in a prison cell, to make decisions for everyone. I was elected at the Industrial Academy to be secretary of the party committee, and I felt myself to be a kind of Pinya. But I never once regretted that I might have told Nadezhda Sergeyevna one thing or another.

In her life she had been a very modest person. She took the streetcar to the Academy. She came and went just like everyone else and never tried to stand out as the "wife of an important person." There is an old and true saying: Fate often deprives us of the best people. As I have already said, Stalin often mentioned particular facts about my activity at the Academy, and I would look and wonder: How does he know that? Later I understood why he knew about certain episodes of my life. Evidently Nadezhda Sergeyevna had informed him about the activities of the party organization at the Industrial Academy when I was a student there and also head of the party organization. Apparently she presented me in a good light as a political activist. And so Stalin came to know about me through her. At first I attributed my promotion to party work in Moscow to Kaganovich, because Kaganovich had known me very well in Ukraine, where he and I had been acquainted literally from the first days of the February revolution. Later I came to a different conclusion: evidently my promotion came not from Kaganovich, but rather it all originated with Stalin. It evidently impressed Kaganovich that Nadezhda Sergeyevna, to put it crudely, had praised me to the skies in front of Stalin.

I liked the way Stalin behaved in everyday life. Sometimes when we met in domestic circumstances, I would hear him joking. For me his jokes were rather surprising. I tended to deify him and therefore didn't expect jokes from him, and so any joke from him seemed unusual to me. How could a man who was "not of this world" be joking?

I also liked Stalin's family. At Stalin's home I met old man Alliluyev.[11] And I met Alliluyev's wife, who was also elderly. Stanislav Redens[12] was often invited there. He was the husband of Nadezhda Sergeyevna's older sister, Anna Sergeyevna. And her brother would also be invited. I liked him a lot, too—he was a young handsome man with the rank of commander, in either the artillery or the armored forces.

Those family meals took place in such a relaxed atmosphere, with jokes and everything. Stalin was very human at those meals, and it impressed me. I was filled with even greater respect for Stalin, both as a political figure who had no equal in the circle around him and as an ordinary person. But I was mistaken. Today I see that I didn't understand everything. Stalin really was a great figure—I would confirm that even today. Within his circle he stood several heads taller than all the others. But he was also an actor, and there was something jesuitical about him.[13] He was able to play a part with great skill, to present himself in a certain light.

I want to describe another meeting I had with Stalin, which made a strong impression on me. This happened when I was a student at the Industrial Academy. The first graduation of students from the Academy was held in 1930. Our director then was Kaminsky,[14] an Old Bolshevik and good comrade. I had a lot of respect for him. We asked him to pass on to Stalin our request that Stalin receive representatives of the party organization at the Industrial Academy in connection with the first graduation. We wanted to hear a graduation speech from Comrade Stalin. We had planned an evening at the Hall of Columns at the House of Trade Unions[15] dedicated to the graduating students, and we were asking that Stalin speak at this celebration. We were told to designate our representatives and that Stalin would receive six or seven people. I, as secretary of the party organization, was one of them. The other participants in this meeting had already graduated from the Industrial Academy, and I ended up part of the group precisely because I was the representative of the organization.

We arrived at Stalin's office. He immediately received us, and a conversation began. Stalin held forth along the following lines: "You need to study, you need to master scientific knowledge, but don't spread yourself too thin. Get to know your specific subject profoundly and in detail. We need well-trained managers to emerge from your ranks. Not some sort of 'experts' who know how to manage in general, but people with a profound knowledge of their own specific field." Then he gave the following example: "If you take one of our specialists, a Russian engineer, you'll find he's a specialist who is very well educated and developed in all spheres. He can carry on a conversation on any subject, whether in the society of ladies or in his own circle; he is familiar with questions of literature, art, and so on. But when you require concrete knowledge from him, for example, if a machine has stopped working, he will immediately send for other people to repair it.

A German engineer, on the other hand, will make for less lively company. But if you tell him that a machine has stopped working, he'll take off his jacket, roll up his sleeves, take a wrench, look into the matter himself, fix it, and start the machine running again. That is the kind of people we need: not with broad, general knowledge, although that too is good, but mainly people who know their special field and know it profoundly and who are able to teach others."

We were pleased by this. I had heard this same point of view before, when I was studying at the workers' school. Back then the idea was widely circulated that we of course needed institutes of higher education, but the main thing we needed was more technical schools, so that we would have, not just well-educated people familiar with one or another field of knowledge, but specialists who had graduated with technical knowledge, or to put it more simply, professionals who would know their subject more narrowly but also more deeply than the engineer in the same field. We didn't disagree. We wholeheartedly supported that point of view. Therefore Stalin's words on this first personal encounter with him made a good impression on me. Here was a man who knew the essence of the matter, and he was pointing us in the right direction, turning our energies toward solving the fundamental problems of industrializing the country, building industry, and on this basis making the borders of our homeland invulnerable to the capitalist world. This was the basis on which a rise in the people's standard of living would be founded.

The meeting came to an end. Stalin said: "I cannot be with you today, but Mikhail Ivanovich Kalinin[16] will come to address you." When the meeting with Stalin ended, we saw that the session in the Hall of Columns had already begun, and we had to run. We arrived from the Kremlin at the Hall of Columns after the general report had already been given. This report, as I recall, was given by Kaminsky.

Then students spoke, and finally Mikhail Ivanovich [Kalinin]. We all respected him and listened to him attentively. But he said the exact opposite of what Stalin had just been saying. To be sure, he also asserted that we needed to study and to master knowledge and become qualified, skilled leaders of industry: "You are the commanders of cadres and you should not only know your specialty but also you should know literature and be roundly developed. You should not just be experts in your field of specialization, knowing your machines and instruments; you should also know literature, art, history, and so forth." Those of us who had been at the talk with Stalin looked at one another. We had just come from talking with him, and here

Kalinin was saying the exact opposite of what we had heard from Stalin. I was on Stalin's side. In my view he was posing our tasks more concretely because above all we needed to be specialists and masters in what we were doing and not to spread ourselves too thin; otherwise we wouldn't have the full value [of the cost of our education]. The person who knew his subject more profoundly was more useful to his homeland and to the cause.

When my party work in Moscow began, in January 1931, a district party conference was held. District party conferences were convened then every six months or every year. It was at that conference that I was chosen secretary of the party's Bauman district committee, and Korotchenko[17] was elected chairman of the district soviet. The man in charge of the organizational department in the district committee was Comrade Treivas,[18] a very good comrade. The department for agitation among the masses was headed, as I recall, by Comrade Rozov, also a very good and energetic person. Then there was Shurov.[19] (His career ended when he was either arrested or committed suicide in Siberia in 1937, I don't remember exactly.)

In the 1920s Treivas had been widely known as an active Young Communist League figure. He had been a friend of the poet and Young Communist League leader Sasha Bezymensky.[20] Together they were among the most active leaders of the Moscow Young Communist organization. Treivas was a very good, capable, and intelligent person. But even then Kaganovich warned me against him. Word had it that he suffered from a serious political defect. At an earlier time, when the sharp struggle with the Trotskyists was going on, he had signed the so-called declaration of the ninety-three Young Communist League members in support of Trotsky. Bezymensky had also signed it. "And so," said Kaganovich, "you have to be on your guard, even though Treivas now fully supports the party line and gives no reason for us to doubt him; he is even being recommended by the Central Committee to take charge of the organizational department." Today when so many years have gone by, I must say that Treivas worked very well, devotedly, and energetically. He was an intelligent man, and I was pleased with him. But I worked with him for only half a year, and then I was elected secretary of the party's Krasnaya Presnya district committee. This was considered a promotion, a step up the party ladder. The Krasnaya Presnya district occupied a more important political position than the Bauman district because of its glorious historical past—it was the working-class district at the heart of the December armed uprising in 1905. The Krasnaya Presnya party organization was the leading district party organization in Moscow. Treivas remained in the

Bauman district, and, as I recall, Margolin[21] was elected secretary of the Bauman district. Treivas's life came to a tragic end. He was elected secretary of the party's Kaluga city committee.[22] The name of the Kaluga city committee resounded everywhere, if I can put it that way. But when the mass slaughter or "meat grinder" of 1937 began, he was unable to avoid it.

I met Treivas again after he was already in prison, because Stalin had proposed the idea that secretaries of the party's province committees should go to the prisons and check on whether the security "organs" were operating correctly. That's why I went. I distinctly remember that Redens was then the head of the OGPU administration for Moscow province. He was also an interesting figure, but his life also ended tragically, poor fellow. He was arrested and shot, despite the fact that he was married to the sister of Nadezhda Sergeyevna Alliluyeva; that is, he was Stalin's brother-in-law. I met Redens many times at Stalin's apartment and at family dinners to which I was invited as secretary of the Moscow party organization, and Bulganin was invited as chairman of the Moscow Soviet.

It was with Redens that I went to check up on the situation in the prisons. It was a dreadful scene. I remember going into the women's section of one prison. It was terribly hot, being summertime, and the cell was terribly overcrowded. Redens had warned me that we might meet so-and-so and so-and-so, that personal acquaintances had ended up there. And sure enough, an intelligent and very active woman I had known was sitting there—Betty Glan.[23] Today [in 1967], it seems, she is still alive and well. She had been a director of Gorky Park in Moscow. But she had been not only a director; she had also been one of the founders and creators of that park. I didn't go to diplomatic receptions back then, but as someone who came from a bourgeois family Glan knew the etiquette of high society, and Litvinov[24] always invited her, so that in a way she represented our government at such receptions. And now here I was encountering her in prison. She was half naked, like all the others, because it was so hot. She said: "Comrade Khrushchev, what kind of enemy of the people am I? I am an honest person, a person devoted to the party." We left and went into the men's section, and there I met Treivas.

Treivas also said to me: "Comrade Khrushchev, am I really one of those?"

I immediately turned to Redens and he replied: "Comrade Khrushchev, they all talk like that; they deny everything. They're simply lying."

Then I understood that our situation as secretaries of the party's province committees was a very difficult one: the factual materials in any investigation were in the hands of the Chekists, who also had the power to shape opinion on the matter. It was they who did the questioning and wrote the official reports on the investigation. And we, as it were, were helpless "victims" of the Chekist organizations and inevitably began to look at things through their eyes. Thus our monitoring turned out not to be that, but a fiction, a veil that covered their activity. Later on I began to wonder why Stalin did that. Today it's clear that Stalin did it deliberately. He thought the matter through, so that, when necessary, he could say: "But the party organization was there. After all, they're following and keeping their eye on everything. They're obliged to do that." But how exactly could we keep an eye on everything in that situation? The Chekists were not under the jurisdiction of our party organization. Consequently who would be keeping an eye on whom? In fact, it was not the party organization that kept watch over the Chekists, but the Chekists who kept watch over the party organization and all party leaders.

At that time I had the chance to meet quite frequently with Stalin and to hear him speak at official party sessions and conferences. I also listened to him and saw him in action during my visits at his home or in the context of the workings of the leadership collective—the Politburo of the Central Committee. Against this background Stalin stood out sharply, especially for the clarity of his formulations. I was very much taken with this. With all my heart I was devoted to the Central Committee of the party headed by Stalin and first of all to Stalin himself.

I was present once at a gathering of a narrow circle of economic managerial personnel. That was when Stalin formulated his famous "six conditions" for the successful functioning of the economy.[25] I was working as secretary of the party's Bauman district committee then. I received a phone call asking that I be present at a Politburo meeting because Stalin was going to speak. I immediately went to the Central Committee offices, which were already full of people. The auditorium in which the conference was held was not large. At the most there was room for three hundred people, and it was full to overflowing. In listening to Stalin, I tried not to miss a single word, and, to the extent that I could, to write down what he was saying. Later this speech was published. I repeat, the brevity of expression and precision of formulation of the tasks that were being posed won me over, and more and more I was filled with respect for Stalin, recognizing his special qualities as a leader.

I also met with Stalin and observed him in the unconstrained circumstances of everyday conversation. Sometimes this was at the theater. When Stalin went to the theater, he occasionally had his people call me up, and I would go there alone or together with Bulganin. Usually Stalin invited us when some questions had come up, and he wanted, while we were at the theater, to exchange opinions with us, most often on questions about the city of Moscow. For our part, we always listened with great attention and tried to do exactly what he advised us. And in those days he gave advice most often in a good comradely manner, expressing his wishes or desires.

One day (as I recall, this was before the Seventeenth Party Congress) I was called up and told to dial a certain number. I knew this was the number of the phone at Stalin's apartment. When I called, he said to me: "Comrade Khrushchev, rumors have reached me that the situation in Moscow is not good as far as public toilets are concerned. People are running around, not knowing where to find a place to relieve themselves. An unpleasant and awkward situation is being created. You and Bulganin should think about creating suitable conditions in this regard in the city." One would think this was such a petty detail. But I was won over more than ever by this: after all, here Stalin was concerned about even such minor questions and was advising us on them. Of course Bulganin and I and other responsible officials immediately undertook frantic activity, ordering that the situation be looked into in every building and courtyard, although this problem mainly had to do with courtyards, and we even alerted the police. Later Stalin outlined the task more specifically. He said it was necessary to create decent pay toilets. And that was also done: separate toilet facilities were created. And all this was thought up by none other than Stalin.

I remember some conference or other where comrades from the provinces came together. Eikhe[26] (who was then, it seems to me, secretary of the party organization in Novosibirsk)[27] asked me a question with his direct Latvian simplicity: "Comrade Khrushchev, is it true what people say, that you concern yourselves with the problem of toilets in the city of Moscow and that you do that on instructions from Comrade Stalin?"

I answered: "Yes, it's true. I am concerned with the problem of toilets, and I consider this to be an expression of how we care about people, because in this big city toilets are an institution that people cannot get along without. That's especially true in cities like Moscow." This incident, which might seem to be so trivial, shows that Stalin paid attention to even the most minor details. He was the leader of the world working class, as we always said, the leader of the party, and yet he didn't lose sight of such a minor but vital necessity for people as municipal toilets, and this kind of thing won us over.

Let me give some more specific instances of actions by Stalin that reveal his character. I remember one day at a Politburo session a rather unusual question came up on the agenda about a person who had been sent by Vneshtorg (the People's Commissariat of Foreign Trade) on a mission to some Latin American country. The man was summoned and came in looking very distraught. He was about thirty years old. The discussion began. Stalin addressed him: "Tell us everything, just as it happened, leaving out no detail."

The man said that he had traveled to the country in question to place certain orders for products. Today I forget exactly where he went, but that's not the important thing. What is interesting is how Stalin reacted. The man continued: "I went into a restaurant to have something to eat. I sat down at the table and ordered dinner. Some young man sat down at my table and asked: 'Are you from Russia?' I said: 'Yes, from Russia.' He said: 'And how do you feel about music?' I said: 'If someone plays well on a violin I love to listen.' He said: 'What did you come to buy?' I said: 'I came to buy some equipment.' He asked: 'In Russia did you serve in the army?' I answered: 'Yes, I did.' He asked: 'What unit were you in?' I answered: 'The cavalry. I was a cavalryman. Even today I love horses, even though I'm no longer in the service.' He asked: 'And are you a good shot? After all you were in the military.' I answered: 'I'm not a bad shot.'"

"The next day people told me that there was a write-up about me in the newspapers. I simply tore my hair. It turns out that this man had been a journalist, a representative of some local newspaper, but he didn't introduce himself as such, and owing to my inexperience I started talking with him and answering his questions. He wrote that such-and-such a Russian had arrived, that he was going to place orders for such-and-such a sum of money (all this was made up), that he loved to ride on horseback, that he was a wild Caucasian horseman, a *dzhigit*,[28] a sportsman, and a good shot, and he shoots in such-and-such a way and hits the target from such-and-such a distance, and on top of that he's a violinist, and so on. In short, so much nonsense was written that I was horrified, but there was nothing I could do. A little while later the embassy suggested that I return to our country. And so I have arrived and am reporting to you what happened. I earnestly request you to keep in mind that this was done without any bad intentions on my part."

While he was telling this everyone chuckled and joked about him, especially people who were not directly involved in the case. But the members of the Central Committee and the Central Inspection Commission,[29] who always attended such sessions, acted in a more restrained manner, waiting to see how things would turn out. When I looked at this man I felt sorry for him. He had been a victim of his own simple-mindedness and naiveté, but what would be the outcome for him in this examination of his case at a Politburo meeting? This man had spoken quite simply and straight from the heart, but he had been embarrassed. Stalin had encouraged him: "Go on and tell your story, tell your story," Stalin kept saying, and he did this in a calm, friendly voice. Suddenly Stalin said: "Well, what is all this? You trusted a man and you ended up a victim of one of these gangsters of the press, a pirate of the pen. . . . Was there nothing more to it than that?"

"Nothing."

"Then let's consider the question closed. See that you act more cautiously in the future." I was very pleased by this outcome of the discussion.

After this a break in the session was announced. The Politburo then continued its session for a long time, an hour, two hours, and longer, and then there was another break, after which everyone went into another large room where there were tables and chairs and tea was served with sandwiches. It was a hungry time back then, even for people like me who held fairly high positions. We were living more than modestly, and even in your own home you couldn't always eat your fill. And so when we went to the Kremlin, we filled ourselves to the brim with ham and sausage sandwiches; we drank sweet tea, and we enjoyed all these good things as people who had not been spoiled by refined cuisine. So when the break was announced, we all headed for the glutton's den, as we jokingly called it among ourselves, and as we went out I noticed that the poor fellow was still sitting there. That's how shaken up he was, evidently, at the surprising outcome of his case. Apparently no one had yet told him that the session was over, and he didn't stir from where he was sitting.

I was very pleased by Stalin's humaneness and simplicity [in this case], his understanding of the man's soul. After all, it might have seemed that this man was already doomed once the question had been brought before the Politburo. It's likely that a report had reached Stalin about this case, and he himself had decided to bring it to the Politburo—to show what he was like and how he resolved such problems.

Here is another incident. This happened probably in 1932 or 1933. In Soviet society at that time there arose a movement of *otlichniki*.[30] Some workers at the Moscow Elektrozavod, who were then considered among the most advanced in the capital city, decided to make a ski trip, to travel on skis all the way from Moscow to Siberia or perhaps the Far East. They accomplished this feat successfully and when they returned were given honorary awards, some sort of badges or even orders. Of course a big sensation was made of this. Then some Turkmen decided to ride their horses at racing speeds from Ashkhabad[31] to Moscow. They too completed their journey, were welcomed with honors, given gifts, and likewise received honorary awards. Then this *otlichnik* movement began springing up in other cities and regions.

Suddenly Stalin said it had to be stopped; otherwise there'd be no end to it. If we started to encourage this movement—and we had already started to—people would be making trips on foot, on horseback, trying to "distinguish themselves," to show that they were "exemplary" in some way; and they would be torn away from productive work. He said: "We would all turn into vagabonds. We would be publicly encouraging vagabondism, and even rewarding people for it." Immediately a halt was called to the *otlichnik* movement. I very much liked this action. First, an unnecessary fuss and uproar was being created. Second, it was really the wrong direction to take—encouraging vagabondism, an endless round of trips and journeys. Stalin, for his part, approached the question in a businesslike way: people's efforts needed to be turned in a different direction, toward activity that would increase production and contribute to unifying the people, meeting their needs, and so forth. It was all right to carry out a ski trip setting a sports record if it was done once, but in principle it really wasn't very important, because if sports were to be developed properly, it would have to be done on an entirely different basis.

On the other hand, one incident struck me as quite unpleasant. It seems to me the year was 1932. Hunger was stalking Moscow. As second secretary of the party's city committee, I put a lot of effort into seeking ways to keep the working class fed. We even began raising rabbits. Stalin proposed this idea himself, and I eagerly undertook the job. It was with great zeal that Stalin's instructions to develop rabbit farming were put into effect. Every factory and workplace began raising rabbits. This was done wherever possible and even, unfortunately, where it was impossible. Then we also began growing mushrooms: organizing mushroom cellars, digging trenches for mushroom beds. Some factories did a good job of providing their dining halls with food products, but every mass movement, even the best, can often give rise to distortions. Thus, many unpleasant incidents occurred. These operations didn't always pay for themselves; some were real money-losers, and not all factory directors supported the effort. A bad joke began making the rounds: instead of the Russian word *gribnitsy* ["mushroom cellars"], people called them *grobnitsy* ["tombs"].

When ration cards with coupons for food and other products were handed out, a lot of swindling went on. The situation was always like this: if ration cards were being handed out, that meant there were shortages, and the existence of shortages prompted people, especially those who were unstable, to step outside the law. Under such conditions thieves flourished. Kaganovich told me: "You should get ready to make a report to the Politburo about the struggle in Moscow to bring order into the ration card system. Cards have to be taken away from people who have obtained them illegally, by thievish methods." Different kinds of ration cards existed—some for people who had jobs and others for people who didn't. For those with jobs there were also different types of cards, and that too was one of the circumstances that enabled people to indulge in all sorts of trickery and outright abuse of the system. We made a big effort then, together with all the organizations—among them the trade unions, the local police, and the Chekists (security police). We cut hundreds of thousands of ration cards out of the budget or took them away from people who didn't really qualify for them. A fierce battle was under way then—for bread, for food products in general, and for successful completion of the First Five-Year Plan. Food had to be provided first of all to those who were contributing to fulfillment of the plan.

The day came when reports on this question were to be heard by the Politburo. Kaganovich said that I would be the reporter for Moscow. This troubled me a lot and even frightened me: the idea of speaking before such an authoritative body, at which Stalin would be passing judgment on my report. In those days Molotov presided at Politburo sessions; Stalin never presided back then. It was only after the war that Stalin himself ran the meetings, [at least] more often than before the war. In the 1940s, a restrained atmosphere usually prevailed at Politburo meetings. But in the 1930s, debate over some questions could become quite stormy, especially if someone allowed himself to express strong emotions. That still happened in those days. For example, Sergo Ordzhonikidze once flew into a rage—by nature he was very hot-tempered—rushed at Rosengolts,[32] the people's commissar of foreign trade, and almost hit him.

So I gave the report, recounting what big successes we had achieved. But Stalin made a comment: "Don't boast, Comrade Khrushchev, don't boast. Many thieves still remain, a great many, and yet you think you've caught them all." This affected me strongly. I actually thought we had unmasked all the thieves, but Stalin, even though he never went outside the Kremlin, could see that there were still a lot of swindlers. In fact, that was so. I very much liked the way he made his comment: with a kind of fatherly tone. This too raised Stalin higher in my eyes.

Let me switch over now to the unpleasant incident I mentioned. After a while I found out that the Leningraders were going to make the same kind of report. I was curious about what work they had accomplished. There was socialist competition between the Leningraders and us Muscovites on all questions, both stated and unstated. The day came when the question was placed on the Politburo agenda. I came to the session and took my seat. (The seats were numbered, but for permanent attendees they were more or less reserved.) A secretary of the Leningrad city party committee gave the report. Sergei Mironovich Kirov was first secretary, but he didn't give the report. Some other secretary, with a Latvian last name, gave it. I didn't know him very well, but after all, he was a secretary of the Leningrad city committee, and for that reason alone I had a duly respectful attitude toward him. He gave a good report, as I saw it. The Leningraders had also done a lot of work, had found ways to economize, and had eliminated many ration cards.

A break was announced, and people began pouring out, heading for the "gluttons' den," but I held back for a while. Stalin was apparently waiting until those whose seats had been in the back passed through. At that point I became an unintended witness to an exchange of remarks between Stalin and Kirov in regard to this secretary. Stalin asked Kirov what kind of person this man was. Sergei Mironovich [Kirov] gave him some sort of reply, probably of a positive nature. But Stalin tossed off a cutting remark, insulting and humiliating to this secretary. For me this was simply a terrible moral blow. Even in my innermost thoughts I could never have allowed myself to suppose that Stalin, the top leader of the party, the leader of the working class, could treat a member of the party so disrespectfully.

I remember [back during the Civil War] we had carried out an offensive and had taken the town of Maloarkhangelsk[33] from the Whites. A local teacher came to see me, a man without much sense, and asked what position he would be given if he joined the party. That made me angry, but I restrained myself and said: "The most responsible position."

"What would that be?" he asked.

"A rifle would be placed in your hands and you would be sent to fight the White Guards. Right now that's the most responsible job. A question is being decided: Will Soviet power exist or not? What job could there be with greater responsibility than that?"

He said: "Well, if that's how things are, I'm not joining the party."

I said: "That would be best. Don't join!"

But I have digressed. Here Stalin, our top leader, from whom it would seem I should be taking lessons on establishing good relations with people and understanding them, had uttered such a cutting remark. So many years have gone by since then, but those words of his stick in my memory like a piece of shrapnel. They left me with a negative opinion about Stalin. Contempt for people reverberated in his words. The Latvian they were talking about was a simple man, apparently from a working-class background. In general, there were a lot of Latvians in the active membership of our party then. One Latvian I met, for example, had headed the 72d Regiment of the Ninth Infantry Division. In official party posts, in economic work, and in the Red Army there were a lot of Latvians, and I always treated them with great respect. Back then, in general, we didn't divide people on the basis of nationality. The line of division was on the basis of devotion to the cause: for or against the revolution. That was the main thing. Later a petty bourgeois attitude toward people began to eat away at us: What nationality was somebody? In earlier times the only thing that mattered was social origin: Did someone come from working-class or peasant origins, or were they from the intelligentsia? In those days the intelligentsia was, as the saying goes, under suspicion. After all, in the early years of the revolution there were in the Communist Party only a relative few who came from the ranks of intellectual labor.

1. Besides the version of the story recounted by N. S. Khrushchev, there was another version according to which Alliluyeva committed suicide following a political argument with Stalin over his harsh policies that she disagreed with. [GS/SS]

2. N. S. Vlasik was the security official responsible for Stalin's personal guard. See Biographies.

3. K. Ye. Voroshilov. See Biographies.

4. A. I. Kork. See Biographies.

5. A. I. Mikoyan. See Biographies.

6. Stalin's government-owned country place, or dacha, in Zubalovo was on a road called Uspenskoye Shosse, about 30 kilometers west of Moscow. Mikoyan had a dacha in the same area. [SK]

7. "Svetlanka" is an endearing form of the first name of Stalin's daughter, Svetlana Alliluyeva. [GS]

8. L. P. Beria. See Biographies.

9. V. K. Vinnichenko was a Ukrainian nationalist activist. See Biographies.

10. "Pinya" was the first name of the main character in the story. [GS]

11. Sergei Yakovlevich Alliluyev (1866–1945) joined the Social Democrats in 1896 while working as a machinist in Tiflis (the capital of Georgia, later renamed Tbilisi). He was active in the revolutionary movement in the Transcaucasus (in Tiflis and in Baku, capital of Azerbaijan) for a decade. From 1907 to 1918 he worked in Saint Petersburg, where his apartment was a secret meeting place for the Bolsheviks and a hiding place for Lenin in July 1917. He was closely acquainted with many leading Bolsheviks. His memoirs, *Proidennyi put'* (The road traveled), were published in 1956. [GS]

12. S. F. Redens was a leading state security official. See Biographies.

13. The term "jesuitical" is used here to suggest a person who employs subtle cunning, false reasoning, and deceptive arguments, qualities attributed to the Catholic order of Jesuits by their opponents. [GS]

14. G. N. Kaminsky. See Biographies.

15. Before the revolution, the House of Trade Unions had been a gathering place for the Moscow gentry. It was used for public events such as conferences, concerts, and lectures. After Stalin's death his body lay in state there. [SK]

16. M. I. Kalinin. See Biographies.

17. D. S. Korotchenko. See Biographies.

18. B. Ye. Treivas was a political party official.

19. V. Ya. Shurov was a political party official.

20. A. I. Bezymensky was a poet and playwright as well as an activist in the Young Communist League.

21. N. V. Margolin. See Biographies.

22. Kaluga is situated about 200 kilometers south of Moscow. [SS]

23. B. N. Glan. See Biographies.

24. M. M. Litvinov was people's commissar of foreign affairs in the 1930s. See Biographies.

25. This was Stalin's speech "A New Situation, New Tasks of Economic Management." It was delivered at a gathering of economic managers convened at the Central Committee of the AUCP(B) on June 23, 1931.

26. R. I. Eikhe. Eikhe was of Latvian origin. See Biographies.

27. Novosibirsk is the main city of western Siberia. [SS]

28. A *dzhigit* (or *jigit*) was a noble warrior in the traditional society of the Northern Caucasus. He adhered to a code of honor similar to that of the medieval European knight and was famed

especially for his accomplished horsemanship. [SS]

29. The Central Inspection Commission was a highly placed party body, elected by party congresses from 1922 onward. It had the nominal authority to oversee the operations and audit the finances of other party bodies, including the Central Committee. In fact, it possessed little real power and was dominated by the top party leadership. [GS]

30. *Otlichniki* (derived from *otlichnyi*, "excellent") were people who performed in an exemplary way or had exemplary accomplishments to their credit. [GS]

31. Ashkhabad was the capital of the Turkmen SSR. [GS]

32. A. P. Rozengolts. See Biographies.

33. Maloarkhangelsk is a town in Oryol province in southwestern Russia. [SS]

## MOSCOW WORKDAYS

In summer 1930 the Sixteenth Party Congress was taking place. I had not been elected a delegate to the congress, because I was a student at the Industrial Academy. The Industrial Academy didn't take a firm political position, and I was not nominated as a candidate for the election of delegates to the party congress: first, because I was a new person, not well known to the party organization; and second, because at the Industrial Academy I represented the new leadership, which held positions in support of the party's "general line." The party's Bauman district committee was then headed by Shirin, and he was insufficiently mature politically; also, apparently there were some other considerations in his case. In short, although I wasn't elected a delegate, I was provided with a permanent guest pass to the congress by the party's Central Committee. As a result I was present when Stalin gave his report and during the various speeches, although not all of them, because a lot of people were asking me to lend them my guest pass, and I wasn't in a position to refuse. Although it was against the rules to give your guest pass to other comrades, I must confess that we did it anyway. It's true that some were caught and even punished, but I got by all right. The comrades who used my guest pass were allowed in, and we were pleased that not only I but others, too, were able to attend the congress using the guest pass that had been written out at the Central Committee for my personal use.

The summer holidays came to an end, and in the fall we got down to our studies again. Our studies proceeded amid great turbulence. We did a lot in the way of reorganizing the educational process. Quite a few loafers were attending the Industrial Academy, people who had come there not really to study but to have a place where they could sit things out in a period of intense political fighting. It was like a political settling tank. The "Rights" had built themselves a nest there and had dug in.

We students had two days off—Sunday, which was normal for everyone, and one other day, a time for processing the material we had gone over. I was living in a dormitory and had a vivid firsthand view of this "processing." Everyone went off somewhere early in the morning and came back who knows when. They were simply loafing. So then we raised the question of how people should study. After all, we had come there not simply to spend time in Moscow, but to acquire knowledge and return to our places in industry, tempered theoretically and practically, to work to better advantage for the party and for the good of the people, in the effort of building social-ism. And so we carried out this measure, and many people threw off the bad habits that had been interfering with the best utilization of study time.

Our party organization soon won great authority in the eyes of the party's Moscow committee and Central Committee. A great many challenging politi-cal situations were coming up then in the course of the struggle against the opposition, situations in which we had to respond, and respond immediately. The Industrial Academy took a more or less leading position in this regard. We met in separate groups and also held general meetings, and the resolutions we adopted on the current situation were immediately published in *Pravda*. Thus they became "common property," an achievement known to everyone.

One of the most burning questions then was collectivization of agricul-ture.[1] We considered Stalin's famous letter "Dizziness with Success"[2] to be a masterpiece. We understood it as a daring action by the leader of the party, who was not afraid to admit mistakes. It's true that he didn't take personal responsibility for those mistakes, but dumped the blame on the party activists. Although local activists had been zealous—to put it crudely, they had been brutally zealous—in carrying out collectivization, still those party activists had been whipped up by *Pravda*. If you look at *Pravda* for that period, it's studded with statistics day after day (telling what percentage of peasants had already been brought into collective farms by which activists in which dis-tricts), and so the local party organizations were constantly being whipped up and spurred on. In 1929–30 I had no direct contact with the rural areas or with party activists who were carrying out this campaign. I nourished myself on the information in the pages of *Pravda*, my only source, and I rejoiced in it. I was heart and soul in favor of the collective farms, and that's why the published figures made me glad.

Then when the thunder rolled—that is, Stalin's letter "Dizziness with Success"—I was somewhat confused. How could this be? Everything had been fine; then suddenly a letter like this? It became clear that this had been necessary because a threat was building up or may even have come to a head. Peasant uprisings had already broken out in isolated cases, and much bigger uprisings were in the offing. The circumstances of collectivization are well described in *Virgin Soil Upturned*, the novel by Sholokhov.[3] To be sure, things were reflected in that novel in precisely the way that Stalin interpreted them. It couldn't have been otherwise. Sholokhov couldn't have written in any other way. Today, however, when Stalin's abuses of power have been revealed, when we analyze the path we traveled, a more analytical and more profound approach is needed. After analyzing everything, we must draw the correct conclusions from our mistakes, above all the mistakes committed by Stalin—when he banged his head against a wall, but couldn't break through that wall, and because of that was forced to retreat. But in retreating, he heaped the blame that belonged to him onto other people, and that cost those people dearly.

I remember the Moscow party organization also being accused of committing excesses. Comrade Bauman[4] was then the head of the Moscow party organization. I didn't know him very well, but he was considered a major leader. Later, when Bauman was relieved of his duties, Molotov was promoted to the post of leader of the Moscow organization. But Molotov accomplished little in that position, and Kaganovich was brought forward to fill the post.

Even then reports began to come through to us that things were not so good in the rural areas, that not everything was going smoothly with the collective farms. A sharp conflict with the "Right" opposition elements broke out. Later, Rykov and Bukharin made a linkup in their oppositional activity with Zinoviev's supporters and even with the Trotskyists. In short, a severe battle flared up. It was at that time, as far as I can now remember, that Uglanov, who was an opponent of that kind of collectivization, was replaced by Bauman; then Bauman was replaced by Molotov, and Molotov was replaced by Kaganovich. Thus the advancement of people in the Moscow organization followed a "rising curve," and that organization itself was pushed to the forefront. It was supposed to serve as a model for others, as collectivization was growing and spreading at the same time.

Later, when I was already working as secretary of the party's Moscow city committee (in 1932), Kaganovich suddenly told me one day that he was getting ready to go on an assignment to Krasnodar.[5] He was not completely candid in telling me his reasons for making this trip. I don't know how long he was away, probably a week or two, but when he came back, he informed us, as leader of the Moscow party organization, about the state of affairs. It turned out that he had gone to Krasnodar because a strike had begun there (or as they said then, sabotage had occurred). The Cossacks of the Kuban[6] didn't want to work the land as members of collective farms, and as a result of his trip they were deported and relocated to Siberia, entire *stanitsas*[7] of them.

We looked at all these events then through the eyes of Stalin and blamed the kulaks, the "Right Oppositionists," the Trotskyists, Zinoviev's people, and everyone else whom it was necessary to blame and with whom the party was then engaged in conflict. One thought simply could not be admitted, that the Central Committee, above all Stalin, could make mistakes. Stalin formulated the political tasks at that time free of any control whatsoever. By that time, as I recall, Rykov, Bukharin, Zinoviev, and Kamenev[8] had been removed from power, and Trotsky was no longer even in the country; he had been deported from the USSR.[9] Thus, it depended on the current Central Committee, on the Politburo, for mistakes to be foreseen or for their existence to be admitted somehow, but Stalin played the leading and deciding role in the Politburo. Hence, if we are to search for those who are to blame, the chief blame must be placed on him.

We didn't see this at the time. We looked at everything through Stalin's eyes: collectivization was proceeding, Stalin had turned the wheel in time, he had seen everything, and published his letter "Dizziness with Success." I don't know even today how real our successes were. Back then, strictly speaking, we didn't even think about it: once Stalin had said something, that meant it was so; we didn't understand and didn't observe the real facts. But the "success" was such that famine arose in the country.

I had friends among the military men. One of them was Veklichev,[10] head of the Political Directorate of the Moscow Military District, a good comrade and a very close and devoted friend of Yakir.[11] He had worked in Ukraine at one time and came from a family of mine workers. He wore three or four rhomboids on the collar of his soldier's blouse.[12] It was Veklichev who told me that things were in a bad way in Ukraine: the peasants weren't working, they didn't want to plow the land, and there were strikes and sabotage everywhere. Suddenly I learned that Red Army men were being mobilized and sent to harvest sugar beets in Ukraine. In those days Ukraine was the main supplier of sugar. It delivered probably 70 percent, if not more, of our country's sugar.

When I had worked in Ukraine I had had some dealings with agriculture and had gained a rough idea of the care and concern that had to be taken with sugar beets. So this news was a terrible surprise for me. Sugar beets have to be weeded, and I was thinking that if Red Army men were going to weed and harvest sugar beets, we couldn't expect any sugar. This is a crop that is quite delicate and requires a lot of labor; it has to be cultivated with knowledge of what one is doing, and it has to be cared for in a timely fashion. It's hard to expect anything of course from people who don't have a direct interest in the results of their labor. Moreover, the Red Army soldiers for the most part were from different regions of the country, not from regions where sugar beets are grown, and they probably would have a poor knowledge of this particular task. Of course this had an effect on the results: there was no sugar.

Later, news leaked through to Moscow that famine was stalking Ukraine. I simply couldn't imagine how there could be famine in Ukraine in 1932. When I left there in 1929, Ukraine was in excellent condition as far as food supplies went. By 1926 we had living standards that were roughly equal to the prewar period, that is, to 1913. There had been plenty of food products in Ukraine then, and all such goods had been inexpensive: a pound of meat was fourteen kopeks, and vegetables cost only a kopek. In 1926 we had reached the prewar level, and after the economic decline resulting from war and destruction, we had taken pride in that success. Now suddenly there was famine!

Much later I learned the real state of affairs. When I came back to Ukraine in 1938, they told me what difficult times there had been earlier, but no one said exactly what the difficulties had consisted of. As it turns out, here is what happened, according to an account later given to me by Comrade Mikoyan. This is what he said: "Comrade Demchenko came to Moscow one time and stopped in to see me. He asked, 'Does Stalin know, does the Politburo know, what kind of situation has taken shape now in Ukraine?' (Demchenko was then secretary of the Kiev province committee of the party, and the provinces were very big in those days.) Some railroad cars had arrived in Kiev, and when they opened them they turned out to be loaded with human corpses. The train with these cars had come from Kharkov to Kiev by way of Poltava. On the stretch from Poltava to Kiev someone had loaded these corpses in the cars and they had come to Kiev. 'It's a very painful situation,' Demchenko said, 'but Stalin apparently doesn't know about it. I wanted you, once you had heard out about it, to bring this information to Comrade Stalin.'"

Here too was a characteristic feature of those times, that even a man like Demchenko, who was a member of the Politburo of the Central Committee of the Ukrainian Communist Party, a prominent official, and a member of the all-union Central Committee couldn't come [to Stalin himself], present his information, and state his opinion in its essentials. An abnormal situation had arisen. One man kept the collective suppressed, and others trembled before him. Demchenko understood everything well, but still he dared only to tell Mikoyan, knowing that Mikoyan at that time was very close to Stalin. In general in the party and among party activists it was often said then that there was a "Caucasus group" in the leadership, and those who belonged to the Caucasus group in particular were Stalin, Ordzhonikidze,[13] Yenukidze,[14] and Mikoyan.[15]

How many people perished then? Today I cannot say. Information about that has leaked out to the bourgeois press, and right up to the last period of my activity [as Soviet prime minister and party leader] articles kept slipping through to the bourgeois press about collectivization and the price paid for collectivization in terms of the lives of Soviet citizens. I talk this way now, but then I knew nothing of this, first, and second, if I had known something, explanations would have been found for it: sabotage, counterrevolution, kulak plots, which had to be fought, and so on. It would not have been possible to deny all that kind of thing, after all, because the October revolution gave rise to a sharp class struggle that shook the whole social system and economic structure of the country and its political foundations right down to the bowels of the earth. Everything imaginable happened. Only it's plain today that you can't use that explanation for everything: it was also necessary to govern the country intelligently.

I met with Stalin regularly when I was working in Moscow as secretary of the party's city committee and was responsible for matters of reconstruction of the city. The first plan for the reconstruction of Moscow was worked out when I was secretary, actually second secretary, of the Moscow city committee of the AUCP(B), and Bulganin was chairman of the Moscow Soviet. As I recall, the main architect of the city at that time was Chernyshev,[16] a very intelligent man. He designed the Lenin Institute building. This architect impressed me as a very modest and shy person. One day an unpleasant incident occurred. We arrived at the square in front of the Moscow Soviet building and began to look over the buildings that surrounded the Moscow Soviet. Kaganovich glanced over at the building of the Marx-Engels-Lenin Institute (the new name for the Lenin Institute; later it was called the Central Party Archive), and he said: "Who the hell designed that freakish-looking building?" The building was in the form of a cube and was painted gray, the color of cement. It's true that the building looked rather gloomy.

The architects were rather embarrassed, and Chernyshev was very, very embarrassed. He answered: "Comrade Kaganovich, I'm the one who designed it." Kaganovich smiled, apologized, and began to speak a little less harshly and insultingly about the architect.

We presented a report to the Politburo about the progress of reconstruction in Moscow. It was Kaganovich who gave the report, it seems, although it might have been Chernyshev as chief architect for the city. I was pleased by the instructions Stalin gave on relevant matters. I don't remember now specifically what he said; the words were not so vivid as to be preserved in my memory, but the general impression remained a good one. This happened in 1934, as I recall. The construction of the Moscow subway system had already begun then. When the question of the subway was being decided, we didn't have a very clear picture of what kind of construction it would really be. We were rather naïve and viewed it as almost a superhuman task. Nowadays people regard sending rockets into space as a much simpler problem than we did the construction of the Moscow subway. But back then times were different of course, and that has to be taken into account.

The best construction manager was considered to be Pavel Pavlovich Rotert,[17] a Russian-born German. He was considered the most significant man among the construction managers. The largest-scale civilian construction project at that time was being carried out in Kharkov, where a building called the House of Industry was going up on Dzerzhinsky Square. That was truly a colossal structure for those days. After the war the House of Industry was rebuilt and enlarged. Previously it had not been as huge as it is now, but for those times it was considered the largest building in the country. It was designed by the same Rotert mentioned above, and that's why the proposal was made that he be put in charge of building the subway.

At first I had nothing to do with the construction project. It was a kind of special project, even though it was in the city itself. But after some time had gone by Kaganovich suddenly said to me: "Things are going badly with the subway construction, and as a former mine worker you'll have to get involved in detailed supervision of it. In the first phase, in order to acquaint yourself with the course of the construction, I propose that you drop your work in the party's city committee, and go to some of the shafts and tunnels being dug for the subway while Bulganin goes to other ones. Stay there for a few days and nights, take a look at everything, and study it all so that you'll be able to direct it in fact and know the whole business."

Kaganovich at that time was first secretary of the party's city committee as well as first secretary of the Moscow province committee, and at the same time he was a Central Committee secretary. Most of his energy was taken up by work in the Central Committee, where he was in fact second secretary of the Central Committee, acting as a deputy to Stalin. Therefore a great deal of the work in Moscow and a great deal of the responsibility was gradually shifted onto my shoulders. This required an enormous exertion of effort if you take into account that I didn't have the knowledge and experience corresponding to these demands. You had to do your utmost with the greatest diligence, exerting enormous effort. The Moscow party organization was a complex organism. I thought, and not without good reason, that it would be a difficult job for me, and I spoke about this directly to Kaganovich. Nevertheless I became second secretary of the Moscow city committee of the AUCP (Bolshevik), and a year later second secretary of the Moscow province committee (after Ryndin).[18] Finally, in 1935, I was elected first secretary, thus becoming a professional Moscow party official. It was a great honor, which brought with it a great responsibility.

Let me return to the question of the subway. We accepted Kaganovich's proposal enthusiastically. I had great respect for Kaganovich then; he was devoted to the party and to practical work. In the work that he did, he "chopped quite a bit of wood," as the saying goes, but he didn't spare his own energies or his health; he was a dedicated and persistent worker. I went to the shafts and tunnels that had been dug for the subway, went down and looked everything over, and began to get a more concrete idea of what a subway was. Previously that word hadn't meant anything in particular to me. But when I looked around, I saw that these were simply tunnels and passageways of the same kind I had encountered when I worked in the coalmines. Of course the scene here in the subway was more impressive. In the coalmines all the work had been done by hand, but to make up for it, by comparison with the subway construction, the work had been more orderly, and, it seems, more highly skilled people had worked there.

Bulganin caught a cold in the subway tunnels and came down with sciatica, after which he had to stay in bed for a long time. Then they sent him to Matsesta[19] for treatment. In short, he was out of action for a long time; I don't remember how long, maybe a month, maybe even longer. In this way the supervision of the subway construction was, as it were, allotted to me, and I became responsible for it. I reported regularly to Kaganovich about the course of the work, and I took a most active part in it all. Above all I suggested to Kaganovich that to build a subway real cadres were needed.

The cadres there were very weak. Of course these people had worked and studied, and that was praiseworthy, but they didn't know the mining business. Yet we had to dig mineshafts and tunnels in the special conditions of the ground beneath the city of Moscow, where we often encountered water-soaked layers of earth that could flood newly dug tunnels. Besides, there were buildings on the surface that could easily be destroyed if the ground caved in, and so forth.

An especially responsible attitude was called for because of this. Therefore I proposed that mining engineers be called in. This was, after all, the kind of digging done in mining, and so mining engineers would do the work much better than those who were now heading up the project. We began looking for miners. As the saying goes, "There wouldn't have been good luck if bad luck hadn't helped out." A glitch had occurred in coal-mining operations in the Donbas. Things turned out to be bad there in the sense that there were growing demands that exceeded our capabilities. The preparatory work, the shoring up, and in general the laying out of new mines was lagging behind the need for coal. Molotov was sent to the Donbas, but he wasn't able to get at the heart of the problem, because he was totally uninformed about the specifics of the mining business.

Operations in the Donbas then were headed by Yegor Trofimovich Abakumov, a veteran mine worker who was widely regarded as highly knowledgeable about the mining industry. He had been a friend of mine. I had made his acquaintance when we worked at a mine together in the years 1912–14. We were together again in 1917, when we welcomed the revolution and became prominent activists at our mine. Later, after the Civil War, we worked together restoring production in the mines. When I had returned from Red Army duty he was director of the work in the coal pits. The party organization had appointed me as his deputy. (Back then the party organization appointed the directors.) I was thrilled at how well he knew the mining business. As a man he was simple and direct, a real worker. It was an excellent combination: he had a superb knowledge of mining and he proved to be an intelligent administrator.

At the Politburo, when they listened to Molotov's report (on the situation in the Donbas), he apparently (although I don't know the details of the matter) suggested that Abakumov be removed. That's the way the wind was blowing. Suddenly I got a phone call. It was Kaganovich calling me: "Do you know Abakumov?"

"Yes, I know Abakumov well."

"I'm calling from the Politburo. Abakumov is apparently going to be removed from his post, and the question is now being taken up where to make use of him. How would you see it if we took Abakumov as assistant director of Rotert in the subway construction? What would your opinion be of that?"

I said: "If Abakumov is removed from his post and assigned to us in the position of deputy director, we couldn't ask for a better deputy director. He would also make an outstanding director."

"No," came the answer, "that's Rotert's position."

Rotert had a reputation as a superb engineer, while Abakumov was neither an engineer nor a construction manager, but simply a man who had come up out of the ranks of the workers, although he had taken a correspondence course as a mining foreman from a special school for such training. There were such people who worked as mining foremen in practice during the capitalist times, men who knew their business even though they hadn't taken regular courses at a school for mine foremen. And so Abakumov was assigned to work with us. When he arrived, things got easier for me, because he and I were friends, and in general we knew and trusted each other. We immediately began bringing in mining engineers. We invited a close acquaintance of ours, a highly respected comrade who was an engineer at the Vishnevetsky coal pits,[20] Aleksandr Ivanovich Sholokhov, a solid and reliable specialist. In this way we assembled qualified cadres, and after that the work on the subway moved ahead more reliably.

Even before Abakumov arrived Kaganovich proposed to me: "How would you see it if we were to confirm you as director of the subway construction?"

I answered, "I'd rather not."

"But look here, you've shown your knowledge and your ability. Strictly speaking, we already regard you as the man in charge of the subway construction. So there would be very little that was new for you in all this."

"If such a decision is made," I answered, "I will do everything in my power, but in that case I would ask to be relieved of my duties as secretary of the party's city committee, because the positions of secretary of the city committee and director of the subway construction can't be combined."

"No," said Kaganovich. "That's not possible."

Later I found out that this was Stalin's proposal. Kaganovich didn't tell me about it, but Stalin had ordered Kaganovich to assign me to two jobs at once, and when I declared that two jobs couldn't be done at once, everything was left that way, just as before. In fact, I devoted 80 percent of my time to the subway then. On the way to work at the city committee and after work I would go through the subway construction sites. It's difficult to tell what kind of workdays we had. I have no idea how much we slept. We simply spent the minimum amount of time on sleep and devoted the rest of our hours to work, to the cause.

The construction was proceeding. I remember the following incident. A young engineer came to see me. I liked him very much. I hadn't known him before that, when he had worked in a planning and design office. A young, handsome fellow, he was the kind of specialist that was coming into existence in our Soviet era. Makovsky,[21] I think his name was. He said to me: "Comrade Khrushchev, we're building the subway in the German way, that is, digging open trenches. This is very inconvenient for the city. There are other construction methods, for example, the closed-tunnel, or English method, using tunneling machines called "tunneling shields." That way you have to dig deeper and it will cost a little more, but if you take into account the possibility of a war, the subway could also serve as a bomb shelter. Besides, in that case construction could be carried out without having to follow the lines of the main transportation arteries; it could be done directly underneath buildings. That method would also be better for the city's transportation system. I ask you to think it over, and if I were given such an assignment, I could present a report on the subject. Another thing: The question of how passengers are to be evacuated is now being decided. Rotert is getting ready to order elevators. That's also the German method. But why not put in escalators?"

I confess this was the first time I had ever heard the word, and I didn't know what it was—or "what you ate with it." I asked him what it meant, and he explained, to the extent that I could understand. It didn't seem to me to be a terribly great complication that he had dreamed up. I said to him: "All right, report to Comrade Kaganovich. We'll have an exchange of opinions, and then I'll reply to you."

He asked me not to say anything to Rotert about it, because Rotert was a very strict and jealous man: "I have come to see you without his knowledge. I didn't inform him. I know it's useless to try presenting this idea to him. He would condemn me without listening, because he is a very self-assured man."

I reported to Kaganovich. Kaganovich replied: "Hear him out in more detail about these escalators, and then we'll either order the elevators or we won't."

Rotert argued that we couldn't make these escalators in our own country, but could only order them from England or Germany. And for that you had to have gold. For us, in those days gold was really "worth its weight in gold." There was very little of it, and so it was spent frugally, and I think that was entirely sensible. For a long time it had been our dream, which we simply assumed would never come true, that we might succeed in having some gold spent on the subway project. First, we were sure they wouldn't give us any gold; and second, we ourselves knew there was hardly any gold to be had. It was spent for necessities that were more important than the subway. Nevertheless we got ready to bring up this question.

When Makovsky had reported to me in more detail I said that now we had to listen to Rotert. Pavel Pavlovich [Rotert] was called in, and so were some other people, and I said: "Here we have Comrade Makovsky who is making such-and-such a proposal." You'd have to see the scene to appreciate it: Makovsky was a young man, elegant, rather fragile, with the good looks of an advertising model, whereas Rotert was already an old man and one of enormous stature. He looked at Makovsky from under his overhanging eyebrows like a crocodile at a rabbit. Makovsky was frazzled, but he didn't lose his head. He began to present his point of view to Rotert very correctly and showing great respect; he said that the way he proposed was more modern and progressive and that we were using an outdated method; he said that some very deep tunnels had already been dug underneath London, and the Piccadilly subway station had had escalators installed. That was the best subway station in London, in an aristocratic part of the city. And so it wouldn't be a bad thing for us to take such a direction in our own work. Rotert looked at him scornfully and called him a baby, declaring that Makovsky was saying things without thinking them through, talking irresponsibly, and so forth. But Makovsky had already sown his seed. I took his side, but when we began to prepare a report to the Central Committee we didn't talk about building stations deep underground, or about escalators for the time being, because we considered it too early to bring up the question of gold, and we couldn't get by without that.

The problem also arose that if we used the new method, the deadlines might be extended somewhat, compared with the deadlines that had been approved for completion of the subway construction. Besides that, it was necessary to allow for a certain increase in the cost of construction. All this required that the decision be made at the top level of the government and in the Politburo. The question was presented first to the Politburo, but before that Kaganovich convened a session of the party's Moscow committee to hear a report from Rotert. Rotert was rather stubborn. For an engineer that is praiseworthy. He had his point of view and he defended it to the end; thus, he did not agree with us.

Kaganovich was troubled and upset: it was necessary to go to the Politburo, to Stalin, with this, but Rotert was opposed. Stalin might not support us. But there was no other way out because Stalin had already been primed on this question: he had been told about the disagreements, and a date for the Politburo session had been set. We went there. Rotert presented his report, and then we began to speak. I don't remember now whether I myself spoke, but the argument became quite heated.

Rotert said: "It's expensive."

At that point Stalin replied to him sharply: "Comrade Rotert, the question of what is expensive and what is cheap is decided by the government. I am asking the question about the technology. Technically speaking, can what the young engineer Makovsky is proposing be done?"

"Technically it can be done, but it will be expensive."

"The government will take responsibility for that. We will undertake the deeper construction."

That's how it was resolved. I was very pleased. Stalin had decided boldly: Yes, it would be more expensive, but at the same time a question relating to military defense was being decided. After all this would be a bomb shelter in the event of a future war. Indeed, the subway played its own significant role not only as a means of transport. During the war the subway stations actually did serve as bomb shelters. At one time the communications center and several other operations of the Stavka (the General Headquarters of the Supreme High Command) were located at the Kirov subway station.[22] That's how a new direction in the construction of the Moscow subway was decided on.

The period of reconstruction of the national economy up until 1935 was a period of great upsurge in the party and in the country. Industrialization was under way, factories were being built in Moscow and other cities—the Ball Bearing plant, the Oil and Gas Refinery, the Elektrozavod, Airplane Factory Number One (Duks)—and then there was the ongoing reconstruction of Moscow. By today's standards, the scale of construction was rather miserly, but the possibilities we had at our disposal then were of a different kind, and everything was therefore more difficult. The subway was built. Construction began on the Moscow-Volga canal. Renovation began on the bridges across the Moscow River. In those days such projects were considered enormous.

All this construction fell precisely to my lot as second secretary of the party's city committee; in effect, I was actually first secretary, because Kaganovich was overloaded with his work at the Central Committee. Even when I refused the position of director of subway construction I didn't gain anything or lose anything by that, because in fact I did direct the work and had to answer for it, not just "in general," but very specifically.

The plan for the reconstruction of Moscow was considered at a Central Committee plenum. I forget whether Stalin spoke on the question, but the main points in the plan had been reported to him before the plenum at a session of the Politburo. Stalin stated his point of view, and later it found full expression in the General Plan for the Reconstruction of Moscow. I will say again that Stalin's participation in deciding concrete questions pleased me. I was a young man who was still only coming into contact with the general problems of municipal planning and administration, let alone the specific problems of Moscow. Moscow was already a big city even then, although its municipal administrative functioning and economic functioning lagged somewhat behind the times: the streets weren't well laid out, there was an insufficient sewage system, the sidewalks were mainly cobblestone and not even cobblestone everywhere, the transportation system was mainly horse-drawn. It's a terrible thing to recall even today, but that's exactly how it was.

The Central Committee plenum laid the basis for reconstruction of the city on new foundations. It was a step forward, a big step. Here again we saw "Comrade Stalin's attention and concern for Moscow and the Muscovites." Yes, that's how people talked then, especially Lazar Moiseyevich Kaganovich, who loved bootlicking epithets of that kind. Such phrases would be taken up by everyone, and like a loud reverberating echo they would roll across all of Moscow. This kind of fulsome praise kept growing as time went on.

Let me recall how things went at the Seventeenth Party Congress, the congress at which I was elected a member of the party's Central Committee. I will tell about the voting procedure when members of the Central Committee were being elected. It made a strong impression on me because of its democratic quality. Candidates were nominated, then the names were written down on a list, and ballots with those names were passed out to the congress delegates. It's true that little possibility of a choice was afforded to the delegates: that is, only as many candidates were listed as there were seats on the Central Committee, counting full members and candidate members, as well as members of the Inspection Commission, and there was not one person more or one person less.

All delegates were given the opportunity to express their attitudes toward one or another candidate, to keep them on the list or cross them off. After receiving ballots for voting, the delegates immediately dispersed, went off and found seats to study the lists of names: each one separately decided who to leave in and who to cross out. Some comrades (judging from personal observation) were pretty zealous in the way they went about this task. But Stalin, in a demonstrative way before everyone's eyes, once he had received his list, walked over to the ballot box and dropped it in without looking. To me this behavior seemed rather peculiar. Only later did I understand that not a single candidate had been placed on those lists without Stalin's blessing; therefore there was no need whatsoever for him to read the list over again.

One incident made a discouraging impression on me. Before the voting Kaganovich instructed us younger delegates on how to deal with the list of candidates, and he did this confidentially so that no one would find out. He recommended crossing out one or another person on the list, in particular Voroshilov and Molotov, and he motivated this with the idea that Stalin should not receive fewer votes than Voroshilov, Molotov, or other members of the Politburo. He said that this was being done from political considerations, and we took an understanding attitude toward this appeal. Still, it made a bad impression on me. How could this be? A member of the Politburo, a secretary of the party's Central Committee and Moscow committee, a big authority for all of us, and suddenly he was recommending that we engage in activity of this kind, which was so unworthy of a party member.

In the voting and the vote counting then the technology of the business was as follows: the numbers of those voting and the number of votes cast for each candidate were announced. I remember that Stalin didn't receive all possible votes: Six people, it was announced, had voted against him. Why did I remember that so well? Because when the name "Khrushchev" was read off it turned out that I, too, was six votes short of the unanimous count. I felt I was in seventh heaven: six delegates had voted against me, and against Stalin there were also six votes, but who was I compared with Stalin? Back then I thought that the vote count actually reflected reality. Many other comrades had several dozen votes, or even, as I recall, a hundred votes against them. Those who received an absolute majority of votes in their favor were considered elected.

During that period I fairly often had the opportunity to communicate directly with Stalin, to listen to what he had to say, and to receive direct instructions from him on one or another question. At that time I was literally entranced by Stalin, by his attentiveness, his considerateness, how well informed he was, and his caring and nurturing attitude, and I honestly felt great admiration for him.

In those days we were all very much caught up in our work; we put a lot of feeling into our work and worked with pleasure, denying ourselves everything. We knew no rest. Very often on our days off, when they still existed (they later disappeared), conferences or assemblies or mass meetings were scheduled. Party and trade union officials were always among the masses. At factories, plants, and other work sites we toiled with enthusiasm and lived rather modestly, even more than modestly. I, for example, was better provided for materially when I worked as a blue-collar worker before the socialist revolution than when I was a secretary of the party's Moscow city and Moscow province committees.

The main thing for us was to make up for lost time, to build heavy industry and equip the Red Army with modern weapons. Because we were surrounded by capitalist states on all sides, we had to turn the USSR into an unassailable fortress. We remembered Lenin's words that after ten years of the existence of Soviet power our country would have become impregnable; we lived by that idea alone and for the sake of that idea. The times that I am recalling were times of revolutionary romanticism. Nowadays, unfortunately, it's not like that. Back then we never permitted ourselves even the thought of having our own personal dacha, or cottage in the country: after all, we were Communists! We wore modest clothing, and I doubt that any of us had a second pair of shoes. And no one had suits the way people do today. A soldier's shirt or *kosovorotka* (a traditional Russian shirt), a pair of pants, a belt, and a cap—strictly speaking, that's all we wore.

Stalin served as a good example in this regard also. In the summer he wore white trousers and a white Russian shirt with unbuttoned collar. The boots he wore were plain. Kaganovich wore a military shirt; Molotov wore a service jacket. To all outward appearances Politburo members conducted themselves modestly and, as it seemed, devoted all their energies to the cause of the party, the country, and the people. There was no time even to read literary works. I remember Molotov asking me once: "Comrade Khrushchev, do you manage to do any reading?"

I answered: "Comrade Molotov, very little."

He answered: "That's how it is with me too; the tasks of the moment swallow up everything. But still, we must read. I understand that we must, but there's no opportunity." I understood what he meant.

When I had come back to civilian life from the Red Army in 1922, what great effort I went to, to try and break free, to go study at the workers' school! But I had been sent off to work for the party before I could graduate. It was only later that I managed to plead with the Central Committee of the Ukrainian party to allow me to study at the Industrial Academy. But there too I worked and studied at the same time. I was a political activist on various levels and rungs of the ladder, energetically upholding the positions of the Central Committee and fighting for the party's general line.

It was as though party leaders in those days found themselves outside the ordinary realm of human existence—they couldn't live their lives for their own sakes. If people pursued their enthusiasm for literature, they would be criticized: "Look, instead of working, you're reading!" If they were studying to obtain a secondary or, God help us, a higher education, that meant they were do-nothings who simply didn't want to work toward the strengthening of the Soviet state. That was what the situation was like back then.

I remember Stalin saying on one occasion: "How exactly has it come about that the Trotskyists and the 'Rights' have got these privileges? The Central Committee doesn't trust them, removes them from official party posts, and they all head off for institutions of higher education. By now many of them have already graduated and are going further, doing research, going into science and scholarship. But the people who have taken a firm stand on the grounds of the party's general line and engaged in practical work haven't had the opportunity to get a higher education, to raise their level of knowledge and skills." He even named a few people as examples. But none of us felt that we were sacrificing ourselves. No! We worked with pleasure, with great enthusiasm, because we considered that the most important thing. We thought that the main thing right then was to strengthen our state. A certain amount of time was required, the amount necessary to build heavy industry, reequip agriculture and collectivize it, create a mighty army, and in that way make the Soviet borders impregnable to the enemy.

In Moscow and Moscow province in those years, as in other provinces, the colossal work of building factories was under way. Moscow itself was being reconstructed, the subway was being built, and there was construction work on the bridges. Work was begun on erecting several bridges at once—the Krymsky, Kamenny, Zamoskvoretsky, and others. All this was done superbly, and it literally transformed the city. In a word, an industrial Moscow was created from the old Moscow that wore cotton-print calico dresses. What was involved politically was the fact that the old cotton-print Moscow conditions gave rise to "Right Oppositionist" moods of the kind reflected by Uglanov, Ukhanov,[23] and other Moscow leaders. Uglanov had headed the Moscow Bolsheviks earlier, but he belonged to the "Rights."

In 1935 the Muscovites celebrated completion of the first stage of the subway's construction. Many received awards from the government. I found myself awarded, all at once, the Order of Lenin. That was my first honorary award. Bulganin received the Order of the Red Star, because he had already been given the Order of Lenin for successfully supervising the work of Elektrozavod, whose director he had been. I remember that Bulganin's Order of Lenin was No. 10. A great deal of emphasis was put on such things in those days. My Order of Lenin had a number something around 110. We had a magnificent celebration of the completion of the first phase of subway construction, which was named after Kaganovich. It was fashionable then among Politburo members (and not only Politburo members) to give their names to factories, plants, collective farms, districts, provinces, and so on. There was real competition among them! This deplorable tendency was born under Stalin.

In 1935 Kaganovich was promoted to the post of people's commissar of railways and relieved of his duties as secretary of the party's Moscow committee. After that I was put forward for the posts of first secretary of the Moscow province committee and Moscow city committee. At the next Central Committee plenum I was elected a candidate member of the Politburo. Of course I was pleased and felt flattered, but felt even more a fear of the enormous responsibility. Up to that time I had constantly carried around with me my own personal set of tools, as every machinist did. This included such items as calipers, a liter measure, a meter rule, a center punch, a marking tool (awl), and various tri-squares (*krontsirkul, litromer, metr, kerner, chertilka, vsyakiye ugolnichki*). In my thinking I had not yet broken my connection with my former profession. I thought of party work as an elective position. At any time I might not be reelected, and then I would return to my main work as a machinist. But gradually I was transformed into a professional party and government official.

As secretary of the party's Moscow committee I was supposed to oversee the functioning of the Moscow agency of the NKVD (People's Commissariat of Internal Affairs). This consisted in my reading reports on the goings-on in the city and province. The reports on life in this large urban area were sometimes quite terrible. The political situation in Moscow was stable, the party organization was solid, although now and then leaflets with Menshevik content appeared and wildcat strikes or even full-fledged strikes took place at factories. The explanation for this was to be found in the very difficult material conditions of the workers. We were doing a lot of building. Construction workers were recruited from the countryside and housed in barracks. In those barracks people lived in unimaginable conditions: filth, bedbugs, cockroaches, all sorts of other foul things. But the main thing was that they were not fed well, and they were not well supplied with work clothes. In general it was hard to get the clothes you needed back then. All that naturally caused discontent.

Discontent also arose when labor contracts were revised, accompanied by changes in work quotas and pay rates. Here the personal interests of individuals came into conflict with the interests of the state. In general these interests merged into one in the consciousness of the masses, but when a specific conflict arose between an individual and the state, naturally the result was a contradiction. For example, there would be a certain work quota at some place; then after the New Year suddenly the quota became 10 to 15 percent higher, with the pay scale remaining the same or even less. This kind of thing could be carried through more easily in places where there was an intelligent director and a sensible party organization that looked into the technical possibilities for increasing production and explained to the workers the situation that had arisen. But in other places most often nothing was done, and administrators tried to cover everything over with the authority of the party and the interests of the state, and this resulted in wildcat strikes in various shops and sometimes in an entire factory.

In such cases we would come from the city committee and explain honestly and openly where the workers were right and where they were not; we would straighten things out and punish those who had committed abuses, or, on the other hand, we would explain the situation to the workers. As a rule they understood quite well that we stood at a lower level in terms of output per worker than the advanced capitalist countries. For that reason it was necessary to tighten our belts to some extent to compete successfully with our opponents and catch up with them. Back then we rarely used the word "surpass."[24] We were afraid to use that word because the gap was much too great. It was so disheartening that we didn't dare even to pronounce that word.

In the NKVD reports about the city quite a few unflattering comments about the party and insulting remarks aimed at its leaders were quoted. The NKVD agents reported about specific people known to them, giving their last names, addresses, and so on. But no measures were taken against such people other than those of an educational kind. We knew that in this place or that place attitudes were bad, and consequently it was necessary to strengthen work with the public, in particular to do party work, to try to influence people through the trade unions and Young Communist League, by having people give lectures and promote the party line. We used every means other than administrative (by which I mean arrests and trials). If that kind of thing existed then, it was only by way of exception, in cases of specific actions of an anti-Soviet character. All that changed after the Kirov assassination.

The head of the Moscow agency of the NKVD was Comrade Redens, a man who was close to Stalin. As I've already said, Redens was a party member (since 1914, it seems to me); by nationality he was Polish; an electrician, he had worked at Dneprodzerzhinsk.[25] In my opinion he was a good comrade. When we met once, he told me he had been given the assignment to "clean up" Moscow. And really Moscow was full of trash. There were many people who didn't work, parasitic elements and speculators of every kind. They did need to be "cleaned out," and for that purpose lists of people designated for expulsion from Moscow were drawn up. That was the first stage of repression following the Kirov assassination, and for the time being it was directed at criminal elements. Where they were deported to I don't know: people stuck to a certain rule back then—to tell you only what directly concerned you. This was a government matter, and so the fewer people who knew about it the better. It was only later that victims of political terror made their appearance.

After I became secretary of the party committee at the Industrial Academy,[26] I was elected secretary of the party's Bauman district committee, then of the Krasnaya Presnya district committee, and finally of the Moscow city committee. I worked in that post until 1935, and then was elected first secretary of both the city committee and the province committee of the AUCP(B). By then I was already a member of the Central Committee, and when I was elected first secretary of the Moscow committee, there and then I was elected a candidate member of the Politburo. Finally, in 1938, when I was sent to Ukraine, at the next Central Committee plenum I was elected a full member of the Politburo. Thus, all the important events of 1934–38 took place before my eyes. Therefore I have the right to make some generalizations.

By 1938 the previously existing democracy in the Central Committee had already been severely undermined. For example, even though I was a candidate member of the Politburo, I didn't receive materials related to Politburo meetings. After the terrible year of 1937 I didn't know, strictly speaking, to whom such materials were distributed in general. I received only those materials that Stalin sent by his own personal order. These materials most often had to do with "enemies of the people": their confessions—an entire book's worth of "confessions," which had already supposedly been checked and verified. These materials were distributed to us so that Politburo members would see how the enemy had entangled us, how we were surrounded on all sides. I also read these materials, and no doubts arose in my mind at that time about the authenticity of the documents: after all, Stalin himself was distributing them! The thought couldn't even have entered my mind that these might be false confessions. What would that be done for? Who would that serve? There was complete trust in the documents, especially because, after all, I had seen Stalin as a different kind of person.

In the early 1930s Stalin was very simple and accessible. When I worked as secretary of the city committee and the province committee of the AUCP(B), if I had any kind of question, I would call Stalin directly. He hardly ever refused to see me, but would immediately receive me or make an appointment. My questions for him were most often concerned with political and practical aspects of resolutions passed at our party meetings, because the Moscow committee always served as an example for other party organizations. Stalin himself spoke to us on exactly those lines, and I understood that a resolution we adopted would later be repeated by almost all the other party organizations, perhaps in different variations, but the essence would be the same.

The domestic side of Stalin's life also pleased me. When I was already working in Ukraine [1938 and after], I'd go to see him (most often at his dacha in Volynskoye, the one closer to Moscow, it was only a short distance away—about 15 minutes from the city), and he would be eating. If it was summer, he was always eating out in the open air, on the porch. He usually sat alone. They served soup, a thick Russian broth, and there'd be a small carafe of vodka and a pitcher of water; the vodka glass was moderate in size. You'd go in and say hello and he would say: "Want something to eat? Take a seat." And "take a seat" meant grab a soup bowl (the soup kettle was right there), fill a bowl for yourself, as much as you want, sit down, and eat. If you want something to drink, grab a carafe, pour yourself a glass, and drink it down. If you want a second drink, you decide that for yourself. The soul knows its own measure, as the saying goes. If you don't want to drink, you don't have to.

Long after that we would reminisce on how good the old times were. But another time came when you not only could not refuse a drink, but they'd simply force it on you, pump you full, fill you to the brim deliberately. Yes, Stalin knew how to do that. It's true that he told me more than once: "Remember back before Beria came to Moscow? We didn't have such drinking bouts then; there wasn't so much drunkenness." And I saw that Beria took the role of instigator to please Stalin. Stalin liked it and Beria sensed that. When no one wanted to drink and Beria saw that Stalin had a need for a drink, Beria immediately organized a round of toasts; he would think up all sorts of pretexts and act as ringleader. I am talking about this because toward the end of Stalin's life this way of spending the time became disastrous both for our work and for our physical health. People were literally becoming drunkards, and the more a person became a drunkard, the more pleasure Stalin got from it. People might say that Khrushchev is washing dirty linen in public. But what can you do? Without washing dirty linen there would be no clean linen. Clean linen gets its cleanness and whiteness by its contrast with dirty linen. Not only that; the conditions of Stalin's home life were closely interwoven with our work life. Apparently this is something that's almost inevitable when a country is actually being run by one person, and, as a result, it's difficult to separate personal circumstances from public affairs.

I recall several instances during our prewar life when I clashed with Stalin on one or another specific economic question. I've already said that on all questions of the rebuilding of Moscow that we brought up ourselves, and where we ourselves had shown initiative, we found support from Stalin. In general he pushed us from behind, urged us not to be afraid to decide difficult problems, break our way through, even if opposition arose among some members of society, including specialists. Architects were sometimes opposed to tearing down structures that had architectural or historical value. It seems that these architects were right in their own way. But after all, the city was growing, its streets had to be widened, new types of transportation were appearing, the old carriage driver was disappearing, streetcars in the center of the city became obsolete, the subway was functioning, trolley buses and new bus lines made their appearance. This was not something exclusive to Moscow: every city on the globe was experiencing such changes and accompanying problems.

The honor of helping lay down the first trolley-bus lines in the Soviet Union, precisely in Moscow, fell to my lot. I spent a great deal of energy introducing them. A great mass of people was opposed to this mode of transportation. When the first trolley-bus line was all ready, it had to be tested. Suddenly the phone rang. It was Kaganovich calling: "Don't do that!"

I said: "But it's already been tested."

"So, and how was it?"

"Everything's fine."

It turns out that Stalin had his doubts; he was afraid that one of these trackless trolleys might turn over during testing. For some reason many people thought that the trolley bus was bound to turn over, for example, on Gorky Street on the downgrade next to the Central Telegraph Building. Stalin was afraid that if something like this went wrong, it would be used by foreign propaganda, and so he forbade the testing of the trolley busses, but he acted too late. The test had been successfully carried out and the trolley bus entered our lives to stay. As soon as it was reported to him that everything turned out all right, he relaxed. He saw that this form of transportation would actually improve city life: it was quiet, and since it used electricity, it wouldn't pollute the atmosphere. A progressive form of transportation had been acquired. Stalin approved it, and in 1934 the first trolley bus line began to operate.

I don't know how things stand with this question nowadays, but at that time people said that the trolley bus was a suburban form of transportation, not an urban one. I didn't agree with that, and Stalin supported me. Once again I was impressed; I admired Stalin for the fact that he looked into matters both large and small and supported everything that was progressive. To be sure, later on, when we bought double-decker (three-axle) trolley busses, Stalin nevertheless forbade their use: again he was afraid they would tip over. No matter how we tried to persuade him of the opposite, it was no use. One day, while traveling through Moscow he saw such a double-decker trolley bus on a test run; he was infuriated by our disobedience and ordered: "Remove it!" It was removed. And so we didn't succeed in putting those into use.

A major opponent of the trolley bus was my friend, now long departed, Ivan Alekseyevich Likhachev.[27] He was a man enamored of the internal combustion engine. So he "pushed" for the use of that kind of motor vehicle everywhere, and in the given instance he said: "A bus can travel down any alley. None of your trolley busses could compare with that. It [the trolley bus] is a hopeless undertaking." I argued with him at great length. Meanwhile everything that he had to do when the first trolley bus models were being readied for use was done with precision and punctuality. But he was doing his duty as director of the factory, and personally he still passed judgment: "All the same, I'm opposed to it because the trolley bus is not a progressive thing." I would argue even today, after so much time has gone by, that his views should be considered incorrect: the trolley bus is a more progressive form of urban transportation. In France experimental lines with monorail electric trains have been introduced. This is also a kind of trolley bus in its own way. The future is in its favor, because it can be raised to a higher level. Hence, the streets can be relieved of some of the load of surface transport. Besides that, rapid transit is needed. Unquestionably technology will create the possibility for us to free ourselves from noise, and this form of transportation will be noiseless. I think that the basis for creating this kind of public transportation system was laid precisely by the trolley bus.

I will also say a few words about the situation at Politburo meetings. I had the chance to attend these meetings when I became a member of the Central Committee after the Seventeenth Party Congress, held in 1934. Good traditions, which had been laid down by Lenin, were still maintained in the party back then. Central Committee members had the possibility, if they wished, of freely attending Politburo meetings. They were allowed to sit there, that is, to listen but not to intervene in the discussion. This was done so that Central Committee members would be up to date on the life of our country and the activities of the Politburo. I personally made frequent use of this right, but not always, because I didn't have time.

Meetings were held at a set time on a set day. There were also closed sessions at which only members of the Politburo were present. But the decisions made at the closed sessions were recorded in a special folder, and all members of the Central Committee could go to the confidential division and ask for this folder and familiarize themselves with the confidential decisions of the Politburo. To be sure, confidential decisions were removed from the minutes that were sent out to party organizations. The fact that any decision was accessible to any member of the Central Committee is very interesting, and I call special attention to it. It was something that remained from Lenin's time. The meetings were chaired in the 1930s not by the general secretary of the Central Committee but by the chairman of the Council of People's Commissars. During my time that was Molotov.

Politburo meetings were also conducted differently from nowadays, when seventy to eighty questions are rubber-stamped in a couple of hours. Back then people were called to appear before the Politburo; questions were asked, people gave special reports, debates and discussions went on, arguments for and against were heard, then a decision would be made, and we'd take a break. During the break we would drink tea. It's said about Muscovites with good reason that they can't have a meeting without tea. Next to the meeting room was a special room where people went to drink tea. The break would last approximately half an hour, and then consideration of a new question would begin. The general meeting lasted three or four hours.

I remember that the discussion of some questions [at Politburo meetings] could be very stormy. Once Sergo [Ordzhonikidze] lost his temper (by nature he was a very hot-tempered man) and flung himself at Rosengolts, people's commissar of foreign trade, and almost threw a punch at him.

After the assassination of Kirov,[28] and especially after the dark year of 1937, everything gradually changed, and the previous way of doing things was eliminated. After the Eighteenth Party Congress in 1939, when I became a Politburo member, I don't recall Politburo meetings being held regularly anymore.

1. The all-out collectivization process that began under Stalin's leadership in 1929–30 involved forcing or pressuring individual peasant farmers to join together in government-dominated collective farms, mainly through a campaign to eliminate the kulaks as a class. (The term "kulak" referred to the minority of wealthier peasants, but it was often used loosely to justify repressive measures against any peasant who opposed collectivization.) By 1933 most of the peasant population of the Soviet Union had been driven into collective farms or state farms, but the price for this was a disastrous blow to Soviet agriculture and to much of the peasantry, with terrible repression and great loss of life. [GS]

2. "Giddy from Success: On Problems of the Collective Farm Movement" was a letter from Stalin to the newspaper *Pravda*, published therein on March 2, 1930. On the basis of the letter, the Central Committee of the AUCP(B) adopted on March 15, 1930 a resolution "On the Struggle Against Distortions of the Party Line in the Collective Farm Movement."

3. M. A. Sholokhov was one of the most famous Soviet writers of the time. See Biographies.

4. K. Ya. Bauman. See Biographies.

5. Krasnodar was the center of Krasnodar territory, a fertile agricultural region in southern European Russia, also including western areas of the Northern Caucasus. [SS]

6. Krasnodar territory is also known as the Kuban, after the main river that flows through the region. [SS]

7. A *stanitsa* is a large Cossack settlement. During collectivization the inhabitants of many such villages were deported. [GS]

8. Rykov, Bukharin, Zinoviev, and Kamenev were all leaders of the revolution and former members of the Politburo. See Biographies. [GS]

9. Trotsky was exiled from the Soviet Union to Turkey in 1929. In 1936, he was given asylum in

Mexico, and in 1940 he was assassinated there by an NKVD agent. See Biographies. [GS/SS]

10. G. I. Veklichev. See Biographies.

11. I. E. Yakir. See Biographies.

12. Rhomboids were diamond-shaped insignia identifying the wearer as the commander of an army or a Front (army group). [GS]

13. G. K. Ordzhonikidze. See Biographies.

14. A. S. Yenukidze. See Biographies.

15. These men came from Georgia, Armenia, or Azerbaijan, the main regions of the Southern Caucasus (also called the Transcaucasus or Transcaucasia). Stalin, Ordzhonikidze, and Yenukidze were Georgians, Mikoyan an Armenian. [GS/SS]

16. S. E. Chernyshev was a prominent architect. See Biographies.

17. P. P. Rotert was in charge of building the Moscow metro. See Biographies.

18. K. V. Ryndin. See Biographies.

19. Matsesta is a health resort near Sochi on the Black Sea coast where patients are treated by immersion in mud baths. The place was considered sacred in ancient times. "Matsesta" means "burning water" in the language of the people indigenous to the area. [GS/SS]

20. Workings of bituminous coal 18 kilometers from the former Cossack settlement of Kamenskaya, where there were mines at the Vishnevetsky Gully by the Donets River (also known as the Seversky Donets River).

21. V. L. Makovsky was an engineer specializing in subway construction. See Biographies.

22. The name of this subway station is now Chistye Prudy (Pure Ponds).

23. K. V. Ukhanov. See Biographies.

24. When N. S. Khrushchev became the supreme Soviet leader, he proclaimed the goal of "catching up with and surpassing" the advanced capitalist countries—above all, the United States. This subject is discussed at length in the article "The Last Romantic," by the writer Anatoly Strelyany, which

is to be included as an appendix in Volume 2 of these memoirs. [GS/SS]

25. Dneprodzerzhinsk is a town in eastern Ukraine to the west of Dnepropetrovsk. It was formerly called Kamenskoye. [GS/SS]

26. Here Khrushchev recapitulates the record of his party career after moving to Moscow. [GS]

27. I. A. Likhachev. See Biographies.

28. S. M. Kirov. See Biographies.

## THE KIROV ASSASSINATION

In [summer] 1934 the Seventeenth Party Congress was held—the Congress of Victors, as they called it then. There was no opposition any longer, neither in the party nor at the congress itself. It was the first congress after Lenin's death that had no opposition. Of course during Lenin's lifetime there had always been an opposition! During the 1930s the five-year plans unfolded, things were going well, and everyone was passionately absorbed with the economic work. That was the main thing then. And it was correct [to focus on the economy]: after all, it specifically confirmed our ideology. If your ideology is not reinforced by material reality, it will not grow and become stronger in the minds of the people. So everything was going well.

It's difficult for me to remember all the details now. One evening in early December [1934] the phone rang. It was Kaganovich: "I'm calling from the Politburo, to ask you to come here immediately." I went to the Kremlin and entered the conference room. Kaganovich met me. He had a kind of dreadful expression on his face that put me on my guard; he was obviously very upset; he had tears in his eyes. He told me: "Something bad has happened. In Leningrad. Kirov has been assassinated. I'll tell you about it later. The Politburo is discussing the question now. A delegation is being assigned to go there: Stalin will go, and apparently Voroshilov and Molotov, along with people from the Moscow party organization and also Moscow workers, about sixty people all together. You need to head up the Moscow delegation. You will be there as part of the honorary funeral guard and accompany the body from Leningrad to Moscow."

I immediately set out for the Moscow committee offices. We put together our delegation, and late in the evening of the same day we left for Leningrad. Stalin, Voroshilov, and Molotov were also going there, but I didn't see them when we got on the train or when we arrived, because they were traveling separately in special railroad cars. All of Leningrad was in profound mourning. (Although it may be that those were just my personal feelings, and I was transferring them to everything else.) We saw the grief-stricken secretaries of the city and province party committees and many other people. I also met old acquaintances there. My relations with Chudov[1] had been especially good. He was the second secretary of the party's Leningrad province committee, a handsome and likable man, respected by all the comrades. We all simply had to shrug; we had no idea what had happened. All we knew was that someone named Nikolayev[2] had assassinated Kirov. We were told that Nikolayev had either been expelled from the party or had been punished for participating in the Trotskyist opposition, and therefore this was the work of the Trotskyists. Apparently they had organized the assassination, and we sincerely felt outrage and indignation over that.

I forget now how many days we spent in Leningrad, while the Leningraders were viewing the remains of Sergei Mironovich Kirov. We also stood in the honor guard, and that happened several times, as I recall. Then there was the transfer of the body to Moscow and the funeral. I cannot say how Stalin and some other members of the Politburo experienced the death of Kirov. But Kaganovich, who I observed firsthand, was shaken to the core by it and, in my view, even felt frightened. I saw Stalin only when he was standing in the honor guard in Leningrad. But he knew how to keep his self-control, and the expression on his face was absolutely impenetrable. And at that time I couldn't even have imagined that he might be preoccupied with other thoughts, not just his feelings about Kirov's death.

I had not been closely acquainted with Kirov. He and I both spoke at someone's funeral at Red Square in Moscow. I don't remember who we were burying then. But Kaganovich said to me at that time: "You have to speak, but keep in mind that Kirov will also be speaking. Kirov is a very good speaker, so you should think out very carefully what you're going to say; otherwise people might get an unfavorable impression of you." I answered that I could do no more than I could do, and that there was no competition between Kirov and me, so that maybe it would be better if someone else spoke instead. "No, the orders are that you should speak." And I spoke. Immediately after I finished Kaganovich came over to me: "Splendid. You spoke brilliantly. Stalin noticed it and said: 'It's hard to speak side by side with Kirov, and Khrushchev did well.'"

My own view of the matter, to speak about myself for a moment, was that I was not a bad speaker. I always spoke without a written text and most often even without notes. Whenever I was getting ready to give a report I made an outline with statistics, because it was hard for me to keep statistics in my head, and my reports came out better that way. I began giving reports only when I became a high-ranking official: there was a lot of responsibility, and once you had said something it was hard to correct it. So I felt obliged to take precisely this line of action. Besides, I saw that everyone was doing it; they were all reading their speeches.

For example, when I was getting ready to give a report at the Nineteenth Party Congress,[3] Malenkov[4] said to me: "So-and-so and so-and-so are preparing your report for you. Don't be offended. You know what I'm saying? Stalin himself, in 1941, when he spoke at the celebrations of the October revolution during the war, didn't even change a comma in his speech. The text of the speech was provided for him. I don't know if he read it beforehand, but he did read the text absolutely without any change. And so you shouldn't feel embarrassed; that's the way it is for leaders."

So then we had gone to Leningrad [after the Kirov assassination]. We were put up in the best hotel. Our delegation numbered about sixty people: blue-collar and white-collar workers. We stood in the honor guard by the coffin, and then at the hotel we sat around and talked. There was nothing else for us to do. Everyone was weeping over the loss of Kirov.

Then the official machinery [of investigation and repression] set to work. Exactly what it did I didn't know; that was not my concern. Stalin himself took charge of that matter. It was outside my sphere. My job was just to join in the general procession when they brought the coffin to the railroad station, and on arrival in Moscow we all marched in a procession from the railroad station. Later the headline was printed in the papers: "The Moscow organization pays its respects to Comrade Kirov." I saw Kirov's wife at the funeral for the first and last time: today I wouldn't even recognize her.

In everyday life Kirov had not been a very talkative man, but when he was out among the people he was like a tribune [i.e., an outspoken advocate]. I myself had never had any direct dealings with him, and later I asked Mikoyan about Kirov. Mikoyan had known him well. He told me: "Well, how can I answer you? At official meetings he never spoke on any question, not even once. He remained silent, and that was all. I don't even know what that meant."

I had also heard that Kirov had the ability to speak in such a way as to inspire even starving people. He did that in Astrakhan in 1919. There had been nothing to eat, and so he got up and gave speeches, and people listened to them and forgot about their hunger.[5] Of course he was an intelligent man and knew what needed to be said. Yes, he was a true tribune of the people! I heard him speak at a party congress. He spoke without any written text and with skilled gestures—an excellent orator.

After the Twentieth Congress of the CPSU [in 1956] a special commission was established to carry out detailed investigations into the cases of innocent people who had been unjustly convicted. Shvernik[6] was confirmed as chairman of that commission. I proposed that the commission also include Shatunovskaya,[7] who herself had sat in prison for sixteen years for no reason and who, in my view, was a very loyal party member who could not be bought. One other comrade, who had been in prison for almost twenty years, was brought into that investigation.[8] The result was a highly responsible commission that was supposed to look into all the cases and present its conclusion: How could it have happened that such a large number of honest people perished, during Stalin's time, as alleged enemies of the people?

Naturally, the commission members first began to look into exactly who Nikolayev had been, how he had carried out the Kirov assassination, and what had prompted him to do it. When they began to study the case, they learned that not long before the Kirov assassination Nikolayev had been detained by Chekists[9] near the building of the Smolny Institute,[10] that is, the offices where Kirov worked. Nikolayev had aroused certain suspicions on the part of the guards of the building; he had been detained and searched. In his possession the Chekists found a revolver. In spite of this evidence (in those days they took a very severe attitude toward such things) and despite the fact that he had been detained in a high security area, an area frequented by a Politburo member—also, the entire leadership of the party's Leningrad province committee and city committee had their offices there—Nikolayev, as the commission reported to us, was set free. And a little while later, he assassinated Kirov. All these details caused both the commission and us to prick up our ears.

After all, Nikolayev had not shot Kirov out on an open city square. No! He had penetrated the grounds of the Smolny Institute. Nikolayev had entered the building using the entrance that only Kirov used and had killed him on a landing of the stairway as Kirov was going up the stairs. All this immediately aroused suspicion that Nikolayev had been sent there to carry out a terrorist act. Before that time Nikolayev had conducted himself in a suspicious way and had been detained, but then he was set free on orders from above. Moreover, Nikolayev gained access to the Smolny building and was able to position himself on a stairway landing in the offices of the party's province committee, where Kirov worked. That's where he encountered Kirov and killed him. Without the help of people in powerful positions it would have been altogether impossible for him to do this, because all the approaches to Smolny were guarded, and the entrance that Kirov used was especially closely guarded. Only those who had access to that particular entrance of the building could have organized this whole affair.

We were all shaken to the core. We began to look into the matter further. It may be that some of those present had known all the circumstances of the case earlier but were now holding their tongues. Certainly Molotov and Voroshilov, who had traveled to Leningrad with Stalin, knew something. The commission reported that it had received information that Nikolayev had been interrogated by Stalin in person. Some Old Bolsheviks said that, but naturally there was no documentary evidence to that effect, nor could there have been.

This is allegedly what happened at the interrogation. When he was brought before Stalin, Nikolayev threw himself on his knees and began to say that he had done this "on instructions" in the name of the party. It should be mentioned that before the conversation with Stalin, Nikolayev had refused to answer any questions from the investigators [of the local Leningrad OGPU] and demanded that he be turned over to representatives of the central apparatus of the OGPU.[11] He asserted he was not guilty of anything and that in Moscow they knew why he had done what he had done. Whether some "instructions" had been given to him or not it's hard for me to judge. If so, then he carried out his instructions. But whose instructions could they have been?

Of course Stalin would not personally have entrusted such a task to Nikolayev. Nikolayev was too minor a figure for that. But I have no doubt that someone primed Nikolayev on orders from Stalin. This assassination was organized from the highest reaches. As I see it, it was arranged by the OGPU head, Yagoda,[12] who in turn could only have been acting on secret orders from Stalin, orders given, as the saying goes, "from eye to eye." If this line of argument is to be accepted, it follows that Nikolayev probably hoped for some kind of leniency. But to count on that was really too naïve on his part. Nikolayev was not an important enough person. He had carried out his orders and thought his life would be spared, but he was simply a fool. Immediately after instructions like that were carried out, it was necessary to destroy the perpetrator in order to keep everything secret. And Nikolayev was destroyed.

When the commission was holding its sessions, Voroshilov was still alive, and Molotov is still alive today.[13] We were not so naive as to ask them about this case. Both would have indignantly rejected such questions, because to admit knowledge would have meant confessing complicity in the conspiracy behind the Kirov assassination. They were not that stupid.

The commission further established that while Stalin, Molotov, and Voroshilov were in Leningrad, and while the investigation into the Kirov assassination was being carried out, Stalin demanded that the OGPU commissar in charge of guarding Kirov on that day be brought to see him. During those same days an announcement was made to the active party membership that when the OGPU commissar was being brought by automobile for this interrogation something went wrong with the steering mechanism of the vehicle (he was being conveyed in a truck), and as a result his head hit the corner of a building and he died. We ordered the commission to question the people who had been driving the commissar and to have them tell exactly what the circumstances were under which this accident had occurred and how this commissar, the head of Kirov's bodyguards, had actually died. A search began for the people involved. There had been three of them, and I was told their names. Two had been sitting in the back of the truck together with the commissar, guarding him, and the third was in the cab together with the driver. It turned out that none of the three was still alive. They had all been shot. This of course made us suspect more than ever that the whole operation had been organized from on high and that the accident had been no accident.

I suggested: "Hunt around and see if the driver might still be alive." I had no great hopes because I saw how the whole business had been organized, and I figured that the driver, too, would have been eliminated as a witness.

But by surprising good luck, the driver was still alive. He was interrogated. He confirmed that he had been the driver of the vehicle, and he said: "We were driving along. The Chekist sitting next to me kept urging me to go faster, to deliver the arrested man quicker. At a certain street, as we were turning, he suddenly grabbed the wheel and ran the truck toward the corner of the building. But I was a strong man and young, and I regained control of the wheel. The vehicle was straightened out and only the fender was bent, there was no real accident. But during our encounter I heard a kind of powerful blow being struck outside and above me. Later they announced that this commissar died 'in an accident.'" Thus the driver's testimony revealed even more details of the plot behind the assassination of Kirov.

Of course Kirov himself was gone, and the threads that might have revealed to us the exact nature of the conspiracy had been broken. All the witnesses had been killed except for the driver. I was surprised by that. The murderers were skilled people, but they hadn't foreseen everything. Almost always a crime leaves some traces behind it, and as a result it can be unraveled. That's what happened in the case of the driver: it's as though [they thought] they had provided for everything; the three Chekists had been eliminated, and the commissar had been killed (the commissar of course could have told a lot: apparently he had been given some orders, because he lagged behind Kirov after they went into the building and Kirov began to go up the stairs), but they forgot about the driver.

Later we began a search for Medved,[14] who had been the chief OGPU official for Leningrad province. He had been, it was said, a very close friend of Kirov's. They used to go hunting together, and their families were friends. Perhaps Medved would have something to say? It was discovered that Medved had at first been deported to the north and later shot. This also destroyed any evidence. As a man close to Kirov, he might have had his own opinion about the assassination. The commission also reported that a certain person had been found who claimed that a woman, a doctor in a hospital where Medved had been a patient, reported that he had told her something, saying that in the future she should pass on what he told her to the party's Central Committee. He had told her: "I won't survive. I'll be destroyed." But we couldn't find the person Medved had spoken with. We came across this thread, but it too was broken. All these things were established by Shvernik through the commission.

Now I'm approaching the main question: Why did the "choice" fall on Kirov? Why was Kirov's death necessary for Stalin? Kirov was a man who had been close to Stalin. He had been sent to Leningrad after the Zinoviev opposition was broken, and he carried out important work there, for the Leningrad organization had consisted mainly of supporters of Zinoviev. Kirov turned the organization around, and it became a bastion of support for the Central Committee and a transmission belt for Central Committee decisions. Stalin himself gave the credit for all this to Kirov. Besides that, Kirov was a big mass leader. I will not try to touch on all his good qualities at this point, which were so highly valued in the party. I will recall only that he was a splendid orator and fought to the best of his ability for the ideas of the party and for the ideas of Lenin; and he was very popular within the party and among the people. For that reason the blow against Kirov reverberated painfully both inside the party and among the people. Kirov was made a victim so that his death could be used to arouse the indignation of the whole country. And then the people who didn't suit Stalin could be dealt with, especially the Old Bolsheviks, by accusing them of raising their hand against Kirov.

Back in those days they said that Nikolayev had once been a Trotskyist. It's possible that that's true, but there was no documentary evidence confirming it—either during Stalin's life or after his death. Although the Shvernik commission had access to all the materials, it did not discover any ties between Nikolayev and the Trotskyists.

A question arises: Why exactly was it necessary for Stalin to take reprisals against the Old Bolsheviks? During its investigation into the circumstances of the Kirov assassination, the commission examined mountains of material and talked with a great many people. In the course of this, new facts came out. The secretary of the party's committee for the Northern Caucasus, Sheboldayev,[15] had been prominent in the party back then. I had known Sheboldayev, although I hadn't been closely acquainted with him. In 1917 he was in the tsarist army on the Turkish front and did a lot of successful agitational work among the troops. As has now become known, the same Sheboldayev, an Old Bolshevik with a prerevolutionary record, came over to Comrade Kirov during the Seventeenth Party Congress and said to him: "Mironych (people close to Kirov called him by that short form of his patronymic), the oldsters[16] are saying that we have to go back to Lenin's 'Testament' and carry it out, that is, remove Stalin, transfer him to some other job, as Lenin recommended, and put someone in his place who would be more tolerant in his relations with those around him. People are saying that it would be good if you were put up for the post of general secretary of the party's Central Committee."

Word of this conversation reached the Shvernik commission, and it reported to the Presidium of the Central Committee on this. What Kirov answered to that remark I don't know, but it did become known that Kirov went to Stalin and told him about the conversation with Sheboldayev. Stalin supposedly answered Kirov: "Thank you, I won't forget you for this favor!" This remark was typical of Stalin. You can't tell from this remark whether he was grateful to Kirov for informing him or whether he was threatening him. This incident lifts the curtain on the reasons why the mass slaughter, the "meat grinder," was organized.

The commission also took an interest in how the voting at the Seventeenth Party Congress proceeded. A search began for the members of the commission that counted the votes. A few of them remained among the living. We found Comrade Andreasyan[17] and several others. I knew Andreasyan well; he had worked as secretary of the party's district committee in the Oktyabrsky district of Moscow at the time when I was secretary in the Krasnaya Presnya district. Andreasyan had been close to Mikoyan: In the old days they had been students at the same seminary. Andreasyan had also "done time" [under Stalin] for fifteen or sixteen years. He and the other members of the vote-counting commission at the Seventeenth Party Congress reported that the number of votes cast against Stalin was not 6, as reported at the congress, but either 260 or 160. Either figure is very impressive, especially taking into account the position Stalin held in the party, his high opinion of himself, and his personality in general. It was announced at the congress, as I have said, that only six people voted against Stalin's candidacy.

Who gave the orders to the vote-counting commission to falsify the results of the voting? I am absolutely convinced that no one would have gone so far without Stalin's backing. If we put together the results of the voting and the talk Sheboldayev had with Kirov, which Stalin found out about, and if we take into account Lenin's well-known warning that Stalin was capable of abusing power, then everything falls into place. We get a logical explanation of the assassination of Kirov by Nikolayev, then the murder of the commissar who was supposed to be guarding Kirov, and the murder of the three security agents who were bringing the commissar to be interviewed and interrogated by Stalin. It suddenly becomes clear why all this happened. Stalin was a smart man and he understood that if 260 or 160 had voted against him at the Seventeenth Party Congress, it meant that discontent was ripening in the party. Who could have voted against Stalin? It could have been only the cadres from Lenin's time. You couldn't even suggest the possibility that a Khrushchev or other young people like him, who had been promoted under Stalin and who idolized Stalin and hung on his every word, could vote against him. There was no way that could have happened.

But as for the older party members, who had had dealings with Lenin, who had worked under his leadership, who had known Lenin well—Lenin, whose testament always remained in their memory—they could not reconcile themselves to the fact that after Lenin's death Stalin had accumulated so much power, that by the time of the Seventeenth Party Congress he had ceased to take them into account, and that he was beginning to display in full all the features of his personality that Vladimir Ilyich [Lenin] had pointed to and warned against. It was they apparently who had decided to speak with Kirov and vote against Stalin. Stalin understood that the older cadres, who were present in the leadership, were dissatisfied with him and wanted to replace him if they could manage it. These people might influence the delegates at the next party congress and bring about changes in the leadership. But then Kirov was assassinated, and the whole mass slaughter began.

Many military men were executed. In regard to the military men I cannot say for certain that there was a direct connection between them and the conversation Sheboldayev had with Kirov. It's possible that the military men fell victim to a provocation by Hitler who managed to foist a false "document" onto Benes, the president of Czechoslovakia, allegedly linking them with the Nazis. Tukhachevsky[18] became the first victim. Tukhachevsky was a very talented military leader. At the age of twenty-seven, during the Civil War, he already commanded the troops of the Western Front. In general he inspired great hopes. On the one hand, this pleased many people; on the other, it put many on their guard: Might not Tukhachevsky follow the example of Napoleon and become a dictator?

Tukhachevsky enjoyed Stalin's confidence to a great extent at that time. It was in fact Tukhachevsky, not People's Commissar Vorishilov, who concerned himself most with building up the Red Army, because Tukhachevsky was better trained and better organized. Voroshilov occupied himself with being the official representative at parades and all kinds of maneuvers, and he was mainly concerned with self-promotion. Therefore Vorishilov also had an interest in the removal of Tukhachevsky.

If we are to bring up the names of all those who were arrested back then, above all it had to do with the Old Bolsheviks, people of the Lenin school, who held leading positions in the party and were assigned to decisive sectors. Stalin determined correctly who had voted against him—the Old Bolsheviks—and so their heads flew. They were proclaimed to be enemies of the people, and all our citizens, both party members and people not in the party, approved it. Today in China Mao Zedong is doing the same thing, except that Mao's victims are called opponents of the Cultural Revolution[19] rather than enemies of the people.

I [recently] read through Krupskaya's reminiscences of Lenin once again. As I was reading, it was as though there passed before my eyes all the people who went abroad to work with Lenin, lived with him, and received his instructions. Those were the people who had been closest to Lenin. And where were they now? They didn't exist. How had they ended their political careers? They showed up on lists of "enemies of the people." Krupskaya wrote about Vareikis,[20] Pyatnitsky[21] (the man who maintained Lenin's ties with Russia), and Peters.[22] I knew Peters very well, because when I worked as secretary of the party's Moscow committee, he headed the party control commission for Moscow province.

Nadezhda Konstantinovna [Krupskaya] also wrote about a certain Bulgarian. An article about this man was recently published in *Izvestia*.[23] It didn't say how he had died; nowadays they take a simple tack. They just say: he lived, and now he is no more; he's gone to heaven. Right now I can't remember his name, but he was the man who provided Bulgarian passports for Ilyich [Lenin] and Nadezhda Konstantinovna [Krupskaya] when Lenin needed personal documents from some country other than Russia. Long after that, after the revolution, Lenin invited him to come to Russia, and he came and worked here. Toward the end of his life he was, it seems, the director of a group of bakeries. This man also perished. Why? Because a purge of everyone who had been close to Lenin had begun—not only people in the Central Committee and among delegates to the Seventeenth Congress, but among all those who might be linked with them or might sympathize with them.

How many people who had had dealings with Lenin turned out to be "enemies of the people"! Kosior, a member of the Central Committee and of the Polituburo.[24] Rudzutak,[25] a candidate member of the Polituburo, an Old Bolshevik, and an influential man whom Lenin had treated with great respect. Mezhlauk,[26] a major economist and organizer, the head of the State Planning Commission (Russian acronym, Gosplan). In my view he was the best chairman of Gosplan after Kuibyshev.[27] Vlas Yakovlevich Chubar,[28] also a highly respected person, an Old Bolshevik close to Lenin. And Petrovsky.[29] He died a natural death, but he was removed from all his previous positions and sent to do third-class work. After the revolution Petrovsky was not considered an active organizer in the party, and he played the role, so to speak, of a party icon. So Petrovsky was no danger to Stalin. It was enough to just hide him away [as the director] of the Museum of the Revolution [in Moscow]. Postyshev, Pavel Petrovich[30]—a very energetic man. Eikhe, secretary of the party's Novosibirsk province committee and later people's commissar of agriculture.[31] When he was arrested, Stalin said: "Here people thought that Eikhe was a Communist, but when they began to interrogate him he said: 'What are you picking on me for? I'm not a Communist, and I've never been a Communist.'" This story was fabricated by Stalin, so that his version of events would be widely circulated among us. Of Vareikis it was also said that he had been a "provocateur." In short, all the people who were arrested were subjected to defamation of character. It was proclaimed that they had not been Communists but provocateurs.

This then is the origin of the mass slaughter that Stalin undertook, thereby confirming Vladimir Ilyich's apprehensions about Stalin remaining in his post, his warning that Stalin was capable of abusing power. The party didn't listen to Lenin and paid for it. But it was not only party cadres who were destroyed. Everyone was mowed down. If someone was in a bad mood and said something wrong, that would be enough for his or her name to end up on the appropriate list and for the person to be deported or destroyed.

I have one more thought that I want to express. Some people in conversations with me have said: "Comrade Khrushchev, what's your opinion? Is it really proper to go on talking about a reign of terror under Stalin, to say that there were no grounds for executing people, that they were innocent? Perhaps it's possible to forgive Stalin and understand him and accept what happened as a historical necessity?" I am categorically opposed to that view. I brought these questions up at the Twentieth Party Congress, and on assignment from the leadership of the party I gave a report on these questions at the Twenty-Second Congress. At various rallies and public gatherings I have denounced and exposed Stalin for the fact that he took reprisals against the builders of the party and the leaders of our Soviet state. I am proud of speaking out, and I feel that in doing so, I have done something useful for the party and for our country.

The evil that Stalin committed did great harm to our country, and every evil should be denounced. You can't put your trust in the idea that all this is supposedly past history. No! To some extent, history can repeat itself. By exposing abuses of power our government is not weakened, nor is the influence of our party reduced. On the contrary, its strength has increased because we cleansed ourselves of the crimes Stalin committed, and we demonstrated that to establish Soviet power and affirm the ideas of Marxism-Leninism that kind of bloodletting was not called for. When the revolution was being made, and when the question of the conquest of power by the working class was posed, that was a different matter. It was almost inevitable then that there would be victims. For four years in the Civil War Russian fought against Russian, brother against brother, son against father, and that was justified: A historical breaking-up process was under way. The capitalist system was being broken up and overthrown; new laws and a new ideology were being established as the working class and the toiling peasants came to power. Those were justified sacrifices: required by revolutionary expediency.

But in Stalin's time there was no longer any need for such sacrifices. The Civil War had long been over, and the same with enemy sabotage or "wrecking." New cadres had grown up, and there was an upturn in industrial production. It's true that agriculture had not yet gathered its forces, not because of "wrecking," but because of our backwardness. We were weak in matters pertaining to agriculture. I am very troubled that nowadays the struggle against the cult [of Stalin] is being blunted and articles are slipping into the Soviet press that seek to hush all this up and have these facts forgotten.

Nothing should be discarded from history! It is possible to throw out people who insist on continuing to expose Stalin's abuses, but that cannot make the facts themselves disappear. The Twentieth and Twenty-Second Congresses cannot be hushed up.

I meet with many people, and many express their gratitude to me; they send me letters and postcards in which they thank me for having raised these questions. They write: "In my family so-and-so perished, and I myself spent time in prison, but now I've come back, and my good name has been restored; previously I was the brother (or the wife) of an 'enemy of the people' but now I have my full rights as a citizen." Well, what can be more pleasant than this kind of acknowledgment? I eagerly accept all this, because, after all, it was I who initiated this process; it was I who did a great deal of work in exposing Stalin. But I was not alone in this. It was done by the Central Committee. And it was done by the Twentieth Party Congress. You can't just say: "Khrushchev wanted this or Khrushchev did that." It's possible, after all, to want something but not to find support, and then nothing will come of it. These questions had come to a head, and it was necessary to place them in the forefront. If I had not brought them up, other people would have, and that would have become a factor in the defeat of a party leadership that wouldn't listen to the demands of the time.

A vivid example of this is Czechoslovakia in 1968. Many times I advised their president, Novotny[32] (an honorable Communist and dedicated proletarian): "Lift the curtain and expose the abuses, if they happened in your country." And they did happen; I know they happened. I myself was a witness when Stalin gave particular orders to Chekists who were sent to Czechoslovakia as "advisers." Such methods had been worked out in detail in 1937, and they were applied in all the socialist countries. We had our "advisers" everywhere.

Novotny got angry and said: "Comrade Khrushchev, we never had anything like that in our country."

I answered him: "If you don't do it, others will, and you'll end up in a very unenviable position." Novotny didn't listen to me, and everyone knows what that led to, both for Novotny himself and for all of Czechoslovakia.

If we had not exposed Stalin, it's possible that events might have taken place in our country that would have been even sharper than in Czechoslovakia. We could not have avoided that. It was necessary to tell the truth to the people and the party. What's really the truth? Had there really been enemies of the people back then? There were enemies then, and there are now. The historical breakthrough, making the transition from capitalism to socialism, cannot occur without conflict, without bloodshed. On both sides sharp measures are taken, up to and including terror and so on. But Stalin directed his blow not against real enemies, which the USSR had pretty well done away with by then and of which only some remnants remained, manifesting themselves feebly in one or another institution. The struggle against these remnants did not require mass terror. Instead, party members were destroyed, above all the topmost layer of the party, people who had laid the foundations of the proletarian Leninist party. The blow was directed against them, and it was they first of all who laid down their lives. These crimes cannot be justified in any way. There was no historical necessity for them. All these people had been socialist organizers among the masses of the workers and peasants.

Why, after all, did Stalin destroy them? He did so because conditions had ripened for the replacement of Stalin himself. In the life of the proletarian party, constructed on the basis of democratic centralism,[33] methods and procedures are followed in keeping with the party rules. That means that the question of replacing one or another individual can always be raised at a party congress or Central Committee plenum. If party members don't have the recognized right to change leadership, then I absolutely don't know what the party would be turned into. Such a party couldn't attract the masses because it would no longer be a dictatorship of the class, but a dictatorship by an individual. In fact that's what it was under Stalin. The party was no longer able to express its will. The Central Committee actually did not function. For years Central Committee plenums and party congresses were not convened. In the outlying areas the party continued to live its previous kind of life, but the leadership was no longer truly elected by the party or the Central Committee. Whatever Stalin wanted he did. If he wanted to execute someone, he did; if he wanted to spare someone, he did.

I remember one other incident that confirms the characterization of Stalin given in Lenin's "Testament." Many times we watched various movies together with Stalin. We once watched a movie based on the life of colonialist England. I remember the movie's plot. Certain treasures had to be transported from India to England, but the ships' passage from India was menaced by pirates. So the authorities turned to a well-known pirate [in an English prison] and proposed that he undertake the risky venture of transporting the treasure. In exchange he was promised some reward. He agreed, but set one condition: that he be allowed to form a team of his own choosing from those who were in prison with him. The English government agreed; he chose a team and was given a ship. He arrived in India, loaded the treasure onto the ship, and set off on the return journey, but on the way to England he began to wipe out his collaborators. The method he used was this: When a victim was selected, he placed the victim's photograph on the desk in his cabin. In this way he gradually destroyed a certain number of his fellow outlaws.

When our viewing of the film was over, Stalin as usual suggested we go to his "nearby dacha" for something to eat. Malenkov and Beria got in the same car with Stalin while Bulganin and I followed in my car. We arrived at the dacha and immediately went to wash our hands, and, as always, remarks were tossed back and forth. Beria said: "Listen, you know what Stalin said while we were driving over here? He said, 'That captain was no fool. He knew what he was doing.'" Then Beria began urging me to bring up the subject at the dinner table, to express the opinion that that captain was a real scum.

I hesitated, but then agreed, and at the table I said: "Comrade Stalin, what a scum that captain was, killing his own closest friends." Stalin glanced at me, but said nothing. I quickly dropped this dangerous subject.

The parallel here is obvious. Stalin, like that pirate, drew up a list for himself (he didn't need photographs) and gave orders to his subordinates as to whose turn had come. What was that bandit compared with him! That "fine young fellow" destroyed ten or fifteen people. But Stalin destroyed hundreds of thousands. I can't say how many exactly, but when Stalin died there were as many as 10 million people in the concentration camps. Of course they included real criminals as well as former prisoners of war, our own servicemen [who had been prisoners of the Germans]—a huge number of people, a number that the English pirate could never have dreamed of.

Stalin called himself a Marxist-Leninist, but he committed atrocities against his co-thinkers, against his party friends and comrades, people from the prerevolutionary underground, people who had engaged in the great and glorious struggle to transform society along socialist lines. When Stalin was exposing "enemies of the people," I had thought him very perspicacious. He had spied out the enemy. But what about me? So many people around me had been "enemies"; there were so many arrested people with whom I had had dealings every day without noticing that they were enemies.

That's why all these abuses by Stalin arouse even greater anger in me today. After all, these people had been extremely honest and devoted. How many of my own friends had perished, as well as people I respected greatly: people like Bubnov[34] and Antonov-Ovseyenko,[35] for example. Antonov-Ovseyenko had been assigned by Lenin to arrest the provisional government at the Winter Palace.[36] Bubnov was an Old Bolshevik who had been people's commissar of education. He was a remarkable man, simple and easy to approach; I liked him very much. And suddenly he turned out to be an "enemy of the people."

I was weighed down by the thought that I had held such a respectful attitude toward Bubnov and hadn't noticed that he was an enemy. So is it possible that I am mistaken now, just as I was then? Back then I was berating myself for having such a poor eye for enemies, while Stalin could sense them and detect them from a distance. No! A murderer should not be placed on a pedestal. Of course, to the dead it's all the same, but the truth is necessary for future generations, which could also end up in the same kind of situation we found ourselves in. If we forgive these crimes (saying that victors should not be judged), a great temptation can arise for persons like Stalin to carry out reprisals against the people, disguising themselves behind high ideals.

Our country has traveled a long road and has accomplished a great deal. For a long time all the credit was given to one person—Stalin. Stalin himself many times condemned this point of view: it was like the position of the SRs,[37] which placed individual heroes in the forefront, while the masses were viewed as just a lowly mob. But the eternal hero is really the people. Who was the "great leader" when the people of Russia fought against Napoleon's invasion? Certainly not Tsar Aleksandr I! No, no, and again no! Perhaps Kutuzov? Again no! Kutuzov[38] was the supreme commander in chief. But if the people had not risen up against the French invasion, no Kutuzov or anyone else could have saved Russia. It was the people who stood up and defended their country, laying down their lives by the thousands. The same thing happened with the invasion of the fascists, who marched against the Soviet Union. The people rose up. And despite the fact that Stalin had destroyed the top echelons of leadership in the party and the economy, despite the fact that great negligence was committed in failing to prepare the army for war, the people thoroughly defeated the enemy, and it was not Stalin who did that.

Yes, the best officer cadres in the Red Army command were destroyed, and no others arose to replace them; there was no time for that. New commanders were promoted to high posts without having the experience and ability to direct large units. Besides that, the army was not supplied with weapons: From the very first days of the war there were not enough rifles and there were no machine guns. It was an impossible situation! We are completely justified today in criticizing Tsar Nicholas II for the fact that the Russian army in 1915 was left without rifles. But we too [in World War II] began the war without the necessary number of rifles. Malenkov said to me then, when I was in Ukraine and was asking for rifles: "Forge bayonets, forge lances." We asked for antitank grenades and special antitank rifles.[39] Malenkov answered: "Make a fuel mixture that you can pour over the enemy tanks [and set them on fire]." Our fighters after that often did pour gasoline over enemy tanks, but they also poured out their blood over the land and lined it with their corpses. Who was to blame for that? Whose negligence was it?

They say that Stalin won the war. But whose were the defeats? The people's? There's an old saying that cities are surrendered by soldiers, but taken by generals. No, no, and again no! It was Stalin who committed so many errors before the war: He weakened the army and the leadership of our industry, and this forced the Red Army to retreat with huge losses, leaving the enemy in control of an enormous territory. The Nazi invaders occupied the breadbasket of the Soviet Union, a densely populated area. But in spite of all that, the people rose up. They found new courage, they went on the offensive, and they smashed the aggressor. New cadres of military leaders were forged in the process of our battles during the retreat. But if the cadres who had gone through the school of the Civil War had been preserved, cadres who had built the new industries, cadres who had been forged in the process of building the economy on socialist foundations (which was an impregnable source of strength!), and if the human and material resources of our country had been used properly, the enemy could never have dreamed of reaching the outskirts of Moscow, occupying the Northern Caucasus, and getting as far as Stalingrad. Today once again some people are starting to shout: "Hurrah for Stalin!" We already had all that, and we paid with too much blood for "hurrahs" like that.

If we don't condemn the abuses of power, if we don't analyze our mistakes, the danger will arise that history may repeat itself. The people must know everything, both about their victories and about their defeats. They must know their heroes, and they must know the reasons for their defeats. The main reasons were Stalin's despotism and abuse of power, the same Stalin who was impatient and intolerant with people, with other leaders of the party, with his own comrades, with people who had once worked together under Lenin's leadership. When those people had the audacity to want a collective leadership and to express their own opinions, he first branded them as political enemies and then began to destroy them.

I think that the Twentieth and the Twenty-Second Party Congresses made absolutely correct decisions, and however much someone might try to minimize or gloss over them, nothing will come of the attempt. No one will be able to palm off the idea that Stalin wasn't guilty of anything, or the idea that if he was guilty, those weren't crimes, but simply mistakes made in the process of transition from one form of social system to another. No, no, and again no! No true Communist will take the side of a man who murdered his own people. To do that would mean to embolden those who might repeat the same thing, which is not at all impossible. It can become possible if vigilance is not maintained.

1. M. S. Chudov. See Biographies.

2. L. V. Nikolayev. See Biographies.

3. At the Nineteenth Party Congress, N. S. Khrushchev delivered the report on a new version of the party rules. [GS]

4. In fall 1952, when the Nineteenth Party Congress was held, Malenkov was a secretary of the party Central Committee.

5. Khrushchev is referring to events that occurred in 1919, when Kirov was the chairman of the Provisional Military Revolutionary Committee of Astrakhan territory as well as a member of the Revolutionary Military Council of the Eleventh Detached Army and head of its Political Department. The political and military situation in Astrakhan territory at that time was difficult, and the Eleventh Detached Army was fighting without success against Denikin's forces in the Astrakhan area.

6. N. M. Shvernik. See Biographies.

7. O. G. Shatunovskaya. See Biographies.

8. Khrushchev has in mind the KGB official Aleksei Vladimirovich Snegov; see Biographies. [GS]

9. "Chekists" refers to officials of the secret police. [GS]

10. Before the revolution, the Smolny Institute in Saint Petersburg had been a school for daughters of the nobility. It was taken over by the Bolsheviks during the revolutionary year of 1917 and remained the party headquarters in Leningrad (the city previously and again currently called Saint Petersburg, renamed Leningrad after Lenin's death in 1924). [GS/SS]

11. The OGPU (Unified State Political Administration) was the state security organization of that time, with headquarters in Moscow. [GS]

12. G. G. Yagoda. See Biographies.

13. When Khrushchev dictated these words, Molotov was still alive. Molotov died in 1986. For more on Molotov, see Biographies. [SK]

14. F. D. Medved. See Biographies.

15. B. P. Sheboldayev. See Biographies.

16. By "oldsters" he meant the party veterans. [GS]

17. N. V. Andreasyan.

18. M. N. Tukhachevsky. See Biographies.

19. In the Cultural Revolution, which was in full swing in China at the time that Khrushchev dictated these lines in the late 1960s, Mao and his inner circle mobilized masses of young people as Red Guards to overthrow Liu Shaoqi and other top officials critical of his policies. [SS]

20. I. M. Vareikis. See Biographies.

21. I. A. Pyatnitsky. See Biographies.

22. Ya. Kh. Peters. See Biographies.

23. *Izvestia* (News) was the official newspaper of the Soviet government. [GS]

24. S. V. Kosior. See Biographies.

25. Ya. E. Rudzutak. See Biographies.

26. V. I. Mezhlauk. See Biographies.

27. V. V. Kuibyshev. See Biographies.

28. V. Ya. Chubar. See Biographies.

29. G. I. Petrovsky was director of the Museum of the Revolution in Moscow. See Biographies.

30. P. P. Postyshev. See Biographies.

31. R. I. Eikhe. See Biographies.

32. Antonin Novotny was the leader of Czechoslovakia from 1953 to 1968. See Biographies.

33. In theory the Bolshevik Party was organized in accordance with the principle of "democratic centralism." This meant that decisions were to be made on a democratic basis following open discussion among party members, but that once a decision had been made it was to be carried out by the whole party in a disciplined fashion without further argument. [SS]

34. A. S. Bubnov. See Biographies.

35. V. A. Antonov-Ovseyenko. See Biographies.

36. Following the overthrow of the tsarist regime in February 1917, an interim government was formed under the leadership of Aleksandr Kerensky. It was known as the Provisional Government because it was intended to remain in power pending the adoption of a new constitution and the conduct of new democratic elections. In fact, it never had a firm grip on power, and its position was increasingly undermined from summer 1917 onward. In the revolution of October 1917, the Provisional Government was overthrown and its members arrested. [SS]

37. The Socialist Revolutionaries (SRs) were members of a revolutionary socialist party that

was based in the peasantry and espoused a populist doctrine. In 1917 they split in two: the Right
SRs opposed the Bolsheviks, while the Left SRs
were temporarily allied with them. [SS]

38. Mikhail Kutuzov (1745–1813) was the general
who led Russia's armies in defeating Napoleon's
1812 invasion. [GS]

39. The antitank rifle was an antitank weapon
larger than a large rifle but smaller than a small-
caliber antitank cannon. Two men could carry it
on their shoulders and use it effectively against
tank treads or tanks with thin armor. [SK]

## SOME CONSEQUENCES OF THE KIROV ASSASSINATION

After Kirov's death, Stalin entrusted the Leningrad party organization to
Zhdanov.[1] At the Seventeenth Party Congress [in 1934], Zhdanov had
been elected a secretary of the Central Committee, and before that he had
worked in the city of Gorky.[2] I was better acquainted with him than with
Kirov. I remember the first time we met. In Moscow [before the Seventeenth
Congress], we had been engaged in competition with the Nizhny Novgorod
region.[3] Now our delegation at the congress invited the Gorky delegation to
be our guests; I don't recall where we gathered. Zhdanov was a cheerful
person. He drank a lot when he was our guest that time, and even before
then he had been drinking. To make a long story short, he got up on stage
and pulled out an accordion. He played both piano and accordion pretty
well. I was pleased by this. Kaganovich, on the other hand, sneered contemptuously: "An accordion player!" But I saw nothing wrong with that. I myself,
as a young man, tried to learn that instrument; I too had an accordion. But I
never played well, whereas Zhdanov did. Later on, when Zhdanov began to
move in Politburo circles, it was evident that Stalin became quite attentive
toward him. At that point Kaganovich's grumbling against Zhdanov intensified. He often made venomous remarks like this: "To be here you don't have
to have a great ability to work; you just have to have a quick tongue, know
how to tell jokes well, and sing ditties. Then you can live high."

I must admit that when I had a closer look at Zhdanov under working
conditions I began to agree with Kaganovich. In fact, when we were at
Stalin's place (Stalin had already begun to drink a lot then, and to make others drink, and that was a weakness that Zhdanov definitely suffered from), it
often happened that Zhdanov would be banging away on the piano and
singing, and Stalin would sing in accompaniment with him. Such songs
could be sung only at Stalin's. You couldn't possibly repeat them anywhere

else. Longshoremen in a cheap bar might sing songs like that, but no one else. More than once I was a witness to this way of passing the time.

But suddenly everything changed. Stalin abruptly turned against Zhdanov and would not tolerate him anymore. During the last days of Zhdanov's life [in 1948] I simply felt sorry for him. He was a charming person in his own way, and I felt a certain respect for him. Before his death, when he went off on vacation, he called me: "I'm sorry I didn't meet with you. I wanted very much to tell you about something, to come visit you and tell you." Not long before his death, I visited him, and he had a lot to say, particularly about the RSFSR: "You know, the Russian Federation (and here I completely sympathized with him)—it's in such a state! In Ukraine you have Central Committee meetings, you hold conferences, plenums, and so on. But here in Russia there is none of that. People are in disarray, no one gets them together for meetings, and no one draws the lessons from their experiences. We need to establish a Russian Bureau of the Central Committee of the AUCP(B)."[4]

I answered: "There was one once, you know. Andrei Andreyevich Andreyev[5] (AA as we used to call him) was its chairman." On this issue I supported Zhdanov with all my heart. Zhdanov later brought the question up before Stalin himself.

When Zhdanov died, work on this problem of a Russian Bureau had begun to move along. Apparently Zhdanov had provided the impetus. But it all ended with the Leningraders being shot as "nationalists."[6] Nevertheless, there was no nationalism involved; it was genuine party work; the question of the fate of the Russian Federation and improving its functioning was being raised. As a result absolutely innocent people perished.

Zhdanov was an intelligent man. He had a certain clever and cutting way of talking. He could comment subtly on another's blunder, slipping in a little irony. On the other hand, to go only by outward appearances, he could be seen sitting and taking notes with his pencil at every plenum. People might think: How closely Zhdanov listens to everything at the plenum, writing it all down so as not to miss anything. But he'd be writing down someone's unfortunate turns of phrase, and then he would go over to Stalin and repeat those for him. For example, there was a speech by Yusupov[7] that made all of us laugh a lot.

Aside from this, Zhdanov really was a musically talented person. He had studied music once with Aleksandrov,[8] the father of the present director of the Red Army chorus.[9] Aleksandrov had taught music at Zhdanov's secondary school. Zhdanov had been a student in Mariupol,[10] graduating from a secondary school there.

Zhdanov's name has caused a lot of talk in connection with the postwar Central Committee resolutions condemning the magazines *Zvezda* and *Leningrad* and Muradeli's opera *A Great Friendship*.[11] In regard to that, I think Zhdanov was assigned simply to give the report. He just said what he was ordered to say. What he himself thought it's hard to make out. Maybe he thought exactly as he spoke, but I doubt it; most likely not. At that time Zhdanov was in total disfavor. The attitude toward him had changed during the war. And why did he fall into disfavor with Stalin?

In the "upper echelons," people had formed a certain impression (how well founded that was—it's hard for me to judge today) that he was a kind of do-nothing, not diligent about his work. To some extent everyone noticed it. He was capable of arriving at a Central Committee session two or three hours late, or he might not even come at all. In short, he was not a person like Kaganovich, for example, who always found something to do, who never had any spare time. Zhdanov was easygoing. If he was assigned a task, he did it, but unless he was assigned to something, he saw no reason to do anything. Stalin formed that kind of impression of Zhdanov, and so did others. It's difficult for me to express an opinion on this. I never worked especially closely with him. That's why it's hard for me to say. But in other respects he was a charming person.

After I was sent to Ukraine—and after he had been sent to Leningrad earlier, that is, from 1935 on—we met occasionally, and now and then we exchanged opinions. He asked me once: "Do you manage to travel around to the factories and plants, and how often?"

I said: "Not that often, but I do go out on such visits."

"Yes," he continued, "I also go out on such visits. I'll tell you what happens sometimes. I went to visit a certain factory once. They showed me everything there, told me about everything. I looked at what I could, asked questions of everyone that was guiding me, then went on to another factory. I arrived. They also showed me everything and told me everything. Then I took my leave. And it had been the same people that had talked to me and showed me things as at the first factory. To double-check on this, I went to a third factory, and the same thing was repeated." I said: "I've had that happen to me too. They've got a defense guard that they 'throw up,' and those guards surround us, and we don't know that's who they are, and we shake their hands as though they were the factory people." Zhdanov told this story with his own kind of, you know, special smile, in his own unique Zhdanov style.

There were other things too. Once after the war when everyone was having dinner at Stalin's place (I wasn't there that time), they ate so much that Zhdanov could no longer even walk. He wanted to stay overnight at Stalin's place, as had happened before, but it didn't happen this time. Stalin said to him: "You have your own apartment." And literally threw him out the door. Malenkov told me about it, but Malenkov put the incident in a different light, as though Stalin was right. As for me, I felt sorry for the man. After all, Stalin made him drink. He should have let him sleep it off, but instead he showed him the door. In general Zhdanov didn't win recognition as a major government figure. That was the opinion of all the people who knew him well.

A little while after Kirov's death, we were shaken by another event: the discovery of a "conspiracy," followed by the trial and execution of Tukhachevsky and a group of other military men.[12] Marshal Yegorov[13] (who himself was later tried) was then one of the judges. I think that the only member of that court still alive is Marshal Budyonny.[14] Tukhachevsky's arrest was very painful for me. But of those who were arrested I had known Yakir[15] the best. We had not met during the Civil War, but I frequently had dealings with him later when he was assistant commander of our forces in Ukraine and Crimea. When I was working in Kiev in 1928, major military maneuvers were held there. Those maneuvers were on a colossal scale, and after the troop movements there were receptions, discussions, and reports. Voroshilov directed it all, but Yakir was there, too.

The military men, back then, did not have a very high opinion of Voroshilov. Formally they accepted him, but they all considered themselves above him, and that really was so, it seems. Even in 1928 there was only great ostentation and a big show [on Voroshilov's part]. Much later when Voroshilov found out that I had been working as an assistant organizer in Kiev at that time, he told me about how they showered him with flowers during those maneuvers. Of course, being showered with flowers was "very important" for the military defense of the country, but not the most important thing.

Before his arrest Yakir had visited me at my dacha. I was living in Ogarevo outside Moscow at the former estate of the governor-general of Moscow, Grand Duke Sergei, uncle of the tsar. The secretaries of the party's city committee and the chairman of the province's executive committee of the Soviets were living there, too. We were modestly occupying an outlying building there (although Kaganovich kept trying to pressure me to go live in the main building). Our building was the place where the Grand Duke's servants had previously lived, and a church had also been located there. I occupied part of the second floor, and Bulganin lived below. In the second half of the upstairs lived a secretary of the city committee, Kulkov,[16] and down below lived Filatov,[17] chairman of the executive committee of the regional Soviets. In the servants' building, secretaries of the district committees spent their holidays; it was a kind of vacation retreat for people when they had a day off. Among the others staying there was Semyon Zakharovich Korytny.[18] Korytny worked as secretary of one of the party committees in the Moscow districts. When I was party secretary in the Krasnaya Presnya district, he had been in charge of organization under me. Later he became party secretary of the Krasnaya Presnya district committee and then secretary of the party committee in the Lenin district of Moscow.

Korytny was Jewish, a practical and efficient man, a good organizer, and a good speaker. He was married to Yakir's sister, who was also a good party activist. Together with Yakir she had gone the whole length of the road of Civil War; she had been a political-education activist in that war. Yakir came to visit his sister in Ogarevo, and he and I went for a long walk in the park among the trees and talked about things. He was pleasant to visit with. Then he was arrested. I felt very upset. First, I felt sorry for him. Second, I also might be affected. After all, people could say that just a few days before he was arrested Yakir had visited Khrushchev, went to see him late at night, and went for a walk with him, talking about something the whole time.

I was not closely acquainted with Tukhachevsky, but my attitude toward him was always one of respect. Once not long before his arrest (I don't know why), he called me and said: "Comrade Khrushchev, would you allow me to send a sculptor to see you?"

I answered: "Why?" He was very much taken with sculpting and loved art in general:

"Oh, you know, no matter what, some sculptor is going to do a bust of you, and the devil only knows how it would come out, so I'll send you a good one."

I said: "I really must ask you, Comrade Tukhachevsky, never to talk to me about such things again." There the matter ended. Later when the trial of the military leaders was reported, I thought to myself: "What the devil, why did he suggest that to me? Was he trying to win me over?" I cursed myself: "What a fine attitude I had toward him! What a stupid shit I was for not seeing anything. And yet, Stalin saw."

After that, the whole ugly business began to unwind. First they dragged in the military men. Then they began to drag in secretaries and members of the Central Committee, at which time things really got nightmarish. What in the world was going on? How had all this mess from alien roots grown up? They had entangled the entire organism of the party, the entire country. It was something terrible, like a cancer.

Yet Stalin "knew" who these people were. He arrested even people's commissars. In particular he arrested Antipov,[19] people's commissar of posts and telegraph, a veteran revolutionary and a well-known person from Saint Petersburg. I have some special memories in connection with that arrest. Stalin played a joke on me then, but it was the kind of joke that could turn your hair gray. They called me from Stalin's office and said I should immediately come to the Kremlin, that Himself was out taking a stroll and wanted me to come. I went to the Kremlin and saw that Stalin was out strolling with Molotov. A park area had just been built inside the Kremlin walls at that time, with walking paths. I walked over to where Stalin was. He looked at me and said: "Antipov is giving testimony against you."

At that time I didn't know that Antipov had been arrested, and I replied that neither Antipov nor anyone else could give any testimony against me because there was nothing to testify about. Stalin immediately switched to some other subject, whatever it was he had summoned me for. Thus, it had been a psychological provocation. Apparently Stalin attributed a certain importance to it. Why did he ask about it that way? Probably he was watching to see how a person would behave (in response to an accusation), as a way of determining whether the person was a criminal or not. But, you know, even an honest person can be thrown off and maybe tremble a little or show nervousness in replying to the leader of the party [on such an occasion], which might give the impression to the person seeking information that he was also involved. This is a dishonest, incorrect, and inadmissible way of trying to find the truth. In fact it's simply intolerable, especially among members of the Communist Party.

That was the kind of situation that took shape then. People grabbed hold of others and dragged them off to the slaughter. People disappeared without a trace, as though the ocean had swallowed them up. When they began to arrest leaders of the party and of the trade unions, military comrades, and factory directors, two of my personal assistants were arrested. One of them, Rabinovich,[20] had general duties, and the other, Finkel,[21] was concerned with matters of construction. Both of them were exceptionally honorable and decent people. I could never entertain even the thought that these two, Rabinovich and Finkel, who I knew extremely well, might really be "enemies of the people." But "factual material" was concocted against all those who were arrested, and I had no possibility of refuting it. All I did then was curse myself for letting myself be fooled. Here were these men who had been closely associated with me, and they had turned out to be enemies of the people!

Then arrests of party secretaries of Moscow district committees began, as well as secretaries of the city committee and province committee. Among those arrested, as I've already said, was Korytny, who I had known back in Kiev. Later he had gone to Moscow to study and after graduating from training courses in Marxism-Leninism, he had worked with me. After he became secretary of the district committees in Krasnaya Presnya and in the Lenin district, he had been elected one of the secretaries of the party's Moscow city committee. He was a man who had been tested and proved in the Civil War, but still he was arrested. How did they take him? He had fallen ill and been sent to a hospital. I went to see him there, stayed a while, and visited with him. The next day I learned he had been arrested. They arrested him right in the hospital, and his wife too, Yakir's sister. In that case, too, I found some sort of explanation. Although I considered Korytny an entirely honorable and irreproachable person, still, if Yakir had turned out to be a traitor, a sellout, and an agent of the fascists, and Korytny had been his close friend, Yakir could have influenced him. So it was possible that I had made a mistake and had wrongly trusted Korytny.

Kulkov was another secretary of the city committee who was arrested. He was a Moscow proletarian, a member of the party since 1916, and although he was not conspicuous for any special qualities, he was a completely honest and reliable person. In short, almost all the people who had worked alongside me were arrested. I hope it's understandable what the general state of my emotions must have been. Another man who worked with me then was Margolin,[22] a member of the party since 1912 or 1914. He had been in the revolutionary underground together with Kaganovich. I also knew him from Kiev. When I had been in charge of organizational matters for the party's Kiev province committee, Margolin had been one of the secretaries of a district committee and later worked as secretary of the Melitopol province committee. After that he was a student together with me at the Industrial Academy. He remained as a secretary of the party's Bauman district committee after I transferred from there to the Krasnaya Presnya district. When I became first secretary of the Moscow city committee he was elected second secretary, then after there had been arrests in Dnepropetrovsk, he was promoted as secretary of the party's province committee there. That's where he was arrested. Margolin had also been a tried and tested comrade, and was well known [in the party], especially to Kaganovich. He was considered a friend of Kaganovich and they often got together at Kaganovich's apartment. I simply couldn't accept the idea that Margolin was an enemy of the people.

The spreading arrests of irreproachable people, people who were well known and generally trusted, created a very painful situation in the party. Today it's hard for me to remember everyone who was arrested back then. It would be necessary to look through the archives for that and study the materials. Probably historians will occupy themselves with this task and put everything in order. I think it's likely that there were three "generations" of party leaders who were arrested; first, those who earlier had been in the leadership; second, those who were promoted to replace them; and third, those who were promoted to replace the second layer. It was an enormous number of people!

Among others, my good friend Simochkin was arrested. He and I had been students together at the workers' school in Donetsk. He had been a Yenakiyevo miner (that is, he worked at what is now called the Rykovo mine).[23] He took part in the Civil War, was the commissar of a regiment, and was given the Order of the Red Banner. After the workers' school, he took courses in Marxism-Leninism and worked as secretary of a district committee of the party in Moscow. Stalin once called me and said: "We're going to take Simochkin away from you (Stalin knew him) and promote him to work on the province level." He was promoted to work at Ivanovo-Voznesensk, but very soon, after working there for no more than a month, he was arrested and shot.[24] That astonished me: "How could it be? Simochkin an enemy of the people? Why did he need to become an enemy of the people when he himself was part of the people?" Some time later Stalin told me that Simochkin had been killed in error, that he had been innocent, and he blamed Zhukov, the head of the province division of the NKVD, saying that he was the person to blame, and that this Zhukov, in turn, had been arrested, condemned, and shot. How could this have happened? Simochkin had held such an important post and had enjoyed people's confidence, so how had some little-known person, Zhukov, been able to fabricate a case against him and arrest him? Where was the oversight, the monitoring, the role of the procuracy, and so forth? This testifies to the kind of procedures that existed in the party (if you could call them procedures): the absence of any norms or standards for defending individual members of the party.

Let me return to Yakir. He had worked in Ukraine. I often met with him in the 1920s at party conferences and congresses on the republic level.[25] In 1928–29 when I was working in Kiev our military people were paying a great deal of attention to Kiev, which was in fact a border city. The Polish leaders couldn't reconcile themselves to the fact that Kiev had not been included in the Polish state (not to mention other cities of Ukraine that were located farther to the west).[26]

Yakir had many occasions to familiarize himself with party work in Kiev, conducting military maneuvers in the region and traveling from garrison to garrison. At that time I was deputy secretary of the Kiev province committee of the party. The assistant commander of the troops in the Ukrainian military district was a remarkable man, Ivan Naumovich Dubovoi.[27] He was distinguished by his handsome red beard. His father was an Old Bolshevik who had been in the prerevolutionary underground, a working-class man from the Donbas. Ivan Naumovich had gone through the Civil War, had been a deputy commander of a division under Shchors,[28] and when Shchors was killed, as I recall, Dubovoi took command of the division. Dubovoi was a tried and tested person, respected by all of us.

[Another military man I knew was] Veklichev, a member of the staff of the Political Directorate of the army in our military district. He himself was from a working-class background, but he had become a professional military man, a commissar in the Ukrainian military district. Thus I always had the opportunity of being in the company of military men.

And now suddenly Yakir was a traitor. Yakir an enemy of the people! Previously Stalin had greatly respected Yakir. Yakir kept in his possession a memorandum in which Stalin had praised Yakir's personal qualities, and, you know, Stalin was very miserly about putting any praise in writing.

Toward Tukhachevsky my attitude had been one of great respect, but I had not been close to him. Sometimes we met or called one another in the line of duty. He would invite me to have a look at some military equipment. It was with him that for the first time in my life I saw a bucket excavator with caterpillar tread. I regarded Tukhachevsky as the heart and soul of the Red Army. If there was anyone who really knew what he was doing and was attending to the needs of the armed forces, Tukhachevsky was that person—along with Gamarnik.[29]

Gamarnik at that time was the first deputy people's commissar of defense and was in charge of military construction and economic matters relating to the armed forces. The story was that the choice of the site for building the city of Komsomolsk[30] was made by Gamarnik. As secretary of the party committee for the Far Eastern territory, he made a trip to Moscow and reported to Stalin that we should build a base there in the event of war with Japan. At that time Japan was acting very arrogantly toward the Soviet Union, trying to provoke us into a fight. The chairman of the executive committee of the Soviets in the Far East was that Gutsenko (who also died at Stalin's hand). The Japanese consul came to a reception Gutsenko held and during a conversation with him stated: "What is the matter with you? You yourselves simply sit there and do nothing in the Far East, and you won't let us do anything. It's time for you to say goodbye." So you see what rudeness he allowed himself. The result was that Stalin paid close attention to Gamarnik's proposal, and soon the construction of Komsomolsk began, along with big industrial enterprises, with the aim of strengthening the Far East and discouraging the Japanese from eyeing our Far Eastern lands so greedily.

Now suddenly Yakir and this whole group of military men were enemies of the people. Back then we had no suspicion that these men might have been victims of slander. The court that tried them was made up of authoritative people; presiding over the court had been Marshal Yegorov. He too fell victim later to all these arbitrary actions. But nothing aroused our suspicions then. The only person I knew who expressed doubt about Yakir's guilt was a member of the Academy of Architecture, Shchusev.[31] As I was told later, he spoke at a meeting of architects and said that he had known Yakir well and felt great respect for him. Shchusev was a remarkable man, but we had a guarded attitude toward him then; we considered him a man of the past, known for having built only churches and having been received by Tsar Nicholas II. He was sharp tongued and always said what he thought, but that didn't always impress people then, considering the mood of the time. In this instance he said that he himself was from Kishinev[32] and had known Yakir's uncle, a doctor and a highly respected gentleman. Therefore he could not entertain the thought that the nephew of this man he had known could turn out to be an evildoer or criminal. And he refused to vote in favor of the sentence against Yakir. All this was reported to Stalin, but Stalin restrained himself and made no move against Shchusev. I'm not saying, of course, that Shchusev saw that the charges were unfounded. It was simply a coincidence, but for Shchusev it was a favorable coincidence.

Later I became closely acquainted with Aleksei Viktorovich Shchusev, when I was back working in Ukraine again. He often came to Kiev, and I visited with him. I remember one spring when it was still too cold to go swimming, he went sightseeing around Kiev, and when I talked to him later I asked: "How are things, Aleksei Viktorovich?"

"Well, I walked around and had a look at Kiev. A beautiful city, beautiful."

"And where did you go?"

"I went to Trukhanov Island,[33] rented a rowboat, took my clothes off there on the sandy beach, and did some sunbathing. Then I went and ate some pirozhki[34] at the bazaar."

Back then of course I felt indignant and denounced all the arrested "traitors." Today the most advantageous thing would be to say: "In the depths of my heart I sympathized with them." But no, the opposite is true. I didn't sympathize with them in my heart. I felt indignant and outraged at them in the depths of my soul because (as we were all convinced then) Stalin could not have made a mistake. I don't recall now how the subsequent arrests went on. They were accompanied by executions. This was not explained or announced anywhere, and therefore there was a lot that even we didn't know. We were informed that such-and-such people had been sent into exile or condemned to such-and-such prison terms.

Nevertheless the Moscow party organization, both on the province level and the municipal level, continued its activity and worked intensely at rallying the people to carry out decisions for building up Moscow and the Moscow region. By that time arrests were being made on a wider and wider scale. We were sometimes informed about the arrests of very prominent people; we were told that such-and-such a person turned out to be an enemy of the people. We in turn informed the district party organizations and the primary organizations as well as the Young Communist League and social organizations.[35] We received all this information with sincere indignation and condemned those who had been arrested. After all, if they had been arrested, that meant their subversive activity, their operations as provocateurs, had been exposed. Isn't that what it meant? Every kind of epithet was put to use, condemning and denouncing these people and branding them with shame.

In Moscow we had a secretary of the province committee of the Young Communist League (I don't remember his name now), a passionate and enthusiastic young fellow who I liked a lot. He was a person who, as they say, was where he ought to be both in education and training, and he had a good personality. Suddenly one morning when I came to work I was told that this secretary of the province committee of the Young Communist League had gone hunting and shot himself. I felt very bad about this incident and immediately called Stalin and reported that this unfortunate event had occurred, that such a fine young fellow, a secretary of the Young Communist League had shot himself. He answered me quietly: "So he shot himself. We understand about that. He shot himself because we arrested Kosarev[36] (first secretary of the Central Committee of the Young Communist League), and some of his other little friends have been arrested."

I was dumbfounded. First, to me Kosarev was a person who did not arouse any suspicion. He was a young fellow from a working-class family; he himself had been a worker, and now suddenly he was an enemy of the people? How could this be? How could he become an enemy of the people? But again, no distrust arose in me. If the party Central Committee had taken this step, if Stalin had done this, then it was already undeniable; it must really be so. Still, all these things lay like a heavy weight on my soul. Of course we assumed that these roots and tendrils of enemy intelligence agencies had penetrated our ranks deeply, working their way into the milieu of the party and the Young Communist League and infecting even the top layers of the leadership.

Events developed very rapidly. They arrested Rudzutak.[37] Rudzutak was a candidate member of the Politburo, a respected and very likable person. He often spoke at factories at the request of the party's Moscow committee. When he was invited to city, district, or factory meetings he always came willingly. Besides, Rudzutak had a particular basis for his good reputation, if not to say his fame, in the party. During the trade union discussion in 1921, many different platforms were put forward, and the debates and discussions shook the party and unsettled it profoundly. Rudzutak had also presented his own platform, and Lenin proposed that this platform be taken as the basis for the party's position. The main forces within the party were able to unite on the basis of that platform, reject other platforms, and thus come to a resolution that was accepted later by the entire party. That was considered no small achievement on Rudzutak's part. Later Rudzutak served as people's commissar of railways. As the economy grew and the amount of freight being shipped increased, the railroads began to have trouble coping with the tasks confronting the transportation system. Therefore Andreyev was sent as reinforcement. But the functioning of the transport system didn't improve, and Kaganovich was sent. With the arrival of Kaganovich, it seemed that the transportation system began to function better. Apparently that was so, because Kaganovich was considered an outstanding organizer, a strong-willed man who didn't spare his own efforts or those of others.

I don't remember the year, let alone the month, but one day Stalin called me and said: "Come to the Kremlin. Some Ukrainians have arrived. Travel around Moscow with them and show them the city." I went right away. There with Stalin were Kosior, Postyshev, and Lyubchenko.[38] Lyubchenko was chairman of the Council of People's Commissars of Ukraine. He had replaced Chubar in that post, and Chubar had transferred to Moscow to serve as deputy chairman of the USSR Council of People's Commissars, that is, Molotov's deputy. "They want to have a look at Moscow," said Stalin. "Let's go." We went out and got in Stalin's car. We were all able to fit in that one car. As we drove around, we talked. There were, it seemed to me, such good comradely relations among Politburo members (although Postyshev at that time was not yet a candidate member of the Politburo). We drove around the streets without of course getting out of the car anywhere; the whole inspection of the city was done from the automobile.

At that point Postyshev raised a question: "Comrade Stalin, it would be a good tradition, and the people would like it, and it would especially bring pleasure to the children if we had Christmas trees. We condemn such things now. But shouldn't Christmas trees be restored for the children?"

Stalin supported him: "Take the initiative yourself. Speak up in the press with the proposal to restore Christmas trees for children, and we'll support you." And that's the way things happened. Postyshev published an article in *Pravda,* and other newspapers took up the idea. This incident shows, in particular, what good relations there were among Stalin, Kosior, Postyshev, and Lyubchenko.

Later Postyshev was transferred to work in Moscow and became a secretary of the party's Central Committee. One day I was taking part in the work of a commission whose chairman was Postyshev. We were discussing the production of consumer goods. One of the people in economic management in the course of this discussion referred to the technical difficulties as well as to the material and production difficulties. Postyshev listened and listened (but he was a harsh and abrupt individual); then he banged his fist on the table and said: "The hell with you! What are all your arguments to me? Submit the plan and that's all there is to it." This made a rather poor impression on me because the man making the report was a respected person, but we went along with it because we all knew that Postyshev was a good fellow, although he sometimes allowed himself to raise his voice too much and, I would say, to behave with undesirable and unacceptable rudeness. But in general my relations with Postyshev were good.

At that time I was poorly informed about the state of affairs in the country as a whole. Details didn't reach me, although I was a candidate member of the Politburo. A bad situation had developed in Ukraine. Kaganovich was sent there, and he spent several days there, and as a result of his trip Postyshev was returned to Ukraine. Kaganovich said that Kosior was a very good political activist, but as an organizer he was weak. And so some weakening and deterioration of the leadership had been allowed to happen; discipline had to be tightened up, and for that purpose it was necessary to send Postyshev to serve as secretary of the Central Committee of the Communist Party (Bolshevik) of Ukraine to reinforce Kosior.

Arrests continued all the while. I found out that Vareikis had been arrested. I knew of Vareikis from party congresses. He had been an official in the Central Black Earth region, then he was a secretary of a province committee. Now it turned out that Vareikis had been an agent of the tsarist Okhranka [secret police]! After some time, major arrests resumed, and another "difficulty" had arisen in the Ukrainian leadership again. After a Central Committee plenum of the Ukrainian party, Lyubchenko shot himself. Later I was told that the plenum proceedings had been very stormy and that Lyubchenko had been criticized. Lyubchenko was a prominent Ukrainian official, but he had big political weaknesses. He had actually been a supporter of Petlyura at one time.[39] I myself had seen a photo of him with the future academician Hrushevsky, Vinnichenko, and Petlyura himself.[40] Everyone there knew about it. For this reason, at all Ukrainian party congresses, the Donbass delegation always opposed Lyubchenko's candidacy in elections to the Central Committee of the Ukrainian Communist Party. But I considered Lyubchenko a capable person, who had come over from Petlyura and had taken a firm stand on Bolshevik positions. I don't know what specific charges were brought against him after so many years of successful work. A break was declared in the plenum sessions. He went home and didn't return to the plenum. They decided to check and see why Lyubchenko didn't come back to the plenum sessions and found the following scene: his murdered wife and he himself were lying on the bed. The assumption was that he and his wife had agreed that he would shoot her and then himself. It was a big blow. The case was explained in this way. He was a former Petlyura supporter; apparently foreign intelligence agencies had found the way to get at him, and he had begun to work for them. But not much news was spread about in regard to this case, because even without it there were too many enemies.

Kaganovich went to Kiev again and brought back information that was not favorable to Kosior and Postyshev. He told the story that when the active party membership had gathered at the Kiev opera theater he literally issued an appeal: "All right now, come forward, report whatever you know about the enemies of the people." A kind of people's court was organized. People came forward and said all sorts of things. Today it's simply shameful and embarrassing to hear this, but that is what happened! I want to tell about these facts, so that correct conclusions can be drawn in the future and the repetition of such phenomena will not be permitted.

It was reported to Kaganovich that there was a certain woman, Nikolayenko, a party activist who worked on cultural matters and who was fighting against the enemies of the people but not finding support. Kaganovich (who was glad to get into such things) immediately summoned Nikolayenko. She came and began to issue denunciations of various enemies of the people. They say it was a terrible scene. Apparently Kaganovich told Stalin about this meeting, and in one of his speeches Stalin commented that there were certain little people who were rendering the party great assistance despite their lack of prominence. One such "little person" was Nikolayenko, who had rendered great assistance to the party in Ukraine in exposing enemies.

Nikolayenko was immediately placed on a pedestal as a fighter for the revolution, a fighter against the enemies of the people. I would like to tell in more detail about this particular individual. When I transferred from Moscow to Ukraine, Stalin warned me that there was a certain woman there, Nikolayenko, and that I should pay attention to her. He said she could help me in the struggle against the enemies of the people. I said I remembered her name from his speech. As soon as I arrived in Ukraine, she came to see me. I received her and heard her out. She was a healthy young woman who had graduated from some institute and was the director of some sort of museum; I don't remember exactly now. She had something to do with Ukrainian folk art, and therefore associated with the intelligentsia. Then she began telling me about the enemies of the people. It was just some kind of mad rambling. She considered all Ukrainians to be nationalists; in her eyes they were all Petlyura supporters, enemies of the people, and they should all be arrested. I was put on my guard. I thought to myself: "What in the world is this?" I began cautiously trying to correct her. (But here great caution was necessary, because it was dangerous even to talk with such people. They would immediately turn all their accusations against anyone who disagreed with them.)

As we were saying goodbye she said, "I will be coming to see you."

I answered: "Please do. I'll be glad to hear you out."

She came to see me many times after that. I could see that she was a sick person and that it was absolutely impossible to believe her. She began discussing her personal affairs with me as well. She said that the party activists had a bad attitude toward her. Earlier she said (she was not married) that Red Army commanders willingly kept company with her, but now they avoided her; they ran across the street to the opposite sidewalk if they saw her coming. She said: "I'm being persecuted because I'm waging a struggle against the enemies of the people."

I told her that she should try to evaluate their attitude toward her more soberly: "People avoid you because, as a rule, those who are acquainted with you get arrested. That's why people are afraid of you and avoid you."

When I arrived in Moscow, Stalin immediately asked me about Niko-layenko, and I told him my impression that no confidence could be placed in such a person, that she was a sick person who was unjustifiably accusing people of Ukrainian nationalism. Stalin flared up, got very angry, and came down hard on me: "Not to have confidence in such a person is wrong." He kept repeating and insisting on his viewpoint: "Ten percent of the truth is still the truth. It requires decisive action on our part, and we will pay for it if we don't act accordingly." In short, he was encouraging me to place confidence in Nikolayenko. I told him also about how offended she was over the Red Army commanders' attitude toward her. Stalin began joking: "What the heck, we have to find her a husband."

I said: "To find a husband for a bride like that would be very dangerous, because the husband would have to be prepared for cooling his heels in prison pretty soon, because without fail she would denounce him."

I returned to Kiev. Nikolayenko came to see me again and reported, with great conviction, that the nationalist counterrevolutionary organization in Ukraine was headed by Korotchenko, that he was a nationalist, and so forth. I replied: "You know, Comrade Nikolayenko, I've known Korotchenko for many years, and Stalin knows him too. Korotchenko is a Ukrainian by nation-ality, but he doesn't even really know how to speak Ukrainian properly. His language is *surzhik* (among the people that's what they call a hodge-podge mixture of Ukrainian, Russian, and Belorussian). For that reason I cannot in any way agree with you." She became very nervous at that point and began narrowing her eyes when she looked at me. I could see that she was starting to distrust me, as if I were covering up for the nationalists, so to speak. She began to cry. I said: "Calm down. You would do better to think things over. You can't talk about people this way, people you don't know. After all, you don't know Korotchenko, and you have no evidence whatsoever against him. You've just come to this conclusion in your mind, and it's absolutely not based on any-thing, and that's not right." She left, but I knew that she would write to Stalin. Before long Stalin's assistant, Poskrebyshev, called me from Moscow about the fact that Nikolayenko had sent a letter to Stalin in which she denounced Korotchenko and someone else. I replied that I was expecting that: "You can now expect that she will write that I too am a Ukrainian nationalist."

Sure enough, after a little time she came to see me again, and again I began to disagree with her, and then she wrote Stalin a statement in which she accused me of covering up for enemies of the people and Ukrainian nationalists. Poskrebyshev called: "Well, there is a follow-up statement and she writes about you."

I said to him: "That's the way it was bound to be. That's what I expected." After that letter, Stalin began to take a trusting attitude toward me in regard to Nikolayenko. I had convinced him that she deserved no confidence, that Kaganovich had been mistaken, and that she was simply a mad woman, an abnormal person. In the end Nikolayenko asked to be transferred from Ukraine to work in Moscow. She came to an agreement with the head of the committee on culture in Moscow (as I recall, he had a Ukrainian last name)[41] and she left.

We breathed a sigh of relief, and I told Stalin that this woman had finally left. He joked: "Well, we survived, didn't we?"

I answered: "Yes, we did." After a while they sent her, it seems, to Tashkent.[42] From there she began to besiege me with telegrams and letters asking to be returned to Ukraine, but I said: "No! We're not about to take her back in Ukraine. Better that she find a place for herself there." I told Stalin about this, and Stalin agreed and even joked about it. Apparently he too had figured her out.

A similar incident occurred in Moscow when a woman named Mishakova[43] came forward to denounce Kosarev and his friends at a plenum of the Central Committee of the Young Communist League. Kosarev was arrested, and Mishakova became one of the secretaries of the Young Communist League Central Committee. She was held up as a model fighter, whose example should be followed. Today many people know that she was not normal. Mishakova was unquestionably a person with a psychological defect, even though she might have been an honest person. As for Nikolayenko, she was simply crazy. I found that out after I had already retired. Among other things, she sent me a New Year's letter. Anyone reading its contents could see that the author was crazy.

I would like to tell about another characteristic episode. I was at Stalin's office in the Kremlin one day, along with some other people; I no longer remember exactly who was there. The phone rang. Stalin went over and picked it up, but because he was a fairly good distance away from where I was, his responses on the phone were hard to hear. As a rule, he generally spoke softly. When the conversation ended he turned and, also in a very calm way, said: "Chubar called. He's crying. He insists that he's not guilty, that he's an honest person." Stalin said this with such sympathy in his voice.

I liked Chubar. He was a simple and honest man, an Old Bolshevik, and he came from a working-class background. I had known him back in the Donbass. He had been chairman of the central administration of the coal industry, replacing Pyatakov[44] in that position. When he came to Moscow, I stayed on good terms with him. Now I was overjoyed that Stalin had spoken sympathetically with him, and consequently I assumed that I needn't believe the compromising materials that apparently existed, but about which I knew nothing. I thought Chubar was in no danger of being arrested, but I was mistaken. (Today I can say that I absolutely did not know Stalin as a person back then.) The next day I learned that Chubar had been arrested, but after that not a word was heard of him. As the saying goes, he disappeared into thin air.

After Stalin's death, I took an interest in this question and asked the Chekists to find the person who had interrogated Chubar, who had been in charge of the investigation. I was curious to know exactly what they had accused him of. Rudenko,[45] the prosecutor general of the USSR, told me that Chubar had not been guilty of anything and that there were no materials that could have served to support the charges against him. Then they found the investigator who had been in charge of Chubar's case. I made a proposal to the members of the Presidium of the Central Committee of the CPSU: "Let's listen to what he has to say in front of the Presidium. Let's see what kind of person he is, and what methods he used to force Chubar to confess to the crimes he confessed to, what the basis was for the reprisals against Chubar." The man who came to our session was not yet old. He was very dismayed when we began asking him questions. I asked him: "Did you conduct the investigation of Chubar?"

"Yes, I did."

"How did you conduct the investigation, and what was Chubar accused of? And how was it that he confessed to certain crimes?"

The man said: "I don't know. They summoned me and told me that I would be in charge of the investigation of Chubar. And they gave me this order: 'Beat him until he confesses. So I beat him and he confessed.'" There you have it. It was that simple!

When I heard that, it made me angry and at the same time filled me with sorrow. I didn't even know how to react. We decided to carry out an investigation of this investigator and to sentence him for having conducted such an investigation. He was sentenced, and then I came to the conclusion that although perhaps legally everything was correct, still if you judged according to the actual circumstances, the situation that had existed in the USSR in those days, this investigator was after all a blind instrument. He was told there were enemies of the people, and he trusted the party and trusted Stalin. Enemies of the people didn't confess to their crimes, and therefore it was necessary to beat a confession out of them. And so he did—not by using honest methods of investigation, but with a bludgeon. Such methods of investigation were used at that time against each and every defendant.

Sometimes Stalin used provocative, jesuitical methods in his conversations. I have already told about the incident with Antipov and myself. At that time Stalin had turned away, lowered his head, and changed the subject of the conversation to Moscow and to the matters for which he had actually summoned me. I don't remember now exactly what those subjects were. We walked around the Kremlin for a while; a new little plaza was being put in there. Stalin said that he had no more questions for me, and I left, but I was troubled. What grounds did Stalin have for this? In general why did he do such things? I think he was curious what my reaction would be when he questioned me, looking me in the eye to see how I would behave. Accidentally, it seems, I conducted myself in such a way that the look in my eyes gave him no grounds for concluding that I had somehow been connected with Antipov. If he had formed the impression that somehow I had "given myself away," then after a little while I would have been another enemy of the people. This method of "exposing enemies" is one Stalin used more than once. Stalin's attitude toward me was better than toward many others. He had greater confidence in me, and consequently I was not subjected to the same sort of thing that came down on the heads of totally honest and reliable members of our Leninist party.

In that painful and difficult year of 1937 new elections were supposed to be held for party organizations—base organizations, district organizations, citywide, and provincewide. Meetings began to be held. They proceeded in a very stormy atmosphere. The party was demoralized. I am now talking about party leadership on a level lower than the Central Committee. What I'm trying to say is that the leaders didn't feel themselves to be leaders. At that time an oral order was given from the top echelons, stating that in the elections all the candidates being proposed for leading party bodies should be carefully examined without fail to determine whether they had connections with arrested enemies of the people. That is, the Chekists had to approve all nominations. All party officials were checked to see how much confidence they deserved, and the governing bodies that were elected depended no longer on those who elected them but on the secret police "organs," on what kind of report they gave about a person. Strictly speaking, candidates were being put forward on an incorrect basis, when viewed from the standpoint of internal party democracy, because the will of the party organizations was restricted in this way.

The security agencies that were supposed to be under the control of the party instead became higher than the party, higher than the elective organizations, and they did what they wanted. I remember a certain sad incident. A citywide party conference of the Moscow organization was going on. I gave the main report. And the conference was proceeding at a high level of activism, but the situation was difficult. Everyone believed that we had reached a stage in our development where our enemies, unable to break us in frontal combat, were directing their efforts at undermining our party from within: recruiting party members, infiltrating agents, and so on. Today we can see how unfounded such reasoning was. After all, it was the veteran party cadres that were hit hardest by the repression, people who had gone through the revolutionary underground, the first years of the socialist revolution, the Civil War, people who had been selected by the very history of the working class struggle in Russia. Therefore it was strange. Why should it be precisely these people who first fell victim to temptation and allowed themselves to be recruited by foreign intelligence agencies? I can talk this way now, but I didn't think this way then. I saw things then through the eyes of the Central Committee, that is, Stalin, and repeated the arguments that I heard from Stalin.

The party conferences in Moscow proceeded with great turbulence. Just to elect a presiding committee, several sessions were spent at district conferences, if not an entire week. For that reason I was troubled about how we might best conduct our citywide party conference and decided to ask Stalin's advice. At that time we already had instructions on how to conduct elections at party conferences. A fairly democratic way of electing candidates was proposed in those instructions. The candidates should be discussed; then there would be a secret ballot, acceptance or rejection of candidates, and so forth. But those instructions were not carried out in fact. Meanwhile at the citywide conference, a discussion of my report was going on. The commissar of the Frunze Military Academy[46] took the floor. I don't remember his name. On the other hand I do remember his black beard. He had served in the Civil War and had a high military rank. He spoke well, and when we began drawing up a preliminary list of candidates for the party's city committee, his name was proposed by the military-academy delegation. Before the actual voting, the phone suddenly rang. They were asking me to call Yezhov,[47] and at that time Yezhov was a secretary of the party's Central Committee and, as I recall, the people's commissar of internal affairs. I was on good terms with Yezhov.

I called him. He said: "Do everything you can not to reject this commissar openly but 'play him along,' because we're going to arrest him. He's linked with the enemies. He's a very well camouflaged enemy." And he went on in the same vein.

I answered: "What in the world can I do? The voting lists have been approved. All that remains is to pass out the ballots and vote. It's something that no longer depends on me."

Yezhov said: "You have to do something so that he's not elected."

I answered: "All right, I'll think about it. And I'll do it."

No sooner had that conversation ended than Malenkov[48] called. He was then Yezhov's deputy, and was in fact in charge of the cadres department of the Central Committee of the AUCP(B). Malenkov said: "Everything must be done so that Yaroslavsky[49] is not elected. Do it without fail."

I answered: "How is that possible? Yaroslavsky is an Old Bolshevik, a man respected by the entire party." Yaroslavsky was working then as a member of the Party Collegium. He was called the "Soviet pope"; that is, he was viewed as the one who protected and maintained the moral and political foundations for party members. Yaroslavsky was in charge of investigating various personal cases of Communist Party members in disputes brought before the Central Committee. And now I was supposed to do what was being proposed!

Malenkov said: "You must do it! We have evidence against Yemelyan [Yaroslavsky], but he must not know about it."

I said: "We have already discussed Yaroslavsky's candidacy, and not a single vote was cast against him."

Malenkov said: "Nevertheless, do it."

I then gathered the secretaries of the party committees together and told them that there were orders about the commissar and Yaroslavsky and that everything had to be done, but in a cautious way, so that their names would be crossed out during the voting. We handed out lists, and the voting began. A commission counted the votes and reported the results to the conference. The commissar did not receive a majority and was not elected. He was astounded, and others were no less astounded than he was. But we told ourselves that the Central Committee had rejected him and therefore felt that we ourselves were to blame: How was it that we had not exposed such a well-camouflaged enemy ourselves, had allowed him to twist us around his finger? We had welcomed him so warmly, yet here he turned out to be an unworthy person. With Yaroslavsky it was a different matter. There was no information that he was an enemy of the people. They informed us only that he was a man the Central Committee did not support, a man who wavered and who was insufficiently active in the struggle against the opposition, that he sympathized with Trotsky.

When we got to Yaroslavsky and counted the votes, we saw that in spite of everything he had been elected a member of the party's city committee by a majority of one or two votes. Well, I reported that the party organization had not demonstrated the necessary understanding of the question and that, as it turned out, I had not managed to cope with the assignment given me by the Central Committee. The orders had really come from Stalin, of course, because neither Malenkov nor Yezhov would have given orders about Yaroslavsky unless there had been instructions from Stalin.

This incident aroused the indignation of Zemlyachka,[50] a person of especially strong character. It was said back then that she was really a man in skirts. She was harsh, abrupt, insistent, direct, and unmerciful in the struggle against any antiparty manifestations. Malenkov and Yezhov told me that Zemlyachka sent a letter to the party's Central Committee. She wrote that she wanted to call attention to an abnormal situation that had developed at the city party conference in Moscow, that an impermissible campaign against Yemelyan Yaroslavsky had been waged among the delegates, that as a member of the party he had been defamed, that people had been urged not to elect him as a member of the party's city committee, even though during the discussion of the candidates no one had raised any challenge or tried to reject his candidacy. It was not up to me to explain anything to anyone, because Zemlyachka's letter had gone to the very people who had given the order to dump Yaroslavsky. I was criticized for not having coped with the assignment given me by the Central Committee. Later I spoke with Zemlyachka and explained to her that there had been instructions from the Central Committee. I also pointed out that every party member and delegate had a right, if he had not spoken at the plenary session of the conference [against someone's candidacy], to express his views informally to the other delegates afterward. She was a sufficiently experienced person. She herself for many years had held leadership positions in the party. She had been a secretary of the Moscow party committee at one time, and she knew all the behind-the-scenes business involved in preparing and conducting party conferences.

Nevertheless these had of course been nonparty methods of operation. People who found themselves in the ruling bodies were using their positions to wage a campaign against others who were simply not to their liking. If Yaroslavsky was to blame in any way, people could have spoken openly about it at the conference. At one time he had been criticized in the press for an insufficiently clear-cut position in the struggle against the Trotskyists and supporters of Zinoviev. But Yaroslavsky enjoyed confidence and respect in the party, and these behind-the-scenes machinations had the aim of getting "one's own people" into the leadership—people who would hang on your every word, who would be thrilled by the genius of your leadership, who would not have their own opinions, but would make good yes-men, with loud, clear voices for saying "Yes."

The Moscow city party conference became, as it were, a model. People began asking me the question, "How did you manage at such a complicated time to hold a conference in just four or five days?" They said that in that amount of time they could have elected only a presiding committee, whereas we had finished up with everything. Actually we had managed to do that only because I had consulted with Stalin about how to act in one or another situation, and this enabled us to fit everything into a definite period because we knew what he would approve at that moment and what he would not.

I would like to pause to dwell on some more of Stalin's personal characteristics. On the one hand there was an Oriental perfidiousness. After speaking courteously with a person and expressing sympathy for him, a few minutes later he could order that person's arrest, as he did, for example, with Yakovlev, a member of the party's Central Committee and of the USSR Central Executive Committee of the Soviets. On the other hand Stalin was often quite attentive and sensitive, and he won over many people because of that. I can relate the following example. This happened, as I recall, in 1937. The Moscow province party conference was under way, and the proceedings were very stormy. It was a terrible time, terrible because we thought we were surrounded by enemies, that these enemies had penetrated not only into our country but above all into the ranks of our own party and were holding prominent positions in the economy and the army and had taken over a majority of the commanding posts. This was of course very disturbing to people devoted to the cause of building socialism and to the ideas of the party.

When the province conference began, a man named Brandt came over to me. At that time he headed the department for agriculture in one of the province committees of the party, and previously he had worked as a secretary of a number of party committees and was considered a very good party official who knew agriculture, especially flax production. I had already received quite a few letters earlier, mostly from military people, stating that the son of an enemy of the people, the son of the White Guard Colonel Brandt, who in 1918 had led an anti-Soviet uprising in Kaluga,[51] was occupying a responsible post in the Moscow province committee of the party. We had checked into these accusations and found they were groundless. But now a very difficult time had begun for anyone who had any kind of "blot" on his reputation. During the province party conference, this Brandt came over to me and said rather calmly (in general he was a solidly built, calm person): "Comrade Khrushchev, I am sick and tired of giving all kinds of explanations and justifying myself. I am thinking of committing suicide."

I answered: "What's the matter? Why are you in such a gloomy mood and why do you want to commit suicide?"

"I think I've told you this before, but let me repeat it. My name is Brandt. My father really was a colonel, and he lived in Kaluga. But the people who think that I am the son of the White Guard leader Brandt have a different Brandt in mind. He also lived in Kaluga, but he wasn't my father. They don't know that even though I am the son of a Colonel Brandt, he was a man who died before the revolution. And so my father could not in any way have taken part in an uprising that actually was led by this other Colonel Brandt, who returned from the front lines in World War I and settled in Kaluga. This is how it all happened: My father Brandt, a retired colonel of the tsarist Army, had his own little house in Kaluga, and the reason he was able to live there, actually, was that he knew how to do very fine embroidery, and he sold this embroidery to supplement his pension. My mother was a cook at Brandt's house and bore him three sons. Brandt legalized the marriage with my mother, adopted us, and we officially became his sons. Then Brandt died, and we were left orphans and lived literally as beggars. I hired out herding sheep, and my brothers did, too, and we scratched up the means of subsistence wherever and however we could. Today my brothers are Red Army commanders, and I am a party official. How many times I've told about this! I've reported on it to every party conference. I'm supposed to keep beating my breast constantly and swearing I'm an honest person. I'm sick and tired of it."

I said to him: "You calm down. If you're an honest person, we'll take you under our wing and protect you."

But I knew that my own words would be insufficient in this case and that the province party conference could become fatal for him. All it needed was for someone to get up at the conference and talk about this matter. All a person would have to do is assert that his father really was the Colonel Brandt who led the uprising in Kaluga, and then it would make no difference whether it was this Brandt or the other Brandt. I was thinking that of course he was not likely to live until a time when this whole matter could be clarified, that the Chekists would drag him off and his fate would be a forgone conclusion.

I decided to tell Stalin about it, which I was still permitted to do then. I called Stalin and asked if he would receive me, and I told him, "Look here, Comrade Stalin, I'd like to tell you about a certain situation and ask for your support." I told him that we had a certain Brandt in our organization and that his fate had worked out in such a way that there had been another Brandt who had led an uprising against the Soviets in 1918 and that the people who fought against that Brandt are taking our Brandt as the son of that Brandt and demanding reprisals against him as the son of that other Brandt. But it was the wrong Brandt, a man who had nothing in common with this Brandt.

Stalin heard me out, looked at me closely, and asked: "You're sure he's honest?"

I said: "Comrade Stalin, I'm absolutely sure. He's a tested person; he's worked in the Moscow province organization for many years." (Incidentally, Kaluga at that time was part of Moscow province.)

"If you're sure he's an honest man, then stick up for yourself and defend him." It was pleasant for me of course to hear that, and I was very glad. He also added: "Tell Brandt about this." As a result, in the elections to the Moscow province party committee, no one tried to pick on Brandt, and he was elected a member of the Moscow committee without any problems.

All of Stalin is contained in this incident. If at a certain moment he had disbelieved me, the man would not have survived! If you succeeded in convincing him, he would support you. Before the province party conference, I also talked with Stalin and asked him to give instructions on how to organize and conduct the conference, taking into account the conditions of sharp struggle and widespread arrests. We of course didn't talk about the arrests, but that was understood. I said: "The Moscow province conference will be a model for conferences in other provinces. A lot of people have been calling me up, even from the Central Committees of union republics, and asking how we think conferences should be conducted. A great deal will depend on our conference." I told him about conditions that had taken shape in the city, and I told him about how the conference was supposed to be conducted according to instructions and what kind of distortions had occurred in the process. I was especially disturbed by the loud and noisy types who liked to attract attention to themselves. We suspected at that time that they might possibly be people who were actually linked with the enemy and were trying to deflect blows from themselves. Stalin heard me out and said: "Be bold and daring in the way you conduct the conference. We'll support you. Stay strictly within the party rules and the Central Committee instructions that were sent out to party committees."

We were able to keep the conference to a short time frame—that is, the way conferences had normally been run before the mass arrests. When we came to the elections a certain question arose in my mind. In 1923, when I had been a student at the workers' school, I had been guilty of certain waverings in a Trotskyist direction. I expected that this matter might be raised at the conference or after the conference, and it would be very difficult for me to give the proper explanations. So I decided to tell Stalin about it. But first I decided to consult with Kaganovich. Kaganovich and I had known each other for a long time, and he had a good attitude toward me and treated me as a protégé. Suddenly he came down on me like a ton of bricks: "What are you saying? Why are you saying that? What's the matter with you? I know that that was just an infantile lack of understanding." That had happened just before a party congress, either the Thirteenth or the Twelfth. I had been elected to a regional party committee then.

I said to Kaganovich: "Still, it did happen, and it's better for me to say something about it than for someone to bring the question up later, and then I would look like someone who was trying to conceal compromising facts about himself. I don't want that to happen. I have always been an honest person, and I also want to be honest in front of the party."

"Well, I don't advise you to do that," said Kaganovich.

"All the same," I said, "I'm going to consult with Comrade Stalin."

I called up Stalin. He said: "Come on over." When I entered his office, he was there with Molotov. I told Stalin everything the way it had been. The only thing he asked was: "When was that?" I repeated that it had probably been before the Thirteenth Party Congress. I had been misled by a man named Kharechko,[52] a fairly well-known Trotskyist. Back before the revolution I had heard that there was a certain Kharechko from a peasant family in the village of Mikhailovka, a student. I knew that village. There were a lot of Kharechkos there. I knew he was a revolutionary, but I didn't know he was a Social Democrat. I had absolutely no idea about the different tendencies in the [socialist movement or in the] Social Democratic Party back then, although I knew that he was a man who before the revolution had fought for the people, for the workers and peasants. When he moved to Yuzovka I naturally felt sympathy with Kharechko and supported him. Stalin heard me out. "Kharechko? But I know him. Oh, he was an interesting man."

"And so I want to ask you what I should do at the provincewide party conference? Should I tell everything the way I've just told you, or should I limit myself to the fact that I've told you about it?"

Stalin said: "Probably there's no need to say anything. You've told us, and that's enough."

Molotov objected: "No, it would be better if he told about it."

Then Stalin agreed: "Yes, better to tell about it, because if you don't tell, someone might grab hold of it, and you'll be hounded with questions, and we'll get a pile of denunciations."

I left. When I returned to the conference I found the following scene. Discussion of the candidates who had been nominated for the province party committee was under way. Specifically they were discussing Malenkov. Malenkov was standing up [in front of the assembly] making explanations. They told me that he had already been up there for an hour or more, and each answer gave rise to new questions about his party loyalty and his activity during the Civil War. The story he was telling was not clear-cut and didn't hang together very well. A situation had taken shape in which Malenkov might fail to be elected. As soon as Malenkov finished and stepped down from the speaker's platform, I stood up and spoke in support of him. I said: "We know him very well, and his past provides no reason for us to have any doubts or suspicions. He's an honest person and has given everything he has to the party, to the people, to the revolution." Malenkov remained on the list of candidates.

My turn came. The Russian alphabet placed me at the end of all the lists. [The letter *Kh* stands near the end of the Russian alphabet.] I told the conference my story, as Stalin had advised, but I made no reference to Stalin. When I finished there were no questions. Somehow everyone was shouting at once: "Leave him on the voting list." I was elected then by an absolute majority of votes. All these things disposed me favorably toward Stalin. It was pleasing to me that Stalin had taken a considerate attitude toward me, had not criticized me, had asked only one or two questions, and even had suggested at first that I say nothing about all this at the conference. I considered it correct that he had recommended I tell everything. Actually, that's why I went to see him. I wanted Stalin to know that Khrushchev had gone to the conference and told about those aspects of his biography. I didn't consider it tactically advisable to do this without warning the general secretary of the Central Committee as long as I had the opportunity to do so. All this further strengthened my confidence in Stalin and gave rise to a feeling of certainty that those who were being arrested really were enemies of the people, although they had operated so skillfully that we had not been able to notice it—because of our inexperience, political blindness, and gullibility. Stalin repeatedly told us we were too gullible. It was as though he himself had risen to a higher position from which he could see everything and know everything, judge people's actions fairly, defend honest people and support them, while punishing untrustworthy people and enemies.

In connection with this episode, I was surprised by Kaganovich's conduct many years later. During the move against me at the Central Committee Presidium in June 1957, one of Kaganovich's main arguments against me was that I was a former Trotskyist. I said to him at the time: "Aren't you ashamed of yourself? Back then you tried to persuade me that I shouldn't tell Stalin about my mistakes, that they didn't deserve to be mentioned, that you knew me, and so on." I appealed to Molotov, and he (for all his failings) was a very honest person: "You remember, don't you, Comrade Molotov, I told Stalin about that in your presence, and how Stalin reacted and what he advised me to do and you advised too?" He confirmed my account. The soul of the bootlicker that Kaganovich was is reflected here as if in a mirror. Back then he had restrained me, but now he dragged out my past error as the main argument against me. The Central Committee plenum that followed after the Presidium session [in 1957] correctly saw through the whole business and rejected the slanderous attack against me.

One other incident—the cutting edge of the struggle of that time was against the Trotskyists, Zinoviev's supporters, and the Right opposition. The fate of Andrei Andreyevich Andreyev is interesting in this connection. He had been a fairly active Trotskyist and at the same time enjoyed Stalin's confidence and protection. Andreyev held fairly high posts as people's commissar of agriculture, people's commissar of railways, and secretary of the party's Central Committee. This was also a kind of plus for Stalin. While speaking out against active Trotskyists like Andreyev, at the same time he took them under his wing. Andreyev did a lot of bad things during the 1937 repression. Possibly because of his past, he was afraid that he would be suspected of having a soft attitude toward former Trotskyists.

Wherever Andreyev went many more people died, both in Belorussia and in Siberia. Many documents attest to this, as does, for example, the following fact: : The Old Bolshevik Kedrov,[53] while in prison, wrote Andreyev a long letter in which he demonstrated that he was absolutely innocent. No consequences resulted from this letter. He was tried (by a troika, a three-member panel; and by a *pyaterka,* a five-member panel), but even the bloody-minded *pyaterka* could not find sufficient evidence to convict him. He was finally killed by Beria at the beginning of the Great Patriotic War without any sentence ever having been handed down against him. All this became known later from the materials in the investigation into Beria's case.

Let me return to 1937, to the province party conference. We finished it up in the normal length of time, probably in five days, maybe even less. Before we adopted a resolution, I looked over the draft. The resolution was ghastly. So much about the enemies of the people had been jammed in there. The resolution demanded that we continue to sharpen our knives and carry out reprisals (against imagined enemies of the people, as has now become clear). I didn't like this resolution, but I was in a very awkward position. What should I do? I was the first secretary; the main responsibility for everything fell on the first secretary, and that responsibility had certainly not become less even then. From the point of view of internal party democracy this was a weakness of ours, in my opinion, because in this way the leader could subordinate the collective to himself. But that's a different subject.

I decided to consult with Stalin once again. I called him up and said: "Comrade Stalin, our province party conference is finishing up its work; a draft resolution has been compiled, but I would like to report to you and ask your advice. After all, the resolution of the Moscow province party conference will be taken as a model for other party organizations."

He said: "Come on over now." I went to the Kremlin, and Molotov was also there once again. I showed Stalin the resolution; he read it, took a red pencil, and began crossing things out. "This should be deleted, and this, and this should be deleted, and this. And now this way you can have it adopted." The political, evaluative part of the resolution was unrecognizable. All the "not yet defeated enemies of the people" had been crossed out by Stalin. Passages about the need for vigilance remained, but they would have been considered fairly moderate for those times. If I had presented such a resolution at the conference myself without asking Stalin, he might have become suspicious of me. The resolution wasn't in keeping with the tone of our party press; it seemed to soften things a little and reduce the sharpness of the struggle that *Pravda* was calling for.

We passed this resolution and published it. After that I was flooded with phone calls. I remember that Postyshev called from Kiev: "How were you able to hold the conference in such a short time and to adopt a resolution like that?" I told him, of course, that the draft resolution had not been like that, but that I had shown it to Stalin and that Stalin, with his own hand, had crossed out passages calling for an intensified struggle against the enemies of the people. Postyshev said: "Then we'll do things that way too, and we'll take your resolution as a model." These events again display the better side of Stalin. He seemed not to want things to heat up unnecessarily, and he didn't want superfluous bloodshed. At that time we didn't know that arrested people were being annihilated; we thought they were simply being put in prison and would serve their sentences. All this aroused still greater respect for Stalin and, I would say, worshipful admiration for his perspicacity and genius.

Our Moscow party organization was solidly united and served as a true stronghold of support for the Central Committee in the struggle against the enemies of the people and in carrying out the decisions of the party on building socialism in the city and the countryside. But bad things kept happening, and people were disappearing. I learned that Mezhlauk,[54] a man I greatly respected, had been arrested. Mezhlauk enjoyed the well-earned confidence and respect of Stalin. I remember the following incident. Some sort of conference was being held in our city, and the prominent physicist Peter Kapitsa[55] came to that conference from England. Stalin decided to detain him and not allow him to return to England. This task was assigned to Mezhlauk. I accidentally happened to be present when Stalin explained how to convince Kapitsa to stay: "Try to persuade him, but if worse comes to worst, simply take away his passport for foreign travel." Mezhlauk had a talk with Kapitsa and reported back to Stalin. Then I found out that they had come to an agreement, that Kapitsa would stay in our country (of course against his will) but with the stipulation that conditions would be created for his work. They wanted to build a special institute for him where he could use his knowledge to better effect for the good of our country. In this connection Stalin gave a rather poor characterization of Kapitsa, saying that he was no patriot and so forth. An institute was built for him—a yellow building at the end of Kaluga Street, not far from the Vorobyov Hills (or Lenin Hills).[56]

But let me go back to Mezhlauk, who had previously worked under Kuibyshev in the State Planning Commission (Gosplan). I knew him because

I came into contact with the State Planning Commission while I was working in the Moscow party committee. Moscow's municipal economy was planned, not through the province or through the Russian Federation, but directly by Gosplan, and so on occasion I had dealings with Mezhlauk. Among other things he often gave reports at Moscow city and district meetings of the active party membership. And now suddenly Mezhlauk was also an enemy of the people! Other Gosplan officials began to disappear, too, and then officials from the People's Commissariat of Heavy Industry. The noose was tightening. Officials who were protégés of Ordzhonikidze himself began finding the noose around their necks.[57]

Ordzhonikidze, or as we called him, Sergo, enjoyed great popularity and well-deserved respect. He was a man of heroic mold. I remember a conference of people in the construction industry being held in the auditorium of the Organizational Bureau of the party's Central Committee. Chairing the conference was Ordzhonikidze, and Stalin was also present. A rather small circle of people had gathered. All together there were probably two or three hundred, no more. I had been invited to represent Moscow, and I spoke there with rather sharp criticism of the course of construction in the city of Moscow. At that time Sergo and a man named Ginzburg[58] were occupied with that construction. Ginzburg was a good construction expert, and Sergo deservedly supported him. But in any big operation there are many short-comings, and in some cases even big shortcomings, and I spoke in defense of the interests of construction in the city of Moscow and criticized Ginzburg and the Commissariat of Heavy Industry. Sergo leaned toward me (he was a little deaf in one ear), listened, smiled endearingly, and made this retort: "And where do you know about construction from? Where from? Tell us, where from?" He said these words in such an amiable way.

My speech was later published in the newspaper of the Commissariat of Heavy Industry; I forget what headline was used. That newspaper was edited then by a very good person and a fine Communist; his name it seems was either Vasilkovsky or Vasilkov. But he perished, the poor fellow, like so many others.

I remember Sergo calling me many times at the Moscow committee on a number of questions. One day he called and said: "Comrade Khrushchev (he spoke with a strong Georgian accent) tell me, why don't you give Lominadze[59] any peace? Why are you always criticizing him?"

I answered: "Comrade Sergo, after all, you know that Lominadze was an active oppositionist and even, strictly speaking, an organizer of the opposition. It is being demanded now that he give clear-cut explanations, but instead he speaks vaguely and by his own doing is creating grounds for criticism. What can I do? After all, those are the facts."

"Comrade Khrushchev, listen, you've got to do something so they don't tear away at him so much." I told him that that would be very hard for me to do, and later I said that I myself considered that they were right to criticize him. Lominadze was a man who was close to Sergo, and Sergo's attitude toward him was one of great respect and great sympathy. Later on I found out about the following incident from Stalin himself.

After Ordzhonikidze had died, Stalin started talking about what kind of man Sergo had been. He said: "I (Stalin) personally found out from him that Lominadze had come to see him and expressed his disagreement with the party line that was being carried out, but persuaded Sergo to give him his word that everything he said wouldn't be passed on to Stalin and consequently wouldn't be used against Lominadze." Sergo had given his word, and Stalin was indignant over this: "How could that be, how could you give that kind of promise? That's the kind of unprincipled man Sergo was!" Ultimately, because of some circumstances, Sergo himself did tell Stalin that he had given Lominadze his word and therefore was telling Stalin about it now on the condition that Stalin not take any organizational measures on the basis of what Lominadze had said. But Stalin didn't honor anyone's word, and in the end Lominadze was sent to Chelyabinsk,[60] where they got him into such a state that he finally shot himself. Before that he had been a secretary of the party committee at an aircraft-engine plant in Moscow.

One day I was at the dacha on my day off. They called me and told me to call the Central Committee. There they told me: "Comrade Khrushchev, Sergo has died. The Politburo is establishing a commission for the funeral, and you're being included in the commission. Please come at such-and-such a time to see the chairman of the commission, and we will discuss questions relating to Sergo's funeral." Sergo was buried in the morning. A lot of time passed. I always spoke of Sergo with great warmth. One day (this was already after the war, it seems to me) I came to Moscow from Ukraine. We were at Stalin's place, engaged in some conversations, which sometimes lacked any real subject because we were just "killing time."

I said: "Sergo—now there was a man! He died before his time, when he was still young. What a shame, such a loss." At that point Beria made an unfriendly remark about Sergo, and no one said anything more. I felt that I had said something wrong, something that shouldn't have been said in that company. Dinner ended and we left.

Then Malenkov said to me: "Listen, why did you talk so incautiously about Sergo?"

"What is there to be cautious about here? Sergo was a respected political figure."

"Yeah, but he shot himself. Don't you know that?"

I said: "No. I helped to bury him, and we were told then that Sergo had died suddenly on his day off (he had, it seems, some sort of kidney ailment)."

"No, he shot himself. Did you notice what awkwardness there was after you mentioned his name?"

I said I had noticed it and was surprised. But the fact that Beria had made a hostile comment was not a surprise because I knew that Beria had a negative attitude toward Sergo and that Sergo did not respect Beria. Sergo was more closely linked with Georgian public opinion and knew more about Beria than Stalin did. If we compare Sergo and Stalin, we can say that they were both Georgians and Old Bolsheviks, but quite different as individuals. Sergo was attentive and a man of great spiritual warmth, although he was very hot-tempered. On one occasion at a Politburo meeting he flew off the handle, and earlier, in Georgia, he had hit someone, when Lenin was alive. A party committee investigated the affair. That's the way it is sometimes—opposite qualities will live side by side within one and the same person. But the main thing that people respected him for was that he was humane, accessible, and just.

I was told in detail about Ordzhonikidze's death by Anastas Ivanovich Mikoyan, but that was much later, after Stalin's death. He said that Sergo, before his death (he committed suicide not on Sunday, but on Saturday or even earlier) had gone for a long walk with Mikoyan around the Kremlin grounds. Sergo had said that he could not live any longer; Stalin had no confidence in him; the cadres that he [Sergo] had selected had almost all been destroyed; he couldn't fight against Stalin, and he couldn't live this way any longer.

As for Sergo's enemy, Beria, I got to know him earlier. It seems to me, the year was 1932. At that time I was working as second secretary of the Moscow city committee. The city committee was located on Bolshaya Dmitrovka. Beria came to our offices as secretary of the Transcaucasian Bureau of the AUCP(B). How Beria got to be a leader there I don't know; I can't say anything about that. But I met with Beria on personnel questions. I don't know why Beria turned to me. After all the first secretary of the Moscow party committee and the regional party committee was Kaganovich. But he came specifically to see me. Could it be that Kaganovich sent him? He came to see me together with Bagirov,[61] a party activist from Baku.[62] He was then taking courses in Marxism-Leninism at a location in the Krasnaya Presnya district. I had made Bagirov's acquaintance when I was secretary of the Krasnaya Presnya district committee of the party. I knew that Bagirov was there, but the history of his activities in Transcaucasia is something I did not know.

We got to talking about Comrade Ruben,[63] secretary of the Frunze district committee of the party, an Armenian comrade. What role they had brought Ruben to play there at that time I don't remember now. I didn't know Ruben very well. I had made his acquaintance when I became secretary of the Bauman district committee and he was the secretary of the Frunze district committee. I ran across him at conferences of secretaries of the party district committees, and at that time there were probably no more than nine people who were party secretaries of districts in Moscow. As a person Ruben distinguished himself dramatically within our circle, and I liked him very much. When Kaganovich called me and said that my candidacy would be proposed for the post of second secretary of the party's city committee, I became embarrassed. I answered that that shouldn't be done because I wasn't a Muscovite, and I knew how difficult things would be for me in Moscow. Moscow was "spoiled" by having so many high authorities, prominent people with big records in the prerevolutionary underground. Besides, Ruben appeared to be a more worthy candidate; if they had asked me, I would have recommended Ruben. But Kaganovich remarked that he had a better opinion of me than I had of myself, and he had decided to propose none other than me for this promotion. He added that Ruben was not a bad party worker, but that it should be kept in mind that Ruben had been an officer in the tsarist army. This of course I had not known.

When I met Beria for the first time, the conversation was formal; after all, it was not I who would decide the question of Ruben; the Central Committee would decide that question. Later I learned that Sergo had advanced Ruben's candidacy. Some little time after that, I encountered Ruben again. Apparently he liked to wear a military uniform. He arrived in Moscow wearing a soldier's blouse with three or four rhomboids on the collar of his blouse.[64] He was being brought in then as a member of the Military Council of the army defending the border, and he had been given a military title. Other party officials were also members of the various military councils, and later I too became a member of a military council. But we didn't wear military uniforms; yet Ruben did. If we put on a military uniform, it was without any insignia, and then only if we were going to some military exercises. [What finally happened to Ruben?] In 1937 he was arrested and annihilated.

After my first meeting with Beria, we became fairly close. I liked Beria. He was a simple, straightforward person, but also quite witty. We often sat side by side at plenums of the Central Committee, exchanging opinions, and now and then we would make fun of the speakers. I liked Beria so much that in 1934, when for the first time I vacationed in Sochi, I went to visit him in nearby Georgia.[65] I arrived in Batum[66] in southwestern Georgia by steamship (there was no railroad back then) and traveled from Batum to Tiflis [Tbilisi, the capital of Georgia] by train. I spent Sunday at Beria's country place. The entire Georgian leadership was there. The country houses of the members of the Council of People's Commissars of Georgia and the Central Committee of Georgian party were there on a mountainside. On my return journey, I took the historic Georgian Military Road[67] and caught a train at Beslan station [on the northern side of the mountains]. As I see it in retrospect, the beginning of my acquaintanceship with this treacherous person was quite peaceful.

In those days I looked at things idealistically: If a person carried a party card and was a real Communist, then he was my brother and even more than a brother. In my view we were all bound by the invisible threads of ideological struggle, the idea of building communism, which was something elevated and holy. Every participant in our movement was for me, if we are to use the language of religious believers, something like an apostle who in the name of the great ideal was willing to undergo any sacrifice. And in truth to be a real Communist then, one had to bear more sacrifices than receive benefits. It was not the same as now among Communists. Now there are ideologically minded people, but also many with no ideological commitment, mere officials, bureaucrats, bootlickers, and careerists. Today membership in the party and possession of a party card offer the hope of positioning oneself better in our society. Slick and clever people manage to get more than others without giving any evidence, either in quality or quantity, that they have contributed a correspondingly greater amount of labor. This is a fact and a terrible scourge of our times. Back then there was less of all that, although it was already beginning.

---

1. A. A. Zhdanov. See Biographies.

2. Gorky was the new name given to Nizhny Novgorod in 1932. The city is now again called Nizhny Novgorod. [GS/SS]

3. The reference is to the Soviet practice known as socialist competition, in which enterprises, regions, or other units were paired to engage in friendly rivalry for the best economic results. The

practice had nothing to do with market competition. [SS]

4. This problem arose because the RSFSR, unlike Ukraine and all the other union republics of the Soviet Union, did not have a Communist Party of its own. Matters pertaining to the RSFSR were the direct responsibility of the All-Union Communist Party, and this could easily result in

the RSFSR's problems being neglected or poorly coordinated. The purpose of forming a special Russian Bureau under the Central Committee of the all-union party was to ensure that the RSFSR would not be neglected. In effect, the Russian Bureau functioned as a substitute for the nonexistent RSFSR Communist Party. [SS]

5. A. A. Andreyev. See Biographies.

6. The advocates of the Russian Bureau were suspected by Stalin of being Russian nationalists whose primary loyalty was to the Russian ethnic group rather than to the Soviet Union as a whole. [SS]

7. The reference is to U. Yusupov, the first secretary of the Central Committee of the Communist Party of Uzbekistan from 1937 to 1950, whose report was delivered at the plenum of the Central Committee of the AUCP(B).

8. A. V. Aleksandrov was a composer who organized the Red Army Song and Dance Ensemble. See Biographies.

9. The reference is to B. A. Aleksandrov, the son of A. V. Aleksandrov, who succeeded his father as leader of the Red Army Song and Dance Ensemble. See Biographies.

10. Mariupol is in eastern Ukraine, south of Donetsk on the shore of the Sea of Azov (an inlet of the Black Sea). [SS]

11. The Central Committee resolution in question was adopted in August 1946. Writers associated with the literary journals *Zvezda* and *Leningrad,* such as Mikhail Zoshchenko and Anna Akhmatova, were accused of insufficient party spirit and deviations from the official cultural doctrine of socialist realism. The campaign was part of the cultural clampdown that accompanied the beginning of the Cold War. For more on the composer Vano Muradeli, see Biographies. [SS]

12. Marshal of the Soviet Union Tukhachevsky, together with other members of the supreme command of the Red Army, was sentenced and executed in June 1937.

13. A. I. Yegorov. See Biographies.

14. S. M. Budyonny. See Biographies.

15. I. E. Yakir. See Biographies.

16. M. M. Kulkov. See Biographies.

17. N. A. Filatov was an official in the Soviet apparatus.

18. S. Z. Korytny was a party official.

19. N. K. Antipov. See Biographies.

20. D. M. Rabinovich.

21. I. D. Finkel.

22. N. V. Margolin. See Biographies.

23. Rykovo had previously been called Yenakiyevo.

24. In 1938, officials of the NKVD administration in Ivanovo province arrested Shultsev, third secretary of the party committee for that province, and forced him to make a deposition about the existence in the province of a reserve Right-Trotskyist bloc. Members of the bloc allegedly included Simochkin and Korotokov, secretaries of the party province committee; Aralov, chairman of the executive committee of Soviets of that province; Karasik, procurator for the province; Volkov, chairman of the province court; and about thirty others. At the same time more than forty members of the command and political staff of the Red Army infantry corps deployed in the province were arrested. Almost all of them were executed.

25. That is, at conferences and congresses of the Communist Party (Bolshevik) of Ukraine, or CP(B)U. [SS]

26. Polish claims to central and western Ukraine were rooted in history. The lands of present-day Ukraine fell under the sway of Poland in the late sixteenth century. In 1648 peasants and Cossacks led by Bogdan Khmelnitsky rose up against Polish rule, and in 1649 Khmelnitsky entered Kiev and proclaimed the Hetmanate, the first independent Ukrainian state. However, a series of military defeats forced him to turn to Moscow for protection. In 1654, Ukraine was united with Russia by the Treaty of Pereyaslav. [SS] During the Polish-Soviet war of 1920, the Polish armed forces initially captured and briefly held Kiev before being driven back. The 1921 peace agreement between Poland and Soviet Russia gave most of the western parts of Ukraine and Belorussia to Poland. [GS]

27. I. N. Dubovoi. See Biographies.

28. Mikola Oleksandrovych Shchors (1895–1919) fought in the Civil War on the Red side in Ukraine. In the mid-1930s he was promoted as a Ukrainian counterpart to the Russian Civil War hero Chapayev and was the subject of a film by the screenwriter Oleksandr Dovzhenko. See George O. Liber, "Adapting to the Stalinist Order: Aleksandr Dovzhenko's Psychological Journey, 1933–1953," *Europe-Asia Studies* 53, 7 (2001): 1097–116. [SS] Dubovoi left behind a book about Shchors entitled *Moi vospominaniia o Shchorse* (My reminiscences of Shchors; Kiev, 1935).

29. Ya. B. Gamarnik. See Biographies.

30. Komsomolsk was built on the Amur River in the Russian Far East, about 250 kilometers from the Pacific coast. It was named in honor of the Komsomol (the Russian acronym for the Young Communist League) because it was supposedly built by young Komsomol volunteers. [SS]

31. A. V. Shchusev was an architect. See Biographies.

32. Kishinev was the main city of the prerevolutionary Russian province of Bessarabia, on the border with Romania. Under the name of Chishinau, it is now the capital of Moldova. [SS]

33. Trukhanov Island is near the eastern bank of the Dnieper River. At that time Kiev occupied only the high western bank, and Trukhanov Island, with its sandy beaches, could be reached only by rowboat. [SK]

34. Pirozhki, a traditional Ukrainian dish, are small pastries filled with mincemeat or cheese and eaten hot. [SS]

35. Social organizations were associations of citizens, such as trade unions or women's organizations, which did not formally belong to the state or party apparatus, although they were under party control. [GS/SS]

36. A. V. Kosarev. See Biographies.

37. Ya. E. Rudzutak. See Biographies.

38. A. P. Lyubchenko. See Biographies.

39. Hrushevsky, Vinnichenko, and Petlyura were all leaders of the Ukrainian national movement and of the independent Ukrainian People's Republic that existed briefly in 1917–18. [SS] In spring 1917 Lyubchenko was elected a member of the Ukrainian Central Rada (of the Ukrainian People's Republic). In fall 1917, however, he was arrested and sentenced to be shot for participating in an uprising against Vinnichenko's government. He was saved by the arrival in Kiev of units of the Red Army on January 26, 1918.

40. S. V. Petlyura was a leading Ukrainian nationalist politician and military figure of the Civil War period. See Biographies. The photograph that N. S. Khrushchev recalls was a group shot of members of the Ukrainian Central Rada, one of whom was Petlyura.

41. Khrushchev is referring to M. B. Khrapchenko, who was chairman of the Committee for the Arts attached to the Council of People's Commissars (Council of Ministers) of the USSR from 1939 to 1948.

42. Tashkent was the capital of the Uzbek Soviet Socialist Republic. [SS]

43. O. P. Mishakova.

44. G. L. Pyatakov. See Biographies.

45. R. A. Rudenko. See Biographies.

46. Mikhail Vasilyevich Frunze (1885–1925), after whom the military academy was named, was a leading Red Army commander in the Civil War. He succeeded Trotsky as commissar of war in 1924. [SS]

47. N. I. Yezhov. See Biographies.

48. G. M. Malenkov. See Biographies.

49. Ye. M. Yaroslavsky. See Biographies.

50. R. S. Zemlyachka. See Biographies.

51. Kaluga is situated about 110 kilometers southwest of Moscow. [SS]

52. T. I. Kharechko, member of the RSDLP from 1914.

53. M. S. Kedrov. See Biographies.

54. V. I. Mezhlauk. See Biographies.

55. P. L. Kapitsa was a prominent physicist. See Biographies.

56. These are bluffs along the east side of the Moscow River, below the Kremlin and near Moscow University. [GS]

57. Ordzhonikidze was people's commissar of heavy industry. "Sergo" was his nickname. [GS]

58. S. Z. Ginzburg. See Biographies.

59. V. V. Lominadze. See Biographies.

60. Chelyabinsk is an industrial city in the southern Urals. [SS]

61. M. Dzh. A. Bagirov. See Biographies.

62. Baku was the capital of the Azerbaijan Soviet Socialist Republic. [SS]

63. R. G. Ruben occupied various soviet, politicomilitary, and party posts.

64. Rhomboids were marks of distinction worn on the collars of the Red Army's highest commanders. They were introduced in 1919. From 1924 they were made from red copper (cuprite). Three or four rhomboids corresponded to the rank of army commander or Front commander.

65. Sochi is a popular vacation resort on the northeastern shore of the Black Sea. Khrushchev crossed the Black Sea to Batum on the southeastern shore. [GS]

66. Batum, also known as Batumi, was the main city of Georgia's autonomous republic of Ajaria (or Adzharia). It is situated on the southeastern shore of the Black Sea, near the border with Turkey. [SS]

67. The Georgian Military Road runs northsouth through Ossetia to Georgia across the main Caucasus mountain range. It was built in the nineteenth century to facilitate tsarist Russia's conquest of the Caucasus region. [SS]

## IN UKRAINE AGAIN

In 1938 Stalin called me in and said: "We want to send you to Ukraine, so that you can head up the party organization there. Kosior is being transferred to Moscow to be Molotov's first deputy chairman of the Council of People's Commissars and chairman of the government Control Commission."

With this, Stalin was expressing obvious dissatisfaction with Kosior. I already knew from things Kaganovich had said that people were dissatisfied with Kosior. Kaganovich had gone, on Stalin's orders, to "help" Kosior and Postyshev "restore order." But restoring order consisted of arresting people. That's when rumors began circulating that Kosior was not coping with his task.

I began trying to refuse because I knew Ukraine and figured I would be unable to cope. The hat was too big for me; it wouldn't fit. I begged that I not be sent because I wasn't trained to hold such a post. Stalin began encouraging me to do it. I responded: "Besides, there's the national question. I'm a Russian. I understand Ukrainian, but not as well as a leader would have to. And I can't speak Ukrainian at all. That's a big negative factor. The Ukrainians, especially the intellectuals, might give me a very cold reception, and I wouldn't want to put myself in that position."

Stalin said: "No, what are you talking about? After all, Kosior is a Pole. Why should a Pole be better for the Ukrainians than a Russian?"

I answered: "Kosior is a Pole, but he knows Ukrainian and can give a speech in Ukrainian. I can't. Besides, Kosior has more experience."

But Stalin had already made his decision, and he stated firmly that I must work in Ukraine. "All right," I answered, "I will try to do everything I can to justify your confidence."

The time for my departure was set. I asked Malenkov to pick out a few Ukrainians from the Moscow party organization for me (there were a lot of them there) or from the apparatus of the party's Central Committee. That was indispensable because I was told that in Ukraine at that time not one of the Soviet executive committees in the provinces had a chairman and even the Council of People's Commissars of Ukraine lacked a chairman (there was only the first deputy chairman); also, there were no heads of departments in the party's province committees or city committees or even in the Central Committee of the Communist Party (Bolshevik) of Ukraine, or CP(B)U.[1] They began looking around for a second secretary.[2] Malenkov named Comrade Burmistenko[3] to be second secretary. Burmistenko was one of Malenkov's deputies in charge of cadres[4] for the Central Committee of the AUCP(B). I didn't know Burmistenko very well, but I got to know him. He made a very good impression on me, and we hit it off well together.

I gave Burmistenko the assignment of choosing people who could be taken with us, about fifteen or twenty. He chose, as I recall, about ten people from Central Committee departments and from the Moscow party organization. From the latter organization he took Serdyuk[5] and some others. Serdyuk was working as first or second secretary of the party committee in

Moscow's Soviet district. He was a native Ukrainian and had an excellent command of the Ukrainian language.

We arrived in Ukraine and went to see Kosior. He informed us about the existing situation and introduced us to the cadres who still survived. We held a republicwide party plenum. Kosior presented Burmistenko and me to the plenum of the Central Committee of the Ukrainian Communist Party. We were co-opted as members of the Central Committee plenum and elected as members of the Politburo and secretaries of the Central Committee. Kosior was relieved of his duties. All these events in Ukraine caused great suffering to Grigory Ivanovich Petrovsky, but he behaved passively, like an old man, although he was not that old then.

We began to acquaint ourselves with the situation. It was as though a modern Mamai had swept through Ukraine.[6] As I've said, there were no secretaries of party province committees in the republic, and no chairmen of Soviet executive committees for the provinces. Soon the secretary of the party's Kiev city committee was no longer among us. A man named Yevtushenko[7] was secretary of the Kiev province committee of the CP(B)U. Stalin's attitude toward him was quite good. I didn't know Yevtushenko very well, aside from some brief meetings in the Kremlin, but in my view Yevtushenko was well suited to the post he held. I liked him. Suddenly a phone call came from Moscow: "Yevtushenko has been arrested." Even today I can't say exactly what the reasons were for his arrest. Back then the standard explanation was given—enemy of the people. In a short time the man had confessed, and a little later he was signing statements with his own hand, statements that were then circulated to whoever was appropriate and the impression was created that there were substantial grounds for the arrest.

Stalin summoned me to Moscow and proposed that I assume two other posts besides the post of first secretary of the CP(B)U Central Committee—[he wanted me to be] first secretary of the party's Kiev province committee and Kiev city committee. That was simply inconceivable. Then Stalin said: "Pick yourself people who can help." I agreed, although, strictly speaking, my consent was not required. The Central Committee had passed a motion, and my job was to carry it out. Serdyuk was chosen second secretary of the party's city committee [in Kiev], and Shevchenko[8] was chosen as secretary of the party's Kiev province committee. Shevchenko was a peasant lad; and he satisfied the demands then being placed on a secretary of that rank. We went to work. The people's commissar of internal affairs in Ukraine was Uspensky.[9] I had made his acquaintance when I was secretary of the party's Moscow committee. He had been the NKVD's official representative for

Moscow province, and I often had dealings with him. He reported to me on the state of affairs and made a good impression on me then. Later he was assigned to be commandant of the Kremlin, and from there he was sent to Ukraine to be people's commissar of internal affairs. I assumed that he would keep me properly informed and assist me.

Uspensky threw himself into feverish activity. As became clear after Stalin's death, Uspensky literally flooded the Central Committee with memoranda about "enemies of the people." Arrests continued. I remember that Uspensky raised the question of arresting Maksim Rylsky.[10] I objected: "What's the matter with you? Rylsky is an outstanding poet. People accuse him of nationalism, but what kind of nationalist is he? He's simply a Ukrainian and is reflecting the national sentiments of the Ukrainians. You can't regard every Ukrainian who speaks the Ukrainian language as a nationalist. After all, you're in Ukraine!" But Uspensky was insistent. I talked him out of it: "Get this. Rylsky wrote a poem about Stalin that became the words of a song. It's a song that all of Ukraine sings. And you want to arrest him? Nobody will accept that."

I didn't know Rylsky personally. I knew him as a Ukrainian poet (it was impossible not to know him); that was all. He was a man of strong character who defended the national interests of Ukraine and the language of the Ukrainian people, a man who spoke energetically and expressed himself boldly on various questions. This of course provided a pretext for accusing him of nationalism and placing him in the category "enemy of the people."

Some time later Patorzhinsky and Litvinenko-Volgemut[11] came to see me. Patorzhinsky I knew. He was also in good standing with Stalin, both as a singer and as a person. They told me that the composer who had written the music for Rylsky's poem about Stalin was sitting in prison. All of Ukraine was singing the song, while he was in prison as an alleged nationalist. I ordered Uspensky to report to me on what grounds the composer had been arrested. When he brought documents, I looked at them and saw that there were no grounds for holding him in prison. I told Uspensky he had been too hasty with this arrest. In my view the composer should be released. I don't remember whether he was released on my instructions or whether I reported to Stalin. But to put it briefly, he was freed and continued his work. Later he became chairman of the Union of Composers of Ukraine.[12] Later I received greetings from his wife and daughter on May Day every year and on every anniversary of the October revolution. I understood this as thanks for having freed him from prison and saved him from the gallows, because that's exactly how things would have ended. That's what the situation was like then.

People in Ukraine back then were being dragged into the ranks of the so-called enemies. There was a splendid man named Tyagnibeda[13] who was deputy chairman of the Council of People's Commissars of Ukraine. I had known him when he had worked as a head miner in the Donbas and was taking engineering courses at the technical school for the mining industry in Yuzovka. Later, at the same time when I was working as secretary of the party's Petrovo-Maryinsky district committee, he was working as director of the Karpovsky coal pits (now the Petrovsky mines in Voznesensk-Donetsky). In a word, he was a good, straightforward person who had even fought in the ranks of the Red Army. Back then, it was a very rare thing for a technician and head miner to share the views of the Bolsheviks and take part in the Civil War on the side of the Reds. Suddenly they were demanding his arrest and presenting "grounds" for it.

When the first deputy chairman was arrested, the Council of People's Commissars of Ukraine was left clean as a whistle: There was no chairman of the Council of People's Commissars and no deputy chairman. I brought the question up with Stalin: Someone had to be found for the post of chairman of the Council of People's Commissars. Some time earlier Stalin had told me that in Dnepropetrovsk there was also no secretary for the party's province committee. At that time Dnepropetrovsk province was huge. It covered almost a third of Ukraine. What today are parts of Zaporozhye and Nikolayev provinces, as well as today's Dnepropetrovsk province, were all part of that one province back then. Stalin was apparently worried about the state of affairs in Dnepropetrovsk and was afraid that the metallurgical industry would be destabilized. The secretary of the province committee there had previously been Khatayevich,[14] but he had been arrested even before my arrival. Stalin suggested: "Perhaps we can send Korotchenko there?" Korotchenko was then secretary of the party's Smolensk province committee.

I of course immediately agreed: "Yes, give us Korotchenko!"

We set up a [Dnepropetrovsk] province committee and city committee of the party. I traveled around to the mills and plants and factories, talked with the active party members, got to know people, and studied the situation. I went to Zaporozhye and to Dneprodzerzhinsk. At Dneprodzerzhinsk I became acquainted with a group of party officials and engineers, one of whom was Brezhnev. We began promoting these people to party work and giving shape to a new party leadership. Korniyets[15] was also promoted at that time. He was secretary of a rural district committee in the Dnepropetrovsk area. In addition to Brezhnev, another man, a secretary of the party's province committee for propaganda, was also promoted from Dneprodzerzhinsk.[16]

In the Donbas the secretary of the party's province committee was Pramnek,[17] a Latvian by nationality. Before the Donbas he had worked, it seems, in Gorky province and was considered a good secretary. Suddenly Stalin called me and informed me that I had to make a trip to Stalino, because Pramnek had been arrested there. I found he was no longer there when I arrived. Shcherbakov[18] had been promoted to his position. He had been a secretary of the party's Moscow committee then.

Here's another example of the situation at that time. A man I didn't know was asking to be received by me. My secretary informed me that the man had just been released from prison, that he was a teacher from Vinnitsa province and wanted to report something important.

I received him. He was a young, healthy, handsome fellow. He introduced himself, told me that he had been arrested, had sat in prison, had just been released, and had come to see me immediately because he wanted to report that he had been beaten and tortured. He said that a confession had been forced out of him, a confession saying that Korotchenko was allegedly an agent of the court of the king of Romania and in our country was the head of a center of spies carrying on work against the Soviet government in the interests of Romania. I thanked him for the information and said that this was slander and the work of the enemy. We would look into the matter, and he should go his way in peace. I informed Stalin about this visit in a memorandum. Stalin got very angry. When I was summoned to Moscow on some other question, there was an exchange of opinions on this subject, among other things. An investigator was immediately sent, an investigator for especially important cases (as I recall, it was Lev Sheinin,[19] who is now deceased), to get to the bottom of the matter. It turned out that three or four or maybe five individuals were mixed up in this business. They had concocted the charge against Korotchenko. In the end, they were arrested and shot.

Stalin was a cruel man. He annihilated the cadres. Yet, on the other hand, what concern he showed in this case! It's true that he also used draconian methods when he showed his concern. Nevertheless, it was concern about saving the lives of cadres. He had no mercy on those Chekists. This also helped dispose me more favorably than ever toward Stalin. His cruelty and injustice, which we see clearly today, were not evident to us then. On the contrary, his actions were seen as expressions of decisiveness, of his unbending will in defense of the Soviet state, to strengthen it against its enemies, whoever they might turn out to be and whatever form enemy activity might take.

Subsequently Stalin often returned to what happened with Korotchenko. In the unconstrained atmosphere when we had been sitting around his table for many hours, again and again he would start to reminisce: "Well, how's the 'samuyar' there where you are?" Instead of calling him Korotchenko, he called him "the samuyar." At the Eighteenth Party Congress the delegates at times would end their speeches with threats aimed at Japan, saying things like, "They have these samurai there, but we'll take care of them!" Korotchenko was rather slipshod in the way he used words. He forgot the last names of people, even those very close to him, and got a lot of things confused. For him it was awkward to say the word "samurai," and so when he ended his speech it came out this way: "We'll make it hot for those there 'samuyars'!" So that name stuck with him—"samuyar." Stalin never called him anything else, right up until his death.

Stalin would turn to me and ask: "Well, how's that 'samuyar' of yours?"

On this occasion I answered: "Well, the 'samuyar' has gone and got involved with the king of Romania."

Stalin joked: "Or with the queen? How old is that queen?"

I answered: "The king there is not yet full grown, still a minor, but there is a queen mother. He seems to have gotten involved with the queen mother." This brought on laughter and new jokes. Of course it was laughter through tears, if you think of the situation at the time. After all, if you looked into it, the people who brought charges against Korotchenko were very simple-minded. Morally speaking, they were totally focused on the search for enemies of the people. They wanted to distinguish themselves, to show initiative, and so they hunted for someone to grab. Why did they specify contacts with Romania? The region in which these false and provocative charges arose was Vinnitsa province on the border with Bessarabia.[20] Our Chekists, in their work in that area, had to counter the work of Romanian intelligence. And so they got the idea of linking this person [against whom they had brought their charges] with Romanian intelligence, but who would they make the head of this group of enemy agents? Why, the chairman of the Council of People's Commissars of Ukraine, Korotchenko! I assume that the only thing that saved him was the fact that Stalin knew Korotchenko personally and knew that he was incapable of treason. If it hadn't been for that, the outcome for Korotchenko would have been a sorry one.

The entire upper echelon of leading officials, several layers deep, was completely destroyed then in Ukraine. Several times the cadres were replaced, and once again they were arrested and annihilated. Ukrainian intellectuals, especially writers, composers, artists, and physicians, were also under surveillance and suffered from arrests and reprisals. Even such a remarkable poet and public figure as Mikola Platonovich Bazhan,[21] who later became a party member—he was an honest and very pleasant person, devoted to the Soviet state and the Communist Party—became the object of attacks, and it was necessary to argue especially strongly in order to prevent his arrest. And what about Petro Panch[22] (also a prominent Ukrainian writer)? I don't know how he survived. The Chekists were on his trail, and those who informed against him were most of all writers, the very writers he worked with. Unfortunately he often drank too much. These other writers provoked him into conversations [when he had been drinking] and then relayed everything he said, so that a case was cooked up against him and documents had already been prepared for his arrest.

Several people were simply charlatans who took up the profession of exposing enemies of the people. They terrorized everyone. They would unceremoniously look a person right in the eye: "Here this one, he's an enemy of the people." Such an accusation would stick to a person, it would attract attention, and the NKVD would start to investigate. The investigation of course was conducted secretly; agents were assigned to follow the person, and later they testified that indeed this was an enemy of the people. I remember there was one such arrogant and insolent person. (I forget his name; he was the head of Kievpalivo, the Kiev Committee for Fuel Supply.) He went around everywhere and accused everyone, one after the other, so that everyone trembled before him. At a session of the bureau of the party's city committee, he brought charges against Serdyuk, who was the committee's second secretary. At the next session I myself was obliged to chair the meeting whose purpose was to look into this accusation. There was no evidence to support the charges that he brought against honest people. But he insisted that there were enemies of the people sitting right there. But back then no factual material, no evidence was required. Just insolence and arrogance were enough.

I was told about another typical incident. There was a certain public figure in Ukraine, a doctor named Medved. After the war he worked in the Foreign Ministry and was part of the Ukrainian delegation at the United Nations headed by Dmitro Zakharovich Manuilsky.[23] He represented Ukraine well there and angered our enemies. Of him they said: "That Ukrainian Medved keeps roaring and roaring." He really did have the voice of a bear[24] and a forceful personality. (Earlier, it seems, he had been deputy chief of a provincewide department for health care either in Kiev or in Kharkov.) The story was told that at a party meeting some woman got up and spoke, pointing her finger at Medved: "I don't know that man, but I can tell from the look in his eye he's an enemy of the people." Can you imagine?

But Medved (and as I say, that's what he was—a *medved*, ["bear"]), without losing his head for a moment, countered: "This is the first time I've ever seen this woman, the one who just spoke against me. I don't know her, but I can tell from the look in her eye she's a prostitute." Only he used a more expressive word. This became an anecdote that circulated throughout Ukraine, passed on by word of mouth. And that saved Medved. If Medved had started trying to prove that he was not some alien creature, not an enemy of the people, but an honest person, that would have aroused suspicion against him. Some sort of confirmation would have been found for the declaration made by this crazy person, who nevertheless was aware that she wouldn't have to take responsibility for what she said, but that, on the contrary, she would be encouraged. That was the kind of horrible situation that existed back then.

Let me go back to my arrival in Ukraine. Kosior left. The leave-taking was rather unemotional; they saw him off rather dryly. Of course this was not the kind of sendoff a figure like Kosior should have been given, after he had worked for so many years and done so much to build the party organization in Ukraine. Kaganovich had told me even before I left for Ukraine that he himself had been introduced to party work by none other than Kosior, who gave lectures on political economy in the Vladimir Hills[25] in Kiev. "We went around together, took a walk, and enjoyed the beautiful view from the right bank [west bank] of the Dnieper River [from the heights of the Vladimir Hills], and I listened to what he had to say. In fact those were training courses. During those walks Kosior was in fact giving lectures on political economy."

In Ukraine at that time, Grigory Ivanovich Petrovsky was feeling very bad as far as the state of his morale went. I had heard a lot about Petrovsky even before the revolution. After all, Petrovsky had been elected to the State Duma from Yekaterinoslav province. The people who had voted for him were the workers of the Donbas region in Yekaterinoslav.[26] Once, before the revolution, I was invited to a meeting—a Sunday get-together in a ravine in the steppes. Petrovsky was supposed to give a speech there. I went to the get-together, but it was called off. The police had gotten wind of it, and people decided it would be better not to go through with it.

A great many things in the Donbas region were linked with Petrovsky's name. The coal mines where I was a secretary of the party district committee in 1925–26 were named after Petrovsky. They're still named after him. It was precisely in the area of those mines that the meeting in the steppes had been scheduled back then.

Grigory Ivanovich Petrovsky's sixtieth birthday was coming up. But an opinion had formed within the party that he did not stand firmly for the party's general line, and so there was a guarded attitude toward him, including on my part. This came from Stalin. I had told Stalin that Grigory Ivanovich's sixtieth birthday was approaching and I thought we ought to celebrate it, and therefore I was asking him how to go about it. He looked at me and said: "Sixty years? All right. Organize a dinner in his honor at your home. Invite him and his wife and members of his family and no one else." And that's what I did. A very difficult situation had developed at that time with Grigory Ivanovich's family—his son had been arrested. I had known his son.[27] He had commanded the Proletarian Division from Moscow. When I was working in Moscow, I went to a celebration in honor of this division at the site of a summer camp. Leonid Petrovsky was considered a good commander then. Grigory Ivanovich's son-in-law (the son of Kotsyubinsky)[28] had been arrested and shot. Petrovsky's daughter (wife of the executed Kotsyubinsky) lived at Grigory Ivanovich's house. You can imagine what kind of situation had developed in his family, what the state of mind and state of emotions were for Grigory Ivanovich himself, and what kind of attitude people had toward him: his son was in prison; his son-in-law had been shot.

I arranged the dinner at my place in the country. I invited Grigory Ivanovich. We all sat down, my family and his family; we sat at the table and drank to his health. Grigory Ivanovich of course looked pretty bitter, and I myself was not cheerful. Everything went along rather formally in a strained atmosphere. Quite soon Grigory Ivanovich said goodbye and left. Our country houses were near each other, five minutes walk from one to the other.

Later on, Stalin informed me that Grigory Ivanovich was being summoned to Moscow. The gathering to see him off was not what it should have been, considering his position. The occasion was purely formal. The Chekists later told me that he was very upset all along the way to Moscow, especially when they were nearing the city—apparently he was expecting to be arrested. And that could have happened. Stalin was capable of anything in those days!

The people we were promoting then were of a different kind. These newly promoted people had no prerevolutionary experience. If we are to speak about past revolutionary activity, it was as though they had "neither kith nor kin." They were simply comrades from the current party membership, virtually rank and filers. And incidentally, everyone promoted then was like that.

Let me say more about the Kiev party organization. The second secretary of the party's Kiev province committee at that time was Kostenko.[29] He was with me only for a very short time, because he was soon arrested. I was surprised. He was a simple person from the collective farm peasantry. What was there in it for him to sneak off and make friends with enemies of the Soviet Union? I simply couldn't understand it and decided to have a discussion about it. I went to the NKVD. They brought him from his cell. I asked him about it, but he kept repeating: "So-and-so and so-and-so collaborated with me in this affair."

I said to him: "And who else was with you?"

"Nobody else." Well, all right, it made me happy that at least there was an end in sight. I no longer had any doubts that he really was an enemy of the people, because he had confirmed this to me in person and in a rather calm frame of mind. The people's commissar of internal affairs told me Kostenko would be sentenced and shot.

At that time instances occurred in which, just before people were shot, they suddenly began to give testimony against others, and in this way an unbroken chain of enemies of the people was created. I said: "If Kostenko starts to give testimony against other people, I ask you in that case not to shoot him, but to keep him alive, so that we would be able to look into the matter." Some time went by, and Uspensky reported to me that Kostenko had been shot but that before his death he had mentioned Cherepin,[30] who was already working as second secretary of the party's Kiev province committee. He was a fine fellow, a shrewd person, who knew his job well, and he also knew agriculture and knew how to approach the peasants. Moreover, he didn't have to put anything on, because he himself was of peasant origin. I asked: "Why have you done this? I asked you to keep Kostenko alive, so we could talk with him in more detail. I doubt that Cherepin could have been involved in any sort of conspiracy. And now I can't find out anything, because the person giving evidence against him is no longer alive. How is it possible to check and verify things now?" I called Malenkov: "Comrade Malenkov, testimony has been given against Cherepin, but I don't believe it; this kind of thing couldn't be true."

"Well, what's the problem? If you don't believe it, then let him keep working."

In those days this was a big indication of support from the Central Committee. Malenkov was in charge of personnel matters, or as the saying went, he "sat on the cadres." A day or two went by, and he called me: "You know, in spite of everything, maybe it would be better to transfer that Cherepin, send him off somewhere. Who knows? Anything is possible. . . . Isn't it possible that he really was recruited [by enemy agents]?" Well, what was I to do? I had to transfer him. I moved him over to be deputy people's commissar of agriculture for livestock, and he worked well, honestly, and devotedly. Some time went by. We needed a secretary for a new province committee of the party. I had proposed that more provinces be created in Ukraine, so that they would be smaller in size—and matters could be dealt with more easily by the leadership. A separate Sumy province was designated.[31]

I called Malenkov: "I still have my doubts that we dealt with Cherepin correctly. He's an honest man. I propose that Cherepin be promoted to sec-retary of the party committee for Sumy province." Malenkov agreed, and Cherepin worked there right up until the war. When the war began we had a need for cadres to be promoted as members of military councils for various units. I named Cherepin member of one of the military councils for a unit operating in the Odessa region.[32]

The war began badly for the Red Army. I learned that during our retreat Cherepin had died. The commander of his unit had been killed or had shot himself, and Cherepin had disappeared without a trace. I think that he too was killed. The general, the commander of the unit, was in military uniform, and the Germans knew that he was the commander. To raise the spirits of their own army, they would bury our generals with military honors. That general was indeed buried with honors, but Cherepin disappeared without a trace. He ended his life as a devoted and true son of the Communist Party, a loyal son of his people, and of his homeland.

How many such people were there? Thousands and thousands! Party members, candidates for party membership, and members of the Young Communist League. Strictly speaking, it was the entire top leadership of the country. I think that the equivalent of three generations of leaders, if not more, was arrested and perished! The leadership was paralyzed; no one could be pro-moted without the approval of the NKVD. If the NKVD gave a positive evaluation of one or another person being proposed for promotion, only that person would be promoted. But even approval by the NKVD provided no guarantees. There were cases where a person was appointed, and within a few days it turned out that he was no longer free; he had been arrested. Explanations were given in these cases, too; further interrogation of such-and-such an enemy of the people had turned up new evidence; so-and-so had given more extensive evidence and testified against this person, who had been well disguised and had not been exposed in time, but instead had been promoted in the leadership. Then it turned out that he was part of a conspiracy and was also an enemy of the people.

Of course that was the standard explanation, but it did have a certain logic of its own, because some arrested person had actually given this testimony. And previously someone else had given evidence against the person who was now giving this testimony. In this way a vicious cycle was created—the result of defective practices by the leadership, which in this way took the road, as it were, of self-annihilation. That's the way things were. On one day a representative of some party organization would speak out, denouncing people who had been arrested earlier, and the next day he himself would no longer be there, and this too found a ready explanation—it was said that he denounced and exposed others zealously because he himself had been mixed up in the affair and was trying to hide the truth. Well, there's an explanation for you!

The most flagrant example of this could be seen in the case of Furer.[33] Furer had worked in Ukraine in 1920. I didn't know him then because he was a big-city man. He worked in Kiev or Odessa or Kharkov, I don't remember exactly now. But his was a famous name, and his name still resonated widely when I was working in Moscow in the 1930s. He was a very good organizer, a good propagandist, and a good promoter; he knew how to publicize things very well, how to "present the material." It was he who "made the arrangements" and laid the groundwork for promoting the figure of Nikita Izotov.[34] I would say that it was Furer who "gave birth" to both Izotov and Stakhanov.[35] Furer organized and with his own hands "made the arrangements" to have the shock-worker Izotov come out of the mine, to have him met by the public carrying flowers, with the press and film people organized to cover the event. In a word, he put on a big promotion campaign, and Izotov became a hero. It was actually with this promotional event that the whole campaign glorifying such production records had its start. Other imitators of Izotov later appeared.

I remember one day Kaganovich asked me: "Do you know Furer?"

"I know him from the newspapers, but I've never met him in real life."

"Well, I know him; he's a very capable man. It would be a good thing if we could get him here to work with us in Moscow."

"I don't know how we would get him, but if it's possible, by all means. This would be a useful person to have working in the Moscow party organization."

Kaganovich was then a secretary of the party's Central Committee, so it wasn't difficult for him to achieve what he wanted. I don't know why he consulted with me about it. Apparently he wanted to "lay the groundwork," so that I would correctly understand the appointment he was planning to make. Sure enough, Furer was transferred to work in Moscow. He headed the department for agitation among the masses and did his job well. I was pleased. His authority in the city organization of the party and in the Central Committee was high. I remember Molotov calling me and asking: "How would you see it if we took Furer from you? We want to put him in charge of radio broadcasting."

I answered: "Of course Furer would be good at such work, or so it would seem. Only I must strongly request that you not take him, because he's working on an interesting and vital task for us. For the Moscow party organization it would be an exceptionally great loss."

Molotov ended the conversation, but I had the feeling he didn't agree with me. In fact I had reinforced Molotov's opinion. His view was that if a good party official showed up [in Moscow] from the outlying areas, he should be promoted as soon as a position became vacant; that was the way people should be promoted.

We were getting ready for some sort of conference. Furer asked me to give him two or three days off to get ready. He wanted to leave the city to go to a vacation place called Osinki in the region of the Khimki reservoir.[36] He was working there for a little while; everything seemed to be as it should be. Stalin and Molotov were not in Moscow right then; they had gone off for a vacation in Sochi.

Sergo Ordzhonikdze and Kaganovich were still in Moscow. I know that for sure, because when I stopped in to see Kaganovich I often found Sergo with him. They often consulted on various questions when preparing reports for Stalin. During one of the trials, either of Zinoviev or of Rykov, or of some other group, I stopped in to see Kaganovich. Sergo was in the office with him, and I decided to stay in the waiting room together with Demyan Bedny.[37] When Kaganovich learned that I had arrived, he immediately came out and asked me into his office. I went in. Demyan Bedny was also called in with me. He had been given the assignment to speak out against the members of the antiparty group that was being tried, to write a fable or poem making fun of them and condemning them. The assignment had been given earlier. He had brought a draft version and then a second variant, but they all proved to be unacceptable. The version that he brought when he came in with me was also not acceptable, in the opinion of Kaganovich and Sergo. They began ever so delicately to criticize him. Demyan, a huge, obese person, began explaining why the poem wasn't coming out right: "I can't do it;

well, I just can't. I've tried; I've put so much effort into it, but I can't. I have something like sexual impotence when I begin to think about them. I don't feel any creative urge."

I was surprised by such outspokenness. Demyan Bedny left. I forget now exactly how Kaganovich and Sergo reacted, but it seems to me that they reacted negatively to the candid admission that he felt impotent and compared the feeling to sexual impotence. That meant he felt some sort of sympathy with the men sitting on the bench of the accused. Naturally I didn't take Demyan Bedny's side then, because I believed in the infallibility of the party's Central Committee and Stalin.

But getting back to the case of Furer: I was suddenly informed that he had shot himself. I was astounded. How could such a young, active, healthy, fervent person, full of the joy of life, suddenly end his life by suicide? His body was soon brought from the vacation place along with the documents that he was supposed to be preparing. A very long letter addressed to Stalin and other members of the Politburo was found. His suicide was preceded by the arrest of Livshits,[38] deputy people's commissar of railways. He was a very active and energetic person and had been a Chekist during the Civil War. I didn't know him, but he had a good reputation as a very energetic party worker. At one point he had supported Trotsky, but during the years when he was deputy people's commissar it was generally considered that he had taken his stand in support of the party's positions. The question of Trotskyism had left the historical stage and was not a subject of dispute; in general it was a bygone stage in Livshits's life, a phase that had been condemned and then dropped from consideration. But it was a fact that continued to hang over Livshits's head, and he and Furer had been great friends. Later on someone else was arrested from a group of people who were close to Furer and Livshits.

Furer's letter was devoted mainly to the rehabilitation of Livshits. Apparently it was preserved in an archive. The author lavished great praise on Livshits, asserting that he was an honest person, had taken a firm stand on party positions, and was not a Trotskyist. In short, in a polite, rather than rude and insulting way (because he was writing to Stalin), he wanted to influence Stalin so that the latter would change his outlook and stop the mass arrests. Furer held that honest people were being arrested. The author closed with the statement that he had decided on suicide because he could not reconcile himself to the arrest and execution of innocent people. He spoke warmly of Stalin. In general in his letter he gave a fairly flattering description of all the members of the Politburo. I took his letter to Kaganovich. Kaganovich read it aloud in my presence. He walked up and down and then began to sob as he read it. He was unable to collect himself for a long time after he read it. How could it be that Furer had shot himself? Evidently he really had a great deal of respect for Furer. At that point Kaganovich said to me: "You'd better send a brief letter to Stalin, and to all the members of the Politburo." That's what I did. Despite the fact that in the case of suicides the party organizations stayed away from the funerals, it was precisely we, the party organization, that is, the Moscow Committee, who buried Furer.

Some time went by and autumn was approaching. Stalin returned to Moscow from his vacation. I was called in to see him. I arrived, suspecting absolutely nothing. Stalin said: "Furer shot himself. He was a useless no-good." I was surprised and disconcerted because I thought that Kaganovich to some extent had been reflecting Stalin's view [of Furer]. Kaganovich had literally sobbed out loud when he read the letter. And now, all of a sudden, *this* turn of events! "He had the audacity to give character assessments of the members of the Politburo, and wrote all sorts of flattering words addressed to the members of the Politburo. He was trying to disguise himself. He was a Trotskyist and a co-thinker of Livshits. I called you in to tell you this. He was a dishonest man, and there should be no regrets about him."

I was very much tormented after that by the fact that I had turned out to be a fool, had believed in Furer, had thought that his letter was sincere, that the man was unburdening himself of his true feelings on the eve of his death. He had said nothing bad about the party or its leadership, but had written only that Livshits and the others had been honest people. With his death he wanted to focus the attention of the party on the fact that honest and devoted people were being killed. For me this was a big blow. As for Kaganovich, after that he never returned to the subject of Furer in our conversations. Furer was erased from his memory. Kaganovich evidently was afraid that I might somehow mention to Stalin how he had wept and that he himself had advised me to send the document to the Politburo members and to Stalin.

I will now say a few words about the public trials of Rykov, Bukharin, Yagoda, Zinoviev, and Kamenev.[39] I don't have very clear recollections of these trials. I attended the court sessions only once or twice. One of the trials was held in a small auditorium in the house of trade unions. Vyshinsky[40] was the prosecutor. I don't know who the defense lawyers were, but they did exist. Also there were representatives of fraternal parties and representatives of the press from the capitalist countries, but I can't recall their names. All this is not so important for my memoirs, because it has been described both in our press and in the foreign press. I listened to the cross-examination of the accused and was astounded and indignant that such prominent people, leaders, Politburo members, Bolsheviks with prerevolutionary records, had turned out to be linked with foreign intelligence agencies and had allowed themselves to act in such a way as to harm our state. I'm trying to tell how I myself perceived the confessions of the accused at that time.

When Yagoda was accused of having taken steps so that Maxim Gorky would die earlier than he might have normally, the proof was as follows. Gorky loved to sit by a campfire. He would often visit Yagoda, or the latter would visit Gorky, because they had become friends. Yagoda built big outdoor fires with the aim of making Gorky catch cold in the outdoors, thus causing him to fall ill and shortening his life. This struck me as rather incomprehensible. I also love campfires, and generally speaking, I don't know anyone who doesn't. A healthy person would simply adjust to the campfire. After all Yagoda couldn't have forced Gorky to sit too close to the fire and get overheated. It was said that someone had caused the death of Gorky's son, Maxim Peshkov, and that later too Gorky had died, and that Yagoda had played some role in all this.

It was difficult for me as a matter of fact to say anything. I simply regretted Gorky's death and took a rather critical attitude toward the testimony that was given. Yagoda for his part agreed that he had pursued this aim in building big bonfires. I remember that the prosecutor asked Yagoda: "What kind of relations did you have with the wife of Gorky's son?"

Yagoda calmly answered: "I have asked that such questions not be raised, and I do not wish to sully this woman's name." The prosecutor did not insist on an answer, and after that the matter was dropped.

It is clear what the culmination of all these trials was—terrible sentences. All of these people were executed; they were destroyed as enemies of the people. And thus they have remained to this day, [officially] enemies of the people. They have remained such because after the Twentieth Party Congress we exonerated almost all the innocent victims, but we didn't clear the names of those who had gone through the big show trials. That was not, however, because any proof of their guilt existed. Considerations of a different kind were involved. We asked the prosecutor then [at time of the Twentieth Congress]: "Was there real proof of their guilt, sufficient to put them on trial?" There had been no proof! And judging from the documentary material that figured in the cases of these people, strictly speaking, not only did they not deserve to be charged; they didn't deserve even to be arrested. Such was the report by Rudenko to the members of the Presidium of the party's Central Committee in the 1950s.[41]

Why, then, were these people not exonerated at that time? Only because, after the Twentieth Party Congress, when we did rehabilitate many unjustly arrested persons, there were stormy reactions among people both inside our country and outside it. The leaders of the fraternal Communist parties were worried because these events had badly shaken their parties. The trials had an especially turbulent effect on the Italian and French Communist parties. At the trials themselves, as I recall, Maurice Thorez, Palmiro Togliatti,[42] and other leaders of foreign Communist parties had been present. They themselves had seen and heard everything; they had, as it were, "touched these cases with their own hands," and they were absolutely certain that the charges were valid. The defendants had confessed their guilt. The charges had been proved, and these observers had returned to their homelands convinced, although there were very stormy discussions about these trials back then, both in the West and in the Soviet Union. Our enemies used them to agitate against the Communist parties, against our ideology, and against our Soviet system. The Communist parties defended themselves. We argued that we were right and that the trials were fully justified; they [the observers from the foreign Communist parties] wrote that everything was well founded; everything had been proved with factual evidence and the confessions of the defendants themselves.

Togliatti (of the Italian Communist Party) and Thorez (of the French Communist Party) appealed to us, stating that if the defendants in the show trials were rehabilitated, it would create unbelievably difficult conditions for the fraternal Communist parties, especially for those representatives who had been present in the courtrooms at the trials. As eyewitnesses they had later reported to their own parties, arguing that the trials had been held on the basis of firm and reliable evidence and were legally valid. We came to an agreement that we would not rehabilitate those victims right then, but we would lay all the necessary groundwork for such rehabilitation. Once the prosecutor general had arrived at the appropriate conclusion, we would pass a secret resolution stating that these people had been victims of arbitrary treatment. We did not publish our resolution for the reasons that I've already outlined. We took sin upon our souls, as the saying goes ["to take sin upon (one's) soul," a favorite expression of Khrushchev's, has biblical overtones; it means simply "to lie"], in the interests of our party, our ideology, and our general working class cause. After all, those people could not be brought back to life! We didn't wish, by publicly admitting that the trials were invalid, to arm our enemies against the fraternal Communist parties, against such leaders of those parties as Maurice Thorez, Palmiro Togliatti, and others who were devoted heart and soul to the workers' cause and who were true Marxists and Leninists.

Trotsky and the question of his death were things we did not take up. We did not lift the curtain on that question and did not want to. We had engaged in an ideological struggle with Trotsky; we had condemned him; we had been and remained opponents of his ideology and his conceptions. He had done considerable harm to the revolutionary movement. Moreover, he had not died on the territory of the USSR; he had been assassinated; and there had been no specific investigation and trial of Trotsky in the USSR.[43] In 1940 an agent of ours had tracked Trotsky down and killed him, it seems, in Mexico. The agent was awarded a medal for this. We did not wish to touch on that aspect of things.

I am talking here only about the supporters of Zinoviev, Bukharin, Rykov, Lominadze,[44] and others. Lominadze committed suicide. An enormous number of people with prerevolutionary records also perished, virtually the entire party leadership. People could ask me: "What are you saying? You 'took sin upon your soul' and didn't publish the truth, that the show trials themselves had no basis in fact, that there was no real evidence in the materials against the defendants? Well, how in fact did things stand in regard to these people in general?"

I think the struggle against them was correct, because there were ideological differences; various points of view about the practical work of building socialism did exist; there were disagreements with the supporters of Zinoviev and with the Right Opposition. I believe that we, that is, the party's Central Committee, and Stalin, who was our leader, carried on the struggle correctly and that it was conducted by party methods, by means of debates, through discussion of the questions, and voting in the party organizations. Here we used precisely party methods, Leninist methods. It may be that on the one side and on the other certain excesses and incorrect actions were committed. I grant that. But in the main, the struggle was conducted correctly and on a democratic basis. But there was no reason to put them on trial, and no grounds for doing so. This was outright arbitrariness and abuse of power. All this confirmed Lenin's view that Stalin was capable of abusing power and therefore should not be kept in the post of general secretary. It demonstrated Lenin's correctness and the accuracy of his forecast.

On the other hand, if we had published truthful materials about the show trials, that would have turned out to be, as it were, an abstract truth. Of course because this had happened, it was necessary to tell the truth. But should this be done with no regard for what ugly blemish this statement of the truth might leave, what kind of harm might be dealt to the Communist movement? After all, what had already been done could not be taken back. If you were to talk about whose advantage publishing the truth would serve, it would be to the advantage only of our enemies, the enemies of socialism, the enemies of the working class. We did not want that, and therefore did not pursue that course. As for the basic questions, we were not afraid to pose them at the Twentieth Party Congress. We published the main decisions [regarding this matter] and told our people, our party, and the fraternal Communist parties everything that needed to be said to exonerate and restore the good names of those who were innocently destroyed, for which Stalin was to blame.

Yes, we did not want to do that without any thought for the consequences. We did not want to do it in such a way as to provide material that could be turned against the revolutionary movement, against our Soviet system, against our party, and against the working-class movement. I think our reasoning was correct.

We believed that some time would pass, during which all those who had lived through these events would, as the saying goes, pass on to the other world, and then documents could be published and would have to be published showing that these people were not guilty, that they had been honest people, devoted to and very valuable for the USSR, that they had simply held some sort of dissenting views. Lenin had made very flattering comments about many of them, although at times he also criticized them.

To argue that the reprisals against them had been correct, some people nowadays accentuate the criticism that Lenin made of one or another figure, while the good things they did and the flattering comments Lenin made about them are completely hushed up. Take, for example, Bukharin. He really was "the favorite of all the party" [as Lenin's "Testament" stated]. My generation was raised on *The ABC of Communism*,[45] written by Bukharin [and Yevgeny Preobrazhensky] on assignment by the Central Committee of the party. It was virtually an official document from which workers in our study circles really did learn the ABCs of Communism. That's why the book was called that. I won't even argue that over the course of many years Bukharin was the editor of *Pravda*. He was a real editor, and a theoretician. His speeches, oral reports, lectures, and articles in the press against the Trotskyists and other enemies of the party were a very big contribution to our victory in the internal party struggle [against the Left Opposition]. Then suddenly he was made out to be some sort of spy, and evidence was presented that he had tried to sell off the territory of the USSR. Today all this looks like fairy tales for little children, and in principle it is totally unfounded slander.

This was the basis of my arguments when we came to an agreement in the Presidium of the party's Central Committee [in 1956] on how to deal with the above-mentioned cases. I regret of course that I didn't succeed in carrying the review of these cases through to the end, along with the gathering of all necessary materials. I received reports about this, but during the years when I participated in the leadership of our country I didn't succeed in concluding this business. Well, what can you do? What one person doesn't complete, others will do later. And if others don't do it, still others will, because a righteous cause will never be lost. It is my opinion that I honestly carried out my duty as a party member in this matter as well. To the extent that I could, I did everything to clear the names of those who, although innocent, lost their lives, people who in fact were irreproachable party members and who had done a great deal for the country both in the years of their underground activity and during the Civil War, the most difficult period after the victory of the Great October Revolution, and in the building of socialism, restoring the national economy, and building our proletarian state.

I want to continue talking now about other facts that show the mechanics of Stalin's approach and his thinking in the era when reaction ran amok without restraint, the era of the cult of his personality. I would like to recall here (and this is also a very telling case) the story of Comrade Zadionchenko[46] (today an invalid). I knew him from the Bauman district of Moscow. When I was elected secretary of that district's party committee in 1931, he was heading, as I recall, the department of culture in the Bauman district Soviet. It seems to me that an organization of that kind existed back then, but I don't recall exactly. In short, I knew him, and knew the good side of him. When we divided the districts, creating a larger number than had existed previously, he became secretary of one of the party's district committees in Moscow, and later he worked as chairman of the Council of People's Commissars of the Russian Federation, and once again he did good work there also. He was promoted to that position when I was no longer in Moscow.

When the decision was made to take Korotchenko from Dnepropetrovsk and promote him to the chairmanship of the Council of People's Commissars of Ukraine the question arose: Who to send to Dnepropetrovsk? Stalin felt that a reliable person and prominent official needed to be there because Dnepropetrovsk had always held a high political and economic position in our country. Besides, the secretary of the party's province committee had been Khatayevich, who was a good organizer and sensible person. We then proposed: "The chairman of the Council of People's Commissars of the Russian Federation, Comrade Zadionchenko, would be a good person to send there." Stalin knew Zadionchenko and agreed: "Well, how about that? He wouldn't be a bad province committee secretary. Let's take him." He was sent to Dnepropetrovsk. I felt that he was in the right place, and I thought he'd be pleased by such a promotion in the line of official party duty, but I was mistaken. He suffered because of this turn of events; he'd already gotten used to a more easygoing way of life. I don't know what specifically he did in the Council of People's Commissars of the RSFSR. In fact the Council of People's Commissars of the USSR took care of all business in the RSFSR, and Zadiochenko simply repeated decisions made by others. His powers there were undeservedly restricted. But that is a different subject.

In spite of everything, Zadionchenko did good work in Dnepropetrovsk and coped with his task. He was an intelligent person, a good organizer, a man who didn't sit still; he wasn't the type to stay in the office all the time. One day an unforeseen incident occurred. A party conference of the Central Committee of the Ukrainian Communist Party was being held in Odessa, and Korotchenko went to it. The conference ended; he returned and told us that during a break a certain comrade had come up to him, a delegate to the conference, and asked: "How's my uncle getting along?"

I asked him: "What uncle?"

"Zadionchenko," he said. Korotchenko looked at him; he seemed to be Jewish from his outward appearance. And Zadionchenko was a Ukrainian. What kind of blood relation could there be here? [But the man said:] "Zadionchenko is my uncle. Send him my greetings." It seems that the man's name was Zayonchik. When Korotchenko returned to Kiev, he told me about this incident. At that time a furious hunting and checking into all kinds of genealogies and family backgrounds was going on, so that people wouldn't be deceived, so that enemies of some sort wouldn't worm their way into our ranks.

I said: "The best thing is to question Zadiochenko himself about this." I asked Burmistenko to do it . (He was an old acquaintance of Zadiochenko.) "Have a talk with him, and tell him that we're asking him to be open with us about everything. That would be best for him."

Burmistenko summoned him and had a talk with him. Burmistenko was a very good comrade and knew how to be delicate in such situations. Then he came to me and said: "He insists that his name is Zadionchenko." In those days we considered it our duty to have such matters clarified, so as not to end up looking like fools. It wasn't that we thought some sort of slander was being cooked up. After all, Zayonchik was proud of his uncle and had sent his greetings. There was no suspicion that some dirty trick was being played on Zadionchenko, implying that the latter was hiding his nationality, was hiding the fact that at some point he had taken a different name to hide behind. The People's Commissariat of Internal Affairs (the NKVD) was brought into the matter. Incidentally, I think the NKVD had already gotten involved, because at that time we party officials were more dependent on the NKVD than it was on us. Strictly speaking, we didn't direct the NKVD agencies; rather, they imposed their will on us, although outwardly all the proper forms of subordination [of the police to the political authorities] were observed. In fact, the NKVD, through its documents, investigative materials, and repressive actions, directed us in whatever way it wanted. For our part, according to the practices that had developed, we were obliged to place confidence in whatever documents the NKVD presented to party bodies.

This case didn't require much effort from the NKVD. We soon knew that Zadionchenko had been born in the small town of Rzhishchev, in Kiev province [at that time a *gubernia*], near Kanev. His father had been an artisan, a tinsmith, and his mother a tobacco worker in Kremenchug.[47] She didn't earn very much, and she was a woman of rather loose habits. The father died, and later the mother came down with tuberculosis and also died. Zadionchenko (who was then really named Zayonchik) remained an orphan, and an artisan or craftsman gave him shelter. He grew up on the streets, fed by kind people. And that's what his childhood was like. Then came the thunder of revolution and Civil War. Zadionchenko told the rest of the story himself. He said that a Red cavalry detachment came through, and he hooked up with it. The Red Army men clothed him, gave him shoes, fed him, and gave him a name. He was no longer Zayonchik, but Zadionchenko. I don't know if that really happened, but that's not the point. The point is, to put it briefly, this is the information we found out.

I have run ahead a little and told what we learned from Zadionchenko himself. I called him in and said to him: "Comrade Zadionchenko! Comrade Burmistenko had a talk with you; you denied everything, but now we've found out all about it. Why are you doing yourself harm, hurting your best interests? We know that you were born in the town of Rzhishchev (a small settlement when he was born, but by then a town). We know about your father and mother, who they were and how their lives ended. The main thing, though, is that there was no need to hide that you were Zayonchik, that your father was an artisan and your mother a worker."

He began to cry; he was simply sobbing: "I didn't have the courage to tell it all right away. It's all true. Now I don't know what's going to happen to me. I confess I hid the truth, but I didn't have any ulterior motives. I hid it, because I've been living as Zadionchenko for so many years and I've gotten used to that name. I've broken all connections with the name Zayonchik. I am Zadionchenko now, and even my wife doesn't know that I'm Jewish. This will be a blow to my family, and I don't know what to do now or what will happen."

I calmed him down: "You should have told us about it long ago, and nothing would have happened. Now of course the business is more compli-cated because the NKVD people have gotten involved and we've received documents from them. Go on now, return to Dnepropetrovsk, do your work; don't say anything to anyone about this, even your wife; conduct yourself as you did previously, and I will report to the party's Central Committee." He was an experienced man—it seems to me he was already a Central Com-mittee member—and he understood the situation. I immediately called up Malenkov: This was a personnel question, and so it concerned Malenkov first of all. I told him the story.

Malenkov knew Zadionchenko very well and viewed him with respect. He said: "This has to be told to Stalin. When you show up again in Moscow do that yourself."

I answered: "All right."

I arrived in Moscow. Malenkov had not told Stalin anything, but he had not been able to restrain himself and had informed Yezhov. (Or was it per-haps that Yezhov found out through Uspensky, the people's commissar of internal affairs in Ukraine?) In short, when I arrived Malenkov warned me: "Zadionchenko, according to you, is Jewish, but Yezhov says Zadionchenko is a Pole." Just at that time there was a "hunt" against Poles; any person of Polish nationality was regarded as an agent of Pilsudski, an agent provocateur.

I answered: "How can you say that? I know for certain that he's Jewish. We even know the synagogue where the Jewish childbirth ceremony was conducted."

I visited Stalin and told him about it. He took it all rather calmly. This encouraged me. "A fool," he said in a fatherly way. "He should have reported it himself, and nothing would have happened. You have no doubts about his honesty?"

I answered: "Of course not. He's an absolutely honest man, devoted to the party. Now they're trying to make a 'Pole' out of him."

"To hell with them," he said. "They should be given a rap on the knuckles. Defend him."

I answered: "With your support I will defend him." Thus a disaster nearly happened for a devoted party worker just because of an innocent change of his last name. I don't know why he changed his last name. Maybe the Red Army men made fun of him because he was a Jewish kid and he wanted to avoid this unpleasant ridicule.

Sometimes there really were unpleasant jokes about Jews, among both Russians and Ukrainians. This happened more often among Ukrainians, not because Ukrainians are more anti-Semitic, but because there were more Jews living among the Ukrainians. The Jews engaged in petty trade and handicrafts more than others did. They often had encounters with Ukrainian working people, and their encounters would be solely on the basis of buying and selling; that is, they rarely worked side by side. In my village you saw a Jew only when he rode into town to buy stuff, offering little candies, rings for the fingers, and shiny earrings in exchange for down and feathers [for making pillows and quilts]. In short, Zadionchenko changed his name without any ulterior motives, and then they tried to make a Pole out of him. After all, if he was merely Jewish, they couldn't make much out of that. And it was well known who his mother and father were. They had to make him out to be, not a Jew, but a Pole—that is, a foreign agent sent into our country by Pilsudski. And so, some people were already reaching out to take Zadionchenko's life.

I have told about this at such length so that people will better understand the times we lived in and the position we were in, those of us who were alive then, and the situation that had taken shape. This was the situation we worked and lived in. But we didn't *only* fight against "enemies of the people"; we also fought to fulfill the five-year plans, and all of them were fulfilled— with the exception of one year of all the prewar five-year plans. That year was the most difficult and the blackest year of all for our party, our cadres, and it was in that year that the plan was not fulfilled. The year was 1937.

When he sent me to Ukraine, Stalin warned me: "I know you have a weakness for industry and the urban economy. I would like to warn you not to get carried away too much, especially with the Donbas, because you yourself are from the Donbas, but pay more attention to agriculture, because for the Soviet Union the agriculture of Ukraine is of the greatest importance. The rural regions of our country are organized poorly, whereas in industry the cadres are organized better, and it doesn't seem likely that any special complications would arise for you in that area." I stuck to this line, although it wasn't easy for me, because I did feel drawn to industry, especially coal, metallurgy, and machine building. But once Stalin had said what he did about agriculture, I began to occupy myself with it more and with the rural part of the country. I traveled through Ukraine, seeking out people who were in the forefront, listening to them, and learning from them.

We promoted new cadres and filled up the ranks of the province committees, the executive committees of the Soviets, and the government bodies on the republic level. These problems were resolved more easily in the collective farms, although the collective farm cadres had also been thinned out.

Burmistenko and I went to Ukraine in January or February [of 1938]. It was time to get ready for the spring sowing. In the south sometimes very early springs come along, when the work in the fields can begin even in February, and without fail it must begin in March. We began to get ready for the spring sowing campaign and suddenly encountered the following phenomenon: In the western provinces (Kamenets-Podolsky, Vinnitsa, Proskurov, Shepetovka), which bordered on Poland, horses were dying on a massive scale. I listened to what they had to say in the People's Commissariat of Agriculture, traveled out into the local areas, listened to what the residents there said, and looked into the matter at length, but I couldn't make sense of it in any way. The horses had become sick, lost weight quickly, and died. It was impossible to determine the reason, because when investigating commissions, including scientists, who were capable of doing something [to solve the problem], began their work, they were immediately arrested and wiped out as alleged saboteurs and wreckers, as though they were responsible for the deaths of the horses.

I remember one incident in Vinnitsa province. I arrived at a collective farm where a great many horses had died and began to question a man who worked in the stables. I was told that he had seen with his own eyes "enemies" poisoning the horses. This is what he told me: "I saw this man pouring out some sort of poison. And we caught him. Who did he turn out to be? A veterinarian." That was how this whole business was explained. The areas bordered on Poland. Supposedly, Germans through Poland, and the Poles themselves, were doing everything they could to undermine our agriculture and deprive us of draft animals.

It's true that the Germans were getting ready for war everywhere. To a certain extent it was logical that they would try to get rid of our horses—to strike a blow at our economy, our agriculture, our military potential, because horses at that time were like tanks and airplanes today. They were used for mobile forces. We had already lived through the events of the Civil War in which horses played a major role, and we assumed the same would be true in a future war. Horses meant cavalry; they meant transport for supplies, without which an army cannot fight. That was why this explanation—that the death of the horses was an act of sabotage by our foreign enemies who had linked up with internal enemies—received a ready reception among our people. But I couldn't completely agree with this explanation. Why was it that the cows and sheep weren't dying, only the horses? I wanted to listen to what scientists, veterinarians, technicians, and experts in zoology had to say, but the ranks had been thinned out drastically, especially those who dealt with horses.

I asked Uspensky, the people's commissar for internal affairs [in Ukraine]: "Do you have any prisoners who have been accused of harming the horses?"

"Yes, we have."

"Who are they?" He gave the name of a professor of the Kharkov Veterinary Institute and the director of the Kharkov Zootechnical Institute. The latter was a Ukrainian, and the former was a Jew. I warned him: "I'm coming to see you. You should have them brought to your office. I don't want to go into the prison. I'll talk with them in your presence."

The reply was: "They have confessed, and they can tell you everything."

Before this meeting, I had told the people's commissar: "If the professor poisoned the horses, let him tell us what poison he used and write down the chemical formula for the poison." I wanted to take that formula and later have some poison concocted and conduct a controlled experiment. The professor gave the formula, and I ordered the experiment carried out. The potion was prepared and was put in the horses' feed. They ate it, but they didn't fall over dead or even get sick. That's when I began to feel a strong desire to speak with the professor in person.

The arrangements were made, and I arrived. The arrested men were called in (one at a time of course). The first was a professor, a man of about fifty, gray-haired. I asked him: "What can you say about this?"

He answered: "I've already made two confessions and can only confirm that we really are German agents. We had the assignment to poison the horses, and we did."

I said: "How could that be? You say you poisoned the horses. I asked for the chemical formula of the poison, and you provided it. We used that formula to mix up alleged poison and gave it to the animals, but they didn't die and didn't even get sick."

He said: "Yes, that's possible, because we mixed the poison that we concocted ourselves with a previously prepared additive. We don't know what the formula of the additive was. We received it directly from Germany." And the man said this himself! He knew that I was a secretary of the Central Committee of the Ukrainian Communist Party. He could see that I had taken an interest in his case, and that I was even suggesting that his confession, from my point of view, didn't stand up, because the animals hadn't died. But not only did he not take advantage of my questioning; he did everything he could do to confirm the confession and prove the correctness of the Chekists who had tortured him, who had forced him to make this false confession.

I was simply astonished: How the enemy had multiplied! But this business didn't make sense: The Germans were such anti-Semites, and here was a Jew working for the anti-Semites? The explanation given for it all was "intensification of the class struggle." I ended the interrogation. Next I called in the director. He also confirmed his confession, although not as solidly [as the professor], but he did confirm it. I understood that to confess to such things was no joke, and I saw that the reason for this was the fact that the prisoners were looking for a chance to obtain better treatment by showing repentance and making a sincere confession. I left to go to a Central Committee meeting, but the idea that something wasn't right stayed with me. I decided to turn to Bogomolets.[48]

I had great respect for Bogomolets, the late president of the Academy of Sciences of the Ukrainian Soviet Socialist Republic. He was a very interesting individual and an outstanding scientist. He once told me about a curious incident. He was filling out a form and had come to the question: "Where were you born?" He wrote: "Lukyanovskaya Prison." Then he told me: "My mother and father were Narodniks.[49] They had just been arrested and were being held in Lukyanovskaya Prison. My mother was pregnant, and I was born there." He was an intelligent man and a very good one; he was not a party member, but that was just a formality, because in general he was a Soviet person, a man of progressive views.

And so I asked him: "Comrade Bogomolets, you know that horses are dying. Something must be done. As I see it, we need to set up a commission of scientists, so they can look into this matter and determine what the cause is. It cannot be that science is helpless and unable to determine the cause of death of these horses. This is unimaginable in our era. I would like you to head up this commission because someone who is trusted, who will be believed both in Ukraine and in Moscow, must stand at the head of this commission. And you are that very person. You must take specialists—zoologists and veterinarians—who can go out to the affected provinces, to the collective farms, and you must preside over this work."

I knew that several commissions had already been formed, but the members of those commissions had been arrested and people had perished. Now everyone was afraid to join such a commission, because if anyone did that, his fate was sealed. Bogomolets agreed, but without enthusiasm. I said to him: "Because previous commissions have been arrested, people are afraid, but if you, the president of the Academy of Sciences, will be chairman, specialists will more readily join in. I promise you that I will come to all plenary sessions, and I myself will listen to the reports of the scientists. The people's commissar of internal affairs, Uspensky, will also come, so as to head off the possibility of members of this commission being accused of anything." He agreed. I made the proposal: "Let's form two commissions that will work in parallel. If one doesn't succeed in figuring out the problem, the other will find the answer."

The aim I was pursuing was to clarify whether there really were wreckers at work. If some wreckers found their way onto one commission, the other might turn out to be all honest people. Besides, two commissions meant two conclusions and two viewpoints. That made it easier for us, the leaders, to figure out a complex, specialized problem. It seems to me that they put Professor Dobrotko in charge of one commission. I don't remember now who headed the other. Bogomolets coordinated all the work. We consulted with the USSR People's Commissariat of Agriculture for approval of the members of the commissions. As I recall, Benediktov[50] was the commissar of agriculture then. I knew him well. When I had worked in Moscow, Benediktov had been the director of the Moscow Vegetable Trust and, before that, the director of the Serphukhov state farm. He was highly regarded as an organizer and a specialist in agronomy. I was one of the people who had helped win his promotion to the post of commissar of agriculture. His commissariat proposed that yet another commission be formed, a third one, consisting of scientists from Moscow. My answer was: "Please do. I would be happy." The third commission was headed by Professor Vertinsky.

All the commissions went to the western regions of Ukraine and set to work. After a little while Dobrotko asked Bogomolets to call him back to Kiev to give a report. This commission completed its work quickly because

Dobrotko had a sense for the correct approach, and he did find out the reason for the death of the horses. He reported that the whole question was now quite clear: The horses were not being poisoned, but were dying because of poor management. The collective farms were not removing the straw from the combines in good time. The combines were left out in the fields, where the autumn rain was falling and wetting the straw. Later the straw was being brought in wet, and because of the dampness a fungus known to science began to grow. (As best as I can remember, it was called stachybotris). Ordinarily in nature it gets dispersed and doesn't end up in large concentrations in the stomachs of animals, so that normally they don't get sick. But under favorable conditions—dampness and heat—this fungus multiplies prolifically and begins to secrete a deadly poison. When a horse eats this moldy straw it takes in a large quantity of fungus and consequently dies. The fungus doesn't affect cud-chewing animals such as cows, sheep, and oxen. Dobrotko ended with this: "When I came to this conclusion I infected myself with this fungus. I came down with an illness similar to the one that affected the horses. To me the question is now quite clear."

Professor Vertinsky refused to confirm this opinion. He held that the investigation was not over, that work should continue. Vertinsky was a professor from Moscow. Dobrotko was a Ukrainian. This had a certain significance. To avoid a clash between them, I proposed that the work continue: "Go out there again, and when you feel the question is completely cleared up, say so. Then we'll call you back and listen to what you have to report." They went their way. Some time passed, and Vertinsky reported that he now agreed with the conclusions of Professor Dobrotko, and with that they could finish their work in the local areas and gather for a plenary session. They gathered in Kiev and made their report. Vertinsky agreed in full with Dobrotko's conclusions. Dobrotko was triumphant. He had deciphered the mystery of the deaths of the horses.

The means for combating the problem turned out to be quite simple. The straw had to be brought in from the fields in good time, so it wouldn't start to ferment and heat up while it was damp. In this way the prime conditions enabling the fungus to grow would be eliminated. We checked into the matter and all the assertions were confirmed. After that, strict instructions were given on how to harvest straw, how it should be kept, and how horses should be fed with it. The animals stopped dying.

Stalin knew that horses were being poisoned in Ukraine and that the republic might be left without draft animals. Therefore when I went to Moscow and reported on the results of the work of the commissions he was very pleased. I proposed that the people be rewarded. Professor Dobrotko was given the Order of the Red Banner of Labor. He deserved an Order of Lenin. But in those days people were miserly about giving out Orders of Lenin. Others were given the Order of Distinguished Service and various medals. I proposed that Vertinsky also be awarded an Order of Distinguished Service (although he had only played the role of a catalyst: he had done nothing on his own, but had merely confirmed Dobrotko's conclusions). After all, at that time it was still a matter of significance whether Moscow or Kiev had figured out the problem, whether it was Ukrainians or Russians. And I felt that there was no need to hurt the feelings of the Muscovites.

This was not just an economic victory—saving the horses was also a political and moral victory. How many collective farm chairmen, specialists in animal husbandry, agronomists, livestock experts, and scientists in general might have laid down their lives as "Polish-German agents"; how many of them might have perished! Later I remembered the Kharkov professor and the director of the institute, who had been shot, and thought: "How could this be? What's going on? It's clear to everyone now that these people were not guilty, and yet they confessed." Apparently I found some sort of explanation for this at the time; I don't recall what it was. I could not then have supposed that it was a hostile act on the part of the agencies of the NKVD; such a thought I could not have admitted. Was it negligence? Yes, it might have been negligence. The NKVD "organs" were considered infallible; they were called the sword of the revolution, which was directed against our enemies.

It's true that when Uspensky was arrested something dawned on us, but once again, in our thinking, we attributed all this to abuses of power on an individual basis. Here's how the Uspensky case started. Stalin telephoned me one day and told me that there was evidence on the basis of which it was necessary to arrest Uspensky. [Because of the poor phone connection] it was hard to hear, and it sounded as though he had said not Uspensky, but Usenko.[51] Usenko was the first secretary of the Central Committee of the Ukrainian Young Communist League. There was testimony against him, and the Damocles sword of arrest was already hanging over his head. Stalin asked: "Can you arrest him?"

I answered: "We can." "But you should do it yourself," and he repeated the name. At this point I understood that it was not Usenko who was to be arrested, but People's Commissar Uspensky.

Soon Stalin called again: "We have had some consultations and decided that you shouldn't arrest Uspensky. We'll call him to Moscow and arrest him here. Don't get involved in this business."

Preparations for the spring sowing had begun. Even before this, I had scheduled a trip to Dnepropetrovsk. I went to see Zadionchenko, and before leaving I said—only to Korotchenko—that Uspensky had turned out to be an enemy of the people and they intended to arrest him. "I'm leaving. You stay here in Kiev. From time to time, find some question of a strictly business nature, so that you won't be suspected, and call up Uspensky."

In the morning I arrived in Dnepropetrovsk and went to the party's province committee, and suddenly there was a phone call from Moscow. Beria was on the phone. Beria was already deputy people's commissar under Yezhov [the people's commissar of internal affairs]. "So you're in Dnepropetrovsk," he said reproachfully, "but Uspensky has run away."

"How do you mean run away?"

"Do everything necessary so he doesn't get across the border!"

"All right. Everything that can be done we'll do right now. We'll close the border and warn the border troops to reinforce the guard along the borders by both land and sea." That night there was a heavy fog. I said: "We have a heavy fog tonight, and so it will be quite impossible for anyone to travel by car from Kiev to the border. He won't be able to get there."

"You evidently ought to return to Kiev," Beria advised. I did go back to Kiev and roused everyone. Divers dragged the Dnieper and the river banks with nets and hooks because Uspensky had left a note indicating that he would commit suicide by throwing himself into the Dnieper. They found a drowned pig, but not Uspensky. He left behind a wife and teenage son, but they could tell us nothing. Apparently they themselves didn't know where their husband and father had gone. We continued to search for the former people's commissar. I don't remember how much time went by—a month, two, or three—when I was told that Uspensky had been caught in the city of Voronezh. It turns out that he had gone by train directly from Kiev to the Urals and from the Urals traveled to Voronezh. He was trying to make arrangements for himself there (or had even done so) but was caught and arrested.

When I arrived in Moscow after Uspensky had fled, Stalin explained to me why the people's commissar had done that: "I spoke with you by phone, but he listened in. Although we were speaking over a special line, and we've even been told that it's impossible to tap that line, apparently the Chekists were able to listen in anyhow, and that's what he did. That's why he fled." That was one version. Another was as follows. Stalin and Beria put this one forward as well. Yezhov had summoned Uspensky to Moscow by phone and apparently had hinted to him that he would be arrested. By then Yezhov himself was suspected of being an enemy of the people. What incredible things! Yezhov, an enemy of the people! There was a slogan based on his name: *Yezhovye rukavitsy* [Hedgehog gloves]; Stalin called him Yezhevika.[52] Yezhov had been made into a hero of the people, the sharp sword of the revolution. And suddenly Yezhov was also an enemy of the people? But at that time he was still working as people's commissar of internal affairs.

Immediately there began to be arrests of security police officials, the Chekists. In Ukraine virtually all the Chekists who had worked with Yezhov were arrested. Now I began to understand some of what had gone on in the matter of the horses. In connection with that case some investigator for especially important cases had come from Moscow to Kiev and conducted an investigation. I had seen that man when I was talking with the professors: A healthy young man of about thirty-five, strong and powerfully built. He was present when I conducted that conversation. I sat at one end of the table, along the side. Uspensky as the "host" sat at the head of the table; the professor was opposite me, and the investigator was behind me. I came to the conclusion later that, when I was talking, this investigator behind me was probably showing his fist to the professor and "encouraging him" to reaffirm his testimony. And that's what he did.

Later this investigator was also arrested and shot. That was the way, by torture and threats and pressure, they forced honest people to confess to crimes that had never happened. I have already said that the crime itself had not occurred because there had been no such action by our enemies. Our enemies of course did everything they could against us, but that did not apply in this case. The horses' deaths were the result of our sloppiness in collective-farm work and our ignorance. That's what the situation was like. How many, many people died then! Uspensky flooded me with documents, and whatever the document, it listed enemies, enemies, enemies. He sent me copies, the originals of these reports going directly to Yezhov in Moscow. Yezhov reported to Stalin, and supposedly I exercised some sort of party control. What kind of control could there be when the party bodies themselves were under the control of those they were supposed to be controlling? The sacred name "Communist" was trampled underfoot, as was the role of the Communist and his position in society. Above the party there arose and stood the power of the Cheka.[53]

---

1. These positions were all vacant because their occupants had been arrested. [GS]

2. As N. S. Khrushchev was going to be first secretary, he needed a second secretary to work with him. [GS]

3. M. A. Burmistenko. See Biographies.

4. That is, in charge of the assignment of party personnel. [GS]

5. Z. T. Serdyuk. See Biographies.

6. Mamai was a fourteenth-century military leader (khan) of the Golden Horde, the Mongol-Tatar state that then dominated Russia and was ruled by descendants of the Mongol conqueror Genghis Khan. Mamai's forces devastated several Russian principalities before being defeated at the battle of Kulikovo in 1380 by troops under the leadership of Grand Duke Dmitry Donskoi of Muscovy. [GS/SS]

7. D. M. Yevtushenko.

8. I. I. Shevchenko.

9. The people's commissar of internal affairs was head of the People's Commissariat of Internal Affairs or NKVD—the secret police. [SS] A. I. Uspensky was people's commissar of internal affairs of the Ukrainian SSR in 1938 and 1939.

10. M. F. Rylsky was a poet, translator, publicist, and public figure. See Biographies.

11. I. S. Patorzhinsky and M. I. Litvinenko-Volgemut were singers. See Biographies.

12. Khrushchev is referring to the composer K. F. Dankevich. See Biographies.

13. Ya. F. Tyagnibeda. See Biographies.

14. M. M. Khatayevich. See Biographies.

15. L. R. Korniyets. See Biographies.

16. Dneprodzerzhinsk is an industrial city on the Dnieper River in central Ukraine, a few kilometers upstream from Dnepropetrovsk. [SS] Leonid. I. Brezhnev, later to become general secretary of the Central Committee of the CPSU and chairman of the presidium of the Supreme Soviet, was until May 1938 deputy chairman of the executive committee of the Dneprodzerzhinsk City Soviet.

17. E. K. Pramnek. See Biographies.

18. A. S. Shcherbakov. See Biographies.

19. L. R. Sheinin. See Biographies.

20. At this time, in 1938, Bessarabia was part of Romania, although it had belonged to Russia under the tsars and was annexed to the Soviet Union after World War II. [GS/SS]

21. N. P. Bazhan. See Biographies.

22. P. I. Panch. See Biographies.

23. D. Z. Manuilsky. See Biographies.

24. His name, Medved, is also the Russian word for "bear." [GS]

25. Vladimir Hills is a hill on the bank of the Dnieper River in Kiev; here a monument was erected to Prince Vladimir (c. 956–1015), who introduced Christianity to Kievan Rus. At the foot of the hill runs the road along which Vladimir drove the people of Rus to be baptized in the Dnieper. [SK]

26. After the revolution, Yekaterinoslav was renamed Dnepropetrovsk.

27. L. G. Petrovsky. See Biographies.

28. Yu. M. Kotsyubinsky was the son of the writer and revolutionary-democratic public figure M. M. Kotsyubinsky. See Biographies.

29. M. V. Kostenko was the second secretary of the Kiev province committee of the CP(B)U from December 1937 to June 1938.

30. T. K. Cherepin.

31. Sumy is in northeastern Ukraine, about 160 kilometers northwest of Kharkov. [SS]

32. Odessa is a large port on the Black Sea coast in southern Ukraine. [SS]

33. V. Ya. Furer.

34. N. A. Izotov. See Biographies.

35. Izotov and Stakhanov (see Biographies) were so-called *udarniki* ("shock workers"), miners who set extraordinary production records by mining huge amounts of coal in one day. They initiated what became known as the Stakhanovite movement, which soon spread to other industries. In reality, the production records of the Stakhanovites were made possible by special conditions. [GS/SS]

36. The Khimki Reservoir is situated on the northern outskirts of Moscow. [SS]

37. Demyan Bedny was a poet and songwriter. See Biographies.

38. Ya. A. Livshits. See Biographies.

39. A. I. Rykov and N. I. Bukharin were sentenced to be shot on March 13, 1938, and G. E. Zinoviev and L. B. Kamenev on August 24, 1936. G. G. Yagoda was executed on March 15, 1938.

40. A. Ya. Vyshinsky. See Biographies.

41. In 1953, R. A. Rudenko became prosecutor general of the USSR. See Biographies.

42. Maurice Thorez and Palmiro Togliatti were the leaders of the French and Italian Communist parties, respectively. See Biographies.

43. In fact, all three major show trials in Moscow, in 1936, 1937, and 1938, were based largely on the defendants' "confessions" of criminal counter-revolutionary acts that they had committed on alleged instructions from Trotsky. [GS]

44. G. Ye. Zinoviev, N. I. Bukharin, A. I. Rykov, V. V. Lominadze. See Biographies.

45. *The ABC of Communism* (Moscow, 1920) was a work of popular sociology widely used in the system of political education. Its co-authors were Nikokai I. Bukharin and Yevgeny A. Preobrazhensky.

46. S. B. Zadionchenko. See Biographies.

47. Kremenchug is situated on the Dnieper River in central Ukraine between Dnepropetrovsk and Kiev. [SS]

48. A. A. Bogomolets was a prominent medical specialist. See Biographies.

49. The Narodnik (Populist) movement was a major social current among the Russian intelligentsia in the second half of the nineteenth century. [GS]

50. I. A. Benediktov. See Biographies.

51. S. I. Usenko.

52. These were both word plays on Yezhov's name. *Yezhovye rukavitsy* means the opposite of "kid gloves." *Yezh* in Russian means "hedgehog,"

and the expression "hedgehog gloves" was meant to suggest how tough Yezhov was in defending the revolutionary cause against so-called or imagined enemies of the people. *Yezhevika* means "thorny blackberry bush." [GS]

53. The Cheka was the first security police agency of the Bolshevik revolution, founded in December 1917. The acronym is derived from a shortened version of the organization's Russian name of Chrezvychainaya Komissiya (Extraordinary Commission); the initial letters of the Rus-sian words are "Che" and "Ka," respectively. The organization's full name was Extraordinary Commission for Struggle Against Counterrevolution, Sabotage, and Speculation. The Cheka was officially dissolved in 1922, after the end of the Russian Civil War, but the term was still used unofficially to designate its successor security organizations, the GPU, OGPU, NKVD, MVD, KGB, and so on; those who served in the security organs were often called Chekists. [GS]

## UKRAINE–MOSCOW (CROSSROADS OF THE 1930S)

I now want to tell about how Beria was promoted in the People's Commissariat of Internal Affairs (NKVD) of the USSR to become first deputy people's commissar under Yezhov. Beria had been working then as secretary of the Central Committee of the Communist Party of Georgia. When I had worked in Moscow, good, friendly relations had been established between Beria and me. He was a smart man, very quick witted. He responded quickly to everything, and that pleased me. At Central Committee plenums we always sat side by side and exchanged cutting remarks during the course of discussion on various questions or in regard to one speaker or another, as always happened among close comrades. I have already referred to this earlier.

In 1934 I was on vacation in Sochi. As my vacation time was running out, Beria invited me to return to Moscow by way of Tiflis.[1] At that time the Russian name Tiflis was still used for the capital of Georgia, which was, properly speaking, called Tbilisi. I traveled to Batumi by steamer, and from Batumi to Tiflis by rail, and spent a whole day there. Then I bought a ticket from Tiflis to Moscow. In those days the only trains from Georgia to Russia went through Baku. I told the conductor that I would take my seat at Beslan in the Northern Caucasus. (That was the name of the station, as I recall.) I traveled by way of the Georgian Military Road and met the train at Beslan.

In Tiflis I became acquainted with the Georgian comrades. Georgia made a good impression on me. I remembered the past, 1921, during the Civil War, when I had been with some Soviet military units in Georgia. Our unit had been stationed in Adzhameti, near Kutais, and our headquarters was in Kutais. Sometimes in the line of duty I rode into Kutais on horseback, most often from Adzhameti, fording the Rioni River.[2] I still had good memories of that time, and it was pleasant to see Georgia again, to recall the past and the year 1921. Stalin jokingly called me an "occupier" when I told him my impressions of how negative the Georgians, especially the Georgian intellectuals, had been toward the Red Army.[3] Sometimes I had to make a trip to the political department of the Eleventh Army, whose headquarters were in Tiflis. It happened that I was sitting in a railroad car together with some Georgians of my age. We were still young. I addressed them in Russian, but they wouldn't answer me. They acted as though they couldn't understand Russian, although I could see that they were former officers of the tsarist army and must have had a good command of Russian.

The Georgian common people behaved differently. The peasants always greeted us very hospitably and invariably treated us to food and drink. If a family celebration was going on, they would arrange an extravagant feast in typical Georgian style. Any Red Army men who happened to arrive at their homes at such times would be literally dragged inside the houses, given something to drink, then be accompanied back to their military unit. But there was never a single case of violence against Red Army soldiers, although such possibilities existed. There were high growths of corn, bushes, and woods all around.

When I told Stalin about this, he seemed to object: "Why are you taking offense against the Georgians? You should understand that you were an occupier. You had overthrown the Georgian Menshevik government."

I answered: "That's true. I understand, and I don't feel offended. I'm simply telling what the situation was like."

Now [in 1934] I was making the acquaintance of Beria and the other leaders of Georgia for a second time. I liked these cadres; in general I liked these people very much. The only thing wrong, I told Stalin, was that they overdid it with their hospitality. It was very hard to withstand their tendency to try and get you drunk. That was no good. "Yes, they know how to do that," Stalin answered. "They're skilled at that; I know them well." In those years Stalin was still drinking moderately, and I liked his moderation.

Once when I was in Moscow, having arrived from Kiev, Beria was summoned from Tbilisi. Everyone gathered at Stalin's place. Yezhov was there, too. Stalin made the proposal: "The NKVD ought to be reinforced, to help Comrade Yezhov. We have to assign him a deputy." He had brought up this question earlier in fact, having asked Yezhov in my presence: "Who do you want as a deputy?"

Yezhov had answered: "If it's necessary, then give me Malenkov." Stalin knew how to pause in the middle of a conversation, as though he were thinking over an answer, and yet he had thoroughly thought out everything well in advance. He was simply waiting for an answer from Yezhov.

Finally Stalin said: "Yes, of course, Malenkov would be good, but we can't give you Malenkov. Malenkov is in charge of cadres at the Central Committee, and so a new question would immediately come up: Who to assign to that position? It's not so easy to choose a person to be in charge of cadres, especially in the Central Committee. It would take a lot of time for him to learn the ropes and get to know the cadres." In other words, he refused Yezhov's suggestion. After a little while he asked again: "So who's to be your deputy?" This time Yezhov didn't give anyone's name. So Stalin said: "Well, how would you look at it if we gave you Beria for a deputy?"

Yezhov shuddered abruptly, but he got hold of himself and answered: "He would be a good candidate. Of course, Comrade Beria could do the work, and not just as a deputy; he could be people's commissar."

It should be mentioned that there were good, friendly relations between Beria and Yezhov at that time. Yezhov invited me and Malenkov to come to his dacha one Sunday, and Beria was there, too. And that happened more than once. When Beria came to Moscow he always visited Yezhov.

[In reply to Yezhov's previous remark] Stalin answered: "No, he wouldn't do as people's commissar, but he would be a good deputy commissar for you." Stalin immediately dictated a draft decree for Molotov to take down. Molotov always wrote the drafts dictated by Stalin. As a rule, sessions like these at Stalin's place ended with all of us having dinner. I went over to Beria and shook his hand in a friendly way and congratulated him.

In a soft voice, not maliciously, but in no uncertain terms, Beria told me to go to hell: "What are you congratulating me for? You yourself don't want to work in Moscow."

He was referring to the fact that Molotov had asked that I be confirmed as deputy chairman of the Council of People's Commissars of the USSR. Stalin had agreed with that and had already spoken to me about it. But the last thing I wanted was an assignment like that, and I began to plead with Stalin not to assign me. Stalin seemed to be listening to what I said, and I tried to persuade him, as follows: "Comrade Stalin, things are heading toward a war. People have more or less come to know me now in Ukraine, and I've gotten to know the republic; I know its cadres. If a new person comes, things will be more complicated for him. It would be more useful for me now to be located in Ukraine than to go work for Comrade Molotov, although Comrade Molotov has many times tried to persuade me to come work for him."

Molotov had a good attitude toward me, and a high regard for my work in Moscow and Ukraine. He often called me up in Kiev and consulted with me on one or another question. For example, when Benediktov was appointed people's commissar of agriculture, Molotov telephoned me and asked: "What's your view of this? After all, you know Benediktov."

I answered: "I know him. He would be a good commissar. Of course that would be moving him up to a high position all of a sudden, from director of a trust to people's commissar, but he'd still be a good people's commissar; he's knowledgeable and knows how to work and organize things."

Or take the case of Malyshev.[4] He was then the chief engineer at the Kolomna steam locomotive plant. I had made a trip to Kolomna[5] and after my return to Moscow had told Stalin a lot about Malyshev, because he had made a very good impression on me. Later Molotov called me and expressed interest: "How would you look at it if we promoted Malyshev to be people's commissar of machine building?"

I answered: "He's a very good engineer. I think he would also be a very good people's commissar."

The same kind of thing happened in other questions involving people I knew. This shows Molotov's confidence in me and his favorable attitude toward me. I appreciated that. I liked Molotov then, but I didn't want to work at the USSR Council of People's Commissars.

Stalin agreed with my argument about the imminence of war and said: "All right, let Khrushchev stay in Ukraine."

When I began congratulating Beria, that's what he was reminding me about: "How hard you yourself scurried to get out of it. You didn't want to, but now you're congratulating me? I also don't want to go to Moscow; it's better for me in Georgia."

"The decree has already been drawn up, and the question has been decided," I answered. "You're now a Muscovite. Say goodbye to your beloved Georgia."

That's how Beria was appointed. In doing this, Stalin had something up his sleeve; he never did anything unconsidered. Apparently he no longer trusted Yezhov, or perhaps it's not that he no longer trusted him, but that he simply felt that Yezhov had done his job and it was time to lay him to rest; it was necessary to make use of someone else. At the time I thought that what Stalin wanted was to have a Georgian in the NKVD. He trusted Beria, and through Beria he wanted to check up on everything Yezhov did. After Beria's appointment to the NKVD I would meet with him when I came to Moscow. Again good relations between us were established. He told me that a lot of people were being arrested, and he complained: "When will it ever end? After all, we have to put a stop to it at some point. Something has to be done, because innocent people are being arrested."

I agreed with him. I had no information, but Beria was the deputy people's commissar of internal affairs, and I trusted and respected him: "Here's an honest Communist," I thought. "He sees that wrongful arrests are being allowed and is upset about it." He had also talked with Stalin about it. I knew this for certain, although he tried to convince me that no conversations on the subject had come up between them. Later I understood that this was a crafty move on his part. He had told Stalin these things as a way of backstabbing Yezhov and taking the position of people's commissar for himself.

Stalin was no longer pleased with Yezhov. The latter had played his part, and Stalin wanted to change horses in midstream, while continuing in the same direction and having the same kinds of actions carried out. But he needed different people to do this. Earlier, when Yezhov had replaced Yagoda, Yezhov had destroyed many cadres, including Chekists who had worked with Yagoda. Now Stalin (as we came to understand after his death) needed to finish off the cadres that had been pushed forward under Yezhov. Beria was designated for this role. But at that time we all thought it was just a matter of his being a Caucasian, a Georgian, a person closer to Stalin not only as a member of the party but also because he was of the same nationality. But Stalin had other goals, as I concluded after his death.

By this time [1938] Yezhov no longer seemed human; he was drunk all the time. He drank so much that he no longer looked like himself. I had made his acquaintance in 1929 when I was studying at the Industrial Academy, and I had often met with him on Academy business. The Academy was under the authority of the party's Central Committee, and Yezhov's assignment at the Central Committee was to be in charge of cadres. The Industrial Academy was considered a center where "cadres were being forged," to use our way of talking at the time, and so I was often called to the Central Committee offices to meet with Yezhov. I always found him to be an understanding person. He was an ordinary fellow, a worker from Saint Petersburg, and that had a lot of importance in those days—to be a worker from St. Petersburg. But toward the end of his activities, at the end of his life, Yezhov had become a completely different person. I think it was the effect on him of everything that he knew, everything that was going on. He understood that Stalin was using him as a club to destroy cadres, the Old Bolshevik cadres above all, and he was trying to drown his conscience with vodka.

Later I was told the following story. In the last stage of Yezhov's life and activity, his wife fell ill. She was put in the Kremlin hospital, but it had already been decided that as soon as she got well she would be arrested. Stalin made wide use of that method of arrest. He tried to use the wives of highly placed officials to discover "conspiracies," to uncover "treason" on the part of their husbands. Supposedly the wives knew the secrets of their husbands and would be able to help the government expose these enemies of the people. The wives of a number of prominent officials were arrested: the wives of Kalinin, Kulik, Budyonny,[6] and later even Molotov's wife, Zhemchuzhina.[7] I don't even know how many cases like this there were: apparently a huge number of innocent women suffered despite the innocence of their husbands. All of them were shot or sent into internal exile.

Yezhov's wife was starting to get well and was soon going to be released from the hospital, but she suddenly died. Later they said that she'd been poisoned, and apparently that was true. Stalin and Beria said that before she was poisoned Yezhov had visited her in the hospital and brought her a bouquet of flowers. This was an agreed-on signal that she was going to be arrested. Apparently Yezhov had guessed what was going on and wanted to eliminate the traces of any possible exposure of his activity. What things had come to! This people's commissar an enemy of the people! Our thinking was that if she had poisoned herself, it was to hide something and to head off the possibility of her companion's being exposed. However, regardless of whether she poisoned herself or not, Stalin had already decided long since, as early as when he promoted Beria as Yezhov's deputy, that Yezhov was done for. Yezhov was someone Stalin didn't need anymore. It was not to Stalin's advantage to have Yezhov continue what he had been doing. Stalin wanted to get rid of him.[8]

Yezhov was arrested. I happened to be in Moscow at the time. Stalin invited me to supper at his apartment in the Kremlin. I went there. As I recall, Molotov and someone else were there too. As soon as we came in and sat down at the table, Stalin said that the decision had been made to arrest Yezhov, that he was a dangerous man, and that he should be arrested at once. Stalin was obviously nervous, which rarely happened, but he did show a loss of self-control in this case; betraying his inner feelings, as it were. After a little while the telephone rang, Stalin went to the phone, talked for a little while, and then said that Beria had called and that everything was in order, Yezhov had been arrested, and now his interrogation would begin. Then I learned that not only Yezhov but also his deputies had been arrested. One of them was Frinovsky.[9] I didn't know Frinovsky very well. They said he'd been a prominent military man in the Civil War, a big, strong man with a scar on his face, a physically powerful fellow. The story they told went like this: "When they [that is, a group of secret police agents] assaulted Frinovsky, one of the attackers, Kobulov,[10] a huge, fat man, grabbed him from behind and threw him to the floor, after which they tied him up." This story was related as though Kobulov had performed some sort of heroic feat. At the time we all accepted that kind of thing as normal and proper.

We believed that we had internal enemies, and the groundwork for exposing them had been laid with the arrest of prominent military men in 1937. They had confessed. It was said that the commander of the troops of the Moscow Military District,[11] when he was brought before the firing squad and asked what government he had been serving, openly stated he had been working for the German army and the German government. That's the kind of demonstrative declaration he made just before his death. Yakir, who was executed in connection with the same criminal case, during the last seconds of his life cried out "Long live Stalin!" just before he was shot. When this information was relayed to Stalin, he cursed Yakir and denounced him: "What a scoundrel. What a Judas. Even when he's dying, he tries to mislead our investigators, tries to make them think he's devoted to Stalin, devoted to our government."

Beria began his work. The meat grinder kept churning, although there was a lot of talk, particularly on Beria's part, which was intended to distract people from the essence of the matter. In our presence he never said anything to Stalin about condemning the unjust acts of repression, but behind the scenes he often discussed it. He didn't speak Russian well, usually he talked something like this: "Lishun, an awful lot of cadres are being destroyed. What's this going to be? What's this going to be? People are afraid to work." He was right in what he was trying to say. Stalin completely isolated himself from the people and had no interaction with anyone outside of his inner circle. But Beria knew the moods and attitudes of the people. He had a huge number of agents, so many that it's difficult even to say how many agents there were. At last Stalin himself said that excesses had been committed.

One day—I forget the reason—Stalin started talking with me on this subject. Apparently it was because there was also testimony against me. When I went to Ukraine there had been no people's commissar of trade. I had great respect for a man named Lukashov.[12] He worked as head of the trade department in Moscow. When Badayev[13] had been in charge of the cooperatives, Lukashov had headed the department in charge of vegetables. He was a very energetic man and knew his business well. Trade was poorly organized then; there was never enough food in the stores, and great resourcefulness was necessary. I asked Stalin: "Comrade Stalin, can I invite Lukashov from Moscow to take the post of people's commissar for trade in the Ukrainian SSR?"

Stalin didn't know him personally but he had heard about him from me. He said: "All right, invite him." I asked about it because when I moved to Ukraine, I set myself the task of not taking anyone from Moscow other than those who were authorized by the party's Central Committee.

Lukashov didn't work with us for very long. He was arrested. I was badly thrown by this, because I had personally proposed his candidacy and had asked Stalin for him. I had gotten to know him earlier in Moscow and respected him greatly; then suddenly it turned out Lukashov was an enemy of the people! This was a blow to my morale. How could this be? I had seen this man, trusted him, respected him.

But what could you do? I don't remember how long Lukashov sat in prison, but later I was suddenly informed that Lukashov had been released. He came to Kiev. I received him and had a talk with him.

"Yes," he said, "I've been released. I'm not guilty. I'm an honest man. I ask you to believe in me the same way you did before my arrest. I want to tell you when they arrested me they beat me unmercifully and tortured me. They stood me up with each foot on a bench; then they moved the benches as far apart as possible. If I made the slightest move, they would beat me until I lost consciousness and fell over. They tortured me by not letting me sleep, and they used other methods of torture. And you know what they were demanding of me? That I testify against you, say that you were a conspirator, and that I had gone abroad on an assignment from you to establish connections."

There actually had been such an incident when I was still working in Moscow. We didn't have enough onions and other vegetable crops, and there wasn't enough seed in the country, especially for onions. I don't remember who told us about it then, but it was possible to buy such seed in Poland and other countries of the West, though foreign currency was needed for that. I asked Stalin to give us some foreign currency and suggested we send Lukashov. Lukashov bought the necessary seed and imported it, and we shipped it off to the republics and farms where they grew vegetables for Moscow under contract.

Just as they arrested wives of prominent men, so they also arrested people who were close to highly placed officials or who worked under them. They had decided to arrest Lukashov, so that he would say something against me.

Lukashov turned out to be a man of strong character, and for that reason he stayed alive. Also, of course, he was just plain lucky. He is still alive today, but he is an invalid on a pension. He became an invalid from what they did to him in prison.

I told Stalin what had happened with Lukashov. Stalin said to me: "Yes, such perversions and distortions do happen. They have even gathered material against me."

Two of my assistants in Moscow were also arrested. I saw this as a personal test. One assistant, Rabinovich, was a good, modest young man. The other, Finkel, was also a very good person, a man of exceptional honesty and modesty. He dealt mainly with matters of construction and was an economist by training. He had been recommended to me by Vasilkovsky,[14] editor of the newspaper *Za industrializatsiyu* (For industrialization). This was the newspaper of Sergo Ordzhonikidze, the people's commissar of heavy industry. Later Stalin asked me: "What is this? They've arrested your assistants?"

I answered: "Yes, they were good men, honest fellows."

He said: "Oh yes? And now they're giving testimony confessing that they are enemies of the people. They have also given evidence against you, that your last name is not your real one. They say that you are not Khrushchev at all, but someone else. All the Chekists have started doing this, and the enemies of the people have wormed their way into this too; they're smuggling in material against us, as though someone had given evidence against us. Even against me there's testimony. Supposedly I have some sort of blot on my revolutionary biography."

Let me explain what he was referring to. There were rumors going around, although it was all pretty vague, that Stalin had collaborated at one time in the old days with the tsarist secret police agency, the Okhranka, and that his successful escapes from prison (he had made several escapes) had been arranged from on high, because otherwise so many successful escapes would not have been possible. When Stalin talked with me about this, he didn't say specifically what people were hinting at, but I assumed that those rumors had reached him, too, somehow. He never said anything to me about them but simply stated that the Chekists themselves were smuggling in false information.

At the Center there was the notion that Beria would clean up the situation. Actually there were new arrests of Chekists. I knew many of these Chekists as honest, good, and respectable people. One of those arrested was Redens, a man who was close to Stalin, because they had married sisters from the same family. Redens was the husband of the older sister, Anna [Alliluyeva], and the younger sister, Nadezhda, was married to Stalin. Redens was often at Stalin's home, and more than once I saw him sitting at the family table with Stalin, to whose home I was also frequently invited. And now, suddenly, he was removed from his post as the authorized representative of the NKVD for Moscow province and sent to Central Asia, to Tashkent. Later he was arrested and executed. Others were arrested as well. There was Yakov Agranov,[15] a remarkable man and a solid security police official of the old school. At an earlier time he had worked in the secretariat under Lenin. He was calm, intelligent, and honorable; I liked him very much. Later he was assigned with special powers to the investigation in the Industrial Party (Prompartiya) case.[16] He really was an investigator. He didn't even raise his voice when he talked, let alone resort to torture. He was also arrested and executed.

Beria completed the purge that Yezhov had begun ("purge" in the sense of annihilation) directed against Chekist cadres of Jewish nationality. They were all good, solid functionaries. Stalin apparently was beginning to lose confidence in the NKVD and decided to assign people to that organization straight from the factory floor, from the point of production. These were inexperienced people, sometimes completely undeveloped politically. It was enough to give them instructions to do something and say: "The main thing is to arrest them and demand a confession." That would be it; they would immediately go and do as ordered.

As I've already related in regard to the interrogation of Chubar, the investigator explained: "They told me to beat him until he confessed that he was an enemy of the people, and so I beat him and he confessed." These were the kinds of cadres coming into the NKVD then. Later they began taking people from party posts to work in the NKVD. The machinery had already been set in motion, and among party officials there was actually no one against whom testimony had not been given.

I remember, for example, the following incident. Vyshinsky called me up and said: "Comrade Khrushchev, we need cadres and I want to promote Rudenko, the prosecutor in Lugansk province,[17] to be my deputy." Rudenko had a good reputation in Ukraine, and I had heard of him, so I asked that he not be taken to Moscow. We had him in mind to be promoted in Ukraine.

Therefore I informed Vyshinsky: "You probably know that there is a fairly large amount of material against Rudenko? Enemies of the people who were arrested and executed testified against him. You know about that, don't you?"

He answered: "Yes, I know, but I think it's slander."

"I also think it's slander. But to promote him to Moscow? You can see for yourself how that would be interpreted."

Apparently Vyshinsky got cold feet, and Rudenko remained in Ukraine. We promoted him to be chief prosecutor of the Ukrainian republic with the qualification that since evidence had been given against him, it had to be looked into. Later he became chief prosecutor of the Soviet Union and to this day works in that position.[18] Many good, honest people were smeared and slandered in this way. I have to say at this point that the people who did the slandering had also once been honest people, but they were crippled both physically and morally by being forced to contribute to such a foul business and to slander their very own friends.

In short, the work of annihilating cadres continued, and it continued right up until Stalin's death, only varying in scale at different times. The Ukrainian leadership of both the party and the government was totally destroyed: officials of the Central Committee of the Ukrainian Communist Party, party secretaries, and heads of departments. The chairman of the Council of People's Commissars of Ukraine, Lyubchenko, shot himself. When Kosior was summoned to return to Moscow, suddenly, a short time later, the radio station that had previously borne Kosior's name stopped being called that and began to be called simply Kiev radio station. This was a signal that Kosior was no longer alive. It was only from that signal that I myself learned that Kosior had been arrested. Yet he had been deputy chairman of the Council of People's Commissars, that is, Molotov's deputy. Postyshev was recalled from Ukraine and sent to Kuibyshev. There he was arrested and later was also destroyed.

Khatayevich, the secretary of the party's Dnepropetrovsk province committee, an official of great merit, was also arrested, and yet Stalin's attitude toward him was one of respect. I remember at one party plenum Stalin called him Genghis Khan[19] for the way in which Khatayevich, when working in Kuibyshev,[20] had solved the sugar problem. There had been no sugar in Kuibyshev, while a train with railroad cars loaded with sugar was heading for Siberia and the Far East. Khatayevich ordered a certain number of railroad cars detached to stay in Kuibyshev, and thus the problem was solved, but actually it was a violation of government regulations. Stalin gave a speech saying: "We have certain Genghis Khans who do not consider the overall interests of the state, but do what it is in the interests of their province, and Khatayevich here is one of them." Khatayevich enjoyed tremendous authority in Dnepropetrovsk. He was a good speaker and a good organizer.

Then there was Pramnek from the Donbass, a prominent official. Before him, as I recall, there was Sarkisyan[21] in the Donbass, also a prominent official, an energetic man who did a great deal for the Donbass. Also Chernyavsky,[22] secretary of the Odessa province committee, and later the Vinnitsa province committee—he too was destroyed. Lyubchenko, before committing suicide, wrote a note to Chernyavsky asking him, if something happened, not to forget about Lyubchenko's fifteen-year-old son. When Chernyavsky was arrested, the note was found, and the boy was also taken away. That's how bad the situation had become.

In Moscow and Moscow province, all the secretaries of district committees of the party were destroyed. I can't list their names specifically now, but practically all of them were destroyed. I was especially shaken when they arrested Kogan.[23] She had been in the party since 1907, a person of exceptional honesty and ability. She was concerned with cultural questions. In the prerevolutionary underground in Kiev, Kaganovich had taken lessons in political economy from Kosior and Kogan. Kogan had been Kuibyshev's wife for a certain time.

She reportedly had confessed to wrecking activities. But when her case was reviewed after Stalin's death, we found that she hadn't confessed to anything, but hurled accusations at her accusers and denounced as fascists those who had arrested her. She too was executed. Also Soifer,[24] secretary of the Lenin district committee of Moscow, an old man already, a member of the party since 1903 or 1905. When the secretary of the Tula province committee[25] had been arrested, a man named Sedelnikov,[26] they took Soifer from us to work in Tula. We sent Soifer there. Then suddenly I found that Soifer too had been arrested, yet Soifer had been the conscience of the party in the literal sense of the word, a man of crystal pure honesty. And suddenly he was an enemy of the people? They also arrested Nikolai Alekseyevich Filatov,[27] chairman of the executive committee of the Moscow Soviet, who had later been an authorized representative of the Control Commission in Rostov.[28]

Then there was Kulkov, an old Moscow activist with experience in underground revolutionary work, who had been promoted to secretary of the party's city committee. He was also arrested. I can no longer remember all of them now, but many Muscovites got that treatment. First they were promoted to replace arrested "enemies of the people," as a support to and reinforcement of other party organizations. Then we suddenly learned that they had been arrested. Simochkin died that way. He had been promoted from Moscow to Ivanovo-Voznesensk[29] province and was arrested there. And what about Margolin? He was a very close friend of Kaganovich. I had known him in Kiev, and later we studied together at the Industrial Academy. He was promoted to second secretary of the party's Moscow Committee when I was its first secretary. Then they took him to Dnepropetrovsk[30] to reinforce the local party organization after the arrest of Khatayevich, and there he was destroyed. If the names of all the party officials executed in those years were listed, they would make a huge book.

I have hardly touched on military officials here because I didn't know them as well, except for Yakir and Belov, commander of the troops in the Moscow military district. The military stayed rather far removed from us party officials at that time; and we rarely had dealings with them, even with the commander of the Moscow military district. Only when certain questions came up did the military address themselves to me. On my part no questions for them ever arose. Of course I also knew Veklichev, who was a military man. He was a close friend of Yakir, and when he showed up in Moscow he would drop in to see me because we had known each other in Kiev. He worked in the army's political directorate for the Kiev military district during the months when I worked as head of the organizational department of the party's Kiev province committee. Veklichev was from the Donbass miners, had gone through the Civil War, and had several rhomboids on the collar of his uniform, three, as I recall. He was also arrested and eliminated.

Later a document appeared. As I recall, it was a letter to the Central Committee of the AUCP (B) and to the party organizations of the USSR. The letter described the struggles against the enemies of the people and presented instances in which this struggle had been distorted. It said that enemies of the people had wormed their way into the Chekist agencies and had destroyed many devoted cadres. Now everything was all confused, and it was difficult to sort out what was what. The main thing for me was that Stalin himself had fouled everything up. In some cases, for example, in the case of the top military cadres, he believed that these military men were enemies of the people who had been recruited by Hitler's Germany and trained by Hitler to carry out treasonous activities once the German armies invaded the Soviet Union. Much was made of the fact that Stalin had been able to expose this state of affairs. It was said to be to his credit. Later we found out that this whole business had been fabricated. The method used is one well known in history. Side A surreptitiously makes available to Side B documents indicating that among those on Side B are people who supposedly have ties with foreign intelligence, and the result is that highly talented leaders of the army and other services are done away with by their own side. In general, this method of provocation is widely used by intelligence agencies. Our intelligence service also used this method against our enemies. It's quite an effective method. I've already mentioned that Hitler's intelligence agency smuggled such documents into Stalin's possession. (As I recall, it was through Benes, president of the Czechoslovak republic.)[31] These turned out to be sufficient grounds [in Stalin's eyes] for the execution of many innocent people.

Now [on January 9–11, 1939] a plenum of the party's Central Committee was being held. The provocative methods of the NKVD were discussed at the plenum, and an appropriate resolution was passed: to put a stop to it! The plenum ended, the resolution was studied in the local areas, but the methods remained the same: above all, the use of the notorious "troikas."[32] People were arrested without a court or investigation, and the same ones who arrested them interrogated and sentenced them. The procurator was reduced to the level of the lowest and most complete insignificance.[33] The procurator had no influence and was unable in fact to look into the legality of judicial proceedings, arrests, and so forth. The situation remained such that it allowed Beria to do what Yezhov had done before him.

After this plenum Beria often said that with his coming to office unjustified repression had stopped: "I had a conversation with Stalin, one on one, and said that at some point this must be stopped. How many officials in the party and the military and the economic administration have been destroyed!" But even after that Beria continued as before, only not on the same scale. Actually, there was no more need for this [repression on the previously massive scale], because by that time Stalin was satiated; he had engaged in these arbitrary actions until he had his fill, and he himself, it seemed, was rather frightened by the consequences. He wanted to curb the vast extent of the repression, and he took some measures to that effect. But even he couldn't put a stop to it, because he was afraid of the enemies that he himself had concocted. Here I am saying that these enemies were simply concocted, but some clever people might say: "What are you saying? That there were no enemies?" No, there were enemies. We fought them and we destroyed those enemies. But that had to be done by proper and permitted methods of government, methods using the courts and honest investigation, not simply breaking into someone's home, grabbing someone by the scruff of the neck, dragging him or her off to prison, and once there, beating a confession out of the person, then on the basis of that confession, not supported by any other evidence, sentencing the person. That constitutes arbitrary rule, and I am absolutely opposed to it.

I remember the first days of the revolution. It's true that I lived in an area where we didn't have any major outbreaks of counterrevolution, aside from the actions of Ataman Kaledin,[34] leader of the Don Cossacks. It was very simple then to figure out who was your enemy and who was your friend. Perhaps there was also sabotage, but it wasn't noticeable. Even without it, industry totally collapsed. Then came the Civil War. It drew a line of demarcation between people and simplified the struggle. Who was on which side, where the Whites were, and where the Reds, were all immediately evident. Life itself drew a class line of demarcation. There were enemies in the rear areas, and we fought against them. This battle was necessary to defend the revolutionary gains, to defend the revolutionary proletarian government.

Then suddenly [much later], when the Industrial Party had been done away with and collectivization had been carried out, when opposition inside the party had disappeared, when total and monolithic unity in the party ranks and among the working people of the USSR was evident, then suddenly this literal butchery began. This was no longer a class approach to the question. In the name of the class, in the name of strengthening the victory of the proletariat, heads were being chopped off, and whose? The same workers, peasants, and working intellectuals.

With Beria's arrival as people's commissar of internal affairs and the removal of Yezhov, the former dumped all the blame for the mass arrests and executions on the latter's head. But what had been done earlier in Georgia? When I traveled to Georgia after Stalin's death, the officials of the Georgian Soviet Socialist Republic (SSR), whose acquaintance I had made in 1934 in Tbilisi, none of them, it seems, was still alive. After Beria's arrest in 1953 a Georgian sent a letter from internal exile to the party's Central Committee, addressed to me. He described what Beria had done in the way of annihilating cadres in the Georgian SSR, and how he had made his way to power over the corpses of his friends and comrades. Beria was a dangerous enemy who had wormed his way into Stalin's absolute trust. I don't know how he cast such a spell over Stalin.

It's difficult for me to explain all of Stalin's actions or motivations. Sometimes he expressed sober judgments about the arrests and several times condemned them in conversations with me, just between the two of us. But nothing changed. What did he seek to accomplish with these arrests? He destroyed cadres who were personally devoted to him, and in their place came scoundrels and careerists of the Beria type. Were they really more reliable? What did he seek to accomplish by destroying Sergo Ordzhonikidze, who was one of his closest friends? In spite of that friendship, he destroyed the cadres at the People's Commissariat of Heavy Industry headed by Ordzhonikidze, cadres whom Sergo trusted. He had Sergo's brother executed and then began to have suspicions about Sergo himself, driving him to suicide.

A person who, in my view, was closest of all to Stalin was a calm and quiet Georgian intellectual, Alyosha Svanidze,[35] the brother of Stalin's first wife, a Georgian woman who had died long before. I of course hadn't known her. Alyosha was often at Stalin's home; I saw him there many times. It was evident that Stalin very much enjoyed conversations with Alyosha. Most often they talked about Georgia, its history, and its culture. I don't remember what kind of education Svanidze had, but he was a cultured and well-read person and a friend to Stalin's children. Uncle Alyosha, as they called him, often stayed overnight at Stalin's. Suddenly Alyosha turned out to be an enemy of the people, that is, also an enemy of Stalin's. After all, Stalin and the people were inseparable. When I learned of Svanidze's arrest, I was aghast. How could this be? Here was a person there was never any reason to suspect; yet he too turned out to be an enemy of the people? That's what Svanidze became in Stalin's eyes when he was arrested. The investigation ended with his being sentenced to be shot. Nevertheless Stalin hesitated. It was hard for him to admit that Alyosha Svanidze, who had been his friend for so many years, was an enemy of Stalin, an enemy of the people, an enemy of the party. Later Stalin often returned to this subject: How in the world had Alyosha suddenly become a spy? (It seems that he had been portrayed as a British spy.) The following version was made up as an explanation, as Beria thought fit. Stalin had well-justified doubts. He asked Beria: "In the materials that have been provided to me it is written, and Alyosha himself confesses, that he was a spy and was supposed to poison me. He could have done that quite easily. This kind of thing was within his reach many times; he spent the night at my place many times. So why didn't he actually do that? Maybe he's not a spy after all?"

Beria gave the following explanation: "Comrade Stalin, there are different kinds of spies, with different kinds of assignments. There are the kind who don't reveal themselves for many years, who worm their way into people's confidence and live side by side with them, people who need to be destroyed at a particular time. Alyosha Svanidze was precisely that kind of agent, who was not supposed to show his hand, but rather to keep quiet. When the signal was given, then he would have done whatever was intended."

Of course, generally speaking, such agents do exist, because the tactics of intelligence agencies are highly diverse. Intelligence agencies use all available methods to do harm to their opponents. But this truism obviously didn't apply to Svanidze. In the end Stalin agreed to Alyosha's execution, but some doubts still apparently remained in his mind. He said to Beria: "You tell him in my name that if he confesses and tells everything, his life will be spared."

A little while later Beria reported that Svanidze had been shot and that before he was shot what Stalin had said was related to him. He listened to it and replied: "I have nothing to confess. What can I confess to if I'm an honest person who never did anything against the party, against the people, against Stalin? I simply don't see what I'm supposed to confess to." And he was shot.

Later Stalin said: "What a man Alyosha was. Just look! He seemed to be such an intellectual, such a softie, and yet he showed such firmness. He didn't even take this opportunity to have his life spared—on the condition that he confess. He refused to confess. What a man."

To what extent Stalin was sincere in saying this, I don't know. As for Svanidze, he was an intelligent man and understood clearly that if he confessed, death awaited him all the same, though perhaps somewhat later, and he simply didn't want to put a blot on his good name as a Communist.

One man who was very close to Stalin and for whom Stalin felt great respect was the party leader of the Abkhazian people, Lakoba.[36] Stalin trusted him completely. When Lakoba came to Moscow you would always see him at Stalin's place, either at the apartment or the dacha. When Stalin went to Sochi, Lakoba, for his part, wouldn't stay in Sukhumi [the capital of Abkhazia] but in [the resort towns of] Gagra[37] or Sochi to be near Stalin. Lakoba was a good billiards player. He would bring his billiards cue with him, make himself at home at Stalin's place, and play against everyone without ever losing. He was not a well man, and he was hard of hearing. I wasn't that close to Lakoba, but he and I were on friendly terms. I even remember once, when I was on vacation either at Gagra or Sochi, he invited me over and I went to visit him at his dacha; and in return he came to visit me with his wife and son. Later he died. Well, what can you say? He died. Everyone has to, without exception. But here's what's interesting. I later found out that when Lakoba's death was reported to Stalin, he expressed regrets about it but not particularly strongly. No one's death seemed to cause him much grief, even that of the people closest to him.

A little while later Beria suddenly instituted a case against Lakoba, who was already dead. Supposedly he had been a conspirator. I don't remember now what facts were cited as evidence that he had been part of a conspiracy, that there was nothing to regret in his passing. And then what did Beria do? He ordered Lakoba's body dug up, burned to ashes, and scattered to the winds: There was no place in the soil of Abkhazia for an enemy of the people! Later, when I got to know Beria better after the war, I began to think that Beria had dug up Lakoba's body not just because of personal envy toward him. It seemed to me that Beria was trying to hide some evidence, from fear that it might occur to Stalin to order the body dug up and have an analysis made, to find out what had been the cause of Lakoba's death. After all, what if he had been poisoned? I think Beria was afraid of that, although Beria and Yezhov knew how to deal with such matters very well. They had doctors who on their orders substituted human organs and inserted either poisoned ones or, if necessary, unpoisoned ones to prove whatever was desired. In the case of someone they had actually poisoned, this was done to make it seem as though the person had died a natural death. They had the possibilities, and their experience in such things was very rich. And here's another low point to which Beria sank, another crime that he committed: Lakoba's son, a young boy, was also shot on Beria's orders. What inspired Beria to get rid of Lakoba? Lakoba was very close to Stalin, closer than Beria, and might inform Stalin behind Beria's back about what was going on in Georgia, revealing Beria's activities in Georgia. And Beria didn't want to let that happen. He wanted the only channel of information about the situation in Georgia to be himself. Thus Lakoba fell, a sacrificial victim. That is my personal conclusion. I can only make assumptions here based on intuition; I don't have any factual evidence.

Then there is the story of [Polina] Zhemchuzhina. She was Molotov's wife, but she was well known, not just as Molotov's wife, but as a prominent person in her own right. When she was young and able, she worked as an active member of the party and was the head of the perfume industry. There was a government trust company, it seems to me, that had the acronym TEZHE. Later she became people's commissar for the fishing industry. She was a woman of strong will. I encountered her many times when I worked as secretary of the Moscow city and province committees of the party. She gave me the impression of a good party worker and a good comrade. And the pleasing thing was that she never made you feel that she was more than simply a party member, but besides everything she was the wife of Molotov. She had won a highly respected position in the Moscow party organization through her own efforts in both the party and the government. Stalin treated her with great respect. I observed this when we met. Several times Stalin, Molotov, Zhemchuzhina, and I went together to the Bolshoi Theater and sat in the government box at the theater. An exception was made for Zhemchzhina: the wives of other members of the Politburo were rarely seen in the government box, together with Stalin. It's true that sometimes Voroshilov's wife, Yekaterina Davydovna, showed up there, but less often than Zhemchuzhina. Zhemchuzhina's chest was covered with medals, but she had earned them all fairly. They provided no basis for gossip.

Suddenly, and even now I can't explain it in any way, Stalin's wrath was turned against Zhemchuzhina. I forget what she was charged with. I remember only that in a Central Committee plenum (I was already working in Ukraine then) the question of Zhemchuzhina was brought up. Shkiryatov,[39] chairman of the Party Control Commission attached to the Central Committee, presented the specific charges against her. Shkiryatov was an Old Bolshevik, but Stalin used him as a club, to do his dirty work for him. He would blindly, and I mean blindly, do everything Stalin said and, like the investigator in charge of Chubar's case, used his jesuitical methods to extract confessions of nonexistent crimes. Sometimes Stalin required the Party Control Commission to look into a case. Then the accused person would be expelled from the party. Thus, suspicions would be confirmed, as it were. After that the person would be seized in Shkiryatov's waiting room and dragged off to wherever he or she was destined to go. The reprisals were already decided in advance. How many such cases there were! Thousands of people perished!

Zhemchuzhina spoke at the plenum in her own defense. Inwardly I admired her, although at the time I believed Stalin was right and I took Stalin's side. But she defended her party record courageously and demonstrated great strength of character. We voted to expel her, as I recall, either from the Central Inspection Commission of the AUCP(B) or as a candidate member of the Central Committee. Of course we voted unanimously for this motion, which was made by the person giving the report. Only Molotov abstained. Later I often heard reproaches directed against Molotov, sometimes directly to his face, condemning him as a member of the Politburo and a member of the Central Committee who did not place party considerations higher than family relations, for not being able to condemn the mistakes of someone close to him.

Matters didn't end there. All sorts of "materials" came pouring out [against Zhemchuzhina]. Stalin made use of very base methods in his attempt to hurt Molotov's pride as a husband. The Chekists concocted an alleged [sexual] liaison between Zhemchuzhina and a factory director of Jewish origin who was a close acquaintance of Molotov's. The man often visited Molotov's apartment. Charges that they were in bed together were dragged into the light of day, and Stalin distributed this material to all members of the Politburo. He wanted to shame Zhemchuzhina and prick Molotov's pride as a husband. Molotov displayed firmness, refused to fall for the provocation, and declared: "I simply don't believe this. It's slander." He apparently was better informed than anyone about the "literary productions" the NKVD had the habit of writing, because he was quite certain that the documents were fabricated. I am discussing this here to show that even such techniques were used. In short, all means to achieve an end were good, the end in this case being the removal of Zhemchuzhina. After the war, repression struck her directly, which I will tell about later. That was a different matter, and I am somewhat better informed about that case.

A further illustration of Stalin's character is the case of Nikolai Alekseyevich Filatov, a Moscow proletarian, a tailor, and a member of the party from 1912 or 1914 on. He and I became acquainted when I was working in Moscow as secretary of the Bauman district committee of the AUCP (B), and he was secretary, it seems to me, of the party's Lenin district committee. When I became secretary of the party's Moscow city committee, Filatov was promoted to the post of secretary of the Moscow province committee. I knew him well. He was a tall, handsome man, with a small goatee. We met not only in the line of duty; we also lived in the same dacha, a house in Ogarevo. I was on the top floor; Kulkov (secretary of the party's city committee) was there, too, on the landing, and Bulganin was below. Opposite Bulganin was Filatov. We met at breakfast and dinner and spent leisure time together.

Stalin treated Filatov well. Filatov had a weakness, as we viewed it then. He always carried a camera around with him. When there was a demonstration on Red Square, he invariably showed up with his camera and took pictures of the demonstration, of the Politiburo members, the members of the government, and of course of Stalin. Stalin used to joke: "Here comes Filatov, and now he's going to take pictures." Filatov would smile and immediately start taking pictures. Everyone got used to it. Later he was sent to Rostov as an authorized representative of the Party Control Commission for the Northern Caucasus region. This was a very high position in those days. Nevertheless, in the end Filatov was arrested and disappeared into oblivion.

These were all people Stalin knew personally, and, it seemed, he had a good attitude toward them. He trusted them—yet suddenly they were destroyed. What were the reasons for that? Had Filatov really become an enemy of the people? If so, what were his motives? He was a working-class person from Moscow who went through the school of underground struggle before the revolution, then through the school of the Civil War, and the school of building a new socialist society, and he had been promoted from the lowest ranks to a fairly high position by the party. Is it possible to speak of certain personal weaknesses of his? Did he suffer a vainglorious lust for power? Hardly. What motive for treason could have arisen in a man like him? There were no such motives. Then why did Filatov perish like hundreds and thousands of others? The reason was one and the same. And I will present my opinion about that further on.

Here is how such cases were fabricated. Probably in 1939 or late 1938, I made a trip to the Donbas. I had a longing to be in my native region, where I had spent my childhood and youth. I wanted to meet my friends, those I had worked with at the Bosse factory and in the mines: Uspenskaya, Podshelkovka, Gorshovsky, Pastukhovka, Mine No. 11, Mine No. 31, and Voznesensk. That's where I spent my youth. My father took me from the village to the Donbas when I was six years old. I spent both my childhood and my youth in the Donbas region. [On this return trip] I went down in a mine. Remembering the old days, I walked along where the men were working, stopped for a while at the coal face, talked with the men who were hewing coal at the face and listened to their conversations; then I went back up out of the mine. Of course there were Chekists with me the whole time. One of them (I forget his name; he had worked in Stalino province) impressed me as an interesting and bright man of the intellectual type, apparently a white-collar worker by origin. He reported to me on all questions.

Shcherbakov was with me there, too. At one time he had been promoted to the Donbas and then transferred to Moscow after the arrest of Ugarov,[40] secretary of the party's Moscow province committee and Moscow city committee, who had gone to Moscow in my place when I was sent to Ukraine. Previously Ugarov, who was himself a Leningrader, had been secretary of the party's city committee in Leningrad, where he worked with Kirov and later with Zhdanov. Ugarov made a good impression on me. When I worked in Moscow we called each other on the phone a lot, and we engaged in a purely friendly form of competition [between Moscow and Leningrad]. He simply appealed to me, this Ugarov. Everything was fine; Ugarov was selected to go to the capital [from Leningrad], and then suddenly Stalin called me up: "Come immediately. Things are going badly for us in Moscow." I went. He told me that Ugarov had turned out to be an enemy of the people, that he had let the municipal economy in Moscow run to ruin; Moscow had been left without potatoes and without vegetables (and it was already autumn). When I had been in charge of Moscow, we had solved such problems successfully and Moscow had been fairly well provided with potatoes and cabbage and other vegetables. True, there had not been great variety, but for the standard of living at the time we provided the basic food products, that is, the food that the workers were used to.

The chairman of the Moscow Soviet then was, as I recall, a man named Sidorov.[41] When I was head of the Moscow party organization, he worked as the director of a dairy and livestock trust [combination or association of enterprises] for the Moscow area. Sidorov was not a bad person, but I'm just making this comment in passing, and I make it simply because it helps me connect things in my memory. Stalin said to me: "Drop everything there in Ukraine. Nothing is happening there. But for us here in Moscow there's a desperate situation. You'll be assigned as an authorized representative of the party's Central Committee for Moscow, and don't leave until you've built up the necessary reserves of potatoes and vegetables for the capital city for the winter." It was a strange conversation, if you will.

But it was even stranger when, after my conversation with Stalin, I got in touch with Molotov and he asked me: "When you left Moscow, did you maintain any connections here?"

I answered: "No, none."

"Why is that?"

"That is our procedure: If you've left a certain party organization, then all ties with it are ended, so that you don't interfere with the new leadership. Contacts should be maintained not with particular individuals but with the Central Committee."

"Ugarov has turned out to be an enemy of the people. If you had been in contact with Moscow, maybe we would have found out sooner and exposed him."

I answered: "For me, when I'm in Kiev, it's more difficult for me to expose Moscow people. You are closer. If we are to talk about who is personally responsible from among Politburo members, it's officially recorded that Zhdanov is responsible for Moscow; he's the secretary of the Leningrad province committee, and he's a secretary of the Central Committee. Besides that, he's secretary of the Leningrad city committee of the party, so that if someone had to keep Moscow under observation, [it should have been Zhdanov]. I think your complaints against me are unfounded." That is also an interesting approach; it was necessary to find someone to blame for having allowed Ugarov to become an enemy of the people, although, of course, he was not any kind of enemy of the people nor could he have been.

After Stalin's phone call, I returned to my former position in the party's Moscow province committee and began to do everything necessary to make sure the task was handled. I had a lot of experience: I already knew Ukraine, and Ukraine was a major source of vegetables. Besides that, I knew the Moscow cadres. I quickly put my weight on the necessary levers and did everything that could be done at that time of year. We ensured a good supply of vegetables, and I stayed in Moscow then approximately half a month. We also held a plenum of the party's province committee. Stalin said: "You conduct the plenum and relieve Ugarov of his duties." (The latter had not yet been arrested.) I asked the question: "Who should be elected?" Stalin thought for a long time, walking around, and then, thinking out loud, he tossed off the name: "Shcherbakov."

Previously Shcherbakov had been a secretary in Siberia in one of the party's province committees.[42] When I went to Ukraine, he was sent to the Donbass as reinforcement. Now Stalin was saying: "We're going to have to take Shcherbakov away from you."

I answered: "If you need him, take him. Only there is testimony against him too. Enemies of the people have testified against him: Testimony that seems to deserve credit. What's to be done about that?"

Stalin again walked around and around, thinking, then he said: "Let's do it this way. We'll go ahead and take Shcherbakov, but we need to send some Moscow person to be a second secretary to Shcherbakov, someone we know well, and we have to tell him that there is material suggesting that Shcherbakov had links with enemies of the people and warn him to keep an eye on him. If something seems suspicious, let him tell the Central Committee about it."

And who would be the second secretary? We asked Malenkov. He answered: "Popov."[43]

Popov was working for Malenkov then in the personnel department, it seems to me as Malenkov's deputy. I met Popov and had a confidential talk with him. "You're going to be in the Moscow province committee," I said. "The Central Committee trusts you, but you on the other hand must be the eyes and ears of the Central Committee, keeping watch over Shcherbakov." Shcherbakov had worked in Moscow before that. He had been first secretary of the Soviet Writers' Union when Maxim Gorky was still alive. Something hadn't worked out between Gorky and him back then, as far as I can recall, and Gorky was opposed to Shcherbakov, because the latter interfered in specific matters of concern only to writers. So he was sent off to be a secretary, first in Leningrad and then in Siberia and Donetsk. But now the plenum was held successfully, and Shcherbakov was elected. And in the Donbass, as I recall, we promoted a local person who had worked under Shcherbakov as second secretary of the party's province committee there.

I returned to the Donbas. I acquainted myself with the operations of the mines and factories and with the cadres. I traveled around my old stomping grounds and recalled the good old days when I had been a worker there and later a party official. I decided to make a trip to Gorlovka. I was told that in Gorlovka things were in a bad way in regard to the secretary of the party's district committee. I told the head of the local NKVD that I would go there and take a look, see for myself, and have a talk with the man. And so I went. The secretary of the district committee was someone I didn't know. There was "material" against him. They showed it to me, and the head of the NKVD told me he had no doubt that this man was an enemy of the people who had not yet been struck down, a remnant of a conspiratorial organization that had been smashed. He had been arrested by the time I came to Gorlovka. The "operational efficiency" was already at a very high level by then. Within a few hours the text of the first interrogation appeared, and the man had already confessed. He testified to this and to that; so-and-so had recruited him, someone else had been connected with them, and so forth.

There were three secretaries of the district committee carrying out their functions then: the first, second, and third. The first secretary testified that the second and third had been recruited along with him. "Well, how could that be?" I asked the NKVD head.

"Well, you know, it's this way," he said, and he went on with his "and so on and so forth." He pretended to be as pure as Christ, but he suggested arresting the second secretary as well. And so he was arrested. After a little while they read me the text of the interrogation. I noted that the confessions of the first secretary and second secretary were phrased in very similar ways, almost word for word, and the same investigator had written down both confessions.

I said: "How could it be that the confessions coincide so closely, word for word? After all, didn't the investigator interrogate them separately?"

"Well, you know, it's all one case, and the investigator's by himself, and so he wrote in a standardized way." This particular detail, as it turned out, sowed doubts in my mind. But an official protocol on the case had already been drawn up, and essentially I did believe that the man had confessed. Also they both testified against the third secretary, Gayevoi.[44] I took a look at his biography: He was a local worker, and everyone around there knew him.

I said: "Let's have a meeting of the district committee." A meeting of the party's district committee was convened. People of a fairly respectable age belonged to the district committee. I said: "Comrades, the first and second secretaries have turned out to be linked with enemies of the people, and the NKVD representative can report in more detail." The main "enemy of the people" at that time in the Donbas region was considered to be the former secretary of the province committee, Pramnek. Supposedly he had established an organization hostile to our government. He had already been arrested by that time.

But now these members of the district committee, these older party members, began to speak up as follows: "Comrade Khrushchev, we don't know those people (the first and second secretaries); they came in from outside; they were sent here to our organization, but Gayevoi grew up right here in our town, in our worker's settlement. We knew him when he was a little kid running around without pants on, and we know his parents. He's one of our people, and we can vouch for him."

I said: "All right. Since you vouch for him, the head of the NKVD who's sitting right here will once again check into the case, and no one will touch Gayevoi, but he will be under your jurisdiction." Gayevoi remained free. Sometime later he was promoted to be second secretary of the party's Stalino province committee and later on, it seems, he even became first secretary. It may be that I'm not narrating this story in the proper order. It may be that the incident with Gayevoi happened before the case of Shcherbakov, because, as I recall, it was actually Shcherbakov who promoted Gayevoi to be secretary of the province committee. But he is not the issue. His colleagues are. These were the methods used to create "enemies of the people." The higher party bodies, as well as leaders in fairly high positions, such as I (at the time I was already a member of the Politburo), proved to be completely at the mercy of the documents presented by NKVD agents, who decided the fates of one or another party member and also of nonparty people.

At that time, also in the Donbas, I learned that some teachers at the Artyom Mining Institute (which had originally been the workers' school I graduated from in 1925), people who I respected very much, had also turned out to be "enemies of the people." One of them, the mining engineer Gerchikov, of Jewish nationality, was a very fine mathematician and besides that had great power as a hypnotist. He had later worked in the coal industry as a mining engineer. Suddenly he fell into the category of wrecker, not in the period when the campaign for exposing wreckers was in full swing, but later, when "enemies of the people" were being exposed. Kaganovich, the people's commissar for heavy industry, came to the Donbas, gave a big speech, listed the names of several dozen enemies of the people who had been exposed, and among the names he mentioned was Gerchikov. It was painful for me that Gerchikov, who I knew well and for whom I had a lot of respect, had also turned out to be an enemy of the people. When I went to the Donbas at the end of 1938, I accidentally encountered Gerchikov, but it was no longer the Gerchikov I had known. Now he was a shadow of his former self. I asked: "How are you doing?" He looked gloomy and withdrawn. He muttered that things were not good, that he had been arrested. Later other people told me he had been beaten terribly; his health had been undermined, and not long after that he died.

It became clear after my arrival in the Donbas that there were no managers of the coal industry left; there were only deputy directors. New people had to be promoted. Kaganovich promoted good, honest people, but they were not well trained, didn't have the appropriate education. One of those promoted was Nikita Izotov, a very good worker, who was justly famous and had been raised to the heights of fame as an outstanding shock worker. But of course he was not suitable as a director of the coal industry. Dyukanov[45] was also promoted, but he too was completely unsuited to the task. People complained to me about Dyukanov: "Comrade Khrushchev, understand what we're saying. He summons the engineers. They report to him. And if something isn't right or some quota hasn't been met, he has only one argument: 'You better look out, or I'll smack your a——' (*zh . . . nashlyopayu).* And we engineers, twice a day, bring him reports, and he hits us." I told Stalin then that this was not the way thing should be done, that we had our own engineers, who were entirely capable of running the industry. Stalin agreed with me. Zasyadko[46] was promoted to head up the Stalino Coal Trust. After the war he became deputy chairman of the Council of Ministers of the USSR, but now he is no longer alive. He was a man who had one great shortcoming. He drank and drank, the poor fellow. But he was a very good administrator and organizer and had an excellent knowledge of the mining industry. At that time, as I recall, there were various conglomerates or associations of enterprises (trusts) in the coal and metallurgical industries. And new engineers were placed at the head of the trusts operating in the Donbas. I won't list all their names, and I don't even remember them all now—those who headed the trusts or who perished at that time.

The situation in agriculture and industry gradually began to straighten itself out. Industry began to fulfill the plans, both the coal industry and the metallurgical industry, as well as the machine industry. Agriculture also began to gain strength. The new cadres proved themselves, and the repression subsided somewhat. It was no longer spreading wider and wider, but was gathering up the leftovers, so to speak, those who had been mentioned in records of interrogation when "enemies of the people" had been arrested and executed.

It happened that the people's commissar of finance called up, a man named Zverev,[47] and he said: "You're not selling enough white bread, especially rolls and buns." The point was that these food products were sold at prices higher than normal because they were goods associated with the Commissariat of Finance. Earnings from their sale went toward the accumulation fund used for industrialization.

I remember also that the situation straightened out in regard to sugar beet production and also for cereal grains: More than 400 millions poods [6.4 million tons] of wheat were delivered. For Ukraine at that time this was a fairly large figure. After the Great Patriotic War, when I was again working in Ukraine, we delivered up to 700 million poods [11.2 million tons] of grain. But by then times were different. In the 1930s Ukraine really was the breadbasket of the Soviet Union as far as grain went, and there is no need even to talk about sugar. Besides that we grew a lot of vegetables, tobacco, and sunflowers.

I also remember that when I had just arrived in Ukraine and first assumed my duties as secretary of the Central Committee of the Ukrainian Communist Party, Academician Paton[48] of the Ukrainian Academy of Sciences called me up one day. I had heard of him but had never met him. I was informed that he was a very interesting man, a major figure in mechanical engineering, who was fascinated with the problem of using welding techniques in bridge construction. He asked if he could come see me, and I agreed. The man who walked into my room was a solidly built figure, well along in years, entirely gray headed, with a face like a lion, and burning eyes. After we had said hello, he immediately pulled a piece of metal from his pocket and put it on the table:

"You see there, Comrade Khrushchev, what our institute can do. This is a piece of bar iron (it seems to me it was about 10 millimeters thick), and this is how I have welded it." I looked at the welding. Since I was a metalworker myself, I had some experience with welding. This was a perfect seam and as smooth on the surface as if it had been cast in a foundry. He said: "That's welding with flux." I was hearing the word "flux" for the first time. Paton had other inventions or innovations. He expounded on the great possibilities of the flux method of welding, what advantages it provided, how it made work easier, increased productivity and the quality of welding work in general, especially its reliability. He was completely absorbed with the idea of welding all ferrous metal structures this way—bridges, roof trusses, and so forth. He argued that it was more advantageous to weld them than to rivet them. He claimed that he would soon develop an automatic process for welding ships. His eyes literally blazed. There was such certainty and conviction in his words that he forced others to believe in his ideas. He was very effective in presenting his views and accomplishments and was able to convince people of the correctness of his views even if they weren't specialists.

I was literally entranced by the meeting and conversation with Paton, by his progressive, revolutionary, technological ideas. Today I can say that Yevgeny

Oskarovich Paton was the father of industrial welding in the USSR. His son, now the president of the Academy of the Sciences of the Ukrainian SSR, is a worthy heir to his father. Even before the death of Paton (the elder), I met many times with the son, Boris Yevgenyevich, and visited the institute that he headed, listened many times to what he had to say, as he showed me new prototypes resulting from progress in the field of welding. A number of these accomplishments had an impact far beyond the bounds of the institute and were widely used in production.

As early as our first meeting Paton the elder said: "I want to make a complaint. The director of the Dnepropetrovsk metal structures plant was in Kiev. I asked him to come see us at the institute and take a look at our work. I wanted to demonstrate our welding of metal structures in order to introduce the method in his plant, above all, automatic flux welding. He couldn't find the time to come visit, and went back to Dnepropetrovsk. That's the attitude our Soviet people are taking toward new things. The introduction of automatic welding would lead to great economizing in metalworking. It would speed up construction and increase the productivity of labor."

I answered: "It's good that you told me. The director of this factory will be at your institute tomorrow." Right then in his presence I called up the secretary of the party's Dnepropetrovsk province committee, Zadionchenko. He was a very efficient man and immediately understood the essence of the matter.

He responded: "I'll call him right away. He'll be at Paton's institute tomorrow." The next day the plant director flew to Kiev. It was a satisfied Paton who soon called me and said that the man had already visited him; he had showed him everything, and they had found common ground.

The conversation with Paton made the most tremendous impression on me. I immediately dictated a memorandum to Stalin reporting everything that the academician had told me and that I myself had seen when I went to visit his institute and got to know the staff there. I praised Paton highly in my memorandum, expressing enthusiasm for his research, and I also wrote about the great future for this method of welding, emphasizing that the work Paton was doing should be promoted, so that it would be introduced as quickly as possible into the practical operations of our factories.

A little time went by. Stalin called me and suggested I come to Moscow. I got on a train immediately. Members of the Politburo and the party's Central Committee didn't fly in those days. That was forbidden. The prohibition arose in an interesting way. On one occasion, Mikoyan, I was told, made a trip to Belorussia, and some pilots there suggested that he take a flight in a plane. He agreed and went for a flight, and later it was written up in the papers. Stalin read that Mikoyan had flown in an airplane and the pilot had performed some advanced, complex flight maneuvers. Stalin proposed that Mikoyan be reprimanded for taking an unnecessary risk. It was officially stated that members of the Central Committee of the AUCP (B) and party secretaries of Central Committees of union-republic party organizations were prohibited from flying because it was considered too dangerous. It was only during the war that we began flying.

I very much liked to fly and often did fly when I held a position of lesser importance, one that Stalin wouldn't be so concerned about. When I worked in Kiev in 1928–29, I flew. A pilot by the name of Deich [Deutsch] was working there. I made a trip to Rzhishchev,[49] and he "treated me" to a flight in an airplane for the first time in my life. It made a powerful impression on me. After that I often flew in what were called Junker planes. The head of the Red Army's air forces, Baranov,[50] also flew in those planes back then. Later he died in an accident. He was a remarkable man, a very close friend of Yakir. During some military maneuvers when he had come to Kiev, he allowed me to fly in his plane. Thus, I was quite the "lion of the air" for those times. Later, when I was working in Moscow as secretary of the party's Moscow city committee, I even took a flight in an experimental plane, the Stal-2. I flew in it together with the people's commissar of the civil air fleet. I also took a flight in a dirigible, again with the people's commissar of the civil air fleet. Although I had flown a great deal, it was now forbidden for us to fly, and so I traveled by train from Kiev to Moscow.

When I arrived in Moscow and met with Stalin, I began telling him again about Paton. He interrupted me: "That's exactly the reason I called you here. I read your memorandum, and it pleased me very much. I completely agree with your assessment of this work and this research, and I would like to discuss it with you and then place this question before the Central Committee and have a resolution written up making it obligatory for welding to be introduced [widely in production and construction]. As for Paton, what kind of man is he? What kind of willpower does he have? Is he strong enough for us to make him an authorized representative of the Council of People's Commissars and give him an unlimited mandate to introduce his welding methods in industry? To force the bureaucrats to introduce welding?"

I answered: "To the extent that I know Paton, if he's given such a mandate, the bureaucrats will have no salvation from him. He'll force them to get a move on. He has the willpower of a real go-getter." At that point Stalin told me not to return to Kiev until Paton had been summoned [to Moscow] and a resolution passed giving him the authority to organize the introduction of this new method of welding into industry. When Paton arrived, Stalin asked him a few questions and got to know him. He made a very good impression on Stalin also, and it could not have been otherwise. Paton was a man who inwardly was entirely calm and collected. He was well organized and formulated his thoughts clearly and concisely. His face revealed a man of strong will, and he had burning, piercing eyes. He forced people to take him into account, and he knew how to influence the people he met. Stalin took a liking to him. The mandate I have mentioned was issued to Paton, and I immediately left for Kiev.

When I had been questioning Paton in detail about the possibilities of his welding method, the idea had occurred to me that we could use his technique for welding tank bodies by assembly-line methods. I asked him: "Could you weld steel for tanks?"

He thought for a little while: "We'd have to study the matter. I can't answer right now. What would be the thickness of the armor?"

I said: "Probably up to 100 millimeters."

He answered: "Complicated, but we'll give it a try. I think it would work." Now I met with Paton again in order to find out more exactly what kind of metals, what metal parts, and what thickness he could weld by his method. I hoped that the technique would be useful for welding tank bodies. After all, war was coming closer and closer.

When I raised the question again, Paton commented that he'd have to know the composition of the steel. I suggested he make a trip to the Kharkov tank factory. Originally it had been called the Gartman factory, and later it was called the Kharkov locomotive manufacturing plant and also bore the name of the Comintern,[51] but a new product was already being manufactured there—tanks and diesel engines. I said: "I'm going to ask the factory directors and the party organizer (the director there was Maksarev[52] and the party organizer was Yepishev,[53] who now[54] serves as head of the Chief Political Directorate of the Soviet Army and Navy). They'll familiarize you with the production process and with the production and design staff. You should study the production technique yourself and after that let me know your opinion." Paton went to Kharkov, familiarized himself with tank production, and then reported that he would need some time to think it over, but he was sure that it would be possible to organize automatic flux welding of tank bodies. I said to him: "That would be a great victory for our entire country and for the army. You would have done a great service."

Together with the tank designers and engineers at the factory, Paton began to work out devices (in the industry they were called conductors, or jigs) by which the parts of the tank were clamped or held together while they were welded.

I am running ahead a little in order to finish my story about the role Paton and the party played in tank production, what a tremendously important part he had in the victories gained by the Red Army, because they really did begin to produce tanks by his welding methods, turning them out like pancakes off the stove, thanks to the help that Paton provided. When the war broke out and events began to develop unfavorably for us, under the blows of the enemy, the Red Army had to retreat, toward Kharkov in particular. We were forced to evacuate industry from Kharkov to the east. Tank production was moved from Kharkov to the Urals region, and the design office was moved there too. And Paton went with it. Tank production was quickly set up once again at the new location. Paton made a tremendous contribution in organizing the production of military vehicles by assembly-line methods. He was a very interesting man, no longer a young man then, and, as the saying went in those days, in spirit he was a man of the old regime, a product of the educational system of the tsarist era.

In 1943 I flew to Moscow after being summoned by Stalin. Stalin rather frequently would call me from the front for various kinds of discussions. At that time Paton also turned out to be in Moscow. He asked if he could see me. I received him and listened to what he had to say. He entrusted to me a letter addressed to the party's Central Committee. He wrote that his father had served as a consul under the tsar; he was a consul in Italy, in Genoa, it seems to me. "When the revolution happened," he wrote, "I had already been fully formed as a person and naturally I did not take a serious attitude toward the revolution. I considered it a phenomenon that was not useful for our country, and therefore I was opposed to the October revolution. But for my part, I never undertook any oppositional measures and did not participate in any anti-Soviet organization. If it can be expressed this way, I expected that this government would not last long, that it would collapse, because I believed it was sterile and lacked prospects. Time went by. I saw that time had tested the government and that the government had held out. Then the new system of power began to grow stronger; it demonstrated its organizational capabilities and showed that it was moving in a direction that impressed me. I liked what the Soviet government was doing. With every passing year I was attracted more and more by the positive activity of the Soviet government. I began to work better and began, as it were, to blend in with the essence of what the Soviet government was creating. Nevertheless, I did not forget the attitude I had had in the first days of the revolution, and therefore I felt that I did not have the right to any kind of protection or sponsorship on the part of the Soviet government, or any special trust in me. I continued to work honestly in my field of specialization. Then the war began, and I was brought in to help with tank production. I think that I have made a big contribution to the defense of our country, organized assembly-line production of tank bodies, and introduced automatic flux welding according to my own technique. Today I am in favor of Soviet power and have been so for a long time. I now feel I have a moral right to address the party with a request that it accept me into its ranks. Therefore I am writing this letter and am attaching to it an application for party membership to be submitted to the Central Committee. I ask that you support me. I would now like to be a party member."

I sensed a profound sincerity in his acceptance of the Soviet government as a government of the people, his acknowledgment that the Communist Party was the organizer of victory over the enemy. I very much liked the desire expressed by Paton to make his participation in the great victory against fascist Germany politically official by becoming a member of our party. I took his document and said I was convinced that he would be accepted in the ranks of the AUCP(B). "I will report to Comrade Stalin and you will know the decision of the Central Committee."

I don't remember how long it was before I met with Stalin, but when I did, I told him everything and gave him the documents. Stalin was also moved, and he rarely showed his emotions. He said: "So Paton has decided to do this. He deserves all possible respect." He immediately proposed that the following resolution be formulated: "To accept Comrade Paton in the party without any trial period as a candidate member."

At the time when Paton was accepted into the party, there existed a procedure under which people coming from bourgeois or intellectual backgrounds had to go through a trial period of two years as candidate members. This was obligatory for them to become party members, but this procedure was not applied to Paton; an exception was made in his case. Because of his special services to the homeland and to the party, he was immediately taken in as a full member. I was very pleased by this. First, I was happy for Paton and for our country and for the work that Paton had done for our country and army. Second, I was pleased that it had fallen to my lot to make his acquaintance, understand the role he could play, and bring him into the tremendously important work of tank production. After the war Paton returned to his duties at the Ukrainian Academy of Sciences, becoming its vice president, and he continued his work in the same fruitful and productive way as during and before the war.

At one point we were all stunned by a terrible misfortune, a misfortune both for Ukraine and for science. The life of the president of the Academy of Sciences of the Ukrainian SSR, Bogomolets, a man whom everyone respected greatly, came to an end. The question arose: "Who would now become the president?" The information was passed on to me that the scientists and scholars of Ukraine were upset. The reason was that many of them assumed the Central Committee of the Ukrainian Communist Party would recommend none other than Paton. Knowing what respect I felt for Paton, they thought that his candidacy would be put forward without question. It should be said at this point that there were differing attitudes toward Paton at the Ukrainian Academy of Sciences. I think that an absolute majority of the academic community had an attitude of great respect toward him as a scientist. But everyone was very much afraid of his personality, and therefore they were frightened by the idea that he might become president of the Academy. Everyone knew how strong-willed he was; he was intolerant of empty talk and insisted on concrete accomplishments instead of talk. He was simply a man of strong, driving will. Arguments reached my ears that if Paton became president, because Khrushchev supported him, he would then drive out this one, that one, and the other one and turn the Academy of Sciences into an experimental proving ground. That is, they were accusing him of excessive pragmatism, an excessive orientation toward the practical application of the sciences. Yes, he was that kind of person. He knew well how to place scientific knowledge at the service of the cause. He did not tolerate abstract talk and sterile phrase-mongering disguised under the label of "science." For people inclined toward such things, he really could be a threat.

We had taken into account such an attitude toward him, and for that reason the idea of recommending him to be president had not occurred to us. It would have been necessary to "put the pressure on," and that would not have been well received when it came to voting. Paton himself did not aspire to the position of president. He was already swamped with the work he was doing and the institute he was in charge of. Today this institute is famous not only in our country; it holds a fairly high place in world science in the field of metal welding.

Another episode gives a better picture of Paton. When I was working in Ukraine, the head of the propaganda department of the Ukrainian Communist Party came to see me with a complaint against Paton. He said that Paton had expressed lack of respect for the Central Committee and that he was outraged by this behavior. Knowing my attitude toward Paton, he had decided to tell me about it.

I asked him: "What specifically did Paton do? What is it that aroused your displeasure?"

"I organized a conference of scientists and invited Paton, among others. Paton sat there for a while; then he got up and left."

I said: "If Paton left, we have to take another look at what was going on. What was the subject of your conference?"

"Questions of ideological work."

"Well, what did you invite Academician Paton to that kind of conference for? He has nothing to do with that subject. He was just sitting there as a kind of ornament. You needed the presences of an academician, and so you invited him along with others, but what good was that?"

Paton's strong character is evident in these events. When he saw that the question being discussed was something he had nothing to do with, and that a lot of people were sitting there wasting their time, he got up and left. What other options did he have? He ought to have given a tongue-lashing to the people who had invited him, but he didn't do that; he simply left. [As I told the party official who had come to me to complain about Paton:] "He was absolutely right to do what he did. The proper conclusions have to be drawn. When you organize a conference, you should invite only people who have some direct relation to the subject under discussion. Then people will be interested and take an active part in the discussion, not get angry that this kind of conference has been organized. Paton expressed his protest in that way, against the fact that he had been invited to a conference that was of no interest to him. He got up and left. He voted, as the saying goes, with his feet. And you should draw the conclusion, by using your brains, not to let something like this happen again in the future, not only in relation to Paton. Every person should be treated with great care, especially scientists and specialists. They should be invited to such things only as a last resort and only when they are necessary for the conference, either when their field of specialization is being discussed, or the subject is something they have to do with."

After Paton's death [in 1963], his institute was run—and quite successfully at that—by his son Boris, who is now[55] president of the Ukrainian Academy of Sciences. When Paton died, construction was being completed on a new bridge across the Dnieper River in Kiev. This was the largest bridge in Kiev. It was welded as an entire unit. It was Paton who accomplished this, and I had supported him in undertaking to create a structure that would be welded in this way. He had been the technical director for welding construction in the building of this bridge. I was visiting Kiev then on some business. The Ukrainians came up with the idea of attaching my name to the bridge. I was surprised by this, especially because by that time the decision had been made in our country to forbid the naming of enterprises, institutions, collective farms, and so forth after party leaders and government leaders who were still in good health. In fact we passed a special resolution to remove some people's names that had already been used this way. As I said jokingly at the time, the people who had "latched onto" factories, plants, towns, and so forth in this way had thereby lost all rights and privileges. There had even been competition over whose name would be attached to the largest number of factories or collective farms. That kind of thing was very unhealthy. It was a barbaric kind of thing! Under Lenin, as far as I know, there was no such thing. Later the name of Budyonny (the Civil War hero), although he was still alive and well, had sometimes been attached to one or another enterprise. The names of people who had died were also used, in honor of the good deeds they had performed for the party and for the sake of the people.

I asked the Ukrainians: "Why do you want to put my name on this bridge? That's a direct violation of a Central Committee resolution. I'm opposed to this, especially because I was the sponsor of that resolution. Don't you understand what kind of position that would put me in? I beg you never to come crawling to me with proposals of this kind again. And is there any need for a lengthy search for a person worthy of having his name attached to this structure? Why, there is Academician Paton right in front of you. I ask you to propose his name, and the government will approve it." And so the bridge was named after Paton. To this day this bridge, as the saying goes, "lives and prospers," and the people traveling across it have kind thoughts and words for the memory of its creator, Academician Paton.

1. Tbilisi was the original Georgian name for the city. In Georgian the name means "warm springs." After the imperial Russian conquest of the region, the tsarist government changed the name to Tiflis. The original name was restored in 1936. [SS]

2. Kutais, also known as Kutaisi, is a major urban center in western Georgia. The nearby Rioni River flows into the Black Sea. [SS]

3. In February 1921, the Eleventh Red Army moved into Georgia from Baku to depose the Menshevik government of the short-lived independent Georgian republic and to incorporate Georgia into Soviet Russia. Later it became part of the Soviet Union. [SS]

4. V. A. Malyshev. See Biographies.

5. Kolomna is situated about 110 kilometers southeast of Moscow. [SS]

6. M. I. Kalinin; G. I. Kulik; S. M. Budyonny. See Biographies.

7. P. S. Zhemchuzhina. See Biographies.

8. Yezhov was replaced by Beria as head of the NKVD in December 1938. [GS]

9. M. P. Frinovsky was a security official. See Biographies.

10. B. Z. Kobulov was a security official and a close associate of Beria. See Biographies.

11. At that time the Moscow Military District was commanded by Army Commander of the First Rank I. P. Belov. See Biographies.

12. P. V. Lukashov.

13. A. Ye. Badayev. See Biographies.

14. G. Vasilkovsky.

15. Ya. S. Agranov. See Biographies.

16. The Industrial Party was a secret opposition party allegedly created by a group of engineers in the mid-1920s. The trial of its supposed organizers was the first great show trial. [SS]

17. Lugansk is in southeastern Ukraine. [SS]

18. As of the late 1960s. Rudenko died in 1981. [SK]

19. Genghis Khan was the founder of the Eurasian empire of the Mongol nomads in the early thirteenth century. [SS]

20. Kuibyshev, now renamed Samara, is situated on the Volga River in the southeast of European Russia. [SS]

21. S. A. Sarkisyan. See Biographies.

22. V. I. Chernyavsky. See Biographies.

23. Ye. S. Kogan. See Biographies.

24. Ya. G. Soifer occupied various administrative and party posts.

25. Tula is an old industrial city situated about 300 kilometers south of Moscow. [SS]

26. A. I. Sedelnikov. See Biographies.

27. N. A. Filatov. See Biographies.

28. Rostov on the Don in the southern part of European Russia. Rostov province is considered part of the Northern Caucasus. [SS]

29. Ivanovo is an old industrial city situated about 300 kilometers northeast of Moscow. [SS]

30. Dnepropetrovsk is a large industrial city on the Dnieper River in east central Ukraine. [SS]

31. Edvard Benes was the foreign minister and later president of Czechoslovakia. See Biographies.

32. Troikas, in the Stalin era, were three-member judicial tribunals with special powers, especially to pronounce the death penalty, without following normal legal procedure. [GS]

33. Under Soviet law, the duties of the procurator (or prosecutor) included monitoring the work of police agencies and preventing or correcting abuses. [GS]

34. A. M. Kaledin. See Biographies.

35. A. S. Svanidze. See Biographies.

36. N. A. Lakoba. See Biographies.

37. Gagra is on the Black Sea coast in northern Abkhazia, about 60 kilometers from Sochi. [SS]

38. That is, at the time this was dictated.

39. M. F. Shkiryatov. See Biographies.

40. A. I. Ugarov. See Biographies.

41. I. I. Sidorov.

42. Shcherbakov had been a secretary of the Irkutsk province committee of the AUCP(B).

43. G. M. Popov. See Biographies.

44. A. I. Gayevoi. See Biographies.

45. M. D. Dyukanov.

46. A. F. Zasyadko. See Biographies.

47. A. G. Zverev. See Biographies.

48. Ye. O. Paton was a prominent specialist in metal welding. See Biographies.

49. Rzhishchev is situated in central Ukraine, about 130 kilometers southeast of Kiev. [SS]

50. P. I. Baranov. See Biographies.

51. That is, the Communist International. [SS]

52. Yu. Ye. Maksarev, member of the RCP(B) from 1921.

53. A. A. Yepishev. See Biographies.

54. That is, at the time this was dictated.

55. That is, at the time this was dictated.

## THE SECOND WORLD WAR APPROACHES

In 1938, when I headed the Communist Party of Ukraine, Stalin proposed that I be made a member of the Military Council of the Kiev Special Military District (Russian initials, KOVO), so that I could be introduced to military matters. A "big war" between the USSR and our enemies was inevitable, and party officials needed to know everything first-hand. Especially because, I should add, there had been so many "wreckers" in the Red Army and so many people had been removed from the command staff. Most of them never returned after being arrested; they were either executed or sent to prison camps. The commander of the troops in the KOVO was Timoshenko.[1] Stalin told me about him. He had known him personally in the First Cavalry Army[2] and spoke well of his character.

When I was added to the Military Council, I always attended its sessions punctually and listened to all the speeches, which dealt with very specific questions. The problem that most concerned everyone at that time was the construction of fortified zones along our western border. Reinforced-concrete pillboxes equipped with machine guns and artillery were being built. Much earlier a fortified zone had been established just outside of Kiev, along the Irpen River.[3] Construction on that had begun in 1928–29 when I headed the organizational department of the party's Kiev district committee. Sometimes I went out to observe military maneuvers and to get to know the troops. Of course my acquaintance with them was fairly limited because I was never directly concerned with military matters, being already up to my ears with party work and problems of economic development: in the coal industry, metallurgy, and agriculture. But the construction of fortified defense zones interested me. In general I had a weakness for questions of construction, and I had a fairly good understanding of construction problems. Therefore it was possible that my participation would be helpful; I traveled out to the construction sites and kept track of how things were going.

Timoshenko informed me about the sessions of the Chief Military Council[4] of the Red Army [in Moscow]. He often traveled there to attend those sessions. Timoshenko was rather shrewd in his own way. I sensed from his manner that he was not pleased with the work of the Chief Military Council, but that he was powerless to straighten things out. He went to Moscow on one occasion (I turned out to be there too), and while there he asked me very insistently to go with him to a session of the Chief Military Council. I had never been there before and really had nothing to do with it. I said: "Why should I go? It would be awkward. And how would People's Commissar Voroshilov look at it?"

He answered: "They're going to be discussing our problems. You're a member of the Military Council of the Kiev Special Military District, and you should be kept abreast of things, know how these problems are being solved. Therefore everything will be properly understood." I wanted very much not to go, but he insisted so much that I understood he had some reason for it, and I decided to give in to him and go to the session. He and I came in and took our seats. He took his usual one, and I found a free chair. The rest of the Chief Military Council gathered. Voroshilov was the chairman, other members were Shchadenko, Kulik, Mekhlis, and I no longer remember who else belonged to the Council.[5] Voroshilov took his seat as chairman and announced the agenda.

Today I haven't the slightest recollection of what specific questions were discussed, but I remember the general atmosphere in which the discussion took place. Timoshenko had evidently invited me precisely so that I would see what kind of atmosphere existed at the Council and how questions were decided. Voroshilov began the meeting. He gave the floor to Kulik, who spoke in a confused, chaotic way. It was impossible to figure out what he was talking about because he got all worked up and began to shout and didn't formulate his thoughts clearly. The level of confusion rose higher, and the atmosphere became hotter. After him Shchadenko spoke even more chaotically. He also began to gesticulate and shout. When Voroshilov stopped him, he shouted at Voroshilov, harshly expressing his objections. When Shchadenko finished, Mekhlis started to speak. I knew Mekhlis well. He was a very honest person, but there was something crazy about him. Even more heatedly than the others, he tried to demonstrate that he was right. Everyone started talking at once, completely at cross-purposes. At one moment Voroshilov would be trying to calm them down; at the next moment he himself would be shouting. The impression all this made on me was that this was not a serious organization, not one capable of solving our country's defense problems in a businesslike way (even though Voroshilov's authority was very high at that time). The discussion ended, some sort of resolution was adopted, and everyone left.

Timoshenko, I repeat, had his own kind of shrewdness. He looked at me and seemed to be asking with his eyes only: Well, did you see what kind of situation this is, where questions of the defense of the USSR are being decided? It was difficult for me, of course, to come to any conclusions or make any generalizations right away, because this was the only time I had been at such a meeting. To state outright that this body was not capable of deciding such questions would have been too brazen. After all, the people who belonged to the Chief Military Council were highly respected: Voroshilov himself; and Kulik, a man who had fought bravely as a soldier and was considered a knowledgeable artillery expert. As for Shchadenko, he had a history of his own. He had been a Communist before the revolution, a tailor by profession. He had distinguished himself at one time in the Don region,[6] in the fighting against Ataman Kaledin. I knew his name from that time because it appeared in many publications, and therefore in my eyes he wore a kind of halo. A man with such a past! The explanation I gave myself for his incoherent behavior at the Chief Military Council was simply that the questions being discussed were very complex.

I was more familiar with Mekhlis. I knew him from [his work at] *Pravda*, and I should say right away that my attitude toward him was one of respect. My acquaintance with him dated from when I was a student at the Industrial Academy during the struggle against the "Rights." Mekhlis, as editor of *Pravda*, helped us greatly in that struggle. After that I kept in touch with him. Whenever we met, we exchanged opinions, and we held each other in high regard. But I remember an incident that revealed a mentally unbalanced quality in Mekhlis. On one occasion, after arriving in Moscow from Ukraine, I was on my way to see Malenkov in his office and met Mekhlis in the hallway. At that time Mekhlis was people's commissar of state control[7] for the USSR. He spoke heatedly, as always: "I've caught a thief!"

I asked him: "You caught only one? There's probably more than one thief still left in the Soviet Union."

He said: "Yeah, but do you know what they were stealing?"

"Well, what?"

"Airplane engines."

I said: "On that point I don't believe you. It's true that people might steal just about anything, but an airplane engine? Who would buy it? Why steal it? You can't eat it. You can't sell it. What would be the point of stealing it?"

I went into Malenkov's office, and Mekhlis went crashing in there too and continued the conversation. Malenkov, it turned out, had already looked into this question. Later I figured out what it was all about. There was a simple explanation. The factories at that time had daily plans they had to meet, and daily reports they had to submit. For example, a factory might be required to produce 100 engines per day, but if it made 101, it reported only 100, and if it made only 99, it would still report 100. In this way, with more on one day and less on another, the monthly production quota balanced out. But Mekhlis was counting all the extra engines that were reported and that didn't actually show up, and he decided they had been stolen. Later Stalin himself looked into the matter, and quite a stormy discussion ensued. I was surprised then that it took Stalin a long time to understand such a simple mechanism. There was a threat hanging over the heads of the factory directors, but in the end it was determined that no thievery had been involved. Mekhlis, of course, had messed up the whole business, and got the Politburo all worked up unnecessarily.

Another incident occurred in 1938, during the military operations at Lake Khasan,[8] When Mekhlis was the chief of the Political Directorate of the Red

Army, he went out to the Far and on his return told about all the wreckers he had found there, and how many enemies of the people there were! And how many people he had arrested. One "scoundrel" he had encountered in the Far East even had the last name Podlas [which sounds like the Russian word for "scoundrel," *podlets*].[9] He too had been arrested. I will tell about Podlas later on, what a remarkable man he actually was, and how splendidly he conducted himself during the Great Patriotic War despite the fact that he had not yet really been exonerated.

I want to tell, while I'm at it, about another episode that dates from 1939, it seems to me. When I arrived in Moscow on one occasion, I told Stalin what I had heard from my driver, Aleksandr Georgyevich Zhuravlev. He had driven for me many years, knew his business as a driver quite well, and loved his work. My attitude toward him was one of great respect and confidence. He said that the tires we were then receiving for our vehicles were quickly getting into a state of disrepair. They were not wearing out; they were breaking. The tread was still good and fresh, but the sides of the tires were bursting. I reported to Stalin that we were losing a lot because of this defect in production. I should note here that Stalin disliked it greatly when we criticized something of our own domestic manufacture. He would always listen with displeasure, and with obvious irritation he would order the defect corrected. In principle, I understand this feeling; it's a good attitude. Stalin didn't want people to grin, as it were, and make fun of our shortcomings. After all, they were short-comings of our Soviet system, and so he reacted to these critical comments in a touchy way and, with a great deal of anger, would order the shortcomings corrected and those at fault to be strictly punished. When I told him about the tires he flared up: "So you're criticizing? Everyone is endlessly criticizing. And who's going to do something? Well, we're going to assign you to look into this. Make proposals that will get rid of poor production and ensure the output of high-quality tires from the factories."

I answered: "I would be happy to undertake this job, but after all, I am totally unfamiliar with this type of production and have never had any dealings with this industry. I know my way around, more or less, in the coal industry, in metallurgy, and in construction, but tire production is completely unfamiliar to me."

[He answered:] "Well, make yourself familiar with it. Take this on right away!"

A government decree was issued, a special commission was formed, and I was confirmed as its chairman. Stalin emphasized: "Don't return to Ukraine until you've worked out proposals that make sense." To tell the truth, I was rather frightened; I didn't know how much time all this would take, and whether I could get to the bottom of the problem at all. Nevertheless I gathered the members of the commission together and summoned specialists from the Yaroslavl[10] tire factory and from Leningrad and from Moscow and invited people from research institutes associated with this branch of industry. In short, I gathered practically everyone who understood the essence of the matter. Officials of the Central Committee apparatus of the party helped me call in whoever I wanted, but I myself didn't really know who would be needed. Then I held a conference at the Central Committee offices and listened to what everyone had to say. An intense debate unfolded. Later I told Stalin what the general lines of debate were. Today I no longer remember who took what position, but the speech by the director of the Yaroslavl factory made an especially good impression on me. During my first meeting with Stalin [on this question], I told him that work had begun, that I had listened to the views of various people and expressed my own thoughts. He answered: "I advise you to go to Yaroslavl yourself and look into things right there on the scene. The Yaroslavl rubber production complex is our biggest plant in this branch of industry." I went to Yaroslavl and took some specialists from Moscow along with me.

In Yaroslavl the secretary of the party's province committee at that time was Patolichev,[11] who later became secretary of other province committees and republic-level committees of the party, as well as minister of foreign trade of the USSR. The chairman of the executive committee of the Yaroslavl Soviet was Gogosov,[12] who was still a young man, as Patolichev was, but he was not trained in chemistry. He was an engineer in the field of metallurgy. They both made a very good impression on me. The first thing I did when I arrived in Yaroslavl was to report to the local comrades about why I had come and ask them to provide assistance. I wanted to see exactly how tires were produced. I went to the complex and said to the director: "Don't tell me right now about your production process; that would be a pointless waste of time. Take me along the assembly line. I want to start from scratch." We went along the whole assembly line. At points in the operation that particularly interested me, we stood for a long time, and I had a thorough look at what the workers were doing.

It wasn't possible to make direct observations of the chemical process of vulcanization, which was carried out under special conditions. Here I relied on specialists, who described the process to me. I was especially fascinated by the techniques used by the workers applying the cord. They did this work artistically, very quickly, and almost without looking. They used their hands almost as though they were musicians. I marveled at them for a while and then began to ask about the technological process. I was told what role the cord played, how many layers of cord were put down, and how that was done. When they told me about it, I understood that this could be a weak point in the process of tire production. After all, I had seen how quickly the workers were doing their jobs. Could they really be laying the cord down carefully, going so fast? The cord needed to lie smoothly, and all the threads in each layer needed to be drawn equally tightly so that they would bear the load, as though, all together, they formed one solid thread. That way the firmness of one thread was multiplied by the total number of threads to make the entire layer resistant to any bursting or breakage. If a layer of cord was laid down unevenly, then each separate thread worked by itself, and the threads would break one by one. That's how the process of deterioration would occur. I had other questions, but this turned out to be the main thing. I had "latched on" to the basic defect in the production of the tires.

I had an exchange of opinions with the leadership of the factory, expressed my views, and then took a walk around the entire complex. Everything there was the same as at any factory: There was a bulletin board with an honor list where the photos of the best workers were posted, the "shock workers" as they were called then. I asked Mitrokhin,[13] the director of the factory: "Let me have the documentation for the technological process of tire production. I need to see what technology is recommended by scientists. After all, we bought this factory in America; and probably the Americans recommended some technological process to us. Get together the main documents for me and let me know what changes might have been made in the technological process." Then the members of our commission were broken down into groups. I assigned Gogosov to carry out the designated task, and Patolichev energetically joined in as well. We studied all the basic aspects of tire production. Soon they reported to me that they had found divergences from the technological process recommended by the firm from which we had bought the factory. One or two layers of cord had been dropped because the view held at the factory was that the quantity remaining was sufficient to ensure the durability of the tires. I felt that, most likely, this was "where the dog was buried," the source of the problem. They also reported that the gauge of the wire around the inner rim of the tire had been reduced in size and one or several rings of wire had been removed to lower production costs. The savings added up to a rather large amount. I asked: "When was this done?"

[The answer was:] "Kaganovich came here. (He was then in charge of the People's Commissariat of Heavy Industry.) He studied the production process and made these proposals." Thus the cause of the decline in quality of tire production became clear.

Sergo [Ordzhonikidze] had also visited Yaroslavl. But he was simply acquainting himself with the factory and encouraging the local people. The specific proposals for "improving" production had come from Kaganovich. I said: "All right, give me an official document so that I can report to Stalin and the Central Committee. You probably keep track of similar production processes in America, right? What is the productivity of labor for workers there?" It was explained that we had gone far ahead and had "surpassed" them. I said: "I need to know specifically, not in general. They have workers who attach the cord to the tires. What is their productivity of labor over there?"

They answered: "But that's precisely what we're talking about [when we say we've surpassed them], because after all this is manual labor." [That is, the Soviet manual laborers were working faster than their American counterparts.] But who needs this kind of "increased productivity of labor"?

A question was then brought up about the quality of the mixture of natural rubber and synthetic rubber. At that time synthetic rubber was not of very high quality, and so it was seasoned with natural rubber. A question was also raised about the quality of the ash that played an important role in the production of these items.

The commission prepared a draft resolution, and I returned to Moscow, where I reported on everything to Stalin, calling his attention to the fact that tires in our country were of poor quality because we ourselves, in trying to economize, had departed from the technical recommendations made by the firm that had sold us the plant. We were "correcting" the American engineers, but on the other hand, one of their tires would do the work of ten of ours. What kind of economizing is that? Then I told Stalin that I considered it a shortcoming to have too high a productivity of labor and too high a production quota, which also reflected negatively on the quality. It wasn't right to lower production costs and increase productivity of labor at the expense of quality. Of course an accumulation of funds did result from this, but in Yaroslavl they had obviously gone too far. More highly skilled workers were needed for laying the cord, and their production quotas needed to be reduced. All these people were on the honor list on the bulletin board—they were Stakhanovites and shock workers – but in fact they were damaging the material and making the work of drivers less successful because the tires were blowing out on the roads and normal work was made impossible. As a result we were not utilizing our pool of motor vehicles to fullest advantage.

Stalin listened to me closely. He was terribly upset, and I understood why. Such news would grate on anyone who cared about the government and the country, especially a person occupying a leading position. This aspect of Stalin's character pleased me. The reason that I have told the story about this particular episode is to show Stalin's statesmanlike approach to the problem. Of course he was a big man, an organizer, a leader. But he was also a terrible despot, and therefore he fought with despotic methods against the barbarism he encountered in our life. Stalin said: "I agree with you. Give us your proposals and we will approve them." There were many proposals for reducing production quotas and increasing pay to the workers, and a number of other measures were mentioned, suggested by specialists at the factory, at research institutes, and at the People's Commissariat [of Heavy Industry]. All the results of the labor of the best minds in this field were included in the draft resolution. Stalin added: "We have to prohibit competition and remove the bulletin board with the honor list at that factory." In principle I felt that this shouldn't be done, that competition was healthy. It was found everywhere in the capitalist countries, but we called it socialist emulation and they called it competition. The increased productivity of labor, which is forced into existence by the compulsion of competition, is the fundamental basis for the development of industry and the accumulation of value.

I was very pleased by the position Stalin took on this question, and it was also satisfying that with the help of specialists who I had brought into the matter, we had succeeded in groping around, feeling our way (and we really were just feeling our way) until we found the weak point in tire production, eliminated it, straightened out the production process, and ensured higher-quality output. Even then we felt the approach of war, and we knew its thunder and lightning would break loose soon. We also knew that the transportation system, which even in peacetime plays a decisive role, was necessary to ensure the mobility of the army in wartime. It was also satisfying that not only had shortcomings been eliminated and the original technological process restored, so that good-quality tires began to be produced, but also that this immediately increased the number of kilometers those tires would last, a figure several times greater than before. Furthermore, we proposed that tests be carried out at special proving grounds to determine how the tires wore, that certain qualities be singled out for testing in local areas and in the normal course of motor-vehicle travel, with strict accounting being made of how long the rubber lasted without need for repair. With the positive results it had achieved, the factory was given a bonus to encourage the workforce there, and measures were taken to improve cultural and domestic life for the employees. Before the war or at the beginning of the war, the director of the Yaroslavl complex became the people's commissar of the chemical industry of the USSR. It was pleasing to me that Stalin remembered him and my favorable comments about him and placed him in such a responsible post. He worked as people's commissar for a long time after that.

Let me repeat that Stalin was a typical despot who did a lot of harm, especially in regard to personnel. In his concern for the success of our state he was ruthless and often excessively so. His ruthlessness was also brought to bear in the elimination of shortcomings, since he took a zealous and proprietary attitude toward the interests of the state and fought against bureaucracy. This was a valuable feature in his character. But a great deal has been written about the positive aspects of his personality, and I am trying to show by certain specific examples the other sides of Stalin as a person. Those aspects did not disappear even when, toward the end of the 1930s, repression subsided somewhat and fewer people were being taken. The mass arrests were not as numerous, and civil society began to calm down somewhat. Most people thought that we had already destroyed all our internal enemies, that we had achieved that goal. In other words, people thought that the repression had been necessary and that our vigilance had helped to prevent counterrevolutionary attempts to overthrow Soviet power. The cadres in the party, in economic and scientific organizations, and in industry and agriculture became more stable, which contributed to the fulfillment of the third five-year plan.

But this good mood was ruined by the fact that a "big war" was inexorably approaching. All our citizens sensed this, but especially the leaders of the country. We made no secret of it. The German fascists and Hitler never stopped proclaiming that their goal was the destruction of the Soviet Union, the destruction of the Communists, the annihilation of the Soviet people, and the enslavement of the Slavs. I remember reading a translation of Hitler's book. When *Mein Kampf*[14] was distributed among us, I also got a copy. I forget how many pages I read, but I was morally unable to go through the whole thing, although I regret it now. I couldn't read it then because it literally repelled me. I couldn't look on calmly at such frothing at the mouth; it turned my stomach; I found it disgusting and had no patience for it. I threw it away without reading it to the end. Still, it was completely clear that Hitler wouldn't give up his main ideas and would, without fail, unleash a war against the USSR.

What was being done in our country to heighten the combat readiness of the Red Army, to improve its arms and equipment, and to provide its troops with the necessary technology? I knew hardly anything specifically, and I don't know how many things other members of the Politburo knew, because Stalin took all this as his own personal responsibility. We trusted Stalin and thought that he knew his way around on such questions and that, besides, he listened to the views of military men, specialists, engineers, scientists, and organizers of the Red Army. I should mention Voroshilov here. Stalin had friendly relations with him then and communicated with him every day. They discussed all questions of the defense of the country with each other directly. Who else might have known about these things? Perhaps Molotov. At that time he was also very close to Stalin. Other members of the Politburo and secretaries of the Central Committee, let alone ordinary members of the Central Committee, I assume did not know much about specific aspects of defense production, except in the case of individuals who were directly responsible for them. Anyone who wants to can look at the books and newspapers to see how our press at that time treated this subject: "The Thunder of Victory, Let It Roll!" Here, there, and everywhere people were repeating [a line from a Soviet song]: "If tomorrow there's war, if tomorrow we march, then today we are ready to go." The main idea was that we would smash the enemy on his own territory without giving up an inch of Soviet soil. Movies with themes corresponding to this were playing, articles in military journals spoke along the same lines, and the military equipment and technology that was paraded on May Day and in the November days [celebrating the Bolshevik revolution] also made quite an impression.

I personally was very pleased with the tank designed by the [American] engineer Christie.[15] It was, for those days, a very fast and highly maneuverable tank, and it made a good impression when the tank crews drove by at high speed in front of Lenin's tomb on Red Square in Moscow during parades. Other tanks and armored vehicles made a pretty good impression, too. But when the war began, these tanks turned out not to be good enough, because their armor was too thin and enemy shells pierced them easily. Our airplanes in general were pretty good, both the fighters and the bombers, but there were too few of them. As it turned out, we should have had many more of them, although in my opinion our technical level in military aviation corresponded to the general level of development of such science and technology at the time, as far as the tactical and technical details went. Perhaps over the course of time our airplanes proved better and the Germans' worse, or the other way around, but in general I would say we were not lagging behind to any great degree.

Our artillery was just fine. Throughout the war, including at the beginning of the war, it was no worse than the enemy's. The artillery troops knew their weapons and equipment well. Our rifles were also good. Our automatic weapons had been produced in good time, but apparently their value hadn't been properly appreciated, and therefore automatic submachine guns had not gone into mass production to be supplied to the army. Only after the war with Finland [in 1939–40],[16] when we saw that the Finns were armed almost to the last man with such rapid-fire weapons, did we take measures to organize mass production of these automatics. This was also done because it didn't require great material expenditure or technical effort. How the process of evaluation of the automatics was carried out, how and by whom the decision was made to produce them, I don't know, because all this was strictly Stalin's concern.

At that time I was absorbed with the idea of increasing the cross-country capabilities of our motor vehicles, and in that connection I proposed that we produce half-tracks. I made a report to Stalin. Stalin supported my idea, and the production of such vehicles was organized at the Likhachev auto plant (which was then called the Stalin auto plant). A large number of half-tracks were produced. But they didn't show themselves to the best advantage. Therefore criticism began to be directed at me. Stalin said nothing, but some other people, opponents of increased cross-country capability for our motor vehicles, who were also the proponents of other ideas, criticized me. It was very painful to me that I had pushed hard for something whose value was not borne out. Then the war began. We began to capture enemy materiel. I was surprised and astonished by something I saw near Rostov. I felt both pleasure and chagrin at the sight. It turned out that the enemy was using half-track vehicles. The enemy had taken into account the higher degree of moisture in the soil of the western territory of the USSR [where there are many marshes] and therefore had employed half-track vehicles. We, on the other hand, had not taken that into account because we expected to fight only on enemy soil, and we paid for that mistake.

In 1938 a military conflict was imposed on us by the Japanese at Lake Khasan. Today I could not relate exactly what the course of the fighting there was, and it was hard to make out the details from newspaper reports at the time. Apparently the fighting was not going exactly in the direction we would have wanted. Therefore we were soon obliged to send reinforcements. I found out about this from Mekhlis in his capacity as chief of the Political Directorate of the Red Army. He went to the Far East as Stalin's authorized representative. Mekhlis was a man whom Stalin trusted a great deal. At one time he had been Stalin's personal assistant, and later Stalin had sent him in to replace Bukharin as editor of *Pravda*. I had very good relations with

Mekhlis. As I've already said, I had made his acquaintance in 1929–30 when I was studying at the Industrial Academy and he was editor of *Pravda*. We were brought together by a friendship based on our joint efforts in combating the "Right Deviationists." Mekhlis gave me a lot of help in my capacity as secretary of the party organization at the Industrial Academy, where earlier the "right deviationists" had been completely dominant. When Mekhlis returned from the Far East I met with him. It's true that I hadn't previously been in touch with him as a friend, and for some time we hadn't even met in the line of duty. We just happened to meet by accident. Mekhlis told me about the events in the Far East. He was extraordinarily expansive and at the same time a rather bilious, irritable person, and when he talked about people he either praised them effusively or covered them with mud. (I remember him telling me about the people he had ordered arrested. I made a positive assessment of his actions at that time, thinking that he had saved our cadres from harm and improved the fighting capacity of the Red Army.)

The Japanese did not achieve their aims at Lake Khasan. The lake was dangerously close to the city of Vladivostok.[17] Their aim was to drive us from that position and from there to dominate the city. Their efforts were not crowned with success, and the conflict was ended. I don't know whether diplomatic steps were taken or whether everything was simply decided by the force of arms.

I don't remember how much time went by after the conflict at Lake Khasan before a new Japanese incursion happened, this time into the People's Republic of Mongolia.[18] Our troops were also stationed in that republic. The most important thing was to defend the region around the Khalkin-Gol River, to prevent the Japanese from moving in the direction of Lake Baikal.[19] The Japanese had even farther-reaching plans than that. They apparently wanted to smash Mongolia's military forces, occupy Mongolia, make a breakthrough to the Lake Baikal region, and cut us off from the Far East. Fighting flared up on a large scale with the use of all kinds of military forces. The Japanese threw a lot of infantry, artillery, tanks, and planes into the battle, and at first things went badly for us. Later, our forces were tightened up and the command structure was reinforced. Zhukov[20] was sent to command our forces there. He conducted that military operation quite well; he really distinguished himself. Later he showed his abilities to the fullest during the "big war" unleashed by Hitler. But at that point [in 1939] the Japanese forces were defeated, and the matter ended there. I don't know what diplomatic steps were taken in that connection, because the matter was not reported to the Politburo. Stalin and Molotov took care of it.

To understand why this was so, one had to know Stalin. Stalin considered the Central Committee and the Politburo as so much furniture, so to speak, necessary to decorate the home properly, but the main thing in the home was the man of the house. He of course considered himself the man of the house (the "master") and did everything necessary so as not to have to consult with anyone else if that didn't enter into his plans. He didn't report to anyone.

The defeat of the Japanese at Khalkin-Gol caused the harmful bacilli of complacency to grow further. It was as though people were saying to themselves: "See, that's our army. It's invincible. We've demonstrated this invincibility in practice. We crushed the samurai[21] at Lake Khasan and Khalkin-Gol." Folk ditties along these lines sprang up, and people began telling jokes and stories to the same effect, sometimes the kind that cannot be repeated in mixed company, "salty" jokes, the kind soldiers tell. This was all in keeping with the mood that arose after our victory over the Japanese.

Meanwhile history was taking its course. Enemy forces were doing everything to prepare for a mighty blow against the USSR. Ties between Hitler and Mussolini were strengthened more and more. Even earlier, as is generally known, the Anti-Comintern Pact[22] was signed. First there appeared the Berlin-Rome Axis. The warlike tendencies of the samurai impressed Hitler and Mussolini, and soon the Berlin Axis was extended eastward and began to be called the Rome-Berlin-Tokyo Axis. The threat to the Soviet Union was becoming more and more immediate. Hitler's Germany and Fascist Italy based their ideology of aggression on the claim that they did not have enough living space (in German, *Lebensraum*). That was the reason Mussolini gave for starting his war against Abyssinia (Ethiopia), and he was successful in defeating the Abyssinians despite the firmness they displayed in the struggle. The army of Abyssinia was weak; the Abyssinians fought mainly with primitive weapons, while Mussolini concentrated his forces, which were armed with modern equipment, and also sent in his warplanes. In fact it was a case of people being slaughtered, but the aim was achieved. Italy seized Abyssinia, and all the Western countries recognized this conquest.[23]

In general the situation that had taken shape was not favorable for us. The USSR, opposed by all the reactionary forces of both West and East, was in a position of hostile encirclement. We were probably going to have to fight alone against the powerful forces of Germany, Italy, and Japan. The Soviet people had not yet forgotten the defeats the Japanese had dealt the armies of the tsar in 1905 in Manchuria.[24] I don't remember exactly what year it was when a certain notorious incident took place, as follows. The

Japanese foreign minister had traveled to Berlin to make an agreement with Hitler on coordinating aggression against us. On his return trip, when this foreign minister, Matsuoka,[25] passed through Moscow, he quite unexpectedly wanted to meet with the Soviet leadership. Something incredible then happened. Stalin went to the railroad station and met with this Japanese envoy, on his way home from Berlin. Soon after that a neutrality pact was signed with Japan. Immediately there arose in us feelings of both satisfaction and the inevitability of war with Japan. We felt this was a foregone conclusion because, as we saw it, Japan regarded the treaty with the Soviet Union merely as something that would calm us down and make us relax our vigilance.

I didn't hear any comments like that from Stalin. Instead, he was carefully calculating what exactly had to be done to protect our borders from the direction of Japan. I assume that he had no confidence in the treaty with Japan. Everything done on both sides then was based on the specific circumstances that had arisen: a war was inevitable and for the time being it was necessary to do everything to somehow win time, everything that could be turned to our advantage. Time was the main thing because we no longer had the power to eliminate the imminent danger of war. We could only look for opportunities to prepare ourselves better for the war and, if we could manage it, to find allies, or at least to neutralize some of our opponents, to weaken the enemy front.

In Ukraine, to be sure, I didn't feel that this was immediately reflected in the situation on our border with Poland and Romania. In political respects Romania conducted itself in an extremely hostile way and rather stupidly besides. There were frequent occurrences of incidents of their border troops suddenly opening fire without any reason, if they saw our border troops on our territory. There were cases of people being wounded, and even some fatalities. Nevertheless, no major border incidents occurred. The explanation for all this was the literally physiological hatred felt toward us, the fear of the Soviet Union and of Soviet power, fear of the Communist Party, its ideology, its strength, and its influence on the masses, because Romania was actually a weak link in the capitalist world.

After Austria was swallowed up by Germany [with the *Anschluss* of March 1938], the fascist threat hung over Czechoslovakia. The Sudeten Germans in Czechoslovakia behaved arrogantly. The government of Czechoslovakia proved to be impotent or too short-sighted, and it took no decisive measures to suppress the antigovernment separatist movement aimed at the secession of the Sudetenland from Czechoslovakia. The final outcome was that Hitler began to threaten Czechoslovakia directly. Out of this came the four-power Munich Conference, which ended with England and France yielding to Hitler, giving him a free hand to take direct action against Czechoslovakia. Even earlier Hitler had won a decision in his favor about territories that after World War I had been under French control. There too France had yielded, so that Hitler was able to move his troops into the Rhineland without any military opposition and establish German sovereignty in that territory. We had a treaty with Czechoslovakia. We were supposed to come to its assistance if our treaty went into effect as part of the terms for fulfilling treaty obligations that existed between Czechoslovakia and France. Therefore when the threat was hanging over Czechoslovakia's head, we demonstrated our military intentions. I know that well, because as a member of the Military Council of the KOVO, I knew about the order to place the troops of the KOVO on a state of alert and to concentrate our main strike force in the Kamenetsk-Podolsky region along the Polish border.[26]

The Polish government displayed frenzied hostility toward us and would not agree to any discussions about heading off the danger we faced in common from the direction of Germany. For the USSR, the fascist danger could make itself felt mainly through Polish territory. The head of the Polish government at that time was Skladkowski,[27] and the foreign minister was Beck.[28] They didn't want to hear about the possibility of a united defense against Germany, and it may be that they were trying to buy themselves off somehow in relation to Germany by displaying their hostility toward the USSR. If they could have thought realistically even a little, they would have seen that Hitler's Germany had aspirations not only to take over Poland but also to claim an enormous *Lebensraum*. Hitler intended at the minimum to seize Ukraine in addition to Poland. The Germans talked openly about this. So circumstances themselves were making allies of Poland and us. However, despite the real threat from the West, the Polish government did not understand the necessity for uniting our efforts against Hitler and in that way perhaps restraining Hitler from attacking both Poland and the Soviet Union.

In view of the situation shaping up it was reported to Kiev (I didn't hear this personally from Stalin; it was transmitted through military men) that it might become necessary for our troops to make their way by force across Polish territory to Czechoslovakia to provide it with assistance. This was a very complicated matter, if you take into consideration the geographic location, the area in which our troops were concentrated. Our army group was, relatively speaking, not that big. If we had moved forward along the indicated route toward Czechoslovakia, the Poles naturally would have hit us in the flanks. It would not have been such an easy matter to suddenly force our way through beyond the Carpathians under such circumstances.[29] In this case Hitler would probably have come to the "aid" of Poland. In short, a complicated situation had arisen.

However, France suddenly solved the problem in a fundamental way. It refused to honor its commitments under the treaty with Czechoslovakia and thereby placed that country in the lion's mouth of Hitler. Hitler was given the opportunity to do as he pleased. At first he seized the Sudetenland; then the Prague government resigned, and the president agreed to the establishment of a German "protectorate." To seize the rest of Czechoslovakia was now much easier. Bohemia and Moravia were occupied, and an "independent" puppet government was set up in Slovakia. Fascists who supported Hitler entered the Slovak government. They in fact were traitors to the Slovak people and allies of fascist Germany. Later they took part in the war against the USSR on Hitler's side.

When military representatives of Britain and France came to the USSR to hold talks on coordinating military efforts in the event of a war that might be unleashed by Germany, it turned out to be pointless for us to have talks with them. In spring or summer 1939, arriving in Moscow from Kiev and sitting at Stalin's table, I heard an exchange of opinions on this subject. The opinion was expressed that the British and French didn't actually want to unite with us, but were intentionally dragging out unproductive negotiations to encourage Hitler to take action against the Soviet Union and to satisfy the fascist demands at the expense of territory to the east. One day in August, on a Saturday, I arrived from Kiev and visited Stalin at his dacha. He told me that all the members of the Politburo were coming to his place then, and he would report to them that on the next day the German foreign minister, Ribbentrop,[30] would be arriving in our country. He looked at me and smiled, waiting to see what impression this news would make on me. I looked at him, thinking that he was joking: The very idea that Ribbentrop would be flying in to visit us! What was this all about? Was he getting ready to flee Germany and seek asylum? Stalin said: "Hitler sent a telegram. Germany's Ambassador Schulenburg[31] delivered it. The telegram says: 'Dear Mr. Stalin, I request that you receive my minister, Ribbentrop, who will bring specific proposals with him.'" Stalin added: "Tomorrow we will meet him."

"Tomorrow" turned out to be August 23, 1939. The date stuck in my memory. I was getting ready to go hunting on that day at the Zavidovo hunting area,[32] which had been established in the Moscow Military District. Voroshilov was in charge of this hunting preserve, and it was used mainly by military personnel. Never having been there, I was preparing for my first visit. Bulganin, Malenkov, and I had agreed to go there as a threesome. I told Stalin I was planning to go hunting the next day. He answered: "All right, go ahead. Molotov and I will receive Ribbentrop and hear what he has to say; then when you come back from hunting I'll tell you what Hitler's aims are and what the results of our talk were." That's what we did. The three of us traveled by night to the hunting preserve. When we arrived at Zavidovo, Voroshilov was already there. Consequently, he too was absent from Stalin's meeting with Ribbentrop. Other military men were there along with Vorishilov. It was quite a crowd. We went hunting, the weather was marvelous, warm and dry, and we had good luck with our hunting. I hope I won't sound like a typical, boasting hunter, but I really did manage to kill one duck more than Voroshilov. Why do I mention this? Because everywhere in our country there was a big uproar about so-called marksmen of the Voroshilov type. Supposedly Voroshilov was a better shot with a rifle or shotgun than anyone else. In fact he was a good marksman, but in the press campaign about this there was a bootlicking spirit of fulsome flattery.

When I returned from the hunting trip, I immediately went to see Stalin. I brought him ducks "for the common soup kettle," as the saying goes. All the members of the Politburo present in Moscow were supposed to gather at Stalin's place. I boasted about my success as a hunter. Stalin was in a good mood and was joking. His attitude toward hunting varied. Sometimes he was eager to go hunting himself, but at other times (apparently depending on his mood) he spoke harshly against hunting, not from the point of view of people who say that all living things should be protected, but from the point of view of someone condemning a pointless waste of time. Well, it may be that he didn't go hunting much, but he nearly always wasted his time more than any other highly placed leader of the country. I am thinking of the time wasted sitting around the table drinking wine, having endless lunches and suppers. Sometimes he even commented in an unflattering way about Lenin in connection with hunting. Everyone knew that Lenin loved to hunt and went hunting a lot. Some people have written that Lenin supposedly went hunting to have direct encounters with ordinary people in an unofficial capacity and have heart-to-heart talks with them. That probably did happen of course. But I don't think that that was the main thing. Lenin was no stranger to the pleasures of human diversion, and he loved to hunt. He simply had a passion for hunting. That's why he went hunting even when he was in Siberian exile and later in Moscow when he was chairman of the Council of People's Commissars. It was his way of relaxing, to go hunting.

It would have been possible to have unofficial encounters with people without taking shotgun in hand and leaving the city.

When I was secretary of the Moscow Committee of the party, I would go hunting in the Ramenskoye district.[33] I don't remember what village the Chekists recommended to me for a hunting place. I was met by a professional huntsman and guide, a tall, old man. I had been warned in advance that he had previously hunted with Lenin in the local forests and marshes. We took shelter for the night in a hayloft, and there he told me about how Lenin had come hunting and what their hunting together had been like. In the morning we went out, but there was a heavy downpour, and I tramped around for nothing all day long without once firing a shot. No game birds were to be seen, and I felt sorry not so much for myself, for not shooting anything, as for the old huntsman. The poor fellow was feeling terrible and kept apologizing, although of course it was nobody's fault. But with this talk about hunting, I have, so to speak, departed from my main theme.

We gathered at Stalin's place on the evening of August 23. While the prizes we had taken during our hunt were being prepared for serving at our table, Stalin told us that Ribbentrop had already flown back to Berlin. He had come with the draft of a nonaggression treaty, which we had signed. Stalin was in a very good mood. He said, "Look, the British and French are going to find out about this tomorrow, and they're going to leave empty-handed." They were still in Moscow at the time. Stalin had a correct appraisal of the meaning of that treaty with Germany. He understood that Hitler wanted to trick us but was just outfoxing himself. He suggested that it was we, the USSR, who had outwitted Hitler by signing the treaty. Stalin then told us that under this treaty in fact Estonia, Latvia, Lithuania, Bessarabia, and Finland would be allotted to us in such a way that we ourselves could decide with their governments the fate of those territories, while Hitler's Germany would stay out of the matter. This would be strictly our business. In regard to Poland, Stalin said that Hitler would attack it, occupy it, and make it his protectorate. The eastern part of Poland, inhabited by Belorussians and Ukrainians would be allotted to the Soviet Union. Naturally we were in favor of this latter arrangement, although we had mixed feelings. Stalin understood this. He said to us: "There's a game going on here to see who can best outwit and deceive the other."

I didn't see the actual treaty with Germany. I don't think anyone among us saw it except for Molotov, Stalin, and some officials of the People's Commissariat of Foreign Affairs who were involved with the matter. In the Politburo we viewed these events as follows: A war was about to begin, with the West encouraging Hitler to go at it with us, one on one. With the signing of this treaty, as it turned out, Hitler would be the one to start the war, which was advantageous for us from the military, political, and moral point of view. By his actions he would challenge Britain and France to declare war on him, because he would be attacking their ally Poland. As for ourselves, we would remain neutral. I think that for us the situation was the best one possible at the time, because Britain and France wanted to send Germany against us for a one-on-one confrontation, so that they could sit back and rub their hands with glee, buying Hitler off from attacking them at the expense of our blood, our territory, and our riches. As for Poland, it had conducted an entirely irrational, unintelligent policy. It hadn't wanted to hear anything about uniting our efforts against Germany, even though that would have been in its own best interests. And so we simply had no other alternative.

If we look at the war as a kind of political game, it could be said that an opportunity had arisen in this game for us to keep our head from being exposed to enemy bullets, and so the treaty with Germany had justification. I still think that's true. Nevertheless it was very painful. After all, we were Communists, antifascists, people who held positions that were absolutely the opposite [of the Nazis']—yet suddenly we were linking our efforts with Nazi Germany. All of our ordinary citizens felt that way. Even for us leaders, it was hard to understand and digest this event, to find justification for what had happened to explain it to other people, basing ourselves on this justification. It was extremely difficult, even with all our understanding of the situation, to argue and try to show others that the treaty was advantageous for us, that we were forced to take this step, and that it was to our benefit.

1. S. K. Timoshenko. See Biographies. At the time of the events described, Timoshenko was an army commander of the first rank.

2. That is, during the Civil War. [GS]

3. The Irpen River is a small river that has its source somewhat to the southwest of Kiev and flowed into the Dnieper River to the north of Kiev. It now flows into the Kiev reservoir. [AH]

4. Until 1934 this body was called the Revolutionary Military Council. Then it became the Military Council attached to the people's commissar of defense. From 1936 it was named the Chief Military Council of the Workers' and Peasants' Red Army.

5. At that time K. Ye. Voroshilov was people's commissar of defense, Ye. A. Shchadenko and G. I. Kulik were his deputies, and L. Z. Mekhlis was

head of the Main Political Administration of the Workers' and Peasants' Red Army.

6. The Don is one of Russia's greatest rivers. It flows through the southern part of European Russia to the west of the Volga into the Sea of Azov, an inlet of the Black Sea. [SS]

7. The people's commissar of state control headed the People's Commissariat of State Control, which was responsible for inspecting state institutions with a view to exposing corruption, theft, and other abuses. [SS]

8. Lake Khasan is situated about 80 miles southwest of Vladivostok in the Primorye (Maritime) Territory of Russia's Far East. It is just east of the Soviet border with China. [SS] N. S. Khrushchev is referring to the armed conflict that took place around the lake in July and August 1938. The

Japanese government had unleashed the conflict after demanding the withdrawal of Soviet border guards from the heights of Bezymyannaya and Zaozernaya west of Lake Khasan in the Primorye (Maritime) Territory of the RSFSR. The aggressor was repulsed by the Red Banner Far Eastern Front.

9. K. P. Podlas. See Biographies.

10. Yaroslavl is situated about 300 kilometers northeast of Moscow. [SS]

11. N. S. Patolichev. See Biographies.

12. V. A. Gogosov.

13. T. B. Mitrokhin. See Biographies.

14. Hitler wrote *Mein Kampf* (My Struggle) in 1924, while imprisoned in the Landsberg Fortress following the failure of the Nazis' Munich putsch. In the book he tells his life story, explains his political philosophy, and sets out the program of the German National Socialist Workers' or Nazi Party. An accessible English-language translation of the book was published in 1999 by Houghton Mifflin Company. [SS]

15. J. Walter Christie was a prominent weapons designer. See Biographies. The Soviet modification of Christie's tank was called the BT. [SS]

16. The Soviet Union attacked Finland following the rejection of an ultimatum from Stalin that Finland cede a portion of its territory west of Leningrad to increase the strategic depth of the city's defense. The Finns put up strong resistance, and the Red Army achieved only part of its war aims and only at the cost of enormous casualties. [SS]

17. Vladivostok is the most important port on Russia's Pacific coast in the Far East. It is situated in the south of the Primorye (Maritime) territory. The name means "ruler of the East." [SS]

18. Khrushchev is referring to the armed conflict that took place between May and September 1939 by the Khalkhin-Gol River in Mongolia to the east of Lake Buir-Nur. Japanese forces from the territory of Japanese-occupied Manchuria tried without success to conquer part of the territory of the Mongolian People's Republic. They were repulsed by Mongolian and allied Soviet forces.

19. Lake Baikal is a large crescent-shaped body of freshwater in eastern Siberia. It is strategically important because it lies abreast the Trans-Siberian railroad and other transportation arteries connecting European Russia with Russia's Far East. [SS]

20. Corps Commander G. K. Zhukov commanded the grouping of Soviet and Mongolian forces from June 1939, while general coordination of combat operations was provided by Army Commander of the Second Rank G. M. Shtern.

21. The samurai were the warrior aristocracy of feudal Japan. [SS]

22. The Anti-Comintern Pact was signed initially by Germany and Japan in November 1936. Italy acceded to the pact in 1937, and Spain in 1939 (after General Franco came to power). The signatories pledged to cooperate against the threat of "communistic disintegration" of their states. [SS]

23. Fascist Italy launched a full-scale invasion of Abyssinia in October 1935. The invasion succeeded despite Abyssinian appeals to the League of Nations. An Italian attempt to invade Abyssinia in 1896 had failed. [SS]

24. The reference is to the Russo-Japanese war in Manchuria in 1904–5, in which tsarist Russia was defeated, the first defeat of a European power in war by a non-European power. The defeat triggered the first Russian Revolution of 1905. [SS]

25. Yosuke Matsuoka was the minister of foreign affairs of Japan in 1940 and 1941.

26. At this time western Ukraine was part of Poland, and the Kamenetsk-Podolsk region was the westernmost section of Soviet Ukraine. [SS]

27. General Felicjan Slawoj-Skladkowski was the prime minister of Poland from May 1936 to September 1939. See Biographies.

28. Jozef Beck was the minister of foreign affairs of Poland from 1932 to 1939.

29. The Carpathian Mountains stretch from southern Poland through western Ukraine into Romania. They formed a natural barrier between Soviet Ukraine and Czechoslovakia. [SS]

30. Joachim von Ribbentrop was the minister of foreign affairs of Germany from 1938 to 1945. See Biographies.

31. Count F. V. von Schulenburg was the German ambassador to the USSR from 1934 to 1941. See Biographies.

32. The Zavidovo hunting area or reserve had been created by the managerial agencies of the Moscow Military District in July 1929.

33. The Ramenskoye district is in Moscow province southeast of Moscow. It is now a suburban area. [SS]

## THE BEGINNING OF THE SECOND WORLD WAR

When the Germans moved against Poland on September 1, [1939,] our troops were concentrated on the border. I was also with the troops then as a member of the Military Council of the Ukrainian Front,[1] with the very units that were supposed to conduct operations in the direction of Ternopol.[2] Also in that area was the commander of the troops of that Front,[3] Timoshenko, who had previously headed the Kiev Special Military District.

As the Germans were approaching the territories that under the August pact were transferred from Poland to the USSR, our troops were moved onto Polish territory on September 17. By then Poland had virtually ceased to resist the Germans. The defenders in Warsaw and some other locations were offering scattered resistance, but organized opposition by the Polish army as a whole had been crushed. Poland turned out to have been completely unprepared for this war. How much showing-off there had been, how much false pride, how much scorn toward our proposal for uniting antifascist efforts—and what a downfall the Polish military machine suffered!

When we crossed the border, we encountered no resistance. Our troops reached Ternopol very quickly. Timoshenko and I traveled through the city and returned from there by way of a different road, which was not very intelligent after all, because some armed Polish units were still active and they could have detained us. He and I traveled this way through several small settlements inhabited by Ukrainians and through bigger towns with a fairly large Polish element; moreover, we were in areas where no Soviet troops were yet present, so that anything could have happened. As soon as we returned to our own forces, we were told that Stalin was asking for us on the phone. We reported to him on how the operation was going.

I don't remember now how many days it took us to actually complete the campaign; it seems to me it took two or three days.[4] If we reached Ternopol on the first day, we arrived in Lvov probably on the second or third day. The Germans were also approaching that city, but we were a little ahead of them, although neither they nor we had actually entered Lvov as yet. The question then arose of how to avoid confrontations between our troops and the Germans. We decided to establish communication with the Germans. For that purpose Yakovlev,[5] who was then commanding the artillery of the Kiev Special Military District, was sent on behalf of the Soviet forces. He knew a little German and personally undertook negotiations with the commander of the German troops approaching Lvov from the west. The commander of our units in that area was Golikov.[6] I went to visit him. His headquarters were located not far from Lvov in a field covered with haystacks. Talks with the Germans ended fairly quickly. They wanted to enter Lvov first; they wanted the chance to plunder the resources of the city. But since our troops were positioned right nearby, they didn't want to demonstrate hostility at that moment; they wanted to show that they were abiding by the August pact, and so they said: "Go ahead, please."

Our troops entered Lvov and then Drogobych and Borislav,[7] from which the Germans retreated, and we finally reached the border that had been specified by the August pact. Some territories that were designated as ours had already been occupied by the Germans, but Hitler was playing for big stakes and did not want to cause conflicts with us over "trifles." On the contrary, he wanted to show he was "a man of his word" and to have us favorably disposed toward him. So the German troops were partially withdrawn, and our troops came up to the borderline designated by the treaty that Ribbentrop and Molotov had signed. That was how the first phase of those events ended.

A big rise in the morale of our troops could be observed, as well as among the Soviet people, in connection with the incorporation of these western lands. Ukraine had long aspired to unite all of the Ukrainian people in one single country. These lands had historically really been Ukrainian and were inhabited by Ukrainians, except of course for the cities. Lvov, for example, had a large Polish population, which constituted a majority there. Sometimes this [Polish presence in the cities] was the result of artificial policies promoting Polish settlement. For example, in Lvov Ukrainians were never hired for jobs, not even for paving the streets. Blatant discrimination was carried out so that there would be a larger Polish population in the cities, serving as a base of support for the Polish government along the border that had been established as a result of the invasion of Soviet Russia by the armies of Pilsudski in 1920.[8] At that time some territories had become part of Poland, although before World War I they had been part of the Russian empire.

Our Soviet land had been weak, back then, and not able to defend the former borders between tsarist Russia and the Austro-Hungarian empire. The Poles had occupied these and other territories inhabited mainly by Ukrainians and Belorussians, and they brought a Polish population to settle along the borders, calling these people *osadniki* (settlers). There were even peasants among them, but they too served as a base of support for the Warsaw government along the border with the USSR.

The unification of the peoples of Ukraine and Belorussia, and later the incorporation of the countries of the eastern Baltic region into the Soviet

Union—these events were correctly perceived by the Soviet people, and they poured out into the streets in a celebration by the whole population. We unconditionally praised Stalin's farsightedness, his statesmanlike wisdom, his concern for our country, his ability to solve problems pertaining to the strengthening of the USSR, making our Soviet borders more invincible than ever. After all, this was no laughing matter. We had established ourselves on the Baltic and moved our borders, which had formerly stood very close to Kiev, far to the west. As for the fact that we had concluded a nonaggression pact with the Germans, I think an absolute majority of party members perceived it as just a tactical measure. This was a correct understanding, although we couldn't talk about it and didn't talk about it openly. Even at party meetings we didn't talk about it. Many people could not accept the idea that there could be some sort of agreement, even the possibility of peaceful coexistence, between us Communists and Hitler, when our ideas were absolutely opposed to those of the fascists. With Germans in general, yes, but with Hitler such a thing seemed impossible.

Stalin's calculation was that with the signing of the treaty we could avoid war for a little while longer. Stalin assumed that a war would start between Germany on the one side and France and Britain on the other. Possibly America would also be drawn into that war. We would have the possibility of maintaining neutrality and consequently preserving our strength. And later on we would see. When I say "We would see," I mean that Stalin did not by any means presume we would remain neutral until the war was over: at some stage we would enter the war, no matter what. That is my understanding of the events of that time looking back at them from the present—or more exactly, looking back from the future.

If we are to speak at this point about the national interests of the Ukrainians, the fact is that they still had not been fully satisfied by the above-mentioned treaty. There is another well-known treaty that was signed after World War I by the former allies of tsarist Russia. It delineated the western borders of Russia as a member of the Entente and an ally of the Western powers, and it was called the Curzon line.[9] Relative to the line designated by the Ribbentrop-Molotov treaty, the Curzon line had been located farther west. Therefore the Ukrainians felt they had been shortchanged somewhat in regard to those territories that were recognized as Ukrainian, even by the former allies of Russia, as a result of the defeat of the German bloc in World War I. Still, the first stage of military-political tension had temporarily passed, and a certain relaxation set in for us. In our estimation that stage had been completed to the advantage of the USSR, even though we had not received everything that we had coming to us historically. The only "extra" we got, it seems, was around the city of Bialystok,[10] where people of Polish nationality had lived since ancient times.

After the defeat of Hitler Germany in World War II, the borderline there was corrected and that region was transferred to Poland. Moreover, some territories with purely Belorussian and Ukrainian populations went to Poland. Apparently Stalin made concessions to "mollify" the touchy pride of the Poles. I would say that this was a case of political game-playing on a new basis so as to minimize the unpleasant aftertaste remaining among the Polish people as a result of the treaty we signed with Ribbentrop. After all, it seemed as though we had handed over Poland to be torn apart by Hitler Germany and had taken part in the operation ourselves. The truth is that Poland acquired at the same time [at the end of World War II] a fatter chunk—to speak crudely—of territory to the west. It acquired enormous and rich territories, significantly in excess of those that had been returned to Ukraine and Belorussia. Those were the western territories along the border formed by the rivers Oder and Neisse, and besides that they obtained the German city of Stettin [Polish name, Szczecin], which was located on the left, or western, bank at the mouth of the Oder River.[11] It too was awarded to Poland as a result of pressure by the USSR on our allies during the negotiations at the Potsdam Conference.

In 1939 we were certain that the Polish people—the workers, peasants, and intellectuals—would correctly grasp the necessity for the Soviet-German treaty. It was not our fault that we signed such a treaty. It was the fault of the unintelligent Polish government of the time, which was blinded by anti-Soviet hatred and was also hostile to the workers and peasants of its own country. Poland was afraid to make contact with the Soviet Union in order not to encourage freedom-loving ideas and strengthen the Communist Party of Poland, which it feared more than anything. If indeed we had united our efforts with Poland and made war jointly against Germany, the fate of the Polish government would have depended on the Polish people. I also think that the 1939 treaty signed by Molotov and Ribbentrop was inevitable for us in the situation that had arisen. And not because it was advantageous to the Soviet Union. It was a move in a chess game. That's how it must be seen, because if we hadn't done that, a war against us would have started all the same, but perhaps in a situation less favorable for us.

So then, the war had already started, but we were able to stay on the sidelines for the time being. We were granted a breathing space. I believe this was a correct step even though it was very painful.

What was especially painful was the fact that it proved completely impossible to explain the advantages of this treaty in a meaningful way. We couldn't say openly that it was just a chess move, because we had to keep the game going with Germany. The game required that we not let Hitler see our cards. It was necessary to explain things in the way that we did at that time, using the language of journalism. This was disagreeable because no one believed these explanations, and some people displayed an outright inability to understand. They really thought that Hitler had sincerely made an agreement with us, and there was nothing we had to explain through the press to suggest that people should not really believe it. In short, a very difficult situation arose from the point of view of our propaganda. Hitler, too, was just making a tactical move. He signed the treaty to gain time and to deal with his adversaries one at a time. The first thing he wanted was to clear a way for himself to the east by destroying Poland and at the same time coming into direct contact with our troops and coming right up to the Soviet border. When he made his blitzkrieg attack on Poland, he apparently thought that England and France would not dare to declare war on Germany, even though they had a treaty with Poland, which stated that if Germany attacked Poland, they would come to its aid.

And indeed, England and France did declare war on Germany. That's what served as the start of World War II, but we were still not taking part in the war. We were only moving our troops to the west, and establishing a new border, that is, as we explained it to people back then, we were taking the fraternal peoples of western Ukraine and western Belorussia under our wing, to protect them.

And so World War II began. But it did not immediately become a major war. The period of what was called "phony war" ensued. The French and British declared war against Germany, concentrated their forces, and brought up their reserves. Britain transferred troops to the continent of Europe and conducted military maneuvers in a demonstrative way. As for the French, they were apparently quite confident about the invulnerability of their reinforced Maginot Line. They had been building it for many years, and it really did have great significance for the way the defense of their country was organized. But a single line of defense fortifications does not ensure the security of a country; it is only one material aspect. A country must be defended by people, such as the ones that would be stationed at this line of fortifications. Hitler also built a line of fortifications, which was called the Siegfried Line. Thus their troops stood face to face with each other. But for the time being, Hitler took no active steps against Britain and France, while they too carried out no active military operations against Germany. Germany had thrown most of its troops against Poland on its eastern front and needed time to regroup its forces.

Then Mussolini began military operations against Greece and got bogged down. Later, Hitler attacked Yugoslavia and made short work of it because Germany was stronger; he occupied Denmark and Norway almost without firing a shot, then seized Holland virtually without resistance, invaded Belgium, and in 1940 seized the greater part of France. Thus he ensured himself a defensive line against the British fleet along a fairly lengthy stretch of seacoast, and in the north he moved right up next to our city of Murmansk [near the border with Norway]. It was natural that the Soviet government at the same time carried out measures flowing from the treaty signed by Molotov and Ribbentrop. We began in the fall of 1939 by holding talks with Estonia, Latvia, and Lithuania and presenting them with our conditions. In the situation that had arisen, these countries correctly realized that they could not stand up against the Soviet Union, and they accepted our proposals, signing mutual-assistance treaties with us. Then changes of government occurred within those countries. This was only to be expected! Some of their leaders, for example, Smetona,[12] the Lithuanian president, fled to Germany. But that was no longer particularly important. In short, governments that were disposed in a friendly way toward the Soviet Union were established. The Communist parties of those countries had the opportunity to function legally. Progressive forces expanded their work among the mass of workers, peasants, and intellectuals in favor of firm friendship with the USSR. This all ended after a little while with the establishment of Soviet power in those countries.

As for western Belorussia and western Ukraine we immediately set about organizing Soviet structures in the areas that became part of the USSR in 1939. At first the new form of power was not given official, legal form because our troops had been there only a short time. Instead we established provisional revolutionary organs of power locally. The people of the western regions of Ukraine greeted us quite warmly. True, the Polish population felt itself oppressed, but the Ukrainian population felt liberated. At public gatherings that we organized, the Ukrainians gave very revolutionary speeches, although not all of them, of course, because the nationalist element was also strong in those areas. The Ukrainian nationalist movement had grown strong under Austro-Hungarian rule, and now it waged a battle against the Communists and against Soviet influence, especially in Lvov, where a large social stratum of Ukrainian intellectuals was located. A special branch of the

Ukrainian Academy of Sciences even functioned in Lvov. It seems to me that it was headed by Academician Studinsky.[13] Pitro Franko, son of the great Ukrainian writer Ivan Franko, also belonged to this group of people. In my view he was the least successful product of Ukrainian classical literature, a very unintelligent person. He behaved in a rather unstable way in relation to us: at one moment he seemed to be supporting us, and the next moment he inclined toward our opponents.

In Lvov and other western Ukrainian cities, there was also a large Jewish element, both among the workers and among the intellectuals. I don't remember whether anything negative or anti-Soviet was coming from that part of the population. Among the Jewish workers and intellectuals there were many Communists. The organization of the Communists there was called the Communist Party of Western Ukraine. Both Ukrainians and Jews belonged to it. When we held a big public meeting in the Lvov opera theater, we invited everyone, Ukrainians, Jews, and Poles, to come there—mainly workers, although intellectuals also came. Jews spoke at that meeting, among others, and it was strange for us to hear what they said: "We *Zhidy* (Jews) proclaim in the name of the *Zhidy*" and so on. It turned out that in Polish the Jews called themselves *Zhidy*.[14] They called themselves that in everyday speech without intending any offensive meaning. But we Soviet citizens perceived it as an insult to the Jewish people. Later, in the hallways outside the public meeting I asked them: "Why do you speak that way about the Jews? You're using the word *Zhid*. That's insulting!"

They answered: "But for us it's considered insulting when we are called Jews." It was very strange for us to hear this, but we got used to it. But if you look at Ukrainian literature, there too the word *Zhid* is not always used in an insulting way; sometimes it just designates a nationality, as it were. There's a Ukrainian song that has the line, "We'll sell to you, red-headed *Zhid*." So the word *Zhid* is also used in Ukrainian. This episode impressed itself on my memory because it contrasted so sharply with our usual practice and what we were used to.

In general there were a lot of good people who welcomed us there; only I have forgotten their names. They were people who had passed through Polish prisons; they were Communists who had been tried and tested by life itself. However, their parties had been dissolved by a decision of ours, both the Communist Party of Poland and the Communist Party of Western Ukraine. Why? According to our understanding, they needed to have their credentials checked, even though their members had been Communists and had won this proud title in the class struggle. Many of them had the experience of

Polish prisons behind them, and so why was it necessary to check their credentials? Well, we had different concepts back then. We viewed them as possible enemy agents who had not yet been exposed. The idea was that not only did they need to have their credentials checked but that this should be done under a special high-powered microscope or magnifying glass. A great many of them, after being liberated from German rule by our Red Army, ended up in our own Soviet prisons. Unfortunately that's exactly the way things were. Without doubt there were provocateurs among them, probably even spies. But you can't look at every person who comes to you with his heart on his sleeve as someone being smuggled in as an agent, who is adapting himself and trying to worm his way into your confidence. This kind of thinking creates a vicious circle. If you base everything on that, what will it lead to? I've already talked about this earlier.

How did the Polish population respond to our arrival? It reacted in a very negative way, which is understandable to me. First, the Poles felt, and it was a fact, that their country had been deprived of its independence. They said: "How many partitions of Poland have there been, and which number is this one now, the fifth or sixth? And who is doing the partitioning once again? Previously we were partitioned by Germany, Austria, and Russia, and now?" This was how the events were viewed by people opposed to our action: "Russia has once again partitioned Poland, suppressed its independence, denied its self-determination, divided it up between itself and Germany!"

I remember traveling from Drogobych to Borislav to look at the petroleum plant there (actually there were two oil refineries) to try to obtain some petroleum and natural gas and at the same time to listen to what people were saying. I arrived at this petrochemical plant. It had been pretty thoroughly battered. The Germans had done this when they withdrew before our arrival, and they knew what they were doing. They destroyed the main systems for the refining of petroleum. When I arrived, there was simply a pile of ashes and debris of some sort that people were walking around. I began talking with them. They turned out to be middle-aged Poles, whose morale was pretty low. I was wearing a semimilitary uniform, that is, a soldier's blouse and a military overcoat, but no insignia, and so they saw me as a military person, no less.

I began questioning them, taking care to be very polite. One of them said in a broken voice: "How did we ever end up in a situation like this? They've really done it to us," and then he stopped. He went on again, expressing by hints and indirection not so much outright anger and dissatisfaction as sorrow and despair over what had happened. I could understand that.

But there was a young man present who started talking in Ukrainian. He joined in the discussion and began arguing harshly against the Pole. Understanding that he was a Ukrainian, I asked him what he did. He answered: "I'm an engineer. The only Ukrainian engineer at this plant. You don't know how hard it was under Polish rule to get an education, and how hard it was once you had an education to find a job."

The Pole looked at the Ukrainian with a pleading, pathetic expression in his eyes and made an appeal to his conscience: "What are you saying here?" He was evidently afraid to have this Ukrainian talking to a representative of Soviet power, and a "military man" at that, in such an unflattering way about the people he had worked with at this plant. Perhaps he feared for his own fate. I also began to counter the Pole's arguments. I don't remember now exactly what I said, but it was something along the lines that the Ukrainian was right because the Poles really had pursued an unintelligent domestic policy toward the Ukrainians. That was understandable to me because Soviet Ukraine was right next to them, a powerful component of the Soviet Union, and the Polish government was afraid of its influence. The Polish government regarded the Ukrainians as agents of Soviet Ukraine, who had not yet been exposed, and reacted accordingly.

We brought together members of the Polish intelligentsia to have joint discussions with them. There turned out to be quite a few of them on the territory occupied by our troops. I found out that among them was the writer Wanda Lwowna Wasilewska,[15] whose voice had been clearly heard among the Polish intelligentsia. Later I got to know her, and we became very close friends. She was a very sweet, intelligent, and decent person. At first she had been a member of the Polish Socialist Party (Polish initials PPS), and later she had become a Communist. This member of the PPS had written books that by no means won the approval of the PPS government of Poland, because she wrote mostly about the Ukrainian and Belorussian poor, spent a lot of time in those areas, studied the life and customs of the people, and reflected this in her writings aimed against the powers that be. This also determined her place in Polish society. As I recall, she even ended up under arrest at one time. Why am I dwelling now on the question of Wanda Wasilewska? Good memories of this woman have stayed with me, a major public figure, a devoted citizen, and a person of irreproachable honesty and directness. I respected her greatly for this. I personally heard her say very unpleasant things directly to Stalin's face. In spite of that, he listened to her, invited her to official discussions, as well as to unofficial comradely suppers and dinners, and he did so more than once. What a strong character

Wasilewska had! Then I was told that Wasilewska was in one of the regions occupied by our troops. She had fled from Warsaw after it had been taken by the Germans and reached our territory by foot. And so we waited for her. I was excited and curious to see what kind of Wasilewska this would be.

Incidentally, besides Wasilewska, there were many other Polish writers whose sentiments were of a different kind. Their views were not the kind we approved of. They carried within themselves vestiges of Polish nationalism and definite views on Ukrainians [i.e., prejudice against them]. Their understanding of the action we had been forced to take was incorrect. They declared that we had made an agreement with the Germans at the expense of the Poles. The fact is that we had never officially renounced for all time the territories that were temporarily part of the Polish state. Actually it had been the Polish government that violated the Curzon line to the detriment of the interests of the land of the Soviets. It did not make sense for Poland to seize those lands and try to hold onto them, having to be always in readiness for some action that would restore justice and establish more reliable borders. While ethnography and history were not on the side of the borders that were established between Poland and the Soviet Union [after the Polish-Soviet war of 1920], many Polish intellectuals did not understand this, and they took an incorrect position. But Wasilewska was an exception.

Wanda Lwowna came to Lvov wearing simple boots under a sheepskin coat.[16] Her outward appearance was quite simple, though she herself was a descendant of a prominent Polish family. She was the daughter of the Wasilewski[17] who had been a minister under Pilsudski and who, besides, had been a close friend of Pilsudski's. Wasilewski, in other words, was one of Pilsudski's trusted intimates. It was awkward for me to ask Wasilewska about this at the time, but there were rumors going around that Wanda Lwowna was Pilsudki's goddaughter. To what extent that corresponded to the truth I do not know, but for her part she never felt ashamed about her past or her father. I also remember the following incident, which took place after the defeat of Hitler's Germany. Wanda Lwowna's daughter Ewa, who had grown up and completed her education, was working in Moscow at some library. Going through the archives, she went to her mother at one point and said: "I found some books by my grandfather and sent them all down into the cellar. Their content is obviously anti-Soviet." I met Ewa while her mother was still alive, when Ewa was a teenager. Today I don't know what subsequently became of her.

Wasilewska immediately took a clearly defined pro-Soviet position. She had an understanding attitude toward the entry of our troops into territory specified by the treaty between the Soviet Union and Germany, and she began to explain our position to the Polish comrades, which was a great service both to the AUCP(B), and to me personally as secretary of the Central Committee of the Ukrainian Communist Party. Soon, for all practical purposes, I had relocated to Lvov and was organizing all the everyday work there. All sorts of Poles who actively collaborated with us appeared later on; nevertheless, none proved to be the equal of Wanda Wasilewska.

As far as the treaty with Germany is concerned, it was not published in full in our country. The only part published was the one that discussed our agreement on nonaggression. In addition to that there were clauses that dealt with Polish territory and our new western borders. Poland lost its independence, which was not something mentioned in the text, but it did follow logically from the spirit of the text. It was transformed into a German protectorate. Thus our border ended up being not with Poland but with Germany. I personally never saw the full text of the treaty, but I know about this from information conveyed by Stalin after the signing of the treaty. Our dealings with Lithuania, Latvia, Estonia, Finland, and Bessarabia also followed logically from the text of the treaty. The fate of those territories was also mentioned, but that part of the treaty was not published either. I am speaking about this because people who want to familiarize themselves with these materials need to look at the diplomatic documents and at the text of the treaty. For my part I consider it my duty to say this, so that everything will be clear, to say what my understanding of the treaty was and what was provided for under the treaty.

In those days I also ran into some situations that were humorous, and even ridiculous. I want to tell about one of them. For a long time we had been under the influence of the work that was carried out in exposing "enemies of the people" and destroying them. Therefore when we occupied the western territories and formed provisional revolutionary committees there, the most significant geographical location for us was Lvov, the capital of western Ukraine. Many Ukrainian intellectuals had previously held Austrian and then Polish citizenship. In their attitudes they were pro-Ukrainian. In Poland they were accused of being pro-Soviet, although that should be understood with some reservations: it was not that they preferred Soviet Ukraine; they simply preferred Ukraine. But if you asked them about the capital, they would say the best place for the Ukrainian capital would be Lvov. The person confirmed as the chairman of the Lvov city revolutionary committee was Mishchenko,[18] the first secretary of the Vinnitsa province committee[19] of the Communist Party of Ukraine. One day in the late autumn I stopped by his office to see how his work was going. A crowd of people was there, because it was necessary to find urgent solutions to problems of the municipal economy—streetcars, the paving of the streets (which had been damaged), water supply, and electricity. The people who had previously worked in the relevant positions, for the most part Poles, wanted to find out their status under the new government. They came to state that they had occupied such and such positions and wanted to receive orders. This was only natural.

What did I find? The chairman of the revolutionary committee was sitting dressed in a sheepskin coat over which he had a greatcoat. I don't know how he managed to do it because he himself was a huge man, enormously tall. He was wearing felt boots,[20] and sticking out from his coat were the large handles of two revolvers. In short, the only thing he lacked was a cannon, which would have been too heavy to carry on his shoulders. People were sitting and looking at him, hanging on his every word. His visiting hours ended, and we were left alone. I said to him: "You're making a bad impression not only of yourself but also of Soviet power and our people. It's as though you're displaying your cowardice. What would you do with those guns if some terrorist came and tried to kill you? Why, he'd shoot you with your own guns. What are you showing off for? Why do you have those gun handles sticking out? Hide them in your pockets and dress more properly." Mishchenko was dismayed and expressed his obvious failure to understand my objections. After all, he was displaying his "revolutionary" qualities, his "unbending firmness"!

After a while we were obliged to revise the appointments we had made. The people who worked there temporarily returned to their previous posts. Mishchenko also returned to Vinnitsa. In Lvov new people were promoted, but this was a complicated business because the local Polish machinery of government was not so much sabotaging things (I have no recollection of any such thing) as that they were simply demoralized and felt paralyzed. Of course our arrival did not inspire them or bring added enthusiasm to their labors. Many years after the war when I was meeting with Gomulka[21] [head of the Polish Communist Party], he told me he had been part of a workers' civil defense unit when we entered Poland and that later on he had been mobilized. But for quite some time he had continued to work in Kiev, helping to build railroad tunnels under the Dnieper River.

Before the war Stalin had proposed that such tunnels be built under the Dnieper: one to the north of Kiev, the other to the south. People who had built the Moscow subway system were working there, but before the war we didn't have enough time to build these tunnels, and after the war the need for them disappeared, and the work was stopped. The remnants of these tunnels even today serve as a reminder of the past.

Our work of Sovietizing western Ukraine continued fairly successfully, and we encountered no resistance then. I don't remember any protests, let alone armed actions, against us. It was only later that Stepan Bandera[22] began his activity. When we occupied Lvov he was in a local prison, after being convicted in connection with the assassination of the Polish minister of internal affairs. I don't remember now what Bandera's role had been in that—whether he himself had shot the minister or had merely been one of those who organized the assassination. We displayed lack of discrimination at that time, freeing prisoners without examining their cases. I don't know, of course, whether we had the opportunity to make any such examinations. All prisoners were freed, and among them Bandera got his freedom. His activities impressed us back then: He had taken action against the minister of internal affairs in the reactionary Polish government. It was not for us to mourn the loss of that minister. But since those actions were carried out by groups that were not friendly to the Soviet Union, groups that were actually our enemies, nationalists who hated the Soviet system, we should have taken that into account. Later on we clashed with Bandera, and he did us a lot of harm. We lost thousands of people; this was after the war, when the intense armed struggle of the Ukrainian nationalists against Soviet power had developed widely. Bandera turned out to be a direct agent of Germany when Germany was preparing for war, and after the war started, the agents of German imperialism, the nationalist supporters of Bandera, actively aided the Nazis.

It's true that when Bandera saw that the Germans had no intention of keeping the promises they had made about the formation of an independent Ukraine he turned his armed units against them, but at the same time he didn't stop hating the Soviet Union. Toward the end of the war he was fighting both against us and against the Germans, and after the war he renewed the fight against Soviet power. Who actually was Bandera? Not everyone in our country knows. Stepan Bandera was from a clerical family; his father had been a priest in Stanislav province, if not in the city of Stanislav itself.[23] Bandera studied at the Lvov Polytechnical Institute, and so he had a university education. At first he became the leader of the Ukrainian nationalists in the western parts of Ukraine and later was the generally acknowledged leader of the Ukrainian nationalist movement.

When Germany began its war against Poland and our troops marched westward to new, enlarged borders, there was a big upswing in the mood of the Ukrainian people and among all the Soviet people. But on the other hand, everyone felt downcast by the premonition that a war would soon break out and the Soviet Union would not be able to avoid it. If the Soviet Union was drawn into a war, these new territories of western Ukraine (or as the Ukrainians said, Zakhidna Ukraina), which had become part of the Ukrainian Soviet Socialist Republic, would come under fire first of all. Attitudes varied among western Ukrainians toward the imminent threat. The Ukrainian nationalists, who were embittered enemies of the Soviet state, looked forward to the war and were getting ready for it. They were happy because Goebbels [Hitler's propaganda chief] had pulled the wool over their eyes by promising that as a result of a German war against the USSR, Ukraine would win its independence as a separate state. They were blinded by nationalism and could not appreciate the magnificence of the progressive Soviet system. These people looked forward to the war and did everything they could to bring it on. They made preparations to facilitate the German occupation of Ukraine, believing that Hitler would clear Ukraine of the *moskali*.[24] They believed that Hitler would triumphantly present to them on a silver platter an independent Ukraine (or as they said in Ukrainian, *nezalezhna Ukraina*).

Later the Ukrainian nationalists saw how this all ended up. Their hopes were dashed, and Hitler began to put them in jail and conduct a merciless war against them. Some of them were even forced to go underground and take up terrorist actions against the Germans, though the terrorist actions they carried out were very rare. They were conserving their strength, calculating that if the Soviet Union began an offensive against Germany, they would need to have their own troops ready so that, at the decisive moment, when the territory was cleared of Germans, they could seize power and establish a Ukraine that would be *nezalezhna* from the *moskali* (independent of the Russians). That was the kind of situation that took shape then, at the time when we were fighting to consolidate Soviet power in western Ukraine and getting ready for the inevitable war.

I want to tell about some tragic occurrences that I had occasion either to observe myself or to hear about, reported to me by officials of the People's Commissariat of Internal Affairs [Russian initials, NKVD]. At that time the head of the NKVD of Ukraine was Serov.[25] He had graduated from a military academy not long before. As part of the reinforcement of the state security agencies at that time, many military commanders were mobilized for war. As one of those so mobilized, Serov ended up with us as people's commissar of internal affairs of Ukraine. He had no experience in this line of work. That was too bad, but it was also all right, because a lot of experience that was harmful for the country and for the party had already been built up, experience acquired as a result of provocations and the arrest of innocent people, interrogation with refined methods of torture to force confessions, the experience of reprisals against the people. Those who did the interrogating were themselves turned into some kind of machine. And they acted that way, guided by thoughts such as, "If I don't do it, others will soon be doing it to me; better that I do it than for it be done to me." It's dreadful to imagine now that Communists felt compelled to be guided in their actions not by political awareness or their own consciences, but by some kind of animal fear, a zoological fear for their own lives, and that to save their own skins, they destroyed honest people who were not guilty of anything.

Serov, in accordance with his official duties, established contacts with the Gestapo at that time. A representative of the Gestapo arrived officially, under mutual agreement, in Lvov, together with his agents. I don't know exactly what kind of network of agents he had, but it was large. The "exchange of people" between us and Germany served as the pretext. People who had fled the area occupied by German troops and who wished to return to the places where they had lived before the Germans seized Poland were given this opportunity. On the other hand, people who had remained on territory occupied by German troops, but who now wished to cross over into territory occupied by Soviet troops, were allowed to return to their places of residence. During this work of exchange, Serov came to me and said: "There are huge lines at the registration center for those wishing to return to Polish territory. When I approached the place I found it very painful, because most of the waiting line consisted of people from the Jewish population. What's going to happen to them? And yet, this is how devoted people are to all kinds of petty everyday things—an apartment, material objects. They give the Gestapo agents bribes to help them leave here sooner and return to their hearths and homes." The Gestapo agents did this quite willingly, took the bribes, enriched themselves, and accompanied these people directly to concentration camps. For our part we couldn't do anything because our words didn't count at all to these unfortunate people: They just wanted to go home. Perhaps for some of them there were still relatives back there. In short, they wanted to return to where they had been born, where they had lived, even though they knew that the Germans back in their own country, in Germany, had committed reprisals against Jews. In spite of that, many Polish Jews, who by the will of fate had ended up on territory occupied by the Soviet Union, were trying by every means legal and illegal to return to the territory where fascism dominated, and where a sorry fate lay in store for them. On the other hand, many people, especially Jews, fled from the fascists over to our side. They were aware of how the fascists dealt with the Jewish population, how they crushed the Jews under foot back in their own country [i.e., in Germany and occupied Poland], making them wear special badges or identification marks, and committing humiliating and insulting acts against them.

I must say something here about Serov. At one time he was punished and relieved of his ministerial duties because he displayed lack of caution. But for all his mistakes he was an honest and incorruptible person. My attitude toward him was one of respect, confidence, and trust.

Here is another incident, the reason for which I did not understand and by which I was greatly saddened. A famous Polish opera singer, Bandrowska[26] (I can't vouch for the accuracy of the name), turned out to be in Lvov. It was reported to me that she was on our territory. I asked people who dealt with cultural questions to negotiate with her and, if she wished it, to provide her the opportunity to sing at the Lvov opera; if she didn't want that, then she should be offered the opportunity to sing at the Kiev, Kharkov, or Odessa opera. I thought that this would entice her and that she would remain on our territory. I didn't want such a famous singer to return to Polish territory under fascist occupation. If she went back to Poland, surely she would sing there, and that would be a blow to the Polish people and the Soviet people. But she didn't want to remain and returned to Poland. While we were negotiating with her, Bandrowska demonstrated some cunning: She kept talking with us and seemed to be showing a desire to accept our proposal, but at the same time she was secretly negotiating with the Germans. They secretly transferred her to the territory they had already occupied. Serov came to me and said: "Bandrowska is not here any more. She's in Krakow[27] and has already performed in a theater for officers of the German army."

Polish intellectuals who found themselves on the territory occupied by the Red Army varied in the way they perceived the arrival of our troops in western Ukraine and western Belorussia. Many intellectuals—and this is understandable—were "literally thunderstruck," as the saying goes. They found themselves in a state of shock. Their country had been attacked with all the power of Hitler's military machine, and Poland had been crushed; Warsaw had been greatly damaged, as had other Polish cities. What would happen next? Having been raised in bourgeois traditions and a bourgeois understanding of the course of events, these people seemed to lose their self-possession, their sense of self. They couldn't understand that Polish culture and the Polish nation would continue to develop on the territory that had come under Soviet rule. True, it was not a large territory, the part inhabited by Poles, compared with the territory and population seized by Hitler Germany. Naturally the Poles saw this and suffered from it very profoundly and tragically. Some of them chose the lesser of two evils. They were opposed to Soviet power, but compared with what Hitler was bringing to the Poles, they preferred the Soviets to Hitler. There were also those who, after finding themselves on territory occupied by the Red Army, fled to German-occupied territory without going through any official "exchange program." Some of them wanted to avoid any contact with the Gestapo in that way.

At that time there were a great many Gestapo agents in Lvov. They came there under an agreement with us, the purpose of which was to facilitate the exchange of populations. But incidents occurred like the one with Bandrowska, where the Gestapo agents did not consult with us or seek agreement on the list of people departing. They simply took advantage of the fact that the border was quite open, and there were no difficulties for people crossing. They fabricated false documents for some people.

The work of establishing Soviet power and normalizing the situation in the western regions of Ukraine continued. This was mainly directed toward establishing local organs of power. Many local activists were brought into the province committees and district committees. There was no shortage of cadres who took their stand in support of the Soviet reality. In spite of strong Ukrainian nationalist sentiments, there were quite a few Communists who sympathized with us, despite the fact that the Communist Party of Western Ukraine (CPWU) had been dissolved and we had expressed our lack of confidence in it. By and large the CPWU had been smashed as early as the time as the "purges" of 1936–37. For all practical purposes the leadership of the Communist organizations in western Ukraine had been transferred to the Communist Party of Ukraine. Back in 1928–29, when I had worked in Kiev as the head of the organizational department of the district committee, Demchenko had been secretary of the Kiev district committee. It was none other than he who, by decision of the Central Committee of the Communist Party of Ukraine, became responsible for ties with the CPWU and for directing its activity. Demchenko met with people from "over there," people who crossed over illegally, received instructions from him, and returned. That's how the organizational work went on.

Demchenko also dealt with cultural questions. The Ukrainian Academy of Sciences was located in Kiev, and the prominent historian Hrushevsky directed the section of the Academy on the history of Ukraine. Supervision of the Academy of Sciences was also entrusted to Demchenko, and he devoted a great deal of attention to that. Through the Academy he was in contact with scholars and scientists located in Lvov on Polish territory. I remember the names of two of these people: Studinsky and Kolessa.[28] They were authoritative figures among the intelligentsia, Kolessa more as an academic and Studinsky as a public figure and fine orator. Speaking out in the Polish press, he made an impression as a significant anti-Polish figure, inclined to be pro-Soviet and pro-Ukrainian. But when we met with him in 1939 it turned out that on political questions he lacked solid convictions. So then, the CPWU had been destroyed and those of its cadres that were within our reach were eliminated as "provocateurs, traitors, sell-outs, and agents of Pilsudski"—even though Pilsudski in fact was already dead.

The Communist Party of Poland was also dissolved by the Comintern[29] and destroyed. Its leaders were eliminated because they lived in Moscow and were actually working for the Comintern. Everyone who lived there was arrested and killed, Lenski[30] and the others. All that was left was the youth. As for Bierut[31] [who later became the head of Communist Poland], he survived because he was not yet well known to us, and in general he wasn't on Soviet territory, but was in Poland. In the case of Gomulka, he was still quite young. But their party was destroyed, their central leadership disappeared, and for all practical purposes there was no leadership of that party for a certain time. Gomulka, before his arrest by the Polish authorities, had worked in Drogobych, as he related to me. Where Bierut worked I don't know. When we occupied Drogobych, Zawadzki,[32] the future chairman of the Council of State of the People's Republic of Poland, a really fine fellow, was in the local prison. He had been in various Polish prisons before that and told me that he knew the prison system well. Jokingly he said that the Drogobych prison was the best of the bunch.

I have already mentioned that during those months we were engaged in establishing elected government bodies representing the inhabitants of the former eastern regions of Poland. It was now time for them to determine their legal status. Who would they be with? Did they want to become part of the Soviet state? Elections for representatives of the people were held. All this time I was based in Lvov and was organizing this work. When the session of people's delegates was held, I sat in an official box and looked on. I no longer remember now what the composition of the presiding committee at that assembly was, but they were people from the western regions of Ukraine, well known to us and with clearly defined political positions. They stated this openly in their public pronouncements, both orally and in the press. These were not some sort of front men that we had put up, to speak crudely. No, they were not some sort of "agents" of ours. They were dedicated Communists. When they spoke I didn't hear a single orator who expressed even the slightest doubt that Soviet power should be established in their region. With joy and enthusiasm they declared it had been their cherished dream to be accepted as part of Soviet Ukraine.

These meetings took place in a spirit of great political enthusiasm. I don't remember how many days they lasted. But it was pleasant to watch what was going on, to rejoice in the fact that this confirmed our point of view: The people—that is, the workers, peasants, and working intellectuals—understood our ideology, accepted it, and wanted to build their future on this basis. That is the power of Leninist ideas! They lived on among the people despite the fact that the Polish authorities had done everything they could to turn people against the USSR, to distort and discredit Leninism, and to frighten people with the idea of Soviet power. It was in those very years that harsh repression had been widespread, and that was also used against us, with suitable interpretations being made. If we wrote and stated that all this was being done only to strengthen the Soviet state and clear the way for the building of socialism, the enemies of the USSR gave their own explanations, of course, which were detrimental to us. Such viewpoints circulated widely in Poland and in other bourgeois countries. However, in spite of such intensified attempts to work on people's minds, when the Red Army arrived the people accepted us, so to speak, as their kith and kin.

The assembly of people's representatives of the areas liberated by the Red Army proceeded in Lvov in an atmosphere of great triumph. People spoke with tears in their eyes about the fact that at last they had lived to see the day when a unified Ukraine could come into existence, and at last they were united with their fellow Ukrainians. Those were triumphant days for us, especially because not only were the national aspirations of the Ukrainians being satisfied but also the western borders of the USSR were being strengthened. The borders had moved far to the west. A historical injustice to the Ukrainian people had been corrected. Never before had this people lived within the context of a united Ukraine. Now its dreams had come true. To be sure, legally, this had not yet been made official because for the time being only the various assemblies in Lvov had been held. For the time being we were observing how the feelings of people who had been liberated from oppression would be expressed, and the acceptance of their territories into the USSR had not yet been officially approved. Besides, there were still Ukrainians who lived in the Transcarpathian region in the Hungarian state. The fact is that after Hitler liquidated Czechoslovakia, Transcarpathian Ukraine became part of Hungary. Our Ukrainians took this into consideration and said: "For now the Transcarpathian Ukrainians do not belong to our Ukrainian Soviet state, but the time will come when they too will be together with us." After the Great Patriotic War that is indeed what happened. After the defeat of Hitler the Transcarpathian Ukraine also became part of the Ukrainian SSR, so that Soviet Ukraine united all Ukrainians living on their historical lands and territories.

After the assembly of people's representatives in Lvov we transferred discussion of this question to Kiev. The session in Lvov was called an assembly of authorized representatives (something like a constituent assembly). It requested that western Ukraine be accepted as part of the Ukrainian SSR. In Kiev a republic-wide Supreme Soviet was convened, and later the matter was brought to a conclusion by a session of the Supreme Soviet of the USSR. Representatives of the western regions came there and presented the same request. This action also took place in an atmosphere of great triumph. I was proud of the fact that from beginning to end I had been present in the western regions of Ukraine and organized this whole business. Analogous events took place in Belorussia, but I don't know the details of how that happened because I had information only from the newspapers. The Belorussians also celebrated their victory; they too rejoiced at this historic measure by which the Belorussian population was united into a single state. Apparently they experienced the same joys and difficulties that we did. That is what I think, but whoever wishes to can find material on this subject in the press.

As for Lithuania, Latvia, and Estonia, I know about the measures we took there only from conversations that Stalin had with me when I came to Moscow. We of course were very happy when the Lithuanians, Latvians, and Estonians were once again to become part of the Soviet state.[33] Here we had an expansion of our territory, an increase in our population, and a general strengthening of the USSR. We obtained a fairly lengthy coastline on the Baltic Sea. Previously we had had only a narrow opening onto the Gulf of Finland, but now we had a real seacoast. Besides, as our reasoning went then, the territory of Latvia, Lithuania, and Estonia, if a "big war" broke out, would become a jumping-off point for foreign troops, whether British, French, or German. So this action improved our position as regards the organization of the defense of the Soviet Union, and this was of great

importance because the unified forces of the imperialist camp were significantly greater than ours at that time. Of course you cannot place an equal
sign between the peoples of Lithuania, Latvia, and Estonia, on the one hand,
and the populations of western Belorussia and western Ukraine, on the
other. After all, the populations living in the Baltic region were distinct
nationalities, not elements of nationalities living in the USSR [as the
Ukrainians and Belorussians were]. But they had now gained the opportunity of living the way all the workers, peasants, and intellectuals in the USSR
lived. For the mass of the people in the Baltic region this was a big gain.

Their government leaders gave up their positions to other people. Smetona,
the president of Lithuania, took off for Germany, as I have said. Not everyone fled, and in fact some people from the former leadership were given
prominent posts. No resistance was offered to us, and as for everything else,
things were carried out differently than they had been in western Ukraine
and western Russia; Sovietization in the Baltic region proceeded differently.
Their own governments came into existence, but now they consisted of progressive people. Not all of their members were Communists. Latsis,[34] who
headed the government of Latvia after Kirkhenshtein,[35] was a Communist
and a well-known writer. As for Kirkhenshtein, he wasn't in there at first. I
don't remember now which of the Estonians and Lithuanians headed their
governments at first. But measures of a similar character were taken there
too. Gradually the Soviet system was introduced everywhere in that area;
Estonia, Latvia, and Lithuania also became part of the Soviet Union, which
was made official by democratic methods, while all legal formalities were
observed, as is required in such cases.

In fall 1939 the problem of Finland also arose. We made contact with
Helsinki to come to an agreement. The question we raised was that in the
event of war it was necessary to protect Leningrad, which was within range
of artillery fire from the Finnish border. A bombardment of Leningrad
could be carried out directly from the territory of Finland. The Finnish
government was then pursuing a hostile policy toward the USSR and was
demonstratively flirting with Hitler Germany. Mannerheim,[36] a former
tsarist general, was the commander in chief of the army in Finland. He took
a very unfriendly attitude toward the Soviet Union. Finland really did represent a threat for us, but not in and of itself. Its territory could be used
against us by enemy forces from more powerful countries. That is why the
desire of the Soviet government to ensure its security in the northwest was
of such great importance.

Negotiations with a Finnish delegation began in Moscow. I don't know the details, because at the time I was in Lvov. Later Stalin told me about them, but the particulars have not remained in my memory. The overall outcome was that the Finns refused to accept our conditions. After that the decision was made to achieve the same thing by means of war. Again I cannot talk about the details. When I came to Moscow from Kiev in those days, I rarely had any time to spare. Most often Stalin would call me and tell me to come see him. Sometimes I would find Stalin alone. It was easier then to have an exchange of opinions and for me to lay out my views and express the needs that I always had to talk about when I came from Ukraine. More often when I ended up in Stalin's presence, Molotov, Voroshilov, and Kaganovich were also there. More rarely Zhdanov, who was usually in Leningrad. Also Beria and Mikoyan on occasion. That was the circle of people I encountered in Stalin's presence more often than others.

One day in late autumn 1939 when I came to Moscow, Stalin invited me to visit him at his apartment: "Come on over and we'll have something to eat. Molotov and Kuusinen will be here." Kuusinen[37] was then working for the Comintern. I went to the Kremlin, to Stalin's apartment. A conversation began, and from the direction it was taking I sensed that it was a continuation of a previous conversation that I knew nothing about. What was being discussed was the implementation of an already adopted resolution to present Finland with an ultimatum. It had been agreed that Kuusinen would head a government of the Karelo-Finnish Soviet Socialist Republic, which had just been established. Before that Karelia had been an autonomous republic, part of the Russian Federation. This new union republic, in Stalin's conception, was intended to unite all of Karelia, to "liberate it" together with parts of Finland and establish a unified state structure [for the Karelians and Finns].[38]

Stalin held the opinion that after Finland was presented with an ultimatum with demands of a territorial nature, if it rejected those demands, it would be necessary to begin military operations. I naturally did not object to Stalin's view. More than that, I considered, as he did, that this position was correct in principle. As far as a war with Finland, I thought that it would be enough to tell them loudly that if they didn't listen, we would fire one shot from our cannons, and then the Finns would throw up their hands and agree to our demands. Stalin commented: "This business starts today."

Kulik[39] had been sent to Leningrad earlier to organize the artillery bombardment of Finnish territory. We stayed at Stalin's place for a fairly long time waiting for the deadline of our ultimatum to expire. Stalin was sure there would be no war, and we also believed that the Finns at the last moment would accept our proposals and in that way we would achieve our goals without a war and ensure our country's security from the north. We had no interest in Finnish territory or its natural resources because it would add little to our vast expanses. Finland was rich in forests, but in that respect it could not rival us. We weren't attracted by that. The question of security stood in the forefront. Let me repeat, Leningrad was under a direct threat.

After a while a phone call came, saying that we had, in spite of everything, fired the first fatal shot. The Finns had replied with artillery fire. A war had begun. I am telling about this because other interpretations of these events exist: some say that supposedly the Finns fired first and we were forced to reply. But, after all, people always say things like that when a war begins, that the other side fired first. In former times, as history testifies, wars began differently. You can see such things in operas; one person throws down his glove as a dramatic gesture; the other picks it up, and a duel begins. In our times, unfortunately, wars begin in a different way. A question comes up: Did we have the legal and moral right to do what we did? Legally of course we did not have the right. From the moral point of view, the desire to ensure our security and reach an agreement to that effect with our neighbor was justified in our eyes.

And so the war began. A few days later I left for Ukraine. We were sure that if the Finns took up our challenge and a war was unleashed, a war in which the opposing magnitudes were simply not comparable, the question would be decided quickly and with few losses on our side. That is what we thought and what we wished. But history went on to demonstrate something quite different.

The war turned out to be a rather stubborn and protracted conflict. The Finns proved to be highly combative and showed great fighting abilities. Their defenses were well organized, and our attempts to break through the Karelian Isthmus, the shortest route into their country, led nowhere. At first this isthmus proved to be beyond our capacity. To our surprise, good reinforced-concrete lines of fortifications had been built there, along with skillfully located artillery positions, and we ran up against an impregnable fortress. As a result many more of our troops laid down their lives than was envisaged in the plan for solving this question by military means. Combat operations lasted into the depths of the winter. The decision was then made to outflank the fortifications on the Karelian Isthmus and to strike at the enemy to the north of Lake Ladoga,[40] where the Finns evidently did not have such fortifications. That is, we wanted to come around into their rear. But when we tried to do that, even more complicated conditions appeared, having to do with the particular features of the natural terrain and the climate. The Finns are people of the north, good athletes and excellent skiers. Our troops encountered mobile units of the enemy on skis, armed with automatic weapons with high rapid-fire capabilities. It was necessary to put our troops on skis as quickly as possible. But that was not so easy to do. Those fighting on our side were ordinary Red Army soldiers without any special training. Then we remembered our people who were specially trained in gymnastics or excelled in that field. Although there were not a great many of them, we enlisted them from Moscow, Ukraine, and Leningrad. We gave them a rather triumphal send-off because there was a feeling of certainty that our athletes would "come and conquer." But they almost all perished in that war. I don't know exactly how many of them actually returned.

Stalin was furious. The military explained to him that they hadn't known about the fortifications on the Karelian Isthmus, the so-called Mannerheim line, and they began directing accusations against our intelligence service. All this blended into one main charge, aimed at Voroshilov. After all, he was people's commissar of defense. Strictly speaking, there was no one else to blame for the military setbacks, certainly not Stalin. So then, Voroshilov was to blame; he hadn't foreseen, he hadn't worked things out, and so on. Shaposhnikov[41] was head of the General Staff then. His people undertook to work out a plan of operations against Finland, and they occupied the top posts among our forces. Shaposhnikov was regarded as a prominent specialist, although he didn't have a decisive voice but rather a consultative voice. Military matters were decided then by Voroshilov in the name of the Red Army.

Those were dreadful months from the point of view of both our losses and our long-term prospects. Take, for example, our navy, which was operating in the Baltic Sea against the Finnish navy. You would have thought the relationship of forces would be not at all favorable to the Finns, but our navy made a poor showing. Here's one of the incidents. A report was made to Stalin in my presence that a Swedish ship was passing by. Our people took it for a Finnish ship, and one of our submarines tried to sink it, but did not succeed. German naval forces observed this and, as a way of needling us, offered to help.

Stalin told us: "The German ambassador, Schulenburg, has passed on a proposal from Hitler. He says that if we are encountering difficulties in the fight with the Finns in the Baltic Sea, Germany is ready to offer assistance."

Stalin of course refused, but he was literally thrown into confusion as a result of this incident; figuratively speaking he turned gray. You can imagine it! This was how our future enemy sized us up. He was openly proposing: "Let's simply set aside any considerations of right or wrong. Once war has begun, it's necessary to use all possible means to solve the problems facing one's military forces in the shortest possible time." Hitler was demonstratively pointing up our weakness, and he wanted us to admit it by accepting his aid.

A feeling of alarm grew in the Soviet leadership. At first this feeling was not very strong, but it kept growing. It was as though the halo of invincibility around the Red Army had been dimmed. How did the song go that we sang then? "If tomorrow there's war, if tomorrow we march, then today we are ready to go." Seeds of doubt began to spread. If we can't deal with the Finns, and we obviously have a much more powerful enemy [in Hitler], how in the world are we going to deal with him? Meretskov[42] commanded our troops on the Karelian Isthmus, and others commanded them farther north.[43] Timoshenko came to me and said: "I'm being called to Moscow. Probably I'll go to the Finnish front." He did go and actually became the head of all the forces of the Northwestern Front with the aim of making a breakthrough in the Mannerheim line. A new decision had been made to strike the main blow not from the north, not going around, but straight ahead, to strike directly at the fortifications on the Karelian Isthmus and thereby decide the outcome of the war.

I remember well what Stalin told me, with bitterness, sadness, and irony, about how the war with Finland had been going to the north of the isthmus: "The snow there is deep; our troops are marching through it; there are a lot of Ukrainians in the units, and they're in a fighting mood, and they ask in Ukrainian, 'Where are these Finns?' Suddenly from the flank come bursts of automatic weapons firing. Our people fall. The Finns have chosen a special combat tactic in the forests: they climb the pine trees, conceal themselves behind the branches, pull white sheets or camouflage garments over themselves, and become completely invisible. As our people approach, they get shot down by point blank fire from the trees. They call these gunmen in the trees 'cuckoos.' And again your Ukrainians are asking (in Ukrainian), 'Where are they? Where are these cuckoos?'" A special struggle had to be waged against these "cuckoos"; we had to train our own marksmen to shoot them down. But all that required time, and the learning process cost us a lot of blood.

A differently conceived [and more carefully planned] operation began. The tactics of the frontal assault were revised; the necessary amount of artillery and air power, the full amount necessary, was concentrated (why in the world wasn't this done the first time?), and a new attack was organized. The Finnish pillboxes were shattered because they couldn't withstand the powerful artillery barrage. Our air power also played a positive role. Stalin said: "Our airplanes flew down on top of them. The assignment was to prevent the Finns from bringing up supplies and ammunition to the front, that is, to knock their railroads out of commission, to bomb their bridges and shoot up their locomotives from the sky. Tactically of course this was correct. So many bridges were destroyed and so many locomotives put out of commission that you would have thought the Finns had nothing left but skis. But no, they kept bringing up supplies."

Finally, the Finns asked for a truce. Negotiations began. An agreement was reached to end the war, and then a peace treaty was signed. The Finns withdrew from the Leningrad region and allowed us to have a military base on the Hanko peninsula in the Gulf of Finland. At that point we began to analyze the reasons why we had turned out to be so poorly prepared for the war, and why it had cost us so many casualties. I don't know exactly how many thousands of fighters we lost there, but I think we lost a great many. Timoshenko told me about this war in detail. It came out that it wasn't true what they said about our intelligence service, that it was of poor quality and therefore had not reported the necessary information for us to know the situation. That all turned out to be lies. Our intelligence service had in fact been right up to the mark. Every pillbox the Finns had built on the whole Mannerheim line—all that was well known and even mapped out. Apparently, the difficulties were simply the result of negligence. I can't even imagine how that could have happened. After all, intelligence information is the holy of holies in working out any military operation. The first thing you do is study the locality where military operations will be taking place. And here we had not just a locality but a fortified zone. For how many years the Finns had been building these reinforced-concrete and granite fortifications! Also, the natural conditions for defense in that area were good: forests, hills, many lakes and marshes, and few roads. The area is difficult to reach by ordinary transport, and it was easy to organize defensive lines there. Besides that, the necessary lumber and granite for building defensive structures were right there on the spot. The Finns made good use of all this. That's why the victory cost us the blood of many thousands of people.

I should say here that the Finnish war in fact may have cost us even millions of lives. Why do I think that? Because if we hadn't touched the Finns, but had come to agreement with them somehow without a war, we would have been viewed differently abroad. After all, if the Soviet Union could barely deal with Finland, whereas Germany would have dealt with Finland very swiftly, what would be left of the USSR if German troops moved against it, troops who were well trained and superbly organized, with good commanders, powerful military equipment, and huge numbers of military personnel? Hitler calculated that he would deal with the USSR in two shakes of a lamb's tail. That's how Hitler's Plan Barbarossa and the policy of a blitzkrieg war were arrived at, based on total self-confidence. That self-confidence was nourished to no small degree by the ill-conceived and poorly executed campaign we waged against Finland. But if we had carried out that campaign differently, as we should have, the subsequent development of historical events might have turned out differently. Of course, one might say that the USSR deceived Hitler by its inept actions in the Finnish campaign, because Germany's overconfidence cost it dearly in the end. But we were not intentionally putting on a false show in 1939–40, because we didn't know in advance how all that was going to turn out, or how events would later unfold. And millions of people were lost in the war with Germany. Our suppositions before 1941, that the government of Finland in the event of a "big war" would offer its territory to our enemies, were indeed borne out. Even before the Great Patriotic War we knew that Hitler would concentrate his troops in Finland along our borders. It could be said, of course, that the Finns took that step because they were angry at us and wanted to get back what they had lost by joining in a war with Germany against the Soviet Union. Such an understanding of the matter is not lacking in good sense either.

Once again I must state my recollection that Kuusinen and I (Kuusinen is no longer alive) found out when we were at Stalin's apartment that the first shots had been fired from our side. There's no getting around that fact. As for Finland, I was in that country more than once in subsequent times and often met with the Finns. I had the very best relations with President Kekkonen and his predecessor, Paasikivi.[44] The former was a "good capitalist," who sincerely wanted peace with us. He actually did make peace with us, since he was the one who initiated the peace agreement. It seems he was the envoy from the Finnish government to our country during World War II. As a result of the negotiations he conducted with us the necessary agreement was reached, and Finland withdrew from the war against the USSR. That was an important victory. Only a great deal of blood was shed to achieve it.

Once again the question comes up: Could the Soviet-Finnish war have been avoided? I will not take it on myself to try to draw a definitive conclusion. If we are to talk about Stalin, on the other hand, the person who decided these questions, he did not begin the war in 1939 in order to seize Finland. We did not in fact try to occupy that country, and when the Finnish army was effectively defeated in 1944, Stalin demonstrated statesmanlike wisdom then, too. The territory of Finland with its population could not decide any fundamental questions of foreign policy for us. It was a small nationality, whose country was not very rich in natural resources; but the signing of an armistice between ourselves and Finland, which then declared war against Germany—that was a good example for other satellites of Hitler's Germany to see. The advantage for us was greater than occupation. Besides, the step that we did take left positive traces as far as prospects for the future were concerned.

I remember the following incident. Once when I came to Moscow from Ukraine I was visiting Stalin. Molotov told about inviting Schulenburg for a visit. Schulenburg, the German ambassador to the USSR, favored the strengthening of peaceful relations between Germany and the Soviet Union and was definitely opposed to war with the USSR. It was not accidental that on August 23, 1939, when the Soviet-German nonaggression pact was signed, Schulenburg, with whom Molotov was working on some incidental problems, was literally radiant with joy and said: "God himself has helped us, God himself!" We regarded his words as part of the diplomatic game back then, but later history showed that this was his sincere sentiment. He understood that it was desirable to improve relations between Germany and the USSR and to place the two countries' relations on a peaceful foundation. Later he reported to Hitler along the same lines, but they paid no attention to his words. Schulenburg was involved in the conspiracy against Hitler in summer 1944. It failed, and Schulenburg was among those who were executed.

But let me go back to the story told by Molotov. While passing through the corridors of the People's Commissariat of Foreign Affairs, Schulenburg saw that we had stenographers sitting by the radio recording relevant broadcasts. He asked in surprise: "What's this? You have stenographers doing transcribing?" And then he bit his tongue. Molotov reported to Stalin about this. Our people decided that apparently the Germans had technical transcribing capabilities. Instead of stenographers, they were using some sort of devices for transcribing. Only after the war did we find out that tape recorders existed. Previously we had not known anything about them. The Germans, on the other hand, had tape recorders even before the war. Thus they conducted their intelligence work in regard to radio broadcasts in a more organized way. Secret radio telegraphic dispatches are sent at very high speeds, and hardly any stenographer can transcribe them, especially if they're coded. But a tape recorder can capture them and play them back more slowly, so that everything can be heard and the key to the code can be found. We didn't yet know how to do this, because we lacked the necessary technical resources. From details like this the fascists also drew their conclusions about our military and technical level, our military technology. They sensed our weakness, which strengthened their desire to unleash a war more quickly. But they exaggerated our weakness.

So then, after winter 1939–40, relatively few people in our country really knew how the military operations against Finland had been conducted and what their results had been politically, how many casualties this victory had required, and how totally incommensurate they were from the point of view of our potential; in other words, relatively few knew what the real relationship of forces was. As for Stalin, in private conversations he criticized our military departments, the Commissariat of Defense, and especially Voroshilov. Sometimes he focused everything on one individual, Voroshilov. I, like others, agreed with Stalin on this, because Voroshilov actually did have prime responsibility for this. He held the post of people's commissar of defense for many years. "Voroshilov marksmen" had made their appearance in our country, and so forth. Voroshilov's boastfulness did lull our people to sleep, reduce their alertness. But other people [besides Voroshilov] were to blame as well.

I remember once that when we were visiting Stalin at his dacha nearer to Moscow, in a fit of anger he began criticizing Voroshilov harshly. He became very upset and stood up and began lambasting Voroshilov. The latter also got angry and red in the face and stood up and in reply to Stalin's criticism threw out this accusation: "You are to blame for this. It was you who destroyed our military cadres." Stalin answered him appropriately. Then Voroshilov grabbed a platter on which a boiled suckling pig was lying and smashed it against the table. This was the only incident of its kind, as far as I know. Stalin sensed above all that in our victory over the Finns in 1940 there were elements of defeat, a very dangerous defeat that would strengthen our enemies in their certainty that the Soviet Union was a giant with feet of clay. The international political consequences could turn out to be highly unfavorable.

The criticism ended with Voroshilov being relieved of his duties as people's commissar of defense, and Timoshenko was appointed in his place. He soon became a Marshal of the Soviet Union. I don't remember now what new post was given to Voroshilov, but for a long time he found himself in the position, as it were, of a whipping boy.

But the statement of how things stood and the anger were justified. I would even say that the anger was insufficient in regard to the war of 1939–40. The proper conclusions needed to be drawn. The conclusions should have been not only to relieve Voroshilov of his duties and appoint another person to the post of people's commissar of defense. What needed to be kept in mind was that a "big war" was inevitable. It was urgently necessary to make up for lost time, to find and fix the holes in our economy as a result of which we had suffered these losses, to raise the fighting efficiency of the Red Army still higher, and most important, to have new cadres ready at hand.

Kirponos[45] was a man I got to know when he commanded the troops of the Kiev Special Military District (Russian initials, KOVO). He was a good commander and an honest man, and he perished as a true citizen of the Soviet Union. In the Finnish campaign he commanded a division, distinguished himself in combat, and later was awarded the title of general and became a hero of the Soviet Union. The KOVO had approximately the same standing in military importance as the Belorussian Special Military District (Russian initials, BOVO). If the BOVO was like a breastwork shielding Moscow from an enemy attack from the west, the KOVO was also located in an area where a vital blow might fall. There were favorable topographical and soil conditions for developing an offensive by mechanized troops from the west in the direction of Kiev: the roads were good, and there were hardly any marshes. Outside our country people wrote that this was like a tank-training ground, that if tank units were deployed there it would be possible to show what they were capable of. This assessment turned out to be correct; that is what happened in the Great Patriotic War. With Kirponos's appointment to this area it was thought that he would have the appropriate moral qualities. That was true. But he didn't have the experience of leading such a large number of troops. Apparently after the bloody meat grinder of 1937–38, the truth was that simply no other more appropriate commanders were left. This lack of experience later made itself felt in the way the fighting was organized during the clashes with Hitler's troops. Kirponos was far from being a Yakir!

After the Finnish campaign it was urgently necessary for us to take another look at how we were supplied with arms and military technology and immediately set about reorganizing industry, placing it on a military footing in order to be completely ready for war. Although we didn't know how much time we would be allowed as a breathing spell or when the enemy would attack us, I think that in fact very little was done that was new in comparison to the amount of time we were granted. This was a terrible oversight, and we paid for it dearly during the first months of the war when we had a catastrophic shortage of weapons and military equipment. Stalin was expecting, I suppose, that prolonged fighting by the British and French forces against the Germans would develop, and they would exhaust Hitler. Thus Hitler's plans to smash the West first and then turn to the East would be thwarted. The strategy that lay behind Hitler's signing of the nonaggression pact with the USSR in 1939—that strategy would fail [or so Stalin expected].

In that period both Stalin and Hitler fulfilled the obligations (or sometimes made it look as though they were fulfilling them) under the August pact and the later border and friendship treaty of September 1939. Molotov often reported [to Stalin]: "Here's what Schulenburg said. . . . Schulenburg has passed on this information." Under the friendship treaty we were supposed to supply Germany with grain, petroleum, and many other products. We punctually fulfilled all these obligations, sending trainload after trainload into Germany. For his part Hitler was supposed to provide us with a battleship.[46] It was already afloat and was delivered to Leningrad, where the completion of the shipbuilding work was organized. Hitler sent his specialists, who helped complete the construction of the battleship. I found out about this in the following way. A high-ranking German naval chief arrived in Leningrad for consultation. He was assigned appropriate premises, and the necessary conditions for his work were created, but then a scandal arose. The Germans caused the scandal, for the following reason. Our intelligence service had set up listening and photographic devices around the apartment of this specialist; in addition, it turned out, he had a passion for the female sex, and our intelligence smuggled a girl into his apartment. One night they photographed the two to have evidence of indecent behavior. But apparently our technology was poor, and he heard the noise—the clicking of the apparatus. He began searching to find out what was going on, and he found it. A large painting hung on the wall, and a small window had been cut in it, and a camera inserted. He made a huge protest. The Germans, it turned out, didn't care about his encounters with female companions, whereas our Chekists had thought the photographs would give them the chance to recruit him. Stalin criticized Beria then for his failure, and that's how I found out about the incident. I don't know how the matter ended. The battleship remained with us until the end of the war, with its construction uncompleted. In sending us an unfinished battleship, Hitler apparently calculated that he would succeed in smashing us and then take the battleship back to Germany.

We had an agreement with Czechoslovakia, with the Skoda firm,[47] which was supposed to supply us with antiaircraft guns. Our 85-millimeter antiaircraft guns, which we used in the fighting later on, were manufactured in many respects on models purchased from Skoda. In addition we purchased some other equipment from Skoda. But that company had not completely filled its orders before Hitler occupied Czechoslovakia. Now Hitler gave the order that Skoda should fulfill its earlier commitment and provide us with a certain number of large-caliber weapons. In regard to the antiaircraft guns, we used them both against aircraft and as antitank weapons. Thus Hitler did everything to create the appearance that Germany was fulfilling its obligations under the treaty with the USSR.

What were our relations with Germany then from the point of view of Ukraine? We had a border that was contiguous with the border of Germany. After the elimination of the state of Poland, along the new border with us, Hitler at first maintained units made up of soldiers who were not the youngest or most recent recruits. These military units were not of the highest quality, though we also saw that the fascists were working intensively at strengthening the borders. If friendship between us had been proclaimed, why this intense work? This looked suspicious. Of course the KOVO reported this to Stalin. Stalin also understood that the threat to the USSR had not been removed, but it seems that he didn't pay attention to the reports, and in reply he gave an explanation that, for those of us in Kiev, by no means strengthened our hopes of avoiding a war with Germany.

At the same time the Ukrainian nationalists became more arrogant and began taking actions against us. Irrefutable documents fell into our hands giving evidence that the Ukrainian nationalists were working with Berlin and were receiving money and instructions from there. This was also a very weighty indication that Hitler was preparing to attack us and was making use of the nationalists as his agents. He wanted, when he broke through into Ukraine, to have a nationalist Ukrainian "spotlight" that would illuminate the situation for intelligence purposes, and he wanted the Ukrainian nationalists to serve as an initial base of support for the Germans. The nationalist gang of western Ukraine took it on themselves to perform exactly those functions.

We began to alter the gauge of the railroad tracks in western Ukraine from narrower to wider—that is, from the European gauge to the Soviet one. Some Germans who visited us in the region near the Carpathians requested on some pretext (through the contacts between their security agencies and ours) that we not do this. Serov reported this. I then said to Stalin: "They think that the previous railroad track will suit them better. That's the gauge they use, and they're asking us not to change it."

Stalin cursed and gave the order: "Change it!" It's true that during wartime it doesn't take long to change a railroad track. The track workers come along directly behind the troops, and if the rails and crossties are in place and the railroad bed has not been destroyed, all they have to do is move the rails apart, take out the old spikes, and drive in new ones.

1. Between September and November 1939 the Belorussian and Ukrainian Fronts were also involved in the liberation of western Belorussia and western Ukraine.

2. Ternopol is about 110 kilometers east of Lvov in the part of western Ukraine that had previously belonged to Poland. [SS]

3. In Soviet military terminology a "Front," which unites two or more armies, is roughly the equivalent of "Army Group" as used in U.S. military terminology. When two or more Soviet Fronts were grouped together under a single command, they were called a *Napravlenie* (literally, a "direction," but also a "sector"). For *Napravlenie,* we have used the term "Area." [GS] For more, see pages xii–xiii.

4. This military campaign was in fact completed by the Red Army in nine days.

5. Major General N. D. Yakovlev was at that time chief of artillery of the Kiev Special Military District.

6. Lieutenant General F. I. Golikov. See Biographies.

7. Drogobych and Borislav are situated about 60 kilometers southwest of Lvov in the foothills of the Carpathians. [SS]

8. The reference is to the Polish-Soviet war of 1920, initiated by Poland with a view to regaining its ancient territories. (See note 26 of the above chapter titled "Some Consequences of the Kirov Assassination.") The Polish armed forces initially captured and briefly held Kiev before being driven back. The 1921 peace agreement between Poland and Soviet Russia gave most of the western parts of Ukraine and Belorussia to Poland. [GS/SS] Jozef Pilsudski headed the Polish state from 1919 to 1922 and was prime minister from 1926 to 1928 and in 1930. See Biographies.

9. Lord Curzon was the British minister of foreign affairs from 1919 to 1924. His "line" was recommended by the Supreme Council of the Entente as Poland's eastern border. See Biographies.

10. Bialystok is about 160 kilometers northeast of Warsaw. It is now situated in eastern Poland, near the border with Belarus. [SS]

11. Thus the Oder and Neisse Rivers, both banks of which had previously belonged to Germany, became the border between postwar Poland and the former German Democratic Republic (East Germany). [SS]

12. A. Smetona was the president of Lithuania in 1919 and 1920 and again from 1926 to 1940. See Biographies.

13. K. I. Studinsky was a literary critic. See Biographies.

14. *Zhidy* (singular, *Zhid*) is an offensive term in Russian, with derogatory connotations similar to those of the term "Yid" in English. [GS]

15. See Biographies.

16. Since Polish culture does not use the patronymic, Wasilewska did not actually have the middle name "Lwowna." Khrushchev usually called people by their first name and patronymic (the polite form of address in Russian culture), and non-Russians had patronymics created for them, a Russian way of showing politeness and warmth. Her father was Leon, the Russian equivalent was Lev, and so the patronymic "Lvovna" (daughter of Lev) was created. [GS/SK]

Khrushchev used last names of people with whom he was on more distant terms. In personal meetings he always used the polite, or formal, version of "you" (*vy* rather than *ty*). [SK]

17. Leon Wasilewski was minister of foreign affairs of Poland in 1918 and 1919.

18. G. K. Mishchenko.

19. Vinnitsa is about 160 kilometers southwest of Kiev. [SS]

20. The felt boots called *valenki* in Russian. [GS]

21. Wladyslaw Gomulka was the Communist leader of Poland from 1956 to 1970. See Biographies.

22. S. A. Bandera was a military leader of the Ukrainian nationalist movement. See Biographies.

23. Stanislav is the name used for the city of Ivano-Frankovsk in western Ukraine when the area was under Polish rule. The city is about 80 kilometers southeast of Lvov. [AH]

24. In Ukrainian, *moskali* became a derogatory term for "Russians"; originally it simply meant

"soldiers" (of the tsarist army) as distinct from the local peasants, *krestyane*. [SK/GS]

25. I. A. Serov. See Biographies. Serov was punished in 1962 after the arrest of Oleg Penkovsky, a Russian who spied for the United States and Britain. Penkovsky had accompanied Serov's wife and daughter on a tourist trip to London. Serov was removed from his post in military intelligence (the Main Intelligence Administration of the General Staff or GRU), demoted from the rank of army general (four stars) to major general (one star), and sent into retirement. [SK]

26. E. Bandrowska-Turska was a Polish singer. See Biographies.

27. Krakow is a major city in southern Poland. [SS]

28. F. M. Kolessa was a composer and scholar. See Biographies.

29. The Communist International.

30. Lensky was the pseudonym of the leading Polish Communist J. Leszczinski. See Biographies.

31. Boleslaw Bierut was the Communist leader of Poland from 1948 to 1954. See Biographies.

32. A. Zawadzki was a leading Polish Communist. See Biographies.

33. Actually, Lithuania, Latvia, and Estonia had been part of the Russian empire, but became independent at the end of World War I. During the Russian Civil War of 1918–20 no stable Soviet presence was established in these three Baltic countries. [GS]

34. V. T. Latsis. See Biographies.

35. A. M. Kirkhenstein. See Biographies.

36. K. G. E. Mannerheim was a prominent Finnish military leader. In the 1930s he created the "Mannerheim line" of fortifications on the Karelian Isthmus along the border with the USSR. See Biographies.

37. O. V. Kuusinen. See Biographies.

38. The creation of a union republic shared by Karelians and Finns could be justified on the grounds that these ethnic groups are closely related. [SS] The Karelo-Finnish SSR was formed on March 31, 1940.

39. Marshal of the Soviet Union G. I. Kulik was at that time head of the Main Artillery Administration of the Red Army as well as deputy people's commissar of defense. See Biographies.

40. The Karelian Isthmus is between Lake Ladoga and the Gulf of Finland, just to the north and northwest of Leningrad.

41. B. M. Shaposhnikov. See Biographies.

42. K. A. Meretskov. See Biographies.

43. Farther to the north, the following armies were fighting: on the Karelian Isthmus, the Thirteenth Army, commanded by V. D. Grendal; on the isthmus between Ladoga and Onega lakes, the Fifteenth Army, commanded by M. P. Kovalev and later by V. N. Kurdyumov; yet farther to the north, the Eighth Army, commanded by G. M. Shtern, and the Ninth Army, commanded by M. P. Dukhanov and later by V. I. Chuikov; and in the vicinity of Murmansk, the Fourteenth Army, commanded by V. A. Frolov.

44. Urho Kalevi Kekkonen was president of Finland from 1956 to 1981; Juho Kusti Paasikivi was president of Finland from 1946 to 1956. See Biographies.

45. M. P. Kirponos. See Biographies.

46. This was the German cruiser *Lutzoff*. In the USSR it was called the *Petropavlovsk* and from 1944 on, the *Tallinn*. During the war it was used as a multiweapon floating battery.

47. The Czech firm Skoda was one of the technologically most advanced armaments producers of the time. [SS]

# EVENTS ON THE EVE OF WAR

In 1940 we carried out an operation to liberate Bessarabia[1] from Romanian troops. This action was one of the results of the treaty we signed with the Germans in August 1939. But we also wanted to return to the historically just situation that had been violated by the Romanian monarchist government after the October 1917 revolution. The Romanians had been allies of Russia against Germany in World War I. But after the October revolution, sensing our weakness, they moved their troops in and occupied Bessarabia and held it until 1940.

As a member of the Military Council of the Kiev Special Military District (Russian initials, KOVO), I took an active part in organizing the liberation of Bessarabia. At that time Zhukov was commanding the troops of the KOVO, and Timoshenko had become people's commissar of defense of the USSR. A plan was worked out in detail for moving our troops forward and occupying jumping-off points—places for crossing or fording the Dniester River[2]—and assault units were organized. In short, everything that needed to be done to carry out the operation successfully was provided for with advanced planning. The only question was whether the Romanian troops would offer resistance. Along the border they had been behaving poorly. They often fired on our border troops without any provocation and also fired on our collective farmers. Among us this border was not considered peaceful. The Romanians were hostile toward us, although we had not allowed ourselves to take any action in regard to the Romanian border and the Romanian border troops. Therefore we did not know how the Romanian troops would behave.

We issued an ultimatum and our troops began to prepare themselves for crossing the Dniester. The Romanians didn't offer any resistance and began to retreat. I don't remember now what diplomatic negotiations were conducted or how they proceeded and what the outcome was, but we began to cross over to the western bank of the Dniester, and the Romanian troops began to pull back from the border. We made the crossing completely unhindered. At that time Marshal Timoshenko and I were in the Tiraspol region.[3] As soon as we had crossed over to the west bank of the Dniester, we began to make contact with the population. They gave us a hearty welcome; one could even say, a very hearty welcome.

On that very same day Timoshenko proposed that we take an airplane and fly into the heart of Bessarabia behind the lines of the Romanian troops and land on a field near the village of Furmanka [his native village].[4] He of course wanted to see his relatives, including his brother and sister. A lot of relatives tend to pile up for almost everyone, but especially if you're a relative holding a high position, as Timoshenko did at the time, people's commissar of defense of a great country. He assured me that we could land safely. He said that there was a good field not far from the village, and then we would walk in or people would come out and give us a lift. This was somewhat risky because the Romanian troops were being redeployed through this area toward the Pruth[5] and Danube rivers, and of course we would be landing in territory that had not yet been liberated from Romanian troops.

We took off and then began to circle. Timoshenko recognized his native Furmanka from the air and pointed through the window of the airplane: "See that lake. What good hunting you could have there!" All sorts of reminiscences about his childhood and youth began then. He had not been in Furmanka since the beginning of World War I when he was called up into the Russian army. Naturally he had a longing to return to his native haunts, to where he had spent his youth. We landed on the field, and immediately from all directions people came running; some on foot, some riding horses or driving horse-drawn wagons. A rally was immediately organized. I remember a bearded peasant who spoke. People told me he was an Old Believer,[6] But one thing seemed not to confirm that he was a strict Old Believer. He was using very choice swear words against the Romanian officer class. It had been a long time since I had heard such choice and unrepeatable Russian swearing. He did this at a big public meeting, and he cursed them for the fact that these Romanian officers used lipstick; he likened them to ladies of loose morals (although he used stronger language than that).

At this rally there also turned out to be a clergyman. Later he came over to us and exchanged kisses with Timoshenko. Later I learned that this man had become a priest during the occupation of Bessarabia by Romania and that he was from a family related to Timoshenko. They gave us horses, as I recall, and we rode into Furmanka. Furmanka gave us an excellent greeting. I say us, because I was there too, but this was really a triumphal welcome for their fellow townsman Timoshenko. Timoshenko's brother immediately invited us to come to his house, and later his sister also arrived.

Treats for the guests were served up. Old acquaintances began to arrive. Soon night began to fall. I saw that there was going to be no end to the reminiscing, the wine, and the heart-to-heart talks. Everyone who came invariably brought a huge *sulei* along. (That's what they call big bottles of wine.) So at that point I said: "You are relatives and friends and know one another, so go on with your conversations, but allow me to take my leave." I went off to a big barn and went to sleep there. In the morning I got up early, although it was already dawn. "How is the marshal doing?" I asked. "Is he still sleeping? Is he up yet?"

"The marshal never went to bed." I went into the house, and they were still sitting around the table talking. It ended with a messenger from Zhukov running in to find us with the report that Moscow was very concerned and was trying to reach Timoshenko.

From Furmanka we flew in the same airplane to Chernovitsy. There, near Kishinev or in Chernovitsy,[7] a headquarters had been organized, and there was a telephone (a special line) over which it was possible to speak with Stalin. We flew there and spoke with Moscow, reporting that everything was fine and that our troops had reached the new border, that is, the Pruth and Danube rivers. Thus we had reoccupied territory that the Romanians had stolen from us after the October revolution, taking advantage of the military weakness of the young Soviet republic. Our troops reached the border that had existed before World War I, except that there were some modifications in the area around Chernovitsy and Ternopol: these territories had been part of the Austro-Hungarian empire before World War I. The border changes were in our favor, and this was historically justified because these lands were inhabited primarily by Ukrainians. Thus, the Ukrainians living on this territory were united with the rest of the Ukrainian nation and became part of the unified Soviet state. In my view, both legally and morally, right was unquestionably on the side of the Soviet government and the AUCP(B), on the side of the actions carried out at that time in the name of the party and in the name of our state by Stalin.

In 1940, a little while after the Germans had crushed the British and French forces and seized Paris and France had surrendered, persistent rumors began to circulate among us—and the Western press wrote openly about this—that the Germans were sending their forces to Romania. Thus, our occupation of Bessarabia pushed Antonescu[8] more than ever into the arms of Hitler. Antonescu ruled the country in the name of the king; he really decided policy there. He was a man of pro-fascist views. Consequently this part of our border had to be watched closely and something had to be done to strengthen our new frontiers in the area. However, very little was actually done on the Soviet-Romanian border along the Pruth and Danube rivers. One could even say that nothing was done. We only brought our troops in and positioned them in the appropriate places, but no work was carried out as far as building fortifications along the border. When the war began, this border turned out to be very weak.

So then, the period of "phony war" by Britain and France against Germany was ending, a period when war was declared, troops were concentrated, but no active military operations were undertaken. This "phony war" instilled a certain uneasiness in the leadership of the Soviet Union. We were afraid that it might end with a deal between Britain and France, on the one hand, and Hitler's Germany, on the other, with the result that Hitler's military machine would turn eastward, against the USSR. This was a very real possibility, although some people in our country would not admit it even in their innermost thoughts. There would have been no special contradiction in such a deal being arrived at, because both sides stood on capitalist foundations, and both sides hated the Marxist-Leninist doctrine and our state, which was an island of socialism in a sea of capitalist encirclement.

Then at last in the West active military operations began. This was in spring 1940. I forget the exact date, but any literate person can look it up in a reference book.[9] The Germans went on the offensive, in an area that was least expected. France's main forces were concentrated along the Maginot line. I haven't studied the specialized literature, and I can't say to what extent this line was really impregnable. But the press claimed it was, both at the time of its construction and afterward. In response to the construction of the Maginot line, Hitler built his Siegfried line. Thus, both on the one side and on the other what people said were impregnable fortifications had been built. This calmed and reassured the French, but it weakened their willingness to organize their forces as needed and prevented them from taking a prudent attitude toward other possibilities that the Germans might use against France and Britain.

The Germans struck through Holland and Belgium. The resistance offered by those countries was weak, and the Germans came out on the border with France and entered French territory. There, without great difficulty, they routed the French and British troops and advanced into the heart of the country. In the region of Dunkirk, they inflicted a major defeat on the armies of their opponents, and the British immediately began the process of evacuating troops to the British Isles, and they did succeed in withdrawing many of their troops. Everything seemed to indicate that Great Britain had abandoned the idea of fighting the Germans on French territory. In the press at that time a great deal was written about the Germans' use of a new method of warfare: landings by parachute troops in the enemy's rear. Such landings caused panic among the French and sent them fleeing. The road to Paris lay open to the Germans.

At that time by chance I was in Moscow. (I forget whether I had gone there with some questions or whether Stalin had summoned me.) I saw that Stalin was very worried by the course of military events in the West, but he didn't unburden himself on the subject or express his point of view. In the course of an exchange of opinions, he said only that the French and British had proved to be very weak, had not successfully resisted the Germans, and the latter were pursuing their offensive and realizing their aims. The news came over the radio that the Germans had entered Paris and the French army had surrendered. At that point Stalin dropped his reserved manner and very irritably gave the French and British governments a good cursing out for the fact that they had allowed their troops to be routed.

Stalin was very quick tempered and irritable at that time. I had rarely seen him like that. At meetings he hardly ever sat down in his chair but constantly paced back and forth. Now he literally ran around the room and cursed like a trooper. He cursed the French and he cursed the British, asking how they could have let Hitler smash them like that. I was still in his presence at that time, and probably Molotov was too. He was always with Stalin. It was rare that I would be in Stalin's office without Molotov or Beria being there. Zhdanov was often there as well, but less often than the others.

Why did Stalin react so strongly to the fall of Paris? The Germans had now realized their aims in the West: they had forced France to capitulate and established a pro-German government headed by Pétain.[10] For them this was the end of the war in France. Only one goal remained for the Germans—to force Britain to capitulate, to organize an invasion of the British Isles. A victory of the Germans in France was a signal that the danger of a war against the Soviet Union had increased. In the West, forces hostile to the Germans had been smashed; consequently, there remained for them a primary task—to crush the Soviet Union, an area that the Germans had found enticing since ancient times because of its riches and vast territory. But the main thing was the clash of ideas. After all, Hitler had assumed the holy obligation of serving as the liberator of Europe and the world from Marxism. Therefore the main enemy, enemy number one, consisted in the ideas of Marxism-Leninism, and the chief proponents of those ideas were the peoples of the Soviet Union who had made them a living reality. A war against us was inevitable. It had already been declared in Hitler's book *Mein Kampf*. This moment was drawing near and Stalin felt alarmed.

He was further alarmed because he understood that our army was not as strong as was claimed in the newspapers and talked about at rallies. The Red Army had shown its weakness in the war with the Finns, in which we had suffered big losses and in which we had realized only with great difficulty the aims we had set ourselves. As a result of the Finnish war, a change of leadership had occurred at the People's Commissariat of Defense: Timoshenko had replaced Voroshilov.

The easy defeat of the British and French troops, accomplished without any special effort on the part of the Germans, frightened Stalin even more. True, there were people in France who refused to recognize the surrender, who fled the country and organized their own resistance movement. This was headed by de Gaulle.[11] We were sure that the French Communist Party was also doing everything it could to organize a struggle against the occupation forces. But that took time, and the Germans of course would use every opportunity to achieve their final goal in the West more rapidly—the defeat of England either by invasion or through diplomatic negotiations. All of that would untie the hands of the Germans in the West. Their rear area would be secure, and this would give them the opportunity to move their troops against the Soviet Union.

With the arrival of Marshal Timoshenko at the People's Commissariat of Defense, the work there began to move forward, according to my observations. Those were rather fragmentary and not fully reliable observations. Only now and then I would hear Timoshenko reporting to Stalin or Stalin calling Timoshenko on military matters. At that time everyone was searching for the possibility of creating a better infantry weapon. After the Finnish war the question was raised of manufacturing a rapid-fire automatic weapon for our foot soldiers. At the same time a new, lighter, rapid-fire rifle with more bullets in each cartridge was being introduced among the troops. People argued a lot about these questions. Some military men expressed themselves sharply; they were opposed to providing our troops with automatic weapons, supporting their point of view with the argument that this would reduce the accuracy with which soldiers aimed their weapons and consequently would reduce the effectiveness of their firing. It took the Finnish war, in which the Finns successfully used German automatic weapons, to decide this argument.

Stalin alone was in charge of all these questions, and no one else was allowed to get involved. The same was true with tanks. I remember that Stalin said to me in 1940: "You should pay attention to the fact that in Kharkov at a former locomotive plant a high-capacity diesel engine is being produced. This is a very interesting diesel engine, being produced in the Soviet Union for the first time. I have in mind the fact that it might be possible to use it for heavy bombers." Stalin's calculation was that if diesel engines were installed in airplanes, less fuel would have to be used and the airplanes' flight range would be increased. Here is another characteristic thing: he told me that at this factory a diesel engine was being made that would be used for military purposes, but even as first secretary of the Central Committee of the Ukrainian Communist Party I hadn't known about it. This was not surprising. To understand this, one would have to know the procedures that were being followed then. We had absolutely no access to military factories; party officials were not admitted there. Even though a party organization existed at the plant, I didn't know about the production of the diesel engine; they didn't report it to me. I knew only that the plant produced locomotives. The shop where the diesel engines were made was blocked off; it was guarded, and people could enter only with special passes; others had no right to stick their noses in this business. Only Stalin and those who had a direct connection with organizing this production knew about it.

It was only after Stalin had called me [and told me about it] that I went to this factory and made the acquaintance of the designer of this diesel engine, Comrade Chupakhin.[12] The engine was indeed very interesting. I couldn't draw any conclusion as to whether it would be suitable for installation in a bomber, but for a tank (and Chupakhin had designed it for a tank) it was an excellent diesel engine. The party organizer for the Central Committee at this plant then was Yepishev.[13] He had just graduated from the military academy, as I recall, and had been assigned as party organizer from the Central Committee; that is, he was not elected by the party organization but simply confirmed by the Central Committee of the AUCP(B) and did not have to report to the local party organizations.

I established communication with the factory and began to observe the course of the work there. I don't remember what month it was, but it was in the summer when they called to tell me that on such-and-such a day near Kharkov, on the Seversky Donets River,[14] a T-34 tank would be tested. This was a new and very promising tank. I immediately went to Kharkov: I wanted to see how the diesel engine worked and what kind of tank this was. I arrived in Kharkov and went out to the testing ground to the east of Kharkov the very same day. The testing area for the tank had been well chosen, with loose sand and marshy areas next to a lake. Observing from an elevated location nearby, I saw this tank run through its paces, overcoming the obstacles of both sand and marsh.

I remember another incident that happened then. I recalled it many times when I later encountered this comrade. Next to me at the testing grounds were people who I did not know personally. One of them was a handsome man of about thirty-eight, perhaps forty, in a dark-blue, well-made, clean pair of overalls. He asked me: "Comrade Khrushchev, what's your assessment of this tank? Is it a good tank?"

I said: "Apparently it's a very good tank; it will really be a menace for our enemies. But a tank is a tank; after all, a tank is a kind of wagon, but the heart of the tank is the motor. Since the motor's good, this tank is really running well."

He was an intelligent man with a sense of humor. He glanced at me and said: "You've apparently made a mistake, Comrade Khrushchev. You seem to think that I'm the designer of the diesel engine, that is, Chupakhin. But I am not Chupakhin. I am Kucherenko,[15] one of the group of engineers who built this tank. But a tank is by no means a wagon!" And he smiled.

I apologized and said: "You guessed right; I really did think you were Chupakhin. It is my opinion—I don't know how right this is—but I still think that the power and maneuverability of a tank depends on its motor." As an engineer and designer he began to explain to me the merits of this particular tank's design. Later I had occasion to be convinced in practice that he was right. These tanks really did prove to be powerful weapons for the Red Army, but unfortunately at the beginning of the war there were still only a very few of them.

After the conversation with Stalin, I often went to that factory and familiarized myself in considerable detail with the production and organization of the factory. Stalin proposed that the factory be expanded, that serial production of the diesel engine be started, and extensive production of T-34 tanks be organized.

War was inexorably approaching. Although Stalin very rarely discussed this question, even avoided the subject, remaining closed off and reserved, it was evident that he was very troubled and that the situation disturbed him greatly. He began drinking then, and he drank a fairly large amount; not only did he himself drink, but he made others drink, too. Invariably if he summoned you, there would be a great many other people with him. It seemed that he gathered as large a group of people around him as he could. I thought that he was troubled because he had been left a widower, that he was feeling bad about it and therefore felt the need for a lot of company to distract himself from thoughts that disturbed him. But those thoughts included the inevitability of war, and the main thing (which he was apparently also thinking about) was that in this war we might suffer defeat. Previously he had not been afraid of a war. On the contrary, he held the view that a war would bring us victory and consequently the expansion of socialist territory, where new socialist relations would be established, where the revolutionary Marxist-Leninist banner would wave victoriously. But in this period he was no longer thinking in that way. On the contrary, he seemed to be troubled by the thought that if a war began, we could lose everything that we had gained under Lenin's leadership.

After the capitulation of the French, the Germans became more arrogant. This arrogance was expressed in unceremonious spy flights by their air force across the borders of the Soviet Union. They went as deep into our territory as Chernigov, and once we intercepted them flying over Shostka.[16] Apparently they were reconnoitering flight paths for bombing the Shostka gunpowder factory. There were cases in which Germans made forced landings. I remember that one of their planes landed in the Ternopol region, and the peasants took the German pilots prisoner. It ended with these pilots being released, the airplane being repaired, and all this passed by quietly without any protest, as I recall. This strengthened the fascists in their certainty that they could act with impunity.

On the border we saw that the Germans were concentrating their troops, that they were getting ready, and that war was inevitable. Naturally we too were worried, no less than Stalin. I remember that the commander of the KOVO troops and I addressed a letter to Stalin. As secretary of the Central Committee of the Ukrainian Communist Party, I proposed to write to Stalin and tell him what was being done by the Germans along our border. We needed to carry out some work to fortify our border so that we wouldn't be caught flatfooted. Work was going on to construct long-term reinforced concrete fortifications, with strong points for artillery and machine-gun installations. This business was moving along very slowly, and it was obvious we would not have time to complete it. That's why I suggested to the commander that we write this letter. He agreed.

We requested that Stalin allow us to temporarily mobilize 150,000 or more collective farmers, bring them to the border, and have them dig anti-tank ditches and other earthworks to help fortify the border. We felt it was necessary to do this. We understood that the Germans would see everything we were doing, and that the German spy network in the western regions of Ukraine was fairly widespread. Thus it was impossible to do anything secretly. The Germans too, for their part, were openly building fortifications along their border, and we needed to do something in response. But Stalin forbade this, saying that it might serve as a basis for provocation. He replied to us very irritably. The Germans continued their work and we did nothing. As a result our border remained open to the enemy, which he took full advantage of later on.

How do I explain this behavior of Stalin's? I think he also saw everything and understood. When the pact with Ribbentrop was signed, Stalin said: "Well now, who's deceiving who? We are deceiving Hitler." He took everything in his own hands. This was his initiative; he decided that he would deceive Hitler. But when we had already learned the lesson of the war with the Finns, a lesson not in our favor, when the Germans so easily crushed the troops of the French and British and continued to conduct air operations against the British fairly successfully, bombing their cities and industry, he was now viewing the possibility of war differently and was afraid of it. As a result of this fear he didn't want to do anything that might disturb Hitler. Therefore he insisted that everything should be exported and delivered to Germany with care and exactitude as provided for under the treaty: oil, grain, and I don't know what other goods.

Possibly he thought that Hitler would see how carefully and precisely we were fulfilling our obligations under the pact with Germany. Perhaps he thought Hitler would give up the idea of a war against us. But that was absurd thinking. It was dictated by uncertainty and perhaps even by cowardice. This cowardice resulted as I have said from the fact that we had shown our weakness in the war with the Finns, while the Germans had shown their strength in the war with the British and French. It was these events that produced such a state of mind in Stalin that he somehow lost self-confidence and lost the necessary drive and energy to lead the country.

By 1940 many matters of dispute had piled up between Hitler and us. After lengthy negotiations it was agreed that Molotov would make a trip to Berlin. He went there by train.[17] I arrived in Moscow after he had already made the trip. This was, it seems, in October or November 1940. I heard discussions in the leadership at that time that I didn't like. Apparently Stalin felt the need to ask Molotov about something. From Stalin's questions and Molotov's replies, the conclusion could be drawn that Molotov's trip had further strengthened the understanding that war was inevitable. It was evident that war was bound to break out in the near future. In Stalin's face and in his manner one could sense agitation and, I would add, fear. Molotov, not a talkative person by nature, described Hitler also as a man who did not say much and who abstained completely from alcohol. In Berlin during the official banquet, wine was served to a small group of people, but Hitler didn't take as much as one glass; he had tea, and he kept the drinkers company by sipping on his tea. I don't know specifically what business matters were discussed in Berlin, what questions were taken up, and what disagreements we had with the Germans. It was very difficult to understand.

A certain practice had grown up among us: if you're not told, don't ask. It wasn't considered essential that people know about these matters. Of course this is not the correct approach. It's fine in dealings with lesser officials. But in regard to members of the government and of the Politburo—the leading bodies of the party and the country—this was a violation of all the rules that were supposed to exist in the party if it was to be truly democratic. But our Leninist party had taken on precisely this character. The restriction and selection of information to be provided to members of the Politburo were decided by Stalin. If we are to talk about rights under the party rules, no such rights existed, nor could they exist. This was a result of the arbitrary rule that had come into being and that had acquired legitimacy under Stalin.

Molotov said that during his trip very strict security measures were taken to ensure the safety of the train traveling from the border to Berlin. Everywhere within his field of vision from the train he could see soldiers standing. He said that during the official discussions someone suddenly came in and reported that the British were making an air raid and their planes were about to appear over Berlin. It was proposed that everyone take refuge in a bomb shelter. They did so, and Molotov understood that it was already a familiar practice to use the bomb shelter. This indicated that the British were giving Berlin fairly solid grounds for concern, so that Hitler and his retinue had to resort to using bomb shelters.

Several months after Molotov's trip to Berlin a peculiar incident occurred. Hess[18] flew to England and parachuted to the ground. Hess was a former pilot, and therefore he could easily have carried out this operation. The Germans circulated the false report, or "canard," that he had fled. But it was obvious that something else was being hidden here and that in the story of Hess's alleged flight some things didn't add up. Suspicion arose that this had not been just an attempt to escape from Nazi Germany. When Molotov was in London during the war, a proposal was made that he could meet with Hess, but Molotov refused. I asked Stalin back then: "Doesn't Hess's flight represent some sort of special mission being carried out on orders from Hitler? Hess took all the responsibility on himself in order not to tie Hitler's hands, but in fact he was acting as an emissary for Hitler. He was not escaping, but in fact he flew there on Hitler's orders to try to come to an agreement with London on stopping the war and untying Hitler's hands for a campaign to the east."

Stalin listened to me and said: "Yes, that's what it was. You understand this question correctly." He didn't go into the subject any further, but simply agreed with me. For Stalin the beginning of the war was a very painful experience. During the first few days, as is generally known, he was completely paralyzed in both his thinking and his actions, and he even made a statement about giving up the leadership of the country and party.

After Molotov's trip to Berlin, there was no longer any question that there would be a war. But the suggestion was that the war could be temporarily postponed. Hitler was getting ready; the war would be unleashed in the near future, but exactly when we of course couldn't know. I don't think that even Stalin knew. It was impossible to know because every country hides from its enemy the time when a war is going to start even if it has decided to start that war.

During the winter, at the end of 1940 or the beginning of 1941, I went to Moscow on one occasion. As soon as I arrived, the phone immediately rang. I was told that Stalin wanted me to come see him at his "nearby" dacha and that he himself was not well. I went to see him. Stalin was lying, fully dressed, on a cot and reading. We exchanged greetings, and Stalin said he wasn't feeling well. Then he began telling me about military matters. This was the only time he started to talk with me about them. Apparently he felt the need for a confidant. It weighed on him very heavily that he was alone. That is what I think. This inner urge to exchange views with someone on questions of a military nature usually did not arise in him. He was usually far removed from such feelings because he apparently had a high regard for his own abilities and a low regard for those of others.

He said that a conference of military people was going on then[19] and that he was deprived of the opportunity to take part. The decision had been made at that conference in favor of a certain weapon. This had angered Stalin, and he immediately made a telephone call, it seems, to Timoshenko, the people's commissar of defense. He began reprimanding him about something, placing special importance on artillery and criticizing the decision that had been made. Apparently there had been broad participation in the conference, with all the commanders of troops of military districts participating. I speak of this to show that at that time measures were already being taken to prepare for the onslaught of Hitler's hordes on the Soviet Union.

The outward signs of deep inner suffering and emotional turmoil on Stalin's part were something I could treat in a human way because our country really was facing the bottomless pit. Hitler had succeeded in subjugating the countries of Europe, bringing his troops right up to the borders of the Soviet Union, and deploying his troops along a line adjacent to the line of our troops. They were separated only by the border established after the downfall of the Polish state. The danger was the greatest, I would say, in all the history of the existence of the USSR. A mortal threat was impending for the Soviet Union. Three major powers—Germany, Italy, and Japan—had united against the USSR. And what about the other powers? America was too far away from us. No one knew what position it would take if the Germans attacked the Soviet Union. Britain was at war with Germany and still preserved its independence, which however was hanging by a thread. The British land forces were weak. Would Britain be able to hold out? Would it be able to beat back the attempts by Hitler's Germany to land an expeditionary force on the British Isles? That still remained unknown.

So Stalin's troubled and disturbed feelings were quite understandable. He felt that danger was imminent. Would our country be able to deal with it? Would our army deal with it? The experience of the Finnish war had shown its weakness. This gave even greater grounds for worry and concern. After all it was no accident that, because of the state of our army, we had suffered huge losses in the war with the Finns. In response, the military leadership had been changed: Voroshilov had been removed from the post of people's commissar of defense, and a new commissar had been appointed, Timoshenko. One has to try to imagine the significance of this, because relations between Stalin and Voroshilov had been, to say the least, very friendly. I always saw them together; they were inseparable. If Stalin had gone to this extent [that is, to replace Voroshilov], one could imagine how deeply affected he was by the weakness our army had displayed in the war with the Finns!

I remember that Stalin said once during a conversation that Hitler, through confidential channels, had asked him for a favor. The German troops had occupied France, and he wanted Stalin as an authority in the Communist world to provide him with some help, that is, to exert influence on the French Communist Party so that it would not take the lead in the resistance movement against German occupation. Stalin was indignant about this insolence. It wasn't even a question of what reply to give. Hitler had descended not just to something vile, but to outright filthiness. How dared he make the assumption that Stalin would agree to a deal of such foul character? A base and unworthy deal. To provide assistance to fascism through the French Communist Party? The very idea!

In another incident, when the Germans were engaged in fighting to take Danzig,[20] the operation was carried out like a theatrical performance. The Germans had set up movie cameras ahead of time. The battles were filmed from both land and sea, and they sought to distribute this film as widely as possible in all countries of the world. Apparently Hitler was pursuing the aim of demonstrating the irresistible might of the fascist forces to make his future enemies tremble and to paralyze their will. Hitler proposed that Stalin take this film and have it shown through our network of motion picture theaters, to show our audiences how the Germans had dealt with Danzig, with Poland, with all of Europe. That's the kind of diversionary action Hitler thought up against our people.

Stalin proposed certain conditions. He said: "If you want to take one of our films (showing very well organized maneuvers, which would have made a strong impression), then we'll take your film." Hitler of course would not agree to such an exchange. That was how Stalin parried the thrust from

Hitler's side, the proposed diversionary act that the latter had undertaken by proposing that we show a film of the Polish forces being defeated. Nevertheless this film was sent to us by the Germans, and we took a look at it together with Stalin. It really did have a depressing effect, especially on people who assumed that those same weapons would soon be turned against them. And that's exactly the situation we were in. In our country at that time a play was being performed, with the title *The Keys to Berlin*.[21] This was also seen as a psychological preparation of our country and our troops for war. In past history there had been occasions when Russian troops had taken Berlin and received the keys to the city gates, which of course upset the Germans. This was a way of psychologically steeling our people against the fascists, who were trumpeting the assertion that everything in the world would soon come under their rule, and that they could smash any opponent army. But in the play Russian troops were shown smashing the Germans and entering Berlin after defeating them.

The prospect of an inevitable war stood out clearly long before the war actually began, and even much earlier than the pact that was signed between the Soviet Union and Hitler's Germany. It was well known from Hitler's own writings that if the fascists came to power it meant war against the Soviet Union. In *Mein Kampf* Hitler laid out his aggressive plans and his misanthropic worldview. He posed the task above all of crushing the Soviet Union and destroying Communism. The stronghold of Communism was the Soviet Union, and when Hitler did come to power, he immediately began to prepare his army for this. This was no secret. With great commotion military parades were held in German cities, and threatening speeches were made against us. But apparently Stalin was under the impression that in our country everything was in good order and that our army and its weaponry were at the necessary level of preparedness, as were the command staff and the mood of the population. And truly the mood of the population testified to its monolithic unity in rallying around the party.

The fascists, like all bourgeois ideologists, calculated that since the Soviet Union was a multinational state, it would therefore fall apart at the very first confrontation, like a giant with feet of clay: ethnic conflicts would arise, the unity and solidarity of the population would fall apart, and consequently our armed forces would lose their solidity. But that turned out to be the delirious ravings of those who took their wishes for reality. The wise Leninist policy toward the non-Russian nationalities after the October revolution during the years of Soviet rule had turned everything around. Of course there was unevenness and roughness. It would take decades to outlive all this. But the main thing had already been done. The various nationalities of our country, the workers, peasants, and intellectuals felt that the only way to have strength was in unity. Our strength was not in our differences or in conflicts among nationalities, but in unity and monolithic solidity. The war convincingly confirmed this and shattered the illusion that our enemies had been cultivating.

The military parades and maneuvers that we held played a major positive role. But they also played a negative role in the sense that they dampened the people's ardor and willpower and had a lulling effect on everyone, concealing the shortcomings that actually existed in the Red Army. Apparently Stalin underestimated this aspect of the matter. He estimated the combat readiness of our army incorrectly, influenced by the impressions made by motion pictures showing our parades and military maneuvers. For a long time Stalin had seen almost nothing of real life. He hardly ever left Moscow. He went outside the Kremlin only to go to his dacha or to Sochi, nowhere else. He received relevant information only through Voroshilov. The latter, of course, reported things as he himself understood them, and he also made a wrong estimation of the condition of the Red Army. He considered it to be on a high level, easily capable of repelling an invasion by Hitler. And so before the war a great many things were left undone.

Would it have been possible, back then, to think that the real state of affairs was different from what was generally assumed? Let me take myself as an example. I was a member of the Politburo and moved in the circles around Stalin and the government. Was I capable of thinking that literally in the very first days of the war we wouldn't even have a sufficient quantity of rifles and machine guns? Why, it's elementary. Even under the tsar, when he was getting ready for a war with Germany, there turned out to be larger quantities of rifles [than we had]. It was not until 1915 or 1916 that the tsar encountered a shortage of rifles. But for us, there was a shortage of rifles and machine guns on the very second day of the war. And after all, our potential in the economic sense was incomparably greater than for the tsarist government.

I was astounded. How could it have been that no one knew? I don't know whether Stalin was aware of this before the war. Probably he, too, didn't know. But Voroshilov couldn't have helped knowing. What was the people's commissar of defense supposed to know, if not that? By this I mean the state of our military equipment and the reserves we had built up in the event of war, military supplies, ammunition, artillery weapons, and infantry weapons. But it turned out that he didn't know. This was a crime! The people who were responsible seemed unconcerned. To them, apparently, it was like water off a duck's back. They smiled in front of the cameras and the motion picture crews. But if Stalin had known about this! It was necessary to bring the whole party to its feet, immediately mobilize industry, work intensively to prepare for war, assign specific factories engage in the production of artillery, rifles, automatic weapons, antiaircraft guns, antitank guns, ammunition, and military supplies. I'm not even talking about tanks and airplanes.

I'm not talking about them, not because I underestimate them as an important armament for the Red Army, but because those types of weapons were more eye catching, more obvious, and they came within the sphere of Stalin's direct attention and concern. For that reason our air power was better prepared. Our tanks were no worse [than the enemy's] and the T-34 surpassed all other tanks in the world. But there were not enough T-34s; more needed to be manufactured. I don't want to talk too much about the T-34 tank right now because we may have been late in constructing and designing it. Our technical thinking may have lagged behind. But after this tank was actually produced, after there had been tests and its excellent qualities had been displayed in those tests, something could have been done at that point. The tests took place in Kharkov, it seems to me, in summer 1940. We still had an entire year. If we had immediately put this tank into production on an emergency wartime footing, established several factories, and organized extensive cooperation among those factories, we could have accomplished a great deal. And the war itself showed that our people, our level of technology, and our engineering staffs were capable of such things.

Under wartime conditions, conditions more difficult than in the prewar period, we actually did organize production of the T-34 quite quickly, starting from scratch in the sense that the factory that carried out this work had never before produced tanks. Yet it began to produce T-34s in fairly large quantities. Consequently the technological and material possibilities, the human resources, the designing skills, and the scientific and technical knowledge were there. If we had evaluated the situation correctly and set ourselves the proper tasks, we would not have had such a disaster as the one we encountered in regard to artillery, tanks, and airplanes in the first days of the war. Later, during the course of the war, we had to make up for this lack. Heroic efforts were exerted, and they were justified. Once it obtained such arms and equipment, our army was able to defeat Hitler's hordes in the war.

I blame Voroshilov first of all for the poor level of preparation of the Red Army. He was the commissar of defense and consequently this was one of his obligations. He should have raised these questions. I don't know of any case in which Stalin refused when a question of providing armaments was brought up. We devoted major resources to arms. Consequently the people who were directly responsible for such matters were guilty of miscalculation. Our weakness was also shown in the following fact: [our shortage of well-trained officers]. I don't know which undermined our army more, the shortage of weapons or the weakness of our cadres. Unquestionably both the one and the other had an effect. Which had more of an effect is hard to say now because even an intelligent commander without tanks, without artillery, and without machine guns would find it hard to lead his forces successfully and have them carry out the tasks that lay before them. On the other hand, even with the best equipment, if an army doesn't have sufficiently trained, educated, and prepared cadres, the effectiveness of having such weapons available is greatly reduced.

But everyone knows about our weakness in regard to cadres and the reason for that weakness. Our cadres had been smashed and shattered as "enemies of the people." Today all over our country there are monuments to those "enemies of the people" who got such a thorough "working over" back then. If those people had been at the head of the army when Hitler was preparing to attack us and even much earlier, long before he attacked us, their intelligence and energy would have been used to prepare the army, to train it, and to build up the necessary reserves for the conduct of the war. Tukhachevsky was especially good at doing this kind of thing. I'm convinced that if he had not been executed, but had continued his activities as deputy people's commissar of defense, the situation we found ourselves in at the beginning of the war in regard to armaments would not have existed. He understood, valued, and loved military innovation.

If we were to weigh on very fine scales, like a pharmacist's, whose guilt was greater here—Voroshilov's or Stalin's—I would say that the guilt was equal, that both Voroshilov and Stalin were equally guilty, perhaps with a somewhat greater degree of guilt going to Stalin. Although Voroshilov did defend people vigorously and disputed with Stalin about them sometimes, at other times he gave in to Stalin's eager desire to exterminate our cadres. I consider both men guilty; each of them is no less guilty than the other.

What can be said about the other members of the Politburo and government? Closest of all to Stalin, in the sense of being admitted to decisions on one or another question, was Molotov. But this was not his field. It's difficult to assign guilt to Molotov. He can be blamed for the fact that he didn't restrain himself, but encouraged Stalin to exterminate cadres. In this respect perhaps Molotov is more to blame than Voroshilov. But Molotov had hardly any influence on questions of armaments and the combat readiness of the Red Army.

I repeat, if we had assessed the situation correctly and placed our industry at the service of the army and the defense of the country, which is after all why we built our industry, many things would have been different. Every blue-collar worker, engineer, white-collar worker, and peasant would have unsparingly exerted every effort; they would have taken their last bit from their families and given it to the defense fund. Fund raising and contributions for the production of tanks and airplanes were organized. The question of issuing war bonds was raised by public opinion. This was a demonstration of the kind of thinking that is incomprehensible to bourgeois historians and ideologists. Soviet citizens, in handing over their savings, were thinking about their country, its defense, and the future, and for the sake of that future they did not begrudge anything, did not spare anything, including their own lives.

Therefore if the question of defense of the country, the question of reorganizing industry to serve military needs, had been posed, and if as a result it had been necessary for people to tighten their belts somewhat, no one would have complained. People understood then the significance of the threat of fascist Germany to the Soviet Union; they sensed it and evaluated it correctly. But unfortunately the leadership did not evaluate it correctly, and the necessary conclusions were not drawn. I think that this occurred as a result of lack of knowledge of the real situation in regard to our military equipment and the state of the army and its cadres, because even in relation to cadres a great deal could have been done if attention had been paid to this matter on a timely basis.

If everything had been correctly evaluated and the proper conclusions drawn about reorganizing our industry and preparing for war, creating military reserve supplies, distributing these reserves geographically in the correct way, [things would have gone better]. Instead, we based ourselves on false slogans, which were made part of Voroshilov's everyday life as defense commissar, I don't know by whom—the slogans, for example, "We won't give up one inch of our land" and "We will fight only on the territory of the enemy." As a result, supply bases were located right at the border, but they should have been moved back, deep into the country, so that if during the war our troops were forced to retreat, those bases would not immediately fall into the enemy's hands.

And why talk about supply bases when Mekhlis, a wild and impulsive person, who enjoyed Stalin's unlimited confidence and therefore became head of the Main Political Directorate of the Red Army, suggested to Stalin the idea that the old defensive lines along our former border should be destroyed, such as the Kiev fortified region and others? The reason for this was supposedly that military personnel were orienting toward defending the country in these locations and were not doing or thinking much about smashing the enemy on our new borders. So these reinforced concrete pillboxes were stripped; the artillery and machine guns were taken out of them. Was it necessary to go to such lengths!? Later when the Germans were approaching Kiev, we had to hunt for anything that we could put into these pillboxes in order to strengthen our defenses.

I want to be understood correctly. What I am talking about now requires no proof. I am speaking to future generations as a witness who was in the thick of things among the people themselves and also was close to Stalin and other leaders of the party and the people. One must try to imagine how we could have organized our industry and what we could have done in a short time! But unfortunately we didn't do it, and we ended up having to retreat as far as Stalingrad and Makhachkala,[22] surrendering almost all of the Northern Caucasus region. A dreadful catastrophe befell the peoples of the Soviet Union, and this could have been avoided. I don't know who among the leaders of the government and the Politburo, other than Stalin, knew about this state of affairs, the condition of the Red Army's equipment, its quality and quantity. Did Stalin know everything? I think that probably Stalin himself didn't know things all that well.

I remember the following episode. Whenever I was in Moscow Stalin always summoned me, and he called me in to see him almost every day. Sometimes I was alone, but more often I was there with other members of the Politburo. I remember that one of our military people, probably Timoshenko, told Stalin that we didn't have enough antiaircraft guns. Stalin looked at us and said that we had to organize their production. That's only natural: if something is in short supply, you have to organize production of it, assign particularly factories to do it, or at least new shops in existing factories. Suddenly an idea occurred to Stalin: a new factory for large caliber machine guns should be built in Kiev. He told me: "Will you undertake to build this factory?"

I said: "If there is a decision to do it, we will build it."

He said: "Then build the factory!" The decision was made then and there; a construction site was designated on the left [or east] bank of the Dnieper River across from Kiev in the Darnitsa region. It's an area of sandy soil, and construction of our factory was begun on that soil. This was in 1940 or perhaps in early 1941. Something was accomplished there; a certain amount of cement was poured to build a foundation. But at the time when the Germans captured Kiev nothing more had been built than that.

Time was allowed to slip by. I don't know how other similar questions were solved, but the main thing is that sluggishness and inertia reigned, along with what I would call a kind of breakdown of morale, because this was not the Stalin I had known. Why couldn't we—at a time when war was going on in the West, and a war against us was about to begin, when we needed antiaircraft guns, without which war can't be waged in modern conditions when a powerful enemy air force is operating—why couldn't we build that new factory? We had so many factories. Some existing factory (or factories) should have been organized to produce antiaircraft guns, as was actually done after the war began. We would have mastered the production of those weapons quickly. But what happened here was that we made only a show of doing something to soothe people's consciences and calm their nerves. That's why they began to build a factory. A year was needed to build it and then still more time to master the details of production. In fact a year wasn't enough. Why do this when the armed forces had urgent needs? Existing factories should have been reorganized, but that was not done, and that made itself felt very substantially in the first days of the war. We turned out to be really without machine guns, without antiaircraft guns, and even without rifles.

Above all this was an oversight by the Defense Commissariat. How could we be preparing for war if we weren't getting the necessary productive capacity ready and weren't producing the necessary reserve supplies and arms? We didn't have enough light arms, items we had learned how to make long before—items like machine guns and rifles. Not to mention that there were no antitank weapons and so on.

The explanation for this, as I see it, was the collapse of Stalin's will, his demoralization over the victories Hitler had won in the West, and our lack of success in the war with the Finns. Stalin was facing Hitler like a rabbit in front of a boa constrictor; he was paralyzed in his actions. This made itself felt both in the lack of production of arms and in the fact that we didn't prepare our borders for defense. We were afraid that our work would be noticed by the Germans, which might cause a war. But you can't think that way! The war was inevitable. When we signed the pact with Hitler, the only question that remained was one of timing; with that pact we had won a little time. The war began in the West instead of the East. But we knew that the war would inevitably come to us. I think that when Stalin signed that pact with Hitler he understood all this, then later he suddenly lost the ability to evaluate events correctly. I think he was demoralized and paralyzed in his actions, and as a result we didn't make full use of our possibilities.

We had a powerful industry then in Ukraine, Moscow, Leningrad, and other parts of the Soviet Union. I have in mind the European part of the Soviet Union, where the heaviest industry was located. But then Belorussia and Ukraine were occupied, Rostov on the Don was occupied, and industry in Stalingrad was destroyed. All of that could have been used to create the necessary reserves of arms and equipment to meet the foe fully armed. I don't remember what proportion of total production was accounted for by Ukraine, but the main metallurgical industry of our country was concentrated there. People who ended up in the occupied territory told me later that when the Germans came to the Donbas and occupied Mariupol they called in their engineers, looked over all the plant and equipment, and kept repeating: "Why it's the Ruhr, the Ruhr!" They were comparing the Donbas region to the Ruhr, and everyone knows that the Ruhr was the biggest industrial base of the German state.[23]

I repeat that in regard to his morale Stalin was simply paralyzed by the inevitability of war. He apparently believed that war would result in the inevitable defeat of the USSR. Later I will tell about how Stalin conducted himself during the first days of the war and what he said at that time. Beria, Malenkov, Mikoyan, and other comrades who were with Stalin at that time told me about this later.

I want to say a few words about a conversation I had with Stalin concerning our tank troops. This was in 1940, as I recall, when I went to Kharkov to observe the testing of the T-34 tank and made the acquaintance of its designer Chupakhin, the inventor of the diesel motor, and one of the tank designers, Kucherenko. I don't remember the name of the main designer,[24] but I knew Kucherenko well. It was not the Kucherenko who was president of the Academy of Construction and Architecture,[25] but his brother, also a talented person, one of the co-designers of the T-34 tank. This tank was tested by none other than the head of the Red Army directorate for motorized and armored vehicles, Pavlov,[26] a celebrated figure and a hero of the war in Spain. He had distinguished himself there as a fighting member of a tank crew, a fearless individual who operated his tank with great skill. As a result Stalin appointed him to command our motorized troops and tank troops.

I had watched with admiration as Pavlov flew over the sandy ground and marshes near the Seversky Donets, east of Kharkov. Then he got out of the tank and came over to us. (We were standing on a small rise, watching.) I had a talk with him. He also talked with the designers and praised the tank, but he made a disheartening impression on me; he seemed to be a person who had not developed very much. I was simply amazed that someone with such a limited outlook, so poorly educated, could be responsible for the good condition of the motorized, armored, and tank forces of the Red Army. Would he be able to grasp everything, and would he actually grasp it all? Would he stipulate the tasks that were necessary to make this armament truly the basic element underlying the mighty power of the Red Army, mobile, armored, and tank forces? He knew that Hitler was putting the emphasis on tank troops. We had to produce antitank artillery, airplanes, and our own motorized and tank troops; we needed to give them high priority so that we could parry the blows of the enemy, using the same means that the enemy wished to use to smash and crush the Soviet Union.

I was very worried about all this. Soon after the tank tests I went to Moscow, and naturally I told Stalin how the testing had gone: I told about the tank's merits, what the designers had reported to me about its operational capabilities, how it traveled over sandy and marshy terrain. I had seen this myself. As for the sturdiness of the armor, that question was also answered [favorably] by the tests that had been carried out. This tank was remarkable! It was the best tank. And sure enough, in the war it made an excellent showing and forced our enemies to admit that this was the best tank in the world. Nevertheless, I decided to tell Stalin my doubts about the abilities of Pavlov as commander of motorized, armored, and tank forces. I had to express these doubts with great caution because my encounter with Pavlov had been brief and didn't really give me the right to argue insistently that he was not fit for the job. I wanted only to express my doubts; I wanted to alert Stalin in this way so that he would take a closer look at Pavlov and then take appropriate measures.

I couldn't proceed in any other way because I didn't know Pavlov very well. I couldn't say right out of the blue that he was unsuitable and so forth. And so I asked: "Comrade Stalin, do you know Pavlov well?"

He answered: "Yes, I know him well." I said: "He made a negative impression on me." And then I told Stalin that to me he seemed to be a fairly limited person, one who knew quite well how to operate a tank, but did he have sufficient intelligence to organize the motorized, armored, and tank troops, provide them with the correct equipment, and know how to utilize them properly? Stalin reacted irritably to my comments: "You don't know him." I said: "I told you ahead of time that I didn't know him very well."

He said: "But I do know him. Do you know how he distinguished himself in Spain, how he fought there? He's a knowledgeable person. He knows what a tank is. He himself fought in a tank." I said: "I simply wanted to tell you that the impression I formed of him was not in his favor. I also wanted to tell you another doubt that I have. Marshal Kulik is responsible for all artillery weapons. (I had observed him more than Pavlov, and I saw that he was very disorganized but very self-assured and willful.) I don't know if he can cope with his duties. War is imminent, and he is responsible for both artillery and infantry weapons. A very great responsibility rests on him, and knowing his personality, I doubt that he can make sure everything is provided for."

At this point Stalin reacted even more violently: "Here you are talking about Kulik, and you don't know Kulik. I know him from Tsaritsyn[27] during the Civil War. He commanded the artillery there. He's a man who knows artillery."

I said: "Comrade Stalin, I don't doubt that he knows artillery and that he commanded the artillery well there, but how many cannons did he have then? Two or three? And here we are talking about an entire country. Under these new conditions other qualities are required of a person who must provide the necessary weapons for our Red Army." He waved his hand at me. He was annoyed that I was sticking my nose in where I had no business. I had foreseen this when I raised the question, because I knew how impatient Stalin could be if comments were made on any questions about the arming and organizing of the Red Army. He considered this his personal specialty, his brainchild, as it were, and he alone was competent to make decisions in this area. And he *was* the one who made the decisions.

Unfortunately my doubts were confirmed by life itself. Pavlov was relieved of his duties as commander of motorized, armored, and tank troops, not because he was unsuited to the task, but because he was given an even more responsible post. He was appointed commander of the troops of the Western Special Military District [in Belorussia], that is, the main central area leading toward Moscow from the west.[28] This was the strongest sector in our defenses, with the largest number of troops. The Kiev Special Military District held second place, and the Odessa district was third. This is understandable, because from Minsk [capital of Belorussia] there was a straight road right to Moscow. As for Kiev, that represented the south, the breadbasket of the Soviet Union, Ukraine with its mighty metallurgical industry, machinery production, and great human resources. Ukraine occupied a very important strategic and economic position. The enemy evaluated things correctly in aiming his blows at Ukraine.

When Pavlov was appointed commander of the troops in Belorussia, I didn't even know about this reshuffling, which was typical, even though I was a member of the Politburo. Stalin asked no one for advice and reported to no one. He reported only to his own conscience. And everyone knows what the upshot was. During the first days of the war Pavlov lost control of his troops. He completely failed to prepare his troops for Hitler's invasion and immediately lost his most important technical equipment: His airplanes were destroyed on the ground at their air bases, as we know. It is evident from German documents how the Germans succeeded in smashing the troops of the Western Special Military District centered on Belorussia. Those documents have now been published in the book entitled *Top Secret!* I have familiarized myself with this book. I haven't read all of it, but I'm familiar with the book. A great deal is written there about this. Stalin condemned Pavlov and his chief of staff.[29] These people were shot during the first days of the war. But the front had collapsed, and the Germans were advancing deep into our country without any resistance, while we were trying to bring up troops from the rear. People like Pavlov were at the helm of the Soviet armed forces, because the cadres trained and tested in the Russian Civil War had been destroyed, cadres who after the Civil War had acquired further education and experience. They were destroyed from top to bottom, beginning with Tukhachevsky and going down to squadron commanders.

And what about Kulik? Kulik was also arrested (although to be sure after the war). During the war he showed himself to be completely insignificant as a military leader, and Stalin reduced him in rank from marshal to major general.[30] I encountered Kulik in 1943 when he came to our Voronezh front. He was then in charge of an army of the guards. Shepilov was a member of his military council.[31] Vatutin and I deployed that army in the Poltava area.[32] Kulik himself came from some village near Poltava[33] and asked that this area be assigned to him. This coincided with the needs of military expediency at that moment. Vatutin and I often visited that army. I remember one occasion when we went and heard a report by Kulik. It was something you simply couldn't convey with words! The way he gave reports and the way he commanded troops could have served as material for a satirical newspaper column. What a totally unfit commander! We were obliged to raise the question with Stalin of relieving Kulik of his duties and assigning a new commander; otherwise he would destroy the army. Stalin resisted, and Kulik actually did mess up this army; he suffered heavy casualties and was unable to carry out the tasks right in front of him. Stalin was forced to agree with us; he relieved Kulik of his duties, recalled him, and sent a new commander to replace him.

The new commander (I should mention in passing) had no sooner arrived and was making his way to his army's headquarters when he was blown up by a mine.[34] Stalin made a big scandal about this, mainly accusing us of failing to protect our army commanders. Just before that, another commander of an army had been blown up; I forget his name; he was a very good commander, although well on in years, a Belorussian by nationality. He had also been riding in an automobile, hit a mine, and was blown up. I reported to Stalin after that: "There is a war on here; we are advancing and liberating territory from the enemy. This territory was under enemy occupation, and therefore it's been 'stuffed' pretty thoroughly [with mines], so there's no guarantee whether you're walking or riding that you won't be blown up by a mine. You propose that we need to take care of our commanders and protect them, but how can we protect them? A commander must go among his troops and command them, and for that he has to move around. It was totally accidental that the vehicle he was riding in hit a mine and blew up."

That's how, literally within one week, two commanders were killed. As far as I know, after that Kulik never returned to direct command of troops; he remained at the disposal of the chief administration for cadres and served as deputy head of the chief administration for the formation and staffing of units. Even before that, in 1941, he was assigned to fortify the city of Rostov on the Don. He stayed there and worked for a long time. It seems that Rostov was fortified fairly well, because there were engineers and sappers working there. Nevertheless Rostov fell to the enemy, and those fortifications played no role whatsoever. Still, that wasn't Kulik's fault, nor that of the sappers and engineers who carried out the work. I will explain later why Rostov fell practically without a shot when the Germans surrounded it from the north.

After Stalin's death and after the Twentieth Party Congress, where Stalin's abuses of power were revealed, there began a rehabilitation of innocent people who had been executed and imprisoned. Military men raised the question of rehabilitating Pavlov and other generals who had been condemned and executed for the collapse of our front lines during the first days of the war. This proposal was accepted, and they were rehabilitated. I was also in favor of that, although with this reservation: if the question is viewed from the standpoint of juridical and factual evidence, which is what the court based itself on when it sentenced them to death, the basis for this sentence was evident. Why did I agree to this rehabilitation at a time when I occupied a post from which I could exert influence in one direction or the other in deciding such important questions? I agreed because essentially it was not

Pavlov and other generals who were to blame, but Stalin. Pavlov was completely unprepared. I could see his lack of preparedness when I made his acquaintance. I had spoken to Stalin about this, and instead of drawing the necessary conclusions and selecting a more qualified individual for that post, Stalin reassigned Pavlov and gave him a promotion. I consider the post of commander of the troops of the Western Special Military District to have been a more responsible post than that of commander of the motorized, armored, and tank troops of the Red Army. I will return later to the question of Stalin's extermination of military cadres.

At the end of 1940 and the beginning of 1941 we felt that we were heading for a war. In my presence Stalin raised the point more than once that war was inevitable, but it was also obvious from his mood and behavior that he felt this and was very troubled and disturbed by it. What were the outward signs? How did they express themselves? In earlier times when I would arrive in Moscow from Kiev, he would immediately summon me to his apartment or dacha, more often to his dacha; he lived there more of the time. It was always pleasant to meet with him in those days, to hear what he had to say and to report to him. He always said something encouraging or explained one or another situation. In short, he carried out his functions as a leader with whom it was pleasant for each of us to converse. (At any rate I can say that for myself.) I was always eager for that.

When war began to approach, Stalin became completely different. Previously vodka and wine were placed on the table at dinner and were served to the dinner guests: you could pour some for yourself or you could choose not to pour. There was no goading or coercion. I remember once when I arrived from Ukraine, Stalin immediately invited me to come to his place. It was in summer 1938 or 1939. He was dining alone on the open porch of his little house. "Sit down," he said. I took a seat at the table. "Do you want to eat?" His dinner was a simple one: potato soup, and there was a bottle of vodka on the table with glasses. "Want something to drink?"

I said: "No." I refused and he said nothing. I found that very pleasing. In addition to the approaching menace of war, the appearance of Beria in Moscow had a big effect on the life of our group. When he showed up in Moscow, the life of Stalin and the group that had formed around him took on quite a different character.

When I talked to Stalin one-on-one, he sometimes expressed his dissatisfaction: "When we didn't have Beria with us here in Moscow, our meetings went along somehow differently; our dinners and suppers were different. But now he invariably introduces some kind of fear or competition over who will drink the most. An atmosphere has been created in which people drink more than they need to, and the orderly situation we used to have has been disrupted."

I completely agreed with Stalin, but I must say that even then I took a distrustful attitude toward such statements; I had seen that Stalin sometimes, to put it crudely, would turn a conversation in one direction or another in order to draw out the opinions of the people he was talking with. I saw that Stalin and Beria were on very friendly terms. To what extent that friendship was sincere I didn't know then. At any rate I saw that it was not by accident that Beria was appointed deputy commissar of internal affairs and soon, when Yezhov was replaced, arrested, and executed, Beria became the lord and master of that commissariat. He assumed decisive influence within our collective group. I saw that the people around Stalin, who held the highest posts in the party and government, were forced to take Beria into account, and they tended somewhat to ingratiate themselves, to fawn on him and toady toward him, especially Kaganovich.

It was only on Molotov's part that I failed to notice such unpleasant, ignoble bootlicking behavior. Molotov gave me the impression at that time of a man who was independent, thought for himself, and had his own opinions on one or another question, who expressed what he thought and told Stalin what he thought. It was evident that Stalin didn't like this, but Molotov still insisted on doing things his way. This, I would say, was an exception. We understood the reasons for Molotov's independent position. He was a very old friend of Stalin. Stalin had known Molotov, and Molotov had known Stalin during the underground days [under tsarist rule]. For many years Molotov had played his role in glorifying Stalin and building him up. Molotov was a bulwark of support for Stalin in the struggle against the opposition. That's why the oppositionists called him Stalin's club. Stalin unleashed him whenever he needed to strike heavy blows against one or another member of the Politburo who had opposed Stalin.

I will tell more about this later when I talk about the Stalin of the later period, after I had the possibility of understanding Stalin more deeply. Especially after his death and even before his death. Immediately after his death I looked at things differently and wept over the death of Stalin. But then, before the Twentieth Party Congress, when Beria had already been arrested, the trial of Beria was held, and we had the possibility of reopening the past and analyzing the reasons for the arrests and executions. This raised doubts in our minds about whether the arrests and the struggle against the enemies of the people had been correctly explained to the party and the people. I will talk about this in more detail further on.

Let me return to my point that on the eve of the war Stalin seemed to become gloomier. The look on his face was more preoccupied; he began to drink more and to make others drink. He literally forced us to drink! Among ourselves we had brief discussions about how to bring the supper or dinner to an end more quickly. Sometimes before supper or dinner, people would say: "Well, what's it going to be today, will there be a drinking contest or not?" We didn't want to have such contests because we had work to do, but Stalin deprived us of that opportunity. Dinners with him sometimes lasted until dawn; often these dinners caused a paralysis in the work of the government and the party leadership because when you left there, after being "tipsy" all night, sitting there pumped full of wine, there was no way you could do any work. We didn't drink much vodka or cognac. If anyone wanted to, he could drink an unlimited quantity. Stalin himself would just drink a glass of cognac or vodka at the beginning of dinner and then wine. But even if you drink nothing but wine for five or six hours, even small glasses, the devil only knows what will come of it! Even if you drink water with the wine, you get drunk from that, not just from the wine. Everyone felt repelled by this; it made you sick to the stomach; but Stalin was implacable on this matter.

Beria would be bustling about at these dinners, full of jokes and witty remarks. These jokes and comments spiced up the evenings and the drinking at Stalin's place. Beria himself would also get drunk, but I felt that he wasn't doing this because he enjoyed it, that he didn't really want to get drunk, and sometimes he expressed himself rather harshly and crudely about having to get drunk. He did this out of servility toward Stalin and forced others to do so as well. He would say: "We've got to get drunk, the sooner the better. The sooner we're drunk, the sooner the party will be over. No matter what, he's not going to let us leave sober." I understood that this atmosphere had been created because of a depressed mood [on Stalin's part]. Stalin saw an avalanche implacably bearing down on us that we couldn't escape, and his belief in the possibility of coping with this avalanche had been undermined. Of course this avalanche was the unavoidable war with Germany.

Hitler was harvesting the fruits of his victories won by force of arms. The entire Western press was trumpeting his victories. I read TASS reports where excerpts from the bourgeois newspapers were printed. They talked maliciously about the fact that when it came to the broad expanses of Ukraine,

Hitler's tanks would display their full strength, that the terrain of the Ukrainian republic was like a testing ground for tanks, and that therefore the German tanks would slice into the body of the Soviet Union like a knife into butter. I remember that expression being used in one of the British newspapers. Of course Stalin read all of this. When I would arrive in Moscow, Stalin would keep me at his place for a very long time. If I was in a hurry to get back, I would ask: "Can I go?"

He would answer: "What's your hurry? Stay here a while. Give your comrades [in Ukraine] the opportunity of working without you. Let them grow stronger; let them build up their strength." It was as though his comments were intended to catch your attention: "You have to give other comrades, who continue to work without your being there, a chance to get used to operating independently, to deciding questions independently, and so forth." All that was fine. But I could see that that really wasn't the issue. After all, there we were, sitting with him again, doing nothing and simply being a presence at all these dinners that had become so repulsive. They were undermining our health, depriving us of clear minds, putting our heads and our entire organisms in an unhealthy condition.

I think Stalin was suffering from the disease of loneliness then; he was afraid of solitude; he didn't want to be alone; he felt an overpowering need to be with people. It seems that the question of the inevitable war was constantly nagging at him, and he couldn't overcome his fear of that war. So then he began drinking and forcing others to drink, with the aim of "drowning his sorrows" in wine, as the saying goes, and in this way relieving his painful state of mind.

That is my impression. But I think it's correct, because earlier I hadn't noticed any such thing about him. I had been at Stalin's dinners when I worked as secretary of the Moscow city committee of the party. Those were family dinners; that's exactly what they were, with myself and Bulganin invited. Stalin always said jokingly then: "Well, here are the fathers of the city. Take your places." That really was a dinner. There was wine and everything else, but in fairly moderate quantities. If a person said that he couldn't drink, there was no compulsion. But on the eve of the war, if someone said he didn't feel like drinking or couldn't drink, that was regarded as totally impermissible. Later if someone didn't participate when a toast was made, he was "fined" by having to drink another glassful and perhaps several glasses. All sorts of other things were invented. Beria played a very big role in all this, and everything was reduced to the question of how to drink more and get everyone drunk. And that was done precisely because that's what Stalin wanted.

People might ask me: "What are you saying? That Stalin was a drunk?" I can answer that he was and he wasn't. That is, he *was* in a certain sense. In his later years he couldn't get by without drinking, drinking, drinking. On the other hand, sometimes he didn't pump himself as full as he did his guests; he would pour a drink for himself in a small glass and even dilute it with water. But God forbid that anyone else should do such a thing. Immediately he would be "fined" for deviating from the norm, for "trying to deceive society." This of course was a joke, but you had to do some serious drinking as a result of the joke. The person who had to drink because of this "joke" was forced to keep drinking seriously. and he paid for it with his health. My only explanation for all this was Stalin's state of mind. As some Russian songs used to say: "Drown your sorrows in drink." Evidently the same thing was true here.

After the war I had kidney trouble, and the doctors categorically refused to let me drink alcohol. I told Stalin about this, and for a while he took me under his wing to protect me. But that didn't last very long. Beria played his role in this, saying that he too had kidney trouble, but he drank anyway and there was no problem. So I was deprived of my defensive armor (that I couldn't drink because of my bad kidneys): no matter, drink! As long as you're walking around, as long as you're alive, drink! But even in those years—it can't be denied—if you went to Stalin with a question, he would listen attentively and would intervene if you needed his support.

While working in Ukraine before the war, I often took initiative on questions of improving the management of agriculture and changing tax policy in the direction of alleviating the system in which taxes were imposed by administrative command. I always took as my basis the interests of increasing production, and therefore I proposed that a system of additional payments for increased production be introduced, and that a new system for meat and milk deliveries be adopted. Previously a set amount of milk was taken from each farm. A farm that had ten cows was given a lower quota, and the farm that had no cows of course did not deliver any milk. I don't know what to call a system like that, but that's what existed. I proposed adopting a method of delivering milk in return for payment using a method based on the number of hectares. The price then being paid was lower than the cost of production of the milk, and thus the collective farms were paying a certain form of tribute to the state because they weren't receiving full compensation for the product they were delivering. But that's how the system of milk deliveries was organized. The collective farms with no livestock were given an exemption. But they did have land, and they were using the land. They were receiving a greater value for whatever items they delivered than was justified in comparison with the collective farms that engaged in all aspects of agriculture, including livestock raising and poultry farming.

When I first made my proposal and then was getting ready to return to Kiev, Stalin called me in and said: "You have reported your proposals, and I would like this matter to be speeded up. So don't leave now, but finish up the business here; preferably, we should pass a resolution." This was in 1939. When I had presented the proposals to him, he had written them down and said: "It's too bad you didn't do this three years ago." He saw that the threat of Hitler's invasion was imminent and that we had no time to make use of this progressive change in the agricultural laws.

I somehow worked out proposals on questions of delivery of leather and wool and sent them to Stalin. He called me in and said: "It seems that you have proposed something new here."

I said: "Yes, that is what I have proposed."

He said: "Well, why did you do this?"

I answered: "Inquiries were sent out to all the regions and provinces so that their opinions could be taken into account." I thought this was the proper procedure. In the Council of People's Commissars Mikoyan was in charge of such matters, and it had been his proposal that these inquiries be sent out. I saw no contradiction here. Surely before making the decision it was necessary to ask the opinion of the people working in the local areas and who knew the local conditions and would have to carry out any resolution.

Stalin saw it differently. Although he wasn't well, he jumped out of bed, and began cursing, called Mikoyan in, and began shouting at him. The draft resolution was to be approved the next day. He told me: "He has sent out your proposal, but he hasn't asked anyone about his own projects, which he is now carrying out. The draft proposals that you have presented are progressive. But they go in the direction of canceling the decisions that had already been worked out and adopted on the basis of Mikoyan's proposals." I don't think that Mikoyan had any ulterior motives. I have the greatest respect for Antastas Ivanovich [Mikoyan]. All of us have our shortcomings, and no one is free of weaknesses. Anastas Ivanovich had them, too. But he was an honorable, good, intelligent, capable person who did much that was useful for our party and our government. Mikoyan evidently was not guided by any desire to slow down or overturn my proposal, but he really did want to test it. It's possible that he regarded my proposal as tending to cancel a law that had been drafted under his direction.

Stalin always supported what was useful for the government and the party. In my work in high positions I had the opportunity to introduce much that, from my point of view, was new and progressive. In such matters Stalin most often supported me. When he did not, it was most often after the war, and usually it was the result of Beria and Malenkov's influence. I am convinced that this negative attitude on their part arose from jealousy.

During the war Malenkov came up in the world; his importance increased. He became a member of the Politburo.[35] At bottom he was a completely sterile person, a typical office bureaucrat and clerk. He could write a good draft resolution himself, or he had people who could quickly work up and put together fine-sounding resolutions. But his documents reflected what already existed in practice, and didn't go one step farther. He never diverged from the path that had been well worn by the existing reality. I consider such people not only sterile but dangerous. They have become petrified themselves, and they stifle everything that's alive and vital if it goes beyond the bounds that have already been set. Later I will return to some specific thoughts on this question.

I have somewhat exceeded the limits of the task I set myself. What I wanted to do was leave behind my memoirs about the path I traveled, together with the party and with Stalin, under his leadership, and to comment on everything positive that I saw in Stalin (I want to be absolutely objective) and also to mercilessly denounce and condemn that which I consider harmful to the party. The harmful practices that Stalin introduced still weigh us down today. They are harmful not only because many good people in the party were exterminated, but also because they left their mark on the consciousness of people and in their minds, especially for limited people. They created certain blinders, as if to say that there is no other way; this is the only way we can achieve victory in building socialism, developing industry, equipping the army, and creating the necessary conditions for the defeat of Hitler's Germany.

This is a rather primitive way of thinking. I would call it slavish. According to this thinking, it was necessary for someone to stand over people with a whip and lash out with it, left and right. Only then would the slaves do something; otherwise they would rebel. This is an amazingly slavish kind of psychology! If one is to take such a position, as some limited people do, it follows that the repression Stalin engaged in was historically inevitable; that all this retribution was justified by the victories the people won. How then can anyone have faith in the people? From this viewpoint, it is not the people who are the creative force in history, but some individual. Only that individual could achieve the stated goal. This shows lack of faith in the people, lack of faith in the working class, lack of faith in the party. I don't know what to call this understanding of things. It flies in the face of all our practical experience in the Soviet Union, the entire history of our people.

The October revolution was accomplished not because of some whip that Lenin wielded, but because of the appeal made by his rational intelligence. People followed Lenin because they believed in him. They believed in him because Lenin understood the aspirations of the people. That's why illiterate people—workers and peasants—listened to Lenin and saw a reflection of their own aspirations in his arguments and appeals. That's why they followed him through to the end. The counterrevolution organized its revolts; the counterrevolution organized the Civil War, and there were generals, officers, and capitalists standing at the head of the counterrevolution. All the capitalist countries gave support to the counterrevolution and sent their troops to support it, but nevertheless our people under Lenin's leadership were victorious. What was the reason for this? As I've already said, Lenin understood the aspirations of the people and expressed their thoughts, and therefore the people followed him, and no one could divert them onto some other road.

1. The borders of Bessarabia, the name traditionally used for the province since tsarist times, correspond roughly to those of the postwar Moldavian SSR, now the independent republic of Moldova. [SS]

2. At that time the Dniester River, which flows into the Black Sea, separated Romanian-occupied Bessarabia from the Ukrainian SSR. [GS]

3. Tiraspol is an industrial city on the eastern bank of the Dniester. At that time the area belonged to the Ukrainian SSR. Later it was transferred to the Moldavian SSR. [SS]

4. Later, Furmanka in the Kiliisky district of Odessa province.

5. The Danube and its tributary the Pruth River marked the new Soviet-Romanian border. [SS]

6. The Old Believers are a Christian sect that broke away from the official Russian Orthodox Church in the seventeenth century in protest against the church reforms introduced by Tsar Peter the Great. [GS/SS]

7. Kishinev was the main city of Bessarabia. Under the name of Chishinau, it is now the capital of Moldova. Chernovitsy is in western Ukraine, near the borders with Romania and Bessarabia. [SS]

8. General Ion Antonescu was the wartime political and military leader of Romania. See Biographies.

9. The invading German armies crossed into French territory on the evening of May 12, 1940. They entered Paris on June 14. [SS]

10. Marshal Philippe Pétain was leader of the pro-Nazi Vichy regime in France. See Biographies.

11. General Charles de Gaulle led the French military resistance to the Nazi occupation and was president of France from 1959 to 1969. See Biographies.

12. T. P. Chupakhin.

13. A. A. Yepishev. See Biographies.

14. The Seversky Donets River is also known as the Donets River. [SS]

15. N. A. Kucherenko was a prominent tank designer. See Biographies.

16. Chernigov and Shostka are in north central Ukraine. Chernigov is about 130 kilometers north of Kiev; Shostka is 160 kilometers or so farther to the east. [SS]

17. This trip to Berlin took place between November 9 and 14, 1940.

18. Rudolf Hess was Hitler's deputy in the Nazi party from 1933. See Biographies.

19. This was a gathering of leading personnel of the Workers' and Peasants' Red Army in December 1940.

20. In the course of the German invasion of Poland in 1939. Today Danzig is called Gdansk. [GS/SS]

21. A play by K. Finn and M. Gus.

22. Stalingrad, a big industrial city on the Volga River in southern Russia, was originally called Tsaritsyn and is now called Volgograd. Makhachkala, capital of the autonomous republic of Dagestan in the northeastern Caucasus, is on the western shore of the Caspian Sea. [SS]

23. The Ruhr is situated along the Rhine River in west central Germany. Its industry, like that of the Donbas, was based on coal mining and metallurgy. [SS]

24. The chief designer of the T-34 was M. I. Koshkin. He took part in trials of the new tank and presented it to Stalin in the Kremlin grounds. During a movement of tanks from Kharkov to Moscow, he caught a chill and died of pneumonia at the end of 1940.

25. That is, N. A. Kucherenko, not V. A. Kucherenko, the deputy chairman of the Council of Ministers from 1955. N. A. Kucherenko, as

Khrushchev recalls, was president of the Academy of Construction and Architecture from 1961. See Biographies.

26. D. G. Pavlov. See Biographies.

27. Tsaritsyn was the city later renamed Stalingrad and then Volgograd. [SS]

28. In July 1940 the Belorussian Special Military District was renamed the Western Special Military District.

29. The chief of staff of the Western Front was Major General V. E. Klimovskikh.

30. Marshal of the Soviet Union G. I. Kulik. See Biographies.

31. D. T. Shepilov. See Biographies. At the time of the events described Shepilov was a colonel.

32. Poltava is in east central Ukraine, about 110 kilometers southwest of Kharkov. [SS]

33. He was born in the hamlet of Dudnikovo in Poltava province.

34. This was Lieutenant General A. I. Zygin, who earlier in the war had commanded the 58th, 39th, Twentieth, and Fourth Guard Armies.

35. From February 1941 G. M. Malenkov was a candidate member of the Politburo of the CC of the AUCP(B). See Biographies.

# The Great Patriotic War

And so we had come right up to the brink of war—not that we ourselves were heading for war [i.e., not that we wanted it], but that it was bearing down on us. We talked about this and did everything we could so that the enemy wouldn't catch us unprepared; that our army would be at the appropriate high level of organization, equipment, and fighting capacity; that our industry would be at an appropriate level of development to ensure the satisfaction of all the army's needs for weapons and equipment if a war started, if our enemies attacked us. And here was the war, implacably bearing down on us.

I can't say specifically what was being done in the army, because I don't know. I also don't know which of the Politburo members was informed about the specific situation, the state of preparedness of our army and its equipment or of our war industry. I think no one knew about this other than Stalin. Or only a very restricted circle of people knew, and even then they didn't know all aspects, but only those of concern to the department under the jurisdiction of one or another member of the Politburo. The assignment of cadres, which was of great importance in preparing for a war, was also Stalin's exclusive prerogative.

The one who "sat on top of" cadre assignments was Shchadenko,[1] a person well known for his peculiar temperament. He was angry and irritable toward people. Later the one who "sat" in the cadres department was Golikov,[2] but he transferred from that department to intelligence. I can't remember exactly now [what his job was], but he too was in Stalin's inner circle and occupied himself with these matters. Mekhlis had a very strong influence on Stalin, but mainly in questions of political work. He was the head of the Chief Political Directorate of the Red Army, but he often exceeded the bounds of his duties, because Stalin very much liked his pushy and aggressive character. He gave Stalin a lot of advice, and Stalin took it to heart. This apparently didn't work out to the benefit of the army.

Shortly before the Great Patriotic War Timoshenko left the Kiev Military District and became people's commissar of defense. I was concerned that the departure of Timoshenko might weaken military work. I had a very high regard for Timoshenko's functioning as commander of the troops of our district (the KOVO). He was strong-willed and enjoyed substantial authority among military personnel; he was a man of firm character, which was necessary for any leader, especially a military leader. He had a lot of authority; he had been a hero in the Civil War, commander of one of the divisions of the First Cavalry Army[3]—and his fame was solidly based and well deserved.

After Timoshenko, Zhukov[4] came to the KOVO. I was pleased with Zhukov, even very pleased. His orderly way of managing things and his ability to solve problems made me happy. This set my mind at rest: it seemed to me that we had a good commander. The war confirmed that he really was a good commander. And I still think so, in spite of sharp differences I had with him at a later time, when he had become minister of defense of the USSR, an appointment I devoted all my efforts and energies to bring about. But he didn't understand his role correctly, and we were forced to relieve him of his duties as minister of defense and we condemned his harmful intentions, which he unquestionably had and which we nipped in the bud.[5] Nevertheless, I had a very high regard for him as a military leader during the war, and I do not renounce that view today, not in the least. I expressed that view to Stalin both during and after the war, when Stalin had already changed his attitude toward Zhukov and Zhukov had fallen out of favor.

So then, in Ukraine in 1940 Zhukov commanded the troops of the Kiev Special Military District (the KOVO). In early 1941 Zhukov was transferred after being appointed chief of the General Staff, and Kirponos[6] was sent to us. I didn't know General Kirponos at all before his assignment to our district. Of course I got to know him when he came to our district and took up his tasks, because I was a member of the Military Council of the KOVO. But I couldn't say anything about him then, either good or bad.

Before Zhukov and Meretskov, the chief of the General Staff had been Boris Mikhailovich Shaposhnikov.[7] He also had unquestionable authority; he was a highly educated military man who was greatly valued in the post he held. Also working in the General Staff were Sokolovsky and Vasilevsky,[8] two capable specialists. But among the military at that time "the word" was that they were former officers of the tsarist army, and therefore they were treated with a certain amount of mistrust. I didn't know either Sokolovsky or Vasilevsky personally then, and for that reason I didn't have an opinion of my own about them. But I listened to the good things said about them by veteran fighters of the Red Army, participants in the Civil War, and I treated them with confidence. When I did get to know them during the war, I of course had no political distrust of these men, nor did any ever arise. I felt very favorably disposed toward them—toward both Vasilevsky and Sokolovsky.

However a certain incident between Vasilevsky and me did occur in 1942, something that I cannot erase from my memory. This has to do with an operation we carried out in early 1942 near Kharkov, at Barvenkovo.[9] Later on I will talk about this operation separately, and then I will certainly not be able to avoid discussing a phone conversation I had with Vasilevsky. He made a very grave and disturbing impression on me then. It was my view that the catastrophe that was played out at Barvenkovo could have been avoided if Vasilevsky had taken the position he should have. He could have taken a different position [from the one he took]. But he didn't do that, and as a result, in my view, he had a hand in the destruction of thousands of Red Army fighters in the Kharkov campaign.

I don't know how Timoshenko managed his new job in the Commissariat of Defense, but I think the work was better organized than before he came. I won't talk about how deeply Voroshilov understood military matters and military work. But he had a reputation as a man who spent more time posing in front of cameras and posing in the studio of the artist Gerasimov[10] than in attending to military matters. On the other hand, he paid a lot of attention to the opera and to those engaged in the theatrical arts, especially the art of opera. He had a reputation as a connoisseur of opera, and he issued categorical verdicts on one or another opera singer. Even his wife talked about that. Once when I was present, a discussion began about a certain female opera singer. Without even raising her eyes, Voroshilov's wife said straight out: "Kliment Yefremovich [Voroshilov] doesn't have a very high opinion of that singer." This opinion was considered to have exhausted the question. What information he had as the basis for these judgments, and why he took on these pretensions, is hard to explain. It's true that Kliment Yefremovich loved to sing, and to his very last days whenever I met him he always sang, even though his hearing was no longer very good. And he sang well. He told me he had had training as a singer, and like Stalin, he had sung in a church choir.

Before the Great Patriotic War began, about three or four days before that, I was in Moscow. I was being detained there, literally suffering from the tedium, but I couldn't do anything about it. Stalin kept urging me: "Stay here with us; you should stick around some more. What's your hurry? Stay here." But I couldn't see the sense of being in Moscow: I wasn't hearing anything new from Stalin. And again, there were those drunken dinners and suppers. By then I found them simply repulsive, but I couldn't do anything about the situation.

Of course I didn't know the war would break out on June 22, but the crackle of prewar tension could be felt in the air. I understood that war could begin at any time. I didn't know what our intelligence service was reporting, because Stalin never talked about the results of our intelligence work. There were generally no meetings on that subject and no discussion of our country's preparedness for war. This was another big shortcoming and, I would even say, a major abuse of power on Stalin's part: he took everything on his own shoulders and decided everything himself. And he decided these things poorly, as the beginning of the war showed.

I saw that I had nothing to do in Moscow, but Stalin wouldn't let me go because he feared loneliness, wanted as many people around him as possible. Finally on June 20, a Friday, I confronted him: "Comrade Stalin, I need to go. A war may start at any time, and I may be stranded in Moscow or along the way." I call attention to the phrase "along the way" because to go from Moscow to Kiev required an overnight trip.

He said: "Yes, yes, you're right. Go ahead."

I immediately took advantage of Stalin's consent and set out for Kiev. I left that Friday, and on Saturday I was in Kiev. This testifies to the fact that Stalin understood that war was about to start. That's why he agreed that I could leave, so that I could be at my post in Kiev the moment the war began. What could be the reason for the claim [now being made] that it was a surprise attack? What is the purpose, and who does it serve, to have this version of events asserted now? The only reason is for people to try and justify themselves. The authors of this version themselves bear responsibility for what happened.

Our situation was very nerve-racking on the eve of the war. It was a hot summer, sultry, as it is before a thunderstorm. I had arrived in Kiev in the morning, as always. I went to the Central Committee offices of the Ukrainian Communist Party and informed the staff about the state of affairs, and in the evening I went home. At ten or eleven that evening, I suddenly got a phone call from the headquarters of the KOVO asking me to come to the Central Committee because a document had been received from Moscow. Accompanying this document was a message saying that the Central Committee secretary Khrushchev should be familiarized with the document. I went back to the Central Committee offices. I don't remember exactly who else arrived there: it was either Purkayev,[11] the chief of staff of the KOVO, or his deputy. It seems to me that Purkayev was in Kiev then, because a few days earlier the commander of the troops had traveled out to a command post near Ternopol. Construction of a command post had been started there, and even though it wasn't finished, it was necessary to go there because people sensed that a war was about to break out. The operations department of the KOVO headquarters was also located there, along with the chief of the operations division, Bagramyan,[12] and the commander of the troops, Kirponos.

Purkayev (or his deputy) read the document aloud. It stated that we had to expect the beginning of the war literally within days or perhaps even hours. I don't remember the exact contents of the document now. I remember only one thing: the note of alarm in its contents and the warning it conveyed. It was thought then that everything that needed to be done to prepare for war had been done—everything up to and including the fact that the commander had moved to the forward command post with his operations department. Consequently we were ready for war.

Then a phone call came from the command post in Ternopol reporting that a German soldier had deserted to our side along our sector of the border. He stated that he had been a Communist and still considered himself a Communist; that he was an antifascist; that he was opposed to the military adventure Hitler was about to undertake. He warned us that the next day at 3:00 A.M. the German offensive would begin. This was consistent with the reports already conveyed to us from Moscow in the above-mentioned document, although I don't remember whether the document named the day and hour of the invasion. It seems to me that it did. In short, this was not news for us, but a more specific and realistic confirmation.

The soldier had deserted from the front lines. He was questioned, and all the indications he mentioned, the facts on which he based his assertion that the offensive would begin the next day at 3:00 A.M., were described logically and seemed worthy of confidence. First, why exactly the next day? The soldier answered that they had just been given rations to last them three days. And why exactly at 3:00 A.M.? Because the Germans always chose an early hour in such cases. I forget whether he said that the soldiers had specifically been told the hour of 3:00 A.M. or whether they heard it through the "grapevine," the so-called soldier's radio, which always reported quite accurately the time at which an offensive was to begin.

What was there left for us to do? The commander was in Ternopol, and the headquarters had also been moved there. The troops were in place, ready to meet the enemy. This was the basis on which we would proceed. I did not return home, but stayed at the Central Committee offices to wait for the appointed hour.

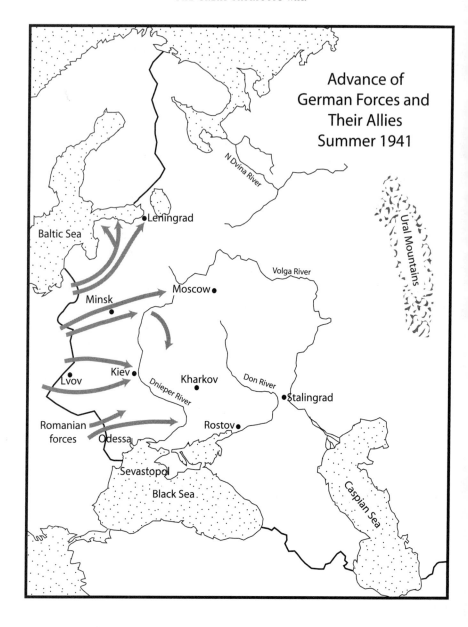

Advance of
German Forces and
Their Allies
Summer 1941

N Dvina River

Ural Mountains

•Leningrad

Baltic Sea

Volga River

Minsk          Moscow•

Kiev•          Kharkov    Don River

Lvov•          •                    •Stalingrad

       Dnieper River

Romanian
forces    Odessa        Rostov•

Sevastopol

Black Sea                        Caspian Sea

Sure enough, as the sky began to lighten around 3:00 A.M., we received news that German troops had opened an artillery barrage and were taking offensive action with the aim of forcing the river barrier along the border[13] and breaking our resistance. Our troops went into battle and were repelling the enemy. I don't remember exactly what time it was, but it was already daylight when we received a report from KOVO headquarters that German planes were approaching Kiev. Soon they were over Kiev, dropping their bombs on the city airport. The bombs hit a hangar, and a fire started. There were only a few U-2 airplanes left in that hangar. Later during the war they were used as communications planes, but at that time they were used for agricultural purposes. There was no military aviation at the airport; all the military planes had been moved up to the border, where they were concentrated and camouflaged.

The Germans did not achieve their intended goal with their first air raid; they were not able to knock our airports out of commission or destroy our aircraft. Nowhere in the KOVO were our planes and tanks destroyed at the first blow. (Although some things may have been kept secret from me, it was reported to me at the time, and I believed it, and to this day I believe it—namely, that nowhere in the KOVO were the Germans able to take full advantage of a surprise attack to strike a crushing blow against our planes, tanks, artillery, supply bases, ammunition dumps, and other weapons and equipment.) Later we received reports that German planes had bombed Odessa, Sevastopol,[14] and some other southern cities. When we first received the reports that the Germans had opened fire, an order came from Moscow not to return the fire. This was a strange order, and the only explanation for it was as follows: It was possible that some sort of provocation by the local command of the German troops or a diversion was involved, rather than orders from Hitler. This indicates that Stalin was so afraid of a war that he held our troops back from returning the enemy's fire. He couldn't believe that Hitler was starting a war, although he himself had said that Hitler would of course take advantage of the situation that had developed in the West and might attack us. This testifies also to the fact that Stalin didn't want a war and kept trying to reassure himself that Hitler would keep his word and not attack the Soviet Union. When we reported to Stalin that the enemy had already bombed Kiev, Sevastopol, and Odessa, that this could not be just a local provocation by German forces in a particular sector, but was actually the beginning of the war, only then was it said: "Yes, this is the war, and the military must take all appropriate measures." Well, after all, they were being fired on and they had to respond.

The war had begun. But as yet there were no statements by the Soviet government or by Stalin in person. This did not make a good impression. Later, in the afternoon on that Sunday, Molotov gave a speech. He announced that war had begun, that Hitler had attacked the Soviet Union. There is hardly any need now to talk about that speech because all this has been described, and people can familiarize themselves with the events from the newspapers of that time. But why did Molotov speak and not Stalin? That made people wonder. Today I know why Stalin didn't speak. He was completely paralyzed, unable to act, and couldn't collect his thoughts. Much later, after the war, I learned that when the war began Stalin was in the Kremlin. Beria and Malenkov both told me about it.

Beria said: "When the war began, members of the Politburo gathered in Stalin's office. Stalin was completely crushed. His morale was shattered, and he made the following declaration: 'The war has begun. It will develop catastrophically. Lenin left us the proletarian Soviet state, but we have sh—all over it' [i.e., made a mess of it]. That is literally how he expressed himself. He said, 'I am giving up the leadership,' and walked out of the room. He walked out, got in his automobile, and went to his dacha nearest the city."

Beria continued: "We remained. What were we to do next? After Stalin had shown his colors in this way, some time went by. We consulted among ourselves, Molotov, Kaganovich, Voroshilov, and I (although I don't know whether Voroshilov really was there because at that time he was in Stalin's disfavor because of the poor showing in the operation against Finland). We consulted among ourselves and decided to go see Stalin, to get him to return to activity, to make use of his name and abilities to organize the defense of the country. When we came to his dacha (so Beria related), I could see from his face that Stalin was very frightened. I suppose that Stalin was thinking we had come there to arrest him for renouncing his role and for not taking any measures to organize resistance to the German invasion. We began trying to persuade him that ours was a huge country, that we had the possibility of organizing ourselves, mobilizing industry and people, summoning them to struggle, and, in a word, doing everything necessary to raise up the people to resist Hitler. At this point it seemed that Stalin regained his senses somewhat. And we began to make assignments, specifying who should be in charge of each particular aspect of organizing the defense, overseeing military industry, and so forth."

I have no doubt that the passage quoted above is the truth. Of course the possibility of asking Stalin himself whether things were exactly that way was not available to me. But I had no reason to disbelieve Beria's account, because I myself had seen Stalin just before the beginning of the war, and what Beria described was just a continuation of what I had seen. Stalin had been in a state of shock.[15]

In the KOVO sector during the first days of the war a difficult but by no means catastrophic situation developed.

I don't remember now on what day Stalin called me, whether it was the first or second day of the war. He said: "Zhukov is flying to meet you, and you should go together with Zhukov to the troops and the headquarters [at the front lines]."

I answered: "All right; I'll wait for Zhukov." Zhukov flew in that same day or the next day. I of course was very glad. I knew Zhukov and had great confidence in him and in his talent as a military leader. I got to know him when he was commander of the KOVO troops and was favorably impressed by the fact that he was coming back to our sector. When he flew into Kiev, he and I tried to decide what would be the best way for us to get to the headquarters. Should we fly there by plane? To go by train would be very slow, and besides the enemy was bombing and might destroy the rail line. That means of travel was generally out of the question. Or should we go by automobile? Both forms of transportation were dangerous. By plane we would be flying into the front-line zone of fire, where enemy aircraft were active. A great deal was being said at the time about enemy paratroops who were supposedly operating in all areas; they were said to be pouring out of the sky like peas from a bowl and cutting all lines of communication. So there was a danger we would fall into the hands of enemy paratroops.

And it was a long way. It took several hours to get from Kiev to Ternopol. At that time of year, the wheat and rye crops had grown high; the enemy could easily hide in the fields, and thus diversionary forces and terrorists could make use of the thick growth of vegetation as much as they wished. It was especially dangerous because we had to travel from our old borders to Ternopol, which was in a region that had come to us in 1939 after the defeat of Poland. The local population was riddled with Ukrainian nationalists who were collaborating with the Germans. We knew this even then. But there was no other choice, and so we decided to travel by automobile. Off we went.

There was a lot of anxiety as we traveled, especially when we stopped and asked questions, seeking to obtain information about the state of affairs. In the end, toward evening, we arrived at the command post, located, not in Ternopol itself, but close to it, to the northwest, in some little hamlet. I looked to see what kind of command post we had. A huge ditch had been dug, and the extracted soil was piled up along the edges. Hardly anything more had been done. The personnel of the headquarters and offices were housed in peasant huts. The commander of the troops of the KOVO had taken shelter in a small cottage typical of the Ukrainian peasants in that area. Our means of communication were located there as well, and people came there to report.

As for the situation on our sector of the front at that time, so far there was no catastrophe! If you took the area toward Peremyshl[16] and farther south, the situation was even quite good. South of Peremyshl, the enemy had not taken any action. The border there was with Hungary, and for the time being the Hungarians had not made themselves apparent in any way. The Germans were making fairly stubborn attacks on Peremyshl itself, but our troops were repelling them. (The 99th Division was located there and had driven the enemy back out of the areas they had occupied as a result of their initial attack.) Our troops occupied a solid position in the city. A great deal was written later about this division, and deservedly so. It was the first division to be awarded the Order of the Red Banner for its combat action during the war, specifically for its actions in the very first days of the war. I can't pass over in silence the fact that right up to the beginning of the war this division had been commanded by Vlasov,[17] the very same man who later betrayed his homeland and became a traitor. He proved to be a very capable commander. In military competition among units of the Red Army on maneuver, his division occupied first place; just before the war began, Vlasov was given a corps and he placed the 99th Division under his chief of staff.[18] That division displayed its heroism under his command and went down in the history of the war as the toughest fighting division.

Stubborn fighting was under way along the road leading to Brody.[19] As we now know from documents captured from Hitler's high command, the main blow of the German armies of Group South was supposed to go in this direction. The Germans were trying to break through toward Kiev in that sector. It cannot be said by any means that the Germans smashed our troops there and put them to flight at the very first encounter. Not at all! Our troops fought stubbornly and beat back numerous attacks. I was very pleased when we arrived to find that Zhukov personally took information directly from the troops and reports from the leadership and began issuing orders. It was pleasant to see how skillfully he was doing all this, and with such knowledge of his job. The estimate we made of our situation then was even quite good; it was our view that we could give the Germans the rebuff they deserved.

I don't remember how long Zhukov stayed with us, a day or two or three. Then there came a call from Moscow. Zhukov told me he was being summoned by Stalin: "He ordered me to leave everything and come immediately to Moscow." Zhukov had been advising us well at that time. I must say that in those days the appearance he gave was one of a bold and confident man. He also said to me then that the commander of our troops was somewhat weak: "But what can you do? There's no one better. You have to give him support."

I also spoke to him candidly: "I very much regret your going. (He and I were on familiar terms, and I used the informal *ty* rather than the formal *vy.*) Now I don't know how things will go with us in this situation and with this kind of commander. But there's no other solution." We said goodbye and he left.

Events soon took a very bad turn in our sector, once again in the Brody region. Hitler's tank troops were attacking there. In that sector, in addition to the troops who were deployed there before the war, we moved up a mechanized corps commanded by Ryabyshev.[20] I don't remember what the number of that corps was. It was a good corps. It had some new KV tanks, several of them, and it also had several T-34 tanks. And there was another corps of mechanized troops; I forget the name of the commander of that corps.[21] He suffered shellshock in those battles, and I don't know what part he took later on in the war. As a corps commander he too gave a good account of himself. We moved these two mechanized corps up to that sector, thinking that would be sufficient to break the back of the enemy offensive, to block its path and to prevent any further advance.

We didn't know the true strength of concentration of the enemy troops. We didn't know that this was the main direction of the Germans' blow in the south, even though the strength of the enemy offensive was somewhat less in the south than in the central part of the front, in the direction toward Moscow. This was natural. We also had more troops in the Belorussian Military District than in the KOVO. It had been correctly determined that the enemy's main blow would fall there, that the main danger would be along the road through Minsk toward Moscow,[22] even though Stalin had thought otherwise.

Still, the Germans did concentrate a great many troops in the sector pointing toward Kiev. The main problem was that the initiative had been left to them. In our sector we were sent a reserve army commanded by Konev.[23] I didn't know him personally, but I had met him once before the war in Moscow. Konev had previously served somewhere in Siberia. Bad relations had developed there between Konev and the secretary of the party's province committee. Relations became so strained that Stalin summoned Konev and the leadership of the province committee to Moscow and personally looked into the conflict that had arisen over some sort of everyday matters. That was when I met Konev for the first time.

Konev arrived in the KOVO; his army was unloaded from the trains, and we were very glad to receive reserves. We immediately assigned this army to the Brody sector. But no sooner did his army make contact with the enemy than a call came from Stalin: "Load Konev's army back on the military trains immediately and see to it that those trains are sent off immediately to be at Moscow's disposal."

I began to plead that Konev's army be allowed to stay with us—our situation was very difficult—and I said: "If Konev's army stays here, we can be sure of stabilizing the situation in the Brody sector and forcing the enemy onto the defensive. We might even succeed in smashing the enemy." Yes, it's true, at that time we thought in terms of smashing the Germans quickly. That was not simply our desire; we believed it was possible, even though the relationship of forces in our sector, even with Konev's army, evidently would still have favored the enemy.

Stalin heard me out and then replied: "All right, I'll leave the reserve army, but the only reason I'm leaving it is for you to go on the offensive." A little while later another call came from Stalin: "Put Konev's army on the trains immediately." The army was already engaged in military operations, but the order was given and the army left us.

Thus we were left with what we had at the beginning of the war. Now the advantage was definitely in the enemy's favor, and a very dangerous situation developed in the area around Brody and Rovno. That meant in the direction of Kiev.[24] Our left flank was thus being bypassed. It became evident that the Germans were driving a wedge south toward Kiev, leaving our Carpathian group behind and not engaging it in combat at all. The Sixth Army was located there, and the Carpathians were being held by the Twelfth Army, it seems to me. There was an imminent threat (and the intention of the enemy was already obvious) that these troops would be surrounded. I don't have any special knowledge that I can present now on this question, but I do want to shed some light on an unpleasant incident that occurred in our area involving a member of the Military Council of the KOVO.

When difficult conditions arose for us in the Brody area, the commander of the troops and I took measures to reposition our forces and to decide exactly where it would be best for our forces to strike in order to counter the enemy troops attacking Brody. We wanted an order to this effect to be received in timely fashion by the commander of the mechanized corps, Ryabyshev, and the commander of another corps, whose name I forget. We decided to send a member of the KOVO Military Council, so that he himself would deliver the order specifying the direction of the blow to be struck. This member of the Military Council went off to the corps.[25] I didn't know this man very well. He had come to us from Leningrad just before the war and gave a good impression. Let me describe his outward appearance. He was still young and looked quite elegant, as though he "had it all together"; he dressed with taste, and attracted attention to himself. And he was strong-minded too. The military men told me that he was a man with aspirations, that he had a low opinion of the commander of the KOVO troops and considered himself a shade above him, and that he could have carried out the functions of commander to better advantage. Of course he was hardly likely to say anything like that openly, but this was the conclusion people working in the headquarters had come to. Well, all sorts of things go on, and whatever desires he had, that was his private business, and for the time being he kept them to himself. I watched him closely: I could see he was no fool, and therefore I had nothing against him, nor could I have.

Before he went off to deliver orders to the mechanized corps he stopped in to see me in the evening. Because the housing situation was poor, both the workplaces and the domestic quarters of the commander of the troops and of myself were in the same room together with the officers on duty. We slept while we were traveling or sitting. We had not yet worked out any daily schedule, and we had not yet grown accustomed to wartime conditions. When this member of the Military Council came to see me, he asked me to step out of the room because otherwise we couldn't discuss things confidentially. I went out. He said to me: "It is my view that you should immediately write to Comrade Stalin that it would be best to replace the commander of the troops of the Kiev district. Kirponos is completely unsuitable for carrying out the functions of a commander." I was amazed and dumbfounded. The war had just begun, and a member of the Military Council, a professional serviceman, was raising the question of replacing the commander.

I answered: "I see no basis for replacing him, especially since war has just begun."

He replied: "He is weak."

I said: "Weakness and strength are tested in action. So I propose it be verified in action whether he's weak or not."

I didn't know the commander any better than I knew this member of the Military Council. I knew him by name and I knew his face, but I had no idea of his operational abilities. For me he was a new man who had arrived to occupy this important position. And just when the first shots were being fired, I didn't want to get involved in leapfrogging, switching commanders around. I added: "This would make a very bad impression on the troops, and I see no basis for it. I'm opposed." Then I asked: "By the way, who do you think is better? Who could be appointed in Kirponos's place?"

He answered: "The chief of staff, General Purkayev."

I had a very good opinion of Purkayev, but I said: "I respect Purkayev and have a high regard for him, but I don't see what would change if we replaced Kirponos with Purkayev. Nothing would be added to our ability to make decisions regarding the conduct of the war, because Purkayev is chief of staff and also takes part in working out those decisions now. (The chief of staff was part of the Military Council of the KOVO.) We are already making full use of General Purkayev's knowledge and experience and will continue to do so in the future. I am opposed."

The member of the Military Council went off to deliver the orders to the troops, and he returned early in the morning and again came to see me. He had a terribly troubled look on his face; he was incredibly disturbed about something. He came in at a moment when no one else was in the room; everyone had gone out; he said to me that he had decided to shoot himself. I said: "What are you talking about? Why are you saying such foolish things?"

He answered: "I am guilty of giving incorrect orders to the commanders of the mechanized corps. I don't want to live any longer."

I continued: "Excuse me, what is this? You did deliver the orders, didn't you?"

He said: "Yes, I delivered them."

I said: "Well now, the orders state what they are to do and how they are to use the mechanized corps. So what does that have to do with you?"

He said: "No, you see, after delivering the orders I gave them oral instructions that were contradictory to those orders."

I said: "You had no right to do that. But if you did give such orders, all the same, the commanders of the corps likewise had no right to follow them; their obligation is to carry out the orders that have been put down in writing and signed by the commanders of the Front and all the members of the Military Council. For the corps commanders no other orders have any authority."

He said: "No, when I was there, I. . ." To put it briefly, I could see that he was trying to start an argument with me, when there was nothing to argue about, and that he was in a state of shock. I thought that if I barked at him instead of trying to reason with him, I might bring him out of his state of shock and he would find the inner strength to return to normal.

So I said: "Why are you talking foolishness? If you've decided to shoot yourself, what are you waiting for?" I wanted to jolt him with some sharp words, so that he would become aware that he was acting in a criminal way toward himself. But he suddenly pulled out his pistol (he and I were standing side by side), put it to his temple, fired, and fell. I ran out. The guards were on duty along the path next to the house. I called them and ordered them to take a motor vehicle immediately and get this man to the hospital. He still showed signs of life. They took him to the hospital, but there he soon died.[26]

Later his adjutant and people who had traveled with him to the corps to deliver the orders told me that when he had returned from the front lines he was very disturbed, wouldn't rest, and frequently went to the bathroom. I assumed that he wasn't doing that for physical reasons but evidently because he was thinking of committing suicide there. The Lord only knows. I can't say what his state of mind was, but clearly he was psychologically disturbed. Then he came to see me and shot himself. But before that he had talked with other people, those he usually had dealings with, and they had heard what he was saying. He thought that everything was going to fall apart, that we were retreating, and everything would turn out the way it did in France. "We are lost!" He actually said those words. I suppose that such thinking put him in a psychological impasse, and the only way out that he could see was to commit suicide. And so he did. Later I wrote a coded message to Stalin describing our conversation. The document exists, but right now I am reproducing it from memory. I think I am speaking accurately except for some possible error in the chronological order of the account. I am describing the essence of the matter, how things were in our lives at that time. Here we had a case where even a member of a Military Council, who occupied such a high position, was shaken. He was not a physical coward. No, his morale was shaken; he lost confidence in the possibility of repelling Hitler's invasion. Unfortunately that was not the only such incident at the time. Such incidents occurred with other commanders as well. That's what the situation was like. And yet we hadn't been at war for even ten days.

Let me return to the situation I was talking about before I described the incident involving the member of the Military Council. We could see that the enemy was conducting virtually no active operations against Muzychenko's Sixth Army and Ponedelin's Twelfth Army.[27] The Germans were deliberately disregarding our left flank. But they were hoping, after driving a wedge with their tank troops, to turn to the right and encircle our troops, and then destroy those two armies. Therefore the commander and I decided to withdraw the Sixth Army, whose headquarters was in Lvov and which was positioned along the border north of Peremyshl. Those troops began to withdraw. I don't remember how many kilometers they retreated, but the enemy didn't even pursue them. Suddenly we received a harsh command from Moscow—a sharp dressing-down for withdrawing the troops. An order arrived that the troops should be returned, that they should occupy their positions along the border, as they had before. We replied: "Why defend that border? No military operations are being conducted against those two armies. The enemy has concentrated his main forces in the Brody area, and his intention is already obvious. He can encircle our troops, and then they would not be able to get out or avoid a flanking attack." But we were ordered to send the troops back, and we did that.

It was a very bitter thing, and I felt deeply offended at having to do that. I had the strong impression that those two armies might perish. Even if encircled, they would still fight, but we could no longer use them with the same effectiveness as we could if we redeployed them to the area where the enemy's main blow was falling. But what can you do? An order is an order, and we carried it out. I assumed then (I don't remember now whether it was Zhukov himself who called up from Moscow in regard to this matter) that Zhukov was wrong. I held to this opinion throughout all the years, and when Zhukov was relieved of his duties in 1957, and I gave a speech criticizing his actions, I returned to that moment in the first days of the war when we were forbidden to withdraw the armies from Peremyshl and Lvov. As a result the Sixth Army later perished after being encircled, as did the Twelfth Army. I said of Zhukov: "There are few such capable military commanders as Zhukov, but even he made an error."

Zhukov replied: "That was not my initiative; that was Stalin's order." Today I cannot get into a debate with him over whether that was actually Stalin's order. Of course it's possible that it was. But [it would have been] on the basis of a report from Zhukov, because Zhukov had just arrived in Moscow from our Front, and so I think he was the chief adviser on this question. If he had said that the order issued by the Military Council of the KOVO was correct, Stalin, to avoid the encirclement of those armies, might not have given the order to send them [to the border]. Today I don't know who actually initiated that order; therefore, the actual person guilty of the destruction of those two armies, after they had been encircled, can't be named with certainty.

Can you imagine what a difficult time it was for us? Hitler had moved full-strength, highly mechanized units against us and we were deprived of the solid force that our two armies, the Sixth and the Twelfth, would have represented. Later they retreated; the Germans besieged them, and ultimately encircled them in the Uman area.[28] Those two armies were taken prisoner together with their headquarters, staffs, and commanders. If we

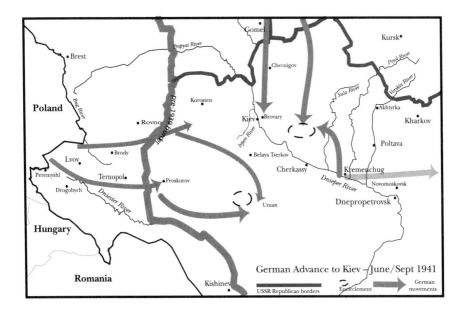

German Advance to Kiev – June/Sept 1941

USSR Republican borders — Encirclement — German movements

could have used the Sixth Army earlier, we might have been able to deploy some of its divisions to strike at the enemy's flank in the Brody area. No one knows how that might have turned out. Even if we hadn't completely stopped the enemy and smashed the enemy's grouping in that area, we would have at least bled him or weakened him considerably and held him back or slowed him down for a time. Quite a different situation would have developed in our area. But we were denied that possibility. Why am I talking about that now? Very little confidence was placed in us. Interference from above occurred frequently, and it was not always intelligent or rational. This interference cost us many lives and a great deal of blood. This is the first case, but later I will cite many more such cases, which also cost thousands and thousands of casualties, but were completely unnecessary, and which could have been avoided if there had been more confidence in the commanders of the Fronts and their Military Councils.

A few days later,[29] again not at our own initiative but on orders from Moscow, we withdrew from our command post. We were ordered to transfer the headquarters to Proskurov,[30] that is, we were to withdraw deep into our rear area. We were astounded, because in our sector the situation was not yet so bad as to force us to take such measures: that is, to withdraw and relocate the headquarters far to the rear, behind our troops. But that was the order from Moscow. I don't remember if any name was mentioned, but everyone considered that if a phone call came from Moscow, that meant it was an order from Stalin. We left our location and began the process of relocating. It was a dreadful scene.

Hundreds of vehicles were moving from the front line toward the rear with the families of officers. Many officers had families in Lvov, Drogobych, and Peremyshl. Refugees moved with them, but there were no peasants among them. The Western Ukrainian peasants did not flee from the Germans. Evidently this was a result of the agitation of Ukrainian nationalists who looked on the arrival of the Germans with sentiments different from ours. The peasants were deceived by the promise that Hitler would bring liberation to Ukraine. That's how the nationalists, the supporters of Bandera, pulled the wool over the eyes of the peasants of Ukraine.

No sooner had we arrived in Proskurov and begun setting up our headquarters than a telephone call came from Stalin. I spoke with him. Stalin said: "You must go to Kiev right away, and when you get to Kiev immediately organize the defense of the city." And that's what we did, although we didn't know in general what was occurring on the right flank of our Front. What the situation was on the Western Front we also didn't know. We arrived in Kiev, but the enemy was almost on our heels, only on a different road. We took the Ternopol road, while the enemy, after smashing our forces in the Brody-Rovno-Korosten[31] area, advanced northward at high speed. Meanwhile outside Kiev a literally hopeless situation was taking shape.

As we retreated toward Kiev, the Germans were devouring the remnants of our troops. We lost our artillery and tanks, and we had no machine guns. Our main forces—two mechanized corps—had been smashed, mainly from the air. The Germans flew with impunity and we had no means of defending ourselves. As for the troops of the Sixth and Twelfth Armies, when the enemy took after them in earnest, they began to retreat in disorganized fashion. The enemy managed to keep them constantly in a state of semi-encirclement, and they had no room to maneuver, which is the most important thing for troops. Nevertheless these armies did not fall apart. They defended themselves and even dealt a blow to the enemy in the direction toward Brody. They were retreating south of Kiev toward an area south of Uman. That was where they were finally surrounded. Both headquarters surrendered: Ponedelin and the commander of the Sixth Army. The commander of the Twelfth Army was wounded. When the Germans drove up, Ponedelin came out of his building and said he was surrendering as a prisoner of war. At that time we didn't know the fascists yet, and we often tried to operate according to the "rules of war."

The fact that our Front was denied the initiative of using our forces as we thought best was of course a foolish thing. The interference by the General Staff turned out the same as with the "good soldier Schweik":[32] everything was fine until the General Staff interfered. That is how our troops perished.

Various generals began to escape from encirclement. Popel[33] arrived, and that not unknown figure, Vlasov, also arrived with his riding crop, but without his troops. Popel returned to our lines after about two or three weeks. He had traveled through the forests of the Polesye region;[34] there were no Germans there as yet; they were taking the paved roads. Popel even brought a wounded colonel out with him and led a small number of troops out of encirclement.

Today I can't say which day of the war this was, but in fact we had no troops and our front lines had been broken. The enemy was rushing ahead with his mobile units while our troops remained far in the enemy's rear, though still engaged in combat. The enemy came right up close to Kiev, reaching the Irpen River. The Irpen is not a large river, but it is swampy. Back in 1928–30 the Kiev fortified zone had been built along this river. There were reinforced concrete pillboxes with artillery there, but I have already mentioned how they were destroyed at the suggestion of Mekhlis. Stalin ordered them destroyed. His intention in doing this was that our command staff would not look back, but would keep its eyes fixed on the fortifications along our new border, which had come to us as a result of the Germans crushing the Polish state. And now when we needed that fortified zone so badly, it had been destroyed. Some reinforced concrete structures still existed, but there were no weapons in them, neither artillery nor machine guns, and there were no troops. And so we began gathering together anything we could: rifles, cannon, and so on, with the aim of building up a defensive line somehow.

General Parusinov[35] was appointed to command this sector. Today I know nothing about what happened to him. At that time he was already well on in years. I had formed a good impression of him, but his job had been in the rear echelons. I don't remember what his title was then. It seems to me he was our Front's chief of supply services,[36] but I'm not sure.

We had no one else [besides Parusinov], so we appointed him. He somehow distributed whatever we had and what we had gathered up and started organizing a defense of the city. But the Germans deployed along the west bank of the Irpen River. They didn't make any attempts to cross the Irpen. There was a bridge there—a rickety wooden bridge, which of course we had blown up. I think that the Germans did break through with a few advance tank units, but they didn't have infantry and they decided not to force this barrier. (I would say it was more the swamps and marshes than the river that deterred them.) They postponed action to a later time.

Our situation was very bad. It was really no joke. The enemy had come right up to Kiev and was poised on the Irpen! A panic began in the city. That was only natural. I remember that late one night (I was sitting on a bench) General Astakhov,[37] commander of the KOVO air force, came in to see me. He was a decent and conscientious man; in his outward appearance he was staid and corpulent; he seemed to embody tranquility itself. He said: "In these battles we have been deprived of virtually all our aircraft. And now the enemy doesn't even let us poke our nose out." And he began to sob.

There were military personnel passing by, and I began trying calm him down. Then I barked at him: "Get hold of yourself, Comrade Astakhov! Look, there are people passing by, and they are going to see a general in a state like this. We need to fight, and so we have to get hold of ourselves." This seemed to have an effect on him, but for a long time, he was unable to regain his self-possession. It was not cowardice that made Astakhov act this way. No, he was a trained military man, and he knew his job very well. But he had been confident previously, as everyone had, that we were unassailable, that our border was "all locked up," and that, as the song said, our only fighting would be on enemy territory. Suddenly here we were a few days after the beginning of the war defending Kiev,[38] and there was nothing with which we could hold Kiev. We had no forces—neither weapons nor troops.

We directed everything we could toward organizing the defense of Kiev. The thing was not to surrender Kiev and to repel the enemy! Defensive positions were erected along the Dnieper River to the left of Kiev, that is, along our left flank outside the city. Our troops were holding a fairly large area to the south of Kiev. It was in this area that the Sixth and Twelfth Armies were retreating. They had already been encircled, but were still fighting and causing fairly heavy losses to the enemy. We began to organize things in such a way as to break through the enemy encirclement from the east and help those armies escape from the trap. The headquarters of those two armies had already been unified during the retreat.

For the defense of Kiev we decided to form a new army and call it the 37th.[39] We began looking for a commander. Kirponos and I proposed several generals who had already lost their troops and were at our disposal. Among them Vlasov made a very good impression. Commander Kirponos and I decided to appoint none other than Vlasov. The cadres department of the KOVO also recommended him and gave a reference in his favor, stating a preference for him over others. I didn't know Vlasov personally or any of the other generals then "at liberty,"[40] and I don't even remember their names now. If I were to appeal to a witness, then I would have a witness who is still alive and healthy today, and I wish he would live another thousand years— Ivan Khristoforovich Bagramyan. He then held the title of colonel and was chief of the operations division of the headquarters staff of the Southwestern Front. A very decent man, a good military man, and a fine operations officer who played a major role in organizing resistance to Hitler's invasion in those sectors where he was assigned to that task.

Nevertheless I decided to ask Moscow. We were under the impression then that there were enemies of the people everywhere, especially in the Red Army. I decided to ask Moscow what documents they had on Vlasov, what character references they had for him. Could he be trusted, and could he be appointed to the post of commander of the army that was to defend Kiev? There were no troops; we still had to gather them together, and all this would have to be done by the new army commander. I called Malenkov; there was no one else I could reach. But since Malenkov was in charge of cadres for the Central Committee, this question was appropriate to present to him. To be sure, he himself knew nothing about Vlasov, but people in the General Staff in charge of cadres would be able to give him their opinion. I asked him: "What kind of references can you get on Vlasov?"

Malenkov answered: "You simply have no idea what's going on here. There's no one and there's nothing available. I wouldn't be able to find out anything from anyone. So take the full responsibility on yourself and do what you think is necessary."

Given this state of affairs, although we had no information on Vlasov, we knew that he was the one whom the military were recommending. And so Kirponos and I decided to appoint him commander of the 37th Army. He began gathering troops together from retreating units or from those breaking out of encirclement. Then he got reinforcements of one kind or another. Soon an entire infantry corps arrived[41] under the command of General Kuleshov. This corps arrived from the Northern Caucasus region. It was a good corps, but it was not fully trained. It wasn't ready for battle as far as its morale went; it had never been under fire, which is only natural as the war had just begun. We deployed the army in the fortified zone and placed it in the most highly threatened sector—defending the Goloseyevsky Forest, the immediate approaches to Kiev from the south.[42] We did not expect the blow to come from the north. The natural conditions there were difficult for the enemy; we were protected there by the Irpen River.

Furthermore, the Fifth Army there was in fairly good shape. It was commanded by General Potapov. His neighbor along our front lines had been commander of the Sixth Army, Muzychenko. Before the war he had been under a shadow: people wondered whether he might be a traitor in the ranks of the Red Army. Why did they think that? Before the war he had gone out among his troops either to conduct maneuvers or simply to inspect his units along the border. The headquarters of the Sixth Army was in Lvov. His wife remained at home alone. He also had a household servant. A young man was courting her, and there was nothing unnatural about that. Apparently Muzychenko and his wife took the same attitude. But as it turned out in this instance, the courting was not just for pleasure.

There were political and intelligence purposes involved. The one doing the courting chose the moment when Muzychenko had gone to visit his troops. (By then he had already won the right to come into the house, and the servants in the house had a lenient attitude about his showing up there.) He arrived at night. Muzychenko's wife was asleep. Suddenly the door opened; this man came in and demanded the keys to the safe. She was frightened. Later she remembered it as follows: "I was sleeping. I didn't have my clothes on. He came in and unceremoniously sat on the bed and in a fairly polite tone, as though he were teasing, began a conversation. He made no attempt on my virtue, and he spoke politely, asking for the keys. I told him I didn't have the keys."

"The commander never left the keys behind, and certainly not with me; he always took them with him or turned them in somewhere. I don't know where. I had nothing to do with the keys, and there was no way I could comply with his demand. For a long time he kept insistently demanding the keys, although he interspersed the conversation with jokes and playful talk, so as not to frighten me and perhaps to get me into a mood more favorably disposed to giving him the keys. The incident ended with him leaving."

Presumably this is all described in detail in the archives of the state security agencies: Muzychenko's wife did present her testimony. The domestic servant who was being courted fled and disappeared. It then became clear that this servant had been sent on the instructions of the Ukrainian nationalists. It was she who had brought in this agent of German intelligence who was trying to get hold of the keys but never got them. When Stalin learned about this incident, he asked me about Muzychenko. I answered that we had absolutely no information that would cause us to mistrust this general. I had asked many of our military personnel, and they all gave very positive references about him—as a military man, an individual, and a party member.

Evidently what was involved here was simply the insolence of the enemy intelligence agencies. Muzychenko's wife could not have been an agent; there was no evidence against her. People who knew her also said she was a decent woman. What had happened was simply a case of their being too trusting [in hiring servants]. The question of Muzychenko's fate stood on a razor's edge. Would he be left in his position, or would he be relieved of his duties as commander of the army? They thought this over for a long time and in the end decided to leave him in his post. Muzychenko continued as commander of the Sixth Army. Full confidence was placed in him, and although this incident undoubtedly left its traces, I don't think it was reflected in our military work. I, for example, continued to treat him with full confidence, as I had done before this incident.

Now his army was fighting south of Kiev. The chief danger for Kiev was precisely from the south, from the direction of Belaya Tserkov.[43] Construction of defensive lines was going on there as well. After a while the Germans brought up their troops and began to undertake operations with the direct aim of seizing Kiev. I remember that when a serious situation developed around Belaya Tserkov, Kirponos and I decided to go visit the troops, evaluate the situation, and take measures so that our troops would not flee. At that time the command post of our Front was in Brovary, that is, on the east bank of the Dnieper River, about twenty-five kilometers from Kiev heading toward Chernigov. The headquarters of the 37th Army occupied a reinforced concrete command post, which had been built in peacetime for the staff of the KOVO, in Svyatoshino.[44] I don't remember the name of the chief of staff of the army now,[45] but he also made a good impression on me.

Kirponos and I arrived at the army headquarters and first met with the chief of staff. For some reason the army commander, Vlasov, was absent. Then he arrived. Vlasov reported on the situation, speaking rather calmly, and that pleased me. His tone inspired confidence, and he spoke with knowledge of the business at hand. We proposed that we travel immediately to the Goloseyevsky Forest, where the newly arrived infantry corps, consisting of three divisions, had been deployed. We traveled out to visit Kuleshov's corps. In their first encounter with the enemy, the troops of this corps had made a poor showing. A panic had begun, and the corps had retreated. There was a danger that people would simply flee. We had gone there at the time to restore order. A military tribunal was set up right on the spot, and so-called barrier units were set up [whose task was to shoot soldiers retreating without authorization]. All the measures taken in such cases to restore order and discipline were carried out. They were stern measures! Courts-martial were held on the battlefield. Strict sentences were carried out right there and then, the kind that are necessary only in such a severe and serious situation. We saw that Kuleshov was doing a poor job of managing his troops. Maybe we were too zealous then, because, after all, he had no experience and neither did his soldiers. He was a man who had not yet been under fire. Be that as it may, we relieved him of his duties and appointed a new corps commander. I don't remember his name now, but he was of Jewish nationality.

When we came there a second time, that new commander was already in charge of the corps. We went there with Vlasov. The Germans were bombarding the area with artillery and mortar fire and they were bombing it from the air. When we arrived, the commander was sitting in some sort of field chair, and there was a red calico cloth over the table and a phone. A foxhole had been dug right alongside, and there were some other people with him. He began reporting on the situation. The Germans were firing at us with mortars and machine guns at the time, but they themselves were not visible; there was just a roaring sound through the forest. They were bombing from their planes. Then the artillery fire grew stronger. Vlasov remained fairly calm. (I glanced at him.) He had broken off a switch from a hazelnut bush and was tapping the toes of his boots with this switch. Then he proposed that to avoid unpleasantness we should get into the foxhole; we might be struck by shrapnel. We heeded his advice and got in the hole. There we listened to the commander's report. The corps commander made a very good impression on me with his calmness, self-confidence, and knowledge of the situation. We left, wishing him success.

During the stubborn fighting for Kiev, Budyonny came to see us. I asked him: "What's going on with the other Fronts? I don't know anything; we haven't received any information. You've come from Moscow, Semyon Mikhailovich, and surely you know, don't you?"

He said: "Yes, I know, and I'll tell you." And privately, one on one, he told me that the Western Front had literally collapsed at the very first shots from the enemy and had disintegrated. The army had not known how to put up the necessary resistance to the enemy. The Germans had taken advantage of our scatterbrained functioning and had destroyed the aircraft of that Front right on the ground at its air bases; the enemy had also caused heavy casualties to our ground forces. As early as June 22, when the very first blow fell, the Front had collapsed. Stalin had sent Kulik there to help bring the Front up to strength. But there was no information or news about Marshal Kulik so far. No one knew what had happened to him.

I expressed regret: "It's too bad. Kulik has perished."

But Budyonny said: "You shouldn't feel sorry for him." And that was said in such a tone as to give me to understand that in Moscow Kulik was considered a traitor, that he apparently had gone over to the enemy. I knew Kulik and considered him an honest person; that's why I said I felt sorry for him. "You shouldn't feel sorry for him. Don't feel sorry for him," Budyonny kept repeating. I understood that evidently he had had some sort of conversation on this subject with Stalin.

Why Budyonny came to Kiev is hard to say. He didn't stay with us long. In the evening he asked: "Where are we going to rest? Let's get some sleep."

I agreed.

"But where?" he asked. "At your place? Where do you sleep?"

I said: "Right here is where I sleep." We left the building. A tent had been put up outside, and hay had been thrown in. "Right here in this tent is where I sleep."

He asked: "What are you saying?" I explained to him that our headquarters was next to a marshy area, and if you dug a hole, water would come up in it. And so during air raids I took shelter in a tent.

Budyonny said: "All right. If you sleep here, then I will too." We lay down and slept a few hours and got some rest. Early in the morning the German planes woke us. The planes were making hedge-hopping flights close above the village and bombing it. Our antiaircraft guns were firing back. But within our range of vision, no enemy planes were being hit—none that we could see. And our planes didn't show up.

I got angry; I felt very indignant about this. I confronted Astakhov: "What's going on? Why is it that they're able to fly and bomb with impunity, and we're not able to do anything?" By then the Germans had already finished bombing and flown away.

Astakhov reported: "So-and-so many enemy planes were brought down."

I asked: "Where were they brought down? I didn't see any fall."

He answered: "They came down on the other side of the Dnieper."

I said: "Well, if they came down on the other side of the Dnieper, you could report that even more of them were knocked down." I think Astakhov "brought sin upon his soul" [wasn't telling the truth]. Maybe it was true that some planes had been knocked down, but for me his statement was not reassuring, and I explained: "After all, our troops can see the Germans flying over us with impunity, and we don't see the enemy suffering any losses."

Budyonny soon left us. He didn't go out to visit the troops but returned to Moscow. He had come on some assignment (it couldn't have been otherwise; he didn't just come on an excursion), but I didn't know what it was.

And he didn't tell me. We simply had a talk together; he listened to our report on the situation, listened to what the commander of the troops and the head of the operations department, Bagramyan, had to say. His conversation with Bagramyan made a painful impression on me. I remember it well. To this day I cannot forget it. It happened after dinner. Budyonny was listening to Bagramyan report on the situation. Bagramyan was a very precise person who reported on everything just as it was. How many troops we had, their positions, and the general situation. Then Budyonny began taking Bagramyan to task. Specifically why I don't know. I didn't attribute any special importance to the conversation at the time. In military language the conversation came under the heading of an inquiry into the situation. The chief of the operations department of the headquarters staff was reporting on the situation to a marshal of the Soviet Union sent from Moscow.

All I remember is that this inquiry ended with the following words: "What's going on here with you? You don't even know your own troops."

Bagramyan answered: "What do you mean I don't know? I have just reported to you, Comrade Marshal."

Budyonny said: "Yes, I've been listening to you, and I'm looking at you, and I think you should be shot. Shot for this kind of a situation." Semyon Mikhailovich said this with a kind of squeaky voice.

Bagramyan said: "What do you want to have me shot for, Semyon Mikhailovich? If you don't find me suitable as chief of the operations department, then give me a combat division. I am a commander; I can command a division. But what would be the advantage of having me shot?"

Then Budyonny in a very crude manner tried to persuade Bagramyan that he ought to agree to being shot. Of course Bagramyan could not agree to such a thing. I was astounded and wondered why Semyon Mikhailovich was so insistently trying to get Bagramyan's "consent." Of course it must be kept in mind that this "polite" conversation was being conducted by this marshal of the Soviet Union and this colonel of our army immediately after an abundant feast with cognac. Nevertheless, in spite of that circumstance, the form this conversation took was impermissible. Budyonny was acting as a representative of the Stavka (the General Headquarters of the Supreme High Command), and of course this conversation had nothing to do with the purposes for which he had been sent there and could not be of any help to our cause or to our troops. But this also testifies to the state of mind of people at that time. Semyon Mikhailovich went completely beyond the bounds of what is permissible. But in those days we didn't take that kind of conversation seriously. Even though a person's life was being discussed, it all passed by without any consequences. Semyon Mikhailovich left, and we remained in the same difficult situation as before. After his visit things were neither any better nor any worse.

1. At the time of the events described, Lieutenant General Ye. A. Shchadenko was head of the Administration for Commanding and Leading Personnel of the Workers' and Peasants' Red Army.

2. Lieutenant General F. I. Golikov was in charge of Red Army personnel in the interval between fall 1939, when he was commanding the Sixth Army, and July 1940, when as deputy chief of the General Staff he was appointed head of the Main Intelligence Administration (GRU; military intelligence).

3. He commanded two divisions: from October 1919, the Sixth Cavalry Division, and from August 1920, the Fourth Cavalry Division.

4. Army General G. K. Zhukov was in command of the Kiev Special Military District from June 1940. He became chief of the General Staff in January 1941, replacing Army General K. A. Meretskov, who had in turn replaced Marshal of the Soviet Union B. M. Shaposhnikov in August 1940. See Biographies.

5. In October 1957, N. S. Khrushchev, suspecting Zhukov of nursing aspirations to political power inappropriate for a military man, removed him from all his official positions and forced him to retire. [SS]

6. M. P. Kirponos. See Biographies.

7. See Biographies.

8. Lieutenant General V. D. Sokolovsky became deputy chief of the General Staff in February 1941. Major General A. M. Vasilevsky was deputy head of the Operational Administration of the General Staff from May 1940. See Biographies.

9. Barvenkovo is a small place in eastern Ukraine, about midway between Kharkov and Donetsk. [SS] Khrushchev is referring to the Barvenkovo-Lozovaya offensive operation in January 1942.

10. Khrushchev is referring to A. M. Gerasimov, the painter of the picture *I. V. Stalin and K. Ye. Voroshilov in the Kremlin*. In 1941 Gerasimov received the Stalin Prize for this work.

11. Lieutenant General M. A. Purkayev.

12. Colonel I. Kh. Bagramyan. See Biographies.

13. Khrushchev is referring to the Western Bug River.

14. Sevastopol was the main naval base on the Crimean coast. [SS]

15. Stalin's absence during the first days of the war is discussed by Anastas Mikoyan in his memoirs *Tak bylo* (That is how it was; Moscow: VAGRIUS, 2000), 388–93. [SK]

16. Peremyshl is about 100 kilometers west of Lvov. It is now situated in southeastern Poland (Polish name Przemysl). [SS]

17. Major General A. A. Vlasov. See Biographies.

18. Major General N. I. Dementyev.

19. Brody is about 80 kilometers northeast of Lvov. [SS]

20. Lieutenant General D. I. Ryabyshev, who commanded the Eighth Mechanized Corps.

21. This was the 22nd Mechanized Corps, commanded by Major General S. M. Kondrusev and later by Major General V. S. Tamruchi. But the Fifteenth Mechanized Corps, commanded by Major General I. I. Karpezo and later by Colonel G. I. Yermolayev, was also fighting in the area.

22. Minsk, the capital of the Belorussian SSR (now Belarus), lies about 650 kilometers west of Moscow. [SS]

23. This was the Nineteenth Army of Lieutenant General I. S. Konev. See Biographies.

24. Rovno (Ukrainian name Rivne) is a city about 200 kilometers northeast of Lvov and about 400 kilometers west of Kiev. [SS]

25. He probably went to the Fourth and Eighth Mechanized Corps. But there still remained the Ninth Mechanized Corps, commanded by Major General K. K. Rokossovsky, and the Nineteenth Mechanized Corps, commanded by Major General N. V. Feklenko.

26. This man was Corps Commissar N. N. Vashugin.

27. Major General P. G. Ponedelin of the Twelfth Army and Lieutenant General I. N. Muzychenko of the Sixth Army.

28. Uman is a city in central Ukraine, about 160 kilometers south of Kiev. [SS]

29. To be precise, three and a half days later.

30. Proskurov is about halfway between Ternopol and Vinnitsa in western Ukraine. [AH]

31. Korosten is situated about halfway between Rovno and Kiev. [SS]

32. The good soldier Schweik is the hero of the satirical antiwar novel of that name by the Czech writer Jaroslav Hasek (1883–1923). The novel draws on Hasek's experience as a volunteer in the Austrian army during World War I. Schweik is a totally undisciplined liar, a drunkard, and apparently a total idiot, but he always manages to outwit his superior officers. [SS]

33. Brigade Commissar N. K. Popel.

34. The Polesye region straddles the border between Ukraine and Belarus. It consists mostly of forest and marshland (the Pripyat marshes). [SS]

35. Lieutenant General F. A. Parusinov.

36. *Nachalnik tyla* (literally, "chief of the rear"). The responsibilities of the officer holding this position included a wide range of duties, such as supply, repair, and maintenance of food, clothing, and so on, for combat troops; provision of weapons, munitions, combat vehicles, fuel, and so on; road building and repair; and medical services such as field hospitals and care of the wounded. For a detailed account of these tasks of supply, provisioning, and other types of support *(tylovoe obespechenie)*, see *Bol'shaya Sovetskaya entsiklopediya* (Large Soviet encyclopedia), 3d ed. (Moscow, 1977), s.v. "Tyl vooruzhennykh sil" (Rear-echelon supply and support of the armed forces). [GS]

37. Air Force Lieutenant General F. A. Astakhov. See Biographies.

38. This took place on July 7, 1941—the sixteenth day of the war.

39. This army was finally formed by August 8, 1941.

40. That is, they no longer commanded units, because their units had been lost when overrun by the Germans. [GS]

41. This was the 64th Infantry Corps, commanded by Major General A. D. Kuleshov.

42. The forest to the south of the village of Goloseyevo, on the road to Vasilkov.

43. Belaya Tserkov (White Church; in Ukrainian Bila Tserkva) is about 80 kilometers south of Kiev. [SS]

44. Svyatoshino was in the Kiev area, to the west of the city center. [AH]

45. Major General A. A. Martyanov.

## PEOPLE AND EVENTS OF SUMMER AND FALL 1941

Today is February 23, 1968. This is a great day, the glorious anniversary of our Soviet Army and of all our armed forces, which were established under Lenin's leadership and which won victory in the very first years of the revolution over the White Guards, our class enemies. Later our armed forces withstood the fascist invasion, a blow directed against our Soviet land and people. Our armed forces withstood and endured everything with honor, smashed all our enemies, and continued to hold high the Red Banner, our banner, which is crimson with the blood of the working class shed in the struggle against its enemies. The Soviet armed forces have traveled a great path, and I am proud of them. I am proud of the fact that I also had the chance to be a part of our glorious armed forces—the Red Army.

I was in the Red Army from January 1919 on, most difficult times for our young Soviet republic. In its ranks I had occasion to travel a long path and to pass through painful experiences; I happened to serve in the Ninth Infantry Division, which at first carried out a fighting retreat, pulling back beyond Oryol, near Mtsensk;[1] later, this division, and I with it, took the road of offensive operations. We marched forward, driving the enemy before us. The Christmas season of 1920 found us in Taganrog.[2] The reason we were in Taganrog was that our infantry division was then attached to the First Cavalry Army, which, as is generally known, was commanded by Budyonny. The

First Cavalry was carrying out an offensive aimed at capturing Rostov while we marched on Taganrog. It's a very long way from Oryol to Taganrog.³ But the Whites were retreating so fast that we had to hurry to keep up with them.

In 1920 as part of that same division I made another march. Beginning on March 1, we carried out an offensive against the settlement of Koshkino (it had a hyphenated name Koshkino-Krym).⁴ It stuck in my memory that the name was Koshkino-Krym. And at the beginning of April we reached the Black Sea, occupied Anapa,⁵ and celebrated our victory, having completely routed the White Guards. We drove them into the Black Sea in that area. During the winter a cavalry group was formed for pursuing the Whites. We mobilized horses from the Cossacks of the Kuban region and put our fighting men on horseback; later we participated in the liberation of Novorossiysk.⁶ But the entire division was not there; part of it had occupied Anapa and stopped there. After five days of rest, spent in Anapa, we moved forward to the Taman peninsula and occupied it that same April, and when we celebrated the May Day holiday we were already in Taman.⁷ This has been a "lyrical digression" in my reminiscences. And yet memories are memories, even if they are not always, unfortunately, presented in chronological order. But then, this is not particularly important.

I will return to the point at which Budyonny left us, left the Kiev area in 1941. On July 8, 1941, I was summoned to Moscow. It was interesting for me to go to Moscow right at that time; I was interested in informing myself and learning the true state of affairs. What situation was our country actually in? What thoughts did Stalin have on stopping the enemy's offensive so that we could then launch our own offensive? We had not been able to establish a firm defensive position; we were in a stage of retreat, in a stage of experiencing defeats on the battlefront. At that time Stalin didn't "come out of the wood-work" anywhere; he didn't come forward with his title of Supreme Commander in Chief, as he was soon to be designated.⁸ Orders were given by the Stavka (the General Headquarters). Nowhere was the term Commander Stalin (or Commander in Chief Stalin) used. This is also evidence of the particular mood Stalin was in. He evidently did not want his name linked with the defeats of our forces.

So then, I had been summoned to Moscow, but I had not been told what questions would be taken up. What I thought was that Stalin was summoning me to learn my view of the state of affairs on our sector of the front. I was then involved only with the territory covered by the Kiev Special Military District (the KOVO), that is, the northern part of Ukraine.⁹ The southern part was called the Southern Front. It was established on the basis of the Odessa Military District. I had no influence on those military forces.

When I arrived in Moscow, I was told that Stalin was at the command post. Moscow was being bombed very frequently then, and headquarters had been moved to the Kirov Gates area, to the offices of the People's Commissariat of Light Industry of the USSR. These premises were occupied and made into a headquarters; also, a command post for the General Headquarters was organized for Stalin and the party leadership in the same area at the Kirov subway station. When I met with Stalin the impression he made on me was discouraging. The man was sitting there as though he had been shell-shocked and couldn't say anything. He couldn't even say a few encouraging words to me, but that is what I needed, because I had come to Moscow to see Stalin, had come to the headquarters, to the leadership of the country and the army. And here I saw a leader whose morale had been completely broken. He was sitting on a couch. I walked over to him and said hello. He was completely unrecognizable. He looked so apathetic and limp. His face expressed nothing. It was written on his face that he felt himself at the mercy of the elements and didn't know what to do, and his eyes were somehow, I would say, pathetic and pleading.

Stalin asked, "How are things with you?" I candidly outlined the situation that had developed in our area: how the population was suffering from what had happened and what shortages we had. There were not enough weapons, not even rifles, and the Germans were giving us a beating. Actually there was no need for me to tell him this because he knew it himself from the reports made by the General Staff: our army was fleeing, the Germans had superiority over us both on the ground and in the air, we didn't have enough weapons, and at that time we didn't even have enough personnel. I told him everything about the situation we were in [on the Southwestern Front].

I remember that Stalin's behavior made a very strong and unfavorable impression on me then. I was standing there, and he was looking at me, and he said: "Well, where's the native wit and inventiveness *(smekalka)* of the Russians? People have talked so much about native Russian wit and shrewdness. But where the hell is it now in this war?" I don't know what I answered or whether I did answer him. What can you say to such a question in such a situation? After all, when the war began workers from the Leninskaya Kuznitsa[10] and other plants and factories [in Kiev] asked us to give them weapons. They wanted to take their place on the front lines in support of the Red Army. We couldn't give them anything. I called Moscow. The only person I could talk with then was Malenkov.

I called him: "Tell us where we can get rifles. The workers are asking for rifles. They want to join the ranks of the Red Army and fight the Germans."

He answered: "I have nothing to tell you. There is such chaos here that you can't make head or tail of anything. There is only one thing I can tell you, about the rifles that the Osoaviakhim[11] had in Moscow (and these were rifles with perforated cartridge chambers, damaged rifles deliberately made unusable)—we ordered them to be made serviceable, to have the perforations filled in, and all these rifles were sent to Leningrad. We can't get anything more."

So it turned out there were no rifles, no machine guns, and no aircraft remaining. We also found ourselves without artillery. Malenkov said: "Instructions are being given to forge your own weapons; forge spears and forge knives. You can fight the tanks with bottles filled with gasoline. Throw them and burn up the tanks." And that was the kind of situation that literally came into existence within a few weeks! We found ourselves without weapons. If the people had been told that then, I don't know how they would have reacted, but the people of course did not find out from us about that situation, although they could have guessed from the actual state of affairs. The Red Army was left without the necessary cover from machine-gun and artillery fire, and was even left without rifles. We were able to hold and delay the Germans outside Kiev for a while, but there was no confidence that we could hold out for long, because we had no weapons and we didn't even have enough troops. We beat the bushes, as the saying goes; we scrounged up people and rifles and organized a very weak defense. But the Germans too were weak by the time they approached Kiev, and that saved us. It was as though the Germans allowed us time, and we made use of it, and with each passing day we built up the defense of the city more. The Germans could no longer take Kiev on the run, although they did make some rather energetic attempts to do so.

I told Stalin that Kiev was still ours and that we were holding firm, building a solid defense. These were the first serious accomplishments in constructing a defense. Attacks were being launched against our troops frequently, and we were repelling them successfully. I told him: "We now feel certain that a frontal assault on Kiev would hardly be successful." That's the word I used, "hardly." I think that people who have even the slightest understanding of the situation at that time will grasp that "would hardly be successful" was an overly optimistic statement.

In the Red Army at that time, unfortunately, more was being said about our fleeing then about our offering resistance, although in the course of flight our troops did stop and deal some rather painful blows to the enemy. I see that clearly now, having read the book *Top Secret! For Command Staff Only!* What was especially interesting for me in this book were the authentic documents from the enemy camp. I don't agree on all points with the notes and commentary in the book: they are not sufficiently profound and not sufficiently objective. Later on I hope to give my views more specifically, stating in what respects I consider this material insufficiently profound and insufficiently objective. But I will say now that the enemy documents give me satisfaction. It's belated, but it is satisfaction.

When I read this book (published by Nauka in 1967), I saw an enraged Hitler writhing in frustration. How he writhed under the blows of our glorious Soviet troops, including in the sectors where I was a member of the Military Council. (In no sense am I attributing this fact to my personal merits. I mention this so that no one will suspect me—or even worse, accuse me—of immodesty.) I am now drawing conclusions objectively based on statements by the enemy, and I see that the greatest resistance was offered, and the greatest losses suffered by German troops, precisely in our sector, in the southern part of the battlefront. In the first days of the war, I was in the KOVO, then on the Military Council of the Southwestern Front, then the Southern Front, then the Stalingrad and Southeastern Fronts, then again the Southern Front, later the Voronezh Front and the First Ukrainian Front. It was pleasant for me to read what I have described.

Today we have gone through more than twenty years since the defeat of Hitler's forces. Documents that had been top secret are now accessible to all who wish to familiarize themselves with how that great struggle of the peoples against the fascist plague was organized and what course it took, the struggle against Hitler's mad ideas of Nazi domination over the whole world and his other delirious ravings that he expressed and in which he believed. It should be stated outright that Hitler misled the German people, but it would be foolish to portray things as though no one supported him. If Hitler had not had support among the German people, he could not have achieved what he did. He deceived the Germans, that's true, but nevertheless even the workers supported him. I know that from questioning prisoners of war. Also, there was no broad internal anti-Hitler struggle by the workers and peasants in Germany that made itself felt. If there had been, then obviously the toughness that German troops demonstrated in World War II would not have occurred. If the German army, which is made up of workers and peasants— if these people had taken a stand against Nazism and against Hitler, they would not have shown such toughness in fighting us. That is why we were obliged to fight to take back every inch of land and to shed a great deal of blood.

All our military people know that [during the war] when we were getting ready for an offensive, the place we chose to strike our blow would be the most advantageous in strategic respects, one that corresponded to our strategic aims—that is, it would be an area without German troops, but with Romanians or Italians instead. Those troops didn't stand up well to our blows. At the very first blow the defensive positions held by those troops would collapse. A different situation took shape in sectors where Magyars [Hungarians] were present in the defensive positions. The Magyars offered very stubborn resistance. Obviously I am digressing somewhat, because what I am saying really relates more to the concluding part of my memoirs. And so I'll return to my conversation with Stalin.

Stalin asked me, and I told him about the situation on our sector of the battlefront. His voice and expression were not those of the Stalin I knew. I was used to seeing self-confidence, a firm, strong expression in his face and eyes, but here was an eviscerated Stalin. It was only the outward appearance of Stalin; the inner content was something different.

I've already said that he obsessively pursued me with reproaches in regard to the Russian people. He said: "Here everyone talked about native Russian shrewdness. Where the hell is the clever inventiveness of the Russians now? Where is it? Why hasn't it made a showing?" I don't remember what I answered. Probably nothing. Because there was nothing I could answer. You can't suck Russian cleverness and resourcefulness out of your thumb. Inwardly I was filled with indignation. As I was leaving Moscow, I felt I was going to burst. How could this be? Stalin was placing the responsibility on the entire Russian nation, saying that the Russians were not displaying their native resourcefulness.

After all, how could you think about people this way, whether they're Russians, Ukrainians, Belorussians, Uzbeks, or other nationalities of our great homeland? How could you accuse them of not showing resourcefulness at a time when the number-one resource needed was weapons, weapons, and again weapons! That's what had to come first. Then people could show their native resourcefulness and could show whether they could use those weapons correctly or most effectively.

Our troops were placed in that situation, in circumstances where they didn't even have enough rifles, precisely as a result of your will, I was thinking to myself, your will, Stalin. I'm not even talking about antitank artillery or about the fact that at first there wasn't even an inkling of our having antitank rifles. We didn't even have automatic weapons. Later the PPSh automatic weapons made their appearance.[12] These weapons had been invented by our weapons engineers and designers soon after the Finnish war, but they had not been produced. In actual practice our first acquaintance with these weapons was in Finland. The Finns made widespread use of these weapons against our troops, and we suffered very great losses. In spite of that, at the beginning of the Great Patriotic War we didn't have such weapons. The reasoning at the time was that these weapons were hard to aim and that they were wasteful of ammunition. This matter was decided in Stalin's inner sanctum; he was the sole judge in such matters. And therefore, the Red Army was left only with rifles.

But life itself proved the opposite. We were forced to return to this weapon. We quickly began producing automatic weapons in sufficient quantity and supplying them to our army. But if this had been done earlier? If this matter had been evaluated correctly? And who is to blame? Stalin is to blame. Stalin and only Stalin! People might say: "But Stalin wasn't in charge of matters involving weapons." Yes, it was precisely Stalin who was! I've said earlier that I tried several times to open Stalin's eyes about Marshal Kulik, that he should make a more sober evaluation of him as a commander. But Stalin wouldn't listen to me. On the contrary, he criticized me. He argued that I didn't know the man, whereas he did know him. Such self-confidence about judging people, and consequently such self-assurance about knowing military matters—this is what it all led to. And how many lives it cost! How much blood was shed by Soviet citizens! Those were the kinds of blunders and oversights that were committed, and Stalin was to blame.

This morning many comrades called me and offered best wishes on the fiftieth anniversary of the Soviet armed forces. My comrade and longtime friend, Serdyuk,[13] also called. I have known him for many years as a party official. He went with me when I moved from Moscow to Ukraine and later became second secretary of the party's Kiev city committee when I was elected first secretary. We lived and worked together. When the war began I recommended him as a member of the Military Council of the Sixth Army. He was confirmed in that post and later remained a member of the Military Council of the army until the complete defeat of the Germans outside Stalingrad. There he was a member of the Military Council of the 64th Army, which was commanded by Shumilov, a remarkable general and a remarkable person.[14] He is retired now.

I've already said that the Sixth and Twelfth Armies retreated after the Germans had penetrated deeply along the flanks of those armies, and later the Germans surrounded them and destroyed them somewhere in the Uman area. These two armies fell into German captivity. Their headquarter staffs were taken prisoner along with their commanders, Muzychenko and Ponedelin. A prewar incident involving Muzychenko was reawakened in my memory at that time, but as the saying goes, no consequences had resulted from it. The only admission we made was that apparently we might have overlooked something and he might actually have been an unreliable person, although his conduct and management of troops remained irreproachable to the end. The Twelfth and Sixth Armies, fighting back from positions of encirclement, caused fairly heavy losses to the German troops, as is now known from captured German documents, and they fought to the last man. Muzychenko was wounded and taken prisoner; it seems he lost a leg. Thus Muzychenko ended up in a bad situation that seemed to offer grounds for believing that he was a dishonest person, that he was a German agent. This was a conclusion that was not confirmed, although there seemed to be indirect indications.

When these generals were taken prisoner the tendency among us was to consider them traitors. By Stalin's order all those taken prisoner by the Germans were to be considered traitors and their families were subject to deportation to Siberia. This measure was actually taken against the families of Muzychenko and Ponedelin. Later these men returned to our homeland. I remember that Muzychenko even returned to some kind of work in the ranks of the Soviet army, and Ponedelin too. Potapov was also taken prisoner and returned later. He later occupied a position of command in the Soviet army.[15] Such were the complicated situations that our commanders sometimes found themselves in.

I would like to tell about another such case. I think it was Sergiyenko who organized this foul business. Sergiyenko was commissar of internal affairs for the Ukrainian Soviet Republic.[16] He was a long, tall man and a crafty person. A slippery person. Later it turned out that he was really sneaky, a very dishonest character. A difficult situation developed in Kiev, and we were forced to transfer the headquarters of the Southwestern Front to Brovary. We did this jointly with the commander of the troops. Suddenly I got a telegram from Stalin in which he unjustly accused us of cowardice and threatened that "measures would be taken." He accused us of intending to surrender Kiev to the enemy. Stalin believed his state security officers, the Chekists; he considered them irreproachable. Of course, he didn't refer to them in his telegram, but I was convinced that no one could have done this other than Sergiyenko. It was a vile thing to do!

When Kiev was outflanked by the Germans, Sergiyenko found himself behind their lines, and he escaped from encirclement by changing his clothes and dressing up as a peasant. After that incident I didn't respect him or trust him anymore. I regarded him as a base individual capable of slandering others. In order to present himself as a hero, he could accuse others of the worst mortal sins. But today history knows that not only did we have no intention of surrendering Kiev, but we caused very heavy losses among the German troops and cooled their ardor about making a frontal assault on the city. Kiev fell, not because it was abandoned by our troops, who continued to defend it, but because of the flanking maneuvers carried out by the Germans from the north and the south, from the Gomel and Kremenchug areas.[17] I am simply recalling this unpleasant episode in passing, one that was a deeply painful experience for me.

One day in late July or early August 1941, Stalin called me in Kiev from Moscow and said that a headquarters for a Southwestern Area (Napravlenie) had been established. Budyonny was appointed commander of the troops of the Southwestern Area.[18] Budyonny would be stationed near Poltava[19] with his small operational staff for directing and coordinating the actions of two Fronts: the Southwestern, whose troops were commanded by Kirponos and where I was also a member of the Military Council; and the Southern Front, whose troops were commanded at that time, it seems to me, by Tyulenev.[20] There was a rapid change of commanders at that time. At first Tyulenev commanded, then Ryabyshev, then Cherevichenko, then finally Malinovsky was assigned.[21] He was the most stable of the commanders and held the post of commander of the troops of the Southern Front for a fairly long time. He got his lumps and he got his plums, as the saying goes. The lumps were from the fact that in 1942 he surrendered the city of Rostov to the enemy a second time. His troops were routed, as were the troops of the Southwestern Front. Malinovsky fell into disfavor and was removed from command. About half a year later he returned to his post and again commanded the troops of the Southern Front. Later he commanded, it seems to me, the Southwestern Front, the Third Ukrainian and Second Ukrainian Fronts, and in the latter post he ended the war in the West, getting as far as Vienna and Prague and celebrating along with others the complete destruction of Hitler's forces.

So then, Stalin said to me: "Budyonny is in Poltava alone, and we think you should go there and be there with him. We have confirmed you as a member of the Military Council of the High Command of the Southwestern

Area, and you and Budyonny together will command two Fronts: the South-western and the Southern."

I answered: "If it's needed, I will go join Budyonny at the headquarters of the Southwestern Area, but to replace me, Comrade Burmistenko could be assigned—the second secretary of the Central Committee of the Commu-nist Party of Ukraine.[22] He's a very fine comrade, an intelligent man, and he is fully capable of handling those duties. He knows people and they know him. People generally have a very good attitude toward him. Kirponos could be left as commander."

Stalin said: "All right. Then you call up Burmistenko and tell him he's being confirmed as a member of the Military Council of the Southwestern Front. But you should immediately remove yourself and get over to Budyonny's headquarters. You will command together with Budyonny."

I summoned Burmistenko. Our headquarters was located in Brovary, 27 kilometers from Kiev and east of the Dnieper River. Burmistenko was on the Central Committee of the party in Kiev. At that time, by decision of the Central Committee, he was engaged in storing ammunition and food and selecting underground party leaders. In short, the technical and material resources for a future underground were being stored away in the forests, where it was felt they would be more secure.. Schools were set up where sappers were trained—people who would know how to place explosives under railroads, highways, and buildings. Burmistenko came to see me. I told him: "Stalin called. You're going to be a member of the Military Council of the Front. Stalin said that you should immediately assume this post now and the order will be issued later. He has ordered me to leave immediately for Poltava, for Budyonny's headquarters. There I will be a member of the Military Council of the High Command of the Southwestern Area." And on that very same day, since Stalin had said it was urgent, I passed on word to the commander that Stalin had given the order to appoint Burmistenko in my place as a member of the Military Council and that now Kirponos should decide all questions together with Burmistenko.

Kirponos was very obliging, and it was easy to work with him. He proved himself to be different from some generals who, unfortunately, were very touchy when it came to comments or suggestions from members of the Mil-itary Council who sought to take a substantial part in decision making, not just a formality. Officially commanders could not do anything without the approval of the Military Council because there was a law that a member of a Military Council was equally responsible with the commander for decisions made. Without the signature of a member of a Military Council any order by a commander was invalid and did not have to be carried out by lower-ranking troops to whom the order was given. This was a formality of a kind that you could not get around if a member of the Military Council demonstrated initiative and really wanted to take part in the decision making, not just to rubber-stamp things with his signature, but some commanders had a hostile response to this.

Konev was especially touchy in this regard. One member of his Military Council[23] complained: "It's impossible to work with him; he slights you and dismisses you." The man who said this was an intelligent and sensible member of a Military Council, a military man by profession, and a man who knew his business, a good man. I don't know if he's still alive today. Unfortunately, many other generals (and I won't name them now) were difficult. Zhukov too was no easy matter. But I think that it was possible to function more freely with Zhukov. He was a highly authoritative person, but when I had occasion to look into one or another matter together with Zhukov (and this happened frequently), I liked his views, his decisions, and his comradely attitude. I respected him, and that respect survives to this day, despite the fact that we had a parting of the ways over certain specific questions. I regret that he allowed this to happen.

Having turned things over to Burmistenko, I immediately set out for Poltava. When I arrived there I soon found the headquarters of the Area Command. It was located to the west of Poltava (about 15 or 20 kilometers, in some state farm or suburban farming operation or truck farm). It was a convenient location. You could travel out to where the troops were, avoiding Poltava, unless you were going to Kharkov, but Kharkov was then in our rear area, and we were not interested in Kharkov. What we were interested in then was Kiev, Dnepropetrovsk, and other cities in the southwest.

When I drove up to Budyonny's headquarters I was surprised to see a tank stationed next to the porch. Noticing my surprise, Budyonny explained: "Things aren't the same now as in the Civil War. The Germans have modern technology, airplanes, and so I hide from them in a tank. I ride in that instead of an automobile."

I set about my duties as a member of the Military Council of the Southwestern Area Command. What kind of a headquarters was it? What kind of an organization is the headquarters of an Area Command? Exactly what we engaged in I can't tell you even today. The Area Command did not occupy itself with matters of providing supplies or ammunition or fighting men. Those questions were taken up by the headquarters of the Fronts themselves; they had direct communication with the Stavka (the General Headquarters) and together with that headquarters they decided all questions, bypassing us. The Area Command interacted with the Fronts only on questions of an operational kind. They reported the situation to us, and the commanders of the Fronts also reported to us, but they did so as equals, so to speak: we could only give them advice of one kind or another. The commanders took our advice and instructions, and if they liked them, they would carry them out. If they didn't like them, they would appeal to the Stavka through their own channels (and they had many such channels).

Budyonny and I had very good relations. He had a positive personality, on the one hand, but on the other, he was quarrelsome. We were returning from Dnepropetrovsk late one evening. It was a painful situation: our troops were abandoning Dnepropetrovsk.[24] The sentry guarding the entrance to our headquarters stopped us. Budyonny began talking to him in an insulting way. The soldier began to respond according to regulations. At that point Budyonny began to "explain" more aggressively, and the explanation ended with his hitting the soldier in the face. I was simply astounded. How could this be? A marshal of the Soviet Union striking a completely innocent person doing his duty according to regulations, striking him in violation of all established norms? We drove up and he stopped us. That was his duty. That's what he was put there for as a sentry. This was sheer arbitrariness! I am citing this incident as an example of what a temper the marshal had. At heart Budyonny was not like that, but apparently he retained the earlier habits of a senior noncommissioned officer, which he had been in the tsarist army, and so he demonstrated this lack of restraint. Later Semyon Mikhailovich [Budyonny] and I had a conversation on this subject, and I felt that he himself was troubled by what had happened. Unfortunately, Budyonny allowed himself such escapades more than once.

Our chief of staff was General Pokrovsky.[25] It seems to me he was a major general. Later (although, to tell the truth, I don't know exactly what post he served in after the war) he was in charge of materials on the history of the war. I think his functioning was useful because he was a professional military man and knew his job. He was very precise and uncommonly punctual. I would also say he was a caustic individual, to an extent that could make you sick. At first I viewed this as a quality that served him well in his job, but later I saw that in the existing conditions it was harmful to our work. There was nothing you could do with him, because having gone through the school of headquarters work and in the interest of meticulous headquarters work and closely organized verification of whether orders were being carried out exactly, he would simply paralyze the functioning of the headquarters of the fronts and the armies. He left no room for the functioning of the chiefs of staff or the commanders of the troops; he kept them all on the phone, demanding that they report continually about the state of affairs, the condition of their troops, the situation on one or another sector of the front, or the situation in one or another unit. This was absolutely intolerable, but people couldn't do anything about it.

As confirmation let me cite the following incident. In the Dnepropetrovsk area a very painful situation had taken shape. The Germans had advanced right up to the edge of Dnepropetrovsk and were bombarding the city. Dnepropetrovsk was defended by an army (or an army group) commanded by General Chibisov.[26] He was a solid, heavy-set former officer of the tsarist army, well on in years. He had gone through the school of the Civil War in the Red Army. Stalin knew him personally, had known him from Tsaritsyn, and trusted him. I told Budyonny that I was going to Dnepropetrovsk to hear what Chibisov and the secretary of the party's regional committee there had to say. The secretary of the committee there was Zadionchenko.[27] I respected him and he deserved it; he was a capable and energetic man.

I made my trip. It was already pretty late when I arrived, either twilight or already dark. I was guided to the location of the headquarters and I went up the stairs. The headquarters was on the second or third floor. When I walked in, the commander was on his feet pacing up and down the room. Right there at the desk, literally on his knees and holding the phone to his ear with his shoulder, was the chief of staff. He was writing something in a notebook and giving answers over the phone. I asked Chibisov what the situation was. "The situation? You can see for yourself what it is." Just then some German shells exploded. The German artillery was bombarding the area where the headquarters was located. I don't know if this was accidental, but the artillery fire was especially intense. Maybe the Germans knew that this was the location of the headquarters. Some of our officers who knew the location had been taken prisoner. Perhaps someone hadn't been able to hold out and had told. Chibisov answered me in a restrained way, but I sensed that he was angry. He said the defense was being organized, but that was just a very general observation.

I've heard this many times from various commanders. When you show up they tell you, "The defense is being organized." Later, when you leave, you look around and the commander is leaving the area right in your tracks, abandoning the defense of that sector. Unfortunately, such things happened. I am not inclined to say that these people were deliberately giving inaccurate reports. No, the situation was such that a commander dared not say he was abandoning a defensive position. This was totally ruled out, because he might have to pay for it later. The standard formulation was to express a kind of hope that perhaps the Germans would not break through here, or even a certainty that they could not, and later to say that under the pressure of superior enemy forces our troops had had to abandon the area after all—that was the standard formulation, and I got used to it in those days. I had asked Chibisov: "What's the situation?" (The situation was, of course, that the Germans had advanced right up to Dnepropetrovsk.)

He had answered: "There, you can see the situation for yourself." I didn't understand:

"What do you mean?"

He answered: "There the colonel sits, the chief of staff; he's already been sitting that way for an hour or more answering the questions of your chief of staff, General Pokrovsky, about the situation on our front. He's completely paralyzed because he's unable to function. If he stops talking, then within ten or fifteen minutes he'll be called again and held for another hour or two. He's not even sitting down. He's on his knees because the place where a person sits has gotten too sore." And he said this in such an angry way!

Unfortunately, everything he said was true, but I must add that at that time my experience in military matters was not very great. So I didn't know to what extent Chibisov was right. It seemed to me that he was right, but on the other hand I had respect for Pokrovsky; he was also guided by good and honorable motives; he really did want to know the actual state of affairs among the troops. Later, after I had been among the troops for many months, and had already grown used to military life, I understood that even though Pokrovsky had good motives, he was objectively hurting the cause. Such constant questioning really was paralyzing the work.

Relations among military people are unique and often incomprehensible to the civilian. A later conversation with Malinovsky[28] stuck in my mind in this connection. As I recall, we had liberated Rostov, and the headquarters of our Front was located in the Cossack village of Sovetskoye.[29] I had known this village back in 1941. After the liberation of Rostov, an operation was begun with the aim of driving the enemy out of Taganrog. The headquarters of the army was also in the village of Sovetskoye. I wanted to make a trip to Rostov and find out what was going on in the city, how restoration of the economy was proceeding, how everyday life was being set to rights, and how party work was being organized. The secretary of the party's regional committee there was Dvinsky.[30] I wanted to hear what Dvinsky had to say about the moods of the people of Rostov. I made my trip, held a conference of party officials of Rostov, and looked into how life was being reorganized and how the party committees and Soviet bodies were functioning. I returned from there late at night. Some question had come up for the commander of the Front, Malinovsky, and I decided to talk with him over the phone. I called him up: "Rodion Yakovlevich, I have a question for you. Are you still up or have you gone to bed?"

He groaned: "You know, I'm already in bed. If there's an urgent need, I can get dressed right away and come over."

I said: "No, what are you saying? Go ahead and rest since you've already gone to bed. My question isn't urgent. We can have an exchange of views tomorrow."

I don't even remember now what my question was. Obviously it was one of a passing nature—maybe a request from Dvinsky to help the city in some way with captured enemy materiel. Malinovsky's answer pleased me. Some other military men who I had occasion to work with, or serve on a Military Council with, always tried to make it look as though they never slept, were always on their feet, were always thinking about military problems and how to smash the enemy. It would happen sometimes that you would drop in to see a commander unexpectedly and he'd be sitting there with his eyes closed in sleep. The adjutants, when they would see me, would immediately wake him up. Supposedly he was always in a "waking state," but in fact he was sleeping. I very much disliked this, but to say something about it and insult a person holding a high post like that—I couldn't do it. And so I was aware of this shortcoming among the commanders.

Of course there is no such thing as a person who can go without sleep, because human beings have an organic need for rest. If a person doesn't sleep, he'll simply end up falling ill. And if he's sleep deprived to the point of illness, he loses his ability to work, especially the ability required of a commander in charge of troops, who is supposed to direct operations and lead the troops against the enemy.

Malinovsky was not that kind of person, and that pleased me very much. He might even have said to himself that he wasn't taking the right attitude toward matters, not acting the way he should, because he was allowing himself to sleep during wartime. We talked many times on various topics, he and I, and once during a conversation he expressed his views on the question of giving orders. His words were especially interesting to me because it was Malinovsky talking, the commander of a Front, a highly experienced military man, who had spent all his life in uniform and been in battle many times: in World War I, in the war in Spain, and in World War II. He said: "Comrade Khrushchev, the proper procedure is as follows: When we make a decision and issue an order to the Front, we have to allow in advance for a certain amount of time. For these orders to be passed along to the armies a certain amount of time is needed; for the order received by the armies to be passed on to the corps another amount of time is needed; for the corps commanders to pass along the orders to the divisions, a certain amount of time, and so on. As a whole it's a very lengthy time. If we immediately, as soon as we've issued an order, start checking to see if it's been carried out, then instead of contributing to this order reaching the troops more quickly, we'll be interrupting people in their work. In reporting to us, they won't say 'The order has *not* been carried out,' but they'll say something else. And so sometimes we would be forcing people to make things up and be paralyzing their work. That's why if an order's given, you have to wait a certain length of time for the order to reach all the military units. Then the officers will begin checking, each in his own line of duty, to see if the order has been clearly explained and whether the regulations are being followed, the regulations that have been taught to every officer."

That's why today I assume that Chibisov was right when he expressed dissatisfaction over Pokrovsky's constantly monitoring the fulfillment of orders. By doing that, he was depriving people of the possibility of properly conducting the work, of organizing the troops and carrying out the orders that had been issued.

Events in the Dnepropetrovsk area were developing in a very turbulent way at that time, and not in our favor. I had occasion to go out to the Dnieper River area several times to find out how the defense was being organized to try to prevent the river from being forced by the enemy. When I had traveled and looked around, I realized that our defense was pretty shaky. Instead of a solid defense line along the riverbank, there were simply the armed riverboats of the Dnieper military flotilla patrolling up and down. Individual military units were stationed in particular areas, observing from the bank, and if the enemy made an attempt to cross, they would try to repel that attempt. This kind of defense did not inspire confidence. If the enemy concentrated his efforts in one particular sector, he could force the Dnieper without any special difficulty.

In those days the Germans were not making any special effort to break through toward Kiev. We felt calmer; we assumed that they had lost their desire to make a frontal assault on Kiev. On the other hand, very active operations were developing to the north of Kiev, around Gomel. Recently I heard a radio broadcast in connection with preparations for celebrating the fiftieth anniversary of the Soviet armed forces. Marshal Yeremenko[31] was speaking. He told about the battles he had been in charge of in the Gomel region. From this I drew the conclusion that it was he, Yeremenko, who had commanded the troops there. But which Front was that? The Western? Or had the Bryansk Front been formed by then? This I don't know. I know only that Gomel for us, that is, for the Southwestern Front, served as the channel through which the Germans poured when they made a breakthrough in our direction, creating the threat of encirclement of our troops around Kiev.

Stubborn fighting broke out in the sector of the front near Dnepropetrovsk. The enemy forced the Dnieper. We had put up a pontoon bridge over which our troops retreated, but our sappers apparently didn't do a thorough job of destroying that bridge, and later the enemy was able to use it. It's hard to figure out how that could have happened, because the command staff reported that the bridge was blown up, but the speed with which the enemy appeared on the eastern bank of the river indicated the bridge was still intact. People fleeing from the western bank reported that the bridge had been blown up but was still floating on the water. It couldn't be used for heavy loads, but infantry could cross it. Apparently the enemy took advantage of that: to move infantry across and then repair the bridge and move heavy equipment across. Once again very heavy fighting broke out.

Budyonny and I went to see Malinovsky. In place of the former Sixth Army, which had been encircled and destroyed, a new one was built and the same designation was given to it—Sixth Army. Malinovsky was appointed commander of that army. Before that I had not known Malinovsky. Previously he had commanded a corps.[32] The army headquarters was located, it seems to me, in a school in the town of Novomoskovsk.[33] We arrived there. The situation was very difficult; the enemy kept the road under constant bombardment so that we couldn't bring up reinforcements. Actually we had nothing to bring up. Budyonny and I went into the school and found the following scene: everything was rumbling and roaring around. Malinovsky, the commander of the Sixth Army, reported on the situation, and as he did the commander of the troops of the Southern Front, Tyulenev, was brought in on a stretcher. His wound wasn't serious, but he couldn't walk because he had been wounded in the leg (a flesh wound). To inspire the troops, Tyulenev himself had gone among the ranks and had led them in an attack on the enemy, and when a mine blew up he was wounded. Zadionchenko, the regional committee party secretary, walked in with him.

After Tyulenev was wounded a new commander of the Southern Front was appointed, a Cossack who before that had commanded a tank corps. His name was Ryabyshev. Everything that was in our power had been done to try to drive the Germans back and not allow them to establish a firm beachhead on the left, or eastern, bank of the Dnieper. But our efforts were not successful. We didn't have the actual forces necessary for that. At the same time we discovered that the Germans had concentrated their forces and were trying to make a forced crossing of the Dnieper to the north of Dnepropetrovsk in the Kremenchug area. Again we did everything in our power: our planes were sent there, and they bombed the tank forces and infantry of the enemy on the approaches to the river to try to prevent them from crossing the Dnieper. Nevertheless, the enemy forced the river and established a beachhead, bypassing the Dnepropetrovsk area and occupying the eastern-bank part of the city of Kremenchug.

When we began trying to guess the enemy's further intentions, a fairly clear picture emerged. His intention was this: to strike a blow from the south, from the beachhead at Kremenchug, and a blow from the north, where the enemy had advanced almost as far as Kursk,[34] and thus break through to our rear (where we had no troops) and close a circle around our troops who were located along the Dnieper near Cherkassy[35] and across the Dnieper around Kiev. We discussed the situation. We had no additional forces at our disposal. Even though we had guessed the Germans' intentions, we could do nothing to paralyze them, to prevent them from carrying out their plans. After considerable thought we arrived at the following decision: to take a certain number of troops and artillery and cover our flank in the direction from Kiev toward Kremenchug, so that there, in the Ukrainian steppe, there would be something with which to block the enemy's path northward and not allow him to close the ring of encirclement. What could we take? It was obvious that the troops we had in Kiev were so far not being used. The situation there was quiet, and the enemy was making no moves against Kiev.

Budyonny and I prepared the appropriate order and sent the text to Moscow to obtain permission. We didn't have the right to redeploy our forces in that way on our own initiative. Moscow reacted very quickly, but in a special way. No answer was given; instead Marshal Timoshenko suddenly flew in with authorization to remove Budyonny as commander in chief of the Southwestern Area. Timoshenko assumed the duties of commander in chief of the troops of the Southwestern Area. Budyonny and I said our goodbyes. Budyonny told me: "This is the result of the initiative we took," and away he went. The commander in chief had been changed, but the situation had not, because the new commander in chief arrived with his hands empty [that is, he brought no new forces with him].

We should grant Timoshenko his due. He understood the situation very well, saw everything, and grasped that for our troops in the region a catastrophe was imminent and that we had no means of preventing it. Several times Timoshenko and I went out to visit the troops, as I had done earlier with Budyonny. For example, as I recall, we went out into the area west of Poltava. There we had a mechanized group commanded by General Feklenko. When Feklenko saw us his eyes literally popped, out of surprise or fear. We asked him to report on the situation. He reported briefly and immediately said: "You've got to get away from here, and hurry!" The situation was so difficult that he could not be sure of our safety. Indeed, we had nothing in that area, aside from the remnants of Feklenko's troops. And flying over them, with complete impunity, was an Italian reconnaissance plane similar to a U-2. The enemy was taking advantage of the impunity he enjoyed, and even in daylight he calmly flew around in such a lazy, untroubled way.

At the end of August or the beginning of September,[36] enemy units, by striking blows from the north and south, linked up to the east of Kiev. Our military group found itself encircled.[37] Among those trapped in the encirclement was the headquarters staff of the Southwestern Front, led by Kirponos, commander of the Front, and Burmistenko, first member of the Military Council. Besides Burmistenko there were two other members of the Military Council. One of them was a young commissar, Rykov, a good comrade and an active and energetic person. He was always rushing about among the troops and doing everything in his power to improve the situation. Colonel Bagramyan, head of the operations department of the Front headquarters, was in the Kremenchug area at that time and escaped encirclement. We asked him to come to the Southwestern Area headquarters to help look into the situation, and we proposed that he immediately fly to the Southwestern Front headquarters to place himself at the disposal of Kirponos and to give him our orders orally. (Because he might fall into enemy hands, no written documents should be on his person.) The orders were: "Break out of encirclement!"

Bagramyan understood our order correctly, and he also understood that he needed to return to headquarters. He said: "The headquarters of our Front is there, and as head of the operations department I should also be there with the headquarters staff." But at that point Kirponos, commander of the troops of the Southwestern Front, received an order from the General Staff to return to Kiev and organize a defense there. In other words, he was

ordered not to break out of encirclement, but rather to go deeper into the
enemy's rear area. The Front headquarters at that time was located approximately 150 kilometers, if not more, east of Kiev. It was a very long way for
the headquarters to travel [back to Kiev], with all its gear and in the absence
of fuel and ammunition and the impossibility of receiving any by air. These
circumstances were ignored by those at the top. Kirponos gave the order,
and the staff headed westward.[38]

I don't know what distance they had managed to cover when they
received a new order from Moscow, to break out eastward. Later, after from
escaping from encirclement, Bagramyan reported to us that the headquarters had already made the decision to turn back, but the staff was completely disorganized by all this. They decided that groups of headquarters
personnel should try to break through eastward by various routes to the
north of Poltava. An armed group was organized to travel ahead of the staff
personnel and break enemy resistance. The enemy had few troops there and
did not expect to encounter our fighters in this rear area, and therefore our
commanders had some hope of breaking through. They began to move. The
entire headquarters staff did not succeed in breaking out of encirclement,
but Bagramyan and his group of fighters did.

A break had occurred [i.e., the forces of the Southwestern Front had
become disconnected]. The Front headquarters remained far behind its
most advanced group, which was commanded by Bagramyan. We [at the
Southwestern Area Command] also lost contact with the [Southwestern]
Front headquarters at that time. Earlier Burmistenko had sent his assistant,
via U-2 plane, to bring out top-secret party documents, in which reference
was made to the locations of secret arms caches, with uniforms, food, and
ammunition for the partisan movement. At that point Shuisky[39] flew out,
on Bagramyan's orders. Later he became my assistant and remained with me
till the end of my party, political, and government work. He was a very
honest and decent person and carried out his orders well. Shuisky told us
that he had flown out before dawn, under machine-gun fire, together with
the pilot, who was Colonel Ryazanov (later the commander of a corps in
the air force). The Germans were already tightening the ring around that
headquarters from all sides, and we had only scanty reports of what was
happening.

Later, one by one and in small groups, people began to emerge, escaping
from encirclement. There were generals, officers, and troops. Each brought
his own personal impressions and later provided information about the situation in which he had been directly involved. After some time we received

information that Kirponos had perished. Some staff member of the special department of the Front headquarters reported to me that he had seen Kirponos's body and had even brought out some of his personal effects: a comb and a little mirror. I did not doubt his truthfulness. He said there was still a chance to penetrate to those areas. I asked him, since there was such a possibility, to go back and remove from Kirponos's service jacket his Gold Star signifying Hero of the Soviet Union. He had always worn it. And the man did go! There were marshes in the area that were hard to cross with mechanized equipment, but this man overcame those obstacles and returned, bringing the Gold Star with him. When he gave it to me, I asked: "How could this be? Surely there are marauders in the area?"

He answered that the commander's service jacket had been covered with blood, that the flap of the commander's breast pocket had turned up and covered the star so that it wasn't visible. He said: "I removed the star from his jacket, as you told me to do."

Burmistenko disappeared without any trace whatsoever. We exerted great efforts in trying to track him down. From people who had been in his body-guard only one thing became known: they had spent the last night in some haystacks. In the evening they noticed that Burmistenko destroyed all his documents, tore them up and buried them. They dug into the haystacks for the night and went to sleep. In the morning when they approached the haystack where Burmistenko had been sleeping he was not there. Later they found the documents he had buried, including personal identity documents. He had previously sent out highly confidential documents with his assistant Shuisky, and we had received them. I concluded that Burmistenko destroyed the documents indicating his identity. He thought that if he fell into German hands, it would come out that he held an important position, so he destroyed all traces of that information. We thought he would break out of encirclement in spite of everything. After all, many generals had escaped. But Burmistenko did not show up. I think that he either shot himself, in order not to fall into enemy hands, or was killed trying to break out of encirclement. As there were no documents on his person to reveal his identity, he could have perished without anyone's knowledge. We waited for him a long time, but unfortunately our waiting was in vain.

Many people did escape from encirclement then. General Kostenko[40] and a group of soldiers escaped. The Front's chief of communications escaped, on his own.[41] And Popel arrived. He returned to our lines two or three weeks later. He had gone through the forests of the Polesye region, where there were as yet no Germans, because they were taking the main roads. Popel even brought a wounded colonel out with him and a small number of other troops. General Moskalenko also escaped. (He previously commanded, it seems to me, an antitank brigade.)[42] We [the Southwestern Area Command] were located to the north of the center of Kharkov, in a place called Pomerki.[43] This had once been an area where people had dachas, the kind beloved by the people of Kharkov.

An unpleasant occurrence with General Moskalenko took place there. He was in a very angry mood toward his fellow Ukrainians; he cursed them, denounced them all as traitors, saying they should all be sent to Siberia. It was unpleasant for me, of course, to hear him saying such absurd things about a population, about an entire nation, just because of the upsets he had experienced. An entire nationality cannot be a traitor. Individuals, yes, but an entire nation, no! I asked him: "And how should people treat you? After all, you're also Ukrainian, aren't you? Your name is Moskalenko, isn't it?

"Yes, I'm Ukrainian. I'm from Grishino."

"I know Grishino," I said. "That's in the Donbas."[44]

He said, "But I'm not like that at all."

I said: "What are you like? Your name is Moskalenko. You're also Ukrainian. You're not thinking correctly and you're not talking correctly."

Then for the first time in my life I saw Timoshenko lose his temper. He and Moskalenko apparently knew each other well. Timoshenko came down hard on Moskalenko and gave him a pretty rough going-over (from my point of view): "What the heck are you doing cursing Ukrainians? What are you saying? That they're traitors? That they're against the Red Army? That they didn't treat you well?" Moskalenko kept cursing them and offered the following as justification: He had hidden in a cowshed, and a peasant woman, a collective farmer, had caught sight of him and chased him out of there, wouldn't let him take shelter.

Timoshenko reacted sharply: "Yes, and she did the right thing. After all, if you had crawled into the cowshed in a general's uniform and with your general's trousers on, it would be different. But you crawled in there all raggedy and tattered. Do you think she really imagined that a general of the Red Army was hiding in her cowshed? She thought it was some thief who had crawled in there. But if you had been wearing your general's uniform, she would have acted differently toward you."

I liked what Timoshenko said. I told Moskalenko: "General Kostenko and a group of troops are still in encirclement now. I'm convinced that they'll break out. Let's hear what he says about the attitude of the Ukrainian collective farmers toward those troops of ours who are still surrounded and in a disastrous situation." One often heard, back then, that Ukrainians displayed an unfriendly attitude toward the retreating Red Army. I gave the following explanation: "Here's what you should try to grasp: Why should Ukrainian peasants welcome our retreat? They feel bitter. How much labor has been lost? Nothing was spared in order to strengthen the army and to strengthen our country. And suddenly this catastrophe has burst on us. The army is retreating, abandoning the population, abandoning the territory. Naturally they display their dissatisfaction toward those who are leaving them to a catastrophe. This isn't betrayal, but a feeling of great grief and affliction."

Several weeks went by. I fell ill and was lying in a little house in Kharkov where the members of the Ukrainian government had originally been located when Kharkov was the capital of Ukraine. At that time this house[45] had been occupied by Kosior, the first secretary of the Central Committee of the Communist Party (Bolshevik) of Ukraine. It was a very nice house, a detached building on its own grounds, with all appurtenances, including a garage, and it was surrounded by a reinforced concrete wall. While I was there, I received the report that Kostenko had escaped from encirclement. I asked that a message be conveyed to Kostenko to come see me immediately and report on events. I knew Kostenko and regarded him with great respect. He arrived and I asked him: "Well, how are things?" He always spoke with humor.

He answered: "Well, nothing special, except that people cried when we retreated."

I asked him further: "And how were the people? Were they willing to help when you needed to feed your cavalry group?"

He answered: "What are you talking about! All you had to do was say something, and they would slaughter chickens, calves, hogs, and provide oats for the horses. They gave everything. That's the way the people are. They wept bitterly, with regret at what had happened, that the Red Army was forced to retreat."

I was very pleased to hear him disprove the assertions made by others who, under the impact of their personal experiences, had formed an incorrect idea about the Ukrainian people. Of course they, too, were honest men; I have not one drop of suspicion about Comrade Moskalenko's loyalty or that of others. I am just comparing how the Ukrainian Moskalenko reacted at that time with the way the Ukrainian Kostenko reacted. Both the one and the other were basing themselves on facts. The one based himself on the fact that a Ukrainian peasant woman chased him out of a cowshed; the other, on what he had experienced in escaping from encirclement with his group of cavalry troops wearing the uniforms of Soviet soldiers. The Ukrainians had done everything for the group led by General Kostenko to help the men escape from encirclement!

When we had been located near Poltava (back before the final encirclement of our troops around Kiev), we had prepared a command post in the Akhtyrka region between Kharkov and Sumy.[46] When we were forced to leave Poltava, we transferred the base for our headquarters to Akhtyrka. Akhtyrka was located in a geographical position where soldiers, officers, and generals, escaping from encirclement and following the course of the Sula to the Psyol and Vorskla Rivers,[47] ended up precisely in the Akhtyrka area. Later our command post was established in Pomerki. Some of the people escaping from encirclement in the direction of Kharkov now ended up at Pomerki. This is where Moskalenko came and Kostenko also.

I don't know now how many days went by after the culmination of this catastrophe—after our troops had either been taken prisoner or annihilated—when it was reported to me that Rykov,[48] a member of the Military Council, had been wounded and had ended up in a hospital that was now in enemy-occupied territory. It was still possible to make one's way there, and therefore Soviet doctors and nurses were working there. I wanted to save Rykov, but I understood that if anyone said something about him openly, he could be killed by the enemy. I sent some people there to try to sneak Rykov out and smuggle him through to territory occupied by Soviet troops. They went off, but soon returned and said that Rykov's life had ended in the hospital and he had been buried.

Now I would like to return to the main subject—the outcome of the fighting in the Kiev area. Budyonny and I had proposed, back then, that we reposition our forces: that we take artillery from the Kiev area and use it to forestall the main danger on our left flank, in the direction of Kremenchug. The direction to the north, from which the enemy was advancing to try to encircle our troops, was in a territory outside our influence—that is, the influence of the Southwestern Area Command. General Yeremenko commanded the troops there.[49] The enemy had broken through our lines in an area southwest of Gomel. But we were not given permission to reposition our forces. Timoshenko arrived [with the assignment] to hold the positions in which our troops were deployed [around Kiev]. Not even a week went by[50] before they were cut off by the enemy. Our proposals, as history has shown, had been correct.

I cannot say now that if we had carried out that repositioning of our forces, catastrophe would have been avoided; probably it would have happened anyhow. But at any rate it might have been less severe, because we would have brought out some of the artillery from Kiev and would have strengthened our left flank in the direction of Kremenchug. Fighting would have broken out that would have been painful for the Germans there, and perhaps they would not have had enough troops to complete the planned operation. Even when they had surrounded us, groups of our troops were able to penetrate the German front lines rather freely here and there. This testifies to the fact that the enemy's offensive lines were not very solid.

As a result of a false understanding of the slogan "Not one step backward!" our troops often remained in disadvantageous positions and ultimately perished, with no tangible benefit resulting from their loss. If we go back for a moment to the Lvov operation, [we can see that] there too, we had wanted to withdraw the Sixth and Twelfth armies to use them in areas where we needed them. We were forbidden to do so. As a result, those troops were surrounded and taken prisoner.

We retreated to Kiev, and our headquarters was established at Brovary. Suddenly General Tupikov arrived there. (I had not known him before that.) He brought instructions that he was to take the post of KOVO chief of staff, that Purkayev was to surrender his duties and place himself at the disposal of the General Staff. That was done. General Tupikov had come to us from Turkey, where he had ended up after the Great Patriotic War began. He had been our military attaché in Berlin.[51] When Hitler attacked the USSR, all Soviet diplomats were removed from Germany; they were placed in special "sealed" railroad cars and sent to Turkey. Tupikov made a good impression on me, although I also had a very good opinion of Purkayev. The new chief of staff [Tupikov] was perhaps a bit younger[52] and a bit more zealous, but I don't know if one of them was more worthy than the other. I wouldn't want to say anything on that point, because I valued both of them highly and respected them both.

Tupikov set to work. I liked his precision and energy. Here's an incident that occurred, involving him. Bagramyan told me about it. Bagramyan had been his deputy, as chief of the operations department. One day German bombers came over the area where our headquarters was located (as was repeated every day). Bagramyan was very tired; he had lain down on a couch and closed his eyes but did not fall asleep. It was impossible to sleep because the ground was shaking and everything was roaring. Tupikov, this whole while, was walking around the room softly singing to himself: "Will I fall pierced with an arrow / Or will it pa-ass me by?" He got a bottle of something out of the desk, poured himself a little glassful, sipped at it, and again continued walking around the room, apparently thinking some matters over. This kind of thing happened more than once. Tupikov was no coward. Alas, when the Front headquarters was encircled, Tupikov did not return. As I recall, even his body was never found. For us he remained one of those missing in action.

Here is another example along the same lines—concerning the Kiev group. The staff of the 37th Army, which was defending Kiev, was also encircled along with many generals, officers, and soldiers. Some of them were taken prisoner, and some escaped. The commander of the 37th Army was Vlasov, who later became a traitor to our homeland and was deservedly hanged after the defeat of Hitler. At that time he did escape from encirclement. (I don't know how long it took.) Timoshenko and I were of course glad to meet him. He showed up in peasant clothing and reported that he had escaped carrying a walking stick, giving the appearance of an ordinary peasant. We set up a new post for him. He won fame as a good general who knew how to command his troops, to construct a defense, and to deal blows to the enemy. But we were not allowed to make use of his abilities. As soon as it was learned that Vlasov had escaped, Stalin personally called us and ordered him sent to Moscow. We did not know that a counteroffensive was being prepared against the Germans near Moscow at that time.[53] Later we found out that in the Moscow operation Vlasov commanded one of the armies, and Stalin praised him highly. This general was given many awards and decorations and was considered one of the best fighting generals, one who demonstrated his abilities on the front lines in the offensive against the German troops outside Moscow.

But let me return to the enemy breakthrough in the Kiev area, the encirclement of our group, and the destruction of the 37th Army. Later the Fifth Army also perished.[54] It was commanded by General Potapov, who was taken prisoner. Other troops perished there also, including the staff of the Front headquarters and all the rear-echelon support services. The rear-echelon units had also been cut off by the enemy, because the Germans penetrated quite deeply, about 200 kilometers to the east of Kiev, and surrounded our group within a large area. You can imagine how much military equipment we lost there! All of this was senseless, and from the military point of view, a display of ignorance, incompetence, and illiteracy. It's hard for me to find the right word. There was an incorrect and false conception embodied in the slogan "Not one step backward!" There you had the result of not taking a step backward. We were unable to save these troops because we didn't withdraw them, and as a result we simply lost them. We were deprived of military equipment, and a huge hole was torn in our front lines, one that we could not close. We had neither the human resources nor the equipment—neither military, economic, nor transport equipment. And yet it was possible to allow this not to happen.

A certain analogy suggests itself—an analogy with what happened, later on, to the fascists themselves. Look at the documents published in the book *Top Secret! For Command Staff Only!*[55] The methods of defense strongly resemble one another. Toward the end of the war, when the Germans found themselves in the same kind of situation we had been in, they made the same kind of foolish mistakes. Just as our lack of good management worked in the enemy's favor, Hitler in a similar way, later on, worked in our favor, facilitating our efforts to destroy his forces.

The headquarters personnel of the Southwestern Area were devoting every effort at that time to the defense of Kharkov. People labored heroically and did everything they could to prevent the further advance of the enemy eastward. Kharkov plant no. 75, where before the war the T-34 tanks had been produced, was now repairing them. Things were organized well, and the tanks were being quickly restored to action. There were spare parts available, and well-trained specialists were at work.

But what happened to the tanks we repaired in our plant? We were ordered to send them to Moscow! Of course we felt offended and even angry over this: we didn't have anything there to stop the Germans with, and they were taking away our tanks. A fairly large number of tanks were taken from us. We began adapting tractors for military purposes: we put armor plate on them and mounted machine guns, so that we could use them in that form against the enemy. Despite the fact that tractors are not really suitable for military operations, it was nevertheless better than nothing: after all, at least there was some metal armor. We wanted to use everything we had at hand, and we used what we could in any way we could. Later the report came from Moscow that the so-called Katyusha was being used—a weapon that launched multiple rockets by jet propulsion. Stalin even criticized us: "Such a weapon exists, and it ought to be used more."

I asked him, "Send us the blueprints, and we'll organize production in Kharkov right away." They sent us the blueprints, and we did immediately organize production at the Shevchenko plant on the Lopan River.[56]

I knew this plant well. Before the revolution it belonged to Berlizov, and in 1912 I had worked there as a machinist for a short time. The plant's workers and engineers mastered the production of the Katyushas quickly. We went out in the fields and fired them, testing the design. We didn't manufacture the rockets for these weapons. I don't know where they were produced. A very limited number of rockets were sent to us.

We didn't know the Germans' intentions then, but after the forcing of the Dnieper and the defeat of our military group near Kiev and Dnepropetrovsk, their aim was to concentrate forces to strike against Moscow. Therefore the enemy forces moving in the direction of Kharkov were apparently not very large. To repel the enemy in the Moscow area, the Stavka was taking everything from everywhere. It took whatever it could, including from us in the Kharkov area, when we ourselves needed every military item. There was a reserve cavalry unit in our area, commanded by Belov.[57] That, too, was taken. The unit had been untouched, and we placed great hopes in it. It arrived in our jurisdiction, but had no sooner made contact with the enemy than the order came to send it off immediately and place it at the disposal of the command staff in charge of defending the Moscow area. This unit later made a good showing outside Tula.

The enemy continued to advance in the direction of Kharkov, but not as quickly as in the first days of the war. Although our forces were small, we did offer resistance. In the Kharkov area the 38th Army was commanded by General Tsyganov,[58] a stout man with some odd caprices. I told Stalin about him, and at dinner on one occasion Stalin later recalled an incident involving this general. As the enemy was threatening Kharkov, Tsyganov came out on a highway down which our troops were retreating, and he set up a desk with a samovar on it and began to drink tea. People ran over to him and said the fascists were approaching the area, but he would not take one step backward. Later he said that this was his way of trying to inspire his troops with confidence, as if to say, "There's no special danger." This was quite a unique way, I would say, of trying to demonstrate that our defenses were impregnable. In spite of that, the enemy kept advancing eastward.

I remember those months: rain and mud—conditions that made it difficult for the Germans to use their equipment. At that time we ourselves didn't have much military equipment. We were repairing tanks, but they were taking them away from us. And so we were making use of tractors. Later they gave us light tanks, the T-50 tanks. This is a very light tank indeed: its armor is no more than 20 millimeters thick, perhaps even less. The Germans could destroy those tanks with their artillery without any special difficulty. We received an order to prepare Kharkov for evacuation, and we concentrated all our efforts on removing the machinery and equipment from the tractor factory. We succeeded in doing this, although I'm not about to say that we took out absolutely all the equipment. We could hardly have succeeded in doing that, but we did clean out all the bays in the Kharkov tractor plant and took those machine tools eastward. There our industry made use of those machine tools to organize production of weapons and military equipment.

Then we received an order with specific time frames for abandoning Kharkov and Kupyansk[59] and retreating to the Don River. I don't remember now what the time limit was, but we were operating according to the plans of the General Staff. When we abandoned Kharkov all the special military trains for this purpose were concentrated at Kupyansk. Timoshenko and I were also riding in one of these troop trains. I don't know why the enemy didn't take advantage of that opportunity to bomb everything we had there. If bombers had flown in, little would have been left. Maybe the Germans were already exhausted or, most important, had set themselves the task of capturing Moscow and had diverted all the forces at their disposal in that direction. Hitler's calculation was that with the capture of Moscow he could end the war and achieve the capitulation of the USSR.

When our troops left Kharkov and retreated to the Seversky Donets River to the east of Kharkov, we came under no further pressure from the enemy. Once the Germans had occupied Kharkov and reached the Donets[60] with their advanced units, they began to take up defensive positions without trying to advance farther. What we were thinking was this: "Why should we retreat farther, as ordered by the directives, if the enemy is not pursuing us?" We then proposed to Moscow that we organize a defensive line along the Donets rather than retreat farther. And sure enough, we received approval of our proposal. We transferred our headquarters to Valuiki,[61] climbed out of the railroad cars, and found lodging for ourselves in peasant huts.

Autumn 1941 in Ukraine was very rainy. The mud was unbelievable, simply impassable. The conditions that arose for the side that was on the offensive were particularly difficult. (When an army is retreating, poor roads to a certain degree tend to hinder the forward advance of the enemy and make things easier for the defending side.) Then snow began falling early in the year, and fairly heavy frosts set in. We began preparing our defenses along the Donets. We gathered that the enemy was settling in for the winter, and we in turn constructed our winter defensive positions. Our military intelligence reported on this to us, as did refugees—our people who had been living in enemy-occupied territory.

After the death of Tupikov a new chief of staff was sent to us, a young, very interesting, learned, and intelligent general by the name of Bodin.[62] I took a liking to this man because of his intelligence and his clear understanding of our situation. He was interesting both as a person and as a military man. It also pleased me that he and Bagramyan became friends. I had felt a great compatibility with Bagramyan from our very first meeting, and now the two of them were working in harmony. They were sober-minded men. They were also sober in regard to the matter of drinking, and they had good minds and an intelligent understanding of the military situation.

I remember one day Bodin and Bagramyan came to see me to present their point of view about our loss of the city of Rostov. At that time the Southwestern Front was operating under the command of Marshal Timoshenko. He was also the commander of all the forces of the Southwestern Area, and therefore the command of the Southern Front was also under him. As for me, I was a member of the Military Council of the Southwestern Area and at the same time of the Southwestern Front.

I am saying this so that it will be clear why Bodin and Bagramyan were reporting to me on the question of Rostov. Rostov always lay within the zone of responsibility of the Southern Front, which had been established at the beginning of the war. Bodin and Bagramyan began demonstrating, with numbers at their finger tips, that the enemy had been able to occupy Rostov because of the extremely unskilled and worthless way in which the troops of the Southern Front had been commanded. The Southern Front had at its disposal sufficient forces to have prevented the capture of Rostov, to have repelled the enemy onslaught. A German tank army commanded by General Kleist[63] had occupied Rostov. Kleist held a high position among German generals because of his skill in leading armored forces. That was the kind of reputation he had.

Bodin and Bagramyan said: "In our estimation, despite the fact that the forces we now have are very weak, they could be bunched together into a fist to strike a blow, and that blow could be concentrated in the direction of Rostov to strike at Kleist. Rostov could be liberated. We are absolutely convinced that this is feasible, but on one condition: that the operation be carried out, not by the commander of the Southern Front, but by Marshal Timoshenko. We have not reported our views to the marshal. We wanted to present them to you first, so that this question could be raised in the Military Council." I forget why they didn't go directly to Timoshenko. Perhaps at that time Timoshenko was drinking. He was a fairly heavy drinker then. (God knows why.)

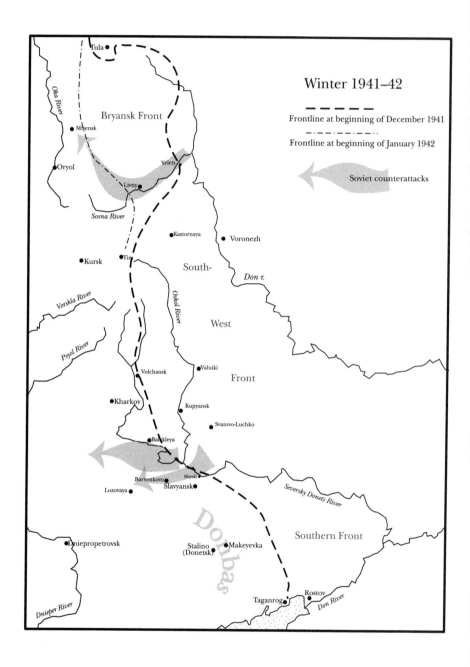

Winter 1941–42

– – – – – Frontline at beginning of December 1941

– · – · – · – Frontline at beginning of January 1942

Soviet counterattacks

Oka River

Tula

Bryansk Front

Mtsensk

Oryol

Yelets

Livny

Sosna River

Kastornaya

Voronezh

South-

Kursk

Tim

Don r.

Oskol River

West

Vorskla River

Volchansk

Valuiki

Psyol River

Front

Kharkov

Kupyansk

Svatovo-Luchko

Balakleya

Barvenkovo

Mayaki

Seversky Donets River

Lozovaya

Slavyansk

Donbas

Dniepropetrovsk

Stalino
(Donetsk)

Makeyevka

Southern Front

Dnieper River

Taganrog

Rostov

Don River

To the extent that I could grasp their arguments and understand them, I found myself convinced that they were arguing realistically, that evidently such a possibility did exist for us. This possibility should be taken advantage of, especially at such a troubled and difficult time. Thus far there had been no instance when, after surrendering a major city to the enemy, we had then taken it back. This would have not just military but also great political importance, both for our troops and for the civilian population. It was important to show that the Red Army could also deal some blows. Here we had a good chance of demonstrating concretely that the Red Army had this capability—by driving the enemy out of Rostov. I took this up with Timoshenko. Timoshenko responded positively to the proposal and replied, "Yes, let's present the question to the Military Council and hear what Bodin and Bagramyan have to say. Let them report to us." They gave their report, suggesting where we could get the units and which units to take and what direction to send them to strike the main blow—that is, these forces should mainly be taken from the Southern Front—in order to concentrate a blow against Rostov, leaving some sectors fairly naked, sectors where we estimated the enemy would remain on the defensive. We reported to Moscow, and Moscow gave its sanction for the operation.

The preparatory work had been carried out. We had gathered together everything we could and transferred it to the appropriate place: ammunition and artillery and whatever tanks we had. The day came that was set for the offensive. Timoshenko and I flew south and established ourselves in some small settlement near Rostov. The operation began, but we were not immediately able to accomplish the task we had set ourselves. The Germans offered stubborn resistance, and we didn't have sufficient forces to drive them out of Rostov. We were compelled to break off our offensive, so as not to wipe out our own troops. But we didn't abandon the operation altogether; we simply interrupted it for a certain length of time in order to bring up new troops, taking them from specific sectors of the Southern Front. Nevertheless, we believed that we could liberate Rostov. A little time went by, and we renewed the operation. I was very pleased by Timoshenko's capable and efficient management. He really shone, as the saying goes, in carrying out this operation, with his sensible deployment of troops and his ability to make people follow orders. And we did take Rostov![64] The enemy was forced to pull back to Taganrog—a fairly good distance.[65]

I immediately went into Rostov. I wanted to look at the destruction in the city and see what damage the enemy had done. Our population had suffered

THE GREAT PATRIOTIC WAR

from what had happened. It's hard even to express with words their joy over the liberation of their beloved city from the German troops. Lying on the streets were many corpses of soldiers as well as of civilians shot by the Germans. The enemy had also abandoned some military equipment. That is when I got my first view of German machine guns and light artillery mounted on half-tracks, which I mentioned earlier. But we didn't capture an especially significant amount of materiel that we could then make use of. Everything that the Germans abandoned either was not working or had been knocked out of commission, evidently during the fighting.

So then, the enemy had been driven back to Taganrog. But, as the saying goes, the appetite grows by what it feeds on. We decided we could take Taganrog, too, without stopping, but actually we didn't have the forces. Later we tried several more attacks there, but they were unsuccessful, and we stopped the offensive. To make up for it, the retaking of Rostov made a very powerful impression on our entire country. A leading editorial in *Pravda* congratulated us and held our success up as an example. Both the military and the civilian forces of the USSR were energized and had their morale strengthened by this example. The possibility that the enemy could be beaten had been demonstrated.

When I flew to Moscow, I saw that Stalin was also very pleased. He praised Timoshenko and me. Our names were mentioned in *Pravda*. In short, all this made a big impression and deservedly so, in my opinion. I'm not speaking here about myself as an individual. But the fact of the liberation of Rostov showed that the Red Army had the capacity not only to offer resistance but also to go on the offensive. The concrete demonstration of this capacity was seen in the liberation of Rostov. I would like to make special mention of the role of General Bodin, who later perished under bombardment in the Caucasus, as well as Bagramyan, who later became a marshal of the Soviet Union. They were the ones who initiated the offensive, and they were the heart and soul of the operation. Here they demonstrated their ability to analyze a situation and deploy troops effectively to destroy the enemy. I want to give Marshal Timoshenko his due also, because he carried out the operation brilliantly.

1. Mtsensk is about 60 kilometers northeast of Oryol. [SS]

2. Taganrog is in the south of European Russia, on the Sea of Azov, about 60 kilometers west of Rostov on the Don. [SS]

3. The distance from Oryol to Taganrog is about 700 kilometers as the crow flies. [SS]

4. The place that N. S. Khrushchev has in mind may be Krymsk, about 50 kilometers northeast of Anapa (see next note). [AH/SS]

5. Anapa is an old tsarist fortress town on the northeastern shore of the Black Sea, to the east of Crimea. [SS]

6. Novorossiysk is a port on the Black Sea, about 40 kilometers southeast of Anapa. [SS]

7. The Taman peninsula is situated 30–50 kilometers northwest of Anapa. It separates the Sea of Azov from the Black Sea proper. Taman is near the end of the peninsula. [SS]

8. Stalin was appointed supreme commander in chief on August 8, 1941.

9. Until September 10, 1941 the Kiev Special Military District was operationally subordinate to the Southwestern Front, which it provided with resources.

10. The name of this factory means "Lenin's forge." [SS]

11. Osoaviakhim is the Russian acronym for Obshchestvo sodeistviya oborone, aviatsii, i khimii (Society to Assist Defense, Aviation, and Chemistry). Officially an independent public civil-defense organization, Osoaviakhim was in practice subordinate to the mobilization department of the General Staff. [SS]

12. The *pistolet-pulemyot* Shpagin or PPSh was a submachine gun designed by G. S. Shpagin and produced in 1941. It was similar in appearance to American submachine guns of the 1930s. See illustration in *Bol'shaya Sovetskaya entsiklopediya* (Large Soviet encyclopedia), 3d ed. (Moscow, 1975), s.v. PPSh. [GS]

13. Z. T. Serdyuk. See Biographies.

14. Major General (later Lieutenant General) M. S. Shumilov commanded the 64th Army from August 1942 until its transformation in April 1943 into the Seventh Guards Army and then (as colonel general) commanded the latter until May 1945. See Biographies.

15. On his return from captivity, I. N. Muzychenko continued to serve in the Soviet Army until 1947. M. I. Potapov continued to serve until 1965, becoming a colonel general in 1961.

16. V. T. Sergiyenko was people's commissar of internal affairs of the Ukrainian SSR from June 1941 to 1943.

17. Gomel is in the southeastern corner of Belarus (then the Belorussian SSR), some 250 kilometers north of Kiev. Kremenchug is on the Dnieper River, about the same distance southeast of Kiev. [SS]

18. S. M. Budyonny was in command of this area from July to September 1941.

19. Poltava is in east central Ukraine, about 130 kilometers southwest of Kharkov. [SS]

20. The Southern Front was commanded by Army General I. V. Tyulenev until August 1941.

21. The Southern Front was commanded by Lieutenant General D. I. Ryabyshev from August to October 1941, then by Colonel General Ya. T. Cherevichenko until December 1941, and then by

Lieutenant General R. Ya. Malinovsky until August 1942 (and again by Malinovsky, now colonel general, in February and March 1943).

22. In August and September 1941 this post was occupied by M. A. Burmistenko.

23. This was Corps Commissar D. S. Leonov, member of the RCP(B) from 1918 and a graduate of the Lenin Military-Political Academy.

24. Dnepropetrovsk was abandoned on August 25, 1941.

25. Major General A. P. Pokrovsky.

26. This was the Reserve Army commanded by Lieutenant General N. Ye. Chibisov. See Biographies.

27. S. B. Zadionchenko. See Biographies.

28. R. Ya. Malinovsky. See Biographies.

29. One of several Cossack settlements named Sovetskoye and located in various parts of the Soviet Union. [SS]

30. B. A. Dvinsky, member of the RCP(B) from 1920, was a secretary of the Rostov province committee of the AUCP(B) from 1938 to 1944.

31. A. I. Yeremenko. See Biographies.

32. He had commanded the 48th Corps.

33. Novomoskovsk (New Moscow) in eastern Ukraine, a few kilometers northeast of Dnepropetrovsk—not to be confused with another town of the same name near Tula in Russia. [SS]

34. Kursk is in southwestern Russia, about 400 kilometers east of Kiev and 200 kilometers north of Kharkov. [SS]

35. Cherkassy is on the western (right) bank of the Dnieper, some 180 kilometers southeast of Kiev. [SS]

36. On August 25, 1941.

37. This took place between September 1 and 8, 1941.

38. The line of the front at that time stretched from Glukhov to Vorozhba. This was a north-south line in the eastern part of Sumy province in northeastern Ukraine, to the southwest of Kursk. [AH/SS]

39. G. T. Shuisky.

40. Commander of the 26th Army Lieutenant General F. Ya. Kostenko.

41. Major General D. M. Dobychin.

42. Commander of the Fifteenth Corps Major General K. S. Moskalenko had previously commanded the First Motorized Antitank Artillery Brigade.

43. Pomerki is now part of the city of Kharkov.

44. The village of Grishino previously belonged to Novocherkassk province. At the time in question it was in the southwestern corner of Sumy province in northeastern Ukraine. [AH]

45. This house was a single-story building in the town center.

46. Sumy is in northeastern Ukraine, 140 kilometers northwest of Kharkov. The village of Akhtyrka (Ukrainian name Okhtyrka) is about halfway between Kharkov and Sumy. [SS]

47. These rivers are Dnieper tributaries that flow through this area. [SS]

48. Divisional Commissar Ye. P. Rykov. See Biographies.

49. This was the Bryansk Front. From August to October 1941 it was commanded by Lieutenant General A. I. Yeremenko. See Biographies.

50. Khrushchev refers here to the week between September 13 and 20, 1941.

51. The Soviet military attaché in Germany Major General V. I. Tupikov served in the Red Army from 1940 and fell on the southwestern battlefront in July 1941. See Biographies.

52. Tupikov was indeed the younger of the two. He was born in 1901, and Purkayev in 1894.

53. On the approaches to Moscow, Lieutenant General A. A. Vlasov commanded the Twentieth Army from November 1941 to March 1942. See Biographies.

54. The 37th Army abandoned Kiev on September 19 and was disbanded at the end of September. The Fifth Army was disbanded on September 20, 1941.

55. Khrushchev is referring to the book *Sovershenno sekretno! Tol'ko dlya komandovaniya: Nemetskie dokumenty o Vtoroi Mirovoi Voine* (Top secret! For command staff only: German documents About the Second World War; Moscow: Nauka, 1967). [SK]

56. The Lopan is a river that flows through Kharkov.

57. Major General P. A. Belov, commander of the Second Cavalry Corps. See Biographies.

58. The 38th Army was commanded by Major General V. V. Tsyganov from September to December 1941. See Biographies.

59. Kupyansk is about 100 kilometers southeast of Kharkov. [SS]

60. Both Donets and Seversky Donets refer to the same river. [SS]

61. Valuiki is just outside Ukraine in Russia's Belgorod province, some 140 kilometers east of Kharkov. [SS]

62. The chief of staff of the Southwestern Area and of the Southwestern Front from October to December 1941 was Major General P. I. Bodin. See Biographies.

63. Commander of the Germans' First Tank Army General (later Field Marshal) E. Kleist.

64. This took place on November 29, 1941.

65. Taganrog is about 60 kilometers west of Rostov. [SS]

## 1942: FROM WINTER TO SUMMER

I want to recall an episode of the war that hardly anyone knows about. Malenkov and Beria told me about this extremely well kept secret, a certain measure that Stalin took. It dates from fall 1941, when the Germans had already occupied the territories of Ukraine and Belorussia. Stalin sought to establish contact with Hitler to come to an agreement on the cessation of military activities on the basis of our conceding to the Germans Ukraine, Belorussia, and the parts of the Russian Federation occupied by Hitler's troops. Beria had a connection with a certain banker in Bulgaria who was an agent of Nazi Germany. On Stalin's personal order one of our people was sent to Bulgaria. His assignment was to make contact with the Germans, begin discussions with them, and to state what the concessions on the part of the Soviet Union would be. But no reply came from Hitler. Apparently Hitler was so convinced then of his victory that in his view the days of the Soviet Union's existence were numbered and he had no reason to make contact and begin negotiating when his troops had already advanced as far as they had. He planned to expand his offensive further, seize Moscow, impose a crushing defeat on all of Russia, and destroy the Russian state.

Of course this episode could be explained by the assumption that Stalin simply wanted to gain time by making concessions. But I don't know how much time we would have needed after cessation of military activities or how much effort we would have had to make to recoup our losses. To give up Ukraine, Belorussia, and the western parts of the Russian Federation under a treaty agreement would have been a very substantial loss from the point of view of our ability subsequently to regroup our forces, break the agreement, and regain what we had lost. I never heard anything more about this episode from anyone. When Beria and Malenkov told me about it they whispered in my ear. Today I don't even remember whether they told me while Stalin was still alive or after his death. but I remember distinctly that such a conversation took place. The conversation involved only the three of us. I don't know whether Molotov, in his capacity as people's commissar of foreign affairs, might also have been aware of this. Perhaps even he was not informed, because the contact was not made through the People's Commissariat of Foreign Affairs but through our intelligence services, that is, through Beria.

Gradually the winter [of 1941–42] came into its own. When we attacked Rostov the ground was already frozen solid. It was cold, but because of the southerly conditions winter had not yet set in firmly. The temperature fluctuates rather widely there, and fairly substantial thaws occur even in the winter. But in 1941 winter came very early, a freezing-cold, snowy winter. We received orders to transfer our Front headquarters to Voronezh, and so we established ourselves there. Then the order came that the territory to our north was being attached to our Front, so that our Front was to be expanded. The area around Yelets was assigned to us. Later after the Bryansk Front was eliminated, we received a new order: that the right flank of our Front would extend almost all the way to Kashira.[1]

After the successful liberation of Rostov, we thought of carrying out an operation to liberate Livny (which was farther north).[2] The enemy had occupied Livny, but his forces were not very large and his front line was not solid. Various groups of German soldiers were spread out at various strong points. If our forces were concentrated like a fist, we could make things unpleasant for the Germans, drive them out of Livny, and disrupt the defense line they had set up for the winter. We began preparations. We pulled together whatever we could—one tree from each forest, as the saying goes—because no one knew how to get reinforcements any other way. From our own internal resources we managed to scrape together an operational group of soldiers, and we got ready to carry out the operation. The general[3] who was entrusted with the command of this military group was Fyodor Yakovlevich Kostenko. He was later killed during the Kharkov operation. He was a very good man and a good general. From being a soldier in World War I, he had become a general. He was from a peasant family, a Ukrainian by nationality, but he came from Martynovka,[4] on a tributary of the Don. Later, when we carried out our offensive from Stalingrad to Rostov, we liberated this Cossack village [Martynovka], but Kostenko was no longer among the living.

We began carrying out the Yelets operation.[5] It was successful, and we took a lot of prisoners right away. As our troops approached Livny, the Germans were to the east of that city. Fearing encirclement, they gave the order for their troops to withdraw. These retreating troops piled into us from the east. The advantage was on the Germans' side, and Kostenko began calling for help. But we had told him even before the operation began that we had no reserves, and therefore he had to count on the element of surprise to create panic among the enemy troops. We encouraged Kostenko, but told him he had to make do with the forces he already had. All in all, the operation proceeded successfully, and the enemy was defeated, but not everything came out the way we wanted. We wanted to destroy the enemy forces completely, but some of their troops managed to break through to the west. Later in Stalin's presence, the joke was often made that Kostenko performed during this operation like a character in a certain anecdote that went like this. A hunter says, "I'm going out today to get me a bear." He goes off, some time passes, and the hunter doesn't return. Then he can be heard shouting that he has caught a bear. They tell him: "Well, bring him on in." The hunter answers: "The bear won't come." The people say: "Then you come yourself." Answer: "Yeah, but the bear won't let me." Kostenko had also caught a bear but couldn't overcome him completely.

Nevertheless, this was a second victory for our Southwestern Area. Of course it was a small victory, but against the background of the preceding retreat of the Red Army even such a small victory was precious to us, and we took great joy in it. I think that people will understand me correctly. It may be that no special notice will be taken of this episode in the history of the Great Patriotic War. But I have told about it because, you know, the fruits of the first victory taste the sweetest. The first *pirozhok* (little pie) that you eat is the tastiest—much tastier than those you eat later on when you've already grown used to the taste and when perhaps your appetite has become jaded. That is why we felt so deeply about what happened and congratulated Kostenko on his victory.

So then, at the end of 1941, this was our second victory, after Rostov. Of course the liberation of Rostov was a much more significant event. Who in the Soviet Union, or even outside its borders, doesn't know the celebrated city of Rostov on the Don River! Yelets is not Rostov. But the situation that developed during that winter, the victory to the east of Livny and the liberation of Yelets, was a great day of celebration for us. A lot of Germans were killed in that operation, and some of them were taken prisoner. I went to visit Kostenko then. I wondered about these German prisoners. What kind of people were they? What was their composition in terms of social origin? How firm was their morale? I also wanted to have a look at the prisoners to see how they had experienced the blows dealt by our troops and our freezing Russian weather.

These troops of Hitler's were a sorry spectacle, including their clothing and footwear. Everything about them made you shiver. Their overcoats were too light and so was their headgear. They had wrapped themselves up with whatever was at hand. Among these prisoners I encountered one whose outward appearance was particularly wild and savage. His photograph was later published in the weekly newsmagazine *Ogonyok,* and his physiognomy stood out because it was so remarkably ugly. We published the photo because the Germans had reproduced and given wide circulation to some photographs of certain Red Army men. They were trying to frighten the Europeans, as if to say, look at these savages who want to rule the world, who want to dominate us. They would often publish photos of our people whose looks were unappealing. Our own journalists in this case, I think, made good use of the photograph of this wild-looking German.

I began to ask which of the prisoners was from where and what their occupations had been before the war. One German, about thirty-five years old, maybe even older, a man of enormous size and a simple, everyday person to judge by his face, said: "I was a foundry worker." I said to him: "Aren't you ashamed of yourself? Here you are a foundry worker, a working class person, and yet you marched against the Soviet Union, against the land of the Soviets, against the working class. Where's your sense of proletarian solidarity?"

He was rather nervous, but he answered candidly; he didn't hold back, and in fact spoke with a certain exasperation: "The devil only knows! You can't figure out who's saying what and who you're fighting for. Here you claim that this land of the Soviets is the country of the working class and the toiling peasantry. But in our country they say pretty much the same thing. And here we are fighting and shedding each other's blood." He said this in such a heartrending way.

Together with Marshal Timoshenko, the commander of our Front, we decided to make a trip to Livny and get to know the leadership of that city and the troops who had liberated it, to make their acquaintance right there on the spot. From our intelligence reports we already had a feeling that the enemy might undertake a counteroffensive against Livny. We were also organizing a strike force [for a further offensive] in the Livny area, but we were behind in our preparations. We figured that the enemy might get the jump on us and break through into Livny a day or two before we were ready, and so we went there to talk with the party and government leaders and warn them that if they retreated they shouldn't destroy anything, literally nothing—neither bridges nor highways nor communications facilities—for we expected to return to Livny in no more than a day or two. We were completely confident of our strength.

We arrived there, held the kind of conversations I have indicated, and then left. Sure enough, a day later the enemy captured Livny. Then, just as we had promised the leaders of the city, we struck back, and the Germans again had to pop right out of Livny like so many corks. Timoshenko and I went there again and met with the local officials a second time. Indeed they had not destroyed anything, nor had the Germans done a great deal of damage as they retreated. I don't know why. Apparently they didn't have time, or perhaps they were also confident that they would soon return to Livny. All of this coincided with the preparations for the great counteroffensive in the Moscow area. We were not informed then that such a counteroffensive was going to take place. It was kept secret.

When we added Yelets to the area covered by our Front and extended our line of defense to the north of Yelets as far as Tula, it was already winter, and a new army, the newly formed Tenth Army, was added to the Southwestern Area. The commander of this army was General Popov, a young, energetic, and capable person.[6] I encountered him again later and had a lot of respect for him. He was an interesting and cultured person. His only shortcoming, which I felt bad about, but couldn't do anything to help him with, was a great weakness for drink. He drank more than you could allow yourself in the middle of a war. Unfortunately this was a source of unhappiness not only for him; it also affected others. Nevertheless, on the whole I treated him with respect then, and today I recall this general and the good work he did with respect.

With the arrival of the Tenth Army (at first commanded by Golikov)[7] we received the news that an offensive was being prepared in the Moscow area, and in that connection we were informed of what direction the actions of our right flank should take, that is, in the area where the Tenth Army was deployed. A cavalry corps commanded by Belov and other units were also located there. The Tenth Army was supposed to go on the offensive toward Mtsensk. The blow struck by the Tenth Army and Belov's cavalry corps[8] coincided with an offensive by the Germans toward Tula. The enemy didn't succeed in taking Tula. The authors of some wartime memoirs explain this by the fact that the people of Tula themselves got organized and defended their city. That's not quite accurate. It's true that the people of Tula heroically defended their city, but the main factors were, first, that this was the last effort made by the enemy forces, who had already been weakened as they approached Moscow; and, second, that the blow struck by our Front helped the people of Tula. For the Germans it was soon a question not so much of reaching Tula as of getting out of there alive. The enemy had to roll back westward. We pursued the Germans as far as Mtsensk, but we couldn't take that city.[9]

Later the Tenth Army was separated from the Southwestern Area, along with the front-line sector where it was deployed, and we no longer were able to know in detail how the fighting was developing in that area as the Germans retreated from Moscow. That was a glorious offensive that the Red Army carried out and a major defeat for the German troops. They were thrown back a considerable distance and lost many lives and a lot of equipment. But as I have said, we didn't know the details of the fighting outside Moscow. The Tenth Army had been transferred to the Western Front, which was our neighbor to the north.

With that the military operations of 1941 in our area came to an end. The enemy took up defensive positions, and we didn't have the forces to continue our offensive. We had to limit ourselves to what we had gained up to that point, and we also organized our defenses, hoping that reserves would be brought up to reinforce us so that we could resume the offensive. Soon after the successfully completed counteroffensive outside Moscow, I was summoned to Moscow for a conversation with Stalin. Here I found a completely "different" Stalin, not the one I had seen at the beginning of the war when I flew to Moscow two or three times. By now he had straightened up and walked around like a soldier, although even then, as I recall, all the orders being issued by the General Headquarters (Stavka) were issued without Stalin's name on them, but simply in the name of the Supreme High Command. There were orders of the High Command, directions and regulations issued by the High Command, and so forth, and it seemed as though Stalin was absent. This of course was not accidental, because Stalin did not do anything haphazardly. He thought through everything he did, measured all his steps, both good and bad.

I decided at that time to make a trip outside the city and find out what line the Germans had reached on the outskirts of Moscow. People recommended that I go in the direction of Solnechnogorsk. Earlier, Solnechnogorsk had been taken by the enemy, and it was only 50 kilometers or so outside Moscow.[10] We went there. Evidence of the fighting could be seen clearly not far from Moscow. When I arrived in Solnechnogorsk, the Red Army soldiers were opening up the graves of German soldiers who had been killed. This was not hard to do because the corpses had been buried in frozen ground and therefore not very deeply, and the ground had not had a chance to harden; in fact in some places the Germans, in their haste, had buried their dead in the snow. Of course it was an unpleasant sight, but there was also a certain satisfaction to it. For one who had seen the sufferings of our people, the corpses of the enemy aroused a certain feeling of gratification, as much as to say: "Well, you wanted to bury us, but instead you found your own graves outside Moscow." If a person is called up in a war, he necessarily carries out his duties as a soldier, which includes punishing and destroying the enemy. After all, the enemy has invaded your territory, with the aim of killing you and those dear to you. It's hard to think about purely human sentiments such as pity in these circumstances and hard to expect that they would arise. I think that lack of pity is only natural for human beings in such a case. On the faces of the Red Army soldiers, I saw expressions of satisfaction: this was the first result of our victory, the result of the efforts of our people and Red Army—the defeat and destruction of major enemy forces.

I returned to our own Front. Our Front headquarters at that time was still located in Voronezh. Now and then the enemy sent reconnaissance planes flying high over the city to reconnoiter. I don't remember particularly that we were bombed. It's true that now and then they dropped bombs, but that didn't make any special impression. Apparently the enemy did not wish to waste ammunition to no purpose. The Germans had taken up defensive positions for the winter and were simply carrying out reconnaissance, without engaging in any active operations from the air. During that time we also built our defenses, reinforced them, received new troops, and armed and trained them. In addition we thought of carrying out a few small operations, for example, in the area around the town of Tim.[11] Tim was then being held by the enemy, and we tried to regain it. We made several such attempts, but they produced no results, and we were forced to call them off.

Soon we got the idea of carrying out an offensive operation in the Bar-venkovo region.[12] Our headquarters staff and intelligence services were hard at work, trying to find out what forces the enemy had there and where they were positioned, and to estimate what our possibilities were, to try to determine what forces we would need for this operation. In a word, we began to prepare for an offensive. When the groundwork had been laid, it was necessary to report to Moscow—to Stalin and the General Staff—to get their "blessing," but the main thing was to have a sufficient quantity of troops and military equipment. The commander and I were summoned to Moscow, and Stalin listened to what we had to say. The report was given by Timoshenko and Bodin, the chief of staff of our Front. We got our "blessing," but unfortunately the men and materiel we asked for to carry out this offensive did not arrive in full, not by any means. The operation had been approved, but the number of troops was insufficient in comparison to what was required according to the estimates of our headquarters staff. The operation was scheduled for January 1942. In preparation for the offensive, we transferred our operational headquarters closer to the front line, to have better communication with the troops. We established ourselves in a large village by the name of Svatovo-Luchko.[13] I knew this village, because in 1919 the Red Army had taken it back from the Whites, and I had been there then. It was a good, strong, prosperous village.

To carry out the operation, as I recall, we were given three cavalry corps. One corps[14] was commanded by General Bychkovsky, an experienced man, well on in years. He had fought in the cavalry in the Civil War. Another corps[15] was commanded by Grechko, who later became minister of defense of the USSR. He was the youngest corps commander at that time. The commander of the third corps was also a man well on in years. I forget his name now, although I knew him well back then.[16] We listened to what they had to say before the operation began. We talked about the assignments set by Timoshenko for each of the corps commanders. Things ended, as was usual then, with a dinner. The one who made the best impression on me then was General Grechko. He had just taken over the corps, and before that he had commanded the unattached 34th Cavalry Division, and since I had heard about him in that capacity I eagerly agreed to his appointment as corps commander. I didn't yet know the other commanders. But Bychkovsky also made a favorable impression on me. Apparently he was a real fighting man, but he didn't seem to me to be sufficiently modern; he was somewhat prim-itive and backward as a person. This made itself evident both in military operations and in his everyday behavior, as well as in his relations with party and government bodies. Wherever his cavalry corps took up position, there were constant complaints about him; people were offended by him. He even allowed himself, for example, to shelter his horses in a school. Probably these were his own horses, the commander's horses, because obviously you couldn't put the horses of an entire cavalry corps in a school. But this set a bad example. The local organizations, on whose territory he had committed such stupidities, complained about him a great deal.

The operation began. The enemy's front line was broken and our cavalry moved forward. I don't remember exactly now the composition of our military grouping. Did we have tanks? Apparently we did, but today I can't remember for sure.[17] The cavalry was our main mobile force and attacking force. We moved forward fairly rapidly, occupied Lozovaya, and then moved forward to the northwest and southwest, making a fairly deep advance. Unfortunately the enemy was able to keep his flanks in position. On the left flank of our offensive, the Germans maintained their position in the Slavyansk area. They also maintained their left flank near Balakleya.[18] Thus the result was a kind of arc penetrating into the enemy's positions, but with no great distance between the ends of the arc, while the extreme point of the arc went a fairly great distance westward. At that time we were happy that this possibility had developed, and from this salient position we hoped to straighten out the front line, as we use to say then, to expand this beachhead. We had the tempting idea of trying to liberate the city of Kharkov in spring 1942, but the operation came to a halt because we were already exhausted and couldn't carry the offensive any further. We did seize a lot of enemy equipment, but this was not of great significance. A lot of it was medical equipment. We also captured stores of goods for German officers, including various delicacies, wine, cognac, and all sorts of canned goods. But it seems to me we didn't obtain anything particularly significant in the way of armaments or military equipment.

We joked a lot then about Grechko's cavalrymen who had captured these supplies and gotten into the champagne. Whether that actually happened or whether someone just made it up, I will not try to judge. But we all enjoyed the joke a lot back then. Later I told it to Stalin, and he liked to repeat it. The situation was as follows. When the Red Army soldiers captured the supplies of wine and began to try it out they didn't know that it was champagne. In general many of them didn't even know what champagne was. A lot of young Ukrainians served in that cavalry corps. They drank it and began talking among themselves, "Hey, what the heck is this? I drink six bottles, and it fizzes, but there's nothing to it." This joke was supposed to indicate the strong and positive mood of our troops.

After calling off the offensive operation we went on the defensive. The headquarters staff—Bodin, Bagramyan, and others—began estimating the results and trying to determine our possibilities for further offensive operations, including the aim of liberating Kharkov. The following plan was worked out: to strike the main blow against the enemy in the spring from the salient we had extended outward, south of Kharkov, and to strike a supporting or auxiliary blow with fewer forces to the north of Kharkov, and thus to "close the pincers" around Kharkov and liberate the city. As we were planning we were sure that this operation would work, that we could accomplish this task and begin military operations for the spring and summer with this kind of effective result—the liberation of a major industrial and political center of Ukraine. We understood that such an operation entailed some danger, because the Germans, on the one hand, had a fairly deep penetration along our flanks, which was rather disturbing because they could use those positions to strike blows at the flanks of our troops during our offensive. On the other hand, there was an enemy grouping near Slavyansk, and the Germans were holding onto those positions very stubbornly. We made numerous attempts to liberate the center of that section of their defensive line—the village of Mayaki[19]—and to test the enemy's strength, but all our attempts ended without positive results: we lost troops but could not move forward and eliminate those German strong points. There was a small stream that flowed into the Seversky Donets,[20] and along its southern bank the Germans had a salient where they had concentrated their forces. We were apprehensive about this sector.

I remember the operation Malinovsky carried out in an attempt to take the village of Mayaki. The Ninth Army was located there, just where the Southern Front and the Southwestern Front adjoined. Kharitonov commanded this army. He died later in the war, as I've been told.[21] He was not a bad general and not a bad person. As the offensive was being prepared, I told Timoshenko I would go visit Malinovsky, look into the situation, and remain on the spot while the operation was being carried out. I made the trip. It was very difficult to move then. The snow was deep, and the roads were not well cleared; so I traveled part of the way by automobile and the rest by sleigh. Malinovsky and I met at an appointed location, and then we traveled, also by sleigh, to the village of Bogorodichnoye, where the headquarters of the Ninth Army of the Southern Front was located, very close to the front lines. Colonel Ratov's artillery was also located there—with heavy guns. I had known Ratov since the first days of the war and it was pleasant to meet him again. His businesslike qualities pleased me greatly. He had not lost a single cannon, and he kept track of every shell. The shell casings were of copper and very close watch was kept over them. New shells could be obtained only in exchange for shell casings turned in.

When we reached the army commander's headquarters he reported that the offensive should begin within a few hours, but he said he was not ready for the offensive, even though the order had been given. Malinovsky immediately took up his pencil and calipers, measured the distance that ammunition had to be brought up (there were not enough shells), determined that the ammunition would not arrive in time for the beginning of the offensive, and therefore said that the offensive should be postponed. I agreed. The offensive was postponed until the ammunition arrived. The operation began the next day, but again there was no success. The enemy resisted stubbornly, and we lost people for no good reason. Therefore we called off the operation in that sector, although previously we had been certain, together with Timoshenko and Malinovsky, that the operation would succeed. What could be simpler, it would seem, than to seize a small settlement? But we couldn't do it. The enemy's defenses had not been studied well, apparently, and our advancing troops were not backed up sufficiently by our artillery. In general there are no strong points that cannot be taken if the appropriate preparations are made and sufficient means are available in advance to suppress the enemy. It seems that our estimates were poor, and as a result we lost people and failed to accomplish the basic task that had been set for us.

After that a number of other offensives were undertaken in the same sector, but also without results. The blatant inexperience of our commanders was reflected in the fact that although we were unable to take this enemy strong point, a decision was made nevertheless to begin an offensive against Kharkov, disregarding the possibility of a flank attack by the enemy. We calculated that when we struck westward and surrounded Kharkov, this sector would simply lose its significance and that it would fall of its own accord as a result of the forward movement of our troops in the main area of operations. As life was to show later, this proved to be a fatal miscalculation, a failure to estimate correctly how important that enemy stronghold was.

Our enemies, while holding on to their flanking positions, had their own plans for encircling our military group that had moved forward into the salient created by our winter offensive. There was only a short distance between those flanks, from which an encircling operation against our troops could be started. But we underestimated the danger at that time and calmly

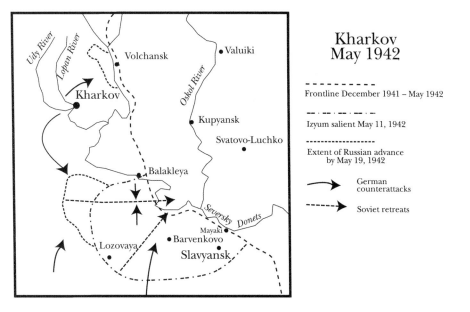

Kharkov
May 1942

- - - - - - - -
Frontline December 1941 – May 1942

-- · -- · -- · -- · --
Izyum salient May 11, 1942

· · · · · · · · · · · · · · · · · ·
Extent of Russian advance
by May 19, 1942

German
counterattacks

Soviet retreats

began preparations for a winter-summer campaign. Our main forces in that area were the Sixth Army under the command of Gorodnyansky[22] and the 57th Army, to which we appointed a new commander, Podlas.[23] He was a very interesting man, and he had an interesting life story. His life had shaped up in quite a tragic way. I have already mentioned that during the Khasan Lake events[24] Podlas was in the Far East, and he saw action there against the Japanese. Luck was not with him. Mekhlis came there, and Mekhlis didn't like him, regarding him as a traitor and a spy. Podlas was removed from his post and put in jail. When the war began, he was released. He showed up in our area when we were still in Kiev. He hadn't yet been officially reassigned, and he wore an old uniform with insignia on the lapels. When he first reported and stated his name, I asked him what nationality he was. You couldn't exactly tell his nationality from his last name. He answered: "I am a Ukrainian from Bryansk province." At first we used him for headquarters assignments. He was a very well organized person. Wherever he was sent he always got a good and intelligent grasp of the situation and made a good impression. As a result he had now been appointed commander of the 57th Army. The composition of this army was fairly good, because at the time when it was formed we had received an additional division and several companies and battalions of reinforcements.

In addition to the Sixth Army and the 57th Army, we also organized a fairly strong army group in that area. As commander we appointed a general who was well on in years, an old fighter from the Civil War. He soon died. He was trapped in encirclement and killed.[25] He had a young fellow with him, his son, who also perished. In addition we also received some tank brigades and antitank brigades then. They gave us everything they could in those days, although it was far from being everything we had asked for. We agreed to carry out the operation with these resources alone. As things were, the High Command never completely met the needs of the Fronts for the forces and resources they needed to carry out one or another operation. One side was always asking for as much as it could, and the other side was always giving less.

We planned our operation to begin in April. By then the ground had thawed and it was possible to use the roads. Timoshenko and I often went out to visit the troops and listen to the reports by the commanders of the Sixth Army and 57th Army right there on the spot. We placed great hopes in this operation because we had been encouraged by the successful offensive at the end of the previous year in the Rostov area, as well as by the operations in the Livny and Yelets areas and above all by the victory outside Moscow. We had no doubt that this operation would also turn out successfully for us.

When the day was set for the beginning of the offensive, Timoshenko and I discussed where we ourselves should take up positions. I proposed to be with Gorodnyansky at the headquarters of the Sixth Army. This was the point of deepest penetration into the German defenses as a result of our winter offensive. Timoshenko proposed something different: "No, I don't think it makes sense to go there. We have two groupings: the southern one, the main one and stronger one; and the other, to the north of Kharkov. In trying to take Kharkov with a pincers operation, it will be more difficult to maintain communications with the northern grouping." Therefore he said: "Let's remain in Svatovo after all, at our old command post. From here it will be simpler to maintain communications with either one of our groupings. And to the Sixth Army sector we can send an influential representative of the command, for example, Gurov, a member of the Military Council." Gurov was a very good comrade in the military council. Later at Stalingrad he became a member of the Military Council under Chuikov. Together with Chuikov, he later retook the city of Stalino, but then he died. In his memory, a monument was erected there.[26]

The operation began quite successfully. We quickly broke through the enemy's front line, and our troops moved forward. But we were concerned that, contrary to expectations, we had broken through that front line a little too easily. We soon realized that there were hardly any enemy forces opposing us and that we had fallen into a trap prepared for us. We began discussing the situation that was developing. Apparently our enemies had certain plans of their own, and that was why our frontal assault had not encountered enemy troops. The fact was that the Germans were also preparing for a spring and summer campaign. We guessed that they had concentrated their forces on our left flank, in a sector that was part of the Southern Front, the Slavyansk area, and we expected that the enemy would strike at our flank from there. An attack from that direction would be very dangerous.

It became clear that it was no accident that the Germans, despite heavy losses, had firmly defended themselves during the winter and had refused to surrender a single position in that area. Apparently even then they were planning to eliminate the salient we had established during the winter campaign by striking at its flanks. The main counterblow threatened to come from the south. We decided to stop our offensive, because it fit in too well with the enemy's plans. The deeper we drove our wedge in a westward direction, the more we would extend our front line and disperse our troops, weakening and exposing our left flank and creating conditions in which the Germans could break through easily with the aim of surrounding and destroying our forces.

So we called off our offensive and issued an order to transfer the tank brigades, antitank brigades, and artillery southward. In a word, we began to reposition our troops toward our left flank, which had been left exposed to the enemy. In our view this was the only possibility for repelling the enemy, the only correct solution to the circumstances that had arisen. Meanwhile to the north of Kharkov we did not undertake anything new. We simply continued the operation in that area. But it was not successful.

Indeed we had correctly guessed the enemy's intentions, but unfortunately too late. It was necessary to take measures to protect ourselves against a flank attack—to stop the offensive and reposition our antitank units, our tanks, and our artillery along our left flank. This was absolutely essential for us, and therefore no disagreements or disputes arose among us on this score. I don't remember who took the initiative in organizing the whole operation [i.e., planning this redeployment of forces]. Later Stalin accused me, saying that the initiative had been mine. I don't deny it. It is possible that I had taken the initiative. My reply to Stalin was this: "What about the commander? The commander and I together made the decision."

He answered: "Well, the commander gave in to you."

I said: "The commander gave in? But you know Timoshenko. Timoshenko is a person of very difficult character, and do you think he would all of a sudden agree with someone if he had a different opinion? Our decision, as the saying goes, was made smoothly and without conflict." It's true that the commander had held the same opinion as I did. The members of the headquarters staff and the chief of the operations department, Bagramyan, also held the same opinion. Bagramyan himself had worked out the details of the operation; it had then been reviewed by the General Staff and had also been approved. So this was not just the fruit of the thinking of the leaders of the Southwestern Area Command. The decision had been approved by the specialists of the General Staff. A single, unitary line had been reached about the measures to be taken, a common understanding of the situation, and a united belief in its success.

So we called a halt to the operation and began taking steps to organize our defenses. That is, from being on the offensive, we went over to the defensive. The necessary orders were given and I went to my quarters. This was probably about three o'clock in the morning. The night sky was beginning to lighten in the east. I arrived at my quarters but had not yet undressed when the door suddenly flew open and Bagramyan came in, very upset. He said: "I have come to see you, Comrade Khrushchev." He was so upset he even began to cry. "Do you know what? Our order to go over to the defensive has been canceled by Moscow. I have already issued the order to cancel our previous order."

I asked: "But who changed the order?"

He said: "I don't know who, because it was the marshal [Timoshenko] who spoke on the phone with Moscow. After the conversation ended, he gave me the order to cancel our previous order, and he himself went off to get some sleep. The marshal didn't say anything more than that. I'm absolutely convinced that canceling our order and issuing a new order to continue the offensive will result in catastrophe within a few days and the destruction of our troops in the Barvenkovo salient. I beg you personally to speak directly with Stalin. The only possibility of saving ourselves is if you can succeed in convincing Comrade Stalin to approve our order and cancel the instructions withdrawing our order and continuing the operation. If you do not succeed in doing that, our troops will perish."

I had never seen Bagramyan in such a state. He was a reflective, thoughtful, intelligent person. I liked him. I had become, as the saying goes, simply enamored of this young general for his sober mind, his party consciousness, and his knowledge of his business. He was a man, I would say, who could not be bought off—in the sense of submitting to someone else's authority. If he didn't agree, he would invariably say so. I had observed this several times when we had discussed one or another operation. If more highly placed people holding key positions at Front headquarters tried to argue something that he did not agree with, he would very stubbornly defend his own point of view. I liked this quality in him. Among the other military leaders I met during the war, this kind of quality was most sharply evident also in General Bodin. I also liked him very much. He too was a capable and sober-minded general. He stood out because of his strong character and party-mindedness, his firmness, his ability to present his objections even to people of higher rank if he thought that their reasoning was wrong, that they were giving the troops wrong assignments, which might cause harm to our forces. I spoke about this to Stalin many times and gave excellent character references for these two comrades.

I listened to everything Bagramyan had to say. His report literally stunned me. I completely agreed with him. In making our decision, we had based ourselves on the very same considerations that Bagramyan was now repeating. But I knew Stalin, and I imagined what difficulties awaited me in a conversation with him. I had to shift his understanding of the situation in such a way that he would believe us. But since he had already canceled our order, that meant he didn't believe us. If he didn't believe us, it followed that we now had to convince him that he was wrong, force him to doubt his own order to cancel our order. I knew Stalin's pride and what I would call his ferocity in matters like this. Especially in phone conversations.

I had had occasion more than once to get into an argument with Stalin on one or another question of a nonmilitary nature, and sometimes I had succeeded in changing his mind. Even though Stalin would rage and fulminate in such cases, I would continue to argue stubbornly that we needed to do one thing and not the other. Sometimes Stalin wouldn't accept my point of view right away, but a few hours would go by, sometimes days, and he would return to the topic and end up agreeing. This was something I liked about Stalin, that in the end he was capable of changing a decision if he was convinced that the person he was talking with was right, if that person stubbornly continued to argue and defend his point of view, and if that person's arguments had solid ground beneath them. In such cases Stalin would finally agree. It happened with me both before the war and after the war that on some particular questions I succeeded in winning Stalin's agreement. But in the given situation, things looked simply hopeless and disastrous, and I had no hope of success. On the other hand, I couldn't refuse to make the most persistent possible attempts not to let a catastrophe happen, because I understood that if Stalin's order was carried out, there would be a catastrophe for our troops.

I don't remember how many minutes I thought about the problem. Bagramyan was right there alongside me the whole time. I decided to call the General Staff first. It was already very late at night; in fact dawn was breaking. I made the call. Vasilevsky answered. I began pleading with him: "Aleksandr Mikhailovich, our order has been canceled, and it has been proposed that the original task approved for this operation still be carried out."

He said: "Yes, I know. Comrade Stalin gave the order. I am abreast of the situation."

I said: "Aleksandr Mikhailovich, you know from the staff maps both the position of our troops and the concentration of the troops on the enemy's side, and you can picture more concretely what kind of situation has arisen for us. More concretely than Comrade Stalin is picturing it."

On some occasions when I had visited Stalin at the Stavka, I had seen him pick up a political map of the world. Once he even came in with a globe and pointed where our front lines were. This was deadly! It was impossible to do that kind of thing. Sometimes he had no idea what was going on. In such cases he saw only where and in what direction we were to strike at the enemy. How deeply we had advanced and what our plans were—he knew all that, of course, very well. But he was capable of not looking deeply enough to grasp what had resulted from the implementation of the planned operation, what complications had arisen; he might not analyze the specific events that had occurred and properly weigh our reasons for changing the original order. As life itself showed, in the given instance that is exactly how he acted.

I continued the conversation: "Pick up the map, Aleksandr Mikhailovich, and take it to Stalin."

He answered: "Comrade Stalin is now at the 'nearby dacha.'"

I said: "Go there. He will receive you at any time. After all there's a war on. Go there with a map—a map on which the position of the troops is plainly evident, and not the kind of map where you can cover the whole front with the tip of your finger. Stalin will see the configuration, the position of our troops, the concentration of the enemy's forces, and he'll understand that we acted quite sensibly when we gave the order to stop the offensive and reposition our main forces, especially our armored forces, on the left flank. Stalin will agree."

He said: "No, Comrade Khrushchev, no. Comrade Stalin has already given the order. I said Comrade Stalin!" People who have met Vasilevsky know how he talked—in such a smooth, droning monotone.

Vasilevsky and I ended our conversation. I put down the phone and again began to think. What to do? Pick up the phone again and call Stalin directly? The phone burned my fingers. Not because I was afraid of Stalin. No, what I was afraid of was that this could be a fatal phone call for our troops. If I called him and Stalin refused me, then there would be no option but to continue the operation, and I was absolutely convinced that would be the beginning of the end, the beginning of a catastrophe for our troops on that sector of the front. For that reason, you know, I looked at that telephone the way a cat looks at boiling porridge, and I drew my hand back in an unthinking reflex action. I had very good relations with Vasilevsky. I respected him. But he had such a soft character. I don't know in general whether he had any enemies and, if so, who they were. Probably he had enemies, but for other reasons [that is, different from the usual ones]. Some military personnel had a very bad attitude toward him. I know this, but I'm not going to get into that subject right now.

I decided to call Vasilevsky once more. I called him and pleaded with him again: "Aleksandr Mikhailovich, you understand perfectly well the position our troops are in. You yourself know how this might end. You must have a clear picture of it. Therefore the only thing to be done now is to allow us to reposition our forces, to put our previous order into effect, the one that was canceled by the Stavka. Otherwise our troops are going to perish. I beg you, Aleksandr Mikhailovich, go to Comrade Stalin and take a detailed map with you." In other words, I began to repeat the same arguments. I had no others. I just stubbornly and persistently repeated the request that he go and report to Stalin and convince him that our order was the only correct decision that could be made, given the existing circumstances.

But all the arguments I brought to bear in the telephone conversation, my persistence, my appeal to his own awareness, his sense of duty and responsibility—nothing had any effect. In the same calm voice (I can visualize the tone of his voice so clearly right now) he answered: "Nikita Sergeyevich, Comrade Stalin has given the order. Comrade Stalin this and Comrade Stalin that." In this phone conversation I couldn't get Vasilevsky to see that in the given instance Stalin was not an authority for me. This was evident from what I was saying, since I was appealing to Vasilevsky and begging him to take an appropriate map and go explain things to Stalin.

It was a very dangerous moment for me. At that time Stalin had already begun to regard himself as some sort of military strategist, as it were—once he had recovered from the shock of our initial defeats. During the first days of the war, he had renounced the leadership and said, "We've made a mess of the state that Lenin created." Now, after all that, he was beginning to feel like a hero. I knew, however, what kind of hero he was from the first days of the war as well as from the prewar period when I had observed him during the months when war was obviously bearing down on us from the direction of Germany.

What options did I have? I had no way of changing the situation other than the arguments I had already expressed and repeated over and over to Vasilevsky, counting on his sense of duty as a military man. At that time he was already deputy chief of the General Staff. It's true that in those days that position had no great importance. This was a time when there was no chief of the General Staff. There was only a man named Bokov[27] who had responsibility for those duties, and Bokov had no authority in the eyes of the commanders of the Fronts. He would issue orders, receive reports, comment on them somehow or other, and report to the Stavka somehow or other. It was a difficult time for the General Staff. I remember Stalin asking me what people were saying about Bokov. This was when we were already fighting the battle of Stalingrad and Bokov had been removed from the General Staff. I answered: "Our Soviet troops have achieved a great victory over the enemy."

He asked: "What victory?"

I said: "Bokov has been removed from the General Staff and someone has been put in who we can talk with and who understands operational matters. That's a great victory for the Red Army." Stalin did not appreciate the joke.

Vasilevsky absolutely refused to do anything in response to my pleadings. He wouldn't express his own opinion but simply referred to the order given by Stalin. Today I must confess that I have somewhat reevaluated my own opinion about this incident. At that time I thought there was a certain lack of will on Vasilevsky's part, that he was too compliant. In the given situation he didn't show strong character as a military man. He was a good man, even very good, and very positive. I considered him a very honest person, and it was easy to talk with him. I had met him many times before this incident. In short, he was a man who deserved respect, but in strictly military matters I of course placed Zhukov on a much higher level always. But now some doubts have arisen in my thinking. In general, in regard to the cancellation of our order, was that really just Stalin's initiative? Today I am more inclined to think this was done on Vasilevsky's initiative. It's possible that Vasilevsky received our order first, because we sent it to the General Staff first, and that he himself did not agree with it, not having looked into the question sufficiently. (I had no possibility of checking into this back then, and today I have even less possibility.) After all, it may have seemed to him that a successful offensive operation by our troops was under way, that our few and rare successes had brought great joy, and that it would be very pleasant to open the 1942 spring campaign with some victories. That would have been pleasing for everyone. It's possible that Vasilevsky received our order, weighed it, got angry about it, and immediately reported to Stalin with appropriate commentary. Then Stalin agreed with Vasilevsky and gave the counterorder or perhaps called Timoshenko himself.

I don't know what the phone call was that Timoshenko received or with whom he spoke. I don't know whether it was with Vasilevsky or with Stalin. From what Bagramyan said, it seemed that it was Stalin. I felt awkward about asking Timoshenko directly. I met him that morning; we looked at each other, and we were both sniffling and breathing huskily. We were both upset, not at each other, but at the circumstances.

Let me return to the conversation with Vasilevsky. More and more I have come to the conclusion today that the decision was one that Vasilevsky put over on Stalin. That was why Vasilevsky stubbornly refused to listen to me, wouldn't take the situation into account or heed my arguments. He must have felt that he couldn't go to Stalin since he himself had advised Stalin on the question and the decision had been made on the basis of his advice. This conclusion has come to me only recently as I have thought over these events, events that for me personally were so horrendous. It was such a terrible time, a turning point for our whole war effort in 1942.

If instead of Vasilevsky Zhukov had been in the General Staff at that time and I had talked to Zhukov about this and he had not agreed, then Zhukov too would have made a mistake, just as Vasilevsky did. But the difference is that Zhukov would have argued against me categorically and wouldn't have referred to Stalin. He himself would have argued that I wasn't right, that this operation would be successful and simply had to be carried through decisively. But if Zhukov had believed me, looked into the matter, and seen that I was right, he would have displayed firmness and insistence in determining the fate of our Front; I'm convinced he would not have hesitated; he would have jumped into a vehicle immediately and gone to see Stalin and would have begun energetically and insistently reporting to him on the need to change the order and confirm the earlier order that we had given. Now, many years later, this is my assessment of the matter. I think about it and remember it constantly. It is a landmark in my life, a very painful landmark. Whenever a conversation about the war starts or when I begin mentally leafing through the pages of that time, especially before the battle of Kursk (because that was the most crucial time, the time of the greatest tension and responsibility faced by our country), I think about the Kharkov operation of 1942. I see it constantly before my eyes, and I immediately begin to think: What if our order had been approved? How would events have unfolded then?

When Vasilevsky absolutely refused to go see him, I was obliged to call Stalin myself. I knew that Stalin was at the nearby dacha, and I knew the situation there quite well. I knew where the dacha was located, and I knew who would be sitting there and where. I knew where the table with the telephones was and how many steps Stalin would take to get to the phone. How many times I had watched him do that when the phone rang. Malenkov answered my call. We greeted each other. I said: "I request to speak with Comrade Stalin." I heard him say that Khrushchev was calling and wanted Stalin to come to the phone.

I could not hear what Stalin answered, but Malenkov, after listening to him, relayed it to me: "Comrade Stalin says that you should tell me and I'll pass it on to him." That was the first sign that the catastrophe was inexorably coming down on us.

I repeated: "Comrade Malenkov, I request to speak with Comrade Stalin. I want to report to Comrade Stalin about the situation that has now taken shape in our sector."

Malenkov again conveyed to Stalin what I had said and immediately responded with the answer: "Comrade Stalin says that you should tell me and I'll pass it on to him."

What was Stalin preoccupied with? He was sitting there, drinking and eating. It would have taken him only half a minute or a minute to get up from his dinner table and come to the table where the phone was. But he didn't want to listen to what I had to say. Why? Apparently the General Staff had reported that the commanders of the Front had responded improperly to the decision: that the operation was succeeding successfully and our troops had encountered no opposition, that they were moving westward, and consequently the offensive should be continued, that the order to reposition our forces was the result of excessive caution on the part of the Front commander and the member of the Military Council, and that pressure needed to be put on them.

During my conversation by way of Malenkov with Stalin, the usual company must have been there in the background: Mikoyan, Molotov, Beria, and I don't know who else. When I asked that Stalin himself come to the telephone, he muttered: "Khrushchev is poking his nose into military matters.

He's not a military man. Our military experts have looked into everything and decided, and we are not going to change the decision." That is what Anastas Ivanovich Mikoyan told me later. He had been present on that occasion. One wonders: Who were those military advisers who knew the situation so well and had given their advice to Stalin? Above all it must have been Vasilevsky and Shtemenko.[28]

What was I to do? Should I plead for a third time? That was not the way to achieve a positive resolution of the matter. Once Stalin had replied to me twice, the third time he would refuse to talk with me at all, and my insistence would just make things worse. So I said to Malenkov that I was no longer asking Comrade Stalin to approve our order but I was explaining the situation and the complications that were now arising for our Front. For us to advance farther westward was to play right into the hands of the enemy; our troops, by moving westward, were taking a shortcut directly into German captivity. I said: "We are stretching our front line too thin; we are weakening it, and we are creating conditions in which a blow can be struck at our left flank. This blow is inevitable, and we will have no means of parrying the blow."

Malenkov passed this along to Stalin. The answer came back immediately: "Comrade Stalin said that we have to carry out the offensive and not to stop the offensive."

Once again I said: "We are carrying out that order. Going on the offensive is easier than anything right now. There's no enemy in front of us. That's what worries us. We can see that our offensive is falling in directly with the wishes of the enemy. I beg that our order be approved. We have weighed all aspects of the situation in making our decision."

Malenkov said: "Yes, a decision was made, but Comrade Stalin says that you imposed your idea on the commander."

I said: "No, we were unanimous in arriving at that decision. We didn't have the slightest disagreement; we didn't even have to vote on it. We studied the situation and saw what a difficult position we were in. That was why we came to that decision."

He said: "No, that was simply your point of view that you were imposing on the others."

I don't know whether Timoshenko really said, in a conversation with Stalin, that the decision to call off the offensive was something I had imposed on the others. I confess that I had my doubts about Timoshenko. He was a man of strong will and great self-esteem. As a commander would he have accepted a decision that he didn't agree with? That was not possible. Nevertheless, might Timoshenko have said something like that in a conversation with Stalin? I find it difficult to agree with that notion. Malenkov had spoken like this to me [about imposing my view on others], and that meant that Stalin had said it to him. I think Stalin simply wanted to needle me a little, to try to put a stop to my insistence. I continued: "You know Commander Timoshenko's character. If he doesn't agree with you, you can't possibly impose your decision on him. Besides, I never had any such aim in mind."

All Malenkov did was to repeat once more: "The offensive must go on." And with that the conversation ended.

Bagramyan had been present the whole time. He was standing next to me, tears pouring from his eyes. If I too didn't cry it was only because I had a less specific picture of the tragedy that was bearing down on us. As a military man Bagramyan understood the situation only too well. His nerves couldn't bear the strain, and that's why he burst into tears. He was suffering for our troops and over our failure. And the catastrophe erupted, literally within a few days, just as we had guessed it would.

There was nothing we could do then, despite all the efforts I made. I don't know how Timoshenko defended the order we favored when talking with Stalin. I was not about to ask him because I could see that he too was suffering. He too could picture the oncoming catastrophe, and I didn't want to return to an unpleasant subject. On the next day Timoshenko and I met and exchanged views but did not reopen the subject of his conversation with Moscow. I also did not tell him about my conversation with Vasilevsky. I didn't say anything about it because Bagramyan had come to see me. The fact that Bagramyan had come to see me and not Marshal Timoshenko might leave its mark on relations between Timoshenko and Bagramyan, or at least that is what I anticipated. I didn't want to set people against one another. On the contrary, I wanted to protect Bagramyan. He was a very calm, sober, and thoughtful person.

Timoshenko and I had breakfast and decided to travel to the area where our forces were holding a crossing on the Donets River. It was the only crossing over which food and supplies could go for our troops who were on the offensive. The crossing was not far from the enemy's airfields. The enemy found no difficulty in keeping bombers and fighter planes constantly poised over the spot. The German bombing of that target was something awful, and we decided to go there because we calculated that it was crucial for us to protect that crossing, to hold onto it and not let the enemy cut off the flow of supplies, ammunition, and fuel to our advancing units, since our troops' staying power and capacity to resist depended on it to a decisive degree.

In 1920, during the Civil War, N. S. Khrushchev was a political worker in the Ninth Kuban Army. He stands in the center of this photograph, wearing a tall black hat.

In 1924, Khrushchev (center) managed to achieve his dream: to study. He was a student at the workers' school in Yuzovka.

In 1922–23, Khrushchev was the secretary of the district party committee in Rutchenkovka, a miners' settlement in the Donbas. He sits in the first row here (fifth from the left).

Khrushchev (third from the left in the first row) with colleagues in the Donbas in 1923.

As a young metalworker, Khrushchev had boarded with the Pisarevs, a family of miners. Yevfrosinya Ivanovna Pisareva, Khrushchev's first wife, is pictured here. Yevfrosinya died in 1919 of typhus, leaving two small children—a daughter, Yuliya, and a son, Leonid.

A wedding photograph from 1924. At the time, Khrushchev was studying at the workers' school in Yuzovka; Nina Petrovna Kukharchuk was a propagandist in the town's party committee.

Khrushchev in 1924 with daughter Yuliya and son Leonid in Stalino (the former Yuzovka).

A family photograph from 1929 shows Nikita Khrushchev and Nina Petrovna Kukharchuk—with children Yuliya, Rada, and Leonid—in Kiev.

Khrushchev visiting one of Moscow's first kindergartens in 1935.

Watching the new sideshows in the Moscow Park of Culture was one of Khrushchev's favorite pastimes. Here, Khrushchev—the first secretary of the city party committee—is pictured with the chairman of the Moscow Soviet, N. A. Bulganin (second from right). Next to Khrushchev stands the first director of the Central Park of Culture and Rest (Gorky Park), Betty Glan, who was repressed during the Stalinist terror.

Khrushchev in 1935 at the "Red Star" collective farm in the village of Korablino, located in the Ryazan district in Ryazan province.

Khrushchev (center), then first secretary of the Moscow city committee of the AUCP(B), at a 1936 exhibition of Ukrainian art in the Central Park of Culture and Rest. Third from the left is A. A. Zhdanov.

This souvenir photograph from December 1936 marked the approval of the USSR's new constitution. Delegates to the Eighth Extraordinary Congress of Soviets included, from left to right, A. A. Andreyev, N. I. Yezhov, Khrushchev, A. A. Zhdanov, and L. M. Kaganovich.

Khrushchev at a housewarming party in Moscow in 1936.

Khrushchev watching a potato-harvesting machine being tested in Moscow province in 1936.

From left to right, J. V. Stalin, G. K. Ordzhonikidze, and Khrushchev by the walls of the Great Kremlin Palace.

Khrushchev, then first secretary of the Moscow city committee of the AUCP(B), visited units of the Moscow garrison of the Red Army in 1936. As a popular Soviet song of that era put it, "If tomorrow there is war, if tomorrow on the march. . . ."

Khrushchev among the workers building the Moscow subway, circa 1933–34.

Khrushchev in the conference hall at the Kremlin, circa 1933–34.

From left to right, G. M. Dimitrov, G. G. Yagoda, G. Ye. Zinoviev, Khrushchev, J. V. Stalin, and A. A. Andreyev on the side rostrum of the Mausoleum in 1936.

Khrushchev and Stalin, circa 1934, on Red Square by the Mausoleum.

Khrushchev at the polling booth in 1937.

Khrushchev, the first secretary of the CC of the CP(B) of Ukraine, in 1938.

Young Pioneers greeting the Eighteenth Congress of the AUCP(B) in March 1939. In the presidium, from left to right, are M. I. Kalinin, Khrushchev, V. M. Molotov, L. M. Kaganovich, K. Ye. Voroshilov, and J. V. Stalin.

Khrushchev, first secretary of the CC of the CP(B) of Ukraine, in Kiev in 1939 at the session celebrating the 125th anniversary of the birth of T. G. Shevchenko. In this photograph, another secretary of the CC of the CP(B) of Ukraine, D. S. Korotchenko, sits to his right in the presidium.

Kiev, May 1941: the leadership of Ukraine on the eve of war with Nazi Germany. Pictured are, from left to right, I. A. Serov, people's commissar of internal affairs of the Ukrainian SSR; L. R. Korniyets, chairman of the Council of People's Commissars of the Ukrainian SSR; M. S. Grechukha, chairman of the presidium of the Supreme Soviet of the Ukrainian SSR; Khrushchev, first secretary of the CC of the CP(B) of Ukraine; D. S. Korotchenko, another secretary of the CC of the CP(B) of Ukraine; M. A. Burmistenko, second secretary of the CC of the CP(B) of Ukraine; K. S. Karavayev, a member of the CC of the CP(B) of Ukraine and deputy chairman of the Council of People's Commissars of the Ukrainian SSR; and K. Z. Litvin, secretary of the Stalino province committee of the CP(B) of Ukraine.

The war with Nazi Germany had been going on for months, but Soviet troops continued to retreat. Khrushchev, a member of the Military Council of the Voronezh Front, talks with a delegation of workers from the city of Tambov. To the extreme left stands front commander Marshal S. K. Timoshenko.

As a member of the Military Council of the Southern Front, Khrushchev addressed a conference of the command staff of the front held in the village of Rubezhnoye on April 23, 1942.

Khrushchev visiting tank units in Voronezh on April 26, 1942.

A conference of the command staff of the Southwestern Front was held in the town of Kupyansk on April 21, 1942. Sitting at the table, from right to left, are Lieutenant General K. A. Gurov; Khrushchev, a member of the front's Military Council; front commander Marshal S. K. Timoshenko; and F. Ya. Falaleyev, commander of air forces of the area. The speaker is the head of the Political Directorate of the Southwestern Front, S. F. Galadzhev.

Stalingrad in the wake of the German air raid of August 23, 1942.

Recalled by the Stavka from the front, Khrushchev was in Moscow in the winter of 1943 to discuss the situation behind the front line with leaders of Ukrainian partisan detachments. Khrushchev remained in charge of matters pertaining to Ukraine throughout the war.

The command point of the headquarters of the Stalingrad Front was located on the lands of the "Red Orchard" collective farm. On October 9, 1942, front commander Army General A. I. Yeremenko (to the right) and Khrushchev, a member of the front's Military Council, observed the battle then under way in Stalingrad.

Khrushchev (center) with comrades from the battle of Stalingrad in the village of Beketovka on February 3, 1943. Commander of the 64th Army of the Stalingrad Front General M. S. Shumilov stands to Khrushchev's right; to his left is Z. T. Serdyuk, a member of the Military Council of the 64th Army.

On February 3, 1943, the army of Field Marshal Paulus surrendered in Stalingrad.

Front commander Army General N. F. Vatutin presenting the Guards Banner to the Fifth Stalingrad Tank Corps on May 7, 1943, at the Rzhava railroad station on the Voronezh Front. To the left stands Lieutenant General Khrushchev, a member of the front's Military Council.

Testing a mobile antitank mine in July 1943.

Khrushchev talking with wounded Soviet soldiers on the Voronezh Front, August 3, 1943.

On August 25, 1943, after the liberation of Kharkov, Khrushchev addressed representatives of that city's intelligentsia.

Leonid Khrushchev, elder son of N. S. Khrushchev, pictured in 1940. He was studying at the Zhukovsky Air Force Academy in Moscow.

Leonid Khrushchev in January 1942 with his younger sister Rada in Moscow. The whole Khrushchev family had evacuated to Kuibyshev. Leonid, a bomber pilot, was in the hospital there, recovering from having broken a leg at the battlefront. At the beginning of January, the Stavka recalled N. S. Khrushchev to Moscow, and Nina Petrovna came to see her husband, taking with her Rada and Leonid (who was already able to walk with the aid of a cane). Each such rendezvous might have been the last.

In August 1943, at the dacha settlement of Pomerki outside Kharkov, a session of the CC of the CP(B) of Ukraine and the Ukrainian government discussed a proposal to introduce a new orthography for the Ukrainian language. Academician L. A. Bulakhovsky (in the center, next to Khrushchev) presented the report.

Khrushchev and V. M. Churayev surveying the ruins of the Kharkov Tractor Factory on August 24, 1943.

In 1943, the Khrushchev family returned to Moscow from evacuation. Pictured in the apartment on Granovsky Street are Nina Petrovna with daughters Rada (to the right) and Lena.

Khrushchev with pupils and teachers from a local school in the city of Chernigov on October 19, 1943, just before the start of the school year.

Khrushchev with three years of war behind him.

On October 25, 1943, Khrushchev spoke at the Brovary railroad station in Kiev province, addressing local inhabitants who had been mobilized into the Red Army.

The same day—at the same Brovary Station. "How are we to go on? The war has left us nothing but ruins and destitution." "We shall rebuild."

General Vatutin's command point during the battle for Kiev at the Bukrinsky bridgehead, October 28, 1943.

M. I. Kalinin awarding Khrushchev the Order of Suvorov First Class in 1943.

On November 6, 1943—the day of the city's liberation—Khrushchev addressed the people of Kiev.

A parade in Kiev on November 7, 1943, received by commander of the First Ukrainian Front N. F. Vatutin and Khrushchev, Military Council member and first secretary of the CC of the CP(B) of Ukraine. In the background stands P. N. Gapochka, who had served as Khrushchev's aide since 1935 and who went through the whole war with him. Many of the photographs that illustrate this book are his. He got into this shot thanks to Yakov Ryumkin, a war correspondent for *Pravda*.

Tears of joy in Kiev on November 6, 1943, when troops liberated the city from the fascists.

Khrushchev at the First Ukrainian Front on July 13, 1944. He flew from Kiev to the front's head-quarters. Khrushchev remained a member of the front's Military Council until the last days of the war.

The First Ukrainian Front, July 22, 1944. Khrushchev is shown talking with German prisoners of war at the settlement of Mostki-Velikiye in Voroshilovgrad province.

Khrushchev in Western Ukraine in 1944 with Generals Moskalenko (to the right) and Yepishev.

The First Ukrainian Front, July 22, 1944. Khrushchev was on the way to Rava Russkaya in Lvov province. He stands by a tree near the soldiers of the 333rd Infantry Division. Next to him is his faithful aide of many years, G. T. Shuisky.

We arrived. Some makeshift shelters had been set up there. Wave after wave of enemy bombers was flying in and "unloading" over that crossing. Still, the crossing had not been destroyed and continued to serve our purposes. Then we received news that the commander of the troops of the Southern Front [Malinovsky] had appeared not far from the crossing [where the Ninth Army of his Front was positioned]. Timoshenko proposed: "Let's go over and discuss our further actions with the commander of the Southern Front, to coordinate our actions. His army is part of the Southern Front, but the enemy is going to make a breakthrough in our defenses and surround our troops by a blow from the south, that is, precisely through the positions of the [Southern Front's] Ninth Army." We left the bomb shelter, made our way to our vehicles, and went to meet Malinovsky. We met in a little village on the Donets and went into a small house where we began to look into the situation. The situation was very tense and difficult. I could see that both Malinovsky and Timoshenko regarded the operation as doomed, but it had to be carried out because there was an order from higher up, and nothing could be done about it. As we were discussing the situation, suddenly one of the guards burst into the room shouting: "Bombers are coming right at us." We were about to go out when they shouted that the bombs were already dropping.

Malinovsky gave the order: "Lie down!" We all lay down. The commander of the tank troops threw himself on top of me. I'm not certain that I remember his name correctly. It seems it was Shtevnev,[29] a good general. He was later killed in action, poor fellow. The bombs exploded right next to the little house we were in, but the house didn't suffer. And neither did we. The bombing ended; we went outside and finished our exchange of views. I don't remember specifically what plans were made. Given the existing circumstances, it was hard to determine the best actions to take. From there we either went back to the crossing area or to our operational command post at Svatovo.

On the second or third day, the enemy began an energetic counterattack against our left flank, broke through our defenses, and closed the circle, bottling up our troops in the salient. The very thing that we had considered inevitable had happened, which showed what unreasonable stubbornness had been displayed in regard to continuing the offensive and carrying out the tasks that had been assigned at the beginning of the operation. Events unfolded very quickly. We could no longer deliver supplies and fuel to the salient, and our military equipment there soon became immobile. Those were precisely the conditions the enemy needed to smash our forces. Later on we went out closer to the Donets and met people who had broken out of encirclement. The enemy hadn't sealed off the area tightly, and our troops were able to break through one by one or in small groups. One of those who escaped from encirclement was Gurov, who was with the staff of the Sixth Army in the main area of the offensive. Riding in a tank, he was able to break through the ring that the enemy had already closed around our forces.

Both writers and generals have given good accounts of how people escaped from encirclement. I cannot describe it better than has already been done in the literature about the war. Gurov reported that he had no choice but to get into his tank and make his breakthrough. If he hadn't done that, he would have been trapped behind German lines. Various voices condemning him were heard at the time. The people behind those voices looked to me with a question: Perhaps Gurov should be tried by a military tribunal for breaking out of encirclement in a tank? But my attitude toward Gurov was one of respect; I valued him highly for his honesty and for his precision and discipline as a military man. My answer to these people was: "No, the number of generals who have already died [in the fighting] over there is enough. Do you want to add the one who broke out of encirclement to make one more? Why, that would be madness. The Germans have destroyed some, and now we're supposed to destroy others who escaped? That would set a terrible example for our troops. It would be like saying it doesn't matter where you die; if the German bullets don't get you, your own people will."

It was all over! Gorodnyansky, the commander of the Sixth Army, did not escape from encirclement. His entire headquarters staff was destroyed. Podlas, commander of the 57th Army, also perished, and all his headquarters people were killed. The commander of the operational group [Bobkin] was killed, and his teenaged son died with him. Many generals, officers, and Red Army men perished. Only a very few escaped, because the distance between the two points at the base of the salient was not very great and the enemy closed up that space solidly. The encircled troops found themselves deep behind enemy lines. They couldn't use their vehicles and heavy weapons because there was no fuel or ammunition. And it was a very long way to go on foot. Some of our forces were killed, but the bulk of them were taken prisoner by the Germans.

I don't remember how many days it was after the catastrophe that a phone call came from Moscow. It was not the commander who was being summoned to Moscow; it was I. Can you imagine? I was in a very downcast mood as I flew to Moscow. It's hardly necessary to talk about what I was feeling. We had lost many thousands of soldiers[30] and had squandered the hope that was keeping us alive: the hope that we would open the year 1942 with offensive operations against the occupation forces. Instead things had ended in catastrophe. The offensive had been an initiative proposed by Timoshenko and myself. That also placed a great responsibility on me. The fact that we had wanted to change the course of military operations and avoid the catastrophe was hard to prove, especially when confronting those who had actually had the power to stop the operation. After all, if they were to agree that our arguments had been correct, that would mean they were saying their own decisions had been incorrect. But such high-mindedness was not for Stalin. He was a treacherous person. He was capable of anything except admitting that he had made a mistake. Therefore I had a clear picture of the tragic position I was in, but I had no other recourse. I boarded the airplane and flew to Moscow, but morally I was ready for anything, up to and including arrest.

But what would be done then with the commander? Did this mean that the commander too would be arrested? Yet the commander had apparently had a different kind of conversation; he had not expressed opposition but had agreed with Stalin. I, on the other hand, had stood my ground and done so fairly stubbornly. Besides, I didn't know in whose presence Stalin might have had his conversation with Timoshenko. When I had had my conversation, the person at the telephone table passing on my remarks to Stalin and Stalin's remarks to me was Malenkov. I was sure that Beria, Mikoyan, and Molotov had been there, too, and possibly Voroshilov as well, but I couldn't be sure of that. Voroshilov was very much in Stalin's bad books at the time. The circumstance I have mentioned worked in my favor but also against me. The witnesses to the conversation were not favorable witnesses for me, but it could also turn out that it was unpleasant for Stalin to have them as witnesses. After all, I had been proved right when I had insistently tried to achieve through Malenkov the canceling of the order Stalin had given, and Stalin wouldn't listen to me. But what significance would that have in the situation that had now arisen? Everything that Stalin said was supposed to be a product of genius. Everything that Stalin spoke against was worthless and insignificant, and people who insisted on something that Stalin was opposed to were dishonest and perhaps even enemies of the people.

At that time there was a theory circulating very widely in our country, a theory dreamed up by Stalin—that the class struggle would continue to intensify and grow more severe in the USSR.[31] This theory confused the thinking of honest people both inside the party and outside it. Stalin succeeded in distorting all concepts. There actually were enemies of the people—genuine embittered foes of Soviet power. But in the course of the repression [of the

1930s] the heads of extremely honest people, devoted to the revolution and to the working class, had been chopped off. These people had demonstrated their loyalty in the Civil War and in the building of socialism. Yet, as "enemies of the people," their heads had been placed on the chopping block. One head more or less, what did that matter to Stalin? But what is to be said about conscience? Stalin's conscience? He would be the first to laugh at that one. That's a bourgeois concept, a survival of the bourgeois past. Everything that Stalin said was justified. What he said was, and could only be, in the interest of the revolution and the interest of the working class.

So then, on my way to see Stalin—riding, flying, and walking—I surrendered, as they say, to the will of fate. I didn't know what would become of me. We met. When I walked into his office, Stalin came toward me—or more exactly, he didn't come toward me, but took a step in my direction. We said hello. Stalin was a great actor. He knew how to control himself and never let on whether he was going to explode in fury or take an understanding attitude. He knew how to wear the mask of inscrutability. We said hello and he said to me: "The Germans have announced that they captured so-and-so many thousands of our soldiers. Are they lying?"

I answered: "No, Comrade Stalin, they are not lying. That figure, if it has been announced by the Germans, is probably accurate. We had approximately that number of troops in that region, even a bit more than that. Partly they must have been destroyed and the rest actually taken captive, as stated by the Germans." Stalin made no reply. I saw that he was fuming, and I didn't know in what direction the boiling kettle might explode. But he contained himself; he didn't say anything more than that to me, and he didn't denounce either the commander or me. He remained silent. Then our conversation passed to other subjects: What would we do next? What were the possibilities of constructing a defense along the Donets to prevent the enemy from crossing the river in that area? How could we stop the enemy's advance, given our very limited resources? Then we went to have something to eat.

I don't remember how many days I stayed in Moscow. The longer I stayed, the more tediously the time went by as I waited to see how things would end up for me personally. How things would end up I simply didn't know. I thought that Stalin could not overlook this catastrophe, especially after our victory at Rostov and the thunderous victory at Moscow, that he could not forgive it and would look for a scapegoat to demonstrate his implacability and firmness of principle. He wouldn't hesitate out of concern for the fate of an individual, no matter how well known that person was or even how close that person might be to him, if the interests of the country were involved. Here he had an opportunity to demonstrate such things. He could say that this catastrophe had befallen us because so-and-so or such-and-such people were to blame. Nothing would prevent the government and Stalin from strictly punishing the individuals who were guilty. I even imagined, basing myself on previous experience, how Stalin might formulate it. He was a great master of such formulations. And in general he was a very talented and intelligent person. The question is, How do you evaluate a mind or an intelligence under differing circumstances? It is one thing when a mind is directed toward serving the interests of the revolution, strengthening and developing the revolution; it's another thing when this mind is directed against the revolution, concealed under fiery slogans about the defense of revolutionary interests. As a result of things like this, many people who to the depths of their being were devoted to the cause of Lenin and the cause of Marxism and Leninism perished.

During one of those agonizing days we were sitting at the dinner table eating. At that time there were no dinners with Stalin at which people did not drink heavily, whether they wanted to or not. He evidently wanted to drown his conscience and keep himself stupefied, or so it seemed. He never left the table sober and still less did he allow any of those close to him to leave sober, including the generals and commanders of troops who came with reports or who were preparing one or another operation. At dinner he began a conversation about the Kharkov campaign in a monotone, but with a fairly steady voice. I was familiar with these cat-and-mouse methods of Stalin's. He looked at me and said: "During the First World War when one of our armies was trapped and encircled in East Prussia, the commander of the neighboring army [instead of coming to the aid of the trapped army] fled to the rear. He was put on trial. He was tried and hanged."

I said: "Comrade Stalin, I remember that case. From the newspapers of course. Our Russian troops had been taken prisoner by the Germans there earlier. The authorities were forced to put Myasoyedov on trial and sentence him and have him hanged. He actually was a traitor, a German agent. The tsar was right to have him hung as a traitor to Russia. But he was only a colonel in the gendarmes, not an army commander." Stalin said nothing more. He did not develop his ideas on this subject any further, but this was enough for me. Can you imagine how I felt after that analogy? The First World War, East Prussia, the disaster suffered by the Russian troops, and then the execution of Myasoyedov. And here it was 1942, an operation in which our troops had been smashed, and a member of the Military Council and member of the Politburo was sitting there and Stalin was reminding him that there had already been "the same kind of case"[32] in our history.

I must confess that I estimated the situation this way: I felt that Stalin was trying to prepare me morally so that I would take an understanding attitude, that in the interests of the homeland, in the interest of the Soviet state, and to soothe public opinion, it would be necessary to demonstrate that all those to blame for the defeats would be strictly punished. There had already been an example of such things during the first days of the war when the Germans broke through on the Western Front and destroyed our aircraft and in general made mincemeat of the entire Front. The Front had collapsed. If it had not collapsed, perhaps the entire war would have taken a different course. At that time Stalin arrested, tried, and sentenced to death the commander of the troops of that Front, General Pavlov, along with his chief of staff and other individuals, so there was already that precedent. I too, as they say, was awaiting my fate. The only difficulty for Stalin, as I saw it, was my telephone conversation in front of witnesses. The conversation had been conducted through Malenkov, and probably there were others present as well. No matter how close those people might be to Stalin, he understood that he couldn't get around the fact that this conversation had taken place. Various viewpoints might be held, and they might leak out either now or later, and this would not be to Stalin's advantage.

I stayed in Moscow for some time, and then Stalin said that I could return to the battlefront. I was overjoyed, but not completely, because I knew that there were cases in which Stalin had given the nod of approval to people, allowed them to leave his office, and then immediately they were sent, not where they were supposed to be sent, but where Stalin had ordered them sent, having instructed those in charge of such matters to arrest them. I left his office. Nothing happened. I spent the night, and in the morning I took a plane and was able to return to the battlefront.

The situation there was very difficult. When we had carried out the Barvenkovo-Lozovaya operation in the winter, the responsibilities had been distributed as follows: the commander of the Southwestern Area was Timoshenko; the commander of the Southwestern Front was Kostenko; his chief of staff was Bodin; and the chief of staff of the Southwestern Area beginning in the spring was Bagramyan. I have already spoken about Kostenko. He was a very fine and pleasant person, a fighting general who carried out his orders, but he was not sufficiently cultivated as a military man to cope with his responsibilities as commander of the Front. Our opinion then was that if Kostenko the commander had Bodin as chief of staff, and if Kostenko was attentive to what his chief of staff said, we would not have to expect blunders. I had especially high hopes for Bodin because of his ability to understand situations. In all circumstances he would be able to come to the aid of his commander. Kirichenko[33] was confirmed as a member of the Military Council.

For some reason Bodin flew to our command post in Svatovo, where the headquarters of the Southwestern Area was located. He told me about the situation at the headquarters of our Front and complained: "I wanted you to know. When we were transferred from Voronezh and established ourselves as the headquarters of the Southwestern Front, abuses began in the matter of drinking: both Kostenko, in whom I had not noticed this earlier, and especially Kirichenko. For me personally, quite a difficult situation has developed. If I propose anything as chief of staff, I encounter opposition when we discuss matters. I don't feel any support coming from Kirichenko. It has become terribly difficult to work, and I cannot guarantee that intelligent decisions will be made."

I was very disturbed by his comments. I had no doubts about Kostenko's honesty, but I valued Bodin more, considering that he had a better understanding of military matters. I assumed that, without Bodin, Kostenko would not be able to cope with the tasks of commanding the Front. When we made these assignments, I had thought that Kirichenko would support Bodin, and here Bodin was telling me the opposite. Kostenko and Kirichenko were drinking together and making all the decisions together without Bodin. Timoshenko and I discussed this and decided that he, Timoshenko, should become commander of the Southwestern Front, combining that position with the one he already held. That was what we reported to Stalin, and he approved our proposal. Later I said to Kirichenko: "Aren't you ashamed? Why did you start listening to Kostenko more than to Bodin on purely military matters? Bodin is both better educated on military matters and superior in his knowledge, his ability, and his sense of tact. Why did you turn your back on him and not give him support? And start committing abuses as far as drinking goes?"

When I went to visit him, the following scene is what I encountered: Kirichenko came out to see me in a light gray overcoat, overcoats of that color having been introduced right at that time for generals. In the tsarist era, that was the color of the overcoats worn by generals. The tsarist police officers and other officials had also worn that color of overcoat. I said to him: "Aren't you ashamed? What kind of general are you? You've dressed yourself up like a peacock. What did you have to do that for? Do you really think that's going to make you look better or raise your prestige in the eyes of the military people? The military still know that you're not one of them. You're here as a representative of the party and a member of the Military Council. Isn't that enough for you? You should value what the party has assigned you to do. You should carry out our political line in support of the army and for the benefit of the party." After that I never saw him wearing that kind of overcoat again. But that was typical. Such trappings had become more important to the man than the political substance of things.

Let me return to the period when we were making assignments for the command of the Southwestern Front and the Southwestern Area. We had suffered a harsh defeat, and people were escaping from encirclement. Timoshenko, drawing on the experience of the Civil War, gave an order: "If the troops are fleeing, then set up field kitchens. The soldiers will come to the kitchens; they'll have no place else to go." And sure enough the soldiers did come to the field kitchens. A certain number were gathered together that way. We also received some units from the reserve of the Supreme High Command: some tank corps and infantry units. We began to construct our line of defense, and we got it set up more or less. When the enemy tried to cross the Donets, we repelled all attacks.

At that point, apparently, the Germans made some different plans. These became evident later, although they continued to make savage attacks in our area. Then they stopped, and soon their intention became clear. The main blow was being directed not at our area but to the north of Kharkov toward Voronezh. The Germans began shifting their infantry and planes to that area. In May or June, a German plane landed at our airfield. The pilot had become disoriented. The German plane was carrying operational documents from their headquarters—maps and so forth. From these documents it became clear that the enemy had intended to carry out an offensive toward Voronezh (and a detailed, officially approved document to this effect already existed). One after the other, two more German planes landed at our airfield, fighter planes. Naturally we took the pilots prisoner, questioned them, and found out that they too had become disoriented. They said: "We were flying to such-and-such an airfield and we landed here [by mistake]. We thought this was our airfield, but it turns out we landed in your territory." Of course we reported to Moscow that the enemy was making preparations for an offensive, gathering his land and air forces together. We reported that these fighter pilots had landed at our airfield, that we had taken them prisoner, and that they had reported such-and-such. The appropriate conclusions needed to be drawn from this.[34]

I remember a phone call from Stalin in this connection. He said to me—either ironically or mockingly: "So what are the Germans trying to palm off onto you? You take it seriously that these are the enemy's intentions? They foisted a map onto you. An airplane has landed; fighter planes have also landed, you report. They're doing this to mislead us and throw us off." In short, he was saying that we didn't understand and that the enemy was doing this deliberately. But in the first airplane, besides the maps, there was also a general! Had they intentionally foisted him onto us? Stalin didn't understand the Germans' intentions. He believed something else. He believed a version that the Germans had fabricated, rumors that the Germans had circulated (I say this now on the basis of documents that have been published in the book *Top* Secret)[35]—rumors that they were preparing to strike in the direction of Moscow, that is, moving again in the direction in which they had suffered defeat in winter 1941–42. Those rumors were intended to disorient our High Command, and they succeeded. Instead of understanding the situation correctly and forming a strong body of troops to the east of Kharkov to be ready to repel the enemy, very little was done. Instead, Stalin fell for the provocation that Hitler had thought up and wouldn't believe any of the information we reported to him. He made fun of us for supposedly being too naive and trusting. He thought the blow would be struck elsewhere, and consequently very little was done to reinforce our area.

I cannot now say what forces the enemy disposed of at the time. But all this information is now known. If Hitler's intention had been guessed correctly, if our proposals had been properly appreciated, and our area had been strengthened, it seems to me that it would have been possible to contain the Germans, and the course of the war would have turned out differently. In all likelihood the German offensive could have been held at the Donets. They would not have been able to advance farther eastward. What is the terrible thing about all this? We lost thousands of people and once again surrendered part of our territory; the war was prolonged, perhaps for a year, perhaps for even two years more.

Thus the appointed hour of the enemy attack came. Timoshenko and I had taken whatever measures we could in our area. We traveled out to our command post, where our 21st Army was located. The commander was Gordov.[36] The Germans began to carry out their operation at precisely the hour indicated. As always, an artillery bombardment began first. Timoshenko, I, and the commander of the 21st Army were at the command post. Some sort of square trench had been dug in an open clearing. That was the entire defensive equipment of the command post. This was very much like Gordov. He scorned danger and made a show of his bravery, and indeed he was a brave man. We were sitting down in this hole with our telephones while the artillery shells flew past us, howling. Fighting began, but the relationship of forces was unequal. We had not counted on success if the enemy actually chose this area to strike the main blow. We did not have the reinforcements to bring up to block the enemy's advance, and the enemy clearly intended to develop his successful offensive in the direction of Voronezh.

Our troops were routed, although not right away. It was the middle or perhaps the end of June when the complete disorganization of our Front finally occurred. I remember only that when our troops did retreat the rye and wheat had already grown quite high. Our infantry and tanks rolled eastward over the croplands. Vasilevsky flew to our headquarters at that point. The most intense pressure from the enemy was being felt in the area of the 38th Army, commanded by Moskalenko.[37] After talking with Vasilevsky, we agreed to take a vehicle and go see Moskalenko. That was where the main location of the fighting was then. When we arrived in the area where Moskalenko's troops were deployed, we encountered a terrible sight. The enemy's planes were flying very low, with impunity, and shooting at everything in sight: our retreating tanks, trucks, and infantry. An unorganized flight was what we encountered. Vasilevsky said: "Let's go to the commander's headquarters." We began searching for him. We knew where his headquarters had previously been located, and we went there first. When we arrived there, we found only the kitchen and canteen staff, and they were getting ready to leave.

We understood from the situation that the headquarters had been here. We encountered a healthy-looking fellow with a ruddy complexion. The soldiers had a saying about such people: "You can tell from their faces that they work in the canteen." Without getting out of our vehicle, Vasilevsky called him over. As I have already indicated, Vasilevsky was a soft-spoken person and he dealt with people in a delicate way. He said: "Listen, comrade! Isn't this Moskalenko's headquarters?"

The other answered: "Yes, Moskalenko's."

"Then where is Moskalenko himself?"

The soldier said Moskalenko was in such-and-such a village not far from there, no more than about 10 kilometers. We started off in that direction. Suddenly the soldier shouted: "Stop! Stop!" We stopped. This puff-faced, insolent fellow, looking right at Vasilevsky, said to him: "Comrade General, you ate dinner at my kitchen yesterday and didn't pay for the dinner."

Vasilevsky looked at me and then at the fellow: "Listen, brother, I don't know what you're saying. That couldn't be. I wasn't here. I just arrived." He looked at me, as though for confirmation, and said: "You know, don't you, that I have just arrived?" The insolent fellow turned on his heel and walked away. Here was a confirmed money-grubber for sure. He had the gall to approach an unknown general and assert that he hadn't paid for his meal, and of all things Vasilevsky had started to defend himself. Another general might have reacted differently. I had good reason to respect Vasilevsky, although I could never forget the defeat of our troops south of Kharkov, the phone conversation I had had with him, and his reaction to my pleadings. To the end of my days it seems, I won't be able to forget that. I'll never be reconciled or find a rational explanation for Vasilevsky's conduct on that occasion.

We went in the direction indicated, arrived at the village, where the headquarters [of the 38th Army] was still being set up, and encountered Moskalenko. Moskalenko was a very nervous man, even more than nervous. He greeted us with these words: "Here you are again coming to visit me at a moment when I can't even lift my head up. The enemy is giving us no rest." He greeted me in the same way on some other occasions when I visited him. Then he told us about the disposition of his forces, although he could not have known this exactly because the enemy was at that very moment bearing down on his fleeing troops. Thus a new catastrophe began, this time to the east of Kharkov in the area around Voronezh and later Stalingrad. In this area we were already retreating, as the saying goes, with no delays. As soon as we would dig in, the enemy would again knock us out of the positions we had occupied, and we would withdraw. We didn't even have a solidly connected front line. Isolated strong points of resistance were fighting, but the enemy was continually driving us farther and farther toward the Don River. We ended up in the Voronezh region. I don't remember the name of the village where our headquarters was established, but I remember that we didn't have the strength to hold that position.

Our intelligence reported that enemy tanks had concentrated northwest of us. It was evident that during the night the enemy would advance with his tanks into the village where our headquarters was located. I cannot say whether the enemy knew that the headquarters of our Front was located there. We warned all members of the headquarters staff that when it got dark we would cross to the other side of the Don River. The village was no more than 20 kilometers from the Don. We recommended that no one spend the night in that village because people could end up being taken prisoner by the Germans. Timoshenko and I, however, waited until it began to get dark: we wanted to make use of the twilight to travel in semidarkness, before night set in completely, because it was impossible to travel at night without headlights, and if the enemy saw headlights, our vehicles would be bombed and strafed. We reached the crossing. Enemy planes bombed us. I don't think the enemy knew that the commander of the Front and a member of the Military Council of the Front were crossing at this location. The enemy was interested in attacking any river crossing. People and various means of transport were always concentrated at such locations, and it was easier to destroy them there.

We made our crossing in some sort of cutter or small motorboat, if not a rowboat, reached the east bank of the Don, traveled a little farther, and set up our headquarters in some village, simply to rest. We had no troops with us. Some scattered elements and units were all that remained. We had no units capable of combat. That was the "cheerful picture" before us. The next day we received orders from Moscow to transfer our headquarters to Kalach on the Don, which is to the west of Stalingrad.[38] Bodin became chief of staff for the area. Timoshenko once again commanded the Southwestern Area and the Southwestern Front, because by then Kostenko had perished in the Kharkov operation, together with the headquarters of the Sixth Army. When we received the order from Moscow to relocate to Kalach I went there along with Bodin and Bagramyan. Timoshenko said that for his part he would remain where he was with Gurov, a member of the Military Council, to try and organize whatever troops were able to cross the Don. We left. In my opinion, this was a very strange decision by the commander. I didn't understand it, but I didn't ask later what the reason for it was. I simply drew the conclusion that apparently Timoshenko's spirits were low; he was feeling depressed, and he somehow wanted to justify himself in his own eyes.

For several days we had no communication with him. He didn't even maintain communications with headquarters. We simply couldn't find him. When Stalin made an inquiry, we were unable to tell him where the commander was. It looked as though we might have abandoned him somewhere. Can you imagine that? This was in the Stalin era when treason was seen at every step! In an extremely difficult time for our army and in the area where Timoshenko was the commander and I was a member of the Military Council there had already been two harsh defeats for our forces.

And now the commander was not to be found. Did that mean he had defected? Divisional Commissar Gurov, a member of the Military Council was with him, and had also disappeared. Really and truly, a thought like that [that he might have defected] occurred to me. I wanted to drive it out of my mind, but it seemed to piece itself together on the basis of the facts. In Stalin's time he hammered his own special way of understanding things into the consciousness of everyone he dealt with. Naturally, negative thoughts about Timoshenko arose in my mind.

We received a new order—to transfer headquarters to Stalingrad. Some group of people was said to be there who would know what would come under our jurisdiction and what the makeup of our new Stalingrad Front would be. Bodin and I set out in a vehicle, and along the way we encountered Timoshenko! Later Gurov told me that they had sat things out in a haystack. They had spread burkas[39] underneath them and had taken command of whoever came by. They had no means of communication and didn't know of anyone nearby. Gurov said: "Timoshenko was in a mood where he was thinking: Why should I go sit in a headquarters? What can I say to Stalin? There are no troops; there's nothing to be in command of. I might be given orders on how to repel the enemy advance, but there would be nothing to repel it with." In short, he was feeling everything at once, bitterness and grief and the damaged self-esteem of a defeated fighting man. Of course he did not suffer any more than I did. It was he (not I) who would be blamed for the new defeat, but in fact the General Staff and Stalin personally were to blame. We did not exchange views on this question. I of course was on my guard because Timoshenko in his conversation with Stalin had apparently agreed that I had put pressure on him about the Kharkov operation, or so Stalin indicated in the phone conversation I had through Malenkov. It was enough for me that, back in May, I had stubbornly sought to have the decision of our headquarters approved, and in so doing, had aroused the dissatisfaction and annoyance of Stalin.

I traveled to Stalingrad together with Bodin. Once again Timoshenko did not come, although he had Stalin's direct order to go there, and his arrival time was set. Bodin and I were traveling together in a motor vehicle. Our mood, of course, couldn't have been worse. We were transferring our headquarters to Stalingrad, and we knew that in the whole area between the Don and Stalingrad we had virtually no troops. There were only some disorganized remnants, which did not represent a fighting force that could be relied on to slow down the enemy. I even remember one little detail. As we were crossing the Khoper River, Bodin said: "Let's take a swim." That was a luxury for those times. There was never any time for that. But under the impact of the southern sun we decided to take a swim.

Then we arrived in Stalingrad. This was the first time I had ever been in this city of the steppes. The impression it made on me was that of a large village except for the part of the city where the tractor plant was located. In that area modern buildings made of brick could be seen, four and five stories high. The Barricades and Red October plants⁴⁰ were in that area, along with a grain mill and other structures, but wooden buildings predominated. I was surprised, because in this steppe area there were no forests at all, except for the oak grove on the east bank of the Volga across from Stalingrad. I wondered how there could be wooden buildings almost everywhere. Later I realized that many a raft was swept downstream on the broad breast of the Mother Volga, and therefore wood was fairly cheap.

We were met by General Tolbukhin.⁴¹ He had been appointed chief of the fortified zone outside Stalingrad and was busy constructing fortifications: digging trenches and antitank ditches. Little had been done so far. It looked as though construction had begun just a short time before. Tolbukhin also had very few fighting units. A representative of the General Staff reported to us (I don't remember who it was) that the 62d Army and 57th Army were located in that area, but they were not up to full strength. The 57th Army was later commanded by Tolbukhin, the 64th Army by Chuikov, and the 62nd by Kolpakchi.⁴² There were some other units there as well, in particular a mechanized brigade.⁴³ It was commanded by Colonel Burmakov, and there was a man well known to me who was a member of the Military Council: when I had been secretary of the Bauman district committee of the party in 1931, this man had been secretary of the party committee of a meat and milk processing complex named after Molotov. He was a very ardent fellow, Jewish, an energetic man, and a good party secretary for the organization, a man of initiative. He conducted himself splendidly and as commissar of the mechanized brigade he bore the title of regimental commissar. There were other military units there, but they were small.

Shortly after Bodin and I arrived in Stalingrad I was summoned to Moscow. Arriving in the capital, I was again expecting any and every kind of unpleasantness. The setbacks at the battlefront promised nothing good for me in Moscow, but Stalin voiced no reproaches against me on that occasion. I even thought that perhaps he had recognized his own incorrectness in not listening to me when I tried to have our order confirmed to shift to the defensive in the Barvenkovo area. Of course Stalin could not say such a thing. If he even thought it, his tongue could not have shaped itself to admit that he was wrong or that someone else was right. I had never heard any such thing from him, and I could not expect to hear anything like that now. But the fact that he greeted me fairly calmly, although a very difficult situation had developed, enabled me then to think along those lines. Stalin questioned me about the events, but there was little I could say because I still didn't know Stalingrad or the situation there. He told me more about what armies were located there and how the defense of the city should be organized. Suddenly he turned to me and asked: "Who should be appointed commander there?" He said nothing about Timoshenko.

Timoshenko was commander of the Southwestern Front, which was now being reorganized as the Stalingrad Front. Therefore it was natural that the question of his candidacy should arise first of all. But I was not going to speak about Timoshenko either. I simply asked: "Well, what do you think?"

He said: "Yeremenko could be appointed commander of the Front, but he's in the hospital and could not take command now." I had only heard about Yeremenko then; I didn't know him personally, had never met him. So I couldn't say anything constructive about Yeremenko. But if Stalin had a high enough opinion of him, I had no reason to object. Yeremenko's name was new to me. I knew only that he had fought the Germans in the Gomel region[44] and on the approaches to Kursk. It was precisely from that area that the enemy had struck southward and closed the ring around our group in the Kiev area. Stalin again began pressing me to name someone to be commander of the troops at the Stalingrad Front. Should I name Timoshenko? [I wondered to myself] For Stalin that would have been no great big find. Stalin himself knew Timoshenko, knew him better than I. He had known him in the First Cavalry Army under Budyonny.[45] Timoshenko in general had been very much in evidence, especially after the repression of the command staff of the Red Army in the 1930s. Against the background of the commanders who remained, Timoshenko stood out fairly prominently.

When I had gone from Moscow to Kiev to be first secretary of the Central Committee of the Ukrainian Communist Party, the commander of the military district had been Timoshenko, and Stalin had given me a favorable report and a good character reference about him. Of course the character reference had consisted primarily in the fact that he was an honest man that you could rely on. Actually Stalin never had a strong or deep trust in anyone. Lodged deeply within him there was always a kind of inner suspicion of everyone. He once said to me in an outburst of candor: "I'm a hopeless person. I don't trust anyone. I don't even trust myself." He said that to me in 1952 in Sukhumi[46] in the presence of Mikoyan.[47] That was something so typical of

Stalin. I don't know what the result would have been if he had suddenly gathered his courage and candidly given a character reference of himself.

But in 1942 I said to him: "Comrade Stalin, I can name only candidates from among the people who have commanded the troops in our area. I don't know any others. Therefore you should name the commander of the Stalingrad Front. You know more people; you have a wider horizon."

He said: "What are you talking about? What's the matter with you? I've already told you about Yeremenko. Vlasov would be a good commander there, but I can't give you Vlasov because he and his troops are trapped in encirclement now. If we could get him out of there, I would confirm Vlasov. You yourself should name whoever you want."[48] I tried and tried to ward this off, but I was placed in the position where I could not leave the room without naming a commander for the troops of the Stalingrad Front.

I said: "Of the people on our Front I would name Gordov, despite all his shortcomings. One of his shortcomings is his roughness; he gets into fights with people. He himself is a frail, small man, but he gets physical even with his officers. Still, he does know military science, and so I would name him."

At that time Gordov commanded the 21st Army and was under our jurisdiction. I was already more familiar with him from the sector of the battlefront that he had held along the Donets. Serdyuk had been a member of his Military Council. I had received a character reference from Serdyuk about Gordov—both good and bad. Good in the sense that he knew his business, was energetic and brave; bad because of his coarseness and roughness, up to and including hitting people. To tell the truth, that was considered to some degree a positive feature in a commander then. Stalin himself, when some commander reported to him, often said: "But did you smash him in the face? You've got to let him have it in the kisser! Right in the kisser!" In short, punching a subordinate in the face at that time was considered a kind of heroic act. And people did hit their subordinates!

Later I found out that Yeremenko at one time had even hit a member of his Military Council. I said to him later: "Andrei Ivanovich, how could you allow yourself to hit another person? After all, you are a general and a commander. And you hit a member of the Military Council!"

He answered: "Well, you know, the situation was like this . . . ."

I said: "No matter what the situation was, there are other means of explaining things to a member of the Military Council besides fisticuffs." He again explained that a difficult situation had arisen, there was an urgent need for shells to be delivered; he had come to see about it, and he found

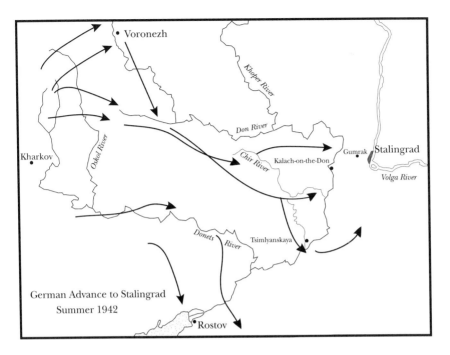

German Advance to Stalingrad
Summer 1942

this member of the Military Council sitting and playing chess. I said to him: "Well, I don't know. If he was playing chess at such a difficult time, of course that's no good. But to hit him does no credit to you as a commander, or as a person in general." Later that member of the Military Council became secretary of the Astrakhan regional committee of the party, but that was after Stalin's death. He's a decent person, well deserving of respect.[49]

Budyonny also used to punch people in the face. I have already mentioned an instance when he hit a soldier who was on guard duty. Georgy Zakharov[50] also would hit his subordinates. Later he became deputy commander of the Stalingrad Front. I had a high regard for him and respected him as a man who knew military matters. He was a warrior devoted to the Soviet state and the Communist Party, but he was very unrestrained about using his fists. At the Stalingrad Front, to tell the truth, I never saw Yeremenko lay a hand on anyone. I only knew of such instances from his life before that.

Meanwhile I had given Stalin the name of Gordov. Stalin said: "All right, we'll approve Gordov." Molotov was sitting there as usual. Stalin said to him: "Take a notebook and pencil, and write an order appointing Gordov." And soon Gordov began taking up the duties of commander of the Front.[51]

We began constructing a defense. After a little while Bodin was recalled to Moscow and appointed deputy to Vasilevsky. Thus he received a big promotion. The character references I had frequently given Stalin about him influenced that appointment. I was simply entranced by Bodin, and even today I would not retract anything good that I have said about this man. He died in battle long ago, in 1942.[52] He was a remarkable general. Today I don't remember who was chief of staff of the Stalingrad Front at first. Bagramyan had already been recalled to Moscow. I was even a little concerned as to whether he had been recalled with considerations threatening to him personally. He left, and after that I no longer encountered Bagramyan on the front lines. I only heard about him, and was overjoyed that he was being appreciated for his worth and was occupying high posts. He distinguished himself greatly during the war.

The Germans began to bring their troops closer to Stalingrad, and our armies began to engage them. This was in July, and the heat was terrible. Gordov and I made a trip to visit the 62nd Army commanded by Kolpakchi. He was reporting on the situation to us when we suddenly heard shooting. It was artillery fire, and this surprised us. We rushed out of the building to look. Our tanks were retreating directly toward us, and they were keeping up a steady fire, but they were also being fired on. In short, it was an incomprehensible scene. What was actually happening at the front lines? Kolpakchi, the commander of the army, had not reported anything alarming to us, and suddenly the enemy was directly approaching the position of the army headquarters. Gordov and I went out. A haystack stood there. It was not very high, but still it was a kind of elevation. We climbed up on it and began looking through our binoculars trying to find out what was happening. But it was impossible to understand anything.

It turned out that the enemy had made a breakthrough and was driving us back. The Germans had forced a crossing of the Chir River,[53] and farther to the south they had taken Tsimlyanskaya[54] and were directly threatening our positions. Something unbelievable must have happened on the Southern Front. We had received no news from there, and so we didn't know what was going on to the south of us. Later we found out that catastrophe had struck us on a much bigger scale than we could have imagined. Not only had our Southwestern Front been smashed, but the Southern Front had also been rolled over by the enemy. We couldn't use our solid defenses around Rostov, because the enemy bypassed Rostov. Our whole line of defense in the area collapsed, and I don't know how many of our people were taken prisoner, how many were killed, and how many fled across the Don.

I had been there earlier when a fortified zone was under construction outside Rostov. It was being built by Kulik,[55] who had been assigned by Stalin. In Rostov he had had his own headquarters, and he carried out the necessary work fairly persistently. A great deal was done: antitank ditches were dug, earthen fortifications were thrown up, and artillery was put in position. All of this was constructed 20 or 30 kilometers from Rostov, and the hope was that the enemy would not be able to take Rostov on the run. The Sea of Azov and the Don River covered the flanks, and the fortifications were built facing north. The command of this fortified zone was subordinate to the Southern Front. How the enemy had reached the Don to the east of Rostov we could not know. What in the world had happened to Rostov? Later we found out that our troops had fled and the enemy had occupied Rostov without a battle. The Germans had reached the Don east of Rostov and had forced the river. As a result we simply abandoned Rostov.[56] Malinovsky was removed from his post [as commander of the Southern Front]. And the threat of Stalin's disfavor hung over him.

After crushing our troops outside Rostov the enemy quickly occupied Tsimlyanskaya. The fall of Tsimlyanskaya was a direct threat to the lower Volga region. From Tsimlyanskaya to the Volga was just a stone's throw. It was only about 150 kilometers from Tsimlyanskaya and Kalach on the Don to the Volga. I've even begun to forget the distances now, although then I measured them fairly frequently, riding in my motor vehicle. Gordov and I relieved Kolpakchi, the commander of the 62nd Army, of his post because of his poor management, and in the next month appointed Lopatin[57] to replace him. Fighting with the Germans was breaking out along the approaches to the Don near Kalach, and at Tsimlyanskaya they were already on the Don.

Gordov and I decided one day to travel to the 64th Army to make the acquaintance of its commander, Chuikov.[58] I had not known Chuikov before then, but had heard that he was a fighting general who had been a military adviser to Chiang Kai-shek.[59] He had just returned from China, immediately taking command of the 64th Army, which had been in reserve. That army was located to the south of us. We drove over the steppe toward it. We had had no alarming reports from that flank, but when we arrived we encountered a terrible scene. Semibarren steppe lands stretch out here, inhabited by the Kalmyk people.[60] Much of the soil is not suitable for cultivation. Across the steppes like white swans against a brown background in scattered formation the soldiers of the 64th Army were heading eastward away from the Don. The enemy had driven them back to the river, and taking off their uniforms, wearing just their underwear, they had swum across—whoever could—and retreated eastward. We arrived at the location of the headquarters. In a small patch of brush and scrub trees, there were vehicles and everything else necessary for a headquarters. There were no buildings. The pathways were well planned, clean and orderly, and there we made the acquaintance of the new commander of the army.

Chuikov was elegantly dressed. His clothing was unusual, not what the other generals were wearing during the war. He was holding a riding crop.[61] He gave the not especially favorable impression of a man who was putting on airs. Gordov went for him with all the rough manner and cursing that he was known for. After all, the army had lost its leadership. In view of the terrible situation and also the fact that Chuikov had just arrived from China and outwardly appeared to have odd mannerisms, he created an unfavorable impression. We were obliged to raise the question of replacing him. Chuikov was relieved of his duties; he was transferred to an operational group, and Shumilov[62] was appointed to replace him as head of the 64th Army. Shumilov had previously been deputy commander of the 21st Army. Chuikov was transferred to the reserve units of our Front. Shumilov, when he took over the army, asked that Serdyuk,[63] a member of the Military Council, be transferred with him. He said that they were used to and respected each other. We conceded to this request and transferred Serdyuk to become a member of the Military Council of the 64th Army. Thus Shumilov and Serdyuk continued to command this army right up until the routing of the troops of Paulus[64] at Stalingrad. Later, after the defeat of Paulus, I met Shumilov and Serdyuk when they came to our positions in the battle of the Kursk salient and were deployed along the Donets. By then their army was called the Seventh Guards Army: because of its success in the fighting at Stalingrad the 64th Army was renamed a Guards unit. It was brought up to full strength and held a sector of the front to the north of Belgorod.[65]

For the time being, Gordov and I assigned Chuikov to gather together whatever remnants of troops could be found and to organize them into units to go into action against the enemy. Chuikov undertook this task. He quickly organized a detachment (I don't remember its size) and distinguished himself by striking blows at the enemy troops who were rushing toward the Volga. This was before autumn began. Meanwhile it turned out that the commander of the 62nd Army[66] had deceived the commander of the Stalingrad Front, who by that time was Yeremenko.[67] Now someone new had to be appointed commander of the 62nd Army, which had retreated directly to Stalingrad and was supposed to defend it. By that time I had formed a very good impression of Chuikov. We called Stalin. He asked:

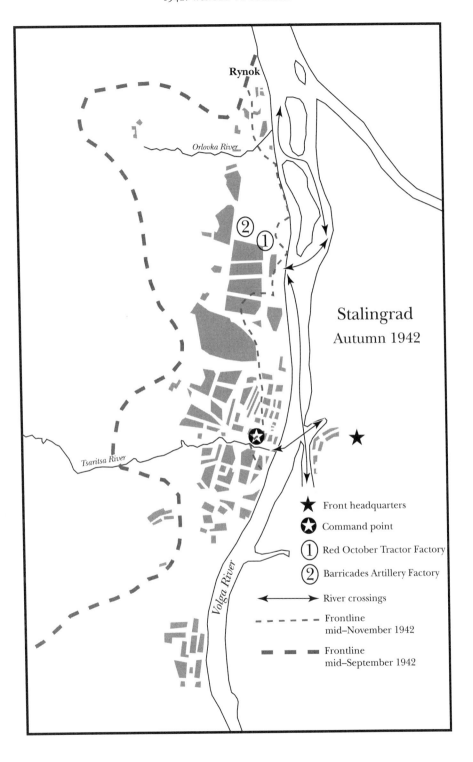

Rynok

Orlovka River

② ①

Stalingrad
Autumn 1942

Tsaritsa River

Volga River

★ Front headquarters

✪ Command point

① Red October Tractor Factory

② Barricades Artillery Factory

⟷ River crossings

- - - Frontline
mid–November 1942

▬ ▬ Frontline
mid–September 1942

"Who do you recommend to head the 62nd Army, which will be right in the city?"

I said: "Vasily Ivanovich Chuikov." For some reason his first name and patronymic were always used, which was rare in the army. I don't know why that happened.

Stalin asked: "But won't he make a mess of this army with his drinking?"

I answered: "Comrade Stalin, I've never heard that he was a drunkard or that he could mess up an army because of his drinking. I don't know what your source is for such reports about Chuikov. Chuikov has shown himself to be a very good commander of a detachment that he himself organized. I think that in the future, too, he will be a good organizer and a good commander of the 62nd Army."

Stalin said: "All right, appoint him. We will approve him."

This happened after Yeremenko was already commander [of the Front]. The enemy was pressing us back at the time. I forget exactly when Yeremenko arrived with his Front headquarters. At first a separate sector was assigned to him and separate troops allocated to him. He was part of the Stalingrad Front with certain special powers. That was incomprehensible to me then, and even today I can't figure out what it meant. He arrived and introduced himself. I made his acquaintance at that time, but I didn't understand what authority he had and what special powers were assigned to him. But once he had reported, that's the way it was. All was well. In war, anyone that can shoot is welcome. And so he began his duties there.

The hot summer of 1942 was ending. It had been hot in all respects.

1. Voronezh is due east of northeastern Ukraine. Yelets is some 130 kilometers farther north, due east of southern Belarus. Kashira is about 100 kilometers south of Moscow. [SS]

2. Livny is in Oryol province, about 120 kilometers southeast of Oryol and 60 kilometers west of Yelets. [SS]

3. His rank was in fact lieutenant general.

4. The village of Bolshaya Martynovka is situated on the Sal River, a tributary of the Don.

5. The Yelets operation was an offensive operation carried out by the right wing of the Southwestern Front between December 6 and 16, 1941.

6. The Tenth Army was formed anew in November 1941. Incorporated into the Southwestern Front in February 1942, it was commanded by Major General V. S. Popov. As for his being "young," he was born in 1894, the same year as N. S. Khrushchev. See Biographies.

7. The Tenth Army was commanded by Lieutenant General F. I. Golikov from November 1941 to February 1942. See Biographies.

8. The First Guards Cavalry Corps, commanded by Major General P. A. Belov. See Biographies.

9. Mtsensk is some 50 kilometers northeast of Oryol in the direction of Tula, which is about 180 kilometers south of Moscow. [SS]

10. Solnechnogorsk is northwest of Moscow, in the direction of the city of Tver. [SS]

11. Tim is in Kursk province, about 60 kilometers east of Kursk. [SS]

12. Barvenkovo and Lozovaya (Ukrainian names Barvinkove and Lozova) are in eastern Ukraine, roughly midway between Kharkov and Donetsk. [SS] Khrushchev is referring to the Barvenkovo-Lozovaya offensive operation of January 18–31, 1942.

13. The village of Svatovo-Luchko (or Svatovo) is in Lugansk province of eastern Ukraine, about

100 kilometers northeast of Barvenkovo and 140 kilometers southeast of Kharkov. [SS]

14. The Sixth Cavalry Corps, commanded by Major General A. F. Bychkovsky.

15. Major General A. A. Grechko commanded the Fifth Cavalry Corps from January to April 1942. See Biographies.

16. It was Major General F. A. Parkhomenko. He commanded the First Cavalry Corps.

17. Several tank brigades—the exact number varied—were fighting in the area.

18. Slavyansk (in Ukrainian Slovyansk) is some 50 kilometers east of Barvenkovo. Balakleya is farther north, about 80 kilometers southeast of Kharkov. [SS]

19. Mayaki is a small village about 15 kilometers north of Slavyansk on the Seversky Donets River. [AH]

20. At that spot the Sukhoi Torets and the Kazenny Torets Rivers converge before flowing into the Seversky Donets River, also referred to as the Donets River. [SS]

21. Major General F. M. Kharitonov, who had commanded the Ninth Army, died on May 28, 1943. See Biographies.

22. Lieutenant General A. M. Gorodnyansky. See Biographies.

23. Lieutenant General K. P. Podlas. See Biographies.

24. On the events at Lake Khasan, see note 8 to the chapter "The Second World War Approaches." [SS]

25. Major General L. V. Bobkin.

26. Lieutenant General K. A. Gurov. See Biographies.

27. Divisional Commissar F. E. Bokov, who had been a military commissar of the General Staff since August 1941. See Biographies.

28. S. M. Shtemenko was at that time a deputy chief of an Area Command in the Operational Administration of the General Staff. See Biographies.

29. Lieutenant General A. D. Shtevnev.

30. The number of troops lost was about 250,000. [GS]

31. The Bolsheviks had previously assumed that the class struggle would grow *less* intense as the construction of socialism proceeded. Stalin's theory to the contrary served to justify increasing repression and prevented anyone from arguing that the time had come to move toward greater legality and democracy. The same theory later served similar purposes in Mao's China. [SS]

32. Here Khrushchev corrects Stalin, who accidentally or deliberately mixed together different events. It was the Second Army, commanded by Cavalry General A. V. Samsonov, which fell into enemy encirclement in August and September 1914. The First Army, commanded by Cavalry General P. K. von Rennenkampf, failed to come to

its aid. Then at the time of the Lodz operation of October and November 1914, von Rennenkampf failed to close off the escape route of a German assault group (commanded by General R. Scheffer) that had fallen into a pocket. After this he was removed from command and retired. It was the Soviet authorities who arrested him around 1918 and put him on trial. He was shot (not hanged) in 1919 in Taganrog, around the time that Khrushchev took part in the liberation of Taganrog from the Whites. Thus Khrushchev could recall the events of 1914 as reported in the von Rennenkampf case in the local newspapers. As for the gendarme officer S. N. Myasoyedov who was exposed in 1915 as an accessory to German spies, he was close to the Russian war minister V. A. Sukhomlinov's wife, who had been recruited by the German-Austrian intelligence service. Myasoyedov and the other "points men" in the minister's case were sentenced. Sukhomlinov himself was arrested only in 1916 and put on trial in September 1917, but in 1918 German agents helped him escape to Germany.

33. Aleksei I. Kirichenko was later, in the 1950s, to become a secretary of the CPSU Central Committee and a member of its Presidium.

34. On June 12, 1942, in Kharkov, General Georg Stumme gave a briefing about the planned offensive at the headquarters of the 40th Tank Corps. Land Forces Staff Officer Major Joachim Reichel flew from Kharkov on the night of June 20 in the small courier plane Feseler-Storch, taking with him secret documents about the operations plan of the German forces for the entire summer of 1942. Near the settlement of Belyanka (Nezhegol), the airplane was shot down by Soviet soldiers of the 74th Infantry Division. The plane landed on its belly. Two officers and the pilot were killed, and Major Reichel tried to run away with the briefcase of documents. He was killed, and the briefcase with its papers was handed over to Soviet headquarters. So the plans for the German offensive to the south were discovered, but Stalin did not trust the information obtained. [SK]

35. These documents were later published in Russian translation in the book *Sovershenno sekretno! Tol'ko dlya komandovaniya: Nemetskie dokumenty o Vtoroi Mirovoi Voine* (Top secret! For command staff only: German documents About the Second World War; Moscow: Nauka, 1967). [SK]

36. Major General V. N. Gordov. See Biographies.

37. Major General of Artillery K. S. Moskalenko commanded this army from March to July 1942. See Biographies.

38. Kalach on the Don was about 80 kilometers west of Stalingrad. [SS]

39. A burka is a broad felt cloak, originally used by native peoples of the Caucasus and later adopted by the Cossacks. [GS/SS]

40. The Barrikady (Barricades) and Krasnyi Oktiabr' (Red October ) plants were in Stalingrad. Barrikady was a machine-building factory that produced artillery pieces, including large-caliber pieces for the navy. Khrushchev is referring to these armaments and this factory (without mentioning its name) in his account of the battle for Stalingrad. Krasnyi Oktiabr' was a metallurgical factory that produced metal from steel scrap. It also produced rolled steel. [SK]

41. Deputy Commander of the Stalingrad Military District Major General F. I. Tolbukhin, who was assigned responsibility for the fortified area. See Biographies.

42. In July and August 1942 the 64th Army was commanded by Lieutenant General V. I. Chuikov and the 62nd Army by Major General V. Ya. Kolpakchi. See Biographies.

43. This was the 38th Mechanized Brigade.

44. That is, in the southeastern part of the Belorussian SSR. [SS]

45. From the time of Budyonny's First Cavalry Army in the Civil War.

46. Sukhumi is a city on the eastern coast of the Black Sea and the capital of Abkhazia, an autonomous republic in Georgia. (Its Abkhaz name is Sukhum.) Many holiday dachas for Soviet leaders were situated there. [SS]

47. A. I. Mikoyan. See Biographies.

48. Colonel General A. I. Yeremenko, to whom Stalin refers, was at that time in the reserve at the disposal of the Stavka. Lieutenant General A. A. Vlasov, at that time in command of the Second Assault Army of the Volkhov Front, did not manage to extricate his army from enemy encirclement, into which it had fallen in the course of the Lyubansk operation, which had been designed to break through the blockade of Leningrad. It was after this, in summer 1942, that he committed treason. See Biographies.

49. F. A. Mamonov was first secretary of the Astrakhan province committee of the CPSU from 1950 to 1954.

50. Lieutenant General G. F. Zakharov. Khrushchev gives his first name so that he should not be confused with Major General M. V. Zakharov, who was at that time chief of staff of the Kaliningrad Front. See Biographies.

51. Lieutenant General V. N. Gordov was commander of the Stalingrad Front in July and August 1942. See Biographies.

52. Major General P. I. Bodin perished in battle near Ordzhonikidze (now again Vladikavkaz) on November 2, 1942. See Biographies.

53. The Chir River is a tributary of the Don. [SS]

54. Tsimlyanskaya was just downstream of the place where the Chir River entered the Don. This is near the place where the village of Nizhny Chir now stands on the shore of the Tsimlyanskoye reservoir, which was created after the war. Tsimlyanskaya may have been flooded by the reservoir. [AH]

55. During these weeks Major General G. I. Kulik was regarded as being "at the disposal of the people's commissar of defense"—that is, of Stalin. See Biographies.

56. This second abandonment of Rostov by Soviet forces took place on July 24, 1942.

57. Major General A. I. Lopatin was commander of the 62nd Army from August to October 1942. See Biographies.

58. V. I. Chuikov. See Biographies.

59. Chiang Kai-shek (1887–1975) led the Chinese Nationalist Party known as the Kuomintang after the death of its founder Sun Yat-sen in 1925. In the 1920s the Soviet Union provided military advisers to the Kuomintang. Later, civil war broke out between the Kuomintang and the Communist Party of China. [SS]

60. The Kalmyks are a traditionally nomadic Buddhist people who live on the northeastern fringes of the Caucasus, in the semidesert steppe near the northwestern coast of the Caspian Sea. They are believed to be descendants of the Oirats or Western Mongols who migrated to the lower Volga region in the seventeenth century. [SS]

61. Chuikov was also distinguished by the fact that he always wore white gloves, not so much because he wanted to look elegant as from the desire to hide the eczema on his hands. [SK]

62. M. S. Shumilov. See Biographies.

63. Z. T. Serdyuk. See Biographies.

64. General (later Field Marshal) Friedrich Paulus commanded the German forces at the battle of Stalingrad. See Biographies.

65. Belgorod is in southwestern Russia, some 80 kilometers north of Kharkov. [SS]

66. That is, Major General A. I. Lopatin.

67. Colonel General A. I. Yeremenko was commander of the Stalingrad Front from August to December 1942. See Biographies.

Enemy forces concentrated their efforts in the direction of Kalach.[1] In the case of our Russian rivers that flow south, the right, or west, bank dominates the left bank. If the Germans were to approach the Don River and occupy the high right bank, that could enable them to force a river crossing. Enemy forces would be able to suppress resistance for a great distance by using artillery and machine-gun fire. Under cover of this fire, they could force a crossing of the Don at Kalach or elsewhere. We did everything in our power to try to prevent this from happening. The Stalingrad tractor factory gave us a great deal of assistance by repairing tanks that had been damaged in combat. Relying on this aid, we gathered together all the damaged and worn-out military vehicles that we had, took them to the tractor factory, and mobilized the workers to repair them.

I use the term "mobilized." This could be misinterpreted, as though I meant that we used some sort of pressure to make the workers and engineers do this repair work. But there was nothing like that. The blue-collar and white-collar workers, the engineers, and all the inhabitants of Stalingrad gave everything they could for the battlefront. We rounded up quite a few of these tanks. As soon as we said that we were making an appeal to them, the workers and engineers immediately got down to it and began repairing the tanks, and there were quite a few of these tanks. From these tanks we later created the material basis for an entire tank army and called it the First Tank Army. I don't know today exactly how many tanks that army had or what tank systems they were. There were only a few T-34s. Most of those tanks were of obsolete design; they didn't really meet the requirements of our tank forces, either in the thickness of their armor or the caliber of their guns. They were rather poor and weak. Nevertheless they were tanks! It was armor of some kind, after all, not just human skin. So we placed great hopes in that tank army.

I remember what joy we felt when we completed the repair work and organized that tank army. General Moskalenko[2] was appointed commander of the army. He was the first of our tank commanders in the USSR. We deployed his army in the direction of Kalach. After crossing the Don, his army spread out along the right, or west, bank to block the path of enemy forces speeding toward Kalach. Today I must confess that our hopes then were somewhat exaggerated—that is, the hopes we placed in that tank army. Once that army had crossed the Don we breathed a little easier because we thought it would prevent the enemy from reaching the Don unchallenged, in one fell swoop.

The commander of the front, Gordov, and I moved the command post of the Front to a small village just outside Kalach, on the east bank of the Don.[3] We occupied a little house on the very edge of the river, actually the second house from the riverbank in the western part of the village. We made this our headquarters because German bombers were constantly flying over and bombing our positions. We had an artillery battery whose guns covered the river crossing, and that attracted the attention of the bombers. They were constantly making turns in the air over that village, right over the building we were in. We hoped that it would never occur to the enemy that the commander of our Front and a member of its Military Council would be located in such a place. Our communications center was set up there as well. All this was camouflaged, and we took up residence in the building.

The following incident occurred. Vasilevsky,[4] the chief of the General Staff, came to visit our Front. We had a little talk, and he acquainted himself with the situation. It came time to retire for the evening. He and I stretched out on some hay. We spread out the hay and rigged up a row of poles and laths overhead to protect ourselves from dampness and from the sun. For a long time we couldn't get to sleep. We were just starting to doze off when I heard a great commotion. It woke Vasilevsky also. It turned out that Moskalenko had arrived. He arrived in a very nervous and excited state. I asked him: "What's the matter?"

In general, Moskalenko was a rather excitable person, and I knew that. But in this case he was more beside himself than usual, cursing the tank troops: "What a bunch of so-and-sos. They don't want to fight. I had to threaten them with a revolver to force them to move forward."

I said to him: "First of all you've got to calm down." But he began getting excited again and couldn't restrain himself in any way. I said: "What exactly is this all about?"

He answered: "Well, we lost a certain number of tanks and now the tank troops are acting up." He spoke very unkindly about them. But he was a very unrestrained person. That was his nature. Nevertheless I held him in high regard because of his unbounded devotion to our homeland and his extraordinary bravery. So I suggested to Vasilevsky: "Let's go have a look at the tank army."

It was a moonlit night. You know what it's like in the south of Russia. You can practically read a newspaper by the light of the moon. We got in a vehicle and drove off. We had to drive all the way through Kalach since the river crossing was there. We went quickly up the steep west bank, where I thought the tank army was located, to the west of Kalach, but it turned out that the army had retreated to the bank of the Don. We were driving without head-lights by the light of the moon. It was quiet, without any gunfire, as though we were in a peaceful, quiet Ukrainian night of the kind whose glories were sung by Gogol.[5] We climbed out of the vehicle to look around. Moskalenko led us to the scene [of earlier fighting]: "Here," he said, "we smashed one of their guns with our tanks." Sure enough, an enemy artillery piece had been put out of commission, and the bodies of the enemy artillerymen were lying around. In short, our tanks had been doing their job. German antitank mines and antipersonnel mines were lying scattered all around. We could see that this meant the enemy had brought up army engineers and was preparing to force a crossing of the Don.

But our tank army was quickly knocked out of commission. We dragged whatever we could into the gullies formed by floods along the bank of the river. As a rule such gullies are overgrown with bushes, which offered favor-able conditions for camouflaging and concealing the damaged tanks. We decided to try repairing the tanks right there and then, not to drag them back to Stalingrad. Better to repair them right on the spot, especially since the [Stalingrad tractor] factory was nearby [and workers from there could be brought to do the repairs]. The workers arrived with their tools, found places to work in the crevices along the riverbank, and began doing repairs. We assigned Kirichenko, a member of the Military Council, to remain with the workers the whole time and help them organize the repair work. Enemy probes located us rather quickly. It turned out that we were visible from the air after all; the camouflage wasn't good enough. After all, these weren't woods, just bushes. The enemy began bombing us and really besieged us with persistent bombing. We suffered losses of both people and tanks. Of course the enemy thought that we had fully intact military vehicles here as well as those being repaired. In spite of all this we did manage to repair some equipment, but the tank army no longer had primary significance for the forces of our Front. That army no longer had any real possibilities because it had lost a major portion of its constituent forces. Besides, its tanks were old, with worn-out equipment. In short, we were left virtually without tanks.

The enemy advanced right up to the Don. Although we still had troops on the right bank, the enemy was already firing on the airstrip on the left bank. We had located our airstrip for communications aircraft not far from our command post. We had U-2 planes[6] based there. The enemy could see this from the high right bank and was firing at the airstrip right over our little building. We had already grown accustomed to artillery fire and to constant bombing from the air, all this being aimed at our artillery battery that was covering the river crossing. It was a small-caliber battery, as I recall, with 37-millimeter guns, but on one occasion we almost suffered a disaster. As an enemy plane was making one more pass over us, we were warned that two planes were heading right for our little building. From the ground it always looks as though planes are flying right at you with their guns firing precisely in your direction.

Knowing this, the commander and I calmly continued our conversation, sitting on the porch of the house. We had a little table between us. Bozhko, a member of our bodyguard, suddenly shouted that the planes were dropping bombs on us. We jumped off the porch and lay down, and an explosion erupted. Bozhko reported that our car had been hit and the driver wounded, my driver Zhuravlev. I went over to where our vehicles were. The drivers had been eating breakfast just then; this happened in the morning. Our camouflaged vehicles were under cherry trees in an orchard. Apparently the enemy pilots had caught sight of them and dropped the bombs.

We were lucky that the building remained intact. Zhuravlev was suffering. He had been cut badly. When the enemy dropped the bombs, the drivers and bodyguards hugged the ground, but the explosion sent fragments flying in a cone-shaped whirlwind and Zhuravlev was hit. Our vehicle had also been badly damaged. No one else suffered. The tenacity of the artillery battery next to us was amazing. No matter how many times the German planes flew over, after the bombing our artillerymen would rise out of the dust and the artillery battery would still be alive, firing away. Those artillerymen showed tremendous perseverance in carrying out their difficult duty as soldiers.

I have already told about Yeremenko joining us. A certain sector was assigned to him, but that didn't last long. Stalin called and said that the decision had been made to appoint him the new commander of the troops of the Stalingrad Front and to assign Gordov to be his deputy. Thus, Yeremenko took command,[7] and Gordov, after surrendering command, began assuming his new responsibilities. The situation around Stalingrad was growing worse all the time. The enemy had superior forces and after forcing the Don, kept up a persistent effort to break through to the Volga. We had done everything we could to make use of the strong defensive position that the Don represented. But with the Germans' obvious superiority in artillery and especially in aircraft, it was not a great difficulty for them to force a crossing of the Don. Soon fighting broke out in the immediate outskirts of Stalingrad, to the south of the city. Stubborn fighting went on both day and night.

I must say that the new commander pleased me because of both his efficient management and, I would say, the military precision with which he directed the troops. I supported Yerememko. Although I wasn't on bad terms with Gordov, I considered Yeremenko unquestionably of higher quality than Gordov as a military leader and commander. Yeremenko and I made use of Gordov later by assigning him to especially dangerous sectors so that he could help the commanders in those places put up more stubborn resistance to the enemy. And Gordov did everything he could. I didn't have any sense that he was particularly dissatisfied, or maybe he was able to suppress such feelings within himself after he had been removed from the post of commander.

But Gordov was soon put out of action; he was wounded. When I received a report of the circumstances under which he was wounded, it troubled me. I was surprised and wondered how Gordov had placed himself in that situation. He had ended up being wounded and was carried away from that location by some communications troops who happened to be there at the time. If they hadn't been there, he would have been taken captive. I didn't want to let myself think that Gordov had somehow done this deliberately. On the other hand, the circumstances of his being there were inexplicable to me. Gordov could not have failed to understand the danger he had placed himself in.

It was reported to me later that in the area to which Yeremenko and I had sent Gordov some very heavy fighting was going on. When he was wounded, we had hardly any troops left in that sector. One or two tanks came by, and the tank men warned him that we no longer had any troops in the area. He paid no attention and continued to occupy a position on some high ground, together with his adjutant. Then an enemy plane flew over and dropped bombs. Gordov was wounded by a bomb, suffered shell shock, and was rendered helpless. The enemy would unquestionably have seized him, but a wagonload of communications troops happened to come by. They were rolling up telephone wire as they retreated, and they found the general. He was loaded onto the wagon and taken away from the front lines. Gordov was placed in a hospital, and the hospital quickly sent him off to Kuibyshev, where his family was located.[8] In Kuibyshev he received medical treatment and recuperated and later returned to the front, but not to the Stalingrad area.[9] I didn't meet him again until, as I recall, 1944, when it seems to me he commanded the Third Guards Army, reaching the border of Poland with that army. He fought well and successfully to the end of the war. He died after the war, in 1951, as a result of an arbitrary act by Stalin. He was arrested and executed.

So that was the unpleasant incident that occurred with Gordov in 1942. The memory of him that remains with me is one of a general with dual, opposing characteristics. I had a high opinion of him because of his tireless energy, quickness to respond and act, and contempt for danger. He carried this literally to the point of irrationality, where he risked his life when it was not required of a commander—he moved around when the bombs and shells were flying. Several times I observed him take off his service cap and walk freely among the bullets. I remember one occasion when he and I were on our way to visit Shumilov, elements of whose 64th Army and of Tanaschishin's mechanized corps were engaged in battle.[10] Tanaschishin was a very brave man. I saw that Gordov conducted himself in an equally courageous manner in the same difficult situation, and I regret the undeserved end that came to this man who gave his whole life, all of his knowledge and strength, to the homeland and to the Red Army. He gave everything he had for our victory, but after the battle with our enemy had culminated in our total victory he was arrested and executed on Stalin's order!

So as not to have to return to this question later, I will now tell what became known to me about the reason for his execution. I learned about this from a conversation Stalin had with Beria. Gordov and Kulik came to Moscow. (Kulik had previously been a marshal of the Soviet Union, but during the war he was stripped of his rank and title as marshal, and at that time [in 1950] he was simply a general.) They were on duty somewhere outside Moscow, but, it seems, they had rooms at the Hotel Moskva. They got drunk. (Both of them were inclined to drink excessively. Kulik especially was a heavy drinker. Gordov was also a drinker, but it seems to me he was less addicted.) They had both fallen out of favor with Stalin, and the war was over, and apparently they felt dissatisfied and stirred up. They got drunk and had a conversation about how the war had been conducted and how it ended. Apparently in their discussion they analyzed why our army had retreated at the beginning of the war. In this connection they dragged Stalin over the coals.

From the conversation between Stalin and Beria I remember that Kulik had said: "A fish starts to rot from the head." It was clear that by the "head" he meant Stalin. Of course Stalin couldn't tolerate anyone talking like that, and this conversation became known for a very simple reason. They were under surveillance, and their conversations were being monitored. When they came to Moscow, they were placed in hotel rooms equipped with listening devices. Thus their entire conversation immediately became known and was reported to Stalin, who then destroyed these men. I think this was extremely dishonorable on Stalin's part. It seems that Stalin was willing to eavesdrop even on himself, never mind those he no longer trusted.[11]

They were honorable men, devoted to the Soviet government. I had a different assessment of each of these two men. I had a very poor opinion of Kulik's abilities as a commander, but I had respect for Gordov in that regard. I felt he had excellent qualities as a commander. He proved this in action both at Stalingrad and after Stalingrad, when he commanded armies. Everybody has shortcomings. Despite all of Kulik's shortcomings as a commander, he was an honorable person. He devoted his whole life to the Red Army and served it to the best of his abilities, both mental and physical. Before the war Stalin overestimated him as an artillery expert and placed him in charge of artillery for the entire Red Army. This was wrong. Kulik was not capable of handling this task. Stalin himself bears responsibility for the fact that he assigned this man to a post that he really wasn't up to. But why execute him when the war was already over? That was both cruel and unjust, an abuse of power. Once Stalin had gained complete power, he was able to do whatever he wanted, and he did. He both killed people and pardoned them.

But let me return to Stalingrad. It was August 1942. The enemy was continuing to attack our troops. We were putting up stubborn resistance. Our headlong flight, or retreat that bordered on flight, which had characterized the situation in 1941—of that there was no longer even a trace. Our troops, if they retreated, did so only because of the pressure of the enemy's superior numbers or as a result of overwhelming artillery fire and the enemy's superiority in the air and in weapons and equipment in general. We were still very weak both in the quality of our armed forces and the number of weapons we had. We didn't have enough field artillery, machine guns, or antiaircraft weapons. The circumstances of this duel were far from equal on the two sides. In spite of that, our troops fought heroically and retreated only when the situation became hopeless. It was no longer headlong flight, but retreat from one position to the next.

The enemy subjected Stalingrad to a very cruel bombing raid. (I don't remember the exact date. It's difficult to keep all this in one's memory when so many years have gone by.)[12] Wave after wave of planes flew in and bombed the city. The entire city was in flames. The commander and I decided to transfer our headquarters and everything that didn't need to be kept in the city to the left, or east, bank of the Volga, but the commander and I and the operational part of our headquarters staff remained in Stalingrad. The head-quarters was located by the Tsaritsa River.[13] There was a deep gully there formed by many years of rainwater and melted snow. This gully surrounded by high banks was used as the site of our command post. I don't know exactly when the command post was constructed. When we arrived there it was already built. I think it was actually organized for some other headquar-ters, not a Front headquarters, but something of much higher rank. Everything was done too much to Stalin's taste. For example, the walls were covered with wood paneling. (Incidentally, all of Stalin's dachas had oak paneling.) Also a long corridor had been constructed—that is, tunnels going deep into the side of the hill. All of this work had been done very skillfully. Even a toilet had been installed. Military men couldn't even think of such a thing. But I never heard any conversation, either before or since, about why such an elaborate command post had been prepared. Opposite the entrance to this underground command post was an old cotton-wool factory, about 100 to 250 meters away. There were defenses around the entrance to protect against shock waves from explosions. Structures to prevent the doors from being blown down were in place, and they were fairly thick and strong.

When the bombing began, the entire city was set on fire. Ordinary civil-ians as well as the municipal defense council (an organization chaired by the first secretary of the party's province committee, Chuyanov)[14] did everything they could. But what could they really do? There were so many fires! The fire-fighting equipment of any city would have been insufficient for this task. The Germans were bombing with virtual impunity. Antiaircraft batteries fired at them, but that didn't stop them, because the antiaircraft fire was not accurate.

The enemy was coming very close to the city. Breaking through our defenses, enemy tanks reached the Volga to the north of the city near the settlement of Rynok.[15] A very dangerous situation had arisen. We had no mobile forces or reserves to prevent the Germans from entering the city from the north. In this case the enemy would immediately seize our facto-ries, above all the Stalingrad tractor factory. The loss of that facility would be a palpable blow. The enemy would then be able to break through into the old part of the city consisting of sturdy stone buildings. The tractor factory itself, with its many workshops, occupied a fairly substantial territory. It was in fact a veritable fortress, and it would be very hard to drive the enemy out of there. At this point the workers of the Stalingrad tractor factory gave tremendous assistance to our army. Tanks were being repaired at the factory, and the workers who tested those tanks were right there on the spot. Military men were there as well, to take charge of their tanks after they had been repaired. It was necessary to make use of these forces. The workers testing the tanks and the military inspectors barred the Germans' way and prevented them from breaking through into the city. They were the ones who in the initial stages organized the defense in that area. Later we transferred units from other sectors of our Front to that area and organized a defensive line facing northward.

By reaching the Volga, the Germans achieved the goal of disrupting navigation on that river—although by then there wasn't really much traffic on it. Nevertheless it was still possible to make use of this means of water transport. When we had just arrived in Stalingrad, the headquarters of a military district was still located there. General Gerasimenko[16] commanded the district. I knew Gerasimenko well from Kiev. Before the war he had been deputy commander of the Kiev Special Military District (or KOVO). I considered him a good general who would do everything he possibly could. When we arrived in Stalingrad, this headquarters organization that I have mentioned was transformed into a command staff for an army, and the proposal was made that Gerasimenko take command of the 28th Army in Astrakhan. He decided to move his base from Stalingrad to Astrakhan by taking a boat down the Volga.[17] He made this trip with great difficulty, undergoing bombing raids more than once, but eventually he made it, and apparently without suffering any casualties, and he set up his new headquarters in Astrakhan.

The enemy very stubbornly pressed his offensive from the north side of Stalingrad. His calculation evidently was that a breakthrough into the city could be made more readily from that direction, and in that way he could achieve the encirclement of our troops in Stalingrad itself. Very heavy fighting broke out in the Rynok area. I remember that General Krylov flew in to join us at that time. Later he became commander in chief of our strategic missile forces. He came to us from Sevastopol.[18] He had surrendered Sevastopol not long before that. The headquarters personnel of the Coastal Army[19] had flown from Sevastopol to Turkey; the Turks had let them pass through, and they had been able to reach our jurisdiction. We assigned Krylov at that point to command a troop formation for organizing our defenses in the Rynok area, where this especially difficult situation had developed.

It was at this same time that the writer Konstantin Simonov[20] arrived. He came to see me and asked which part of the front lines he could go to. I told him that right then the most dangerous sector, where the enemy was most stubbornly attempting to break through into the city, was the area around Rynok, that our forces there were not very numerous, and that we had just sent General Krylov there to organize the defenses and prevent the enemy from achieving his aims in that area. Simonov said: "All right, I'll go there too." And he went.

Krylov organized a good solid defense, and the Germans were not able to take the whole area around Rynok, although they drove a wedge into our defenses in some places at the cost of heavy casualties. And to the north of Rynok the Germans had broken through to the Volga. We were in a situation of semi-encirclement. We no longer had rail links with the sector to the north of us; in our rear was the Volga River, and we had no substantial means for making a river crossing, if necessary. Transport facilities for crossing the river had either been removed by us or sunk by the enemy. The only river craft at our disposal were of small size; only small boats or cutters were being used to cross the Volga. When this difficult situation arose, we did organize a means of crossing the river [a pontoon bridge] to reach the east bank of the Volga, and it was actually in the Rynok area. But after the enemy had broken through to the riverbank in that area, we exerted every effort, which was not easy, to destroy our own system for crossing the river. Otherwise the enemy might have made use of those transport facilities and crossed over to the east bank himself.

The loss of an efficient means of crossing the river was a serious blow to us. The possibility of receiving military supplies and reinforcements for our troops deployed in the city had effectively been eliminated. Our pontoon bridge was destroyed. It was during these days that Malyshev[21] (the people's commissar of the tank industry) came to join us. I knew Malyshev well and respected him. But for what purpose he had been sent and what he was supposed to do was something I couldn't understand then and still don't understand. We met and had a talk, but what could he do concretely to help us? Nothing, of course.

One day the following incident occurred. I want to relate it because it's typical of Stalin's behavior, especially at that time. Stalin suddenly called me up and rather irritably and rudely asked me: "Why have you begun the evacuation of the city there?"

I began to express my displeasure rather sharply. I answered him: "Comrade Stalin, who is reporting this to you? There's no evacuation of the city going on; there's nothing of the kind. I don't know where you're getting such information from, but it's absolutely untrue." He hung up.

I began wondering who could have told him such rubbish, and who could have attributed such intentions to me personally. I decided to call up Malyshev, who had come to visit us and had already left, although I never thought Malyshev would stoop to anything so low. And in fact there had been no conversation between us on such a subject. Neither he nor I had brought up any such topic. I said: "Comrade Malyshev, Comrade Stalin has just called me." And I told him why he had called.

Malyshev answered: "Yes, he just called me, too, and expressed his dissatisfaction in literally the same terms. I have no idea who could have made up such lies."

Then I thought to myself: "The devil only knows what's going on. Could it have been Chuyanov? But Chuyanov could hardly have done such a lowdown thing." I called Chuyanov and asked him: "Comrade Chuyanov, would you happen to know whether anyone has brought up the question of evacuating the city? Stalin has called to ask me about this question."

Chuyanov said: "He called me, too, and expressed his displeasure very angrily." Once I had sounded these men out I didn't bother calling anyone else. I understood that Stalin had made this up to test us, apparently as a preventive measure.

No one was thinking about evacuating, and no one had done anything along those lines, although someone should have thought about it. Yes, they should have! But I already knew that taking that kind of initiative meant that you could run into very unpleasant consequences. Stalin himself did take this initiative, but belatedly.

Stalin called up again much later, when any possibility of evacuating equipment from the plants and factories of Stalingrad had already been lost. He said: "There's a factory in the east that we need to get running. Isn't it possible to evacuate some machinery from the tractor factory, the gun factory, and other factories and send it there?"

I answered: "Comrade Stalin, it's absolutely impossible now to evacuate anything. We don't have any [normal] river-crossing facilities. We're barely able to feed the army, and the only thing we can get across the river are light loads."

He said: "Well then, do what you can."

I said: "We'll try." We began to dismantle some of the machinery and move it to the riverbank, in the landing-stage area by the river, but it seems that nothing was taken across. The machinery simply sat there, and only after the defeat of Paulus's army group was it sent east.

That was the kind of incident that took place. To act otherwise would not have been in our interests. Yet if we actually could have removed the machinery and equipment from Stalingrad, as we had done from Kharkov, how useful that machinery could have been! We evacuated a lot of machinery from Zaporozhye,[22] from under the enemy's nose. We assigned Korniyets to carry out that operation. In those days he was either a member of the Military Council of the Southern Front or, it seems to me, a representative of the government of Ukraine.[23] Korniyets played a major role in evacuating equipment, and that equipment immediately went east and played a very positive part in the establishment of a defense industry in the new location. But this was not done in Stalingrad, because of Stalin's wrong understanding of the situation. He tied us down and blocked our initiative. He wanted to regulate everything from Moscow, and this excessive regulation caused us harm because it paralyzed our initiative and left no room for maneuver, even in questions of redeploying our troops, let alone the question of evacuating equipment. This was a case of the Center running everything. Locally we couldn't do anything without orders from the top.

Malenkov[24] flew into Stalingrad then. I don't know why he did that or how he was supposed to help us. But, after all, he had flown in from Moscow, and as the saying went, Moscow sees things from higher up and sees farther. And so he found himself among us, and he spent days and nights there without doing any good for himself or us. Later, when enemy forces had come right up to Stalingrad and were beginning to penetrate the city, when the bombing had intensified and many fires were burning, several more top officials flew in, including Vasilevsky; Novikov, commander of the Soviet air forces; and Voronov, the chief of artillery.[25] Voronov had flown in to visit us several times earlier and had stayed for a few days and then flown away. I didn't have a very high opinion of the people who came from the Stavka. They couldn't do anything concrete to help us, except on those occasions when Voronov or Novikov or someone else arriving on orders from the Stavka actually brought something with them—something real, such as aircraft we could use, infantry, artillery units, and so forth. If they came by themselves, gracing us, so to speak, with their personalities, which we already had a perfectly good sense of, because all these people were well known to us, it didn't make us happy. They simply took up our time without bringing anything of benefit to the cause.

And so Vasilevsky, Malenkov, Voronov, Novikov, and other representatives of the Stavka had gathered, in short, quite a large number of people. Since the city was burning and was constantly being bombed, the municipal leadership also moved to our command post. Things got pretty crowded there, so crowded that you couldn't turn around, as the saying goes. And the situation kept getting worse.

Precisely then (and this always happened at the most critical moments) I felt that Stalin was putting me under more intense scrutiny. Several times, when events took a sharp turn for the worse, I saw Vasilevsky and Malenkov whispering to each other. Evidently they were trying to protect their own positions. Apparently they were getting a report ready, so that in event of failure they could place the blame on someone else. But on whom? Of course it would be the commander of the Front and the chief member of the Military Council of the Front first of all.

I didn't sense any wrong understanding of our situation on the part of Vasilevsky. When they were whispering among themselves, I figured that Malenkov had taken the initiative. He himself understood nothing about military questions, but when it came to questions of intrigue he had a good chance of succeeding. After all he had to return to Moscow and report something to Stalin, to explain why he had come and what he had done. And if he returned without accomplishing anything and the enemy broke through into Stalingrad, this would have to be explained somehow. But how? Of course he would say that the people commanding the troops were to blame. Perhaps I am exaggerating in attributing such thinking to him, but I am sure that whatever was reported to the Center about the course of events in our area was approximately along those lines.

Later Vasilevsky and Malenkov told me they had received orders from Moscow to fly out. They crossed the Volga to the east bank and drove to the airfield there. Then everyone else left, too. After the terrific crowding we had experienced at the command post an eerie silence set in, as sometimes happens when you're deep in the forest. There was no one left! Only Yeremenko and I and a small operational staff. The headquarters of the Front had been transferred to the east bank in order to be able to receive reports, maintain communications with the armies, and provide them with ammunition and other supplies necessary for the troops. All those operations were transferred to the east bank, and so all the people were there, too. The enemy was keeping up the pressure on our forces and, as before, was trying to break through into the city. Our troops were stubbornly holding their defensive positions. There was a moment when I thought that Stalin might have reconciled himself to the idea that the Germans would occupy the city. I think that's why he ordered everyone withdrawn who wasn't needed and who wasn't doing any good. Only the commander and I remained. We understood that that's where our place was.

It was already late summer (but it was still hot), when General Golikov arrived. Stalin called and gave us advance warning that Golikov was coming. Golikov was in Stalin's good books, and he placed some sort of special hopes in him. He apparently thought that Golikov could help organize the fighting in the city itself. Golikov was appointed first deputy commander of the forces of the Stalingrad Front.[26] His functions consisted in the following: The commander and I would send him to places where we felt the troops needed to be encouraged by the presence of someone from the command staff of the Front.

I had some acquaintance with Golikov. I got to know him back in 1939, when the Red Army was approaching Lvov and getting ready for a battle to seize the city. But as we approached Lvov, it turned out that the enemy—the Polish army—was no longer there. The Germans were also coming up close to Lvov, and so it was possible that there could be clashes between our troops and the Germans. We held talks with the Germans, and that was when I made Golikov's acquaintance. I recall that he had an observation post under a haystack. That's where I went when I came to visit him, and that's where we waited to hear the results of the talks with the Germans. Those talks ended favorably, and our troops were able to enter Lvov without resistance. I also met Golikov when he was the head of the Chief Administration for Personnel of the Red Army. He had also been chief of intelligence for the Red Army. But in those days I met him only in Stalin's presence, and there was no possibility of getting to know Golikov as an individual and as a Communist. I knew of course that he had been a member of the party virtually from the first days of the Civil War, and I had never heard any bad reports about him.

Meanwhile the fighting in Stalingrad was continuing. The enemy was besieging us, but by then our troops were putting up a tough defense, fighting for every inch of ground, as the saying goes. The enemy paid with much blood for every advance he made. Some famous slogans applied to us: "Not one step back!" "There is no place for us on the other side of the Volga," and "Fight to the death, but don't give up Stalingrad." We were regularly receiving reinforcements in the form of small units, and we were receiving weapons. When we found ourselves in a position of semi-encirclement, we discovered at the gun factory that many pieces of field artillery were still there. It was impossible to ship them out, as we had been ordered to do. The commander and I decided to place these weapons in firing position. We had no means of transporting the guns, but we decided simply to drag them to the front lines, set them up, and fire as much as possible. And if we had to retreat, we would, without fail, blow them up. We made pretty good use of these weapons. We organized a lot of gun crews, and we had the necessary ammunition. These guns played a positive role. And we had no other choice: we couldn't ship them out, as we had been ordered to, and we couldn't leave them at the factory, where the enemy might break through and capture them.

It was just then that a new division arrived, headed by Rodimtsev. It was a very solid division, of good composition,[27] but it was quite poorly equipped; it had no artillery and not even machine guns. Fighting in the ranks of this division, among others, was the son of Dolores Ibarruri.[28] When this division went into battle it suffered very heavy casualties. It could have played more of a role if it had had better weapons. I received the report that Ruben Ibarruri had been killed. The following incidents in relation to him have remained in my memory. He was wounded during the first days of the war. My son Lenya had also been wounded. They were in beds in the same ward in a Kuibyshev hospital. The second episode has to do with the time when Ibarruri's death was reported. I was also informed then that the son of Anastas Ivanovich Mikoyan, a fighter pilot, had been killed in an aerial battle. Such things were familiar to me. There was a war on, and as in every war, people were dying, a great many people, especially in the desperate situation in which our Red Army found itself, not having been prepared as it should have been for the war and not having enough weapons.

I remember the following painful scene. Gordov and I had gone forward into an area of fighting by a gully near the settlement of Nariman, southwest of Stalingrad.[29] The army commander, Shumilov,[30] and a member of his Military Council, Serdyuk,[31] had also gone there. The scene that I observed there was very unpleasant for me. Our PE-2 bombers were attacking enemy positions. They were similar in appearance to the German ME-110s. As our planes approached the front line some Messerschmitts suddenly appeared and before our eyes sent one after another of our Petlyakovs down in flames. Their pilots parachuted out. What was especially painful to see was that our troops, our Soviet infantry, as these pilots descended to the ground, opened fire on them. Our infantry thought these were enemy bombers and that it was German pilots coming down in parachutes. To this day I remember one of the pilots, who was already close to the ground. He began shouting: "I'm one of yours. I'm one of yours!" Suddenly there was a burst of submachine gun fire and that was the end of him. In regard to the PE-2 planes, our pilots, I was told, did not have a very high opinion of them. These airplanes had good flight qualities, but their fuel tanks were positioned in such a way that literally any bullet that hit them would set them on fire.

Once again let me repeat that all representatives of the Stavka had abandoned us, and Yeremenko and I were left alone. The only thing that remained for us, as Andrei Ivanovich [Yeremenko] joked, was the fancy toilet. But the truth is that after the representatives of the Stavka had left, it became impossible to use that toilet, although previously it had been in prime condition.

I don't remember when this happened (and it would have been useful if I had noted down the date), but Stalin called me (and I was surprised at how calmly he spoke, which was a rare thing for that time). He said: "How are things there? Can you hold out for three more days or so?" This happened soon after Vasilevsky, Malenkov, and the other Stavka representatives had flown out.

I answered: "Comrade Stalin, I don't know why you have chosen such a deadline for us. We think that we can hold out not just for three days, but much longer. I can't say exactly how long, because in a war you can't be sure of anything, but at any rate, we now feel that our troops have had their baptism of fire, and this provides the assurance that in the future they will defend their positions just as stubbornly."

He said: "Well, that's good!" Then he continued: "Be sure that you hold out for at least three days. Right now we are organizing a blow from the north to relieve you, and we are either going to cut off that left wing of the enemy that broke through to the Volga on the north or else we're going to drive them back from the Volga. When the fighting begins to the north of you, you should organize a blow from Stalingrad, with whatever forces you have, to prevent the Germans form transferring reinforcements against the troops that will be striking the blow from the north."

I answered: "All right, we'll do that."

The blow was struck from the north. But our efforts didn't result in the destruction of the German forces, nor were they driven back from the Volga. That is, the main task that had been set for our troops was not accomplished. I don't know what forces were at the disposal of our northern area, but the desired results did not materialize. After that, new troops were sent by the Stavka to the northern sector to prevent the enemy from exploiting his success and moving farther up the Volga. These troops in principle became part of the Stalingrad Front. Armies under the command of Moskalenko and Malinovsky[32] were brought up to that position. Preparations were again made for a blow that had the aim of cutting off the northern wing of the German forces that had reached the Volga and of restoring the positions that we had previously held. When a fairly solid force had been concentrated in the area, Yeremenko and I went to the command post to direct the operation. Several prominent figures from the Stavka also came to direct this operation, including Zhukov, Novikov, Malenkov, Golovanov,[33] commander of our long-range air forces, and Voronov, chief of artillery for the Red Army. We hoped for success.

At the appointed hour, an artillery barrage began, and then we started our offensive. Unfortunately this offensive, too, was unsuccessful despite the highly concentrated forces we had there. It was said that these forces had been brought from the Far East. They were fresh and young, well-trained troops. But our attack misfired, and the enemy didn't move back even a little bit. How is this to be explained? We all know and have often repeated, and correctly repeated, that there are no fortresses that cannot be stormed. But you have to have the necessary means to do that! It's true that the field fortifications that the Germans had put up were not all that powerful, not such mighty fortresses. Evidently we had not properly calculated everything; an insufficient number of troops had been brought up and above all an insufficient quantity of artillery.

I would not say that we underestimated the role of artillery. Not at all. Even before the war we called artillery "the god of war." I don't know who used that expression first or where it came from. It seems that it comes from olden times, from the Napoleonic era.[34] And Napoleon certainly did value artillery highly. At any rate, Stalin and our military men did correctly evaluate artillery at its worth. If an insufficient quantity had been concentrated, that meant we simply didn't have enough artillery. And so our offensive, which was not supported by a good artillery effort, did not succeed.

Why am I talking about this? I valued Georgy Konstantinovich Zhukov very highly, and I still value him. (I have repeated this more than once.) I respect him for his sober-mindedness, audacity, simplicity, and aggressiveness. In my opinion he possesses the highest qualities of a commander. Back then I also valued him as a fighting comrade. He and I were on the best of terms. Nevertheless, in spite of what seems to have been all the most favorable circumstances, with the presence of Zhukov and representatives of all the various forces and other strong commanders, we still did not accomplish our tasks. What it comes down to is that personal qualities alone are not enough. What is also needed, and the war showed this clearly, are the means of mass destruction of the enemy's military equipment, the means of destroying his living forces, and the means of destroying his fortifications. And that means artillery, tanks, machine guns, antiaircraft guns—that is, antiaircraft cannon and machine guns to cover our troops against air attack so that the enemy could not with impunity seek to disorganize our attacking troops. And we still did not have those things.

Zhukov told me something then (and we shared impressions in a comradely way; he went forward to one sector of the battlefront and returned and shared with me what he had seen): "You know, I went up near the front, and our wounded troops were coming back from the front lines. A group of these wounded men were heading toward our rear area, and I cursed them. I called them left-handers." That term was much in use then. It was said that people deliberately put up their left hands to be hit by bullets. Once they were wounded, they could go back to the rear area. Unfortunately, that expression was used fairly widely, and sometimes undeservedly; it was an insulting expression to use for our troops. [Zhukov continued:] "One of them looked at me and said: 'Comrade General, we left-handers are walking because we still can walk, but those who got bullets in the head are still lying there. I have seen just how many are still lying there.' And he gave me such an expressive look, and you know, he was telling the truth. I can't forget how piercing that look was—the look he gave me." That soldier made quite a strong impression on Zhukov.

The offensive sputtered out, and soon that sector was detached from our Front. That was the right thing to do, because we were in Stalingrad, after all, and that sector lay to the north of Stalingrad, and communications with it were very poor. Besides, a specialized task had been set for those troops—to prevent the enemy from developing his success northward up the Volga. A new front was established there, the Don Front. Rokossovsky[35] was appointed commander. Direct communications between them and us were broken off, and our only contacts with them were as a neighboring Front. Kirichenko became a member of the Military Council of the Don Front. Previously he had been a member of the Military Council of the Stalingrad Front, and later he was with the Southern Front. I don't remember who was the primary member of the Military Council, but Kirichenko was appointed as the second-ranking official of that council. The number-two council member was concerned with questions of the rear areas and supplying the troops; the first member of the Military Council decided operational matters.

At that time I was summoned to Moscow again. What I heard there was undoubtedly fabricated by Malenkov. It was said that the commander and the command staff of the Southwestern and Southern Fronts, which had retreated from the Don to Stalingrad and taken up defensive positions there, had grown used to doing nothing but retreating during 1941. Therefore, supposedly the defense they were organizing was not strong enough; they were giving in to panic and retreating. The word was that the entire command staff had to be replaced. And they began to replace it. They replaced many people. But this viewpoint was absolutely groundless; it was simply a philistine way of looking at things. Malenkov began circulating this view in order to justify his trip to Stalingrad, to divest himself of any responsibility and dump it on others. He made up this worthless theory and later it spread all over the place.

There were other bad attitudes that arose among military personnel [along the following lines]: "Here we are retreating. Why are we retreating? Because the soldier doesn't have a sense of what he's fighting for, what he's willing to die for. Take World War I, for example. Back then the soldier had land; he owned his own farm. He fought for Russia as a whole, but he was also fighting for his own home. But now everything is owned in common; all the farms are collective farms. And there's no particular incentive." In my opinion this was an anti-Soviet and antisocialist theory. It placed the blame for our setbacks on the Soviet system itself and on the socialist foundations that had been laid in the USSR. Of course this was an invalid theory; it was a theory held by people suffering from a collapse of morale, who were beginning to make up wrong explanations for our defeats. Life refuted these theories. If some people who today hold fairly high military rank were reminded that this kind of thinking affected them at one time, they would probably get angry and say that this was lies and slander. Unfortunately, though, that's the way it was! That's how it was, and there's nothing to be done about it. But we survived this, and the defeat of Paulus's troops at Stalingrad put an end to such "explanations."

As stubborn fighting continued, the enemy kept pressing our troops back step by step, and from the west our troops retreated deeper into the city. The enemy began to make incursions past the city limits. Our defensive positions were already being set up directly inside the city, making use of its buildings—homes and other structures. Being in the command post located on the Tsaritsa River was not without its dangers now. We looked into the possibility of moving farther to the rear. But we couldn't find anything suitable in the city except for a location right on the riverbank of the Volga. (Today a wharf has been built there, and no traces remain of our command post of that time.) Two holes had been dug into the sloping riverbank. The Stalingrad security police (the Chekists) had started to build a shelter for themselves, but they had no time to complete the work; they had only dug these holes. The two tunnels that they had started were supposed to have linked up deeper in the hillside to form a horseshoe. But that work had not been completed; they had simply dug two holes and reinforced them with timbers. We occupied those tunnels in the form in which they had been abandoned during the process of construction. Yeremenko and I took one tunnel, and a small staff of service personnel was situated in the other.

The working conditions there were very poor: a primitive table as a desk, at which the commander and I sat, and next to us a young fellow in a dirty summer uniform operating a communications station. He would sit there and monotonously repeat: "This is lily of the valley. This is lily of the valley. Over." He kept repeating these words the whole time, without stopping for a minute, so as to keep the communications line open in case it was necessary to send some order. The deputy commander of long-range aircraft, General Skripko,[36] was also with us then. He received orders about what areas to bomb and immediately transmitted these orders to the air-force units that would then send in the bombers to our location. Signal fires were set to show where air strikes were needed. This was a big help to our infantry.

We made extensive use of 85-millimeter antiaircraft guns. They were valuable as antiaircraft weapons and as antitank weapons. Part of our artillery was on the east bank, camouflaged by the woods. This artillery gave substantial aid to our infantrymen fighting directly inside Stalingrad as the Germans kept coming closer. The Volga flotilla also provided some resources for our Front. Rear-Admiral Rogachev[37] commanded the flotilla in our sector. Later we discovered two long-range artillery pieces manufactured at the Stalingrad gun factory that had not been removed because of the Germans' swift advance to the Volga. We decided to give Rogachev an order to find personnel who could service these two cannon and to deliver artillery shells from Kamyshin [across the river] so that fire could be directed at the enemy directly from the place where these cannon were located—on the territory of the gun factory. The cannon were too heavy to move, and they fired directly from the factory grounds until they were knocked out of commission by enemy air raids.

I remember the following incident. Later on, we joked about it a lot. One afternoon Skripko came to take a rest. We had an iron bed at our location. He stretched out on the bed and fell asleep because he was a "night person"; he was connected with the long-range bombing branch of the air force, and so he slept during the day. At one point Yeremenko and I had called Rogachev in and asked what direction it would be best to aim these two huge cannon. He brought the artillery commanders of the cannon in to consult with us. When the necessary instructions had been given, the rear-admiral, I don't know why, gave an order to the sailors: "About face!" The tunnel floor was covered with boards, over which the sailors began marching out, in step. A roaring sound echoed through the tunnel. Skripko jumped up and quickly slung the belt of his map case over his shoulder [ready to go off to work at the airfield, thinking he had been awakened to report to duty]. He looked at us, wondering why we were just cheerfully sitting there. I calmed him down. I said it wasn't bombs exploding, but just the sailors' boots resounding in the tunnel. Without saying a word, Skripko put down the map case, fell onto the bed, and in a moment was asleep. He was completely exhausted.

The commander and I considered it inexpedient to remain in Stalingrad any longer. Our communications with the "outside world" had been cut, and communications with the east bank of the Volga were very uncertain; we didn't have a reliable cable connection. There was a lightweight cable that we had laid by hand across the Volga, but that communications link was extremely unreliable. And we ourselves couldn't keep crossing over to the east bank. That was simply impossible because we'd have to cross back to work with our staff. The same difficulties would be encountered when commanders or messengers tried to reach us with their reports. So we decided to transfer our entire command post to the east bank. When we were drawing up the next military report we included the point that we were requesting permission to transfer the command post to the east bank. A real command post had been set up there, and it had a communications center linking us with all the armies of the Front. We sent our report. A day went by and we didn't hear a mumbling word in reply. We repeated our message. Today I don't even know how many times we kept repeating that message, but still no answer came. We were neither given permission to take this action nor forbidden to do so.

This was a typical tactic of Stalin's. He was probably against our proposal, but he wouldn't say so directly. We of course could not leave our previous command post without his permission and make the crossing to the east bank. Later on, Stalin called up in regard to some other question. During the conversation I said to him: "Comrade Stalin, we have already asked more than once for permission to transfer to the east bank. The General Staff is not giving any reply. I request that this question be resolved for us because the interests of proper command of our forces require that we transfer over there."

He answered: "No, that's impossible. If the troops find out that the commander and his staff have left Stalingrad, Stalingrad will fall."

I said: "No, Comrade Stalin, I don't see it that way, because the fighting is being done by the troops and not by the staff of the Front. The staff of the 62nd Army is right here alongside us, and it's commanded by Chuikov. The

62nd Army is defending Stalingrad. We have appointed Gurov, a member of the Military Council of the Front, to serve as a member of the Military Council of the 62nd Army to reinforce its leadership. We are absolutely certain that Chuikov and Gurov can fully cope with their task and will do everything necessary to prevent the enemy from taking Stalingrad."

Stalin said: "Well, all right. If you're sure the front lines will hold and the defense won't be disrupted, I'll let you cross over to the east bank. Only you should leave a representative of the Front headquarters in Stalingrad so he can report to you, so you'll know the state of affairs through one of your own people and not just through Army Commander Chuikov."

I answered: "All right. We'll leave General Golikov, the first deputy commander of the Front."

Stalin knew Golikov well and agreed. We began to get ready for the crossing. It took us a day to get ready, and at dawn the next day we crossed to the east bank in small boats. We had very few people with us. The chief of staff of the Front had already been on the east bank for a long time. At that time the chief of staff was Zakharov.[38] He had come to us together with Yeremenko. Yeremenko had a lot of respect for him, and I, too, respected him. He deserved respect except for one failing: he would get rough with his subordinate officers and hit them. This defective behavior was encouraged both by Stalin and by Yeremenko, who knew Stalin's attitude. When talking with Yeremenko, Stalin often said it was necessary to "smash people in the face." When people of limited horizon carried out such orders, that was one thing, but Zakharov was an educated man. He had a good military education[39] and a good understanding of military manners. When you talked with him you got the impression of a capable person who reasoned sensibly and accurately. Nevertheless he did have this failing.

The air army assigned to our Front [the Eighth Air Army] was commanded by Khryukin.[40] He was young, such a tall man, and a very pleasant person. He had won the title Hero of the Soviet Union. In my view he was where he was supposed to be. I respected him and supported him. He had won his title participating in China's war of liberation against Japan. He fought in the skies of China on the side of Chiang Kai-shek. (Back then we were supporting Chiang Kai-shek.) He was an experienced man, who had previously served as a fighter pilot. But the forces in his air army were fairly limited; he didn't have very many planes. Nevertheless, he fought the enemy in a self-sacrificing way. His deputy was also a good pilot, Naneishvili, a Georgian.[41] He had also been a fighter pilot previously, but now he was well on in years, quite a heavy-set man, who could no longer fly. But as an organizer he was very good, and besides that he was a decent, conscientious person and a capable general.

Yeremenko and I summoned Golikov and told him that we had obtained permission to transfer the command post of our Front to the east bank and we wanted him to stay on the west bank at the previously existing command post, maintain communications with the commander of the 62nd Army, and report to us from there about the state of affairs. We also told him that he wouldn't be staying there long. We assumed there would be no reason to keep him on the west bank for a prolonged period. Besides, Chuikov might take it badly. As commander of the 62nd Army he might think that we had left this man to nag him on behalf of Front headquarters. Commanders don't like such people. They give the impression of being tiresome spies on behalf of the higher-ups. It's often said that such people simply interfere and prevent effective functioning. Besides, I had already seen that Chuikov was a man of abrupt character, and all imaginable excesses might be expected of him. Golikov was beside himself over our recommendation. There was a frightful change of expression on his face, but he restrained himself and left the room. Later he found a moment when I was alone and appealed to me, literally pleading with me not to leave him there. I had never seen anyone in such a state, during the entire war, no one—neither civilian nor military. He pleaded not to be left there, and the motivation that he gave for this request was that everyone was going to perish; they were all doomed: "Don't toss me aside, don't leave me here, don't destroy me. Let me leave, too." He pleaded in a tone that was totally unacceptable.

I said to him: "Listen to what you're saying. Try to grasp this, Comrade Golikov, an entire army is positioned here and it's putting up a very stubborn fight. You yourself can see how staunchly it's holding its positions. How dare you say that everything is doomed, that everyone is going to perish? That conclusion cannot be drawn from the situation that we now have on our Front. You can see how firmly our troops are fighting. After all, this is not the same situation as before, when we were surrendering a good dozen kilometers of territory to the enemy every day. That's not happening here, and it's not going to happen. What's the matter with you?" But then he repeated the same things. I said to him: "Look how you're behaving." But nothing had any effect on him. Then I added: "Comrade Golikov, a decision has been made by the Stavka, a decision that must be carried out. Do what has been ordered!" With that the conversation ended. This conversation made a dreadful impression on me. Later Golikov repeated the same thing with Yeremenko.

In short, we left him behind, along with several communications officers, and we ourselves moved over to the east bank of the river. I don't remember how many days went by, but then we received a note from an officer attached to Golikov, who informed us that Golikov had completely lost his head, was out of control and behaving like a person who had lost his senses, that he was crawling up the walls, and that therefore his continued presence in the army was not only doing no good but was actually harmful: he was infecting others with the poor state of his morale. This officer begged us to take appropriate measures. When we received this report, we ordered Golikov to leave the former command post and come over to us. After that the attitude that Yeremenko and I had toward Golikov changed sharply. His behavior and his state of mind were the cause. Soon another incident occurred that put Golikov in a quite unfavorable light.

We faced difficult conditions in ferrying ammunition and reinforcements across the river to our fighting forces. Maintaining the link with Stalingrad across the Volga was very difficult. The river crossing was under constant enemy artillery fire and was being bombed from the air in all sectors. We took special measures to ensure normal delivery of ammunition, food, and reinforcements. One day we ordered Golikov to go to the river to make sure supplies were getting across. Of course I understood that the conditions were very difficult, but when he went there he didn't carry out his orders. He did nothing at all, then came back, and reported that the enemy was bombing very heavily and bombarding the river crossing with artillery so that nothing could be accomplished. Previously we had sent other officers with the same assignment, and they had accomplished something, although with difficulty. We reprimanded Golikov for failing to carry out orders to ship ammunition across the river. Apparently Golikov complained to Stalin about us, but neither of us ever had a discussion about this or tried to explain our different points of view.

One day another incident involving Golikov occurred. Yeremenko and I had gone to the Volga riverbank where our river flotilla was located. We arrived in the area across from Rynok and observed how the flotilla was making use of its artillery. It wasn't playing any special role because there was so little artillery. But as the saying goes, when there are no fish a crayfish will do. We considered the artillery of the river flotilla one of the bases of our strength. As we were returning, we saw Golikov coming toward us. We stopped and he got out of his vehicle: "Where are you going?" we asked him.

He said: "I'm going to the airfield; I'm flying to Moscow. It's a good thing we met, because I wanted to say goodbye to you."

We asked: "How is it that you're leaving all of a sudden?"

He said: "I just received orders from Comrade Stalin to go to Moscow."

We said: "But we only happened to meet you by accident. What if you had left, and we hadn't known where to find you or where to look for you?"

He said: "I have my orders and I have to go!" And off he went. Of course we gossiped among ourselves about this later, and what we had to say was by no means favorable to Golikov. After all, if he had been in the position of the commander of the Front, he too would have reacted sharply to anyone behaving the way he had. But what could you do? Once he had gone he had gone, and there was no use talking about it. In essence we weren't opposed to his leaving. Our objection was really over the way he did it.

A little while later a new deputy commander was sent to us, General Markian Mikhailovich Popov. Earlier Popov had commanded an army, but I don't remember that army's number.[42] I have good memories of Popov. I worked with him a lot during the time when the decision had been made to prepare our troops to encircle Paulus's forces. We concentrated these troops and went to visit them together with Popov—all these preparations were carried out together with him. Yeremenko was unable to recover from an old wound. His leg kept going bad on him, and it was difficult for him to either walk or ride, and so he couldn't go long distances. When we did go on long trips I could see that it was hard for him, and I didn't want to encourage him to make such trips or to go somewhere when we could get by without his going. Popov, on the other hand, was a healthy man who was still young. As the saying goes, he still had all the cards in his deck. And he was a man who knew military science well.

A telephone call came from Moscow ordering me to go there. I arrived in Moscow and met with Stalin. Stalin began rebuking me, accusing me of having the wrong attitude toward generals, not defending them, and so forth.

"What exactly and who exactly are you talking about? Which general? What do you have in mind? I know of no such cases myself."

He said: "Golikov, for example. We sent you Golikov, and suddenly you have this attitude toward Golikov." In this conversation Stalin put the emphasis mainly on Yeremenko, saying what a difficult person he was, and so on. I was surprised. Previously Stalin had literally idolized Yeremenko, made a big fuss over him, and portrayed him as the best fighting general we had. That's what Stalin himself told me when we were looking for someone to appoint as commander of the Stalingrad Front! Of course some time had gone by since that conversation; the enemy had penetrated Stalingrad, and fighting was going on in the city itself. It was very heavy fighting. We were suffering a lot of casualties, but so was the enemy. Stalingrad had not been taken, and it would not be—that is, of course, as long as we were given the assistance we needed.

I replied to him: "Comrade Stalin, I don't know what Golikov has told you, but I must say that if Golikov told you that a certain attitude was taken against him, then I am obliged to explain to you the reasons for our negative attitude toward Golikov." I told him about the events connected with our leaving the command post in Stalingrad: what our conversations had been, how Golikov had conducted himself, how he had expressed absolute lack of confidence in our victory, had even said we were doomed, and literally with tears in his eyes had pleaded not to be left behind. Stalin looked at me with surprise. I understood that no idea of any such thing had occurred to him, that he didn't know about it. I continued: "That's why the reprimand we gave Golikov was justified. I actually don't understand why you were coming down on Yeremenko and me. I defend people who deserve to be defended, but I can't defend those who deserve condemnation."

He said: "Well, now we have gone and decided to remove Yeremenko."

I said: "Comrade Stalin, if you have decided to annul our decision, of course you will do that, but it would be incorrect."

"Why?" he asked.

I said: "There are various opinions about Yeremenko. As is true of almost anyone, he has opponents who don't respect him. But as for me, as a member of the Military Council, I have gone through crucial times with him and in my opinion as a commander (I'm not talking about his other qualities, because in wartime military qualities are the main thing) he corresponds fully to the position and situation to which he has been assigned. He has energy and drive, and he knows how to lead troops. You can see how the defense of Stalingrad has been organized, and this is still being done well. The commander should be given credit for it." I presented other arguments as well.

At first Stalin kept pressing the attack, but after a while he began to subside, to back off, and finally he stopped attacking me altogether. The time had come for me to leave and he said: "You have permission to take your flight." When we said goodbye he shook my hand: "It's a good thing we called you here. If we hadn't called you, we would have removed Yeremenko. I had already decided to remove him. Your arguments and your objections have convinced me. We must leave him where he is."

I answered: "What you are doing is very correct, Comrade Stalin, very correct." Today I will not go into the details of how I contrasted Yeremenko's good military qualities with other qualities that Stalin called bad.

He said: "All right, we'll leave him where he is." And I flew off. Thus, as it turns out, all this trouble was stirred up by Golikov's stories. I was simply amazed. I had a high regard for Golikov's qualities as a party member, and I had previously no reason to doubt him. But when he allowed himself to do this kind of thing, reporting very subjectively about his own actions, I changed my opinion about his qualities as a party member. If he had said to Stalin even one-tenth of what he had said to Yeremenko and me when we were leaving him on the west bank, Stalin would not have deigned to speak with him any longer. Golikov, instead of correctly acknowledging his own weaknesses, tried to place the blame on the commander and me. I think Stalin probably asked him: "Well, all right, so much for Yeremenko, but what about Khrushchev?" Golikov must have said: "Khrushchev also failed to defend me. He's in full agreement with Yeremenko." If Golikov did answer that way, it was true, because on that question I was in full agreement with Yeremenko. In fact that was the only position an honest person could take.

I returned to the Stalingrad Front. We were continuing preparations for encirclement of the German army group. How did the idea arise of surrounding the enemy there? I will not say that we—that is, Yeremenko and I—were the only ones to whom this idea occurred. Of course it's possible that it occurred to others as well. Because in general matters were coming to a head. How so? Here's how. The fighting on the Stalingrad Front kept being drawn out longer and longer. The Germans were concentrating their efforts along a fairly narrow line, which testified to their weakness. They couldn't carry out offensive operations on a broad front and were throwing their living forces into the city like meat into a grinder. The heaviest fighting was in the heart of the city, where things were easier for the defenders than for the attackers. We received reports from our troops that along the enemy's flanks his defenses were very thin. We sent our reconnaissance scouts there. They crossed the Don and penetrated fairly deeply behind enemy lines. They didn't always report accurately. We took them at their word sometimes when the scouts were simply lying and hadn't been in the places they reported on. But that was an exception. As a rule the reconnaissance people worked conscientiously and reported accurately. They reported that the Germans had virtually no forces on the other side of the Don. Our 51st Army was on our left flank [to the south]. Enemy defenses were weak in that area, too. It was mostly Romanians that were positioned there—a very unreliable force. The commander of the 51st Army reported that the enemy's forces were quite weak there and that he could make short work of them.

We decided to make a "reconnaissance by combat" to find out how solid that part of the enemy lines was, and we ordered the commander of the 51st Army to make a probe.[43] In addition we specifically summoned a commander of one of the divisions and gave him the assignment to strike at a particular area and told him what forces to use. We gave him strict orders that if the strike proved successful, he should not advance deeply and that he should go no deeper than such-and-such a distance behind enemy lines. If he took prisoners, he was to treat them properly, so as not to leave behind any "evidence" that the enemy could use against us later. The commander of the division, a fine fellow of about forty-five, a stocky, heavy-set man, whose hair was completely gray, nevertheless a strong and bold fellow, answered: "All right, I'll do everything you say." He quickly organized the attack, easily overran the enemy, and penetrated deep behind enemy defenses, even farther than we had specified, that is, he "overfulfilled the plan,"[44] although we had warned him not to do that. He took many prisoners and shot them all. Subsequently the enemy made use of that as propaganda against us. When we found this out we criticized him sharply.

He answered: "What else could I do with them? Where could I take them?" It was wrong, of course, for him to do that.

Later the Germans took soldiers' representatives from their various divisions to that location and showed them, saying: "Here, you see? The Russians aren't taking prisoners. They're shooting the soldiers they capture." The Germans of course blew this incident out of all proportion in order to frighten their troops and prevent them from surrendering to us.

In general our troops were holding our defense line pretty firmly, and it was a fortified line. This encouraged us. We saw that we had the chance to strike at the enemy's flanks and thus change the entire state of affairs in the Stalingrad area. Yeremenko and I wrote a memorandum to Stalin at that point expressing our opinion. What this came down to was approximately the following. "According to our information—including information coming from reconnaissance scouts sent behind enemy lines and from our own reconnaissance by combat, by which we have tested the firmness of the enemy's defenses—the Germans' area beyond the Don is virtually empty; they have no forces there that they can rely on. We do not know what the Stavka has at its disposal, but if the troops can be found and concentrated on the east side of the Don, so as to strike a blow from there to Kalach, and if at the same time we could strike a blow from the south against the enemy's southern flank, it would be possible to encircle the enemy forces that have broken into the city and are now fighting in Stalingrad itself."

We didn't know what the Stavka had at its disposal or what its possibilities were at that time. We knew only that things were very hard for us and that we were being given very few reinforcements. And if we were not being given much, presumably that meant there wasn't much to give. That's what we thought. It also occurred to us that perhaps we were asking too much because we didn't know the real situation in the country as a whole.

A little while later Zhukov came to visit us. He told us that the Stavka had a plan similar to the one that Yeremenko and I had proposed in our memorandum, and he warned us that no one should know about this operation. He said he had flown in especially to warn us about that. In this instance Stalin's suspiciousness was useful. The fewer who knew about the operation in the making, the better for the operation itself. Zhukov showed us on a map the sector in which the Stalingrad Front should strike its blow. It was precisely the area of operation of the 51st Army. We, too, had thought that the blow should be struck from there, in the area where we had already carried out a successful reconnaissance in force. Lake Tsatsa[45] was located there. South of the lake along the defensive positions being held by the 51st Army there was an elevated position. It was held by Romanians, and our defense line was at the foot of these hills. This didn't disturb us. The hills were not very high. In that area, the flat, bare Kalmyk steppes spread out in all directions.[46]

Anyone who has been in this locality knows that you can see for a distance of some 20 kilometers with the naked eye, that everything there is quite transparent. I asked Zhukov: "What are they giving us to carry out this task?"

Zhukov answered: "You'll get a mechanized corps of a hundred tanks or more, and infantry with trucks, and enough artillery to correspond to the number of troops. In addition you'll get a cavalry corps. It's just arriving now. General Shapkin[47] is the commander. Also there's ammunition. And you'll be given some infantry units, but not very many." He told Yeremenko and me all this. Then we went with him to the area specified for the offensive to familiarize ourselves with the topography. Everything there was plainly visible, and there was not a bush or tree anywhere.

I said: "If the troops you say will be given to us actually arrive, plus what we have ourselves, I have full confidence that we'll break through the enemy defenses, that we'll trounce the enemy and accomplish our task."

Our first task was to take the small village of Sovetsky not far from Kalach on the Don. I knew the village of Sovetsky, because it was not that long before that we ourselves had been in that village. Vatutin[48] was supposed to come down with his troops along the Don and occupy Kalach. By striking our blow at Sovetsky, we would facilitate fulfillment of the task set for the Southwestern Front. That was the plan that took shape. There was no reason to doubt the success of the operation. We were certain that the Germans in Stalingrad would be surrounded. Let me repeat once again that Zhukov and I were on very good terms. I said to him: "Comrade Zhukov, we will do our part and surround the Germans. We must assume that the enemy troops, when they find themselves surrounded, will try to break out. Which direction will they take? They won't try to break out to the north, but to the south. What are we going to use to hold them? We don't have anything to hold them with. They'll roll right over us, break out, and get away."

Zhukov looked at me with a smile and responded with some Russian words of a rather strong nature and sharp content. Then he added: "Let them get away. That's all we want—that they go away, so we can liberate Stalingrad and the Volga region."

I said to him: "That's true. That's our main goal. But if we were given more resources, we could also pulverize any force that attacked us in an attempt to break out."

He answered: "We don't have any more to give you." I said: "Well, all right then." And Zhukov left.

A very limited number of people knew about the operation. You could count them on two hands. We continued our preparations and awaited the arrival of the mechanized corps commanded by General Volsky.[49] The corps was in the process of arriving. I got acquainted with Volsky. He made a very good impression on me as a man who knew his business. Other people had also given good recommendations about him. They said he was a strong advocate of the use of armored forces and had a good knowledge of modern methods of tank warfare. It was said that he could be relied on and would give a good account of himself in this situation. His corps was arriving. We designated a crossing point [over the Volga] for the corps near a large village where the riverbanks were high. An assembly area had been prepared there, and a steam ferry was ready for use. The crossing was made, and the corps was able to move forward from there to an area of concentration near the Sarpinsky Lakes.[50]

Then Timofei Timofeyevich Shapkin arrived. He was an old Russian soldier, well on in years, of medium height, with a full beard. He had sons who were already either generals or colonels. He had served in the tsarist army and fought in World War I. Yeremenko told me that Shapkin had earned four Crosses of Saint George. In short, he was a real fighting man. When he introduced himself, there were no Crosses of Saint George on his chest, but it was decorated with three or four Orders of the Red Banner.[51] I greeted him with great respect and deference. I regarded him with a feeling of great tenderness and was ready to listen to the tales told by this old military man. The assistant who arrived with him was a young, handsome, very well trained man, a Turkmen by nationality.[52] He was a completely modern person. He was the heart and soul of the cavalry corps, but he didn't succeed in fighting for very long; he was killed. By the time the main battles began, he was already dead. As the operation was being prepared he was riding among his units, and at one crossing point a Messerschmitt strafed the motor vehicle he was in. I felt very bad about this general, but he was not the first and he would not be the last to fall. The enemy killed many of our people that way.

How were the preparations for this operation carried out? Vasilevsky flew in to be with us. By then Volsky had arrived, and Shapkin with his cavalry corps. We had accumulated ammunition and artillery. In short we had already received basically everything that we were supposed to receive. Vasilevsky, Popov, and I went to see Volsky. His mechanized corps was our main force. We went to inform ourselves and see how things stood in his sector. Autumn had come. In the southern region around Stalingrad autumn is sometimes quite cold and rainy with a piercing wind. Volsky's units had already crossed the Volga and taken up their positions in the designated village. The enemy was bombing them, but not very heavily. Apparently the enemy didn't notice that Volsky was crossing the river with his tanks. Otherwise the Germans could have struck a substantial blow during the crossing. The Volga is pretty wide there; the banks are steep, and it is not so easy to get across to the high western bank. The report Volsky gave made a good impression on us. We talked to the tank troops. It was evident that people were ready for the operation and were anxious to go into battle.

On the way back, it was freezing cold, and we stopped to see Popov and get warm. Popov had his command post not far from the point of disembarkation to the right of the mechanized corps. Right then he was having his birthday. In principle Vasilevsky and I were on our way to visit Tolbukhin at the 57th Army.[53] The Front headquarters was to the east of the Volga, near the Akhtuba River,[54] in the small settlement of Raisky Sad. I rarely went to the Front headquarters in those days because it was so far away; more often I was at Tolbukhin's, which was right near the river crossing on the Volga. The troops being concentrated for the offensive were also located in that region. So it was most convenient to make ourselves comfortable at Tolbukhin's. But

Popov had pleaded with us: "Hey, just stop by for half an hour. It's my birthday. I really want you to come by today, and then you can be on your way." So we stopped by.

It's well known what happens on a birthday, especially on the eve of an offensive! We wished him well and had a fairly large amount to drink. I saw that Markian Mikhailovich [Popov] was pleased with his birthday. Unfortunately, he got carried away, drinking more than his health would permit and more than was good for the interests of the cause. If not for that shortcoming, he might have used his abilities for the good of the armed forces to greater advantage. I considered him a very talented person, a marvelous, interesting man, but he drank too much. He himself was aware of this shortcoming, and everyone knew about it. We didn't stay long with Popov. We got in our vehicle, wrapped ourselves in burkas (a good way of protecting yourself from the Stalingrad winds), and went on to Tolbukhin's. We arrived late and warmed ourselves up. Tolbukhin had a good Russian sauna, dug into the side of the riverbank.

Preparations for the offensive were going full blast. Every day our confidence of success increased. We were just waiting for the day of the offensive, as though for a celebration. We were absolutely convinced that this offensive would bring us happiness, although we couldn't specifically picture how great that happiness would be. It turned out to be an occasion for happiness for all of progressive humanity, which was making every effort to win the victory over Hitler. I was surprised at the early frost. Ice began to appear on the Volga early, very early. It was cold, especially at night and in the morning. In the afternoon the sun warmed things up. The offensive was supposed to start on November 19, but later the date was moved to November 20 for our Front, and that is when it happened. On November 7, in the evening, Vasilevsky and I traveled to Tolbukhin's headquarters, where we learned that a great meeting of celebration had been held in Moscow the morning of November 7,[55] and that Stalin had given a speech. This encouraged us. We were happy that life in the capital city was returning to normal, that the capital felt confident, and that Stalin himself had given the main speech.

[As I've said] preparations for the offensive were in full swing. Everyone was hurrying; troops were being concentrated and learning to handle their equipment better, especially the armored forces. The tank crews were being given practical instruction in preparation for the coming operations, not out in the field, but with maps, because you couldn't take tanks out in the field. If that were done, it would attract the attention of enemy aircraft and we would suffer losses, but even more importantly, it would alert the enemy prematurely. The chief condition for success was that our attack be a surprise. Every branch of our armed forces, every military unit was getting ready so that the designated task would be carried out as quickly and efficiently as possible with the fewest possible casualties. Popov and I frequently went out to visit the units. Yeremenko also went despite the difficulties he encountered traveling with his bad leg. He and I even went to the most distant location, to the 51st Army. Its commander was General Trufanov.[56] I met him again later, long after the war, when Mikoyan, Bulganin, and I flew to the island of Sakhalin.[57] Trufanov commanded the troops there.

When we arrived, we again looked into everything relating to the forthcoming operation. Trufanov reported on the plan of operations that he was to carry out. We checked on what units had arrived and what state they were in. In short, we looked into all questions related to the successful accomplishment of the tasks set for our front. Trufanov was to strike in a southwesterly direction and break through the Romanian defense line. The main forces in our 51st Army were Volsky's mechanized corps, Trufanov's infantry divisions, and the cavalry corps. These forces were insufficient to contain the enemy in the encircled area after we had surrounded him, if the enemy brought all his weight to bear for a breakthrough to the south. But these forces were quite sufficient to pierce the enemy's defenses and carry out the main task: to reach the village of Sovetsky with the mechanized corps and link up there with Vatutin's troops from the Southwestern Front, who were supposed to move southward along the west bank of the Don.

Everything had been calculated carefully. Today I don't remember how much time was planned for the preliminary artillery fire [to soften up enemy positions]. Perhaps two hours, perhaps even less. Nor do I remember how many "units of fire" *(boye-komplekty)* we had in terms of artillery shells, but we considered the amount allotted to us enough to do the job. A diversionary attack was organized in the sector of Tolbukhin's 57th Army. Our forces in that area were small. The task was to pin down the enemy and, if we could, to mislead him and cause him confusion. The main thing was to prevent him from moving troops from that sector to the area where our main blow would be struck. We decided that General Popov and I would go to where the 51st Army was, the sector where the main blow would fall, and Yeremenko would go to where Tolbukhin was. His army was closer than the others in relation to our Front's headquarters, although it's true that his action would be only an auxiliary one. Meanwhile the chief of staff, Zakharov, would go to join the 28th Army in Astrakhan.[58] The intention was to make a show of an offensive in that area, in order to pin down enemy troops there also.

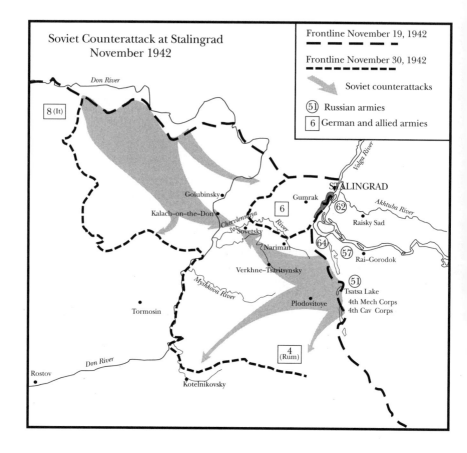

We discussed a great deal with Vasilevsky then and thought out the details of this operation. He was a pleasant person to talk with. You could talk with him about any and every question. Suddenly, a day before the beginning of the operation, Stalin called. On the night of November 19 we were supposed to go to the jumping-off points, each to his own, to the locations from which each grouping would begin its offensive. Stalin asked me: "Where is the chief of staff, Zakharov?"

I said: "We decided he should go to Astrakhan. That sector is quiet, but he should go to Gerasimenko's headquarters all the same, to double-check on everything and make sure the operation there begins successfully. Popov and I are going to the sector where the main blow will be struck, to the 51st Army, to General Trufanov. Yeremenko will go to Tolbukhin's sector, where the auxiliary blow will be struck."

Stalin made no comments. He said only: "You should warn General Zakharov not to get into fights when he's there." It was rather strange for me to hear this from Stalin. It was the first time he had spoken like that, and I never heard that kind of thing from him again. Apparently some change of mind had come over him just then. He had always said you have to "smash people in the mouth." He would say things like, "What are you listening to him for? You should smash him in the mouth!" Such "mouth smashing" practices were instilled in the command staff. Zakharov and other people acted on these recommendations from Stalin and Yeremenko, as I've already said. Many officers did that. And now suddenly Stalin was saying: "You should tell him not to start hitting people."

I told Vasilevsky what Stalin had just said. We laughed at this because Vasilevsky also knew Stalin's views on this question quite well. Stalin didn't like his instructions on this matter to be publicized, although he encouraged everyone he encountered to "smash people in the mouth." Later we began thinking: How should we raise this question with Zakharov? How present this bitter pill to him? I made this suggestion: "Comrade Vasilevsky, let's recommend that Yeremenko tell him. Not you or me, but Yeremenko. Yeremenko himself has encouraged such actions and has done such things himself. Therefore let him say it."

Zakharov was a big favorite of Yeremenko's. And I should mention that as a military man Zakharov deserved a lot of respect. My attitude toward him was also positive—except for this shortcoming, which I knew about and which made me angry. So I reported to Andrei Ivanovich [Yeremenko]: "Stalin just called to ask where we were all going to be. He has probably talked with you too?"

He said: "Yes, he also talked with me."

I said: "I don't know whether he said this to you, but he also said to me that General Zakharov should be warned that he should not allow himself to hit people when he goes to the 28th Army, and if he allows himself to do this, he will be punished. It would be best, Andrei Ivanovich, if it were you that told Zakharov about this and warned him."

Yeremenko was very guarded in the way he took this advice from me. I don't know whether he really had spoken with Stalin and whether Stalin had mentioned this. Stalin might not have said anything about it. Perhaps he had said it only to me. I don't know what Stalin's reasons were for all this. In the evening we gathered at Yeremenko's bunker: Yeremenko, Zakharov, Vasilevsky, and I. The final details of the plan for the offensive were being put in place. Zakharov gave a report. After we had discussed every question, it came time to leave. We all had long distances to travel, especially Zakharov. I looked at Yeremenko. There was only one thing left—for Yeremenko to pass on to Zakharov what Stalin had indicated. But he wasn't saying anything; his tongue was stuck. I said to him: "Well, Andrei Invanovich, we have to be going."

He said: "Yes, we have to be going."

I said: "So then we're off. I'm wondering, Is everything clear?"

He said: "Yes, everything." In short, he was stalling, and I began to get worried.

I said: "Well, Andrei Ivanovich, it's time for us to get going, and something should be said to Comrade Zakharov. So how about it?"

He said: "Yes, yes." And Yeremenko suddenly assumed an official posture and turned toward Zakharov. They were actually great friends.

Yeremenko said: "Look here, Comrade General, you're going to the 28th Army and while you're there—uh—don't—uh, don't go smashing anybody in the mouth. Otherwise things will turn out badly for us."

At this Zakharov raised his head slightly but kept his eyes lowered: "What do you think? That I need to persuade people that way to go on the offensive?"

Yeremenko again said: "Comrade General!" I made some sort of a comment to Zakharov that he should restrain himself; otherwise there could be unpleasantness for him. He muttered something under his breath in reply. It was hard for him to take these comments. I understood that he felt it was an insult to his human dignity and his dignity as a general, but these comments were the result of actions he had allowed himself to commit. And after all, such actions are the most insulting of all to human dignity and the dignity of a soldier.

1. There are two towns called Kalach. The one to which N. S. Khrushchev refers is Kalach on the Don, a town in the Stalingrad area, and not Kalach in Voronezh province. [GS]

2. This was the First Tank Army, formed in July 1942 from the 38th Army and placed under the command of Major General of Artillery K. S. Moskalenko (see Biographies). However, after three weeks it was disbanded when its field command was reassigned to the new Southeastern Front. The First Tank Army reappeared in January 1943 as the First Guards Tank Army, but with different personnel. As for Moskalenko, in August 1942 he was placed in command of the First Guards Army.

3. In Ukraine and the Don and Kuban regions, the term khutor was often used to designate a farming settlement, regardless of the number of households; elsewhere it designated a single-household farm. [GS]

4. Colonel General A. M. Vasilevsky, chief of the General Staff from June 1942. See Biographies.

5. Nikolai Gogol (1809–52) is known for his short stories and novels. He was also a playwright. Though of Ukrainian origin, he wrote in Russian. [SS]

6. The U-2 was an old biplane, designed in 1928 and used as a courier plane and a light night bomber.

7. This change of command took place in August 1942.

8. Kuibyshev (now again known by its old name, Samara) is in the southeastern part of European Russia, between the Volga River and the Urals Mountains. The families of many high-ranking officers and officials, including Khrushchev's own family, were evacuated there during World War II. [SS]

9. From October 1942 he commanded the 33rd Army on the Western Front.

10. The Thirteenth Mechanized Corps, commanded by Major General T. I. Tanaschishin.

11. After the war, Colonel General V. N. Gordov commanded the Volga Military District, but was later demoted and reassigned. Major General G. I. Kulik served as his deputy in the Volga Military District before being retired in June 1946. They were both arrested in 1950 and executed. In 1957 Kulik was posthumously restored to the rank of Marshal of the Soviet Union. See Biographies.

12. Khrushchev is referring to the air raid of August 23, 1942.

13. The Tsaritsa River, a small tributary of the Volga, flowed through Stalingrad.

14. First Secretary of the Stalingrad province and city committees of the AUCP(B) A. S. Chuyanov.

15. The name "Rynok" means "marketplace" in Russian. [GS]

16. Until September 1942, Lieutenant General V. F. Gerasimenko commanded the Stalingrad Military District. See Biographies.

17. Astrakhan is downstream from Stalingrad, at the mouth of the Volga, where it runs into the Caspian Sea. [GS]

18. Major General N. I. Krylov was chief of staff of the Coastal Army at Sevastopol in Crimea. On the approaches to Stalingrad in September 1942 he was appointed chief of staff of the 62nd Army. See Biographies.

19. The Coastal Army, under General Ivan Yefimovich Petrov, defended Odessa for many months in 1941, then was transferred to the defense of Sevastopol on the Crimean peninsula. Except for the evacuated leaders mentioned here by Khrushchev, this army was essentially destroyed during the long siege of Sevastopol, in which Soviet forces fought to the death. The Germans finally took Sevastopol in July 1942. The Coastal Army commander, General Petrov, later headed the Black Sea Coastal Group fighting against the Germans in the Northern Caucasus. [GS]

20. Konstantin Simonov was a prominent Soviet writer who wrote several novels about the battle of Stalingrad. See Biographies. [GS]

21. People's commissar of tank industry V. A. Malyshev. See Biographies.

22. Zaporozhye is a large industrial city in the eastern Ukraine. It is situated on the Dnieper River about 80 kilometers south of Dnepropetrovsk. [SS]

23. Korniyets was a representative of the government of Ukraine, having previously, before the German occupation of Ukraine, been chairman of the Council of People's Commissars of the Ukrainian SSR.

24. G. M. Malenkov, a secretary of the party Central Committee. See Biographies.

25. Air Force Lieutenant General (soon to be promoted to Colonel General) A. A. Novikov became in April 1942 deputy people's commissar

of defense of the USSR and commander of Air Forces. Colonel General of Artillery N. N. Voronov was from July 1941 deputy people's commissar of defense of the USSR and chief of artillery of the Red Army. See Biographies.

26. F. I. Golikov. See Biographies. He occupied this post from August to October 1942.

27. The Thirteenth Guards Infantry Division, commanded by Major General A. I. Rodimtsev. See Biographies.

28. Ruben Ibarruri was the son of Dolores Ibarruri, a prominent Spanish Communist politician and orator during the Spanish civil war of 1936–39, who had taken refuge in the Soviet Union following the victory of General Franco. [SS] See Biographies.

29. Nariman was a settlement on the Chervlennaya River, southwest of Stalingrad.

30. Lieutenant General M. S. Shumilov was at that time in command of the 64th Army. See Biographies.

31. Major General Z. T. Serdyuk.

32. That is, the First Guards Army and the 66th Army.

33. Air Force Major General A. E. Golovanov.

34. At the beginning of the seventeenth century, Diego Uffano, author of The Treatise on Artillery, understanding "artillery" as "the art of shooting" (arte de tirar), introduced the expression "artillery, the goddess of shooting." In the eighteenth century, the outstanding master of artillery armaments J.-B. Baquette de Griboval altered this expression to "artillery, goddess of the battlefields." In this form it was widely used during the Napoleonic Wars. The expression "artillery, the god of war" is a further modification of the expression. It seems to have first appeared in the Soviet press at the time of the Finnish campaign of 1939–40.

35. Lieutenant General (soon to be Colonel General) K. K. Rokossovsky commanded this front from September 1942 to February 1943. See Biographies.

36. Air Force Major General (later Lieutenant General) N. S. Skripko was deputy commander of Strategic Air Forces from March 1942.

37. Rear Admiral D. D. Rogachev commanded the Volga Naval Flotilla from February 1942 to May 1943.

38. Lieutenant General G. F. Zakharov was chief of staff of the front from August to October 1942. See Biographies.

39. Zakharov had already graduated before the war from the Vystrel ("shot") courses (the Higher Courses in Shooting and Tactics for Red Army Command Personnel Named After the Comintern), the M. V. Frunze Military Academy, and the Military Academy of the General Staff.

40. The Eighth Air Army, commanded by Air Force Major General (later Lieutenant General

and Colonel General) T. T. Khryukin from July 1942 to July 1944.

41. Hero of the Soviet Union, Air Force Major General V. V. Naneishvili.

42. Lieutenant General M. M. Popov had previously commanded the Leningrad Military District, the Northern Front, the Leningrad Front, the 61st Army, and the 40th Army. He took up the post of deputy commander of the Stalingrad Front in October 1942.

43. This was an application of the Soviet military tactic of *razvedka boyem* ("reconnaissance by combat"). Combat is initiated with the purpose of discovering the location and strength of the enemy's positions. [SS]

44. Khrushchev here draws a parallel with the way enterprise managers would strive to exceed the output targets set for them in the annual plan. In the context of reconnaissance by combat (see preceding note), such "overfulfillment"—continuing combat operations after the goals of reconnaissance had already been achieved—could have undesirable consequences. [SS]

45. Lake Tsatsa is a small lake about 50 kilometers south of Stalingrad. [SS]

46. The Kalmyks are traditionally nomadic people of Mongol origin who live in Kalmykia, a region of semidesert steppe abutting the northwestern shore of the Caspian Sea. The northern border of the Republic of Kalmykia, which is part of the Russian Federation, lies just south of Lake Tsatsa. [SS]

47. Lieutenant General T. T. Shapkin commanded the Fourth Cavalry Corps.

48. That is, Commander of the Voronezh Front and later of the Southwestern Front Lieutenant General (later Colonel General and Army General) N. F. Vatutin.

49. This was the Fourth Mechanized Corps, commanded by Major General (later Lieutenant General) of Tank Forces V. T. Volsky.

50. The Sarpinsky Lakes are a chain of small lakes stretching south from Lake Tsatsa to Lake Sarpa, lying just north of Sarpa in central Kalmykia. [SS]

51. The Cross of Saint George was a medal awarded in tsarist Russia for outstanding courage. The Order of the Red Banner was a Soviet medal. [SS]

52. The Turkmen are a traditionally nomadic people of mixed origin who speak a Turkic language. Their mostly desert homeland—in Soviet times the Turkmen SSR, known also as Turkmenia, now the independent state of Turkmenistan—stretches eastward from the southern part of the eastern shore of the Caspian Sea. [SS]

53. Major General F. I. Tolbukhin did indeed command the 57th Army at this time. See Biographies.

54. The Akhtuba River, 530 kilometers long, is an arm of the Volga that branches off to the east above Stalingrad and merges with the Volga again south of the city. The floodplain between the Volga and the Akhtuba is an important agricultural area, where especially vegetables and melons are cultivated. In 1942–43 there was also a town named Akhtuba, now part of Akhtubinsk, some 30 kilometers east of Stalingrad. [GS/SS]

55. November 7 is the anniversary of the Bolshevik Revolution of 1917. [GS]

56. Major General N. I. Trufanov commanded the 51st Army in July 1942, then again from October 1942 to February 1943. He served in the Far East from 1950 to 1957.

57. A. I. Mikoyan and N. A. Bulganin. See Biographies. Sakhalin is a large island off Russia's Pacific coast. The island came under Russian rule in the mid-nineteenth century. Its southern half, ceded to Japan after the Russo-Japanese war of 1905, was taken by Soviet forces at the end of World War II. After Stalin's death, Khrushchev, Mikoyan, and Bulganin, as part of their assertion of leadership in the Soviet Union, made a much-publicized trip to the Soviet Far East, including Sakhalin, during their return trip from a visit to Mao in China in 1954. Those journeys are recounted in later volumes of Khrushchev's memoirs. [GS/SS]

58. Lieutenant General V. F. Gerasimenko was there in command of the 28th Army from September 1942 to November 1943. See Biographies.

## TURN OF THE TIDE AT STALINGRAD

Being on the verge of our counteroffensive gave a big boost to our morale. We said goodbye, wished one another well, and went our separate ways. I got into a vehicle with Popov, while Vasilevsky headed off to Tolbukhin's command post. Toward dawn we reached our destination. The roads were good and level. It was steppe land. We were familiar with the route and we hurried along at high speed. We arrived at Trufanov's command post.[1] Everything was ready, strictly according to schedule. The men were in their places, every unit having received its orders. We only had to wait for the appointed time to begin the operation and then go to it. We had decided to limit the preliminary bombardment to artillery alone. We couldn't use airplanes because there was heavy fog in the morning, which made flying impossible. Also, we were afraid that air strikes might hit our own troops.

It was of course a big loss for us that we couldn't use air strikes against the enemy lines. That would have disorganized the enemy more and sown panic among the Romanian troops,[2] making the task of breaking through their defenses easier. But we didn't have that possibility. Besides, we thought that our artillery would enable us to break through the enemy defenses; then we would immediately send our tank forces into the breach, and after the tanks spread out, we would throw the cavalry corps into the battle to disorganize the enemy's rear.

November 20 came. The army commander and I were sitting at his command post. Everything was ready. The artillery had its guns cocked, as one might say. The infantry, the mechanized corps, and the cavalry corps had all taken their positions. The flare of a rocket gave the signal and our artillery opened fire. I had the impression that the earth itself was shaking. It was very intense fire. I don't remember now how many artillery pieces we had per kilometer along the front line. Later, when we were fighting outside Kiev, we had more than three hundred artillery pieces per kilometer in the main area of battle. Later on, even that magnitude was exceeded. We didn't have even half that amount here [that is, in the counteroffensive around Stalingrad], but for those days it was considered a lot. It was considered a tremendous artillery force. And sure enough, it thoroughly disorganized the enemy. The artillery bombardment stopped and the infantry were ordered to occupy the enemy trenches. The infantry immediately began moving forward and did not encounter any great resistance on the part of the Romanian troops. The Romanians held fairly advantageous positions. First, they had had plenty of time to dig in. Second, they were in an elevated position. The height was not great, but nevertheless it was an elevated position, from which they could more easily see the area around the front lines, whereas our troops had to climb to reach the enemy positions. The topography was on the enemy's side, and the enemy had been able to choose his position when he constructed his defenses.

Our troops broke through to the enemy trenches and began hand-to-hand fighting. The enemy retreated. We ordered Volsky[3] to send his mechanized corps into the breach. We waited, but no tanks came. We began to get worried. What was this? We were losing time. After all, the enemy might reorganize and set up a new defense line farther to the rear, after abandoning his front-line positions. We assumed that the Germans had some previously constructed defensive positions, and still there were no tanks. What was this? Dawn had already come. The sun had risen. You couldn't actually see the sun because the fog was too heavy, but by all indications the fog would soon disperse. And the mechanized corps didn't seem able to make it into the breach! Popov[4] and I decided to get in our vehicle and go to Volsky's command post. We knew where he was located. We would drive around among his brigades and, as the saying goes, give them a poke in the back, or elsewhere, to get them going and speed them up.

When Popov and I arrived in the area where the tank troops were deployed, the way they were organized gave me a bad impression. It was like some sort of bazaar. Everything was plainly visible. Our troops were out on the open plain without even a bush around. All the tanks and other vehicles and the men were right out in the open. We were lucky it wasn't good flying weather, and enemy planes weren't in the sky. If enemy aircraft had come, I don't know how badly they might have damaged the tank corps, not to speak of the cavalry. Of course the enemy would not have stopped our offensive, and our tasks would have been accomplished nonetheless, but we would have suffered considerable losses. What we saw there was simply a Sorochinsky Fair,[5] a real bazaar. Of course you can't dig a hole and hide horses and wagons in the earth. Everything was standing out on the open ground. It was a dreadful scene. Volsky was still fussing around with the commanders of his brigades, giving them orders. We began telling them to hurry up—it was time to stop this; the orders should have been given much earlier.

We drove around among the units and began urging the mechanized corps to carry out the offensive. At the time I thought this had been an oversight on Volsky's part, that he had not prepared his brigade commanders on time. Later I came to understand that apparently there was something else going on. The brigade commanders had actually received their instructions. In fact they had received their orders in plenty of time.

Later I observed this kind of thing not only in the case of Volsky but with other tank commanders as well. They were deliberately slow about getting started, waiting for the infantry to clear a path, so that the tanks wouldn't come under fire and they wouldn't have any losses when they went through the breach. They were waiting for the breach to be widened further, so that it would be easier to send the tank troops through. Unfortunately this line of reasoning is something I often heard after that. And I not only heard it; I also encountered it directly in the case of many tank troop commanders. I'm not going to name any names. Some of these men hold fairly high positions even today [that is, in 1968]. They fought well and completed the war with good records, but I observed this failing on the part of many of them.

Finally Volsky began to move, and we all started driving over the fields through this bazaar. The sun was starting to break through the grayness. The fog was rising and dispersing. I could see that there were two airplanes flying over the enemy's front lines and bombing them. I said: "Look, Comrade Popov, what in the world is that? Whose are those planes? It seems like they're ours. But there's no enemy over there any more. The enemy has been smashed in that area. So how can this be? Maybe it's enemy planes bombing our troops?" I couldn't figure it out, and neither could Popov. Of course, on the whole we were quite happy. We were in a good mood because we were winning! We had broken through the enemy's front line. The infantry had gone to work with a will. But these two airplanes troubled us. Then we saw that the planes had turned and were heading in our direction. They were coming in very low over the scene of this vast bazaar with all its tanks and horses, with everything out in the open, as though on the palm of your hand. Then the pilots noticed our jeep and came flying straight at us. They seemed to be our planes.

Popov said: "We'd better jump out. Run for it and flatten out. Or else God only knows what'll happen." We jumped out of the jeep, he on one side and I on the other, and the airplanes strafed us with their machine guns. Later Popov said that a burst of machine-gun fire had come very close to him. It came fairly close to me, too, but not in my immediate vicinity, because I didn't hear the smack of bullets in the ground. Then the planes flew off.

I said: "Those are our planes sure enough. What the heck are they shooting at us for? How could they get this so mixed up? This area is marked on all the maps that our pilots might use. It's clearly designated as the area of concentration for the tank troops and cavalry before being sent through the break in enemy lines."

We got the mechanized corps moving forward and returned to Trufanov's command post. He made us happy by presenting us with the first prisoners of war. They had seized a couple of dozen to begin with, and more were to come later. I remember that among the prisoners was one man with the last name Chaikovsky. He was a Russian, he told me—from Kishinev. Another prisoner was a very interesting Romanian. I interrogated him; it was not necessary to force anything out of him. He himself understood what a rotten position the Romanian forces had been placed in. He understood that the war was not being waged in Romania's interests, but in the interests of Germany, and that the Romanian military dictator, Antonescu,[6] had sacrificed his country to the Germans. We didn't have to use any propaganda on this man. He said that he was the son of a priest and that his attitude was not peculiar to himself alone, that many commanders he had had a chance to talk with shared the same sentiments. I said to him: "Would you perhaps agree to write a leaflet or an open letter then, to these commanders, so that they would stop resisting Soviet forces and would surrender to us and thereby help Romania in the struggle against the common enemy, against Hitler?"

He said: "Yes, I would agree to that willingly. Give me some paper and I'll do that."

As for a leaflet signed by Chaikovsky, that didn't interest me. After all, he was Russian. The name Chaikovsky would not impress the Romanians if he was calling on them to surrender to the Russians. On the other hand we had a native Romanian, son of a priest, and an officer of the Romanian army. (It seems to me he was a company commander.) All that could make an impression on the Romanians, especially religious ones. I said to Chaikovsky: "How could you go and discredit such a famous name?"[7]

He answered: "Yes, I understand. I know who that name belonged to. But you should understand, too. It was not only me they drafted, but other Russians as well. We didn't want to fight. The proof of it is that we surrendered to you as soon as the fighting began. This by itself tells you that I didn't want to fight and at the first opportunity I did everything I could to surrender to you. And other Russians did likewise." These prisoners were placed at the disposal of our intelligence service, and we went forward with the troops.

It was necessary not only to move forward but also to do everything possible to speed up the advance. We were interested above all in Volsky's mobile forces, and we traveled over to where he was. Today it's impossible to relate what happened day by day. (I think that anyone can understand my situation.) I remember only the general panorama of events or some particularly striking incidents.

Volsky moved his tanks forward. Enemy resistance turned out to be weak. You could say that in general there was no really organized resistance. In the sector where our main forces were in operation, Volsky took many prisoners. Many of the enemy were killed, a great many. We warned Volsky that in no case should he allow violence toward prisoners of war. First, that was immoral. Second, it was dangerous, because the enemy would use that against us in his propaganda, saying, "Don't surrender to Soviet troops; they're shooting prisoners!" But when we started moving forward, I saw many large groups of enemy soldiers who had been shot. Our people were standing nearby. I said to Volsky: "This is strange. I saw many scenes where enemy soldiers who had been shot were lying around."

He said: "No, they were all killed in battle." I don't rule out the possibility that perhaps in some places our directive was violated by people influenced by hatred and bitterness. Every one of our soldiers had strong reasons to feel that way. When we were retreating, we saw what was being left behind for the enemy. We also had information about the reign of terror on enemy-occupied territory. In Soviet Ukraine, on occupied territory of the RSFSR, in Belorussia, and in the Northern Caucasus—wherever the enemy showed up he ruthlessly massacred all "undesirables," recognizing no moral criteria. Hitler openly mocked moral considerations. To the victor everything is permitted! The Russians had to be destroyed, demoralized, intimidated, terrorized.

Our soldiers knew this. And if, in violation of our orders, abuses were committed in some places, may these people be forgiven for it, as the saying goes. This was not an expression of some organic character trait of our people. It was the result of the war that had been imposed on them, which brought human feelings to the breaking point. Of course people who fought in the war understand this, as does anyone who takes a careful and objective attitude toward the regrettable acts that were sometimes committed then.

Some amusing incidents from this time come to mind. As in any tragedy, so too in the course of the war there were also some comic moments. I remember once after the offensive had been carried out, we were traveling late at night, across the open steppe. There were no roads. Driving was dangerous because there was always the chance that you could hit a mine in some unexpected place. We were driving along, not sure that we were going in the right direction. There were no landmarks, no settlements, not even a bush. The naked steppe. We had to get our bearings from the stars. But even on the open steppe you can't fight a war steering by the stars. Then we saw a light flashing. We immediately headed our jeep toward that light. Popov jumped out of the car. He was a man who enjoyed life greatly, and he laughed with all his might: "Comrade Khrushchev, come here and take a look. You'll see some real live devils."

I got out of the jeep and went over. Some of our soldiers were sitting around a small campfire they had built. You couldn't get a large campfire going because there was very little firewood. The soldiers had gathered everything they could find out on the steppe that would burn. And they had water from somewhere and were making tea as they huddled around the fire.

They were so black with soot it was frightening. All you could see was their eyes and teeth shining. They really did seem like devils, there in the middle of the night, but these young fellows just smiled when they saw that "some generals" had arrived. I didn't have any military rank then, but I was wearing a military uniform. They saw immediately that some military big shots had arrived. We questioned them. Something in their vehicle had broken down, or else they had run out of fuel. "We're waiting for help to come," they said. They were artillerymen with antitank guns—one or two guns. We joked with them a little. They couldn't tell us anything that made any sense; they themselves didn't know what was going on; the only thing they could tell us was what military unit they were with.

The next day again we were traveling along the front lines and came across another amusing scene. I told Stalin about it many times. An *arba*[8] was bumping along. In it were sitting five or six Romanian soldiers, with one of them driving the horses. They were heading east. Popov asked them: "Where are you going? Who are you?"

One Romanian soldier handed us a piece of paper with a note scribbled on it. Popov took it and read: "This is to state hereby that so-and-so many Romanian soldiers, horses, and an *arba* are traveling east toward the Volga, to surrender as prisoners of war." And there was a signature: Lieutenant So-and-So. We had to laugh. The Romanians saw that our mood was not hostile, and they too became cheerful.

Popov handed the note back to them and said: "Keep going in the direction you're headed." Of course they didn't understand a word. So he waved his arm in the direction of the Volga, and they headed off to surrender, and we continued on our way toward the front lines.

We came to the village of Plodovitoye [which could be translated as "Place of Fruitfulness"].[9] It was a sorry little village. Everywhere around there the settlements had such interesting and life-affirming names. Apparently when this dry semidesert steppe country was being settled, the people arriving there chose these beautiful names as a kind of compensation. A lieutenant came up to me and said: "I want to ask what to do with my prisoners."

"How many do you have?"

"About three hundred."

"Where are they?"

"Over there, not far away."

Popov and I went over. We saw a huge crowd of prisoners standing around. We began questioning them through an interpreter. At that very moment another lieutenant rode up on horseback: "May I speak with you? I would like to know what to do with my prisoners and where to send them."

"How many do you have?"

"Probably about three thousand."

"Where are these prisoners?"

"Over there beyond the church."

We went over there, too. An enormous file of people, maintaining some kind of order, was stretched out on the steppe. The lieutenant told us that this was an entire Romanian regiment, equipped with large-caliber artillery. The regiment had surrendered with its commander taking the lead. I thought to myself: "An entire artillery regiment here behind our lines. The devil only knows what unpleasantness it could cause for us." I said out loud: "Issue a command that all the officers should come forward. We need to separate the officers from the soldiers and take them separately back to the rear to some receiving station for prisoners of war. There's an awful lot of weaponry lying around out here on the plains, from rifles to cannons. They could do quite a bit of damage to us, because they're a full-strength artillery unit." We had no forces in that rear area.

The Romanian officers came forward. The lieutenant invited the commander of the regiment to approach. A middle-aged man walked over and calmly stated: "I am the commander of the regiment. I never even ordered the coverings removed from our guns. I decided not to open fire but to surrender the full strength of the regiment with all its arms and equipment. I am hereby surrendering everything to you: officers, soldiers, and artillery."

I said to him: "Colonel Sir, wouldn't you agree to issue an appeal to the Romanian soldiers and officers to cease their resistance and surrender? Since you yourself have done this, you understand correctly that the war against us was imposed on you by Hitler. You don't want to fight in this war and for you this war is already over. So please help us and help those who are still on the other side of the front line so that they will follow your example."

He answered: "Willingly! Just give me the chance, and I'll write that kind of letter." Later when I was questioning him further I told him about the officer I had spoken with previously who had signed a similar leaflet addressed to the Romanian troops. It turned out that he knew the other officer, and I later found out that the other officer had addressed his leaflet precisely to this colonel.

Sure enough, when I reread the leaflet of that other officer, the son of the priest, who I had spoken with earlier, he had literally addressed this colonel: "Do not fight against your own conscience! I know your sentiments. We must end this war!" When I returned to headquarters, they showed me this leaflet, which I had ordered to be printed. But it turned out there was no need for it: the unit to which it had been addressed had surrendered and was already in our hands. We ordered the Romanian officers to be taken away separately from the soldiers.

The operation proceeded successfully. Our troops were moving forward and we were enjoying the sweet taste of our first big victories. It's hard to convey in words how happy we felt then and how we rejoiced. This was the first time on our part of the battlefront that we had successfully broken through enemy lines, and having smashed everything that stood in front of us, we were now developing our offensive and encountering no resistance. Of course we understood that these were Romanians and not Germans. They were not resolute fighters because they knew this war was not in the interests of Romania. Nevertheless it was the enemy. There were Romanians and Romanians, as the saying goes. There were Romanians of quite a different kind from those I have described. We knew how they had behaved when they were on the offensive. How arrogantly they had treated civilians and how they had killed our people. They had marched into our country together with Hitler's troops and had also committed atrocities against Soviet soldiers. And so the joy and exultation that our soldiers and officers felt must be correctly understood. Our people were simply glowing with happiness.

I don't remember which day of the offensive it was, the third or fourth, when we completed our military operations, having accomplished the task that had been set for us. Our tank troops had reached Sovetsky and the Don River, and Vatutin's troops had come down the Don to Kalach. We were supposed to meet up there, so Popov and I traveled to Kalach. I'm not speaking very precisely here. Generals who took part in this operation have been more exact in their memoirs because they had access to materials of the General Staff, official documents. With this help they could reconstruct everything exactly as it had developed, including the chronology of the events. I don't have that possibility. At any rate, Popov and I went to meet the commander of the tank corps of the Southwestern Front. The commander was Kravchenko,[10] a general who I knew. I met with him frequently during the war and after. Today he is dead. But he was such a strong and healthy man.

He didn't even seem to show any wear and tear, and yet he is dead. And he was such a good fighting man back then.

When we reached the place where he had taken up his headquarters he said that he didn't feel well, that he was sick. He had something like the flu, but he was bearing up, staying on his feet. We greeted each other and expressed our mutual joy at the link-up of our Fronts. Kravchenko suggested: "Let's drink a bottle of champagne to celebrate our meeting. I have some French champagne captured from the enemy."

I said: "Well, let's do it." We opened the champagne and each had a glassful, but drank no more than that, not because we didn't want to, but because we had no "reserves" other than that one bottle of champagne for celebrating the linkup between the Stalingrad and Southwestern Fronts.

Kravchenko addressed me formally: "Comrade Khrushchev, please accept a gift from me in memory of our meeting, a German dagger. True, it has a swastika on it, but by now the swastika is a bit mangled. This souvenir will be a reminder of our meeting."

I said: "All right, I'll take it. I have a little boy, Seryozha [nickname of Sergei], and I'll send it to him. It will be tangible proof that our troops are beating the Germans, and on top of that, it will be a nice gift."

We didn't stay long at Kravchenko's, just long enough to inform one another about the situation. The situation was a good one. We felt no threat from the enemy and had crushed all opposition. We didn't know what the enemy might try next or what we would encounter next. That was in the future, but for the present we had carried out our assignments brilliantly. Kravchenko said that he had marched along the west bank of the Don and had not encountered much resistance. The enemy's rear areas had been pretty weak, not secured by troops [in any large numbers]. As I've said, we rejoiced at our success. When we first thought about this operation, in our letter to Stalin, we had proposed the plan cautiously. We hadn't known what our reserves might be, whether the Stavka had any reserves at its disposal, and we hadn't known how insubstantial enemy strength was in the direction we chose to strike. It may not have been our specific recommendations that became the basis for the plan of operation, but at any rate our recommendations did not conflict with the plan that was carried out or the proposals possibly made by other commanders. The main thing was not who first made the proposal but the fact that our attack had succeeded. The enemy had been defeated, and the German troops in Stalingrad were surrounded. Now the thing was to hold them there and defeat those forces also.

Later we were to encounter difficulties. I talked about these with Zhukov, who came to our headquarters and reported on the Stavka's thinking about a plan of operation. I told him that we sensed that the reason we had been able to accomplish our task was that the enemy was weak in the area. I said: "But unless you give us reinforcements, we won't be able to hold the surrounded enemy. They'll roll right over us and break out of Stalingrad."

I have already mentioned Zhukov's reply to me: "Let the enemy go off somewhere away from Stalingrad. That would be a big victory for us—to have driven the Germans back from the Volga." I agreed with Zhukov, but I wanted more. Besides, I don't think there could have been any disagreement between us on this point. Zhukov had the same desire I did, but the problem was how to hold the Germans and defeat them.

That evening Popov and I decided to go to Tolbukhin's headquarters instead of returning to the 51st Army headquarters. Tolbukhin was closer to Sovetsky. Besides, the 51st Army had accomplished its task; the enemy's troops had been defeated and many taken prisoner, and no immediate danger seemed to be looming ahead of us. Meanwhile the enemy's main forces were in Stalingrad. Tolbukhin's army—that is, the 57th Army, not the 51st—was the weakest of all on the Stalingrad Front, with the smallest number of troops. That's why we decided to go to Tolbukhin's headquarters and inform ourselves in greater detail. As we were on our way we learned that Tolbukhin had moved his command post to some gully near Nariman, closer to the Don. So we headed in that direction.

It was an autumn night typical of southern Russia. No matter how hard you screwed up your eyes, you couldn't see any landmarks. We began hunting for the gully, circling around for a while. I expressed my doubts to Popov: "Markian Mikhailovich, I don't think we're going to find that gully tonight. There are no roads. We haven't been there before. We don't know of any landmarks. It's going to be very hard to get there."

He answered boldly: "Well, Comrade Khrushchev, the main thing for a general is to have a map, a compass, and a speedometer, so you can tell how far your car has traveled. We'll find it!" We kept searching. Later this incident became a full-fledged anecdote for us. Many times later, when I met Popov, I would remind him about it, and he would smile.

We had just set off again when we came across the naked corpses of two German soldiers. They were plainly visible despite the darkness of the night. A little farther, the corpse of a gray horse was lying there. Of course this was not any kind of a landmark. But there were also some German signposts. We could read what was written on them. Popov had two adjutants, one of whom

knew German. But what good did that do us? Whichever way we went—
every single time—we eventually found ourselves back where these two
corpses lay. It was like some strange place with a hex on it! Over and over,
endlessly, we kept coming back to these corpses, the two naked soldiers and
the gray horse. What kind of hallucination was this? It was like something
out of Gogol! Some evil spirit was leading us round and round and bringing
us back to this place. Finally we heard voices. Someone was coming. We too
let out a shout.

A vehicle was approaching. A man got out and said: "I am Colonel So and
So, commander of such-and-such tank unit."

He recognized me and asked where we were going. "To the gully at Nariman," I told him.

He said: "Comrade Khrushchev, you're not going to find that gully. After
all, there's nothing but flat steppe country all around. And what do you
want to be driving around here for? There you can see the German front
lines where the rockets are flaring. (The Germans kept their front lines well
lit up at night.) You're liable to hit a mine in this area. I suggest that we travel
together. I'm heading for a first-aid station. I was wounded in the arm. At
first I thought I would just bear with it, but now the wound is starting to
bother me. I'm afraid it may be starting to fester, that gangrene might set in.
I want some qualified person to dress the wound and do everything that's
supposed to be done for this kind of injury."

I agreed, but Popov said: "No, we're going to keep hunting on our own."
We said goodbye and went on our way. Again we heard voices. Another
vehicle came up. We stopped and got out of our vehicle.

It turned out that a representative of the Stavka was on his way through, a
general whose job was communications. He said: "I'm heading for Tolbukhin's
headquarters on the Volga. I also wanted to find the gully at Nariman, but I
couldn't find it, and you won't be able to find it either. Shall we travel
together?" Again we refused. We still hoped to find the gully. Again we started
hunting for it, but kept circling around, ending up next to those two corpses. It
seemed to us that we had been traveling a long way in a certain direction when
suddenly it would turn out that somehow we had made another circle and had
ended up in the same place again. There lay the two corpses and the gray horse.

I was shivering from the cold despite the burka I was wrapped in. Popov
was, too. The cup of our patience was running over. We came up to some
sort of road crossing and saw several signs in German. An officer [one of
Popov's adjutants] ran over to them and began to translate from German to
tell what these signposts were pointing to. Popov was cold. He couldn't keep

one tooth next to the other; his teeth were chattering so. He shouted to the adjutant: "Bring it here."

The man pulled the sign off the post and brought it over. I said: "Well, he's read you what was written on the sign, but now you don't know what direction the post was pointing in because he's taken the sign off the post."

Popov agreed: "Yes, I guess we're not going to find that Nariman gully tonight. Let's go to the headquarters on the Volga."

We knew quite well where that headquarters was located. Soldiers say that a horse will barely drag itself along when it's heading toward the front. But when it's heading away from the front it goes full speed. Our situation was not exactly like that. We were hunting for [Tolbukhin's] field headquarters [not heading toward the front lines], back toward the Volga. We knew that Tolbukhin had a solid and well-equipped army headquarters. Now we were filled with anticipation, frozen as we were, at the thought of getting into Tolbukhin's Russian sauna when we arrived. Tolbukhin loved saunas, and he had built some good ones. When we got to the Volga, General Popov said to me: "Well, Comrade Khrushchev, I don't think you are ever going to forget how we wandered around this night. I think you'll remember the rest of your life the corpses of those German soldiers and that gray horse and our adventures, trying to find our way using a map, speedometer, and our watches."

I said: "Yes, I'll remember this a long, long time." And that was the end of the adventure we had returning from our joyful celebration with Kravchenko.

The defeat of the enemy, the linkup of our two Fronts, the successful encirclement of the Germans in Stalingrad—all that was certainly something to be happy about. We had earned that happiness by all our suffering during the course of the war, the dreadful retreats, the defeats we had suffered, and our other bitter experiences. The Don Front, commanded by Rokossovsky, had also accomplished its tasks. I won't say anything about that here because I don't remember specifically what Rokossovsky's assignments were. But the Don Front was securing its new positions against the Germans. The task of the Stalingrad Front was to direct its main forces to the south to strengthen the defenses there in case the enemy tried to break out. We already understood that if the surrounded troops did not try to break out, that meant they had received an order from Berlin not to abandon Stalingrad but to wait until help arrived and their former positions could be reestablished. We understood from the enemy's actions that, indeed, such a decision had been made. Consequently we had to expect that the enemy would try to strike blows from the south and west. But any help that might come from the west would have to come from beyond the Don. The task of stopping any such forces was on the shoulders of the Southwestern Front commanded by Vatutin. Our duty was to block the path from the south, so that any troops sent from that direction to help Paulus could be stopped. Rokossovsky's Don Front, together with us, had the task of keeping the enemy encircled.

Operating along the sector of the front in the direction of Kotelnikovsky[11] were the 51st Army, Shapkin's cavalry corps, Volsky's mechanized corps, and other units. I went out to visit that group of forces because a serious situation had developed there. We knew from our intelligence data that the German field marshal, General von Manstein, was commanding the forces moving toward us with the aim of liberating the group we had surrounded.[12] He began to push us back. His troops were already within 50 kilometers of Paulus's front line. The headquarters of Tolbukhin's army, where I stayed most of the time (I went to the headquarters of our Front very little at that time), was located then at Verkhne-Tsaritsynsky, directly between Paulus's troops and the troops of Manstein, who had reached the Myshkova River[13] in the first days after Paulus was encircled. Tolbukhin's forces were so few that one sector of the front, about 6 or 7 kilometers long, was completely bare. We had nothing there at all. But because of an order issued by Hitler, which doomed the surrounded German troops to inaction, ordering them to stay where they were and wait for help, the enemy missed a chance to break out. If Paulus had struck at us to the south, as he wanted, he undoubtedly would have had the chance to break out. We would not have been able to hold Paulus. But as the saying goes, although we didn't have good luck, Hitler's stupidity helped out. He condemned Paulus's forces to immobility even though they had great strength in weaponry and a large number of troops. They sat and waited, and during that time we took measures to solidify the circle we had closed around them.

Soon after we had surrounded the Germans a decision was made to try to break through the defenses of the surrounded troops and smash them. Our forces were not strong enough for that, but our desire to do so was great. And so we tried to do that with Tolbukhin's divisions, after giving him some reinforcements. We wanted to break through Paulus's defenses in the region of the Chervlennaya River,[14] where there was broken terrain cut by many streams. Popov and I went to Tolbukhin's command post. Its position was advantageous. You could see literally everything in front of you, as though it was on the palm of your hand. The command post was on a hill; there was a valley below, and then there was another hill. We were visible to the enemy, as though on the palm of his hand, just as he was to us. I even saw a German soldier walking across the field and suddenly disappearing, apparently into a bomb shelter. We sent tanks in that direction. I don't remember now who the commander was. At that point Tanaschishin, commander of the 13th Mechanized Corps, had been sent back for rest and recuperation, and Volsky's mechanized corps was located farther south near Kotelnikovsky.

We used all our forces, but the fighting brought us no success. By the end of the day we saw that we couldn't continue such intensive fighting on the next day, despite our desire to break the enemy's resistance. The Germans had tanks there and heavy artillery. It's true that no aircraft were operating on their side. On our side some fighter planes were active, but not very many. They couldn't really help the ground forces very much. With the onset of darkness we called off the attack, especially as we had suffered losses, particularly tanks. We didn't have many tanks. If you compared our losses to the number of tanks we had, these losses were appreciable. Still, we didn't lose hope of breaking through the enemy's defenses and penetrating Paulus's positions. We figured that every day the enemy was being exhausted further; every day was weakening him physically, because after all the surrounded army wouldn't have enough food. We didn't have any specific information about this. We simply calculated that this was so. And it is now evident from published material about Paulus that we were right. We made a second attempt to break through, but it too was unsuccessful.

I remember the following incident. We were in a command post. It was just a hole in the ground covered with a layer of beams and camouflaged with dirt spread over the beams. Army Commander Tolbukhin was there, along with Popov and myself as representatives of the Front. Suddenly we saw an airplane descending in our direction. It looked like it was going to land right on top of the command post and destroy everything there. "Whose plane is that?" we wondered. It was hard to make out. In the end the plane landed (even today I find it hard to believe) about 10 meters or maybe even less from the command post. The explanation for this was not that the pilot was highly skilled; it was purely an accident. Such incredible accidents do happen in wartime and also when you're out hunting. I came out of the shelter. The airplane turned out to be Soviet. The pilot was still in his cockpit in a state of shock. They began pulling him out of there, and he regained his senses. They sent him off to the hospital, but the airplane stayed where it was.

I went back into our shelter. A little while later when I came out again, the airplane had already been stripped bare. Our people had been at work.

Everything that could have had value to a soldier had been taken: the clock, the window glass, and so on. All sorts of knickknacks and contraptions could be made out of the things that were stolen. Soldiers found a use for everything. I was amazed and angry. That airplane could have been repaired and put back to use! Such an attitude toward military property depressed me, but no one else paid any special attention to the incident.

As darkness set in, we saw German transport planes flying over with supplies for Paulus's troops. They flew in, in big waves, as though they were on parade. Our antiaircraft guns went to work, but we had a very low percentage of success in hitting these targets. Only two enemy planes were knocked down in our sector on the first day, and on the second day the number was also very small.

When we later interrogated captured enemy soldiers I was curious about what cargo they had been flying in. Was it food for the soldiers? Weapons? Fuel? Ammunition? As it turned out, they brought a little of everything. Later when our troops advanced further into the encircled area, German cargo planes were no longer able to land, and instead they dropped cargo by parachute. But that was much later on. The point here is that our first efforts at eliminating the surrounded German forces were not successful.

General Shumilov,[15] commander of the 64th Army, had the assignment to go on the offensive from the south. Everything in that area had been destroyed. Shumilov reported to us that his troops had occupied such-and-such a place. We congratulated him. Later Yeremenko and I thought it over, exchanged opinions, and called Shumilov: "You should double-check all the same to make sure your report was not mistaken." "No, no," he assured us. You had to know Shumilov to know what he was like. He was a very honest and conscientious person. Still, on the next day, when he checked into things, it turned out that he had been misled. He explained to us that the Germans had counterattacked after he had already sent his report, and they had retaken their positions. I talked with him about this more than once after that. The point is that this was how people who deceived you would justify themselves; they would dream up the story that the enemy had counterattacked. This was a typical explanation when it was inaccurately reported that one or another place had been taken. People would say, "The enemy counterattacked and drove us out." But there was no counterattack. People simply reported prematurely, thinking they were about to take such-and-such a village, and then they wouldn't succeed in taking it.

As time went on, the enemy began to increase his pressure from the Kotelnikovsky area in the direction of Stalingrad. Once again our troops put up stubborn resistance, but we suffered heavy losses. I went to that area several times. We sent Zakharov there as a superior officer who would coordinate the efforts of our people right on the spot. We began to be seriously worried about this area because we kept backing up and backing up toward Stalingrad. A real danger arose that Manstein would break through. At that point we received word that the Second Guards Army, commanded by Malinovsky,[16] was being transferred to us. I knew Malinovsky and had a high regard for him. Yeremenko and I were very happy to hear this news and looked forward to the arrival of the Guards Army. It soon arrived and was placed at our disposal, and we immediately sent it into battle against Manstein's troops. This force was a saving grace. It consisted of fresh, strong, well-trained, and well-armed young men. The Second Guards Army had three infantry corps, and each corps had three divisions and a tank regiment, with twenty-two to twenty-four tanks in each regiment. For those days that was a powerful force—in short, an army with its full complement. Its deputy commander was General Kreizer,[17] who had been awarded the title Hero of the Soviet Union. A young military man, he made a very good impression on me. That army's chief of staff was Biryuzov,[18] also a young man and a good general. In short, the commanders and the troops were top-notch.

This army came into contact with enemy forces in December on the Myshkova River. Intense fighting flared all along the line, and the enemy advance was stopped. We began driving the enemy back. At that point Vasilevsky flew in once again. We traveled with him up to the front lines and saw how stubbornly the fighting was going on. There were heavy losses on our side. Sometimes he and I would "make estimates" (as the military men put it). We would stand at a certain point and look to see how many dead there were within our range of vision. Alas, we counted a great many bodies from our side, mostly young men. I retrieved a Young Communist League booklet from the body of one young man who had been killed. There was a hole right through the booklet. A bullet had hit him in the chest.

We soon received an additional tank corps as reinforcements. Its commander was Rotmistrov.[19] It was a good tank corps, made up of people "fresh off the assembly line," who knew tank operations superbly. This substantially strengthened our Front.

I spent most of my time then at Tolbukhin's headquarters in Verkhne-Tsaritsynsky. Malinovsky also set up his headquarters in Verkhne-Tsaritsynsky. So there were two army headquarters in one place: Tolbukhin's, which was holding the line facing north and keeping Paulus's troops encircled; and

Malinovsky's, which was holding back Manstein's troops from the southwest. Several times I visited Shapkin's cavalry corps. One day when I arrived at his headquarters I encountered a very bad scene: many of our cavalrymen and horses were lying dead near the settlement where Shapkin had his headquarters. As I went over a little bridge, I saw the body of an officer lying there, and marauders had already taken his boots. I told Shapkin about this, and he looked into it. "Yes," he said, "that was a squadron commander."

"How can this be?" I asked. "Don't you retrieve your dead? People are stealing from their own dead comrades. It's true that they're dead, and to them it doesn't make any difference, but it's still pitiful and unpleasant to see." That's how it was in the war. Shapkin was doing everything he could to withstand the enemy's pressure, and when Malinovsky arrived we beat back the enemy and counterattacked.

Before Malinovsky's army came up the following incident occurred. A representative of the Stavka, an expert on cavalry utilization, arrived at our headquarters—Oka Ivanovich Gorodovikov.[20] Where could we send him [to be of use]? He was inspector general for cavalry then, and so of course we sent him to the only cavalry corps we had in that sector. I was at Tolbukhin's headquarters and then at Popov's. A new army had been formed by that time, and Popov had become its commander. It was a "shock army,"[21] to be used as a strike force aimed at Tormosin[22] on the west bank of the Don. Suddenly Oka Ivanovich arrived at Popov's, very upset and angry. He didn't speak very pure Russian, but expressed himself this way: "What sort saber this is? This saber to slice shish kebob, not to cut down enemy! Lousy saber. Not saber, no!"

To be sure, our cavalry did not have first-class equipment, and that went for the sabers, too. Oka Ivanovich told me: "I was sitting in trench looking to see where enemy is, and I see them—there's the enemy, right there. And I said: 'Popov, what are you doing? Do you want to surrender me to the enemy?'" Manstein's offensive was under way (this was before Malinovsky's Second Guards Army had arrived) and evidently made a powerful impression on our gallant cavalryman. Later he asked me: "Comrade Khrushchev, when are you going to the Front headquarters? Where is the Front headquarters?" I told him that the Front headquarters was back where he had landed when he arrived from Moscow, that is, in the settlement of Rai-Gorodok [Rai-Gorodok means "Paradise Town."] I don't know why it had that name. It was actually just a large village, and all its buildings were made of wood.

Colonel General Gorodovikov continued: "Are you going to be going there?" [A native Kalmyk, he spoke poor Russian.]

I answered: "Yes, I am."

He said: "Let's travel together."

I said: "All right, let's. But when do you want to go?"

"I want to go now."

"I wouldn't advise going now. It's a very bad business traveling at night. You can't put headlights on, because the German planes will fire at them. And if you drive without headlights, you can have a smashup—that's more likely even than being hit by enemy machine-gun bullets. It would be better if we traveled tomorrow just at daybreak, when visibility is still low and enemy planes are not yet flying their daytime sorties, and when it's also dangerous for their nighttime bombers to fly, because they fly at low speed and low to the ground. When dawn is starting to break, it's easy to hit them with a machine gun or even a rifle. So we would do better to choose that time of day."

He said: "All right, let's call each other." But in the morning when I called him, the duty officer who answered told me that Oka Ivanovich had already left.

I asked: "When did he leave?"

"Yesterday evening."

Apparently Gorodovikov was so upset and shaken that he couldn't wait for morning. I never met Oka Ivanovich again after that. At one time he had commanded the Second Cavalry Army[23] and had been a hero of the Civil War. But the military operations carried out in that war were different, and the conditions were different. He obviously felt that he had no particular help to offer us and that his arrival at the front lines was not contributing anything. All he could do was demonstrate his good intentions, his honesty and devotion to the Soviet state. He was a good fighting man, but his time had already passed. His physical condition and his knowledge of military affairs no longer enabled him to play the necessary role.

I have already mentioned that I was spending more time at Verkhne-Tsaritsynsky than at the Front headquarters. I even had my own personal quarters there. One day I went there on my regular visit, and after I had received an update on the situation, everyone went off to get some rest. Suddenly Malinovsky came bursting into my apartment, still wearing his overcoat. He was very upset. I looked at him and saw tears streaming down his face. "What is it? What's happened, Rodion Yakovlevich?"

He said: "Something awful has happened. Larin has shot himself."[24] Larin was a member of the Military Council of the Second Guards Army. He and Malinovsky were great friends and had worked together before the war. When Malinovsky had commanded a corps Larin had been his commissar.

Malinovsky always requested that Larin remain with him either as chief of the political department of his unit or as commissar. He had earned his respect as a political worker.

Before all this happened, Larin had been wounded. I had gone to his quarters to visit him. He was lying there, but it was not a serious wound, a flesh wound in the leg. The bone had not been damaged, the bullet having only grazed the shin. Larin conversed with me and was fully conscious. A woman was looking after him, an Armenian doctor. Later I was told that before he shot himself he had been chatting rather cheerfully with her. Malinovsky was terribly upset, sobbing over his lost friend Larin. I didn't know how to console him. But what had caused him to take this action, I wondered. Why had Larin shot himself? Later his adjutant gave a report describing the circumstances under which it had happened.

The circumstances were rather unclear. Larin had gone up to the front lines and was observing the course of the fighting, hiding himself behind a haystack. But he also walked around in the open as though he were making himself visible to the enemy, evidently seeking to be killed. There was no need for him to behave that way. He was simply drawing the enemy's fire toward himself. Of course he was soon wounded. Although the wound turned out not to be serious, he suddenly shot himself. What was going on here? At the beginning of the war there were instances of people shooting themselves when we were retreating. But now we were on the offensive; we had surrounded Paulus's forces, and we were engaged in a battle with Manstein that, you could say, marked a major turning point. We had long since stopped running away, and a whole new stage in our military operations against the enemy had begun. Also, the Second Guards Army was a sturdy and powerful army and was successfully repelling Manstein's offensive. And suddenly at that point Larin shot himself.

Larin left a note behind that was also quite strange. I can't reproduce its contents exactly now, but the gist was simply that he was ending his life by suicide, and then came the words "Long live Lenin!" followed by his signature. We immediately sent this note to Moscow. The head of the Chief Political Directorate of the Red Army at that time was Shcherbakov.[25] One should not speak ill of the dead, but what can you do? Shcherbakov was an official who for many years had worked at the level of secretary of a party province committee. Later I had occasion to experience his unpleasant personality, but at that time, when he received that note, he began "playing it up," making a big thing out of it. I don't even know what goal he had in mind. After all, Larin was already dead. Either he was after Malinovsky and trying to arouse Stalin's anger against him or he was trying to "dig a hole" for me as a member of the Front's Military Council, because this incident had occurred in my jurisdiction. I was immediately summoned to Moscow. The usual dinner, many hours long, was held at Stalin's place with all the usual "appurtenances," so to speak: drinking and everything that went with it, and at the same time an inquiry into the events that had taken place during the previous few days.

Stalin asked me: "Now, who exactly is Malinovsky?"

I answered: "I have reported to you about Malinovsky many times. He is a well-known general who commanded a corps at the beginning of the war and after that an army and then the Southern Front. He had some setbacks there, as you know." Stalin of course knew that the Southern Front had had its flanks turned, had been overrun by the enemy, and had fallen apart. The enemy had easily captured Rostov, a failure for which Malinovsky was relieved of his duties and transferred to the rear. Later he commanded the 66th Army and was deputy commander of the Voronezh Front until the Second Guards Army was formed. I was reminded where Larin had served, of the fact that Malinovsky always requested that Larin serve with him, and how he succeeded in getting people to go along with him on that.

It must be said that Shcherbakov was a past master at playing up such things and turning them to his own advantage. His aim was not to calm Stalin down somehow but, on the contrary, to slyly place material in front of him to get him worked up and make him angry. Shcherbakov understood that anger at Malinovsky would also be aimed, directly or indirectly, at me as well. Shcherbakov said: "Ah, this is not accidental. Why did he write 'Long live Lenin' and not write 'Long live Stalin'?"

I answered: "I can't tell why he did that. Apparently he shot himself under the influence of some sort of abnormal psychological state. If he had been in a normal frame of mind, he wouldn't have shot himself. He had no reason to shoot himself." It would have seemed that everything was clear and straightforward, but no. Shcherbakov kept chewing the thing over, pouring salt on the wound. I suffered a lot of unpleasantness as a result.

Of course the most advantageous thing for me might have been to say that Larin was a no good so-and-so and that Malinovsky was the same. But I didn't agree with that and I couldn't tell Stalin that. But Stalin asked again: "Who exactly is this Malinovsky?"

I answered: "I know Malinovsky, and I know only good things about him. I cannot say that I have known him for a great many years, but I have known him since the beginning of the war. He has conducted himself well that whole time. He has behaved in a solid and steadfast way both as a man and as a general." A threat was plainly hanging over Malinovsky's head. The fall of Rostov and Larin's suicide were being woven together and tied into a single knot.

Stalin said: "When you return to your Front, you'll have to watch Malinovsky closely. You'll have to stay at the Second Guards Army headquarters all the time. Follow his every move and review all the orders and commands that he issues." In short, I was going to be personally responsible for Malinovsky and his army. I would be the eye of the party and of the Stavka watching over Malinovsky.

I said: "Comrade Stalin, all right, as soon as I return to the Front I'll make myself inseparable from Malinovsky."

I flew back to Verkhne-Tsaritsynsky, and it was as though I had forgotten the way back to Front headquarters. I was always at the headquarters of the Second Guards Army, staying at Malinovsky's side, and moving with his headquarters whenever it moved. Malinovsky was an intelligent man. He understood that this was the result of lack of confidence in him on Stalin's part. He saw in me a person assigned to monitor his activities. Whenever we relocated the headquarters, my living quarters were set up right next to Malinovsky's. It was as though I were more a member of the Military Council of the Second Guards Army than of the Front as a whole. In fact that army constituted our main force in the area for which our Front was responsible, so that essentially there was no real contradiction in this situation. Before signing any orders or commands that he had prepared, Malinovsky invariably consulted with me and made sure we were in agreement. I didn't sign them because that was not part of my duties, but I knew all his orders and commands and he reported to me about everything.

Things in our area were moving forward well. I was satisfied with the state of affairs of our Front and with Malinovsky—I was pleased by his abilities, his efficient management, and his tact. In short, as I saw it, he really stood out by comparison with other commanders, and I had great respect for him. It was good to work with him.

In those days Comrade Ulbricht[26] flew into our area and with him two other German Communists. They came to carry out antifascist propaganda, using loudspeakers along the front lines and calling on the German troops to surrender. This work was carried out mainly at night. Ulbricht would crawl along the front lines with his loudspeakers, directing his message to the soldiers and officers of Paulus's army group. Ulbricht and I always ate together, and I joked with him: "Well, what is this, Comrade Ulbricht? You haven't earned your daily bread today. No one surrendered." He calmly continued doing what he was doing.

One day it was reported to me that a soldier from the surrounded enemy forces had defected to our side. I said: "Well, bring him in so I can find out what kind of person he is. I want to find out what frame of mind he's in and how he sees the state of morale among his comrades." They brought him in. I asked: "What nationality are you?"

"Polish."

"How did you end up in the German Army?"

"I'm from the part of Poland that became part of Germany [after 1939], and I was drafted."

I said: "A new Polish army will probably be organized in our country. After all, Poland must be liberated. What is your attitude toward that?"

He said: "Yes, it must be liberated."

I asked him: "And will you sign up with this new Polish Army? Will you join it?"

He said: "No, I won't."

"But how is Poland going to be liberated?"

"The Russians will liberate it." And he made that reply in a rather arrogant way. I didn't like it.

Later I said to Ulbricht: "This soldier of yours, he's not even a German. He's a Pole. He defected from the Germans, but he's not on our side. He doesn't even want to fight to free Poland."

Later some full-blooded Germans were taken prisoner, just before Christmas. I said that they should be placed at the disposal of Malinovsky's headquarters, and we began questioning them. This was not really an interrogation session but more of a propaganda discussion. Walter Ulbricht and I led the discussion. First I ordered the soldiers taken to a bathhouse so they could be bathed and deloused and given new clothing. They were each given 100 grams of vodka (after all, it was Christmas!), and they were fed. After that we began our discussion with them.

One of these prisoners stood out in particular. As I saw it, his attitude was especially good, from our point of view, of course. He was opposed to the Nazis, opposed to Hitler, and opposed to the war. Ulbricht said to him: "We want to send you back. Would you agree to be sent?"

He answered: "Yes, I would. I would even ask you to send us. We'll go back and tell our fellow soldiers everything [i.e., about being well treated]."

But suddenly there was a split in the ranks of these prisoners. One of them remarked: "What do you want to send us back for? If you do that now, they'll just shoot us. No one will believe that we escaped from you or any other story that you might think up." Some rather serious squabbling broke out among these prisoners.

"Our" German said: "You're a coward! But I'll go. Let them shoot me. Even that will have an effect."

Ulbricht and I had already agreed to send this group of prisoners back over to the enemy's side, but when Tolbukhin heard about it he came to see me: "Comrade Khrushchev, I've heard what you and Ulbricht have dreamed up. I beg of you not to do it. These prisoners of war know the position of our headquarters. They'll give the information to their people, who will then bomb us. At least don't send them back until I've moved the headquarters to a new location. I don't want to subject my people to any danger."

I said: "How can you talk like that? These prisoners were brought here blindfolded, and when we take them away they'll be blindfolded. They don't know what your location is."

He said: "No, I can't take the risk." I could see that if he told Stalin about this, Stalin would not support me. I didn't tell Ulbricht about Tolbukhin's attitude.

I said simply: "Comrade Ulbricht, apparently our operation will have to be put off for a while because there is a risk that the prisoners might reveal the location of our headquarters."

He said: "Well, if we can't, we can't!" And he went on with his work. How serious were the dangers that Tolbukhin was afraid of? Even today I don't agree with him. He was being overly cautious. I don't think there would have been any danger to the headquarters if we had sent those men back into the surrounded "pocket" of German troops.

The fighting continued. We began pressing Manstein's troops back in the direction of Kotelnikovsky. The situation was such that it would have been difficult for the headquarters of the Stalingrad Front to direct the operations of both the troops who were immediately holding Paulus's surrounded forces in their "pocket" and the troops that were on the offensive against Manstein, driving toward the Manych River[27] and Rostov. The proposal was made that we divide our Front. The proposal came from the Stavka. I don't know if this was on Stalin's initiative or if it came from someone in the General Staff. But they understood the complications that had arisen for our Front. The armies that were facing directly toward Paulus, it was proposed, would be transferred to the Don Front, and the troops that were driving toward the south and looking westward would become part of the Southern Front.

We felt bad about taking our leave of units like the 62nd Army, whose troops had placed their lives on the line to defend Stalingrad; the 64th Army, commanded by Shumilov; the 57th Army, and other units. These military units had truly made a record of great significance in history. The 62nd and 64th Armies had formed a semicircle, fighting off the German troops seeking to break through into Stalingrad. The 57th Army had started out fighting in Stalingrad itself, but later was moved to another part of the Front. Our lives had become intertwined, and we had become very closely attached to these people. But when Stalin called up I said to him: "We will do what you say. I think it is correct and in the interests of the cause. Things will be better this way." Stalin also called Yeremenko. I don't know what his conversation with Yeremenko was like or how Yeremenko responded to him.

I found Yeremenko almost in tears. I felt sorry for him: "Well, Andrei Ivanovich," I said. "What's the matter? After all, this is in the interests of the cause. You can see for yourself that our armies are now facing south. Our task is to continue the offensive, striking at the flank of the enemy forces located in the Northern Caucasus to press them back to Rostov [and cut off their retreat from the Northern Caucasus by way of Rostov]. As for Stalingrad, everything there has already been decided; the outcome is foreordained. The only thing necessary there is to keep the enemy firmly hemmed in. He is going to perish from hunger by himself. He doesn't have any ammunition, food, or clothing."

Yeremenko said: "Comrade Khrushchev, you don't understand. You are a civilian, and apparently you don't have a feeling for how much we military men suffered to win this victory. We ourselves were almost doomed. Do you remember when Stalin called us and asked if we could hold out for three more days? Do you remember how it was almost like a wedding party, so many people had come from the Stavka, and then suddenly they disappeared—like they had been swept away by a broom. They thought the Germans were going to take Stalingrad, and we were left there to be scapegoats. And now look what has happened! You may not know it, but I know, I can foresee that all the glory of Stalingrad will go to the Don Front!"

I tried to calm him down: "The greatest glory will be the victory of our people. That has much more importance than the personal satisfaction of one or another military man or commander. Remember the main thing!"

But there was no way that I could convince him. He really had suffered a great deal to accomplish what he did. He contributed a great deal of strength, energy, military talent, knowledge, and perseverance to our victory. I don't know how many words one would have to use to properly express full appreciation for the exertions Yeremenko made as commander of the troops of the Stalingrad Front. I want to be correctly understood on this point. I am not trying in any way to diminish Rokossovsky's merits. He is an extraordinarily talented military leader and a remarkable party comrade. I did not have many dealings with him, but every encounter with him always left me with the very best impression of Rokossovsky. However, on the historical plane, I think that what was most important occurred not in his area: it was not the Don Front whose name resounded throughout the world. It was Stalingrad. But what can you do? That's the way it was fated to be.

In principle the functions of the Don Front were different from those of the Stalingrad Front. If the Germans had taken Stalingrad, they then would have turned to strike northward. That means that the Stavka was correct in establishing another Front [the Don Front, to the north of Stalingrad] and in appointing a most worthy general, Rokossovsky, as commander. But now the situation had changed. The Germans were no longer deciding the direction in which the main blows would be struck. We were. The direction we were sending our troops was toward the south, to drive out and crush the German forces located in the Northern Caucasus. This of course was the only correct decision to make. Every honor would be paid to those who finally crushed Paulus. The commander who had carried the whole burden of the defense of that city earlier wanted to be the one to finish up this operation and to harvest the laurels of victory. But in fact it was not the Stalingrad Front that was going to do this. There was now the Southern Front, commanded by Yeremenko, carrying out an offensive toward the Northern Caucasus and westward from there. And there was the Don Front, which would finish off Paulus. Yeremenko could not be consoled by these arguments. No way could he be consoled!

Such were the collisions in our ranks as the epic of the fighting at Stalingrad ended. A new stage of the war had begun—the stage of our war of liberation advancing westward.

---

1. Major General N. I. Trufanov was at that time (until February 1943) in command of the 51st Army.

2. The Fourth Romanian Army was deployed in the sector where the Soviet offensive was launched.

3. Commander of the Fourth Mechanized Corps Major General V. T. Volsky.

4. From October 1942 Lieutenant General M.

M. Popov was deputy commander of the Stalingrad Front.

5. The allusion is to the fair described in the story "Sorochinskaya Yarmarka" (Sorochinsky Fair), by the writer Nikolai Gogol. [SK]

6. The Romanian leader General Ion Antonescu. See Biographies.

7. The man had the same surname as the famous Russian composer Peter Ilyich Chaikovsky (1840–93), known for his concertos, symphonies, operas, ballets, and other musical works. [SS]

8. An *arba* was a cart or wagon, usually two-wheeled with high sides, of a kind originally used by nomads of the steppes. [GS]

9. Plodovitoye was about 50 kilometers south of Stalingrad in an outlying section of the Republic of Kalmykia just west of Lake Tsatsa. [SS]

10. Commander of the Fourth Tank Corps Major General A. G. Kravchenko.

11. Kotelnikovsky was about 160 kilometers southwest of Stalingrad, near the River Don. Today it is called Kotelnikovo. [AH/SS]

12. General Field Marshal E. Manstein von Levinsky, who was in command of the Army Group Don (the Hollidt operational grouping, the Third Romanian Army, the Army Group Goth, and the Sixth Army, thirty-three divisions in all) tried to break through the ring of encirclement at Stalingrad from November 1942 to February 1943. The Army Group Goth, fighting on the right wing of his forces, included the Fourth Tank Army and the Fourth Romanian Army and confronted the forces of the Stalingrad Front.

13. The Myshkova River was an east-bank tributary of the Don. It now flows into the Tsimlyanskoye Reservoir. [AH]

14. The Chervlennaya River was a tributary of the Don that formed a southern arc around the Stalingrad region. It largely disappeared under the Volga-Don Canal built in the 1950s. [AH]

15. Lieutenant General M. S. Shumilov commanded the 64th Army from August 1942 to April 1943, when it received the title of the Seventh

Guards Army, and continued to command the Seventh Guards until the end of the war.

16. Lieutenant General R. Ya. Malinovsky commanded the Second Guards Army from November 1942 to February 1943.

17. Major General Ya. G. Kreizer was eleven years younger than Khrushchev. He commanded the Second Guards Army before Malinovsky took up the post and again after Malinovsky departed from the post—that is, in October and November 1942 and from February to July 1943.

18. Major General S. S. Biryuzov became chief of staff of the Second Guards Army in December 1942.

19. Major General of Tank Forces P. A. Rotmistrov was at that time (from April 1942) in command of the Seventh Tank Corps.

20. General Inspector of Cavalry Colonel General O. I. Gorodovikov, deputy commander of Red Army cavalry from 1943.

21. This was the Fifth Shock Army.

22. Tormosin stood on a small west-bank tributary of the Don. It now stands on the shore of the Tsimlyanskoye Reservoir. [AH]

23. That is, the Second Cavalry Army that fought in the Civil War. [SS]

24. Divisional Commissar I. I. Larin.

25. Lieutenant General A. S. Shcherbakov. See Biographies.

26. Walter Ulbricht, later the leader of the German Democratic Republic (East Germany), was at this time one of the leaders of the National Committee Freies Deutschland (Free Germany). See Biographies.

27. The Manych River is a tributary of the Don, which it enters a few miles upstream from Rostov.

## THE ROAD TO ROSTOV

We began to drive the enemy toward the southwest. Then the right wing of the Southern Front crossed the Don and began to advance along its west bank. I don't remember now at exactly what place or exactly what time we crossed the Don (and that's not necessary; I haven't set myself that kind of task for present purposes). It seems to me it was somewhere in the vicinity of Tsimlyanskaya. We drove Manstein's troops back from the right bank (or west bank) of the river there. This meant that the Germans had to abandon their wish to save Paulus. Paulus was doomed. The Germans needed Manstein's troops now to block the advance of our Southern,

Voronezh, and Southwestern Fronts.[1] (It may be that, besides the Southern Front, only the Voronezh Front was involved then; the Southwestern Front may not have been there.) Our forces were moving westward. The Germans had no forces in the area to our west at that time. Their front lines were practically deserted there.

When I was summoned to Moscow and flew off to the capital, I stopped along my way to visit my Stalingrad comrades Shumilov and Serdyuk. They told me about the following incident. We wanted very much to know what the German generals we had taken prisoner were talking about with Paulus. For this purpose we took some of our officers who knew German, dressed them as ordinary Soviet soldiers, and placed them as guards in the presence of the German generals. They heard nothing special, but one day one of the generals asked Paulus: "Herr Feldmarschall, what do you think? When will the German troops be able to stop the westward advance of the Soviet forces after the defeat of our troops in Stalingrad?"

Paulus thought for a while, then answered: "The hole that was created as a result of the defeat of our troops—there is no way to close it up now. Perhaps it can be done somewhere along the Dnieper River, at a very great distance from the present front lines. Gathering up new troops in Germany and delivering them to the front, so they can stop the Russians, is a difficult task. It requires time and great effort to gather together the necessary number of troops." This was correct. Our troops had advanced rather deeply into the occupied territories, almost as far as Dnepropetrovsk. We had liberated Kharkov and Pavlograd and were approaching Novomoskovsk.[2] So Paulus was more or less accurately describing how deep our breakthrough was after the Germans and their allies had been defeated at Stalingrad.

As we advanced toward the south we encountered more stubborn resistance than we did to the west. This is understandable because our advance southward toward Kotelnikovsky and the Manych River along the left, or east, bank of the Don posed a threat to the entire German group in the Northern Caucasus. Although the enemy had transferred Manstein's forces to a different sector, the Germans were apparently now withdrawing their troops from the Northern Caucasus and throwing them against the Southern Front. Stubborn fighting was going on, and we were suffering heavy casualties and causing even greater losses to the enemy. What were the particular features that could be observed in that fighting? For one, the German planes, which in the first period of the war and even during the second year of the war had been quite active—we hardly felt their presence anymore. Enemy planes were mostly conducting reconnaissance flights, and of course they did bomb us, but not with the same intensity as before. We managed to knock down some reconnaissance planes, and I questioned the captured pilots. I was interested in the Germans' fuel situation. Actually the Germans were having great difficulty with fuel supply then, but the prisoners of war were trying to reply to my question on this point in an optimistic way, declaring that they hadn't met with any difficulties, that they were getting the fuel they needed in the necessary quantity and quality, fuel not only for their airplanes but also for their tanks and motor vehicles. But the documents that have been published now by the Germans themselves make it clear that they were already experiencing severe difficulties with fuel by that time, although of course they still did have fuel.

I was summoned to Moscow. I flew there in February or perhaps the end of January 1943. Stalin gave me a good welcome. His mood now was quite different from what it had been. He had straightened up and was standing tall. He was not the same man I had seen at the beginning of the war. He greeted me with the words: "We have made the decision after all to relieve Yeremenko of his command of the Southern Front."

I answered: "Well, what can I say? Once a decision has been made, it has been made. Nothing to be done about it. But I don't think it should have been made."

Stalin said: "But he himself asked to be relieved." And he read me a telegram in which Yeremenko requested Stalin to relieve him of the command of the Southern Front and give him the chance to recuperate and heal from his wounds. Stalin continued: "He asked to be relieved, and we granted his request."

I said: "I understand why he asked. He needs rest and recuperation badly. He really does have something wrong with his leg. He limps and is not as mobile as is desirable and necessary for a commander. In general he is a very mobile person [if not for the bad leg]. Nevertheless, hidden behind all this is his feeling of being offended. He can't stand it because he feels that an insult has been dealt to him personally, since he was denied the possibility of completing the victory by crushing the enemy troops in Stalingrad. It was our Stalingrad Front that bore the burden of the fighting, but the glory is being given to another commander, that is, Rokossovsky."

Then Stalin said in a bitter and angry way: "Rokossovsky has already taken command of the Don Front. And as for Yeremenko, we have relieved him."

Why he got angry and showed such impatience I don't know. It was hard for me to understand, but then, you couldn't expect sincerity from Stalin.

Again Stalin asked me: "Who shall we appoint as the new commander [of the Southern Front]?"

I said: "I don't know. Who do you think is appropriate to appoint as commander?"

He said: "No, you should name someone."

I said: "It's hard for me to name a commander. The position of commander of a Front is something of such magnitude that it really comes under the jurisdiction of the Stavka."

"No," Stalin put the pressure on again, and he was very stubborn about it: "You say."

Of all the army commanders that we had in our Front the most fully prepared, the one who could cope with this task best, was Malinovsky. But I couldn't bring myself to mention Malinovsky's name. All the dogs were being hung on Malinovsky at that time [that is, everything that went wrong was being pinned on him]: Malinovsky had surrendered Rostov; a member of Malinovsky's Military Council, his friend Larin, had written a note whose content was politically questionable, ending with the words: "Long Live Lenin!" and then he had shot himself. I have already told how Shcherbakov played up that suicide note. And Shcherbakov was always right there, always at hand, dancing attendance on Stalin, obsequiously bringing all sorts of questions to Stalin and giving them his own "interpretation." In essence he was encouraging the wrath of Stalin. And this made me very angry.

I would ask those who subsequently acquaint themselves with my memoirs to keep in mind that, although this was perhaps a weakness on my part, the situation aroused a feeling of indignation in me. Possibly I was overly sensitive toward the line of action Shcherbakov was pursuing, but I felt it was unjust. Although it was aimed against Malinovsky, it undermined my authority even more. After all, I had given Stalin a good recommendation in regard to Malinovsky, and suddenly it turned out that Malinovsky was virtually an enemy of the people. But what can you do? The people in Stalin's immediate circle were much less concerned about the interests of the state than about themselves. As for Stalin, he portrayed himself as the alleged founder of the Red Army. In what way was he the founder? He was as much the founder of the Red Army as I am a chemist. Stalin had become, as the saying went, the one who issued the death sentences and granted the pardons. Actually he could do whatever he wished. Sometimes even the men in Stalin's inner circle became exasperated; they would splutter and grumble among themselves, but there was nothing to be done about it. That's the way things were!

In the end Stalin forced me to name someone from among the leading military men in the Southern Front to be its commander. I said: "Malinovsky, of course. You know him and I know him."

He said: "Malinovsky? You're proposing Malinovsky?"

I said: "Yes, I am proposing Malinovsky."

He said: "All right! I approve Malinovsky!" Then he said to Molotov: "Write it down!" Molotov immediately picked up a notebook and pencil, and Stalin dictated an order appointing Malinovsky commander of the Southern Front.[3]

Then the discussion turned to me [and my assignment]. When we were in Stalingrad and the enemy was besieging us and trying to force us out of the city Stalin felt during those months that Stalingrad might be lost. And his attitude toward me would shift abruptly, depending on the state of affairs of our Front, and the front-line situation as a whole. The enemy was very active in the Northern Caucasus then also. If you compare the balance of forces between the enemy and us at Stalingrad, on the one hand, and in the Northern Caucasus, on the other, there really is no comparison. Our superiority in the Northern Caucasus was substantial. I remember that Bodin[4] said at the time: "It's surprising that our troops are conducting themselves so poorly in the Northern Caucasus. After all, the balance of forces there is in our favor. Our intelligence services report that the enemy has such-and-such forces there, whereas we have so-and-so many. And yet the enemy still keeps advancing."

I had a very high opinion of Bodin. He was a talented, well-educated military man, as I have already mentioned. But the problem was that Beria was in the Caucasus. Stalin had absolute confidence in Beria, and Beria was also able to influence Stalin. Thus everything became explicable to me, since the specific balance of forces in one or another sector of the battlefront was something Stalin could never know exactly or in detail, in my opinion. He lived by what the General Staff reported to him, and this of course was correct. But as supreme commander in chief he should have been able to look into the question of the real balance of forces himself, to study and weigh that question. This is something that is accessible even to a person without military training. Weighing the balance of forces is a question of arithmetic. Any rational or intelligent human being could do it, and Stalin was a very intelligent person.

At that time Stalin said to me: "We consider it necessary to relieve you of your duties as member of the Military Council of the Southern Front and appoint you as member of the Military Council of the Voronezh Front. That front is advancing through Ukraine, and you should be there. You also need to attend to the problems of restoring the economy in Ukraine."

I was surprised, but I said: "That is up to you, Comrade Stalin. I will go where you send me if that is what is needed."

I was additionally surprised because when we were at Stalingrad and I went to Moscow on one occasion, Stalin said to me: "You should not occupy yourself with Ukrainian matters anymore." I, along with others, was involved then with the partisan movement in Ukraine. General Strokach[5] was chief of staff of that partisan movement. He oversaw all operational questions and reported to me. Together we made the necessary decisions and gave orders to the partisans.

Stalin said: "These questions will now be taken over by Korniyets. You are a Russian, not a Ukrainian."

I said: "Yes, I am a Russian and not a Ukrainian."

In my heart I was simply astounded. After all, he had known this all along. He knew that I was a Russian when he sent me to Ukraine to begin with. I had asked him not to send me precisely because of the fact that I was a Russian. At that time he had said to me: "Kosior was in charge of Ukraine, and he's a Pole. In what way is a Russian worse than a Pole?"

I answered: "Kosior is a Pole, but only by national origin. He grew up in Ukraine, was raised there and worked there in the underground. He was a Ukrainian Pole, a Ukrainian from a Polish family." I should add that Kosior had an excellent knowledge of Ukrainian culture and was an acknowledged leader of the Communist Party of Ukraine.

Now Stalin began to relate—using an insulting tone, in my opinion—how he had summoned Korniyets[6] and given him the following assignment: "Ukraine is beginning to be liberated. Find out what is required and make a list of what you are going to need now for Ukraine." Korniyets put forward his requests accordingly, but he only asked for things in miserly, trifling quantities. Now Stalin was making fun of him. "The man has absolutely no idea what he's going to need when he has to start running everything. So you are going to be a member of the Military Council [of the Front] in that area. Take it upon yourself to organize the administration and leadership for the parts of Ukraine that the Red Army liberates. And for now, since we have relieved Yeremenko of his duties and appointed Malinovsky at your suggestion, you'll have to go back to Malinovsky for the time being. Don't let him take one step out of your sight; keep a close watch on him and check on everything he does." He had said the same thing to me after Larin shot himself. I was to be in Malinovsky's presence at all times.

To strengthen our Front and reinforce its ranks, we were sent General Rotmistrov, who commanded a tank corps. At that time he was supporting the attack on Kotelnikovsky with his tanks. Kotelnikovsky was liberated. Vasilevsky and I went there, to Rotmistrov's headquarters (Vasilevsky had also flown in to visit us), and we acquainted ourselves with the situation. Our position then was very solid, and the mood among the troops was cheerful and optimistic. Manstein's forces had been broken, and we were confidently moving forward. The troops of the Southern Front had advanced by then to the Cossack *stanitsa* of Martynovskaya.[7]

At this point I want to make a few favorable remarks about Rotmistrov. After the war he was promoted to the rank of chief marshal of our armored forces. Later he served as head of the Military Academy for Armored Forces.[8] I will begin my remarks with winter 1943. When we began our counter-offensive the Cossack village of Verkhne-Chirskaya was like a toothache to us. Or maybe it was Nizhne-Chirskaya, I don't remember exactly now. There was a bridge across the Chir River.[9] I drove across the bridge and stopped to have a talk with the construction crew that was working to restore the bridge. This was truly a labor of heroism because the enemy frequently "dropped in to make a call," bombing the position, not just to hinder restoration of the bridge but also to inflict further damage. In that situation our engineers and the Red Army crewmen from the department for bridge restoration had to keep working very persistently. We had to keep hold of this Cossack village in to ensure our advance along the west bank of the Don. For a fairly long time we kept making attempts to drive the Germans out of that village, but every attempt failed. Then we decided to concentrate one of our armies on this point together with a tank corps. The tank corps arrived and was placed at our disposal. It was a brand-new tank corps with a full complement of tanks and troops.

Vasilevsky and I scheduled an operational conference in some little hamlet on the banks of the Don. Rotmistrov came there too with his people and the commander of the army[10] that was supposed to go on the offensive the next morning. The army commander reported that he was ready for the offensive and was sure they would take the Cossack village. I didn't know him, and, as I recall, some doubt arose in my mind as to whether he had assessed the situation correctly. It seemed to me that he was approaching the problem too lightly. Then we began making calculations about how long it would be before the arrival of the troops who were going to take part in the attack. We estimated that in the best of cases the troops wouldn't arrive until early morning, toward dawn, and in that case it would be necessary to send them into battle without letting them stop to rest. The men would be tired,, and it was obvious that this could cost us dearly; the attack might fizzle, and the job would not get done.

Rotmistrov took the floor: "Comrades, I urge you to trust me and not organize the attack for tomorrow morning. The troops will be too tired; they'll be worn out. They won't be able to carry out the offensive. We'll just be sending them to their destruction. Give me a day or two, and I'll give you my word that I will capture that village with my tank corps." He went on to present a vivid picture: on the appropriate day we would begin at dawn, just before sunrise when there would barely be light from the sky, only enough to see by, so that the tanks wouldn't end up in a ditch somewhere or sink into something. We would deploy our tanks from three directions, and at dawn the tanks would suddenly open fire and charge the village. He said: "I'm convinced that the enemy will lose heart and go running out of there. The Germans don't have many troops in the village. They've dug in and built fortifications, but their numbers are not large."

Vasilevsky and I agreed with Rotmistrov and decided not to attack the next morning. Let the new army commander bring up his troops and put them in order. As for Rotmistrov and his tank corps, they were already there, and he would carry out some preparatory operations with his tank forces, mainly working with the commanders of the tank brigades who would participate in the operation. We set the date and time for the offensive. Vasilevsky and I told Rotmistrov that we would come to watch at the time when the tank corps was to attack the village.

That's what we did. It was a freezing cold morning. We arrived at Rotmistrov's command post. At dawn he gave the command, and the tanks moved toward the village. It seemed to us that the firing was very heavy for those days. Of course, if you compare that with later times, when our strength had grown much greater and the number of weapons we had was larger, the scale of the firing at Nizhne-Chirskaya was really trifling. But the enemy there was also weak, and success was achieved, just as Rotmistrov had proposed. Enemy planes suddenly appeared. The weather was exceptionally favorable for bombing, but there were not many planes. They flew over, dropped their bombs, and that was all. Our tanks burst into the village, and the enemy retreated, abandoning it. We all congratulated Rotmistrov because he had preserved and protected the infantry by using his tanks in an intelligent, bold, and well-thought-out operation. Even earlier I had great respect for Rotmistrov's skill at leading armored forces, and after that my respect grew even greater. Later in 1943 I met him again during the battle of

Kursk. Rotmistrov also arrived with his tank unit for that battle. But I'll tell about that in another part of my memoirs.

The offensive of the Southern Front continued successfully. The Germans retreated, although fighting as they went, and step by step we advanced closer and closer to the Manych River and the *stanitsa* of Bagayevskaya. This large Cossack village is not far from Novocherkassk.[11] Novocherkassk is on the right, or western, bank of the Don, and this village is on the left bank. We took Bagayevskaya, and then we took Manychskaya, which is also a large Cossack village. From there we planned to make a powerful thrust with our tanks. If successful, we thought, we could break through to Bataisk[12] and Rostov. For this operation the main forces we used were Rotmistrov with his tank corps and Bogdanov,[13] who also commanded a tank corps. We did everything in our power to make this operation a success, but it didn't succeed. The enemy acted before we did and started an offensive toward Manychskaya. Malinovsky and I went there right at the most difficult moment to help bring Rotmistrov's tank corps into action sooner, but the fighting was already going on in the village. By the time we arrived, the enemy had counterattacked and occupied half the village. That's why our planned offensive didn't take place.

When we reached the Manych River we decided to transfer the Front headquarters to the small village of Vesyoly on the Manych. It was closer to our troops, and it was more convenient for maintaining communications and going to visit the troops. An incident occurred there that was fairly typical of the situation and the relations among people at that time. Discipline requires that great precision be observed, but sometimes precision and accuracy are replaced by a good effort at making things up, not out of any evil intention, but simply for "professional reasons." Our troops had taken Salsk.[14] I told Malinovsky I wanted to go to Salsk while the "tracks were still fresh." The city had just been liberated, and I wanted to talk with the inhabitants and find out how people's lives had been under the enemy and what they needed now. I also wanted to meet up with the commander of the 28th Army, Gerasimenko,[15] who commanded the army that liberated Salsk after advancing from Astrakhan through Elista.[16] On the way there I passed through the Cossack village of Proletarskaya.

I was told that Budyonny was from one of the hamlets of this *stanitsa* and Gorodovikov from another.[17] I was also told that the White General Kornilov[18] came from this *stanitsa*, but it's not true. Budyonny once told me the following story. A teacher in that village, while conducting class, said: "Children, our village holds a special position. Here you see what prominent

Kalmyk people[19] there are holding high positions in our government who came from here. For example, there is this general here [he was pointing to a picture of Kornilov]; he is from our *stanitsa*. And Oka Ivanovich Gorodovikov is also one of ours. These are our hometown heroes." The portraits of both men were hanging in the schoolhouse. I don't know how true this story is, but this odd mixture of pride for both Oka Ivanovich and for the White general is typical. On the one hand there was a hero of the Civil War and the pride of the Red Army, and on the other a general who had been a stalwart supporter of the autocracy, who had taken part in a rebellion against Soviet power. Everything here was all mixed together. Each man was considered as much a celebrity as the other.

To get back to the question of accuracy and making things up. I arrived in Salsk, a small city in the steppes. There was a railroad depot there, so that in effect this was a proletarian center for the steppe country around Salsk. Gerasimenko arrived there with his staff at the same time I did. He said: "Come with me over to my headquarters. We're just setting it up. I myself haven't been there yet." We went to the premises where the headquarters were being set up. It was already getting dark.

I asked Gerasimenko about Salsk: "How did the liberation of the city go? Was there heavy fighting?"

He said: "Yes, we had heavy fighting and we broke into Salsk literally on the heels of the enemy."

I said: "It's a good thing that you're setting up your headquarters, and I won't hold you up. I want to get back to the Front headquarters as soon as I can, and I still have a long way to go. There's a crowd of people standing out there on the square. I'll go talk with them, listen to what they have to say, and get some idea of what mood they're in, how they're feeling."

I went out. They addressed me: "Comrade Khrushchev, how could this be? For three days we were sitting here waiting and waiting for our people to arrive. Time went by and still they didn't come. The Germans had left; they abandoned the city. But our troops didn't arrive." I looked around, and Gerasimenko was standing behind me. I gave him a look, but said nothing. He also said nothing to me. We understood each other right off. After all, he had just told me that they had broken into the city hot on the heels of the enemy, the kind of thing fighting men always say, but here the workers were telling me they had had their eyes peeled for three days waiting for our troops to arrive. That's the kind of thing that happens in war! Where is the truth? I think that the workers were telling the truth, and Gerasimenko was adding a little adornment to his victory.

Our troops continued to advance successfully toward Rostov and Novocherkassk. They took Novocherkassk. Malinovsky and I went there, and we decided to go among the troops right there on the spot to inform ourselves about the situation. I forget now the name of the commander in that area, nor do I remember the number of his army.[20] But I remember that he was a good commander, who made a good impression, and in my opinion he was coping with his task. From Novocherkassk we went to Shakhty,[21] also a sector of our front. And so we were carrying out our offensive against Rostov simultaneously from the south and from the east, as well as bypassing it and surrounding it from the north. But Rostov was still a long way away, and we received an order to attack Rostov from the south. That was a very difficult assignment.

I knew this from as far back as the Civil War. Back then our infantry division was attached to the First Cavalry Army and was fighting in the area to the west of the Don River in the direction of the railroad junction Kushchevskaya, from which the railroad went to the town of Azov.[22] This is flat country, the floodplain of the Don River, but in contrast Rostov is situated on high ground. Therefore it's easy to defend: all approaches to it are easily covered by machine-gun and artillery fire. And now once again our infantry would have to cover a great distance under enemy fire. We didn't like the look of it, but an order is an order. Certainly we thought that a different solution might have been sketched out, one that would have made it possible to take Rostov at less cost, with fewer casualties.

Let me repeat: All sorts of curious things happen in war. Some tank and cavalry units were transferred to our Front at that time. It seems to me that there was one tank corps and two cavalry corps. These units were commanded by General Kirichenko,[23] a man completely unknown to me. Malinovsky and I decided to travel to Kirichenko's headquarters and get to know him better. Malinovsky said: "I know him, but I'd like you to make his acquaintance in person. We'll return from there to Bataisk and spend the night with Gerasimenko." I don't remember now the name of the Cossack village where Kirichenko's headquarters was located. It was in the southern part of Rostov province. Evening had come, or it may even have been late at night. It was cold. We burst into the headquarters building and caught the adjutant and the general's orderlies by surprise. High-ranking officials had arrived, and they hadn't had a chance to report to their commander in advance. We asked where he was. They answered that he was resting and indicated his room. Malinovsky went striding right in there, and I behind him. We hadn't even taken our coats off because we had agreed that we'd be leaving soon. We were wearing heavy winter greatcoats. We went in. Kirichenko had lit a candle, having heard the noise outside. In our presence he got up and dressed and began reporting on the situation, the condition of his units, and everything else that one usually reports to the commander of the Front.

The light from the candle was fairly weak. It surprised me that he had nothing better and that he was reporting to us by candlelight. Then I glanced toward the bed from which he had just arisen and noticed that the bed covers seemed to be breathing. "What is this?" I thought to myself. I looked again and no doubt remained in my mind that these covers were concealing another person. We listened to his report, said goodbye, and left. Then we got in our vehicle. (We were traveling together in one vehicle.) I asked Malinovsky: "Have you known this general long?"

He said: "Yes, a long time."

I asked: "Didn't you notice, or was I just imagining because the room was dimly lit, that there seemed to be another person breathing under the covers?"

He said: "Of course I noticed." Well, we had a few laughs over this, made a few jokes, and drove off. Such things happen, as the saying goes—even in the case of a corps commander. But later when we met him we didn't bring up the incident.

Kirichenko performed fairly well in battle. He did not have a full complement of troops, because earlier he had been engaged in battles with the German Army Group A in the Caucasus. By this time the enemy was already retreating from the Northern Caucasus to Novorossiysk and Taman.[24] From Kirichenko's headquarters we went to Gerasimenko's and then to Azov. We had already taken Azov,[25] and the headquarters of the 44th Army was there. It was commanded by General Khomenko.[26] I knew Khomenko and had a good opinion of him. Before the war, as I recall, he commanded border troops in the Kamenets-Podolsky region.[27] He made a good impression both as a soldier and as a party member. He asked us to stay at his headquarters, as it was already late, but we said no and returned to Gerasimenko's.

We generally made our trips to Gerasimenko's headquarters more frequent at that time because that's where the operation for taking Rostov was being prepared. But it kept being postponed and postponed. It was felt that conditions were not yet ripe. I would arrive at Gerasimenko's headquarters and say: "Well, Vasyl Pilippovich, how's Rostov?" (I always used the Ukrainian form of his name, even though he spoke Russian well.) He was a dear fellow who I had known well in the prewar era, when he had served as deputy commander of the Kiev Special Military District (the KOVO).

He would answer: "Well, what about Rostov? The damn place is still standing there."

Once Malinovsky and I agreed, as a joke, to bring Gerasimenko a bottle of cognac, but to make it a condition that he couldn't drink the cognac until he had taken Rostov. We would dangle the cognac in front of his nose. A gypsy would hang a carrot or a clump of hay in front of his horse's nose to make it run faster. So we were using this gypsy method. We decided, as it were, to hang this bottle of cognac in front of his nose, so that its aroma would encourage our army commander to speed up the taking of Rostov.

I've already said that the enemy was not especially active in the air during the day by then, but he was still very active at night. His small planes, similar to our U-2s, were lambasting every road, shooting at motor vehicle headlights, and causing us fairly painful losses both in men and equipment. The main thing was that this interfered with our troop movements at night. One night when we were getting ready to leave Gerasimenko and return to our own headquarters in the small village of Vesyoly, Gerasimenko reminded us that we shouldn't travel at night. You couldn't drive without headlights, and with your headlights on the Germans might strafe your vehicle. But we had constantly been traveling at night, and we told him this wouldn't be our first time. We set off, and sure enough we ended up in a tight spot. Evidently Malinovsky and I had both been dozing. Suddenly there was machine-gun fire. I opened my eyes and saw streaks of multicolored lights spraying across the road in front of our vehicle, the tracer bullets from an enemy plane. Then a bomb exploded. The bomb exploded fairly far in front of us, but the machine-gun fire was almost on target, just a little ahead of us. Malinovsky and I often joked about that close call, reminiscing about that incident.

There was some military transport in that same area. Some peasants were bringing up loads of shells for our troops in carts and wagons. When our vehicle was fired on, we got out. We looked around and saw some carts standing there. One driver of a cart with a load of artillery shells had been frightened by the gunfire and had hidden under his cart. What was the meaning of this? Instinct! He had to find some sort of cover, so he crawled under a wagon loaded with artillery shells. A sorry kind of cover that was! But that's the unthinking way instinct works in a human being.

We were preparing for an offensive. As it turned out, there was no need for us to attack Rostov from the south, because our troops to the north of Rostov had begun a successful offensive and had advanced well to the west of the city. The Germans were forced to clear out of there without any particular force having to be applied from the south. Thus the enemy withdrew, and Gerasimenko was able to enter Rostov with his units and liberate it virtually without a fight.[28] Of course all honor and praise is due to the 28th Army and its commander for taking Rostov. But if you look at the essence of the matter, who really took the city? Supposedly it was Gerasimenko, because his troops were the first to enter Rostov, although they didn't have to do anything special to accomplish that. On the other hand, the general who led the offensive farther north and forced the Germans to abandon the city remained in the shadows and was not given any particularly honorable mention.[29]

Malinovsky and I arrived in Rostov. Gerasimenko met us and immediately pulled out the bottle of cognac. We joked that maybe we should drink the cognac, not with him, but with the general who commanded the troops to the north. Gerasimenko also understood this, but he was quick-witted and joked his way out of it.

For us this was a huge victory! We had taken Rostov back for the second time. The first time was in 1941 when we took it together with Timoshenko, and now we were doing so together with Malinovsky. For Malinovsky this was especially pleasing. After all, it was he who had left Rostov in 1942 when the Germans broke through our front lines, routed our troops, and advanced past Rostov to Stalingrad and the Northern Caucasus. It's true that they didn't actually break through at Rostov but forced the Don to the north and east of the city. Now we held a victory parade with our troops marching in formation. This made a powerful impression not only on the inhabitants of Rostov but on all the citizens of the Soviet Union. It was a genuine demonstration of our new success: after we had liberated Stalingrad from our enemies, we had also forced them to abandon Rostov. This fact, in my opinion, had great international significance.

Although by that time I was no longer a member of the Military Council of the Stalingrad Front, I had a strong yearning to go back and look at Stalingrad and see how things were there now, to see how the city looked. I decided to take a flight there. A rally had been scheduled there just at that time. I took a plane and flew to Shumilov's headquarters and stopped over, staying with him. Then I spoke at the rally and drove around and looked over the places that I remembered from the time when we had first arrived to organize the defense of Stalingrad. The panorama that spread before me was both a happy and a sad one, because literally the entire city lay in ruins. There was nothing but heaps of debris. I don't know if there were any houses that remained intact. I went to the Stalingrad tractor factory, to the gun factory, and to the riverbank. Broken and ruined equipment was lying around everywhere, mainly German. When the Germans attacked here, they lost a lot of planes and tanks. There were quite a few corpses lying around, too. They hadn't been cleared away. But very few living people were evident. The residents of the city, hungry and emaciated, moved around like shadows.

I stopped at one place to look over the scene of the former fighting. A youngster of about twelve or thirteen appeared from nowhere. He saw that some military men were standing around, and he broke into our conversation with his comment: "Yeah, and I bumped off one of the Fritzes myself."

We said: "You did what? How?"

He said: "Yeah. Here's how it happened. When the Germans were already in a panic, I picked up a rifle. There were lots of rifles lying around. I knew how to shoot. I aimed and bumped him off."

We said: "Well, you may have fired a shot, but you don't know if you hit the target or not."

He said: "No, I hit him. He fell over. And then I checked him out. I had bumped him off all right."

We asked: "And how was it that you were living here?" (He was completely black with dirt and grime and dressed in rags and tatters.)

He said: "You know how I lived? I ate dead things. Later at the leather factory I found all sorts of leather still lying around. I took the leather, sliced it up and boiled it, then I ate it and drank the bullion. That's how I lived."

The city was a dreadful sight. Shumilov, Serdyuk, and other generals told me many interesting things. It was at that time I heard an anecdote that I later told Stalin, but he didn't like it. If you told this anecdote to military people, they would catch on immediately that it was a story made up by troops who had been part of the Stalingrad Front. It went like this: "Some hunters went hunting. They hunted and hunted and finally they had good luck. They caught a live wild hare, a very hardy hare, with a strong will to live. They tied it to a tree. The wild hare just sat there. The hunters decided not to waste ammunition on the hare and began beating it with sticks. They hit it and hit it, and they got tired, but the hare was still alive. They rested and began to feel angry. Why was it that they couldn't kill this hare even when it was tied to the tree? They picked up their sticks and began whacking away at it again. They hit it and hit it and still they didn't kill it. They quit. They thought, why wear yourself out and keep hitting without taking a break? After all the hare is tied there and isn't going to go anywhere. Time is working in our favor. And so some time went by, and then the hunters gathered up all their strength and again began to beat the hare. They beat him and beat him and at last they killed him."

When I told Stalin what I had seen in Stalingrad and related this anecdote, he gave me a sharp look: "The wild hare is Paulus after he'd been surrounded, right? We hit him several times, and he still remained alive. And it was only when we brought up more forces, artillery, tanks, and after our troops had advanced 250 to 300 kilometers to the west, that we were finally able to kill the hare, right? This anecdote was obviously made up about Stalingrad." Well, after all, we're human and we have our human weaknesses. Actually I was impressed by this anecdote. I guess I was infected by what Yeremenko was feeling. Shumilov, commander of the 64th Army, who told me the anecdote, was a great friend of Yeremenko's, and Yeremenko was right. He and his troops had withstood the main attack of the Germans and then had tied up the hare. But other people came and finished it off. Of course this doesn't in any way diminish the credit that goes to the Don Front, which fulfilled its mission very well.

I saw a very gruesome sight in Stalingrad. Of course in war everything is gruesome, but still. . . . Our people in Stalingrad were busy gathering up the corpses of the German soldiers. We feared the onset of a warm spring and hot summer. If corpses were still lying around and began to decay, an epidemic could break out. So we were trying to round up all the corpses and burn them as soon as possible. The ground was frozen; it was hard to dig into, and that was also dangerous. There were too many corpses, thousands of them. The corpses were stacked up in rows. Two layers of railroad ties were placed between each layer of corpses, and then they were set on fire. Enormous funeral pyres were blazing. Later I was given some photographs of this, and I looked at them once but never returned to them. The effect they had was too disheartening. They say that Napoleon or someone else once said that it's pleasant to smell the corpse of the enemy. I don't know how it is for other people, but for me it was not a pleasant smell and it was also not pleasant to see that picture!

I would like to relate another comic incident, which is also typical of that time and the people of that time. It was a good time, heroic, tragic and in its own way triumphant. We suffered tragedy during our retreat, and then we triumphed with our offensive, dealing retribution to the Germans for their insolent incursion across the borders of the USSR. I was flying once from Rostov to Moscow, having been summoned by Stalin. Airplanes in those days often had to be refueled along the way and so we landed at Stalingrad. I stayed over with the 64th Army. There were army celebrations going on then. It seems that some orders or honorary decorations were being awarded. A dinner was given for the command staff by the army headquarters in a rather large meeting hall. I took part in the ceremonies and sat at a table with the commander. Tables were small, seating only a few people each. Sitting next to us were a general, a colonel, and two other people. A conversation started up among them. Since people had been drinking, the tone grew more heated and the conversation turned into an argument between the general and the colonel. The colonel was chief of staff of the unit commanded by the general. I had known the general even before Stalingrad; I had met him near Kharkov, where he commanded a division and had a good reputation. His division was honored with the title of Guards division. I'm not going to mention his name now, although I do remember it. I had good relations with him. I felt that he was in the right place and was coping with his task. When the argument flared up between them, apparently the colonel had a stronger argument, and the general really had nothing to counter him with, so he decided to make use of his position. When the colonel had finally irritated the general thoroughly, the latter suddenly barked out in Ukrainian using his full commanding general's tone of voice: "Comrade Colonel, do not forget yourself!" He pronounced these words in such an intimidating way. The colonel answered: "Yes, sir," and subsided. I didn't interfere in the conversation, of course. I was just looking on from the sidelines, but this incident remained in my memory.

After I had arrived in Moscow when we were sitting around the table with Stalin talking about various incidents, I told about this one also. Stalin liked it very much. Many years later he would still smile and say in some appropriate situation: "Comrade Colonel, do not forget yourself!" Why bother to force yourself to think up arguments to convince your opponent when you have power and a powerful position? I am the general; you are the colonel. The junior officer must subordinate himself to the senior. A colonel cannot be smarter than a general. He doesn't have the right to be. He should do his duty more and talk less. In my life I've met many people along the way, of various callings and different characters, but unfortunately I've often encountered incidents when for lack of an intelligent argument people fell back on their superior positions or titles and put down their subordinates.

I remember another anecdote that circulated widely, one brought into existence by life itself. "A subordinate was reporting to a superior officer and, in so doing, was arguing quite cogently for his own point of view on the course of a military operation. He was arguing that such-and-such should be done, or that it would be better to do so-and-so. In reply there came a shout, "Don't try to argue with me. Just listen and carry out your orders. Your job is to carry out orders. You don't need to think." Unfortunately I don't know when or how such things will change. Military men say that that's the way military discipline works. The senior officer decides questions, and the junior officer carries them out. There is a formula that says: "Don't try to be intelligent; just be good at carrying out orders." This kind of thing often boomeranged on us, and I would like that to be taken into account. Today times are different, the people are different, and there's a different culture. But I don't think this depends on culture. Military conditions left a certain imprint on our lives. I don't know if this is because of military discipline or merely because there was a kind of caste system. I find it difficult to define the problem any more precisely.

The troops of the Southern Front, having taken Rostov, advanced westward and reached the banks of the Mius River to the north of Taganrog.[30] I was familiar with these places from 1941. That year we had driven the Germans out of Rostov, and our troops—that is, our main force, the 56th Army—had operated in this area. The remnants of General Tanaschishin's tank corps had also fought in this area. At the end of 1941 the commander of the 56th Army had been General Tsyganov,[31] a heavy-set man. He himself, as I recall, had not been a front-line commander but had graduated from the Military Academy in the department of material supply. He was very witty and original. The following incident comes to mind. In 1941 after we had liberated Rostov, we wanted to take Taganrog immediately, and so we hurled our troops against that position over and over but had no success. At one point we captured two prisoners. I decided to interrogate them. One turned out to be a Czech. When they brought him in and I began to question him, he told me how he had become a prisoner: "I have brought you a submachine gun. I decided to cross the front line and surrender myself. After I arrived in the position held by your troops, I hunted and hunted for a long time to find someone I could surrender to." This made our general angry and he began explaining something to me to counter this assertion.

I said to him: "But you weren't there. Why should this soldier lie? Evidently that sector, the sector where he crossed the front line, was bare, so he went hunting for people and finally found some that he could surrender to." Of course it had been reported to me earlier that our forces had captured this man. It turned out that this was not so; he himself had come over to our side. Military men may want to dispute this, but in war all sorts of things happen. Sometimes our reconnaissance scouts would cross the front line, and the enemy would simply not notice them. The enemy would also find weak spots in our lines and penetrate to our rear areas. Evidently something like that happened in the case of this Czech.

The second prisoner was a Romanian, a tall young man wearing a Romanian black sheepskin cap. I asked what his name was, and in reply he immediately said: "We Romanians will not make a revolution. We will fight!" Here was a man who as far as his political views went was still wet behind the ears.

I said to him: "In your case you've already made your revolution and finished with your fighting. Your job now is to go to a prisoner of war camp. You can wait it out there in captivity until the war ends."

Back then, in 1941, when the first fighting began near Taganrog on the Mius River, the army headquarters had been located in the village of Sovetsky, a small village with rather unimposing peasant houses. I no longer remember any of the local inhabitants. In 1943 when we took Rostov we once again established our Front headquarters in Sovetsky. It was a very convenient location because it was in the middle of our forces, and we could easily organize communications with the various units from that position. That's why both in 1941 and in 1943 the choice fell on the village of Sovetsky.

Recently a teacher from that village wrote me a letter asking me to tell what the settlement was like back then, when we occupied it. Unfortunately, a lot of time has gone by, and I really have nothing to say right now. I had very little contact with the population. The residents had been cleared out of the building we occupied as a command post; the people had been relocated. The headquarters was guarded rather tightly, and there was nothing really to distinguish this village from a multitude of others that we were forced to abandon and later recaptured. So no special memory or impressions of any kind have remained with me of that village. It was simply a small village and a poor one from its outward appearance. Besides, both in 1941 and in 1943 everything was covered with snow. Moreover, in 1943 I was not in the village itself very much. No sooner had we moved our headquarters to Sovetsky than a phone call came from Stalin ordering me to fly to Moscow. I immediately made the flight, and in the process I was warned that I should fly out keeping in mind that I would not return to the Southern Front, because I was going to be given a different assignment.

I arrived in Moscow and reported to Stalin on the state of affairs of the Southern Front, and about Malinovsky, who had already, as it were, been rehabilitated. The very fact that I was recalled from the Southern Front and confirmed as a member of the Military Council of the Voronezh Front testified to that. Kirichenko was appointed second member of the Military Council of the Southern Front; I don't remember who became the first member.[32] As I recall it was also someone from the military. I felt sorry to leave Malinovsky. It had been pleasant to work with him, and he and I had had no disagreements or conflicts on any question. We had decided all questions jointly, as would normally be done by a commander and the first member of a Military Council. We also consulted with other comrades who belonged to the Military Council, but for the most part the main questions were decided by two people: the commander and the first member of the Military Council. In those days in general there were no questions that needed to be discussed at conferences. To have someone chair a meeting, to have a discussion and arguments pro and con—all that kind of thing took place only in rare instances when an operation was being worked out or something new was being undertaken. Ongoing military questions were decided on the run, and various orders and commands were issued immediately, right on the spot.

It was also good to work with Malinovsky because he was a well-organized person. He never tried, from a feeling of false pride, to give the impression that he never slept or never rested. Many generals during the war tried to give that impression, to make it look as though they never slept, were always on their feet thinking about one thing or another, so that they never had time to sleep. Of course that is the purest kind of lie and fabrication. A human being is simply not capable of functioning properly without a minimum amount of sleep. You can go for a certain number of days without sleep, but the work of a person who does that will not be productive and in military respects it could even be dangerous. One must always be prepared to think sensibly about questions on which the lives of hundreds of thousands of people depend. Malinovsky conducted himself like an ordinary mortal. Actually he did do a great deal of work. He was a man with a great capacity for work and a good head on his shoulders. I liked the way he reasoned about military questions and not only military ones. But when he needed to, he rested. He always rested a certain amount of time every day, if of course the situation allowed. It's a different matter if a dangerous situation has developed. Then you can't go to sleep. Certainly you can't just go off and sleep at your regularly scheduled time. But other people simply tried to make it look as though they never slept, that they had an eternally vigilant eye, that they saw everything and heard everything. That was just foolishness!

Malinovsky told me a lot about his life. He hadn't known his father. His mother, it seems, had not been married, and she didn't raise her own son. He was raised by an aunt, and spent his childhood in Odessa. He spoke very unrestrainedly, even insultingly, about his mother. Not only did he not love her; he had a strong sense of injury that survived from his childhood years. He spoke of his aunt with great tenderness, but about his mother he was very bitter. He also said that as a young man he had worked in Odessa as a shop assistant or salesman, and then World War I had begun. He ran away and found a spot for himself on a military train heading toward the front. Soldiers adopted him as one of their own. And that's how he landed in the army. Later he ended up as part of the expeditionary force of Russian troops sent to France, and he fought there as a machine gunner. That's where he was when the revolution found him.

Much later, when he was already minister of defense of the USSR, Mali-novsky accompanied me to a meeting of the heads of state of the four great powers in Paris: a summit meeting of the United States, the Soviet Union, Britain, and France. The meeting collapsed.[33] It was called off because just before it was to be held the Americans sent a spy plane over Soviet territory. This is a fairly well known fact in the history of our struggle against American imperialism, which had organized the so-called Cold War. The opening day of the summit conference was postponed, and so we had a "window of time." Malinovsky proposed: "Let's make a trip to the village where our unit was once stationed, not far from Paris. I can find the village, and I can find the peasant woman in whose house we lived. It may be that the husband has already died because he was old, but the wife was young. She is probably still alive." So we did. We got in a car and headed down the French highways. The roads there are excellent. We found the village without any trouble. Malinovsky remembered its location exactly. We also found the home of the peasant woman, who actually was still alive. She had a son of about forty, a daughter-in-law, and grandchildren. "But my old man," she said, "died long ago." Her son greeted us very politely and immediately began to organize a treat for his guests, bringing out the wine.

We drank, and Malinovsky began to reminisce about the old days and ask questions: "What happened to the tavern that was here, where the peasants used to gather?"

Our French hosts said: "You remember that?" "Yes, I remember it very well." They said: "Well then, you probably remember so-and-so." And they named some young woman. Malinovsky said: "Yes, I remember."

They said: "Ha, ha, ha. Of course he remembers. She was the local beauty. But she's no longer with us and hasn't been for a long time. She died long ago."

Other French people also arrived. They had heard that the minister of defense of the USSR had been a soldier in a Russian unit stationed at that village fifty years earlier. They said: "How is this possible, how could it be! We remember, too. You had the bear with you."

Malinovsky answered: "Yes, we had the bear." Malinovsky explained that when they went to France they had gotten a little bear cub from somewhere. The bear cub stuck close to the soldiers and later even went with them to the front. That was a detail that the peasants particularly remembered.

Malinovsky told me about other events in his life. He said: "The fact that I had been in the Russian expeditionary corps in France was like a cloud that hung over my head." I can't remember now exactly what he told me, but I know from history that the expeditionary corps had great difficulty returning to Russia. It seems it was sent back from France in such a way that the soldiers ended up on territory occupied by the Whites. Malinovsky had to travel a long road before he found himself with the Red Army. The episode in question is important for an understanding of the atmosphere of the Stalin era. There always hung over Malinovsky, like the sword of Damocles, the fact that he had been in the expeditionary corps in France and on territory held by the Whites before he joined the Red Army. I once told him about how General Popov and I had wandered aimlessly around Kalach and kept coming back to the corpses of the two German soldiers and the gray horse. I also told him how we had met a general from the signal corps that night, and I mentioned his name. Malinovsky immediately reacted. I asked: "Did you know him?"

He said: "What do you mean? I knew him very well. I served together with him." Later he gave me some more details: "The following incident occurred. Once when I went to Moscow I was supposed to make an appearance at the department of cadres of the People's Commissariat of Defense. The officer who greeted me at the department of cadres, through his own inadvertence or inefficiency, handed me my personal file. I leafed through it, and it was like little ants were crawling over my skin; it gave me goose bumps. How could it be that I was still walking around on this earth, still alive? There were so many false, vile things gathered in that file against me. You could only be amazed that I had not been arrested and shot like so many of the others. And among all the other foul things there was a denunciation against me by that very same general. Apparently he was a secret agent. The foul things he wrote about me were really gruesome. After that it was repulsive even for me to shake his hand or hear his name mentioned.

He really is a vile man. The things he dreamed up about me. The awful slander! I don't know what kept Stalin from arresting me and having me shot like he did so many other honest people. People who were more prominent than I was, with more distinguished service in the Red Army. It seems that I drew a lucky ticket in the lottery of life. That's the only way I can explain the fact that I'm still alive."

After Stalin's death, when Malinovsky and I met on a hunting trip in circumstances where we could relax and talk at our ease, I told him how Stalin had reacted to Larin's suicide and how I had been ordered not to leave Malinovsky's side, to keep an eye on him and watch to see whether he really closed his eyes when he went to bed, whether he was really sleeping or just putting on. In short, my job was to dog his footsteps and never let up. It was unpleasant for me to perform this surveillance, because I knew he sensed it; he understood why this member of the Military Council and of the Politburo was following his tracks so persistently and was showing up at his side without fail, no matter where he went. And if I didn't insist that all of his orders and commands be reported to me, it was only because he himself displayed a certain amount of tact and reported to me of his own accord. He didn't force me to demand anything of him, and thus he actually put himself in a more favorable position.

Malinovsky replied: "Yes, I saw that, and I must say sincerely that I was very pleased that you stayed with me all the time. After all I was an honorable person and I was doing everything that from my point of view needed to be done. And so I was pleased that you would see all that and understand it correctly." I agree with him, because that meant that the proper kind of reports would be made to Stalin. And that's how I did report to Stalin. As for Stalin, during the war, it seems that life itself forced him to restrain the wrath that drove him to have people arrested and destroyed.

On the other hand, I really don't know. Perhaps I should take some credit because of my influence on the Politburo (and evidently my influence was not small) and the character reference that I gave in favor of Malinovsky back in 1941, when I met him and when Timoshenko and I appointed him commander of the Sixth Army. That may also have had some influence. He was fighting the enemy then in the Dnepropetrovsk area. And so to sum up, that's what my joint work with Malinovsky was like. Now he is dead, and what else can I say about him? Nothing beyond the good things that I have already said. We are all mortals. You have to watch what you're getting into when you start reviewing someone else's life. In every individual you can discover a great many different qualities. It depends on the character of the person making the assessment. The thing is to set aside all secondary matters, all kinds of trash, and look at a person the way he mainly was. To look at his actions and the main direction of his thinking and his energy, what things he applied his energy to. Malinovsky's energy was positive and served the Soviet state. His energy was directed toward building up our Red Army, and during the war it was directed toward crushing the enemy. Things don't always work out for any of us the way we might have liked. Malinovsky and I had occasion to swallow some things that were pretty hot and sometimes pretty repulsive during the first and second years of the war. Later he and I had the chance to enjoy the sweet taste of victory, the success of the Red Army, and to rejoice in having driven the enemy from the territory occupied by Hitler.

What else can I say about Malinovsky that is good? I will return to him again later, when I tell about how Malinovsky and I in the 1950s and 1960s directed our efforts toward reequipping and modernizing the Soviet armed forces. I think that was a very interesting stage in our lives, which gave us a lot of satisfaction. Even today I live on memories of that creative period, the time when the Soviet army was being reequipped. I am proud that it fell to my lot at that time to be chairman of the Council of Ministers of the USSR and first secretary of the Central Committee of the party.

And so I have digressed in giving a description of Malinovsky's character. I left off at the point when I was summoned to Moscow. When I flew there from the village of Sovetsky I felt different about myself on arriving in the capital, and Stalin's attitude toward me was different from what it had been a little earlier. After all, we were no longer the same people who had surrendered Ukraine to the enemy. Back then, Stalin had been ready to dump all the blame on me. He was always ready to blame someone else, anyone, as long as it was not himself. In the period when the Red Army was retreating, no documents that you could find anywhere, and no orders, were published over his signature. Things were always signed by the Stavka or the General Staff—a nameless, faceless signature—but never by Stalin! Later, when we went on the offensive, the situation changed completely. His signature glittered on every document then. He took no responsibility, as it were, for the retreat, but when there was success and the enemy was being smashed, then he took the credit for it. Some miserable so-called historians even today when Stalin is no longer alive march in his footsteps in their descriptions of that era. I will express my point of view on that again later on. There is a good joke that I have mentioned before. They say that it's the soldiers who surrender the cities but the generals who retake them. Stalin operated according to that principle. The soldiers retreated, and Stalin wasn't there, but when we began to retake our cities it was as though the soldiers weren't there anymore, that Stalin alone was retaking them, because there were the orders with his signature on them, the initiative belonged to him, and all that sort of thing.

1. During the retreat of the Red Army, various formations were repeatedly incorporated into these fronts under new names. At the time of the events here described, the Voronezh Front was advancing along the Oskol River from Kastornoye (on the nearby Orlym River) toward Kupyansk, the Southwestern Front along the Seversky Donets River from Svatovo-Luchko toward Kamensk-Shakhtinsky, and the Southern Front along the Lower Don River (the section between the Donbas-Stalingrad railroad and the town of Azov).

2. All these places are in the eastern Ukraine. Novomoskovsk is some 30 kilometers northeast, and Pavlograd (in Ukrainian Pavlohrad) about 60 kilometers east, of Dnepropetrovsk. [SS]

3. Malinovsky took command of the Southern Front again in February 1943.

4. Lieutenant General P. I. Bodin was chief of staff of the Transcaucasus Front through October 1942. He was killed November 2, 1942.

5. Major General T. A. Strokach was head of the Ukrainian staff of the partisan movement from 1942 to 1945.

6. Lieutenant General L. R. Korniyets, at that time chairman of the Council of People's Commissars of the Ukrainian SSR, was transferred in 1943 from the Northern Caucasus Front, where he was the second member of the Military Council, to the Voronezh Front, where he and Khrushchev shared the post of first member of the Military Council. See Biographies.

7. In Cossack regions of Russia, the term *stanitsa* designated an administrative district as well as the capital of that district—presumably the largest village in the area. A *stanitsa* encompassed a number of *khutora,* smaller villages or farming communities, and *posyolki,* which were settlements of an urban type. (Russian geographic-administrative terminology makes a distinction between settlements "of a rural type" and those "of an urban type.") We have sometimes used the term "hamlet" for smaller settlements, whether in Cossack regions or not. [GS]

8. Rotmistrov, being chief marshal of tank forces, headed this academy from 1958 to 1964, after which he occupied the post of assistant to the minister of defense.

9. It was probably Nizhne-Chirskaya, because at Verkhne-Chirskaya the bridge was too small.

10. This was the Fifth Shock Army, under the command of Lieutenant General V. D. Tsvetayev.

11. Novocherkassk is an industrial city about 30 kilometers east of Rostov. [SS]

12. Bataisk is just south of Rostov. [SS]

13. Lieutenant General of Tank Forces S. I. Bogdanov was at that time commander of a mechanized corps.

14. Salsk is about 160 kilometers southeast of Rostov. [SS]

15. Lieutenant General V. F. Gerasimenko commanded the 28th Army from September 1942 to November 1943. See Biographies.

16. Elista is the capital of the Republic of Kalmykia. It is about halfway between Astrakhan and Rostov. [SS]

17. S. M. Budyonny came from the hamlet of Kozyurin, O. I. Gorodovikov from the hamlet of Mokraya Yelmuta.

18. General (of the tsarist army) L. G. Kornilov actually came from the Cossack settlement of Karkaralinskaya in Kazakhstan.

19. Not only ethnic Russians but also many Ukrainians, Kalmyks, and members of other ethnic groups became Cossacks. The inhabitants of Proletarskaya were evidently Kalmyk Cossacks. [SS]

20. The commander Khrushchev has in mind is Ya. G. Kreizer. See Biographies. The Second Guards Army under his command liberated Novocherkassk on February 12, 1943.

21. The town of Shakhty is about 30 kilometers north of Novocherkassk. [SS] It was liberated on February 13, 1943.

22. Azov is a few kilometers west of Rostov, on the shore of the Sea of Azov (an inlet of the Black Sea). [SS]

23. Lieutenant General N. Ya. Kirichenko commanded a mobile mechanized cavalry group consisting of the Fourth Guards Kuban and the Fifth Guards Don Cavalry Corps and a tank formation. This group had previously been part of the Northern Caucasus Front.

24. Novorossiysk and Taman are on the northeastern shore of the Black Sea, south of the Sea of Azov. [SS]

25. This took place on February 7, 1943.

26. Lieutenant General V. A. Khomenko was in command of the 44th Army from November 1942. He perished on the approaches to Nikopol (in

south central Ukraine) on November 9, 1943. Before the war he had commanded the border guards of Moldavia and the adjacent section of Ukraine.

27. Kamenets-Podolsky is in Ukraine, in the south of Khmelnitsky province on a tributary of the Dniester River called the Smotrich, not far south of the little town of that name. It is just east of the old 1939 border. [AH]

28. This took place on February 14, 1943.

29. The Second Guards Army and the 51st Army

were advancing from the north, bypassing Rostov on the Don.

30. The Mius River flows south and enters the Sea of Azov at Taganrog. [SS]

31. Major General V. V. Tsyganov commanded the 56th Army from December 1941 to July 1942. See Biographies.

32. A. I. Kirichenko. The first member of the Military Council was Lieutenant General K. A. Gurov.

33. This summit meeting was to take place in May 1960.

## BEFORE THE BATTLE OF KURSK AND AT ITS BEGINNING

I arrived in Moscow and told Stalin about the situation on the Southern Front. We were in a good mood then, enjoying the taste of success. The Northern Caucasus was also being liberated quickly, but that was not part of our Front; it belonged to another Front altogether; and I was reporting on the situation of our Front. Stalin said: "We have confirmed you as member of the Military Council of the Voronezh Front. Kharkov has been taken by our troops.[1] Do you know about that?"

"I know. The Red Army has advanced quite some distance to the west of Kharkov."

"So, you should now fly to the headquarters of the Voronezh Front. You will function not only as member of the Military Council but also as secretary of the CP(B)U, as previously."

Stalin again began ridiculing the leaders to whom he had entrusted Ukrainian affairs, just as he had on my previous visit. On that occasion—back during the battle of Stalingrad—he had told me that since I was not a Ukrainian, Ukrainian affairs would be taken over by Korniyets, who was then chairman of the Council of People's Commissar of the Ukrainian SSR.

As I have already related, I conceded in the conversation back then that indeed I was not a Ukrainian. Everyone knows both from my passport and from my birthplace that I am a Kuryanin [a person from the Kursk region] and my village was a Russian village, although it was right smack up against the border with Ukraine. A border is a border. As for me, I didn't attribute any importance to whether I was Ukrainian or Russian. I am an internationalist and my attitude has always been one of respect toward every nation. But of course those closest to me are the ones among whom I spent my childhood and youth. They were Russian and Ukrainian workers and peasants, and also the Ukrainian intelligentsia with whom I worked when I was head of the organizational department of the party's Kiev district committee in 1928–29 and especially when I was first secretary of the Central Committee of the CP(B)U. For thirteen years I worked in Ukraine, not just with satisfaction, but with great pleasure, and I am very happy with the attitude of all its people toward me—workers, peasants, and the Ukrainian intelligentsia.

I answered: "All right, Comrade Stalin, I will be glad to go to the Voronezh Front. And who is commanding that Front?"

He said: "General Golikov."[2] I immediately remembered that Stalin had criticized me for not supporting Golikov when he was deputy commander of the troops at Stalingrad. Then (as I have already related) Golikov had written some sort of foul thing to Stalin against Yeremenko, and Stalin criticized me for supporting Yeremenko too much and not supporting Golikov. Could it be that he also wrote something foul about me? It's possible. In my life, unfortunately, I've seen a lot of foul things. It's true that I've seen good things, but I've also seen foul things. Sometimes foul deeds have been done by people who from their outward appearance seemed rather nice and decent. I am not a person who holds grudges. But I wonder how others would have acted, for example, if they had had this kind of run-in with Golikov. After all, he had not acted decently; he had written some sort of foul denunciation of Yeremenko and also, directly or indirectly, of me as member of the Military Council of the Stalingrad Front. It was due to me in large part when later, in my era, Golikov was confirmed as head of the Chief Political Directorate of the Red Army and when he was awarded the rank of marshal—the highest rank in the Soviet armed forces.

I asked Stalin: "How is he as a commander? What is your impression?" I said nothing more than that, but Stalin immediately understood that I was asking this question because we had different assessments of Golikov's behavior as a representative of the Front with Chuikov's army, when Golikov had failed to carry out the order to organize the shipping of munitions and reinforcements to Stalingrad [across the Volga]. I thought then and I still think now that the commander of the Stalingrad Front and I reacted correctly. But now a different situation had arisen. The enemy troops at Stalingrad had been taken prisoner, and everyone was carried away with the joy of victory. It was a joy not only for our people but for all of progressive humanity, which understood the significance of our fight against the fascist plague.

Stalin looked at me again: "You remember what you told me about Golikov?"

"Yes, I remember."

"What was it you said then?"

"Well, but why are you sending me to be a member of the Military Council with Golikov?"

"We're soon going to make a new decision and reassign him." I don't know why he told me that. Was he perhaps feeling the pangs of conscience? He said: "We were thinking about appointing Vatutin to be commander of the Front there. You know General Vatutin, don't you?"

I said: "I know General Vatutin. I know him very well, and I have a high opinion of him."

This general was a special case. He was virtually a nondrinker. I never saw him drink even wine. Besides, he had a great capacity for work, and he was very well trained in military matters. At one time he had been chief of staff in the Kiev Special Military District, and then he had been deputy chief of the General Staff.[3] This testifies well to his military knowledge. I said: "I have great respect for him as chief of staff, as a man who knows military science, and as a party member. But I don't know what qualities he would show as a commander. What's required in this sphere is not only knowledge but also efficient management and the ability to exercise the powers of a commander, the ability to give orders and see that they are carried out. He can work out and plan a military operation. I have no doubts about him in that respect. But his other qualities are completely unknown to me. So for me, in this sense, he is an entirely new person. I have never had any dealings with him in this area." I don't remember what Stalin said in reply, but I was satisfied with the new appointment.

A day or two later I flew out of Moscow. As I was getting ready for my flight, it was reported to me that the Germans had assembled many Schutzstaffel (SS) troops and tank divisions[4] in the Kharkov area and they were pressing our troops back toward Kharkov. Our troops had already retreated eastward a fairly good distance, and the enemy had once again come right up to the outskirts of Kharkov. I flew out in the evening, before twilight. My personal pilot, Nikolai Ivanovich Tsybin,[5] and I had chosen precisely that time of day. As long as I live, I will always have a good word to say about this remarkable pilot, a Soviet general, and a very honest and sober-minded man who had, I would say, such a delicate, almost maidenly quality about him. In this case it was he who planned that we would fly into Kharkov just before evening, because at that time of day there was less likelihood of encountering enemy fighters. And that's what we did. We landed just when lights were starting to come on.

We drove from the airport into Kharkov. I was given alarming news: Kharkov was being threatened; the enemy might take it once again. I went to the Front headquarters and met with the commander there. He reported on the situation at the front lines. Sure enough, the situation was very unstable. The enemy had superiority over us in both troop strength and quality of weapons and equipment. The enemy had armored forces and elite infantry troops. At the present time I have learned from reading the book *Top Secret!*[6] that the Germans had taken these forces from Italy. The best SS divisions and armored forces had been transferred precisely to this location, to throw them against us in the Kharkov area.

We had to make an immediate trip out to Merefa, 25 kilometers from Kharkov.[7] I had been in Merefa often, back before the revolution. Whenever I chanced to travel from my native Kursk region to the Donbass, to Yuzovka, I invariably passed through Merefa. Now I was going there in a different capacity. General Kozlov[8] commanded our military group in this area. I had not known Kozlov before that. Earlier he had commanded our military group in Kerch. We had landed an expeditionary force on the Kerch peninsula, part of the Crimea,[9] which was under enemy occupation, but that operation had been unsuccessful, and many of our troops had perished there. As I recall, Voroshilov was also sent there at one time to command the troops. After that, it seems, he was recalled, and Mekhlis was sent to be commissar there.[10] As a representative of the Stavka, Mekhlis actually acted as commander of that military group. He dominated Kozlov and in effect took charge, and as a result our forces were destroyed. I remember how Mekhlis cursed and thundered against all the peoples of the Caucasus at that time. He said that the main reinforcements and in general the troops of that front were made up of people from the Caucasus and that they were completely unreliable. From the point of view of our nationalities policy he took an absolutely incorrect position. He himself was a mentally unstable individual, but Stalin had complete confidence in him.

Mekhlis had, in effect, assumed command and prevented Kozlov from really acting as commander. I had no possibility of observing that operation in detail then, because of my own position. That was not one of my functions. But I heard what the military specialists said when they discussed and analyzed what had happened with the Crimean Front. Of course this is only what I heard in passing. They laid the blame for the disaster there on Mekhlis and to a certain extent on Voroshilov. But mostly they blamed Mekhlis and the fact that Kozlov did not display any strength of character as commander. He had immediately fallen under Mekhlis's influence instead of

asserting his will as commander and using his military knowledge to organize the troops as they should have been. He began listening obediently and
carrying out the orders and suggestions made by Mekhlis. In short, Kozlov's
reputation had been tarnished. As a commander, he had displayed, to a certain extent, both lack of principle and lack of character.

I had gone to Merefa together with Golikov. In general, Kozlov did not
make a bad impression on me. I tried not to be influenced by what I had
heard about him earlier. I wanted to evaluate him on the basis of the facts
that I could currently observe. He reasoned quite intelligently. The orders he
gave seemed to me sensible. In short, I didn't form a negative impression of
Kozlov.

And yet we were retreating. Well, what of it? Whether Kozlov had been
there or some Petrov or Ivanov it would have made no difference. We would
still have had to retreat because the enemy had superior forces. We already
sensed, and even spoke of it openly, that we were going to have to surrender
Kharkov again, that we would not be able to hold it. I felt very sorry about
this. I made a trip through the city. It hadn't suffered especially great damage.
The tractor factory, for example, was generally still intact, with no major

destruction! Earlier [in 1941] we had removed our equipment from the factory, but the Germans had been doing some repair work there. They had brought in some equipment and organized repair shops. The factory was still almost as good as new, you might say. Just bring in some machine tools, raw materials, and workers, and you could start production of tanks, motor vehicles, tractors, or whatever you wanted. But I also knew that now that we were going to abandon Kharkov again, the next time (we were confident that we would return; we had no doubt that the enemy would not be able to hold the city for long) the enemy would do everything in his power to smash and destroy the city, especially its factories. I was sure that the enemy would not leave the tractor factory behind again in this condition but would wreck it completely. Still, there was nothing to be done about it. We were once again forced to abandon Kharkov.

I decided then to gather the Ukrainian intelligentsia together and talk with them. A meeting was called in the evening for the intelligentsia who had remained in Kharkov and who had lived there under the Germans. That very same night or the next morning we were going to move the Front headquarters out of Kharkov. The event was organized by the Ukrainian intellectuals who were associated at that time with the Front headquarters, or more exactly, associated with me as a member of the Military Council and, more important, as secretary of the Central Committee of the CP(B)U. Intellectuals were there and also leading officials of the Council of People's Commissars of Ukraine, in short, the party's active members. We gathered up the appropriate people so that when our troops advanced westward we could immediately assign cadres and organize government institutions on the republic, province, and district levels. A great deal was done then by Nikolai Platonovich Bazhan[11] and other writers. It was through them that I asked the intellectuals to gather and told them that I would be coming to talk with them and listen to them. Primarily I wanted to listen and get a sense of their moods and attitudes.

The meeting went very well. I had warned my own people: "Be very cautious in the statements you make. We have always said 'not one step backward' and so forth. But that kind of talk would make a bad impression now, because we've already decided to retreat. There is no way that we can hold Kharkov. We are going to abandon Kharkov. And so your speeches should be geared toward inspiring hope. Our retreat should not be seen as some sort of incomprehensible maneuver. We will move forward again, in spite of everything, and the enemy will be defeated and driven from the territory of the

Soviet Union." I wanted to bolster their morale. I couldn't say directly that we were going to retreat. In general nothing was said about retreating. But I hinted indirectly and tried to instill confidence in them so that they could endure the new arrival of the enemy more steadfastly. In my speech I tried to steer them toward the idea of retreating together with the Red Army. I didn't literally say that that they should, but I wanted to convince them not to place any trust in the Germans, to assure them that we would not be arresting intellectuals, that we would not criticize people if they remained on the territory occupied by the enemy, but we would like to see them retreat together with us.

That possibility concerned me most of all. I was afraid that we would retreat and they would stay, and that is exactly what happened! But if I had given the slightest hint that I would condemn their behavior if they remained, it would sound like a threat. And then they would flee to the west with the Germans. That's what I was afraid of. I wanted the rumor to get around Kharkov that, no matter what, there would not be any repression. I wanted this word to reach the people who were not at the meeting (and there were not many there). For example Gmyrya[12] was not there, yet his voice as a famous singer resounded throughout Ukraine. He was a splendid master of his art. He remained in Ukraine under the Germans. Later he explained that he remained because his wife was ill. We won't try to go into that now. I had already grown accustomed to explanations that a wife or a mother or a father was near death and a person could not evacuate and leave a family member alone. Whether that was really so is difficult to judge. It was a tense situation, and there was no time to check on such statements. Later on there was no sense trying to look into such things.

So then, the meeting was held. A certain artist was present at the meeting (I forget his name). He was considered a fairly good artist. But he spoke in such a free and easy way about how he had lived under the Germans, and how he had "done business" with them, that it made a very unpleasant impression on me. I tried not to show it. I acted as though it didn't bother me. He was boasting about dealing in icons. "We would take some ordinary icons," he said, "and treat them with chemical reagents so as to age the material and, taking advantage of the ignorance of the German buyers, we would sell them the icons as ancient treasures having special value." He spoke like a swindler, portraying himself as such a clever and resourceful tradesman. Evidently he didn't make a bad living from this. Other people spoke differently, but he spoke with a kind of proud passion, as though to say, "Look what a clever fellow I am. I knew how to survive in such a milieu and even to make fools of the Germans." A clever man, he seemed to be saying, can always swindle fools, and I too have shown my talent.

After we held the meeting, I said goodbye and left. We had to retreat that very night or the next day. Our entire headquarters staff moved out of the city the next morning, and soon the Germans entered Kharkov again.[13] I wanted this artist to retreat with us and the other intellectuals as well. I didn't want them to remain under the Germans any longer. I wanted to think the best of them—that they would not stay. But no. In the case of this artist, he was not a man of good spirit. In his makeup and in his character he was closer to our enemies than to a true Soviet intellectual or Soviet artist. Later on I asked Bazhan and other comrades where this man was. They answered: "He's not with us any longer." It was hard to find out whether he could have retreated or could not have. It turns out that he could have if he had wanted to, but he didn't go with us. When we liberated Kharkov again, I assigned someone to find this artist, to check and see whether my evaluation of him was correct, but no, he had left with the Germans. He, having the soul of a wheeler-dealer, a merchant, and a self-seeker, was more inclined toward the Germans than toward us and he went with them "to the other side." When the war ended I asked if there were any traces of him. No, he couldn't be found. But to me it doesn't seem possible that the Germans might have done something to him. After all, he served them well. Perhaps he was one of the so-called displaced persons who refused to return. There were many of them back then—Russians, Ukrainians, and others. A lot of them were Ukrainians! Especially residents of western Ukraine. There were a lot of nationalists there who had been taken in by enemy propaganda or were simply supporters of Bandera.[14] They had faith in the enemy, remained in the West, and broke from their native land. Perhaps that artist went off to Canada. In short, I would say that he was a typical second-hand goods dealer, a speculator in works of art.

And so we retreated. The Front headquarters withdrew to Belgorod.[15] We expected to hold Belgorod, but our forces were too weak and we didn't succeed. Our headquarters was located in a small building with a garden. Every night the enemy bombed Belgorod, including the location of our headquarters. It's not excluded that some German agents or traitors may have been left behind in Belgorod to provide information about targets for enemy aircraft. It's true that Belgorod is not a large city, but the enemy planes were literally circling right over the area where our headquarters were located. One day when Golikov and I were standing at the map analyzing the situation, a bomb exploded in the courtyard. A lampshade broke, the lights went out, and glass sprinkled all over the map. We went out and looked at the bomb crater. Apparently only a small bomb had fallen. If it had been a large one, our little house would probably have no longer been standing. We put everything back in order, but that same night we were hit by another air raid.

Another incident occurred there. The commander had to use the toilet. There was no warm toilet in the house, only a cold one out in the yard. The commander was out there when another bomb hit, but everything came out all right except that Golikov returned to the house—all covered with some refuse. We joked about that a lot with him afterward. But what can you do? Everything happens to people in this life, both traumatic and humorous.

We were hard pressed by the enemy, who had already come right up to Belgorod. We were unable to bring enough forces against the Germans to stop them, and we were now forced to abandon Belgorod, too.[16] In the morning Golikov and I chose a new location for our headquarters, either in Stary Oskol or Novy Oskol, somewhere beyond the Seversky Donets.[17] We decided to make the trip at dawn to avoid bombing. It was a fairly good distance to the new headquarters. I don't remember if we were in a motor vehicle; perhaps it was a sleigh, because there were deep snowdrifts everywhere then. We were feeling very distressed over what had happened. We had surrendered both Kharkov and Belgorod. Of course the enemy would now exert every effort to retake Kursk,[18] which we had won back in February.

We began constructing a line of defense. We dragged everything we had to the front lines and everything that the Stavka could send our way. The enemy apparently was also exhausted by that point and stopped advancing. Our troops stopped to the north and east of Belgorod on a line from Sudzha to Volchansk. We moved the Front headquarters to Oboyan.[19] This was the southern edge, or face, of what had now taken shape as the Kursk salient. At that point Vatutin arrived with orders to take over as commander of the Front. Golikov was given written instructions to surrender the command and place himself at the disposal of the Stavka. We took leave of Golikov, and Vatutin assumed his duties as commander. We couldn't undertake any active operations at that time, and we had no intention of trying. All our efforts were directed toward straightening out the line of our front and choosing the most advantageous positions for building field fortifications. We wanted to prepare as well as we could for springtime, because we were sure that in the spring the enemy would again go on the offensive, but we too would take the offensive and hit hard at the enemy.

We were given a tank corps. I have forgotten the name of the commander right now. He was a good tank commander, who had earlier led a brigade.

Now, in 1943, he was given a corps. He moved his forces up to the front line in the area where he was supposed to take up position. And then for the first time since the beginning of the war, we found the enemy employing a new device. The enemy managed to destroy almost that entire tank corps as it was marching. How was this done? From the air, using low-speed, low-flying aircraft similar to our U-2s, only somewhat more powerful. They were armed with cannon.[20] They would swoop down on our tanks and strafe them from the air, taking advantage of the fact that the armor on top of our tank turrets wasn't very strong. Therefore it was not difficult, using a small-caliber cannon or even a large-caliber machine gun, to set a tank on fire. I remember how the general of that tank corps arrived at our headquarters without his tanks, "with nothing but his stick." They used to joke about gypsies who had lost their horses and were left with nothing but the stick they used to drive the horses. And so this general showed up at our Front headquarters "with nothing but his stick." He was terribly upset—to the point of tears. After all, he had lost an entire corps and accomplished virtually nothing.

He didn't even have antiaircraft machine guns to protect his tanks against air attacks. After that incident Soviet designers took this inadequacy into account and began to produce tanks with antiaircraft machine guns. I don't remember whether every tank after that had a machine gun or just a certain number of tanks, so that in a sense we could maintain our order of march, so that one's own tank and the neighboring tanks could be protected against air attack while on the march. For the time being, however, the Germans had taken advantage of the element of surprise and had dealt us a substantial blow. Vatutin and I had placed such great hopes in that tank corps. And we were left with nothing but the command staff and the tank troops; the tanks themselves had been burned to bits along the line of march.

A lull descended on the Voronezh Front. The Germans were getting themselves in order, equipping their front-line forces and strengthening them, and we were busy doing the same. Spring was already upon us. It greeted us at Oboyan and outside Belgorod, but the snow was still very deep. There was an unusually snowy winter in 1943, more snowy than cold. But Vasilevsky, as a representative of the Stavka, soon appeared at our headquarters. He often visited us. By that time the pain I felt in regard to him had abated, the pain I had carried with me since winter 1942 when Vasilevsky, acting incorrectly, refused to perform his duty as a soldier and failed to report to Stalin during the first Kharkov operation. But to this day when I remember that time I experience strong feelings. I experienced a lot of pain and it put me on guard against Vasilevsky, who in his own right, as I've already said, was a kind and easygoing man. He was someone you could get along with. He often came to our Front headquarters, and it was always pleasant to talk with him and discuss matters that had become urgent for us.

Let me repeat that we felt no special need for representatives of the Stavka to come visit us—from the standpoint of assisting on strictly military matters. In my opinion the staff of the Voronezh Front and the commander were sufficiently well trained and prepared to carry out their functions. They understood them correctly and appraised the situation accurately. On the other hand, every time a representative of the Stavka came to visit, our hopes would rise that we might succeed in obtaining reinforcements or ammunition or "tear loose" some overcoats and shoes from supply services. In short, we took a rather mercenary approach. Sometimes we succeeded in this but not always. The representatives of the Stavka themselves understood this. They came because they were ordered to. They were told things such as: "Go there. It looks like the Germans are going on the offensive again. After all, our people out there have already surrendered Belgorod." It's possible that the impression had been formed in Moscow that if a representative of the Stavka arrived, the enemy offensive would be stopped and the front would be stabilized. But that's not how things worked out. It was not because someone from the Stavka arrived, but because the enemy was worn out and was forced to stop of his own accord in order to get himself back in order. Or it may be that we ourselves had received reinforcements and forced the enemy to stop.

At that time there was only one sector where the enemy continued active operations and was still on the offensive. That sector was being held by the 38th Army.[21] We made a trip to that sector. It was a sunny day, and the deep snow reflected the sunlight. It was so blindingly white that it hurt your eyes to look at it. Leaving the snowy open country, we arrived at a settlement whose name was Yam [meaning "Gully"]. Sure enough the settlement was down in a gully, and just then one or two enemy planes dived at us and began bombing our vehicles. Vasilevsky and I jumped out. We must have presented a humorous spectacle for the enemy pilot. After all, he could see everything. We ran from the vehicle, and the pilot faced the choice of either bombing the vehicle or strafing the "living forces of the enemy" with his machine gun. That meant Vasilevsky and I, our drivers, and accompanying personnel. But apparently the pilot had already fired all his ammunition at the vehicles in front of us. He turned and flew away. He flew pretty low and affected our nerves quite badly. Anyone who has been under fire from enemy aircraft knows what I mean.

We arrived at the headquarters of the army commander and listened to his report on the situation. The enemy had tried, but had not taken the above-named settlement [Yam]. The Germans had probably just been trying to improve their own position. It was an offensive of purely local significance—to straighten out the front line, to make it more suitable for defense, or to make use of it later, to establish suitable jumping-off points for a future offensive.

[To sum up] that is how the operations of winter and spring 1943 ended, the operations in which I participated. We had liberated Rostov and approached Taganrog; we had almost reached Dnepropetrovsk; and we had liberated Kharkov. Then under pressure of enemy counterattack, we were forced to abandon Kharkov again, as well as Belgorod and some other towns. After that, the front lines were stabilized, and in our area a bulge in the front lines had been formed, which was given the name "Kursk salient." It was a salient of fairly great depth. The left face, or edge, of the salient began in our position on the upper reaches of the Seversky Donets. The outer edge of the salient was to the north of Sumy near Rylsk.[22] And the northern edge of the salient ran between Kursk and Oryol.[23] Kursk remained in our hands. To the north of Ponyri[24] and to the east of Oryol, another zigzag in the front line wound back in the reverse direction. The commander, Comrade Vatutin, and I were of course concerned above all with the sector for which we were responsible: from Volchansk to the Seym River.[25] And we took measures so that the enemy could in no way advance through this sector. If he tried to move forward, for example, in a northerly direction, that is, toward Kursk, he would threaten our 38th and 40th Armies, positioned near Sumy, and we would lose favorable positions for an offensive toward Romny and Lebedin.[26] At that time we moved our headquarters to the northern outskirts of Oboyan at some depth from the southern edge of the salient. The name of the place we chose was some sort of military term. It was called Company Such-and-Such. This was a reminder left over from former times, from the Middle Ages, when the borders of the Russian state passed through Oboyan. Military settlers had lived there who performed military service, defending the borders from nomadic raids from the south. That is why the villages in that area had military names. I don't remember now what the number of the company was in that place where we moved our headquarters.

Spring was coming, and with the spring we knew that heavy fighting would also come. Our thinking was that until the enemy had "dried himself out" and built up sufficient forces he couldn't begin any significant operations against us. And we ourselves were absolutely incapable of undertaking any active operations. We simply didn't have the forces. I don't remember exactly when new military units arrived at our location or which ones they were. But we did receive the Sixth Guards Army as reinforcement. This had previously been the 21st Army, which had fought in the battle of Stalingrad as part of the Don Front. It had subsequently been reinforced and retrained and given a new name. It arrived at our positions after the snow had already melted. Its commander was General Chistyakov. I hadn't known him personally before that. But when he arrived and we got to know each other he made a good impression. In our opinion this army was a force to be reckoned with! The main thing is that the cadres of this army for the most part had already gone through the fighting at Stalingrad. They had been steeled and had acquired experience and perseverance in defensive fighting. In view of the oncoming summer that is exactly what we needed, an army that would be strong in defensive fighting. We deployed it to the north of Belgorod.[27] It straddled the paved road that ran from Belgorod to Kursk to Moscow.

The Seventh Guards Army, also from Stalingrad, likewise arrived at our positions. At Stalingrad it had been called the 64th Army. Its commander had been Shumilov,[28] and Serdyuk had been the first member of the Military Council. It had the same commander when it reached us. This army was deployed to the east of Belgorod beyond the Donets. It was supposed to offer resistance to the enemy if he tried to advance toward Novy Oskol, and at the same time the Seventh Guards could strike to the south of Belgorod. In our second echelon of defense, between the Sixth and Seventh Guards Armies, was the 69th Army commanded by General Kryuchenkin. I knew Kryuchenkin. He had been a fighter during the Civil War.[29] His face was covered with scars that he had received fighting the Whites. He had been a cavalryman. His army headquarters was established in Stary Oskol. On the right flank of the Sixth Guards Army, the 40th Army was deployed. Its commander was a general well known to me, Moskalenko.[30] Much later the 47th Army arrived at our positions. At first it had been part of the reserve forces of our Front.[31] Alongside Moskalenko's army was the 27th Army. Its commander was General Trofimenko.[32] Those armies faced toward the south; that is, they were positioned along the part of the front line that formed the southern edge of the salient. Facing westward was the 38th Army commanded by Chibisov. It was deployed on the right wing of our Front, and its right flank touched the left flank of the Central Front.

Behind Shumilov, beyond his left flank, were the reserve troops commanded by Ivan Stepanovich Konev. This body of troops was called the

Steppe Front. Later it took the name Second Ukrainian Front. The troops of the Southwestern Front, which adjoined the Voronezh Front on the south, were commanded by Malinovsky. That Front was then aimed at Kharkov and Dnepropetrovsk. That is how the troops were deployed in the area that directly or indirectly came under my jurisdiction at the time. As for the headquarters of Shumilov's army, it was established to the east of Belgorod in a forest. We often traveled there to check up on how his army was getting ready for an offensive and to listen to the reports of the army commander and the corps commanders as well as the division and brigade commanders.

The assignment set for all the troops of our Front was to learn how to fight well and work out effective tactics; soldiers were to learn to operate their weapons in exemplary fashion. The party organizations and the political departments of the army were oriented toward solidifying the troops politically and morally, so that every soldier would understand his mission and do everything he could not to retreat a single step and to prepare for a counteroffensive. Actually no special agitation was needed to convince the troops to defend their positions staunchly and take the offensive courageously. Everyone was eager for battle. I don't remember that any particular excesses occurred. I never heard of any desertions. Of course when you have a mass of people there are always deviations from the average in the behavior of one or another person, but on the whole the troops were in a very good state of mind. They were ready to fight, and die if necessary, but they would drive the enemy from their country. Drive him out! The Guards armies distinguished themselves especially. Even then the slogan could be heard among them, "On to Berlin! From Stalingrad to Berlin!" Later there were a lot of jokes on that subject. It seems that one general, partly joking and partly serious, had said: "Well, we're going to take Berlin, and I want to be commandant of Berlin." That kind of desire took hold of everyone. People who had suffered through the war, who had seen how many disasters and what misery it had brought us, wanted to show the enemy that the war could bring some disaster to him, too, and that he would have to pay for this war that he had started.

The Sixth Guards Army was ordered to dig in, to dig antitank trenches, and to establish three echelons of defensive fortifications. We built our defense lines in great depth in case the enemy, after beginning an offensive, might succeed in taking our first positions. Three more defense lines were built behind the first one, and they were well equipped and armed to the fullest extent possible. Fortifications were dug into the ground. For the most part

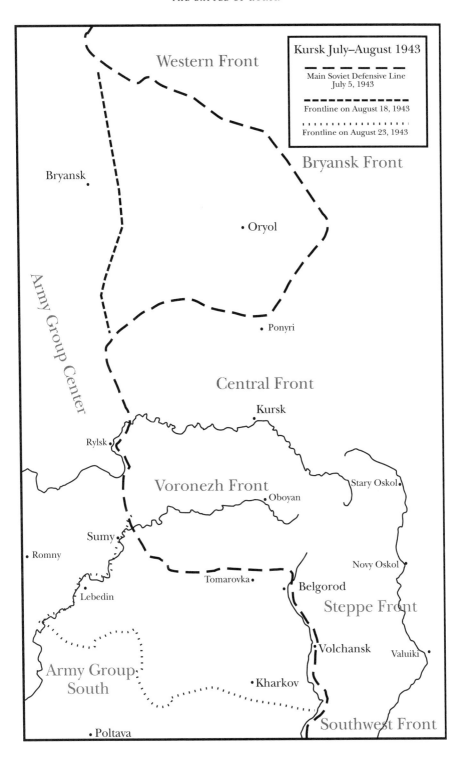

Western Front

Kursk July–August 1943

- - - - Main Soviet Defensive Line
July 5, 1943

━ ━ ━ Frontline on August 18, 1943

· · · · · · Frontline on August 23, 1943

Bryansk Front

Bryansk

• Oryol

Army Group Center

• Ponyri

Central Front

Kursk

Rylsk •

Voronezh Front

Stary Oskol •

• Oboyan

Sumy •

• Romny

Novy Oskol •

• Lebedin

Tomarovka •

Belgorod

Steppe Front

Army Group
South

• Volchansk

Valuiki •

• Kharkov

Southwest Front

• Poltava

they were pillboxes built of timbers and covered with dirt. All these fortifications were built by using an unfailing "mechanism"—the soldier's shovel. Behind us the defense line of the Steppe Front was built, reinforcing our rear echelon, and beyond it, along the Don River from Lebedin to Pavlovsk,[33] stretched another defense line, the so-called State Line of Defense. We had had nothing like this previously. The soldiers did an enormous amount of work. There was no need to especially try to persuade our soldiers. They themselves understood everything. By then they were already tough, old "wolves" who had gone through two years of war. They all knew that the better the antitank defense they built, the more strongly the trenches were equipped and the more effective the artillery and machine guns were deployed, the less blood would be shed by Soviet soldiers and the harder it would be for the enemy to knock us loose and drive us back.

General Chistyakov and his chief of staff Penkovsky[34] knew their business exceptionally well and carried out tremendously useful work. Penkovsky is still alive and well [in 1968]. I wish him long life and health for a hundred years. He is a good man and a general who knows his business. He took a diligent attitude toward his complex duties and complemented the commander of the army well. The other armies were also constructing defensive fortifications but not to such a great depth as the Sixth Guards Army did. In those days we frequently traveled to visit that army and to hear the reports from the commanders and to see how every day was being used to expand our defenses. One day we arrived at General Moskalenko's headquarters. He was in a small room in a peasant house with rather poor lighting. His subordinates were sitting around on wooden benches, like the council of the tsar in the old days in the Granovitaya [Palace of Facets] of the Kremlin in Moscow. In the old days there had also been wooden benches in the Kremlin on which the boyars[35] sat when a council was in session. Silence reigned. Moskalenko began to give a report. Suddenly a loud snore echoed in the room. Vatutin immediately straightened up, pricked up his ears, and ran his eyes over those sitting on the benches. It was half dark and you couldn't see clearly who was sitting where. Vatutin figured out the direction the sound was coming from, and when it was repeated a second time the commanders saw that the snore was coming from the army chief of staff, Batyunya, a good comrade and a good general, but a man who was exhausted beyond his limit. It was warm in the room, and that had put him to sleep. Vatutin shouted: "Batyunya!" He started and looked around. The report continued, but Batyunya dozed off again. Incidents like that broke the routine of our daily lives and introduced a little humor and liveliness.

In April or perhaps May the Front headquarters moved from Kazachyi (a settlement to the north of Oboyan) and was relocated to the southeast of Oboyan in a large village.[36] The strengthening of our defensive fortifications continued, but our headquarters was already busy working out an offensive operation. It had been determined that if we counterattacked, the Sixth Guards Army would head toward Belgorod, turning toward Kharkov, that is, moving from north to south. The chief of staff for our Front was Ivanov.[37] He was a very decent man who was conscientious about his duties. But since Front Commander Vatutin had previously been more of a headquarters person than an army commander, it was not so easy for Ivanov to display his talents as chief of staff. Vatutin not only gave the general outlines of how plans of operation should be drawn up, but he himself would often sit down at the table, pick up ruler, pencil, and map, and begin to sketch out the arrows and make calculations. In short, he took on himself the work of chief of staff, sometimes even chief of the operations department. As I saw it, there were both positive and negative aspects to this. Of course he was over-burdening himself and taking on work that should have been done by the chief of staff and other staff officers. So then we began to prepare for an offensive operation. Several variants were worked out. We recognized that the best variant would be a counterblow toward Belgorod.

At this point I would like to make a digression. I have referred to Ivanov. In the years 1959–62 he worked as deputy chief of the General Staff, and we had to relieve him of his duties in that post. I was then chairman of the Council of Ministers of the USSR and commander in chief of the Soviet armed forces. I felt sorry about it, but a situation had arisen in which considerations of state required us to make this sacrifice in spite of my great personal respect for General Ivanov. Today I no longer remember exactly what the problem was. He had committed some serious oversight in regard to documents. This happened at the very time when a spy in our ranks had been exposed, Penkovsky, but not the same Penkovsky mentioned above, a different one, a colonel.[38] I ask that people not confuse the honest soldier devoted to his homeland with another man of the same name who was a traitor to his country. At any rate something had happened in the General Staff in regard to documents, and it was necessary to remove Ivanov from his position. That was especially painful for me because I respected him for his past service and valued his diligence and capacity for work. I had no doubts about his honesty, nor do I have any doubts now. But military matters require not only honesty but also accuracy and precision, especially in confidential staff work. You can be an honest person, but if you don't follow the proper procedures, you can do harm without meaning to. The enemy takes advantage of sloppiness and any other oversight we might commit. So we punished General Ivanov, making him chief of staff of the Siberian Military District.

I recall another unpleasant incident. It dates from the early period of the defense of the Kursk salient. Vatutin and I went to visit army commander Chibisov. I didn't like the report Chibisov gave, or that of the member of his Military Council. The question they raised was as follows: They said they had been given reinforcements consisting of local Ukrainians who had been living under the German occupation. These men had shown up for duty, but they were not trained, and—even worse—unkind accusations of a political nature were leveled against them. The member of the Military Council said: "What kind of order is this to have in an army? There was a battle, and after the fighting the mothers, wives, and sisters of those who had died came out on the battlefield to gather up the corpses of those who had been killed."

I got angry: "Comrade, this is your own doing. Why are you blaming people who you drafted? Although you gave them no training and their ranks had not been solidified, you immediately threw these units into battle. There they died, and they died honorably. The fact that their wives, sisters, and mothers came out to find the corpses of their relatives is only natural. Your duty is not to allow things that will undermine the morale of the troops to happen." But the member of the Military Council was particularly stubborn, and he wouldn't back down from his point of view. After Vatutin and I left we talked things over and decided that this member of the Military Council had too negative an attitude. We proposed that he be relieved of his duties and that a new member of the Military Council be assigned who would concern himself with his actual duties and who would understand his work and organize it correctly.

It was not only in Chibisov's army, unfortunately, that we encountered such attitudes. In the Kursk salient at that time, everyone was engaged in mobilizing men of draft age from the local population, and for a while this kind of attitude was widespread—that the locals who had been under fascist occupation were some sort of second-class people. It was necessary to fight against this point of view. Such moods were essentially incorrect and harmful. Before us lay the task of waging an offensive to liberate all of Ukraine. Undoubtedly in the future too we would have to get reinforcements by mobilizing people who had remained in occupied territory. Such people later played an important part in the defeat of the enemy. Such "local resources" became the main source of reinforcements during our offensive. That method of acquiring reinforcements was the predominant one.

We had worked out our plan for an offensive operation. We had calculated what forces and what military equipment we would need and what material resources would be necessary to break through to Belgorod and through Belgorod to Kharkov. Then Vatutin and I were asked to come report to Stalin. Stalin said: "Fly in and report." Before we made the report to Stalin, our draft plans were studied by the General Staff, and after the report, as usual, everything was put into final form. We reported to Stalin. He had a different sense of himself now. He was glowing with confidence. I would say that at that time it was pleasant enough to report to him, not the way it had been a year earlier. He himself displayed a better understanding of the situation and a more correct attitude toward the questions posed by the various Fronts. A date was set for us—July 20—and our orders were to prepare for the beginning of the offensive. The direction for the attack that we had chosen was approved. Then the most important question was "trading" or "dealing": what reinforcements could we obtain for carrying out this operation? It was always that way. The needs that the commanders expressed were never fully satisfied. They gave us a lot, but they still didn't satisfy all our needs. But they said to us: "Here are the forces that you will have at your disposal. And standing behind you will be further reserves of the Supreme Command."

I think that we prepared well for the operation in the Kursk salient— that is, both the Front headquarters and the General Staff. When we left we felt very pleased about the meeting with Stalin and about the results of our report. Today I no longer remember why the date for our offensive was specifically July 20. Evidently that was determined by the fact that we couldn't receive everything we needed before that date. Stalin told us that Rokossovsky's Central Front would begin an offensive operation about six days earlier than us, and then we would begin our operation. I remember that, because a reserve corps of heavy artillery attached to the Supreme High Command was sent first to Rokossovsky to help ensure a breakthrough of the fascist front lines there, and when that corps had done its job in that location it was going to be placed at our disposal and it would assist our offensive. Incidentally this might have been artillery not of the Central Front but of the Bryansk Front, which operated farther to the north. I also remember General Korolkov very well. He was the commander of that corps. I liked him very much. I met him again later during the liberation of Kiev. He commanded the same artillery corps there as well.

As we continued to build fortifications and prepare our troops for the defense of our positions, we were also coordinating the actions of our troops with the adjacent Fronts. For example, we held a conference with our southern neighbor. It was held in an oak forest. We arrived there, and so did Malinovsky with his generals. There were no leaves on the trees because some gypsy moths specific to oak trees had eaten all the leaves. Everything was visible from the air. There was no cover. The commander of the army in the zone where we held the conference said: "As soon as the conference is over I'm getting out of here. I expect that at any moment the Germans can make an air raid and destroy my headquarters." At the conference we exchanged opinions and worked out joint operations for the area where the two fronts met, so that the enemy would not be able to drive a wedge between our positions.

Zhukov and Vasilevsky came to see us before our offensive was to begin. We went with them to visit all our armies. The delivery of ammunition and the arrival of military units to be placed at our disposal were proceeding according to the plan that had been approved for the conduct of the operation, and everything was being accomplished more or less on time. We drove the Stavka representatives from our headquarters located southwest of Oboyan. Our headquarters had been in the same place for a month or a little more. Discipline was not being observed quite strictly enough. Various vehicles were sitting around the area of the headquarters when they should not have been visible, and enemy air reconnaissance must have noticed that a headquarters was located there. We were aware that the Germans had intensified their air reconnaissance. German planes began circling above the position of our headquarters.

Since we had a backup location prepared in the neighborhood of a small junction to the north of Prokhorovka,[39] we decided to move the headquarters there. We warned all the staff personnel that at dawn the next morning we would be moving to the new location. We moved some "household goods" earlier so that there would not be too large a "wagon train" during the transfer period that might attract the attention of the enemy aircraft. Vatutin and I also moved to a state farm 2 or 3 kilometers from the railroad junction where our new headquarters would be located. All we had there were temporary structures built out of boards. They turned out to be full of bedbugs. It was terrible! These hardy creatures had managed to survive in empty barracks and had grown hungry, and now they threw themselves on us and fed on our blood.

Near that state farm a small wooded area was visible—a small ravine overgrown with oak trees. Whenever I hear people singing that song by the composer Solovyov-Sedoi,[40] which goes, "O nightingales, nightingales, don't disturb the soldiers," I always remember that ravine. How many nightingales it had in it! It was like nightingale heaven. We set up a bunker for ourselves in case of an air raid, and we also placed all vitally necessary headquarters elements there so as not to lose control of the troops and not to have communications disrupted. The bunkers of Vatutin, myself, and several others were in that woods.

We had just settled in and still had some things at the old command post, when we received the report that at dawn an enemy air raid had struck the old headquarters. But we didn't suffer any losses; the bombing raid proved to have no negative consequences. The enemy destroyed the village but not completely. A day or two later a German reconnaissance plane was downed, and the pilots were taken prisoner. Vatutin and I interrogated them. I asked one pilot: "Did you take part in the bombing of such-and-such location?" We had downed his plane directly over the settlement where our headquarters had previously been located.

He said, "Yes."

We asked: "What assignment had you been given?"

He said: "We were told that a major Russian headquarters was located in that settlement." Well, that's the way things went. Later we often recalled how our "presentiment of danger" had saved us.

It is customary among military men as soon as a headquarters is set up at some location immediately to prepare a reserve command post as a backup. This time we chose one a little to the north of our headquarters. We picked out another wooded area for ourselves and sent the engineering personnel there. By the beginning of the German offensive on July 5, 1943, this command post was ready. Our plan was to move there before the start of our operation scheduled for July 20. We wanted to move there just before the start of our offensive, so that the enemy wouldn't have time to find the new location of our headquarters. From there we could be sure of maintaining communications and directing the troops.

I don't remember whether it was on our own initiative or on the initiative of the Stavka, but we traveled to Moscow once again and met with Stalin. I asked that General Popel be assigned to one of our armies as a member of the Military Council. I had made his acquaintance in the first days of the war when he was a commissar of the corps commanded by General Ryabyshev.[41] I liked Popel very much because of his calmness, efficiency, and courage. In 1941 the staff of the mechanized corps [to which he was attached] was broken into two parts. One part was with Ryabyshev and the other with Popel. They were communicating by radio. Ryabyshev began asking questions because he wasn't sure whether it was actually Popel who had answered or someone the enemy had put there to pretend to be Popel. He asked for the names of his daughters and what they had done to his dog. It was such an entertaining conversation! For a long time afterward the story of this conversation kept spreading among the command staff and was repeated many times in meetings with Stalin. We made a joke of it, but this method for verifying identity was essentially correct. Now I was asking for Popel to be assigned to us again, and Stalin agreed.

While we were in Moscow we were told we would also be receiving the First Tank Army commanded by General Katukov.[42] We were very glad of that. I had not met Katukov before, but I knew him from his accomplishments. He was considered a good tank strategist, a stubborn fighter who knew his equipment, and an efficient commander. When Katukov was giving a report to Stalin about the condition of his army, he made a request: "Comrade Stalin, I ask that you give me Popel as a member of my Military Council." Stalin immediately glanced at me. Katukov said: "I know him and he knows me. We trust and understand each other. I beg you to let me have him."

Stalin said: "What can I say? Yes, we'll send him to you." And he said to me: "You hunt for another." And we found another: Krainyukov,[43] a good member of the Military Council who was already present in another army of our Front.

The First Tank Army arrived. Its ranks included approximately a thousand tanks as well as motorized infantry. To be sure, there was not a large number of motorized infantry. We assigned it to the same location as the Sixth Guards Army, so as to create a defense in depth with more than just the digging of antitank trenches and the construction of other field fortifications. We decided to deploy the tank army at a certain depth and to dig Katukov's tanks into the ground in case the enemy broke through and we had to switch to a defense in depth. That is, we decided to use the tanks "as casemate" [that is, in a fixed position] and at the same time as mobile artillery. We dug special gun emplacements for these tanks[44] but with no covering over the top. This was a fully justified measure. From these positions Katukov made good use of his forces and played a major role in the defeat of the fascist offensive in the Kursk salient.

We received other tank reinforcements in the form of detached corps. I remember now that when we made a count of our strength at the moment when the enemy offensive began, we had approximately 2,500 tanks. That was an enormous power! Our intelligence services reported that the enemy had approximately the same number of tanks. This meant that on this narrow sector of the battlefront, taking the one side and the other together, there was a total of between four and five thousand, and I'm not even talking about artillery, of which we had quite a lot on our side. On the German side there was even more artillery. Today I don't remember all the figures that our intelligence people reported, but we were waiting expectantly. We had fifteen days before the beginning of the operation. We were confident that we would be successful, that we would smash the enemy here and move westward, liberate Kharkov, and reach the Dnieper. This desire was something we had suffered and paid for, that we had won through suffering by years of war.

Suddenly a call came from the Sixth Guards Army. The commander reported that a German soldier from one of the SS divisions had defected to us across the front lines. There were a number of SS divisions in that sector. I had already told Vatutin that, no matter what sector of the front I was on, it seemed that the SS Death's Head Division was invariably pursuing me. It was always in operation there, across the front lines from me. The Sixth Guards Army commander reported that this soldier claimed that on the next day, on July 5 at 3:00 A.M., the Germans were going on the offensive. We ordered the soldier brought to us right away. We questioned him. He repeated the same thing to us. We asked him: "Why do you think that? "

He answered: "Of course I haven't seen an order for the offensive, but there is the soldier's grapevine and the soldier's feeling for these things. First of all, we have been given three days' worth of dry rations. Second, tanks have been brought right up to the front line. Third, there was an order to build up supplies of artillery shells next to the guns. Everything has been made ready so there won't be any delay."

We asked: "Why do you say precisely at 3:00 A.M.? What is your source for that exact time?"

He said: "You yourselves could have noticed this by now. If we go on the offensive at this time of year, it's always at 3:00 A.M., that is, as the sky is beginning to lighten. I'm sure things are going to be as I'm reporting to you." This defector was a young fellow, handsome, elegant, well groomed, obviously not from the working class.

I asked him: "How is it that you have crossed the front lines and have reported to us about this offensive when you yourself are an SS man? How is that to be understood? After all, you're a Nazi."

He said: "No, I'm not a Nazi. I am against the Nazis, and that's why I came over to your side."

I said to him: "But only Nazis are taken into SS units, isn't that so?"

He said: "No, that was before, during the first and second years of the war. Now they take anyone they think is appropriate. They took me because I'm the right height, and I look like an Aryan. That's how I ended up in the SS forces. But I'm against Nazism. I am a German, but my parents are from Alsace. We were raised in the tradition of French culture, and we are not like the Nazis. My parents are opposed to Nazism, and so am I. I made a difficult decision for myself and defected, so as not to take part in this offensive, not to expose my head to your bullets for the sake of Hitler. That's why I defected. I'm telling you all this openly because I wish to see Hitler defeated. That would be in the best interests of the German people."

We called Moscow and passed along a warning about what we had heard. Later Stalin called me. I don't know whether he had spoken with Vatutin before that. We [that is, Vatutin and Khrushchev] were at different locations just then. Sometimes Stalin called me before he called the Front commander, and sometimes the opposite. There was no "established procedure" in this respect, nor could there have been. I want to be understood correctly on this point. Some people might say, when I report that Stalin called me, "Look, Khrushchev is giving himself a buildup." No, I'm not. I was, after all, first member of the Military Council of the Front and a member of the Politburo. Stalin knew me well and took me into account, in spite of the rages he got into at especially difficult moments for our country, when he would undeservingly vent his moods on me and others, searching for a scapegoat. And here I was, first secretary of the CP(B)U Central Committee, a member of the Politburo and of the Military Council of our Front. Here was someone you could dump blame on for all the disasters. The supreme commander in chief would certainly not take the responsibility on himself for all the failures we had suffered before Stalingrad. But by now the bitterness of our defeats was already beginning to fade away.

In principle Stalin's attitude toward me was one of confidence. He often called me and asked me for my opinion. That's how it was at Stalingrad, and in the south, and at the battle of Kursk. At the Kursk salient a decisive battle took place, a turning point that switched the arrow of history in the Red Army's favor, and from then on the arrow did not change direction. It firmly pointed toward the road of complete defeat for Hitler's Germany, the path toward the triumph of our people, the Red Army, Soviet ideology, and our Communist Party! I've allowed myself to digress from the subject here so that my words would be understood correctly and that people wouldn't say, "Well, he's just yakking about himself." No dear friends, I am not yakking. I am simply telling exactly the way things were.

When Stalin called, I told him again what news the German soldier had given us. Stalin listened to me calmly, and that pleased me; he didn't display any rudeness or abruptness. He was usually abrupt and abrasive, even when he was in a good mood. The devil knows why. It was as though something was constantly eating away at him, tugging at his nerves, and disturbing his equilibrium, although sometimes he managed to restrain himself and conceal his mood. Both the one ability and the other were very strongly developed in him. It was constantly made evident that one element in his character was in conflict with the other. But he could control himself when he wanted to. In short, he was a man of great willpower.

Stalin asked me: "What is your sense of the situation there? What confidence do you have of success?"

I answered: "The commander and I have exchanged views, and we agree that we feel good about the situation and are confident. We are even pleased that the Germans are going on the offensive tomorrow."

He asked: "Why?"

I said: "Because they will have to run up against our fortifications and our fortifications are solid and we are confident that we will force the enemy to expend his strength and powers against these fortifications and shed his blood. For the time being we don't have enough forces for an offensive. We haven't received everything we were supposed to by July 20, according to the plan. And so we're not yet ready to go on the offensive ourselves, but we're ready to maintain a strong defense. It's possible to defend ourselves successfully with fewer forces. We've already learned how to do that in practice, not just in theory. That's why we're confident. It's a good thing the enemy is going to take the offensive, because we're going to smash him."

He said: "We also have information that an offensive is going to start against you tomorrow." And with that the conversation ended.

Let me repeat (as I've already mentioned) that, according to the plan, Rokossovsky's troops were supposed to go on the offensive first, and a short time after that it would be our turn. The reserve artillery corps of the Supreme High Command had already taken up positions to the north of us. The enemy began his offensive simultaneously against both Rokossovsky and us. Thus Rokossovsky turned out to be in a more advantageous position. Because he was supposed to attack first, according to the plan, he had therefore received reinforcements and ammunition and everything else first.

Why do I mention this? So that the reader will understand why things went badly for Vatutin and me for a certain length of time. When the Germans began their offensive, they broke through in our area and drove more deeply than in Rokossovsky's area, which was better prepared. For us fifteen days still remained before the time of our offensive, and according to the plan, we still had time to spare. Suddenly the available time was cut short. The enemy moved before we did. Fifteen days is quite a long time from the point of view of bringing up reinforcements, materiel, and so forth to the front line.

Who were the commanders of our Front? The commander of the artillery was General Varentsov, chief of staff of the Front was Ivanov, and the chief of the air forces was General Krasovsky.[45] Just yesterday when the Red Banner Badge of Distinction was awarded to the Gagarin Air Force Academy, I had the opportunity to see how our Air Force Marshal Krasovsky has put on weight. He is already more than seventy years old, and he is still the director of that Academy. Who was the commander of our tank forces? In 1942 it was a certain Armenian, a good general. Later he was arrested for no reason, and, as I recall, he was shot. I had a very high regard for his work and respected him. His name was Tamruchi.[46] I asked him once: "Judging from your name, you're either Italian or Greek, right?"

He laughed: "Armenian, comrade member of the Military Council." Many Armenians took part in the fighting on our front. They were good generals.

Later the chief of our tank troops was Shtevnev.[47] He was killed, and to a certain extent it was his own fault. He was supposed to make a trip several kilometers in depth toward the rear from the road on which he was traveling. The road he chose to travel from one unit to another was under fire by enemy artillery. But with a wave of his hand he said: "I'll make a jump for it!" But he didn't get through. The enemy artillery hit him at short range. Shtevnev was also a good general. In general the chiefs of the tank forces and other kinds of troops that I encountered on our Front were worthy of their rank, understood their business, and handled their weapons and equipment properly. It bothers me that I can't right now recall the name of the next commander of tank troops on the Voronezh Front. In general I always had a great weakness for the tank troops. They were among my favorites, but it happens sometimes that a name just slips your mind.

Vatutin and I were reviewing the plan of operations for repelling the enemy offensive and discussed a proposal made by Chistyakov, the commander of the Sixth Guards Army. He proposed: "At 2100 hours let's direct an artillery barrage at the enemy positions, to cause them some damage shortly before their offensive."

I disagreed and expressed myself as follows: "It would be better if we didn't launch an artillery barrage at 2100 hours. How much of a barrage can we maintain, considering the ammunition we have on hand? Only for several minutes. We're not in a position to fire for a long time and waste our shells. We're going to need them tomorrow when the enemy begins his offensive. In this case we would just be firing in a general direction. That's not a useful expenditure of ammunition. By all means let's fire an artillery barrage, but do it just a few minutes before the enemy offensive, right around 3:00 A.M." The considerations I had in mind were these: the enemy soldiers would already be in their jumping-off positions then, not sitting in the trenches; they would have no cover. The artillerymen would also be in place next to their guns. All the enemy's forces would be out of their underground shelters, standing in the open, waiting for the signal to attack. If we fired a good strong artillery barrage at that time, it would have more effect, causing more injury to the enemy's "living forces" and putting some of his equipment out of commission. Some communications would also undoubtedly be disrupted, which would have great importance for the conduct of operations. Vatutin agreed with me, and that's what we decided to do. We got ready and waited for the three o'clock hour.

I would like to make a slight digression at this point before describing the decisive duel between the two sides in 1943. This duel took place in our area, and as regards its overall military significance and immediate results this battle became historic, not only for our sector of the battlefront but in general for the entire Red Army and the fate of the USSR. I want to mention how we all felt, and I include myself, when we read in the newspapers about how on such-and-such sector of the front in such-and-such military units a concert was given for the troops and that such-and-such performers or writers took part. Mostly this had to do with the troops of the Western Front, who were virtually in the same positions from which they had defended Moscow in 1942–43. We felt envious of them and we didn't understand how, when there was a war going on, they could be listening to songs and watching dances. We couldn't raise our heads long enough to look at the sky because the enemy was constantly engaged in active operations, raining heavy blows on us and constantly moving forward. We had defended ourselves, retreated, and sometimes even ran. The enemy had driven us back to the Volga and advanced almost as far as the Caspian Sea. But now on the eve of the German offensive of July 5—and it was rather gratifying to taste this fruit—we were holding fortified defensive positions and working hard to reinforce those positions.

Now people from the Center were starting to come visit us and make speeches. There was an established phrase for all these speakers—they were called "fiery orators." It was only "fiery orators" who came to visit us. But you needed a bellows to heat up their "fires." Their speeches didn't come off well in every case. Still, these speakers were called fiery! I don't know who thought up the expression "fiery orator." Later, musicians and singers began to arrive and they gave some concerts. In short, mass cultural work was being carried on. At that time the head of the political directorate of our front was General Shatilov.[48] I knew Shatilov well from my work in Moscow. Back then he had worked at Elektrozavod[49] and was engaged in mass propaganda work there. Later he worked in the Moscow city committee or in the party committee of the Stalin district. In short, he was a Moscow party official. He became head of our Front's political directorate later, and the mass work of party propaganda fell on his shoulders to a large extent. Only in 1943 could I understand what it meant to stay for a long time in defensive positions and what possibilities that situation provided for organizing mass party propaganda work among the troops.

July 4 arrived. It was getting toward evening. Vatutin and I were waiting impatiently for the fatal hour set by Hitler for our Front. At that point I recalled General Tupikov. When our Front headquarters was outside Kiev in 1941 and the German planes were bombing that position, our chief of staff, Tupikov, pacing up and down the room, kept singing an aria from a Chaikovsky opera.[50] The aria asked: "What has the coming day in store for me?" Now Vatutin and I might well start singing that aria. Of course we were sure that the coming day had success in store for us. But as the Ukrainians say, "Don't say 'I hopped' until you've made your jump."[51] Therefore it was natural that we all felt alarm and concern over the beginning of the enemy offensive. How well would we manage in stopping the offensive and then going over to a counteroffensive ourselves?

At five minutes before three o'clock in the morning, Varentsov gave the order for an artillery barrage against the enemy positions, firing a certain number of shells from every gun along the front lines of the Sixth and Seventh Guard Armies. We found out about the results later. And then exactly at 3:00 A.M.—the punctuality of the Germans didn't let us down—the earth began to tremble and the air began to roar in our ears. I had never seen anything like it. I had experienced retreats, and we ourselves had carried out offensives, but I had never encountered such massive fire before. Later we ourselves perhaps laid down even heavier fire. But for 1943, it must be admitted, the enemy organized an extraordinarily powerful artillery bombardment to soften up our positions. German planes also began to smash away at our front line. The Germans used all their planes during those initial hours at the battlefront with the sole aim of breaking our resistance, turning our fortifications to dust and rubble and mixing everything together with the earth, so as to clear a way for their tanks to go charging toward Kursk, with the aim of surrounding the Soviet troops within the salient. They wanted to repeat what they had done to our troops in 1942 in the Barvenkovo-Lozovaya area, to do what they had done then and even more.

Sometime later, after we had already gone on the offensive and crushed an enemy tank division and captured its headquarters, the commander of that division managed to hide in the wheat fields. We didn't catch him, although we hunted for him intensively. To make up for it, we captured enemy headquarters documents and a map. The disposition of our units was marked on the map, and a tiny flag had been stuck at the place where our headquarters had been detected, a flag marking the headquarters of the Voronezh Front. Although the Germans had known the location of our headquarters, they didn't drop a single bomb there or send a single plane to make an air raid. My explanation for this is that the Germans were so confident of success that they ignored the fact that the headquarters would be left in a condition to carry on its work normally; its functioning would not be disorganized, and its communications would not be disrupted. They calculated that the main thing was to destroy our defensive positions, break through our front lines, smash our troops there, and clear the way for their tanks, so that everything else would collapse of its own accord. Certainly they did charge forward furiously, using all their potential, betting everything on a single card, with the aim of accomplishing the task assigned them. The earth shook from the explosions of bombs and artillery shells. The air was filled with the roaring sound of bombers and fighters. But our troops were ready to repel the blow. Fighting began, very heavy fighting. The Germans kept moving forward, as only they are able, the highly disciplined people that they are. Or else they were using some sort of narcotics on their soldiers (people talked a lot about that back then), but they did show great perseverance in their attack. At first our troops held their positions, but the sheer quantity of enemy fire would have eventually shattered steel, let alone people who were dug into the ground. And so our first line of defense was broken through. We had foreseen this. That's why we had built three lines of defense. We still had the second and third lines, and we were not discouraged by the beginning of the battle. We knew that the enemy would deploy many troops and a great deal of equipment to try to break through our front line. No question ever arose of our troops running away. Our troops fought to the last and died, but they didn't run. True heroism was displayed here, not the kind you read about in newspapers, but genuine heroism.

Vasilevsky flew in again to our headquarters. It seems this was on the second day of the offensive. We always greeted him warmly because he was a man of special qualities. It was pleasant to talk with him. He didn't raise his voice or shout, and he always conducted a discussion, not just in general, but about the essence of the matter at hand. It was pleasant to have a feeling of human understanding, and a humane attitude toward you, especially in the difficult moments of defensive fighting. Meanwhile we had begun to take a few prisoners among the attacking Germans. I received a report that an artillery officer had been captured, among others. I said to Vasilevsky: "Let's question him." They brought in a tall, well-built young man who apparently had poor vision. He was wearing pince-nez. I wanted to make him feel more comfortable, so that he might speak more freely. I asked: "How did you happen to blunder and end up being taken prisoner?"

"Well, what happened is that I don't see well. I was preoccupied with trying to get my artillery across one of your antitank ditches, and your infantrymen grabbed me. That's how I ended up being taken prisoner."

Then I began asking him questions about the composition of the German forces.

He looked at me and said: "I am an officer of the German army and I would ask you not to ask me such questions. I will not answer a single question that might be used to harm Germany."

Vasilevsky and I stopped asking him questions and said: "You will be sent where you belong." He got frightened. He probably thought that meant he was going to be shot. But he was sent for further questioning by our field intelligence and from there to a prisoner of war camp. Actually, that didn't particularly concern me. I didn't even know exactly where prisoners were sent then. It didn't especially interest me.

The fighting became very hot. Vatutin and I began to feel alarmed. In spite of everything, we had not expected such heavy pressure. It was extremely alarming for us to hear the news that a new kind of tank had shown up on the enemy's side, with armor that our antitank shells couldn't pierce. A shudder passed through my body. What to do? We gave orders that the artillery of all calibers should fire at the tank treads. The treads on a tank are always vulnerable. Even if you can't pierce the armor, an artillery shell can always take out the treads. Once you've knocked out the treads, it's no longer a tank, but a kind of immobile artillery piece. A feeling of relief came over us. Our men started doing exactly this and pretty successfully, too. At the same time we began bombing the enemy tanks from the sky. We also immediately reported to Moscow that we had encountered new tanks. The enemy called them Tigers.

We also reported to the Center about the technical details of these tanks. We learned what these were because our troops captured one or several damaged Tigers. The Center soon sent us new antitank thermite shells that had a cumulative charge,[52] which would burn through the metal and thus pierce the armor of the Tigers. Meanwhile the Tigers had succeeded in shaking our confidence, making us wonder about the effectiveness of our antitank artillery. We had thought there would be nothing to it, that we would simply smash the German tanks, but the new tank compelled respect. Our troops had to give it their undivided attention.

In general the events unfolding then were extremely important. The outcome of the war was being decided, along with the fate of our country. There are many unpleasant things that can be recalled today. Now the situation is different, the times are different, and my situation is different. Today I am not what I was then, when after receiving a report I had to react quickly and find some solution, to make a decision or make some move to counter the enemy. Nowadays I don't hurry like that.

The fighting in the Kursk salient grew more and more intense. The enemy displayed stubborn persistence and kept moving forward, however slowly. He forced our troops to retreat. It's true that Soviet soldiers stood their ground and fought to the death, but at first the enemy's strength was greater. We couldn't hold the first line and had to retreat to the second, where we continued to offer stubborn resistance. By then our troops had learned how to put the Tigers out of action. They were the most powerful type of tank known up to that time. They were rather cumbersome, but their frontal armor was tremendously strong. At first we began firing only at the tank treads, and later, as I have said, thermite shells were sent to us that burned through the armor. We began using our aircraft intensively against the Tigers. Especially our *shturmovik* planes (low-flying attack planes used for ground support). The first shock caused by these new tanks was over. We saw that the Tigers could be made to submit to our firepower.

Nevertheless the enemy did drive us back to the third line of defense. All three lines, including the last one, had antitank trenches and various earthen fortifications and field fortifications, special positions for infantry, artillery, and tanks. And within a week the enemy had overcome almost all of these until he ran into our army's backup defenses. An especially critical situation had developed at Prokhorovka junction in the direction toward Kursk.

Approximately at that time or a little bit before then, the Stavka made a request to us (it was Vasilevsky who talked with me, but he referred to Stalin): Army General Apanasenko needed to go through some field training together with us. We were asked to let him come to the Voronezh Front. But Vatutin objected, and Vasilevsky started trying to persuade me: "None of our commanders wants to accept him. Everyone refuses, and so I've decided to call you and ask you to agree to take him. Apanasenko is a man with great experience, a hero of the Civil War, but his is a difficult personality. He has a very high opinion of himself. That's why all the commanders refuse to take him." Actually Apanasenko regarded all the Front commanders as people who were beneath him, at least in revolutionary merit. He had fought through the entire Civil War on horseback. He was a real fighting man. And who were these Johnny-come-latelies? They all held high positions now, while he was stagnating with nothing to do in the Far East.[53] This was a factor in the attitude he took toward people. I had never met him, although I had heard about Apanasenko. I said: "Let him come." And soon he arrived.

When I had worked in Kiev with Timoshenko—and Timoshenko had known Apanasenko well in the First Cavalry Army—he told me about him. As far as the details have stayed in my memory, it seems that when Tukhachevsky and the other glorious Red Army commanders were executed, Apanasenko was also interrogated. He had come under suspicion for something. Timoshenko said that Stalin had a talk with Apanasenko and that Apanasenko admitted to being part of some sort of conspiratorial group. Stalin accepted his word of honor, pardoned him, and sent him off to Central Asia. There he occupied a high position as a commander. Later he became commander of the troops in the Far East. That meant that he was being trusted [by Stalin]. And now he came from there to our headquarters.

Apanasenko made a good impression on me. He was a man of enormous size, heavyset, with big shoulders, but already well on in years. He took the post of deputy commander of the Front, but at first he was attached to the commander for special assignments, which in effect was the same thing. We were warned that he needed some training in the field, to get to know the smell of powder in World War II. He had known World War I and the Civil War, but he didn't yet know World War II. And this was a completely different war; it was taking a different course. The weapons were different, the tactics were different, and conditions had changed. We sent him out to visit the armies, to get to know them, so to speak. First we sent him to the Sixth Guards Army because the situation there was especially tense. He surprised me somewhat by his behavior, and Vatutin and I joked about him behind his back. Once he arrived at some unit, acquainted himself with the situation, and sent a telegram: "I have looked over such-and-such and so-and-so and have tested the borscht that the soldiers are making. The borscht is excellent. Signed, General of the Army Apanasenko." We laughed over that one for a long time. This was the first time I had encountered this kind of playacting, an actor's way of behaving. I had never noticed such mannerisms in anyone. He was always, so to speak, posing a little. But let him! Later we sent him to other sectors of the battlefront where intense fighting was going on. We sent him wherever the situation was most dangerous. That was only natural. A military leader of such prominence might provide some assistance to the army commander.

We needed a lot of reinforcements, and in those days the Stavka immediately provided them. We received the Tenth Tank Corps and then another tank corps commanded by Poluboyarov. But he was operating along the line held by the Steppe Front. Today Poluboyarov is the chief of the armored forces of the Soviet Army. At that time we deployed his corps at first in our rear echelon to the west of Voronezh. Then they gave us the Fifth Guards Army, a strong army with a full complement of well-trained young men. Its commander was General Zhadov. We deployed it for use against the right flank of the German offensive. We also received the Fifth Guards Tank Army. Its commander was General Rotmistrov.[54] I have already told about him in connection with the battle of Stalingrad. He arrived in our area as an old acquaintance. I had great respect for him and valued his knowledge and military abilities highly. We deployed the Fifth Guards Tank Army alongside the Fifth Guards Army in such a way that it, too, could strike a blow at the flanks of the German forces. When the enemy displayed such stubborn persistence in his offensive and our troops were equally stubborn in holding their positions, giving a terrible beating to the living forces and equipment of the enemy, we made a decision to strike at the Germans' flank, not to attack them head-on but to turn their flank, so as to disrupt their offensive from the side and then go on the counteroffensive ourselves.

But there was a coincidence, and such coincidences happen. The Germans also decided to strike at our flank, only they were going to strike at our left flank, that is, toward the east. At first we had not had very strong forces there, only the 69th Army, positioned along the Seversky Donets. As it turned out, our decision and the enemy decision coincided territorially. A head-on tank battle resulted. Zhadov's army was fighting alongside as well. I found myself at his headquarters. I had met Zhadov earlier but didn't know him well. Very stubborn fighting broke out along the upper reaches of the Psyol River.[55] Zhukov came to visit us. He and I decided to make a trip to Rotmistrov's tank army in the Prokhorovka region. We arrived at the location of the headquarters, which was right out in a field in a planted area or in some bushes. There were no headquarters services there—only Rotmistrov himself and some officers to take assignments and some communications people with them. There was a smooth road leading to that headquarters, but we were warned that the enemy was shelling and bombing it intensively. Zhukov and I looked at each other, but there was nothing to be done. We decided to make a run for it. We ordered the driver to give it all the gas he could, and we made it through. The dangers we were warned of didn't materialize.

A very hot battle was raging in Rotmistrov's area. Many destroyed tanks could be seen in the fields—both the enemy's and ours. A disagreement arose on how to count the losses. Rotmistrov said he saw more destroyed German tanks, whereas I saw more of ours. Both reactions are natural, by the way. There had been appreciable losses on both sides. Later I went there again, but this time without Zhukov because he had returned to Moscow. Apanasenko had come to Rotmistrov's headquarters a little bit before me. I encountered him there when a signal corps officer led me to a small hamlet in a hollow near some water. From ancient times the peasants chose places for themselves near the water. The scene I encountered made an impression on me as a kind of theatrical performance. Next to a peasant hut stood a little table covered with red calico cloth. On the table was a telephone. Apanasenko was sitting at the table with a burka thrown over his shoulders, and all this was right near the front lines. Enemy shells, live ones and duds, were flying over the houses of that hamlet, screaming and howling. The dud shells had a characteristic howling sound, and then they would hit the ground without any explosion.

At that time our situation was getting worse. We had exhausted our reserves, although we didn't know there were still more reserves at the disposal of the Supreme High Command. Later we were told that behind us stood the armies of the Steppe Front commanded by Konev. We learned that the 47th Army of that Front would be placed at our disposal. This happened when the enemy had already driven us back 35 kilometers to the north and we were exhausted.

I made a trip to Katukov's headquarters. His forces straddled the Belgorod-Kursk road and were holding that position to the south of Oboyan. The headquarters of the Sixth Guards Army was also located there, because Katukov and Chistyakov were holding the same line, both at the front line and in depth. The tank army was added to strengthen the Sixth Guards Army in the capacity of mobile artillery. When I got there I immediately met with both commanders. A very difficult situation had developed, and Moscow was displaying nervousness.

I remember before I went to Katukov's headquarters, Vatutin and I had had a talk with Stalin. Then Molotov had taken the phone. In such cases Molotov always talked more coarsely and rudely than Stalin. He allowed himself to use insulting expressions and to get out of control with his verbal attacks. But we didn't hear anything specific or useful from him, only cursing. He had nothing to help us with because when it came to military questions he was an empty vessel. Stalin simply used him in such cases as a whip or a club. He spoke with the commander in an insulting tone and then with me. I am not going to permit myself to use disrespectful phrases in retaliation because despite all his negative qualities Molotov was in his own way an honorable person, and his devotion to Soviet power is such that I have no right to comment on him negatively in connection with the war. At moments of crisis, he displayed rudeness and coarseness, but not in calm situations. I understand that at times like that, all he knew to do was curse.

A threatening situation really had arisen. That's why I had gone to the main area of fighting, where Chistyakov and Katukov were in position. They didn't have enough forces. Katukov's army had been shattered. I don't remember how many tanks it had at that time, but the situation was no joke. The enemy had chewed up three lines of defense, where our tanks had been deployed almost solidly. But behind the last line, our troops held firm, and the enemy could advance no further. The Germans themselves were exhausted. It was not so much that the front became stabilized, because neither side was trying to shift over to defensive positions; it's just that both sides, by then, were equally powerless.

Two German pilots ended up as our prisoners. They had both been flying planes in the same area. I don't remember what make they were; they were old and slow, low-flying planes armed with low-caliber cannon. Their purpose was to destroy our tanks from the air. One of the pilots was over forty

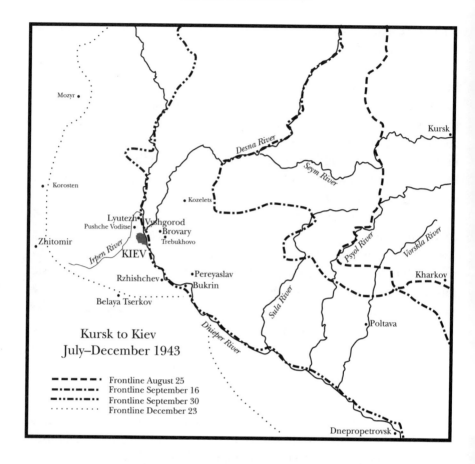

Kursk to Kiev
July–December 1943

- - - - - Frontline August 25
-·-·-·- Frontline September 16
-··-··- Frontline September 30
·········· Frontline December 23

years old, and the other was young and probably a wealthy person, because everything he had on him, judging from its quality and type, was not standard issue but acquired at his own expense. The first pilot was simpler, although he held a higher rank. He had been burned. There were burn marks on his fingers and face, but the other had come through unscathed. I questioned them both. But the "resistance" they offered to the questioning differed. Our intelligence people reported to me that the younger man, who they had questioned earlier, wouldn't tell anything. He was a fascist who believed in Hitler and in the victory of the German army. They had even tried to frighten him to make him give in, but he answered that he was ready to die for Hitler, that the German army would win and we would be defeated. He repeated the same thing to me. I didn't waste much time on him, and he was taken away.

I began a conversation with the older man. He was different. His morale was broken. I suggested to him: "Couldn't you write a letter to your fellow pilots, address them in a leaflet, the content of which would be against Hitler?"

He answered: "How can I write?" And he held up his hands. "I can't use my hands; they're all burned."

I said: "You can dictate." He agreed. Actually I don't think we printed up that leaflet because we were trying to solve the main problem of physically crushing the enemy, and we didn't place much hope in leaflets. I mention this only to show that at that time even among the pilots of the German army there were people whose morale was low and whose spirit was broken. They had lost faith in the victory of German arms.

There are a lot of things I don't remember any more, and I'm not trying to give an exact picture of how military units were moved around or the chronology of the operations. All that is described in memoirs by our generals, each one taking up his own sector, and also in operational documents that have been published. From those materials it is known exactly when the enemy spent his strength, when we stopped his forward movement, and when we ourselves went over to the offensive. What I want to talk about is my perception of those events and about some incidents that remain in my memory about interesting people and about how I felt in those days.

So then, we began driving the enemy back in the main area of the fighting, and that determined the situation for the entire battlefront. I don't remember how many kilometers we advanced when we moved our headquarters and I moved with it. The new field headquarters was organized in a dugout. The headquarters of the Sixth Guards Army and the First Tank Army were located almost at the same place. Our headquarters' dugouts were located in the side of a hill, and we could follow the course of the battle, being located at the flank of the troops who were directly engaged. Chistyakov, Katukov, Popel, and I watched from up there, and everything was visible, like on the palm of your hand: the operations of our tanks and the enemy tanks and the infantry movements. Enemy aircraft circled overhead. I don't know whether they noticed us but they did drop bombs. To be sure, they didn't hit any targets and we escaped with just some strained nerves.

I remember the first night at the new location. The enemy was very close. Our dugout was literally under the enemy's nose. The artillery commander of the Sixth Guards Army has stayed in my memory. He was a very good artilleryman. Unfortunately he was killed, poor fellow, when we were liberating Kiev. He died foolishly. He was riding on a motorcycle and turned over, got a concussion, lay in the hospital a few days, and died. I felt very sorry for him and went to the hospital to see him then. He was a good general. I forget his name, but his words have stuck in my mind. He said [on that first night in the new headquarters]: "Well, Comrades, how shall we sleep? Shall we take off our pants or sleep with them on?" He said that with the meaning that during the night anything was possible. The enemy might try to make a new attack, in which case we would either perish or get out of there quickly. I don't remember, incidentally, which of our generals took off their pants and which went to bed fully clothed. The soldiers had gathered some worm-wood branches for us (a good antidote for fleas in the summer), and we lay down on them.

We had taken a lot of forces from the 38th and other Armies and moved them over to the main sector. The 38th Army was to the west, on our right flank, where there had been no active operations. Nevertheless we were terribly exhausted and had suffered heavy casualties. After each trip to visit the troops, I returned to the Front headquarters, where Vatutin was. He sat there like a sentinel and directed the troops. I trusted him, respected him, and knew he was doing everything that a commander should.

I remember another episode. Now that the war is over this incident, when I tell it, will probably sound rather amusing. Apanasenko was at the command post of the Sixth Guards Army. Suddenly Chistyakov called up and said the enemy was approaching very close to the location of the command post, and he was asking permission to move the command post to the reserve post that they had established earlier. However, there were no communications links with the reserve post as yet, and therefore Vatutin and I told him: "No, stay in your defensive positions and don't move the command post!"

A little while later Chistyakov called again and made the same request insistently. Again we refused. Then Apanasenko called and said that he was there standing next to the commander and he was adding his voice and also asking permission to move the command post: "I myself can see the enemy tanks literally heading right for our command post. We might be taken prisoner."

We had an exchange of opinions. "Don't they have anything they can drive off that tank attack with?" "Maybe all their people are up on the front line. They can see what's going on better than we can." And so we decided to let them move the command post. But the chief of staff should stay where he was until reliable communications were working at the new command post. The chief of staff stayed; Apanasenko and Chistyakov left.

As soon as Apanasenko and Chistyakov arrived at the new command post, they were supposed to establish communications with us and report that their communications were working and that they could direct their troops from the new location. But there was no call from Chistyakov or Apanasenko. On the other hand, the chief of staff of the Sixth Guards Army kept regularly reporting to us from the old command post about what he could see himself and what was being reported to him. This went on for many hours. Then it became clear to us what was going on. It turned out that it was our own tanks retreating, and they had been mistaken for enemy tanks. It's a good thing, by the way, that the chief of staff, Penkovsky, survived intact. I am far from intending to cast suspicion on Chistyakov and Apanasenko. I don't want to be understood that way. All sorts of things happen at the battlefront. It happens sometimes that people of heroic mold, who have distinguished themselves in more than one battle, suddenly lose their nerve and make a mistake. In general, a simple mistake could have happened.

When we were already driving the enemy back on all sectors, cleaning them out as though with a plunger from all the places they had penetrated after July 5, there occurred an unfortunate and incongruous incident. Apanasenko was on his way to Rotmistrov's headquarters, and suddenly we received the report that Apanasenko had been killed. It was reported that he died under the following circumstances: Apanasenko and Rotmistrov were standing out in the field conversing, with their staff people standing nearby. A German plane flew over and dropped a bomb. It exploded a fairly good distance away, but a piece of shrapnel struck Apanasenko and killed him instantly. Of the whole group he was the only one injured. A note was found in his pocket, something that remains incomprehensible to me. It contained assurances of his devotion to the Communist Party. He went on at some length, expressing his feelings on this subject. I didn't understand this. In the middle of a war, why carry a note around in your pocket stating assurances of your loyalty? I never ran into anything like this either before or since. Apanasenko himself always gave me the impression of an actor who was constantly playing a part, admiring his own actions. It's possible that he gave some thought to the impression this note would make on the person who read it once the note had fallen into other people's hands. Is that possible? Or was it a result of those terrible upheavals of 1937 involving Apanasenko, the things Timoshenko had told me about?

Apanasenko's wife came. I made her acquaintance. I was told that she was an actress in a theatrical group. She insistently requested that his remains be sent to Stavropol[56] to be buried. That was his birthplace. For a long time I tried to persuade her not to do that. I said: "It's better to bury him here in the Prokhorovka region. A great battle was fought here that will be remembered for centuries." Perhaps it was somewhat immodest of me to talk like that because I, too, had been in the "company" that fought there, and a soldier always says that the hardest fighting was where he served. I said to her: "What could be a greater honor for a combat general, as Apanasenko was, than to be buried here? Our people will be coming to this place and paying their respects to those who fell here." His wife at first agreed and we buried the general where he had fallen. But later she raised this question again and his body was finally moved from there and reburied in Stavropol.

Let me return to the military operations. The Germans had also advanced against the Central Front, against the troops of Rokossovsky, but not as far as they did in our sector. In those days some people drew an incorrect and insulting conclusion from this, as if to say: "Look, on your part of the battlefield—look how much farther the enemy was able to advance!" But it's not enough just to point out things like that when talking about a commander's ability to organize defenses and direct troops. Today I can't say exactly what the balance of forces was in our sector compared with that in Rokossovsky's sector. I had great respect for Rokossovsky and I respect him now. I consider him one of the best commanders of our troops, and I also liked him as a person. I especially liked his orderly work habits. I don't want to extol anyone in order to thereby belittle someone else, or vice versa. All should be given credit for their part in the great and grand event that was the battle of Kursk.

1. This took place on February 16, 1943.

2. Lieutenant General F. I. Golikov commanded the Voronezh Front until March 1943, when he was appointed deputy people's commissar of defense with responsibility for personnel.

3. Lieutenant General N. F. Vatutin was chief of staff of the Kiev Special Military District in 1939. Before the war he was head of the Operational Administration of the General Staff.

4. These troops belonged to the Waffen-SS (Armed SS), a special elite military formation created by Hitler in 1940 under the umbrella of the SS organization. [SS]

5. Later Air Force Major General N. I. Tsybin.

6. The book to which Khrushchev is referring is *Sovershenno sekretno! Tol'ko dlya komandovaniya: Nemetskie dokumenty o Vtoroi Mirovoi Voine* (Top secret! For command staff only: German documents about the Second World War; Moscow: Nauka, 1967). [SK]

7. Merefa is about 30 kilometers south of Kharkov. [SS]

8. Lieutenant General D. T. Kozlov commanded the Crimean Front from January 1942. Following the abandonment of Kerch, he commanded the 24th Army from August 1942 and from October 1942 was deputy commander of the Voronezh Front.

9. Kerch and the Kerch peninsula are at the far eastern extremity of the Crimea, on the strait connecting the Sea of Azov with the Black Sea. [SS]

10. K. Ye. Voroshilov and I. Z. Mekhlis. See Biographies.

11. N. P. Bazhan, who since 1943 had been deputy chairman of the Council of Ministers of the Ukrainian SSR, during these months was editing the newspaper *Za Radiansku Ukrainu* (For Soviet Ukraine). See Biographies.

12. B. R. Gmyrya, a bass soloist at the Kiev theaters of opera and ballet. See Biographies.

13. Kharkov was abandoned to the German forces for the second time on March 16, 1943.

14. The Ukrainian nationalist insurgent S. A. Bandera. See Biographies.

15. Belgorod is about 60 kilometers north of Kharkov, no longer in Ukraine but in southwestern Russia. [SS]

16. Belgorod was abandoned on March 18, 1943.

17. The Seversky Donets flows south through Belgorod into Ukraine. Stary (Old) Oskol and Novy (New) Oskol are on the Oskol River, which flows roughly parallel to the Seversky Donets farther to the east. Novy Oskol is about 80 kilometers east of Belgorod, and Stary Oskol about 110 kilometers northeast. Both are in Belgorod province. [SS]

18. Kursk lies about 140 kilometers north of Belgorod. [SS]

19. Oboyan is south of Kursk province, about midway between Belgorod and Kursk. Sudzha is some 60 kilometers farther west, very close to the border with Ukraine and roughly equidistant between Belgorod and Kursk. Volchansk (Ukrainian Vovchansk) is about 40 kilometers southeast of Belgorod, just over the border in Ukraine, on a small tributary of the Seversky Donets. [SS]

20. At that time, the German aircraft Messerschmidt-109E, Fokke-Wulf-190A, and Henschell-129 had armaments with gunfire adequate for attacks on tanks from the air.

21. The 38th Army was at that time commanded by Lieutenant General N. Ye. Chibisov. See Biographies.

22. Sumy is on the Ukrainian side of the border, about 110 kilometers northwest of Kharkov. Rylsk is in Kursk province on the Seym River, some 80 kilometers north of Sumy and 100 kilometers west of Kursk. [SS]

23. Oryol is about 130 kilometers farther to the north from Kursk. [SS]

24. Panyri is in the north of Kursk province, about midway between Kursk and Oryol. [SS]

25. The Seym River flows westward, passing a little to the south of Kursk, then past Rylsk and into Ukraine, where it eventually joins the Desna River, a tributary of the Dnieper River, north of Kiev. [SS]

26. Romny and Lebedin are in Ukraine. Romny is about 100 kilometers west, and Lebedin 50 kilometers southwest, of Sumy. [SS]

27. The Sixth Guards Army under the command of Lieutenant General I. M. Chistyakov had been occupying positions at Tomarovka and Butovo since April 16, 1943.

28. Lieutenant General M. S. Shumilov. His army received the title of Guards Army in April 1943.

29. Major General V. D. Kryuchenkin. During the Civil War he had fought in the First Cavalry Army.

30. Lieutenant General K. S. Moskalenko. See Biographies.

31. When the 47th Army was in reserve, it was commanded by Major General A. I. Ryzhov. In July 1943 it was headed by Major General P. M. Kozlov.

32. Lieutenant General S. G. Trofimenko.

33. Pavlovsk is in the south of Voronezh province, on the Don River, about 250 kilometers east of Belgorod and about 320 kilometers southeast of Kursk. [SS]

34. Major General V. A. Penkovsky. He was no relation of Colonel Oleg V. Penkovsky, who later became famous as an American spy. [SS]

35. The boyars, Russia's upper nobility from the tenth to seventeenth centuries, owned vast tracts of land and occupied the highest state offices. A council of boyars advised the ruling prince. Later their position became much weaker, until finally the rank and title of boyar were abolished by Tsar Peter the Great, who replaced the boyars by a dependent service aristocracy. [SS]

36. This was the village of Bobryshevo.

37. Lieutenant General S. P. Ivanov.

38. This was Colonel Oleg V. Penkovsky.

39. Prokhorovka, also known as Aleksandrovsky Station, is in the north of Belgorod province, a few kilometers southeast of Oboyan. [SS]

40. The composer Vasily Pavlovich Solovyov-Sedoi (1907–79), a graduate of the Leningrad Conservatory, was during the war the organizer and musical director of a variety show called *Yastrebok* (Fighter plane). He was made a People's Artiste of the USSR in 1967. He is remembered mainly for his patriotic and nostalgic songs, the most widely known of which is "Podmoskovnye vechera" (Evenings near Moscow). [SS]

41. Lieutenant General D. I. Ryabyshev, commander of the Eighth Mechanized Corps (see Biographies), and Brigade Commissar N. K. Popel.

42. Lieutenant General M. Ye. Katukov commanded the First Tank Army from January 1943.

43. Major General K. V. Krainyukov was serving at that time in the 40th Army.

44. A Russian variant of the French term *caponnière* is used for such emplacements. [GS]

45. Lieutenant General S. P. Ivanov, Lieutenant General of Artillery S. S. Varentsov, Air Force Lieutenant General S. A. Krasovsky.

46. Major General V. S. Tamruchi.

47. Lieutenant General of Tank Forces A. D. Shtevnev.

48. Major General S. S. Shatilov (up to December 1942 brigade commissar).

49. Elektrozavod was a new electrical engineering plant in Moscow. [SS]

50. The opera was Chaikovsky's *Yevgeny Onegin* (1879). [GS]

51. In other words, don't count your chickens before they hatch. [GS]

52. Thermite, which was discovered by Hans Goldschmidt in 1895, is a mixture of finely powdered aluminum and iron oxide. When the mixture is ignited, the iron oxide oxidizes the aluminum, leaving a residue of pure iron. The aluminum burns at temperatures of 2,000 degrees C and upward, emitting bright light (including ultraviolet light) as well as heat. Used as an incendiary device, thermite is held in a magnesium casing, the ignition of which sets off the reaction. [SS]

53. From January 1941 Army General I. R. Apanasenko commanded the Far Eastern Front, which was formed in 1938. From 1943 he was deputy commander of the Voronezh Front.

54. The Seventeenth Tank Corps, commanded by Lieutenant General P. P. Poluboyarov, became in January 1943 the Fourth Guards Tank Corps. The 66th Army, commanded by Lieutenant General A. S. Zhadov and from February 1943 by Lieu-

tenant General P. A. Rotmistrov, became in April 1943 the Fifth Guards Army.

55. The Psyol River flows west through Oboyan to Sumy in Ukraine and eventually joins the Dnieper River. [SS]

56. Stavropol is in southern Russia, some 320 kilometers southeast of Rostov, on the approaches to the Northern Caucasus. [SS]

## TO THE DNIEPER!

I have already told about how we prepared for the battle of Kursk. The Voronezh Front was supposed to go on the offensive on July 20, but instead the enemy went on the offensive as early as July 5. That was one thing. We had not yet received a significant part of the reinforcements that were due to us according to the plan. That is another thing. Rokossovsky's offensive was supposed to begin sooner than ours, and he was supposed to attack northward to extend the right, or northern, edge of the salient. It seems to me he was supposed to begin his offensive on July 15 or perhaps even earlier.[1] Reinforcements for the Central Front, which were provided to him in the form of an artillery corps from the reserves of the Supreme High Command, after they had been used in his sector, were supposed to be transferred to us. A certain amount of time was required for that. Of course, since the Central Front was beginning earlier, it received everything it was supposed to under the plan earlier than we did. Thus, at the beginning of the German offensive, Rokossovsky's forces had more and we had less, because we still had time remaining [before our offensive]. The artillery corps was already in its firing positions in Rokossovsky's sector, so that ideal conditions were created there for repelling the enemy with artillery fire.

I want to make an objective assessment of the situation that developed then and not simply justify myself as a member of the Military Council of the Voronezh Front. I want to explain what happened, so that it will be correctly understand why the enemy penetrated less deeply in Rokossovsky's area than in ours. There was another reason. It seems to me that the enemy concentrated a stronger military group opposite us. It was precisely in our area that the Germans directed their main blow. Therefore larger enemy forces were deployed in our area. But I don't have exact knowledge of this;

still less do I know what forces Rokossovsky's Front disposed of. Today it would not be difficult for a military historian to investigate the matter because all the documents on troop strength and weapons, both of our side and the enemy's side, are available. These can be analyzed and a more objective approach made in evaluating the situation that arose then, as well as evaluating our ability to utilize available resources during the battle. Back then some people tried (not in the press but in private conversations) to needle us a little in regard to our morale, but today all that has become irrelevant. Many years have passed, and after all, the main thing is that we won the battle!

I don't know how to put together the appropriate phrases to express the grandeur of our success, the smashing of the enemy in the Kursk salient! After the defeat of the Germans outside Moscow [in November–December 1941], the Germans began to spread the word that the Russians' main ally was the winter. It was said that the Russians win in the winter because winter is their ally. Supposedly it was "our" winter! Supposedly it was easier for us to conduct winter operations than for the Germans, because for us those were familiar conditions—the usual climate where we live. They say that Napoleon was also defeated by the Russian winter. Previously the Russians had defeated Napoleon's army in the winter, and now the Russians had driven the Germans back from Moscow in the winter. Hitler removed his commander in chief, Brauchitsch, because of this failure.[2] Later at Stalingrad, when we smashed Paulus's enormous group, the Germans also said the winter was to blame for it all. We surrounded Paulus in the late autumn, and it was in the winter that we finally defeated him; therefore the winter was at work here, too. In addition the fighting at Moscow and at Stalingrad was very long and drawn out.

But the conditions in the battle of the Kursk salient were completely different. [First], it was summer! In fact the best time of summer—July 5. Everything was flowering and ripening, to use some fancy words. Second, the initiative was taken by the Germans themselves: they chose the direction in which to strike and struck at a time of their choosing. Therefore all the resources they wanted to concentrate to try to achieve the goals set for their troops in the Kursk salient had been gathered together. Thus, the Germans could no longer say that the Russians had an ally in the form of winter. Of course even earlier that had not been the main thing, but they had circulated that kind of talk by way of justification. Now the arguments they had used in Berlin to justify themselves to their own people for their defeats in 1941, 1942, and 1943 would no longer work. The initiative was theirs in all respects. The time and place and the buildup of the necessary resources—literally everything was in the hands of Hitler's High Command. In spite of that, and in spite of the advantage of firing first, the enemy was defeated.

The concentration of troops and especially of artillery and tanks and other equipment in that area was colossal. Unfortunately I don't have the figures at my disposal now, and I don't know which works by our military historians contain the appropriate information and comparisons of relative strengths. When I held the position of first secretary of the party's Central Committee and chairman of the Council of Ministers of the USSR, I always warned the military that when they studied the past and analyzed battles they should rely least of all on memory. One must be guided strictly by factual material. And all that material is available now: you can pick up the maps, compare the relative strengths of the opposing forces, see how they were deployed both on our side and on the enemy's side, weigh the outcome, and it will be evident where and how the knowledge and ability of one or another commander was displayed. But if you rely only on memory, you must know that it's very difficult to expect objectivity, even from those who personally took part in these operations.

I spent a lot of time at war, knew many of the commanders, and had good relations with the absolute majority of them, although disputes did arise. You can't avoid such things, and I, too, am no saint. All people are mortal, and we all have our shortcomings. Not everything runs smoothly in this life, as the saying goes; when you try to plane a piece of wood you're always going to run into knots and snags. But in general I was satisfied with the people I worked with at the battlefront. We almost always found a common language. I say almost, but I could even say always. Now and then some disagreements would arise, but I won't start talking about those specifically now, because I don't want to go into the negative aspect of things. People who took part in those battles were decorated and appropriately honored, and so there's no point in "washing dirty linen in public."

I repeat it was a colossal battle. Because of it the enemy lost the strategic initiative once and for all. The fortunes of war never again favored the German side. I remember once when I went to visit Rotmistrov's headquarters[3] he showed me a German document that had been seized when some German unit was smashed. It contained the following words addressed to the German troops: "You are now going to carry out an offensive, and you have weapons that are superior to the Russians' weapons. Our tanks are superior to the Russian T-34 tanks, which until now have been considered better. You have now received the German tank Tiger, which has no equal in the world.

Therefore you, soldiers of the German army, having received such weapons, will be able to crush the enemy, . . . " To be sure, the Tiger tank was monstrous and intimidating. We must grant it its due. But it didn't play the role that Hitler hoped it would. Our forces quickly learned how to smash the Tigers. Even when our shells couldn't pierce their armor, our soldiers found their weak points and fired at the tank treads.

Not long ago I saw a movie. It showed a young woman who had been assigned—get this—to crawl up to the front lines and photograph a Tiger tank. But this is artistic license. The author is free to put anything he dreams up into a movie. But when we encountered the Tigers in the battle of the Kursk salient, the conditions were such that photography didn't enter into it. I don't even know what the point would have been to photograph those tanks. According to the movie script, the young woman wanted to photograph them to show which part of the tank was best to fire at. The conclusion was that our people should fire at the side of the tank. But when a tank moves toward you it usually comes straight on. It doesn't show its side. That's why we gave the order to fire at the treads. The treads are not only the most vulnerable part of a tank but they also offer a good target because the Tigers had very wide treads. Of course it's also a good thing to fire at the side of a tank. The armor on the side is weaker than the frontal armor, but the enemy didn't always show you his side. I don't want to go on at length about this, even though the artistic license in this case, from my point of view, contradicts the real facts. After all, it's not good for a movie if the spectators start talking about how this was not so or that was not so. Opinions do coincide on the fact that the German tank really was a terrible menace, but then our artillery forces managed to cope with the problem superbly.

Let me return to the question of the significance of the battle of the Kursk salient. The first appreciable victory in an area where I was present occurred in 1941. At Rostov. Then there was a successful operation in the area around Voronezh, Kursk, and Yelets. Then, another area of victory [where I was not present] was Moscow. That really was a colossal victory. The Germans were totally confident that they would seize Moscow, but they suffered a huge defeat and were thrown back a great distance. Then we suffered new setbacks in 1942 with our defeats near Kharkov and the enemy's renewed advance, the fall of Rostov, and the enemy's advance into the Northern Caucasus and to the Volga. Once again came our successes and the defeat of the enemy at Stalingrad, and as a result Hitler's planning on a grand scale collapsed, including his plan to break through to Iran and to India.⁴ But the fascists still did not admit they had been defeated. They decided to restore the former glory of German arms and take back the strategic initiative. They chose the appropriate place and time, concentrated all the best forces they could against our troops, and carried out the operation against the Kursk salient. But all they achieved was the defeat of their troops, and after that they began rolling back before the blows of our forces along a vast front.

Let me go back to Stalingrad. There we chose places where it was convenient for us to strike [when we counterattacked]. Although this really was not the main thing, it was a significant additional help to us that we could decide the direction in which to strike our blow and choose the troops that we would attack in that sector of the front. We preferred that there not be German soldiers, but Romanians or Italians, their allies. When we went on the offensive at Stalingrad, there were mainly Romanian troops opposite us; their resistance was not as tough; they were less organized, and they were more poorly armed [than the Germans]. They didn't have inner firmness either. They didn't really know what they were fighting for; they were just an appendage to the Germans, German satellites, who were treated insultingly and condescendingly by the Germans. This also had an effect on the morale of the Romanian troops, and they didn't display the same refusal to yield that the Germans did. In the battle of the Kursk salient, there was no question of anything like that. In front of us there were no troops other than Germans. The question of what nationality was opposite us did not arise—whether they were Germans, Romanians, Italians, or Hungarians. But since they were Germans, then all the better; smash them, since they were the main forces of the enemy, their shock troops. After the battle of the Kursk salient, this kind of question lost its significance altogether because the initiative after that was entirely in our hands.

After the battle of the Kursk salient, I continued to be a member of the Military Council of the Voronezh Front, which later became the First Ukrainian Front. We fought the battle for the liberation of Kiev and advanced farther west. Of course I have no lack of human feelings and frailties. I'm glad that in those colossal battles fought by the Red Army at Stalingrad and the Kursk salient I was a member of the Military Council of the Fronts involved. That is why I felt insulted and I suffered inwardly (another human frailty, but perhaps also a protest against injustice) that at the ceremonies held recently on the occasion of the twenty-fifth anniversary of the enemy's defeat at Stalingrad I was not invited. In the historical films and parts of films shown on that date everyone who knew me well and saw those films noticed how everything was done to keep the viewer from seeing that Khrushchev took part in that battle as a member of the Military Council of the Stalingrad Front. I was told about another unpleasant, I would even say shameful, fact. When a session was held in Moscow on the occasion of the anniversary of the defeat of the enemy at Stalingrad, at the end of the ceremonies one officer addressed a question to a general who was there. I asked the comrades who were there what the name of the general was. It turned out to have been General Batov.[5] An officer asked him: "Comrade General, tell me please, was Stalin at Stalingrad when the great battle was being fought?"

There was a pause and then Batov said: "I don't know."

Again the officer asked Batov: "Was Khrushchev at Stalingrad?"

Again a pause, and then came the answer: "I don't know."

I respected Batov. The pause he made before replying testified that some remnant of conscience or shame or what have you remained in him. Batov told the officer that he didn't know, but surely he knew he was telling a lie. He knew very well that Stalin was never there during the battle. All right, let's suppose that that was top secret. Yet I knew. As a member of the Military Council I knew that Stalin was not there, and Batov knows it too. He brought sin on his soul [that is, he lied] and not without his conscience bothering him. That's why he paused before answering. The same thing happened with his answer to the question: "Was Khrushchev there?" Again there was a pause, also a sign that there were some remnants of decency. He couldn't answer right away. And the answer he did give was evasive. "I don't know." After all, that's better than saying Khrushchev wasn't there, which would have been a barefaced lie. But even that kind of evasive answer is no credit to a man and a general who in essence is not speaking the truth to a young officer. And that officer is nevertheless going to find out who was there and who was not. He will find out because some time will go by and one or another person who has an interest in enormously overemphasizing or distorting the facts will have died, and the same for people who had an interest in grossly exaggerating certain facts or individuals who played a definite role in the events while belittling and trampling under foot the actions of other people. Time, the great restorer, will clear away all the layers and encrustations of falsehood and slander. All of that will be cleared away, and every true fact will be seen in its proper light, and all participants in the events will take their proper place. I am deeply convinced of this. I believe in people, I believe in the justice of people, and for me, nowadays, that is a consolation and a reassurance.

Let me return to the defeat of the enemy troops at Kursk and our triumph. It's a sweet thing to remember! After prolonged suffering, bitterness, torment, trouble, and concern for the fate of our country, each of us then felt that victory was assured, that this was the beginning of the end for Nazi Germany, the beginning of our victorious march on the road to Berlin and the complete rout of the German forces. You can imagine how people felt who had lived through those times. Here at last was their triumph. The threat to the country had been warded off and eliminated. We were heading toward final victory and would be able to enjoy a peaceful life and continue the successful construction of socialism and communism.

It's possible that not all those who read my memoirs will understand this. Here it's necessary to enter into another person's soul, so to speak, to understand him, and to understand the threat that hung over our country. Our people had undergone shortages in their daily lives without complaining, and then they had died on the front lines of the war or under Hitler's bombs, but they did everything they could to ensure victory and they achieved this great turning point in the war. By then we were sure that, as the soldiers said, Hitler was now "Kaput." We experienced all those feelings then, and even now as I begin to recall the past, straining my memory, I once again live through the sorrows and joys of that time.

So then, we went on the offensive. It was not so much that we were on the offensive as that we were pushing the enemy back, bit by bit, because we still didn't have the strength for a real offensive, although the enemy had suffered heavy losses. The Germans not only lost the possibility of advancing farther, but even the possibility of holding the line that they had reached as a result of their earlier offensive in the Kursk salient. For several days we kept pushing the enemy back. We drove the Germans back probably 20 kilometers or more, maybe 30. We didn't have enough strength to push them back to the old line they had held on July 5, and we had to suspend our attack. We were exhausted and began trying to assess our possibilities, to calculate when we might be able to renew the offensive. It was determined that we could resume on August 3. I remember that day perfectly. What makes it memorable is that it felt as though we were lifting up our heads, spreading our wings, straightening our backs. We were getting ready to strike a blow not only to drive the enemy back to his old lines. No, by then we were already prepared to drive forward and liberate Belgorod and Kharkov and head west to reach the Dnieper.

The Steppe Front, which had previously been a reserve force, was sent toward Belgorod. Its commander was Konev.[6] Kharkov was also part of the Steppe Front's zone of responsibility. By August 3 we had brought up reinforcements, received ammunition, and were ready for the offensive. At this point we ourselves were choosing the time and the direction in which we would strike. While the plan for the offensive was being worked out, and the sector where we would strike the main blow to break through enemy lines was being chosen, Zhukov came to visit us. We had several variant plans. We were racking our brains over which variant to choose, whether to strike head-on against the same sector from which the enemy had begun his offensive against us or instead to shift our blow to the right, that is, farther to the west, with the idea of breaking through the German defenses there. The latter variant was considered easier. There was a possibility of breaking through to the enemy's rear and perhaps even surrounding the enemy group in that area. This was very tempting. But we hadn't carried out such an operation except at Stalingrad, and we were not yet accustomed to that kind of thing.

We discussed for a long time, hesitated, and in the end decided to make a head-on attack. Zhukov made the suggestion, and I agreed with him then. Even today I still think that that decision was the correct one. It was more difficult in the sense that we were forced (and we understood this) to exert greater efforts and to take more casualties than if we had succeeded in striking at the enemy's flank. Why then did we renounce the flanking attack? The forces we had at our disposal were relatively not very large. It was dangerous to carry out this kind of maneuver with relatively small forces. Our reasoning went along the following lines. In making a flanking attack, we would strike from our right flank and hit the enemy's left flank. We would evidently be able to break through the enemy defenses. But what guarantee was there that the enemy would not counter with the same thing, that is, make a flanking attack against our new flank? Then it might turn out that in trying to encircle the enemy, we ourselves would be encircled and suffer casualties. The fact that we were driving the enemy back was not yet sufficient proof that the Germans might not have brought up reserves, as we had done, or that they didn't have the capability of striking a counterblow. We decided, as Zhukov suggested, to make a frontal attack, grinding up the enemy's living forces. After all they had to be ground up at some point; otherwise our forward movement could not be assured.

A frontal attack was organized. By then we had fewer forces than we had had on July 5, when the German offensive began. But we felt that even with those forces we could deal a blow to the enemy. And we did hit the Germans hard. They were shaken and began to back up. I say "back up." I don't say, "They ran." Pushing them back, we forced them in a southwesterly direction. We took Belgorod and then Kharkov.[7] The retaking of Kharkov was a great victory. I made a trip to Kharkov, either in my capacity as member of the Military Council of the Voronezh Front or possibly as secretary of the Central Committee of the CP(B)U (because Kharkov at that time was not part of the zone of responsibility of our Voronezh Front).

A big celebration was held in Kharkov. The people gave a good greeting to the Red Army on its reentry into the city. We held a large rally. Everything was very triumphant; people were simply glowing. But there were dark moments at the rally. I don't remember what square the rally was organized at, probably the square in front of the Gosprom [State Industry] building or perhaps it was on Sumskaya Street. A speaker's platform was made by putting some trucks together. A lot of people gathered. I remember we were standing around waiting for the city authorities to declare the meeting open, and suddenly one or two enemy reconnaissance planes appeared and began circling over the city. Like sparrows that immediately start hiding under the eaves when a hawk appears, the people began running for the nearest buildings. I saw that unless steps were taken, we might end up with no one at the rally. People were running off in all directions. I was standing next to Zhukov and I said to him: "Let's go up on the speaker's platform. That will immediately stabilize the situation." He said: "Yes, let's." We climbed up on the speaker's platform, and when the people saw that we were up there on top of the trucks, they began coming closer and finally crowded around the improvised platform. Meanwhile our fighters appeared in the sky and chased the enemy planes away.

Later Zhukov and I often reminisced about the conditions in which we were obliged to hold that rally, when Kharkov had been taken, but the enemy was still right at our side. We also held a meeting for the Kharkov intelligentsia in a theater. As I recall, enemy shells were still falling in that district. The enemy was still very close. This testifies to the fact that we had enough strength to drive the Germans out of Kharkov, but not much farther. That was the kind of thing we experienced back then.

Several other episodes have stuck in my memory. The Ukrainian government organized a dinner for the military men who had taken part in defeating the enemy and liberating Kharkov. There were not that many people at the dinner. Zhukov and Konev were there. But Vatutin was not, because his sector had been transferred from the Voronezh Front to the Steppe Front, where Konev was the commander. We were having our dinner. A hundred grams of vodka were allotted per person on that occasion, and those who wished to could obtain even more. I remember an artist named Laptev[8] who evidently had obtained more than a hundred grams. Otherwise he would not have made the request he did after approaching us. I was sitting next to Zhukov, and he addressed Zhukov: "Well now, you are a general, and I, too, would very much like to be a military man. I earnestly beg of you, won't you please award me the rank of colonel. I want so badly to have the rank of colonel." The man was tipsy. I knew Laptev, and if he had not been inebriated, he would hardly have been so persistent, trying to show how badly he wanted to be a military man and hold the rank of colonel. The rank of general would of course have been even better. But he wasn't trying for general. Evidently he thought he could try that at the next dinner, after he had won the rank of colonel.

I tried to talk him out of it jokingly, but he continued to beg. And then, what a surprise it was to me. In some sort of special mood—perhaps under the influence of a hundred grams himself—Zhukov suddenly turned to me and said: "You know (he spoke to me using the familiar form of "you" because we were on very friendly terms), I do have the right as deputy supreme commander in chief to award ranks, up to and including the rank of colonel." I answered: "Let's discuss these things tomorrow." And I began insisting more firmly that Laptev should stop making these requests and go back to his seat. And that's what he did. Of course the next day no one brought it up again, neither Laptev nor especially Zhukov, and I didn't remind him. Just imagine if something like that had happened, what an unbelievable scandal there would have been. And a scandal would have been justified. After all, you can't go throwing military ranks around, especially at the request of anyone who approaches you. You can't just go handing out military ranks like that, especially not such a high rank as colonel.

I got busy with matters in Kharkov. Even before the liberation of Kharkov and of all the major cities in the provinces and districts of Ukraine in general, we had created organizational committees in advance and appointed the necessary people to particular posts. As soon as the next city was liberated, they would assume their responsibilities and begin to get things running again, providing public services for the population, putting production back in order, and in general ensuring that people had everything they needed. First we organized food supplies and restored the public water systems, the electric power plants, the streetcars, and the sewage system. I had a strong urge to see how the Kharkov tractor factory had fared. It had been built [in the 1930s] not long after the Stalingrad tractor factory and had the same large capacity. I wanted to see how quickly the factory could be restored, because unless we restored tractor production it was not possible to think about success in restoring agriculture in Ukraine, thereby ensuring food for the people, first of all bread and sugar.

I went to see the tractor factory and encountered a sorry sight. In winter 1942–43, when we had first liberated Kharkov, the tractor factory was empty, but its buildings were still in good shape to receive machinery and equipment. Just give us the raw materials and send in your orders and we could start producing right away. But in August 1943 the factory lay in ruins. Other factories had also been destroyed, as had residential areas. A great deal of damage was done to Kharkov. But war is war! We of course wished that things were better. But we were also prepared for what we found in Kharkov, left in ruins by Hitler's hordes.

The person we appointed secretary of the party's province committee, as I recall, was Churayev.[9] When we retreated, it seems that Svinarenko was chairman of the executive committee of the Kharkov Soviet, but he had been killed during the bombing of Valuiki, where our Front's headquarters had been located. He was walking down the street at night; a bomb exploded, and he was gone. He was a good, young, energetic man, either an agronomist or a livestock expert by training.[10] I don't remember who we appointed to replace him in August 1943. It also slips my mind who was the chairman of the executive committee then, who was the secretary of the party's city committee or the chairman of the city soviet. After all, people moved around, but we had cadres in reserve, and we immediately organized a local leadership, which saw to it that the normal life and functioning of the city and province were restored.

During that time the Voronezh Front was continuing to straighten out the line from the Kursk salient. The extreme point on the southern edge was near Sumy, and that is where we struck. But we struck at the enemy's flank more toward the south. The enemy was threatening us from that direction and we needed to smash him there; otherwise, after regrouping his forces he might do us some harm. Moskalenko's 40th Army remained there in our area, along with Trofimenko's 27th Army and Chibisov's 38th Army, and adjoining us on the right was the 60th Army, which was part of

Rokossovsky's Central Front. As the fighting proceeded our armies of course kept changing position.

We began thinking about organizing a new attack with the aim of crushing the enemy forces deployed opposite Moskalenko's army. We wanted to drive the enemy from his positions there with fewer casualties as compared with our offensive of August 3, even though the enemy was still offering fairly strong resistance. We encountered especially strong resistance around Tomarovka.[11] There the enemy refused to retreat. We surrounded the enemy forces, but we spent quite a lot of time and effort before finally crushing them. The Germans were holding on tightly, refusing to yield, refusing to run, and fighting for every inch of ground. Then the 27th Army continued the offensive. It had a fuller complement of fighting men, because it had been less involved in the main arena of fighting earlier. In addition we received reinforcements—a tank corps under the command of Poluboyarov.[12]

By then we were deciding the time and direction for our next blow. We were absolutely certain not only that we would organize the offensive successfully but that it would end with the enemy's defeat. Vatutin, Ivanov,[13] I, and other members of the Military Council and commanders of various forces decided the direction of our main blow, and we began to prepare for the offensive, bringing up everything we needed for that purpose. Then we received an auxiliary corps from the Supreme High Command, a strike force to hit the enemy's front line and enable us to break through. I don't remember whether we all went to Moscow to have that plan approved or whether we simply sent the chief of staff of our Front. That kind of thing did happen, because this particular offensive was not considered a major battle. It was simply that, as a result of the overall defeat of the enemy, we were able to start chipping away at his flanking positions along the Kursk salient.

Then Zhukov flew in. I was very glad that he had arrived because he always introduced something new to every operation. He was a man who felt sure of his abilities, and he intervened decisively in the preparation and implementation of operations. He always made an intelligent analysis of where and how the enemy forces were deployed and then expressed a definite opinion on how to use our forces in a given sector. I had confidence in his intervention. Not only did it not hurt my pride; it made me happy. I don't know what the Front commander thought. Perhaps he showed some hurt feelings, although I didn't notice anything like that on Vatutin's part.

We made preparations for the operation, hung the maps up, and discussed what direction to strike our blow. Zhukov, Vatutin, Ivanov, and I were sitting there. Zhukov went over to the map, poked his finger at it, and said: "What if, instead of striking our blow here, we drove in a little deeper?" That is, we were returning to the same question that had arisen earlier, when we were preparing our offensive of August 3. Should we make a frontal attack or a flanking attack? If we made another frontal attack, as we were proposing, the front line would not be straightened to any significant extent. I don't remember now how many kilometers. Zhukov had pointed to a position much farther to the west. There was a large settlement there, a district capital. A rush of strong feeling came over us then. Why not? After all, we had broken the enemy's main forces. Maybe we should strike more boldly. We decided to aim our blow in that direction and immediately assigned a chief of staff to work up an operations map and assign targets for the troops and give the necessary orders to Commander Trofimenko, in whose sector this offensive would take place. No special changes were made except for the direction of the attack.

Some time went by. Our rear-echelon supply services did their work and brought up everything needed for the coming battle. Not long before the scheduled start of the operation, Vatutin and I went to Trofimenko's headquarters to hear his report on the spot and to work out the details more concretely at the actual location in order to be more certain of success. Trofimenko's headquarters were located in a field, in a small wooded area or among some bushes. There were not many woods around there. This was in the south of Kursk province on the border with Ukraine, and it may even have been Ukrainian territory. His headquarters was in a tent. He unrolled a map and began reporting how preparations were proceeding. I had a lot of respect for this general. He was younger than the other army commanders, but he was well educated and experienced. Suddenly Trofimenko began arguing that the new direction in which we were to strike our blow was worse than the one that had originally been designated.

Vatutin stiffened. He very much disliked changing orders once they had been made. He had argued with me more than once that military men should not change orders after they had been given. I objected to his argument: "Comrade Vatutin, if a military man or even a nonmilitary man, after making a decision, sees a new or more interesting possibility shaping up, which would allow him to win a battle with fewer losses, then it would be foolish to stick to the old way. It's as though you were saying, 'Once I've said something, I have to do it.' That's foolish and I don't understand it. Whether a military man or a civilian, this is a principle of donkeylike stubbornness and not of searching intelligently for the best solution." A rather strained conversation ensued, which had never happened for me with Vatutin before, and it never happened again afterward. I not only respected him, but simply liked the man very much.

I didn't want to get into an argument, so I simply asked Trofimenko: "Why do you think the original direction is better?"

Trofimenko said: "Here, look at [the original direction on] the map. I've crawled around this area on my belly late at night and at dawn, and I've studied the sector very thoroughly. Here in front of me there is no populated area, not right nearby. The front line runs through a lowland, and there is a marshy area in that lowland that tanks can go through. I am certain of that. If the tanks couldn't make it through on the run, it would still be possible, without much effort, to make the area passable for tanks. I can actually see the enemy front line because our position is a little higher than the enemy's." And sure enough, when we went to his command post, the spot that had been chosen for it was such that the enemy trenches were visible. He went on: "Over here is the new direction. Here there is the district capital with a lot of brick buildings. I think the enemy would turn them into fortified bunkers, setting up machine guns in them and maybe even artillery. Great efforts would have to be made to drive the Germans out. Besides, in front of the district capital there are three ponds. They aren't deep but they're full of water. Although the water could be drained, there would still be mud, and the tanks would hardly be able to get through. I'm convinced that even if we stay with the second direction, I will be able to drive the enemy out, but it will take greater effort and more casualties. I would request, if possible, to have the old direction assigned to me."

I was not about to express my opinion because the Front commander had already expressed his, and I didn't want us to have a difference of opinion in front of the army commander. But also I didn't want to support Vatutin in this case. I said: "All right, let's go back to our headquarters."

We left. We got into our jeep, and Vatutin and I were riding along. I began arguing that, as I saw it, Trofimenko was right, that his arguments made sense, especially since that was the direction we ourselves had originally chosen, and we changed it on Zhukov's advice. He had only given us that advice; he hadn't ordered us to do it. We had taken up his proposal because it seemed to offer more; it would allow us to straighten out our line more fully and knock a deeper piece off the enemy's flank. It was now evident that we hadn't studied the region very carefully, although we had no complaint against Zhukov for that. He, too, hadn't studied the region at all, but had simply poked his finger at the map. I thought that we should support Trofimenko. Vatutin again began arguing that a decision should not be changed:

"We've issued all the necessary orders. We have assigned positions for the heavy artillery corps, and it's already on the march."

I responded: "Yes, we have chosen new positions for the artillery, but we also have the old ones that we had chosen. The artillery corps is moving in from the east, so that the old positions are even closer for them by several kilometers. I don't think that would be an obstacle." He disagreed with me. We arrived at our headquarters. Nothing remained for me but to write to Stalin. I sent him a coded message.

Much earlier than that, Stalin had suggested to me: "Pick a code and take a code technician with you so that I can receive, directly from you, anything you consider necessary to report, bypassing Front headquarters." Now I took advantage of that, composed a coded message, and sent it to Stalin. On the next day the commander and I were getting ready to make a trip to the 38th Army. Its commander was General Chibisov. It was a long way to his head-quarters. Along the way a jeep suddenly caught up with us, with a staff officer. He said there was a call for me from Moscow, from Ivanov. Front-line pseu-donyms were being used then, and Stalin's pseudonym was Ivanov. "Ivanov has ordered you to call him by special telephone[14] from the nearest point." The closest thing for us was to keep going to Chibisov's headquarters.

I understood that Stalin had read my coded message and wanted to have our disagreements made more precise and clear to him, and therefore I con-sidered it my duty to warn the Front commander [Vatutin] so that he would not be caught off guard. I said to him: "Nikolai Fyodorovich, I think Stalin will be asking about this question. I informed Stalin about Army Comman-der Trofimenko's opinion, and I wanted to warn you so that you would be prepared and would have a chance to think over answers to questions that he may ask." I again said that I thought we should accept Trofimenko's proposal and return to our old variant. He fell silent, thinking the matter over. Evidently he was disturbed. Undoubtedly my position caused him dissatisfaction, but this was a step I had felt obliged to take.

I had good friendly relations with the commander, but after all, there was a war on. You can't, just for the sake of maintaining friendly relations, disregard a danger and expend more resources and shed more blood than necessary. I felt I had no other choice. We arrived at Chibisov's headquarters and called Moscow. Stalin answered. I don't remember whether he first called me or the commander to the phone. I was standing alongside and heard Vatutin say: "I think that if we again change the direction of our attack, we cannot arrange things in the time frame that has been set for the offensive. I request that the second direction be left as is, and then we can ensure the beginning of the operation at the scheduled time."

Stalin told him to pass the phone to me, and he said: "Did you hear?"

I answered: "I heard, but I think that that is not exactly correct." And I began to argue that the artillery corps was still on the march and if we immediately made the decision to return to the old direction, the positions for the artillery had already been set, because the corps commander had already reconnoitered the area, and it was even closer for the artillery corps to reach those positions. I didn't think that any disruption of the timing would occur.

Stalin said: "I support you. If it becomes necessary to extend the deadline, I consider that it can be extended."

I replied: "It would be best if we now spoke with Trofimenko, then we can call you again to tell you his opinion." Stalin said that that was all right.

We immediately called Trofimenko on the phone. Vatutin talked with him. Trofimenko said that everything would fit in the same time frame, that he would not need any additional time. Then I took the phone and Trofimenko repeated the same thing to me. We called Stalin again. It seems to me that I was the one who spoke with him: "We have talked with Trofimenko, and he is not asking for any additional time. He's ready to carry out the operation on the schedule that has been set and is absolutely certain of the success of the operation." Stalin said: "I agree. I am in favor of your variant." But it was not my variant. It was the original variant worked out by the Front headquarters and approved by the General Staff, and consequently, by Stalin himself. I handed the phone to the commander, and Stalin said that he supported Khrushchev's variant. With that the conversation ended.

We had already looked into the situation of the 38th Army. We had come to see Chibisov to hear what he had to report because the next operation after Trofimenko's offensive was scheduled to be an operation by the 38th Army [of Chibisov]. We had not yet worked out that operation, and we listened to the commander so that he could express his opinion about whether it was possible to organize a blow that would strike directly westward. We had already, as one might say, turned our face toward the Dnieper and toward Kiev. We listened to his report and went back to our headquarters. Along the way we stopped to see Trofimenko and told him we had satisfied his request, we had changed the orders, and the blow would be struck in the direction that had been originally decided on. Trofimenko literally beamed and began to assure us that the operation would be carried out successfully. I was pleased that the man had been concerned about carrying out an operation with the fewest possible losses.

Preparations continued. We had come right up to the time set for the beginning of the offensive. At that point Zhukov came to visit us again. He already knew that we had changed the direction of our attack. I told Zhukov: "You stuck your finger on the map and evidently didn't really look into it, and the army commander was critical of that decision. We studied the situation again and became convinced that the direction that had been chosen earlier for the offensive was better. Therefore we changed the decision that was made during your earlier visit. The army commander insisted it was better to go back to the first variant. That's what we have done and that has been approved." I was glad that he agreed without any display of false pride.

He was calm and even somewhat cheerful about it. He said: "Apparently it's better that way. Since Trofimenko says so, then evidently it's better that way." Zhukov and I decided to visit Trofimenko, who was already prepared for the offensive. Everything that needed to be put in order for the beginning of military operations had been done. When we arrived we saw that even the Katyushas[15] were in position. That is the number one preparation for battle, so to speak.

The following incident occurred there. We drove up close to the front line so as not to come under the enemy's high-angle fire, when suddenly Zhukov, in a curt and abrupt manner, addressed a question to the officer accompanying us: "What's going on here? Where are we headed?"

The officer answered: "Over there, onto that little hill."

We arrived. There were Katyushas on the hill. Their fire is effective only at a fairly short range, so it turned out that we had come very close to enemy lines when we ran up on this little hill with our jeep. As we were getting out, the enemy immediately showered us with mortar fire, but no one was injured. We quickly got away from the jeep. There was a communications trench right alongside, and we dove into it. Zhukov gave that officer a good cursing out: "What do you think you're doing, exposing us to mortar fire? Are you making experiments or something?" The officer should have warned us that if we went up on that little hill, the enemy would see us and of course wouldn't forgive us for such audacity and would at least try to scare us with some mortar fire.

We followed the communications trench to the command post, which was also on the little hill and was covered with layers of timbers, and one thing or another. It stuck up like a belly button and was plainly visible to the enemy. But the command post was well equipped. It had optical equipment for observation, and from it you had a good view of the front lines and the low-lying area that we needed to push through with our tanks. Trofimenko gave a report, fully confident that he was ready for the offensive, and sure enough, the offensive went well. After a preliminary artillery bombardment our troops attacked the enemy. Everything was visible from the command post, which was ideally located to oversee the field of battle. But there was a delay with Poluboyarov's tank corps. Trofimenko turned to me and said: "It's time for the tanks to go into the breach, to develop the success achieved by the infantry, but they're delaying." We ordered the corps commander, who was right there with us, to have the tanks move forward, but they didn't move.

Again we said to him: "What's the matter with you?"

He said: "There's marshland there. It has to be reinforced, or else the tanks won't get through." In short, he was stalling.

I said to him: "You better take measures right away. We're losing time, and the enemy may be able to do something, to bring up some forces to the area where we've broken through. And if the enemy has tanks, he'll throw them into the battle. We have to take advantage of our success, which the infantry has achieved." His delay made me very angry.

Later I reproached this general: "You're trying to save your tanks, but you're not saving the blood of the soldiers. You wanted the infantry to enlarge the breach and provide the best possible circumstances for your tanks to move forward." And sure enough none of the tanks got stuck in the marshes. Trofimenko was right when he said that the marshy area was passable for tanks. Evidently Poluboyarov suffered a lot from that incident. In general he was a conscientious person. I remember even after the war he came to visit me in Kiev to explain again. He said he wanted to be correctly understood. There had been such-and-such obstacles that he had to overcome before sending the tank corps into the breach made by the infantry. But I had the impression that he was feeling sorry for his tanks, and I told him: "It's a thing of the past. The war is over. The enemy was smashed. Your tanks did well when they went into battle, but I still think you were slow about sending your tank corps into the breach made by the infantry. Nevertheless, victors are not judged." (That was a popular phrase with the military.)[16]

Success was achieved. Our armies had gone on the offensive and were developing their successes. No specific memories about the operations of the 27th Army come to mind. The 38th Army was the last to go on the offensive. There was stubborn fighting, but we kept moving ahead, straightening out the front line, especially the part of the enemy's salient that threatened us from the south. Now the front was moving straight westward all along the line. Rokossovsky was doing the same thing. He pushed out the right edge of the salient, straightening out his front line also, and turned westward. When we were getting ready for the offensive, I went to visit him at his headquarters and had a talk with him. This was not the first time I had met him. We had met when he commanded the troops of the Don Front. It was always pleasant to meet with Rokossovsky. He was a good commander and an intelligent man.

We headed westward. Another army joined us, the 4th Guards Army. Its commander was General Kulik.[17] He had been reduced in rank during the first year of the war, being stripped of his title as marshal. I don't remember exactly what his general's rank was then. It was either lieutenant general or major general. The first member of his Military Council was Shepilov.[18] It was a Guards army, with shoes and clothes that were brand-spanking new, as the saying goes, and it was armed with everything we had then to arm it with. We of course were glad to receive such an army, but neither Vatutin nor I deceived ourselves. Its commander inspired neither confidence nor respect in us. I was familiar with him from earlier times, I knew his poor character, and I simply felt sorry for this army. Such a splendid army, and yet Kulik had been appointed its commander. Why Stalin appointed him is hard for me to explain. Stalin himself had reduced Kulik in rank earlier, but I don't know to what extent Kulik was to blame or how justified it was for him to be stripped of his marshal's rank. He must have been punished for some specific action. He always was a limited individual. The real reason he was given the rank of marshal was because Stalin knew him from Tsaritsyn in 1918.[19]

This army arrived and began to carry out operations, as I recall, in an area pointing roughly in the direction of Poltava or a little north of Poltava. Kulik himself was from a village near Poltava.[20] Vatutin and I went to visit his army. I wanted to meet Kulik again. We went into his headquarters, and just then he was talking on the phone. As I listened to him, I felt very disturbed and even upset by his conversation. His phrases were rather incoherent in their content, and I felt sorry for the corps commanders. They, too, apparently felt that their army commander was insufficiently qualified. We then sent a memo to Stalin saying that we were dissatisfied with the army commander and that he should be replaced because we feared for his army. We feared that there would be unnecessary losses, and that they could be quite heavy, as a result of his unskilled handling of the troops. Stalin finally agreed with us, and we were told that Kulik was being recalled and a new commander was being appointed.

Shepilov on the other hand made a good impression on me. He was an intelligent man, and I thought he was in the right place as a member of the Military Council of the army. But however good he was, he was not the commander. The commander decides everything. He does the commanding and he gives the orders. That's why it's important to choose a good commander. Today I don't recall the name of the new commander.[21] I didn't know him and actually was never able to meet him. He died. He flew directly to the location where his army was deployed and for some reason didn't come to the Front headquarters. As he was riding in his jeep from the airfield to his army headquarters he was blown up by a mine completely by accident. So we didn't get a new commander after all, and Kulik remained for a while. Then someone else was sent.[22] I don't remember who replaced Kulik as commander of that Guards army. That army's ranks had been thinned by fighting, but to some degree its losses were greater because of Kulik's unskillful leadership.

Stalin was furious. He called up and very harshly expressed his dissatisfaction with the fact that the new commander had been blown up by a mine. You can imagine. A brand new commander arrives and, as he's traveling down the road, hits an enemy mine. And that supposedly means that the first member of the Military Council of the Front is to blame! Stalin accused me of not taking proper care of army commanders. But I couldn't imagine how it was possible to protect army commanders against mines. We were all driving around in vehicles—soldiers and officers, generals and marshals. After all, it was a war, and an enemy mine doesn't tell you where it's located. Such losses were inevitable, as in any war. But in our case this was made worse by the fact that, not long before that, the commander of another army had also been blown up by a mine, a man who had been appointed to replace Chibisov. Chibisov had been relieved of his duties because Vatutin and I were dissatisfied with him and told Stalin about it. A new commander took charge of the army and within a week was blown up by a mine. Both of these generals were killed by mines during the course of one week. Once again Stalin's accusations went like this: "Here now, two commanders have been blown up in your sector. You're not taking proper care of them." This made me angry. How could he, sitting there in the Kremlin, demand that I give orders to my commanders on how to drive their jeeps so as not to hit mines placed by the enemy? After all, we had entered a new phase of offensive action, and these might even be our own mines that we had laid earlier before abandoning the area. Both we and the enemy laid mines, and there really ought to be no complaint about this fact of life.

(I remember two years after the war in Kiev, a tractor blew up alongside a road that had been open for traffic and cleared by minesweepers. A person driving along on a tractor turned off the road and blew up on a mine.) Going back to the conversation with Stalin, of course I was angry that Stalin was voicing dissatisfaction this way, and I replied that there was no way I could take on myself the blame for the deaths of those two generals. These deaths were unforeseen, as is always possible at the front lines.

The commander of the air force on our front then was General Krasovsky.[23] Today he's the head of the Gagarin Air Force Academy. By nationality he's Belorussian. He's a decent man, who puts his heart into his work; he always tried to make things go as well as possible. One day he approached me with a suggestion, something new he had thought of on how to destroy the enemy. He told me: "I want to equip our planes with incendiary powder, which we would spray from the air. It would set fire to grass and crops. If we spray this incendiary powder on an airfield, the grass, since it's dry now, will immediately start to burn and consequently the airplanes will also burn." Listening to him, I was reminded of the first year of the war.

How many times we had tried this kind of mixture, but I know of no case when it produced results. I said: "Comrade Krasovsky, in my opinion nothing will come of it. We would just be consoling ourselves and feeding ourselves on illusions and false hopes that the grass would catch fire. How many times in the past we've tried to do this. Sometimes it would happen that a section of grass would start to burn, but the enemy quickly put it out. We also set fields of ripe wheat on fire so as not to leave them behind for the Germans, but there were people who stayed behind, and it was their wheat. They had their own way of looking at things; they themselves put out the fires. Besides, generally speaking, it's not a very effective method. Before trying to use it at the battlefront, make some tests. Spray the powder somewhere and see how it works, so you can be sure it really will destroy enemy aircraft at airfields."

He tested the powder and, being an honest and conscientious man, came to see me and said: "Yes, you're right. The game's not worth the candle, and I'm giving it up." Sometimes after that we would joke with Krasovsky on the subject. He was a very pleasant man and I respected him.

Here is another incident. It dates from an earlier time, the second year of the war. The air force commander of our Front then was General Falaleyev.[24] He was a good general. At a difficult moment during the enemy's offensive, when we were completely exhausted and had no prospects before us other than to retreat and retreat, because we were unable to contain the enemy, he brought us a combat report from the air force requesting that this report be included in a general combat report from our Front and sent to the General Staff. The report stated certain losses that we had caused the enemy in the course of a day. Falaleyev reported that our planes on that day had knocked out five hundred enemy tanks. I looked at him: "Comrade Falaleyev, five hundred tanks? There is no way I can accept that and I can't agree to it. Five hundred tanks in one day? Do you know what kind of strength that is? Well, all right, you're the deputy commander of our Front and commander of the Front's air forces. What do you think? If we've knocked out five hundred tanks today, what will the situation be tomorrow? Will we hold the positions our troops are in now? Or will we have to retreat?" And I knew that we would have to retreat, that our troops couldn't hold on.

He also said: "No, our troops will not be able to hold on."

I said: "Then what view do you think the Stavka is going to take of our report? We say we've destroyed five hundred tanks in one day, and yet we're fleeing from the enemy? There's no logic to it. I think people are bluffing you when they report so many direct hits. They even report that some tanks were overturned. I advise you, Comrade Falaleyev, to carry out an experiment. Have your pilots fire at any tanks you want with these jet-propelled rockets from our attack planes and announce a reward for a direct hit. You will see how difficult it is to achieve a direct hit from the air. It's possible that none of your pilots will win the award. And the claim that some rockets hit directly under the tank and turned the tank over—that's absurd. I recommend you take one of these rockets and put it right under a tank and set it off. I don't think it has the explosive strength to turn over a tank. And what we're talking about is not a rocket that someone has placed under a tank, but one fired from the air. This is a very unlikely event. Let's write two hundred fifty, all right?" I don't remember what figure we finally agreed on. You could write down some figure based on the theory of probability. But Falaleyev said that his figures had all been checked and carefully counted. For my part I didn't believe in that count.

We sent in the report, and then, sure enough, we were forced to retreat. Later Falaleyev told me he had carried out an experiment: "I set up a table and announced a reward for anyone who could make a direct hit on that table from the air. No one was able to claim the reward." Of course our attack planes were hitting the enemy tanks. But to destroy five hundred of them in one day? Even the enemy couldn't do that back then, and at that time German air power was greater than ours. Unfortunately we were not able to do that kind of thing at all, especially in 1942, when our forces were basically battered and exhausted. That's how things happen in war. They say that Suvorov, when he took the Turkish fortress of Ismail,²⁵ wrote a report to the Empress Catherine informing her that he had destroyed seventy thousand Turks. An adjutant said to him: "Your Highness, there were not that many Turks there." Suvorov answered: "No mercy on the infidels! Write it down!" Probably that kind of thing happened even before Suvorov.

To return to the account of our offensive drive to the Dnieper, after the fighting near Poltava, our soldiers, officers, and generals were sure of our strength. Whereas previously it had seemed to us that when the Germans stood opposite us it would be difficult or even impossible to drive them from their positions, now in everyone's consciousness, from soldier to general, the point of view had changed. We were sure of our capabilities and even our superiority over the enemy. This was a very pleasing time. We continued to move forward toward the Dnieper. I remember Krasovsky came in once and reported that his pilots had returned from an operation. On their way they had seen a vast sea of fire. The wheat had ripened, the rye had ripened, and the barley had ripened, and all of them were burning. It was painful for me to hear him say this. Of course it had nothing to do with him; he was just reporting what his pilots had seen. I answered: "I can't agree with this. I don't think it's so." I simply didn't want to believe it. Somehow, I told myself, this was impossible. I said: "Your pilots were returning from battle at high speed. Maybe there was an area on fire, and as they rushed past their eyes formed the image of a vast sea of fire. But that just can't be!" I very much wanted it not to be true.

We were on the offensive. We wanted to obtain grain for our country and our army. And we did bring in a relatively large amount of grain from the areas liberated in 1943. In Ukraine the harvest was downright excellent. I said to Krasovsky: "We'll continue our offensive and see." And when our offensive continued and we liberated those areas nowhere did we find that very much grain had been burned. I joked with him later: "Comrade Krasovsky, where are those burned-out fields, that vast sea of fire that your pilots saw?" My guess turned out to be correct. In war sometimes the pupils get dilated [distorting the pilots' vision].

I also remember a report about bombing at night. At that time General Skripko²⁶ joined our Front. He commanded our long-distance bombers for nighttime bombing. He was a good general. I had known him at Stalingrad, and he had worked well there. He was an experienced "night fighter." Having been placed at our disposal, he was now working in the interests of our Front. It was reported to us that near Poltava (and I remember perfectly well now the name of the village there—Machokha) there was either an ammunition dump or an enemy repair base located in a village. We were getting ready to resume our offensive, and it's always a cherished dream for any commander to deprive the enemy of ammunition, fuel, and other means of waging war. We called Skripko in and showed him the report from our intelligence people and gave him the order to bomb the village! Of course it could be said now that there were people living in that village. Yes, there were people living there, but there were also people carrying out an offensive. In war one is always faced by very difficult choices. If you spare one person, you may lose more. Therefore we decided to bomb the ammunition dump, which the Germans would use to strike at our people.

The next morning Skripko reported: "Everything there has been leveled to the ground. Everything has been destroyed." But I already had some experience, and not just a little bit. I looked at him and said: "Keep in mind, now, that we're on the offensive and we'll soon be in Poltava and will liberate Machokha. Then I will tell you to what extent your report corresponds to reality—this report you received from your people who bombed the ammunition dump." How chagrined Skripko was after we liberated the area. I said to him: "Comrade Skripko, you can go to Machokha. Not a single house was burned there. Machokha generally suffered no damage. I wonder where your pilots actually dropped their bombs. I wonder what it was that was burning when you reported that everything there had been destroyed." Later when I would meet him, I would often ask: "Comrade Skripko, how are things at Machokha?" Machokha became for him a term of opprobrium. Of course all sorts of things happen in military operations. We bombed and we set things on fire and we destroyed things and we laid waste to enemy territory. But there were also cases when things were reported that were based on God only knows what. Was this conscious lying or did they actually drop those bombs that night, but had been disoriented and had lost their exact location? It's hard to say. Today I don't even remember whether anything near Machokha or around it had been destroyed or burned.

Here's another incident. I heard about this from Stalin's own lips. When we were fighting Finland in 1939–40, there were reports that our pilots had destroyed the enemy's locomotives. There was an order to destroy the Finnish locomotives to make it more difficult for them to use their rail transport system. It was reported that so many locomotives had been destroyed that they couldn't possibly have any locomotives left.[27] But when we finally reached that region we didn't find any damaged locomotives. Stalin said bluntly: "They lied!" I can't put things that crudely. It's one thing to lie and it's another to make a mistake. After all, it was war. I don't think people lied deliberately. No, I think they made mistakes, and mistakes are certainly possible, especially when you're bombing at night.

1. On July 12, 1943, the Western and Bryansk Fronts began their offensives, followed on July 15 by the Central Front.

2. General Field Marshal V. von Brauchitsch was commander in chief of the German ground forces from 1938 to 1941. See Biographies.

3. Lieutenant General P. A. Rotmistrov was at that time in command of the Fifth Guards Tank Army. See Biographies.

4. Hitler hoped to capture the oil fields of the Caucasus and from there to move his forces into the Middle East. [SS]

5. Hero of the Soviet Union Four-Star Army General (at the time of the events described Lieutenant General) P. I. Batov was at that time in command of the 65th Army, which took part in the battle of Stalingrad as part of the Don Front.

6. Marshal I. S. Konev. See Biographies.

7. The second liberation of Belgorod occurred on August 5, 1943. The second liberation of Kharkov followed on August 23.

8. N. S. Khrushchev is referring to the baritone singer K. A. Laptev, soloist at the Kiev Theater of Opera and Ballet (from 1957 People's Artiste of the USSR).

9. In 1943 A. A. Yepishev was for a short time first secretary of the party committee for Kharkov province, but his appointment was not confirmed by the Central Committee of the AUCP(B). After his departure, only the second secretary I. I. Profitilov and the third secretary M. D. Maksimov remained in position. In 1944 V. M. Churayev became first secretary.

10. P. G. Svinarenko perished in May 1942. When in August 1943 Kharkov was liberated, nobody was at first appointed chairman of the province executive committee, and the duties of this post were carried out by the military commandant, Deputy Commander of the 69th Army Major General N. I. Trufanov.

11. Tomarovka is a village a few kilometers west of Belgorod. [SS]

12. The Fourth Guards Tank Corps of Lieutenant General of Tank Forces P. P. Poluboyarov.

13. Chief of Staff of the Voronezh Front Lieutenant General S. P. Ivanov.

14. Literally, high-frequency telephone (in Russian, *vysokaia chastota*, or VCh). High frequencies were used to ensure secrecy. [SS]

15. "Katyusha" was the colloquial name for a multiple rocket launcher mounted on a truck. The name is a diminutive form of Yekaterina (Catherine), something like "Katie." [SS]

16. The first time that this expression seems to have been used in Russian history was in 1773, when during the Russo-Turkish war the detachment of General A. V. Suvorov carried out a successful raid on Turtukai, crushing superior enemy forces by means of a sudden attack. In doing this, Suvorov exceeded the limits of his orders. His immediate superior complained to Catherine II, but the empress wrote on the report: "Victors are not judged." After this the expression entered general Russian usage.

17. Lieutenant General G. I. Kulik commanded the Fourth Guards Army from April to September 1943. See Biographies.

18. Colonel D. T. Shepilov, member of the AUCP(B) from 1926.

19. That is, Stalin and Kulik had served together at Tsaritsyn during the Civil War. [SS]

20. Poltava is in the east central Ukraine, some 130 kilometers west of Kharkov. [SS] Kulik came from the hamlet of Dudnikovo in Poltava province.

21. The person whom Khrushchev has in mind is Lieutenant General A. I. Zygin.

22. This was Lieutenant General I. V. Galanin.

23. Air Force Lieutenant General S. A. Krasovsky. See Biographies.

24. In 1942 Air Force Lieutenant General F. Ya. Falaleyev was in command of air forces in the Southwestern Area.

25. Field Marshal Aleksandr Vasilyevich Suvorov (1729–1800) is one of the most celebrated Russian generals. He commanded the Russian army during the reign of the Empress Catherine II, including the Russo-Turkish wars of 1768–74 and 1787–92. His troops took Ismail in 1790. [GS/SS]

26. Air Force Lieutenant General N. S. Skripko was at that time deputy commander of Strategic Air Forces.

27. Khrushchev is referring to the bombing of the section of railroad northwest of Vyborg, between the Ixpya and Vainikkala Stations. Vyborg, on the northern shore of the Gulf of Finland, is about 130 kilometers northwest of Leningrad (Leningrad, now St. Petersburg). Before the Soviet-Finnish war it belonged to Finland. [SS]

A nd so we had lived to see the day when our troops once again stood on the middle reaches of the Dnieper, and we had seized some small beachheads on its west bank.¹ Can you imagine what joy we felt? Possibly I am exaggerating, but I felt a special joy. After all I was "responsible" for Ukraine, being the secretary of the Central Committee of its Communist Party. Besides, I had spent my childhood and youth working in the factories and mines of the Donbass, and I was very much attached to this part of our country. Not so long before, I had suffered greatly from the experience of the Red Army's retreat. To this day I remember that terrible panorama: the flood of refugees with their children, their chickens, geese, goats, cows. It was a terrible sight! But now we were moving forward to the west.

The year 1943 was a year of joy, the year of our forces' victorious offensive. We reached the Dnieper and took Pereyaslav,² that historic city. It was there that Bogdan Khmelnitsky received the Russian emissaries and signed a treaty making Ukraine a part of the Russian state, placing it under the authority of the Russian tsar. The bourgeois nationalists curse that day and that treaty, calling it merely a "treaty of convenience." Supposedly Pereyaslav was a treaty of bondage imposed on Ukraine.³ Well, so much for the nationalists. The actions of Bogdan Khmelnitsky, in my opinion, were progressive. They played a positive role in the history of both the Ukrainian and the Russian peoples. Two great nations, closely related, the Russians and the Ukrainians, had united, and after that they went through all joys and sorrows together.

Vatutin and I were triumphant. Before the war Vatutin was chief of staff of the Kiev Special Military District (KOVO)⁴ and had lived in Ukraine a long time. He and I had visions of again seeing the Monastery of the Caves overlooking the Dnieper in Kiev. Even today I joyfully remember those days when we were driving the Germans out and approaching the Dnieper. During that approach it happened that we took some Russian soldiers prisoner (or else they defected to our side from the enemy; in general they were Soviet citizens). I remember questioning one of them. He himself had crossed the front lines and surrendered to us. He was a young man and seemed to be a fairly decisive person. He told us that among the German forces there were Russian units consisting of prisoners of war. They were called Vlasovites because they were commanded by Vlasov. Not in our sector, but overall, Vlasov was their commander. His units were not concentrated in one place, but were more or less dispersed among the German troops; still, their commander in

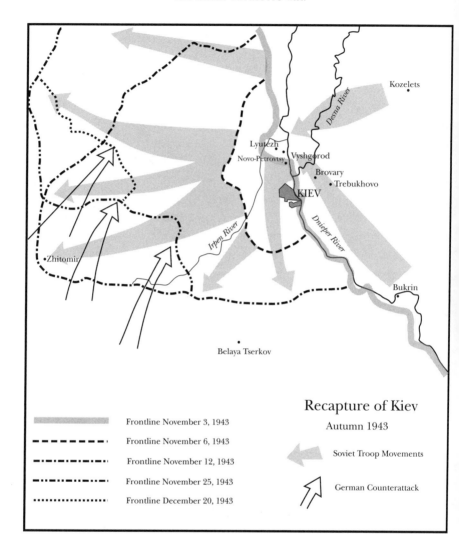

**Recapture of Kiev**

Autumn 1943

Frontline November 3, 1943

Frontline November 6, 1943

Frontline November 12, 1943

Frontline November 25, 1943

Frontline December 20, 1943

Soviet Troop Movements

German Counterattack

general was considered to be Vlasov.[5] I asked this young fellow to tell me in detail how he had crossed over to our side and under what circumstances. He said that he had crossed over alone, but that there were others who were also looking for a suitable moment to defect to our side. They had signed up with Vlasov's army so as to be sent to the front lines and not be left in prisoner-of-war camps, where they were doomed to certain death.

Our intelligence service worked with this young fellow. He was sent back across the front lines to the enemy's side and returned to our side, bringing several Vlasovites with him. The German command showered our soldiers with leaflets urging them to surrender and telling them that a Russian general, Vlasov, was conducting operations on the German side along with another former general of ours whose name I don't remember. He was also a traitor to his homeland who had defected to the enemy. Previously that defector had been a secretary of a party district committee in one of the districts of Moscow.[6] This was simply unbelievable, but such things did happen. I saw captured enemy photographs, a great many of them. They showed these two individuals: the former district committee secretary and Vlasov wearing a German uniform. The Germans had awarded the rank of general to the former party secretary, who had not had any such rank in the Red Army.

The Germans spread many other leaflets around as well as postcards with a photograph of Stalin's son. I was acquainted with Stalin's son Yakov, but not all that closely, although I had met him at his father's apartment when I had been there. I had heard only good things about him. He was a serious person. He had graduated from some institute and was an engineer, but I don't know in what field. Stalin criticized him: "Here you've gotten yourself an engineer's degree, but what we need is military cadres." He suggested that Yakov enter the Artillery Academy. He did and graduated. When the war began he was already an artillery officer. He fought on the Belorussian sector, where he became a German prisoner. After the war a great deal of effort was made to try and find some trace of him. We were unable to find anything. Apparently he was destroyed. At any rate he disappeared without a trace. The photographs [on the postcards circulated by the Germans] showed Yasha walking along and at a certain distance from him a German officer walking. There were other photographs as well, and even an appeal signed with his name. All this was of course fabricated by the Germans. It didn't make much of an impression, and no one who had known Yasha placed any confidence in this propaganda, and neither did our soldiers in general.[7]

One day I was summoned to Moscow. I went there most often after being summoned, that is, on the initiative of Moscow itself. I don't remember whether there ever was an instance when I went there on my own initiative. Discussions were usually held around the table at Stalin's place, and unfortunately there was a lot of drinking at that table. The most urgent and burning questions were brought up when it was late at night and a lot of time had been spent sitting around the table, which meant that a lot of drinking and eating had gone on. One time (this was a little bit before the events I have just described) Stalin turned to me and said: "What about this Vlasov? What the devil is he? A traitor? I don't believe it."

I answered: "I also find it hard to believe." Two or three times after that, Stalin returned to the subject of Vlasov. At first this happened when we had just heard the claim that some Russian general by the name of Vlasov was fighting on the German side. At that time we thought it was merely German propaganda, that they were just trying to bait us.

After a while we began actually taking Vlasovite prisoners, and when I went to Moscow again Stalin returned to the subject of Vlasov: "What the hell is this? Is he really a traitor?"

I answered: "There can no longer be any doubt about it. We're taking people prisoner who call themselves Vlasovites and who wear German uniforms. Apparently Vlasov really is fighting on the enemy's side."

Stalin said: "Then we have to issue a declaration that he is an outlaw and a traitor."

I answered: "Undoubtedly. We have to do that now, so that our propaganda will counter German propaganda, so that their propaganda won't turn out to be one-sided. If we keep quiet about this and take no countermeasures, it will look as though we have no arguments on our side." The appropriate publications were produced, and a campaign of counterpropaganda was begun in the ranks of the Red Army and in our party organizations on this subject.

Once, after a fairly long "session" at Stalin's table, he brought up the question of Vlasov again. Everyone present at that table remembered that it was a particularly "heavy" table. These were hard to wait through, and no one ever knew how one of them would end. Once Bulganin said to me in private: "You get an invitation, you go as a guest to visit him, they give you food and drink, and afterward you don't know where you're going to end up: whether you're going to go back to your own home or whether they're going to take you off somewhere and put you in jail." There was no lack of truth in what he said. Each of us experienced that kind of thing back then, it seems. Stalin had outbursts of anger, sudden, unexpected, and unbelievable eruptions. His naked power and unlimited, unchallenged authority went to his head. Sometimes he "awarded" the most indecent and inappropriate epithets, even to the people who were closest to him. Before the war the people closest to him were considered to be Voroshilov, Molotov, and to some extent Mikoyan. At a later stage Beria was included in that number. Other people were considered close to him in the second or third rank, so to speak, because they belonged to a younger generation and had not spent such a long time in joint work with Stalin. Molotov, for example, had known him from a very early time, and Voroshilov also, from prerevolutionary times. During the Civil War, when Voroshilov commanded an army and retreated to Tsaritsyn, he and Stalin developed very close ties there, at Tsaritsyn.

That was the circle in which Stalin raised the question: "Why did Vlasov become a traitor?"

I answered: "There is no longer any question now that he really is a traitor."

Stalin said: "But you praised him and promoted him."

I answered: "That's true. I promoted him to be commander of the 37th Army. The defense of Kiev was entrusted to him, and he coped with the task brilliantly. The Germans never took Kiev. Kiev fell because, much farther to the east of Kiev, our troops were surrounded. But then Vlasov escaped from that encirclement. Yes, I did praise him and told you about his merits many times. And how many times did you praise him, too? After all, when Kiev had fallen and he had escaped from encirclement, you appointed him commander of a new army, and he distinguished himself in the defense of Moscow.[8] You decorated him, Comrade Stalin, for the Moscow campaign, and then you assigned him to a critical sector, the Valdai region.[9] He was surrounded and trapped again there, but once again he escaped from encirclement and returned to our lines. You even proposed that he be appointed commander of the Stalingrad Front. You told me that I should name the commander and at the same time said that the most appropriate commander would be either Yeremenko, who was in the hospital, or Vlasov. You said that you would appoint Vlasov, but he was not available [being trapped in enemy encirclement]. So then, both I praised him and you praised him. His deeds were such as to deserve praise. But after that he became a traitor, and now there can no longer be any doubt about it."

I should say, in addition, that Stalin had previously talked about Vlasov in front of everyone, and everyone had heard Stalin praise him and assert that he would have been the best commander for the Stalingrad Front. So after these comments of his at the table and my reply, Stalin never raised the question again in my presence, although of course the Vlasov case was a source of great chagrin and bitterness for me as well. It was very hard to explain, and even today it's simply impossible for me to understand how this could have happened. The man fought steadfastly, did things well, made a favorable impression, won the sympathies of those ranking above him, and then suddenly turned out to be a traitor. Why didn't he turn traitor right at the beginning when he was caught in enemy encirclement while commanding the 37th Army in the defense of Kiev? But no, he escaped from encirclement! He escaped literally on foot and reached our lines when we were already outside Voronezh. This happened on the eve of our offensive in the Moscow area. No sooner had he escaped from encirclement, and we reported it to Stalin, than immediately we received the order to send him by plane to Moscow. We sent him off, and I must confess, at that time I thought perhaps there was some information compromising Vlasov and that they wanted him in Moscow to interrogate him. Later we found out that he had also commanded an army outside Moscow, that that army had performed very well, and that he had been decorated for that.

What was going on here? People encountered difficult and painful experiences in those days. Some were unable to withstand the impact of those trying experiences. I don't think Vlasov had previously been recruited by the Germans and had become an enemy agent. It seems that by nature he was an unstable person, lacking in strong character. He was considered a decent Communist, but there was no deep-seated ideological conviction in him. By education and training he had been a teacher. He probably had a loyal attitude toward Soviet power in the early years. It may be that he had self-seeking motives for remaining in the Communist Party with the hope of obtaining an advantageous post. Unfortunately we had quite a few such people, and I think that nowadays there are even more such careerists. I must qualify my use of the term "careerist" because Vlasov's careerism culminated in outright betrayal. And that is something of a different order.

You don't encounter many people like Vlasov, but on the other hand Vlasov was not an exception. Later there was Colonel Penkovsky, who also held a high post, working in our intelligence services. He was entrusted with the task of keeping track of other intelligence personnel outside the Soviet Union. For that purpose he often traveled abroad, and suddenly he went over to the enemy. Unfortunately, Penkovsky was not an isolated case. But the most flagrant of all the cases of treason was that of Vlasov. He was punished as he deserved to be. After the war he was tried, condemned, and hanged.

So then, our troops had reached the Dnieper and seized several beachheads on the right, or west, bank. However, the Dnieper is a substantial obstacle, and we wanted to establish a really large beachhead to get large numbers of troops and equipment across. As a start in this direction, we decided to carry out a major parachute landing on the right bank. We made preparations for this, and it seemed that everything was going well. But the question of the weather came up. On the recommendation of the General Staff a meteorologist came to our sector to help choose the best time for the paratroop landing. We of course were glad to have him. Using his data on the strength and direction of the winds, we chose a day and hour for the parachute drop.

General Skripko,[10] commander of our heavy bombers, flew the paratroops across the river. It was precisely the heavy bombers that we used for this paratroop drop. But after the paratroops had been dropped, we soon learned that they weren't landing on the right bank, but either on the river or on the left bank, literally on top of the trenches of our front-line troops. There were incidents in which our troops seized the paratroopers and strangled them. The paratroops began to explain in Russian, but our soldiers took them for Vlasovites and said: "You're traitors!" and dealt with them all the more savagely. They kept shouting: "No, we're Soviet paratroopers!" Can you imagine how many people perished for no good reason on the Dnieper? It was such a shameful thing. Meanwhile this "weather god," as he had been recommended to us, immediately "broke into a sweat" and fled to Moscow. Our anger at him was pretty intense, but I never had a chance to meet him again after that paratroop drop. Sad cases like this did happen in the war. Everything was possible, because in real life that's what war is like.

Later when the situation was calmer, and I recalled this incident, I could put myself more easily in his difficult position, because at that time he had only very limited information to draw on in trying to determine what location and what time would be best and what the direction of the wind currents and the speed of the wind would be at that time. For an accurate answer to that problem a great deal of meteorological data from a very extensive area is necessary. Of course we didn't have such data or information. What the weather was like on the other side of the Dnieper we simply didn't know, and so I understood that he was not personally to blame, that he was an honorable man, and his mistakes can be explained by the fact that he didn't have enough accurate data.

We began to make preparations for the crossing of the Dnieper. Meanwhile we walked along the river, gazed at it, and simply rejoiced. We sang a beautiful song, which I still love very much. I have a tape recording of it. The poet Dolmatovsky wrote the words. Its title was "O Dnipro, Dnipro." It's an excellent song.[11] During the most difficult times of our retreats and defeats and our abandonment of Ukraine, many Ukrainians drew from this song the hope that we would someday return to the Dnieper. And here we had returned to this river sacred to the Ukrainian people.

The 38th and 40th Armies had come out on the Dnieper to the north of Kiev, while the Third Guards Tank Army and 27th Army were a little south of Pereyaslav. The 40th Army of General Moskalenko (which was later com-

manded by Zhmachenko) had reached the area of Rzhishchev.[12] The 38th
Army of General Chibisov (later commanded by Moskalenko) had established a beachhead for itself in the Mezhigorye area.[13] After the fighting in
the Kursk salient, some of the other armies in our Front were withdrawn
and placed in the reserves of the Supreme High Command. They were given
the opportunity to rest and recuperate, since the extent of our Front had
narrowed after the battle of Kursk.

Later Moskalenko told me he crossed the Dnieper on a raft without a
motor. The raft had been built from the remnants of wooden buildings.
When he reached the middle of the river, some German planes flew right
overhead. They were bombing everything that was floating on the river, and
Moskalenko found himself in a difficult situation, but he reached the right
bank safely without suffering any losses. Vatutin and I crossed over to the
right bank in a cutter. In the middle of the river the motor suddenly died on
us. Enemy planes were flying over, but they weren't bombing, and the German
artillery was keeping up a blind fire at the Dnieper to try and interfere with
the crossing of our troops. We soon expanded our beachhead and moved our
forces over to the right bank. The Third Guards Tank Army, commanded by
General Rybalko,[14] a remarkable military leader who I respected, was at first
brought across the river to the Bukrin beachhead[15] with the aim of striking
north toward Kiev. We had thought the ground there was fairly level, but it
turned out to be rather broken ground, difficult to launch an offensive over,
but good for defense.

We twice tried to start an offensive there, but had no success, and after
losing a certain number of tanks, we called off the offensive.[16] At that time
autumn was already setting in. It was the second half of October, heavy rains
had begun, and the ground had turned to mud. In a certain sense this was
favorable for us because the rain and bad weather prevented the enemy
from carrying out air reconnaissance. We decided to call off the offensive
from the Bukrin beachhead and transfer the tank army and infantry back to
the left bank in order to redeploy those troops to the north of Kiev, to the
Mezhigorye region, where the villages of Novo-Petrovtsy and Staro-Petrovtsy
were located.[17] That is what we did. And luck was with us. The weather was
completely unsuitable for flying during the time when we were redeploying
the tank army to the north. The tank army moved a distance of about 100
kilometers probably and had come right up to the Dnieper in some places,
and the enemy had still not noticed this redeployment.

Now we began preparations for an offensive from the region of Vyshgorod,
to the north of Kiev. The beachhead there was fairly bare and open.[18] Farther

along there were forests and the mouth of the Irpen River.[19] In general, the area was not large, but it was quite sufficient for concentrating our troops and striking a blow at the Germans. On the extreme right wing of our front, as we approached Kiev, the Supreme High Command transferred the 13th and 60th Armies to us from Rokossovsky's Central Front. The commanders of those armies were two very good generals, Pukhov and Chernyakhovsky,[20] and we were pleased to have received these armies on the eve of our offensive at Kiev. The Stavka had proposed that we start our offensive not from the place we had chosen, in the area of Novo-Petrovtsy, but farther to the north, closer to the town of Kozelets. That's about 60 kilometers from Kiev. It was exactly there that the 60th Army was deployed, and it was supposed to start the offensive, and then the 38th and other armies would join in. They were positioned farther to the south. We did begin preparations that way. We went to visit Chibisov at his 38th Army headquarters. His headquarters was located in a forest not far from the Desna River. I have forgotten the name of the village, but it was a poor one. The soil there is sandy and not very fertile.

When Vatutin and I were on our way to visit Chibisov, we saw two people who had been hanged. An order had been issued permitting local inhabitants to hang traitors, to give vent to their anger, because [during the German occupation] these traitors had lorded it over them. If they were caught, they could be tried right there and hanged immediately. So there were two bodies hanging, one with a great full beard, a thick black beard that overshadowed the face. Evidently this had not been an old man, but one who had allowed his beard to grow. Perhaps he used it as a kind of mask?

When we reached Chibisov's headquarters, after he had reported on the situation, I asked him: "Comrade Chibisov, we saw two men who had been hanged. What does that mean? What people were these? What crimes had they committed and who hanged them?"

He answered: "Yes, that's what things are like now. They were given the right to do that, so they went and caught these people and hanged them." I didn't like his answer. He apparently hadn't looked into the question of who had been hanged and what for.

I went out of the headquarters building (there were people walking by), and I asked them: "There are some people hanging back there. Who were they? Do you know them?"

"How can you ask? Of course we know them."

"Well, who were they?"

"Our blacksmith was hanged. We hanged him ourselves." The man I was talking with then told who the other hanged man was.

"What did you hang them for? What crimes had they committed?"

They answered: "When the Germans came, the blacksmith ratted on the Communists and Komsomol members. He ratted on our teacher and the Germans hanged her. That's why we hanged him as a traitor."

"And what about those who were village elders under the Germans? Did they run away?"

"No, our village elder didn't run away. He was a good, honest man. He helped the partisans, and we are protecting him in spite of the fact that he was a village elder, serving under the Germans. He held that position because he was appointed to it; someone had to be appointed. In our opinion he did everything within his power to save the village and its people."

I went back into the headquarters building and said: "Comrade Chibisov, here you are implying that illegalities are being committed, but you haven't listened to the people. They say that the punishment was deserved. And as far as the village elder goes, the one who had served under the Germans, they consider him worthy to be defended and they are protecting him. So things aren't the way you said, that people are just grabbing others without any investigation and hanging them. No, they are making distinctions between who to defend and who to punish." In general I didn't find Chibisov to be a very sympathetic person. I had an extreme dislike for him. I have spoken about this earlier, and I repeat it now.

So then, we had received the order to attack to the west of Kozelets. This was just a general orientation, not literally a command; it was based on the fact that we had troops there. Our troops of course had already crossed the Dnieper. We also went to visit the 60th Army. I wanted to make the acquaintance of its commander, General Chernyakhovsky. He had attracted a great deal of attention to himself. The rumors that had reached me told of a man of great vision, quite a young man to be a general.[21] We arrived. He impressed us with his intelligence, and the report he gave showed his knowledge of the situation. This disposed us even more favorably toward him. As for going on the offensive, he knew when it was the right time for that! An order had been given, and he was diligently preparing for an offensive, but at the same time he said categorically that the amount of time allowed him for preparing for the offensive didn't seem right. An additional three days were needed.

I've already talked about the way Vatutin reacted when Trofimenko asked for a change in the direction of an attack that had already been decided earlier. Now here was Chernyakhovsky asking that the offensive be postponed for three days, although the Stavka had set a definite date for it. Vatutin flared up and began arguing that an order had to be respected and obeyed. But I could see that he was simply not listening to Chernyakhovsky and I said: "Nikolai Fyodorovich, let him give his report on why an additional three days are needed." I saw that Chernyakhovsky's eyes were already starting to flash and that he, too, could display some character.

He answered: "Here's why. My companies have so many soldiers. Our reserve regiment is in such-and-such a location. It is on the march and will arrive at such-and-such a time. The companies that are going on the offensive—I can give them reinforcements, but that would be literally on the evening before the offensive. And then the next morning they're supposed to attack. The commanders of the companies will have absolutely no time to get to know the people they have received as reinforcements. The soldiers won't have gotten to know one another, and not only will the commander not know the newcomers; he won't even have met them. How can you go on the offensive under such conditions? You'll just suffer casualties and not carry out your assignment. Give me three days. The new people will arrive, I will work with them, and then I will be sure that the task will be carried out. I will break the resistance of the enemy forces standing in front of me and expand the offensive in the direction indicated in the order."

I said: "Let's take a break and have a little rest." We took a break. It was a beautiful day. We went outdoors, and Vatutin and I went off to the side. I said: "Nikolai Fyodorovich, let's give him his three days! Let's call Stalin. I'm convinced that Stalin will agree with us. What difference will it make to Stalin whether we start the offensive now or three days later? If the commander says he can't vouch for success now and that we could be placing our troops in danger, then it's better to do as the general recommends."

Vatutin agreed: "All right, let's make the phone call." He evidently gave his consent because of the incident involving the 27th Army. In that case he had disagreed with me, and I had sent Stalin a coded message. Of course I would have done the same thing in the present situation, because what the army commander [Chernyakhorsky] had said meant a great deal to me. I saw that he was on the right track and was reasoning correctly. How could I, a member of the Military Council of the Front, not support an intelligent decision, especially since I was free of any false notions, as some military men have, that once an order is given it has to be carried out, no matter what. My view is this: So what if an order has been given? If the situation requires a change in the order, the most rational and intelligent thing is to change it, to take into account things that have become evident after the order was given. Then later, either continue in the same direction or change the direction of the offensive, depending on the situation and the circumstances.

In the given instance I was pleased that Nikolai Fyodorovich [Vatutin] agreed. I said: "You call Stalin. You're the commander of the Front; you're the one that should make the phone call." This pleased him. I myself never liked calling Stalin. The commander was the one who should call him. If I called, it would only be in situations when I considered it necessary to make a personal report to Stalin. Most often Stalin himself called me. In short, the phone call to Stalin was made, and Stalin agreed without any resistance: "All right, we'll allow the offensive to be held over for three days." The offensive was to be carried out by our Front alone, and therefore Stalin had no other special concerns in that area. Of course there were other matters of concern to him, because the war was still on, but for all practical purposes it was only in our area that active operations were being conducted.

We had lunch with Chernyakhovsky and told him that his request had been granted. He would be given three days to prepare his troops for the offensive. We also said that we would come visit again at the beginning of the offensive. We said goodbye and left. We were traveling through a forest. We came to a large clearing, which was covered with German graves. The Germans had divided it into neat squares, and each grave had its own cross of birch wood. This scene gave an eerie impression. How many people had been killed there! But I won't hide the fact that I also felt a certain satisfaction: as much as to say, so you came here looking for Lebensraum, for "living space" at the expense of other people, and you found your "space" in these graves in the forest. Later I recommended: "Don't destroy those graves. Preserve them in the form they're in. Let our people see what the aggressors have conquered for themselves (3 arshins of ground, as they used to say in the old days—that is, a few square feet)." I think this graveyard was the result of the "work" of our Fifth Army commanded by General Potapov, which fought in this area when the Germans were attacking in 1941.[22]

Soon we received an order to abandon the offensive by the 60th Army and to attack instead in the direction that we had proposed earlier, in the Novo-Petrovtsy area. Novo-Petrovtsy is about 27 kilometers [north] from Kiev [on the west bank of the Dnieper]. We would have to fight our way forward through a forest held by the enemy, whereas our troops were out in an open space. When we had chosen the place for forcing the Dnieper and establishing a beachhead, I said to Chibisov: "Look, this is the best sector of all." I pointed in the direction leading through Novo-Petrovtsy. I knew the area well because that was where our government dachas had been located previously. In olden times a Cossack monastery had been built there.

Zaporozhian Cossacks had lived there when they got old.[23] They left their wealth to orphans and lived out the remainder of their days in that monastery. After the Ukrainian government was moved from Kharkov to Kiev,[24] dachas were organized at Novo-Petrovtsy for government officials. Kosior lived there, and so did Petrovsky and Postyshev. When I went to Ukraine [from Moscow], I also lived there, together with Burmistenko, Korniyets,[25] and other comrades, and so I knew the locality. It was a small, level area, "the size of a pocket handkerchief," as the saying goes. It was surrounded by hills, with an orchard and a fairly steep, paved exit road. It occurred to me that if we forced the river at this place, we would have a ready-made road that our tanks and infantry could travel on. The main thing was that this area was inaccessible, because it was bounded on the west by a deep ravine, which was absolutely impassable for tanks. There was only a narrow road [across the ravine], which could easily be covered by artillery fire. You could literally withstand a siege in that location.

Chibisov reported to me: "We have taken the government dacha." (He even said: "We took your dacha." But actually none of us owned personal dachas; these were government dachas, and I had lived there together with other individual leaders of our republic.) So we began preparations for an offensive from this beachhead. When preparations were completed, Vatutin and I decided to go visit Chibisov at the headquarters of the 38th Army. His headquarters was located a great distance away, on the east side of the Dnieper. We told him: "Move your headquarters to either Staro-Petrovtsy or Novo-Petrovtsy [on the west side of the Dnieper]. You should be closer to the troops during the offensive."

"Yes, sir," he answered like the old tsarist officer he had been. "It will be done." In general he loved to answer with such standard phrases, but I had no confidence in him.

The headquarters of our Front was a little to the southeast of Brovary in the village of Trebukhovo. This is not far from Kiev, that is, it is on the east bank of the Dnieper in a marshy area. Before making the trip to the new location of the 38th Army headquarters of Chibisov, I said to Vatutin: "Nikolai Fyodorovich, call up Chibisov and ask if he has moved out of his former quarters. Where is he? At his new quarters or somewhere else?" Vatutin made the phone call, and I was standing right next to him. We had already put our coats on in order to make the trip.

I heard him say: "Where are you, Comrade Chibisov? Where are your quarters? Are you at your new quarters?"

"Yes, I'm at my new quarters."

"All right, I and the member of the Military Council are coming out to see you now. Organize things so that we meet up with you as quickly as possible."

Vatutin hung up the phone and I asked him again: "Nikolai Fyodorovich, did you find out the exact location of his new quarters?" He called again. We got exact directions. It turned out there was some sort of island or peninsula in the Dnieper with some sort of farming settlement on it. That's where he had set up his headquarters instead of within the beachhead itself. I simply looked at Vatutin without saying anything. Nikolai Fyodorovich turned green and began cursing. I said: "You see what kind of man this is? He's not a reliable person. He's as tricky as a gypsy."

The reason for my lack of confidence in him and the reason I began asking for precise directions was that this was not the first time such an incident had occurred. During the battle of the Kursk salient, when we were preparing our offensive and when it was the 38th Army's turn to go into action, we had also decided to visit that army on the eve of the offensive and hold a conference.

We had told Chibisov a specific place—a certain village—where he should establish his headquarters. All the villages then were deserted, because an order was in effect relocating all peasants from the front-line areas. Chibisov was supposed to set up his headquarters near the front line. His wife and daughter used to travel with him, and he also brought along with him either a goat or a cow. His adjutant was his son-in-law. In short, his headquarters was like some sort of mobile Cossack family farm. He himself was a Cossack. Because his family was with him, he was reluctant to get too close to the front line. On that occasion, too, when we were on our way to visit the 38th Army, I said to Vatutin: "Call him and ask him if he's at his new headquarters?"

Chibisov said: "Yes, at the new headquarters." We went to this new location. When we arrived we found the village completely deserted. The doors of the peasant huts were locked and their yards were overgrown with weeds and nettles. Usually a headquarters is easy to find. There are always officers going in and out, guards visible, and a communications line. But there was none of that. Back and forth we went along the roads, but he wasn't there. That's all there was to it! We stopped next to one of the houses, went and sat on the porch, started talking things over, and sent an adjutant to look once more. Then we saw a general coming. It was Chibisov.

Vatutin lit into him: "How come we arrived before you did? You said you were at your new headquarters, didn't you?"

"No, not at all."

I was astounded by this barefaced insolence. An army commander answering a front commander this way! I myself had been a witness when Vatutin got exact directions for Chibisov's location. Later I reported this to Stalin. But for some reason Stalin was much more tolerant toward Chibisov than toward others who didn't do even one-hundredth of what he did. Stalin had known him at Tsaritsyn as a Cossack officer who served in the Red Army. Of course that is a great merit, especially for those times, when for the most part the Cossacks were in rebellion against Soviet power. But still. . . .

Let me return to the offensive operation at Kiev. We arrived at Chibisov's headquarters in the farming settlement [on the island or peninsula] and said that he should set up a new headquarters on the west bank of the Dnieper in order to be in direct contact with the troops when they began their offensive, not here on the river. What kind of command and control of troops could there be from across the river? We came to agreement on when the offensive would start, and we left. We went to our own headquarters, and I said to Vatutin: "The offensive is going to begin in this sector, and if Chibisov is going to be the commander, I'm worried about the outcome. Chibisov will not make sure that Kiev is taken. Even though we will be with him, still, he commands the army. He will be giving the orders, and we can't replace him."

"Yes that's true, but what should we do?"

"Let's ask for Moskalenko to be put in charge of this army. Let's raise the question with Stalin—that Chibisov should be relieved and Moskalenko put in." Vatutin agreed. We immediately wrote a coded message. Then Stalin called, and I explained the situation to him over the phone: "How can we rely on this kind of commander?"

Stalin said: "I agree. We will confirm [a new commander]." We immediately called Moskalenko and ordered him to turn his army over to his deputy commander and come at once to Front headquarters. From there we immediately sent him to the 38th Army so that he could begin preparations for liberating Kiev.

I had confidence in Moskalenko. Everyone has shortcomings of one kind or another. Only God is perfect and free of faults, as the saying goes. Everyone has "black marks." I won't talk about Moskalenko's shortcomings at this point. I've already talked about them before. The positive thing about him, however, and something I valued highly, was his inexhaustible energy. His energy manifested itself sometimes quite tempestuously, "laying waste to the crops," like a storm wreaking havoc. But his energy was directed above all toward smashing the enemy. When Moskalenko's army was on the offensive, if there were three days of intensive fighting, he would not eat for the entire three days. In his appearance he was always something like the ferocious wizard of Russian fairy tales—Koshchei Bessmertny [Koshchei the Deathless]:[26] fierce and gaunt, with nothing but skin and bones.

Moskalenko was happy to receive our order. For him it was an honor to liberate the capital of Ukraine. He said: "I will do everything in my power. I am convinced that we will carry out the task and take Kiev. I ask only that you transfer Yepishev to be a member of my Military Council."[27] Yepishev was a member of the Military Council of the 40th Army, which Moskalenko had commanded previously. We called Stalin. Although Stalin didn't know Yepishev, it wasn't a problem for him.

"You can transfer him," he said.

We transferred Yepishev and appointed him a member of the Military Council of the 38th Army. Further preparations were made. Rybalko's tank army was transferred to this area. There was also a tank corps in that sector, a very weak one, but still it was a corps. Its commander was General Kravchenko.[28] In short, the forces we had there were not bad at all.

On the front line, in the sector where our main blow would fall, we concentrated more than three hundred artillery pieces per kilometer, including mortars, for a length of 4 kilometers along the front line. In my opinion, we had never had such a concentration of firepower in a single sector. We were absolutely convinced of our success.

There was a Czechoslovak brigade among the troops of our Front. Recently on the radio, I heard a broadcast celebrating the fighting that had gone on near Sokolovo outside Kharkov. At that location among the troops of our Front, there had been only one Czechoslovak battalion.[29] What good fighters they were! We went to visit them when the battalion was expanded into a brigade. It was not a large brigade as far as numbers went. Its commander was Colonel Svoboda. Vatutin and I had a talk with him and the other officers. He made a good impression on us. Although he was not a party member—he had formerly been an officer of the Czechoslovakian army—he was considered close to the Communists. He knew that a party organization existed in his brigade and that it was doing its work, but he took no measures against it. Svoboda and I were on good terms, and when we carried out our offensive against Kiev his brigade was also ferried across the Dnieper and deployed on the left flank of the beachhead in the area of Vyshgorod,[30] where the Kiev hydroelectric power plant is now located.

So then, everything was ready. An army command post had also been set up. We knew that if Moskalenko set up a command post it would be literally under the enemy's nose. Zhukov had told me once that when the fighting was going on at Stalingrad, and Moskalenko was positioned somewhat north of there, Zhukov had decided to visit him and see how the fighting was proceeding. Zhukov said: "I arrived at the command post at night along a communications trench. We were waiting for an offensive to begin at dawn. It began to grow light. I could see people through my binoculars. 'What in the world is this?' I asked. Moskalenko said, 'Those are Germans.' I said to him: 'What the devil do you think this is? Do you want the Germans to take me prisoner?'" Zhukov was very upset and cursed the army commander. He said that headquarters shouldn't be located right under the nose of the enemy. And it's true that from a certain point of view it's not a good thing, but on the other hand, having the command post so close inspired confidence among the troops. They felt that the commander was right there at their backs. And the main thing was that he directed the entire course of the preparatory bombardment and the offensive itself, not by reports and telephone conversations, but by personally observing everything that was going on.

Vatutin and I arrived to check up on the preparedness of the troops for the offensive. Everything was ready. The offensive would start the next day. We scheduled everything in exact detail. We allowed two hours, as I recall, for the artillery bombardment, which was pretty intensive. On the flanks, of course, the artillery fire was less intensive. We wanted to cut a "window" into which we could send our tank army. The tank corps on the right sector of the beachhead was supposed to move forward to the Irpen River. We warned Moskalenko that we would be coming early the next morning at the beginning of the offensive. When preparations were being made for the offensive, we had been told that a separate dugout had been prepared for us at the army command post so that we would not interfere with the army commander. He would have his own dugout and we would have ours. But Moskalenko overdid it somewhat. He had separate dugouts made, one for Vatutin and one for me. In fact, there was an entire city of dugouts: one for Krasovsky, commander of the Front's air force; one for Varentsov, commander of the Front's artillery; one for Korolkov, commander of the artillery corps from the reserves of the Supreme High Command;[31] and of course one for Moskalenko himself.

We arrived at Novo-Petrovtsy at dawn. The duty officer met us and said we couldn't approach the front line, but that we should walk along a communications trench and keep bent over because the trench wasn't very deep.

We reached the command post. It was well furnished, and we were pleased. Vatutin looked at his watch and said to the adjutant: "Run a little way down the communications trench and set off the standard signal—that is, send up a flare to signal the beginning of the artillery bombardment." The flare went flying up, off to the side as he had ordered, so as not to reveal the position of the command post and not to attract enemy artillery fire to our position. The ground began to shake. Our artillery had opened fire. It was like a symphony of war. For us it was a very joyful and pleasant occasion. Everything was shaking and trembling and shuddering. There was return fire from the enemy, but not intensive. At the height of the artillery bombardment our bombers flew in, in waves, and behind them came Ilyushin attack planes.[32]

I came out of the dugout and saw a group of planes flying toward us. I don't remember how many there were. I saw that they were our Ilyushins. I said: "That's the culminating phase. Soon the infantry will start to move forward." Suddenly the Ilyushins, before reaching our command post, began to fire. Shells and tracer bullets began tearing into the lines where our command post was located and our artillery positions. I thought to myself: "What the devil is this? What's going on?" I looked over to where the air commander was, Krasovsky. He wasn't there! I thought to myself: "Probably the Germans have some captured Ilyushins that they're putting to work. By pretending to be our planes, they've broken through here, flying low and shooting up our artillery." I shouted: "Where the devil is Krasovsky? Call him!" He came up. I said: "Comrade Krasovsky, are those Germans?"

He said: "No, Comrade Khrushchev, those are ours."

"How could they be ours? How do you know that? Maybe the Germans have fixed up some captured planes of ours?"

"No those are ours. They're right on schedule. I have the schedule here. This is the time when our Ilyushins are supposed to arrive and attack enemy positions. And there they are, attacking."

I was indignant. This incident testified to the low level of training in our air force. It would seem simply impossible to confuse our positions with those of the enemy. The Dnieper was just to our left. You couldn't imagine a better landmark. The enemy was to the south, and we were attacking from the north. The forest up to the Dnieper was held by the enemy, and in front of the forest was this small, clear area held by Soviet troops. I don't know how there could be any confusion. But in war, even the unbelievable sometimes becomes believable. Here it was that, by the clear light of day in a position of very distinct landmarks, our attack planes, in spite of everything, were firing at the wrong troops. But that too came to an end. The attack planes flew away. Truly that had been the last wave. Our infantry rose from their trenches and moved forward. German resistance was weak. Everything in their positions was weak. It had simply been mowed down, and our tanks moved forward.

Along the main line of our attack, we had mowed down everything and swept it clean. But the enemy's right flank hadn't come under such intense fire, and there the Germans were still holding on. They decided to make a counterattack against us, striking at the left flank of our advancing troops. Watching from the command post,[33] we saw the Germans rise to their full height and come running toward us. All this was happening very close to us. In that direction, near Vyshgorod, was the Czechoslovak brigade. Vatutin ordered Svoboda to counterattack against the Germans. He carried out the attack and disrupted their offensive. That was the enemy's last effort in the area around that beachhead. The Czechoslovaks were a great help, and our position was stabilized. The offensive continued.

It was a triumphant moment! Fighting began to the west of us, a new stage in our offensive. We had reached the west bank of the Dnieper and were fighting to liberate Kiev, the mother of Russian cities and the capital of Ukraine. Each of us felt a lump in his throat and tears of joy welling up. At last the time had come! Since 1941 we had been thrown so far back, as far back as Stalingrad. Our planes hadn't even been able to fly as far as Kiev. And now we were just outside Kiev, and tomorrow or the next day we would be in Kiev itself. At that point Zhukov arrived as a representative of the Stavka. As I recall, no one else from the Stavka was there. He appeared on the second or third day of the offensive. I remember that a dugout had been prepared for him and me at Novo-Petrovtsy, where we slept at night and where during the day we sat and exchanged opinions and joked. On the third day of the offensive, when we left our dugout at night, the previous front line no longer existed. We had driven the Germans far into the woods, as far as Pushcha Voditsa.[34] Fighting was going on already in some places just outside Kiev. From our beachhead we had struck in the direction of Svyatoshino,[35] that is, to the west of Kiev, so as to prevent the enemy from taking up defensive positions straddling the road from Kiev to Zhitomir.[36]

Grechko[37] became deputy commander of our Front. Before the offensive we had sent him to Mezhigorye so that he could set up a command post for himself and observe the course of the fighting from there and help to organize the troops. I remember the sun was setting, it was a warm evening, but still it was autumn, and we had burkas thrown over our shoulders. Grechko came over and reported to me. He was a man of enormous size, and I had known him a long time and respected him, so I made a joke: "Comrade General, please stand back a little. It's hard for me to see your face when you give your report so close up." He laughed and stepped back a little but continued to give his report. The essence was clear: the enemy had been smashed. But I knew that as well as he. Suddenly, in the distance an explosion and a column of smoke rose from the city. Knowing the location in Kiev I said: "The Germans are blowing up the Bolshevik factory in the western part of the city near Svyatoshino. If they're blowing it up, that means they're on the run."

Before the beginning of our offensive, I had asked the generals and all the commanders of attacking units to assign special groups so that when our troops broke into Kiev they could go immediately to particular buildings—the party's Central Committee building, the headquarters of the Kiev Special Military District, the Council of People's Commissars building, the Academy of Sciences, and other key locations in the city—so that if the Germans hadn't blown them up or burned them down but had placed explosive charges in them, those charges could be defused. That order played its intended role later on. When these explosions began, I turned to the commander of the Front's artillery and said: "Comrade Varentsov, I request that you have the artillery rake Kiev quickly with volley fire." He knew what a patriot of Kiev I was and how much I loved that city, yet here I was ordering him to fire on Kiev. I explained: "Why do I want to do this? If you fire on the city now, that will speed up the German retreat. It will help sow panic among the enemy, and they'll do less harm to Kiev. Our shells won't do much damage. It won't be a big bombardment, but some quick volley fire, and we can easily repair the damage. But if the Germans hold on, they may plant charges and do much worse damage to Kiev." Varentsov gave the order, and the bombardment of Kiev began.

That day ended; the fighting was over for the day. Vatutin and I went back to our dugouts to review matters, to plan out our actions for the next day, and then to rest in the dugouts that had been built for us. The Red Army entered Kiev during the night of November 5–6. This turned out to be an especially triumphant day, right on the eve of the anniversary of the October revolution [that is, November 7]. People now might say that we timed the liberation of Kiev to coincide with our official holiday, and I might agree for the sake of boasting, but to be honest, it was not that way at all. Circumstances simply worked out that way. Nevertheless it was a happy coincidence. We didn't have any official celebration right then of course, but it was pleasant to feel that we were the victors.

Our troops advanced successfully toward Zhitomir. The enemy was broken and offered no particular resistance. The road was wide open, although the forces we had for developing and expanding the offensive were not large. I evaluated it as a great success that we had broken through the German defenses, defeated them, and taken Kiev. We were helped by the fact that we had tried to make an offensive from the Bukrin beachhead to the south of Kiev. We had tried that twice, and evidently the enemy had concentrated his troops in that area and didn't notice our redeployment, when we switched the offensive to the north, to Staro-Petrovtsy and Novo-Petrovtsy, that is, the Lyutezh beachhead. The Germans' main forces remained around the Bukrin beachhead, where they expected our offensive to continue. Instead we struck from the north quite suddenly. The Germans had not been expecting an attack there, and the forces they had there were not large. As they were trying to regroup, we smashed the enemy forces in that area and reached the road from Kiev to Zhitomir and cut the path of retreat for the enemy forces still in Kiev, so that the Germans were forced to leave the city and head toward Belaya Tserkov.[38]

Thus our unsuccessful attempts at an offensive from the Bukrin beachhead played a positive role by misleading the enemy. That helped us defeat the Germans with less effort from a different direction. Early on the morning of November 6 I sent my chauffeur, [Aleksandr] Zhuravlev, into Kiev. For many years he drove the vehicles I rode in, literally until the last day of my activity as first secretary of the party's Central Committee, right up until my retirement. All together, it was probably thirty-two or thirty-three years that I rode with him. So this was the driver—Uncle Sasha, as my children called him—who I sent. I said to him: "Go into Kiev and report back on the best way to get into the city." Our troops were already in Kiev, and so the path was clear. He took the old familiar road that we used to travel before the war, going from the dacha to the city. He quickly returned and said that Kiev was absolutely clear of the enemy, and in general there was no one around; the place was empty; hardly anyone was visible on the streets.

I immediately went into the city together with representatives of the Ukrainian intelligentsia, Bazhan[39] and others. There are simply no words to describe the joy and emotion that overcame me as I made that trip. We passed through the suburbs, then there we were on the Kreshchatik, Kiev's main avenue. I went up the steps to the building that had housed the Council of People's Commissars and looked it over. On the outside it was intact. The Central Committee building had also not been destroyed. We looked at other buildings, such as the Academy of Sciences and the theaters.

From their outward appearance everything was intact. Then we went to the building that had housed the headquarters of the Kiev Special Military District. That building had been constructed just before the war. After the war that's where the Central Committee of the CP(B)U was located, and that's still its location. The Bolshevik factory had been badly damaged, and the Kreshchatik was in ruins. When we arrived at Bogdan Khmelnitsky Square, some buildings were still burning.

The city made an eerie impression. It had once been such a large, noisy, cheerful southern city, and suddenly there was no one on the streets! You heard only your own footsteps when you walked down the Kreshchatik. Then we turned up Lenin Street. You could hear the echoes in the empty city. Or maybe we merely got that impression from the tremendous pressure and tension. At any rate it was a very painful impression. Gradually people began to appear. It was as though they rose out of the earth. From the Kreshchatik we went in the direction of the Opera Theater along Lenin Street (its old name was Fundukleyevskaya Street). We walked along, talked, and exchanged impressions. Suddenly we heard someone crying hysterically. A young man was running toward us. I don't know what state of mind he was in. I remember only that he kept repeating: "I'm the only Jew in Kiev still alive."

I tried to calm him down as much as I could. I asked him: "What else can you tell us?" But he just kept repeating the same thing. I saw that he was in an abnormal state of mind, close to psychological derangement.

I asked him: "But how did you survive?"

He said: "My wife is Ukrainian. She worked at a dining hall, and she kept me hidden in the attic. I spent this whole time sitting in the attic. She fed me and saved my life. If I had gone out in the city, they would have grabbed me as a Jew and destroyed me right then and there."

A man with a gray beard, obviously no longer young, came along. He was carrying a workman's shoulder bag. When I had worked at a factory, I used to bring my breakfast and lunch to work in that same kind of bag. He threw himself on my neck, began to hug me and kiss me. It was a very touching moment. Some photographer managed to take a picture of it, and later that photograph found its way into many magazines and newspapers.

We rejoiced and celebrated our victory, the liberation of our native Kiev. Our troops continued their offensive, while my colleagues and I took up the urgent task of restoring production and reestablishing government and party bodies, so that normal work could be resumed. Above all, grain procurement had to be organized. The entire country needed grain. The people were starving. Maximum effort had to be made to obtain as much grain as possible. In 1943 there was a very good harvest in Ukraine. There had been a snowy winter and a normal amount of precipitation during the summer; therefore the harvest was good. It was necessary to organize the harvesting and procurement of grain as quickly as possible to provide the country with the relief it so badly needed.

I received reports during this time about the special groups that I had ordered to be organized during the taking of Kiev. Each group had a specific address and its own assignment, which building to pay attention to, to see to it that explosives were defused and fires put out. For example in the Council of People's Commissar's building, where it seems the Germans had a hospital, they set fire to the straw as they were leaving, but our people broke into the building quickly and put out the fire. Only some traces remained. The parquet floor was burned in some areas. The same fate befell the new headquarters building of the KOVO.⁴⁰ Our people saved many buildings at that time because they had been assigned to specific objectives in advance, and they immediately went there before the fires spread too far. The Opera Theater had not been touched. I went into it, although I was warned that it might be booby-trapped. (The enemy did play such tricks on us.) I was drawn to that place. It turned out to be free of booby traps. The special box for government officials was still there, along with the same furniture, the same wallpaper on the walls, and in general everything remained as it had been.

Later, after the taking of Kiev, Moskalenko told me the following story about how he and his troops entered the city: "I entered Kiev at night with our tanks. I walked in front of the tanks, lighting their way with a flashlight, and led them into Kiev." He asked me not to let Stalin know about this. At that time an order had been issued strictly warning generals not to risk their lives for no reason and not to expose themselves to enemy fire. Of course there was no necessity for such behavior; it was simply a kind of heroism bordering on madness. But then, that was Moskalenko! You could expect anything from Moskalenko. I gave him my word that I wouldn't tell Stalin, because I knew that Stalin would condemn him and might even punish him harshly as an example for violating an order. And after all, why should I say anything about it? The city had been taken, Moskalenko had led the tanks into the city and lived through it, and victors are not judged.

That is how Kiev was taken. I drew up a short memorandum on how the fighting had proceeded and how stoutly and steadfastly our troops had fought. I gave special mention to the artillery troops. The artillery bombardment preceding the offensive had made a very strong impression on me then. It certainly was the most powerful barrage I had seen since the beginning of the war. The infantry had also performed well, you couldn't deny it, and the tank troops had fought gloriously, but the work of the artillery particularly impressed itself on my memory. That's why I singled out the artillery. I sent this memorandum to Moscow, simply wishing to cheer up Stalin. I was happy and I wanted him to be happy that we had taken Kiev by November 7. But I was surprised when a day or two later I picked up our central and most important newspaper and saw that my memo had been published in full in *Pravda*.

Later, when I arrived in Moscow, Stalin gave me something like a fatherly lecture: "Here you sent a coded message, top secret, and it ended up being published."

I said: "Comrade Stalin, who gave you the report that the message was coded? There was no code at all. I read the message over the phone. We sent it from Kiev by the special government phone line. Poskrebyshev [Stalin's secretary] wrote it down and reported it to you."

Stalin asked Poskrebyshev, who confirmed that it was so: "Yes, yes, Comrade Stalin." It seemed to me that Stalin felt rather awkward. He wanted to needle me for supposedly making a secret of things that had nothing secret about them, and instead his attempt to rebuke me ended up making him look foolish.

1. This was at the end of September 1943.

2. Pereyaslav (or Pereyaslav-Khmelnitsky) is about 80 kilometers southeast of Kiev. [SS] It was liberated on September 22, 1943.

3. In 1648 the Cossack leader (Hetman) Bogdan Khmelnitsky led a peasant uprising against Polish rule in Ukraine, and the next year the first independent Ukrainian state, the Hetmanate, was proclaimed. A series of defeats by the Polish army subsequently forced Khmelnitsky to turn to Moscow for protection. The Treaty of Pereyaslav was concluded in 1654. Although Ukraine was thereby incorporated into the Russian empire, Ukraine was allowed a certain autonomy for more than a century. However, this autonomy was whittled away and finally abolished in 1775, when serfdom was imposed on Ukraine. Soviet historiography regarded the union of Ukraine with Russia as "progressive" from a long-term perspective because it facilitated the inclusion of Ukraine in the Soviet Union. [SS]

4. Brigade Commander N. F. Vatutin was chief of staff of the Kiev Special Military District from November 1938 to September 1939. See Biographies.

5. Lieutenant General A. A. Vlasov, commanding the Second Shock Army of the Volkhov Front, after completion of the Lyubansk operation that

aimed to break through the blockade of Leningrad, did not manage to extricate his army from German encirclement. A partial breakout by formations of this army was organized in June 1942 by the reappointed commander, Volkhov Front Army General K. A. Meretskov (after the previous commander, Lieutenant General M. S. Khozin, had "overlooked" the enemy encirclement of the Second Shock Army) and the representative of the Stavka and Chief of the General Staff Colonel General A. M. Vasilevsky. Meretskov and Vasilevsky, from outside the encirclement, widened the corridor through the ring that had been pushed through by the 59th and 52nd Armies (commanded by Major General I. T. Korovnikov and Lieutenant General V. F. Yakovlev, respectively). However, many soldiers of the Second Shock Army were taken captive by the Germans, while Vlasov voluntarily gave himself up to the enemy. Subsequently he set about organizing the Russian Liberation Army to fight against the Red Army, although only in 1944 did Berlin gave Vlasov official permission to fight. See Biographies.

6. The associate of Vlasov to whom Khrushchev refers is evidently G. N. Zhilenkov, who had been secretary of the Rostokinsky district party committee. When war broke out, he became an

army commissar and was captured in autumn 1941. He joined Vlasov's Committee for the Liberation of the Peoples of Russia and was made head of its propaganda section. He also served as an intermediary between the Vlasovite movement and the German authorities. He was hanged with Vlasov. See Catherine Andreyev, *Vlasov and the Russian Liberation Movement: Soviet Reality and Émigré Theories* (Cambridge and New York: Cambridge University Press, 1987), 84. [SS]

7. Yasha is a diminutive form of Yakov. [SS] On being taken prisoner, Stalin's son Yakov I. Dzhugashvili was put in the Nazi concentration camp of Hammelburg. From there he was taken to the Lübeck camp for Polish prisoners of war and finally ended up in Sachsenhausen, where he was killed, allegedly while attempting to escape. Yakov was survived by his widow Yu. I. Meltser, together with his daughter Galina and his son (by another wife) Yevgeny.

8. During the battle for Moscow, from October 1941 to March 1942, Vlasov commanded the Twentieth Army.

9. The region to which Khrushchev refers is that of the Valdai Hills, which straddle the border between Tver and Novgorod provinces, 300–400 kilometers northwest of Moscow. This Valdai is not to be confused with another place called Valdai in the Republic of Karelia. [SS]

10. Air Force Lieutenant General N. S. Skripko was deputy commander of Strategic Air Forces.

11. Dnipro is the Ukrainian form of Dnieper. [GS] "The Song of the Dnieper" was composed in 1942, with words by Yevgeny Aronovich Dolmatovsky and music by M. G. Fradkin.

12. Rzhishchev is on the west bank of the Dnieper, about 60 kilometers southeast of Kiev. [SS]

13. Mezhigorye is a village on the west bank of the Dnieper beyond Vyshgorod, north of Kiev. From October 1942 to October 1943 Colonel General K. S. Moskalenko was in command of the 40th Army, succeeded by Lieutenant General F. F. Zhmachenko, who was in command from October 1943 to May 1945. Lieutenant General N. E. Chibisov commanded the 38th Army from August 1942 to October 1943.

14. Lieutenant General P. S. Rybalko commanded the Third Guards Tank Army from May 1943 to May 1945.

15. The Bukrin bridgehead (named after a local village [SS]) on the west bank of the Dnieper River, 80 kilometers to the southeast of Kiev, was created on September 23, 1943.

16. Fighting continued there until November 3, 1943.

17. The villages of Novo-Petrovtsy and Staro-Petrovtsy are situated close to each other on the high west bank of the Dnieper.

18. Khrushchev is referring to the Lyutezh bridgehead, 30 kilometers north of Kiev, which was created on September 26, 1943.

19. The Irpen River is a west-bank tributary of the Dnieper, which it enters about 30 kilometers north of Kiev. [SS]

20. Lieutenant General N. P. Pukhov commanded the Thirteenth Army from January 1942 to May 1945. Lieutenant General I. D. Chernyakhovsky commanded the 60th Army from July 1942 to April 1944.

21. At that time Chernyakhovsky was thirty-seven years old.

22. This took place at the end of August and the beginning of September 1941, when the Fifth Army fell into encirclement at the mouth of the Desna River (where it enters the Dnieper just north of Kiev [SS]).

23. The Zaporozhian Cossacks were members of a Cossack community established in 1540 by Prince Dmitry Vyshnevetsky (ruler of the Grand Duchy of Lithuania, later included in Ukraine) on Hortytsa Island in the Dnieper, where the city of Zaporozhye now stands. The Cossacks lived an austere life in a military camp without women or families, which explains why they went to live in a monastery when they grew old. [SS]

24. The capital of the Ukrainian SSR was moved from Kharkov to Kiev in 1934. [SS]

25. S. V. Kosior, G. I. Petrovsky, P. P. Postyshev, M. A. Burmistenko, L. P. Korniyets. See Biographies.

26. Koshchei the Deathless is a powerful wizard or demigod in Russian mythology. He holds death at bay by keeping his soul hidden inside an egg, which is inside a duck, which is inside a hare, which is inside an iron chest, which is buried under a green oak tree on the island of Bujan on the wide ocean. Though sometimes obliterated by powerful forces, his dry bony body reconstitutes itself over and again so long as the soul-bearing egg is safe. His undoing is Marena, the goddess of death, who coaxes out of him the location of his soul, enabling her son or husband to crush the egg. At the moment of destruction, a cleansing fire from the egg envelops the Earth, wiping it clean of all its old evil. [SS]

27. A. A. Yepishev became the first member of the Military Council of the 38th Army in October 1943. See Biographies.

28. The Fifth Guards Tank Corps, commanded by Lieutenant General A. G. Kravchenko.

29. Sokolovo is about 40 kilometers south of Kharkov on the Mzha River, a west-bank tributary of the Seversky Donets River. [AH] Colonel L. Svoboda was in command of this battalion (later a brigade) from February 1942. See Biographies.

30. Vyshgorod is about 15 kilometers north of Kiev on the Dnieper River. [AH]

31. Commander of the Second Air Army Air Force Lieutenant General S. A. Krasovsky, Commander of Artillery of the First Ukrainian Front Lieutenant General of Artillery S. S. Varentsov,

Commander of the Seventh Artillery Break-through Corps from the Stavka Reserve Major General of Artillery P. M. Korolkov.

32. The Ilyushin aircraft design bureau was established in Moscow in 1932. Named in honor of the aircraft designer Sergei V. Ilyushin (1894–1977), it remains one of the leading Russian design bureaus for both military and civilian airplanes. [SS]

33. The command post was in Novo-Petrovtsy.

34. Pushcha Voditsa is about 10 kilometers southwest of Vyshgorod. [AH]

35. Svyatoshino is near the western edge of the city of Kiev. [AH]

36. Zhitomir is about 130 kilometers west of Kiev. [SS]

37. Lieutenant General A. A. Grechko took up the post of deputy commander of the First Ukrainian Front in October 1943. See Biographies.

38. Belaya Tserkov (White Church; in Ukrainian Bila Tserkva) is about 80 kilometers south of Kiev. [SS]

39. N. P. Bazhan was at that time editor of the newspaper *Za Radiansku Ukrainu* (For Soviet Ukraine). Later he was appointed deputy chairman of the Council of Ministers of the Ukrainian SSR. See Biographies.

40. KOVO stands for the Kiev Special Military District.

## WE LIBERATE UKRAINE

Around this time [fall 1943] our fronts were given new names: the First, Second, Third, and Fourth Ukrainian Fronts. (Also, there were either three or four Belorussian fronts; I don't remember exactly now.)[1] Our Front became the First Ukrainian Front. Konev's front became the Second Ukrainian Front; before that it had been called the Steppe Front. Fighting farther south was the Third Ukrainian Front, and southernmost was the Fourth Ukrainian Front. The latter was commanded by Tolbukhin, and the commander of the Third Ukrainian Front was Malinovsky.[2] Not long before we liberated Kiev, Dnepropetrovsk had also been liberated.[3] Our troops were successfully advancing westward. The Donbas was also liberated. When the fighting for the Donbas was under way, I made a special trip there. I remember that a battle was going on for Makeyevka.[4] I arrived when the Second Guards Army was carrying out an offensive. Previously its commander had been General Kreizer. He had been Malinovsky's deputy commander and later became the commander of this army.[5] I had known Kreizer a long time and considered him a worthy commander. By nationality he was Jewish. As early as 1941 he had been awarded the title Hero of the Soviet Union. He made a very good impression on me. After the war he commanded a number of important military districts. Today I don't know where he is or what post he holds.

When I reached the outskirts of Makeyevka, the fighting was still going on. The Germans were bombarding the outlying district where I arrived, but they couldn't hold their positions. Our troops moved forward, and I entered Makeyevka along with them.[6] I was in a hurry to enter Makeyevka because I wondered what condition the metallurgical plants and coal mines would be in. What I saw was a very sad sight. First, when we retreated we had blown things up; and then the Germans retreated and they also blew up everything they could. It was such a sad sight to see—nothing but ruins. We had to think about restoring our ruined industries, above all the coal mines. I don't remember whether it was right at that time or a little later that my old and dear friend Yegor Trofimovich Abakumov arrived. We had known each other since 1912, when we worked together at Mine No. 31—the property of some French company. He began pleading with me to help get people demobilized from the army to work in the mines. It turned out that a great many miners and other workers were needed.

Tolbukhin, who was commanding the army that was on the offensive there, had drafted the workers into the Red Army. I immediately sent a coded message to Stalin asking that miners and metalworkers not be called up. Coal and metal would be needed now, just as before, because, after all, the war was still on. Without a labor force we couldn't provide the country with coal and metal. Later I was summoned to Moscow in connection with this telegram. Stalin asked me: "What forces are we going to have to do the fighting? How are we going to reinforce our units?"

I answered: "I understand. Let's mobilize the collective farmers for service in the army. We need skilled workers here [in these industries]. If we draft collective farmers to work in the plants and mines, it will be very difficult to train them quickly for industrial production, especially in the metallurgical field."

He said: "Well, all right. The people that Tolbukhin has already drafted—I won't give them back to you, but I will send him an order not to draft any more miners and metalworkers." Well, that suited me! At least it was a small victory.

At the same time Stalin said to me: "It seems that you should focus your attention now on party work and the work of reestablishing government institutions in the republic, in its provinces and districts. The main thing now is crops, grain, sugar, coal, and metal. You will remain a member of the Military Council of the First Ukrainian Front, as you were, and from time to time you can visit the front lines, but your main efforts and your main energy should be devoted to the reconstruction of the republic."

I said, "All right." When I arrived back in Kiev from Moscow, I told Vatutin about this decision. Vatutin expressed his regrets. He and I were used to working together, and we respected each other. I too felt sorry about leaving Vatutin.

After that I would make visits from Kiev to the Front as a guest, to put it bluntly. I don't really like using the word "guest," because I was still a member of the Military Council and had the authority corresponding to that position, but I could no longer be involved in any systematic way with the problems of the Front because I had to concern myself with the problems of the Central Committee of the CP(B)U and of the Council of Ministers of Ukraine. Still, I did go out to the front lines fairly often.

I want to be understood as a human being. After our troops reached the Dnieper a satisfying phase began. Previously we had fled [from our borders] back to the Dnieper, retreating, and now we had placed the enemy in the same kind of position. It was a bitter thing to retreat and all the more pleasant to attack. Although we did suffer losses, we experienced joy and pride in the USSR, in our party, in the ideas of Lenin, and in everything our people had done in building this powerful country. Then suddenly, at a time like that, I was deprived of the possibility of actively participating in the further offensive against the enemy.

But I understood that while it was a good thing to fight and defeat the enemy, the home front also needed to be organized and the army needed to be supplied, not only with the means by which the troops were literally nourished, that is, the food they ate, but also with ammunition, equipment, and so forth. In this matter Ukraine needed to make its own weighty contribution. We had cadres and we had factories. Although they were ruined and destroyed, it is easier to restore ruined factories than to build new ones. We undertook this task. We restored the mines, the metallurgical plants, and the factories.

Winter set in early in 1943. Our troops either had reached the outskirts of Zhitomir or had even entered that city. Just then the enemy brought up troops from the west, including from Italy, and forced us to retreat from Zhitomir. We had relatively few forces there. A cavalry corps had attacked Zhitomir, but it was only the vanguard of our forces.[7] Naturally when it encountered tanks it couldn't hold its positions. The Germans began to pursue our troops, who withdrew to Kiev. The Germans hoped to drive us into the Dnieper. I remember at that point Anastas Ivanovich Mikoyan visited us and spent a day or two. He came to organize grain procurement. He told me: "Stalin sent me for grain. Let's get busy with that job." While we were investigating the possibilities for obtaining grain (and we had sent people out into the local areas for that purpose even before Mikoyan arrived), the Germans began to threaten Kiev again. Residents who had already returned to Kiev did not wish to fall into their clutches again. They began to flee the city, but this danger passed quickly. Our troops coped with the situation and contained the enemy. So the Germans did not succeed in driving us out of Kiev a second time.

Anastas Ivanovich asked me to show him the area from which our troops had liberated Kiev. I said to him: "Let's go there. It will take about thirty-five minutes." We made the trip. I showed him where the enemy troops had been deployed, where our troops had been, along with our artillery positions, and our dugouts.

He went into the command post, looked around, and asked: "Where did you say the enemy was?"

"Right over there."

"Well, that was very close."

"Yes, we could not only sense the enemy's presence nearby but could even see them." Now Mikoyan had a more concrete idea of how we had carried out the offensive at Kiev. Then we went back to the road. We usually didn't go off the roads much because we didn't want to hit some stupid mine. As we came up to the Pushcha Voditsa forest, Mikoyan glanced over at an area where some newly grown pine trees had stood, but they had literally been mowed down. I said: "Our artillery swept all this area clean." It was as though people had come there with axes and chopped down all the trees. Everything was either reduced to splinters or torn out by the roots. I told him: "There were 307 artillery pieces per kilometer. Can you imagine what a slaughterhouse it was? It pulverized and tore apart everything living or growing here. Everything was destroyed."

Mikoyan left us and went to Poltava, because Poltava was an important grain-growing region.[8] The western part of Ukraine, on the other hand, was still held by the enemy. Fighting was still going on there, and there was no question of obtaining grain from that region. Questions there were being decided by machine guns, artillery, and planes. But on the left bank of the Dnieper [that is, to the east of the Dnieper], it was already possible to obtain grain—although it's true that on the lower reaches of the Dnieper, in the Kherson area, Tolbukhin had still not crossed the river.[9]

That's the kind of situation that had shaped up at the end of 1943. All our front-line fighters and all our patriots on the home front were tasting the joy of victory, the emancipation of our native land. There was no longer any question of whether we would reach Berlin. We were absolutely sure that we would not only rout out the enemy but would completely defeat him. The military men were saying seriously: "I want to be commandant of Berlin." There were a fairly large number of candidates for this position, and everyone who sought that title was worthy of it. They had earned that title through suffering and pain.

Some military men might say that Khrushchev is using nonmilitary terminology. It's true that I'm not a military man, and I use the language of the people. It might be said that the concept of earning something through suffering is not appropriate. But I think that all our people, both military and nonmilitary, suffered in the war, and therefore this phrase is appropriate. I very much liked Zhukov's candor in such matters. When he and I were at the front lines together, on one or another occasion, and when he ended up in a dangerous situation, he would get very angry at those who placed him in that situation. He would curse and say: "I'm scared! Christ knows, you can get killed, you know. The bastards can kill you, and I'm scared. I don't want them to kill me." I don't see anything humiliating or degrading for such a thoroughly military man as Zhukov to talk like that. This is a basic human feeling. It's one thing to give in to fear and another thing to correctly assess a dangerous situation and refuse to do what Chapayev[10] used to say: "To stick my foolish forehead in front of a foolish enemy bullet." People have different ideas about these things. That's why I say that the war brought suffering to all our people. The person who was fighting suffered, and so did the person who was not fighting. That's why, when we began to move forward, we were happy because we could see that the war's end was near, that the enemy was going to be defeated, that our country would be freed from the incursions of this fascist plague, and that our victory was assured.

Another incident from the military operations at that time has stuck in my memory. After enemy resistance to the west of Kiev was broken, heavy fighting broke out to the southwest of Kiev, northwest of Uman.[11] This happened along the juncture between two Fronts: the First Ukrainian and the Steppe Front (or Second Ukrainian Front). The commander of the last-named Front was Ivan Stepanovich Konev.[12] As a result of the fighting there a fairly large German group had been surrounded. It had established an all-round defense and was stubbornly resisting. The Stavka assigned our two Fronts, the First and Second Ukrainian, to destroy this group and not let the Germans break out to the west. I remember Vatutin saying to me then that this was an assignment of great responsibility and that he was getting ready to travel out to be with the troops. I said: "I'm going with you."

We made the trip. There was a big thaw going on and the roads were bad, but we also encountered snowdrifts here and there. There were some days when the old snow was melting and new snow was falling. We flew to Belaya Tserkov and from there made our way with difficulty to the location of our troops who were holding the enemy group in a "pocket." Specifically we were heading in the direction of a tank army then commanded by General Kravchenko.[13] I've spoken about him before. At Kiev he commanded a tank corps that did not have a full complement and later received a higher appointment; he was given an entire tank army. We reached the headquarters of the tank army with difficulty and met with Kravchenko there. The member of his Military Council was Tumanyan,[14] who I later found out was a relative of Mikoyan's wife. I had not known Tumanyan before that. He made a good impression on me.

Stubborn fighting developed. The enemy desperately defended himself and kept trying to break out to the west. In the end in spite of everything some elements of the surrounded group did succeed in breaking out. They came at us in a wave. They were mowed down as much as possible by every means of destruction that we had, but a certain percentage of them broke through. Many civilians also turned out to be trapped in this encirclement— our own Soviet people, men and women of various ages. As the Germans were retreating, they took Ukrainians with them, driving them westward. Later we watched as these exhausted people made their way back through snowstorms and in the face of heavy winds, back toward the east from which they had been taken. It was a ghastly scene, which remains vivid in my memory.

Stalin was furious that the enemy group had not been entirely destroyed. The way in which a report would be presented to Stalin was very important; one had to know how to report these things. By nature Vatutin was very modest and conscientious. He was unable to embellish things or shift the blame onto others to protect himself or to show himself in a better light by belittling others. Everyone knew about these decent qualities of Vatutin's, and I liked this about him very much. But if a person had such good qualities, it was not always the best accompaniment for a successful career. Everyone would praise him and honor him in words, but they didn't always follow his good example. And it turned out that Stalin got into a rage against Vatutin.

It was almost as though Vatutin was to blame for the fact that the entire group of Germans was not destroyed. And this had its effect on Vatutin's later career. He suffered an insult that is particularly painful to a military man. Konev was awarded the rank of marshal for his success at Korsun-Shevchenkovsky [that is, in the battle of the Korsun salient].[15] But Vatutin was left only with the rank of army general, and he died with that rank. I never spoke with Vatutin on the subject. I considered it unnecessary. It would have been like pouring salt on an open wound, and so I never raised the question of why Vatutin was passed over when higher military ranks were given out. We have only now returned to this question, and our government has posthumously awarded Vatutin the title Hero of the Soviet Union.[16]

The defeat of the German group made a great impression. The entire world press wrote about it. I remember our own correspondents and foreign correspondents coming to the area. They wanted to see the results of this German group's defeat. The body of a German colonel-general was found among the dead. The Western correspondents wrote a great deal about it then, stressing the fact that when this general's body was found there was a gold ring on his finger. The correspondents stressed in particular that even a gold ring had remained untouched! This was beyond their comprehension. After all, marauders were common in all the armies of the world. For example, at Stalingrad the corpses of German soldiers were stripped bare. And of course it wasn't the wolves that did it! If their trousers had been removed, it was clear who had done it—marauders. Was this the work of civilians or military people? I think, unfortunately, both categories were capable of such behavior.

The defeat of this large German group was completed, although it required much persistence on the part of our troops and a great deal of time. We returned to Kiev. I don't remember exactly now, perhaps I returned to Kiev and Vatutin went to the Front headquarters, which was located to the west, probably the latter because I remember well that I returned to Kiev alone. I traveled through Belaya Tserkov but could go no farther because from there halfway to Kiev the road was totally blocked by snowdrifts. There was a heavy snowfall, and I couldn't make my way any farther. I decided to spend the night in the nearest village and stopped at the first peasant hut that I came to. I knocked on the door. It was already late at night. A woman's voice answered and the door was opened. I went in with the comrades who were accompanying me and said I'd like to stay in the hut until morning. The woman was alone with a little child, a son of about eight years old.

This peasant hut was more poorly kept up than is usual in Ukrainian huts. Usually Ukrainian peasant homes are very clean, spick and span. This house was below the average level of cleanliness and tidiness of that area. I said: "Would you allow us to spend the night?"

She said: "Please. *Bud' laska* (Please do)." She spoke only in Ukrainian. [Literally the expression means "Be so kind."] I didn't introduce myself or tell her my name because we had just liberated this area and we still didn't know what the people there were like. As far as she knew, some military man in a general's uniform had come into her home, and she accepted me as such, as a military man. We had something to eat (we had our own rations), and we treated her as well.

Then she began to talk and told me something I hadn't known before. When the German offensive had come through here in 1941, a Red Army man found himself a place to live there in the village with them. When there were many Soviet troops still in the village, he took his meals with the rest of the military men, but when the Soviet troops retreated he remained, and everyone found out that he was a Bandera supporter, a nationalist. He became the village commandant under the Germans and told people that he had undergone some training in the West, where he and others had been students, trained both by Germans and by Ukrainian Bandera supporters. He had been brought by plane and dropped by parachute much earlier than the Soviet troops who retreated from this village. For a while he hid in a potato field.

She also told about life under enemy rule, but her accounts of daily life were not especially interesting. What was of interest to me was the fact that the Germans had made advance preparations for all this. We had known earlier that they had come to an understanding with the Bandera supporters. Bandera's people were a source of supply of German agents. They provided people who could be dropped by parachute in the rear of our forces, and they determined in advance who would become commandant in which village. This so-called Red Army man waited until the German troops entered the village. Then he made his appearance (that's how things happened), stated that the village commandant was already in place, and began to carry out his duties.

This peasant woman told us: "He was a very foul man." I had no doubt that he was pretty foul. She said they could tell by his accent that he was from Western Ukraine: "He didn't talk like us Kievan Ukrainians." In short, he was a man who had been sent in from the ranks of Bandera's agents who had become servants of Hitler. Bandera at that time believed that Hitler would "liberate" Ukraine and that a Ukrainian national government would be established. Ukraine would become independent of Moscow. But Hitler put an end to those dreams. He showed them what kind of an independent Ukraine they would have! In fact the Nazis didn't allow any Ukrainian government bodies to be established; instead they appointed their own commandants and bailiffs.

After we liberated Kiev the nationalists began to act in opposition to the Nazis. This shows that Hitler was so convinced of his victory that he thought he had no need for local satellites or allies of any kind, even if they were nationalists who were confirmed enemies of the socialist system. He thought that everything would be decided by the force of German arms, and therefore everything was for the Germans. Everything should be subordinated to the Germans, including the Ukrainian nationalists. They should know their place, and the fascist leadership would decide the fate of Ukraine.

The Central Committee of the CP(B)U and the government of the Ukrainian SSR were located at that time in Kharkov. As soon as we had liberated Kharkov, we set about the task of reestablishing Soviet government and party bodies. The necessary buildings were taken over, and technical personnel were brought in temporarily to flesh out the Central Committee and the Council of People's Commissars of Ukraine. Work was begun on getting the everyday functioning of the republic back in order. I had to travel around a lot then. Beginning in fall 1943 I was constantly going back and forth between Kharkov and Kiev. After a little while I raised the question with Moscow and Stalin of transferring the Ukrainian government to Kiev. I would also feel better about being closer to the front lines, because from time to time I could travel out to Front headquarters to inform myself of the situation and find out how military matters were proceeding. So it was also more convenient for me.

I forget now what month it was, but we did make the transfer to Kiev. Some people in Kiev still didn't feel very good about the situation. The Germans often flew over the city, especially reconnaissance planes. They didn't bomb Kiev much. It was only the Darnitsa railroad station that was bombed very heavily. The Germans had left many spies behind, and when the First Polish Corps[17] was being sent across the Dnieper [to the west bank] in special troop trains they were bombed heavily. Instances when the Germans bombed the rest of the city were more rare. Usually they flew over Kiev to Darnitsa. Darnitsa is on the east bank of the Dnieper across from Kiev. The explosions and flames from there lit up the Kiev Monastery of the Caves. The enemy planes flying over Kiev wore on the nerves of the population. The people who worked in the party's Central Committee and at the Council of People's Commissars of course felt the same way.

I remember some military men coming to me all of a sudden and reporting: "An underground command post needs to be built in Kiev."

I didn't understand them and said: "Why do we need an underground command post now, when the front lines have moved far to the west and we're sure the enemy won't be back in Kiev?"

They answered: "There's an order. Let's choose an appropriate site." They began hashing things over. There were many places in Kiev you could choose, because the city is hilly, with many suitable places for the construction of underground installations. At first I thought the command post should be located on the banks of the Dnieper. Then I abandoned that idea because of the shifting and unstable ground. If we began digging tunnels there, the ground might shift. Besides, we were told that the underground shelter should have an exit leading into a building of good quality. The decision was made to locate the underground post close to the building of the former headquarters of the Kiev Special Military District. The Central Committee of the CP(B)U later had its offices there. Some sort of structure was built. I would say it was insufficiently equipped. Later I found out that this was Stalin's undertaking. After our troops had liberated Kiev, he began, as it were, looking at himself in the mirror to see how he might appear as commander of the liberating troops, and so forth. He decided to make a trip out to be closer to the troops. For that he needed a place for his headquarters, and he decided to locate it in Kiev.

This was a very foolish undertaking. I don't know why he thought he had to do this. It was not required for the convenience of the command staff. If a place needed to be found from the angle that Stalin was thinking about, the command post should have been established much farther west. In general this undertaking was thought up after the usual dinner, abundantly provided for, with bottles of the Georgian wines Tsinandali and Napareuli, and there was no good sense to any of it. I knew that Stalin really had no great desire to visit the front lines. The undertaking was pointless, and Stalin of course never showed up there. During the time when I was first secretary of the Central Committee of the CP(B)U, Stalin never visited Ukraine at all. He traveled through Ukraine only when he was on his way to vacation in Sochi,[18] and once when he took his vacation in the Crimea he also traveled through Ukraine. Besides that, the meeting with Roosevelt and Churchill was held in Yalta [also in the Crimea], and on that occasion he traveled through Kharkov (where I met him). Of course during the Civil War he had been in Ukraine when he was a member of the Military Council of the Southwestern Front, whose commander then was Yegorov.[19]

As for the command post, we later had to fill it in because we were afraid the soil would give way. There is that danger in Kiev. As I said, it is a hilly region. We were afraid that if the soil gave way, nearby buildings could be destroyed, including the Central Committee building and the Ivan Franko

Theater.²⁰ Besides, this underground post had served its purpose before it was eliminated. People had taken shelter there from enemy air raids.

I forget the exact dates, but it was probably in March (I am orienting myself by the thaw; there was an incredible thaw with the accompanying impassability of roads) when our troops undertook the next stage of their powerful offensive and again drove the Germans out of the positions they were holding. The enemy could not withstand the pressure and had to flee, leaving behind enormous baggage trains of military equipment and also many people who the Germans had been dragging along with them. Some of these were people who had committed crimes against the Ukrainian people and were fleeing with the Germans of their own accord; others were being forcibly evacuated westward. It was difficult for us to tell who was guilty and who was not, because in such cases even if people were fleeing to save their own skins, they would nevertheless conceal themselves behind the verbal claim that they had been dragooned, that the Germans had rounded them up and ordered them to leave, and so on.

Suddenly it was reported to me that among the people found in wagon trains abandoned by the Germans was Gmyrya, the celebrated bass singer, a man with a marvelous voice.²¹ I have already mentioned that during the German occupation he had remained in Kharkov. Later he explained that someone close to him had been sick. It's very difficult to determine the truth even now. And I don't even want to try, because all those who stayed behind [under German occupation] justified their behavior in the same way: saying that his wife was sick or his father or mother, and he couldn't abandon whoever it was, and so forth. In short I was told that Gmyrya had been found in a German wagon train with all his goods and possessions. I ordered him brought to Kiev immediately, and he was brought there.

Then I had a special phone conversation with Stalin on this subject because I couldn't decide it on my own. After all, Gmyrya was a very big name! When the Germans took Kharkov we received a report (it may be that the enemy broadcast it over the radio) that Gmyrya had sung in a concert hall to an audience of officers of the German army. Possibly that didn't really happen; the Germans may have been trying to make propaganda by claiming that a famous Ukrainian singer had performed for German officers. I told Stalin that we needed to decide what our attitude toward Gmyrya should be. He was a very fine singer. I didn't know his biography, but it seems to me he graduated from the conservatory in 1939. I said: "We would like to have him remain as part of the Kiev opera company. But we can expect great objections from Ivan Sergeyevich Patorzhinsky."²² Stalin had strong sympathies for Patorzhinsky, and he deserved respect. Patorzhinsky was a good singer and a good performer, excellent in both regards. He combined a powerful voice with an effective stage presence.

Nevertheless, Stalin agreed with me: "Yes, you can have Gmyrya in Kiev." I wasn't mistaken. Voices were immediately heard saying that they wouldn't sing alongside a traitor to the homeland! I knew where this was coming from. There were patriotic feelings, yes, but also rivalry. We explained that Gmyrya was at fault for not retreating with us if he had been able to; but it was difficult to investigate this matter now, and we didn't want to, because it was difficult to come to a clear conclusion as to whether he really wanted to stay behind. The fact [that he had stayed behind] was evident and that of course was bad. "But," I said, "after all, we abandoned all of Ukraine. Those who stayed behind do have a certain right to blame us for going off and leaving them. Therefore it's better not to dig into this matter, trying to apportion who's to blame and punishing everyone that remained under German occupation. If that's to be done, it needs to be done intelligently. Otherwise, millions would have to be punished. They stayed behind because they had no other option. We need to approach this question more seriously, evaluate the facts more sensibly, and determine our attitude toward each individual case separately—that is, each individual who remained behind on German-occupied territory."

And so Gmyrya remained with the Kiev opera theater. I met with him toward the end of the war. He had wanted to meet during the war, but at that time I didn't think it was appropriate for me to do so. It was only later, when I was in Transcarpathia,[23] and it turned out that Gmyrya was there too, that I said he could come see me at my apartment. He wanted to pour out his soul to me, but to discourage him from doing that (and that kind of thing is unpleasant for anyone) I treated him to a good dinner and asked him to sing. Only after he had sung did I ask: "Was there something you wanted to say?"

He said: "After everything that I've heard from you, I have nothing to say except to express my gratitude. I am very grateful to you and will never forget your attitude toward me at a moment of great difficulty for me, the difficulty that arose after people found out that I had remained on German-occupied territory." Again Gmyrya took an honored place in the Kiev opera theater. He resumed his proper position as a performer and as a human being. He did very useful work and often gave concerts and still gives them today [i.e., 1969]. Whenever I hear he's going to be featured on a radio or television broadcast, I take advantage of that opportunity to listen and enjoy his voice.

There was another prominent singer in Ukraine at that time—Donets.[24] He sang in accompaniment with Patorzhinsky. He also had a fine voice. I don't know why, but for some reason among party activists and especially among the Chekists his "fame" was firmly established as a man of alleged anti-Soviet views and a nationalist. He had never been arrested, but in 1941, when the Germans were threatening to take Kiev, he finally was arrested. There was no specific evidence against him aside from people's intuitive feelings. My place in society was pretty far removed from his, and so I didn't know him well enough to gauge his inner feelings and sentiments. It was only the security agents who reported that his sentiments were anti-Soviet and that he was a Ukrainian nationalist.

He was arrested on the grounds that the Germans supposedly knew about his anti-Soviet political views and would make use of him after they took Kiev. To prevent the enemy from having that opportunity, he was arrested, and he soon died. It may be that, if not for the war and his arrest, he would have lived a long life and worked for the benefit of his people. Even after the war I returned to the question of Donets several times. There was the thought that slander might have occurred—the result of artificially stimulated suspicions. Everyone was seen as an enemy who had not yet been exposed. In his character Donets was quite abrupt and distinctive. As I was told later, he refused to bow down to authority; he bore himself with dignity and perhaps even seemed to display arrogance. Evidently this was the basis for judging him as an anti-Soviet figure.

In fall 1944 our armies continued their offensive, and we were approaching Odessa.[25] I was very concerned about Odessa, about what condition it would be in and what destruction might have taken place there. It is of course a major city. I also simply wanted to visit Odessa immediately after it was liberated. With the agreement of the commander of the troops there (the Front was then commanded by Malinovsky), I flew to his headquarters. He reported on the situation, and we traveled together into Odessa right after it was liberated.[26] We immediately went to see whether the building of the party's province committee on the shores of the Black Sea was still intact and whether the Odessa opera building was still all right and to look over the condition of the city in general. The favorable impression I got was that the damage Odessa suffered was relatively not very great. The opera theater was intact. Only one corner of the building had been damaged by a shell. A great many anecdotes of all kinds were told about the enemy occupation. Odessa had been taken by the Romanians, and as a result many anti-Romanian anecdotes were making the rounds, and of course the people of Odessa are skilled at making up funny stories.

Nowadays I'm wondering how it happened that Malinovsky liberated Odessa, and not Tolbukhin. Apparently Tolbukhin was left to liberate the Crimea, and Malinovsky, that is the troops of the Third Ukrainian Front, moved westward, and thus he had the honor of liberating Odessa, the city in which he had spent his youth, living with his aunt. I can't say for sure that this is what happened. A lot of things run together in my memory now, and I don't think it's worth the effort to hunt through printed materials to check on this.

By March 1944 our First Ukrainian Front had reached the pre-1939 border between the Ukrainian SSR and Poland. A place was still assigned for me wherever the Front headquarters was established, but I went there only from time to time. In general I wasn't able to visit our armies, however much I wanted to. I understood that Stalin's instructions were correct, that I had to concentrate my efforts on organizing the reconstruction work in our republic's industry and agriculture. That was the main thing necessary for Ukraine at that stage, whereas the question of attacking and defeating the enemy was, as the saying goes, already in the bag. In that department everything was assured.

I don't remember the exact date but it was before the springtime when I received a report that Nikolai Fyodorovich Vatutin had been wounded.[27] I was very distressed at this news, although at first they said the injury was not life threatening. He had been wounded in the leg, but under what circumstances they didn't tell me. Some time went by and I received a report that Vatutin was coming to Kiev in a railroad car. I met him. He felt as any wounded person does, but he was certain he would soon be returning to his job. It seems that the proposal had been made for him to go to Moscow for treatment, but he decided to stay in Kiev because it was closer to the Front and he might not have to discontinue his activity as Front commander. Doctors arrived, including Burdenko, a very prominent surgeon.[28] You couldn't wish for anything more or better in those days. After looking at Vatutin, Burdenko told me: "Nothing to be afraid of. His wound isn't dangerous. It seems we'll be able to put him back on his feet, and he'll soon be fulfilling his duties as usual." Zhukov[29] had taken over command of the First Ukrainian Front after Vatutin was wounded. He took command temporarily while Vatutin was recovering.

Then it was reported to me under what circumstances and where Vatutin had been wounded. It turned out that he had been wounded by Ukrainian nationalists, Bandera supporters. They had taken advantage of a lack of prudence and caution not only on Vatutin's part but also on the part of those responsible for guarding him. He was in some settlement from which he was supposed to travel to another place. He decided to travel at night. Mud made the roads impassable. At the front lines most often we traveled from place to place at dawn or in the evening twilight, but here he was traveling late at night. A jeep carrying tommy-gunners was traveling ahead of him, and Vatutin also had guards carrying submachine guns in his vehicle. At a fork in the road the vehicles got separated. The one in front took one direction, and Vatutin took the other. Vatutin was passing through a village when there was a burst of machine-gun fire and the commander was wounded. I don't remember now whether the attackers seized the vehicle or just ran away. Later we caught the men who had shot Vatutin, but that was already after the war. It was reported to me that during interrogation they said that they had found out that the person they had wounded (or killed) was Vatutin. They were able to find that out because certain documents and materials to that effect had fallen into their hands.

The commander's treatment was coming along fairly well. I went to see him every day. He felt fine and was recovering confidently. He was already beginning to take up his job again, and the day had already been set when he could officially resume his former duties and return to Front headquarters. But one day he said to me: "My temperature has gone up a little and I don't feel well." The doctors examined him and said that apparently an old case of malaria had revived. He had contracted malaria earlier, and even at the battlefront, when he and I were together, he suffered from it.

I replied: "That's too bad. It's apparently wearing you down, but there's nothing to be done about it."

Within a day or two he began to get worse. Then the doctor said: "It's not malaria; it's something more serious. The wound has become infected." Everyone was alarmed by that. If the wound was infected, that could lead to gangrene and amputation of a limb or even death. The infection had to be cured quickly.

The doctors thought penicillin should be used, but I was told they couldn't use it at that time without Stalin's consent, and that Stalin was opposed. I didn't talk with him personally about the question of penicillin, but the doctors told me that Stalin rejected its use in general for this reason: Penicillin was not a Soviet medication (we had none); it was American.[30] Stalin thought the American penicillin might be infected. They might send infected penicillin from the United States to weaken our forces, and so it would be an impermissible risk to use this medicine to treat such a prominent military figure as Vatutin.

It was not for me to judge. The doctors had to decide this. The doctors told me that if he were given penicillin, the illness might take a different course and Vatutin's life might be saved. But without it the doctors were unable to help him recover, and the wounded man's condition grew worse. One day when I went to see him, Burdenko took me aside and said that the only solution was an operation as soon as possible. They would have to remove the leg. He said: "We're placing great hopes in you. You need to speak with Vatutin before we do. You can refer to us and tell him about this necessity. He has great respect for you and confidence in you, and you can find the right words to convince him to agree to this operation."

And so I had a talk with Vatutin: "Nikolai Fyodorovich, there are complications in regard to your wound. The doctors say that amputation is necessary. The leg will have to be removed. I understand what that would mean for any human being. But it's possible to be a general without a leg. And if you feel sorry for the leg, you could lose your head. There's only one choice: amputation or your life. Amputation will save your life. If that isn't done, death is all that remains. I beg you to agree to the operation."

He replied rather calmly: "Yes, I agree. Tell the doctors they can do what they consider necessary. I am ready even if it's done right now."

I immediately informed Burdenko what Vatutin had said. He had an assistant who was also a prominent surgeon. I don't remember his name now, but he is the one who actually amputated the leg, with Burdenko overseeing the operation. The operation was carried out. I went there after the operation and was told the results. To speak in human terms, it was a dreadful sight, not only to see this man without his leg, but also the open wound. Even for medical personnel this is a fairly impressive spectacle from the professional point of view, and for others it makes quite an unpleasant impression. Vatutin's treatment resumed again. All the doctors did everything they could so that the state of his health would improve. I don't know how many days he continued in stable condition when Burdenko called me again (or maybe it was his assistant) and asked me to come because Vatutin had taken a turn for the worse. He was tossing around, lifting himself up on his elbows, demanding a notebook and paper, trying to write some sort of telegram asking Stalin to save him, and so on.

As I was coming to see him, he flung himself at me, embraced me, kissed me, and seemed to be only half-conscious. But he wanted to live and was begging everyone who could help in any way to save his life. I said to him:

"Nikolai Fyodorovich, Stalin knows and is doing everything that needs to be done." I had made a special point of calling Stalin to speak with him about Vatutin. Later Stalin rebuked me for having allowed Vatutin to die. But I didn't cause his death! Even Burdenko was unable to do anything, and what could I do, just an ordinary person, not a physician? It was Stalin himself who had forbidden the use of penicillin, but he didn't say anything about that. He understood that that might make a bad impression. Subsequently I didn't ask Stalin about it because I didn't want to seem to be criticizing him.

When I was getting ready to leave the hospital, I said to Burdenko: "My impression is that Nikolai Fyodorovich is dying." Burdenko answered that the patient might live a few more days. I repeated: "I think he will die tonight or even this evening." Sure enough, a few hours later, I received a phone call: "Please come. Vatutin is in very bad condition. We would like you to come." When I arrived, Nikolai Fyodorovich was already at death's door. So ended the life of a remarkable man,[31] devoted to the Communist Party, to the Soviet state, and to his people, a very honorable and sober-minded man in all respects, an intensely principled man. I have not seen many military men who were such good Communists as Nikolai Fyodorovich Vatutin. So I took my leave of him, having lost a good comrade and a true friend. I had not been especially close to him before the war, but during the war we had become very close. I respected him greatly and I respect his memory.

When he was buried, I raised the question of erecting a monument to him. Stalin agreed. Work on the monument was begun. What inscription should it have? I proposed something along the following lines: "To General Vatutin from the Ukrainian people." I thought that would be the best way of honoring him. After all, he had fought in Ukraine and had liberated Ukrainian territory from the Nazis. This proposal was accepted. As the inscription was being made, suddenly some question was raised in Moscow. Cultural matters in our country then were being directed by someone with a Ukrainian name, although he himself was not Ukrainian.[32] He suddenly called me up and said that the inscription I proposed should not be used.

I asked: "Why?"

He said: "That would be a nationalist inscription. Probably Bazhan thought it up, and after all, Bazhan is a nationalist."

I said: "Wait a minute. It wasn't Bazhan who proposed it. It was I. Bazhan was also pleased by it, I don't deny that, but what kind of nationalism is there in this—an expression of gratitude from the Ukrainian people to a Russian? This honor—this statement of gratitude—will have the opposite effect. The Ukrainian nationalists will go out of their minds if an inscription is dedicated in the name of the Ukrainian people to a Russian." A lot of effort was required from me in defending the wording of the inscription, and I won out only when I appealed to Stalin and said that the whole thing was outrageous.

Stalin answered: "Tell them to go to hell! Do what you propose, and that's all there is to it." And that's what we did. The monument stands to this day in memory of Vatutin's life and work, an acknowledgment by the Ukrainian people of the services he rendered in the struggle against the aggressor.

There are educated people who concern themselves with problems of culture in the Soviet Union. But that man showed his ignorance and lack of political education. Things were the opposite of what he thought. I repeat, a real Ukrainian nationalist's eyes would glaze over and his head would swim if a message was chiseled onto a monument "from the Ukrainian people" to a Russian general. Moreover, this inscription testified to the merging of the thoughts and actions of both the Ukrainian and the Russian people in a single effort, in the common struggle against the invaders. And that's actually the way things were, because not only Russians and Ukrainians but also Tatars, Jews, Bashkirs, Belorussians, and representatives of other nationalities died on the same battlefields and for the same cause. Their political and moral unity was displayed in this effort, when all the peoples of the USSR rose up against the enemy to defend our homeland. Whenever I'm in Kiev I always go to visit the monument to Nikolai Fyodorovich [Vatutin], and I pay the respects that are rightly due to this man, expressing my esteem and gratitude for all that he did.

After Zhukov, the First Ukrainian Front was commanded by Konev.[33] I first met him before the war. Stalin was looking into some sort of case involving Konev, and I happened to be there on that occasion. Konev had become involved in a dispute with the secretary of the party committee in some territory or province. Later I met him after the war had already begun. During the first days of the war he arrived with his Nineteenth Army in our military district when we were still on the border, but his army was quickly transferred from our district to Belorussia. Then I met him at the battle of Kursk. Quite recently he and I had celebrated our joint victory—the liberation of Kiev. I knew only good things about Konev and was pleased that he had taken over command of the Front. Of course Zhukov had a stronger personality, and, to tell the truth, by that time he was actually doing all the preparatory work and deciding all questions in the Stavka. And what about Stalin? God forbid that someone should start huffing and puffing over my saying that Stalin didn't decide matters, but that Zhukov did. At any rate, that is what I thought at the time, and I believe it really was so.

Under Zhukov I remained a member of the Front's Military Council, but continued my work aimed at restoring the ruined economy of Ukraine, and as before I went to Front headquarters from time to time, and was there together with Zhukov sometimes for several days. By that time our troops had already reached Ternopol.[34] I remember that Zhukov called me and said that an offensive was just beginning then and he would like me to come to his headquarters. I was glad to go there. I myself wanted to watch this offensive by our troops in the victorious year of 1944. We already had absolute confidence of our success. I arrived at Front headquarters, spent more than a day there, and familiarized myself with the situation, as I was supposed to do. Early in the morning on the day of the offensive, we were supposed to be at the command post to monitor the progress of the operation. We got in a jeep and set off. I don't know why, but we were a little late for the beginning of the preliminary bombardment.

As we hurried toward the command post, we drove past some bushes and suddenly the loud, deep bang of an artillery piece came from behind us. We were virtually shell-shocked by the power of the explosion and the impact of the blast. That was the beginning of the preliminary bombardment. All our artillery began to roar, and then the planes flew in and the Katyushas went to work. It was a very impressive spectacle. The Germans were knocked to pieces, and our troops rushed into Ternopol and Chernovtsy.[35] For a while Ternopol was surrounded and under siege, because the Germans had turned it into a well-fortified strong point. As a result Ternopol suffered a lot of damage. I would say that of all the Ukrainian cities Ternopol suffered most. The Germans there were surrounded, and we bombed them from the sky. Bombs destroy urban structures more than artillery does, because their explosions are more powerful and they cause the ground to shake. As a result buildings are destroyed not only by direct hits but also by cracks and breaks appearing in their structures.

When we moved forward, I remained at Front headquarters for several days. Later it was reported that right next to the place where my quarters were located a hiding place of the Bandera men was found. Of course we hadn't seen any of them and knew nothing at all about this hiding place. They had dug a hole like a root cellar and camouflaged it. It seems that our reconnaissance men who chose that place for a headquarters didn't check out the area with sufficient care. I doubt that Bandera's men were present when we were. That would have been difficult for them. After all, they would have had to obtain food, water, and so forth. But the fact that they had a hiding place there was definitely confirmed.

While I remained at the headquarters and continued to work, our troops advanced successfully to the south and west. At the upper reaches of the Western Bug River stubborn fighting again broke out. The Germans wanted to give battle using that river as a defense line to stop the advance of our troops toward Lvov and Peremyshl,[36] and they fought very stubbornly. Nevertheless the left wing of our Front advanced quite far, and an enemy group to the north of Kamenets-Podolsky[37] was smashed, leaving many corpses and much armament behind. In one place I saw something new in the way of German military equipment—a large quantity of handheld antitank grenades in a row against a wall, partly still in boxes. It was a virtual ammunition dump. It seems they had brought this materiel up to the front lines, but had not had time to distribute it to the troops and abandoned it.

The tank army commanded by Rybalko[38] was operating there, and doing very good work. I remember that as early as the summer we had begun discussing plans of how to move against Lvov.[39] I knew the approaches to that city. It was difficult to attack Lvov from the north or east. It is in a hollow among hills, and from the north it's protected by [rough terrain,] the bottomland of two rivers, the Southern Bug [actually, the Western Bug] and the Poltva.[40] An absolutely flat area stretches out farther north. There are also plains stretching to the east. But closer to Lvov there are hills. Thus, the city lends itself readily to the organization of a defense. At first we tried to take Lvov by luck, hoping to catch the defenders off guard, but we didn't succeed. The enemy fought back. We decided not to persist and waste time, not to expend our vital forces trying to overcome a well-organized defense line. Instead we struck directly at Peremyshl. If we let Lvov end up behind our lines, we could force the enemy to leave Lvov without a fight [after being outflanked], and that is how things worked out.

For this purpose it was necessary to turn Rybalko's tank army to the north. It had to be pulled back from the fighting it was engaged in at the approaches to Lvov and sent north and then west through Zholkva and Yavoriv toward Peremyshl.[41] Together with this tank army an offensive would have to be undertaken farther to the north by the Thirteenth Army commanded by Pukhov,[42] a fine person and a good military man. He had commanded that army in the battle of Kursk. I took part in reviewing and approving this plan. Then I went to visit Rybalko to familiarize myself with the condition of his forces right there on the spot. As I was approaching, there were tanks coming toward me. They had already been withdrawn from the fighting and were heading in the new direction. Suddenly some planes swooped down and began bombing them. I was riding with the secretary of the party's Lvov province committee (he is now chairman of the Committee of People's Control in Ukraine, a sensible and energetic man). He was a general then, a member of the Military Council of some army, and during our advance on Lvov, I asked that he be relieved of his military duties and be placed at our disposal so that we could confirm him as secretary of the Lvov province committee of the CP(B)U.[43] Suddenly this bombing began and some of our tanks started to burn. We jumped out of our vehicles. There was a hole that had been dug in the ground alongside us. This general, a very thin man, threw himself sideways right into this hole and hugged the ground intently. I laughed: "Your instinct of self-preservation is working well." He said: "Yes, no matter how long you've fought, all sorts of things still happen."

I reached Rybalko's headquarters. General Ryazanov[44] was standing on the porch of the small house where the headquarters was located. I had known him back at the beginning of the war when he was a colonel and had removed the Ukrainian party's secret papers and documents from Kiev [in a small U-2 plane], having been entrusted with that task by Burmistenko. Now he was in charge of the attack planes of our Front and, as I recall, had Ilyushin-2s in his arsenal. I asked him: "What planes are those that are bombing our tank column?"

He said, "Those are our planes!" and immediately established radio contact with the leader of the squadron, ordering him to turn the planes aside, to call off the attack.

Later I asked him again: "How could it be that our planes bombed our own tank column?"

He said: "We were wondering about that ourselves, and we came to the conclusion that the pilots were given orders to bomb the front lines and anything that was moving against us near Lvov. When we turned our tanks around, they were coming toward us from a northeasterly direction, on the road that leads directly from Lvov. Our pilots probably took them for enemy tank columns and began to bomb them." In such cases, when you came under fire from your own side, people always said: "Thank heavens, as usual, their bombing wasn't very accurate!" I don't remember what casualties we suffered. If there were any, they were insignificant, because the tank crews managed to jump out and run away. There were really no substantial losses of tanks either, as I recall; I saw only two or three vehicles enveloped in flames.

I went in to see Rybalko. His headquarters was located not far from the rail junction of Krasne, to the east of Lvov. When I came in, he was receiving a report on the situation. The mood then was quite different from what it had been in 1942—complete confidence that we would quickly move ahead.

The repositioning of our forces was under way, the direction of our attack being changed, and I went to visit the Thirteenth Army of Pukhov. I hadn't seen him since 1943, the previous year, when we were still fighting near Kursk. I arrived at his headquarters just when our tanks were moving full force behind the infantry toward Peremyshl. I asked him: "Where are our troops?"

He showed me on the map: "They're already approaching Peremyshl."

I asked: "And what's in front of you? What's holding you up now?"

He said: "There's nothing in front of us. There's no enemy there. The tanks need to move ahead as quickly as possible so as not to give the enemy a chance to collect himself. But there's a marshy area there, difficult for the tanks to cross. Our engineering crews are working there now to make the area more solid. Then Rybalko's tanks can move ahead and we'll take Peremyshl." He had no doubts about this, and it was pleasant for me to hear it. I wished him well and returned to headquarters.

Meanwhile, as I was on my way to visit him, I had passed either a company or a battalion on the march. The men were taking a break, and I went over to them to have a talk. It was an interesting conversation. The mood you could sense among them was totally different from 1941. Humorous catchphrases and soldier's jokes were being bantered about. Practically every company had its own Vasily Tyorkin.[45] Tvardovsky captured very accurately and well this characteristic figure among our front-line troops, and he wrote a remarkable narrative poem, whose content was very powerful and which reflected, as clearly as in a mirror, the life, the battles, and the sentiments of our fighting men of the Red Army.

Our troops soon took Peremyshl.[46] The Germans, feeling a threat from their rear, quickly left Lvov of their own accord, and our troops entered it. I went there immediately. This city was of special interest to us. An absolute majority of the city's population was Polish. There were very few Ukrainians. The peasants around Lvov were all Ukrainians, but the people living in the city were mostly Polish, the result of a special policy pursued by the Polish government. I was told that previously Ukrainians had not been able to get work even cleaning or paving the streets of Lvov. A policy of Polonization of Lvov was pursued to strengthen the Polish side in the dispute that had gone on for a long time in that area between Ukrainians and Poles. The Polish government had done everything it could to create a base of support for itself in Lvov, relying on a mostly Polish population. For this reason we feared that some sort of local administrative bodies might arise that would turn out to be hostile to Soviet power. We had to hurry to be sure that our people came into positions of leadership in the city. And that is what we did. We immediately confirmed the secretary of the party's province committee and the chairman of the local Soviet executive committee, and we began to gather together cadres for the districts and to establish other government and party bodies. The necessary meetings and popular assemblies were held.

I remember someone came to see me in Lvov and reported: "Comrade Khrushchev, I just went past the railroad station and saw civilians carrying away weapons. One man was even carrying a light machine gun." I immediately took a car and went there. Here's the scene I encountered: people completely unknown to us were actually making off with rifles and machine guns. As I have said, most of the population of Lvov was Polish. The Germans had been routed and had withdrawn from the city, but still the population was arming itself. Who was it arming itself against? Certainly not against those who had withdrawn from the city. In other words, they were arming against us. Urgent measures were taken at once to put an end to this disorder and to round up unauthorized weapons. Nevertheless quite a few weapons had been carried away. Some of them evidently fell into the hands of Bandera's men later on.

As for the Polish population, it really couldn't create any kind of nationalist military organization of its own in Lvov. The Polish Home Army, the Armia Krajowa, which took orders from the émigré Polish government in London, was of course getting ready to fight the Red Army and to oppose Soviet power. But for them Lvov was an outlying area.

Our offensive in the foothills of the Carpathians was carried out by Moskalenko's 38th Army, Grechko's First Guards Army, and another army commanded earlier by the Georgian Leselidze.[47] I didn't know Leselidze very well, because his army had joined us after I was no longer participating actively in the work of the Military Council of the Front. And so I was not able to have a close acquaintance with him. These three armies on the left wing of our Front were lagging behind. Defensive conditions in the hills and mountains were favorable to the enemy, and he waged a tough and lengthy battle there. In this connection Stalin praised Pukhov's Thirteenth Army highly—this was when I made a trip to Moscow—while strongly criticizing those who were lagging behind: "Why are these highly placed so-and-so commanders of yours standing there, marking time?"

I said to him: "Well, I have a lot of praise for Pukhov and for others. But Comrade Stalin, I visited Pukhov and I know personally, firsthand, that there was nothing in front of Pukhov. The enemy wasn't there. That's why he was able to move ahead quite freely. Besides, the ground is level there, a flat plain, and Rybalko's tank army was accompanying Pukhov across that ground, so all of that [their quick advance] is only natural. But the others are advancing into foothills and mountains. It's easier for the enemy to organize defense lines there and harder to drive him out, especially when he's putting up such stubborn resistance."

Stalin didn't look into such questions closely. He didn't really want to investigate. I don't know if he did this consciously or simply didn't understand. In other words, if you didn't move forward, that meant you were bad; if you moved forward, that meant you were good. And what the conditions were for one or another army or in one or another sector, he sometimes didn't even want to hear about that, and in such cases he made no special study of the conditions and particular circumstances, and he never asked why certain conditions had arisen on some sector of the front lines.

The reorganization of life in Lvov continued. Among the Poles some activists distinguished themselves. They cooperated well with the Communist organizations and became excellent agitators. I recall one man who particularly distinguished himself, a doctor by profession, a really smart man. I myself heard him speak when we held a rally in the city. He gave a remarkable speech, a very intelligent one. I warned our security people then: "You better create appropriate conditions for him and guard him without making it obvious. I'm afraid the Polish nationalists will assassinate him." Alas, that is what happened.

They sent a "gift" from a friend in Warsaw. As he started to open the package—his wife told us later—he remarked to her: "What kind of package is this? Maybe it's a bomb? Some sort of infernal machine?" Just then the package exploded, killing him instantly. His wife was shell-shocked, but she survived. The assassin of course was never found. Thus we lost a good friend, one who was especially valuable because he was Polish. There were not that many supporters of ours among the Poles in Lvov, especially not active agitational speakers[48] and good orators of the kind that we needed badly.

After taking Peremyshl and Lvov, our armies continued on the offensive. The left wing of our troops advancing on the Carpathians took Drogobych with its oil fields and refineries. I immediately went to Drogobych and then to Borislav,[49] on the heels of the retreating enemy. This area—Borislav and the area to the south of it—was soon transferred to the Fourth Ukrainian Front. Its commander was Petrov, a former teacher and good commander.[50] He died soon after the war. He had a characteristic habit of twitching his head as though he had a tic, and during those months a member of his Military Council was Mekhlis,[51] an extremely energetic person. His energy, like a whirlwind, sometimes swept everything before it, both hostile and useful. When operations were analyzed, Mekhlis usually gave the report rather than the commander. He stifled the commander's initiative. The second member of the Military Council of that Front was a general whose last name I have now forgotten.

Mekhlis and he on one occasion decided to visit the troops and got into an argument. The second member of the Military Council said: "I suggest that we take this road and not the one that you suggest, Comrade Mekhlis. That road is under artillery fire and we can't travel there."

Mekhlis lit into him: "What are you saying? That's exactly the road we're going to take. It's shorter, and we'll get there quicker." They traveled in different vehicles. As it turned out, Mekhlis got there safely, but the other general's vehicle suffered a direct hit by an artillery shell and he was killed. So, as a result of Mekhlis's stubbornness and stupidity, we lost a general. That was the price we paid for his provocative bragging: "I'm not afraid of anything!" It's true that Mekhlis was a very brave man. You have to give credit where credit is due. But bravery that passes over into recklessness results in unnecessary losses and cannot be justified.

When I arrived in Drogobych and Borislav I found great destruction in the oil fields, but two oil refineries, which we had closed down temporarily even before the war (they belonged to some foreign company), remained completely intact. We would be able to start them up quite quickly, as soon as the need arose. But that need would arise only when the oil wells were restored to operation and oil was successfully being extracted again. These refineries were antiquated, and I don't know their subsequent fate.

During those weeks our troops continued their offensive, across the Carpathians, and had already descended into the valley of the Tisza River.[52] When I found out that fighting was going on in the area of Mukachevo,[53] I decided to set out for the headquarters of the Fourth Ukrainian Front, to meet with the commander and with Mekhlis. We in the Ukrainian leadership had had our eyes on the Transcarpathian region because Ukrainians lived there. From ancient times their homeland had been called Chervonnaya Rus (or Ruthenia). Therefore as soon as I learned that our troops had entered Mukachevo I immediately went there to look into things on the spot. I wondered what our party activists were like there, what other political parties there were, and what the composition of the population was— what percentage Ukrainians, Hungarians, Czechs, or other nationalities, if they existed. In principle they probably did exist, because this region for many years had been part of the former Austro-Hungarian empire, and after World War I it had been part of Czechoslovakia. Each new government had tried to suppress the national sentiments of the Ukrainian part of the population, claiming they were not Ukrainians. Sometimes they were called Ruthenians or something else, but they were never called Ukrainians or Russians. Actually they were different from the Hutzuls of the Carpathian Mountains, although in their clothing and the culture of their daily life, their daily habits and customs, they were quite similar to the Hutzuls of the mountains.[54]

Before the war I had been in that area, but not in Transcarpathia, although I had crossed the mountain passes and went right up to the [Czechoslovakian] border. There were two fairly good roads that ran through that area. I had traveled over both of them to the border that ran along the mountain passes, and now I hoped I could remember them and therefore didn't take a guide. But I made a mistake, took the wrong road, and instead of traveling on the westernmost road across the mountain pass that led to Uzhgorod[55] I ended up on a road to the southeast. Late at night when I reached the mountain pass, I was surprised that there was no one there, not a soul; nothing was stirring, and there was such an eerie silence in the forest. We stopped, started up again, stopped again, and listened. No one was there! With me there were only the guards who usually accompanied me. It took a long time to make the trip back. It was quite late at night when we came down out of the Carpathians. Finding the Front headquarters, I told the commander why I had come. He reported on the situation. Then Mekhlis came in. We were old friends and acquaintances, having known each other in Moscow when I was a student at the Industrial Academy and he was editor of *Pravda*. Mekhlis said: "We are fighting in Uzhgorod. The enemy is resisting, but we'll probably drive him out of there by tomorrow morning."

I stayed overnight with them and in the morning I went to Uzhgorod. The enemy was still holding on in the western suburbs of the city and firing mortars at the center. I had seen Mukachevo when General Petrov and I passed through it. It was a nice, clean little town with marvelous buildings. I also liked Uzhgorod very much. The villages along the way did not seem to be typical of the Hutzuls, but they also had good buildings. Later I learned that these were Hungarian villages. They were of quite a different type, brick and stone houses built on foundations. The Hungarians had driven the Hutzuls farther back up into the mountains. The Hutzuls had wooden houses without chimneys; the smoke from the stove simply came out from under the eaves. This reminded me of my childhood. We had had those same kinds of chimneyless huts in my native village in Kursk *gubernia.*

In Uzhgorod I made the acquaintance of Ivan Ivanovich Turyanitsa,[56] a Communist tobacco worker from Mukachevo. He was the local leader then, and he pursued a policy favoring the incorporation of Transcarpathian Rus into the Ukrainian SSR. He was establishing new party and administrative bodies in the liberated territory. A special governing body of the Transcarpathian region, the People's Council, was established on a preliminary basis. I liked Turyanitsa. He was a well-known figure in the Czechoslovakian Communist Party. When Transcarpathia had been part of Czechoslovakia, Turyanitsa had carried on party work among the Transcarpathian loggers. In general there were a lot of working-class people there. Manuilsky told me that back in the 1920s, when he had begun work in the Comintern, he had gone to Czechoslovakia as an emissary from the Comintern[57] and had also met with the loggers of Transcarpathia. "I held a meeting with the loggers," he recalled. "It was either 1928 or 1930. The line of the Comintern at that time was that as long as a revolutionary situation did not exist, we had to switch from calling for insurrection to other methods of conducting work among the masses. I gave a speech on the subject to the Communist loggers. They listened to me, but then began to huff and puff and began making speeches themselves. They spoke in Ukrainian (Manuilsky himself was a Ukrainian and spoke the language well), and said: 'The speaker says that we don't have a revolutionary situation. But we need weapons.' I argued with them that if there was not a revolutionary situation, there was no point having weapons, but they insisted: 'Give us guns.'" In short there was a very militant spirit among those loggers. The people there lived in great poverty, and in their living standards they were considerably worse off not only than the Czechs but even the Slovaks, who were also not at all wealthy. There was no comparison with the Hungarians. The Hungarian part of the population was very well off.

Of course I encouraged Ivan Ivanovich Turyanitsa, considering his political line to be correct. But as the saying goes, the appetite grows by what it feeds on. Turyanitsa organized armed detachments and took over several regions, which before the war had belonged to the kingdom of Romania. It is true that the inhabitants of those regions, mainly peasants, had come to us themselves and asked to be included in Soviet Ukraine. I, too, met with them. They argued that they were Ukrainians. But we ourselves couldn't take any specific initiatives in this area. As for Turyanitsa, he sent his representatives into those areas at his own risk.

The Romanian leaders were very displeased by this. These regions were remote, up in the mountains, and it was hard to get to them. To put it jokingly, Ivan Ivanovich Turyanitsa was beginning to engage in expansionist activity. When the government of Czechoslovakia was reestablished and its representatives were sent to Mukachevo, he drove them out of there. After our troops had passed through, these people moved farther west, it seems, to Kosice.[58] In general a strong desire for unification had grown up among Ukrainians at that time. Representatives from a certain area in Slovakia, an area mainly inhabited by Ukrainians, even came to see me in Kiev and asked that their district be included in the Ukrainian SSR. I said to them: "That's impossible. If you Communists have organized your life in common together with the Czechs and Slovaks, then this would hurt the feelings of the Czechs and especially the Slovaks because it would mean that the territory of Slovakia was diminished. I want you to understand me correctly. Build socialism and create a government of the working people together with the Communist Party of Czechoslovakia. You should unite with them and build a future together with the other nationalities inhabiting Czechoslovakia."

They left Kiev dissatisfied. Of course I reported this to Stalin.

One day he called me up and said: "Have you got a man out there named Turyanitsa?"

I said: "No, he's not one of ours. He has nothing to do with us. He's our neighbor."

"Well, they tell me that you have influence on him all the same. Let him know that he should call off his armed units, withdraw from the territory of the kingdom of Romania. Not only that, he's even taken some districts on the left bank of the Tisza. And that territory belongs to Hungary." I passed all this on to Turyanitsa. We had established communications with him. Of course I couldn't give him any orders. I could only advise him. And he immediately did as we advised.

I was already working in Moscow after the war when I found out that Turyanitsa had died.[59] I regretted his loss very much. He was still young and could have done splendid work. I recommended to Kiev: "Give it some thought. He deserves to be acknowledged in some special way for his work in the Transcarpathian region. He played a positive role there toward the end of the war." His services to the Communist Party of the Soviet Union in general and to the Communist Party of Ukraine in particular were substantial. But I don't know what was done along those lines.

When Transcarpathia became a province of Soviet Ukraine the people there did good work. Collective farms and state farms were established, and a new industry was built up, including an electric power plant. The Terebly and Rika Rivers flow from the Carpathians down into the Tisza. A considerable distance separates the two rivers.[60] A tunnel was dug to connect them, and a hydroelectric power plant was built, which utilized the increased force resulting from the combined flow of the rivers. Today I don't remember what the power plant's capacity was, but it did temporarily meet the energy needs of that region.

And that is how all of Ukraine was liberated.

1. There were three Belorussian Fronts. [SS]

2. Major General F. I. Tolbukhin commanded the Fourth Ukrainian Front from October 1943 to May 1944. Major General R. Ya. Malinovsky commanded the Third Ukrainian Front from October 1943 to May 1944. See Biographies.

3. Kiev was liberated on November 6, 1943, and Dnepropetrovsk on October 25, 1943.

4. Makeyevka was an industrial town just east of Stalino (present-day Donetsk). It is now a suburb of Donetsk. [AH]

5. Lieutenant General Ya. G. Kreizer commanded the Second Guards Army from February to July 1943.

6. Makeyevka was liberated on September 6, 1943.

7. Zhitomir was first liberated on November 12, 1943 and then again on December 31, 1943. On this section of the front, the advance was led by the First Guards Cavalry Corps, commanded by Lieutenant General V. K. Baranov.

8. Poltava is in east central Ukraine, between Kiev and Kharkov. [SS]

9. Kherson is in southern Ukraine, near the estuary of the Dnieper. [SS] It remained under enemy occupation until the end of 1943.

10. Vasily I. Chapayev (1887–1919) was a Red commander in the Civil War. He was much celebrated as a hero in Soviet literature and film, especially because of his peasant origins. He epitomized the peasant leader of peasant soldiers in the Red Army, an embodiment of the worker-peasant alliance in the Soviet armed forces. [SS/GS]

11. Uman is about 160 kilometers south of Kiev. [SS]

12. Lieutenant General I. S. Konev commanded the Steppe Front from July to October 1943, when this front was renamed the Second Ukrainian Front.

13. This was the Sixth Tank Army, commanded by Lieutenant General of Tank Forces A. G. Kravchenko from January 1944 to September 1945.

14. Lieutenant General G. L. Tumanyan.

15. Korsun-Shevchenkovsky (shortened form Korsun) is in Cherkasy province, about 150 kilometers southeast of Kiev, on the Ros River, a west-bank tributary of the Dnieper. [AH] The Germans had tried to hold a salient along the Dnieper, centered on Korsun. The encirclement and successful reduction of this position, involving the destruction of nearly 80,000 German troops, is often referred to as the battle of the Korsun salient. [GS]

16. Vatutin was made a Hero of the Soviet Union in 1965.

17. From May to August 1943 this formation was the First Kosciusko Polish Division. Then until March 1944 it was called the First Polish Corps and thereafter the First Polish Army. In July 1944 it merged with the Armia Ludowa (People's Army; the Communist partisans) to form the two Polish Armies (under the provisional pro-Soviet Polish government in Krakow).

18. Sochi is a popular resort on the Black Sea. [SS]

19. A. I. Yegorov. See Biographies.

20. This theater was named in honor of Ivan Franko (1857–1919), a Ukrainian poet, short-story writer, and socialist activist.

21. B. R. Gmyrya was a singer at the Kiev Opera Theater. See Biographies.

22. I. S. Patorzhinsky sang at the Kiev Opera Theater. See Biographies.

23. Transcarpathia includes the central stretch of the Carpathian Mountains and adjacent lowlands to the southwest. Between the wars it belonged to Czechoslovakia. Following the occupation of Czechoslovakia by Nazi Germany, a separate Transcarpathian state existed for a short period (October 1938–March 1939). After the war Transcarpathia was annexed by the Soviet Union and became the southwestern corner of the Ukrainian SSR, bordering on Poland, Czechoslovakia, Hungary, and Romania. [SS]

24. M. I. Donets was a soloist in the theaters of Moscow, Kharkov, Sverdlovsk, and Kiev. See Biographies.

25. Odessa, in southwestern Ukraine, was the largest port on the Soviet Union's Black Sea coast and a major economic and cultural center. [SS]

26. Odessa was liberated on April 10, 1944, by the Third Ukrainian Front commanded by Major General (later Marshal of the Soviet Union) R. Ya. Malinovsky. See Biographies.

27. Vatutin was wounded on February 29, 1944.

28. Colonel General of the Medical Service Academician N. N. Burdenko was at that time the chief surgeon of the Red Army. See Biographies.

29. G. K. Zhukov commanded the First Ukrainian Front from March to May 1944.

30. Stalin's perception of penicillin as an American medication was at variance with the facts. Natural penicillin—that is, the fungus of the blue mold *Penicillium*—was first observed in 1928 by the British bacteriologist Sir Alexander Fleming, while the development of artificial penicillin over the next decade was the work of scientists in a number of countries. [SS]

31. Vatutin died on April 15, 1944.

32. Khrushchev has in mind M. B. Khrapchenko, chairman of the Committee for the Arts attached to the Council of People's Commissars. He came from Smolensk province.

33. I. S. Konev commanded the First Ukrainian Front from May 1944 to May 1945.

34. Ternopol is about 110 kilometers east of Lvov in western Ukraine. [SS] Soviet troops reached the city on March 23, 1944. (Previously the city had been named Tarnopol; it was renamed Ternopol in 1944.)

35. Chernovtsy is in western Ukraine, southeast of Lvov near the border with Romania. [SS] Khrushchev is referring to the Proskurov-Chernovtsy offensive operation, which took place between March 4 and April 17, 1944.

36. In this area the Bug (or Western Bug) River flows northwest, passing about 50 kilometers northeast of Lvov. Later it flows north along the Soviet-Polish border established after World War II, then west into Poland to the Vistula River, and thence to the Baltic Sea. Peremyshl (Polish name Przemysl) is about 80 kilometers west of Lvov, just west of the post–World War II Soviet-Polish border. [SS]

37. Kamenets-Podolsky is about 220 kilometers southeast of Lvov, near the border with Romania. [SS]

38. The Third Guards Tank Army of Colonel General of Tank Forces P. S. Rybalko.

39. Khrushchev is referring to the Lvov-Sandomir offensive operation, which took place between July 13 and August 29, 1944. (Sandomir, in Polish Sandomierz, is in Poland, about 200 kilometers northwest of Lvov, on the Vistula River. [SS])

40. See note 36 on the Bug (or Western Bug) River. Khrushchev is confusing this river with the Southern Bug, which rises in the same area but flows south to the Black Sea. The Poltva River is a west-bank tributary of the (Western) Bug River. [AH/GS/SS]

41. Zholkva is about 25 kilometers north of Lvov, Yavoriv about 40 kilometers west—that is, about halfway to Peremyshl. [SS]

42. Lieutenant General N. P. Pukhov.

43. The man to whom Khrushchev is referring is Ivan Samoilovich Grushevsky. See Biographies.

44. Air Force Lieutenant General V. G. Ryazanov, twice Hero of the Soviet Union. He commanded the First Guards Shock Air Corps.

45. Vasily Tyorkin was the hero of a long narrative poem of the same name by the popular poet Aleksandr Trifonovich Tvardovsky (1910–71). The poem portrayed the simple Russian soldier in an idealized but humorous light. Tvardovsky was to play a crucial role in the post-Stalin cultural thaw as editor of the leading "liberal" literary-political journal *Novy mir* (New world). [GS/SS]

46. This took place on July 27, 1944.

47. Colonel General K. S. Moskalenko commanded the 38th Army from October 1943 to May 1945. Colonel General A. A. Grechko commanded the First Guards Army from December 1943 to May 1945. The third army to which Khrushchev refers here was the Eighteenth Army, commanded until February 1944 by Colonel General K. N. Leselidze and thereafter by Lieutenant General E. P. Zhuravlev.

48. In Soviet usage dating back to Lenin, a clear distinction was drawn between "agitation" and "propaganda" and correspondingly between "agitators" and "propagandists." Both agitators and propagandists spread officially approved ideas, but propagandists appealed to people's intellectual faculties while agitators appealed to their emotions. [SS]

49. Drogobych and Borislav are about 80 kilometers southwest of Lvov, on the slopes of the Carpathian Mountains. [SS]

50. Colonel General (from October 1944 Army General) I. Ye. Petrov commanded the Fourth Ukrainian Front from August 1944 to March 1945.

51. Colonel General L. Z. Mekhlis was a member of the Military Council of the Fourth Ukrainian Front from August 1944 to July 1945. See Biographies.

52. The Tisza River flows southwest and south from the Carpathian Mountains past Uzhgorod, then through eastern Hungary and into northern Yugoslavia, where it joins the Danube River. [SS]

53. Mukachevo is one of two towns in Transcarpathia; most of the population lives in mountain villages. The town lies just southwest of the mountains, near the postwar border with Hungary. [SS]

54. The precise ethnic or national identity of the indigenous inhabitants of Transcarpathia was and remains a matter of acute controversy. They speak an East Slavic language close to but distinct from both Russian and Ukrainian. Many of them regard themselves as belonging to a separate ethnic group called Ruthenians or Rusyns. (Other names are also in use.) Khrushchev, like many Ukrainians, regards them as a branch of the Ukrainian nation (Carpatho-Ukrainians). Ruthenian peasants who

lived in the Carpathian Mountains were known as Hutzuls. [SS]

55. Uzhgorod is about 40 kilometers northwest of Mukachevo, very close to the post–World War II border with Czechoslovakia. It is the administrative center of Transcarpathia. [SS]

56. I. I. Turyanitsa was at this time the leading Communist of the Transcarpathian Ukraine. See Biographies.

57. D. Z. Manuilsky was a prominent official of the Communist International from 1922 to 1943. See Biographies.

58. Kosice is a town in southeastern Slovakia, about 80 kilometers west of Uzhgorod. [SS]

59. Turyanitsa died in 1955. [SS]

60. The Tereblya and Rika Rivers are in fact only a few kilometers apart as they flow down the mountains, but the points at which they enter the Tisza River are separated by a distance of about 25 kilometers. [AH]

## FORWARD TO VICTORY!

In summer 1944 our troops had already reached the former western border of the USSR, which had become our border in 1939 after Poland's eastern territories, inhabited mainly by Ukrainians and Belorussians, were merged with the Belorussian and Ukrainian Soviet Socialist Republics. The First Belorussian Front (it was the first counting from the north) was initially our main force operating in this sector. Rokossovsky was commanding that Front in 1944, and Malinin was the chief of staff. I went to visit them.[1] Why?

The First Army of the Wojsko Polskie[2] was part of that Front. Its commander, General Berling, had written a letter to Stalin complaining that the Ukrainians were treating his army badly, and Berling spoke with me over the phone rather harshly, declaring that the Ukrainians did not understand what was going on and were displaying an unfriendly attitude toward the Polish armed forces (Wojsko Polskie). I decided to go visit this general to talk with him personally. I had made his acquaintance earlier, and we had been on good terms. I informed Berling that I had also called Stalin. Berling apologized: "I didn't want to cause any difficulties or unpleasantness for you. Actually what has happened is nothing special, and I will take the necessary measures." I replied: "I too will take measures on my side."

I spoke with him after telling Stalin (without complaining) that there had been incidents in which Polish soldiers had arbitrarily taken hay or allowed their stock onto the fields where crops were growing, and that was the cause of the conflict. Any war is conducted at the expense of the peasants. Evidently some Polish soldiers had also behaved badly toward the Ukrainian population, and the latter had replied in kind. Our conversation with Berling ended on a fairly friendly note, and we maintained good relations after that to the very last days of the war, as long as he was commander of that army.

After the war, in my opinion, a lack of tact was displayed toward Berling. He was pushed aside and even slighted. He sent me letters in which he poured out his feelings and his bitterness. He wrote that even though he had commanded the First Army of the Wojsko Polskie, he was undeservedly being regarded as a person who would not support a new order in Poland.[3] It's true that he was a man who had been shaped in former times and had been left over to us as a legacy, as it were, from the collapse of the Polish armed forces in 1939. He had become one of our prisoners of war and had been in one of our detention camps somewhere. When he was appointed commander of the new Polish army he still did not really sympathize with the idea of building a new socialist Poland. He remained a bourgeois intellectual and favored the previously existing system. But time marches on, and as I recall, he later changed his views.

In general I met with the Polish comrades quite often when they came to Kiev. Some of them managed to cross the front lines and come directly to Kiev. The Second Army of the Wojsko Polskie was formed in our area, and I knew many of the people in that army. Its commander was General Swierczewski.[4] I also met with Bierut[5] as well as with other Polish comrades. Living in Kiev at that time was Wanda Wasilewska, who headed the Union of Polish Patriots.[6] The Wojsko Polskie was subordinated to the Union of Polish Patriots in ideological respects. Thus Kiev became a kind of government center, or simply a guiding center for the Polish armies, but only nominally, of course, because military orders were received directly from the commanders of the Fronts to which those armies belonged.

After my talk with Berling, I went to Rokossovsky's headquarters. Zhukov was there too. Our troops were outside Kovel[7] and were getting ready for an offensive. The weather was beautiful. It was either late spring or early summer. I really had no official business there. I had nothing to do with that Front, because I was a member of the Military Council of the First Ukrainian Front. So when I arrived I told the commander jokingly: "I've come on an inspection tour. There are complaints by the collective farmers that your troops are trampling on their crops. Is that so? We have to look into this."

They all understood the joke. "Go ahead. Look into it," they said. They joked lightheartedly. After all, this was a "different time" altogether. It was we who were now sitting in the saddle, as the saying goes, and swinging our legs across our western border. A great deal was being written in the Western press then: "Will the Soviet troops cross the border or will they stop? Will they pursue the enemy or call off the war?" Those were the concerns they had in the West. For us such problems did not arise. We all agreed and stood in favor of battering the German forces thoroughly, no matter on what territory, until they surrendered.

Evening had come. I asked: "Where can I find some sleeping quarters here in your area?" In those days you often had to sleep under the nearest bush.

They said: "Zhukov is gone. You can sleep in his quarters. He doesn't have a bad arrangement there at all." I went to the place where Zhukov had been sleeping. He had hung gauze around his bed to keep off mosquitoes. Peasant women cover their cradles with the same material to keep flies off their babies.

I said to them: "Not bad. This is what it means to be on the offensive, to be driving the enemy back. It's not the same situation Zhukov and I faced in the first days of the war, when we were at the front near Ternopol. We couldn't arrange any comforts then, to sleep peacefully and not be bitten by mosquitoes." The changed situation could be seen even in this small detail.

From Rokossovsky's headquarters I called the chief of staff of the First Ukrainian Front, Sokolovsky.[8] I don't remember now what necessitated that phone call. Sokolovsky always made a very good impression on me. I first met him in 1944, when we were getting ready for some military operation, and Sokolovsky made a report on the preparations. He immediately impressed me favorably. He gave a well-grounded report on the plan of operation. His report was given in a highly skilled way and he showed a profound knowledge of the situation. Ever since then and to this very day I have great respect for this man. And I always listened to his opinions with respect when he was working as chief of the General Staff after Stalin's death.

Undertaking the latest stage of our offensive, our troops entered Polish territory, and in July, the First Belorussian Front liberated the town of Chelm and then Lublin.[9] The new Polish government—the Polish Committee of National Liberation[10]—moved to Lublin and established itself there. Stalin told me: "You should maintain contact with the Poles. Wasilewska is there with you, and you should give her all possible support." I felt that this was absolutely correct, and we did everything that was in our power. When the Polish leaders needed something, and in the event that they appealed to us, we tried as much as we could to meet their requests.

It was just then that the question arose among us of what procedure to establish for an exchange of populations between Poland and the Ukrainian SSR, so that Poles living in Ukraine could move to Poland if they wished to and Ukrainians living in Poland could move to Ukraine. The city of Lvov was of course affected by this,[11] and it was necessary for me to travel to that city several times in that connection. At the same time I was chairman of the Council of People's Commissars of the Ukrainian SSR and secretary of the Central Committee of the CP(B)U. In this capacity I also traveled several times to Lublin, where we had talks with the Poles and then signed the appropriate agreement. I signed for the Soviet side and Bierut for the Polish side. Belorussia was also negotiating with the Poles, Ponomarenko then holding the same post in Belorussia that I held in Ukraine, that is, chairman of the Council of People's Commissars and secretary of the Central Committee of the Communist Party (Bolshevik) of Belorussia.[12] He also came to Lublin.

When I flew there to sign the agreement it was August, and the watermelons in Ukraine had already ripened. Various Polish leaders and representatives of Polish parties had gathered in Lublin. I flew in with gifts, bringing watermelons in particular and treating them to watermelons and cantaloupes. That was a great delicacy for all of them back then. They didn't raise melons or similar crops. This made a good impression on them. I remember a humorous incident connected with this. A representative of the left wing of the Peasant Party, Witos, was there. His brother previously had been the leader of that party.[13] He himself was from the wealthier upper stratum of peasants. He owned a flour mill and was, they said, fairly secretive and close-mouthed. Evidently he was simply being used for his prominent name. He collaborated with us, but not sincerely. When we were having dinner, I presented him with a muskmelon: "Here, Comrade Witos, take a muskmelon. This variety is called Kolkhoznitsa." [The term means "collective farm woman."]

He looked at me, screwed up his eyes, cut the melon, and repeated: "Kolkhoznitsa?"

"Yes."

"Then why isn't this melon red?" Well now, I ask you, just because a melon is called "collective farm woman" why should it be red? Apparently he was trying to needle me, make fun of me. Of course he was opposed to collective farms and opposed to socialism, but he was going along with us because we were helping to liberate Poland and drive out the Germans.

These were internal matters, however, and they were the business of our comrades of the Polish Workers Party,[14] which was headed by Gomulka and later by Bierut. Gomulka was not in Lublin.[15] He was in Warsaw in the underground. All the questions I am talking about were taken up by Bierut, who was president of the new government. General Rola-Zymierski[16] was appointed commander in chief of the Wojsko Polskie. He was on good terms with us, and his sentiments were pro-Communist, although he himself was

THE GREAT PATRIOTIC WAR

not a Communist. We didn't have any disagreements with him. It's true that the poor fellow later fell out of favor, but he made a good impression on me. Later on, in Poland, he was arrested and even served a term in prison. I don't know what he was accused of. I heard rumors he was supposedly accused of being a foreign agent. I am stating something unconfirmed. This Zymierski was a very good friend. He and I maintained friendly relations even after the war when he had already been given the rank of marshal in Poland.

As I said earlier, an agreement was reached between the Soviet government and the Poles as to which territory would be granted to Poland and which would become part of the USSR. Among the territories ceded to Poland, some were inhabited by Ukrainians. The Ukrainians living in those areas felt that this was very painful news, especially in the Chelm region. That region had been part of the Russian empire before World War I, and there was a strong Russian influence. The population there was Ukrainian. Bulganin[17] was an official representative from Moscow at that time, something like an ambassador to the new Polish government. When I flew to Lublin, I always stayed with Bulganin. After all, we were old friends. I suggested to him: "Let's make a trip to Chelm."

We made the trip. We went into a cathedral. A clergyman of some sort met us, a beaten-down, cowed person. We were wearing generals' uniforms, and he pleaded with us: "They're handing Chelm over to the Poles. All the cathedrals here were built by Russians, by Orthodox people. Now we are going to be stripped of everything." He wasn't asking for anything, but with tears in his eyes he was complaining that it was unfair, that it was unjust, that it was wrong. He wanted his region to be united with the Soviet Union, with Russia, to preserve the Russian Orthodox Church, so that this cathedral would not be turned into a Catholic church. We simply took a look around and then left. We knew that the question had already been decided, and we didn't want to get into an argument with him.

When I was in Lublin, I saw for the first time the ovens in which the fascists had burned the corpses of dead prisoners in their concentration camps. That was not Auschwitz; it was some other camp.[18] But it, too, had several ovens. Bulganin and I arrived there just when they were digging up the mass graves filled with corpses. It was a ghastly sight! Barns or warehouses were also located there, in which mountains of shoes were piled up. I saw a huge barn that was filled with braids of women's hair. In short, the Germans had sorted everything out with great precision, and this made an especially grisly impression. You look, and somehow you can't believe your eyes: Could people really have committed such crimes? A commission was in operation just then investigating, examining all this, and recording the information. But that was the first time I personally saw this gruesome sight. I didn't go in and look at any of the other slaughterhouses like this one, but I did read about them.

The First Ukrainian Front had reached the Vistula River.[19] Front Commander Konev called me on the phone and reported that on such-and-such a date we would go on the offensive in the direction of Sandomierz, heading for the Vistula.[20] "Come and see!" he said, and I immediately flew there. I had a strong urge to watch this offensive and familiarize myself with the situation. The main thing was to watch, because in my opinion my participation was not required for analyzing and approving this operation. Everything had already been thought through. Konev enjoyed complete confidence at that time as a good fighter who knew how to command and to organize an offensive. I arrived early in the morning and went out to Konev's command post while it was still dark. The preliminary artillery bombardment began at the appointed hour. I had not observed such tremendous firepower before. An especially strong impression was made on me by the salvoes from the Katyusha rocket launchers. These massive volleys were fired as the concluding stage of the bombardment. Literally the entire battlefield lit up when the rockets hit their targets. Our planes were also operating with impunity. We had already achieved full mastery in the air. When the preliminary artillery bombardment ended and our troops moved forward, Konev and I came out of the command post. Some scattered, uncoordinated artillery fire could still be heard.

I asked: "Is there some army commander located nearby?"

Konev said: "Yes, the command post of General Zhadov.[21]

I said: "I'm going to visit Zhadov. Give me a guide, so I don't hit a mine." I went to Zhadov's command post. I asked him: "What's out there in front of you, Comrade Zhadov?"

He said: "In front of me? Out there are Soviet soldiers, who have gotten up and moved forward at full height, as the saying goes. They're not crouching down. There is no resistance. There's only one enemy gun still firing over on the left flank." Everyone on the enemy side who was still alive had fled. For me that was such a joyful thing to see. We had outlived them, we were defeating them, and we were crushing them underfoot!

And now let me talk about something else. It was 1944. Late spring or early summer. On one sunny day, of the kind that Kiev has in great numbers, I suddenly heard a roaring sound and saw a large group of planes flying over, stretched out in a column and glittering with an unusually bright white color. I had never seen such planes before. Before the war we had white airplanes, front-line bombers called SBs, but there had been very few of them during the war. And these were much larger. I realized that these were American planes flying over. I had read that the United States was producing "flying fortresses." They were flying in the direction of Kiev. I of course wanted to believe that these were American planes, but I also felt some alarm and concern: "The devil only knows," I thought, "those might be German planes." The planes flew by, a little north of Kiev, heading in the direction of Poltava. Later I found out that under an agreement with President Roosevelt an American military air base had been established near Poltava, and the American planes landed there.[22] They took off from Africa, bombed enemy troops and military targets, then landed in our area, made repairs, took on new loads of bombs, and flew off again on their military assignments. These operations by the U.S. bombers were called shuttle flights.

At one point the Germans tracked down where these American planes were flying to after their bombing raids. Evidently they were somehow able to tail these bombers and determine the exact location of the air base near Poltava. Maybe the Germans also had spies there. Both things are possible [that is, that they followed the bombers and that they had spies]. In short, they found out the American planes were based near Poltava, and they made a bombing raid on that air base.[23] I head a report that the Germans destroyed many planes there and many people suffered. It was mainly our people, because the service personnel at that air base were ours, Soviet forces. But that was one of the episodes of war. Often after that we observed these planes flying over Kiev. They flew out at night and returned by daylight after their bombing runs.

Through the headquarters of our partisans in Ukraine, we learned that the Bandera forces were forming their own guerrilla detachments. More precisely we were informed that they were based in the area around Rovno.[24] Thick forests are found there in the remote, marshy Polesye region. Our large Ukrainian partisan units were also in the Polesye. Their commander was Begma. He died about two years ago. For some time before the war, he had worked as first secretary of the party's Rovno province committee.[25] That's why he was sent there during the war, so that he could organize partisan units. He did his work well. It was he who reported that there was a very large Bandera unit in the forest near him, a unit headed by a man who called himself Taras Bulba. That is, this guerrilla leader had taken the name of the hero of Gogol's novel *Taras Bulba*.[26]

Begma even had contacts with these people. Some of them had come over and invited our troops to join them. We assigned Begma to find out in more detail what the plans of the Bandera forces were, how they were operating, and so forth. We said: "You can invite Bulba himself [for talks], if of course he shows up in your area." The invitation was sent, but Bulba never came.

When we had scouted things out in more detail, it became clear that the Bandera detachments were simply standing around, not doing anything, taking no action against the Germans. We understood that they were gathering people together who were dissatisfied with the German occupation and who might otherwise have joined our Soviet partisan units. They were thus providing a safety valve, a way for these people to vent their dissatisfaction. They took such people into their ranks, but still were doing nothing. We ascertained that they were building up forces to fight against the Red Army, not when our army was on the offensive and clearing the enemy out of our territory, but rather when our army had already moved forward. They planned then to develop their activity in our rear, behind our lines.

When we liberated Rovno, I went there to have a talk with Begma and with the commander whose troops had liberated Rovno. I don't remember now the name of that commander.[27] I arrived in Rovno at the end of the winter in early 1944. The fields were still covered with snow and it was cold. I arrived and talked to the military men. (The army headquarters was not there; only the headquarters of a division.) They told me the enemy was still nearby and was bombarding Rovno with artillery. In the evening I decided to return to Kiev. They tried to persuade me to stay over, but I was not agreeable to that. I headed north, traveling along the old border that had previously separated us from Poland.

One of our supply bases was located somewhere in that area, and I arrived there late at night. There were a great many people on the premises. I took them all in at a glance and thought to myself: "What a lot of Bandera men who have changed their uniforms! And they're getting fed, staying warm, and spying on us at the same time." I had been warned in advance that although there had been no alarming incidents, it had been observed that the Bandera forces were arming themselves in this area, and that therefore the road was not safe. Nevertheless I decided to travel farther that very same night, so as not to spend the night at that base. I reached a small town on our old border and there I spent the night. Apparently I did the right thing.

In summer and fall 1944 our troops successfully advanced westward. I visited the Front's headquarters more rarely by then. There was a lot of work to do in the Ukrainian republic. I wanted to visit, but I couldn't tear myself away to visit the front. I very much wanted occasionally to take a look at the territories we had liberated. These were no longer formerly Soviet lands, but Poland. January 1945 arrived. Stalin called me up: "Can you come here?"

I said: "Yes, I can."

He said: "Then, come. You are very much needed." I immediately flew to Moscow.

Stalin was in a very elevated mood when he met me: "The Polish comrades are asking us to give them help in setting things right in everyday life and restoring the normal functioning of city institutions. They're especially asking for help in fixing up the water supply and sewer systems, without which a city cannot live. We have liberated Warsaw, but the situation they're in—they're really helpless. All of Warsaw is lying in ruins and they can't do anything. You on the other hand have built up some experience in quickly restoring the most essential and necessary things in the cities that have been liberated." I answered: "All right, I'll be glad to go to Warsaw. Let me take along some engineers who know about municipal services and electric power plants. Electric power and water have to be provided first of all, and the functioning of the sewage and drainage systems has to be restored. Without those three components no city can live."

I invited Stramentov to come with me.[28] I knew him as an energetic organizer and a good engineer. Then I invited other engineers who specialized in electric power, water supply, and sewage systems. I took these people, as I recall, from Moscow and perhaps some from Kiev, and together with them I flew to Warsaw. At that time the provisional Polish government, the Committee of National Liberation, as it had previously been named, had established itself in Praga, a suburb of Warsaw on the east bank of the Vistula. The premier was Osobka-Morawski, and Gomulka was the secretary of the Central Committee of the Polish Workers Party, while the president of Warsaw, the title then in use, was Spychalski, who held the rank of general.[29] He made a favorable impression on me. He was a young, active, and energetic man, an architect and engineer by education. It was a good combination to have an architect as the head of the city of Warsaw as it was being restored.

Previously Spychalski had held responsible posts in the Gwardia Ludowa (People's Guard) and the Armia Ludowa (People's Army), which had been organized by the Polish Communists. He was one of the organizers of their armed detachments. Even when he held the civilian post of president of the capital city, Spychalski went around wearing a military uniform. Bierut was head of the People's National Council, the Krajowa Rada Narodowa. I had met him more than once before that, but this was my first meeting with Spychalski.

We agreed that our engineers, together with Polish engineers, would break up into groups according to sector. Some would take the job of examining what condition the electric power plant was in, how quickly it could be restored and electric power be provided; a second group would deal with the problem of the water supply system; the third, the sewage system: all the most important things for people. The cleaning of the city was undertaken by the Poles themselves, on their own. Our services were not needed in that area. I put Stramentov in charge of the whole operation. He was a theoretician and practical expert in urban construction and city management. He dealt with the Polish specialists and with our own. When specific problems came up, the Soviet engineers discussed them first with Stramentov, and then Stramentov reported to me, while our specialists discussed the course of the work further with the Polish comrades. Soon some encouraging news was reported to me. At the electric power plant, which according to the Poles had been completely destroyed, actually only the outer building had been destroyed, while the equipment inside could be started up, and we could immediately have electric power. A surface examination had shown that the machinery was working. The mechanisms that provided water were in the same condition, and so water could be supplied quickly. The sewer system, it seemed, had not been destroyed either. These were indeed glad tidings, and it was a joy to hear them.

A few days later, after the condition of the machinery had been checked out in detail and the turbines had been tested, I joked a little with Bierut: "Wouldn't you give us, in repayment for our consultation and assistance, half the electric power that we restored in Warsaw so we can use it in Kiev?" Things were in a bad way with electricity in Kiev. The electric power plant there had been destroyed. We did have light in the city, but not everywhere. The situation turned out to be better in the case of the Poles. Their electric power plant had not been destroyed as badly. Warsaw got electric power and it got water. Bierut was radiant. He was beaming. He thanked us and asked us to extend his gratitude to Stalin also. He spoke very sincerely. I think that he was an honest Communist, devoted to the cause of Marxism-Leninism. But he had one weakness: he was overly kind, trusting, and gentle. This got him into complications. People who worked alongside him took advantage of these traits of his character.

Bierut made a suggestion to me: "Our party is being led by a major figure of the Communist movement, Comrade Wieslaw, that is, Gomulka. I would like to ask you to visit him at his apartment, because he is very ill and is not going out."

I answered: "All right, I'll be happy to go visit him and make his acquaintance." They gave me a guide, and we set out for Gomulka's place. I don't remember of course what street he lived on. I remember only that it was a large room, with the shades drawn, and with walls and ceiling blackened by smoke. There was a little fireplace in the room so that you could warm yourself, but the regular large heating stove was not working. His wife was doing laundry by hand when I arrived. Gomulka was sitting in an armchair, his cheek wrapped in a black bandage. We talked for a little while. Gomulka did not have an especially good command of Russian at that time, but we were able to explain ourselves to each other, and the translator helped.

"Comrade Wieslaw" gave his evaluation of the situation in the country and of how the work of the Polish Workers Party was being organized. Gomulka impressed me as a man with a sober mind who knew where to begin and how to organize his party's activity as well as the machinery of government. In short he gave the impression of a major political figure and government leader. He said: "Right now I am not well, but I will be back on my feet soon, and then I will get fully involved." When I told Stalin about my trip, I also informed him about Gomulka. We had not known about this man previously. Actually I don't know whether Stalin had heard about him before. Probably he had not. To Stalin I conveyed high praise and a good character reference about Gomulka.

I wanted to make a trip to Lodz. It had already been liberated from the fascists. The textile mills of Lodz had been famous throughout Russia even before World War I. (Warsaw and Lodz had previously been part of the Russian empire.) Lodz was a major proletarian and industrial center, so that's why I wanted to take a look at it. I had mentioned this to Gomulka also. He had said: "All right, make a trip there."

Apparently the Polish leaders had come to an agreement among themselves, because Osobka-Morawski made the suggestion: "I'll come with you."

I said to him: "Please do." We set off for Lodz in an automobile. It was a fairly good distance from Warsaw[30] but the road was very good. Along the way I of course saw much of the destruction that the war had brought to Poland, but I didn't notice any particularly massive scenes of destruction. We arrived in Lodz and went to a hotel, which was well equipped. It had at one time been quite a prosperous hotel, but now it was cold. The heating system wasn't working, and yet we had to spend the night in this hotel. The building protected us from the wind but gave us no warmth. It was a real icicle, and we had to put on every piece of clothing that we had available. In the evening Rola-Zymierski showed up, and we had supper together. The next day I looked around the city. The factories of Lodz were not working. Nothing in the city was functioning. Everything was disorganized, although I didn't see a great deal of destruction in Lodz either. At any rate no such thing has stuck in my memory. Comparing the destruction suffered by Kiev, Kharkov, the cities and mines of the Donbass, and Poltava with what I noticed there, I came to the conclusion that Poland got off fairly lightly, with the exception of Warsaw.

Warsaw lay in ruins. Only a few isolated buildings remained intact. People lived in cellars and in the ruins. Everything was covered with debris, the rubble from upper stories that had collapsed. People dug openings in the ruins and somehow made places for themselves to live in. I went up in a plane to view Warsaw from the sky. It was really hard to imagine the scale of the destruction. When you traveled through the streets all you saw was ruins, on your right and on your left—it was as though you were traveling in the mountains between cliffs. When I went up in the plane and made a few circles over Warsaw, a terrible spectacle unfolded beneath me. Everything was smashed to bits, especially the Warsaw ghetto area, where the fascists had corralled the Jews and then killed them all, literally destroying everything that could be destroyed. Other districts of the city suffered less perhaps, but they also lay in ruins.

One Sunday the people of Warsaw organized a massive street cleaning to make it possible to use the streets for walking and driving. Bierut suggested to me: "Let's work with them a little, even if it's just symbolic." We went on the appointed day to a district that had been assigned in advance, where industrial workers and office workers had already gathered. Actually, at that time no such distinctions were made. They spoke of everyone as Varsovians together, not in the sense that we say Kievans, simply meaning "residents of Kiev." There was a special meaning and social significance invested in the word "Varsovian." People came with posters and banners with slogans calling for Warsaw to be completely restored, and they set about that task. Everyone worked in harmony, but the people were not well nourished and it was hard to expect great success. We worked with them for a little while; it really was just symbolic.

Spychalski and other leading comrades were there, together with Bierut. I don't remember them all now. There was one elderly gentleman who I especially remember. They told me he was an architect by training. He was then one of the active Communist Party members, but later he more or less disappeared from the scene rather quickly, and when I went to Warsaw again later I no longer encountered him. What happened to him? He was notably older than the others. Perhaps his years told on him. I had an impression of him as an intelligent man, judging from his remarks.

That's how I was included, on Stalin's orders, in the process of restoring Warsaw immediately after the Germans were driven out. When I departed from the Polish capital, it was pleasant to feel that I was leaving behind me some work well done.

I suppose that the Polish specialists could have done everything by themselves, and they apparently would have, but Stalin sent me there to help. That meant that the question had been settled beyond dispute. Besides, we really did have the necessary experience. We had restored the Donbass, as well as Kharkov, Kiev, and other cities. We knew where to begin. The sight of ruined cities no longer made a devastating impression on us, sapping our morale and preventing us from working. You look around and say to yourself, "Everything has been destroyed, everything is in ruins, and the machinery is totally unfit for use." But then you clean things up, take away the broken bricks, sweep up the dust, get down to repairing the machinery and other aspects of the municipal economy, and soon you get things running. You look around and the city has taken on a normal aspect again. The Polish electric power plants were all also restored quickly and began to provide electric power, meeting the needs of Warsaw in full, in fact, not only satisfying the demands of the city and its industry, but with reserves to spare.

After returning to Moscow I reported to Stalin on the results. Stalin was very pleased with my report. He was also glad that we had given assistance to Poland and felt it ought to leave good memories in the minds of the Polish people, especially the inhabitants of Warsaw. Of course Stalin did not discuss any other considerations with me, but I myself understood that after the Soviet-German treaties of 1939 the fresh wounds that the Polish people felt had not yet been healed and Stalin wanted somehow to alleviate those by doing everything possible to help Poland heal its former wounds.

Osobka-Morawski, as the Polish Communists told me, had been a member of the Polish Socialist Party (PPS), and they did not have complete political confidence in him. Nevertheless along with a certain number of other PPS members, he had agreed to collaborate with the Polish Workers Party and had been promoted to a high government post, the post of prime minister. He had been part of the cooperative movement and concerned himself very much with questions of the cooperatives. It's difficult for me to judge him as an individual, although I did meet him after the war. He was my guest in

Kiev then. Stalin at one point suggested to me: "Invite Osobka-Morawski together with a Polish delegation to visit you in Ukraine and give them a good warm reception." In addition to Osobka, those who came to visit us then included Berman and, as I recall, Minc.[31] They visited Kiev and Zaporozhye, and then I flew with them to Odessa. We did literally everything we could to dispose them favorably toward us and create good conditions for favorable relations between the leaderships of the USSR and Poland, to lay the groundwork for friendship and mutual respect between our two nations.

Incidentally, compared with Bierut and especially with Gomulka and Spychalski, Osobka did not make a very strong impression on me. I also heard about Cyrankiewicz[32] then. He was a young and prominent member of the PPS, but I had no occasion to meet him in person. He was not in Warsaw in 1945, because he was in one of Hitler's concentration camps. I made his acquaintance later. Wasilewska told me about Cyrankiewicz. She was a remarkable Polish woman, an interesting person, and a good writer with great willpower and profound intelligence as a political activist. I had great respect for her, but in this conversation about Cyrankiewicz she caused me some distress. I said to her: "Wanda Lwowna, I am sorry that the time is soon going to come when it will be a rare thing for you and me to meet."

She asked in her strong Polish accent: "Why do you think that?" She was not especially fluent in Russian.

I said: "What do you mean why? Poland is being liberated, Warsaw will soon be free, and evidently you will have to go there to help with the work." At that time she was the head of the Union of Polish Patriots, and as I have said, the Wojsko Polskie was subordinated to it in ideological respects.

"No," she replied, "I'm not going anywhere. I'll leave Kiev only when Poland becomes the seventeenth republic of the USSR." (At that time there were sixteen union republics in the USSR.)

She repeated this to me later many times. And sure enough, she never did leave Kiev. I even felt a little sorry that she didn't leave because I felt that she would be more useful in Poland. But evidently the Ukrainian writer Korneichuk[33] was the big obstacle to her leaving. She and Korneichuk had become very close. It was almost as though she had become his wife, but officially there was no government document attesting to such a marriage. Wanda was a good influence on Korneichuk and restrained him from many inappropriate actions, especially connected with heavy drinking. In the latter respect Korneichuk had always been unrestrained. It's true that during the first period of the war she too abused alcohol. Evidently that was because of the painful experiences of losing her homeland, retreating with the Soviet troops, and losing Ukraine. Later she regained her former willpower, took herself in hand, and was a good influence on Korneichuk. When at a meal he would reach for a second glass of cognac, Wanda would give him just one look and he would pull his hand back. I liked that. It was good for both of them.

I also want to touch on the Warsaw uprising of 1944. Much has been written about it. It is said that we of the Soviet Union were to blame for the defeat of the uprising. Political leaders in the West have frequently returned to this episode to try to incite the Polish people against the USSR. They say that the Russians didn't extend a helping hand when Bor-Komorowski[34] was fighting the Germans, with Soviet troops right alongside. Komorowski was taken prisoner by the Germans, but despite the fact that he was the organizer of an uprising in Warsaw that occurred at the most critical moment for the German occupation forces in Poland, he got off with only a bad scare, and later he was active in the West in opposition to the Soviet Union and People's Poland.

The opinions I can express on this question now are strictly my own. I do not know any concrete facts in regard to how this question was resolved, the question of our aid to the insurgents, or how much basis there is for the accusations made in the West against Stalin in this connection. I cannot even confirm that they took place [i.e., the things Stalin was accused of], although the opposing side may be able to substantiate them fully. What were the general circumstances that arose at that time?

Soviet troops had come up close to Warsaw, leaving a new Polish government behind them in Lublin. The Polish government-in-exile in London was headed by Mikolajczyk.[35] It was natural that the West, primarily London, should be preparing a government of its own for Poland. These people wanted to defeat the Germans and liberate Poland, using our troops, our strength, and our blood, but they wanted Poland to remain a pro-Western capitalist country. They wanted to deny to the Polish people the possibility of building a new socialist People's Poland of the workers and peasants. That was Churchill's intention. Naturally on this question Stalin was heart and soul in favor of Poland becoming socialist. It might not literally imitate our Soviet form of socialism, but in essence the working class would come to the fore in alliance with the peasantry, so that Leninist politics would be victorious there.

As our troops were approaching the Vistula, and an uprising broke out in Warsaw, a great commotion began to the effect that we should give some assistance to the insurgents in Warsaw. But after all, there was a war going on. What does it mean to give assistance? The Germans were there, defending their positions, and the broad and deep Vistula River lay in front of us. This is not such an easy thing to deal with. You can't just say "I want to," and there you've gone across! I remember that when we were approaching Kiev we also had to stop at the Dnieper River. We first had to make a number of attempts to cross the Dnieper, and only after we succeeded in crossing were we able to deal a crushing blow to the German forces and drive them out of Kiev. We spent quite a bit of time trying to accomplish that. I have already told about how we undertook offensive operations from the Bukrin beachhead and then had to regroup our forces and strike a blow from a different beachhead.

Evidently in front of Warsaw we encountered difficulties of the same kind. We were not able to take Warsaw head on. We were unable to cross the river from Praga, the suburb on the east bank of the Vistula. We had to force the Vistula farther north, bypassing Warsaw, and eventually forcing the Germans to abandon the city. I don't know what the specific circumstances were during those days when the enemy was still in Warsaw and we were more or less looking across the river at each other, situated on opposite banks. But I understand the arguments of the opposing side. They had every opportunity of drilling it into people's heads that we, the Soviet authorities, deliberately refused to take action because it was not in our interests to reinforce Bór-Komorowski. After all, he would fight against us in Warsaw if we didn't recognize his authority. And of course we would not have recognized it.

Churchill was the real instigator of this uprising, acting through Mikolajczyk. He wanted to confront us with an accomplished fact. It might be true that we had shed a lot of blood and consequently were approaching Warsaw after driving the Germans back, but in the capital of Poland he would already have the country's government, a new government headed by Mikolajczyk. Then if we had removed such an already existing government, it would have meant creating complications with our allies—harsh disputes, which of course were not desirable. That was the situation then, as I understand it. But I repeat, I do not know of any particular facts supporting one point of view or another.

When the Germans were driven out, Mikolajczyk came to Warsaw and became deputy prime minister. I made his acquaintance in Moscow when the Polish leaders arrived for discussions with Stalin. Later Stalin gave a dinner in their honor. The truth must be stated here, that the Armia Krajowa, the "Home Army," which had been organized by people headed by Mikolajczyk, was a complex and powerful organization.[36] We had clashes with that army, and it caused us a lot of worry and trouble. As early as our occupation of Lvov we ran into active operations by the Armia Krajowa.

During winter 1944–45 our troops successfully continued their offensive and entered the territory of Germany itself. Konev, the commander of the First Ukrainian Front, and I called each other on the phone quite often. He kept me up-to-date, but of course there was no need for my immediate presence at the Front headquarters. At that time I was up to my ears in civilian tasks in Ukraine, although I had a very great longing to be with my military comrades from time to time, to hear what they had to say and take a look at the land of Germany. I had never been in Germany, and I wanted to look the Germans right in the eye, to read their faces and see how they felt about our troops entering their territory and how it tasted to them now, the war that Hitler had imposed on them. Now the war had been brought to the territory of Germany itself, and the German people were suffering from what they had done to us.

One might say that Hitler was to blame, not the German people, and that is true. I understand that. I always understood it and made a distinction between Hitler and the German people. The German people were deceived and made fools of, or else they were intoxicated with chauvinism (I don't know which expression is most appropriate here; evidently both are appropriate), and they supported Hitler. If the German people had not supported Hitler, Hitler could not have stayed in power. The German army not only fought against us but displayed very great persistence and stubbornness in its fighting, and after all, it was composed of Germans. The ideas that Hitler put forward about the need to conquer more "living space" and the superiority of the German nation—this Nazi narcotic blinded the people. That's why I wanted to see how the sobering-up process was going on among the Germans, and in general whether it actually was going on.

On one occasion, after talking with Konev on the phone, I flew to visit him. The Front headquarters was located in some settlement inside Germany along the Oder River.[37] Our troops were fighting in the Breslau region.[38] Breslau had been surrounded, but the Germans were putting up stubborn resistance, and rather prolonged fighting was going on.[39] While I was at the Front headquarters, I decided to talk with the commanders and other comrades of long standing. I wanted to visit Silesia,[40] because Moskalenko's 38th Army was operating there. Then I wanted to visit the 60th Army, commanded by Kurochkin.[41] Chernyakhovsky had commanded that army earlier, and later had been appointed Front commander, but he was killed in East Prussia. He was a young general, full of great promise.[42] And so I flew to Germany. Krasovsky,[43] the commander of our air army, informed me where I could land. Our people met us and directed us to the headquarters. It was located in a German settlement. As we were driving there I could see that all the roads were covered with feathers and down. I asked: "What's the meaning of that?"

They explained: "When the Germans were fleeing, they threw out their belongings, including pillows and quilts. Evidently the soldiers let the stuffing out and took the cloth to make foot bindings."[44]

I saw no Germans near the area where the headquarters was located. Either they had fled or been deported. I was familiar with the structure of German houses. The main house would have stables, a cowshed, and other outbuildings attached to it, and a manure pile in the middle of the yard. I had seen such arrangements in the settlements of German colonists in Ukraine. Large German colonies had lived there since long ago. From the Front headquarters I went to visit Kurochkin and Moskalenko. I don't remember which headquarters I spent the night at, but I remember that the headquarters of one of the armies was located in a miners' settlement next to some coal pits. I compared them with what we had in the Donbass. To a miner's eye this was truly a paradise on earth. The coal pits were in a forest, a beautiful spot, and the buildings for the workers and for the white-collar employees provided much better domestic arrangements than the mines where my father had worked and where I spent my childhood and youth.

The army commanders reported to me on the situation. Everywhere the situation was superb. Our troops were moving forward, and their mood was as good as could be. Victory was already rising up before their eyes. They could picture it and taste it. I made my trip actually more for the purpose of looking at living conditions in Germany and meeting the local population than occupying myself with military matters. But I didn't meet any of the local population. They had all fled or been deported. As a rule, even in our own country, we usually removed local residents from the area where our headquarters was established. Stalin had set down strict rules on this matter. To what extent that was really necessary is hard to say. It was done so that spies could not lurk nearby.

At that time of year there was snow remaining only in the woods. The rest of the ground was clear, and I saw a huge a number of storage piles out in the fields. I asked: "Are those potatoes?" It was well known that the Germans loved potatoes and were good at growing them. They made storage piles right out in the fields, where the potatoes were kept for a very long time. I also knew this from the experience we had in Ukraine. But the storage piles we had in Ukraine were not like the ones I saw in Germany. Nowadays, as a retired person, I occasionally go cross-country skiing. While skiing one day, I saw a pile of fodder beets out in a field. The beets had been placed in a storage pile the previous autumn, but it was really painful to see how ignorantly and carelessly this had been done. A huge number of beets were rotting because the storage piles had not been set up properly. I told the local officials: "Do you really make your storage piles without allowing air to get in?" They had put a light covering of straw over the beets and then thrown dirt on top without allowing any ventilation. Of course everything down inside suffocated and began to rot. The Germans, on the other hand, did everything in their efficient German way. You have to give credit where credit is due, as far as German agricultural skills go. And in general the level of German culture is quite high. I looked at their fields and felt envious that everything there was so fine. They had plenty of potatoes, even though it was 1945, the year of Germany's defeat.

Konev told me the Front's further plans. At that time he had nothing to complain about. He felt that his troops were fighting well and were supplied with everything they needed, so that they could successfully carry out their assignments. I returned home from the front lines by way of Poznan[45] and some other [former German] cities that have now been turned over to Poland. These cities had been damaged very badly. Then I went to Krakow, from which I returned to Uzhgorod, and from Uzhgorod I flew to Kiev.

I had decided to travel through Polish territory by car. As I was going along, being able to study the situation better as I traveled, I came to the realization that I was taking a serious risk. We didn't have our own troops in the area; there was not much traffic on the roads, and the Armia Krajowa was beginning to expand its activities. Closer to the border of Soviet Ukraine, the Bandera forces were active. This was only the beginning as yet, but there had already been incidents in which our people had been attacked and killed, assassinations of party and government officials and especially of security personnel. The security police were hot on the trail of Bandera's men and paid with their lives for pursuing these enemies of the Soviet Union.

I can't say anything about Krakow now except that it was a city that had been completely untouched. The Polish activists gave the credit for the saving of Krakow to Soviet troops. Much has been written about this. On the road from Krakow to Uzhgorod I didn't see a lot of destruction either. I got the impression that as a result of the rapid advance of our troops [in 1944], and the weak resistance of the Polish army in 1939 when the Germans had come through, there had been no prolonged fighting and consequently no major destruction. That was the last time I flew out to Front headquarters. I celebrated the favorable course of events together with the Front commanders, the army commanders Moskalenko and Kurochkin, and other commanders. They all felt they were in seventh heaven. Not only was our side winning, but we were also close to the end of the war, the complete defeat of Hitler's armies. We were close to entering Berlin, close to victory! This was our reward for all we had suffered, for all that our country had endured until then.

I returned to Kiev. Zhukov, who was commanding the First Belorussian Front,[46] often called me in Kiev. He and I maintained friendly ties. He rejoiced over the telephone: "That so-and-so Hitler. I'm soon going to put him in a cage and bring him to you. When I deliver him to Moscow, I'm going to come through Kiev, so you too can take a look at him." For my part, I wished Zhukov success and rejoiced with him. I was sure that if he commanded the troops, the success of our offensive was assured. When Germany surrendered, Zhukov called me again: "I can't keep my promise [about Hitler]. He's dead— the filthy rat, and they burned his body. We found the charred corpse."[47]

I also talked with Konev on the phone at that time, and he told me what was going on with him. But I had more contact with Zhukov than with Konev then, because I had much closer personal relations with Zhukov. I had made Konev's acquaintance only at the beginning of the war; before the war I had met him only once. Zhukov, on the other hand, had been commander of the troops of the Kiev Special Military District. He and I met not only in the course of our work, but he also came to visit me at my dacha and we used to go hunting together. So he and I had established good relations. I had great respect for him and valued him as a commander, and he deserved that.

And so we came to the culmination of a great epic—the war of the peoples of the USSR against Hitler's invasion. Joy at the destruction of our enemy was combined with a tremendous feeling of moral satisfaction at our victory. A passage from the Holy Scriptures came to me, one that was repeated by Aleksandr Nevsky: "All they that come against us with the sword shall perish with the sword."[48] That saying was on everybody's lips, and at last it had come true in the form of our victory. When I heard that Germany had surrendered, the joy I felt was unbelievable. And all of us rejoiced. This has been described many times, and I cannot describe it better than our writers and artists have done, especially the victory parade that took place in Moscow on Red Square. People were suffocating our military men with embraces of joy. Victory! A universal celebration! People hugged and kissed one another and celebrated. And I too experienced and felt all of that.

Although I knew Stalin well and I knew what kind of response I could expect from him, I still hastened to call him on the phone and congratulate him on our victory. I made the call. I was quickly connected, and Stalin picked up the phone. I congratulated him. I said: "Comrade Stalin, allow me to congratulate you on the occasion of the victory of our armed forces, the victory of our people, the complete defeat of the German army, and so forth." I don't remember what I said word for word.

But what was the response? What Stalin said to me in reply was some sort of rudeness. I simply turned to stone. How could this be? Why? I knew his character very well, and I knew that you could expect virtually anything from him. I knew that he would want to demonstrate to me that what had happened was for him already a bygone stage, that he was already thinking about great new things. It was as though he were saying, "Why should I think about what happened yesterday?" Supposedly he was already racking his brain about what was to come tomorrow. In my opinion this was play-acting. Stalin knew very well how to perform this kind of role, and since he was also a coarse and rude individual, this was how it came out. (I am not the first one to speak about his rudeness. In his "Testament," Lenin, who had a superb knowledge of what Stalin was really like, referred to Stalin's rudeness and his lack of patience and tolerance.)[49]

I suffered and felt hurt for a long time about what had happened. How could this be? Did he really lack any feelings of joy? Or was he just pretending? Well, he had not been lacking in feelings of fear. I had seen the state that Stalin was in during the first days of the war. He had been completely demoralized then, like a formless mass of protoplasm. He nearly renounced all his posts and all active duties. To the members of the Politburo he said the following words: "Lenin created our state, and we have sh—all over it. Everything is ruined. I am resigning." He got in his car and left the Kremlin and went to his private dacha. Later the others went there to seek him out, as Beria told me later. They tried to persuade him. They urged him to resume his former duties and authority and set to work, because victory was possible; all was not lost; we still had an enormous territory and great resources.

And here at last was the long-awaited victory! But he acted as though it was nothing to rejoice over. He put on a show, as though to say: "What are you congratulating me for? I knew long ago that this was exactly how it would be." But the truth is that I had seen him in a different situation, and I knew for certain that at one time he had not thought this way. His thinking had been much more negative than that of the people around him. Yet now he was pulling a stunt like this, refusing to accept congratulations.

1. Marshal of the Soviet Union K. K. Rokossovsky commanded the First Belorussian Front from February to November 1944. Thereafter and up to June 1945 this front was headed by Marshal of the Soviet Union G. K. Zhukov. The chief of staff of the front remained Colonel General M. S. Malinin.

2. Lieutenant General Z. Berling (see Biographies) served in the Polish armed forces (Wojsko Polskie) of General Anders and later in the formation that in July 1944 became the First Polish Army. From October to December 1944 this army was commanded by Lieutenant General W. Korczyc and thereafter by Lieutenant General S. G. Poplavsky. (Poplavsky was a Russified Pole. He was born in 1902 to a Polish peasant family in Podolia, and his original name was Stanislav Poplawski; his father's name was Hilary. He joined the Red Army in 1923 and pursued a successful military career in the Soviet Union. He took command of the First Polish Army at the request of the pro-Soviet Polish government. [GS])

3. Z. Berling. See Biographies.

4. From July to September 1944 the Second Polish Army was commanded by Lieutenant General K. Swierczewski. Thereafter it was headed by Lieutenant General S. G. Poplavsky and from December 1944 again by Swierczewski.

5. From 1944 to 1947 Boleslaw Bierut was chairman of the provisional supreme body of power in Poland, the National People's Council. See Biographies.

6. From 1943 to 1945 the writer Wanda Wasilewska was editor in chief of the newspaper *Wolna Polska* (Free Poland) and chair of the Union of Polish Patriots in the USSR. See Biographies.

7. Kovel is in northwestern Ukraine, near the postwar Soviet-Polish border. [SS]

8. Army General V. D. Sokolovsky served as chief of staff of the First Ukrainian Front from April 1944 to April 1945. Thereafter up to May 1945 he was deputy commander of the First Belorussian Front.

9. Advancing west from Kovel, Chelm and Lublin were the first two towns on the Polish side of the postwar border. Chelm is about 90 kilometers, and Lublin about 160 kilometers, west of Kovel. Lublin is about 160 kilometers southeast of Warsaw. [SS]

10. The pro-Soviet Polish Committee of National Liberation was formed in July 1944 on the basis of the Union of Polish Patriots. It was one of two provisional Polish governments in existence at this time. Its rival was the Polish government-in-exile based in London. [SS]

11. Lvov was affected because of its large Polish population. [SS]

12. P. K. Ponomarenko occupied these posts from 1944 to 1948.

13. The Polish Peasant Party (Polskie Stronnictwo Ludowe) was led by Wincenty Witos from 1931. Its left wing, People's Freedom (Wolia Ludu), joined the National People's Council and the Polish Committee of National Liberation.

14. The Polish Workers' Party was the name of the Communist party in Poland at that time. In December 1948, the Polish Workers' Party absorbed the social-democratic Polish Socialist Party and was renamed the Polish United Workers' Party (PUWP). [SS]

15. Wladyslaw Gomulka (whose party name was "Wieslaw") was general secretary of the Central Committee of the Polish Workers' Party from November 1943 to August 1948. Then up to December 1948 this post was occupied by Boleslaw Bierut. Gomulka was imprisoned in the postwar era, as hard-core Stalinist elements took control; he was released in 1956 and again became party leader, remaining first secretary of the Central Committee of the PUWP until December 1970. [GS]

16. Tank Forces General Michal Rola-Zymierski commanded the Polish armed forces under the pro-Soviet provisional Polish government in Krakow from July 1944.

17. N. A. Bulganin. See Biographies.

18. This was the Nazi concentration camp of Maidanek, near Lublin.

19. The Vistula River (in Polish the Wisla) is Poland's longest river. It flows north from the Carpathian Mountains in southern Poland through Krakow, Sandomierz, and Warsaw and empties into the Baltic Sea. [SS]

20. Sandomierz is on the Vistula River about 200 kilometers south of Warsaw and 150 kilometers northeast of Krakow. [SS]

21. N. S. Khrushchev is referring to the Fifth Guards Army under the command of Major General A. S. Zhadov.

22. They landed at three airfields: one on the approaches to Poltava, another near Mirgorod, and a third near Piryatin. (These places are in central Ukraine, about midway between Kiev and Kharkov. [SS])

23. As a result of this incident, which took place on June 22, 1944, near Poltava, forty-seven American airplanes were destroyed and twenty-one American and twenty-four Soviet airplanes were damaged. On June 23 there was a raid on the airfield near Mirgorod, resulting in the destruction of three and the damage of thirteen American airplanes. Altogether thirty Soviet and two American servicemen were killed, and eighty Soviet and fourteen American servicemen injured.

24. Rovno is in northwestern Ukraine, about 140 kilometers northeast of Lvov. [SS]

25. From 1942 to 1944, V. A. Begma was secretary of the underground committee of the CP(B)U for Rovno province (with the rank of major general). See Biographies.

26. Gogol's novel *Taras Bulba* is about an imaginary Cossack hero of the struggle for independence in Ukraine in the sixteenth century. [SS]

27. Rovno was liberated by the Sixth Guards Cavalry Corps commanded by Lieutenant General S. V. Sokolov.

28. A. E. Stramentov, author of a number of monographs on city planning and the development of urban transportation.

29. E. Osobka-Morawski was chairman of Poland's provisional government from January 1 to June 28, 1945. General M. Spychalski was mayor of Warsaw in 1944 and 1945, then deputy minister of national defense of Poland. Previously he had been chief of staff of the People's Guard (Gwardia Ludowa) and deputy chief of staff of the People's Army (Armia Ludowa).

30. Lodz is about 120 kilometers southwest of Warsaw. [SS]

31. After the war Jakub Berman was a member of the Central Committee of the Polish Workers' Party and a leading figure in the Polish government. Hilary Minc was a member of the Central Committee of the Polish Workers' Party and minister of trade and industry.

32. Jozef Cyrankiewicz was in Nazi concentration camps during the war. He was general secretary of the Polish Party of Socialists from 1945 to 1948, when he joined the Politburo of the Central Committee of the Polish United Workers' Party. He was premier of Poland from 1947 to 1952 and from 1954 to 1970. See Biographies.

33. The dramatist A. E. Korneichuk was chairman of the Union of Writers of Ukraine from 1946 to 1953.

34. General Tadeusz Komorowski, also known as General Bor, was a leader of the Armia Krajowa (Home Army; partisans loyal to the Polish government-in-exile in London). He led the Warsaw uprising of August and September 1944. See Biographies.

35. Stanislaus Mikolajczyk was vice premier of the Polish government-in-exile from 1940 to 1943, then from 1945 to 1947 vice premier of Poland and chairman of the Polish Peasant Party.

36. The Armia Krajowa (Home Army) emerged in 1944 through the unification of various Polish underground military organizations. It was the largest resistance organization in Nazi-occupied Europe, with up to 300,000 members at its peak. It had close ties with the Polish government-in-exile in London. The Warsaw uprising is considered its greatest achievement. [SS]

37. The Oder River flows north to the Baltic Sea, passing about 100 kilometers east of Berlin. It was inside Germany's pre–World War II borders. After the war it formed part of the new German-Polish border (the Oder-Neisse line). [SS]

38. Breslau is the old German name of this city. It was later renamed Wroclaw. It is on the Oder River, about 300 kilometers southwest of Warsaw. [SS]

39. The fighting for the city of Breslau lasted from mid-February until May 6, 1945.

40. Silesia is a highly industrialized region in southwestern Poland, along the border with the Czech Republic. Before the war it belonged to Germany. [SS]

41. From Silesia the 38th Army moved toward the town of Moravska Ostrava in Czechoslovakia. Colonel General P. A. Kurochkin commanded the 60th Army from April 1944 to May 1945.

42. Army General I. D. Chernyakhovsky commanded the 60th Army from July 1942. Then from April 1944 he headed the Western Front and the Third Belorussian Front. He perished (at the age of thirty-nine years [SS]) on February 18, 1945, near the town of Melzak (now in Poland). (Melzak, now called Pieniezno, is in the Masurian marshes of northeastern Poland, some 50 kilometers northeast of the town of Olsztyn and about 200 kilometers north of Warsaw. [AH/SS])

43. Air Force Lieutenant General S. A. Krasovsky commanded the Second Air Army from March 1943 to May 1945. The headquarters of the First Ukrainian Front was situated in Schönwalde (on the railroad line from Poznan to Katowice). (This is a very small place about 100 kilometers northwest of Katowice, about halfway between Wroclaw and Czestochowa. [AH/SS])

44. Foot bindings were used in the Russian army instead of socks or stockings. [SK]

45. Poznan is in western Poland, about 300 kilometers west of Warsaw. The former German name of the city was Posen. [SS]

46. Marshal of the Soviet Union G. K. Zhukov commanded the First Belorussian Front from November 1944 to June 1945.

47. Hitler committed suicide on April 30, 1945, in his Berlin bunker. The corpse was burned with gasoline and buried in the garden of the bunker. Following the partial recovery of the remains by Soviet troops, an autopsy was conducted on May 8, 1945. The autopsy indicated that in addition to shooting himself in the head Hitler had poisoned himself with cyanide. [SS]

48. Khrushchev's words are not a literal quotation of the Bible. According to the King James version, Jesus said: "All they that take the sword shall perish with the sword" (Matt. 26:52). Variations on this phrasing are commonly encountered in modern English, such as: "Those who live by the sword shall die by the sword." The version of the quotation used by Khrushchev is similar to the proclamation made at the end of the film *Aleksandr Nevsky* (1938) by the Soviet director Sergei Eisenstein, and it may be from this film that Khrushchev recalled the saying. Aleksandr Nevsky (1219–63) was a prince of Novgorod who defended Russia from invasion by the Swedes, the Lithuanians, and the German Teutonic Knights. Eisenstein's film is devoted to the battle at Lake Chudskoye (now Lake Peipus along the Russian-Estonian border) on April 5, 1242, at which Nevsky's

troops defeated the Knights of the Teutonic Order. [SS/GS]

49. The passage of Lenin's "Testament" to which Khrushchev refers was dictated by Lenin on January 4, 1923, as an addition to his "Letter to the Congress" of December 24, 1922: "Stalin is too rude, and this defect, although quite tolerable in our midst and in dealings among us Communists, becomes intolerable in a Secretary-General. That is why I suggest that the comrades think about a way of removing Stalin from that post and appointing another man in his stead who differs from Comrade Stalin only in having one advan-

tage, namely, that of being more tolerant, more loyal, more polite, and more considerate to the comrades, less capricious, etc." (See *Collected Works* [Moscow: Progress, 1966], 36:596.) After the consolidation of Stalin's power in the late 1920s and early 1930s, Lenin's "Testament" was suppressed; people were arrested by the security police for simply having a copy of the document. Only after Khrushchev's "secret speech" at the Twentieth Party Congress in February 1956 was Lenin's "Testament" published in the USSR. [SS/GS]

## POSTWAR REFLECTIONS

A victory parade was scheduled for Moscow for June 24, 1945. I also went to Moscow. I wanted to see the troops parade across Red Square and to celebrate together with all of our people in the capital of our homeland. I don't remember whether Stalin called me to tell me to come, or whether I simply went on my own. General Eisenhower came to visit us. He too stood on top of the Lenin Mausoleum. That was the first time I met Eisenhower, who of course was not the president of the United States then, but the commander in chief of Allied forces in Western Europe.

It is not up to me today to describe how the parade went. Many people saw it and it is recorded in films and paintings. It really was a parade of great joy. Afterward Stalin gave an official dinner. Eisenhower was there, and all our most prominent military people, but it seems that the British commander was not there. Stalin was on good terms with Eisenhower and on even better terms with Roosevelt, but relations with Churchill were poor, and with the British military leader Montgomery[1] they were very bad. Stalin had a poor opinion of him, and I think Stalin had good reason for that.

I want to express my views about relations with our allies—that is, the countries we were allied with in the fight against Hitler's Germany. After 1940 France did hardly any fighting, and after it was liberated it still didn't take a major part in the war because the war ended so soon after France's liberation. The only real wartime allies that remained from 1941 to 1945 were the United States and Great Britain. I think Churchill played a major role in the course of the war. He understood the threat to Britain and did everything he could to turn the Germans against the Soviet Union and draw the USSR into the war against Germany. Then when Hitler considered it possible to attack us, Churchill was the first to declare that Britain would necessarily have to conclude a treaty of alliance with the USSR and organize a united military effort. Stalin did the right thing; he accepted this offer and established the appropriate contacts, which were then made official through treaties. A little later the United States entered the war. Thus there came into being a coalition of three great powers—the Soviet Union, the United States, and Britain.

In late 1941 Japan went into action against the United States, Britain, the Netherlands, and other countries that had colonies in Asia and the Pacific. This made the military situation easier for us because we could move our troops from the Far East with the assurance that Japan would not go to war against us. Our Far Eastern territories were no longer under immediate threat. This gave us room to maneuver and to make better use of our armed forces, although even in that situation we had to allow for the possibility of a blow from Japan. At the beginning of the war Japan's offensive actions were successful, and Japan felt confident that it would soon win a decisive victory. But its initial victories were "fool's victories," and later when it got bogged down in the war and the Americans were able to stop Japan's advance, it became clear that Japan was no longer in any position to try and organize an attack on the Soviet Union.

Britain and the United States did everything they could to provide us with material aid of all kinds, above all military aid in the form of arms and other materiel necessary for waging war. The aid we received was very substantial. Of course this was not an expression of magnanimity on the part of Britain and the United States, nor of their desire to help the peoples of the Soviet Union. No, not at all. They gave us aid so that we might do a better job of pulverizing the living forces of our common enemy. Thus, they were using our hands and letting us shed our blood to fight Nazi Germany. They paid us so that we could keep fighting; they paid us with weapons and other war materiel. This made sense from their point of view, and it really was a sensible policy and one that benefited us. Things were difficult for us then, and we paid a very high price in the war, but we were obliged to follow that course because otherwise we would not have been able to fight at all. Thus there was a situation of mutual interest and mutual advantage, and so good relations and mutual trust were established and improved as time went on.

I would like to express my candid opinion about Stalin's views on whether the Red Army and the Soviet Union could have coped with Nazi Germany and survived the war without aid from the United States and Britain. First, I would like to tell about some remarks Stalin made and repeated several times when we were "discussing freely" among ourselves. He stated bluntly that if the United States had not helped us, we would not have won the war. If we had had to fight Nazi Germany one on one, we could not have stood up against Germany's pressure, and we would have lost the war. No one ever discussed this subject officially, and I don't think Stalin left any written evidence of his opinion, but I will state here that several times in conversations with me he noted that these were the actual circumstances. He never made a special point of holding a conversation on the subject, but when we were engaged in some kind of relaxed conversation, going over international questions of the past and present, and when we would return to the subject of the path we had traveled during the war, that is what he said.

It was hard to expect objectivity from Stalin. He was a very subjective person. Incidentally, the subjective factor and individual personalities in general do play a big role in politics. Sometimes it is useful to evaluate what was done right and to take an objective approach toward the past, to weigh all the factors influencing the situation, so as to assess more accurately the path we traveled and to arrive at correct decisions for the future. In the given instance, I think, Stalin's conclusion was correct. When I listened to his remarks, I was fully in agreement with him, and today I am even more so. Therefore, I want to present my own arguments in support of what Stalin was saying, based on what I myself saw and understood back then.

How did the war proceed? You have to try to put yourself in our position, to try and analyze in your thinking the path we had taken and the position we were in after Germany had attacked us, especially after Hitler had forced us to abandon Belorussia, Ukraine, and vast portions of the Russian Federation, including the Northern Caucasus with its oil-producing regions. It is true that the main oil-producing regions remained in our hands, but in effect they were out of commission. The equipment in the oil industry was dismantled, and both the extraction of petroleum and its refining were stopped.[2] Our industry found itself in very difficult conditions. Besides that, we were denied the possibility of making economic use of the territories taken from us by the enemy. Let me return to the subject of Ukraine, if nothing else. What was the relative weight of the Ukrainian metallurgical industry in the Soviet economy in 1941? I don't have the statistical data at hand at the moment, but I think Ukraine was producing at the minimum 50 percent of all the steel in the Soviet Union, if not more.[3] Ukraine held a leading position in coal production, and its relative importance in the production of grain, vegetables, and meat was great. Ukraine also had powerful machine-building and chemical industries.

The industry of Leningrad was also effectively out of service. That included shipbuilding, tank construction, and the making of special technical instruments. Leningrad was an industrial city with a highly skilled workforce and a large number of scientific institutions—in effect, the nerve center for the technical sciences in the Soviet Union. It was paralyzed and disorganized, and in effect it wasn't functioning. Industrial production was no longer a key question. Instead the main question was the physical survival of Leningrad's people. Many thousands of Leningraders died, and only part of the population was evacuated.[4] In the city of Gorky,[5] industry was functioning only intermittently because it was within range of German air strikes. Industry in Moscow was disorganized for the same reason. The production of airplanes and of airplane engines was moved out of Moscow, and motor vehicle production in Moscow essentially stopped. And, you can be sure, a great deal was previously being produced in Moscow, with its powerful and highly skilled workforce and great potential.

What about Kharkov? This city had a major tractor factory, whose strength was second only to the tractor factory in Stalingrad. There were also machine-building plants and plants where locomotives were manufactured. Kharkov's industry provided many resources for waging war, and all of it had fallen into enemy hands.

Voronezh[6] was also an important industrial city. A big aircraft factory was located there, but it too had effectively stopped production, not when the enemy entered Voronezh, but earlier, when its machinery and equipment were removed. That factory did remain in use as a kind of front-line workshop for aircraft repair, but it was no longer used for aircraft production.

Thus we had been deprived of some of our most powerful bases for the production of airplanes, tanks, and engines for tractors and other motor vehicles. And what about the Stalingrad tractor factory? A major gun factory was also located in Stalingrad, producing light and heavy artillery for the army and navy, including long-range coastal artillery. Can you imagine what a disaster this was! We found ourselves without transport facilities; we didn't have the factories that had provided us with motor vehicles, especially the towing equipment for transporting artillery, and without such facilities you can't wage war. There was no towing equipment! We had to orient ourselves toward using horses, returning to the past. A substantial part of our artillery depended on horses for towing. We were the only country in the war other than the Romanians that fought with artillery that was pulled around by oxen. A question arose: Would we have to switch over entirely to horse-drawn and ox-drawn artillery? That was the kind of position we were placed in.

Facing the modern technology and weaponry of the German army, with the Germans having occupied practically all of Europe, with its great industrial potential, a terribly difficult situation had arisen for us. Looking back, I can say that when we were retreating I couldn't imagine how we were going to get out of that situation. Part of our machinery and equipment had been evacuated to the east, but it was still necessary to find buildings in which to set up and get this equipment working, and that required a lot of time. Our people coped with these difficulties heroically. They accomplished miracles. Sometimes they set up machinery and equipment literally in barns and began producing weapons. Be that as it may, we were still inevitably losing time.

At that point the Americans and British made every effort to help us, so that the enemy would not crush us completely, to keep us from being rendered totally helpless. They gave us aircraft, motor vehicles, and weapons. When I saw the vehicles we were beginning to receive, I couldn't believe my eyes, and we received them in fairly large quantities. The figures for the exact amount of equipment we received have not yet been published. The repository for these figures, if not in written form, at least in memory, is Mikoyan. He carried out the relevant functions. As the representative of the USSR he dealt with the United States and Britain in regard to the delivery of lend-lease military and industrial equipment and supplies.[7] Lend-lease was a special form of credit granted during the war, which provided for repayment on favorable terms after the war was over.

In short, we received a flood of all sorts of goods and equipment. On one occasion, Anastas Ivanovich [Mikoyan] recounted how much duralumin, steel, gasoline, aircraft and materials for aircraft manufacture, and other military materiel, arms, and equipment he had received. This was very substantial aid. Above all there were the motor vehicles. We acquired the possibility of providing mobility for our troops, which is decisive for successfully waging war under modern conditions. The Germans made wide use of troop mobility against France and against us. They struck their blows in the form of wedges to splinter enemy forces and then surround and destroy or capture them. They would then move farther ahead, accomplishing forced marches of great depth to carry out a new encirclement. This spread panic in the civilian population, and it was also intimidating for the military personnel, who were traumatized by the fear of encirclement. Incidentally, all this was reflected later on, in our military literature and in our imaginative literature.

And what about long-range bombers? At the beginning of the war we actually didn't have any. Or what we did have was, so to speak, purely symbolic. Some of our planes sometimes reached as far as Berlin, but it was not at all a systematic bombing campaign. You can't disrupt the enemy's industrial potential with that kind of bombing. It was a drop in the ocean, mere pin pricks, when what we needed were heavy air raids on the enemy's industrial centers. We had no possibility of doing that. I'm not even talking about the fact that after we retreated and Leningrad was besieged we lost any possibility of bombing Germany's administrative center—that is, Berlin. (Only the Baltic Fleet had planes capable of flying as far as the capital of Germany, not to mention the western parts of Germany.) The Germans were safe, and we presented no threat to them. The British air raids on Germany were a different matter. And when the United States entered the war, placing its industry on a wartime footing, America's enormous industrial potential created a genuine threat for the Germans. I think that Hitler probably realized that was the beginning of the end for him.

In these memoirs I have been referring to Stalin and criticizing him, but there were two sides to what Stalin did. He did a lot that was good and useful for our country. This is acknowledged by everyone, and I too am acknowledging it now. I am obliged, as a person who was placed in the very high position that I held, to analyze everything and to disclose shortcomings, oversights, and cases of abuse of power, or cases where Stalin exceeded his authority. That is one side of the story. Now I will take up the other side, a positive one. When the United States entered the war, Stalin said in conversation: "Now the war of motors will begin." He had said the same thing even earlier. Whether these were his own words or they had been spoken by someone else before him, I don't know. But it's plain to anyone of even average development that war today, in the modern era, actually is a war of motors. Whoever has the largest number of motors or engines and has the best chance of keeping them going, that is, has sufficient fuel, will win the war. Disruption of U.S. economic activity [by bombing] was of course excluded. The United States had enormous economic potential, and it made use of that potential.

This was to our advantage from the point of view of the supply of arms and war materiel. Of course the delivery of these supplies made the capitalists richer. The monopolies in the United States made big profits from all this. But they were helping us. The United States built up a powerful air force. There was an airplane that made its appearance in their country, the so-called flying fortress, a remarkable airplane, the best in the world. Using these planes, the Americans were able to penetrate enemy airspace even without the accompaniment of fighter planes, whereas our bombers could do that only at night. During the day they had to have fighter protection. Without such cover they could operate only along the front lines, using the method of surprise attack. We suffered fairly heavy losses from enemy antiaircraft guns and fighter planes. But the Americans flew without fighter-plane protection right into enemy territory and bombed German industrial centers, which was something of great importance. These bombers were equipped with large-caliber machine guns—in the tail, in the nose, and along the sides.

In 1943 during our offensive at Kiev, enemy airpower was already rather spotty. It was not such a serious danger as it had been at the beginning of the war. In 1944 I rarely went out to the front lines, but in general I no longer heard complaints about the German planes giving us no rest. My front-line friends (who I kept in touch with by phone; also they would come to Kiev, or sometimes I would visit the battlefront) told me: "You can't imagine. We're able to travel both day and night, and enemy planes don't bother us." Who gets the credit for that? American airpower. Their bombers had knocked out the German factories that produced airplanes. The Germans had the metal needed to build planes and the gasoline to power them, but their airplane factories were destroyed. Is this really such a small thing? Was this just a minor form of military assistance? As for the other German factories that produced armaments, the United States bombed them very stubbornly and persistently with knowledge of how to go about this task. This was a big help to us.

And what about the assistance we received in the form of battle-ready tanks? I remember we received British tanks during the battle of Stalingrad. (I've forgotten their name.)[8] Their combat capabilities were not very great; nevertheless, a tank is a tank. With armor to cover them, the infantry attacked more boldly and was better able to deal blows to the enemy. The armor in those tanks was not as good as ours, but they had a better undercarriage [the part of the tank with the treads providing mobility].

In this connection I recall some disgraceful and exasperating incidents having to do with our tanks. During the battle of Stalingrad we received some tank reinforcements, but before they had gone 100 kilometers they stopped in their tracks because their tread mechanisms stopped working. I wrote a memorandum to Stalin then, and Stalin took stringent measures. There was a reshuffling of part of the leadership, and Malyshev[9] was made responsible for tank production from then on. Closer attention was paid to the quality of the undercarriage of our tanks, not just to producing them in greater quantity. But the quality of the tank-tread mechanisms continued to be abominable. In winter 1943, when the Germans were trying to break out of encirclement at Stalingrad, Malinovsky arrived and joined us with his Guards Army. There were three corps in that army, and each corps had a tank regiment. Not one of those tank regiments made it to the front lines. All the tanks were just sitting there on the roads, waiting for repairs to make them mobile again. If even one tank out of three could have been brought up to the front lines, we would have had a tank regiment, but because of the poor quality of undercarriage production we didn't receive a single tank regiment. And yet there was fighting to be done!

The enemy had a sufficient quantity of weapons. Sometimes they were not as good as ours, but they had substantially more, and not all the German armament was worse than ours. Simple-minded patriotism can have a harmful effect if you base your policy on that alone and don't analyze the real facts. And so we shouldn't create illusions in the future either. We need to proceed from the facts as they are.

We don't have adequate and proper information. From a feeling of false pride, information is kept out of our press. This is wrong. I think it would be useful if appropriate information was published. Perhaps some research institution could even prepare such material and do a probing scientific analysis of the past. We need to study the past so that mistakes that were committed earlier will not be committed again, so that they will be excluded in the future as well as the present. Unfortunately, Stalin took an incorrect position back then. He admitted many things, but only to himself when he was behind closed doors in his bathroom. He considered it humiliating to express such things publicly so that others could hear them. It does not diminish our worthy achievements simply to acknowledge the merits of our partners. On the contrary, an objective statement of the real facts would raise us higher in the eyes of other countries and would in no way diminish our successes, our achievements, our merits, our victories, and the significance of the decisive blows we dealt to the common enemy.

But for Stalin such a thing was impossible. He tried to cover up our weaknesses, supposing that somehow that made us stronger than our enemy; so that we would be more greatly feared. This is a foolish position to take and a wrong one. You can't deceive the enemy that way. He knows how to count and how to analyze. But meanwhile our own people would be able to understand everything correctly.

It's possible that Stalin was afraid that openness on such questions would at some point boomerang against him. People would ask why he hadn't foreseen things. That is another question entirely. I think it's necessary to admit things openly and not to spare oneself, because the best help you can give to your country and to the cause you serve is not to cover up shortcomings but to bring them out into the open, even if it's painful, so that the people can see everything. Then the people will understand you correctly and evaluate things correctly and support you, if that's necessary, and forgive you for mistakes that have been made. If people sincerely analyze past mistakes, they won't repeat them. Some people might say: "Here's Khrushchev criticizing Stalin, but he's quoting Stalin in support of his position on these questions of analysis and criticism." That's right. Besides, I assume that my colleagues, with whom I worked under Stalin's leadership, will also leave memoirs behind. If they are objective, they will not be afraid to tell about Stalin's shortcomings before the eyes of history and to tell about everything they know.

Stalin usually said the kind of thing I've been talking about not in one-on-one conversations but in discussions in which as many as five, seven, or ten people participated. Not all members of the Politburo took part as a rule in meetings with Stalin. Stalin always chose a group of people that he would bring closer to himself, while not inviting another group for a certain length of time, as a sign of punishment, as it were. Anyone at all might fall into either group. He'd invite one group to come see him today, and tomorrow he'd invite those he hadn't invited yesterday.

What Stalin said at those meetings constituted an accurate, profound, and sober admission based on a comparison of all the facts, all the decisive facts that would determine whether we would continue to exist in the world or not, whether we would win the war or lose it. When Stalin gave a positive assessment of the role of our allies at those meetings I agreed with him absolutely and considered it a correct analysis of the facts. It is never too late to speak of this. After all, the new generations, which will take the place of the present leadership of our country, will necessarily find the courage to shine an objective spotlight on the initial phase of the war. Today this is no longer of fundamental importance. Our former allies have today become our adversaries. Acknowledging the aid they gave us in the form of arms and war materiel is no reflection on the present state of affairs, because today we find ourselves in a new and different situation. It's no small thing, after all, that we have lived to see a time when we are considered the second greatest power in the world as far as industrial potential goes! And we really are the second greatest power.

British Prime Minister Macmillan[10] told me once when I was talking with him: "What is Britain today? It is no longer what it was when Britannia ruled the waves, no longer a decisive force in world politics. Today everything is decided by two other countries—the United States and the USSR."

President de Gaulle of France, a sober-minded man, said the same thing to me, using practically the same phrases. He said: "Mister Khrushchev, today the United States and the Soviet Union are the two great powers. France no longer has the greatness that it had in the past. Today it cannot decide the course of world politics." That is the kind of general recognition that exists about our strength, our role and significance in world politics. Therefore, our merits are not at all minimized when we admit that in the past these countries gave us the kind of military assistance that had a substantial effect on the outcome of the war.

Let me repeat: they did not give us aid for the sake of the victory of socialism or the ideas of Marxism-Leninism. For them it was a question of life or death. They helped us so that our army would not collapse under the blows of Hitler Germany and so that, relying on more advanced arms and equipment, our army could crush the living forces of the enemy, while weakening itself in the process. After all, that too was in the interest of our allies. They wanted to choose an appropriate time before taking an active part themselves in the war against Germany, a time when the Soviet Union would no longer have great strength and could not occupy a decisive position in solving world problems after Germany's defeat. Therefore, their military aid was not a sign of love for our people or of respect for our system of government. It was the result of a sober estimation of the situation that had arisen for the Western countries.

The situation was such that we became allies in order to win the war against a common enemy. Britain and the United States wanted to take advantage of the situation and use our country's resources, primarily our human resources, so that the living forces of the common enemy would be ground up by the hands of others, to win victory and put themselves in a position to decide the fate of the world. Those were the considerations that guided them when they gave us military aid. They were not ashamed to make an alliance with a socialist government—an avowed enemy of capitalism. And Stalin—we must grant him his due—also agreed to this arrangement, not of course because it meant a good life for us, but because there was no other way out. We had no alternative. But that was the path to salvation, the only path by which we could survive and win the war. That is how I view the question, and I heard the same opinion expressed by Stalin. He didn't go into detail about that period of the war, but it doesn't take great effort to arrive at such a conclusion. He understood this and spoke accordingly.

I hope that my viewpoint will be reflected in the research of historians who will try to objectively examine the situation that arose in the years 1941–43. Incidentally, the Americans also gave us a lot of aid in 1944 and 1945. Even after the war Zhdanov traveled to the United States and told me that we subsequently received, on a lend-lease basis, a huge American rolling mill and that this mill was set up on the grounds of the Ilyich factory in Mariupol, which was later renamed Zhdanov.[11] I made a trip there myself. There were Japanese prisoners of war working on the installation of the rolling mill. The installation was organized unit by unit so that the rolling mill would be put into commission more quickly. I remember talking with these Japanese and asking them about their lives. Later we joked about the fact that these former Japanese soldiers, prisoners of war, had told us they had come there to help the Russians on orders from the Mikado. They didn't consider themselves prisoners of war but emissaries of the Japanese emperor, the Mikado.[12]

To sum up, we did receive equipment, ships, and large quantities of weapons from our allies. This played an important part in the war. Almost all our artillery was pulled by American towing equipment. On one occasion after Stalin's death I proposed: "Let's give all the transport equipment that we produce to the military because it's simply embarrassing to see a parade going by and all the artillery is being towed by American trucks." Almost all the military equipment we had in East Germany was also being towed by American Studebakers. This was an awkward and shameful situation for us. So many years had gone by since the end of the war, and we were still using American trucks.

At this point I want to stress the quantity of the machinery and equipment we received, as well as its quality. Just imagine! How could we have carried out an offensive without this materiel? How could we have moved forward from Stalingrad to Berlin? I can't imagine it. Our losses would have been colossal because our troops would not have had the same maneuverability. Besides, we received a lot of steel and duralumin.[13] Our industrial production had been disrupted, and part of it had been lost to the enemy. Under those conditions the military assistance from the United States was of tremendous importance.

The British demonstrated great persistence in providing us with aid. They delivered aid by cargo ship to Murmansk and suffered heavy losses in the process. It was a long way for ships to travel, and German submarines patrolled the route with impunity.[14] The Germans had also taken Norway and had brought their troops right up to our border, near the city of Murmansk. For this reason the British and Americans delivered many vehicles by driving them through Iran.[15] This worked out better, because this southern route was safe. The ships unloaded in the Persian Gulf and then the vehicles drove under their own power until they reached us. In addition, airplanes reached us from the United States by flying across Alaska, Chukotka,[16] and Siberia. A fairly substantial flow of cargo was received in that way as well.

Of course this did not decide everything entirely, but without it the most decisive aspect of the whole situation would not have come about. The blood shed by our fighting men and the equipment from the United States and Britain together combined to ensure victory, to ensure the successful operations and actions of the Red Army, which did most of the fighting and caused the heaviest losses to our common enemy.

We also received food products in large quantities. There were quite a few jokes, including off-color jokes, about American Spam. Nevertheless, it was tasty. Despite the many humorous comments about the Spam, we still ate it. It would have been very hard to feed our army without it. After all, we had lost our most productive agricultural land—Ukraine and the Northern Caucasus. One must try to imagine how difficult it was to organize food supplies for the entire country under such conditions.

Besides that, we received many new instruments and technical devices from our allies that we had had no idea of before then. We received an electronic device, a radar, for our antiaircraft forces. The commander of our air force told me that this device came from Britain. Previously we had equipped our antiaircraft defense forces only with searchlights and listening devices that were fairly crude and difficult to use. We had no concept of modern electronic equipment, but the British did, and they passed on a certain amount of this equipment to us. The military personnel at our air force command center showed me how you could follow the movements of enemy aircraft by looking at the screen of this radar detector.[17]

In short, we must honestly acknowledge the contribution our allies made to the defeat of Hitler. We should not go around boasting that supposedly we drew our swords and won the victory, and the others arrived only when the fight was over. That point of view is accurate if you look only at the contributions of our allies in terms of expeditionary forces, that is, the direct part played by American and British troops in the fighting against Germany on the European Continent. In that regard this is true. But the assistance they gave us in war materiel and equipment is another matter. If they had not given us that assistance, we might not have been victorious. We might not have won the war, because the losses we suffered in the first part of the war were too great.

Now for a few words about the expeditionary forces of our allies. All through 1942 and 1943 we were waiting for them to open a second front in

Europe. This was especially necessary in 1942, when things were going very badly for us. I am talking mainly about our area—the Southwestern Front and the Southern Front, where the enemy's main blow fell in 1942. The enemy's goal was to deprive us of our oil and to break through to Iran by way of the Caucasus region. And the Germans came close to realizing their plans. To be sure, if our allies had landed expeditionary forces at that time, our losses would have been much fewer.

It's hard for me to judge now about our allies' intentions then. Was their decision not to land expeditionary forces dictated by the desire to put a heavier load on the Soviet Union's back and bleed us even more? I don't rule out that possibility. On the other hand, is it true, as they explained, that they were not yet sufficiently prepared, that their war production had not yet expanded enough, so that they were not ready for a large-scale landing? They said they needed more time. I think that both considerations applied, but the first one was stronger. The desire to let us bleed was greater. Their thinking was to let their ally bleed, so that when they joined in the battle good and proper at the climactic point they could then decide the fate of the world. They could take advantage of the war's outcome and impose their will not only on the enemy but on their ally as well. I grant this possibility entirely. And evidently such thinking played a considerable role.

If you look at it from a class point of view, our allies had no interest in strengthening us. It was in their interest to make use of the USSR for a time despite the fact that our country was organized on a socialist basis. Our common fate worked out in such a way that we were forced to unite our efforts. Each of us alone could not have won the war at all, or could have won it only with enormous losses and over a much longer time span. Thus the various sides agreed to this alliance, and while combining their efforts in the struggle against the common enemy, they at the same time remained on separate class foundations.

We also felt that it would be to our advantage if we could come out much stronger than our allies at the end of the war, so that our voice would be heard more strongly when international questions were decided. If we had succeeded in this, the question of Germany would not have been decided the way it was at Potsdam. The decision made at the Potsdam Conference[18] was a compromise. It was based on the balance of forces that had taken shape at the end of the war. This affected the status of Berlin and Vienna in particular. These cities were in the zone occupied by Soviet troops. It would seem that they should have become fully a part of our zone, but our allies did not turn them over to us entirely. These cities were divided into four sectors. We received one quarter and the other three parts went to Britain, France, and the United States. This also testifies to the balance of forces that existed at the end of the war.

The Americans and British had a lot to think about, of course, when they agreed to an alliance with us. This problem began to trouble them especially when our army withstood the blow from the Germans, and when, straining every nerve and exerting every effort, our army went on the offensive and gained a solid sense of itself, placed itself on a firm footing. When we had already advanced westward and were approaching Germany, our allies were forced to hurry up and open a second front in Western Europe because they were afraid we would move considerably farther west than the boundaries designated when the zones of occupation for each of the countries participating in the war were demarcated.[19] All this must also be taken into account in specifying the merits of our allies, their contributions to the common cause of defeating Hitler's Germany, and their class position.

Now I want to tell about statements by Stalin pertaining to relations with our allies during the war, specifically with Roosevelt and Churchill. France had no major forces in Europe, and Stalin began to pay attention to France only later, in fact, beginning with the Potsdam Conference and after it. Before that his attention was centered mainly on Roosevelt and Churchill. Stalin, according to his own words, had more sympathy for Roosevelt because the U.S. president had a more understanding attitude toward our problems. Roosevelt's dislike for the British monarchy and its institutions also brought him closer to Stalin.

Stalin once related the following episode. During the Teheran Conference, when the heads of state met during dinner, Roosevelt raised his glass and proposed a toast to the president of the Soviet Union, Kalinin. Everyone drank the toast. A little while later Churchill raised his glass and proposed a toast to the British monarch. Roosevelt said he would not drink to that. Churchill reacted in an offended way, but Roosevelt would not be moved: "No, I won't drink. I can't drink to the king of England. I cannot forget my father's words." It turns out that when Roosevelt's father left Europe, while they were still on a ship heading for America, he said something to his son about the British monarch: "He's our enemy."[20] The son never forgot that and, regardless of proper etiquette, would not raise his glass to drink this toast.

In the discussion of practical matters, and in the disagreements that arose, Stalin frequently found himself being supported by Roosevelt against Churchill. Thus, Stalin's sympathies plainly favored Roosevelt, although he also esteemed Churchill and treated him with respect. He was a major political figure not only for Britain. He held a leading position in world politics. During the setback in the Ardennes region in 1944 [also known as the Battle of the Bulge], when the Germans were seriously threatening Allied troops on the second front that had been established in Western Europe,[21] Churchill asked Stalin to help by diverting the German armies in our direction. To do that, we had to carry out an offensive operation ahead of schedule, before we were prepared. We carried out this operation, although we were planning it for a later time.[22] This was a demonstration of friendship, helping an ally out of a difficult situation. Stalin carried out this operation quite well. He knew how to understand such situations and do something about them in real life.

I remember Stalin several times returning to the subject of Eisenhower's personality. He commented on Eisenhower's noble traits and chivalrous attitude toward relations with an ally. I heard such comments from Stalin several times when we were conversing with him in the inner circle. This was after the war but before I moved back to Moscow.

When I was working in Moscow again and was in Stalin's presence more often, he began inviting me to go with him on vacation to the Caucasus. I sensed that he simply could not stand being alone and was actually afraid of it. He developed a physical fear of being alone. This was pretty costly for all of us. (I'm talking about members of the leadership who were in Stalin's immediate circle.) It was a great honor to go on vacation with him and to share meals with him, but it was also a heavy physical burden.

Once I vacationed with him for a whole month. He put me in a room right next to his. I had to live next to him and have lunch and supper with him all the time, but that was only the outward aspect of the matter. If people only knew what that meant in fact, what a physical burden it was, how much you had to eat and drink, in general how much you had to consume regardless of whether it was harmful or unpleasant, simply for the sake of keeping personal relations on an even keel! The warmest and friendliest attitude was being demonstrated toward you, and you had to make sacrifices accordingly. But that kind of life was useful in part because conversations were held from which you could derive some advantage for yourself and draw some political conclusions.

In the course of these conversations I frequently heard Stalin make very flattering remarks about what a decent man Eisenhower was. Stalin said that when we were carrying out our offensive at Berlin, if the commander in chief of allied forces had been someone other than Eisenhower, we would certainly not have taken Berlin; we simply wouldn't have gotten there soon enough. The Americans would have taken it before we could get there. And that really was so, because the Germans were concentrating their main forces against us and were only too willing to surrender to the Western Allies. Stalin appealed to Eisenhower in a letter, stating that according to the terms of the Inter-Allied Agreement, and considering the blood that our people had shed, we wanted our troops to be the first to enter Berlin, not our allies. Stalin said that at that point Eisenhower did hold his troops back and stopped his offensive. He gave our troops a chance to crush the Germans and take Berlin. Thus we were allowed to have priority in occupying the German capital. A different commander in chief would not have agreed to that. And if Berlin had been captured by the Americans, the question of the fate of Germany would have been resolved differently, according to Stalin, and our position would have been much worse. Eisenhower displayed such chivalry and nobility, said Stalin, and was true to the promise that Roosevelt had given us. He respected Roosevelt's memory.

By that time Truman had become the new president of the United States, and Stalin didn't have the same respect or esteem for him. Evidently Stalin was right because Truman did not deserve respect and esteem. Here is another fact Stalin mentioned, one that also relates to the end of the war, when the Germans had been backed up against the wall by our forces and were being forced to surrender because they could no longer put up any resistance. They had to lay down their arms and become prisoners of war. Many of them did not want to surrender to our troops, and they headed west to surrender to the Americans. Again Stalin appealed to Eisenhower. He said that Soviet troops had shed their blood to defeat the enemy, and now the enemy was surrendering to the Americans. This was unjust. Eisenhower then issued an order [to his forces] not to accept surrendering Germans. (It seems that this was in northern Austria, where Malinovsky was commander of our offensive.) Eisenhower told the German commander to surrender to the Russians because it was Russian arms that had defeated the German army. And that's how the surrender was in fact made.

Stalin said he made a similar request to Churchill. In the part of northern Germany occupied by Montgomery, the Germans were also fleeing from Rokossovsky's troops and surrendering to the British. Stalin requested that the British not accept these prisoners but order them instead to surrender to our troops. "Absolutely not!" Stalin related indignantly: "Montgomery took all those prisoners into his fold and their weapons too. So it was our troops who defeated the Germans, but Montgomery reaped the fruits of victory." Both Eisenhower and Montgomery were representatives of the capitalist class. But they differed in the way they made decisions and in the way they observed the principles of partnership, treaty agreements, and their word of honor. When I had dealings with Eisenhower [in the 1950s] it was as though I always pictured to myself those noble actions of his in the past. I remembered what Stalin had said about him, and I trusted him. After all, there was no way you could suspect Stalin of having sympathy for someone. On class questions he seemed to us incorruptible and irreconcilable. This was one of his strongest political features, for which he enjoyed great respect among us.

Toward the end of the war Stalin became very worried that the Americans might cross the boundary lines established for the various Allied forces. As I have already said, the Germans maintained an organized resistance to our advance, whereas the Americans were able to advance with less difficulty and could easily have crossed those lines of demarcation. Stalin doubted that the Americans would yield to us and abide by the promises Roosevelt had given. After all, they could simply say that their troops stopped at the point they happened to reach and that the dividing line between the occupation zones would be established accordingly. But no, the Americans pulled their troops back and deployed them along the lines established at the Teheran Conference in 1943, long before the victory over Germany. This also testifies to Eisenhower's decency. It was on such facts that Stalin based his good attitude toward Eisenhower. That is why Stalin invited Eisenhower to our victory parade and expressed our acknowledgment of his services by awarding him the highest military honor in the USSR, the Order of Victory. This is a very high honor. To be sure, Field Marshal Montgomery was awarded the same order, but in that case we were merely carrying out a formal obligation to an ally, because the British had also decorated our military leadership with their orders and medals. In that case it was official reciprocity, but in Eisenhower's case Stalin singled him out specially. Later I met with Eisenhower many times, but I will tell about that elsewhere.

For now I want to express my views on the question of whether there existed the conditions necessary in the USSR to provide our Red Army with everything it needed to effectively resist the enemy. More specifically, the question should be asked as follows: Could the Red Army by itself have stood up against Hitler's army and, as Stalin and Voroshilov said at the time, not give up one inch of land to the enemy? Could the war have been fought and the enemy defeated entirely on enemy territory? That had been one of our slogans. The whole world sensed that this was a false slogan, that the actual strength of the USSR was rather precarious. Could we have turned this slogan into a reality? There is no question that we could have [if things had been done differently]. There is another question besides the economic one. This whole question depended very crucially, especially during the initial phase of the war, on the matter of military personnel. We could have dealt with the fascists much more easily if our military cadres had not been annihilated in the 1930s. The essential cadres of the Red Army command staff, to a very large extent, had been exterminated.

I don't have the exact figures for the number of officers of various ranks who were eliminated. But if you look at the top command staff, you can see that almost all the top commanders—from the commanders of military districts to divisional commanders—were exterminated. But these were people who had good knowledge and abilities; some of them had graduated from military academies, and some had even had training at both specialist and generalist military academies. The command staff at the middle level had a medium amount of military education. But the most valuable thing about these cadres was that they had gone through the school of the Russian Civil War and other wars and possessed valuable experience. They had not held important titles when they fought in the Civil War, but after that war they had received both theoretical and specialized military training and acquired a great deal of experience commanding troop units. Before that, many of them had gone through the school of World War I as soldiers or officers. In the Red Army they had become commanders of various rank and degree and had taken part in military games and maneuvers. Everything had been done in our country that could have been done to educate and train these cadres in the proper way. They were entirely suited to the task before them and they were ready to perform their duty for their homeland.

Unfortunately these people were exterminated, after which people who had neither knowledge nor experience were promoted to commanding positions. Therefore it was during the war itself, out on the battlefield, that they got their training and learned how to lead troops. That is not at all the same thing as being trained under peacetime conditions. To be sure, they may have matured more quickly, but the cost to our people was greater. When one or another military operation is played out, using maps, they then make a count, or estimate, that so many thousand people would have died. But these are only nominal or symbolic losses. The deaths at the front lines were not symbolic or "conditional." They were absolutely unconditional; they were very real. If our cadres had survived, that is, the cadres who had received the necessary schooling long before the war, we would have suffered many fewer casualties. That must be clear to everyone, and it should be taken into account without fail in any analysis of the initial phase of the war. Unfortunately, no one dares to lift this curtain even a little. The people who were destroyed in the 1930s were considered "enemies of the people." That is why the blame for these deaths was not placed on those who were at fault for killing them. On the contrary, their extermination was held up as an alleged example of great service.

Well, all right, we were all taken in back then. We all believed that Stalin's perspicacity, the penetrating insight of the "father and great leader of the Soviet people," had saved us from the enemy. But later, at the Twentieth Congress of the CPSU, all these questions were brought up and dealt with irrefutably. The irrefutable facts can be placed at the disposal of anyone who wants to make a deep analysis of what happened. However, even today there remain people who tremble worshipfully before the soiled underpants of the great leader Stalin. They stand at attention in front of him, as they did before, and they consider the losses we suffered back then to have been historically unavoidable. They talk about the greatness of the man who did not stop short in the face of these losses, but carried our country though to such-and-such a place, reaching such-and-such a great new frontier, achieving so-and-so and such-and-such. I don't even know what to call people who think like that. What if we had not suffered those losses? What if those abuses of power had not occurred? Would that really have been worse? Let us remember what Lenin said about Stalin. He said that Stalin was intolerant (*neterpim*) and that he should be removed from his position of power in the party. If that had been done, the war to save the USSR would have cost us much less than it did under the leadership of "our dear father, the great leader and genius Stalin."

Preparations for the waging of war require more than just war games, military exercises, operations carried out with the use of maps, and the training and drilling of troops, although one cannot prepare for war without these things. If the necessary material conditions are not created, if the economic foundation is not properly laid, no war can be won. The main thing is to ensure sufficient supplies of war materiel and the production of weapons and equipment: aircraft, artillery, tanks, small arms for the infantry, and engineering and other equipment—to ensure the provision of everything necessary to defeat the enemy and repel enemy attacks. One must have certain kinds of military technology in reserve, just in case—that is, chemical and bacteriological weapons. Fortunately, such weapons were not used in World War II,[23] but in World War I poison gas was used. If we had not had such weapons or materials in reserve and if the enemy had used such devices against us, that would have created a disastrous situation for our army. Consequently, it is necessary to have such weapons in reserve. They have been indispensable in the past and, alas, they are indispensable in the present and will be in the future as long as antagonistic social systems exist. To some extent we are simply forced to accumulate such instruments of war and keep them in reserve.

So then, I was expressing my views on the military personnel who were subjected to repression. It would be difficult for me to list them all. I would like to pause for a more detailed discussion of some of them. Take Gamarnik, for example, the deputy people's commissar of defense of the USSR.[24] He was a major political figure and a very good organizer, a man who directly participated in creating the Red Army. His role as deputy people's commissar was also very important. People will object that Gamarnik was not executed. I know that he shot himself. But he thought that he was going to be executed. They were coming to arrest him when he shot himself. The executioners were going to drag him off and put his head on the chopping block, and he decided it would be better to end his own life by suicide. He was an extremely honest and worthy man.

Yegorov[25] was also a major military leader. In the Civil War he commanded the Southwestern Front. As for Tukhachevsky,[26] at the age of twenty-seven he commanded several Fronts. Lenin personally entrusted several major operations to Tukhachevsky. Which were they? Kronstadt, the campaign against Antonov, the one against Kolchak, the one against Denikin, and the one against the Poles.[27] When he was executed, how much petty muttering of every kind was directed against him by people who didn't even come up to his kneecap, let alone his belly button. How they kicked him around for all they were worth. If some military operation was carried out under Tukhachevsky's command in the Civil War, any failures in that operation were personally attributed to Tukhachevsky. Nevertheless even after such operations—which failed, these critics claim, because Tukhachevsky was not "up to the mark"—in spite of that, Lenin invariably entrusted to Tukhachevsky other even more complex operations, involving matters of life and death for our Soviet land. Lenin valued and esteemed Tukhachevsky, and rightly so. I used to meet with Tukhachevsky, although I didn't know him well. Still, our relations were not very distant either. When I worked as secretary of the party's Moscow city committee, and Moscow province committee we used to call each other and meet, not only at major plenary sessions. More than once I traveled with him out into the field, where he showed me certain military innovations in practice. I am talking about innovations pertaining to the Red Army's weapons and engineering equipment. Very good memories of Tukhachevsky have stayed with me.

Now let's talk about Yakir.[28] Before 1917 Yakir had been a student. He had no military education. He didn't serve in World War I, but began his military career during the Civil War by forming some sort of armed detachment. People armed themselves in those days with whatever they could. The main weapon the workers had was their hatred for the old system and their devotion to building a new one, and that was the cause they fought for in the Civil War. Yakir's detachment eventually grew to become a division. He commanded that division, operating in the south of Russia, where he had been cut off from the main forces of the Red Army, but he broke through to join up with our main forces. It seems he was able to go right through the lines of the White Guards, leading his division out of entrapment and joining up with our forces. Later he successfully led large military groups. After the Civil War ended he held high positions in the Red Army, commanding the troops in Ukraine and the Crimea and other districts, but after that he was arrested and executed.

And what about Eideman?[29] He was a poet as well as a military man. He too distinguished himself as a major military commander. He headed the organization called Osoaviakhim[30] when he was arrested and executed. Today I have forgotten the name of a military man, an Estonian by nationality, who had been an officer in the tsarist army, but later went through the whole Civil War with us and then commanded the Moscow Military District and other military districts. I knew him in Moscow. He was also considered a major military leader, was arrested along with Tukhachevsky and Yakir, and executed together with them.[31]

And what about Blyukher?[32] Today the newspapers are endlessly repeating things like: "Blyukher received the very first Order of the Red Banner, Blyukher did such-and-such, Blyukher did so-and-so," but no one dares tell how Blyukher's life ended. Where was he when the war with Hitler was going on? He was already dead. Why? Did he die a natural death? No, he too was executed as an "enemy of the people." He had been a worker, a machinist by trade; he got his military experience in World War I as a noncommissioned officer and later developed into a major military leader, commanding military formations in the Civil War [for the Red Army], and he was our adviser to Chiang Kai-shek,[33] when we still had confidence in Chiang as a military and political figure. Blyukher commanded the Far Eastern Military District. Our enemies regarded him with dread, but for the land of the Soviets he was a sturdy shield. A monument is now being erected in his memory. How is it now that they are not ashamed—the people who don't want to tell the truth about Blyukher—that he fell at the hand of the same man [Stalin] about whom Lenin said that he was not to be trusted? Yes, a monument to Blyukher is necessary, but the monument should be erected in such a way that everyone would know that we were deprived of the possibility of using Blyukher and his talents in the war against the Germans, that it was not a natural death that deprived us of his talents.

I recently saw a movie that I've seen before. It's called *The Iron Flood*, based on the book of the same name. That was the first book about the Civil War that I ever read. It was written by a talented author, Serafimovich,[34] and now they have made a movie of his book. This was not the first time I had seen the movie, but as always I was deeply moved and felt great pain as I remembered the brave and intelligent man who commanded the vanguard of the Taman Army. In the book he was given the name Kozhukh, but in real life he was Kovtyukh, a man who displayed a great deal of intelligence, military talent, and courage. He led the Taman Army in a breakthrough after it had been surrounded by the Whites.[35] In the movie theater the viewers were thrilled and delighted by the talent of this man and his troops—peasants and Cossacks from the Kuban region who broke out of encirclement together with their families. One wonders where Kovtyukh is. What did he do during World War II? He was no longer alive then. He was numbered among the "enemies of the people." He too was shot. Can you imagine? And yet, if Kovtyukh had been alive and had commanded military units in the fight against the Germans, how much good he could have done, what benefits there would have been for us. When he was arrested, he bore the title of corps commander, a high military rank. And did this happen just to Kovtyukh? How about the others?

They too died at the hands of Stalin as "enemies of the people." Today they have all had their good names restored. This was done after the Twentieth Party Congress. But now a lot of things are being hushed up. I think it is necessary not only to restore their good names but also to point out that all of them were martyrs to the reign of terror Stalin carried out under the pretext of fighting "enemies of the people." What was Stalin's true worth? What kind of genius was he? He was proclaimed the "father of our people" at mass rallies, and that was repeated wherever it was necessary and even when it wasn't necessary. In literature he has also been portrayed as "the father of the people." No, this former cloak of greatness will be torn from him, and Stalin will be revealed before the Soviet people in all his nakedness and will take the place in history that truly belongs to him.

Another prominent military leader, also a man of the people, was Fedko. And he too is no more. In the final period of his activity, he commanded the troops of the Kiev Military District and become deputy people's commissar of defense. Then he was arrested in 1938 and perished, like other honorable men, after being declared "an enemy of the people."

I don't remember now whether I have spoken earlier about Ivan Naumovich Dubovoi.[36] Dubovoi came from a working class family. His father was a Donetsk miner with a prerevolutionary record in the Communist Party. I have been told that during World War I Ivan graduated from a school for ensigns of the tsarist army and became an officer. Then the Civil War began, and before long he was assistant to the head of a division, and that division head was Shchors.[37] I became acquainted with Dubovoi later at congresses of the Communist Party of Ukraine. He always took part in those congresses. I got to know him especially well in 1928–29, when I was working in Kiev as head of the organizational department of the party's district committee and Dubovoi was assistant commander of the Ukrainian Military District. He was a very good friend of Nikolai Nestorovich Demchenko, secretary of the party's Kiev district committee.[38] Demchenko had a lot of respect for Dubovoi, met with him frequently, and traveled with him to visit the troops. Dubovoi was also a close friend of Yakir. I was happy that we had commanders like these in the Red Army, men who were devoted heart and soul to the cause of the revolution, Soviet power, and socialism.

When the exposure and denunciation of "enemies of the people" began, Yakir, Tukhachevsky, and others perished, and a little while later Stalin circulated their "confessions" among us. He did this several times, rarely, but he did circulate them. And I happened to read Dubovoi's "confession." It was written in Dubovoi's own handwriting. In it he wrote that he had killed Shchors, describing the locality where a battle was being fought by the division that Shchors commanded. Dubovoi wrote: "Shchors and I were lying on the ground observing the battle. Suddenly an enemy machine gunner began firing in our direction. The bullets were hitting home among our troops. We too came under fire from this machine gun. I was behind, and Shchors was in front. He turned around and said: 'Vanya, the Whites have a good machine gunner there. Look what a good shot he is.' Then he turned around again and said something to me. That is when I killed him—shot him in the temple. I killed him so that I myself might occupy the post he held after he was gone, that is, take command of his division."

You can imagine how indignant I was at reading this. I had respected this man, and suddenly it turned out he had committed such a foul deed. I cursed myself. How could I have been so blind? How could I not have seen! Why, when I had known him in Ukraine, I thought I knew him so well, and all the time he had been the murderer of Shchors! Today after the Twentieth Party Congress, after we had opened the archives and looked at the cases in which people had been declared "enemies of the people," people who had been shot and otherwise put to death, I came to see that all this had just been lies and deception. And so it turned out that I had been deceived for a second time. The first time the deception was false, when Dubovoi supposedly "confessed" to crimes when I had been considering him an honest person. The second time when I really found out that I had been deceived, it turned out that the one who deceived me was the murderer of Dubovoi, that is, Stalin.

I am entirely willing to grant that Dubovoi's confession was written in his own handwriting, that he himself told this story about his "crimes," confessing that he had killed Shchors, who was his closest friend. Then I found out what methods had been used to make an "enemy of the people" of another man, Meretskov.[39] He also wrote his confession in his own handwriting, admitting that he had been a British spy, an enemy of the people, and so on. I didn't actually read Meretskov's confession. This was in 1941, and Stalin no longer needed other people in the leadership to support his actions in executing Soviet leaders. By then he simply ran the trial himself and had people destroyed. By then the war was going on. And it was Beria[40] who told me the story about Meretskov—that is, a fairly reliable source. It used to be that when people would say that someone was pretty steadfast, that a person could hold up pretty well, Beria would say: "Listen, let me have him for just one night, and in my hands he'll confess that he was the king of England." Beria knew quite well how to accomplish such things, and he accomplished them more than once. At that time, when Stalin was still alive, he simply talked about it that way, but later, when we opened up the archives, and when we arrested, tried, and condemned Beria himself, we saw what methods he had used to achieve his ends.

So then, back when Stalin was still alive, Beria was telling the story of Meretskov's arrest, and Beria himself took the credit for having Meretskov released: "I went to Comrade Stalin, and said, 'Comrade Stalin, Meretskov is sitting in prison as an alleged British spy. What kind of spy could he be? He's an honest man. There's a war going on, and he's sitting there in prison. He could be commanding troops. He's no British spy, not at all.'"

Even today I can't understand who it was that arrested Meretskov. Beria tried to dump all the blame on Abakumov.[41] But who was Abakumov? Beria's own man. In the work that he did he reported first of all to Beria and only after that to Stalin, so Abakumov could not have arrested Meretskov without consulting with Beria and without sanction from Stalin.

And yet, according to Beria's account: "Stalin replied, 'You're right. Have Meretskov brought to you and have a talk with him.' I had him brought to me and said: 'Meretskov, what you have written is nonsense. You weren't a spy. You're an honest man and a good Russian. How could you be a British spy? What does Britain mean to you? You're a good Russian, an honest man.' Meretskov looked at me and answered: 'I have told you everything. I wrote in my own handwriting that I am a British spy. I have nothing to add, and I don't know why you have called me in for further interrogation.' I said (and this is still Beria talking): 'This is not an interrogation. I just want to tell you that I know you're not a spy. Go to your cell, sit there for a while and think about this, sleep on it, and I'll summon you again later.' They took him off to his cell. The next day I had Meretskov brought to me, and I asked him: 'Well, comrade, what do you have to say? Did you think about it?' He began to cry: 'How could I be a spy? I am a good Russian, I love my country and people, and I believe in them.' He was released from prison, dressed in a general's uniform, and went off to the battlefront to command troops."

When I saw Meretskov for the last time [in 1968], it was no longer the Meretskov I had known, but only a shadow of his former self. Previously he had been a young general, physically strong, a powerful man, but now he could barely walk; he was just "scraping along." I found out that he had been awarded one more honor after a great many on the occasion of the fiftieth anniversary of the Soviet armed forces. Of course this was an honor that he deserved. But Stalin had robbed him of his health. He had been transformed from an honest man into an "enemy of the people," a British spy, and it was only by a miracle that he was saved. I don't know why Beria happened to take it into his head to save him. I think he wanted to get him back into service as a talented military leader, to restore him to his place in the army where he could do his job, command the troops, and trounce the enemy hordes who had invaded our country.

But Beria was such a beastly person. I don't rule out the possibility that he did what he did with some long-range goal in mind. After all no one lives for two centuries, whereas a talented military leader like Meretskov, once he had regained his rightful position in the Soviet armed forces, might turn out to be personally useful for Beria. Beria was a very crafty man, and I don't rule out the possibility that on his part he was taking a step in the game of big-time politics, that he foresaw the possibility that he might rely on Meretskov and other military leaders who he could count on as "his own people" in the future when he might need them.

It would require a lot of time for me to list everyone who died as a result of Stalin's ruthlessness, his reign of terror. (And I still wouldn't be able to do it.) Besides it really isn't needed for my memoirs. Perhaps some day historians will dig into the archives and bring everything out into the light for the sake of our descendants. All this material will become open to the public, and historians will publish the formerly secret information, so that people will know about it and will not allow such things to be repeated.

Sometimes history does repeat itself, especially in such matters. Here it's not good enough just to be good humored and have an easygoing attitude about life. We can't simply say this was a bygone era that will never be repeated. Foul deeds that were committed must be exposed and denounced; the authors of those foul deeds must be revealed. These events should not be hushed up. History should not be glossed over. On the contrary, a sense of responsibility among the people and in the party should be raised higher and made more acute, so as to exclude the possibility of what Stalin did being repeated. After all, Lenin warned us about Stalin, and his warning was extremely accurate; in fact Stalin went far beyond what Lenin warned against. In spite of Lenin's warning, Stalin won his way into the confidence of the people and later made a rapid about-face and resorted to those methods Lenin referred to when he warned that Stalin was capable of abusing power. That is what happened.

Let me return again to the point I was making—that if the cadres that had been trained and developed by the party and that went through the school of the Civil War—if those cadres had remained alive and had been in the appropriate places as commanders of the troops, things would have gone quite differently when Hitler attacked the Soviet Union. It was not by chance that we had to promote new commanders during the war. Probably there were two, three, and in some places four changes, new generations brought into the command staff. I even know people who came in as replacements in the fifth wave. Many of them were thrust forward deservedly. They were capable and honorable men, devoted to their homeland. But they needed experience, and that experience was something they acquired during the course of the war at the expense of blood shed by many soldiers and great material damage to our country's resources. That kind of military training cost a huge number of lives and terrible destruction for our country. In the end we survived and were victorious, and we learned from our mistakes how to command troops properly, and we smashed the enemy. But what did that cost? If what Stalin did, when he dreamed up all these "enemies of the people" and destroyed loyal military men—if that had not happened, I am convinced that our victory would have cost us many fewer lives. Our victory would have been cheaper, if it is morally permissible to use that word in view of the vast amount of blood that was shed, the human lives that were lost, the people who were forced to lay down their lives during the war. Everything would have happened at much less cost and much more easily for our people.

Works on this subject have not been written [in the Soviet Union], and no one has gone into such an analysis. Many historians have received candidate degrees and doctoral degrees[42] for making scholarly analyses of events that are not very interesting. Sometimes you look and you see that a dissertation is being defended on such-and-such a subject, one of very dubious value for science. You come across such subjects at times. But if someone would only write the kind of historical work I'm dreaming of! That subject is still waiting for its researchers, and of course this is work that can't be carried out all at once.

Returning again to the subject of our former military cadres, I would suggest possibly that if those cadres had still been with us, the enemy might not have decided to go to war against us. And if a war had broken out nevertheless, it actually would have been fought much more on enemy territory than on ours. So then, one of the most decisive conditions for victory is the ability to make use of one's human resources, to organize one's military forces properly and command them correctly so as to be on top of the situation as far as military tactics and strategy go.

But that is only one thing. There is another aspect of the matter—economics. In modern conditions of warfare, victory also depends on the extent to which a country is developed economically, and the extent to which the economy can serve as a basis for mechanizing one's forces and providing weapons and equipment to the army. The olden days are long gone when princes led their fighting men to battle with pitchforks, lances, axes, and maces. Today we have mechanized warfare, a "war of motors," a war of artillery, aircraft, tanks, antitank guns, and engineering corps. Modern warfare is conducted on land

and sea and under the land (land mines and bomb shelters) and under water (submarines), and in the air. If one side in a war possesses everything that modern science and technology have produced, while the other side continues to rely solely on the muscular strength and willpower of the human individual, the conditions of battle will be completely unequal.

So then, did the Red Army have the necessary technical and engineering material base before the war? If not, the next question arises: "Did we have the possibility in general of creating the appropriate military-technological base, the necessary arms and equipment, the means for defending and attacking?" I can answer without any hesitation: "Yes, we did!" Our people regarded the end of the Civil War as a breathing spell in the struggle against the imperialists and sought to make use of that time to create a powerful industry, to reorganize the national economy, and to cover in a short time the same distance the capitalist countries had taken decades to pass through. Our people tightened their belts, endured hunger and cold, and lived in poverty, but they did not begrudge the resources necessary to create a powerful industry and to provide arms and equipment to the army, so that the enemy wouldn't even dare to approach our borders.

I remember when I returned from the front lines of the Civil War in early 1922. As soon as I returned to civilian life, the party organization sent me to be assistant manager at some coal mines formerly run by a French company, the same mines where I had worked as a machinist in 1912–14. The manager of those [Rutchenkovo] mines was my close friend Yegor Trofimovich Abakumov. That is not the same Abakumov who was minister of internal affairs,[43] but a different man who became one of the leaders of the coal industry in the USSR. We experienced a difficult time in the 1920s. There was hunger as we worked at the mines, and in 1922 there were isolated incidents of cannibalism. The countryside had been ruined; agriculture suffered even more than industry. But the people had confidence in the party, because they knew that this ruin and destruction had been imposed on us by our own capitalists and by the capitalists around the world who supported the counterrevolution and organized foreign military intervention. Even illiterate people understood the party's slogans and demands. In those days we not only pledged our lives for the sake of the new world, but sometimes took sin on our very own souls [that is, lied] and said that in the old days we had lived even worse.

That was a sin and a lie because highly skilled workers before World War I and before the revolution—not everyone, but highly skilled workers in the Donbass region, where I worked before the revolution—actually lived better and even substantially better. In 1913, for example, I personally was better provided for than in 1932, when I worked as second secretary of the party's Moscow committee. You could say that other workers [workers other than the highly skilled ones in the Donbass] lived worse. Probably they did. After all, not everyone lived the same. . . .

In the 1930s we consciously accepted deprivation because we were literally squeezing out everything we could for the sake of speeding up industrial development. We had to take full advantage of the time we had. Sometimes this required sacrifices that were virtually beyond human capability. But the people accepted that too and built up a modern industrial base. However, as it turned out, we didn't know how to use that industrial base as it should have been used. At the beginning of the war, our army turned out to be lacking in both qualified commanders and the kinds of weapons necessary to repel the enemy attack and defeat the enemy at the borders of the USSR.

I think that our historians will need to analyze the impact of the losses we suffered not only because of the military cadres destroyed by Stalin but also the cadres in our national economy that he destroyed. How many honest people died then! Party, trade-union, and other officials working in industry. Thousands and thousands! The most qualified people of all were wiped out: the directors of factories, chief engineers, the heads of major subdivisions in the factories, secretaries of the party's district and citywide committees, chairmen of district and citywide Soviets, and secretaries of base-level party organizations. Hundreds of thousands of perfectly innocent people died. Of course I cannot list them all. I can name only some of the individuals from among those I knew.

For example, Ivan Tarasovich Kirilkin, director of the Rutchenkovo mines, where I once had been an ordinary worker and later an assistant manager. As I have already said, I went to work in those mines in 1912. At that time they belonged to a French company, which later sold them. (It seems to me that its name was the Bryansk Joint-Stock Company.) After the revolution those mines became government property and were called the Rutchenkovo mines. At one time they were given the name Krasnotvorcheskiye [literally the "Red Creative Mines"], but that name didn't catch on. The coal pits were named after a prominent local landowner, Rutchenko. Kirilkin was the manager of those mines in 1925–26. Later Ivan Tarasovich [Kirilkin] was appointed director of the Makeyevka metallurgical works, and he showed a good knowledge of the business in the way he ran them. Meanwhile, the manager at the Yuzovka metallurgical works, which had earlier belonged to the British capitalist Hughes, was Bazulin, a local worker. Everyone knew Vasya Bazulin. He didn't do a bad job at managing those metallurgical works, relying on the support of the active party membership and the engineering staff. Then came 1937. Ivan Tarasovich [Kirilkin] perished. I couldn't find any traces of where and under what circumstances he died. Bazulin also vanished from the horizon.

And what about in Moscow? How many directors of factories and how many engineers perished? It used to be that people would simply report to me: "Hey look, here are some 'enemies of the people' that we overlooked!" The party organization would pound itself on the chest with shame and remorse: "We didn't see them before!" The number of such "enemies of the people" grew so large that even Ordzhonikidze[44] could no longer stomach it, and he shot himself. Thus an extremely honest man, a man of truly chivalrous character, took his own life.

Anastas Ivanovich Mikoyan told me once, in a private conversation, that before Sergo [Ordzhonikidze] shot himself he went for a walk with Mikoyan during the evening along the tree-lined pathways of the Kremlin grounds. Sergo said: "I can't take it anymore. I can't resign myself to what's going on. I also can't fight Stalin, and I don't see any possible way to go on living." And then Sergo shot himself. And how did Stalin react to this?

Stalin got around this incident in his own clever way. At that time I was secretary of the party's Moscow city committee and Moscow province committee. On one of my days off, I received a phone call from Avel Sofronovich Yenukidze,[45] who said: "Comrade Khrushchev, please come to see me at the Kremlin. It's urgent."

I went there, and I asked: "What's going on?"

He said: "Sergo has died."

I said: "How could he have died? I saw him just recently."

He said: "His life ended suddenly. You yourself know that he was not a well man. A government commission has been established to arrange his funeral. You are part of that funeral commission, and I am the chairperson. We now need to prepare proposals for the Central Committee on how the funeral is to be conducted." There was a standard procedure for such ceremonies, and we quickly discussed the question and submitted our proposals. I don't remember now exactly, but it seems to me that I spoke at the funeral on behalf of the party's Moscow committee.

I felt very bad about Sergo. He had enjoyed great respect among the people, and I personally regretted his loss because I had always felt that he had a warm and kindly attitude toward me. He treated me in a sort of fatherly and protective way, and I needed that. Besides, it was a pleasant thing. After all, no matter who you are, a kind word is more pleasant than being yelled at and treated rudely, as was very much the fashion in those days.

We held the funeral and buried him. So then, at that time I did think that Sergo's life had ended suddenly on that day off. They said that he had eaten breakfast, lay down on the sofa, and never got up again. It's true that he lay down on the sofa, but that's when he shot himself.

For so many years both I and others were deceived on this subject by Stalin. Why did he need to practice this deception? Apparently so as not to arouse unnecessary thoughts in the minds of our people about why such an outstanding man as Sergo, a man who was very close to Stalin, had suddenly shot himself. Obviously he didn't do this because life was so good. And this was a man who had lived through the trying experiences of underground struggle against the tsarist regime, having been sent to Siberia several times. And yet, at a time when the USSR was advancing, when it might seem that the only thing one needed was to do one's work and take pleasure in his country's progress, he suddenly decided to leave this life and put an end to himself. This means that there was a real reason for it. Without a good reason, a man like this could not go and kill himself, because he was a Communist of high principle, exceptionally well trained and educated, with a highly developed sense of honor. I say this on the basis of opinions expressed by Stalin himself, but Stalin was quite unprincipled in matters of morality. Stalin condemned Sergo precisely for his high principles. When I finally did find out that Sergo had shot himself, many things that I had heard from Stalin about Sergo became clearer to me. Stalin had always tried to belittle Sergo's role in the revolution and in the effort to develop the USSR economically.

And what about Avraamy Pavlovich Zavenyagin, my friend, whose acquaintance I made in 1922 when I returned from the Red Army? He was the secretary of the party's district committee in Yuzovka then. Later I went to study at a workers' school in Yuzovka, while Avraamy entered the mining academy and graduated from it with honors. He was an interesting man and a good hard worker. He worked hard in many different posts. Ordzhonikidze promoted him to be his deputy for ferrous metallurgy.[46] Then suddenly Zavenyagin disappeared. I was concerned. I wondered, "Where in the world is Avraamy?" There had been neither sight nor sound of him, but after a certain length of time Zavenyagin reappeared. Later he became deputy chairman of the Council of Ministers of the USSR. The last post he held (and he was holding more than one) was that of minister of medium machine building for the USSR. In other words, he was involved with our atomic energy and atomic weapons program, and he died as a result of exposure to atomic radiation. Where did Zavenyagin disappear to for that length of time? It turned out that he was serving a term of internal exile.

I was later told that Stalin called him in and expressed his lack of confidence: "There's testimony against you, Zavenyagin." And he sent him off to the other end of the world.[47] He worked hard and distinguished himself there. He was an honorable man who knew how to use his knowledge and energy. Later Stalin brought him back from exile, and he again began to work as an official in Moscow.

I am not about to try right now to name all the names of those who suffered for no reason. First, I have forgotten the names of many factory directors, engineers, and shop foremen who were destroyed during those years in Moscow. There were probably thousands of them. Second, I am simply not informed as to where these people are or what became of them. But I can draw the following conclusion: If these cadres had not been destroyed but had continued their work to our country's advantage, creating industrial resources and weapons for the Red Army, making use of our industrial potential intelligently and with their knowledge of what they were doing, we could have made good use of the circumstances to produce the necessary weapons in the necessary quantity so that the Red Army would have been equipped no worse than the Germans, and even better. We had every possibility for doing that.

I would like to demonstrate this in a vivid and graphic way. For example, we did manage to produce the necessary quantity of weapons during the course of the war, by the middle of 1943. It was at that very time that we crushed Hitler's enormously powerful army in the battle of the Kursk salient. Hitler's forces were armed to the teeth with the latest weapons. I don't remember whether our ground forces in that battle were using foreign materiel and weapons other than motor vehicles. At the battle of Stalingrad I saw some individual British and American tanks, but the Soviet tank crews always placed our own domestically manufactured tanks, especially the T-34, in the first rank for combat capabilities. The artillery, machine guns, rifles, and submachine guns were all ours, of domestic manufacture. Thus we actually were capable of producing remarkable weapons in the necessary quantities to equip our army by mid-1943. Later our own weapons were supplied to us in increasing quantities, even though we had previously abandoned an enormous territory to the enemy—all of Ukraine, including the Donbass, Belorussia, and other regions with their factories and raw material.

But still that is not everything. At that time we were deprived of the industrial, scientific, and technological resources of Leningrad, which was under blockade and of Moscow, which had been evacuated—two industrial centers of nationwide importance. We were also deprived of Rostov, Voronezh, Stalingrad, and the Northern Caucasus. If we could now draw on statistical data, [we could show that] the areas occupied by the Germans provided considerably more than half of all the iron, steel, coal, and oil produced in the USSR. Probably it is more like 60 or 70 percent if we take into account the metallurgical industry. So then, deprived of this industrial base, our people, after evacuating personnel and equipment as much as they were able, found it possible to set this equipment up again, sometimes in the middle of nowhere in some sort of barns, and they again organized the production of tanks, artillery, automatic weapons, rifles, machine guns, mines, explosives, and so on. A colossal amount of work was done in order to provide the army with everything necessary.

What is the point? Why were we not able to do all this before the war? As soon as it became clear that we were going to have a war with Nazi Germany, and this became clear with Hitler's rise to power in 1933, we should have constantly expanded our production of arms and military equipment and prepared ourselves for the inevitable war. From 1936 to 1939, when the Civil War was going in Republican Spain, we confronted our enemy face to face as we provided aid to the revolutionary forces in Spain. Our people in Spain directly encountered the German and Italian fascists, who were fighting there on the side [of the right-wing insurgency] led by the rebel general, [Francisco] Franco. Then came the year 1939 and the signing of the Ribbentrop-Molotov pact, as it is sometimes called in the West. And Stalin told us: "I am deceiving him. I am deceiving Hitler." That means he expected that Hitler would attack us all the same, but he was playing for time by signing this treaty. Instead of clashing head on with Hitler right then and drawing his fire on ourselves, by signing this treaty we pulled back from this dangerous edge and created conditions in which Hitler could first engage with the Western European countries. That was what Stalin meant when he said he was deceiving Hitler; he wanted to win some time.

That is precisely how Stalin evaluated the situation then. At least I want to think that is how he understood things then. But in that case he should have exerted every effort—after signing the nonaggression treaty and then another treaty, a friendship and border treaty with Hitler—he should then immediately have started everything working at full force, our industry, our scientific institutions, and our design offices for production of the required armaments, to get everything running at full steam. We had enough time from August 23, 1939, to June 22, 1941. I consider that the immediate prewar period.

The inevitability of war was clear to everyone, to anyone who thought even the slightest bit. It was only a matter of time, and Hitler was deciding the timing of events. It was necessary to use our time to the fullest advantage and to develop to the maximum our production of the means of waging war.

If we had done this when we had the time (I am counting 1939, 1940, and almost half of 1941, that is 2.5 years, which was exactly equal to the amount of time that we later lost, when half of our country's industrial potential was taken, when we were forced to retreat), we would have been able to organize weapons production earlier and provide our army with all the means of waging war. If we had made intelligent use of the breathing spell we gained, by mid-1941 we would have had what we finally received in 1943, and the Red Army would have found that sufficient, and even more than sufficient, to crush and defeat the Germans right at our borders and not allow the fascist hordes to penetrate the Soviet Union.

Of course we weren't sitting around doing nothing; we were working hard. But we didn't make use of the breathing spell as we should have. This is known to history. I was in a position close to the army, and I know very well that as soon as the war began workers in Ukraine came to the offices of the party's Central Committee and demanded: "Give us rifles!" And I couldn't give them anything because there were no rifles. I called Moscow to ask for some.

Moscow said (it was Malenkov who came to the phone): "There are no rifles. The rifles we had in Moscow belonged to the civil defense organization and had holes in the barrels. We filled in the holes, fixed the rifles, and sent them to Leningrad. But you'll have to forge your own weapons. Make knives, spears, and so forth." Can you imagine? The Germans were crashing down on us with all their advanced military technology, and we were told: "Forge spears, forge knives." We were supposed to use these to defeat an enemy who was attacking us with tanks? Only our people, our army, and our party could have withstood this experience! In spite of the very difficult conditions, our army resisted as it retreated, and even though we were retreating, we gave a good mauling to the German armies and equipment. We made use of Molotov cocktails, mines, booby traps, and anything else our people could think of, the people who were defending their native land, their wealth, and their honor.

But what if we had used the breathing spell to full advantage? Did Stalin have the right to ignore the danger and limit the pace of arms production to the same old tempo, keeping production at the same level as when he signed the treaty with Germany? No, he had no such right. He himself said he was deceiving Hitler. That meant he was certain that Hitler was still the enemy, that he could attack us. And if he was going to attack us, then we had to use the time, while Hitler was tied up in the West, to our own best advantage, to develop the production of all possible means for destroying the enemy, to turn them out in the necessary quantity, and to build up reserves. It really is necessary at this point to cite statistical data on production levels for iron, steel, rolled stock, machinery, and so on, but I don't have those figures at hand.

Of course what I have said does not contradict my earlier arguments about the role that aid from our allies played in our victory. It also doesn't contradict the fact that we actually did produce a huge quantity of weapons to defeat the enemy. I don't know whether we received artillery from our allies. As far as I know, we didn't. We received motor vehicles and airplanes. We equipped our army with these motor vehicles, and even after the war a great many American vehicles were being used in our industry. Our maritime transport was also American to a significant degree. We returned some of these ships to the United States after the war.

In principle the fact that we retreated so far from our borders and allowed the enemy to occupy and destroy Ukraine, Belorussia, and part of the Russian Federation was the result of miscalculation and incompetent leadership. A lot of people who were rather primitive in their makeup were given important assignments. Let me refer once again to Kulik.[48] Kulik was in charge of supplying our army with weapons, but he was actually a very primitive individual. Later Stalin had him shot. I repeat for the umpteenth time that that was a crime. He did not deserve to be shot. But there is no question that Kulik also did not deserve to be appointed to such a high post. I had no doubt of that, and I spoke to Stalin about it even before the war.

And now to speak about our military technology. In 1940 the T-34 tank had already been adopted and put through tests. Since we found ourselves in a situation in which war was about to break out, production of this tank should have been undertaken not just at Kharkov factory no. 75. Mass production of this tank should have begun immediately; the machinery and equipment should have been provided, and a number of factories assigned to develop mass production of the T-34. Then at the beginning of the war we could have delivered T-34 tanks, as many as were needed each month, to meet at least the minimum demand for them. We also did not have enough antiaircraft machine guns, although we knew how to manufacture machine guns, and our industry was capable of producing as many as were needed. Instead, we just sat on our hands.

I already said earlier that after the nonaggression treaty with Germany, Stalin raised the question of building new factories to produce antiaircraft machine guns. Of course these factories were not built by the beginning of the war, nor were they built during the war. The production of these machine guns was assigned to other factories, so that our army's requirements were eventually met. But why was this not done in 1939 and in 1940? After all, there was enough time. We also had a shortage of divisional artillery. At Stalingrad we received reinforcements without artillery. I remember one division that arrived (the son of Dolores Ibarruri was serving in that division), and it had no artillery. It wasn't even equipped with a sufficient number of machine guns. Who was responsible for that? Some people say that Stalin was misled, that people reported to him inaccurately. Does this mean that when Stalin destroyed our military, economic, party, and scientific cadres, and our intellectuals, he was being inspired by his own great genius? But when he allowed the army to be left without a sufficient supply of rifles at the beginning of the war, not to mention other types of weapons, he was being let down by other people? Where does this come from, this unequal and inconsistent approach to evaluating the genius and the mistakes of the "great leader"?

For my part, I consider what happened to be a crime. [In the attitude that I have described] there is an element of overindulgence, of making allowances on ethical questions, a kind of slave mentality. It is an attitude of forgiving the "strong man" for anything he does and searching for some "weak person" who misinformed or misled the strong man, so that then the weak one can be thrown into the meat grinder to add to those who had already been ground up earlier. I think that the party will come to the correct conclusions and complete the work that was begun at the Twentieth and Twenty-Second Party Congresses; that all those who were guilty will be named, so that Soviet public opinion will be correctly informed, and so that this kind of thing will not be repeated in the future. That is my opinion about the defeats we suffered during the first years of the war, our losses and our retreats. Those were defeats that seemed to have been prepared "in alliance with Hitler." Hitler took advantage of Stalin's suspiciousness, mistrust, and his treacherous nature and foisted off on him materials suggesting that our well-known military leaders were actually German agents. Stalin believed these materials, and the machinery of destruction went to work. Thus the enemy was able to deprive us of our best military cadres. And we even helped do this. The high point in the destruction of honest Soviet people was reached in 1937, the only prewar year in which the five-year plan for industrial production was not fulfilled. And Hitler, preparing for war against the USSR, also took note of that slowdown in our industrial development.

I know that in the future the term "Stalinist" will become the most offensive and insulting of all terms. Today the Stalinists are trying to purify and varnish Stalin, portraying him as a "great genius and great military leader." These are very harmful people. Whether they mean to or not, they are simply covering up crimes that were committed, and they are laying the groundwork for the same kind of methods that Stalin used to be used again in the future. It was Marshal [Matvei] Zakharov who began this pro-Stalin movement in the 1960s. Marshal Konev has taken the same road, and behind them, bringing up the rear, is Marshal Grechko[49] on his long stilts. Shame on them all!

Zakharov may have some feeling of personal bitterness toward me, although I never had any clashes with him and I never said a bad word about him during the war, nor did I ever hear anything bad from him. In the 1960s I did say to Malinovsky that Matvei Zakharov should be relieved of his duties as chief of the General Staff, but after all, I did not do that unilaterally. God forbid! When I stood at the head of our country's leadership, all questions were taken up at sessions of the Presidium of the Central Committee. All important questions were discussed there, and this was a proposal that everyone agreed with. What was my motivation for this proposal? The man's age and physical condition. You can't have as chief of the General Staff a man who starts to nod off five minutes after a meeting begins and falls fast asleep. How can the defense of the country be entrusted to people who are physically worn out? It is not their fault. Age is age.

You can't keep people in office who are physically not capable of working in the interests of the army with the required energy. That's why I said it was necessary to find some other honorable post for Zakharov. And so he was appointed chief of the General Staff Academy, which is not only an honorable position but also one of great responsibility—training cadres and teaching people. His age would not be a hindrance there, because the actual teaching is done by the staff of professors and instructors, while he himself, an honest and devoted man who knows his subject, would understand what general directions to give. Apparently the human feeling of being slighted sometimes drowns out one's sense of reason and intelligence and prevents a person from correctly understanding some measure, which may not necessarily seem very pleasant. But it is necessary to understand when things are being done in the interests of the cause!

Marshal Biryuzov[50] was appointed his successor, but he died in a plane crash as part of a delegation flying to Yugoslavia. The level of Zakharov's military knowledge was higher than his, but Biryuzov was younger and more energetic. Now Zakharov has returned to his former post. In my opinion this has been done against our country's best interests. It doesn't improve the leadership and it doesn't improve the work of training the army. Because, alas, Comrade Zakharov is old.

But why has Konev taken this pro-Stalin position? Konev is a man of special makeup, with special qualities of mind and character. He is the only one of the prominent military leaders who "responded" favorably to the material Stalin circulated in regard to the so-called Doctors' Plot.[51] These doctors were arrested just before Stalin died. In response to these falsified materials, Konev sent Stalin a letter expressing his agreement with the information that had been circulated, even though it was a frame-up. He strengthened Stalin's belief that it was right to arrest the doctors and even provided personal confirmation from his own experience, alleging that he had suffered harmful treatment at the hands of these doctors. This was a shameful thing for an honest person to do! I cannot accept the idea that a decent person could agree with these delirious charges that Stalin dreamed up. After his death all this was swept away like so much smoke. No crimes had been committed at all, and these prominent doctors were set free.

What about Grechko? He is a "KVD." [Russian initials for the phrase "whichever way the wind blows."] I put in a lot of effort to have him promoted. The same Konev accused me of covering up for Grechko and making him my protégé, promoting him and supporting him. Konev claimed that it was Khrushchev who wanted to give Grechko the rank of marshal of the Soviet Union after the war and so forth. And then comes this surprising transformation of Grechko! I have seen a lot of things. It is not only Grechko who has passed before my eyes. But I can say that of all the chameleons I have seen he takes his place as the archetype of chameleons. Yes, my dear sirs, whatever post you hold, whatever personal services you have to your credit, you can only take the wrong road this way. History will not forgive you for it. You are only leaving behind a bad memory of yourselves, because you were not true to your own selves and you misled the people by covering up for Stalin's abuses, and now you are trying to whitewash him by saying that after all our country did win the war!

Yes, the people and the party did achieve victory. But Stalin? In his ideas, in his outlook on the world, in his understanding of things of course he was a party man. But his methods, his ways of working, were based on such destructive things as killing people, having them shot, having them tortured, forcing confessions from them for nonexistent crimes. There cannot be two different opinions about Stalin's personal activity, the details of which have been fully revealed since his death. Many aspects of his activity and work deserve moral condemnation and should surely be condemned by history.

We achieved great successes in socialist construction; we built up a mighty industry, reorganized agriculture, and raised the level of culture, science, and the arts. The latent forces of the people were awakened, and they created the powerful country that is the Soviet Union today. We are now no weaker than any other country. Although the industry of the United States is more powerful than ours, our armed forces are equipped no worse and perhaps even better than the Americans. May this serve as a stern warning to all adventurers, militarists, and advocates of aggression! If they want to unleash a war, that war might come back to haunt them. And I'm not even talking about the European opponents of the USSR, such as West Germany. By comparison with us, any European country without the United States is simply not a factor. Today no sensible person, however blinded he might be by hatred of the Soviet Union, can think about aggression against our country. And that is ultimately the result of the victory of the October revolution in 1917.

With that I want to end this part of my memoirs about those striking and vivid times, when our people were struggling to transform our society along socialist lines.

1. Viscount Montgomery of Alamein commanded armies in North Africa from 1942 and in France, Belgium, and Germany in 1944–45. He headed the British General Staff from 1946 to 1948. At the time of the events being described, he was commander of the British occupation forces in Germany. See Biographies.

2. In July 1942, the delivery of oil products from the Caucasus along the railroad through Rostov on the Don came to a halt. Soon thereafter delivery along the Salsk–Stalingrad route also came to a halt. Oil products from Krasnodar and Grozny (in Chechnya) were brought out on the rail shuttle between Grozny and Makhachkala (in Dagestan) and then by sea along the Caspian coast to Astrakhan. Later they were shipped across the Caspian Sea to Krasnovodsk (in Turkmenia) and thence in a loop through Central Asia to the Urals and the Volga. In August 1942 the country was receiving 48 percent of its fuel supply by rail directly from the Caucasus, while by the end of the battle of Stalingrad in winter 1943 the figure was down to only 17 percent. The relative weight of the

Caucasian supply points fell by two-thirds. As a result, the tank cars on the Caucasian rail lines were at a standstill. To relocate the tank cars to places where the railroads were still in Soviet hands, their wheels were removed in Makhachkala, and then the tank cars without wheels, partly filled with water to improve their equilibrium, were lowered directly into the sea and towed across the Caspian to Guryev (now Atyrau, in Kazakhstan [SS]) or to Krasnovodsk (Turkmenbashi, in Turkmenistan [SS]), while trolleys holding the wheels were loaded on barges or steam tugs. The tank cars were then reassembled and placed on the railroad.

3. Of the 18.3 million tons of steel smelted in the USSR in 1940, Ukraine's share was 8.6 million tons. But in the first half of 1941 the rate of growth of smelting increased both in Ukraine and in the country as a whole. Of the 166 million tons of coal mined in the USSR in 1940, just over half (83.73 million tons) was mined in Ukraine.

4. N. S. Khrushchev is referring to the long siege of Leningrad by German forces. During the siege, which lasted from September 8, 1941, until

January 27, 1944, more than half of Leningrad's prewar population of 3 million perished, mainly from starvation and exhaustion. The classic account of this traumatic experience is Harrison Salisbury's *The 900 Days: The Siege of Leningrad* (Cambridge, MA: Da Capo Press, 1985). [SS]

5. Gorky has now been given its old name of Nizhny Novogord ("lower new town"). It is on the Volga River, about 400 kilometers east of Moscow. [SS]

6. Voronezh is in southwestern Russia, about 500 kilometers south of Moscow. [SS]

7. Mikoyan was a deputy chairman of the Council of People's Commissars and a member of the State Defense Council. He had some relevant experience as people's commissar for foreign trade. See Biographies.

8. The tank to which Khrushchev refers may be the Valentine, the standard British infantry tank in 1942. Of 4,260 British tanks delivered to the Soviet Union under the lend-lease program, 3,000 were Valentines. However, other British tanks, such as the OT-34 Flamethrower, were also used in the battle of Stalingrad. [SS]

9. Colonel General of the Engineering Service V. A. Malyshev was people's commissar of tank industry from 1941. See Biographies.

10. Harold Macmillan was leader of the British Conservative Party and prime minister of Great Britain from 1957 to 1963. See Biographies.

11. Mariupol is in southeastern Ukraine, south of Donetsk on the Sea of Azov. "Ilyich" was Lenin's patronymic, commonly used to refer to him in an affectionate though respectful way. [SS] Mariupol was renamed Zhdanov in 1948 and is now again Mariupol. Khrushchev is referring to a factory built in 1897 by the Nikopol-Mariupol Mining and Metallurgical Society.

12. Mikado, "exalted gate," is an archaic term for the Japanese emperor. In Japan his usual titles are Tenno ("heavenly sovereign") or Tenshi ("son of heaven"). [SS]

13. Duralumin (or duraluminum) is an especially hard and strong alloy of aluminum, used in the construction of aircraft. [SS]

14. To reach Murmansk, a port on the Barents Sea at the northwestern extremity of the Soviet Union, British ships had to travel around the western and northern coastlines of Nazi-occupied Norway. [SS]

15. This operation was carried out by the Soviet Transportation Administration in Iran from February 1942. The American military administration was responsible for the section from the Persian Gulf to Teheran by rail and on to Qazvin by road. (Qazvin is in Iran, about 150 kilometers northwest of Teheran on the main road and railroad line from Teheran to Tabriz and the Soviet border. [AH]) Taking the goods farther north from Qazvin into the USSR was the task of the Soviet

Transportation Administration. The crews of two Soviet fighter squadrons flew the American planes from Qazvin to airfields in the USSR. The total freight transported through Iran into the USSR between 1941 and 1945 (taking reloading into account) amounted to 10.5 million tons. Repair and maintenance of the roads along which vehicles and other goods from the Allies were delivered were provided by the Soviet Military-Vehicle Roads, a subdivision of the road troops.

16. Chukotka is a peninsula at the northeastern extremity of Siberia, directly across the Bering Straits from Alaska. [SS]

17. "Radar" is an acronym derived from the initial letters of "*ra*dio *d*etection *a*nd *r*anging." Radar ascertains the direction and range of aircraft and other objects by reflecting electromagnetic waves against them. Radar was developed and used in air defense during the war by Britain and Germany, but not by the Soviet Union. [SS]

18. The Potsdam Conference was a summit meeting of the three Allied powers—the United States, Britain, and the Soviet Union—which was held between July 17 and August 2, 1945, following Germany's unconditional surrender. The United States was represented by President Harry S. Truman, Britain at first by Winston Churchill and then by the new prime minister, Clement Attlee, and the Soviet Union by Joseph Stalin. Potsdam is near Berlin. [SS]

19. Khrushchev refers to agreements reached at the Teheran Conference of the three Allied powers. The conference, the first three-way meeting between Roosevelt, Churchill, and Stalin, took place in Teheran, capital of Iran, between November 28 and December 1, 1943. [GS/SS]

20. This anecdote is of course erroneous. The Roosevelt family had been in America for many generations before the time of FDR. Whether the source of the error was Stalin or Khrushchev is not known. [GS]

21. The Ardennes are a range of hills in southeastern Belgium. Khrushchev is referring to the Battle of the Bulge, which took place in the Ardennes between December 16, 1944, and January 28, 1945. It was one of the bloodiest battles of World War II, with more than half a million American and British soldiers fighting on one side and more than half a million Germans on the other. The battle was the result of a German offensive planned by Hitler as a last-ditch attempt to avert defeat. The offensive was followed at the end of December by a successful Allied counteroffensive. [GS/SS]

22. Khrushchev refers to Churchill's appeal to Stalin on January 6, 1945. The Soviet offensive in East Prussia and Poland began on January 12. It had been planned to begin on January 20.

23. Japan had used some forms of bacteriological weapons against Mongolian and Chinese

troops. (Japan had also made extensive use of chemical and bacteriological weapons against the Chinese civilian population and had tested bacteriological weapons on prisoners of war.) However, it is true that chemical and bacteriological weapons were not used in Europe. [SS]

24. In this section of the chapter, Khrushchev discusses ten military commanders who were unjustly arrested in the purges of 1937–38 (or, in the case of Army Commissar Ya. B. Gamarnik, who committed suicide to escape arrest). Four of these commanders—Tukhachevsky, Yakir, Eideman, and Kork—were among eight who were court-martialed and executed for treason in August 1937. [SS] For Gamarnik, see Biographies.

25. Marshal of the Soviet Union A. I. Yegorov. See Biographies.

26. Marshal of the Soviet Union M. N. Tukhachevsky. See Biographies.

27. The military operations that N. S. Khrushchev lists here all belong to the Civil War period (1918–21):

The Kronstadt operation was carried out in March 1921 to crush a rebellion against the Bolshevik regime by sailors at the naval base of Kronstadt on Kotlin Island in the Gulf of Finland, about 30 kilometers west of Petrograd (Leningrad, Saint Petersburg).

The "operation against Antonov" was carried out in August 1920 to suppress a peasant rebellion (led by a man named Antonov) in Tambov province, about 500 kilometers southeast of Moscow.

Rear Admiral Kolchak and General Denikin commanded White forces in 1919 and the first part of 1920. Kolchak was active in Siberia, Denikin in southern Russia.

The "operation against the White Poles" refers to the campaign waged against Poland between April and October 1920. [SS]

28. Army Commander I. E. Yakir. See Biographies.

29. Eideman was a well-known military strategist and for a time was director of the Frunze Military Academy. [SS]

30. Osoaviakhim was the Society to Assist Defense, Aviation, and Chemistry. Officially an independent public civil-defense organization, it was in practice subordinate to the mobilization department of the General Staff. [GS/SS]

31. Khrushchev is referring to Army Commander of the Second Rank A. I. Kork. See Biographies.

32. Marshal of the Soviet Union V. K. Blyukher, commander of the Far Eastern Army. See Biographies.

33. Chiang Kai-shek headed the Chinese Nationalist Party, the Kuomintang. [SS]

34. A. S. Serafimovich (1863–1949) was a writer and playwright. His novel, rendered into English variously as The Iron Flood or The Iron Torrent,

was published in 1924. Later he wrote a play based on the novel, which was staged at the Realist Theater in Moscow in 1934. [SS]

35. The Taman Army, a 30,000-strong force, was trapped on the Taman peninsula (in the Kuban region of southern Russia, just east of the Crimea) by the advance of General Denikin's Volunteer Army in summer 1918. In August and September 1918 Kovtyukh led the Taman Army on a 500-kilometer march around the White lines. Ye. I. Kovtyukh (1890–1938) is also known for the daring raids he led against the expeditionary force of General Wrangel in the same region in August 1920. [SS]

36. I. N. Dubovoi. See Biographies.

37. Mikola Shchors was a Red Army commander in the Civil War in Ukraine. Later he was much celebrated as a hero. [SS]

38. N. N. Demchenko. See Biographies.

39. From the end of June to the end of August 1941 Army General K. A. Meretskov was under investigation.

40. L. P. Beria. See Biographies.

41. V. S. Abakumov was a highly placed secret-police official. In October 1946 he became minister of state security. [SS] See Biographies.

42. The kandidat nauk ("candidate of sciences") degree corresponds roughly to a Western Ph.D. The doktor nauk ("doctor of sciences") degree is at a higher level than the kandidat and has no Western equivalent. [SS]

43. In fact, V. S. Abakumov was not minister of internal affairs but minister of state security. [SS]

44. G. K. Ordzhonikidze, whose nickname was "Sergo." See Biographies.

45. A. S. Yenukidze. See Biographies.

46. Ordzhonikidze at that time was in charge of the People's Commissariat for Heavy Industry. [SS]

47. Stalin sent Zavenyagin to Norilsk (in north-central Siberia [SS]), where he was chief of construction and director of the mining and metallurgical nickel combine. [SS]

48. Marshal of the Soviet Union G. I. Kulik. See Biographies.

49. M. V. Zakharov, I. S. Konev, A. A. Grechko. See Biographies.

50. S. S. Biryuzov. See Biographies.

51. In January 1953, it was announced that nine physicians had been arrested on charges of plotting to poison and kill top Soviet leaders. Following Stalin's death on March 5, 1953, the physicians were declared innocent and released. The affair of the so-called Doctors' Plot had anti-Semitic overtones—six of the nine doctors were Jews—and it was feared that it might be the prelude to broader repressive measures against the Jewish population, possibly including deportation. [SS]

## THE FAR EAST AFTER THE GREAT PATRIOTIC WAR

The year 1969 is now close at hand, and I want to dictate my recollections about the end of the war and the victory over Japan and about how our rather complicated postwar relations with Japan took shape.

Our rights to property in Manchuria and Korea—property that had been lost as a result of the Russo-Japanese War of 1904–5—were restored to us. That war had ended in the defeat of tsarist Russia, and as is generally known, Japan imposed an onerous peace treaty back then [in 1905].[1]

[After World War II] in the San Francisco Peace Treaty with Japan, appropriate clauses relative to the USSR were included in the text of the treaty, but not all the proposals the USSR made were taken into account, and so in 1951 we did not sign that peace treaty.[2] It is very difficult, in my opinion, to find any logic in our approach to the question of signing the treaty. One thing was of primary significance: We had to recognize that the main effort in defeating Japan had been made by the United States. Every thinking person familiar with the facts knows this. As a result of Japan's treacherous attack, the United States had suffered serious losses, although the interests of Britain, the Netherlands, and other European colonial powers were also affected. Japan seized a number of colonies formerly belonging to those countries. We had no reason to suffer over that.

What we were concerned about was that Japan had conducted a hostile policy toward the USSR during the whole period leading up to World War II. It was not only a hostile policy; it was arrogant, intransigent, and extortionist. Nevertheless we were forced to put up with it. Besides, we understood that it was not just a question of Japan. Japanese militarism was expanding in the East, but in the West was Nazi Germany. We had to play a diplomatic game and maneuver between these two forces in order to ensure peace and not provoke our enemies into war. We could not allow the USSR to be drawn into a two-front war, both in the West and in the East. We were still too weak for such a war. Even in 1945 we allowed ourselves a three-month interval [after the defeat of Germany and before declaring war on Japan]. Incidentally, I never heard from Stalin (he never talked about it in my presence) what exact agreement had been made between the USSR and the Allies about our participation in the war against Japan after the defeat of Nazi Germany.

When that moment came, our troops crossed the Manchurian border.[3] Vasilevsky was appointed commander in chief of our forces. The commanders of our Fronts were Malinovsky, Meretskov, and Purkayev.[4] Malinovsky's troops accomplished more than the others. We smashed Japan's Kwantung

Army. It's true that this happened after Japan had actually been defeated, because the Americans had already dropped the two atomic bombs on Japan.[5] Japan had been thrashing about in a kind of death agony, looking for some way to escape from the war. It was literally the last month of this situation when we joined the war against Japan.

I was present in Moscow during a conversation in which Stalin was urging our military leaders to hurry up and begin operations against Japan as quickly as possible; otherwise Japan would surrender to the United States, and we would not have joined the war in time. Stalin had his doubts then as to whether the Americans would keep their word, which they had given earlier. He thought they might go back on their word. The terms that had been agreed on between us were as follows: We would receive back the territory taken from Russia by Japan in the war of 1904–5 as long as we immediately joined in the war against Japan. And what if we had not taken part? What if the Japanese had surrendered before we entered the war against them? A different situation would have arisen, and the Americans might have revised the commitment they made earlier. They could have said: "Since you didn't participate, we are not obliged to give you anything."

If President Roosevelt had remained alive, Stalin would have had greater hopes. Roosevelt was an intelligent leader and took the Soviet Union into account. Stalin had dealings with him more than once, and as Stalin himself said, good relations had been established between them. (And apparently this was actually so.) Those relations were much better than the ones with our other ally, Britain, including personal relations with its leader, Churchill. But in summer 1945 Roosevelt was no longer among the living. He had died that spring,[6] and it was Truman who finished off the war with Japan. Truman was not an intelligent man, and he became president really by accident. He pursued an unbridled reactionary policy, and his policy toward the Soviet Union became simply intolerable.

I don't remember now on exactly what date Japan surrendered, but our envoy, it seems, was not present for that; he arrived only for the official formalities when a statement of surrender was signed.[7] That was not accidental. It was not we, after all, who had fought on the islands of the Pacific (aside from the island of Sakhalin and the Kurile Islands). Our troops had not been there. Our claim to a voice in deciding the postwar fate of Japan caused our allies to become irritated with us, and Stalin, overestimating what was possible for him, responded with equal hostility. In short, relations with the United States began to go bad. We were often ignored. Sometimes we were

THE GREAT PATRIOTIC WAR

not taken into account, and attempts were made to slight us. Truman was the first to mistreat us in this way. This was a product of his personality and his limited mental capabilities. An intelligent president would not have conducted himself in such a provocative way and would not have turned the Soviet Union against the United States.

As far as territorial questions went, the Americans kept their word. They must be granted their due. When a draft peace treaty with Japan was drawn up, a line where we could sign was also included. Consideration for our interests was provided for, as had been stated in a protocol signed earlier by Roosevelt. We should have signed that treaty. I don't know what played the main role in our refusal to sign: whether it was Stalin's vainglory, his pride in our success during World War II, or whether Stalin overestimated what was possible or the extent to which he could influence the course of events. But he took the bit in his teeth and refused to sign the treaty. Who benefited from our refusal to sign? It is true that in fact we were given the territory of southern Sakhalin and the Kurile Islands; our troops had already occupied those territories, and so it was as though those clauses in the treaty had already been put into effect. But this reality was not confirmed juridically and was not reinforced by an official peace treaty. Since we had refused to sign the treaty, we could not use it as a basis of justification for decisions we made.

Stalin was displeased with Truman's policies, and rightly so. But it was one thing to be displeased and another to take incorrect actions harmful to the Soviet state. We were invited to sign the peace treaty with Japan, and we refused. An unclear situation resulted, which continues to this day.[8] For me personally this is completely incomprehensible. I couldn't understand it then and I still can't. Stalin didn't consult with us, and in general he didn't take other people and their opinions into account. He was too self-assured, especially after we had defeated Nazi Germany. Here, as was said earlier, he imitated the dashing Cossack soldier Kuzma Kryuchkov. People of the younger generation might not know this newspaper hero. During World War I an army hero was created, the Don Cossack Kuzma Kryuchkov. He was depicted in illustrations in magazines and newspapers lifting up ten German soldiers at once on the point of his lance. It would have been better if Stalin had not tried to imitate him, but had imitated Vasily Tyorkin, the modest hero of the long narrative poem of the same name by Aleksandr Tvardovsky, if we were to search for an analogy rather than an exact comparison.[9] But Stalin was imitating none other than Kuzma Kryuchkov. He thought the ocean would bow down before him, that he could do anything, that whatever he wanted he would get. But by then the war was over. The main enemy whom the West needed our help in defeating had been smashed. Now the West had already begun to mobilize and rally its forces against the Soviet Union. And when we refused to sign the peace treaty with Japan not only did that in no way distress our former allies; it also turned out to be advantageous for them.

A Far Eastern Commission and Allied Council for Japan were established. Their purpose was to keep watch over the state of affairs in that country after the surrender of the Japanese army.[10] There were Soviet representatives on these bodies, but in my opinion we were placed in an unenviable position, like a beggar at a rich man's banquet.

Our representatives on the Far Eastern Commission and the Allied Council for Japan had no influence on the course of events, and they were slighted by the Americans. I cannot cite specific instances confirming this. The details have gone from my memory, but that is the way things were. This upset and angered us, all of us, not only Stalin. But there was nothing you could do. The United States had taken first place there. You couldn't declare war on them over that. That would have been unthinkable! And we had no such capabilities. Intelligent government leaders in general do not declare war over such things. But relations between the Allies grew cold; and later, hostile relations heated up.

But what if we had correctly evaluated the circumstances arising after the defeat of Japanese militarism and had signed the peace treaty? It had been drafted by the American side without our participation, but they had taken our interests into account. In that case we could have sent a diplomatic delegation and immediately established an embassy in Tokyo. Our people would have had contacts with the Japanese on a new basis. Our influence would have increased somewhat. I think that at that time, when the peace treaty had just been signed, better conditions existed for establishing contacts with progressive sections of society in Japan and for bringing the essence of our policies to the awareness of the Japanese public—more so than today. To repeat, the main force that had defeated Japan and crushed its military machine was the United States. But the United States caused unnecessary injury to Japan materially and morally with their actions, especially their use of atomic bombs. This was the first time in history that such a monstrous thing had been done against human beings! We did not take advantage of the favorable moment then. We isolated ourselves and thereby allowed the aggressive forces in the United States to turn the Japanese against the Soviet Union.

After our diplomatic representatives withdrew from Japan, we did not have such representatives in that country for many years. This was a great loss. We ourselves displayed thickheadedness and an incorrect understanding of things in this case. We created the most favorable conditions for anti-Soviet propaganda on the part of our enemies in both Japan and the United States. The huge propaganda apparatus that existed on the Japanese islands was directed against the Soviet Union. That is how we paid for our totally inexplicable stubbornness in not signing the treaty, and there is no way I can understand now what the reason was.

I remember that after the war a delegation from the United States came to visit us for some reason. Secretary of States Byrnes[11] was the head of this delegation. I was in Moscow at that time and I was present at a dinner that Stalin gave in honor of Byrnes. The head of the British Labour government, Bevin,[12] was also present at this dinner. Earlier he had been part of Churchill's war cabinet. He was an influential man. What was the atmosphere at this dinner? As the host, Stalin was the one who proposed the toasts, and in doing so, he deliberately slighted Bevin. Later when we exchanged opinions among ourselves, we were outraged about this. After all, Bevin was a man with a working-class background; he had been a truck driver and a dockworker. And at the dinner table, when Stalin directed totally inadmissible insulting hints at him and needled him, Bevin put Stalin to shame: "I was the first one to raise his voice in the defense of Soviet Russia," he said. "In my day I organized a strike of British dockworkers with the slogan 'Hands Off Soviet Russia.'"[13] And that really was so. He was telling the truth. All the newspapers were writing about it.

What was the reason for Stalin's behavior? It's hard to explain. I think it's just that Stalin had taken the bit in his teeth, as the saying goes [that is, he got carried away]. He began to think of himself as the ultimate authority in world politics. That's why he behaved in such an unrestrained manner toward this representative of an allied country, our partner in the war. On the other hand, he was very polite toward Byrnes. To be sure, his politeness had another side to it. Stalin was courting Byrnes and making all kinds of pleasant remarks to him, but at the same time he allowed himself to make unpleasant jokes disparaging the president of the United States, Truman. This was absolutely inadmissible—to pay all sorts of compliments to Truman's representative right to his face and at the same time to disparage Truman himself. Byrnes, for his part, "wriggled out" of the situation somehow. He didn't accept the compliments addressed to him. Stalin even compared Truman and Byrnes to the disadvantage of the president.

When we were talking things over after the dinner, Beria was outraged: "Listen, how is this possible? How can this be? You know, this very day, as soon as Byrnes leaves us, all this is going to be made known to Truman." Evidently that is what happened. In effect, Truman, with his anti-Soviet sentiments and his antipathy toward Stalin, was thus stirred up against us even more.

After the signing of the peace treaty with Japan, the bodies that had been established to oversee matters in that country were gradually eliminated.[14] We had been part of those. Even if our status on them did not correspond to what we deserved as a great world power, nevertheless we were present there. After the signing of the peace treaty regular diplomatic relations were established with all the countries that had signed the treaty.[15] Our diplomatic representatives did remain for a certain time in Tokyo. They didn't want to leave, and they remained on the basis of their rights as one of the powers that had been present at the time of Japan's surrender. Finally the Americans requested that we leave. We put up resistance. In the end our people there were literally blockaded. Intolerable conditions of life were created around them. Besides, they were really unable to do anything, not allowed to go anywhere, and not taken into account at all. As a result our people finally went home.

What was the result? After the defeat of Japan we regained what tsarist Russia had lost.[16] Our honor as a great power was restored. Our troops took part in the final phase of operations and helped defeat the Japanese armies. We should then have displayed sobriety. It was the United States, after all, that had expended itself the most, in terms of both material resources and human lives, in the war against Japan. If comparisons are to be made, we expended less in the war against Japan than the Americans and British expended on the defeat of Hitler Germany. Their contributions to the victory over Germany were relatively greater than the Soviet contribution to the war against Japan, even though the victory over Germany was mainly won by the USSR, as a result of the blood shed by the Soviet people and the expenditure and depletion of our resources. Of course under the lend-lease program, they had provided us with essential aid. Even Stalin admitted this in private conversations in the Soviet leadership. Several times I heard him say: "If the Americans and British had not helped us with lend-lease, we would not have been able to deal with Germany by ourselves. We had lost too much."

Almost every soldier knows how things went in Manchuria toward the end of World War II. Our planes landed with an expeditionary force at Mukden,[17] and the so-called emperor of Manchuria was taken prisoner. He was a puppet ruler installed by Japan, the "Emperor" Henry Pu Yi.[18] This incident by itself testifies to the condition the enemy was in. The so-called emperor was not even able to flee from Manchuria and was captured by our soldiers, who arrived on transport planes! Is this at all comparable to what happened on the German front? Of course it is also true that we shed quite a bit of blood in other parts of Manchuria, but that is a different matter.

Then after the signing of the peace treaty, our diplomatic representatives were in effect evicted. From then right up until Stalin's death, it seems that there were absolutely no contacts between Japan and the USSR. And who did that benefit? It was our fault that it happened. If we had signed the treaty, we would have established our embassy in Japan, established contacts with Japanese society, organized trade and business relations with Japanese companies. But we were denied such possibilities. That is exactly what the Americans wanted. They wanted our representatives not to be there and in general tried to isolate us. In fact this kind of policy was pursued from the very first days after the emergence of the Soviet state: hostile encirclement, foreign intervention, and nonrecognition of the Soviet government. But now we ourselves were falling for this bait, which was quite pleasing to the aggressive forces in the United States. And not only the United States, but all the anti-Soviet forces in the world. That is the kind of situation we created through our own thoughtlessness as a result of some kind of dimming of the consciousness and overestimation of our possibilities. Our enemy, which at that time was the United States, took advantage of this.

In the mid-1950s, after Stalin's death, we began to clear away the political battlefield and remove the fragments and remnants that remained from World War II in Europe and Asia. We immediately encountered the problem that relations with Japan were still not normalized. We had no direct contact with Japan, and this was harmful to our foreign policy and our economy. The Americans were represented in Japan not only by an embassy. As an occupation force they were virtually the masters in that land. They conducted themselves arrogantly, built bases, carried on an anti-Soviet policy, and tried to incite the Japanese against us. In short, they did everything dictated by the unbridled and frenzied monopolies and militarists, who breathed hatred for the socialist countries, above all for the country that had first raised the banner of Marxism and Leninism, the banner of working class struggle, and that had achieved great successes in that sphere.

Now I want to tell about how we decided to eliminate the legacy of the Stalin era, clearing away the fragments and remnants of a mistaken policy. Stalin had worked out that mistaken policy together with Molotov. The foreign policy views of Stalin and Molotov were the same as the other views they held in common. Who played first violin in this duo? Unquestionably Stalin, but Molotov played his part as hard as he could, with all his might. Incidentally Molotov did play the violin. I can't judge how well he played, but I heard that he did play. Stalin sometimes teased him about this, sometimes mocking him outright. Before the revolution Molotov was in internal exile in Vologda or some other place.[19] (Molotov told about this himself and I was a listener; I heard what he said.) Hard-drinking merchants used to invite Molotov to come into a restaurant. He would play the violin for them and they would pay him. Molotov said, "It was a way of earning some money." When Stalin got angry, he would make gibes at Molotov: "You used to play for drunken merchants. They were rubbing hot mustard in your face." I must confess that on this subject I was more on Stalin's side, because I thought it was demeaning for a person, especially a political exile, to behave as Molotov had. Playing the violin for the pleasure of drunken merchants! After all, there are other ways of obtaining the means of subsistence. But enough of that. It is beside the point.

[After Stalin's death] when I raised the question of the abnormal situation with Japan, I discussed it with Mikoyan, Bulganin, Malenkov, and others. It turned out that we were all of one mind on this question. We needed to find some way to sign our country's name to that peace treaty and thus officially end the state of war between the USSR and Japan. We wanted to have the possibility of sending an ambassador to Tokyo who could then conduct the necessary work in Japan. Only Molotov displayed a failure to understand. He displayed the same quick temper and abruptness he had shown in regard to the peace treaty with Austria:[20] "How could this be? They didn't do this and they didn't do that . . . and so we can't do it!" In short, he repeated all the arguments that Stalin had presented earlier when he refused to place our signature on the peace treaty.

We tried to persuade Molotov: "Vyacheslav Mikhailovich," we said, "try to think in terms of what we can accomplish now in the existing situation, what influence we can have on Japan. We cannot correct what is already behind us. The past is gone, irreversibly so. The only thing that can be corrected is for us to have our signature accepted on the peace treaty. Then everything will move into its proper place." After all, we had received everything promised to us under the [Yalta] protocol.[21] Our interests had actually been taken into account and we had already made that a reality. Only one problem remained. We were still technically, in terms of international law, in a state of war with Japan. There was no Japanese embassy in Moscow, and we did not have ours in Tokyo. Who benefited by our absence from Tokyo?

It had to be understood that this was only to the advantage of the United States. They had been the master and continued to dominate in Japan. Our return would be to the advantage of progressive Japanese and to the disadvantage of the Americans. As soon as our embassy could be reopened in Tokyo, it would be like a magnet attracting those forces that were dissatisfied with the existing reactionary policies. Thus we would begin to exert some influence on Japanese policy.

After all, there was great dissatisfaction with the Americans in Japan, which was only natural. It is sufficient to recall Hiroshima and Nagasaki! There were people suffering from radiation who were still alive. The dead of course could not express dissatisfaction. But what about their relatives?[22] The Japanese could not do anything in this area because they had been rendered powerless. After the war the Americans had conducted themselves arrogantly in Japan. Their soldiers displayed rudeness, committed acts of violence, and engaged in all sorts of escapades. And such things are still going on.

I said to Molotov: "If we continue to be stubborn and refuse to seek out contacts and the possibility of signing the peace treaty, which would work out well for us, that would simply be a gift to the Americans. They could want nothing more from us. That would be the best thing we could give them. We could express our dissatisfaction, but we would be providing them with absolute freedom of movement in conducting their policies. They would turn Japan against the USSR to an even greater degree, pointing out that the Soviets had taken this or that piece of Japanese territory, but had refused to sign a peace treaty with Japan. They would say that this evidently means that the Soviets have certain intentions. But in fact even under Stalin we did not have any particular intentions in regard to Japan!"

These were the kinds of difficulties we encountered with Molotov and the kind of opposition we met with on his part. But we didn't get angry: I simply felt sorry for Molotov. I was dismayed. How could this be? After all, this man had been in charge of Soviet diplomacy under Stalin. He had represented our country for so many years in foreign policy matters in the most critical situations. He had been people's commissar of foreign affairs and even head of government [prime minister]. And yet he displayed such a limited outlook, such a failure to understand the simplest things. Yes, he displayed narrowmindedness. I myself was surprised. Where did this come from? If you were simply having an ordinary conversation about something with him (and I had been on friendly terms with Molotov earlier), it was evident that he was an intelligent person. It gave me pleasure to talk with him. The following fact testifies to the good relations that existed between Molotov and myself. I had always used the polite form of you in talking with him. But one day he said to me: "Listen, let's use the familiar form of 'you' [*ty* rather than *vy*]. Let's call each other by our first names and use the informal 'you.'" At first I felt rather awkward about this,[23] but later I got used to it. He was especially well disposed toward me after the removal of Beria. When a banquet was held in honor of my sixtieth birthday within the inner circle of the top leadership of our country, Molotov gave a friendly speech about me, stressing in particular my role and the services I had performed in organizing the removal of Beria.

I don't want to pretend any false modesty, and so I must say that Beria was removed in a timely way. If we had not done that, all aspects of internal and international Soviet policy would have developed in a completely different direction. This man was a monster and butcher, and he would have taken reprisals against all of us, and he was close to doing that. He had already gathered together in Moscow all the professional killers who had carried out his secret assignments, and evidently they had already received their orders or were about to receive their orders. After Beria's arrest, investigators presented us with the names of all these people. I don't remember their names now. But those events drew Molotov and me very close together, because Molotov understood Beria very well and knew what he was capable of. He understood that if Beria went into action, the heads of Molotov and Khrushchev would be the first to roll. Beria would have seen to it that our heads rolled in order to free himself for other things. A sea of blood would have been shed, even more than under Stalin.

I have digressed from my subject to emphasize what kind of relations I had with Molotov, relations not merely of trust but very friendly relations. And so I had no reason to be dissatisfied with Molotov. But the facts of politics, and such a divergent understanding of the simplest things, fundamental truths for everyone, even for people who were not experienced in politics— all this discouraged me. It seemed that we could find no other way out. The only solution would be a completely rational one, but there could also be compromise decisions, a compromise, taking into account conditions in which the only correct solution could be carried out. In the given instance signing the peace treaty would actually require no compromise. Refusing to sign showed a dimness of the mind and downright thickheadedness. In the end we began to take diplomatic steps toward establishing contacts with the

Japanese government. We could not go around the United States or avoid it because the actual text of the diplomatic document was located in the United States, and the possibility of signing the treaty largely depended on the United States. When we informed the Americans that we wanted to sign the peace treaty they refused. After all, the text of that diplomatic document had been drawn up by American hands, and a line on which we could sign had already been included—or whatever diplomatic terminology is used in the chancelleries of foreign affairs. All we had to do was sign in the prepared place. But we had refused to do that.

The Japanese also pursued a policy line in opposition to our signing the treaty. I am talking about the Japanese whose policies were anti-Soviet. Those were the forces in power then in Japan, people suitable to the United States. America in fact had a determining part in choosing the people who constituted the higher government bodies in Japan and exerted a decisive influence on the Japanese position. Of course the Japanese began a struggle against those clauses of the peace treaty that authorized the transfer of the Kurile Islands and southern Sakhalin to the Soviet Union, and other aspects of the treaty that provided things that were to our advantage. That is why we still did not gain the opportunity to sign the treaty. Neither the Japanese government nor the American government wanted our signature. What position Britain took on this question has not stuck in my memory. Evidently it took a subordinate position, not a decisive one. The United States was the determining force behind the anti-Soviet policy on the Japanese question. And our relations with the United States were strained to the utmost at that time.

It would seem to be a simple matter: To correct the mistake made by Stalin and Molotov, express our desire to sign the peace treaty with Japan, and sign it. It turned out in fact that our desire by itself was not enough. And that was understandable. Why? Because it was to the advantage of our adversaries that we not have an embassy in Tokyo, not have the opportunity of influencing Japanese public opinion and the Japanese government. To the contrary, the United States was energetically engaging in activities aimed at strengthening its position in Japan. A treaty on military bases was signed.[24] The American presence on Japanese territory was reaffirmed in very harshly expressed form. Right after the war passions were still inflamed, and the United States was savoring its victory over Japan, but by 1950 Japan was already being "protected" by U.S. forces, allegedly against the Soviet Union. The main enemy of Japan was made out to be the Soviet Union. That's how things had turned out!

When Molotov reared up on his hind legs on the question of signing the peace treaty with Japan I absolutely could not understand him. I looked at him and thought: "What in the world is this? Why?" Then after we made the decision Molotov no longer objected. After all, a party decision now existed on the question. But did he understand the essence of the matter or not? I didn't return to the subject afterward or to these unpleasant kinds of discussions. He was such an experienced diplomat, we thought, and yet here he was doing our country a disservice. We nipped his opposition in the bud and decided the matter our own way. And now life itself has shown that we acted correctly, even though we still have not been provided a chance to sign the peace treaty.

We signed a declaration ending the state of war between the Soviet Union and Japan,[25] and that was all there was to it. Legally this could be interpreted as an armistice. Of course it would have been better if we had signed a peace treaty. It's true that now our relations have been normalized and are developing as they would have developed if we had signed the treaty, but the legal aspect of the matter remains as before.

And so we established an embassy in Tokyo and obtained equal rights with other countries who were officially at peace with the Japanese government. Thus a normal situation was restored, various contacts began to develop well—even very well, I would say. I forget the name of the Japanese prime minister at that time, a liberal. When he came to power, he visited us in the Soviet Union.[26] It seems to me his minister of agriculture and fisheries came with him, not an old man; in fact you could say he was a young man and very energetic.[27] We had discussions about the possibility of signing the peace treaty with Japan after all. I don t remember exactly whether we talked about that with the prime minister or with the other government minister, who was a very influential man. I try, but I can't reconstruct that in my memory, and I'm not in a position now to look up references in the newspapers.

We started negotiations. The prime minister paid a lot of attention to this matter and directed all his efforts toward the normalization of relations with the USSR. He advocated the signing of the peace treaty. But domestic forces in Japan and, most important, the influence of the United States, which exerted its pressure on public opinion and the government of Japan and kept blinders on Japanese foreign and domestic policy, would not allow that to happen. The Japanese could do only what the Americans secretly advised. To be sure, the very fact that the Japanese prime minister had come to the USSR established a basis that promised to bear good fruit.

Unfortunately, the improvement of relations did not go any further. The reactionary side in Japan was strong, and the United States kept pursuing its policy aimed at isolating the USSR. Even today it continues to pursue that aggressive anti-Soviet policy. Perhaps if that prime minister had lived longer and strengthened his hold on power, public opinion in Japan might have changed. But he was already an old man and quite ill. Soon after returning to Japan he died.[28] Thus his efforts toward normalizing our relations, and officially establishing good new relations with the signing of a peace treaty, were not crowned with success.

During his visit, the Japanese side also raised the question of our yielding control of two small islands in the Kurile group, which were immediately adjacent to the main Japanese islands.[29] We consulted among ourselves in the Soviet leadership for a long time then and came to the conclusion that it would be worthwhile to move in the direction of the wishes expressed by the Japanese and agree to turn over these islands. (I don't remember the names of the islands now.) But we set the condition that a peace treaty be signed between Japan and the USSR and that U.S. troops be withdrawn from the Japanese islands. Otherwise it would not make sense. It would simply be foolish to hand over these islands to a Japan that in fact was under American occupation and control. Despite the peace treaty, Japan was in effect occupied by U.S. troops. We would hand over these islands to the Japanese and the Americans would turn them into military bases. We would want to achieve one thing and something else would result. Therefore we said: "Please try to understand that we cannot grant your request now. When U.S. troops are withdrawn and when the military treaty between Japan and the United States ceases to be in effect, so that there is no longer an alliance aimed against the USSR, then we can talk about handing over these islands to you."

I want to say a few more words on this subject, so that it will be understood why we decided to move in the direction of concessions to Japan in those years—or more exactly, concessions to that prime minister, who had come to visit us and who was pursuing a policy of détente and friendship with the Soviet Union. Our calculation was that this kind of concession would not be of any importance for the USSR. These were deserted islands, used only by fishermen and by the military. Given contemporary military technology, these islands did not have much military significance either. By then we had missiles that could strike an enemy 1,000 kilometers away, so that these islands had lost the importance they might have had as locations for coastal artillery. They also had no economic importance. As I recall, no useful minerals were found on them.[30] On the other hand, the friendship of the Japanese people, which we hoped to win, the mutual friendship of our two countries, was of tremendous importance. Thus, the new relations that would be established between the Soviet Union and Japan would more than make up for these territorial concessions.

We wanted to strengthen the influence of this prime minister [Hatoyama] in Japanese domestic and foreign policy, considering that such influence was bound to develop in the direction of strengthening friendly ties with the Soviet Union. That was the main consideration that guided us when we were threshing out this question. Even today I would argue that this was a correct decision, that it would play a favorable role if we were to further develop our policy of peaceful coexistence and strengthen friendship with Japan. Governments come and go. They change, but the people remain.

This whole business has been drawn out much too long. Today the latest Japanese prime minister, Sato,[31] during his visit to the United States and his meeting with President Nixon, arrived at some sort of agreement on the withdrawal of American troops from Japan. It's not clear to me exactly what kind of agreement was reached, but part of the agreement had to do with Okinawa.[32] We will have to see how this works out in practice. There will be no hurry to withdraw U.S. troops. At any rate the United States will not depart entirely from the territories of Japan, will not remove its troops altogether, and the military treaty with Japan, aimed against the USSR, will stay in effect. Our earlier agreement with the Japanese prime minister, then, will evidently not be implemented. I cannot say anything more on the subject because it is a question of how things will shape up in the future in the process of development of our relations with Japan. It will also depend on the leadership of the Soviet Union and how it evaluates changing situations.

But many things testify to the fact that a crude error was committed when we failed to sign the peace treaty with Japan. In the 1960s when our relations with China went bad (I was then part of our country's leadership), I heard that Mao Zedong had received some Japanese delegation. I don't remember whether these were industrialists or political figures. In the meeting with Mao the Japanese raised the question of their complaints against the Soviet Union, including in regard to the southern part of Sakhalin and the Kurile Islands. Mao agreed with their complaints. He said: "Yes, we support you. Your complaints are compelling and legally justified." I saw some materials published after that delegation returned to Japan. The Japanese published reports in their press to the effect that Mao took an understanding attitude toward their national aspirations and complaints against the Soviet Union. There you have the concrete results of our past mistakes. Of course this was an outrageous thing for Mao to do. Not only did he fail to support the USSR, but he provoked Japanese public opinion against us and supported the Japanese desire to take the Kuriles and southern Sakhalin back from us. Yet, after all, Japan had no historical basis for these claims. At one time, when Russia was weak, the Japanese had seized these territories.[33]

United efforts by such powerful and wealthy countries as the Soviet Union and Japan could provide many possibilities for expanding and deepening our relations and, on that basis, expanding friendship and strengthening fraternal ties between our two peoples. The Japanese people have lost Okinawa. The Americans have occupied it. A step by us in the opposite direction, our return of two islands to Japan, could have mobilized public opinion in Japan in favor of friendship with the USSR, or so we thought, and that would have directed the efforts of the popular forces in Japan against the American occupiers, against those who had drawn Japan into a military alliance and were pursuing militaristic aims. Taken all together, these were the considerations that guided us when we moved toward taking such a step. We felt that the concession we would make to Japan was politically justified and would more than repay itself. There is one more confirmation that our approach was correct. It is not by accident that Mao Zedong tried to incite Japanese political figures against us (the ones he met with), reinforcing their complaints against us. In this case an effort was being made for Japan and China to come to a mutual understanding at least on these questions [territorial claims against the USSR], and the aims being served in all this were by no means peaceful. This only revealed Mao's true personality and character. Unfortunately even today he has remained true to this negative precedent. He is running the show, not for the benefit of socialism, but in a direction harmful to the fraternal relations we had established with China. All the nationalities of the USSR would like to see those relations restored, and I think that will happen. All that is needed is time and patience.

Today, from reading the newspapers and listening to the radio, I would judge that economic ties and diplomatic relations between the USSR and Japan are developing normally. In our day we spent a lot of time holding talks about a direct air connection between Europe and Japan by the shortest route, that is, across Soviet air space. We were not successful in resolving this question. At the very end of my work [as party and government leader] we reached an agreement in which we would act as a kind of surrogate for the Japanese airlines. Nevertheless we were approaching the reality that there would be flights from Japan. They would be in our planes and under our control.[34] But here, too, the United States put pressure on the Japanese. The Americans didn't want this to happen. But there was another factor. We ourselves were holding back, as a result of the practices imposed on us in Stalin's time and the incorrect understanding of things from that time. Some people will say: "Here he goes again, dumping all the blame on Stalin!" No, I am not dumping blame. It must be admitted, after all, that for many years we were trained in the spirit that even the slightest weakening was impermissible. How could we allow a foreign power to enter our air space and fly across the Soviet Union? These flights would cover the entire length of the USSR, from its eastern to its western border. We thought that foreign intelligence services would literally "turn our pockets inside out," find out everything about us [as a result of such flights]. To be sure, we too looked at things in an oversimplified way then. We were condemning Stalin, but still looking at things through his eyes, guided by the habits and practices established under him and governed by his false, incorrect, and unhealthy understanding of events.

Our sovereignty must be protected. The imperialist intelligence agencies cannot be allowed to work against us. This is always a correct and appropriate way of thinking. Still, it is necessary to have a sense of proportion. Intelligence agencies will remain as long as differing social, political, and economic state structures exist, as long as the world is divided as it is now. As long as antagonistic social structures exist, the conflict between them will continue, and intelligence agencies will try to do their job. Here, as the saying goes, we have to keep our eyes and ears open, stay alert. But that does not mean that we should isolate ourselves, which would only be to the advantage of the major capitalist powers and leaders of the Western world such as the United States. That is what I wanted to say. I think that this subject is of general interest because we are talking about major signposts along the road of our developing relations with Japan.

Japan today is the third country in the world in industrial production. It is just behind the USSR and is rapidly developing its economy. So Japan has to be taken into account, and efforts must be made to establish normal relations between us, to the extent possible, given our differing social and political systems. It is to Japan's advantage to strengthen economic and diplomatic ties with us. There is no question about that, because we are the closest major country to the islands of Japan. Besides, we are rich in natural resources and would be able, to a significant extent, to meet the demands of Japanese industry for raw materials.

For example, when I was still part of the Soviet leadership, the Japanese expressed a special interest in our forest industry. People would say that this is not surprising. Japan needs raw materials, and we need Japan as a customer and for the manufactured goods that Japan can supply us. At that time the Japanese proposed that they provide us with equipment for processing forest products, for producing cellulose, and for obtaining a synthetic fiber derived from that cellulose. In its technical specifications this kind of fiber would be the best for making cord for automobile tires, the best of all that is produced around the world. These terms were truly advantageous both for our country and for Japan. Japan would supply us with the equipment on credit. After the equipment had been set up in the Soviet Far East, we would pay Japan back in cellulose from the wood that we processed. What could be more advantageous? The interest rates, as they say in the capitalist world, were fair. Also there were other raw materials that we could supply to Japan.

In general Japan is a very interesting country with strongly developed industry. And I repeat this now with a kind of bitter taste in my mouth. After all, if we keep in mind that Japan was defeated in the war, doesn't have any raw materials, and has a much smaller population than ours, how is one to assess the fact that it has taken so many strides forward not only in the production of manufactured goods but also in technology and the production of extremely sophisticated and refined instruments? I don't know the level of Japanese achievements in optics now, but at the end of my work [as part of the Soviet leadership] Japan held one of the foremost places in the world (perhaps even first place). I remember that our optical engineers traveled to Japan, brought back samples of their output in this field, and showed them to us. Our specialists gazed at these with their mouths open. I asked: "How much did those cost?"

The answer I heard was: "Nothing. They simply gave us these as gifts."

I said: "If they gave them as gifts, then bear in mind that whatever they gave us is no longer being produced. No company will give samples of their new products because that might create competition for them." All this is quite in keeping with the economic laws of competition and profit!

There is much evidence testifying how far technology and technical thinking have advanced in Japan. What about transistor radios? The Japanese ones are considered the best. It is said that their only rivals are the West German radios. But that too was a ruined country after the war! All this makes us think about our own forms of organization, about the functioning of our research institutes, and many other things. It is evident that some sort of major defect exists. In our country the number of engineers and scientists, if you approach the question purely arithmetically, is apparently no less than in West Germany or Japan. Statistics even proclaim that we produce several times more engineers and technicians than they do. And look how many holders of doctoral degrees and candidate's degrees we have in science. Nevertheless you have to go outside our country to find the kind of technical and scientific thinking on whose basis the most advanced machinery, equipment, and devices are produced. And this situation persists. This forces us to think, and not only to think but to really analyze the situation well in order to correct the situation.

Victory will go to that social system which is able to take best advantage of scientific and technological thinking, the major advances in the fields of engineering and design. Whichever system can ensure the highest level of production and the highest productivity of labor is the one that will win. The material goods that people can obtain under one or another social system, whether capitalist or socialist, are determined by the level of development of science and technology, engineering, machine tools and instruments, and the increased productivity of labor. I do not conceal the fact that I am speaking now with envy. I feel envious and aggrieved that we have lived through fifty-two years since the October revolution, and although we have achieved great successes and transformed our country, to this day we cannot boast of having the most advanced position in technology and science. Our science and technology have made incredible leaps forward. But still, our scientists probably know better than I, and feel it too, that the scientists in capitalist countries are walking all over us. This is not some quality inherent in socialist or capitalist conditions. There is no way one can agree with the idea that the capitalist order creates better conditions for developing science and technology. I could never agree with that argument. No, we have some organizational defects in our country that we need to probe and correct so that the thinking of our scientists can be given practical application and placed at the service of socialist society.

The interests of the Japanese people are consistent with those of the Soviet people. If Japan became a friendly country in relation to the USSR, that would only be to its benefit economically and politically. Today the U.S.-Japanese treaty that is in effect pursues primarily military aims. Treaties like that lead to the exhaustion of material resources and could draw Japan into a military catastrophe more horrible than the one the Japanese people experienced in World War II, when two atomic bombs were dropped on them. After all, if a war breaks out, who knows how many bombs or what kind might fall on the islands of Japan? What then will remain of Japan? Friendship with the Soviet Union and the removal of U.S. military forces from the islands of Japan would relieve tensions. Possibilities would arise for using our natural resources to develop the economy and raise the living standard of the people. Japan would gain the opportunity of obtaining from a neighboring country—right next door—such raw materials as forest products, oil, natural gas, coal, and various kinds of ore. And there are many other things I could name.

1. N. S. Khrushchev is referring to the Treaty of Portsmouth, concluded on September 5, 1905 in Portsmouth (New Hampshire) in the United States. (The treaty ended the Russo-Japanese war of 1905. The negotiations were facilitated by U.S. President Theodore Roosevelt. [SS])

2. The reference is to the peace treaty between Japan and the Allied powers. [SS] The USSR proposed eight new articles in addition to the twenty-seven American articles, but they were not discussed. The treaty was signed in San Francisco on September 8, 1951, by forty-nine countries, not including the USSR.

3. Khrushchev is referring to the Manchurian strategic offensive operation, which began on August 9 (simultaneously with a Soviet declaration of war on Japan) and was completed on September 2, 1945. The Red Army defeated the Japanese forces and occupied the whole of Manchuria, the island of Sakhalin and the Kurile Islands, and Korea down to the thirty-eighth parallel, which later became the dividing line between North and South Korea. [SS]

4. General M. A. Purkayev. See Biographies.

5. The atomic bomb was dropped on Hiroshima on August 6 and on Nagasaki on August 9, 1945. [SS]

6. President Franklin Delano Roosevelt died of a cerebral hemorrhage on April 12, 1945. [SS]

7. Emperor Hirohito announced the unconditional surrender of Japan to the Allies in a radio broadcast on August 14, 1945. A formal ceremony of surrender was held on board the battleship USS Missouri in Tokyo Bay on September 2, 1945. [SS]

8. This was true at the time that Khrushchev dictated it in the late 1960s, and it remains true in 2004). [SS]

9. See Khrushchev's comments on the poem Vasily Tyorkin in the chapter "We Liberate Ukraine" (page 605). [GS]

10. The Far Eastern Commission and the Allied Council for Japan were formed after the Moscow meeting of the ministers of foreign affairs of the

USSR, the United States, and Great Britain, held between December 16 and 26, 1945.

11. James Francis Byrnes was U.S. secretary of state from July 1945 to January 1947.

12. Ernest Bevin was minister of labor and national service in Churchill's war cabinet and foreign minister in the Labour government of Great Britain during 1945–51. See Biographies.

13. The strike was organized to impede British military intervention in support of the Whites in the Russian Civil War. British troops were landed at Arkhangelsk on the White Sea coast in northern Russia in spring and summer 1918. [SS]

14. The Americans disbanded these bodies on April 25, 1952.

15. This took place after the official end of the occupation of Japan on April 28, 1952.

16. Khrushchev is referring to Russia's loss of Sakhalin and the Kurile Islands as a result of its defeat in the Russo-Japanese war of 1905. [SS]

17. The city of Mukden, in southern Manchuria, is now called Shenyang. [SS]

18. On August 17, 1945, at Shenyang (Mukden) a Soviet paratroop force took Henry Pu Yi ("emperor" of the Japanese puppet state of Manchukuo [SS]) prisoner together with the Japanese generals Yosioka and Hasimoto. (Henry Pu Yi later, under the Chinese Communist regime, became a gardener. [SS])

19. From 1909 to 1911, V. M. Skryabin (Molotov) was in exile in Totma, Solvychegodsk, and Vologda, all towns in Vologda province. See Biographies.

20. The reference is to the State Treaty of May 15, 1955, which restored Austria as a sovereign state subject to certain conditions. Austria was to be a neutral state without foreign military bases on its soil, and it was not to unify with Germany. The neutrality provisions were incorporated into a new Austrian constitution on October 26, 1955. [SS]

21. Khrushchev is apparently referring to a secret protocol signed at the Yalta conference. [GS]

22. A nationwide association of hibakusha (atomic bomb survivors), the Japan Confederation

of Atomic and Hydrogen Bomb Sufferers' Organizations (Nihon Hidankyo) was set up in 1956. *Hibakusha* have also taken an active part in general movements of protest against nuclear weapons, such as the Japan Council Against Atomic and Hydrogen Bombs (Nihon Gensuikyo), established in 1955. [SS]

23. Khrushchev was accustomed to addressing colleagues by first name and patronymic and the polite form of "you" (*vy*). [SK]

24. The number of U.S. bases in Japan eventually reached 282. On February 28, 1952, an administrative agreement was signed to regulate the implementation of the Security Pact, which entered into force on April 28, 1952. On March 8, 1953, the U.S.-Japan Mutual Security Assistance Agreement was signed. On June 2, 1953, the Defense Administration of Japan was established.

25. The stages in the normalization of relations between the USSR and Japan were as follows. On October 11, 1954, the Chinese People's Republic and the USSR published a joint declaration that they were prepared to normalize their relations with Japan. On January 29, 1955, the Soviet government published a declaration that it was prepared to establish diplomatic relations with Japan. On June 3, 1955, negotiations were held in London between representatives of the USSR and Japan on the normalization of Soviet-Japanese relations. On October 19, 1956, a joint Soviet-Japanese Declaration of the Normalization of Relations was signed in Moscow, and on December 12, 1956, the latter entered into effect.

26. This prime minister was Ichiro Hatoyama, who held office from December 10, 1954, to December 20, 1956. He arrived in Moscow on October 19, 1956. (When Khrushchev calls Hatoyama a "liberal," he means specifically that Hatoyama belonged to the Liberal Democratic Party. [SS])

27. Prime Minister Hatoyama was accompanied by the Japanese minister of agriculture and fisheries Itsero Kono and also by a member of the Japanese diet (parliament), Tsunitsi Matsumoto. A joint declaration was signed by Hatoyama, Kono, and Matsumoto on the Japanese side and by Bulganin and Shepilov on the Soviet side. [SK]

28. Hatoyama died in 1959. [SS]

29. The two islands in question were Habomai and Shikotan. The USSR agreed that they would be returned to Japan following the conclusion of a peace treaty between Japan and the USSR. But after the signing on January 19, 1960, of the U.S.-Japan Mutual Cooperation and Security Treaty, which replaced the preceding Security Pact (the series of agreements made in 1951 and 1952), the Soviet concession was retracted. (There has been much speculation about the willingness of Presidents Gorbachev, Yeltsin, and Putin to make the same concession. [SS])

30. At the present time the economic zone around the two islands under discussion, Habomai and Shikotan, is estimated to be worth many billions of dollars. There are major fishing banks and other ocean resources in the area, which are being exploited jointly by Russia and Japan. [SK]

31. Eisaku Sato was prime minister of Japan from November 9, 1964, to June 17, 1972.

32. The chain of small islands called the Ryukyu Islands (known as the Nansei Shoto in Japan) stretch southwest over 1,000 kilometers from Kyushu, the southernmost of the main Japanese islands, to Taiwan, separating the East China Sea to the west from the Philippine Sea to the east. The most important of the islands, in the middle of the chain, is Okinawa. In 1949 President Harry Truman decided to retain the Ryukyu Islands under U.S. control, although Japan was recognized as having "residual sovereignty" over them. Okinawa became home to a large U.S. military base, and there have been persistent popular protests against U.S. control. In 1969 President Richard Nixon opened negotiations with Japan for the return of the islands. [SS] Between November 19 and 21, 1969, negotiations were held, in which Japan guaranteed to support American policy in Asia, and in exchange the United States agreed to return the Ryukyu Islands to Japan. The agreement came into effect on May 15, 1972.

33. Southern Sakhalin was really transferred to Japan in accordance with the Peace of Portsmouth—that is, as a result of Russia's military defeat. But the Kurile Islands were transferred to Japan in accordance with the Russian-Japanese border treaty of May 7, 1875, and not as a result of military conquest.

34. Negotiations on this matter took place during the visit of A. I. Mikoyan to Japan between May 14 and 27, 1964. An agreement about direct air flights between Moscow and Tokyo came into effect in April 1967.

## WAR MEMOIRS

A few days ago, purely by accident, I ran into Ivan Khristoforovich Bagramyan. I was very pleased to see him. After all, I hadn't seen him for many years. He and I briefly exchanged opinions on various topics. Unexpectedly, he raised the question of Zhukov's book of memoirs, made a few comments, and stated that some very big distortions and departures from the truth had been committed in that book.

At the same time, he said that Marshal Moskalenko had also written his memoirs, and in so doing had written a very foul book. I didn't ask him to be more specific on how the foul qualities in this book were expressed. In general, I knew that Moskalenko was capable of such things. I know both his good sides and his bad sides. I know his good sides as a man devoted to the cause, who fought well, displayed energy and perseverance, and did not spare himself. His bad sides were his nervousness, his instability, his hot temper, and his coarseness and rudeness, and sometimes even worse than rudeness. It is well known what insulting and offensive behavior he dealt out to his subordinates. People who served under him often complained to me that he was rude and insulted them. His usual vocabulary consisted of things like this: "Enemy of the people! Traitor! Scum! Ought to be put on trial! Ought to be shot!" He was a man of moods, very subject to outside influence. He was capable of anything, especially if he felt it was to his advantage. If some foul action would somehow pay off for him, then he would go ahead and do it.

His lack of principle struck me especially during the business involving Zhukov's retirement in 1957. I had a trusting attitude toward Zhukov during the war and did a lot to raise his reputation and authority in Stalin's eyes. In 1957 when we discussed the question of nipping in the bud Zhukov's attempts to organize a military takeover, with the aim of putting power in the hands of a military junta, Moskalenko came out energetically with accusations against Zhukov. It was not at a general plenary session of the Central Committee of the CPSU, but in a smaller circle of people, that Moskalenko passionately accused Zhukov of having the intention to seize power, while Zhukov with the roughness and directness of a soldier (and I believe that Zhukov was telling the truth) hurled this reply at him: "What are you accusing me of? You yourself said to me more than once, 'Why are you standing there looking around? Take power in your own hands. Take it!'"

---

This text was tape-recorded in November 1969.

When I heard that, I was astounded. I never expected anything like that from Moskalenko. Zhukov had no reason to lie. And Moskalenko himself was unable to refute this serious charge, which in effect amounted to high treason. When I told Malinovsky about it, Malinovsky, on his own initiative, made the proposal that Moskalenko be relieved of the posts he held.[1]

But I said: "Rodion Yakovlevich, it's hardly necessary to take such action. After all, this is Moskalenko! If the situation was normal (and I was sure it would become normal again), Moskalenko would carry out his duties honorably." Malinovsky gave me a surprised look. I could read in his expression that he was surprised, because after all, what Zhukov had said, and what Moskalenko had not denied, was grounds for legal action. But at that time I said to the members of the Presidium of the Central Committee: "Let's not be governed by strict considerations of state, even though it would be appropriate to have an investigation and try Moskalenko. We should keep in mind the role he played in the arrest of Beria, when we turned to him for help, and he honorably carried out everything assigned to him. So let's forgive him for the present incident."

I have recounted this to show what kind of person Moskalenko was. There are really several Moskalenkos. One is a general who honorably commanded his troops but got into every possible kind of mess in the initial period of the war. Later he commanded an army, and his energetic role was deservedly acknowledged. I personally made a proposal that he be promoted—this was already after Stalin's death—to the rank of Marshal of the Soviet Union. There is another Moskalenko—a thoroughgoing hysteric. I have already told the anecdote about how during our retreat a woman collective farmer chased him out of a cowshed, where he had hidden after changing into peasant's clothing, and how after that, even though he himself was Ukrainian, he spoke harshly against all Ukrainians, asserting that they were all traitors and should all be deported. That's an example of his lack of equilibrium. But there is a third Moskalenko—the timeserver, a man without logic or principle. That's what he showed himself to be in the Zhukov case. But the foulness [in Moskalenko's memoirs] that Bagramyan was talking about, and what specific form it took, I do not know.

As for Zhukov, during my encounter with Bagramyan, the latter spoke about Zhukov's book and said it contained an inaccurate, distorted account of how the Barvenkovo operation was carried out in 1942. Zhukov wrote that when the operation was reported to Stalin, he himself had been present, as had Timoshenko and Bagramyan. Ivan Khristoforovich [Bagramyan] indignantly objected: "Nothing is said there about your being present."

It further surprised me that Zhukov wrote that he himself had been present, although I remember perfectly well that Zhukov was not there. Why did he write that way? Zhukov himself could hardly have written that he was present. My guess is that it was *not* Zhukov who wrote that. After all, I know the man. Zhukov does not stoop to lies. Evidently, this was the work of the editors who "assisted" him. The book is filled with such "assistance," distorting the facts and sometimes doing so in defiance of common sense.

"And here's another thing," Bagramyan continued. "The book describes Stalin calling the Front and talking with you in Zhukov's presence, warning you that according to the information of the Stavka, there was the danger of a breakthrough by the enemy on the left flank of our Front, that is, in the direction from Slavyansk to Barvenkovo. For my part," continued Bagramyan, "I remember that no such phone call happened. I remember very well how events unfolded for our Front. This is a fabrication!" Yes, it was a pure fabrication. But it was not of any advantage to Zhukov. Consequently, once again, this was not Zhukov's fabrication but someone else's, someone who found it convenient to insert such an incident in describing the operation. All this is very typical.

Who were these editors? I wonder. After all it was not Stalin who called me then, but on the contrary, it was I who called Stalin, after he canceled the decision of our Front command to stop the offensive and reposition our forces to cover our left flank in the Slavyansk area. At that time Stalin didn't even come to the phone but suggested that I pass along whatever I wanted to say through Malenkov. I presented our arguments to Malenkov and again raised the question that our decision be confirmed as the only possible correct one. Stalin passed it along through Malenkov that the previous decision of the Stavka should be carried out. I argued again that this should not be done. Stalin conveyed to me, through Malenkov, the assertion that the decision to cancel the offensive had been made by the Front commander, Timoshenko, as a result of my pressure on him. In reply I argued that Comrade Stalin knew very well what Timoshenko's character was like. You could not put that kind of pressure on him. You could not force him to say something he didn't agree with. Besides, there was no disagreement between us on that question. Our opinion was unanimous on that point. "No!" was their only answer to me, and the conversation ended with that. The whole conversation took place in Bagramyan's presence. And the next morning when we met with Timoshenko, he didn't say anything to me. Evidently it was unpleasant for him to return to the subject. We got into our vehicle and went to the front lines.

That is what really happened on that disastrous day during our offensive toward Krasnograd. It's well known how it all ended. It ended in the destruction of our troops.

One wonders why Zhukov today had the need to return to this incident. He personally took no part in it, but as the saying goes, was just looking on as a bystander. Evidently it was in someone's interest to put falsehoods in Zhukov's mouth about how, supposedly in Zhukov's presence, Stalin had called Khrushchev and warned him about the danger of the Germans on our flank. If such a phone call had really been made, why was it that Stalin called Khrushchev and not the commander of our Front? This question relates to the proper jurisdiction of the commander. Of course there were cases when Stalin would call me on one or another question of an operational character. But in the given instance it was not Stalin who called me, but I who was trying to get through to have a conversation with Stalin. And there were witnesses to this—Molotov, Malenkov, and others. At one point—and this was after the war—Mikoyan said during conversation at Stalin's table, and Mikoyan was fairly well under the influence at the time: "Comrade Stalin, after all, Khrushchev warned you correctly back then."

Stalin gave him such a look that I even got frightened and replied: "What are you bringing that up for, Anastas Ivanovich?" It really was a bone in Stalin's throat. He knew very well how many thousands of lives his stubbornness had cost.

Anastas Ivanovich [Mikoyan] told me that while I was speaking with Malenkov on the phone, Stalin made the comment: "What is Khrushchev, a civilian, doing poking his nose in this business? What does he understand about military matters? The military have reported to me on the situation." One wonders who "the military" were that gave Stalin the kind of advice that cost many thousands of casualties. I think it might have been Vasilevsky, who I pleaded with urgently at that time to help. Vasilevsky has now written his memoirs. I haven't read them, and I won't read them. He is hardly going to tell the truth, although he always impressed me as a very decent person. Still, he is hardly going to gather up the courage to tell how that operation really was conceived and carried out and what measures our Front command took. He will not have the courage to admit that he, while working at the General Staff, did not figure out [what was really going on] and reported to Stalin that it was necessary to cancel the decision of the Military Council of our Front and continue the offensive. But other people were there, too, because Vasilevsky did not personally keep track of the situation of every Front. He had "area people," which was the name for the generals who kept watch over particular areas along the front lines as a whole, and they reported to Vasilevsky. Who were they specifically? Today it's hard to say. It might be that Shtemenko was one of them. Was Shtemenko assigned to the area in question? My guess that he was is based on the fact that Shtemenko today strongly defends the point of view of the General Staff about that operation and accuses the Front command of every kind of sin.[2]

Now these men of the General Staff are putting cosmetic touches on Zhukov's memoirs, imposing a point of view that is really foreign to him, correcting and editing his text. They evidently were mixed up in this business, and now they want to go down in history as simon-pure, to shift the blame from the sick person to the healthy one, in this case myself. For some reason Timoshenko has been left aside in this matter, and Khrushchev is made to figure in it alone. This also is not accidental. Of course as a member of the Military Council I had equal rights with Timoshenko in deciding one or another question, but in a case like this, the commander should not be just some sort of passive onlooker, not if he's the commander of the troops.

I want to call attention to another fact. The people who are now editing and rewriting history and touching it up to suit their own taste—they knew Stalin, and they knew his harsh and abrupt character. They have Zhukov writing that supposedly Stalin called me and warned me that the enemy was threatening our left flank and that allegedly I didn't listen to him. That means that I bear the responsibility for the failure of the operation. But that contradicts Stalin's words that were passed on to me by Malenkov accusing me of allegedly "imposing my ideas" on Timoshenko, "imposing" on him the decision to cancel the earlier orders of the Stavka to go on the offensive. Even if one were to suppose that my guilt had been proved, a question arises: Why did Stalin draw a conclusion of an opposite kind? After all, Stalin's anger was not directed at me but at Timoshenko.

And this was soon made evident. When our troops were forced to retreat beyond the Don, and the enemy, after taking Rostov, broke through across the Don into the Northern Caucasus and also began to develop an offensive in the direction of Stalingrad, at that time Stalin called me (and here I am saying that he did call me in this case), and he said: "You have to get yourself together right away and move your headquarters, together with your headquarters staff, to Stalingrad. There the Stalingrad Front is being organized, and we have confirmed you as a member of the Military Council of the Stalingrad Front. But you must name the commander for the troops of this new Front." I kept refusing to suggest a commander, referring to the fact that that was the function of the Stavka, but Stalin said: "I would appoint Yeremenko, but he's in the hospital. Vlasov would be suitable, but he's been encircled and is trapped. Therefore you should name someone."

I kept refusing and refusing [but Stalin kept insisting], and in the end I named Gordov. Gordov was confirmed as the commander of the troops of the Stalingrad Front. Stalin didn't say a single word about Timoshenko. What was that all about? The defeat on the Don [the failure after the Barvenkovo offensive] ended up being a kind of disgrace for Timoshenko, putting him out of favor. This means that Stalin, remembering how I insisted that the decision to carry on the offensive at Barvenkovo should be canceled, must have thought things over after the disastrous failure of that operation and realized that Khrushchev had been right. Then he transferred his anger to the commander of the Front for not having displayed firmness, although in fact there was no lack of firmness in Timoshenko's character. As a result Stalin evidently drew the conclusion that the Front commander should be changed. As for me, the first member of the Military Council of that same Front, on whom the editors of military memoirs now want to heap all the blame for the failure of that operation, Stalin went ahead and confirmed me as a member of the Military Council of the Stalingrad Front.

I was part of the Stalingrad Front as long as it existed. Then I was con-firmed as [first] member of the Military Council of the Southern Front, and I, together with Yeremenko, and then with Malinovsky, who replaced Yere-menko as commander, liberated Rostov and advanced as far as Taganrog. Then I was taken from the Southern Front and appointed first member of the Military Council of the Voronezh Front. When it was reorganized as the First Ukrainian Front, I remained first member of the Military Council. We carried through the Kursk operation, and we carried it through well. That was the decisive turning point in the war. Then we liberated Kiev, and I remained a member of the Military Council of that Front to the end of the war and the complete defeat of Hitler. If Stalin considered me guilty [of the failure at Barvenkovo], he would never have forgiven me and, as the saying goes, would have blamed me for everything. At the same time, I am not saying that that was just my personal point of view back then. It was also the point of view of the commander of the troops and of the chief of staff of the Front at that time, and of all the leadership of the Front, first of all Bagramyan, who displayed great persistence in the attempt to persuade Stalin to cancel the decision of the Stavka. I am sure that objective people will be found who will look into the whole course of that operation, investi-gating primary sources. It is true that there are no written records of the telephone conversations I had with Stalin by way of Malenkov, but the written record of our order exists, the order to reposition our troops [and call off the offensive], an order that Stalin canceled, although he did that only orally, not in writing.

Once again to comment on war memoirs. I don't these days read the memoirs of military men very much. I don't want to and I can't read them. I can't endure these lies with equanimity. I know very well how the war began and how it proceeded, what the difficulties were and what the casualties were, and when I read such literature my nerves just can't stand it. Nevertheless I do know some things. I know that there's a great deal of baloney in the descriptions of the course of the war, a lot of blarney and a lot of inaccuracy. Evidently there are people who have an interest in this sort of thing. They shuffle facts around to suit themselves, to show themselves off, to show supposedly how wise they were and how they foresaw everything. But actually they don't write that they "foresaw everything," because after all we proved to be unprepared for the war, even though these same people at that time were sitting in the headquarters staffs and giving shape to the policy of our country's defense along the lines that they chose.

At my advanced age I constantly look back over what I have lived through. I don't have anything else now. The only thing that has remained for me is the past. The only thing the future holds for me is the grave, and I am not afraid of that. Not only am I not afraid; it is what I desire. It is dreary, dreary to live in a situation like mine.

1. At the time of the events described, Marshal of the Soviet Union R. Ya. Malinovsky was minister of defense. [SS]

2. Colonel General S. M. Shtemenko occupied senior positions in the General Staff throughout the war. He too has written memoirs: *The Soviet General Staff at War, 1941–1945* (Moscow: Progress Publishers, 1985). [SS]

APPENDIXES

# A Short Biography of N. S. Khrushchev

NIKITA SERGEYEVICH KHRUSHCHEV was born on April 15, 1894 (April 3 according to the old style),[1] in the village of Kalinovka in Kursk *gubernia,* to a peasant family. He worked there for hire as a shepherd and in the winter months studied at an elementary school.

In 1908, when Nikita was fourteen years old, his family moved to the Donbas, to the Uspensky mine, not far from Yuzovka (later Stalino, now Donetsk). Here Nikita was again hired to herd cows and to clean cauldrons in the pits. Soon he was taken on at a factory as a metalworker's apprentice. He learned his trade and helped repair equipment at the local mines.

In 1912, the eighteen-year-old Nikita Khrushchev took part in collecting donations at the factory in aid of the families of the workers killed at the Lena goldfields. The news of the Lena shootings set off strikes in Yuzovka, too. On orders of the police superintendent, Khrushchev, together with other strike activists, was fired from the factory. He began to work as a metalworker at Mine No. 31, a large mine for that time.

In 1917–19, Khrushchev was elected chairman of the committee of poor peasants of the village of Kalinovka. He participated in the Civil War. In 1925 he graduated from the workers' school at the Donetsk Industrial Institute, and in 1929 he became a student at the Industrial Academy in Moscow. Then there was state and party work:

1924–30: Party work in the Donbas, Kharkov, and Kiev.

1931–32: Secretary of the Bauman and Krasnaya Presnya district committees of the party in Moscow.

1932–34: Second secretary of the Moscow city committee of the party.

1934–35: First secretary of the Moscow city committee and second secretary of the Moscow committee[2] of the party.

1935–38: First secretary of the Moscow committee and of the Moscow city committee of the party.

1938–49: First secretary of the Central Committee of the Communist Party (Bolshevik) of Ukraine and of the Kiev province and city committees of the party.

1944–47: Simultaneously chairman of the Council of People's Commissars (from 1946 the Council of Ministers) of the Ukrainian Soviet Socialist Republic.

1941–45: Member of the Military Councils of the Southwestern Area and of the Southwestern, Stalingrad, Southern, Voronezh, and First Ukrainian Fronts; did much work organizing the partisan movement in Ukraine.

In 1943, he was given the military rank of lieutenant general.

1949–53: Secretary of the Central Committee of the Communist Party of the Soviet Union (CPSU); simultaneously first secretary of the Moscow committee of the party.

1953–64: First secretary of the Central Committee of the CPSU.

1958–64: Simultaneously chairman of the USSR Council of Ministers.

1956–64: Simultaneously chairman of the Bureau of the Central Committee of the CPSU for the RSFSR.[3]

From 1964: on pension. On October 14, 1964, a plenum of the Central Committee of the CPSU released him from the duties of first secretary of the Central Committee of the CPSU, member of the Presidium of the Central Committee of the CPSU, and chairman of the USSR Council of Ministers.

Deputy to the USSR Supreme Soviet of the first to sixth convocations; deputy to the Supreme Soviet of the RSFSR of the second to fifth convocations.

Member of the party from 1918. From 1934, member of the Central Committee of the party. Between 1938 and 1939, candidate member of the Politburo of the Central Committee of the All-Union Communist Party (Bolshevik). Between 1939 and 1952, member of the Politburo of the Central Committee of the CPSU. Between 1952 and 1964, member of the Presidium of the Central Committee of the CPSU.

Thrice Hero of Socialist Labor. Hero of the Soviet Union.[4] Laureate of the international Lenin prize "For the strengthening of peace among peoples." Awarded orders and medals of the Soviet Union.

Wife, Nina Petrovna, lecturer, died in 1984. Son, Sergei Nikitich, Doctor of Technical Sciences, electronic and control systems engineer. Daughters Yuliya, Rada, Yelena. Son Leonid perished in the war.

1. "Old style" refers to the Julian calendar, introduced by Julius Caesar in 46 B.C.E., and "new style" to the Gregorian calendar that replaced it and remains in use today. The Gregorian calendar was introduced by Pope Gregory XIII in 1582, but was adopted in Russia only in 1918. [SS]

2. The Moscow committee stood above the Moscow city committee in the hierarchy of party committees and was responsible for both the city of Moscow and Moscow province. [SK]

3. Russian Soviet Federated Socialist Republic.

4. "Hero of the Soviet Union" was the highest Soviet military decoration, "Hero of Socialist Labor" the highest civilian decoration. [SK]

# The Khrushchev Family Line: A Historical Note

THIS INVESTIGATION IS based on *The Memoirs of N. S. Khrushchev*, the biographical references in the second and third editions of *The Great Soviet Encyclopedia*, and the book of the publicist Fyodor Burlatsky, published in 1990 and entitled *Vozhdi i sovetniki* (Leaders and advisers), where facts are cited pertaining to the Kursk period of the life of N. S. Khrushchev.

The second edition of *The Great Soviet Encyclopedia* (1957) states: "Nikita Sergeyevich Khrushchev was born on April 17, 1894, to the family of a mine worker in the village of Kalinovka in Kursk *gubernia*." The date of birth is given according to the new style. In the third edition of the encyclopedia (1978), the date of birth is given according to the old and new styles—April 5 and 17—and we are told that N. S. Khrushchev was born to the family of a miner. In *Vozhdi i sovetniki*, Burlatsky gives the date of birth (according to the old style) as April 4, supposing that an error had been made in transposition from the new style (April 17) to the old. However, in transposing dates from the nineteenth century, twelve days are added; thirteen days are added only in transposing dates from the twentieth century.

In the archive *Churches of Kursk Gubernia*, I was able to find the birth registers of the Arkhangelsk church for 1894. This church was situated in Nikita Sergeyevich's native village, Kalinovka, in the Dmitrievsky (Dmitrosvansky) district of Kursk *gubernia*, and it is here that we should find a record of the birth of a baby boy to the Khrushchev family. The record tells us that on April 3 (according to the old style, or April 15 according to the new style) a son was born to the peasant of the village of Kalinovka Sergei Nikanorovich, son of Khrushchev, and his lawful wife Aksinya, daughter of Ivanov. On the same day, the baby was baptized Nikita. His godparents were "the peasants of the same village Stefan Nikolayev, son of Zuyev, and Varvara Vasilyeva, daughter of Khudyakov."

Thus the archival documents bear witness to the fact that Nikita Sergeyevich Khrushchev was born not to the family of a miner, but to the family of a peasant, and not on April 4 or 5, as official publications indicate, but on April 3 (according to the new style, April 15), 1894.

Having discovered this first birth-register record, I decided to trace back the genealogy of the peasant family line of the Khrushchevs.

*Pages of the Birth Register of the Arkhangelsk Church for 1894 Showing the Day and Year of the Birth of N. S. Khrushchev*

My basic source in searching for this information was the census records stored in the archive of the Chamber of the Kursk Treasury, that is, the documents of the population census of prerevolutionary Russia. I also made use of surviving documents of the Arkhangelsk church, to which reference has already been made; these documents have been preserved in part for some years. The problem was that the last, tenth census had been carried out in 1858, and this meant that at best I might discover information pertaining to the grandfather of N. S. Khrushchev. In the confessional records of the Arkhangelsk church for 1866, I found a record of only one family of Khrushchevs, the head of which was Sergei Fyodorovich Khrushchov (spelled that way in the text), seventy years of age; his wife was Ulyana Yermolayeva, fifty-four years of age; their children were Ivan, Nikolai, Maria, and the fourteen-year-old Nikanor. Consequently, Nikanor was the grandfather of Nikita Sergeyevich. We may consider this reliable, because the father of N. S. Khrushchev was called Sergei Nikanorovich.[1]

The next step takes us deeper into the past. In the census records for 1858 (the tenth census), among the peasants of the village of Kalinovka, who were serfs of the woman landowner and privy counselor Yelizaveta Fyodorovna Levshina, there is once again information about only one family of Khrushchevs, the head of which, one Andrei Fomich Khrushchev, died in 1851 at the age of seventy-two years. Apparently he had no children, but mention is made of a nephew, Sergei Fyodorovich, the nephew's wife Ulyana Yermolayeva, and their children Ivan, Nikolai, Maria, and Nikifor. That means that the census records and the confessional records are referring to one and the same family. There is, however, one discrepancy: the fourteen-year-old boy identified in the confessional records as Nikanor is entered in the census records as Nikifor. This is clearly a slip of the pen. There is no doubt that we are dealing with the same family.

In the census records of the ninth census (1850), and then of the eighth census (1834), two interesting points are revealed. First, it turns out that the family of Andrei Fomich Khrushchev was transferred to Kalinovka in 1834 from the neighboring village of Khomutovka, likewise in Dmitrievsky district, evidently on the orders of the landowner. Second, Sergei Fyodorovich and Fyodor Fomich Khrushchev, according to the census of 1834, "are shown as fugitives" since 1816.[2] True, in a separate part of the census record, devoted to "persons who have been from among the fugitives," mention is made of Fyodor Fomich Khrushchev, fifty-three years of age. No mention is made, however, of his son Sergei. Apparently he returned to his native village after 1834.

Information about Fyodor Fomich and Sergei Fyodorovich Khrushchev can be traced back to 1811, when the sixth census was carried out.

The Khrushchevs continued to live in Kalinovka until 1908.

As in many of Russia's villages, there was in Kalinovka, as already mentioned, a church, built as early as 1760. Among the local sights might have been counted also the landowner's house. Nikita Sergeyevich was later to recall it as the "palace," the only structure of the landlord's estate to survive the revolution, when the rest of the estate had been destroyed and "dismantled brick by brick."

In 1906, a zemstvo[3] school was opened in Kalinovka. It was here that the little herdsboy Khrushchev studied. Nikita Sergeyevich recalls the Kalinovka school and his classmates Alyuskin and Slobodchikov. And in his speeches he more than once recalled his first teacher Lidiya Mikhailovna Shevchenko. There are even shots from a cinema documentary of the 1950s showing Lidiya Mikhailovna with Khrushchev attending a students' New Year's fir-tree celebration in the Saint George's Hall at the Great Kremlin Palace.

Nikita Sergeyevich was briefly in Kursk province in 1919, during the Civil War. He was fighting in the ranks of the Red Army's Ninth Rifle Division and returned to his native Kalinovka to visit his wife and children, who were living with his parents. The reunion turned out to be a tragic one: he saw his young wife Yevfrosinya in her coffin. She had died of typhus.

In 1943, on the eve of the battle of Kursk, Khrushchev, as a member of the Military Council of the Voronezh Front, saw with his own eyes how the land of his native region had been scorched and devastated by war. Khrushchev's postwar visits to the Kursk region were both official and private in character. In the archive, photographs have been preserved of his visits to Kalinovka, to the Mikhailovsky Ore-Concentrating Combine, and to the Kursk Production Association Khimvolokno.[4]

—L. Lasochko, *staff member of the State Archive of Kursk province*

1. The middle element in a Russian name is the patronymic, derived from the father's personal name—in this case, Nikanorovich, that is, son of Nikanor. [SS]

2. Serfs were not allowed to leave their village without the consent of the landowner. Runaway serfs were regarded as outlaws. [SK]

3. The zemstvos were bodies of local self-government created under Tsar Aleksandr I. [SS]

4. An enterprise for the production of synthetic thread. [SS]

# The History of the Creation and Publication of the Khrushchev Memoirs, 1967–1999

IN THE 1970S my father's memoirs were published in sixteen languages. People around the world have been reading them for more than thirty years. Right up until 1999, however, there was no complete Soviet or Russian edition, despite the fact that the former archive of the CPSU Central Committee, now the presidential archive, contained the whole text of the memoirs recorded on tapes, about three hundred hours of dictation. Moreover, by 1990 transcripts of the tapes had been typed, edited, and fully prepared for publication. Between 1990 and 1995 they even appeared in the Russian scholarly journal *Voprosy istorii* (Questions of history). But a journal, after all, is only a journal. Not everything can be squeezed into it, and it is much less permanent than a book. All I needed to do, so it seemed, was to stretch out my hand and the book would be in my grasp, but it wasn't there—a typical example of our thoughtless and "don't give a damn" attitude to our own history.

The history of the creation of these memoirs, and of the intrigues about them among the powers that be, is full of the most unexpected twists and turns, from the first day of Father's work on the memoirs until the end of Gorbachev's perestroika. And then they were practically forgotten. Once again, and for the umpteenth time, Russia tries to begin anew and write its history on a blank page.

We first began to talk about Father writing memoirs in 1966, when he was recovering from his pancreas trouble. At that time neither Father nor anyone else had any idea of their content or length or of the role they were to play in our lives. We just wanted to distract Father's attention by encouraging him to embark on some project. None of us foresaw the uproar that his decision to start work on his memoirs was to cause.

Besides, Father was not the first to unsettle the people at the top by aspiring to contribute to history. When he himself had been in power, the "furious zealots" of the KGB had reported to him that Marshal Zhukov had begun writing his memoirs. They proposed stealing what Zhukov had written and obstructing further work by him.

Father reacted otherwise: "Well, so what? Let him write. He has nothing else to do now. Don't interfere. Let him do what he considers necessary. It's very important for the history of our state. Zhukov was retired for certain things he did, but that has nothing to do with his previous activity or with his present work on his memoirs."

In suggesting to Father that he write his memoirs, we reasonably expected that the people on top would take a similar attitude. We were wrong.

At first Father did not respond to our suggestions. Sometimes he laughed them off. More frequently he remained silent, not even saying, in the way he usually did: "Don't bother me!" Time passed; life settled into a new routine. Yuliya's[1] husband, the journalist Lyova Petrov, somehow brought up the subject of memoirs once more. We decided to tempt Father by encouraging him to read the memoirs of others. I took an active part in this effort, seeking out and bringing him the memoirs of Churchill and de Gaulle. Alas, our efforts had no effect.

The days passed. Almost everyone, acquaintance or stranger, who met Father asked him whether he was writing his memoirs. Upset at hearing "no" for an answer, they all told Father that it was "a crime," for he held in his memory remarkable facts that should become part of the historical record.

At long last we began to make some progress. In August 1966 Lyova brought a tape recorder, and Father started dictating. The weather was warm. They sat together in the garden and talked. At first Father did not want to dictate inside the house because of the listening devices. So on the earliest tapes his words are often drowned out by the noise of planes passing overhead. Later he contemptuously ignored the bugs and went on dictating indoors.

There was no plan for the memoirs. We had no idea of the immensity of the project that we had undertaken. It was not real work yet, but just a trial run, simply a recording of the stories that Father so generously shared with his visitors.

The first recording was devoted to the Cuban missile crisis. At that time it was still recent history. Everyone was worried by the dramatic sequence of events that had almost led to a clash between the two great powers. Even today the matter has not lost its topicality. Lyova insistently asked Father to talk about this historical episode in particular. He took the tape home, transcribed it, and a week later brought back the edited record. Father did not like it. Lyova had not confined himself to transcribing what he heard, but had in effect rewritten it. It was no longer Khrushchev, but rather Petrov on a theme by Khrushchev. Nuances had been lost; the style was radically changed, and some facts had been distorted beyond recognition.

For almost a year we marked time. So that he could apply himself seriously to the memoirs, Father needed a good push from without. And the push came.

Father's hopes that his successors would continue to reform the country came to naught. His former colleagues, who only yesterday had so "unanimously" supported all his initiatives, now increasingly slid back. It became ever clearer that they preferred the old pre-Khrushchev ways. But they could not make up their minds to turn the clock back openly. They were afraid of something and acted in an underhand fashion. The most that they dared was to accuse Father of voluntarism and subjectivism. As if a person taking even the simplest decisions, let alone decisions on which depends the fate of a country, can be anything but a voluntarist. Otherwise he turns into an opportunist, constantly shifting his position in search of consensus. Not only do the threads of government slip from his grasp, but he even ceases to understand where he is leading—or misleading—the people who have entrusted themselves to him. As for the accusation of subjectivism, a person is not a machine, especially a person who takes a position of his own. He is obliged to have his own opinion, and it is always a subjective one.

But it was just words. The criticism of Father went no further than vague accusations. But all his innovations and experiments, especially those pertaining to the structure of government, were immediately curtailed. Everything returned to the old pattern. Provincial party committees were reunified, and the ministries reestablished.[2] Economic reform bogged down. There was talk of rehabilitating Stalin, of restoring his "good name." The vain Brezhnev very much wanted to feel that he was sitting in the armchair of "the brilliant leader of all times and peoples," and not in that of the restless "corn promoter," the *kukuruznik* Khrushchev.[3] But that required a whitewash of Stalin. The operation was to be carried out on the fiftieth anniversary of the Soviet regime, in fall 1967.

Father was distressed at what was happening in the country, but he kept silent even with us, his close relatives, and on his Sunday walks talked only about the past. If one of our guests had the misfortune to raise a contemporary issue with him, he would sharply interject: "I'm a pensioner now. My business is with the past. About the present you should talk with those who make the decisions, and not just chatter." After such a rebuff the curious guest would fall silent, and the conversation would turn back to the war, Stalingrad, the Battle of Kursk, or Stalin's death.

Father would constantly return to the subject of Stalin. It was as though he had been infected by Stalin. He tried to rid himself of the infection, but could not. He tried to understand what had happened to the country, to its leaders, and to himself. How had the tyrant managed not only to subject the country to his rule, but even to make its inhabitants deify him? He sought an answer and found none.

The news of the forthcoming rehabilitation of Stalin stunned Father. Even in a nightmare he could not have foreseen such a thing. How could it all be justified—the concentration camps, the executions, the humiliations heaped on people? Father resolved that he had no right to remain silent. He had to tell the story of those times and warn people, even if the chance that his warning would reach people was negligible. Now he began to apply himself seriously to the dictation of his memoirs: memoirs that were to become the pivot of the remaining years of his life; memoirs that gradually grew from an exposé of Stalin and Stalinism into reflections on the fate of the country, on reforms, and on the future.

However, Brezhnev's rehabilitation of Stalin ran into serious obstacles. How was such a sharp change of course to be explained to people and to the world? Although Father's "secret" report to the Twentieth Party Congress had never been published in the USSR, everybody knew what it contained. It was not possible to shrug off or ignore the monstrous crimes that were public knowledge. A way out was needed—and it was found.

The disinformation specialists of the KGB proposed to reduce the matter to Khrushchev's personal resentment against Stalin. The egoistic "pygmy" upstart had taken his revenge on the "titan." One of the authors of the idea is said to have been Filipp Bobkov, who later became head of the KGB's Fifth Administration (which carried out actions against dissidents) and its first deputy chairman. But how was this disinformation campaign to be carried out? A hook was needed: in other words, facts from Father's life susceptible to such an interpretation. And they were found in the tragic story of the wartime death of my brother Leonid.

Before the war Leonid had graduated from a training school for pilots. He began his war service in bomber aviation. At the beginning of the war, flying a bomber was considered equivalent to suicide. There were practically no fighters to provide cover, and the Germans fired point-blank at the slow and unwieldy bombers. According to the testimony of those who served with him, Leonid fought well. He did not hide behind others' backs or take cover behind his father's name. Here is what his commanding officer, Commander of the 46th Air Division Colonel Pisarsky, wrote about him on July 16, 1941, when recommending him for a decoration:

Crew leader Leonid Nikitich Khrushchev . . . has twelve combat flights to his credit. His performance in carrying out all combat missions is excellent. He is a courageous and fearless pilot. In air combat on July 6, 1941 he bravely fought the enemy's fighters until their attack was repulsed.

Khrushchev returned from battle in a plane riddled with holes. He shows initiative. . . . More than once he has gone into combat substituting for crews that were insufficiently prepared. . . . I recommend that Comrade Khrushchev be awarded the Order of the Red Banner.

Leonid had ten days left to fly. "On July 26," so it is recorded in the battle dispatch, "the remaining planes of three squadrons of the 134th Bomber Regiment went to bomb an airfield in the area of the Izocha Station [and] artillery emplacements in the area of Khikalo. On their way back, the undefended bombers were attacked by eight German Messerschmidt-109 fighters. Four of the six planes were lost."

Leonid's plane barely managed to reach the front line and landed in no man's land with its chassis missing. One of the crew members had already been killed in the air, and Leonid broke his leg on landing. Red Army men arrived in time to rescue the crew of the knocked-out plane. At the field hospital they wanted to amputate Leonid's leg, but he wouldn't let them, threatening them with his pistol. The leg healed very poorly, and for more than a year Leonid lay in the rear hospital in Kuibyshev. It was there that I saw him for the last time—pale, smiling, with his new medal on his chest.

When his leg had knitted back together, Leonid strove to return to the front, but now as a fighter pilot. Using all the means open to him, my brother got what he wanted. And then misfortune struck. Naturally they did not tell me, a six-year-old, what happened. But at home I heard whispering in the corners about Leonid killing a man. Much later I was to learn about those events from the memoirs of General Stepan Mikoyan, who as an air lieutenant had met Leonid in Kuibyshev. "Once," writes Mikoyan, "we happened to find ourselves in the company of some sailor from the front. We were all the worse for drink. Someone remarked that Leonid was a very good shot. The sailor demanded that Leonid prove it by knocking a bottle off his head. For a long time Leonid refused, but eventually he gave in. He took a shot and knocked the neck off the bottle. The sailor said that wasn't good enough: he had to hit the bottle itself. So Leonid took a second shot and hit the sailor in the forehead."

The court found Leonid guilty. At that time they sent offenders not to prison, but to penal battalions at the front. Leonid was allowed to remain in aviation, though with penal status. So again he ended up on the front line, in a fighter regiment, as he had so wanted. However, he did not have long to fight. Leonid completed only six combat flights. On his seventh flight, on April 11, 1943, he was shot down as he approached the town of Zhizdra, on the border of Kaluga and Bryansk provinces. Such was the typical fate of all the young pilots who had had too few training flights and had not adequately mastered the technique of air combat. It happened over German-occupied territory. Below there stretched out the marshes. In the heat of battle, the pilots of the other planes flying in the same formation did not even notice his disappearance. The commander of the front sent Father his condolences and proposed to send a search group into the area where the plane had gone down, but Father, thanking him for his sympathy, asked him not to risk people's lives in vain. It would not help matters and would not bring back his son. That is how Leonid Khrushchev came to be listed as missing in action.

In 1995 there appeared in the Russian newspapers a report to the effect that the remains of another Soviet fighter had been found in the Bryansk marshes by a local schoolteacher together with a search team of pupils. In the pilot's cabin they had found the skeleton of the pilot in a frayed lieutenant's uniform and a fur helmet with earphones. According to the testimony of other members of Leonid's regiment, Leonid was the only man in the regiment who wore such a helmet. The number was still there on the plane's motor. It remained only to check it against the service record in the military archive. If the service record was preserved, one name could be removed from the list of those missing in action.

Shortly after Leonid's death, his widow Lyubov Illarionovna was arrested in Kuibyshev. The accusation made against her was the standard one—that is, that she had worked for foreign intelligence, as the diplomatic corps had also been evacuated to this city on the Volga. Whose spy she was supposed to be I no longer remember—perhaps the British, perhaps the Swedes. Only in 1956 was she released, having suffered her full share of grief in the Karaganda camps.[4]

Their one-year-old daughter Yuliya remained on my mother's hands. She was brought up together with us. She very much disliked being singled out from the other children as our parents' granddaughter. Mama was the first to notice the problem that had arisen, and Yuliya became in effect our parents' daughter.

It was the uncertainty surrounding the fate of my brother, the fact that his death had never been registered, that the KGB decided to use for its own selfish ends. It was 1967.

As is the custom among professionals, they acted in a cautious and roundabout fashion. The task of telling the story was assigned to the deputy head of the personnel department of the Ministry of Defense, Colonel General Kuzovlev. He held the cards in his hand, for Leonid had been a military man. Rumors spread around Moscow to the effect that the general had discovered documents—nobody had seen them, of course—proving that Leonid did not perish, but gave himself up to the Germans, began to collaborate with them, and betrayed the motherland. Subsequently, either at the end of the war or after it ended, he allegedly fell into the hands of Soviet counterintelligence, admitted to the crimes he had committed, and was sentenced by the court to death. Father allegedly begged Stalin on his knees to have mercy on his son, but Stalin refused, saying: "My son too was taken prisoner. He conducted himself as a hero, but I refused to exchange him for Field Marshal Paulus.[5] As for your son, . . ."

The KGB's "creators of history" accomplished their mission. They explained how Khrushchev had exposed Stalin's crimes to get personal revenge for his son. It may seem that this fiction did not deserve attention. But what makes a professional a professional is knowing better than anyone else how rumors spread. The fable passed from mouth to mouth, acquiring more and more new details as it went. Then it was published in the newspapers and was recounted in the memoirs of Stalin's murderer in chief, KGB General Sudoplatov, who in Father's time had been sentenced to a long prison term. Finally, it started to be discussed—cautiously at first, then more and more boldly—even in the scholarly literature. And all without a single proof or document!

Fortunately, Father did not learn of this dirty fabrication.

And now we, his descendants, have to look for arguments to disprove the slander. We need not look very far. Even if we suppose that Leonid had been taken prisoner, what kind of treason could a senior lieutenant possibly have committed? What did he know? The answer is obvious: nothing of importance. The only way in which he could have been of use to the Germans would have been by appealing to Soviet troops to surrender. Such leaflets, bearing the signatures of Stalin's son Yakov, of Molotov's nephew, of General Vlasov,[6] and of many others, were scattered in large numbers from German planes over the positions of Soviet troops. There is no record of any leaflet signed by Leonid Khrushchev, nor do war veterans recall such a leaflet. The Germans simply did not suspect his existence; otherwise they would have made use of his name. My brother perished in anonymity on the approach to Zhizdra. What a miserable and unpleasant story it is! I don't think that my explanations will put an end to it. Fighting against slander is a difficult, almost an impossible, task, but a necessary one.[7]

Yet another myth about Father was circulated in those years and for the same purpose. The same KGB specialists let loose the rumor that Khrushchev had tried when he was in power to conceal and erase the traces of his own participation in Stalin's repressions, and that he had ordered all pertinent documents and evidence removed from the archives. This accusation is more difficult to disprove. First, Father himself never denied that he had to countersign orders prepared by the NKVD for the arrest of people with whom he worked. That is how things were in those times. And just let anyone try not to countersign such a paper! Father would also visit prisons and meet with arrested people. Nevertheless, an important distinction needs to be drawn. Some of Stalin's comrades-in-arms, such as Kaganovich, Voroshilov, and Molotov, not to mention Beria, did all they could to shed a sea of blood as soon as the boss called them to attention. Others—and Father was one of them—did not display zeal, and tried when they could to reduce the number of victims and ease their plight. He talks about this in his memoirs.

At the time of the Twentieth CPSU Congress, Father openly declared that all members of the country's leadership had been involved in Stalin's crimes, but to different degrees, and that it was up to the people to determine the guilt of each person. Toward the end of his life, Father used to repeat: "I shall die, and my deeds will be put on the scales. On one scale the evil I did, on the other the good, and I hope the good will outweigh the evil." But even after his death the devil's servants try to throw their false weight on to the "evil" scale. They do it so skillfully that doubts arose even in my mind, and I admitted the possibility that Father really had "corrected" the past. With great reluctance—but I admitted the possibility.

I thought that it did not correspond to Father's inner nature, but I know that people are weak. And we all want so badly to improve our image after the event and to forget the unsightly things we have done. And he had such opportunities! It would have seemed a sin not to make use of them. Truthfully speaking, I resigned myself. But His Majesty Chance intervened. In December 1994, when I was already in the United States, at Brown University, there was a conference devoted to the 100th anniversary of Khrushchev's birth, and some speakers made reference to Father's "purge" of the archives. I resolved to examine the primary sources. The accusations pertained to two periods of Father's life: the Moscow period (up to 1938) and the Kiev period (after 1938). So if anything had been "purged," it must have been the Moscow and the Ukrainian party archives.

I began with the Ukrainian archive. In his lecture at the conference, the historian Yuri Shapoval, who specializes in the life of Khrushchev, had categorically declared that many documents relating to Father's activity were missing from the Ukrainian archive. They had been "purged." I asked him to go back to the primary sources. The issue interested Shapoval. He was a relatively young man had not been not "infected" with contempt for Father by the party apparatus, which never forgave him for exposing Stalin's crimes. And what did the facts turn out to be? The Ukrainian archive indeed lacks a great deal connected with Father's name. The reason is that Father had his own archive. When he went to Ukraine from Moscow in 1938, he took it with him. His assistants placed in it what they considered to be the most important documents. All these folders—there were more than two hundred of them—Father (or, more likely, his assistants) brought back to Moscow when he returned there in 1950. After Father's retirement they lay in the archive of the Politburo of the CPSU Central Committee. Now the archivists of independent Ukraine are arguing with the guardians of Russia's presidential archive over who has a right to the documents. Yuri Shapoval discovered no sign that any documents had been destroyed in Kiev.[8]

Encouraged by the results of the Ukrainian investigation, I turned my attention to the Moscow period of Father's activity. I sought help in this part of the research from another participant in the conference at Brown University—Vladimir Pavlovich Naumov, secretary of the commission headed by Aleksandr Yakovlev that was responsible for the rehabilitation of the victims of political repression in the pre-Stalin, Stalin, and post-Stalin periods. By virtue of his position, Naumov has access to archives, including the presidential archive. For a long time Vladimir Pavlovich did not respond to my request. However, after repeated reminders, he sent a reply through William Taubman, a professor at Amherst College: "Please excuse the delay in my reply. It took me time to try to clarify the circumstances of the purge of the former archive of the Moscow city and province party committees. It turned out to be a very difficult task. There are various versions of what happened, all to one degree or another connected with N. S. Khrushchev. But nobody was able to confirm his version with documents."

Translated from bureaucratic jargon, this meant that, as in the Ukrainian archive, nothing in the Moscow archive had been burned on Father's orders. Such orders do not remain without trace. For documents to be destroyed, there must be an instruction. A document is drawn up, or at least a letter is written, giving its bearer freedom of action. Otherwise the whole responsibility would have lain on the guardians of the archive, and they would have been unwilling to take it on themselves without a written instruction.

The only documents the destruction of which could really be confirmed were those discovered in Beria's safe in 1953 after his arrest. The members of the Presidium of the Central Committee unanimously resolved to burn them unread. That was understandable enough: who knows what kind of compromising material Lavrenty Pavlovich had accumulated about them? But Father mentions this episode in his memoirs.

So that disposed of yet another myth, although I think that we shall yet encounter new attempts to reanimate it. However, my historical digression has dragged on for too long.

When after a year Father resumed the dictation of his memoirs, Mama began to help him. She knew how to type, at the same time editing the text. The work now went better, and its quality improved, but the rate of progress was unsatisfactory: there seemed to be no prospect of completing the job in the foreseeable future. That was when I too was brought in to work on the memoirs. At first I proposed to Father that he ask the Central Committee to assign him a typist and secretary.

"For this isn't a private matter. The Central Committee should be interested in the memoirs. This is history," I urged him.

But he refused to ask them. "I don't want to ask them for anything. If they themselves offer me help, I won't refuse it. But they won't offer. They don't need my memoirs. They will only obstruct me."

We decided not to ask for help. Soon all the transcription and editing work landed on my shoulders. While Father was alive I managed to prepare 1,500 typed pages. Gradually a certain rhythm was established. In one day, without letup, I could handle no more than ten pages. And although I made a great effort, the results, in Father's opinion, were not too impressive.

From the very start problems arose. The main problem was where to find an experienced and trustworthy typist. For we had to make sure that no material would be lost or fall into the wrong hands. It was no easy task. I shared my concerns with my friends Semyon Alperovich and Volodya Modestov. Together we found a suitable person—Leonora Nikiforovna Finogenova. She was working at the time at our enterprise in the final assembly workshop, and often came with us on expeditions to testing ranges.[9] She was an excellent specialist and an extremely honest person. I put the proposal to her, and she agreed. It remained to sort out the technical side of the matter. I bought a typewriter in a store on Pushkin Street. I already had a four-track Grundig tape recorder. We just had to attach earphones to it. We decided to work at my apartment, because I did not think I should let the tapes out of my hands.

I remember the evening in fall 1967 that Lora [nickname of Leonora] first came to my place on Stanislavsky Street. We spent a long time adjusting the tape-recorder and the typewriter so that the typing could be conveniently synchronized with the playing of the sound track. Neither she nor I had any experience of such work. The adjustments took a lot of time. At last every-thing was in place and the work could begin.

Well qualified as she was, Lora was clearly unable to keep up with the tape. Moreover, some words on the tape were garbled. Then we had to stop and go back. After an hour it was obvious that we would never get the job done that way. We might do a few dozen pages or at best a hundred. But we had before us hundreds, even thousands, of pages. Our spirits fell. Imper-ceptibly night crept on. We took our first break and went to drink some tea. The conversation revolved around the problem that was worrying us. There was no alternative: the work had to be transferred to Lora's home, where she would have more time.

In this early period of the work on the memoirs, the KGB was not yet interested in us, and nobody paid any attention as we carried the equipment to Reutovo.[10] We began to make faster progress. Father dictated three to five hours a day in two sessions, one in the morning and the other after lunch. Although Lora typed fast, she could still not keep up with him. I was quite out of breath. I spent every free minute editing, at home and at work, on workdays and on holidays, from morning until late at night. I could not keep up with them—but I hurried Lora on all the same, fearing that we would not manage it. Something prompted me to expect that the work would not always go so smoothly.

Father dictated without referring to any documentary sources. He relied solely on himself, on his own memory. And it must be admitted that he had a phenomenal memory. How was he able to hold in his head such a vast quantity of information—events, places, names, figures? And then to record it on tape with almost no repetition or muddle?

Gradually Father got used to our work. More and more often there appeared in the dictated text asides giving me various instructions: "I talked about our trip to Marseilles, but forgot the name of the government official accompanying us. Now I remember. Joxe. Is that right? Yes, yes, Joxe. When you edit it, put the name in the right place."

Or:

"At the congress of the Bulgarian Communist Party I was approached by a member of the Romanian delegation, but I've forgotten his name. (There followed a description of his appearance.) You'll have to look into it and put in the name."

In the section about the war it was necessary to check the names of the military formations referred to. There were not many errors with these. Father was astonishingly accurate. Only one thing can explain it: the deep impression left in his memory by the events of those years. The figures, the names, the dates were all correct.

He did make mistakes when he tried to reconstruct from memory the sequence of events during a state visit. For instance, in the account of the visit that he made with Bulganin to Burma in 1955, Father tried to recall their itinerary and who received them and where. A person usually does not remember such details. Father retained a general picture of the visit in his memory, but he got in a muddle when it came to remembering in which town they watched the national rowing race and in which town they saw a parade with elephants. It was my job to check the text against published press reports and put everything in the right place.

Father looked through the edited transcripts and made his remarks, which I immediately noted down on the back of the pages of the initial text for use in the next retyping. Occasionally I suggested to Father my own additions and clarifications and entered into the text those that he approved.

Father preferred to have a listener present while he was dictating into the tape recorder. "It goes better when someone is listening," he complained more than once. "You see in front of you a live person and not just a stupid box." When Father was on his own with the "box," his voice became less lively. There were hesitations and long pauses.

It was not always possible, however, to find somebody to listen. It is true that when one did turn up—usually it was some old acquaintance, a pensioner come to visit us for a week or a little longer—it did go better and more quickly. You could hear a dialogue on the tape.

Not that dialogue was always an unmitigated blessing. When I now, many years later, listen to the tapes of Father's memoirs and recognize the voice of Vera Aleksandrovna Gostinskaya, I know that the dictation is gradually going to give way to talk about prices in the stores, followed by discussion of Polish affairs. Another visitor who was not satisfied with the role of passive listener was Pyotr Mikhailovich Krimerman. He asked questions about Egypt and Israel, about the Six-Day War, and in general about everything under the sun. At Father's request, I edited the dialogue into a monologue—to no purpose, in my opinion. But Vera Aleksandrovna and Pyotr Mikhailovich were exceptions. The majority of listeners sat with bated breath and did not interfere with Father's work.

Father worked most productively in the fall and winter. In the summer his gardening came first, and he dictated in fits and starts.

Father prepared himself seriously and over a long period for work on each new theme. While on his walks, he thought over what to say and how to say it. The most dramatic events of his life were branded into his memory for life. He recounted them many times. Among such events were the defeat on the approaches to Barvenkovo in 1942, the arrest of Beria, Stalin's death, and the Twentieth Congress. In recounting them he hardly diverged a step from the initial version. The way he recounted a given event sounded the same in 1967 as it had in 1960, even though Father would complain: "I'm growing old; my memory is starting to fail."

As kilometers of the tapes accumulated, Father grew increasingly tormented by the question of what fate awaited his memoirs. "It's all in vain, it's all futile. All will be lost. When I die they'll take it all away and destroy it, or else they'll bury it so deep that not a trace will remain," he said more than once during our Sunday walks.

In the house we never talked about such matters, bearing in mind the bugs. I reassured Father as well as I could, although in my heart I was inclined to agree with him. I understood that if all was quiet today that did not mean it would always be so.

Just in case, we decided to duplicate the tapes and the text and to store them separately in reliable places.[11] Deciding was easy, but when we asked ourselves what places might be considered reliable, an answer did not immediately occur to us. In my mind I went through the list of my friends and acquaintances, weighing up who could be relied on. Who could be trusted not to gossip? It was vital not only that he himself not gossip, but also that his wife not gossip, and his mother-in-law, too. Who, in the event of my failure, would not attract to himself the heightened attention of the professionals? Who? Who? Who?

At last, my choice rested on Professor Igor Mikhailovich Shumilov, a colleague of mine at Moscow Technical University. He was the son of General Shumilov, who had commanded one of the armies that had taken Field Marshal Paulus prisoner in Stalingrad in 1943. During the hard times of retreat, Shumilov senior had been close to my father, and now I was friends with his son.

Igor responded to my proposal without hesitation: "Let's do it!" He would hide everything in the numerous attics, cluttered with odds and ends brought from Germany, of the general's big apartment in a building not far from the metro station Sokol. He resolved to tell neither his father nor his wife anything. True, he added: "They'll probably guess, but they won't ask questions." On that we agreed. In the best traditions of detective novels, I handed Igor transcripts, reels with newly dictated tapes, and sheets of prepared text during the intervals between lectures, when we "accidentally" ran into each other at the university department. We decided to reduce our social contacts to the minimum, just in case.

The problem appeared to be solved, but Father and I knew only too well the powers of detection available to professionals in such matters. There are no absolutely reliable places. During one of my conversations with Father while out walking, the idea occurred to us of looking for a safe place of storage abroad. At first Father was doubtful, fearing that there the manuscript might escape from our control and be used in a distorted form to harm our state. On the other hand, it would be preserved more reliably abroad. After weighing all the pros and cons for a long time, Father did all the same ask me to give further thought to this option. Of course, we kept this decision strictly secret. But, to be honest, I was at that time quite unable to think up any plan of action to implement the decision.

Father began his memoirs with the 1930s, the period of his work in Ukraine and in Moscow. Then he went on to tell about the preparation for war, about the tragic beginning of the war, and about the retreat under German attack. What he said diverged widely from the version of the history of the first period of the war that was officially recognized at that time and presented in the numerous publications on the subject. His descriptions of the tragic events of 1941 made a powerful impression on me as a reader. In editing them, I tried not to lose a single word or to distort his thoughts in any way. For me Father was the sole true source of information. And now the preservation of these memoirs for future generations had become my life's work.

After dealing with the war, Father proceeded to the postwar period—the restoration of the Ukrainian economy, famine, intrigues, how Kaganovich was appointed party leader in Ukraine and then recalled, Father's transfer to Moscow, the "Leningrad affair," the preparation of a "Moscow affair," and much else besides. An enormous amount of material accumulated. We started to get confused: what had already been dealt with, and what had not? We resolved somehow to get the work better organized. I spent a whole week putting together a plan—a list of those questions to which in my view priority should be given. On Sunday, Father and I discussed it, and he took the papers to think it all over at leisure. Within a week we had the first version of our plan ready. In the years that followed, we worked in accordance with this plan, crossing out points that had been covered and inserting new points that had been overlooked.

Our intention was to cast light on all the main issues of contemporary life—the Virgin Lands campaign and other agricultural problems, the development of industry, strategies for reorganizing the national economy, questions relating to the armed forces and military industry, means for democratizing our society, and Father's relations with the intelligentsia. Nor did we forget international affairs—the struggle for peace, Father's first meetings with Western state leaders in Geneva, various contacts and visits, the problem of peaceful coexistence, and questions of disarmament and the abolition of nuclear weapons.

Father did work in accordance with the plan, but being easily distractible he would wander far off the subject, recalling other events analogous to those being recounted. Unfortunately, we did not manage to carry out all that we had planned. Father's thoughts remained unrecorded on many topics, including the democratization of our society, the setting of maximum limits to the periods for which one person could occupy a state or party position, openness and use of the electoral principle in the work of state and party, and the establishment of constitutional guarantees of citizens' rights that would prevent any repetition of the terror of the 1930s. Nor did we manage to create the planned section on the creative intelligentsia, in which Father wanted to assess the events that took place toward the end of his period in power. He very much wanted to explain the motives underlying his behavior. But time did not suffice. The last recording, taped shortly before his death, was devoted to this matter, but it left Father dissatisfied.

"Scrap the whole thing," he told me. "I'll dictate it again." But time no longer remained for dictating again. I disobeyed Father and did not erase the recording. It is now the sole reminiscence on this theme that has been preserved. He himself entitled it: "I Am Not a Judge."

Now the work went smoothly. It became more productive. The three of us—Father, Lora, and myself—worked well together. But where were our family's numerous journalists? I have already mentioned Lyova Petrov. He continued to help Father. True, his collaboration did not last long. Lyova fell seriously ill and died soon afterward. Yuliya was occupied with her small daughters—and besides, by professional inclination she was far removed from political journalism.

My sister Rada did not involve herself in matters to do with the memoirs. She acted as if they simply did not exist. She was fully occupied by her work at the magazine *Nauka i zhizn* (Science and life). On her not too frequent visits to the dacha, she would comfortably settle herself down on the settee underneath a picture of the spring flooding of the Dnieper River. There she would go through galley proofs and edit articles for her magazine. The cat would lie in bliss next to her. Father would take offense at her failure to pay any attention to his work.

By that time I had been deeply drawn into the work on the memoirs, even though it was activity of a kind with which I had previously been quite unfamiliar. I was constantly thinking about the memoirs and pressing on Father my suggestions and advice. I dreamed of beautiful published volumes. Regarding the memoirs as my own project, I would have looked jealously on any interference in my new "diocese," as on the invasion of an uninvited guest. For that reason my sister's indifference suited me.

Father had a special regard for Aleksei Ivanovich Adzhubei [Rada's husband and a prominent Soviet journalist.]. At first it was on him that he set his hopes, and it was he whom he saw as his main assistant. That was natural enough. In the not so distant past, Adzhubei had constantly accompanied Father on his journeys, and together with other prominent journalists he had belonged to the working group that assisted the first secretary in preparing speeches, documents, and drafts of new laws. And indeed, Adzhubei himself, who had been chief editor of the newspaper *Izvestia,* wrote a great deal and was regarded as a capable journalist. Now they were both in disgrace, and who if not a son-in-law should help his father-in-law in his literary work?

At first it seemed to be going that way. Aleksei Ivanovich actively supported the idea of Father working on the memoirs. True, he himself did not offer to help , but at that time the project was just getting started. Over time his attitude began to change. He stopped referring to the memoirs, and began to avoid talking about them with Father. Evidently he had decided to be cautious, for his highly developed political intuition warned him of the danger inherent in the undertaking. At that time, in the mid-1960s, Aleksei Ivanovich had yet to lose hope of resuming his political career. He had recovered somewhat from the shock of the 1964 plenum of the Central Committee[12] and sought ways of returning to political activity. He put all his hopes on Shelepin. Not long before he had hung his head, but now he straightened his shoulders once more. On his visits to Petrovo-Dalneye,[13] he would take first one person, then another, out on to the street and secretively inform them: "Soon everything will change. Lenya won't keep his place for long. Shelepin will replace him. Shurik[14] won't forget me. He can't manage without me. I just have to wait a little."

Rumors really were circulating, and such a scenario seemed by no means improbable. Adzhubei backed up his words by referring to conversations with his old friends from the Komsomol—with Grant Grigoryan, perhaps, or with Dmitry Goryunov.[15] Once he even told us confidentially that he had met with Aleksandr Nikolayevich [Shelepin] himself.

I believed and did not believe what he said. Of one thing I had no doubt: without Khrushchev, Shelepin had simply no need of Adzhubei.

Should we condemn Aleksei Ivanovich for his attempt to return to the political scene? I don't think so. He was then only just over forty years old. Naturally, in the situation that had arisen he considered it wise to distance himself somewhat from Khrushchev and to do it in a way that would be noticed. Participation in work on the memoirs could only harm him. However, it turned out that Brezhnev was by no means a transitional figure, and that he knew how to hold on to power. The possibility of Shelepin coming to power receded. But then new events occurred that put paid to any inclination Aleksei Ivanovich may still have had to take part in the work on the memoirs. These events affected us all, including Father and myself, and to some extent influenced the fate of the memoirs.

In summer 1967, when Khrushchev had apparently been well and truly forgotten, his name suddenly again shook the world. Nothing special had happened. It was simply that the Americans had decided to make a biographical film about the former Soviet leader. In the USSR, however, this was viewed as a provocation, almost as an anti-Soviet attack.

The problem was that by 1967 Brezhnev found it hard to bear even the mention of Khrushchev's name. People of his temperament relive their evil deeds in their own special way. They transfer all their hatred onto the victim, trying in that strange fashion to prove, both to themselves and to those around them, that they were right. Any mention of Father's name to some degree impeded the consolidation of Brezhnev's own image in history—for Leonid Ilyich wished to claim for himself the credit for much that had been initiated long before he came to power and that had indeed under his leadership lost momentum. Of course, the moods of the boss were transmitted to his subordinates.

Sometimes this reached laughable extremes, or it would have been laughable had it not involved people vested with practically unlimited power. In the Crimea, on the road from Simferopol to Yalta, there was a village spread out on the slope of a hill that bore the name of Nikita. Since olden times it has been the home of the famous Nikitsky Botanical Garden. Once, as he passed through the village on the way to his dacha, Brezhnev threw a glance at the roadside sign "Village of Nikita" and involuntarily made a wry face. His scowl did not go unnoticed, and a few days later a new sign appeared at the same spot: "Botanical Village." The botanical garden kept its old name, but it now sounded almost surreal: the Nikitsky Botanical Garden in Botanical Village. And this was not the only such episode. Gradually the contempt for Father that had built up in Brezhnev's soul turned into open hatred.

It was against this background that the scandal blew up about the appearance in the West of the film about Khrushchev. Nobody in our country had yet seen this film: there was only information about it. They said that it was based on shots taken at the dacha. In it Father gave a number of interviews, one more terrible than the next.

Unfortunately, I had a chance to see this film only after Father's death. As was to be expected, it contained nothing sensational or seditious. It was based exclusively on archival photographs and film clips. The whole brouhaha was stirred up over two or three minutes at the end, where Father is shown sitting in the garden in his "Boussac" cloak[16] by the open fire, and by his side Arbat, Father's beloved dog, an Alsatian. Father is recounting something, but the sound of his voice is muffled, overlaid by that of the narrator. He is saying something about his youthful years, then about Cuba. There were many such fireside scenes in Father's life.

At that time I was an enthusiastic cinematographer and was always dragging around with me an 8-millimeter movie camera. Many of our guests also came with cameras and movie cameras. Not to mention the people vacationing at the neighboring vacation center: a souvenir photo with Father was part of their "cultural program." Photos and movie shots could easily—had anyone so desired—have ended up abroad. There was nothing reprehensible in that. Had I been asked, I myself could have filmed that sequence. But it was not my shot on the film.

As became clear much later, the shot was taken by Yuri Korolyov, a professional photographer who at the time worked together with Adzhubei at the magazine *Sovetskii soyuz* (Soviet union). Besides that, the Korolyov family was on friendly terms with Yuliya and Lyova. From time to time Yuri visited Father, took photographs, and buzzed his movie camera. His shots were apparently supplemented by archival material, including fragments of tape recordings of Father's voice made before 1964. At that time he would quite often talk about the Donbas period of his life and about the miner-poet Pantelei Makhinya. But they also might have been contemporary tape recordings. When guests came, Father loved to reminisce about his youth. The Cuban missile crisis was another of his favorite themes.

We did not have to wait for the reaction to the film. They did not touch Father or ask him any questions. Their ire descended on those around him. First to be called to account was Melnikov, the chief of Father's guard.

They had long been displeased with Melnikov. They considered him too much of a "pro-Khrushchev" person, who always tried to please and help Father and did whatever he could to make him happy. His behavior was not in the spirit of the times. The film provided a good pretext to take reprisals. Melnikov was accused of loss of vigilance. How could he have permitted a foreign journalist to interview Father? The fact that no foreign journalist had ever been at the dacha was naturally of no interest to anyone.

As a result, Melnikov was removed from his position and dismissed from the KGB. Later I met with him again. He was working as a manager in a vacation center. He was getting old and going gray, and his eyesight was poor. I saw him for the last time at Father's funeral. He had come to say goodbye.

Melnikov's place was taken by Vasily Mikhailovich Kondrashov—a different kind of person altogether. Kondrashov, unlike Melnikov, acted in the spirit of the times. He "needled" Father about trifles and to Father's requests gave the standard reply that he would check with his superiors. Within a few days there usually came the answer: "No, you're not allowed to."

It may be that this was not a trait of his character. Remembering the fate of his predecessor, he may simply have been fulfilling his instructions to the letter. The replacement of the chief of the guard was intended by the higherups as a warning to Father, to remind him in whose hands power now lay.

However, Father kept up the appearance that the changes taking place were no concern of his. Even in conversation with us he hardly mentioned the subject. This action of the authorities did not affect our work on the memoirs. Not only did Father not give up his dictation: he went on with redoubled energy.

Our work on the memoirs peaked in winter 1967–68. By that time Brezhnev had already consolidated his position and was beginning to devote his attention to ensuring that his personality would be appropriately reflected in the mirror of history. The writing of *Malaya zemlya* (Little land) and *Vozrozhdenie* (Rebirth)[17] was still apparently a matter for the distant future, but the first shoots of the new cult of personality had already matured.

When Brezhnev was informed that Khrushchev was dictating his memoirs, he was extremely worried. It was decided to make Father stop the work. But how? In all likelihood, various methods were considered. Should the dacha be searched? Should the tapes be removed by force? No. That won't avoid a scandal. The whole world will regard Brezhnev as an ogre, and Khrushchev as a martyr. So what was there to do? Only one remedy remained—to meet with Khrushchev and persuade him to stop writing his memoirs and to hand what he had already written over to the Central Committee. If he can't be persuaded, then he can be forced. As a last resort, he can be scared.

Brezhnev did not want to meet with his former patron himself. The meeting in 1965 had been quite enough.[18] He gave the job of summoning Khrushchev, talking with him, and trying to put a stop to the memoirs to his first deputy at the Central Committee A. P. Kirilenko, a crude and impudent man who could be relied on to give no quarter. Kirilenko was to be joined by A. Ya. Pelshe, chairman of the Party Control Committee, who would exert pressure by the very fact of his presence: one does not play games with the Party Control Committee. A third person was brought in—namely, P. N. Demichev. He had been close to Khrushchev in the past, so if necessary he could defuse tension and also persuade Khrushchev not to do anything foolish. Some such decision must have been taken in spring 1968. It remained to act on it.

In April 1968, on the eve of Father's birthday, I went as usual to Petrovo-Dalneye for the weekend. Father was not at home. Mother said that he had gone to the edge of the forest to sit a while in the sunshine. "Father is very upset. Yesterday Kirilenko summoned him to the Central Committee and demanded that he stop work on the memoirs and hand over what he has done already. Father lost his temper and started to shout. It ended in a big scandal. He'll tell you all about it himself," she went on. "Only try not to bother him. He's very overwrought and doesn't feel well."

Alarmed, I set off down the path. Father was sitting on the bench. Next to him lay Arbat. Father did not notice me approaching, and when I sat down without a word next to him did not immediately turn his head. We sat a while in silence. Father looked tired. His face had grown gray and old.

When he did turn to me, he asked: "You know already? Mother told you?"
I nodded.

"The bastards! I told them everything I think of them. Perhaps I said too much, but never mind—it'll do them good. Do they think I'm going to crawl on my belly in front of them?"

I decided to make things clearer. "Mother told me practically nothing. Only that Kirilenko summoned you and demanded that you stop work on the memoirs."

"That's right. What a bastard!" Father repeated. He began to tell me the whole story. As he proceeded, his face grew animated and a mischievous glint came into his eyes. It was obvious that he was reliving every sentence, every riposte.

Recalling that Father was not feeling well, I tried to divert the conversation and calm him down somehow. But Father did not want to be diverted. Boiling with indignation, he was intent on recounting to me the outrageous exchange that had taken place at the Central Committee from beginning to end. Later he was more than once to return to the events of that day. I remembered well the whole exchange and even made some notes while my memory was still fresh. Here is what happened.

In Kirilenko's office, there sat, besides Kirilenko himself, Pelshe and Demichev. Kirilenko went straight to the point, without asking—as is customary in such situations—how Father was feeling. He declared that it had become known to the Central Committee that Father had for a long time been writing his memoirs, in which he described various events in the history of our party and state. In essence, he was rewriting the history of the party. But explaining the history of the party and of our Soviet state was the job of the Central Committee, not of individual persons, let alone of pensioners. For that reason the Politburo of the Central Committee[19] demanded that he stop his work on the memoirs, and that he hand what had already been dictated over to the Central Committee.

As he finished his speech, Kirilenko looked around at those present. It was obvious that this declaration had cost him no little effort. Pelshe and Demichev remained silent. Kirilenko had worked alongside Khrushchev for quite a long time in Ukraine and here in Moscow, where he had been his first deputy in the Central Committee Bureau for the RSFSR, so that he was familiar with Father's explosive temperament. He understood what an insult his words represented for a man who only four years earlier had occupied the posts of first secretary of the Central Committee and chairman of the USSR Council of Ministers. Evidently he hoped that Father's situation as a pensioner, dependent on them for every trifle, would make him more compliant and tractable and force him to obey.

Father paused before replying, and looked at his former colleagues. After a few moments he began to speak, at first calmly and then getting more and more excited. He said that he could not understand what it was that Kirilenko, and those whose instructions he was carrying out, wanted of him. An enormous number of people in the world, and in our country too, wrote memoirs. It was a normal thing. Memoirs were not history, but a particular person's view of the life that he had lived. They supplemented history and could provide good material for future historians of our country and our party. And he therefore regarded their demand as a violation of the personality of a

Soviet person and as an infringement of the constitution and refused to comply with it.

"You can use force to put me in jail or to remove these materials. Now you are in a position to do all that with me, but I protest categorically," he added.

"Nikita Sergeyevich, what I have conveyed to you is a decision of the Politburo of the Central Committee, and you are obliged as a Communist to comply with it," insisted Kirilenko. "Otherwise. . . ."

Father did not let him finish. "What you are permitting yourself in dealing with me is something that the government would not have permitted itself even in tsarist times. I recall only one similar case. You want to deal with me in the way that Tsar Nicholas I dealt with Taras Shevchenko when he sent him into the army[20] and forbade him to write or draw there. You can take everything away from me—my pension, my dacha, my apartment. It's all in your power, and I won't be surprised if you do it. It doesn't matter: I'll find a way to feed myself. I'll go back to working as a fitter. I still remember how. No I won't. I'll go begging with a knapsack on my back. People will give to me."

He glanced at Kirilenko and said. "But no one will give you a crumb. You'll starve to death."

Realizing that Khrushchev was not going to go along with Kirilenko, Pelshe intervened in the exchange. He said that Politburo decisions were obligatory for everyone, Father included. These memoirs might be exploited by hostile forces. Raising this point was a mistake on Pelshe's part.

"If only the Politburo would assign me a stenographer and a typist to record my dictation," said Father in a calmer tone. "Then I could work in a normal fashion. They could make two copies: one to be kept at the Central Committee, and the other for me to work with." But then, remembering something, he added in irritation: "You've installed listening devices all over the dacha. That's an infringement of the constitution, too. You haven't even overlooked the lavatory. You waste the people's money just so you can listen to me shit and fart."

It had become clear to everyone that the conversation needed to be brought to an end. Father was not going to cede anything voluntarily.

As he departed, Father repeated that as a citizen of the USSR he had the right to write his memoirs, and that they could not take that right away from him. His memoirs were intended for the party Central Committee and for the whole Soviet people. He would like them to be of benefit to the Soviet people, to our Soviet leaders, and to our Soviet state. Let the events to which he had been a witness serve as a lesson for the future.

On that note ended Father's second, but unfortunately not his last, visit to the Central Committee since his retirement.

This encounter had an unsettling effect on Father. He was continually dwelling on it, reliving the experience over and over again. Only episodically would he return to work on the memoirs. In 1968 he dictated very little, so in that regard Kirilenko had achieved the desired result.

Father was once more tormented by the same problem. What was the point of it all? On our walks, far from the microphones recording every word, he again began to repeat: "We're just wasting our time. They won't leave us alone. I know them. Now they won't dare, but as soon as I die they'll take the memoirs and destroy everything. I can see what is going on these days. Genuine history is of no use to them."

I tried to reassure him, but was unable to reassure myself. It was necessary to seek out a way of reliably preserving the materials until better times. Wherever we might store the tapes and transcripts inside the country, they could not be absolutely safe. When the professionals got down to the job, all our amateurish secrets would be exposed.

We returned to the idea of smuggling the manuscript abroad. It was then that there first occurred to us the thought that under extraordinary circumstances, such as the removal of the dictated materials or other punitive measures, we should respond by having the memoirs published. Publication would be the ultimate solution to the problem of preserving the materials. What would there be to look for if the book could simply be bought in a store? No secret repositories would prevent it from being read. There is no paper shortage in the West.

Having calmed down somewhat after the stormy conversation at the Central Committee, Father got busy with his gardening. May was approaching, and it was time to prepare for planting. At the same time I managed to find a way of sending a copy of the materials abroad.

Lyova Petrov had once introduced me to his old friend Vitaly Yevgenyevich Louis. For some reason, many people called him Viktor. Louis had spent ten years in jail on the kind of nonsensical political charge that was typical in Stalin's time. Released after the Twentieth Congress, he took a look around and decided to start a new life.

The way in which Louis's new life took shape was most unusual for a time when any contact with foreigners was equivalent almost to a great feat or at least to a dangerous expedition into the jungle. He fixed himself up with a job as the Moscow correspondent of a British newspaper, *The London Evening Standard*. This gave him a freedom to travel and make contacts that

ordinary Soviet citizens could hardly dream of. His position was strengthened even further by his marriage to an Englishwoman named Jennifer, who
was working in Moscow.

Of course, the KGB demanded certain services from Louis in exchange
for permission to work for the British. After brief negotiations a mutual
understanding was established. Soon Vitaly Yevgenyevich became an unofficial liaison between Soviet officialdom and corresponding circles abroad.
He found himself carrying out delicate assignments at an ever higher level
and began to communicate even with state leaders.

At the end of 1967, several months before Father's summons to the Central
Committee, Lyova had suggested to me: "Let's go visit a friend of mine. He's
an interesting man. His home is a place where some curious people gather.
He himself works for a British newspaper."

At that time I was light on my toes and very willing to make new acquaintances. I loved parties frequented by members of the intelligentsia, with
their talk and arguments on the most unexpected subjects. So I would have
been quite prepared to accept the suggestion, but his last words alarmed me.
I worked at a missile design bureau and was categorically forbidden to have
contact with foreigners. I shared my doubts with Lyova.

"Trifles," he assured me. "Would I really suggest to you anything of the
kind? We won't be meeting any foreigners, and our host is a loyal Soviet
person, tried and true."

Lyova himself did not just work as a journalist at the Novosti press agency.
He was also an officer in military intelligence and of no mean rank.

At the door we were met by a hospitable man in his middle years, who
took us into the house and showed it to us from top to bottom, from the
attic to the basement. It was obvious that he took great pride in his household
and his prosperity. We chatted pleasantly. The conversation turned to political
problems. I myself listened more than I spoke. It was very interesting for me.

That was how I came to be acquainted with Louis. I started to visit his
house quite frequently. I was especially attracted by Louis's extensive library,
overflowing with books that one would never find elsewhere. On his shelves
stood the works of Solzhenitsyn and Western studies of Stalin and Khrushchev. Some of the books were in Russian; others in English. This library
played no small part in the formation of my political outlook.

In the course of our talks together, Louis and I got to know each other
better. He told me about himself, his hard and poor childhood, and his
imprisonment. He spoke warmly of Nikita Sergeyevich, which in that period
meant a great deal to me. Besides his journalism, Louis was involved in various

other activities. He had traveled as a "tourist" around South Vietnam during the war there. Without any fuss he would go to Taiwan. After the Six-Day War he had made a visit to Israel. He had gone around Orthodox monasteries in Greece when that country was under the regime of the "black colonels." He had met with the Chilean Communist leader Luis Corvalan, who was being held at the time in one of Pinochet's concentration camps. His adventures were without end. But that part of his life is not the subject of my story.

What really interested me was his involvement in the semilegal publication in the West of manuscripts forbidden in our country. First he had sent to the West the book by Tarsis, whom the KGB—also on Louis's recommendation—decided to exile abroad instead of to Siberia. When I made his acquaintance, Vitaly Yevgenyevich was "handling" the book by Svetlana Alliluyeva.[21] She had almost finished preparing for publication her *Twenty Letters to a Friend,* in which she promised to describe some hidden aspects of her father's life. Svetlana had only recently fled to America, and every step that she took there resonated loudly in the corridors of power in Moscow. The book had been due to come out in October, on the eve of the celebration of the fiftieth anniversary of the Soviet state. Neither cautious diplomatic and nondiplomatic soundings nor direct appeals to Svetlana, to the publishers, and to Western governments to defer the date of publication by a few months produced any positive result. Then Vitaly Yevgenyevich proposed, on his own responsibility, as a private person, to make some cuts in the book to remove those passages that most alarmed the Kremlin and to bring the book out a few months earlier than the official launch date.

He set the following conditions. He needed to have the manuscript. The cuts were not to distort the meaning of the book and were not to be detectable by the reader. The proceeds from the publication were to belong exclusively to Louis, just as it was he who would bear the inevitable inconveniences. His conditions were accepted. Vitaly Yevgenyevich was supplied with a copy of the manuscript that was in the safekeeping of Svetlana's children.

The operation began. A publisher willing to undertake the piratical venture was found without difficulty. The book came out in summer 1967 and did to a certain extent subdue the growing hullabaloo. Louis received a substantial honorarium, as well as a subpoena to a Canadian court. His authority in the eyes of the Soviet power elite grew.

When I learned of this side of Louis's activity, I thought that he was the person who could help us smuggle Father's memoirs abroad. In London Louis had a mother-in-law: the materials could be kept in her home or deposited in a bank. And the honorarium from the publication of Khrushchev's memoirs, even if he were to get it only in the distant future, would be out of all comparison with the sums he had earned from the publication of Alliluyeva's book.

Of course, as in any business, there was some risk, and no small risk. But storing the manuscript and the tapes only at home, in our own country, was even riskier.

However, besides the technical aspect, there was also a moral aspect. It was no longer 1958, but 1988 and 1998 were still far off. It was ten years since lightning bolts had been hurled at Pasternak for handing his manuscript to an Italian publisher. Only recently Sinyavsky and Daniel had been sentenced for a similar offense.[22] Father did not approve of that judicial spectacle, but all the same. . . . More distant events also came to mind—the letter in which Fyodor Raskolnikov exposed the horrors of the Stalin regime.[23] Had that letter not been published in France, there is much that we would not have learned at that time. And what about Lenin's letters and articles? After all, they too were often published abroad before the revolution.

Nevertheless, the stereotype had a powerful effect on me. As soon as one's book is published in the West, that means one is an enemy. It's a hostile gesture.

Father was bolder than I. He took the view that the memoirs of the first secretary of the Central Committee were the testimony of a man who had devoted his whole life to the struggle for Soviet power and for a communist society. They contained the living truth, warnings, facts. They had to reach people. If they reached people in the West first, then let it be so. Eventually they would reach people here too. Of course, it would be better the other way around, but how were we to endure until those times?

We really had no choice. Either we could avail ourselves of Louis's services, or we could wait in torment for the KGB and the authorities to take serious action with regard to the memoirs. I believed—or, rather, I very much wanted to believe—Louis, although I had heard many scurrilous things about him. He was inclined toward adventures. He might let me down, and later he did let me down—true, in a matter of secondary importance.

I went to Bakovka, where Louis lived. I was in no hurry to begin the conversation. Indeed, I didn't know how to utter the first words. This conversation was a watershed dividing my "legal" from my "illegal" activity. I didn't feel good inside myself. Who could tell how it might end? With arrest, exile? I didn't want to think about the consequences. I had to act.

Chatting about trivia, Louis and I went down into his garden, through a wicket gate, and onto a nearby knoll. Here, outside the house, we both felt calmer. When we were quite alone, Vitaly Yevgenyevich himself unexpectedly raised the subject of getting the memoirs published abroad. Cautiously, as if

by the way, in general terms: "It would be good. . . . That way they'll be preserved for the world and later they'll return to Russia. . . . When the conditions are ripe. . . ." I listened in silence. The first step had been taken and not
by me. Now it was easier.

When it was my turn to speak, I said to Louis roughly the following:
"Work on the memoirs is in full swing. Or rather it is still in its beginnings.
Far from the whole text has been dictated, and even less has been transcribed and edited. We still have several years of work ahead of us. We need
not a sensation but a completed work. It makes no sense to think about
publication now. But there is another problem, a more important one for
the time being—how to keep the material safe."

"Well, you're no fool, after all. You must have more than one hiding place."
He naturally guessed what I was leading up to, but wanted me to spell it out
myself.

"I'd like to find a place that would be as safe as possible—like a Swiss
bank, for instance," I joked. "You never know how thoroughly they may
search, and there is always the danger that they'll find it."

"Yes, they'll probably find it. They know how to do it," he confirmed.

There was no point in dragging things out any further. I made up my
mind. "I wanted to ask you to keep a copy. It needs to be taken abroad, to
England perhaps. The mother of your wife Jenny is there."

"The chest of one's mother-in-law isn't the safest place," parried Louis.

"A safer place might be found," I went on. "The main problem is how to
get it out."

"No simple problem, of course, but it can be solved. Of course, certain
expenditures will be required." Vitaly Yevgenyevich was energetically pushing
the conversation in the direction of business.

"In the event of publication," I quickly responded, "the honorarium will
be very great, while for us the main thing is keeping the material safe, not
making money. We can discuss all the practical issues later. I repeat: for the
time being it isn't a question of publication, it's a question of security."

"In matters of money it's best to get things clear from the start," my interlocutor thoughtfully but firmly declared.

"That isn't the main thing. We'll agree to any arrangement you propose.
It goes without saying that such a venture requires large expenditures. On
money matters you will have the last word."

I had made it as clear as could be.

"All right, I'll do all I can. I think it will work out. And does Nikita Sergeyevich know? Has he authorized you?" he asked.

"No," I answered without hesitation, "but he and I have an agreement that I am responsible for security. There's no need to involve him in this business."

"That's your business," declared Louis. "I'll try to arrange everything. But it's better not to drag out the matter of publication. In ten years' time the world will have forgotten who Khrushchev was. New people will come onto the scene. Then publication of the memoirs won't arouse the same interest as it would now."

"We're going around in circles. I repeat once again: it's a question of safeguarding the manuscript, not of publishing it. We have agreed on that!" I was starting to get angry.

"Yes, of course." Vitaly Yevgenyevich did not insist.

When I told Father about the conversation, he agreed after a brief discussion that the intermediary should not be fully trusted. The less informed he was, the better. Let him be acquainted with me alone. Nor did I fail to mention Louis's wish to get the memoirs published. I emphasized that I had categorically rejected his proposal. At that the exchange broke off, Father making no further comment.

A few days later, I brought Louis at his dacha the reels of tape and the text edited by me in a sealed box. Vitaly Yevgenyevich took offense: "You can't do it that way. I have to see what I am taking with me."

For a second I wavered. The cardboard box, one of those used for pastries, the thick brown packing paper, the string tying it all up—they created an illusion that the contents inside were safe. Only an illusion, of course. The materials were passing into the hands of an outsider, and it made not the least difference whether they were sealed or not. I opened up the box. Louis took a look at the contents, counted the cassettes, and "sealed" the box again.

"Now everything is in order," said Louis, hiding the box away in a big cupboard carved in black wood. I did not feel my usual self. From that moment it had all begun in earnest. The talking was over.

Some time passed by. Louis went abroad, and there was no news from him. A month later he returned. "It's all in a safe place. Just don't ask how I did it. That's my secret. Of course, I didn't carry it out in a suitcase," he merrily remarked. "Now IT is safe—not at my mother-in-law's but in a safe in a bank. No one will get to it there."

The next time I was at Petrovo-Dalneye, I told Father everything in detail. He nodded in reply. From that time on, as new materials were prepared, they were spirited away to the safe abroad.

Some time later, Father suddenly returned to the subject of having the memoirs published abroad. He had evidently been pondering and weighing up the matter all this time, trying to guess what might await us in the future.

"I think," he began, "that the proposal of the intermediary is not so very stupid. The situation may take such a turn that not only you and I but even he will be unable to get to the safe. Against us there are people capable of anything. You can't even imagine what they are able to do. Talk with the intermediary. Let him come to an agreement, for the time being a conditional agreement, with some well-established publishing house that it will get the right to publish the book, but only after we give it the signal from over here."

Father fell silent. We were going along the path leading to the meadow. In front of us, Arbat was trotting along.

"We must be ready for anything," Father suddenly said. "They won't give up. Any kind of knavery can be expected. They'll either steal the material secretly or simply take it away. Apparently they won't take the risk of arresting us. It isn't in the spirit of the times, and they aren't up to it. But they'll try to take the material away."

At that time Brezhnev was extremely worried that Father might be writing something bad about him. But what irritated him even more was the fact that Father, according to the reports of the guards, had never once so much as mentioned Brezhnev's name. Without doubt, more trouble was in store for us. On another front, we had to clarify our relations with Louis, who kept returning to the issue of publication. For him it was his commercial interest in the matter that came first, and he yearned for a definite decision.

"When?" he would repeat. "In a year's time? Two years? Ten? You have to make up your mind. It won't be of any use if you wait until we're all dead."

I avoided a direct reply, but I couldn't drag it out indefinitely. At our next meeting, I told Louis of Father's decision, presenting it as my own. He was overjoyed:

"I'll find a publisher." I was stupefied but kept my silence, thinking that now was not the time for clarifying relations. "They will probably agree even to your conditions, if you don't drag it out for too long. Besides, they have no choice," continued Louis. "If they won't agree, then I'll find other publishers who will. The main thing is to deflect the blow from ourselves as best we can. We must have a plausible story to explain how the materials ended up abroad. And another thing—someone over here has to provide us with cover. All right, I'll think up the story myself, and as for cover I'll seek advice."

I don't know the details of what happened. Vitaly Yevgenyevich told me only that he had begun "from the top." By that time he had established relations of trust with Andropov himself. They had met more than once—not in Andropov's office on Dzerzhinsky Square,[24] but informally, as if by chance, at the home of one or another mutual acquaintance. During one of these conversations, Louis had brought up the subject of Father's memoirs. He had decided to take a risk and tell Andropov everything or almost everything. Andropov heard him out without interrupting, just nodding in satisfaction. Asked whether he wouldn't like to see the memoirs, he smiled and responded with a single word: "No." Henceforth we could count if not on the help of the KGB, then on its neutrality—or at least on that of some of its departments. True, the KGB's Second Directorate would do all it could to thwart us, but we had reason to think that the First Directorate was surreptitiously helping us.

On the American side, Vitaly Yevgenyevich and his "friends" were assisted by Jerrold Schecter, who represented *Time* magazine in Moscow. I won't try to guess why their choice fell on him in particular.

For some reason, the Americans decided to hold the negotiations in Copenhagen. Why Copenhagen rather than London or New York is hard to say. At the beginning of the talks, the publishers were in some doubt about the authenticity of the text presented to them. A scandal had recently blown up surrounding the publication of fakes purporting to be the diaries of Adolph Hitler. The publishers were afraid of a provocation. The question came up of how to confirm the authenticity of the material. We didn't want to write to them, judging that the danger of a mishap was too great. Then our helpers found a way out. They decided to resort to the aid of photography.

From Vienna they sent Father two hats—bright cherry plum and black with enormous brims. To confirm Father's authorship and his consent to the publication, they asked to be sent photographs of Father wearing these hats. When I brought the hats to Petrovo-Dalneye, they attracted everyone's attention by their extravagance. I explained that they were souvenirs from one of Father's foreign admirers.

Mother was astonished: "Does he really think that Father will wear such things?"

Father and I set off on a walk. When we were by ourselves, I told him what the hats were for. He laughed for a long time. He loved sharp-witted people, and the scheme appealed to him. When we got back from our walk, he joined the game. Settling himself down on the bench in front of the house, Father loudly ordered me: "Well then, bring me these hats. I want to try them on."

Mother was horrified: "Surely you don't intend to wear them?"

"And why shouldn't I?" Father egged her on.

"They're too bright," replied Mother, shrugging her shoulders.

I brought the hats. At the same time I brought my camera with me.

Father put on one of the hats and said: "Take a photo. I wonder how it'll turn out?"

And that was how he was photographed, with one of the hats on his head and the other in his hand. Soon the publishers received the snapshots. Now they could rest assured that they weren't being led around by the nose.

Preliminary agreement was reached about the possibility of publication of the memoirs by the American publishers Little, Brown and Co. Louis signed the contract with the publishing house in his own name, and it was to him that the royalties for the book were due. At that time the Soviet Union did not recognize the Convention for the Protection of Authors' Rights, so that publishers would lightheartedly sign contracts with whoever might turn up. Indeed, this contract remains binding even today. When a few years ago I visited the publishing house and tried to demand my own rights, I was politely but firmly shown the door.

The job of preparing the manuscript, and of putting it into a shape that would suit American readers, was entrusted by the publishers to a very young man, a student at Oxford University whom nobody had yet heard of by the name of Strobe Talbott. The work absorbed him totally. Strobe had no time left either to cook his meals or to clean the hostel. To his good fortune, all his daily cares were assumed by his roommate Bill—the future president of the United States, Bill Clinton.

It was not Louis's intention to hand the whole text over to the Americans. He proposed removing from the text those passages that were liable to irritate Brezhnev or other members of the Politburo too much. Mainly this concerned the extremely rare references to their own persons and a few odious facts—for instance, how the Rosenbergs[25] helped the Soviet Union master American atomic technology, some "secrets" to do with missiles, I don't remember what else. "If too big a noise is raised," Louis explained to me, "they won't be able to provide us cover." There weren't many such passages, and Father gave his consent. Later, in 1990, Louis and Schecter published in the United States, on the basis of these deleted passages, a slim third volume of Father's memoirs under the title *Khrushchev Remembers: The Glasnost Tapes.*

Talbott prepared the text on his own. We couldn't dream of making contact with him. For that reason, the American text did not closely correspond to the original. Paragraphs of the original text were put together in an arbitrary fashion. A great deal of material was omitted. Moreover, without our permission Louis and Schecter added several pages about Father's youth, thereby introducing a fair bit of confusion. For example, not knowing the name of Father's first wife, they "rechristened" her Galina rather than Yefrosinya. And as this was presented as text dictated by Father, it looked as though he had forgotten the name of his own wife.

I discovered other curiosities, too. Comparing the book to my copy of the manuscript before it was edited and printed, I found an amusing misprint in the comments about Mao Zedong. Father recalled that Stalin had a poor opinion of Mao's theoretical training and called him a *peshcherny* ("cave") Marxist. In the edited English text this had turned into *peschany* ("sand") Marxist. I laughed. When I next met Vitaly Yevgenyevich, I mentioned it to him. I was astonished when he slapped himself on the forehead and began to roar with laughter! It turned out that Talbott had asked him to explain how the term "sand Marxist" was used in Russia, as he had not encountered such a term in the literature. Louis did not know how to reply and off the bat thought up the explanation that it meant an unsteady or wavering person, someone standing on sand.

But in those years before the American publication, we knew nothing or almost nothing about what was going on in America. Father continued to dictate, Lora typed, and I edited.

Notwithstanding everything, in my heart I very much hoped that we would not have to resort to the ultimate measure of having the book published in the West.

During the summer Father was occupied with his gardening, which took up practically all his time. There was little time left over for the memoirs, and in any case Father didn't want to get down to them. For such work one needs the right mood, the desire. And now he only needed to think of the memoirs, and in his mind there would surface the image of Kirilenko's face and he would hear his words. However, his "well-wishers" were not dozing. As they had got nothing from their talk with Father, they decided to take a different tack. They began to work on his children and their families, starting with the Adzhubeis.

Aleksei Ivanovich Adzhubei, who was now in charge of a department at the magazine *Sovetskii soyuz* (Soviet union), was summoned somewhere, and it was suggested to him that he leave Moscow and go to work at a publishing house in the Far East. Aleksei Ivanovich took fright and made a big fuss. He declared that he wasn't going anywhere, and that he would immediately send a complaint to the secretary-general of the United Nations. Unexpect-edly his threat had an effect. They didn't bother him anymore. Apparently they talked with him about other matters too. In any case, from then on, he had even less contact with Father. A number of times he brought up the subject of the memoirs, on which his opinion had diametrically changed. Now he thought that Father's work on the memoirs was useless and unnec-essary. Father's deeds, he declared, speak for themselves and require no additional explanations. Father kept his silence or made neutral replies that meant nothing. Adzhubei turned to me also, proposing that I persuade Father no longer to occupy himself with the memoirs. I did not agree and said in reply that the memoirs were important both for history and for Father himself.

I too did not escape their attention. I'll tell about that in more detail.

I was working at Experimental Design Bureau No. 52 (OKB-52), an orga-nization dealing with missile technology. I liked my work. I liked my boss, too—Academician Vladimir Nikolayevich Chelomei. At that time I was in charge of a section responsible for the guidance systems of several cruise missiles and spacecraft. There was a lot to do, but I grabbed every free minute for work on Father's memoirs. I always dragged along with me the folder containing the next batch of typed sheets to edit.

Soon after Kirilenko's conversation with Father, the telephone in my office rang, and an unfamiliar voice informed me: "Sergei Nikitich, I am speaking with you from the personnel department of the Ministry of Instrument Building. We have been informed that you are making a transfer to our ministry's Control Computer Institute. Come around to us, and we'll sort out all the formalities."

I understood nothing. "It seems that you have made a mistake," I replied. "I have no intention of making any transfer."

"I don't know, I don't know," my interlocutor continued. "I have before me the transfer documents for you. Anyway, it's your affair. Make a note of my telephone number just in case." And he dictated his number.

I didn't know what to think. It was an unpleasant situation. Academician Chelomei had greatly changed his attitude toward me in recent years. On the one hand, he tried to preserve friendly relations with me. On the other hand, he wanted to make me less visible to people outside the design bureau. Once he had even told me in a fit of frankness: "Don't let them see you. Stay here; don't go visiting other organizations."

The first person whom I met after the strange telephone conversation was Chelomei's deputy for personnel Yevgeny Lukich Zhuravlev. I told him everything straight off. Suddenly he interrupted me: "And I was just going to tell you what I think of your treachery. Here I have the order for your transfer. I thought that you had fixed it all up behind our backs. I reported to Vladimir Nikolayevich, and he instructed me to talk with you."

That was a plain lie. Later I discovered that representatives of the KGB had approached Chelomei about me shortly before. They had suggested that for certain reasons I felt offended, and that it was therefore advisable to transfer me to nonsecret work. Had Chelomei replied that that was nonsense and that I was needed in the design bureau, the conversation would have remained without consequences. In any case, so I was later told by well-informed people.

But Chelomei acted otherwise. An opportunity had arisen for him to get rid of me. It was a welcome opportunity, because in his talks with Brezhnev and with Ustinov, the Central Committee secretary in charge of military industry, my name might always come up—they knew very well who I was, and where and on what I worked—and evoke displeasure.

But at that time I was aware of none of this. I told Zhuravlev that I had no plans to go anywhere. Such thoughts hadn't even crossed my mind. I immediately went up to the sixth floor to see Chelomei. Vladimir Nikolayevich heard me out attentively. He didn't pretend that he knew nothing about it.

"The whole problem is Ustinov. He doesn't like you." Chelomei was riding his favorite hobbyhorse. He hated Ustinov, and Ustinov hated him in return. "He's the one behind it all. Serbin[26] has already called me about you. He asked when you were leaving. You have no idea what a low-down person he is. He's capable of any dirty trick."

I wasn't sure to whom he was referring, Ustinov or Serbin, but I knew very well that Vladimir Nikolayevich was in the habit of describing many people with whom he had to deal in such terms, so that I didn't attach any great significance to his words.

I was at a loss and expected his help. "What on earth am I to do? I don't want any transfer."

"You know what." He drawled out his words as he thought. "Write a letter to Leonid Ilyich.[27] Apart from him, nobody will do anything. But he knows you and has always had a warm regard for you."

It was impeccable advice. Chelomei had put the matter out of his hands. If Brezhnev deigned to make a favorable response to my plea, then my future at the design bureau would have approval from above, and Chelomei would no longer need to worry. And if Brezhnev said no, that would be the end of the matter.

Vladimir Nikolayevich mentioned that he had an urgent summons to see the minister and left me alone with my thoughts. I had no desire to write to Brezhnev, especially after Father's clash with Kirilenko. It was useless, and I didn't feel like it. I decided to undertake nothing on my own initiative. Perhaps they would just forget about the whole business.

Two weeks went by. I had a call from Zhuravlev: "Well, what are you going to do? They just called me about you."

"Actually I haven't done anything."

"It won't help you to wait around. You've been given time to make up your mind. Now it's time to act. You'll have to go to that organization."

I resolved on a last attempt: "Lukich, what will you do if I just refuse and go nowhere? After all, according to the law you have no grounds for firing me."

"You're wasting time. You and I are old friends, but I must carry out orders from my superiors. And there are laws and laws. For example, perhaps the staff of the design bureau needs to be reduced. Or your position might disappear as a result of reorganization. Here's my advice: either accept the proposal or take measures. Time isn't on your side."

"Thank you for the advice. But couldn't you put me in touch with whoever is giving you orders?"

Half an hour later, Zhuravlev gave me a name and a telephone number. From the first digits, it was obvious that it was a KGB number and not a number belonging to our ministry. My talk with the unseen interlocutor was a brief one. He was able to tell me nothing new. I simply asked what I should do if the proposed organization didn't suit me. Could I fix myself up somewhere else?

I naively supposed that I might be able to transfer to the "firm" of one of the other famous chief designers in my existing field of work—Pilyugin, Kuznetsov, or Petelin. I was told that there were no alternatives. If the proposal did not suit me, there was no way that the KGB could help. I put down the receiver. I had no choice but to comply or to appeal to the very top.

That very day I was summoned to see Chelomei.

"Have you made contact with Leonid Ilyich?"

"Not yet. I've been trying to sort it out without his help. I really don't want to write to him."

"You'll get nowhere. Apart from him, nobody will do anything about it. I've already been called by Serbin twice. I stalled as well as I could, but I get the feeling that his patience will soon run out."

There was no way out. That evening I wrote a short appeal addressed to the general secretary, setting out the facts and requesting that I be left at my old place of work, where as a specialist I could be of the most use. I got hold of the telephone number of Brezhnev's aide A. M. Aleksandrov-Agentov and called him. I wasn't very well informed about the duties of Brezhnev's various aides and didn't realize that Aleksandrov dealt with international affairs.

Aleksandrov answered the telephone himself. He heard me out and suggested that I come there at a time convenient for me. We agreed to meet the next morning. I was received with the greatest of courtesy. Aleksandrov said that he would put the matter before Brezhnev in the nearest future, and that he hoped it would all sort itself out.

He closed the conversation on an encouraging note: "Call me in a couple of days."

I calmed down somewhat. I must admit that I did not expect such promptness. Evidently, I thought, Brezhnev used to have a lot to do with our work, so he knows our bureau well and me, too. Probably it will all sort itself out. I "obligingly" forgot about Father's meeting with Kirilenko. I also forgot that after 1964 Brezhnev had become quite a different person.

Two days later I called Aleksandrov. Humming and hawing, he told me that he had drawn my appeal to the attention of Leonid Ilyich, but that the latter had not commented on the substance of the matter, saying only: "This is a matter for Ustinov. Let him decide."

"Call Dmitry Fyodorovich," concluded Aleksandrov. "Here is the telephone number of his aide."

I did not call Ustinov. Such an answer on Brezhnev's part amounted to an unambiguous and dismissive refusal.

I dialed the telephone number that had been given me of the director of the organization at which I would henceforth be working, Boris Nikolayevich Naumov.

The secretary connected me immediately. In response to my confused explanations, Naumov amiably assured me that he had heard of me, knew all about the transfer, and was confident that I would find work to my liking at his organization. He suggested that I come there. Two hours later I was at my new place of work. I passed through the entrance gates and came into a small courtyard, where there stood a single five-story school building. After the vast territory of our bureau and its numerous multistoried blocks, my new workplace looked shabby.

On the second floor, a plump blonde secretary greeted me with a smile: "Sergei Nikitich? Boris Nikolayevich is waiting for you. Please go in."

In the office I was met by a big man. It was as if the whole of him was one big smile. He radiated goodwill. I began to talk, trying to keep it as brief as possible.

"Wait a minute," he interrupted me. "Tell me, if you can, in a little more detail. I've heard a lot about your work." And he spoke to the secretary through the intercom: "Lyuba, bring us tea, and don't put anyone through to me. Anyone."

Over tea we talked for about two hours. At our parting, Naumov invited me to give some thought to which field of scientific activity was most to my liking. He would make me a section head in whichever department I might choose. "I have received such an instruction," he explained.

We agreed to meet again in a couple of days. That is how I began work at the Computer Institute.

All these stormy events distracted me from helping Father with his work on the memoirs, but the summer of 1968 was unproductive for him as well. Fall came, and Father got back to his dictating. It went slowly. He had fallen out of rhythm and forgotten what he had intended to talk about. We went back to our initial plan. We would select a theme for the week, and on my next day off I would help him put the material in order.

At first Father would get angry, responding to my questions about what he had dictated over the preceding week with his usual "Don't bother me!" But gradually he got carried away again; the work picked up speed, and there was no longer any need for me to pester him.

When 1969 came, all was tranquil. It appeared that they had forgotten about us at the top. The rebuff suffered by Kirilenko had had its effect. Apparently they had decided to have nothing further to do with Father. Everything proceeded according to the set timetable: work on the memoirs, gardening, walks, photography, again memoirs, television, reading. So it went from one day to another. By spring Father was working no less intensively than he had in 1967, when the epic of the memoirs was just beginning.

But as it turned out, we had no good reason to stop worrying. Father's memoirs remained under vigilant observation. In the summer there occurred an event that seemed on the surface in no way connected to the subject of this narrative, but that for various reasons suddenly interfered with our work on the memoirs and had a big influence on our future.

My younger sister Lena had always suffered from poor health. On her return from the south as a child, she had contracted lupus, a serious and incurable disease not understood by contemporary medicine.[28] What did

Mother and Father not try! Neither appeals to the luminaries of science nor the remedies of folk medicine gave results. The disease progressed inexorably. In the second half of the 1960s, Lena's condition seriously worsened. She could no longer work and could walk only with difficulty. However, buoyed up by her courage and optimism, Lena managed to busy herself around the dacha with the bees and the flowers. In the summer her condition deteriorated further, and she was taken to hospital. The disease had entered a frightening new stage. Her arms were immobilized; she couldn't walk. The situation was very serious. Moscow's most prominent physicians—Academician Tareyev, Professor Smolensky, Professor Nasonova—had long been observing and treating my sister, but there was no improvement.

Yuliya's husband, Lyova Petrov, who had worked for several years in Canada as a correspondent for *Novosti* and had come to believe in Western medicine, suggested that we have analyses done abroad. Perhaps there had suddenly appeared there a diagnosis and cure of which we had no inkling. Lena's physicians were skeptical, but did not object. They knew that the situation was hopeless, and in such cases it was customary to give the relatives a completely free hand. The question arose of how to put the idea into practice.

An occasion presented itself. Happening to run into my friends Volodya Baraboshkin and Revaz Gamkrelidze, the mathematician and future academician, I asked their advice. After a little thought, Revaz made a proposal: "I think there is a way. A delegation of American mathematicians is at present visiting Moscow. I'll talk with them. Perhaps one of them will volunteer to arrange for the analyses to be done in some hospital in America."

I didn't want to deal with foreigners at all. I would have preferred one of our own people to volunteer for this mission. But I had no choice. A few days later Gamkrelidze hosted the American guests at his home. I too was invited. There I made the acquaintance of Dr. Jeremy Stone, president of the Federation of American Scientists. "This man can help you," said Revaz.

We talked. It turned out that Stone had been close to the late President John F. Kennedy. He spoke warmly of Father. Revaz had already told him about the problem, and he was willing not only to take the trouble to arrange the analyses but also to seek out—and, what is more, try to send to Moscow— a specialist in collagenoses, which was the scientific term for my sister's illness. Before his departure, Dr. Stone took material for analysis and promised to call soon.

A couple of weeks later, he informed us that a prominent American specialist in this field (I've forgotten his name) was currently in Europe, and that he had agreed to come to Moscow if he was given a tourist visa. The matter had to be resolved quickly, in one or two days. The American physician was near the end of his trip to Europe. From Vienna he intended to return home.

To be honest, until I got that call, I had not taken the talk of bringing a foreign physician to Moscow seriously. It was outside the range of what I, as a Soviet citizen, assumed feasible. I felt as if a jet of icy water had struck my head. My first impulse was to thank him and say no. But I remembered that this might be our last chance—and said yes.

How in my present position was I to arrange a visa? And in a couple of days? The solution came to me unexpectedly. I had to go to the top. The only person who could help was Andrei Andreyevich Gromyko.[29] I had no doubts about his decency, but he was extremely cautious and that might be a problem.

Gromyko and I lived in the same apartment block—also a circumstance of no little importance, giving me a better chance of meeting him. Mustering my courage, I called him at home that evening and asked if I could come to see him on a very important matter.

Of course, my call had been a surprise for him, and my request to meet him could hardly have been welcome, but he revealed no external sign of such feelings. Calmly and benevolently, as though we had conversed many times in the years since Father's retirement, he invited me to come round there right away. I went down to the floor where he lived. Gromyko received me in the hall of his large apartment. With him was his wife, Lidiya Dmitryevna.

I briefly set out the essence of the matter. Andrei Andreyevich knew our family well, and was informed about my sister's illness. His reaction to my request was positive: "Well of course, it's a humanitarian matter. I'll try to help. Call me tomorrow."

Lidiya Dmitryevna, who always tried to shield him from possible trouble, interjected: "Andrei, you can't decide this matter on your own. It has to be agreed."

Andrei Andreyevich refused to give way and repeated: "Call me tomorrow." He knew better how these things were done, and what needed to be agreed with whom. The audience was at an end.

The next day I called him at the Ministry of Foreign Affairs. I had not been mistaken about Gromyko's human qualities. Even before my call the matter had been resolved, and a telegram had been sent to the Soviet embassy in Vienna instructing the officials to give the American professor a visa.

The plan, however, fell through. The physician was apparently afraid of traveling to an unfamiliar city. Whatever the reason, he didn't use the visa and went straight home from Vienna. It was all reported to Gromyko. When I called again to thank him, he said that if needed he was willing to help in this matter again. As I later heard, Gromyko on his own initiative sent a telegram to the Soviet ambassador in the United States, Anatoly Dobrynin, requesting him to help in the event that he was approached about a visa for an American physician. He did much more than I had asked of him.

I called Stone in the United States and told him what had happened. He didn't lose heart. He assured me that he would find another way. "I was at your embassy, and they promised to regard the matter favorably. That's the main thing," he concluded.

At that time we didn't know about Gromyko's telegram. A few days later Stone called again. Harvey—the world's most prominent specialist in the field of collagenoses, formerly personal physician to Jawarharlal Nehru—was willing to go to the Soviet Union. He would come with his wife. His mother-in-law had died, his wife was very upset, and a change of scene would be very welcome to them.

"The matter of visas has been seen to. In your embassy they told me that visas would be provided without delay. By way of honorarium, you'll have to pay the cost of their travel and their stay in Moscow, as well as arranging their cultural program," explained Stone.

I gladly agreed. The formalities were quickly seen to, and at the end of October I met at Sheremetyevo Airport a short and rather thin Dr. Harvey and his wife. They were put up at the Hotel Natsional.

Unexpected problems arose in setting up the conference of medical specialists. Tareyev and Smolensky were disinclined to meet an American, and only with great difficulty were they persuaded to do so. After careful questioning and assessment of all the available results, both ours and the American ones, Professor Harvey arrived at the same medical prognosis as the Soviet physicians had reached. From that moment on, relations between them noticeably improved.

The American specialist cheered us up a bit. He thought that the situation was not as bad as all that. He declared that the disease could still be held in check, and that Lena might yet live to a ripe old age. Unfortunately, the illness is incurable: they don't know how to cure it in either America or Europe. Lena did not live to a ripe old age. She died three years later, in summer 1972. The professor was either mistaken or trying to comfort us, in accordance with medical ethics. There is no way of telling now.

After the first conference, additional analyses were ordered, with a new meeting to follow when the results came back. Harvey asked to send more blood samples from my sister to his laboratory in the United States, where they could make use of the most up-to-date equipment and obtain new, more precise results. However, from the expression on his face, it was obvious that he didn't expect to discover anything new. It was all clear to him.

I admit that I was rather disappointed and discouraged. Such a lot of bother, such fantastic efforts, and still no miracle had happened. The professor had only confirmed what we already knew.

The cultural program proceeded without a hitch. Our guests visited theaters, museums, the Palace of Congresses, and the Armory in the Kremlin. They went to Leningrad for two days, and through the Chancellery of the Patriarch we managed to arrange an excursion to the monastery complex at Zagorsk.[30]

The interpreter assigned to us by Intourist could not understand who we were. Lena's husband Vitya and I tried not to leave our guests on their own. Lena was especially uncomprehending when from time to time we took them off somewhere—for medical conferences. These trips evidently struck her as suspicious.

The Harveys' visit to Moscow was nearing its end. For the sake of politeness, Father invited them to the dacha. After consulting with Vitya—we didn't ask Father—we decided not to bring the interpreter along with us. We had no special reasons: we simply didn't want to drag an outsider into the house.

That day, arriving at the hotel in the morning, we told the interpreter that we would be taking the guests for the whole day, and that she was free. She took offense, but we didn't regard that as of any importance. In accordance with the planned program, we first went to Arkhangelskoye and visited the palace. We had lunch in a nearby restaurant. Only then did we tell the Harveys that Khrushchev's dacha was not far off, and that if they had no objection he would like to meet them. They gratefully accepted the invitation.

Father had put on a jacket for the occasion. We hadn't seen him dressed like that for a long time: usually he went around in a dressing gown. He greeted the guests joyfully. You could see that Harvey made a pleasant impression on him, and that it was a pleasure for him to receive him in his home. Mother invited everyone to sit at the table. Food and drink had been prepared for the guests. We had not taken this into account, so we all had to eat a second lunch.

Conversation at the table was not restricted to medical matters. Father first thanked Harvey for agreeing to come to Moscow for a consultation. Then, in accordance with tradition, we talked about the Russian winter: deep snow lay in the courtyard. As might have been expected, the conversation turned next to Soviet-American relations. Father reminisced about his visits to the United States. He spoke warmly of the country and its people. He recalled his meetings with President Eisenhower. The conversation was relaxed. To celebrate the occasion, Father even allowed himself to drink a glass of cognac with the guests in honor of friendship between our peoples.

Father had two favorite glasses. One of them was tall and rather narrow, holding 15 grams: I remember it from the time we lived in Kiev. The other glass was big and solid. He liked to boast of it. (There was also a German tea glass with a handle of which he was very proud.) Inside it was almost completely filled with glass, leaving just a few millimeters on top for the fluid. From a distance it looked as though the glass were full to overflowing. This glass had been given to Father by Jane Thompson, the wife of the American ambassador, on one of her visits to us at the dacha. She had said that Mr. Khrushchev often had to attend receptions, and that this glass would come in very handy when he had to drink a lot of toasts. Father would frequently retell this story and demonstrate the glass. He did so this time as well.

After lunch we all went out onto the porch. It was already starting to get dark. Harvey wanted to take advantage of the fading sunlight and take some snapshots to remember the occasion. He also photographed us sitting around the table.

Of course, not a word was uttered about the memoirs. Harvey did not know about them, and the very idea of mentioning them would never have entered Father's head. By the time we got back to the hotel, it was already dark. The guests were extremely pleased with their reception by the former prime minister and asked us to convey their most heartfelt gratitude.

We had no inkling of the storm clouds that were gathering over our heads.

The Harveys had enjoyed their stay in the Soviet Union. Mrs. Harvey had cheered up and was her old self again. The November 7 holiday was approaching. Right from the start, I had tried to persuade them to extend their visit by a couple of days so that they could see the parade and demonstration, and finally they did agree to postpone their departure from November 6 to November 8. Their visas would still be valid, and Aeroflot changed their tickets without a fuss.

But everyone still thought that the guests were departing on November 6.

I had told Louis that, too. To be more precise, I had mentioned in passing that an American professor had arrived, that he would be staying until November 6, and that until then I would be busy and we wouldn't be seeing each other. I mentioned it and forgot. The postponement of our guests' departure passed unnoticed. After all, I thought, to whom could that be of any interest—one day earlier, one day later? Naturally, I didn't tell Louis either. I couldn't get hold of him, and anyway what business was it of his? As it turned out, however, something special had been prepared for these two days.

I didn't manage to get hold of tickets for Red Square for the Harveys, but I told them not to worry. The windows of their hotel faced onto Gorky Street, and they would be able to see almost everything without leaving their room. I intended to bring along a portable television, on which we would be able to follow events on Red Square. (At that time far from all hotel rooms were equipped with televisions.)

We had to get to the hotel early on the 7th, before seven in the morning, because after that we would not have been allowed through without passes. I brought with me many things: besides the television, there were two samovars—our souvenirs for the Harveys and for Stone. Everyone was staying home for the holiday; Vitya was busy too. A friend of mine had offered to come along and help. At the last moment I took a book with me as well, so that if the guests were still asleep I could sit and read in the foyer.

Harvey was already waiting for us. We drank some coffee and began to look at the samovars, but at that moment the duty woman[31] came in and warned us that during the military parade we were not allowed to remain in the room: we had to leave the hotel and go out on the street. She did not explain why, but being in a holiday mood we were not particularly upset. We all set off to see the parade from the hotel porch. We stood around in the cold for quite a long time and got frozen. When the military parade was over, we were allowed to go back to our rooms. The Harveys were very pleased. They excitedly exchanged their impressions and joked. Mr. Harvey looked forward to showing his friends at home his interesting snapshots from Russia. To warm ourselves up, we ordered a bottle of Armenian cognac and some snacks to be brought to the room. We plugged in the television. It was cozy and tranquil. Soon Dr. Harvey would be seeing his patient for the last time and giving his final advice. That evening our guests planned to go to the Bolshoi Theater and the next day—back home.

Suddenly the harsh shouting of an unfamiliar voice shattered the tranquility. "Everyone stay where you are!!! We have information that you are engaged in activity harmful to the Soviet state! Don't move!!!"

Through the doors, which had been opened wide, several men flew into the room. Accompanying them was a woman, the hotel manager. The man in charge displayed his identification, showing that he worked for the KGB and that his name was Yevgeny Mikhailovich Rasshchepov. More calmly now, he repeated: "In connection with your antistate activity, we must conduct a search of your room. Show me your documents and stay in your places."

No order for the search was produced. I forgot that such a formality was required, while the Harveys didn't know what our rules were. The grimmest stories about how things were in Soviet Russia had just been confirmed for them. At that moment they probably regretted that they had agreed to take the trip.

Recovering his bearings sooner than the rest of us, Dr. Harvey politely but firmly demanded that he be allowed to make contact with the embassy of the United States. His request was resolutely denied.

They put us up against the wall and searched us. They pulled all our personal belongings out of our pockets and examined them carefully. Then they began a thorough search of the hotel room and of our guests' luggage. Coming back to myself, I inquired what it was that they were looking for. Rasshchepov did not honor me with an answer.

They turned the beds and suitcases inside out, rummaged through all the cupboards, made a careful inspection of the lavatory pan, and leafed through the book that I had brought with me. They evinced an interest in the television and wanted it dismantled. I refused to do this, and they were reluctant to do it themselves. Finally they satisfied themselves with a close examination of what they were able to see by peering through the grill in the frame. The resolve of our uninvited guests showed no sign of diminishing. The man who had felt around inside the lavatory pan spat out maliciously: "Nothing. We're late. They managed to hand it over."

The telephone rang. It could have been about the tickets for the Bolshoi Theater, or it could have been Mother, with whom the Harveys were supposed to be meeting.

"Don't move, don't pick up the receiver!" roared Rasshchepov. Nor did he go to answer the telephone himself.

At this point my friend came to life. "But isn't that what you're looking for?" He pointed to some piece of paper that was protruding from the keyhole in the door.

Rasshchepov glanced at him furiously.

My friend tried to justify himself. "Well, how should *I* know what you're looking for? I just wanted to help."

At last Rasshchepov deigned to answer my question. Pointing at Harvey, he solemnly informed me: "This man is an agent of the CIA. He is engaged in spying."

The most interesting thing is that I believed him! Not completely, but I believed him.

The search ended, naturally, without results, unless one counts the confiscation of the film from Dr. Harvey's camera, which was so precious to him. Our unexpected "visitors" now seemed to feel uncomfortable, and their tone changed sharply. Rasshchepov excused himself. He said that they were only doing their duty. Then he invited everyone to sit at the table and started to write something. As a result, there came into the world a short chit saying that we, so-and-so and so-and-so, had no complaints to make against the security organs in connection with the search that had been carried out.

My friend and I were stunned by what had happened, and at the same time happy that it had all ended "well." We nodded in agreement. Following our lead, the Americans also reluctantly agreed. Rasshchepov asked me to write out the statement again in my own hand. I automatically complied. We all signed our names. Our "guests" departed. Rasshchepov pulled me along with him into the corridor. "You understand, we did our duty. These are dangerous people," he repeated.

I nodded.

"We shall return to them the exposed film, if there is nothing forbidden on it, tomorrow. And I shall call you in a few days." His voice became firmer. "I ask you not for any reason to invite them to your home. Goodbye."

I went back into the room. My friend hurriedly said his goodbyes and left. Depressed, we sat down around the table. I don't know which of us was most upset. I tried to reassure the Harveys, waffling about how after all everyone makes mistakes. The security services must do their job, but they can make mistakes too.

Apparently my words did not sound very convincing. Nor, I think, was the way I looked very reassuring. Harvey in turn tried to reassure me: "Mr. Khrushchev, I worked for some years in Peru. I saw such things there too. Don't you worry. I understand that you wouldn't want any publicity, and I promise you that back home I'll give no information to the press."

Publicity really was something that I didn't want. I gratefully smiled. Gradually we calmed down, but Harvey didn't want to stay in the room. "I don't feel like sitting in the midst of all this mess. Let's go somewhere else. And your mother and sister. . . . It's terrible that they should have to come here. Let's meet with them in your apartment instead."

I recalled the parting words of Yevgeny Mikhailovich: "Not for any reason. . . ." I dared not defy his order, so I mumbled: "I haven't tidied up there, and Mother was planning to come here. Let's not change our plans."

He understood everything. He smiled sadly with his eyes alone.

We sat in silence waiting for Mother. Each of us thought his own thoughts. The final conversation with Mother and Lena was hurried—or so at least it seemed to me. I was preoccupied with what had just happened. We didn't talk about the "guests." Even afterward I didn't tell my relatives about their visit, as I didn't want to worry them for no good reason. They had enough troubles as it was. Both Father and Mother, and my sister too, died without ever finding out what had happened.

Before we left, Harvey reminded me that it would be a good idea for him to make yet another analysis in his laboratory. He asked me to send him a blood sample when the opportunity arose.

In the morning, Vitya and I took our guests to the airport. The film, as Rasshchepov had promised, had been returned to the Harveys exposed. Only one film—the one taken at Father's dacha—had been "spoilt." The practical and conscientious Vitya carefully packed the samovars so that they would withstand the long journey.

But at customs . . . at customs the Harveys' suitcases were turned inside out. They began to shake them up in the general hall; then the Americans were led off somewhere, probably to be searched. In the old airport at Sheremetyevo, the whole inspection procedure was clearly visible through the grill barrier that divided the hall. They returned the samovars to us, saying that they couldn't be taken out of the country without a certificate from the Ministry of Culture. It was necessary to provide confirmation that they were of no artistic value.

Harassed and worn out, the Harveys finally got through. They sighed with relief and waved goodbye to us as they set off for the plane. Their "Russian ordeal" was over. Now they could recount it all to their friends back home in graphic detail, comparing police methods in Latin America and in Russia, while we still had unfinished business and problems. We had to find a way of getting a blood sample to Harvey for analysis.

At first it all seemed simple. At the beginning of December, Yuly Vorontsov, the second man at our embassy in the United States, was flying to Washington. I was slightly acquainted with him. Vorontsov willingly agreed to fulfill my request, all the more so as he had been involved in arranging Harvey's trip to Moscow. Difficulties arose unexpectedly. On the very eve of Vorontsov's departure, his wife Faina told me in surprise and alarm: "An unheard-of thing! We were specially gathered together in the Ministry of Foreign Affairs and warned that none of us was allowed to take any packages to the States for other people. I just don't know what to do."

True, there had always been a prohibition on taking packages for third persons, but a blind eye was usually turned to the practice. Unlike Faina, I immediately understood what was behind it. Rasshchepov's agency had put up a new barrier. It was not packages from third persons in general that they had in mind, but packages from me in particular, because a blood sample, they thought, could be only a pretext. What I really wanted to smuggle out was something else entirely. I managed to persuade the Vorontsovs all the same. They took a thermos flask containing the blood, and it reached its destination.

A few days later I telephoned Harvey. He said that he had found nothing new. He sent the results of the analysis in the mail. Our paths were not to cross again. However, we were to feel the reverberations of the Harveys' visit for a long time to come.

I was no longer able to get through to the United States on the telephone. The very next day, automatic dialing no longer worked for international calls. Day after day, the Moscow telephone operator informed me in a melancholy voice that all lines to America were busy and that she did not know when any of them might become free. I guessed what the problem was and stopped trying. Of course, I never received the results of the analysis. They were presumably kept in my dossier at the KGB.

Soon the rumor was put into circulation—its echoes can be heard even today—that as an honorarium for his visit Harvey asked Father for his memoirs. Father allegedly agreed. The books published in the West (and in the East) did, it is true, contain passages pertaining to the period after the Harveys' departure, but presumably it was felt that that fact could safely be overlooked.

In certain circles there circulated for a long time a version according to which the cunning Khrushchev had deceived everyone by taking advantage of Lena's illness and the credulity of those around him to smuggle the memoirs abroad.

Without a doubt, what happened can be attributed neither to chance nor to the KGB's routine suspicion of all foreigners. The key to the puzzle is the day on which the search was carried out. At the moment that Rasshchepov and his team broke into the Harveys' room, they should, in accordance with their initial plan, have already been beyond reach, on their way home.

One is forced to conclude that the KGB was fed information "at the last minute" by someone who knew the Harveys' original date of departure but was not aware of its postponement. What was the informer's purpose? If his information was taken into consideration, then a simple answer would appear to the question of how Father's memoirs ended up abroad, an answer that could not be verified.

Such an answer was needed by everyone. It was needed both by those who really did smuggle out the materials and by those who covered up for them. It gave the KGB bosses an official pretext not to initiate an investigation or at least to close it in time. I cannot with absolute certainty name the person responsible for this adventurous undertaking.

At the end of December I met with Yevgeny Mikhailovich Rasshchepov. He again warned me that both Stone and Harvey were inveterate intelligence agents. If I noticed anything suspicious about them, then I should promptly inform him, for which purpose he gave me his telephone number.

The November events caused a lot of trouble not only for us, but also for those who were involved in inviting Harvey, and even for people who were in no way involved. Academician Gamkrelidze was not allowed to go abroad again, and Dr. Stone was not allowed back into the Soviet Union. It was only with the start of perestroika that these bans were lifted, and I read with satisfaction in the press that among the American scientists received by Mikhail Sergeyevich Gorbachev was Dr. Stone. Times had changed, and no longer was he considered "an inveterate CIA agent."

Information reached me that completely innocent people in our embassy in Washington, who had assisted in preparing the Harveys' entry documents, suffered. I think that Andrei Andreyevich Gromyko too must have found himself in a difficult position, for after all it was he who had approved the invitation to the physician. I didn't have the chance to apologize to him—and that grieves me to this day.

Acquaintances of mine who were at that time serving in the KGB were fired, although they had never heard of either Stone or Harvey. True, they were given good positions in other government departments.

I would like to offer all these people my belated apologies.

The samovars never did reach their destination. For a long time Vitya could not get the needed certificate. He was messed about with and kept running back and forth from one office to another. The next time I met Rasshchepov, I made passing mention of Vitya's odyssey to send the samovars to America. His reaction took me by surprise. He went all gray and spitefully exclaimed: "Those samovars were given to you! Why are you so keen to send them to your Americans?"

Evidently he was still sure that these were not ordinary samovars. They mustn't be allowed to reach America. I couldn't guess what it was that our guardians feared. Perhaps they suspected that tiny tapes were hidden in them.

By 1969 the memoirs had acquired a recognizable shape. They were no longer a miscellaneous collection of pieces or chapters. In our hands we had a manuscript of about 1,000 typewritten pages, edited by myself, covering the period from the beginning of the 1930s up to the death of Stalin and the arrest of Beria. In addition, there were accounts of various episodes from Father's later life and work—the Twentieth CPSU Congress, the Geneva summit, the Cuban missile crisis—and reflections on various subjects, such as relations with China, the General Staff, and military memoirs. All this was kept in a number of folders.

In summer 1969, Father again reread the edited text and made new remarks. Far from everything was to his liking, especially as regards the literary quality of the text.

I resolved to find a real writer who would take on the task of improving the literary style. It was a big job and entailed a certain risk, and far from every writer would be willing to take it on. I was friends with the famous scriptwriter Vadim Vasilyevich Trunin. I happened to mention our difficulties to him. He offered to take on the task. Although, he noted, it was an enormous job and such work was normally very well paid, he would do it for free. The solution was at hand. I gave Vadim the edited text. After reading it, he asked for the original text. I gave it him. Vadim tore my editing to pieces. He said that it would all have to be done anew. Having devoted so much time and effort to the editing, I was a little offended. But I understood that it was hard to compete with a professional. Trunin set to work. I continued to edit new material typed by Lora.

When I told Father about the arrangement I had come to with Trunin, he was rather worried: "Are you sure he isn't an agent? It's as if everything that has fallen into his hands has disappeared from the face of the earth."

I assured him that I had known Vadim a long time, and that he was an honest person, tried and true, my friend, and sympathized with us. Father was relieved, relying on me.

Let me note in passing that in those days I made no secret of our work. Thanks to the listening devices, I thought, the authorities knew about the dictating anyway, so what was the point of being conspiratorial about it? Lora and I—by that time she had moved to a new job—regularly called each other on the telephone to discuss all matters pertaining to the work.

There were practically no changes in Father's life in the new year (1970). It appeared that they had forgotten about him. Alongside his other customary activities, he continued to dictate. His health, it is true, had somewhat deteriorated: he was noticeably weaker. Vladimir Grigoryevich Bezzubik, the physician who regularly examined Father, warned us that he was developing severe sclerosis. "He could live on for many years like that," he declared. After this standard reassurance there usually followed a terrible warning. "Or he may die at any moment. Here medicine is helpless."

Father paid no attention to his state of health, and tried to ignore his ailments. When spring came, he turned to the cares of spring. He intended to install a water pipe leading from the house down to the meadow, thereby solving the problem of watering the kitchen garden. He got started on the job, as on all his undertakings, with great enthusiasm. All day long he was dragging along sections of pipe, winding flax around them, painting them, screwing them together. The work brought him joy. He joked as before: "My trade as a fitter has come in handy. You couldn't do it. What did they teach you?"

With the arrival of fine weather, the memoirs were almost completely thrown aside.

And all that time storm clouds were gathering above our heads. As has only now become known, as early as March, the 25th to be precise, Andropov submitted to the Politburo a top-secret memorandum. It was about Father's memoirs:

*N. S. Khrushchev has recently begun working more intensively on the preparation of his memoirs concerning that period of his life when he occupied top party and state positions. In the dictated memoirs he presents detailed information comprising party and state secrets concerning such crucial matters as the defense capability of the Soviet state, the development of industry, agriculture, and the economy as a whole, scientific and technological achievements, the work of the security organs, foreign policy, and relations between the CPSU and the fraternal parties of socialist and capitalist countries. He also reveals the way in which issues are discussed at closed sessions of the Politburo of the CPSU Central Committee. In view of this situation, it is absolutely essential to take prompt operational measures to control the work of N. S. Khrushchev on his memoirs and to prevent the quite likely leak of party and state secrets abroad. It would be expedient in this connection to establish secret operational surveillance over N. S. Khrushchev and his son Sergei Khrushchev. . . . At the same time, it would in our opinion be desirable again to summon N. S. Khrushchev to the CPSU Central Committee, to warn him that he is responsible for any revelation or leak of party and state secrets, and to demand that he draw from this the necessary conclusions.[32]*

In Andropov's conduct there is much that I find hard to explain. He knew from the very start about the sending of copies of the tapes to the West. And now what a turnabout! Apparently what had happened with the Harveys had frightened Andropov, and he decided to insure himself. However, those people in the KGB who were helping us received no new instructions. Instead, new old players, from another department, were introduced into the game. But about that a little later.

May 29 was as hot as any day in July. It was hard for Father to work, but the time had come to weed and hoe. Father took a chopper, went down to the kitchen garden, and busied himself there until the middle of the day. In the afternoon he came back. He didn't eat lunch. He complained that he didn't feel well: his heart hurt. He walked around the house, hoping that the pain would go away. It didn't. The physician was summoned. Vladimir Grigoryevich [Bezzubik] diagnosed the onset of a major heart attack. Father was taken without delay to the hospital on Granovsky Street.[33] There followed anxious days of waiting.

Vladimir Grigoryevich explained that Father would have to stay in the hospital for a long time, for several months, but that the critical period was the first ten days. Anything might happen. He might die at any minute. "We're doing all we can," he concluded. Stereotyped officialese as they were, his words had a calming effect on me. Making use of his rights as the chief physician of the hospital, he wrote me out a pass allowing me to visit Father every day at any time. He warned me only that Father must not be upset. Any agitation might have a pernicious influence on the course of the illness.

Every day—sometimes in the afternoon, sometimes in the evening—I visited Father and spent an hour and a half with him. Outside it was hot, but in the hospital room an air conditioner kept the air cool. It was an old building, constructed at the beginning of the 1930s for the Administration of Medical Treatment and Sanitation. It had undergone extensive reconstruction not long before.

Father lay motionless on his back. They did not allow him to read, and he got lost in his own thoughts. I tried to distract him, told him various pieces of news from home, and told him how work was going on the memoirs, what I was doing, and what Trunin was doing.

Next to the bed there stood a monitor, from which a cord led to Father. The screen displayed the moving jagged green line of the cardiogram. A nurse was constantly on duty in the room, as the patient was in critical condition. Only when I arrived did she leave the room for a short time.

Father did not, as he used to say, like empty pastimes. Apparently he regarded my visits too as such a pastime. He would pretend to get angry: "Well, why do you keep on coming here? What's the matter? Don't you have anything else to do? You're wasting your time and getting in my way. They keep me busy here all the time. First they set up the medicine drip, then it's time to give me an injection, then the doctors come to examine me, then they take my temperature. I have no time to get bored."

But it was obvious from the expression on his face that my visits pleased him. Of course, Mother also visited him, and my sisters did, too.

Time passed, and Father's condition improved. There was no more talk of death. I kept in mind Bezzubik's warning to shield Father from anything that might upset him, so that whenever I was with him I was full of optimism.

Meanwhile, there began a new stage of the hunt for the memoirs, or perhaps the hunt had never ceased since the Harveys' visit. The first warning signs had appeared in the spring, when Father was still in good health. At first I didn't take them as seriously as I should have. It was all too much like a bad movie. I realized that something was wrong at the end of April. In our section there worked an amiable, smiling young man by the name of Volodya Lisichkin. When he flew into our room on that sunny day, Volodya was looking perplexed. Pulling me off into a corner, he informed me without any preamble in a secretive whisper: "You know, you're being followed!"

I didn't believe him. And although preceding events should have taught me to be surprised at nothing, I could not get such a thing into my head. They follow spies and criminals who are in hiding from the law. But why would they want to follow me?

On account of the memoirs? Without a doubt!

Volodya went on: "An hour ago you were driving along Lenin Prospect—over that way, at the end, right?"

"Right."

"See here. I had no time, I was in a hurry. I took a taxi. The driver happened to be a talkative fellow. And he says: 'Would you like to see how they follow a car? See, that car over there is being followed by these two Volgas.' I looked and was stupefied. The numbers on the plate were yours. We were following behind: I could see it all clearly. One car chases you while the other hangs behind. Then they change places. Are they after the memoirs?" he asked with the curiosity that was characteristic of him.

Everyone at work knew that I devoted my free time to editing Father's memoirs. There was nothing provocative in Lisichkin's question. I didn't answer, but just thanked him for the warning. Had it not been for Lisichkin, it would never have entered my head to keep track of the cars that swarmed around me on the street. It would have all gone unnoticed. Knowing that I was being followed did not, it is true, change anything. There was nowhere to hide, and I had no intention of running away. I decided to make no changes in my conduct. There was no need to let my tails know that they had been found out. There was no doubt about who they were. This was Yevgeny Mikhailovich Rasshchepov in action.

My reaction to Volodya's warning was, I admit, a childish one. I failed to grasp the seriousness of the situation. Seized by curiosity, I decided to check whether I was being followed. It would be very interesting to see how they did it. Would I be able to notice it straight away? How could I distinguish my tails in the flow of traffic?

With episodes from detective movies spinning around in my head, I drive along Lenin Prospect—slowly, then still more slowly. I'm going no faster than 25 miles per hour. There it is! A gray Volga with two antennas is right behind. At my snail's pace everyone else is passing me, but the gray Volga is sticking to my rear like glue. Eventually it loses patience and passes me, too. I memorize the plate number. I pull up to the side of the road. Behind me a dark blue Volga, also with two antennas, turns leisurely into a side alley. In a minute I set off again. I keep my eye on the rearview mirror. There it is—the same dark blue Volga creeping out of the alley.

I went on treating it all as a game. I started to drive slowly and was always looking out for when "it" would appear. Usually I did spot it, although there were often several cars that I suspected.

The tails would also play tricks with their appearance. One day in May I was driving to the Moscow Technical University for a lecture. (I was lecturing there at the time.) Behind me was the suspicious Volga. I take a glance. Behind the wheel is a man. Next to him sits a girl wearing a blouse, her hair folded smoothly over her head. Is it them or not? I break away, swing left, cross the Yauza River by the Hospital Bridge, and come to a halt in the parking area by the college. I get out and wait. Nobody. Suddenly the familiar car passes by. Behind the wheel is the same girl, but now she's wearing a sweater and her hair is hanging loose. The young man sits next to her. I recognize the girl: it's them! My curiosity satisfied, I set off for the lecture.

Not wishing to upset Father, I decided not to tell him for the time being. There was nothing he could do to influence events, and it didn't seem reasonable to stop working on the memoirs. All the more so considering that such a step would show that we were afraid.

Events gathered pace. It appeared that my place of work had been searched. I noticed that a roll of Kodak colored film taken at the dacha had disappeared from the drawer of my writing desk. Nobody in our country had been able to develop the film, and it had already lain there for almost a year. I decided to pretend that I hadn't noticed anything. Quietly, without a fuss, I closed the drawer. Perhaps there was an informer among my colleagues. That was quite possible.

Suddenly instructions came from the management of the institute. We were immediately to check and report whether the typists were typing any unofficial material. They had failed to take into account the fact that in our section the instruction would pass through the hands of the section head—that is, through my hands.

With a clean conscience I reported: "They are not typing any unofficial material. I have explained the prohibition to the staff."

Our typists really weren't typing any unofficial material. One of them whom I knew well told me about some strange things that had started to happen around her. A few days before, realizing on her way to work that she had forgotten something, she had gone back to get it. By the door to her apartment some people she didn't know were pottering about. When they saw her, they hastily climbed up to the floor above and began to ring a doorbell there. I reassured her: there was nothing to be afraid of, she had imagined it.

For me, of course, there was no mystery. They wanted to check whether the memoirs were in her apartment. They were not

With each day my mood grew worse. So far they had found nothing, but they knew how to search. In our case they didn't even need any special professionalism. They would soon get to Lora—for it was she who was storing what they were looking for so stubbornly. At that time Lora happened to be ill and was in the hospital. Naturally, she wasn't doing any typing there. At the end of June I intended to visit her and while I was about it warn her about what was going on. The day that I went to visit Lora, the dark blue Volga was following me. I noticed how it came to a halt by the fence of the hospital. Its passengers remained inside. Lora and I strolled in the park that surrounded the old building. I told her about what had happened, trying not to frighten her. I concluded by pointing out the car parked behind the fence.

"But I know that car," Lora suddenly interjected. "I've seen it here before. A couple of days ago we were playing ping-pong. Right away I spotted a stranger. He stood out like a sore thumb among all the familiar faces: a tall thin man in a gray mackintosh and a broad-brimmed hat. He looked strange, like a detective in a movie. He hung around a bit and then quickly disappeared. I'd never seen types like that around here before. Then I quit playing and ran to the fence. I looked and there was the dark blue Volga with this guy in the hat and mackintosh sitting in it. He drove off immediately. Yes, it's the same car all right."

Lora had taken fright. I tried to reassure her: "There's nothing to be frightened of. They'll do it for a while and then they'll stop. We're doing nothing wrong. If they want to know who is typing the memoirs, let them find out. It's no secret. If instead of acting like idiots and playing at detectives they'd just ask me, I'd give them a straight answer. What is there to hide?"

At that we parted. I wasn't really as calm as I had made out. They were cooking something up. But what? One thing was clear: they already knew about Lora.

A few days after my visit to Lora, I had another telephone call from Yevgeny Mikhailovich Rasshchepov. He politely asked to meet with me: there were some details that needed to be clarified. I had nothing against the meeting and readily agreed. "It will be more convenient not to meet at our place," said Yevgeny Mikhailovich. He meant the KGB building on Dzerzhinsky Square. "If you don't mind, we'll wait for you at the Hotel Moskva."

He told me which floor and suite to go to. This was the first time I had gone to a meeting in such a place. I was curious and a bit frightened. I went up to the floor that he had indicated. The duty woman showed me to the right door. The suite was in no way different from other luxury suites that I had seen in this hotel—a bedroom and a room for receiving guests.

There was a second man with Rasshchepov. He introduced himself as Vladimir Vasilyevich. During the conversation he attentively followed my every movement. The questions were routine in nature. It was obvious that my answers were not of great interest to my interlocutors. I don't recall the whole exchange, but parts of it seemed to me worthy of note. "Don't you have any new information about Stone and Harvey? Aren't you in touch with Harvey?" asked Yevgeny Mikhailovich.

I had nothing to hide. "There has been no news from Stone. I think he has enough to do without bothering with me. As for Harvey, we sent him, as agreed with him in Moscow, a sample of my sister's blood for analysis. I tried to call him, but I could hardly make out anything he said—only that he'd send the results of the analysis by mail. However, I have received nothing from him. That worries us greatly. It's a matter of Lena's health."

Yevgeny Mikhailovich expressed his sympathy, but did not offer to help. "Tell us, Sergei Nikitich," his colleague suddenly asked. "Do you know a man by the name of Armitage? Hasn't he met you?"

"I did once meet a man with that name. Of course, I can't say whether it was the same man as the one in whom you are interested. Eleven years ago, when I was accompanying Father on his visit to the United States, a representative of the U.S. State Department by the name of Armitage took me to Brooklyn in New York. A butterfly collector lived there whom I very much wanted to see. Butterflies are a hobby of mine," I explained. "I haven't seen him since, nor have I heard anything about him."

I was astonished. Why should they be bringing this up? I should add that later they were to ask me about Armitage again. Why my contact with him should have been of such interest to my interlocutors I don't know. Even if he belonged to one of the secret services—and there would have been nothing out of the ordinary in that—his conversation with me was strictly within the limits of the permissible. True, in Stalin's time even such an innocent "connection" would have been quite enough to get you shot. In any case, I had not met Armitage since 1959.

"He's working in Moscow now," continued my interlocutor. "In the embassy. An inveterate spy, like Stone. Both of them are active CIA agents. If he suddenly makes contact with you, tell us immediately."

I agreed.

"Journalists have taken an interest in you, haven't they?" inquired Rasshchepov.

"No."

"If they do, tell us."

"All right."

And that was all. Only as we said goodbye was the main question put, as if in passing. "By the way, how is Nikita Sergeyevich's work on the memoirs going?" asked Yevgeny Mikhailovich. His companion fixed his glance upon me.

"Thank you, but at present he is sick, in the hospital. What work can he do there?"

At that we parted.

About two weeks went by. On July 11, 1970, a Saturday, my wife and I had been invited to visit friends. Evening was approaching when the telephone rang: "Hello, Sergei Nikitich, this is Yevgeny Mikhailovich speaking. We need to speak with you very urgently. Couldn't you meet with us?"

That day I had no time for a meeting. And anyway, we had spoken quite recently, although there had really been nothing of significance to talk about. "Yevgeny Mikhailovich, today is a day off. You caught me at a bad time: I'm about to go to a party. Let's meet next week."

"No, no," he rushed on, "it's a matter of extraordinary importance. Certain things have happened. I can't tell you on the phone. Please do come."

I gave in. "All right, I'm on my way."

"Thank you," gushed Rasshchepov. "Come straight to the entrance. You'll be met there."

Indeed, by the enormous marvelously engraved metal doors of the massive building on the Lubyanka, so familiar to all Soviet people, I found waiting for me my recent interlocutor from the Hotel Moskva. He took me through all the checkpoints to the right floor. We entered the small office of Yevgeny Mikhailovich. I had already been here after the business with the Harveys.

Rasshchepov rose from behind the table. He was cordiality itself. We exchanged greetings and sat down. My escort took the seat opposite me. All these methods were already familiar to me. Yevgeny Mikhailovich struck up an old song. We had talked about all that a few days earlier. Again about Stone, again about Armitage. How was Nikita Sergeyevich? He asked something about the memoirs.

I didn't understand. What was so urgent? What had happened? What was the matter with them? Didn't they have anything else to do? Needless to say, I didn't utter any of these thoughts out loud, but obediently answered their questions and waited to see what would come next.

"Sergei Nikitich, our boss wanted to speak with you. You don't have any objection, do you?"

"Of course not. And who is that?"

"The deputy head of the directorate."

"Of the Second Directorate, right?" I was trying to show how well-informed I was.

He made no reply. We left the office and climbed up several floors by the stairs. Yevgeny Mikhailovich knocked on a firmly closed door and propelled me forward. This office was a bit bigger, but still not large. To the right by the window stood a writing desk, while to the left along the wall was a long conference table of walnut wood, a green cloth stretched down the middle—typical Stalinist style. From behind the desk there rose a thin man in his late forties. He looked like an intellectual. "Good day. My name is Viktor Nikolayevich. Please be seated."

We sat at the long table. Now it was Yevgeny Mikhailovich in the third position. Again a mundane conversation began about life and work. I mentioned that two years previously I had been transferred against my will from the design bureau to the institute.

"And how are you getting on at the new place?" inquired the host. I felt that he knew all about me. Indeed, he had apparently played some part in arranging my transfer. By that time I had settled in at the institute. I liked the work, and I liked the people, too. I replied that I had no complaints, and that in a way I was even glad about the change. I didn't go into details. My answer pleased him. It would have been harder to reach a mutual understanding with a discontented and embittered person.

Finally, he got to the point: "Tell us, Sergei Nikitich, where are Nikita Sergeyevich's memoirs kept at present?"

I pricked up my ears. It had begun. Even earlier, pondering how to behave, I had decided not to lie. Getting entangled in lies would only make matters worse. What was more, the role of a naïve dull-witted simpleton better suited my appearance. And the main thing was that I had nothing to hide.

"Part of the memoirs is at my apartment, and part is at the dacha, in Nikita Sergeyevich's safe."

"You know," Viktor Nikolayevich lowered his voice and put a secretive expression on his face, "we have received information that agents of foreign intelligence services are plotting to steal your material. Where do you keep it?"

All became clear. I was struck by the primitive nature of the argument. "I keep it in a closed bookcase. But that, of course, is not the main point. I live in a building where members of the Politburo live. The building is carefully guarded by the KGB. There is a checkpoint by the entrance, and a sentry patrols around the building." I permitted myself a little joke. "Foreign agents would find it just as difficult to get into the building to steal my material as they would find it to get into this building of yours here."

"We-e-ell, you know, for professionals there are no such things as guards and locks. Even my safe isn't a hundred percent guaranteed." He proceeded in an official tone of voice to say that inasmuch as these memoirs were of great importance for the state a decision had been taken in the Central Committee that on the recovery of Nikita Sergeyevich he should be assigned a secretary and a typist to help him continue the work. Then in the name of the Central Committee he requested that I hand the material that I was holding over to the KGB, because—as my father also had pointed out more than once—the organs of state security were the right hand of the Central Committee. Everything that they did was done solely with the sanction, and on the instructions, of the Central Committee. In the safekeeping of the KGB, the material would be more secure, and one could be confident that it would not fall into the hands of foreign intelligence services.

"I can *officially* assure you, as a representative of an organ of the Central Committee, that all the material, preserved in its entirety according to the inventory, will be returned to your father to enable him to continue the work," concluded my interlocutor.

I feverishly racked my brains. What should I do in this situation? Then, remembering, I replied that he was placing me in a difficult position, as Nikita Sergeyevich was at present in the hospital. I could not consult with him, because the doctors had categorically forbidden me to bring up any subject that could make him agitated. The memoirs were his property, and I could not give them away without his permission.

But this was obviously what they had been counting on all along—that I wouldn't want to bother Father while he was sick, and dealing with me on my own was not so hard for them. Viktor Nikolayevich firmly declared that he understood my difficulties, but that after all it was not a matter of giving the memoirs away. It was only a matter of handing the material over for temporary safekeeping until Father had recovered.

In reply, I repeated that I did not have the right to dispose of the material myself. But if it was a decision of the Central Committee and if such importance was attached to the matter, then in any case I requested a meeting with Yuri Vladimirovich Andropov [head of the KGB]. I would like to hear about the guarantees directly from him. All the more so considering that he and I were well acquainted. I added that I had always had great respect for Andropov, that I valued him as a wise and intelligent person, and that I was therefore sure that he would not break his word.

As it turned out, this request did not take Viktor Nikolayevich by surprise. "There is no possibility of a meeting with Yuri Vladimirovich. He is traveling. He went to meet with his electors." He shrugged his shoulders.[34]

I nodded silently. They both looked at me expectantly.

Of course, I thought, the word of Viktor Nikolayevich could not be trusted, but neither could I dismiss his proposal out of hand. Suppose that I refused, and that they, against all probability, gave way. After all, I knew what these people were like. At any moment the material might be stolen by "foreign intelligence agents." And then there would be no end of trouble for me. I myself might be accused. On the other hand, the offer of help from the Central Committee was tempting. Father and I had more than once discussed that idea. And he had spoken with Kirilenko about it. But all the same, how could I take such a decision without Father's permission? To take such responsibility on myself! After all, Father had said "no" to Kirilenko. But then it had been a matter of prohibiting work on the memoirs, while now. . . . But who could provide guarantees?

The prolonged silence was broken by Yevgeny Mikhailovich. "Why don't you speak?" he sullenly asked.

"I'm pondering what I should do."

He exploded. "You have no other way out!"

Viktor Nikolayevich gave his assistant a reproachful look. I smiled. "Well, for the time being I do still have another way out," and I pointed to the door.

Viktor Nikolayevich took alarm. "Sergei Nikitich, the decision is up to you. We're simply warning you about the situation that has arisen and the possible consequences." They both looked very worried.

Viktor Nikolayevich changed the subject. He talked about the United States, where he had worked for many years and whence he had only recently returned home. He began to describe his impressions. They boiled down to the view that it was worse to live in the United States than in the Soviet Union. And the food there was less tasty: it was all frozen. I nodded automatically. My mind was occupied with a different problem.

I weighed up all the possible consequences. If I didn't hand the material over now, they wouldn't give up. They'd go on searching, and God alone knew how it would end. They wouldn't let us continue the work. Of course, they knew about Lora. We would hardly manage to find another typist. They would go to any lengths to prevent it. If I did hand the material over, they'd probably search no further. We could wait a while and then resume work. And perhaps it was time to give the signal for publication. If only I could talk with Father! But no, I'd have to decide by myself. If I handed the material over, they'd be pleased. They'd have won. And somehow or other I'd explain it all to Father. In short, after pondering it over like this, I resolved on this difficult step, and suddenly I felt easier.

"All right," I said. "I've thought it over. If foreign intelligence services are really after the material, then let it stay with you for the time being. If, as you say, it's safer that way."

At this point I realized that now we would have to go to my place to collect the folders and tapes, and that my wife was waiting for me there so that we could go out together. I'd have to explain things to her, which I didn't want to do. Naively I asked whether the transfer of the material could be postponed until the next day. My request, naturally, was categorically refused. Reference was made to the monstrous intrigues of our enemies, who were just waiting to put their evil plot into effect that very night. There was nothing to be done. I agreed. I also mentioned an unforeseen circumstance: part of the material was at the home of the typist Lora Finogenova.

I was calmly informed that that part of the material was already in the possession of my hospitable hosts. They had just gone to her home and asked her to hand it all over.

"That is dishonest," I exploded. "You didn't have the right. You should have acted only through me."

Viktor Nikolayevich tried to smooth over the awkward situation. He said that he understood my indignation, but that time did not wait. Every minute was precious. They had reliable information that foreign intelligence agents might be just about to steal the material.

This last argument finally "convinced" me. Now that I had begun to "cooperate," I added that another part of the material was undergoing literary revision by my friend, the scriptwriter Vadim Trunin. It turned out that they didn't know about Trunin! True, he and I had rarely met in recent months.

My interlocutor was worried: "And where does he live?" he asked.

Trunin used to rent apartments now in one part of the city, now in another. Recently he had again changed his address, taking up residence somewhere near the Warsaw Highway. I had only his telephone number. Yevgeny Mikhailovich made a note of it and left the office. A few minutes later he came back and told us that Trunin was not in Moscow, but would return the next week. Then they asked me how long ago I had given him the material.

"In the fall of 1969."

Viktor Nikolayevich nodded and paused for thought. Then he suggested that the building where Comrade Trunin lived be placed under guard. And as soon as he returned, I was to retrieve the material from him and hand it over to my interlocutors. I agreed.

There remained the final operation—handing over my material and obtaining a receipt for it.

"Yevgeny Mikhailovich will go with you," decided Viktor Nikolayevich.

Ten minutes later we were at my apartment block. I went up to the sixth floor and—unobtrusively, trying not to make a noise, as I didn't want to explain it all to my wife—entered the room. I opened the bookcase, and my heart tightened with bitterness as I thought of how much time and effort, how much of my own soul, had gone into those folders. It was almost more than I could bear to hand them over. But . . . I filled two big bags with folders and reels and brought them down to the car in which Yevgeny Mikhailovich was waiting for me.

When we got back to Viktor Nikolayevich's office, the material taken from Lora already lay on his table. And there among the large reels containing Father's memoirs, I noticed another, smaller one. I had quite forgotten about it. About a year previously, I had dictated from my rough notes into the tape recorder an account of the events of October 1964, to which I had by chance happened to be a witness [the removal of N. S. Khrushchev from his positions of leadership in the party and government]. And now this very tape lay on the table before Viktor Nikolayevich. How could I have forgotten! I was sure that the authorities would not react negatively to the contents of Father's memoirs. In his recounting of times past, there was not even passing reference to today's leaders. But as for my tape, that was another matter altogether. I had spoken of quite recent events and of the part played in them by all the current top leaders. Even worse, I had drawn what seemed to me the obvious conclusion: that what had happened had nothing in common with principled party policy, but was simply a "palace coup."

At that moment I naturally assumed that Father's tapes would be transcribed and carefully studied, if not at the Central Committee, then at least at the KGB. And then my tape too would not escape attention. Feverishly I racked my brains. What should I do? I could only hope for a miracle.

I made, I must admit, a hopeless attempt to take back my tape, declaring that this little reel had ended up here by mistake. "This is a record of my notes, please let me have it back," and I even stretched out my arm toward the box. But nobody had the least intention of giving anything back. What was worse was that by my false step I had inadvertently drawn attention to this reel. Thanks to my own stupidity, out of the whole mass of material it was my little tape alone that was examined. Of that I was later to become convinced.

Together the three of us sorted out the material, separating the pages of edited text from the original transcripts and reels of tape, which I had numbered in chronological sequence. We counted the total number of pages and of reels.

I was tired. "Write out the receipt, let's sign it and be done with it."

"No, no," objected Yevgeny Mikhailovich, "write it out yourself, in your own hand."

I agreed and proposed roughly the following formulation: "In order to ensure safekeeping and to prevent seizure by foreign intelligence services, the organs of state security demanded that I hand over to them the memoirs of my father Nikita Sergeyevich Khrushchev."

However, my wording did not suit Yevgeny Mikhailovich. He suggested his own instead. Here is what the final version looked like:

*On July 11, 1970, at the request of representatives of state security, for the purpose of ensuring safety and security, Sergei Nikitich Khrushchev handed over for safekeeping tape recordings and text containing memoir material of Nikita Sergeyevich Khrushchev. The materials were handed over to Viktor Nikolayevich Titov and Yevgeny Mikhailovich Rasshchepov in person. Tapes on reels 13 cm. in diameter—18 items. Tapes on reels 18 cm. in diameter—10 items. Typed material in 16 folders, in all—2,810 pages. In addition, Lora Nikiforovna Finogenova, who worked on the memoir material at my request, handed over to the KGB 6 large reels containing dictated text and 929 pages of typed material. In the fall of 1969, I handed over for literary revision part of the typed material, in 10 folders, making up about one and a half copies of the memoirs, to the writer Vadim Vasilyevich Trunin, which part on his return to Moscow will also be delivered for storage at the KGB. Apart from the persons indicated above, material has not been handed over to anyone. All enumerated material will be returned to the author upon his recovery. July 11, 1970.*

*Signatures: V. Titov, Ye. Rasshchepov, S. Khrushchev*

Titov summoned a secretary and told her to type out the receipt. While we waited for her to finish the job, we sat drinking coffee and made small talk. Viktor Nikolayevich could not conceal his satisfaction at the successful completion of the operation, but it was Yevgeny Mikhailovich who most openly rejoiced.

Speaking of the memoirs, we all agreed that they were of great historical and political interest. Viktor Nikolayevich again stressed that the KGB acted only on the instructions and full authorization of the Central Committee. Once more he brought up the point that Nikita Sergeyevich himself had always put special emphasis on the KGB being the right hand of the Central Committee.

Suddenly Viktor Nikolayevich, as if on impulse, asked whether I was acquainted with Louis. I tensed up. I had not anticipated such a turn in the conversation. I did my best to hide my internal agitation. "Yes, we meet from time to time. Vitaly Yevgenyevich is an interesting man. . . . It was Lyova Petrov who introduced us," I added. "As you probably know, he worked in military intelligence."

Viktor Nikolayevich did know that, but Lyova, who had died not long before, was no longer of interest to him. He was not going to let me off the hook. "Well, and what's your opinion of Louis?"

I resolved not to get deeply entangled in such a dangerous subject.

"It's not for me to judge him," I parried. "You know much more about Louis than I do. After all, he works for you."

"Well, so to say, " drawled Viktor Nikolayevich and said no more on the slippery matter.

Then we returned to talking about the United States. Viktor Nikolayevich again complained that the food in America was less tasty than in the Soviet Union. And in general it was uncomfortable working there—all the time being followed, living one's whole life in a state of tension.

"Never mind being followed," I egged him on. "That's not so terrible. You just have to get used to it. See how long you've had me followed, and I have come to no harm, have I?"

The faces of my interlocutors registered alarm. "No, what are you talking about? We've never had you followed. You were imagining it."

I wasn't going to argue about it. "Well, let's not aggravate the issue. Let each of us stick to his own opinion."

Time passed. The secretary was still typing out the receipt. Now I touched on a sensitive subject. Not long before our meeting, a KGB captain by the name of Nosenko, son of the former minister of the shipbuilding industry, had asked the American authorities for political asylum. There had been a big stir. I was curious to know how it could have happened and what he was doing now.

Viktor Nikolayevich frowned. He declared that Nosenko was a corrupt character who broke the law for his own personal purposes, believing that as a KGB officer he could get away with anything. And you see how low he sank—to treason.

I agreed that treason could not be justified. But breaking the law in the interests of the state—that too was a very slippery path. One didn't know where one would stop.

On this point, for some reason, my hosts were not in agreement with me. My remark hung in the air. The conversation died. Fortunately, the typed text of the receipt at last arrived. We all signed it. Then they took me back to the entrance and we parted.

I returned home for my wife, and we set out for the party. We were, of course, hopelessly late, as the visit to Viktor Nikolayevich had taken up several hours. I was unable to enjoy myself. Again and again I went over what had happened in my mind. Now they should leave us alone.

But what about Lora Finogenova? What situation was she in? I need not worry about myself, but who knows how they had behaved with her? I was very worried. And besides that, I was tormented by the main question: what to do now? Alas, there was no one with whom I could consult. Father was in the hospital: I couldn't talk about it with him. I had to decide for myself.

And so—should I give the go-ahead for publication, or should I wait a little? It was obvious that publication of the book would cause a big stir. True, Father and I had discussed all the details two years before. But was this the critical moment? And on the other hand, publication would show the whole world that the memoirs did exist, and that meant that they would not perish without a trace. It would certainly raise quite a commotion among my new "friends." They were so sure that they had won complete victory, the poor devils, and now what an embarrassment!

Then I began to wonder how they interacted with one another at the KGB. My new acquaintance Viktor Nikolayevich has me followed and "guards the material from American spies," while at the same time some other "Viktor Nikolayevich" in some other office helps us send the material to those same Americans. I pushed these thoughts aside. I had no time now for empty speculation.

In short, having agonized about it at the party and then in the middle of the night at home, I decided that this should be considered the critical moment. That meant I should not await the further development of events, but without delay have the book published in the West. There was clearly nothing more to wait for. The situation would not change for the better. Of course, I was in a delicate position: the author should really have made the decision himself, but Father would not be coming out of the hospital until the end of summer or even until fall. Time would be irreversibly lost. Who knew what Titov and Rasshchepov might think up next?

Finally I had made up my mind. The surveillance over me had not been lifted, but I no longer paid it any attention. My contacts with both Louis and Lora had long ceased to be a secret. In the morning, without calling him in advance, I set off for Louis's house at Bakovka. Along the Minsk Highway, the now familiar Volga relentlessly followed me.

There was the turn for Peredelkino. On the usually empty intersection there loomed a police officer. A second later I noticed another, hiding in the bushes. He was peering attentively at the car, trying better to make out the number on the plate; then he literally rushed after the wheels of my passing car [to get a closer look], but he made not the slightest attempt to stop me. I happily swerved onto the narrow forest track leading to Bakovka. A few more twists and turns, and there I was already approaching the familiar gates. Fortunately, Vitaly Yevgenyevich was at home. He liked to lead the life of a sybarite, and used to get up late. I had to drag him out for his morning stroll: I was determined not to utter a single word while in the house. When we came out onto the familiar hillock where we usually conducted our confidential conversations, I spotted in the distance two characteristic male figures. Without a doubt, they were observing us even here. But there was nothing to be done about it. Falling out of step, I began to tell Louis about what had happened the day before. He listened without interrupting. When I said that the time had come to publish the book in the West, his satisfaction was apparent. Naturally—he had his own interest at stake.

He decided to set off on his mission to the United States without delay. He went the very next week. When he got back about ten days later, Louis informed me that the matter had been seen to. The first volume would be coming out at the end of that year or at the beginning of the next year. Preparation of the second volume would require much more work, so it would not be appearing for several more years. But at that moment this didn't worry me. The important thing was to make a start.

The publishers had decided to announce the forthcoming publication in October, and the first extracts from the memoirs would be appearing in the magazines in November. "But rumors may leak out as early as September," Vitaly Yevgenyevich warned me.

I had no problem with the timing. Somehow or other I would manage to warn Father. I had no doubt that Father would approve of my decision about publication, for we had discussed this possibility many times and I was now acting strictly in accordance with the plan we had worked out. But as for his reaction to the fact that I had handed over the material—that, to be honest, gave my mind no rest, although from the point of view of logic I had acted correctly. Nevertheless, the feeling never left me that what I had done did not look very good from the ethical point of view. After all, Father had not given the memoirs to Kirilenko. These thoughts never left me. And, I must admit, they still torment me to this day, many years after the events.

What else was I thinking at that time? Father had gone through the revolution, the Civil War, World War II, the Lenin, Stalin, and post-Stalin periods in the development of our state. His mistakes were no longer of any significance. He had devoted the whole of his long and active life to the common cause. Now, in his retirement, he was trying through his memoirs to bring history back to life, to make sense of what he had lived through, and to warn those who came after him. All of this was needed by society, for without knowledge of the past it was impossible to see clearly into the future.

And there was a paradox. Not only did it turn out that nobody to that day had felt any need to learn from Father's experience, but the memoirs were hunted down as if they were subversive literature and turned into an illegal work that could be published only abroad, while we had been reduced virtually to the position of criminals.

Father's memoirs were a party document to the highest degree. Of that there could be no doubt. Then what was all the fuss about? At that time I was seeking a reasonable answer to that simple question, but did not find one.

I had no sooner got home after meeting with Louis than the telephone rang.

It turned out that Yuliya had been trying to get through to me ever since morning. They had called her from the KGB and told her to meet them that afternoon. I hurried over. Yuliya looked scared. I reassured her as best I could. "The main thing is to tell the truth. After all, you took no part in anything. Lyova did not let you in on these matters. They know all that," I instructed her. We talked in the public garden next to her home.

"But I still have two reels with Father's dictation," complained Yuliya. "What should I do with them? Hand them over perhaps?"

I categorically objected. That would only complicate matters and give rise to suspicions that others too were still storing the material.

"Erase them and forget about it," I ordered.

Yuliya obediently nodded.

Her meeting at the KGB went by without any problems. Her interrogators also knew that Yuliya had kept her distance from the work on the memoirs. They questioned her about Lyova, about me, about Father—and then left her alone. In general, it all ended well, and I regretted that I had been in such a panic and asked Yuliya to erase the recordings from the tapes. Now they were lost to history without a trace.

After meeting Yuliya, I went looking for Lora. As I was to discover, they had dealt with her much less politely than they had dealt with me or Yuliya. She had long been kept under surveillance. During the last few weeks some suspicious-looking characters had been wandering about her building and making inquiries of her neighbors. My visit to her in the hospital had only made her pursuers all the more certain that the surveillance was not in vain. Her neighbors told her that the secretive visitors were very interested in learning what kind of tape recorder she had, where she had got it from, and what it was that she was typing. They also tried to strike up an acquaintance with Lora herself, but got nowhere with her.

Once, while she was away on a work trip, someone had tried to break into her apartment. But the uninvited visitors ran into a problem: Lora's mother was sick and at home in the apartment. Then they used a tested expedient. Lora was summoned to the personnel department—by that time she had a job in our institute—and asked to fill in a long questionnaire. They hinted that they wanted to assign her to some interesting but top-secret work. By that means she was kept away from home for at least a few hours. Her sick mother was urgently admitted to the hospital for observation.

People had clearly been in the apartment in their absence, declared Lora. They had enough time to conduct a thorough search. True, they didn't need to be all that thorough. They must have discovered at once the typed pages of memoirs lying in the cupboard together with the tapes of Father's voice. That day, Lora told me, only two pages of used copy paper had disappeared. The "guests" were apparently trying not to leave behind obvious traces. The observant Lora, however, did not fail to notice even such a small change, as she was psychologically prepared for just such a "visit."

On the morning of July 11, Lora went home. Outside the building they were waiting for her. Three of them approached her and displayed their identifications. Not especially standing on ceremony, they sat her in the Volga parked not far from the building. Two sat on either side of her, the third next to the driver. They brought her to the Lubyanka and immediately put her under interrogation. A cursory initial interrogation, just—so far as one could judge—to get acquainted. Lora concealed nothing: "Yes, I typed Khrushchev's memoirs. Is that really forbidden? How was I breaking the law?"

Then they went back to her home with her. They carried out a thorough search—without, moreover, showing any order for the search or bringing in witnesses. They took both the tapes and the typed pages. No record of the search was compiled.[35] And they went straight back to the KGB, this time to Titov and Rasshchepov.

The interrogation was conducted by Rasshchepov. Seeing no need to restrain himself, he immediately declared that she evidently did not understand that she had been taking part in a plot against the Soviet state. She wouldn't get out of it that easily. She should, they told her, have come and reported right away that she had been asked to type anti-Soviet material! But instead she had allowed herself to be drawn into anti-Soviet activity.

That was the kind of accusations they threw at the poor woman! Fifteen years after the Twentieth Party Congress, she was accused of anti-Soviet activity merely for typing the memoirs of the former first secretary of the CPSU Central Committee! Mysterious are Thy ways, O Lord.

This "rendezvous" put Lora into a state of nervous shock, from which it took her a long time to recover.

A few days later, the last of the characters in the drama returned to Moscow—Vadim Trunin. Who informed me of his arrival? The KGB! I called him in the morning, rousing him from his bed. I didn't mention what had happened, but asked only whether I could come see him. He lived near the Warsaw Highway, in the vacated apartment of his friend, the movie director Andrei Smirnov.

I told him about the events of the last few days. In conclusion, I said that I was taking the folders, as I had promised to hand them over for safekeeping at the KGB. I had to repeat the explanations of Viktor Nikolayevich: it was a temporary measure, after Father's recovery it would all be returned, and then we would resume the interrupted work. I wasn't at all sure that I believed my own words. Vadim, too, skeptically hemmed.

"Anyway, the material is yours. If you want, go ahead and take it." He neither argued with me nor tried to dissuade me.

I collected the folders and took them to Rasshchepov. He didn't give me a separate receipt for them, pointing out that the material had already been mentioned in the last receipt. I could have objected that the number of pages had not been indicated there, but I didn't insist. After all, these were only copies. I wanted to get this whole nightmare over and done with as soon as I could. But there still remained the question of my own tape.

Yevgeny Mikhailovich excused himself, saying that he had a lot of work on his plate and that they hadn't yet listened to it. He asked me to wait a bit and promised that the tape would be returned in the nearest future.

I lost my temper. "Why do you have to drag it out? Make a copy and listen as much as you like. It isn't hard to make a copy."

This subject was clearly of interest to Rasshchepov. He asked me how easy it was to make a copy from a tape. I realized that behind his interest in my knowledge in this field there lay some ulterior purpose. I replied that one needed only two tape recorders—and plenty of time, because the copying took exactly the same time as the original recording had taken. In other words, to copy all of Father's tapes I would have needed about two hundred hours. Being under unremitting surveillance, there was no way I could have done it without being noticed. I very much hoped that that would be the conclusion drawn by Rasshchepov, although in fact I had done the copying in much less time by playing the recording at maximum speed. I also copied simultaneously onto both of the two sound tracks that were on each side of the tape. This worsened the quality of the recording and broke the text up into fragments, but given the situation as it was, it never even entered my head to bother about such "trifles."

Next Rasshchepov wanted to know whether a member of the family could have made a copy.

"Impossible," I replied categorically.

Finally, he inquired whether Nikita Sergeyevich could have made a copy.

I shrugged my shoulders. "I don't know. That's his business. I have never asked him such questions."

At that we parted.

The next day Vadim told me that as soon as the door had closed behind me a stranger had burst into the apartment, introduced himself as Vladimir

Vasilyevich, shown his identification, and hauled Vadim off to the KGB. There they had messed him about for a long time. They had asked who else had seen and read the memoirs. Where were they kept? And so on for many hours nonstop.

"And it was you who dragged me into this whole affair," grumbled Trunin good-naturedly. "They'll give you nothing back, you mark my words."

Titov and Rasshchepov brought in a great number of people in connection with the memoirs. Apparently the interrogations went on for weeks. Moreover, some of the people interrogated were quite unknown to me. For example, the movie director Andrei Smirnov got caught up in the affair because of letting his apartment to Trunin. My friend Baraboshkin was questioned about me and about the tape-recorders. There were other "participants" in this KGB operation, too, some of whom in all likelihood remain unknown to me to this day.

My sister Rada and her husband Adzhubei were not touched. Their loyalty was evidently in no doubt. In his own memoirs, Aleksei Ivanovich [Adzhubei] alluded in passing to the writing and publication of Father's memoirs. He remarked that he personally was not involved in this work and that he did not know how the memoirs came to be published. He expressed the hope that in time an answer would be found to this question.[36]

All this time Father remained in the hospital. He knew nothing of what was going on. I continued to visit him regularly. I tried to convey the impression that nothing had changed, although I no longer gave him detailed accounts of work on the memoirs. I didn't want to lie, for soon I would have to tell him about everything. Father himself asked me no questions about the manuscript. His health was on the mend.

Every so often I would call Rasshchepov about my tape. At last, in the second half of August, Yevgeny Mikhailovich told me to come in. He was ready to return the tape. Viktor Nikolayevich also wanted to speak with me.

At that time Father was preparing to leave the hospital. The day for his checkout had already been set—a week and a half or two weeks later. He refused to go to a sanatorium to recuperate. He said that he would feel better at the dacha. I had still not told him what had happened. I decided that I would tell him after his return to Petrovo-Dalneye. I wanted to put off the difficult and unpleasant conversation.

So here I was once more at the KGB building, now so familiar to me. And here were Yevgeny Mikhailovich and I again climbing the stairs to Titov's office. Viktor Nikolayevich greeted me amiably, took out of his safe a little gray plastic box with my reel inside, but did not give it me. He said that they had listened to my recording, and that they had found it very interesting and vivid. Evidently it had been dictated in the immediate aftermath of the events described. Was that not so?

I nodded. Viktor Nikolayevich suggested that the feelings I had at that time accounted for my very harsh, and not in all respects correct, assessment. Probably, now that some time had passed, I had a more objective view of those events.

I said nothing and shrugged my shoulders.

Viktor Nikolayevich smiled. "We shall return to you the tape, but let us erase the recording—right here in the office, in your presence."

Naturally, there was no point in objecting. And anyway, I could restore it word for word.

As if he had read my thoughts, Titov continued: "You could, of course, restore the recording, but we are counting on your good sense."

A man came into the office. It was Vladimir Vasilyevich, whom I had already met. In his hands was some sort of unwieldy gray apparatus, clearly a homemade product. The cord was plugged into the socket. The apparatus hummed. Vladimir Vasilyevich ran it over the reel and held the reel out to me. The operation was complete. By destroying the memory of the events, the "surgeons" obviously intended that it should be as though those events had never occurred. Something like a tape-recorder lobotomy. In any case, I felt very sorry about the erasure of the recording. It was as if a part of myself had been extinguished. Of course, I would restore it, but the new recording would inevitably not be exactly identical to the old one.

"Well, there you are then." Viktor Nikolayevich smiled again. "Take your tape. As you see, we always keep our promises to the letter."

He was clearly pleased with the spectacle. But I was in no hurry to leave this "hospitable" office. "Thank you for the tape," I began. "But there is another of your promises that you have forgotten."

Viktor Nikolayevich raised puzzled eyes.

"You promised me—and it is recorded on the receipt—that as soon as Nikita Sergeyevich came out of the hospital all material that you have taken from me would be returned. He is being checked out in a few days' time and will be moving back to the dacha. I would like both the tapes and the typed pages to be lying there in their proper places when he arrives. As regards the secretary and typist that you promised him," I finished, "you will have to talk with Father about them."

Viktor Nikolayevich looked at me with a big smile and declared that he had no material in his possession. I, of course, was expecting a refusal and was ready for an argument, but this was a turn of events I had not anticipated. I was at a loss.

"How can that be? After all, both Yevgeny Mikhailovich and you yourself repeatedly told me that you were holding the material in your office, in your personal safe, that you would hand it over to nobody, as you were afraid for its security even within these walls." I nodded at the safe in the corner. "So where is it then?"

They informed me that the material had been handed over to the Central Committee. Shrugging my shoulders, I pointed out that it had been in the name of the Central Committee that the promise had been made to me. Viktor Nikolayevich readily confirmed his promise, but immediately referred to the order to hand the material over to the Central Committee, which they were obliged to carry out. My confusion clearly amused him.

Then I repeated my request to meet with Comrade Andropov. They replied that this was impossible, as Andropov was away on an official trip, after which he would be going to the south for his vacation. It would be quite a while before he was back in Moscow.

There was nothing more to say. I left.

I found myself in an extremely invidious position. Father was coming out of the hospital, and the material had disappeared. Was it really at the Central Committee, or had it simply been destroyed? And to whom at the Central Committee was I to turn?

Now I understood that I had been absolutely right to give the signal for publication. Being in a combative mood, I went through in my mind all the ways in which I might rescue the memoirs from the depths of the Central Committee. However, I didn't have to go to any trouble. The Central Committee officials found me themselves.

The next day after my talk with Titov, the telephone rang at work. The person asking for me was an official of the Party Control Committee at the CPSU Central Committee. He gave me his name, but I've forgotten it. He asked me to come the next day to the Party Control Committee and told me the number of the room. "A pass will be made out for you. Don't forget your party card," he reminded me severely.

I was not told the reason for the invitation and didn't ask. All was clear without asking. The way that I had demanded my rights in Viktor Nikolayevich's office showed that I had not yet "matured," and it would do no harm to press me a little harder. When I turned up at the Party Control

Committee, I was received by the official who had called the day before. He was quite an amiable man. He said that he was acquainted with the story of the memoirs and asked me to write down a detailed account of everything that had happened. I wrote for a long time, trying to leave nothing out.

He attentively read through the pages that I had written and went out without a word. I did not have long to wait. A few minutes later, I was invited in to see Melnikov, a deputy chairman of the Party Control Committee. In the half-dark office behind an ordinary writing table, there sat a tall and rather angular man with crude facial features. Before his appointment to the Party Control Committee, he had been the second secretary of the Central Committee of the Communist Party of Uzbekistan.

Melnikov began to question me about the work on the memoirs. How had the work been organized? What were the accompanying circumstances? It was obvious that apart from anything else he was simply curious. He wanted to find out details of Father's life that were hidden from outsiders.

I recounted everything that Titov already knew, but in addition described in detail the surveillance to which I was subjected. I especially stressed the point that Titov had taken the memoirs into safekeeping in the name of the Central Committee, and that it had been in the name of the Central Committee that he had promised to return them. Now he was declaring that they were not in his possession, and that where they were he did not know. I naively supposed that all these abuses would disturb my interlocutor, that an investigation would be initiated—and that justice would triumph.

However, he told me that at the Central Committee nothing had been promised to me. The material really was at the Central Committee, but it was not at Melnikov's disposition. At present there could be no question of returning it. The Central Committee would take a decision on the matter, which would be communicated to us in due course. Thus ended our meeting.

At the end of August, Father came out of the hospital and went home to the dacha. He was weak and pale. He did not go walking much. Mostly he sat on the terrace or dozed in his armchair. The days followed one another, and his strength gradually returned to him. He began to venture down the slope to his beloved forest edge, to take a look at the kitchen garden, and to enjoy the view over the river.

We did not yet speak of the memoirs. Perhaps Father guessed that something had happened: I was trying too hard to avoid the subject. I tried to distract his attention with light news from Moscow.

The refusal to return the material, while not totally unexpected, depressed me greatly. It got harder and harder to hide from Father the unpleasant truth,

He could have found something out from someone else. Or he could have simply asked me directly: "How are things going with the memoirs?" On the other hand, he was still weak. If I told Father how things stood, he would get agitated, and his heart wasn't yet very strong. But sooner or later I would have to tell him.

Bit by bit Father returned to his old self. One day, as we were leisurely strolling toward the edge of the forest, I made up my mind to tell him everything. I talked about the KGB and the Party Control Committee and mentioned also that the book was soon to be published. He approved my decision to give permission for the book to be published. The unpardonable way in which they had behaved toward him gave him, too, a free hand to do as he thought best.

"You can't keep the truth hidden. If for the time being the book isn't published here, let it be so. . . . It's bad that it has to be abroad, but what can we do about it? Sooner or later the book will come out here as well," he lamented.

But for handing the material over to Titov he gave me a good dressing-down. Until his dying day Father never forgave me for this fault. He declared that I had no right to hand it over under any pretext. It was a matter of principle. They were violating the constitution. And I dared take it upon myself to dispose of what I had no right to dispose of. He told me to contact Titov immediately, to register in his name an unequivocal protest, and to demand everything back. There was no point in going to the Central Committee. I would get nowhere with them. After all, they themselves, as they said, had promised me nothing. I must demand the material from those who gave me the receipt for it. Otherwise he threatened to create a scandal.

Father was very agitated. He took out his Validol—now he always kept it with him—and put a tablet in his mouth. I was afraid that another heart attack might be on its way, but this time he was spared.

"Of course," he said, calming down a little, "it's a good thing that there are backup tapes. Our work hasn't been in vain. But we can't put up with this kind of behavior. We can't let them get away with it." Father was starting to get agitated again. Suddenly he broke off: "Let's end this discussion."

We walked on a bit further, talked about something or other, but did not return to the subject of the memoirs.

As Father had demanded, I tried to make contact with Titov. Of course, Titov knew about my visit to the Party Control Committee and realized why I was looking for him. Naturally, he became inaccessible.

"Viktor Nikolayevich has gone out. . . . Viktor Nikolayevich will call you back himself. . . . Viktor Nikolayevich is off on a trip. . . ." That is what I heard whenever I called. There would, it seemed, be no end to it. But I understood the situation very well and was extremely persistent, calling several times daily. At last—what a miracle!—Viktor Nikolayevich just happened to be there when I called. We agreed on a meeting. Evidently he realized that I would not give up.

When I met Titov, I made an official declaration in which I included everything that Father had told me to convey. Viktor Nikolayevich merely reiterated that he had nothing and that the KGB was subordinate to the Central Committee, on whose demand the material had been transferred. The KGB was not in possession of it and could not dispose of it. True, he did express regret that the Central Committee had not fulfilled the obligations that they had taken on themselves, and he offered his personal apologies.

When I recounted the exchange to Father, he had such a fit of temper that he spat. "Them! . . . You can't get anywhere with them nowadays! You won't get anything out of them!!! And don't go there any more," he growled.

Life was to decree otherwise. My acquaintance with Yevgeny Mikhailovich and his "team" dragged on for many years. Their interest in me would seem to die out altogether, only to flare up once more with renewed strength. At the beginning of October, I had yet another meeting with Yevgeny Mikhailovich and Vladimir Vasilyevich. In the West an announcement had been made of the forthcoming publication by the publishers Little, Brown & Co. of Father's memoirs under the title *Khrushchev Remembers*. It was stated that the publishers had at their disposal a typewritten text and tapes with recordings of Father's voice. Experts had confirmed the authenticity of the tapes. The title of the book had been agreed in advance with us. It was modest, unpretentious, and dignified.

This time Rasshchepov looked despondent. That was understandable. After his "brilliant" operation in July, suddenly such a denouement in October!

We met in the familiar suite of the Hotel Moskva. The conversation was brief. It wasn't hard to guess the one thing that interested them. How had the memoirs ended up in America?

My reply was simple: "So long as we had the material, there was no question of publication. Now it is you, not me, who must explain how they ended up in America."

And, broadly understood, my words were not dishonest. At the conclusion of the conversation, I again demanded that the material be returned to its owner. Under the circumstances, its retention had lost all point, as it would soon be published anyway. Rasshchepov maliciously replied that under the circumstances he did not advise me even to raise this issue.

But even with that our trials were not at an end. Father, as we were to discover, faced a new meeting with his former colleagues. The book had yet to come out. Nobody had yet seen it with his own eyes, let alone read it. And nonetheless, Father, still not fully recovered from his illness, was rudely summoned to the Central Committee. Nobody was interested in what was written in the book, in what it was about. Nor, so far as I am aware, was anybody interested in the contents of the material taken from me. And all the same, on November 10, straight after the October holidays, Father had a call from Pelshe's secretariat. He was ordered to come right away to the Party Control Committee.

Brezhnev was constantly gaining in strength. His days as a wolf cub were behind him now. He increasingly felt that he could act with impunity. This was not yet, of course, the end of the 1970s, but nor was it any longer the liberal 1960s, when nobody would have dared act in such a fashion. Father replied that he couldn't come at once, as he had no means of transportation on hand.

"A car has already been sent out to pick you up," came the answer.

At the Party Control Committee, Father found waiting for him Pelshe, Melnikov, and—as I realized when he told me about it—the same official who had dealt with me there two months before. In the very first minutes the prepared scenario for the conversation was blown to smithereens.

Father had already been angered by the outrageous way in which he had been treated—by the confiscation of the memoirs, by the crude deceit, by Titov's unhelpful reply. Pelshe's summons had been the straw that broke the camel's back. It was hard for Father to restrain himself. The state of his health did not permit any acrimonious encounter, but it had not been Father who started it. And now all the good advice of Dr. Bezzubik—not to get agitated, to stay calm, not to take things too much to heart—flew out the window. Father went into battle, as always, without a sideways glance.

In short, the "educational" conversation on which those who had invited Father had evidently counted did not take place. I certainly wouldn't have wanted to be in the shoes of the "educators" that day. No record had been taken of Father's first meeting with Kirilenko. But this time everything was officially set up, like an interrogation. The stenographic record prepared at the Party Control Committee has now become available. It has been published. Nevertheless, I shall leave my own record, made immediately afterward on the basis of Father's account, as it stands, without any changes.[37]

Father was presented with the text of a prepared declaration, saying that he, Khrushchev, had never written any memoirs, nor had he handed any memoirs over to anyone, and that the forthcoming book was a fake. Father immediately rejected the draft out of hand, declaring that he would not put his signature to such a document. It was a lie, and it was a sin to lie, especially at his time of life. It was time to think of a better world. And it wouldn't hurt them either to give some thought to their souls. He *had* written memoirs. Everyone had such a right. His memoirs were intended for the party and for the people. In Father's opinion, they would help people to understand the era in which he had lived and worked. His memoirs were a contribution to history. And at this point he assured his critics that he would continue working on his memoirs. Then he said that he was willing to sign a document saying that work on his memoirs was not yet complete and that they were therefore not yet in a form suitable for publication.

As concerned the publication of the book abroad, Father was willing to write that he himself had not handed over material for publication abroad. This compromise suited Pelshe. A new text was quickly drafted, typed out, and signed by Father.

Here there is a discrepancy—the only serious one—between the official stenographic record and my own. From the official record it appears that there was no text prepared in advance, only the declaration dictated by Father. I believe Father, and not Pelshe. Prudent officials could not have left such an important matter to Father's spontaneous decision. It would have been easy enough to dictate an amended record. The Kremlin fakirs had performed just such a conjuring trick with Father once before. In October 1964, he had signed a prepared declaration in which he asked to resign from all his posts, but in official documents it was stated that he himself had dictated the declaration. But that doesn't affect the essence of the matter.

The text signed by Father was published in *Pravda* the very next day. I cite it in full:

*Declaration*

*As is evident from information appearing in the press of the United States of America and of some other capitalist countries, the so-called memoirs of N. S. Khrushchev are currently being prepared for publication. They are a fabrication, and I am indignant at this fabrication. I have never handed any memoirs, or any material pertaining to memoirs, over to anyone—neither to* Time *nor to any other foreign publishing houses. Nor have I handed any such material over to Soviet publishing houses. I accordingly declare that all this is a fabrication. Such lies of the venal bourgeois press have already been exposed more than once.*

*N. Khrushchev*
*November 10, 1970*

The word "fabrication" grated on my ears, but Father did not object to its insertion in the text. Otherwise he would have had to go too far and to say too much, thereby placing in danger others who had put their trust in him.

However, the meeting did not come to an end with the signing of the declaration. Father's anger had burst into the open, and he decided to say everything he had on his mind. Father reminded Pelshe of the confiscation of the memoirs. Pelshe did not have a reply ready and said that he knew nothing about it. Melnikov did not come to the aid of his boss. By that time Father had gone on to another and even more contentious subject.

Six years, said Father, had passed since his retirement. For six years they had been working without him. At that time they had hung the blame for each and every problem on him. They had said: "We'll get rid of Khrushchev, and everything will go without a hitch." Father had warned his former colleagues that they had to reform the way in which they managed the economy, or else nothing worthwhile would be achieved. But they had re-established the ministries and destroyed what little progress had already been made.[38]

Agriculture was in a state of collapse. In June 1962, under Father, prices for butter and meat had been raised with a view to stimulating higher output, but that had not happened, and there was nothing in the stores. In 1963, again during his term in office, grain had been bought in America, but as an exceptional measure. But his successors had made this into a regular practice. Shame! For the Soviet Union to be buying grain! That meant, continued Father, that it hadn't been he who was to blame, but the faulty system of economic management. They had grown complacent and didn't want to do anything. They were sitting in a quiet bog when it was necessary to act and seek out solutions.

And what about international relations? Khrushchev, they had said, has got us into a quarrel with China. Six years had gone by, and our relations with China had only deteriorated. Now everyone could see that more complex processes were at work. Relations would normalize with time, but for that new people would have to come, people able to look at the problem with new eyes and throw off accumulated dross. As Father later recounted, Pelshe had got worked up and wanted to make objections, but Father had not let him interrupt and had continued to lay into his former colleagues.

In Egypt, he said, everything had been allowed to go to pieces. (He used a stronger expression.) How much money, how much effort had been invested in that country! And they had let an ally of ours lose a war, even though it had been fully prepared for war, with an up-to-date, excellently equipped army.

Father touched also on a number of other matters of foreign and domestic policy. At last he finished his accusatory speech and fell silent.

The whole angry tirade used up a lot of Father's strength. The meeting had not been easy for him. He had had to be evasive and prevaricate, which went against his nature. But that he could bear. He did not fear for himself, but behind him stood not only I but all those who had taken risks, albeit not without selfish motives, to smuggle out what he had dictated.

What had made the conversation real torture for Father was the fact that his untalented successors were undoing everything that he had begun, and that there was nothing he could do to put things right. By the end of the duel, he felt himself enfeebled once and for all. He said that he had done what they demanded and signed the declaration. And now he wanted to go home.

Arvid Pelshe hurried to report his "victory" to his Politburo colleagues. I cannot resist reproducing his report word for word. It speaks for itself.

*To the Central Committee of the CPSU*

*On the instructions of the Central Committee of the CPSU, in connection with the forthcoming publication in the USA and a number of other Western countries of "the memoirs of N. S. Khrushchev," a conversation with Comrade N. S. Khrushchev took place on November 10 of this year at the Party Control Committee.*

*During this conversation, Comrade Khrushchev conducted himself in an insincere and incorrect fashion and avoided discussion of the issue of his incorrect actions. He asserted that he had not handed over his memoir material to anyone for publication. As a result of the conversation, he agreed to make a declaration for the press.*

*We attach the stenographic record of the conversation with Comrade Khrushchev and the declaration signed by him.*

*A. Pelshe*
*November 13, 1970*

This was the last meeting that Father ever had with the party leadership. He gave voice to everything that had grieved his heart in the years since his retirement, to all the thoughts that tormented him in his solitude.

Mother called me the same day to tell me that Father had been summoned to the Party Control Committee and questioned about the memoirs.

I came to the dacha right away. Father was sitting at the edge of the forest that surrounded the dacha. I sat down next to him. We sat in silence for a long time. Then he told me all about it, getting more and more agitated as he did so. He finished, paused a moment, and suddenly added, apparently in response to his own thoughts: "Now I am finally convinced that the decision to have the book published was right. What they have taken away they will destroy. They fear the truth. The decision was right."

Again we fell silent, each in his fashion thinking about one and the same thing. In the evening I left, as it was a working day. At home, while my memory was still fresh, I made a written record of Father's account.

Father's visit to the Party Control Committee took its toll on his health. Thanks to Pelshe, Father had to go into the hospital again. Vladimir Grigoryevich Bezzubik declared that Father had had a minor heart attack. He tried to reassure us. "It's nothing like what he had in the summer. There's no comparison. All the same, the cat's claws have scratched him."

An apt metaphor, but too weak, I think.

Father was a wise man. There was a great deal that he foresaw. At the very start of our work, he had instructed me that in the event of his illness and hospitalization I was to remove everything connected with the dictation and keep it in a reliable place. Just in case.

Once more I came to visit Father every day. As usual, he grumbled at me. And, just as before, the endless green line moved across the screen. Father had greatly aged and not only on the outside. The shower of blows that had recently descended on him had done their work. He recounted the scandal at the Party Control Committee to everyone—to the doctors, to the nurses, to visitors. He didn't expect any reaction: he just needed to speak out and relieve the tension.

Shortly before the new year of 1971, the last new year of Father's life, he was discharged from the hospital. He celebrated the holiday at the dacha. On the surface, life returned to its customary routine: the same walks, the same meetings with people staying at the local vacation center, who had resumed their excursions to Petrovo-Dalneye, familiar questions and familiar answers.

But some new themes had now made their appearance. Many people asked him about the memoirs, having learned of their existence by listening to various foreign radio stations. Father would reply that how the memoirs had ended up abroad was none of his business. He had dictated his memoirs and saw no reason to hide the fact. He had revealed no secrets. There was nothing there of which it was forbidden to write.

It was, naturally, not only Muscovites who took an interest in the memoirs. Their publication gave rise to a stream of correspondence from abroad. People wrote to Father from all over the world. But these letters never reached Father. The stream of correspondence arriving at the dacha dried up almost completely. Why? The authorities reacted to the memoirs in their own spirit. A proposal made its way from the KGB to the Central Committee: "On restricting the delivery of foreign correspondence to N. S. Khrushchev."

3502-A

Special Folder<br>Top Secret

December 25, 1970

*Recently a large quantity of correspondence of various kinds from private persons in the capitalist countries has been sent to N. S. Khrushchev.*

*The greater part of the correspondence consists of postcards with New Year and Christmas greetings. On some of them there are expressions of a religious character, comparing N. S. Khrushchev with biblical "heroes."*

*The authors of letters appeal to N. S. Khrushchev as "a fighter for peace and an opponent of anti-Semitism," express sympathy in connection with his illness, in some cases approvingly mention the appearance in the West of his "memoirs" or ask his opinion of certain former Western statesmen. There are also magazines containing photographs of N. S. Khrushchev and articles mentioning his name.*

*Taking into account the tendentious character of such correspondence and the possibility that it may be inspired by foreign subversive centers, we suggest that it would be expedient to restrict its delivery to N. S. Khrushchev.*

*We request authorization.*

Chairman of the KGB ANDROPOV

A note in the margin, dated December 31, 1970, confirms that "Comrade V. A. Kryuchkov (KGB) has been notified of authorization by secretaries of the Central Committee." The secretaries in question were Mikhail Suslov and I. Kapitonov.

They were panic-stricken. They were afraid of Father. A helpless sick old man, isolated from the outside world, and nonetheless they were afraid of him.

The events of the last few months had noticeably undermined Father's moral and physical powers. This time his recovery progressed very slowly. He quickly got tired. He was no longer able to walk to the edge of the forest without taking a rest. On the way he would sit down for a while on the little folding stool that he always took along with him. Arbat was no longer around. He had died at a very advanced age, and there was no one to drag along the stool. Father got himself a new dog, a mongrel. He called her Squirrel because of her reddish-brown fur and lively temperament. She would run after him everywhere, devotedly gaze into his eyes, and lick his hands. She obviously lacked Arbat's tact and good training. We suggested that he get a purebred dog.

Father refused. "A mongrel is cleverer, and more devoted, and less pretentious. What would I want with a blockhead with a pedigree?"

Although the conversation at the Central Committee had taken its toll, Father was not broken. As early as February he said to me: "Let's continue with the work. Make all the arrangements."

But now Father found it difficult to dictate. He had to force himself into the necessary frame of mind. No longer did he live by the work. Rather, he was fulfilling obligations that he had laid on himself. Through his work he proved, both to himself and to his persecutors, that he had not resigned himself and that he had no intention of surrendering. Thus by sheer force of will he dictated three incomplete reels. He spoke of his meetings with airplane and missile designers, with scientists, in particular with Pyotr Kapitsa, and with cultural figures. He also spoke about excessive military expenditures and about how in his opinion the vicious circle of the arms race could be broken.

In January Louis brought me a long-awaited copy of the memoirs—a black volume with a title in red and yellow lettering and a photograph of Father smiling on the dust cover. I immediately rushed over to Petrovo-Dalneye to show the book to Father. He leafed through it, looked at the photograph, and handed it back to me. He did not read English. For him the book remained alien. If only it had been a Soviet book.

Also in January, I was yet again summoned to the KGB. Yevgeny Mikhailovich told me that I had been asked to familiarize myself with a translation of the English-language edition of Father's memoirs and to provide a report about the extent to which it corresponded to the original.

I was astonished: "But I don't have the memoirs. Everything is with you. The easiest thing is to compare the two texts. Any discrepancies will be immediately obvious."

He reminded me that it had already been explained to me more than once that the memoirs were not at the KGB. They had been handed over to the Central Committee. The KGB had nothing to compare the translation with. That was why they had turned to me, as a person well acquainted with the text.

It was, of course, hard to believe that they were unable to get hold of the material. I could not guess what they were after in asking me to provide a report. Nevertheless, I willingly agreed. I had a decent reading knowledge of English, but a professional translation enabled me to make a more accurate assessment of the authenticity of the text. I was entrusted to the care of

Vladimir Vasilyevich and assigned a room, where I got down to work on the typewritten translation of the book.

It's a long time since I last read the book, but I clearly recall my feeling of annoyance at the short commentaries by the well-known Sovietologist Edward Crankshaw that introduced each chapter. The rest of the book was all right. The text did not differ in meaning from what Father had dictated, nor was it much different from the stories that we had heard Father tell so many times.

In my report I noted that the material had been greatly reduced in length. In particular, almost everything relating to the war, apart from a few isolated episodes, had been omitted. Some other facts relating to various periods of our history had also been omitted. I gave my report to Vladimir Vasilyevich. He thanked me, and we parted. As we had expected, publication of the book dissipated the tension. Nobody bothered Father about the memoirs again.

That same year (1971), the Progress publishing house issued a reverse translation from English into Russian. This publication, marked "For Service Use," was for the benefit of a restricted circle of readers. Thus although greatly reduced in length and translated from the English, this second publication was at least in Russian.

Khrushchev's memoirs have now been published in fifteen more languages. They have been read in practically all the countries of the world. On my bookshelf at home, the English edition was successively joined by a German, a French, an Italian, a Japanese, and even a Turkish edition.

Of course, Father need not have written memoirs. He had other favorite pastimes: growing vegetables, walking, photography. Had it not been for the memoirs, his lifestyle would have suited the authorities very well and would in all likelihood have enabled him to live several years longer. But he chose another path—in the certainty that our people needed his words and that, whatever happened, those words would eventually reach the reading public. And the resonance that the publication of his memoirs evoked in the world confirmed that Father had been right.

On Sunday, September 5, 1971, Father and Mother went to visit Rada and her husband at their dacha. It was a long and arduous journey, about 40 miles altogether, but it made a welcome change for Father, giving him the chance to meet new people and absorb new impressions. Unfortunately, the trip did not work out as planned. Father felt unwell. His heart ached. Mother gave him a tablet, and he went to sit by himself on the little stool, which he had brought along with him. They set off for home earlier than usual. Father took some more medicine, and although it didn't help, at least he wasn't getting any worse. They decided that there was no need to bother the doctor on a Sunday.

The night brought Father no relief. The darkness seemed to press down on his chest and he had difficulty breathing. He called Mother. The door to her room was never closed, just in case. "Sit a while with me. I feel a weight pressing down on me. I don't think I'll survive the fall," said Father in the voice of a frightened child.

In the morning Bezzubik arrived. He examined Father and listened to his heart, found no foreboding signs, but advised Father to go into the hospital all the same. Father didn't want to go, and Vladimir Grigoryevich didn't insist. But in the afternoon Father suffered a new bout of pain, and Bezzubik became implacable. At this point Father gave in, asking only to be taken in the Volga. He hated ambulances: he used to say that inside them he already felt almost like a corpse. Vladimir Grigoryevich gave his consent. They waited for the car.

Mother called me at work. She told me that Father was being taken to the hospital. I threw all my things aside and rushed to the dacha, but I didn't get there in time: Father was already on his way to the hospital. Only Mother was at home. She had accompanied Father to the hospital and had already got back to the dacha. She was in a confused, pitiful state. As if trying to reassure herself, she explained to me that Father had not had a heart attack, which was good, but that he didn't feel well. "Perhaps it will get better," she concluded uncertainly.

By force of habit, I removed the reel with the latest dictation from the tape recorder and put it in my briefcase. I inserted a fresh reel in the tape recorder. I sat down in Father's armchair. Cats screeched in my soul. On the other side of the wall, Lena and her husband Vitya huddled quiet as mice in their room.

"What if . . . ?" An idea flashed across my mind. "Now I am the weakest link in the chain. They'll be looking for the tapes at my place."

The decision came to me spontaneously. With the reel in my hand I knocked on Lena's door. As I entered, I saw my sister and her husband sitting on the bed. In the corner by the wardrobe stood wide open the spacious briefcase that Vitya took with him to work at Academician Semyonov's Institute of Chemical Physics.

I put a finger to my lips and silently dropped the precious little cardboard box with the reel into the briefcase. Then, equally silently, I beckoned Lena and Vitya to follow me. We went out into the courtyard. When we were at a "safe" distance from the house, I explained what it was all about and asked them to hide the tape, just in case. Vitya said that he knew a safe place. I didn't ask him where.

On September 11, 1971, Father passed away. After Father's death, I gave Lena and Vitya the other two reels that remained in my possession. These were originals. Because of my nervous state, I was wary of making copies.

Yevgeny Mikhailovich and his "team" had, it seemed, forgotten about me. Only occasionally, during important state visits such as the visit to Moscow of the Secretary-General of the United Nations, did I notice the familiar Volga in my rearview mirror. Now and then information reached me about the preparations for the publication of the second volume of the memoirs. Admittedly, no longer was anything required of me, and no longer did anything depend on me.

In 1974, three years after Father's death, there at last appeared the second volume of the memoirs under the title *Khrushchev Remembers: The Last Testament.* The white dust cover had mournful red and black lettering on the front and spine, and on the back there was a photograph of Father sitting in winter on his favorite bench by the edge of the forest.

That was when they again remembered about me. Once more Yevgeny Mikhailovich and I met in the same suite of the Hotel Moskva. He was accompanied, as always, by Vladimir Vasilyevich. The subject under discussion was also the same: how the memoirs had ended up at the publishing house Little, Brown & Co.

They showed me a prepared text purporting to be a letter from me to a well-known American editor, Mr. Norman Cousins [editor of *The Saturday Review of Literature*]. Recently, as I was going through old papers, I found a copy of this draft. Here is the text that Yevgeny Mikhailovich asked me to sign:

*Respected Mr. Cousins!*

*It has become known to me that material purporting to be the memoirs of my father has been published in the United States. In fact, this is nothing other than a provocative action of the reactionary Western press designed to discredit Soviet reality and raise obstacles to the further improvement of Soviet-American relations.*

*It is well known that N. S. Khrushchev regarded the first version of his "memoirs" published in the United States and some other capitalist countries as just another fake fabricated by the bourgeois press, and that he made an official declaration to that effect in the newspaper* Pravda.

*My father is no longer among the living, so naturally he is not able to issue a similar declaration today. For that reason I consider it my duty to declare, in my own name and in the name of the other members of our family, that no memoir material of N. S. Khrushchev was ever handed over to anyone, and also to express my indignation at the unseemly conduct of certain American publishing houses with regard to the USSR, the Soviet people, and our family in particular.*

*I hope that through your magazine you will draw the content of my letter to the attention of American public opinion.*

*Yours sincerely,*
*S. Khrushchev*

The intention was that my letter should create a scandal and discredit the memoirs. It was a simple plan, but an effective one. As a competitor of Time Corporation, to which the publishing house Little, Brown & Co. also belonged, Cousins would be only too pleased to take advantage of the opportunity offered him to get his rivals into hot water.

I could not of course give my consent to the proposed text, but I also thought that it wouldn't be sensible to refuse right off the bat. I decided to play for time. I said that I would have to consult with Mother, as this was a matter that I couldn't decide all by myself. We arranged to meet again in a few days' time.

That same day, I told Mother all about it. She was interested in knowing whether I had read the book. "No," I replied, "I haven't even laid my eyes on it."

"So how can you write that it's a fake, without even seeing the text?" she objected, logically enough. "You mustn't make such a declaration about a book that none of us have seen with our own eyes. You can write what Father wrote: that we don't know how this material ended up in the West."

With these words in mind, I turned up for the next meeting. Realizing that it would not be an easy conversation, I had ready an irrefutable argument: Mother had forbidden it. It was true, and Nina Petrovna was someone they would leave alone. Besides, from the behavior of my interlocutors, I inferred that the issue was no longer as sensitive as it had been four years earlier.

Once again I read through the prepared text and requested that it be revised in accordance with Mother's point of view. There was an argument. I held firm. "Give me the book. Both Mother and I read English. Not too fast, I admit. It will take us a couple of weeks to study the text. If the text of the book does not correspond to the memoirs, then I'll denounce it as a fake at every street corner. And I'll write about it to whomever you like. But to do it this way—spare me, I can't."

"How can we give you the book?" exploded Yevgeny Mikhailovich. "We don't yet have a single copy. We haven't seen it ourselves."

I jumped at these words: "So how on earth can I declare anything about a book that, as it turns out, neither I nor anyone else has seen?"

Rasshchepov realized that after his slip of the tongue I wasn't going to agree to the prepared text. We had to mess about for a long time with the text of the letter to Cousins, arguing over each word. At last we managed to reach agreement on a version modeled on the declaration that Father had made four years before. They asked me to write out the letter again and to address the envelope in my own hand. And so the letter was sent off to Mr. Cousins, Washington, D.C., United States of America.

Since then I have not had the occasion to meet again with Yevgeny Mikhailovich Rasshchepov or with his faithful friend and colleague Vladimir Vasilyevich.

My letter reached Mr. Cousins. Finding it of interest, he sent his representative to Moscow with instructions to meet me and find out whether I was willing to write for publication a series of articles exposing the fake memoirs.

At that time I was occupied with the question of Father's gravestone, which was being created by the outstanding Russian sculptor and artist Ernst Neizvestny. Around Neizvestny there were always a lot of foreign correspondents. Mr. Cousins's emissary easily found a way to make contact with him and asked him to pass on a request to meet me. Not knowing this whole story, Ernst Yosifovich took the emissary for a novice who wanted to get an interview with me. He warned his interlocutor that I didn't give interviews. The emissary replied that he wasn't after an interview, but just wanted to discuss with me an exceptionally important matter of which I was well aware.

Neizvestny recounted the conversation to me in detail and suggested that we all meet in his studio. It was not a particularly pleasant prospect, but in a way I was glad that events had taken this turn. The letter to Cousins had worried me, and now I had the chance to get the situation back under my control.

I was a frequent visitor to Neizvestny's studio, and my visits had long ceased to evoke the professional interest of Viktor Nikolayevich's colleagues. But this time Ernst Yosifovich warned me that there was a car with special antennas parked outside his studio. Clearly they would be eavesdropping on us. "That car is always there when I have foreign visitors of interest to them," Neizvestny blithely informed me.

I felt that Yevgeny Mikhailovich would be a trifle out of place at our get-together. Neizvestny and I had hardly settled ourselves down in the small room when the doorbell rang. It was the emissary. He was in a businesslike mood. We greeted him in high spirits and invited him to take a taste of what God had sent. On a little table stood a bottle of vodka and some simple snacks. Our guest's Russian wasn't bad, which of course made communication easier. We all downed a glass and nibbled on the snacks. We learned how things were in America. Then we talked about art and religion. Downed another glass. Discussed recent world events. Talked about the dissidents. Downed a third glass. The conversation turned to Neizvestny's creative style. Opened a second bottle. Looked at the sculptures in the studio.

Our guest understood nothing. He tried to raise the subject for the sake of which he had come to the Soviet Union, but every time I switched the conversation to some other subject. At last he evidently got fed up with all this nonsense. The expression on his face eloquently bespoke his perplexity. He decisively stood up and thanked us for receiving him so warmly. We exchanged good-byes. His perplexity deepened. I went with him to his car.

I didn't know whether they were still listening in on us now that we were on the street. The car with the antennas was standing about ten yards from the emissary's Volvo. I didn't want to upset Yevgeny Mikhailovich, so I would have preferred that he not know about our brief exchange. However, it was impossible to delay any longer.

Our guest opened the door to his car. I put my hand on his arm. "Please forgive me. Inside they were listening in on us."

He smiled in delight. At last the situation was beginning to make sense.

"Please convey to Mr. Cousins my deepest apologies. For various reasons I was forced to deceive him. Such things happen in life. The memoirs are genuine. I have read them, so there is nothing to expose."

After that we said good-bye.

That was the KGB's last attempt to intervene in the life of the Western edition of Father's memoirs. Since then the memoirs have lived a respectable life, as befits the memoirs of a retired head of government of a great state. Reference is made to them. They have become part of world history.

True, in our country they continued to spread the idea that the memoirs were a fake.

At the end of the 1970s, I decided to return to the notes that I had made in October 1964. I had immediately restored the tape that the KGB had so obligingly erased, while my memory remained fresh. Now I felt that the time had come to put everything down on paper, using my old notes from 1964, even though I couldn't ask anyone to type up my story. By that time my wife and I had divorced, and I had gone to live with Mother on Old Stables Alley. Father had died, and a year later so had Lena, so Mother was now living there on her own.

By cast of mind I am a lark. I find it easiest to work early in the morning. One morning I laid out my papers on the dinner table, opened the window, which looked out on the well of the Arbat[39] courtyard, and got down to work. It was the middle of May, the height of spring. Below, under the windows, the blossoming lime trees spread their greenery. At first I had difficulty stringing the words together. Then it became easier. I even began to feel satisfied. Taking courage, I inserted my first adjective and then added more. Imperceptibly three hours flew by. My morning time had run out. It was time to get ready to set off for work.

I left Mother a note asking her not to touch anything, not to put the papers on the table into order. I knew that Mother could not tolerate things being out of their right places and would put the scattered papers neatly back into their folders.

Within a month I had accumulated a couple hundred handwritten pages. I was describing, trying not the leave out even the smallest details, the dramatic events of September and October 1964, Father's life after his forced retirement, his first steps at his newly assigned place of residence at Petrovo-Dalneye.

I did not make up my mind to hand the manuscript over to anyone to be typed. In those days I saw no chance of putting my notes to any practical use, and I didn't want to take the risk. I stowed the manuscript away in a small suitcase, which I put against the wall behind the bedside table.

Amid the bustle of everyday cares, it was not often that I recalled my notes. From time to time I glanced into the corner to check that the little suitcase was still in its place and immediately shifted my attention to something else.

There was plenty going on in my life. Work took up most of my time. Nor were things going well at home. Mother had arthritis. It was hard for her to walk. Her legs refused to move. She courageously endured the illness, as she had endured all the trials in her life. She wouldn't let anyone look after her, but tried to do everything by herself. Most of her time she spent at the little country house in the little village of Zhukovka outside Moscow, which the government had assigned her after Father's death.

In the first years after Father's death, Mother liked to take walks and to gaze into the pine woods adjoining the house. She would cut through the previous year's branches of wild raspberry cane that encircled the house in a dense ring to make room for the new berry-bearing branches. For hours Mother would busy herself on the two small vegetable patches that I had at her request cleared right in the forest. All summer long she grew strawberries there. Mother took great satisfaction in regaling with berries her children and grandchildren on their weekend visits.

Gradually all this receded into the past. Now she had strength left only for a few steps along the path, and even for that she needed the assistance of a walking stick. Mother would spend the rest of her time sitting on a folding linen stool on the porch of her house. And then ill fortune struck. Suddenly, as often happens in old age, Mother's organism started breaking down, and illnesses engulfed her from all sides. For half a year Mother hardly left the hospital. On August 9, 1984, she passed away.

Several years went by. I was still living in the same apartment that had once been assigned to Father. One day I had a call from a neighbor in the apartment block. Her name was Jane Tempest. Her father had been a British Communist, a poet, connected in the past with Kim Philby and the "Cambridge five."[40] He had worked in the Soviet Union for many years. Jane had been born in the USSR and had grown up a real Muscovite. Our families often met together. Now she lectures at an American university.

"A new acquaintance of mine wants to meet you," said Jane. "He's had a lot to do with the memoirs of Nikita Sergeyevich."

I invited them to visit me the next day. That was how I first made the acquaintance of Strobe Talbott, a likeable young man with an excellent knowledge of Russian. I have already mentioned him in connection with the preparation of the first edition of Father's memoirs for publication. Strobe had devoted a substantial part of his life to Father's memoirs and had made a journalistic career for himself out of them. He had a splendid grasp of the nuances of our life. Khrushchev became for him a person whom he understood and to whom he felt close. He told me how work on the memoirs had been arranged in the United States, what he had left out and why. The sections that had been abridged were those on the war, on construction, and on agriculture, which had been especially "unlucky."

"He talks a great deal there about corn, trying to persuade the reader of its advantages. That is incomprehensible to us. American farmers don't need persuading about the advantages of corn," explained Strobe.

Before this meeting I had known practically nothing about who had worked on the memoirs in the United States and how they had gone about it. It was a pleasant surprise for me to discover the attention that the staff of the publishing house had devoted to Father's recordings—and, I would say, the respect that they had for them. In our conversation we did not touch on matters about how the memoirs had been smuggled out. It was the last part of the stagnation period,[41] and it was still dangerous to speak of it.

I thought that we would not meet again. However, fate saw fit to decree otherwise. In 1988, Rada Nikitichna received a call from the Moscow office of *Time* magazine. They requested a meeting to discuss an important proposition. In mid-June, Rada and I met with representatives of *Time* at the apartment of my niece Yuliya Leonidovna, daughter of my brother Leonid.

From *Time* had come Ann Blackman and Felix Rosenthal, who worked at the Moscow office, and also Strobe Talbott. We were in a state of perplexity. What was it that they wanted of us? Talbott recalled our previous meeting and much else besides. He said that *Time* was extremely proud to have had the honor of being the first to publish the memoirs of this great man. Then he said that they could not consider their mission complete until Khrushchev's memoirs had been published in Russian and belonged to the people for which they had been intended. He added that they were prepared to make whatever efforts might be necessary and to give our family whatever help we might need to accomplish this goal.

Strobe explained that when he read my interview with the Yugoslav magazine *Vjesnik* he had called his bosses and told them that the time had come to act. He had to go to Moscow. They had approved of his idea. And here they were. All was now clear. In spring 1988, I had been asked for an interview by Milan Bekesh, a correspondent of the Croatian magazine *Vjesnik*. In reply to his question about the Khrushchev memoirs, I had explained that they were in the possession of the CPSU Central Committee, and that under conditions of perestroika and glasnost they could, in my opinion, be published without difficulty in the Soviet Union. This interview received wide publicity in the world. It was distributed by the leading press agencies.

In the name of our family I thanked the representatives of *Time* for their kind words and intentions. I said that what could help us most would be the Russian text of the memoirs, as typed up from the tapes. Talbott replied that *Time* had handed all the tapes over to the Harriman Institute of Columbia University in New York, which maintained a collection of tape recordings of the voices of the most outstanding statesmen. "These recordings are accessible to any researcher. We shall have no difficulty obtaining them for you," he assured me.

We agreed on our next meeting. At the beginning of July, less than a month later, we had a visit from the executives of Time, Henry Muller and John Stacks, accompanied by the three whom we had already met—Strobe Talbott, Ann Blackman, and Felix Rosenthal.

Muller and Stacks had not been involved in the publication of the memoirs. They had joined the company later. They presented us with copies of the English-language editions of the Khrushchev memoirs. I had copies already, but it was the first time that Rada and Yuliya had received copies. Once more we were assured that *Time* considered it a matter of honor to bring the publication of the Khrushchev memoirs to a successful conclusion. They said that we would very soon have transcripts of the tapes.

I should point out that despite the sharply negative official attitude to Khrushchev during the Brezhnev period there had been signs of a cautious revival of interest in Father long before we met with the Americans. At the end of the 1970s, I had a call from Aleksei Vladimirovich Snegov, who as a KGB official had worked with Father on rehabilitating victims of Stalin's repressions. Snegov informed me that the historian Roy Medvedev was writing a biography of my father. Aleksei Vladimirovich told me everything that he knew himself and at Medvedev's request asked me to meet with the historian.

I had heard a great deal about Roy Medvedev. I had read his book about Stalin, *Let History Judge.* To write such a book was for those days an extraordinarily bold act that could not but evoke respect. Ernst Neizvestny had in his time also spoken well of Medvedev. In fact, Neizvestny had intended to introduce us to one another, but had not managed to do it before his own departure abroad.

I had also read Medvedev's books about Father that had been published in English in the West. To be honest, I didn't like them. I felt that they lacked deep analysis of the historical period. Many events were explained in a superficial manner. Some facts had been distorted. As for Medvedev's assessments of Father, however I might try to be objective and overcome my filial feelings, I could not bring myself to agree with them. They too closely resembled the standard accusations of those times about Khrushchev's voluntarism and subjectivism. But we should not forget the situation in those not-so-distant years. Nowadays one frequently comes across features about my father in the press. But in those days just referring to his name in print might be fraught with unpleasant consequences for the culprit.

Medvedev and I agreed to meet. And here was a gray-haired man of intellectual appearance sitting opposite me. We talked about his intentions for the biography, about the need for an objective view of history. It appeared that we fully understood each other, and our meetings continued. I told him stories about Father, and he made use of these stories in writing many chapters of his book.

At last, Roy Aleksandrovich [Medvedev] brought me his final draft. He said that the book was already being prepared for publication in London, where his twin brother Zhores was now living. This event happened to coincide with Brezhnev's death.

The book was not to my liking. Some sections were pervaded by rejection of Khrushchev's reforms. Only such indisputable achievements as the Twentieth Congress and disarmament escaped being torn to pieces. Especially harsh treatment, as I recall, was meted out to Father's "incorrect" policies in the field of agriculture, which had led to a reduction in the output of tractors, combine-harvesters, and other agricultural machinery. And yet now, in the light of sober analysis, it turns out that our world leadership in the output of tractors and combine-harvesters was of no use to anyone. Father said exactly the same thing. A considerable part of the book was given over to a critical review of school reform, an issue that was naturally close to the heart of Medvedev, with his professional background as a specialist in education, but that was not a high priority for Father.

In short, however I might try to compensate for my subjective reaction as Khrushchev's son and look historical facts soberly in the face, I still ended up disliking the book. I frankly told Roy Aleksandrovich all this when we met in December. We parted coldly. Roy Aleksandrovich said that every historian had his own view on past events, and anyway the book was already in production.[42] There was no arguing with that. In these pages I also give my personal view of the events of past years.

Snegov called me a few days later. He was even more categorical than I in his negative assessment of Roy Medvedev's book. I was soon to hear from Roy Aleksandrovich again. We met once more. We made no reference to our last conversation. Medvedev gave me the Russian-language edition, also published abroad, of his book *A Political Biography of Khrushchev*.[43] It bore scant resemblance to the preceding English-language edition, although it still, in my view, contained a whole series of inaccuracies.

We renewed our acquaintanceship. Roy Aleksandrovich said that he was now writing a book about Brezhnev and asked for my help. Naturally, I agreed to help.

Whatever may have been the shortcomings of his work, Medvedev was the only Soviet scholar to concern himself with Khrushchev in those dark times, and for that I am grateful to him.

The changes that began after Brezhnev's death allowed me to give serious thought to the possibility that Father's good name might be restored and work on his memoirs conducted in our country. I was thinking of writing a letter to Yuri Vladimirovich Andropov, but did not manage to do it before

Andropov died. Twilight once more descended over our country. To appeal to Chernenko would have been not merely senseless but dangerous.[44]

Fortunately, the retreat did not last long. After long pondering and hesitation, I resolved to write to Mikhail Sergeyevich Gorbachev. Gorbachev's speeches and actions inspired optimism, encouraging one to believe that changes for the better were on the way. The whole style of his activity, his dynamism, his sociability, his striving for something new—all reminded me of Father.

I spent a long time working on the letter, writing and rewriting in an effort to get the text just right. So much depended on it. At last I made up my mind. I was able to get through quite easily on the telephone to Gorbachev's aide Anatoly Sergeyevich Chernyaev. He received me the next day. With trepidation I passed through the first entrance of the familiar Central Committee building on Old Square. How long it was since I had last been here.

Anatoly Sergeyevich questioned me in detail about everything. He promised to put the matter before Mikhail Sergeyevich within the next few days, which astounded me beyond words. I had not expected a response in less than a few weeks and had thought it might take months. Evidently these really were new times.

Indeed, three or four days later, when I got through to Chernyaev again, he told me that Mikhail Sergeyevich had consulted with the other members of the Politburo, and that they had decided that work on the memoirs of Nikita Sergeyevich would be timely and in accordance with current priorities in historical scholarship. Chernyaev added that all necessary conditions would be created for me, and that practical implementation of the decision had been entrusted to Aleksandr Nikolayevich Yakovlev. He proceeded to give me the telephone number of Yakovlev's aide Valery Alekseyevich Kuznetsov, suggesting that I call him if I ran into any difficulties. I was in seventh heaven! So that's how it was! And I had been expecting our usual red tape. That's what new thinking meant!

People spoke in Moscow of A. N. Yakovlev as a man of a new cast of mind, a democrat, the complete opposite of Suslov.[45] I was very much hoping that Aleksandr Nikolayevich would receive me, that we would discuss our plan of action together, and that he would take the publication of the memoirs under his supervision. It took me a long time to realize that the differences among the "ideologists" between the "liberals" and the "reactionaries" were illusory. None of them, the old ones or the new, had ever forgiven Father either for his speech against Stalin at the Twentieth Congress or for his intentions to restrict the total power of the bureaucracy. They had not forgiven him, the only difference being that some of them openly admitted it, while others did not admit it, sometimes not even to themselves.

Many years later, in April 1994, at the commemoration of the centenary of Father's birth, I first met Aleksandr Nikolayevich face to face. To my question why he had not helped me obtain the manuscripts of Father's memoirs—why, in effect, he had not fulfilled the task entrusted to him by Gorbachev—Yakovlev began to explain that the KGB had expressed a negative opinion of me, not only from the political point of view but also in regard to my work at the institute. Some time later, Aleksandr Nikolayevich conveyed to me through shared acquaintances that it had not been his fault, but the fault of the wily Boldin, the head of the General Department of the Central Committee. It was in his department that Father's material was kept, and it was he who did not want to return it.

Probably all of this is true. The KGB can hardly have forgiven me for outwitting them in 1970 and smuggling out Father's memoirs under their very nose. And at work too I didn't always behave correctly. For example, whatever pressure was put on me, I would write in references for colleagues applying to emigrate to Israel what I thought of them rather than what was required of me. And Boldin was indeed by no means keen to give up Father's memoirs, which he was keeping in the General Department.

All that is true. But it is also true that, as I was told by his aide, Aleksandr Nikolayevich did not find the time to deal with the matter himself [in 1985] and redirected it to the head of the Propaganda Department Yuri Aleksandrovich Sklyarov. Sklyarov got in touch with me without delay. The conversation was amiable in the extreme. Yuri Aleksandrovich assured me that he would sort it out within a few days. He would call me himself.

A month passed. Silence. . . . I called again. It turned out that not only had nobody in all these years taken an interest in the content of the memoirs, but nobody even knew where they were. They would have to be searched for in the archives. Yuri Aleksandrovich once more assured me that he would call me himself as soon as he had any news.

And so it went on for two years. In August 1987, I had to appeal again to Mikhail Sergeyevich [Gorbachev]. There followed a new instruction confirming the previous one. With renewed determination I got down to trying to reach Yuri Aleksandrovich again. First I was given the explanation that the archives were under repair. Then I was told that they were being transferred to a different location.

In August 1988, they finally found something. I had a call from the Central Committee inviting me to come see Comrade Sklyarov the next morning. A few minutes later the telephone rang again. This time a thick male voice belonging to a person named Smirnov from the magazine *Ogonyok*[46] was looking for photographs of my father's funeral. They were planning to publish an article about this sad event, but they didn't have any illustrations because not a single Soviet journalist had been present.

Smirnov and I agreed to meet the next day outside the Central Committee building, by the tenth entrance. On the fifth floor Sklyarov was waiting for me, and not only he. Perhaps I would at last manage to get back the memoirs of my father that had been taken away more than fifteen years before. I naturally had no idea that my meeting with Smirnov was going to open a new stage in the struggle for the publication of the memoirs.

I was late. I had difficulty in finding the tenth entrance: I had to keep on checking where I was against the piece of paper on which I had marked the route. Beside the entrance there stood a tall man, shifting from one foot to the other. That was Smirnov. He had a prepossessing face. I handed him the photographs and took hold of the massive door handle. Smirnov, however, held me back. He was curious to know why I had come here, to the Central Committee department in charge of ideology. I very briefly explained that I was fighting to get my father's memoirs published in our own country. There was no time for a detailed discussion. Smirnov did not let me go and proposed straight off the bat that *Ogonyok* publish the material. I didn't have the time to explain all the complications to him, and suggested that we meet at the beginning of September, after my leave.

When I finally got to the office of Yuri Aleksandrovich Sklyarov, my sister Rada was already sitting there. There was one more person at the table— Vasily Yakovlevich Morgunov, who had been assigned by the leadership to help us in the work on the memoirs. Yuri Aleksandrovich opened up a sturdy cardboard folder, or rather a box, and said that he had been brought four hundred pages and that we could start working on them.

"Why four hundred? And where is the rest? Where are the tapes?" I asked anxiously.

I took a look at the text. It was not the version edited by me, but neither was it the translation from the English. Evidently someone besides us had been engaged in this work. But who? The first page was defaced with sinister blood-red stamps: "Top Secret, Do Not Copy; To Be Returned to General Department of Central Committee." Smiling, Yuri Aleksandrovich pushed the box of papers across to me: "Take it, work on it." I recalled Rasshchepov, Titov, and Melnikov. There was no doubt about it: they were still playing the same game. As soon as I touched these sheets, the trap would slam shut, and

I'd never be able to make use either of the copy of Father's memoirs buried in Shumilov's attic or of the copy that the Americans had promised to send me. They would both automatically become top secret, to be returned to the General Department of the Central Committee.

Rada kept her silence.

"But they took from me about 1,500 pages," I said. "Here we have only four hundred. To put together the book, we need to have the whole of the original text and in addition the tapes for checking. Only then can we be sure that nothing has been left out, and that the original text has not been distorted."

Sklyarov looked in alarm at Morgunov. Morgunov remained silent.

In preparing for this meeting, I had reread the receipt that Titov had given me for the material and written out a copy of it. I showed them the copy of the receipt and explained that it would help them find all the material. Yuri Aleksandrovich displayed genuine astonishment. They had not known here about the existence of the receipt.

Sklyarov again suggested, less confidently this time, that I take at least the four hundred pages while they undertook a search for the rest. I politely refused. The conversation was over. We agreed to call one another . . . in September.

I left the Central Committee building, said goodbye to Rada, and then from a pay-phone—it was quicker and safer that way—called Rosenthal at the *Time* office to find out whether the promised transcripts had yet arrived from the Harriman Institute. It turned out that they were already in Moscow. Rosenthal and I agreed to meet.

Soon there turned up at my apartment a beaming Rosenthal, followed by his driver, holding in his hands a large cardboard box. "I couldn't lift it myself," explained Felix Rosenthal. "Here it all is, as we agreed. My bosses in New York send you their best regards and wish you all success."

Rosenthal left. After a long journey and so many years away, the memoirs had come back home. There they were before me.

I opened the first folder. Yes, it was without a doubt the real thing. Father's words, so dear to me, and my amateur but diligent editorial corrections: *"For a long time now my comrades have been asking me whether I was going to write my memoirs (and not just asking, but urging me to). Because I, and my generation in general, lived in very interesting times. . . ."*

Once again I had this priceless—not only, I hope, to me—historical testament. Strictly speaking, I needed neither the copy buried in the depths of the Central Committee nor the American copy. I intended to work with the material being kept by Igor Mikhailovich Shumilov and by Vitya—that is, Viktor Viktorovich Yevreinov, the husband of my late sister Lena. By that time, he was no longer just "Vitya," but a solid doctor of sciences,[47] but he still worked at the same Institute of Chemical Physics. (However, the former director of the institute, Nobel Prize winner Academician Semyonov, was no longer alive.) What I needed was a cover story, an answer to the question: "Where did you get all this from?"

I had not forgotten how I had assured my interlocutors at the KGB and the Party Control Committee—and signed my name accordingly to the records of my interrogations—that I had given up all the material, that I had nothing left, that I had fully "disarmed." The thought that I might be called to account if events took another turn occurred to me more than once.

There began the second and last period of work on Father's memoirs. I spoke with Lora Finogenova, and we concluded that our old arrangement was still the most convenient. We just had to bring the equipment back into working order. After twenty years it was well and truly worn out. We repaired the tape recorder and bought new earphones—one blessing of those years was that earphones had ceased to be a rarity. As for the typewriter, Lora's basic work tool, it was always on the go.

At last the first transcripts made their appearance. Assisted by my wife Valentina Nikolayevna (I had remarried in 1987), I divided between us the precious sheets and took pencils in hand. The work was moving ahead, but my heart was unquiet. We were still, as in the old days, preparing a manuscript to leave on the shelf, counting on better days in the future.

That was the time I also decided to return to my notes. From behind the bed I pulled out the cherished little suitcase, shook off the dust, and took out the sheets, now slightly yellowed with age. I worked on the notes in fits and starts. At work I had become deputy director, and concerns related to the institute swallowed up all my time.

During August and September 1989, the situation about the memoirs changed. Two magazines, *Ogonyok* and *Znamya,* had simultaneously expressed the desire to publish them. Everything, however, depended on the censorship, and whether we had enough strength to break through it. I began my tour of the editorial offices in good time. Now there lay in my briefcase not only Father's memoirs but also my own manuscript about Father, *A Pensioner of Union Significance.* Over the past year it had acquired clear contours. It was published in the United States in 1990 by Little, Brown under the title *Khrushchev on Khrushchev.*

I started with *Znamya*. As they had recently published the memoirs of Adzhubei, I perceived them as being bolder than the others. So here I was climbing up to the third floor of a dilapidated old building, hidden away in the depths of a courtyard off October 25th Street. (It has now been given back its prerevolutionary name, Nikolskaya Street.) The chief editor of the magazine, Grigory Yakovlevich Baklanov, was busy, but the amiable secretary nonetheless showed me into his office without delay.

Grigory Yakovlevich was talking with a visitor. He looked harassed. A stout lady with a thick manuscript in her hands was putting pressure on him. At last the lady left. Defenselessly screwing up his eyes, Grigory Yakovlevich spread out his arms, as if to say: "That's how it is."

We discussed my problem over a cup of tea. The conversation was not very constructive and left behind a feeling of hopelessness. We agreed that it was necessary to wait for a decision from the top. The conversation was nearing its end, so I hesitantly mentioned that I had written something myself. Digging into my bag, I clutched a voluminous, poorly shuffled bundle of papers. I had not yet got around to retyping the manuscript, the pages stuck out on all sides, and the size of it looked frightening. Grigory Yakovlevich looked at me with apprehension. I remembered the woman who was there before me, and sighing, I crammed the bundle back into my bag.

"So I, you see. . . . Maybe sometime in the future," I forced out.

"Of course, of course," Baklanov hastened to say.

A few days later, I called Smirnov. I learned that his first name was Kostya and set off for *Ogonyok*. While anyone could walk into the *Znamya* offices, here a pass had to be made out. One could see that it wasn't a literary magazine but a political one.

After a short conversation, Smirnov took me off to see Gushchin, the first deputy chief editor. "He's called Lev Nikitich. He decides everything here," Kostya admonished me.

We were already passing through the door of the office, but I managed to whisper: "And Korotich?"[48]

Kostya nodded his head. "Korotich too."

The still young man who came out to meet us radiated goodwill. We sat down around a big table. After a brief pause Lev Nikitich began to set out his thoughts about the possibility of publishing Father's memoirs. He spoke crisply, without going into any inessential details. One felt that he knew not only what he wanted but also how to get it. His attitude boiled down to the following: "If you have something to publish, then let's publish it. When they forbid it, that's when we'll ask permission."

If the flabbiness of *Znamya* had depressed me to the utmost, the forcefulness of this place even frightened me somewhat. The tension dissipated when the door opened and Korotich rolled into the room. It looked as though he consisted wholly of curves. There was a sly smile on his ball of a face. "What are you up to here?" he asked, taking a look round at us all, as if he knew nothing about it and had glanced in here quite by chance.

Gushchin explained the essence of the matter to him. "With the memoirs of Nikita Sergeyevich we'll get nowhere. There's a decision of the Central Committee—true, from the stagnation years, from 1973—to the effect that memoirs of top leaders can be published only with the permission of the Secretariat of the Central Committee. Nobody will let us do it. No point in even trying," he summed up.

Gushchin nodded. Smirnov opened his mouth, thought a bit, and cautiously closed his mouth again. The smile didn't leave Korotich's face. He turned to me again: "But if you have something of your own for us. . . ."

Kostya raised his hand, in the way that a hunting dog that smells prey raises its paw. While we were waiting to see Gushchin, I had managed to tell him about my notes. I dug into my bag for the papers. To be honest, I was almost certain that the story of Father's ouster would be much harder to publish than his memoirs. "Here, for example, is a story about how Father was retired in 1964. Only I don't know whether you have the determination. . . ."

They were instantly excited at the idea. With hardly a glance at the bundle of sheets that I was holding out, Korotich exclaimed: "We'll publish it!"

A few minutes later, Korotich gave us a parting smile—he had a mass of things to see to, they were already expecting him somewhere else—and rolled out of the office. Kostya and I got to work.

At the beginning of September 1989, I resolved to write a new letter, my third, to Gorbachev. In it I informed him of the changes that had taken place in the last year and of the circumstances now surrounding Father's memoirs. It was no longer a matter of obtaining them from the archives. It was a matter of getting approval for the publication of what I had personally managed to get hold of. (Of course, I still did not reveal that I had any material apart from what I had received from *Time*.) Rada suggested that I convey the letter through another aide of Mikhail Sergeyevich, Ivan Timofeyevich Frolov. She was well acquainted with him, and it was only now that she had decided to share with me her precious contact in the highest echelon of the Central Committee.

We arranged to meet with Frolov in the last week of September 1989, on a Monday or a Tuesday—I no longer remember exactly. He received us very warmly and promised to put the matter before Gorbachev on the first possible occasion. I complained that the whole business of Father's memoirs had been outrageously dragged out. Remembering what had happened with Sklyarov, I was insistent and asked when we might learn of the result. A worried look came on to Frolov's smiling face. He suddenly began to complain about the extraordinary burden on Gorbachev and the difficult situation. Then he fell silent. It wasn't clear what difficult situation he had in mind. Did he mean in the world? In the country? In the Central Committee?

He made another exclamation that, so it seems to me, had some special meaning. "You can't imagine what is going on here!"

And really, we couldn't imagine, try as we might.

"So I won't be able to put it before Mikhail Sergeyevich this week," declared Ivan Timofeyevich. "Call me early next week—on Tuesday or Wednesday."

After waiting a decent interval, I called Frolov at the Central Committee. I called at just the right time. My request had been placed before Mikhail Sergeyevich, and he had expressed his support. Gorbachev had not, however, taken the responsibility for making the decision on himself: "The comrades exchanged opinions in the Politburo and approved the idea of publishing your father's memoirs." Implementation of the decision was entrusted to the newly elected member of the Politburo Vadim Andreyevich Medvedev.

"There, you see, everything is in order," finished off Ivan Timofeyevich. "In the next few days you'll get a call from Comrade Medvedev's people, and you can reach an agreement with them about starting the work." Speaking more slowly, he added: "If they delay things a bit, don't get upset. They're facing big changes there. They may not get around to you right away."

I was not upset. I was in raptures. I dreamed of typists, editors, proof-readers—and, at the end of the process, volumes fresh off the press. Then I read over again the brief announcement in the press with biographical information about the newly elected member of the Politburo, and my enthusiasm began to wane. For some reason I did not think that he would call me. I did not intend to call myself any more: the business with Sklyarov had taught me a good lesson. Negotiations with the apparatus sucked one in like a quagmire. Telephone calls, shuttling from one office to another, where they always promise this and assure that but never finally decide.

On the last Saturday of September 1989, just after Rada and I had gone to see Frolov, there appeared the issue of *Ogonyok* containing my story about Father's ouster from power. The effect it produced was like an exploding bomb. In a single day I became what is called a celebrity. On that very same day, the press carried a communiqué about the Central Committee plenum that had just ended, at which Gorbachev had forced the resignation of the majority of his opponents. This was probably what Frolov was alluding to when he mentioned the difficult situation in the Central Committee.

Accustomed to the idea that nothing in Moscow ever happens by chance, foreign correspondents immediately postulated a link between these two events. A correspondent of the Japanese newspaper *Asahi* asked me straight out whether it was true that Gorbachev had personally ordered the publication of my story in *Ogonyok.*

However that may be, from that moment on there was a big change. The taboo on Father's name was not officially removed, but less attention began to be paid to infringements of the taboo. There began to appear—at first, it is true, infrequently—articles that mentioned the forbidden name. Institutions began to vie with one another in inviting me as a visiting speaker to share my reminiscences of Father. During one such meeting in October 1989, televised for the program *Good Evening, Moscow,* I referred for the first time to Father's memoirs, saying that they did exist. After the broadcast I felt like a hero and prepared myself for possible sanctions. No sanctions followed, which I considered a good sign.

On Old Square, however, everything remained as it was. I had no calls from the Central Committee. Apparently the Politburo decision had got lost between buildings. I waited patiently. Yuri Aleksandrovich Sklyarov was replaced by Comrade Kapto, who was put in charge of a single consolidated Central Committee department responsible for supervising all ideological issues in the country.[49]

At that time it again became fashionable to hold meetings between the party leadership and prominent members of the intelligentsia, somewhat similar to those that Father had arranged in the 1960s. Baklanov was invited to one of these meetings. He decided to make use of the opportunity to feel out the situation by taking part in informal discussion in the corridors. Baklanov returned discouraged. During the intermission he had managed to catch hold of Vadim Medvedev and ask him about Father's memoirs. Medvedev had been unwilling to talk about the matter. "This isn't the time," he had growled with displeasure.

And then he had walked away.

By spring [1990], as information about Father's memoirs percolated through the country, I was receiving a growing number of proposals for their publication. I had telephone calls from various provinces of the Russian Federation and republics of the Soviet Union, from thick journals and from thin journals.[50] But nobody seemed able to overcome the barrier of censorship. *Argumenty i fakty* (Arguments and facts) tried to insert extracts from Father's memoirs dealing with the Twentieth Congress, but time and again the censorship removed the material, requiring that permission be obtained from the CPSU Central Committee. Finally, after a prolonged siege, there appeared on the third page of this weekly newspaper, with the highest circulation of all periodicals in the country, a few paragraphs from Father's memoirs.

We celebrated victory. Now there was a real possibility of getting sections of the memoirs published in *Znamya* and *Ogonyok*. But as before I dreamed of publishing the entire text, and such an opportunity presented itself. I had a call from Akhmed Akhmedovich Iskenderov, corresponding member of the USSR Academy of Sciences[51] and chief editor of the scholarly journal *Voprosy istorii* (Questions of history). He proposed to begin the publication of Father's memoirs in his journal.

A coherent strategic plan took shape in my mind. First *Ogonyok*, with its enormous print run but small size, would draw public attention to the fact that Father's memoirs existed. Then more substantial publications would follow in a variety of outlets, including the thick literary journal *Znamya*, culminating in scholarly publication of the entire text in *Voprosy istorii*.

It was a good plan, but I was worried by the lack of coordinated action between *Ogonyok* and *Znamya*. After the appearance of my story in their magazine, the *Ogonyok* people regarded me as "theirs" and asserted their preferential rights over everything connected to my name. Baklanov in his turn regarded Father's memoirs as belonging to him and him alone. I found myself between two fires. When I urged Smirnov and Gushchin to liaise with Baklanov and agree with him on a joint plan of action, Smirnov pretended that he had no influence on such decisions, while Gushchin smiled sweetly and promised to call Baklanov but never did.

Nor was I happy about the way in which Kostya was adapting the material to the *Ogonyok* house style. He cut, rearranged, and condensed passages in an effort to compress the text as much as he could. I timidly objected and proposed that instead he select specific excerpts for inclusion as they stood, leaving the rest for other periodicals to publish. I did not, however, have the strength to stand up to Kostya's irresistibly insinuating forcefulness. If he couldn't convince me, then he'd simply go ahead and do it his own way.

Thus *Ogonyok*, *Voprosy istorii*, and *Znamya* were all urgently preparing material for the press in parallel. Publication in *Ogonyok* was to begin in mid-summer 1990. In fact, I was to read the first excerpt published in the magazine on my birthday, July 2. *Voprosy istorii* planned to start in August, but this journal was always behind schedule. *Znamya* put off the beginning of publication until September for internal reasons.

There was no immediate reaction from the leadership to the first publication of an excerpt in *Ogonyok*. Nonetheless, the feeling of danger didn't leave me. As it turned out, I wasn't wrong. In the middle of July, my wife and I set off for London. Since 1964 I had not been allowed to visit capitalist countries. Now things were easier, and we, like many of our fellow citizens, had got ourselves a private invitation that enabled us to travel to a Western country. The invitation came from our good acquaintance Brigitte Yosifova, formerly a Muscovite and now the London correspondent of a Bulgarian newspaper. It was all splendid—the hospitality of our hosts, the city, the hot, dry weather. For several decades Londoners had not known such a summer. We were already into the second half of our stay when one morning our hostess lifted the receiver of the desperately ringing telephone and called out in a perplexed voice: "Sergei, there's some Gushchin asking for you."

I took the receiver.

"The censorship has removed Khrushchev." Gushchin audibly exhaled. "What shall we do?"

I was thunderstruck. The very thing that I didn't want to think about had happened. Everything had been going just too smoothly in the last few months. There was no point in trying to do anything from England. I had to wait until I got home.

On arrival in Moscow, I hurried over to *Ogonyok*. Korotich was waiting for me in his office. Gushchin and Smirnov joined us. We crowded around the writing table, as close as we could get to the telephones. Korotich suggested that we try to find out what was going on, working from the bottom up. I supported him. Kostya was raring to call Gorbachev right away.

On his "Kremlin" telephone,[52] Korotich dialed the number of a highly placed official. There was no answer. He called another. Still no success. At last he got through to the censorship office. In an oily voice, feigning utter bewilderment at the misunderstanding that had occurred, Vitaly Alekseyevich asked for advice. What should he do? Readers were confused. The last issue of the magazine had announced continuation of the Khrushchev memoirs, and there was no continuation. An explanation was needed, and in the era of perestroika one couldn't get away with an allusion to a censor's ban of an author who not so long ago was our leader.

At the other end of the line, reference was made to the resolution passed in 1973 by the Secretariat of the Central Committee.

"But who nowadays," cooed Korotich, "can be guided by that document? It was adopted in the stagnation period, whereas now we have perestroika. We can't give an answer like that to our readers."

They agreed to give some thought to the matter, and to seek advice. They wouldn't leave it on the back burner and would be back in touch.

Having finished his conversation with the censorship, Korotich dialed the telephone number of *Znamya*. Baklanov answered. He told Korotich that he had sent the material off to the censorship and was awaiting the result. He had, of course, heard of the ban, but did not intend to call or appeal to anyone. When they banned it, then he would see. *Znamya* had plenty of time, and Baklanov could allow himself to wait and see what would happen with *Ogonyok*. They agreed to keep each other informed.

In the evening Kostya called me. He told me that Korotich had decided to make use of his rights as chief editor. The new instructions that had been introduced under perestroika envisaged that in the event of disagreement with the censorship the chief editor had the right to include the forbidden material on the responsibility of the editorial board. "The material has gone in!" Kostya was again full of optimism.

And so the next issue of *Ogonyok* came out with Khrushchev's memoirs. So did the issue that followed, and the one after that. Every Sunday I would open up my *Ogonyok*, look for Khrushchev, and finding it remark with satisfaction: "Here it is. Everything is in order."

September arrived. Finally, in its ninth issue of the year, *Znamya* too contained material from the Khrushchev memoirs. *Ogonyok* had finished publication of the part of the memoirs devoted to the period of the war. Kostya sent me the section about Stalin's death as they had prepared it for the press and then the section about the arrest of Beria. The section about the Twentieth Congress was to follow.

At the end of September I had a call from Baklanov. He told me in an irritated tone that he had received some very unpleasant telephone calls from readers annoyed at the repetition in *Znamya* of passages from Father's memoirs that had already appeared in *Ogonyok*. Grigory Yakovlevich laid down an ultimatum: Either I was to forbid *Ogonyok* to publish the part of the memoirs relating to the postwar period, or *Znamya* would forbid *Ogonyok* to do so, or else he would stop publishing the memoirs, informing his readers about my improper behavior.

I could not do as Baklanov demanded. At the critical moment only Korotich had fought for the continued publication of the memoirs. Now that he had achieved a positive result, I could not, for both moral and pragmatic reasons, cut short the work that he had successfully begun. Otherwise, if the attack were renewed, I would find myself standing alone, for the preceding events had shown that Grigory Yakovlevich was no fighter. On the other hand, it didn't require any special perceptiveness on my part to realize that there was no way I could reconcile the two editorial offices. So I didn't call Baklanov back. I had nothing to say to him.

That night I slept badly. I took Validol. Finally I decided. Let publication in *Ogonyok* continue, even if that had to mean losing *Znamya*. I telephoned *Ogonyok* and through Smirnov informed them of my decision. Unfortunately, this painful decision turned out to be in vain. A couple of days later, Kostya asked me in a depressed tone of voice to come to the editorial office. The censorship had again removed Khrushchev.

It had all begun with the receipt by the censorship office of a brief but expressive instruction from Comrade Medvedev, who was on vacation at the time. The instruction consisted of all of two words: "No Khrushchev"—and his signature. The disobedience of *Ogonyok* had caused serious irritation. Evidently it was no laughing matter.

The next issues were to have contained material about Stalin's last days. Korotich set off for the Central Committee to explain himself. Having met with Kapto, he came back with bad news. He had been categorically forbidden to continue publication on the basis of that same notorious resolution of 1973. In reply to Korotich's tirade about the stagnation period, he was shown a new document confirming the old one. It was dated the week before. With difficulty Korotich managed to persuade Kapto to permit another two issues so that the ban wouldn't look too obvious. But that was to be all.

In the course of the conversation, Kapto had complained that Khrushchev had worked in isolation. He might have made mistakes in describing certain facts, and it had not been possible for him to check. "It wouldn't be good if untrue statements were to be discovered in the memoirs. We must take care to uphold Nikita Sergeyevich's authority. Now we already have a transcript here in the Central Committee, about four thousand pages. We'll hand it over to the Institute of Marxism-Leninism. There they'll check it all out and make any corrections that may be necessary. Then it can be published. Such serious documents shouldn't be published just anywhere. The memoirs will be put out by Politizdat,"[53] he concluded.

As they parted, Kapto had tried to reassure Korotich. In a couple of days, at the beginning of the next week, Vadim Andreyevich would be back from leave and would invite Sergei Khrushchev to come and see him, and they would reach an agreement on how to conduct the work on the memoirs from then on.

These words evoked in me sad recollections of my conversations at the KGB with Viktor Nikolayevich Titov. I recalled how he, in the same oily way, had promised to return all the material as soon as Father came out of the hospital. One day followed another. There was no call from the Central Committee. Smirnov impatiently suggested that I call Medvedev myself, but I refused. I understood that this was no chance forgetfulness.

By this time even the irrepressible Korotich had lost a large part of his optimism. Baklanov finally made good his threat, declaring that he was breaking off publication of the memoirs, of his own free will. In any case, the censorship would undoubtedly not have let through the section of the memoirs planned for the tenth issue of *Znamya*.

The censorship acted in analogous fashion with regard to *Voprosy istorii* and removed the memoirs from the eighth issue. Iskenderov went to see Kapto. Like Korotich, he too was shown the paper confirming the notorious decision of the stagnation period.

"There were several signatures on it," recounted Iskenderov. "I couldn't make out whose they were. There was only one that I recognized—Medvedev's."

The conversation continued along the same well-beaten track. Kapto mentioned the four thousand pages of Father's transcribed dictation in their possession, the need for careful verification of facts, and the subsequent publication of Father's memoirs under the aegis of the Institute of Marxism-Leninism. Akhmed Akhmedovich, however, had no intention of giving in. He prepared to put up a fight with thoroughness and academic rigor. "If verification is what they want, then I'll send my material to the Institute of Marxism-Leninism," he explained to me on the telephone. "I told them at the Central Committee that in the era of glasnost we have just as much right to publish historical material as Politizdat has. So let them check and make their report. I've already been in touch with Georgy Lukich Smirnov, the director of the institute."

Documents have now become available that give us more insight into the political background of the ban on the publication of Father's memoirs. In the CPSU Central Committee they had for some time been unable to agree on how they could neutralize me and how, if the publication of the memoirs could not be prevented altogether, they could at least take the process under their control.

As early as July 1989, the heads of the Ideological Department and the General Department of the CPSU Central Committee, Comrades Kapto and

Boldin, had sent the leadership, and in the first instance the secretary of the CPSU Central Committee for ideology Vadim Medvedev, a verbose memorandum. In it they stated that they had obtained from the KGB 3,926 typewritten pages of the memoirs of N. S. Khrushchev, that these memoirs "suffer from substantial deficiencies and contain factual inaccuracies" (as Kapto told Korotich), that N. S. Khrushchev "demonstrates personal biases and displays lack of objectivity in his assessments," and that therefore "the statements and conclusions of the memoirs, in many ways subjective as they are, need to undergo careful expert examination."[54] Kirilenko had used exactly the same expressions when he upbraided Father twenty years before. It was as if nothing had changed in all those years. But no, something had changed. It had now become impossible simply to ban the memoirs. The authors of the memorandum proposed that the memoirs be published, but only after the Institute of Marxism-Leninism had brought them into a form acceptable to the authorities—in other words, had falsified them.

However, Academician Smirnov, the director of the institute, was in no hurry to salute *Yes, Sir!* He understood with what all this was fraught. Iskenderov was putting pressure on him. The situation was constantly changing. He played for time. Only on July 17, 1990, did Georgy Lukich reply to the Central Committee. In his reply, he rightly noted that "S. N. Khrushchev questions the legality of the confiscation from him of the tape recordings containing his father's memoirs and intends to assert his rights to them." For that reason Smirnov proposed that a full and proper agreement be reached with the heirs.

His proposal was rejected out of hand. On August 24, 1990, the deputy heads of the Ideological Department and the General Department of the CPSU Central Committee, Comrades Degtyarev and Solovyov, wrote a report in which they argued that "it is hardly expedient to provide legal arguments in support of the right of the CPSU Central Committee to the memoirs of N. S. Khrushchev that are at its disposal. There has been no such practice, and the need for it has not arisen. The right of the archive to publish documents at its disposal has never been placed in doubt." All true enough. But then times had changed.

The furthest that the Central Committee—in other words, Medvedev—should go by way of concessions, proposed Degtyarev and Solovyov, was to invite the daughter of N. S. Khrushchev, R. N. Adzhubei (Khrushcheva), and his son S. N. Khrushchev to take part in preparing the official edition of the memoirs for publication . . . and also to come to a decision about publication in the journal *Voprosy istorii.*

How Medvedev reacted to this we know: "No Khrushchev!"
But another Central Committee secretary, Valentin Falin, a more farsighted person, expressed doubts about the expediency of such a frontal strategy. He asked:

*1. What is it proposed that we do if:*
*(a) the heirs of N. S. Khrushchev refuse to cooperate with us? Or*
*(b) the heirs put forward unacceptable conditions? It is not clear.*
*2. The question of the right of the Central Committee (or of the archive) to the memoirs of N. S. Khrushchev is more complicated than the report suggests. The recordings and manuscripts were confiscated by administrative order, and there is no court decision changing the status of the property. Legally ownership was vested in the author so long as he was alive, and in his heirs after his death. The administrative order did not create any rights, and does not guard the Central Committee from possible complications.*

*V. Falin*
*September 12, 1990*

In reply to Falin, Degtyarev and Solovyov proposed on September 19, 1990, that negotiations be opened with the heirs of N. S. Khrushchev with a view to working out a solution acceptable to everyone.

While the party bureaucrats intrigued against one another, life moved forward. As early as February 1990 *Ogonyok* had resumed publication of Father's memoirs. In the same month, *Voprosy istorii* had also started to publish the memoirs. Georgy Lukich Smirnov decided not to get involved with Iskenderov, and in response to his inquiry said that he had not seen the Khrushchev memoirs and that he therefore had no comments to make about them. The censorship office also preferred not to interfere. The CPSU Central Committee was fast losing its authority, and the threads by which it used to run the country were slipping from its hands. People had simply stopped paying attention to the cry: "No Khrushchev!"

However, some parts of the rusty mechanism still creaked along. The transcripts of Father's memoirs that had been made at the KGB were at long last delivered to the Institute of Marxism-Leninism. The task of dealing with them was assigned to two of the institute's historians, Nikolai Barsukov and Vasily Lipitsky. In winter 1991, Lipitsky called and asked me to come around for a talk. The discussion was not a great success. In reply to Lipitsky's proposal that we work together, I asked him just one question:

"And do you have the original tapes?"

Lipitsky shrugged his shoulders. "No."

"So what kind of historian are you if you're prepared to work with material the reliability of which has in no way been confirmed?" I angrily objected. "Perhaps someone has changed the text, and you have no inkling of it?"

Lipitsky again shrugged his shoulders. We both knew very well what was going on. I got the impression that Lipitsky did not seriously count on drawing me into this adventure and was simply going through the motions of carrying out an instruction received from above. We parted for good. Soon events were to take such a turn that the CPSU Central Committee would no longer be up to falsifying history.

But the KGB transcripts did not disappear without a trace. They were picked up by another player in the game—Lipitsky's colleague Barsukov, a person already well advanced in years. Later I was to get into an argument with him. When he left the Institute of Marxism-Leninism, Barsukov took with him, among other documents, the transcripts of Father's memoirs. He strenuously insisted that his was the only true version of the memoirs. In his articles he would cite Father by sole reference to his own transcripts, demonstratively ignoring the text published by *Voprosy istorii*. I could, of course, have paid no attention to his cranky eccentricity. What concerned me was that by his actions Barsukov was intentionally or unintentionally prolonging the life of the fake manufactured in the depths of the security organs. As for whether the text had been edited before its delivery to the Institute of Marxism-Leninism—those pages that I saw showed clear signs of an editor's hand—or whether the job of bringing it into "a suitable form" had been entrusted to Barsukov and Lipitsky, that isn't so important.

Both texts are now kept at the Russian Center for the Preservation and Study of Documentation in Moscow.[55] A copy of the tapes is also there. It remains to find a conscientious historian prepared to undertake a comparison of the two texts, the genuine one and the one from the CPSU Central Committee, and pronounce his verdict.

In 1991 the work of editing the memoirs was approaching completion. My wife and I polished up the last sections and made the necessary number of copies. We had to decide what to do next, and not only with regard to the memoirs. The year before, to continue work on the memoirs without hindrance and to write two books that I had planned,[56] I had resigned from my position as deputy general director of the computer company Elektronmash.[57] The time had come to seek new work. During one of my trips to the United States, Brown University offered me the opportunity to work there for a time. I agreed to spend the 1991–92 academic year at Brown. Who could have guessed what was going to happen to our country in the space of that year? According to my contract with Brown, I was obliged to arrive at the university in early September, for the beginning of the academic year. Before leaving Russia I had to settle the fate of the memoirs.

I came to an agreement with the Moscow City Archives Association—that is, with the association's director Aleksei Samoilovich Kiselyov and his deputy Vladimir Aleksandrovich Manykin—that they would take into their safekeeping the complete set, including a copy of the tapes, the original transcripts from the tapes, the transcripts as edited by myself, and the final text. I attached special importance to the completeness of the set, as by this means I wanted to make the whole editorial process transparent for future researchers. The association for its part promised to publish the full text of the memoirs. Just to be on the safe side, I prepared two more such complete sets, one for the Harriman Institute at Columbia University in New York[58] and the other for my hideaway in Professor Shumilov's attic. In August 1991, for the first time in many years, all the copies were collected together in one place, heaped up in a mountain in a room at my dacha. Before being placed in long-term storage, everything needed to be carefully sorted out.

You can imagine my state of mind when I turned on the television early in the morning of August 19, 1991, and heard that an attempt was underway to return to the old days. Looking at the mountain of folders, I thought to myself: "THEY will soon be here to get me. For all these years I've been hiding the stuff, and now I myself have brought it all together in one place for their convenience." My confusion didn't last long. There being no way in which I could influence events, I decided to get on with my task. The next day I had everything in order—three complete sets. I handed one set over to the Moscow City Archives Association and then took Shumilov his set. The third set I brought with me to the United States.

Unfortunately, more mishaps were still to come. The Moscow City Archives Association was not able to publish Father's memoirs. Its money had run out. The search for a publisher had to start anew. All these troubles now lay on the shoulders of my son Nikita. I still teach at Brown University.

I am very glad to report that in 1995 *Voprosy istorii* completed publication of the memoirs.

In 1997, the Russian publishing house VAGRIUS put out a one-volume collection of chapters from Father's memoirs, selected by Nikita and myself. It was a success. It even became a bestseller. There was a lot of talk about the memoirs. In one newspaper they were even described as a textbook for future politicians. Soon after the VAGRIUS publication, Nikita was approached by people from the Democracy Foundation, headed by Aleksandr Nikolayevich

Yakovlev, the same Yakovlev whose path I did not manage to cross ten years before. The foundation proposed to publish the full text of Father's memoirs.

From that point on, everything happened as it does in a good fairy tale. To publish the memoirs Yakovlev needed money. The foundation did not intend to finance the project itself. Nikita (who was then working at *Moscow News*—and still is) turned to the president of the *Moscow News* publishing company, Aleksandr Lvovich Vainshtein. Would Vainshtein make a contribution to the project?

Aleksandr Lvovich reacted instantly: "And what do we need Yakovlev for? We'll do the whole job ourselves."

Nikita couldn't believe his ears. At the turn of the century one could not expect to make a profit from publishing the memoirs of Nikita Sergeyevich, and a publisher could well end up losing money. In Russia today, four volumes are beyond the pocket of the majority of potential readers, and as for those who could afford them—if they read anything at all, it isn't political memoirs.

*Moscow News* spared no expense. It bought the best paper and sought out the best printer. The first volume came out in March, the fourth and last in May 1999: reddish-brown volumes with gold lettering against a black background, in boxes on the front covers and spines—just as though they were asking to be placed on the bookshelf. It gives me a feeling of satisfaction to turn the smooth pages, pleasantly cool to the fingers, and to examine the clear photographs.

At long last, life brings my journey to its end. The memoirs of my father, the person who led our country through the stormy decade of the late 1950s and early 1960s, have seen the light of day. The story of their dictation and publication has gone into history, where it should have been long before. The last full stop has been set in this affair.

—Sergei Khrushchev

1. Yuliya is Khrushchev's granddaughter, the daughter of his son Leonid, who died as a pilot in World War II. [SK]

2. N. S. Khrushchev had abolished economic ministries in favor of a system of regional economic management and was in the process of dividing the province party committees into separate committees for industry and agriculture. [SS]

3. The sobriquet "corn promoter" (*kukuruznik*) had its origin in Khrushchev's enthusiasm for corn. He regarded it as the best feed for livestock and the only feasible means by which the production of meat could be increased. [SS]

4. Karaganda, in central Kazakhstan, was in Stalin's time the location of a large complex of forced-labor camps. [SS]

5. Field Marshal Paulus was taken prisoner by the Red Army at the battle of Stalingrad. The Germans offered to exchange Stalin's son Yakov for him. [SS]

6. Andrei Vlasov, a prominent Soviet general taken prisoner by the Germans, recruited other prisoners of war into an army that fought alongside the Germans against the Stalin regime. [SS]

7. Only in the year 2000, when Russian journalists got around to looking into the archives, did

articles that reestablished the truth appear in the Russian press. See, for example, "Khrushchev's Son Not a Traitor" (*Komsomolskaya Pravda*, April 14, 2000); "Label of Traitor Removed from Khrushchev's Son" (*Novoe Russkoe Slovo*, April 4, 2000).

8. To those who wish to verify my explanation, I recommend the book *Khrushchev i Ukraina* (Khrushchev and Ukraine), published in 1995 by the Institute of the History of Ukraine in Kiev. The whole history of Father's personal archive is recounted in detail by R. Ya. Pirog, Doctor of Historical Sciences, in "The Archive of First Secretary of the Central Committee of the Communist Party (Bolshevik) of Ukraine Nikita Khrushchev: Problems of Reconstruction," *Khrushchev i Ukraina*, 181–85. [SK]

9. Sergei Khrushchev was still working in the field of missile production at this time. [SS]

10. Reutovo, where Lora lived, is an urban settlement a few kilometers east of Moscow. [SS]

11. I did not immediately realize that the tapes might have a historical value in themselves. Magnetic tape being in short supply, I returned the first reels to Father for reuse as soon as the text had been typed. Only with the fourth reel did I reconsider. From then on, three copies were made of each tape and preserved for posterity. [SK]

12. The plenum at which the removal of Khrushchev from power was confirmed. [SS]

13. The settlement where Khrushchev's dacha was situated. [SS]

14. "Lenya" refers to Leonid Brezhnev. Aleksandr Shelepin was known by the nickname of "Iron Shurik." [SS]

15. Shelepin had been head of the Komsomol (Young Communist League). Grigoryan was a middle-ranking official at the Central Committee. Goryunov was director general of the TASS news agency. [SK]

16. The "Boussac" cloak, a warm woolen cloak greenish-beige in color, was a gift from Marcel Boussac—a French millionaire, textile manufacturer, and owner of the "right-wing" (as reported to Father at the time) newspaper *L'Aurore*. During Khrushchev's official visit to France in March 1960, Boussac took a liking to the Soviet leader. Afterward, he sent to Moscow fruits, French wines, and other tokens of his respect. The cloak pleased Khrushchev so much by virtue of its rational simplicity that he never parted from it in the cold and rainy spring and autumn weather. [SK]

17. These works were ghostwritten to glorify Brezhnev's role in the Great Patriotic War and in the postwar reconstruction, respectively. [SS]

18. Brezhnev had met with Khrushchev at the beginning of 1965. At that meeting he had informed him that the Presidium of the CPSU Central Committee had assigned him a personal pension, an apartment in Moscow on Starokonyushenny (Old Stables) Alley, a dacha at Petrovo-Dalneye, and a

Volga automobile for his use. He had also demanded that Khrushchev vacate his house on the Vorobyovsky Highway. [SK]

19. At the Twenty-Third Congress of the CPSU in 1966, the Presidium of the CPSU Central Committee was renamed the Politburo. The first secretary of the CPSU Central Committee was given the new title of general secretary. [SK]

20. Taras Shevchenko (1814–61), a famed Ukrainian poet. During the nineteenth century, being conscripted into the Russian army was a form of arrest and exile, as the period of army service was twenty-five years. [SS]

21. Valery Tarsis, one of the first dissident Soviet writers, was confined to a mental hospital following the publication of his work in 1962. On his release, he described the experience in the short story "Ward 7." Tarsis was deported to England in 1966. Svetlana Alliluyeva was Stalin's daughter. [SS]

22. The Soviet poet and writer Boris Pasternak (1890–1960) attracted worldwide attention when his novel *Doctor Zhivago*, which had been refused publication in the USSR, appeared in Italy in 1957 (and thereafter in other Western countries). Pasternak was awarded the Nobel Prize for literature in 1958. These events set off a hysterical official campaign against Pasternak, who died in 1960.

Andrei Sinyavsky was a Soviet literary scholar and Yuli Daniel a translator. They were arrested in 1965, put on trial for having their work published abroad, and sentenced to camp terms of seven and five years, respectively. The case became a cause célèbre, and protests against the trial stimulated the growth of the dissident movement. [SS]

23. Fyodor Raskolnikov was a leader of the Kronstadt sailors in the Russian Revolution of 1917 and a commander in the Red Navy during the Civil War. Later he served as Soviet ambassador to Spain and France. During the purges of 1936–37 he was recalled to Moscow, but knowing the fate that awaited him there he defected instead. He then wrote an open letter to Stalin, the publication of which drew the attention of world opinion to the purges. [SS]

24. Yuri Andropov was chairman of the KGB. Felix Dzerzhinsky was founder of the Cheka, the first Soviet secret police created in Lenin's time. [SS]

25. Julius and Ethel Rosenberg were Americans who spied for the Soviet Union in the late 1940s and early 1950s. Accused of providing the Soviet Union with important information about the atomic bomb, they were convicted of treason and sent to the electric chair. [SS]

26. Ivan Dmitriyevich Serbin was head of the Central Committee department responsible for defense industry. [SK]

27. That is, Brezhnev. [SS]

28. It is now believed that lupus is a disorder of the human immune system, which loses the capacity to distinguish between invading viruses and

bacteria and the body's own tissues and attacks them all indiscriminately. Lupus is still incurable, although new drugs have been developed that mitigate the effects to some extent. [SS]

29. Minister of Foreign Affairs. [SS]

30. The reference is to the patriarch of the Russian Orthodox Church. The town in which the monastery complex is located has now been given back its old name of Sergiev Posad. [SS]

31. On every floor of a Soviet hotel, at a table near the elevator, a *dezhurnaya* (duty woman) was inevitably posted. She was in charge of room keys, enforced instructions from the hotel administration, sorted out guests' everyday problems, and kept an eye on the comings and goings of guests and visitors. [SS]

32. From the Archive of the President of the Russian Federation, Special Folder, KGB Memorandum of 3.25.70, No. 745-A/ov, the Kremlin, Moscow. [SK]

33. This was the Kremlin Hospital, which served members of the power elite. [SK]

34. As a member of the Supreme Soviet, Andropov was expected to attend meetings with his constituents. This was somewhat of a formality. [SS]

35. An order for the search, the presence of witnesses, and the compilation of a record were all required by official regulations. [SS]

36. A. I. Adzhubei, *Te desyat' let* (Those ten years; Moscow: Sovetskaya Rossiya, 1989).

37. See "Conversation at the Party Control Committee." [SK]

38. Khrushchev had abolished the central economic ministries and devolved economic management to *sovnarkhozy* (regional councils of national economy). The *sovnarkhozy* were disbanded and the central economic ministries reestablished as soon as he lost power. [SS]

39. The Arbat (after which Khrushchev's dog was named) is a fashionable thoroughfare in central Moscow. [SS]

40. The "Cambridge five" refers to a circle of Cambridge University graduates—Kim Philby, Donald Maclean, Guy Burgess, John Cairncross, and Anthony Blunt—who spied for the Soviet Union between the 1930s and the 1960s. [SS]

41. Under Gorbachev the term "stagnation period" was used to refer to the whole of the period from Khrushchev's retirement in 1964 up to the coming to power of Gorbachev in 1985. [SS]

42. Roy Medvedev and Zhores Medvedev, *Khrushchev: The Years in Power* (Oxford: Oxford University Press, 1979). [SS]

43. Roi Medvedev, *Khrushchev: Politicheskaya biografiya* (Khrushchev: A political biography; Benson, Vt.: Chalidze, 1986). [SK]

44. Yuri Andropov came to power after Brezhnev's death, on November 10, 1982, but died fifteen months later, on February 9, 1984. He was succeeded by Konstantin Chernenko, who died on March 10, 1985. After Chernenko's death, Mikhail Gorbachev came to power. [SS]

45. Yakovlev under Gorbachev, like Suslov under Brezhnev, was the secretary of the Central Committee responsible for ideology. [SS]

46. The mass-circulation popular magazine *Ogonyok* was famous in the late 1980s for exposés that pushed forward the limits of glasnost. [SS]

47. Doctor of Sciences was the highest Soviet scholarly degree, well above the level of Western doctoral degrees. [SS]

48. Vitaly Korotich, the chief editor of *Ogonyok*, was a well-known "democrat" and a highly controversial figure. [SS]

49. Previously responsibility for ideology had been shared among a number of Central Committee departments. [SS]

50. The main Soviet literary journals were bulky and thus known as "thick journals." [SS]

51. Corresponding members of the Academy of Sciences had a status just below that of full academicians. [SS]

52. People occupying the most important positions had access to an especially secure and high-quality telecommunications system known as the *kremlyovka* ("Kremlin line"). [SS]

53. Politizdat was one of the official Soviet publishing houses for political literature. [SS]

54. The Central Committee archival documents to which reference is made in the following discussion were published in the Russian newspaper *Segodnya* (Today; Moscow), October 14, 1994, p. 9. [SK]

55. The official name of the Russian Center for the Preservation and Study of Documentation is the Rossiysky gosudarstvenny arkhiv sotsial'no-politicheskoi istorii (Russian State Archive of Socio-Political History), at Bol'shaya Dmitrovka 15, 103821 Moscow. The fax number is (7095) 292 9017. The director is Kirill Mikhailovich Andereon. [SK]

56. One of the two books was published in 2000 by The Pennsylvania State University Press under the title *Nikita Khrushchev and the Creation of a Superpower*. The other book that I planned, on reforms in the Soviet Union, remains unfinished. [SK]

57. The NPO Elektronmash (Nauchnoproizvodstvennoe ob"edinenie Elektronnye mashiny, Scientific-Production Association "Electronic Machines") was created in the mid-1980s on the basis of the Control Computer Institute where I used to work. It included a computer factory in Moscow (Energopribor) and two software organizations, in Voronezh and Kazan, respectively. My position there was first deputy director in charge of research and development. [SK]

58. Another copy of the tapes on compact disks and of all the transcripts is now in the archive of the John Hay Library at Brown University, Providence, Rhode Island. [SK]

# Conversation with N. S. Khrushchev at the Party Control Committee

*To the Central Committee of the CPSU*

*On the instructions of the Central Committee of the CPSU, in connection with the forthcoming publication in the USA and a number of other Western countries of "the memoirs of N. S. Khrushchev," a conversation with Comrade N. S. Khrushchev took place on November 10 of this year at the Party Control Committee.*

*During this conversation, Comrade Khrushchev conducted himself in an insincere and incorrect fashion, and avoided discussion of the issue of his incorrect actions. He asserted that he had not handed over his memoir materials to anyone for publication. . . .*

*We attach the stenographic record of the conversation with Comrade Khrushchev. . . .*

*November 13, 1970*
*A. Pelshe*

TOP SECRET

Stenographic Record of the Conversation with Comrade N. S. Khrushchev at the Party Control Committee under the Central Committee of the CPSU on November 10, 1970

Present:     Comrades Pelshe, A. Ya.; Postovalov, S. O.; Melnikov, R. E.;[1] and Comrade Khrushchev, N. S.

*Com. Pelshe:* On the instructions of the Politburo, we've invited you to the Party Control Committee for you to give an explanation about a matter of foreign policy connected with your memoirs, a matter that may cause our party and country great political damage. Possibly you have up-to-date information on the matter, possibly you don't. According to a communication from our ambassador in the United States, Comrade Dobrynin, on November 6 representatives of the American magazine-publishing concern *Time* in New York officially announced that they are in possession of "the memoirs of N. S. Khrushchev," which will first appear in the magazine *Life*, starting on November 23, and will then come out as a separate book under the title *Khrushchev Remembers*. The book will be put on sale on December 21. In the last few days, information was obtained through TASS[2] to the effect that information agencies and the foreign press are widely advertising the forthcoming publication of "the memoirs of N. S. Khrushchev" in the USA and a number of other Western countries—in particular, Britain, West Germany, France, Italy, and Sweden.

You recall that some time ago we had a conversation with you in the office of Andrei Pavlovich Kirilenko, in which we told you that the way you were producing your memoirs, involving a broad circle of people in the process, was not in accord with party principles. You were warned that it didn't exclude the possibility of a leak. You see, the leak has occurred, and you must understand that you bear full responsibility.

We would like to hear your explanation of this matter and to know what attitude you take. Perhaps you'll tell us directly to whom you handed over these materials for publication abroad.

*Com. Khrushchev:* I protest, Comrade Pelshe. I have my human dignity and I protest. I didn't hand over material to anyone. I'm no less a Communist than you are.

*Com. Pelshe:* You must tell us how they ended up over there.

*Com. Khrushchev:* You tell me how they ended up over there. I don't think they did end up over there. I think this is a provocation.

*Com. Pelshe:* You are in a party office.

*Com. Khrushchev:* Never before have I been at the Party Control Committee. I find myself in such a situation for the first time now, at the end of my life. I don't say at the end of my activity. My activity is over. And you demand explanations from me.

*Com. Pelshe:* Correct.

*Com. Khrushchev:* I've explained it to you.

*Com. Pelshe:* You haven't yet explained anything to us.

*Com. Khrushchev:* There's nothing more to explain. I have never at any time handed over any memoirs to anyone. I would never permit it. As for what I have dictated, I consider that to be the right of every citizen and party member. I remember very well what I've dictated. Not everything can be published at this time.

*Com. Pelshe:* That's your opinion. We had a talk with you and told you it wasn't appropriate to involve a broad circle of people in the writing of your memoirs, and that the secrets you were setting out might end up abroad. And that's where they did end up. It disturbs us greatly.

*Com. Khrushchev:* That was not, if you recall, what I was told. I was told not to write and not to dictate. And I said it was Nicholas I who forbade Shevchenko[3] to write or draw. I was astonished that in my party, to which I had devoted my life, we were returning to his methods.

*Com. Postovalov:* That's an inappropriate comparison. An incorrect one.

*Com. Khrushchev:* I was treated in the same way as Shevchenko.

*Com. Postovalov:* Why draw such a parallel?

*Com. Khrushchev:* I'm against such a parallel.

*Com. Pelshe:* You didn't accept the advice we gave you.

*Com. Khrushchev:* No. Please arrest me, shoot me. I'm fed up with life. When people ask me, I say that I'm not glad to be alive. Today the radio reported the death of de Gaulle. I envy him. I was an honest and devoted person. Ever since the party was born I've worked for it.

*Com. Pelshe:* That we know. You tell us, how shall we get out of this situation?

*Com. Khrushchev:* I don't know. It's your fault—not yours personally, but the whole leadership's. If the leadership had been attentive and reasonable, they would have said: "Comrade Khrushchev, . . ."

You recall that Comrade Kirilenko asked: "Are you dictating?" I replied yes. I understood that before summoning me they had sent agents to observe me.

*Com. Pelshe:* Many people in Moscow already know that you're dictating.

*Com. Khrushchev:* I'm seventy-six years old. I'm of sound mind, and responsible for all my words and actions. I thought Comrade Kirilenko would give me people to whom I could dictate.

*Com. Pelshe:* Why didn't you turn for help to the Central Committee earlier? When you were summoned by Comrade Kirilenko, you had already dictated a great deal.

*Com. Khrushchev:* How did you hear about it? You say you learned about it from the radio. Who reported it to you?

*Com. Pelshe:* Our ambassador officially informed us.

*Com. Khrushchev:* It may be a provocation on the part of the bourgeois press. As my name makes a sensation, perhaps they fabricated material about me.

*Com. Pelshe:* How shall we get out of this situation?

*Com. Khrushchev:* I don't know. I am completely isolated. I find myself in effect under house arrest. Both gates, entry and exit, are under surveillance. It's very shameful. I'm fed up. Help me in my suffering.

*Com. Pelshe:* Nobody is hurting you.

*Com. Khrushchev:* Moral torments are the most painful.

Com. Postovalov: You say you haven't handed anything over to anyone. That's very important in the current situation.

*Com. Khrushchev:* I think you and Comrade Pelshe understand very well that I haven't handed anything over to anyone, and that my convictions don't permit me to hand anything over. You remember, Comrade Pelshe, in Comrade Kirilenko's office I said: "If only I had been given help."

*Com. Pelshe:* That wasn't what you said. You said: "When I'm finished, I'll hand the material over to the Central Committee."

*Com. Khrushchev:* That wasn't what I said. Comrade Kirilenko proposed that I stop writing. I said: "I can't stop, it's my right." We're politicians. I shall die.

*Com. Pelshe:* We shall all die.

*Com. Khrushchev:* The chairman of the Supreme Soviet—I don't recall his name—has died.

*Com. Pelshe:* Ignatov?

*Com. Khrushchev:* Yes, Ignatov. We don't know who will die first. And he was a fool.

*Com. Postovalov:* That isn't the point, Comrade Khrushchev.

*Com. Khrushchev:* Yes it is.

*Com. Postovalov:* The point is the serious situation that will arise if the materials are published. In all likelihood they will be published. And you yourself don't know how they ended up over there.

*Com. Khrushchev:* I know our ambassador in the United States very well. I have the highest respect for him.

*Com. Postovalov:* All the more so.

*Com. Khrushchev:* He reported what the press is reporting. I've never trusted the bourgeois press. That's why I say he himself knows nothing. Perhaps by summoning me here you'll help me die sooner.

*Com. Pelshe:* We don't want you to die. Live in good health.

*Com. Khrushchev:* I want death.

*Com. Melnikov:* Perhaps someone tricked you?

*Com. Khrushchev:* My dear comrade, I take responsibility for my words. I'm not a madman. I haven't handed materials over to anyone and couldn't have done so.

*Com. Melnikov:* To whom did you entrust the materials? Might not those to whom you entrusted them have handed them over?

*Com. Khrushchev:* No.

*Com. Melnikov:* It wasn't only your son who handled your materials, but also a typist who you don't know, and a nonparty writer whom you also don't know, and other people as well.

*Com. Khrushchev:* They are Soviet people, people I trust.

*Com. Melnikov:* There are all kinds of people. They might have tricked you.

*Com Khrushchev:* I don't believe that the materials ended up in the hands of the Americans. It's a hoax, a lie, a fabrication. I'm sure of it.

*Com. Melnikov:* But if they are published you'll answer for it.

*Com. Khrushchev:* You don't scare me. At the age of seventy-six, I take responsibility for my actions. In no way will you scare me.

*Com. Melnikov:* Don't you bang your fist and don't shout. You are at the Party Control Committee. Behave in an appropriate fashion.

*Com. Khrushchev:* You too behave in an appropriate fashion. I'm still a party member. Don't deprive me of my rights.

*Com. Postovalov:* Nobody is being rude to you. We've informed you of the situation that has arisen in connection with your memoirs. And you shout and bang your fist on the table.

*Com. Khrushchev:* It's my nerves. I'm not shouting. My position is different from yours. So is my age.

*Com. Pelshe:* Every party member, whatever his age and the state of his nerves, must take responsibility for his actions.

*Com. Khrushchev:* You're absolutely right, Comrade Pelshe. I do take responsibility. I'm ready to bear any punishment, up to and including the death penalty.

*Com. Pelshe:* The Party Control Committee doesn't impose the death penalty.

*Com. Khrushchev:* It used to. How many thousands of people perished! How many were shot! And now memorials are being erected to those who were branded "enemies of the people"—to Postyshev, Blyukher, Stanislav Viktorovich Kosior.[4] It makes me glad, and it pains me.

*Com. Pelshe:* This is superfluous talk.

*Com. Khrushchev:* It's directly relevant to what we're discussing. I told Comrade Kirilenko, Comrade Demichev, and yourself that I stood, and still stand, on the decisions of the 22d Party Congress, and so long as I live I shall remain a supporter of those decisions. The murderers must be exposed. They are dead, but if the murderers are now put up on a pedestal, then perhaps someone will feel inclined to repeat what they did. I'm against that. At the Twentieth Party Congress, I said nothing about the cult of personality in my report, and in the course of the congress it was decided to speak about it separately. Material on this question had been prepared by a commission chaired by Comrade Pospelov. But then it turned out that we had one general report and another on Stalin. If the two reports had been presented by different speakers, it might have given rise to misunderstanding. I agreed to present the second report as well.

*Com. Pelshe:* That report is well known. The party has drawn the necessary conclusions from it. But how shall we get out of today's situation?

*Com. Khrushchev:* Comrade Pelshe, the best way out is not to place Khrushchev in the conditions in which he has been placed, but to create for him the conditions to which he has a right. I thought and said that at sixty-five years of age, or even at sixty, we must give up leading positions in favor of the younger generation.

*Com. Pelshe:* But you didn't put this issue on the agenda.

*Com. Khrushchev:* I did.

*Com. Pelshe:* I don't know.

*Com. Khrushchev:* You didn't know because at that time you occupied a different position. When Mzhavanadze reached sixty, I told him: we must transfer you from the post of chairman of the presidium of the Supreme Soviet of Georgia.

*Com. Pelshe:* But that isn't the subject of our conversation today. If you think that this is a provocation on the part of the *Time* agency, then could you make a declaration to that effect?

*Com. Khrushchev:* Nobody is asking me about it.

*Com. Pelshe:* You could declare that you have written no memoirs.

*Com. Khrushchev:* That I cannot say. I did dictate them.

*Com. Melnikov:* You haven't finished them?

*Com. Khrushchev:* They're still unfinished. I've been sick.

*Com. Postovalov:* An agency couldn't have obtained unfinished memoirs from you.

*Com. Khrushchev:* As is well known, in any country an author must conclude a contract with a publishing house, which thereby acquires the right to publish his work. Otherwise the publisher has no such right.

*Com. Postovalov:* That's why we have to find a way out of this situation. They can't be allowed to treat you in that way. Respond to what the enemy has done. It will all be right and sane.

*Com. Khrushchev:* Every madman thinks he is not a madman. I don't think I'm insane. Perhaps you see my condition differently.

*Com. Postovalov:* So the problem must be solved in a sane way.

*Com. Khrushchev:* I say that in my memoirs there is information that is secret and cannot be published either in my lifetime or for some time—for how long we don't yet know—after my death. Although, you know, there is in general no such thing as a secret. In the conspiracy to murder Paul, his son Aleksandr took part.[5] And everyone knew he was one of the murderers.

*Com. Postovalov:* What you've written is not secret?

*Com. Khrushchev:* But when to publish this material must be decided by the party. Many people surely believe, for instance, that the Americans began the war in Korea. But I know it was Kim Il-Sung who began it. I was with Stalin at the time. But there's no need to reveal that at present.

*Com. Melnikov:* But you dictate it.

*Com. Khrushchev:* I dictate it because it happened in my presence. I know about it. That is my right.

*Com. Postovalov:* And if it's published?

*Com. Khrushchev:* I say that cannot be, from my point of view.

*Com. Pelshe:* Your dictation has passed through many hands on tape and in typescript, and you are unable to provide any guarantee that it hasn't somehow ended up where it isn't supposed to be. You are responsible for what you dictate.

*Com. Khrushchev:* That, Comrade Pelshe, is another matter. You mean to say that I shouldn't write.

*Com. Pelshe:* You must answer for your actions.

*Com. Khrushchev:* Do as you must.

*Com. Pelshe:* If you think you're doing everything in the interests of our country, then it would now be expedient to make a declaration to the effect that you have written nothing and handed nothing over to anyone, and that the forthcoming publication of your memoirs is a libel, a fabrication.

*Com. Khrushchev:* I repeat that I want to die an honest man. What I have written I have given to nobody. That is so.

*Com. Melnikov:* But if they publish it, it will be a fabrication?

*Com. Khrushchev:* From my point of view, yes. You too understand. Why interrogate me, go after me, catch me on a fishhook? I'm an old man. Who needs me? No fishhook works on me. So I say to you, Zinoviev—

*Com. Pelshe:* That's another matter. Give us an answer on the substance of the question put before you. We must act to prevent the foreigners from publishing your memoirs in the nearest future.

*Com. Khrushchev:* I know nothing of these memoirs. Where do they come from? What memoirs are they?

*Com. Pelshe:* We're talking about your memoirs.

*Com. Khrushchev:* You're speaking on the basis of the ambassador's report.

*Com. Pelshe:* But on November 23—that is, in thirteen days from now—they will be in print. They are now in press.

*Com. Khrushchev:* Nobody, including myself, has seen these memoirs.

*Com. Postovalov:* What will be your attitude if they appear?

*Com. Khrushchev:* Like you, I am indignant.

*Com. Postovalov:* That's not saying much.

*Com. Khrushchev:* I'm prepared to declare that I have not given, and have no intention of giving, any memoirs either to Soviet or to foreign publishers. Write it down please.

*Com. Postovalov:* If they are written only in rough draft, then it can't be said that they are written.

*Com. Khrushchev:* There are no such documents. That's why I think my materials were removed. These methods are an infringement of Leninist norms and of the standards of party life. I protest, Comrade Pelshe. I ask that my materials be returned.

*Com. Pelshe:* You protest in vain. You say there are materials that must not be published. And what if they're wandering around Moscow?

*Com. Khrushchev:* Where are they wandering? That shows we're returning to Stalinist surveillance.

*Com. Pelshe:* No surveillance is being conducted against you.

*Com. Khrushchev:* This material is mine. Nobody has a right to take it. This is like the time of Nicholas. It's a lawless reprisal. It's a disturbing thing.

*Com. Pelshe:* A disturbing thing!? Your secret materials are in broad circulation, and you bear party and state responsibility for this.

*Com. Khrushchev:* I'm ready for the cross. Take the nails and hammer.

*Com. Pelshe:* We don't need these phrases.

*Com. Khrushchev:* They aren't phrases. This is what I want. The Russians say: From the begging bowl and prison there is no escape. I've always been in a different position. Throughout my whole political career I've never been under interrogation by party agencies.

*Com. Postovalov:* You're here not for interrogation, but for a conversation. We're discussing with you what is to be done. But there's no point in your saying it's a hoax, for the materials are already at the editorial office. You can believe the ambassador.

*Com. Khrushchev:* I have the highest respect for Ambassador Dobrynin. He's the cleverest ambassador we have abroad.

*Com. Postovalov:* So we have to think, and first of all you have to think, what kind of declarations need to be made about this. And they will have to be made—if, as you say, you are indignant.

*Com. Khrushchev:* I'll say just one thing. Everything I've dictated is the truth. There are no inventions or exaggerations. On the contrary, in places I've softened things down. I counted on being invited to write. After all, Zhukov's memoirs have been published. Zhukov's wife called me and said: "Georgy Konstantinovich is lying sick and cannot speak with you personally, but he asks you to give your opinion of his book." "Have you read it?" she asked. I said I haven't read it, but people have told me about it. I said that what Zhukov has written about Stalin is repulsive, and I can't read it. Zhukov is an honest man, a military man, but he's a madcap. Zhukov described the episode about how Vatutin was killed,[6] and claimed I was also there at the time.

*Com. Postovalov:* But you said you hadn't read the book.

*Com. Khrushchev:* But people told me about it.

*Com. Pelshe:* How can you make judgments about a book you haven't read?

*Com. Khrushchev:* Such an episode is described.

*Com. Pelshe:* You don't know how it is described.

*Com. Khrushchev:* You talk to me in the proper way. I'm no dimwit who can be pulled along by a thread. I'm a human being and I have my dignity. You're exploiting your position. But so long as my heart beats I shall defend my human dignity.

*Com. Postovalov:* You must defend the interests of the party.

*Com. Khrushchev:* What I write doesn't diverge from the interests of the party.

*Com. Postovalov:* It isn't Zhukov we're talking about.

*Com. Khrushchev:* Comrade Pelshe didn't let me finish my thought. Cutting people short—that was Stalin's style.

*Com. Pelshe:* Those are your habits.

*Com. Khrushchev:* I was also infected by Stalin. I have freed myself of Stalin, but you haven't done so.

*Com. Pelshe:* You don't know that.

*Com. Khrushchev:* I have the right to speak.

*Com. Pelshe:* I too have the right to speak.

*Com. Khrushchev:* I didn't read it, and I won't read it. It disgusts me. I said to Zhukov's wife: "How could Zhukov write such an episode about Vatutin's death? As though Vatutin leapt out of his vehicle and gave my vehicle cover with his machine gun." I said: "Vatutin was wounded in the groin. He couldn't leap out. But the most important thing is that Khrushchev wasn't there." And in the second edition it was corrected. And you said that I say what isn't true.

*Com. Pelshe:* Let's think how to put the matter right.

*Com. Khrushchev:* You are now stronger than I am. You can do it.

*Com. Pelshe:* We can't do it through diplomatic channels.

*Com. Melnikov:* Comrade Khrushchev, you can come out with a protest and express your indignation.

*Com. Khrushchev:* I tell you, don't push me into lying in my old age.

*Com. Pelshe:* It's a matter of what needs to be done to lessen the political damage.

*Com. Postovalov:* So there were memoirs?

*Com. Khrushchev:* I can't say I didn't dictate anything.

*Com. Melnikov:* It's up to you to decide.

*Com. Khrushchev:* Now this material must be returned.

*Com. Pelshe:* That's a different issue.

*Com. Khrushchev:* I wanted to appeal to Comrade Brezhnev, but I was summoned to you. After all, the Party Control Committee is an agency of repression. When Shkiryatov was in charge here, how many people passed through.

*Com. Postovalov:* Don't you talk about that. Your material, as you said, is of such a kind as cannot be published for many years. And if it is published, what indignation that will arouse among Soviet people!

*Com. Khrushchev:* I am indignant.

*Com. Postovalov:* That's the point of our talk. What is your attitude?

*Com. Khrushchev:* My attitude is a fully party attitude.

*Com. Postovalov:* So it should be. You should be extremely indignant.

*Com. Khrushchev:* I'll agree to anything. In my time I used sharp words. I knew how to do it.

*Com. Postovalov:* And you need to use them now, to hinder the publication.

*Com. Khrushchev:* Agreed. That's right.

*Com. Postovalov:* If you say you are indignant in the extreme, then you must speak out.

*Com. Melnikov:* While the material has not yet been published, it could have some effect.

*Com. Khrushchev:* You understand, as there is no contract and I've seen nothing.

*Com. Postovalov:* Haven't you even seen the material from TASS?

*Com. Pelshe:* When they already intend to publish the material, you must say you have had no intention of writing or publishing anything.

*Com. Khrushchev:* So far I've read nothing anywhere. In the old days, even those of us who were not members of the party Central Committee—I was secretary of the Bauman district committee[7]—used to receive material from TASS. Party members would come and read it to familiarize themselves with the position of our enemies. When I was secretary of a district committee of the party in the Donbas, we used to receive *Socialist Courier*.[8] Lenin was dead, but Lenin's spirit was still alive at that time.

*Com. Postovalov:* So you don't believe us about what they intend to do with your material?

*Com. Khrushchev:* You yourselves have seen nothing.

*Com. Postovalov:* What they are broadcasting on radio and television is sufficient. You must be indignant at this.

*Com. Khrushchev:* I am indignant.

*Com. Pelshe:* It became known to us today that the American magazine-publishing concern *Time* is in possession of Khrushchev's memoirs, which they will start to publish over there. That's a fact. And you must declare your attitude toward it. From the reports it's clear that the American press, and the German and British press too, have raised a hullabaloo about it. We'd like you to make clear your attitude, without speaking about the substance of the memoirs, to say you are indignant at this, and that you have handed nothing over to anyone. That will to some extent reduce interest in the publication of the materials, and will expose its organizers.

*Com. Khrushchev:* Let the stenographer take down my declaration:

*From reports appearing in the foreign press, mainly in the United States of America and other bourgeois European countries, it has become known that some memoirs or reminiscences of Khrushchev are being published. I am indignant at this fabrication, because I have handed no memoirs over to anyone—neither to the* Time *publishing house, nor to any other foreign publisher, nor even to a Soviet publisher. Therefore I consider this to be a lie and a falsification, of which the bourgeois press is capable.*

*Com. Pelshe:* If we help and suggest channels through which you could bring your declaration to the attention of the American press, would you agree to use those channels?

*Com. Postovalov:* In view of your indignation.

*Com. Pelshe:* Let's suppose a correspondent came to see you. Could you repeat this to him?

*Com. Khrushchev:* Yes. If you would like, I can hold a press conference. I still have enough gunpowder and dignity to defend the honor of my regiment, the honor of our country and party. I know, and I repeat it to you, that the statements I've dictated are true. I vouch for them absolutely.

*Com. Postovalov:* All the same, somehow this has leaked out, and you need to give that some thought.

*Com. Khrushchev:* I place the responsibility on those comrades who didn't want to help me. They wanted to settle the matter by shouting an order, and that leads to no good.

*Com. Postovalov:* It is easiest of all to place responsibility on someone else.

*Com. Khrushchev:* The comrades who talked with me placed the responsibility on me. You remember, Comrade Pelshe, our talk in Comrade Kirilenko's office. A record of that meeting wasn't taken. I said: "If you had helped me, given me a typist, the Central Committee would have obtained those materials."

*Com. Pelshe:* That is, from the very start you acted illegally.

*Com. Khrushchev:* Don't scare me with talk about illegality. You shouldn't approach the issue in an oversimplified way.

*Com. Pelshe:* What, would they really not have given you a typist had you from the very start appealed to the Central Committee?

*Com. Khrushchev:* They summoned me to the Central Committee.

*Com. Pelshe:* That was in 1968.

*Com. Postovalov:* And you began to write earlier.

*Com. Khrushchev:* At that time I'd only just begun writing. And straight away a young man came to see me, and straight away I guessed he'd been sent to spy on me. I've never kept the fact that I was dictating secret. It isn't an underground activity. They didn't help me. They didn't create the right conditions for me. I thought that this was a long-term project, and that I wouldn't resume dictating for a long time. And do you know how many of the people who meet me ask: "Are you writing?" I say no. "You must write. How valuable it is for us!" Don't think I want to exaggerate my own importance. We lived in the same era. I was near Stalin. This will have great value for future generations.

*Com. Postovalov:* The Central Committee has party periodicals. There is the Institute of Marxism-Leninism. They study and elucidate the history of the party. But memoirs are quite another matter.

*Com. Khrushchev:* Popov wrote a history. A good history. A clever man. He worked in the Comintern.[9] Stalin shot him. Pospelov was a sycophant. He wrote to Stalin's dictation. History is constantly revised, because it is written by people. Memoirs are a completely personal matter. And you will never take away from me my point of view. In memoirs a person sets out his point of view. He writes of the time in which he lived.

*Com. Postovalov:* You must keep secrets.

*Com. Khrushchev:* I was told straight out: "Don't dare to write." I don't agree.

*Com. Pelshe:* You were obliged to inform the Central Committee that you'd begun writing memoirs.

*Com. Khrushchev:* I didn't realize. You were there at the time, Comrade Pelshe, and you know that I asked.

*Com. Pelshe:* There was no such clear request from you.

*Com. Khrushchev:* How could I ask when they refused me? I couldn't imagine such a thing. No organization is as dear to me as the Central Committee. I want to end my life devoted to the Central Committee, and to serve as I am able to the benefit of my party, to which I have given so many years. True, on the party's fiftieth anniversary they were giving out medals to good and deserving people. People asked me: "Have you received one? Well, you will." But I didn't.

*Com. Pelshe:* That's another matter.

*Com. Khrushchev:* That's the attitude taken toward people, toward party members who have traversed the long road—the road of the Civil War, the Great Patriotic War, the restoration of what was destroyed, the five year plans. When I was first secretary in Ukraine, how much effort I put in! In Moscow and Moscow province I put in no less effort. So why is the attitude taken toward me different? You yourselves think about it. I don't want to call things by their names. I'm indignant not because they didn't give me the medal, but because there is no objectivity, only subjectivity. I'd like to appeal to you, as chairman of the Party Control Committee, to come to the defense of an honest party member.

*Com. Pelshe:* We still have to examine the matter that's on the agenda today.

*Com. Khrushchev:* Don't scare me, I'm not afraid. What I have now is not life but suffering. I envy De Gaulle. He was a healthy fellow. I now have a hard life.

*Com. Melnikov:* And what's so hard about it?

*Com. Khrushchev:* When you're pensioned off, then you'll learn that those are hellish torments.

*Com. Pelshe:* That comes to everyone. We all have to retire.

*Com. Khrushchev:* They deprived me of the rights of a member of the Central Committee. They stopped inviting me to plenums. Is that really proper? I called Malin.[10] He says: "I can't." Everyone retires. Shvernik is also retired. He lies like a corpse. But the attitude taken toward him is quite different. Why one attitude toward him, and a different attitude toward me? In what way have I done less for the party than others? That creates special conditions for me. You try my life. You won't frighten me with anything.

*Com. Pelshe:* We don't intend to frighten you with anything.

*Com. Khrushchev:* Anything. Because everything now is hard for me.

*Com. Postovalov:* You're not speaking seriously.

*Com. Khrushchev:* Try it yourself. You'll learn.

*Com. Postovalov:* This isn't a serious conversation.

*Com. Khrushchev:* Comrade Pelshe, how many people they executed! How many friends of mine they executed, the most loyal members of the party! How many enemies of the Cultural Revolution has Mao Zedong now executed! Mao Zedong and Stalin.

*Com. Postovalov:* You draw such a parallel in vain.

*Com. Khrushchev:* Stalin and Mao Zedong.

*Com. Postovalov:* That isn't what we are talking about now.

*Com. Khrushchev:* For three months I was in the hospital on Granovsky Street. Three months I was lying there. Now I've begun to walk. I don't know what will happen after my appointment with the chief party physician. What will you say about me, Comrade Pelshe? I won't talk about you under any circumstances. [*To Melnikov*] Your face seems familiar. Where did you work?

*Com. Melnikov:* In Uzbekistan.

*Com. Khrushchev:* I want to say something about the depot that supplies people receiving special food rations. I think it does enormous harm. Our families—I too benefit from these special supplies—don't know the real state of affairs. Take, for instance, the fact that ordinary people can't even buy dill. That's just poor organization of trade. Essential products are missing from the stores. There's no meat.

*Com. Pelshe:* In Moscow there is.

*Com. Khrushchev:* People say: "Can a camel get from the Far East to Moscow? No it can't—it will get eaten."

*Com. Postovalov:* And did people really not tell such anecdotes in your time?

*Com. Khrushchev:* Six years have passed since I left office. After Stalin's death, our country found itself in a difficult situation with regard to defense. Now the situation is different. We must devote greater attention to consumer goods. Try to buy yourself a cap. You won't find one.

*Com. Postovalov:* You're telling us fairy tales. See, I did buy myself a cap—true, not a deerskin cap, just an ordinary one.

*Com. Khrushchev:* What can I say? We have very many deficiencies.

*Com. Pelshe:* Per capita consumption of meat has increased. Wages have increased. The people have more money than before. They have begun to live better.

*Com. Khrushchev:* Does your working day end at six o'clock? It's getting late, but that isn't my fault.

*Com. Postovalov:* Again. Why shift the blame to others?

*Com. Pelshe:* If you had respected your Central Committee, you would immediately have informed it of your decision to write memoirs.

*Com. Khrushchev:* The Central Committee deprived me of my right to attend its plenums. Stalin himself would not have permitted such a thing. Stalin acted directly—he would arrest someone as an enemy of the people. That's a fact. As a member of the Central Committee, I wanted to come to the Mausoleum on the anniversary of the October revolution. I ordered a car, and the man[11] told me he didn't recommend that I go there. How is that possible?

*Com. Pelshe:* You might have complained.

*Com. Khrushchev:* Again it's my fault.

*Com. Pelshe:* I don't know what they said to you.

*Com. Khrushchev:* I'm dead, and your conscience can't reconcile itself to that. Vera Zasulich[12] told the tsarist court that she had killed. The court heard her out and vindicated her. And that was a tsarist court! An interesting thing! I find it hard to explain how it could have happened.

*Com. Postovalov:* It's all on record.

*Com. Khrushchev:* How could the court have vindicated her? You're not a jurist yourself?

*Com. Postovalov:* No.

*Com. Pelshe:* He's a party official.

*Com. Khrushchev:* There are some party officials who are also jurists. I want to ask about something else, as a human being and a party member. How could we, with such military might, allow Egypt to be crushed?[13]

*Com. Melnikov:* The struggle continues. Egypt hasn't been crushed.

*Com. Khrushchev:* Then you've heard nothing of what I've said, and you've said nothing to me. In 1956 we were very weak with regard to defense.[14] I recall the hardest time of the Cuban crisis. We won the battle without fighting. We resolved the problem correctly. I'm often asked questions about the Israeli aggression. I reply that now I don't know everything, I am a pensioner.

*Com. Pelshe:* On that note we shall bring the conversation to an end.

1. Pelshe was chairman of the Party Control Committee under the Central Committee of the CPSU. Postovalov and Melnikov were members of the Party Control Committee.

2. Telegraph Agency of the Soviet Union, the official Soviet news agency.

3. A nineteenth-century writer, the Ukrainian national poet. Tsar Nicholas I officially forbade him to write or draw and exiled him to Kazakhstan.

4. Postyshev, a former general secretary of the Communist Party (Bolshevik) of Ukraine, was arrested and shot in 1938. Marshal Blyukher was also arrested and shot in 1938. Stanislav Vikentye-vich (Viktorovich is an error) Kosior, another former general secretary of the Communist Party (Bolshevik) of Ukraine, was arrested in 1938 and shot in 1939.

5. The reference is to the assassination of Tsar Paul I in 1801.

6. In 1943, after the liberation of Kiev, while moving from one command post to another, Commander of the First Ukrainian Front Vatutin was killed by Ukrainian nationalists.

7. A district of Moscow. N. S. Khrushchev held this post in 1931–32.

8. Khrushchev held this post in 1925–26. *Socialist Courier* (Sotsialistichesky Vestnik) was the periodical of the Mensheviks in emigration.

9. The Communist International.

10. V. N. Malin was head of the General Department of the Central Committee of the CPSU.

11. The KGB officer assigned to N. S. Khrushchev.

12. Vera Zasulich (1851–1919) was a prominent Russian revolutionary. In 1878, she shot and seriously wounded General Trepov, the military governor of Saint Petersburg, in retaliation for an incident in which he had a political prisoner flogged for not removing his cap in his presence. At her trial Zasulich was acquitted and released. The tsar set the verdict aside and ordered her rearrest, but with the help of friends she escaped to Switzerland.

13. In the Six Day War of 1967.

14. Khrushchev is explaining his own failure to come to Egypt's aid at the time of the joint British, French, and Israeli attack on the Suez Canal in 1956.

# Biographies

**Abakumov, Ye. T.** (1895–1953). In 1932–33 director of the Stalinougol (Stalino Coal) trust in the Donbas. From 1933 to 1938 first deputy director of construction of Metrostroi (the body in charge of building the Moscow metro), in 1938 director of Metrostroi. In 1938–39 head of the Main Administration of Mine Construction of the People's Commissariat of Coal Industry, from 1939 to 1947 deputy and then first deputy people's commissar of coal industry. Thereafter occupied senior government posts with responsibility for inventions and discoveries, technological innovation in industry, and standardization.

**Abakumov, V. S.** (1908–54). From 1941 to 1943 deputy people's commissar of internal affairs and head of the NKVD Administration of Special Departments. From 1943 to 1946 head of the Main Counterintelligence Administration "Smersh" (acronym for *Smert shpionam*, "Death to spies") of the People's Commissariat of Defense (Ministry of Armed Forces). From 1946 to 1951 deputy minister and then minister of state security. In June 1951 arrested by Stalin, and in December 1954, under Stalin's successors, tried by the military collegium of the Supreme Court, and executed.

**Agranov, Ya. S.** (1893–1938). From 1919 an official of the All-Russian Cheka, the GPU, and the NKVD. From 1934 first deputy people's commissar of internal affairs, then secretary of the Small Council of People's Commissars (a permanent commission of the Council of People's Commissars established in early 1918 for the preliminary examination of governmental issues). Last post before being arrested was head of the Saratov administration of the NKVD. Fate unclear, probably shot.

**Aleksandrov, A. V.** (1883–1946). Composer. Major general. People's Artiste of the USSR from 1937. In 1928 organized the Song and Dance Ensemble of the Red Army.

---

Some biographies have been translated from the Russian edition of the memoirs. Others have been compiled with the aid of various other sources. In the biographies taken from the Russian edition, frequent use is made of the word "repressed," meaning "victim of Stalinist repression." This term refers to the arrest and imprisonment—and in many though not all cases the execution—of individuals on fabricated political charges, especially in the years 1936–39.

Where not otherwise indicated, "people's commissar," "minister," and similar designations refer to "people's commissar of the USSR," "minister of the USSR," and so on. The same applies to people's commissariats, ministries, and other government bodies. [SS]

**Aleksandrov, B. A.** (1905–?). Son of A. V. Aleksandrov. Composer. Major general. People's Artiste of the USSR from 1958. Succeeded his father as leader of the Song and Dance Ensemble of the Red Army in 1946.

**Andreyev, A. A.** (1895–1971). Worker. Member of the RSDLP from 1914. After 1917 occupied party and trade union posts. From 1920 secretary of the All-Russian Central Council of Trade Unions. From 1922 chairman of the CC of the Union of Railroad Workers. From 1924 to 1925 secretary of the CC of the AUCP(B). From 1927 secretary of the Northern Caucasus territory committee of the AUCP(B). From 1939 chairman of the Central Control Commission of the AUCP(B). People's commissar of workers' and peasants' inspection and deputy chairman of the USSR Council of People's Commissars. From 1931 people's commissar of communications. From 1935 to 1946 secretary of the CC of the AUCP(B). From 1939 to 1952 chairman of the Party Control Committee attached to the CC of the AUCP(B). From 1943 to 1946 people's commissar of agriculture. From 1946 deputy chairman of the USSR Council of Ministers. From 1953 member of the presidium of the USSR Supreme Soviet. From 1962 an official in the apparatus of the presidium of the USSR Supreme Soviet. Member of the party CC in 1920 and from 1922 to 1959. Member of the Politburo of the CC of the AUCP(B) from 1932 to 1952.

**Antipov, N. K.** (1894–1938). Worker. Member of the RSDLP from 1912. Participated in the revolutions of February and October 1917. Thereafter deputy chairman of the Supreme Council of National Economy, chairman of the Petrograd Cheka, and secretary of the Kazan province committee of the RCP(B). From 1920 member of the presidium of the All-Russian Central Council of Trade Unions. From 1923 secretary of the Moscow committee of the RCP(B). In 1925 secretary of the Urals province committee of the party. From 1926 secretary of the Leningrad province committee and of the Northwestern Bureau of the CC of the AUCP(B). From 1928 people's commissar of posts and telegraphs. From 1931 deputy people's commissar of workers' and peasants' inspection. From 1935 chairman of the Soviet Control Commission attached to the USSR Council of People's Commissars and deputy chairman of the Council of People's Commissars and of the Council of Labor and Defense. From 1924 member of the party CC. Member of the All-Russian CEC and of the CEC of the USSR. Victim of repression; arrested, posthumously rehabilitated.

**Antonescu, Ion.** (1882–1946). Romanian. General. From 1938 minister of defense, and from September 1940 prime minister of Romania. Marshal of Romania from 1941. Organizer of war against the USSR. Executed as a war criminal.

**Antonov-Ovseyenko, V. A.** (1883–1939). Son of an officer. Member of the RSDLP from 1903. Had an active role in the armed uprising of October 1917 in Petrograd. Thereafter member of the first Soviet government and leader of combat operations in Ukraine and against the Antonov rebellion. From 1922 head of the Political Administration of the Revolutionary Military Council. From 1924 to 1934 engaged in diplomatic work. From 1934 public prosecutor of the RSFSR. From 1936 general consul of the USSR in Republican Spain. Shot 1939, posthumously rehabilitated.

**Apanasenko, I. R.** Russian. Army general. From January 1941 commander of the Far Eastern Front (formed in 1938). From 1943 deputy commander of the Voronezh Front. Perished at the battlefront.

**Astakhov, F. A.** (1892–1966). In Red Army from 1918. From 1940 deputy chief of staff of the Main Administration of Air Forces of the Workers' and Peasants' Red Army. From June 1941 air force lieutenant general. During war commanded air forces of the Southwestern Front. From May 1942 to end of war, head of the Main Administration of the Civil Air Fleet and concurrently deputy commander of Red Army Air Forces (from May 1942 to August 1943), then deputy commander of Strategic Air Forces (August 1943 to December 1944). Air force marshal from 1944. After war, head of the Main Administration of the Civil Air Fleet.

**Badayev, A. Ye.** (1883–1951). Peasant. Member of the RSDLP from 1904. Worked as a fitter in Saint Petersburg. Deputy to the fourth State Duma. From 1913 official publisher of the newspaper *Pravda*. From 1917 occupied leading posts in food-supply and cooperative agencies. From 1921 worked in the consumer cooperative movement. Chairman of the Central Union of Consumers' Societies from 1930 and of the Moscow Union of Consumers' Societies from 1931. Deputy chairman of the Moscow Soviet. Member of the CEC. From 1935 deputy people's commissar of food industry of the USSR. From 1937 to 1938 people's commissar of food industry of the RSFSR. From 1938 to 1943 chairman of the presidium of the RSFSR Supreme Soviet, then member of the collegium of the People's Commissariat (Ministry) of Food Industry. Member of the CC of the AUCP(B) from 1925.

**Bagirov, M. Dzh. A.** (1896–1956). Azeri. Member of the RSDLP from 1917. From 1920 deputy chairman of the revolutionary committee of Karabakh province, chairman of the Azerbaijan Cheka and GPU, people's commissar of internal affairs, deputy chairman and chairman of the Council of People's Commissars of the Azerbaijan SSR. From 1933 to 1953 first secretary of the CC and of the Baku committee of the CP(B) of Azerbaijan. In 1953 chairman of the Council of Ministers of the Azerbaijan SSR. Member of the party CC from 1939. Candidate member of the Presidium of the CC CPSU from 1952 to 1953. Executed for criminal activity.

**Bagramyan, I. Kh.** (1897–1982). In Red Army from 1920. Head of the operational department, then deputy chief of staff and (from April 1942) chief of staff of the Southwestern Front. From July 1942 commanded the Sixteenth (later the Eleventh Guards) Army, from November 1943 the First Baltic Front, from February 1945 the Zemland Troop Grouping, from April 1945 the Third Belorussian Front. Took part in battle of Kursk and in Belorussian, Polotsk, Riga, Memel, East Prussian, and other military operations. After war occupied leading army posts. Twice Hero of the Soviet Union. Marshal of the Soviet Union.

**Bandera, S. A.** (1908–1959). Ukrainian. During the 1920s took part in the Ukrainian underground military organization created in Poland by E. Konowalcz. From 1929 member of the Organization of Ukrainian Nationalists. From 1933 chairman of the Organization of Ukrainian Nationalists in the western Ukraine (at that time belonging to Poland). Participated in terrorist attacks on Polish statesmen, imprisoned, and freed in 1939 during the German-Polish war. After 1941 led the anti-Soviet activity of the Ukrainian Insurgent Army on Ukrainian territory under temporary fascist occupation. In winter 1945 moved to Germany, whence continued to lead anti-Soviet activity. Remained in the Federal Republic of Germany under the pseudonym Stefan Poppel. Killed in Munich by a Soviet agent.

**Bandrowska-Turska, E.** (1899–1979). Polish. Singer. Performed in operas and concerts from 1918 to 1960. Professor at the Krakow and Warsaw Conservatories.

**Baranov, P. I.** (1892–1933). Member of the RSDLP from 1912. After 1917 in the Soviet armed forces. Fought in the Civil War. From 1923 deputy chief, and from 1924 chief, of the air forces of the Workers' and Peasants' Red Army. From 1925 to 1931 member of the Revolutionary Military Council of the USSR. From 1932 deputy people's commissar of heavy industry and head of the Main Administration of Aviation Industry. Member of the All-Russian CEC and of the CEC of the USSR.

**Batov, P. I.** (1897–1985). Lieutenant general. In Red Army from 1918. At start of war commanded the Ninth Unattached Infantry Corps in Crimea, then from November 1941 the 51st Army, and in early 1942 the Third Army. From February 1942 assistant commander of the Bryansk Front. From October

1942 until the end of the war, commander of the 65th Army, which took part in military operations of the Don, Stalingrad, Central, and First and Second Belorussian Fronts, including the battles of Stalingrad and Kursk, the battle for the Dnieper, the liberation of Belorussia, and the Vistula-Oder and Berlin operations. After war occupied important military posts. Twice Hero of the Soviet Union.

**Bauman, K. Ya.** (1892–1937). Peasant. Member of the RSDLP from 1907. Active participant in the revolution of October 1917. From 1920 secretary of the Kursk province committee of the RCP(B). From 1923 an official in the apparatus of the party CC. From 1928 member of the Orgburo of the CC of the AUCP(B) and second secretary of the Moscow city committee of the party. From 1929 secretary of the CC and first secretary of the Moscow city committee of the AUCP(B). From 1931 first secretary of the Central Asian Bureau of the CC of the AUCP(B). From 1934 head of the Department of Science and Scientific and Technological Discoveries of the CC of the AUCP(B). Candidate member of the Politburo of the CC of the AUCP(B) from 1929 to 1930. From 1925 member of the CC of the AUCP(B). Member of the CEC. Shot 1937, posthumously rehabilitated.

**Bazhan, N. P.** (1903–83). Poet, translator, and public figure. Son of a serviceman. Member of the AUCP(B) from 1940. During the Second World War editor of the newspaper *Za Radiansku Ukrainu* (For the Soviet Ukraine). From 1958 editor in chief of the Ukrainian Soviet Encyclopedia. Secretary of the USSR Writer's Union from 1967. Academician of the Academy of Sciences of the Ukrainian SSR from 1951. From 1943 to 1948 deputy chairman of the Council of People's Commissars (Soviet of Ministers) of the Ukrainian SSR.

**Bedny, Demyan.** (Pridvorov, Ye. A.) (1883–1945). Poet, writer of songs and fables. Member of the RSDLP from 1912. Actively served as a Bolshevik party propagandist.

**Begma, V. A.** (1905–65). From 1939 to 1941 first secretary of the Rovenky province committee of the CP(B) of Ukraine. From 1942 to 1944 under Nazi occupation, secretary of the underground Rovno province committee of the party (with the rank of major general).

**Beck, Jozef.** Polish. Minister of foreign affairs of Poland from 1932 to 1939.

**Belov, I. P.** (1893–1938). Hero of the civil war. Played a prominent role in the creation of the Workers' and Peasants' Red Army. From 1935 army commander of the first rank. Member of the Military Council attached to the people's commissar of defense. Before being repressed, commander of the Moscow Military District. Shot 1938, posthumously rehabilitated.

**Belov, P. A.** (1897–1962). In Red Army from 1918. In June 1941 colonel general. Commanded the Second (later the First Guards) Cavalry Corps from June 1941 to July 1942. From June 1942 to end of war commanded the 61st Army. After war in command posts in the army. Hero of the Soviet Union.

**Benediktov, I. A.** (1902–83). Son of a white-collar worker. Member of the AUCP(B) from 1930. Agronomist. From 1931 director of the trust of vegetable-growing state farms of Moscow province. From 1937 people's commissar of state farms of the RSFSR. In 1938 and from 1943 to 1946 first deputy people's commissar of agriculture. From 1938 to 1943 and from 1946 to 1947 people's commissar of agriculture. From 1947 to 1955 minister of agriculture. Thereafter minister of state farms, deputy chairman of the State Economic Commission, minister of agriculture of the RSFSR, and deputy chairman of the State Planning Commission of the RSFSR. Soviet ambassador to India in 1953 and from 1959 to 1967, ambassador to Yugoslavia from 1967 to 1970. Member of the party CC from 1939 to 1941 and from 1952 to 1971.

**Benes, Edvard.** (1884–1948). Czech. From 1918 to 1935 minister of foreign affairs of Czechoslovakia. From 1935 to 1938 and from 1946 president of Czechoslovakia.

**Beria, L. P.** (1899–1953). Georgian. From a peasant background. Member of the RSDLP from 1917. From 1918 to 1920 a specialist employee of the customs office. From 1921 to 1931 worked in agencies of the Cheka and GPU in the Transcaucasus. From 1931 second secretary of the Transcaucasus territory committee of the AUCP(B) and first secretary of the CC of the CP(B) of Georgia. From 1932 first secretary of the Transcaucasus territory committee of the AUCP(B). From 1938 first deputy people's commissar, then until 1953 (with an interval) people's commissar (minister) of internal affairs. From 1941 deputy chairman of the USSR Council of People's Commissars and general commissar of state security. Member and deputy chairman of the State Defense Committee. From 1945 Marshal of the Soviet Union. In 1953 first deputy chairman of the Council of Ministers and minister of internal affairs. From 1934 member of the CC of the AUCP(B). From 1939 candidate member, and from 1946 member, of the Politburo of the CC of the AUCP(B). From 1952 member of the Presidium of the CC of the CPSU. Executed in December 1953.

**Berling, Z.** (1896–1980). Polish. Lieutenant general. While still lieutenant colonel, headed a base of the Polish armed forces in exile of General V. Anders, but remained in the USSR when Anders and his army left for Iran in spring 1942. From 1943 to 1944 (as colonel) commanded the Kosciusko Division, then (as major general) commanded the First Polish Corps and then the Polish armed forces (Wojsko Polskie) in the USSR. From July 1944 commanded the First Army of the Polish armed forces. From fall 1944 studied at the Military Academy of the General Staff in the USSR. From 1948 to 1953 chief of General Staff of the Polish armed forces. Thereafter in civilian service.

**Bevin, Ernest.** (1881–1951). British. In his youth an errand boy, tram driver, salesman, and chauffeur. Later led the dockers' trade union and the trade union of transport and general workers. A leader of the Action Council that protested against British intervention in the Russian Civil War in 1919–20. Minister of labor and national service in Churchill's war cabinet. Foreign minister in the Labour Party government of 1945–51.

**Bezymensky, A. I.** (1898–1973). Member of the RSDLP from 1916. Poet. Active participant in the Communist youth movement. Author of collections of verses, poems, and plays.

**Bierut, Boleslaw.** (1892–1956). Polish. Member of the Communist Party of Poland from 1918. From 1944 to 1947 chairman of the National People's Council (provisional supreme body of power in Poland). Chairman from 1948 to 1954, and first secretary from 1954, of the CC of the Polish United Workers' Party.

**Biryuzov, S. S.** (1904–64). Major general. Joined Red Army in 1922. At start of war commanded the 132nd Infantry Division. In May 1942 appointed chief of staff of the 48th Army, in December 1942 chief of staff of the Second Guards Army, in April 1943 chief of staff of the Southern Front (six months later transformed into the Fourth Ukrainian Front), and in May 1944 chief of staff of the Third Ukrainian Front. From October 1944 until end of war commanded the 37th Army, while serving as chief Soviet military adviser to the Bulgarian army. After war occupied important military positions. Marshal of the Soviet Union.

**Blyukher, V. K.** (1890–1938). Metalworker. Junior officer in World War I. In March 1918 chairman of the Chelyabinsk soviet, then commander in Red Army, making important contributions to victory. Minister of war 1921–22. Under his command the Red Army of the Soviet Republic of the Far East defeated White and Japanese forces. Military adviser to Kuomintang in China 1924–27. Commander of the Far Eastern Army 1929–38. Commander in chief of Far Eastern Front during its victorious clash with Japanese forces at Lake Khasan in July 1938. Shortly thereafter arrested and executed.

**Bodin, P. I.** (1900–1942). In Red Army from 1919. In June 1941 major general. Chief of staff of the Ninth Army from June to September 1941, then of the Southwestern Area from October to December 1941, of the Southwestern Front from October 1941 to March 1942 and in June and July 1942, of the Stalingrad Front in July 1942, and of the Transcaucasus Front from August to October 1942. Perished in battle on November 2, 1942 near Ordzhonikidze (now Vladikavkaz).

**Bogdanov, S. I.** (1894–1960). Joined Red Army in 1918. Unjustly imprisoned in 1938 and released in 1939, but rehabilitated only after his death. At start of war, colonel in command of the 30th Tank Division, then commander of tank and mechanized corps. From September 1943 until end of war, except for six months from July 1944, commander of the Second Tank Army (later named the Second Tank Guards Army). This army took part in the battle for Moscow and in several offensive operations in the final period of the war. In 1945 promoted to marshal of tank troops. Twice Hero of the Soviet Union. After war occupied important army posts.

**Bogomolets, A. A.** (1881–1946). Pathophysiologist. From 1911 professor at Saratov University. From 1925 professor at the Second Moscow University. From 1928 to 1931 director of the Institute of Hematology and Blood Transfusions. From 1930 to 1946 president of the Academy of Sciences of the Ukrainian SSR. Full member of the Academy of Sciences of the Ukrainian SSR (from 1929), of the Academy of Sciences of the Belorussian SSR (from 1939), and of the USSR Academy of Sciences (from 1942). Honored Scientist of the RSFSR from 1935. Member of the CEC of the Ukrainian SSR and of the CEC of the USSR. Author of important works on endocrinology, physiology, and gerontology.

**Bokov, F. Ye.** (1904–84). In Red Army from 1926. In June 1941 division commissar. From August 1941 military commander of the General Staff. From July 1942 deputy chief of the General Staff. Member of the Military Council of the Northwestern Front (May–November 1943), of the Second Baltic Front (November 1943–February 1944), of the Second Belorussian Front (February–April 1944), and of the Fifth Assault Army (July 1944–May 1945). After war, occupied command posts in the army.

**Bor-Komorowski.** See **Komorowski.**

**Brezhnev, L. I.** (1906–82). Until May 1938 deputy chairman of the Executive Committee of the Dneprodzerzhinsk City Soviet. Later to become general secretary of the CC CPSU and chairman of the presidium of the USSR Supreme Soviet.

**Bubnov, A. S.** (1884–1938). Son of a government official. Member of the RSDLP from 1903. Participated in the revolutions of 1905, February 1917, and October 1917. A leader of the armed uprising of October 1917 in Petrograd. Thereafter occupied leading Soviet, party, and military posts on the Don, in Ukraine, in Moscow, and in the Northern Caucasus. From 1922 to 1923 headed the Department of Agitation and Propaganda of the CC of the RCP(B). From 1924 to 1929 head of the Political Administration of the Workers' and Peasants' Red Army. In 1925 secretary of the CC of the RCP(B). From 1929 to 1937 people's commissar of enlightenment of the RSFSR. Member of the party CC in 1917 and from 1924. Member of the All-Russian CEC and of the CEC of the USSR. Arrested, shot 1938, posthumously rehabilitated.

**Budyonny, Semyon M.** (1883–1973). From a Cossack background. Member of the RCP(B) from 1919. In Civil War commanded cavalry units, the First Cavalry Army, then various military districts. From 1924 to 1937 inspector of Cavalry of the Workers' and Peasants' Red Army. From 1939 to 1941 deputy and first deputy people's commissar of defense. From 1941 to 1945 commander in chief of the Southwestern, Northern Caucasus, and Reserve Fronts, representative of the Stavka. Member of the CC of the AUCP(B) from 1939 to 1952. Member of the All-Russian CEC, of the CEC of the USSR, and of the presidium of the USSR Supreme Soviet until 1973. Marshal of the Soviet Union from 1935.

**Bukharin, Nikolai I.** (1888–1938). Son of a teacher. Member of the RSDLP from 1906. One of Lenin's closest associates and one of the leaders of the armed uprising in Moscow in October 1917. From 1918 to 1929 editor of the newspaper *Pravda*. From 1917 to 1934 member of the party CC. From 1919 candidate member, and from 1924 to 1929 member, of the Politburo of the party CC. From 1926 one of the leaders of the Communist International. In 1929 elected a full member of the USSR Academy of Sciences. Thereafter repeatedly subject to party and state persecution. From 1929 member of the presidium of the Supreme Council of National Economy. From 1932 member of the collegium of the People's Commissariat for Heavy Industry. From 1934 chief editor of the newspaper *Izvestiya*. From 1935 member of the CEC and of the Constitutional Commission. Author of numerous works on economics, sociology, politics, literary criticism, theory of science, and other subjects. Unjustly repressed and defendant in the third major Moscow trial (1938); rehabilitated posthumously under Gorbachev.

**Bulganin, Nikolai A.** (1895–1975). White-collar worker. Member of the RSDLP from 1917. From 1918 official of the All-Russian Cheka. From 1922 official of the Supreme Council of National Economy. From 1927 director of the Moscow Electrical Factory. From 1931 chairman of the Moscow City Soviet. From 1937 chairman of the RSFSR Council of People's Commissars. From 1938 deputy chairman of the USSR Council of People's Commissars. Between 1941 and 1943 member of a number of Military Councils in the field forces. From 1944 deputy people's commissar of defense and member of the State Defense Committee. From 1947 minister of the armed forces and deputy (from 1953 first deputy) chairman of the Council of Ministers. From 1955 to 1958 chairman of the Council of Ministers. From 1947 to 1958 Marshal of the Soviet Union. In 1957 joined the so-called antiparty group inside the CPSU CC. In 1958 was demoted to colonel general. From 1948 to 1958 member of the Politburo (Presidium) of the party CC. Member of the party CC from 1939 to 1959. Until 1960 was chairman of the Council of National Economy of Stavropol territory. Thereafter a pensioner.

**Burdenko, N. N.** (1876–1946). Colonel general of the medical service. Full member of the USSR Academy of Sciences. Chief surgeon of the Red Army. Hero of Socialist Labor from 1943.

**Burmistenko, M. A.** (1902–41). From a peasant background. Member of the RCP(B) from 1919. During the 1920s engaged in Communist youth, military, and journalistic work. From 1932 second secretary of the Kalmyk province committee of the AUCP(B). From 1936 an official in the apparatus of the CC of the AUCP(B). From 1938 second secretary of the CC of the CP(B)U. From 1939 member of the CC of the AUCP(B). From 1941 an organizer of the partisan movement in Ukraine and member of the Military Council of the Southwestern Front. Perished at the battlefront.

**Chernyakhovsky, I. D.** (1906–45). Army general. Commander of the 60th Army from July 1942. Commander of the Western and Third Belorussian Fronts from April 1944. Perished on February 18, 1945 near Melzak (now in Poland).

**Chernyavsky, V. I.** (1893–1939). Member of the RSDLP from 1911. Participated in Civil War in Ukraine. Party official in Kiev, Poltava, Vinnitsa, Dnepropetrovsk, and Odessa. From 1930 secretary of the CC of the CP(B)U. Until

1937 candidate member of the Politburo of the CC of the CP(B)U. Fate unclear, probably shot, posthumously rehabilitated.

**Chernyshev, S. Ye.** (1881–1963). Architect. After 1917 lectured at the All-Russian Artistic-Theatrical Workshop University (until 1930) and at the Moscow Architectural Institute (until 1950). From 1934 to 1941 chief architect of the city of Moscow. From 1944 to 1948 chairman of the Administration for Architectural Affairs of the Moscow city executive committee. From 1950 to 1955 first secretary of the Architects' Union. After 1931 took part in creating the General Plan for the Reconstruction of Moscow.

**Chibisov, N. Ye.** (1892–1959). In Red Army from 1918. From June 1941 lieutenant general. During war commanded the Odessa Military District, the Maritime Troop Grouping, and the Reserve Army of the Southern Front (1941). Deputy commander of the Bryansk Front from July 1942. Commanded the 38th Army (from August 1942), the Third Assault Army (from November 1943), and the First Assault Army (April and May 1944). From 1944 to 1948 head of the Frunze Military Academy, then in other command posts. Hero of the Soviet Union.

**Chistyakov, I. M.** (1900–1979). Joined Red Army in 1918. At start of war, colonel, promoted in 1944 to colonel general. In 1941 and 1942 commanded the 64th Infantry Brigade on the Western Front, then the Eighth Guards Infantry Division and the Second Guards Infantry Corps on the Northwestern and Kaliningrad Fronts. In October 1942 placed in command of the First Guards Army, later in command of the 21st Army (renamed in April 1943 the Sixth Guards Army). In June 1945 appointed commander of the 25th Army, which took part in the defeat of Japanese forces in the Far East. After war held command posts in the army. Hero of the Soviet Union.

**Christie, J. Walter.** (1865–1944). American. Prominent tank designer. In the 1920s built the first prototype amphibious landing vehicle and in 1932 an experimental tank faster than any previous model.

**Chubar, V. Ya.** (1891–1939). Peasant. Member of the RSDLP from 1907. From 1911 a worker, participated in the revolutions of 1905, February 1917, and October 1917. From 1918 to 1922 an official of leading economic agencies. From 1923 chairman of the Council of People's Commissars of the Ukrainian SSR and deputy chairman of the USSR Council of People's Commissars. From 1934 deputy chairman of the Council of Labor and Defense. From 1937 people's commissar of finances. From 1938 first deputy chairman of the Council of People's Commissars. Member of the party CC from 1922.

Member of the Politburo of the CC of the AUCP(B) from 1935. Unjustly arrested and executed, rehabilitated posthumously.

**Chudov, M. S.** (1893–1937). From a peasant background. Worker. Member of the RSDLP from 1913. From 1918 held a number of leading Soviet and party posts. From 1928 to 1936 second secretary of the Leningrad province committee of the AUCP(B). Member of the CC of the AUCP(B). From 1925 member of the All-Russian CEC and of the CEC of the USSR. Arrested, shot 1937, posthumously rehabilitated.

**Chuikov, V. I.** (1900–1982). In Red Army from 1918. From December 1940 to March 1942 Soviet military attaché in China. In June 1941 lieutenant general. From May 1942 commander of the First Reserve Army, from July 1942 of the 64th Army, then of the operational grouping of the 64th Army. From September 1942 commanded the 62nd Army (from April 1943 renamed the Eighth Guards Army), which fought from Stalingrad all the way to Berlin, distinguishing itself especially in the heroic defense of Stalingrad and (as part of the First Belorussian Front) in the Vistula-Oder military operation. After war, deputy, first deputy, then commander in chief of the Group of Soviet Forces in Germany, then in leading posts in the army. Twice Hero of the Soviet Union. Marshal of the Soviet Union.

**Curzon, J. H.** (1859–1925). British. Minister of foreign affairs of the United Kingdom from 1919 to 1924. His "line" was recommended by the Supreme Council of the Entente as Poland's eastern border.

**Cyrankiewicz, Józef.** (1911–89). Polish. From 1941 to 1945 in Nazi concentration camps, then general secretary of the Polish Party of Socialists. From 1948 member of the Politburo of the CC of the Polish United Workers' Party. From 1947 to 1970 premier of Poland (from 1952 to 1954 vice premier).

**Dankevich, K. F.** (1905–84). Composer, pianist, conductor, and educator. Member of the AUCP(B) from 1946. Professor at the Odessa Conservatory from 1948 and at the Kiev Conservatory from 1953. People's Artiste of the USSR from 1954. Headed the Composers' Union of Ukraine from 1941 to 1944 and from 1956 to 1967.

**de Gaulle, Charles.** (1890–1970). French. Military man. From June 5, 1940, deputy minister of national defense of France. On June 18, 1940, in exile in England, founded the movement "Free France" (from 1942 "Fighting France"). From 1941 leader of the French National Committee (from 1943 the French Committee of National Liberation). From 1944 to 1946 head of the provisional government of France. Founder of the party "Assembly of the French People." In 1958 prime minister, and from 1959 to 1969 president, of France.

**Demchenko, N. N.** (1896–1937). From a lower-middle-class background. Member of the RSDLP from 1916. Occupied a number of party and state posts in the Ukrainian SSR. From 1929 to 1932 people's commissar of agriculture of Ukraine. From 1932 secretary of the Kiev, then of the Kharkov, province committees of the CP(B)U. In 1936 first deputy people's commissar of agriculture. In 1937 people's commissar of grain and livestock state farms. Member of the Politburo of the CC of the CP(B)U from 1931. Fate unclear, probably shot, posthumously rehabilitated.

**Donets, M. I.** (1883–1941). Singer. People's Artiste of the Ukrainian SSR from 1930. Member of the AUCP(B) from 1940. Soloist in the theaters of Moscow, Kharkov, Sverdlovsk, and Kiev.

**Dubovoi, I. N.** (1896–1938). From a peasant background. Member of the RSDLP from 1917. In Civil War commanded divisions and also occupied political and military staff posts. From 1924 commander of an infantry corps. From 1929 assistant, and from 1934 deputy, commander of the Ukrainian Military District. From 1935 commander of the Kharkov Military District. Member of the Military Council attached to the People's Commissariat of Defense. Army commander of the second rank from 1935. Shot 1938, posthumously rehabilitated.

**Dvinsky, B. A.** Member of the RCP(B) from 1920. Secretary of the Rostov province committee of the AUCP(B) from 1938 to 1944.

**Eikhe, R. I.** (1890–1940). Latvian. From a peasant background, then a worker. Member of the RSDLP from 1905. Member of the Social Democracy of the Latvian territory. Participant in the struggle for Soviet power in the Baltic region. In 1919 people's commissar of food of Soviet Latvia. Until 1924 worked in the RSFSR People's Commissariat of Food. From 1925 to 1937 chairman of the Siberian territory executive committee and first secretary of the Siberian and West Siberian territory committees of the AUCP(B). From 1937 people's commissar of agriculture. Member of the CC of the AUCP(B) from 1930. Candidate member of the Politburo of the CC of the AUCP(B) from 1935. Member of the CEC. Shot 1940, posthumously rehabilitated.

**Falaleyev, F. Ya.** (1899–1955). Joined Red Army in 1919. At start of war, air force major general, promoted in 1944 to air force marshal. In 1941 and 1942 commanded in turn the air forces of the Sixth Army, the Southwestern Front, and the Southwestern Area. In October 1942 appointed deputy commander of Red Army air forces and held this post until 1946. For part of this period (until May 1943 and again from April 1945) simultaneously chief of staff of Red Army air forces. As representative of the Stavka for air forces coordinated action of air armies in the liberation of Ukraine, Crimea, Belorussia, and the Baltic and in the assault on East Prussia.

**Filatov, N. A.** (1891–1941). Member of the RSDLP from 1912 to 1938. After 1917 engaged in administrative party work. A well-known official in the Soviet apparatus. From 1930 to 1934 secretary of a district committee of the AUCP(B) in Moscow. From 1934 to 1937 chairman of the Moscow province executive committee.

**Frinovsky, M. P.** (1898–1940). From 1919 an official in the Cheka. From 1930 chairman of the GPU of the Azerbaijan SSR. From 1933 head of the Main Administration of Border Guards of the OGPU. From 1936 deputy (from 1937 first deputy) people's commissar of internal affairs. From 1938 people's commissar of the Navy. Arrested in 1939, shot in 1940.

**Galanin, I. V.** (1899–1958). Lieutenant general. Joined Red Army in 1919. Appointed commander of the Twelfth Army in August 1941 and of the 59th Army in November 1941. Between May and September 1942 commanded troop groupings of the Western and Voronezh Fronts. In October 1942 placed in command of the 24th Army, in April 1943 of the 70th Army. From September 1943 to November 1944 commanded the Fourth Guards Army (except for a short period in early 1944 at the head of the 53rd Army).

**Gamarnik, Ya. B.** (1894–1937). From a white-collar background. Member of the RSDLP from 1916. Participant in the revolutions of February and October 1917. In Civil War, was active in the struggle for Soviet power in Ukraine, occupied politicomilitary posts. From 1920 chairman of the Odessa and Kiev province committees of the CP(B)U and of the Kiev province revolutionary committee and province executive committee. From 1923 chairman of the Primorye (Maritime) province executive committee and of the Far Eastern revolutionary committee and territory executive committee. Secretary of the Far Eastern territorial committee of the AUCP(B). Member of the Revolutionary Military Council of the Siberian Military District. From 1928 first secretary of the CC of the CP(B) of Belorussia and member of the Revolutionary Military Council of the Belorussian Military District. From 1929 head of the Political Administration of the Workers' and Peasants' Red Army, member of the Revolutionary Military Council, and editor in chief of the newspaper *Krasnaya zvezda* (Red star). From 1930 deputy chairman of the Revolutionary Military Council, deputy people's commissar of military and naval affairs,

first deputy people's commissar of defense, and member of the Military
Council attached to the people's commissar of defense. At time of death
member of the Military Council of the Central Asian Military District.
Member of the CC of the AUCP(B) from 1927. Member of the Orgburo of
the CC of the AUCP(B) from 1929. Army commissar of the first rank from
1935. Committed suicide in 1937 to avoid arrest.

**Gayevoi, A. I.** (1907–62). Member of the AUCP(B) from 1930. From 1939
chairman of the Stalino province executive committee in the Ukrainian
SSR. From 1940 to 1951 first secretary of the Voroshilovgrad province committee of the CP(B)U. From 1952 to 1957 first secretary of the Zaporozhye
province committee of the CP(B)U. From 1957 to 1961 first secretary of the
Dnepropetrovsk province committee of the CP(B)U, then secretary of the
CC of the CP(B)U.

**Gerasimenko, V. F.** (1900–1961). In Red Army from 1918. During war commanded the 21st Army, then in June and July 1941 the Thirteenth Army. From
September to November 1941 deputy commander for the rear of the Reserve
Front, then assistant chief of the rear of the Red Army. From December 1941
commander of the Stalingrad Military District. From September 1942 to
November 1943 commander of the 28th Army. From January 1944 commander
of the Kharkov Military District. From March 1944 to October 1945 people's
commissar of defense of the Ukrainian SSR and commander of the Kiev
Military District. After war, occupied command posts in the army.

**Ginzburg, S. Z.** (1897–?). From a lower-middle-class background. Member of
the RSDLP from 1917. During 1920s and 1930s worked in Soviet and economic bodies. People's commissar of construction from 1939 to 1946, then
minister for the construction of military and naval installations and minister
for the building materials industry. From 1950 deputy minister in a number
of ministries.

**Glan, Betty N.** (1905–?). From a white-collar background. Member of the
RCP(B) from 1924. In 1920s an official of the Communist International and
Communist Youth International. From 1929 to 1937 director of the Central
Park of Culture and Rest in Moscow. Arrested but survived to be released.
After rehabilitation in 1955 an official of the USSR Composers' Union, the
All-Russian Theatrical Society, and the RSFSR Actors' Union.

**Gmyrya, B. R.** (1903–69). Bass singer. Graduated from the Kharkov Conservatory in 1939. From 1936 soloist at the Kharkov, and from 1939 at the Kiev,
theaters of opera and ballet. People's Artiste of the USSR from 1951.

**Golikov, F. I.** (1900–1980). From a peasant background. Member of RCP(B) from 1918. Fought in Civil War. During 1920s engaged in political work in the Red Army. Graduated from Frunze Military Academy in 1933. Commander of the Sixth Army from 1939. From 1940 to 1941 deputy chief of the General Staff and chief of military intelligence. Headed military mission to London and Washington in 1941. Commanded Tenth Army in the battle of Moscow 1941–42. Commanded the Voronezh Front from 1942 until March 1943, then deputy people's commissar (minister) of defense of the USSR for personnel. From 1950 commander of the Special Mechanized Army. From 1957 head of the Main Political Administration of the Armed Forces. From 1962 official in the Ministry of Defense. Marshal of the Soviet Union. Hero of the Soviet Union.

**Golovanov, A. Ye.** (1904–75). Spent most of career in Red Army, which he joined in 1919. In August 1941 appointed commander of the 81st Long-Range Bomber Division. In February 1942 put in command of all long-range air forces, a position he held until 1948. In 1944 made chief air force marshal. In December 1944 appointed commander of the Eighteenth Air Army. Took part in the bombing of Berlin, Königsberg, Danzig, and other targets deep in the Germans' rear. Provided air support to ground troops in several important offensive operations in the later part of the war, also assisted partisan fighters in the Crimea, Belorussia, the Baltic, and Yugoslavia. After war, occupied command positions in the air force.

**Gomulka, Wladyslaw.** (1905–82). Polish. Member of Communist Party of Poland from 1926. General secretary of the CC of the Polish Workers' Party from November 1943 to August 1948. First secretary of the CC of the Polish United Workers' Party from 1956 to 1970.

**Gordov, V. N.** (1896–1950). In Red Army from 1918. In June 1941 major general, promoted in 1943 to colonel general. From June 1941 chief of staff, and in August 1941 and from October 1941 to June 1942 commander, of the 21st Army. Commander in July and August 1942 of the Stalingrad Front, from October 1942 of the 33rd Army, and from April 1944 of the Third Guards Army. Took part in the battle of Stalingrad and in the Rzhevsk-Vyazemsky, Spas-Demensky, Smolensk, Berlin, and Prague military operations. In 1945 Hero of the Soviet Union. After war occupied command posts in the army. Executed in 1950.

**Gorodnyansky, A. M.** (1896–1942). In Red Army from 1918. In June 1941 major general. During war commanded the 129th Infantry Division in the Western Front, then from August 1941 the Thirteenth Army and from January 1942 the

Sixth Army. Perished in battle on May 27, 1942, at the Barvenkovo bridgehead during the battle for Kharkov.

**Gorodovikov, O. I.** (1879–1960). Colonel general. Joined Red Army in 1918. During war inspector general and commander of Red Army cavalry, entrusted with the formation of cavalry units. In summer 1941 and during the battle of Stalingrad, he represented the Stavka at the battlefront on matters involving the use of cavalry. Deputy commander of Soviet Army cavalry between 1943 and 1947.

**Grechko, A. A.** (1903–76). In Red Army from 1919. In June 1941 colonel. From July 1941 commanded the 34th Detached Cavalry Division on the Southwestern Front, from January 1942 the Fifth Cavalry Corps on the Southern Front, from April 1942 the Twelfth Army, from September 1942 the 47th Army, from October 1942 the Eighteenth Army, and from January 1943 the 56th Army. From October 1943 deputy commander of the First Ukrainian Front. From December 1943 to May 1945 commanded the First Guards Army. After war occupied command posts in the army, later minister of defense. Marshal of the Soviet Union.

**Grushevsky, I. S.** (1904–82). From 1929 to 1937 in leading positions in the Zaporozhye Province Soviet. In 1938 secretary of the Dnepropetrovsk province party committee. In 1939 second secretary of the Stanislav province party committee. In 1940 first secretary of the Chernovtsy province and city party committees. From 1941 to 1944 member of the Military Councils of the 40th Army and of the Second Ukrainian Front with the rank of major general. From 1944 to 1951 and in 1961–62 first secretary of the Lvov province party committee. From 1951 to 1961 first secretary of the Volyn province party committee. From 1962 to 1966 chairman of the Commission of Party-State Control of the CC of the CP(B)U and of the Council of Ministers of the Ukrainian SSR, secretary of the CC of the CP(B)U, and deputy prime minister of the Ukrainian SSR. From 1966 to 1972 chairman and then deputy chairman of the Party Commission of the CC of the CP(B)U. From 1972 to 1976 chairman of the presidium of the Supreme Soviet of the Ukrainian SSR. Hero of Socialist Labor 1974. From 1976 in retirement.

**Gurov, K. A.** Lieutenant general. Member of the RCP(B) from 1921. Member of the Military Council of the Southwestern Front from January 1942. Member of the Military Council of the 62nd Army (commanded by V. I. Chuikov) from July 1942. Died September 1943.

**Hess, Rudolf.** (1894–1987). German. Hitler's personal secretary from 1925 and his deputy in the Nazi party from 1933. After war condemned to life imprisonment as a Nazi war criminal.

**Hrushevsky, Mikhailo S.** (1866–1934). Ukrainian. Prominent historian, literary critic, and statesman. Played a central role in the rise of the Ukrainian national movement. From 1917 to 1918 chairman of the Central Rada (parliament of the short-lived independent Ukrainian People's Republic). Full member of the Academy of Sciences of the Ukrainian SSR from 1924, and of the USSR Academy of Sciences from 1929. Author of numerous scholarly works.

**Ibarruri, Dolores.** (1895–1989). Spanish. One of the founders of the Spanish Communist Party in 1920. Elected to Spanish parliament in 1936. During Spanish civil war gained fame as an orator and was given the name of *La Pasionaria*. After Franco's victory took refuge in the USSR. Returned to Spain in 1977 and won reelection to the National Assembly.

**Ivanov, S. N.** Member of the RSDLP from 1920. Engineering, economic, and party official.

**Ivanov, S. P.** (1907–93). Staff officer and author of works on the art of war. At beginning of war lieutenant colonel and head of the operational department of the staff of the Thirteenth Army. Later chief of staff successively of the 38th Army, the First Tank Army, and the First Guards Army. Between end of 1942 and mid-1945 chief of staff successively of the Southwestern, Voronezh, First Ukrainian, Transcaucasus, and Third Ukrainian Fronts. In July 1945 appointed chief of staff of the Supreme Command of Soviet Troops in the Far East. After war occupied command posts in the army. Hero of the Soviet Union.

**Izotov, N. A.** (1902–51). Member of the AUCP(B) from 1936. Face worker at the coal mine No. 1 Kochegarka in the town of Gorlovka. In 1932 initiated the "Izotov movement," in which experienced workers trained young workers in shock-work techniques. Then became a participant in the Stakhanovite movement (see **Stakhanov**). Continued to set records for the extraction of coal until September 1935. From 1937 occupied leading posts in the coal industry. Member of the CEC.

**Kaganovich, L. M.** (1893–1991). Shoemaker. Member of the RSDLP, AUCP(B), and CPSU from 1911 to 1962. Before 1917, participated in underground party activity as a member of the Yekaterinoslav, Kiev, Melitopol, and Yuzovka party committees and as chairman of the illegal leatherworkers' trade union. From 1918 to 1921 engaged in party and Soviet government work in Moscow, Nizhny Novgorod, Voronezh, and Tashkent. From 1924 secretary of the CC of the AUCP(B). From 1925 to 1928 general secretary of the CC of the CP(B)U, then worked again in the CC of the AUCP(B). In 1930 elected first secretary of the Moscow committee and Moscow city committee of the AUCP(B) and a member of the Politburo of the party CC. In 1933 headed the Agriculture Department, and in 1934 the Transportation Department, of the party CC. From 1935 to 1937 people's commissar of communications, then people's commissar of heavy industry. In 1938 deputy chairman of the Council of People's Commissars. From 1939 to 1949 people's commissar of oil and fuel industry. From 1942 a member of the State Defense Committee. After war occupied a number of leading party and state posts in Ukraine, in the Council of Ministers, and in union ministries. Member of the party CC from 1924 to 1957. In 1957 belonged to the so-called antiparty group inside the CC CPSU. Thereafter a pensioner.

**Kaledin, A. M.** (1861–1918). Cossack. Cavalry general in the tsarist army from 1916. Ataman of the Don Cossack Army and leader of the uprising on the Don after the October revolution. Committed suicide.

**Kalinin, M. I.** (1875–1946). Peasant, then a worker. Member of the RSDLP from 1898. Active participant in the working-class movement and in the revolutions of 1905, February 1917, and October 1917. In 1917 city head of Petrograd. In 1918 commissar of municipal services of Petrograd. From 1919 chairman of the All-Russian CEC. From 1922 chairman of the CEC of the USSR. From 1938 chairman of the presidium of the Supreme Soviet. Member of the party CC from 1919. From 1926 member of the Politburo of the party CC.

**Kamenev, L. B.** (Rozenfeld). (1883–1936). Member of the RSDLP from 1901. Active participant in the revolutionary movement. Chairman of the All-Russian CEC in November 1917. Chairman of the Moscow Soviet from 1918 to 1926. Deputy chairman of the Council of People's Commissars from 1923 to 1926. Chairman of the Council of Labor and Defense from 1924 to 1926. Director of the Lenin Institute from 1923 to 1926. Member of the party CC from 1917 to 1927 and of the Politburo of the CC from 1919 to 1926. Member of the All-Russian CEC and of the CEC of the USSR. Defendant in the first major Moscow trial (1936). Shot 1936, posthumously rehabilitated under Gorbachev.

**Kaminsky, G. N.** (1895–1938). From a working-class background. Member of the RSDLP from 1913. From 1917 to 1921 occupied leading party and Soviet posts. From 1922 to 1929 a leading official in the trade unions, the coopera-tive movement, and the All-Russian Union of Agricultural Collectives. From 1930 secretary of the Moscow city committee of the AUCP(B). From 1932 chairman of the Moscow province executive committee. From 1934 people's commissar of health of the RSFSR. From 1936 people's commissar of health. Candidate member of the CC of the AUCP(B) from 1925 to 1927 and again from 1934. Member of the All-Russian CEC and of the CEC of the USSR. Imprisoned, shot 1938, posthumously rehabilitated.

**Kapitsa, P. L.** (1894–1984). Physicist. Until 1935 worked in Cavendish Labora-tory directed by Sir Ernest Rutherford at Cambridge University, England. From 1935 to 1946 and from 1955 director of the Institute of Problems of Physics of the USSR Academy of Sciences (dismissed 1946 for refusal to work on atomic bomb, reinstated 1955). Full member of the USSR Academy of Sciences from 1939. Awarded Nobel Prize for physics in 1978.

**Katukov, M. Ye.** (1900–1976). Joined Red Army in 1919. At start of war colonel and commander of the Twentieth Tank Division. Given command of the Fourth Tank Brigade, and in 1942 of the First Tank Corps and then the Third Motorized Corps. At beginning of 1943 appointed commander of the First Tank Army (in 1944 renamed the First Guards Tank Army), remaining in this post as marshal of armored forces until end of war. Took part in the battles of Moscow and Kursk, in the liberation of Ukraine and Poland, and in several of the major offensive operations of the last phase of the war. After war occupied command posts in the army. Twice Hero of the Soviet Union.

**Kedrov, M. S.** (1878–1941). Son of a government official. Member of the RSDLP from 1901. Active participant in the Bolshevik movement and in the revolutions of 1905, February 1917, and October 1917. After 1917 occupied leading military and party posts. During 1920s worked in the Council of Labor and Defense, the Supreme Council of National Economy, the People's Commissariat of Health, the public prosecutor's office, and the Red Sports International. From 1932 member of the presidium of the State Planning Commission of the RSFSR. From 1934 director of the Military Sanitation Institute. Author of works on history of the Communist Party and on Civil War. Shot 1941, posthumously rehabilitated.

**Kekkonen, Urho Kaleva.** (1900–1986). Finnish. Prime minister of Finland from 1950 to 1953 and from 1954 to 1956. President of Finland from 1956 to 1981. Known for his policy of maintaining good relations with the USSR on the basis of neutrality.

**Khakharev, K. G.** Member of the RSDLP from 1905. After 1917 an active party figure. Occupied a number of leading posts.

**Kharechko, T. I.** Member of the RSDLP from 1914.

**Kharitonov, F. M.** (1899–1943). In Red Army from 1919. In June 1941 major general. During war deputy chief of staff of the Southern Front. From September 1941 commanded the Ninth Army, and from July 1942 the Sixth Army. Died May 28, 1943 from acute illness.

**Khatayevich, M. M.** (1893–1937). Son of a trader. Member of the RSDLP from 1913. Participant in the revolutions of February and October 1917, then engaged in party work in Belorussia, in Samara, and on the western battlefront. From 1921 secretary of the Gomel, Odessa, and Tatar province committees and of the Middle Volga territory committee of the party, then secretary of the CC of the CP(B)U. From 1933 first secretary of the Dnepropetrovsk province committee, and from 1937 second secretary of the CC, of the CP(B)U. From 1930 member of the CC of the AUCP(B). Member of the All-Ukrainian CEC and of the CEC of the USSR. From 1932 to 1937 member of the Politburo of the CC of the CP(B)U. Arrested, shot 1937, posthumously rehabilitated.

**Khomenko, V. A.** Lieutenant general. Before war, commander of border guards in Moldavia and adjacent part of Ukraine. Commanded the 44th Army from November 1942. Perished on the approaches to Nikopol on November 9, 1943.

**Khryukin, T. T.** (1910–53). Joined Red Army in 1932. At start of war, air force major general, promoted in 1944 to air force colonel general. Commanded in turn the air forces of the Karelian Front (from August 1941), the air forces of the Southwestern Front (in June 1942), the Eighth Air Army (from June 1942), and the First Air Army (from July 1944). Helped organize air cover for the Kirov Railroad and for Murmansk. Led air combat on the Stalingrad Front, during the liberation of Ukraine, the Crimea, Belorussia, and the Baltic, and in the assault on Eastern Prussia. After war occupied command posts in the air and air defense forces. Twice Hero of the Soviet Union.

**Kirkhenstein, A. M.** (1872–1963). Biologist specializing in vitamins. State official. Member of the AUCP(B) from 1941. Prime minister and president of Latvia in 1940, then until 1952 chairman of the presidium of the Supreme Soviet of the Latvian SSR. From 1946 director of the Institute of Microbiology of the Academy of Sciences of the Latvian SSR.

**Kirov, S. M.** (1886–1934). From a lower-middle-class background. Member of the RSDLP from 1904. Participated in the revolutionary movement. After 1917 occupied leading military party posts. From 1921 secretary of the CC of the Communist Party of Azerbaijan. From 1926 first secretary of the Leningrad province committee of the AUCP(B) and of the Northwestern Bureau of the party CC. From 1930 member of the Politburo, and from 1934 member of the Orgburo and secretary, of the CC of the AUCP(B). Murdered on December 1, 1934.

**Kirponos, M. P.** (1892–1941). Member of the RCP(B) from 1918. Occupied various command posts. Before Finnish campaign was head of the Kazan Military College. During Finnish campaign commanded the 70th Division, which attacked Vyborg. Then commander of the Leningrad and Kiev Special Military Districts. In 1941 commanded the Southwestern Front. Perished in battle.

**Kobulov, B. Z.** (1904–53). From 1922 an official in the Cheka. From 1938 deputy people's commissar of internal affairs. From 1943 deputy people's commissar of state security. In 1953 first deputy minister of internal affairs. Executed in 1953 together with L. P. Beria.

**Kogan, Ye. S.** (1886–1937). From a lower-middle-class background. Member of the RSDLP from 1907. In 1918 secretary of the Samara province committee of the RCP(B), thereafter engaged in important party and lecturing work. From 1930 to 1936 secretary of the Moscow committee of the AUCP(B). Member of the Central Inspection Commission from 1934. Arrested, fate unclear, probably shot, posthumously rehabilitated.

**Kolessa, F. M.** (1871–1947). Composer, literary critic, and ethnographer. Professor at Lvov University from 1939. Full member of the Academy of Sciences of the Ukrainian SSR from 1929.

**Kolos, G. A.** Member of the RSDLP from 1917. Active participant in the peasant movement in Ukraine.

**Kolpakchi, V. Ya.** (1899–1961). In Red Army from 1918. In June 1941 major general. During war chief of staff, in October and November 1941 commander, of the Eighteenth Army. In December 1941 and January 1942 chief of staff of the Bryansk Front. Commander in July and August 1942 of the 62nd Army, from November 1942 of the 30th Army, from May 1943 of the 63rd Army, and from April 1944 of the 69th Army. After war, occupied command posts in the army. Hero of the Soviet Union.

**Komorowski, Tadeusz.** (1895–1966). Polish. General. From 1943 to 1944 member of the leadership of the Polish Home Army. Official leader of the Warsaw uprising between August 1 and October 2, 1944. Also known as General Bor.

**Konev, I. S.** (1897–1973). From a peasant background. Lumberjack. Non-commissioned officer of tsarist army during First World War. Member of RCP(B) from 1918. Commissar of an armored train during Civil War. Thereafter commissar, regimental and divisional commander. Graduated from Frunze Military Academy in 1934, then divisional and corps commander. From 1938 commander of Second Far Eastern Army and of the Transbaikal and Transcaucasus Military Districts. Commander of the Nineteenth Army in the battle for Moscow in 1941, then of the Steppe and Second Ukrainian Fronts. From May 1944 commander of the First Ukrainian Front. From 1945 commander in chief of Soviet occupation forces in Austria and Hungary. From 1946 commander in chief of ground forces and deputy minister of defense. From 1951 commander of the Carpathian Military District. From 1955 first deputy minister of defense and commander in chief of Warsaw Pact Forces. From 1961 commander in chief of Soviet occupation forces in Germany. From 1962 inspector general of the Ministry of Defense. Marshal of the Soviet Union. Twice Hero of the Soviet Union.

**Kork, A. I.** (1887–1937). Peasant. Served as an officer in tsarist army. Member of the AUCP(B) from 1927. Commander in Red Army from 1918. Commanded a number of military districts. Before being arrested and executed was head of the Frunze Military Academy. Shot 1937, posthumously rehabilitated.

**Korniyets, L. P.** (1901–69). From a peasant background. Member of the AUCP(B) from 1926. From 1931 engaged in party and state work. From 1938 second secretary of the Dniepropetrovsk province committee of the CP(B)U, then chairman of the presidium of the Supreme Soviet of the Ukrainian SSR. From 1939 to 1944 chairman, then until 1953 first deputy chairman, of the Council of People's Commissars (Council of Ministers) of the Ukrainian SSR. During the war, member of the Military Council of the Northern Caucasus Front and from 1943 of the Voronezh Front (with the rank of lieutenant general). From 1953 minister of procurements, minister of grain products, and chairman of the corresponding state committees. Member of the CC of the AUCP(B) from 1939 to 1952.

**Korotchenko, D. S.** (1894–1969). Peasant, then soldier. From 1918 member of the RCP(B) working in various party posts in Ukraine. From 1931 to 1934 chairman of the Bauman district executive committee in Moscow, then secretary of the Bauman and Pervomaisky district committees of the party in Moscow. From 1936 secretary of the Moscow province committee of the AUCP(B). From 1937 to 1938 first secretary of the Western, then of the Dnepropetrovsk, province committees of the party and chairman of the Council of People's Commissars of the Ukrainian SSR. From 1939 to 1947 secretary of the CC of the CP(B)U. From 1947 to 1954 chairman of the Council of Ministers of the Ukrainian SSR and thereafter chairman of the presidium of the Supreme Soviet of the Ukrainian SSR. Member of the CC of the AUCP(B) from 1939. From 1952 to 1953 member, and then candidate member, of the Presidium of the CC CPSU.

**Korytny, S. Z.** Member of the RCP(B) from 1919. Later mainly a party official.

**Kosarev, A. V.** (1903–39). From a working-class background. Member of the RCP(B) from 1919. Participated in Civil War. From 1921 occupied leading posts in the Russian Young Communist League. In 1926 secretary of the Moscow committee of the All-Russian Young Communist League. From 1927 secretary, and from 1929 to 1939 general secretary, of the CC of the All-Russian Young Communist League. From 1934 member of the CC of the AUCP(B), of the Orgburo of the party CC, and of the CEC. Shot, posthumously rehabilitated.

**Kosior, S. V.** (1889–1939). Worker. Member of the RSDLP from 1907. After 1917 a prominent party official, one of the organizers of the CP(B)U. Secretary of the CC of the CP(B)U from 1920. Secretary of the Siberian Bureau of the CC of the RCP(B) from 1922, thereafter general secretary of the CC of the CP(B)U until 1938. Member of the party CC from 1924. Member of the Politburo of the CC of the AUCP(B) from 1930. At time of arrest, deputy chairman of the Council of People's Commissars and chairman of the Soviet Control Commission. Shot 1939, posthumously rehabilitated.

**Kostenko, M. V.** Second secretary of the Kiev province committee of the CP(B)U from December 1937 to June 1938.

**Kotsiubinsky, Yu. M.** (1896–1937). Son of M. M. Kotsiubinsky (1864–1913), the writer and revolutionary-democratic public activist. Member of the RSDLP from 1913. Member of the first government of Soviet Ukraine. In 1918 commander in chief of the armed forces of the Ukrainian SSR, then engaged in state, diplomatic, and economic work. From 1934 chairman of the State Planning Commission and deputy chairman of the Council of People's Commissars of the Ukrainian SSR. Shot 1937, posthumously rehabilitated.

**Kozlov, D. T.** (1896–1967). Lieutenant general. Joined Red Army in 1918. In late 1941 and early 1942 commanded in turn the Transcaucasus, Caucasus, and Crimean Fronts during the operations to liberate Rostov on the Don and in defense of Sevastopol and the Kerch peninsula. In August 1942 appointed commander of the 24th Army. In October 1942 became assistant commander and later deputy commander, of the Voronezh Front. Between May and August 1943 was plenipotentiary of the Stavka assigned to the Leningrad Front, as deputy commander of the Transbaikal Front took part in the Soviet-Japanese war of 1945. After war occupied command posts in the army.

**Kozlov, P. M.** (1893–1944). Joined Red Army in 1918. At start of war, major general, promoted to lieutenant general. In first year of war, deputy commander in turn of the Eighteenth Army, the Ninth Army, and the Eighth Guards Army. In May 1942 put in command of the Ninth Army, then the next month in command of the 37th Army. In May 1943 returned to command the Ninth Army, but in July 1943 appointed commander of the 47th Army. From the fall of 1943 until his death, a corps commander in the First Ukrainian Front. Hero of the Soviet Union.

**Krainyukov, K. V.** (1902–75). Joined Red Army in 1919. During war a brigade commissar in the Southern Front. From August 1941 to October 1943 a member of the Military Councils of the Sixth, Ninth, and 40th Armies and thereafter until end of war a member of the Military Council of the First Ukrainian Front. Took part in border fighting on the River Pruth (against Romanian forces) and in the battle for the Caucasus, the battle of Kursk, the battle for the Dnieper, the liberation of Ukraine, Poland, and Czechoslovakia, and the assault on Berlin. After war, occupied important army posts.

**Krasovsky, S. A.** (1897–1983). Joined Red Army in 1918. At start of war, air force major general, promoted to air force marshal. During first year of war commanded the air forces successively of the Northern Caucasus Military District, of the 56th Army, and the Bryansk Front. In May 1942 placed in command of the Second Air Army. In November 1942 appointed commander of the Seventeenth Air Army, but in March 1943 returned to command of the Second Air Army and remained in that post until end of war. After war occupied command posts in air force. Hero of the Soviet Union.

**Kravchenko, A. G.** (1899–1963). Joined Red Army in 1918. At start of war, colonel and chief of staff of a mechanized corps. Participated in the battle for Moscow as commander of a detached tank brigade. In March 1942 appointed chief of staff of the First Tank Corps. In June 1942 placed in command of the Second Tank Corps, then in October 1942 of the Fourth Tank Corps (later renamed the Fifth Guards Tank Corps), fighting as part of the Western, Bryansk, Stalingrad, Voronezh, and First Ukrainian Fronts. Took part in the encirclement of enemy forces at the battle of Stalingrad and also in the battle of Kursk and the battle for the Dnieper. In January 1944 appointed commander of the Sixth Guards Tank Army with the rank of colonel general of tank forces and in this capacity took part in offensive operations leading to the liberation of Romania, Hungary, Czechoslovakia, and Austria. Fought in campaign against Japanese forces in Manchuria in 1945. After war occupied command posts in the army. Twice Hero of the Soviet Union.

**Kreizer, Ya. G.** (1905–69). Joined Red Army in 1921. At start of war, colonel in command of the First Moscow Motorized Infantry Division on the Western Front. In July 1941 led his division in a well-organized counterattack near Borisov in Minsk province (Belorussia), which succeeded in halting the enemy advance for two days on the banks of the River Berezin. Also achieved success in fighting near Orsha, inspiring his troops by his personal courage. For his achievements in the initial period of the war named Hero of the Soviet Union—the first man in the infantry forces to receive this honor. In late 1941 commander of the Third Army, then deputy commander of a number of armies. In October 1942 placed in command of the Second Guards Army. Between August 1943 and end of war, commander of the 51st Army. After war occupied command posts in the army.

**Krupskaya, N. K.** (1869–1939). Daughter of a government official. Member of the RSDLP from 1898. Lenin's spouse and one of his closest associates. Active Communist Party figure. Organizer of the women's movement. Leading official in the agencies of political enlightenment and popular education. Honorary member of the USSR Academy of Sciences from 1931. Author of numerous works on the history of the AUCP(B), political work, and pedagogy.

**Krylov, N. I.** (1903–72). In Red Army from 1919. In June 1941 colonel. Chief of staff from November 1941 of the Maritime Army, from September 1942 of the 62nd Army, and from April 1943 of the Eighth Guards Army. Commander from July 1943 of the 21st Army and from October 1943 of the Fifth Army. Took part in the defense of Odessa and Sevastopol, in the battle of Stalingrad, and in the Belorussian, East Prussian, and Harbin-Jilin offensive operations. After war, in command posts in the army, commander in chief of Strategic Missile Forces, and deputy minister of defense. Twice Hero of the Soviet Union. Marshal of the Soviet Union.

**Kryuchenkin, V. D.** (1894–1976). Joined Red Army in 1918. At start of war major general, promoted in 1943 to lieutenant general. Initially in command of a division, then of the Fifth Cavalry Corps (at the end of 1941 renamed the Third Guards Cavalry Corps). In July 1942 appointed commander of the 28th Army, then in August 1942 of the Fourth Tank Army, in March 1943 of the 69th Army, and in April 1944 of the 33rd Army on the Southwestern,

Voronezh, Steppe, and Second Belorussian Fronts. In 1945 deputy commander of the 61st Army and then of the First Belorussian Front. After war, occupied command posts in the army.

**Kucherenko, N. A.** (1907–76). Member of the AUCP(B) from 1942. Colonel-engineer from 1945. One of the designers of the Soviet tanks T-24, BT-2, BT-5, BT-7, BT-7M, T-34, T-44, and other models. President of the Academy of Construction and Architecture from 1961.

**Kucherenko, V. A.** (1909–63). Deputy chairman of the Council of Ministers from 1955.

**Kuibyshev, V. V.** (1888–1935). Son of an officer. Member of the RSDLP from 1904. Participated in the revolutions of 1905, February 1917, and October 1917. After 1917 a prominent politicomilitary official. From 1921 member of the presidium of the Supreme Council of National Economy. From 1922 secretary of the CC of the RCP(B). From 1923 people's commissar of workers' and peasants' inspection and deputy chairman of the Council of People's Commissars and of the Council for Labor and Defense. From 1926 chairman of the Supreme Council of National Economy. From 1930 chairman of the State Planning Commission and deputy chairman (from 1934 first deputy chairman) of the Council of People's Commissars. From 1934 to 1935 chairman of the Soviet Control Commission. Member of the party CC in 1922 and from 1927. From 1923 to 1926 chairman of the Central Control Commission of Workers' and Peasants' Inspection. From 1927 member of the Politburo of the CC of the AUCP(B).

**Kulik, G. I.** (1890–1950). During Civil War fought in the First Cavalry Army. Thereafter occupied a number of high posts. Member of the CC of the AUCP(B) from 1939 to 1942. From 1939 head of the Main Artillery Administration of the Workers' and Peasants' Red Army and simultaneously deputy people's commissar of defense. Marshal of the Soviet Union and Hero of the Soviet Union from 1940. In March 1942 demoted to the rank of major general. From April to September 1943 commanded the Fourth Guards Army. Thereafter at the disposal of the Main Cadres Administration of the Workers' and Peasants' Red Army. Worked as deputy head of the Main Administration for the Composition of Troop Units. After war, deputy commander of the Volga Military District. Retired in June 1946. Falsely accused of treason and executed in 1950. In 1957 posthumously restored to the title of Marshal of the Soviet Union.

**Kulkov, M. M.** (1891–1938). Worker. Member of the RSDLP from 1915. After 1917 occupied leading Soviet and party posts. In 1935 headed the Department of Party Cadres of the Moscow city committee of the AUCP(B). Thereafter second secretary of the Moscow committee of the party. Fate unclear, probably shot, posthumously rehabilitated.

**Kurochkin, P. A.** (1900–1989). At start of war, lieutenant general. In the first months of war commanded the Twentieth Army and then the 43rd Army. For most of the period between August 1941 and November 1943, involved with the Northwestern Front, either as its commander or deputy commander or as representative of the Stavka. For some months in late 1942 and early 1943 in command of the Eleventh and 34th Armies. In December 1943 appointed deputy commander of the First Ukrainian Front, then in February 1944 commander of the Second Belorussian Front. From April 1944 until end of war commanded the 60th Army. Took part in several offensive operations in the last phase of war and in the liberation of Poland and Czechoslovakia. After war occupied command posts in the army. Hero of the Soviet Union.

**Kuusinen, O. V.** (1881–1964). Finnish. Member of the RSDLP from 1904. From 1911 to 1917 chairman of the Executive Committee of the Social-Democratic Party of Finland. A leader of the Finnish revolution of 1918. From 1921 to 1939 member and secretary of the presidium of the executive committee of the Communist International. From 1940 to 1956 chairman of the presidium of the Supreme Soviet of the Karelo-Finnish SSR (set up by Stalin with a view to the absorption of Finland into the USSR). Member of the CC of the AUCP(B) from 1941. From 1957 secretary of the CC CPSU. Member of the Presidium of the CC CPSU from 1952 to 1953 and from 1957. Full member of the USSR Academy of Sciences from 1958. Author of works on the history of the international Communist movement.

**Lakoba, N. A.** (1893–1936). Abkhazian. From a peasant background. Member of the RSDLP from 1912. After 1917 participated in the struggle for Soviet power in the Transcaucasus. In 1921 chairman of the revolutionary committee of Abkhazia. From 1922 chairman of the Council of People's Commissars of Abkhazia. From 1930 chairman of the CEC of Abkhazia. Member of the CEC of the USSR. Poisoned by Beria in December 1936.

**Larin, I. I.** (1903–43). Joined Red Army in 1921. At start of war, regimental commissar, then commander of a corps. From September 1941 member of the Military Council of the Sixth Army, then from December 1941 to July 1942 (as division commissar) member of the Military Council of the Southern Front.

From October 1942 to January 1943 member of the Military Council of the Second Guards Army (with the rank of major general). Took part in border fighting, in the battles for the Donbas and for Kharkov, and in the Soviet counteroffensive at Stalingrad. Perished in 1943.

**Latsis, V. T.** (1904–66). Latvian. Writer, political and state figure. Member of the AUCP(B) from 1928. People's Writer of the Latvian SSR from 1947. From 1940 to 1959 chairman of the Council of People's Commissars (Council of Ministers) of the Latvian SSR.

**Leonov, D. S.** (1899–1981). Member of the RCP(B) from 1918. Joined Red Army in 1922. Graduated from the Lenin Military-Political Academy. At start of war, corps commissar, promoted in 1942 to lieutenant general. Member of the Military Council of the 22nd Army, then from October 1941 of the Kaliningrad Front and from October 1943 of the First Baltic Front. Took part in the battles of Smolensk and Moscow and in several military operations conducted in the Baltic region and East Prussia. In November 1944 appointed deputy chief of the General Staff for political work. Between May and September 1945 member of the Military Council of the Far Eastern and Second Far Eastern Fronts. After war engaged in political work in the army.

**Leselidze, K. N.** (1903–44). Joined Red Army in 1921. At start of war, colonel, promoted in 1943 to colonel general. During the first year of war chief of artillery of an infantry corps and then of the 50th Army in the Western Front. In June 1942 placed in command of the Third Infantry Corps. Appointed commander in turn of the 46th Army (in August 1942), of the 47th Army (in January 1943), and of the Eighteenth Army (in March 1943) in the Transcaucasus, Northern Caucasus, and First Ukrainian Fronts. Took part in the battle for Moscow, the defense of the Caucasus, and the liberation of the Caucasus and Ukraine. Died from wounds in February 1944. Posthumously named Hero of the Soviet Union.

**Leszczinski, J.** (1889–1937). Polish. General secretary of the CC of the Communist Party of Poland from 1929. Member of the presidium of the executive committee of the Communist International from 1929. Victim of Stalin's repression.

**Likhachev, I. A.** (1896–1956). From a peasant background. Worker and sailor. Member of the RSDLP from 1917. Fought in Civil War, thereafter a trade union official. From 1926 to 1939 and from 1940 to 1950 director of the Moscow Automobile Factory. From 1939 to 1940 people's commissar of machine building. From 1950 director of the Moscow Machine Building

Factory. From 1953 minister of automobile transportation and highroads. Member of the CC of the AUCP(B) from 1939.

**Litvinenko-Volgemut, M. I.** (1892–1966). Singer and educator. Member of the AUCP(B) from 1944. Soloist from 1914 in Petrograd, Vinnitsa, and Kharkov and from 1935 in Kiev. From 1944 professor at the Kiev Conservatory. People's Artiste of the USSR from 1936.

**Litvinov, M. M.** (1876–1951). From a white-collar background. Member of the RSDLP from 1898. Participated in the revolutions of 1905 and October 1917. Active figure in the Bolshevik movement. From 1918 in various diplomatic posts. From 1921 deputy people's commissar of foreign affairs. From 1930 to 1939 people's commissar (and from 1941 to 1946 deputy people's commissar) of foreign affairs. From 1941 to 1943 Soviet ambassador to the United States. From 1946 on pension. Member of the CC of the AUCP(B) from 1934. Member of the CEC of the USSR.

**Livshits, Ya. A.** Member of the Socialist Revolutionary Party from 1913 and of the RSDLP from 1917. From 1919 an official in the Cheka and the GPU. From 1924 engaged in economic work. Deputy manager of the Kharkov trust Donugol (Don Coal). Head of the Southern, Northern Caucasus, and Moscow–Kursk railroads. From 1935 deputy people's commissar of communications. Arrested in 1936 and shot in 1937. Posthumously rehabilitated.

**Lominadze, V. V.** (1897–1935). Son of a teacher. Member of the RSDLP from 1917. Until 1924 occupied leading party posts. From 1925 to 1929 a prominent official of the Communist International, then occupied various party posts. Secretary of the Magnitogorsk city committee of the AUCP(B). Member of the party CC from 1930. Committed suicide 1935, presumably to avoid arrest.

**Lopatin, A. I.** (1897–1965). In Red Army from 1918. In June 1941 major general. During war commanded the 31st Infantry Corps on the Southwestern Front, then from October 1941 the 37th Army, from June 1942 the Ninth Army, from August 1942 the 62nd Army, from October 1942 the 34th Army, from March to July 1943 the Eleventh Army, and in September and October 1943 the Twentieth Army. From January 1944 deputy commander of the 43rd Army. From July 1944 commanded the Thirteenth Guards Infantry Corps on the First Baltic and Third Belorussian Fronts. Hero of the Soviet Union.

**Lyubchenko, A. P.** (1897–1937). From a peasant background. Medical assistant. Member of the Ukrainian Social Revolutionary Party from 1913, of the Struggle (Borotbist) Party from 1918 and of the CP(B)U from 1920. Participated in the struggle for Soviet power in Ukraine. From 1921 occupied leading posts in the Soviets and in the cooperative movement. From 1927 secretary of the CC of the CP(B)U. From 1934 chairman of the Council of People's Commissars of the Ukrainian SSR. Member of the CEC, arrested and executed, posthumously rehabilitated. His personal name, Afanasy in Russian, is often written in Ukrainian as Panas.

**Macmillan, Harold.** (1894–1986). British. Leader of the Conservative Party and prime minister of the United Kingdom from 1957 to 1963. From the mid-1960s headed an important publishing house.

**Makarov, I. G.** Member of the RSDLP from 1905. Director of the Yuzovka (Stalino) Factory from 1922 to 1924 and again from 1932 to 1936.

**Makovsky, V. L.** Engineer working for Metrostroi (the organization building the Moscow metro). Subsequently a prominent expert on metro construction. Author of a number of specialized works.

**Maksarev, Yu. Ye.** Member of the RCP(B) from 1921.

**Malenkov, G. M.** (1902–88). From a white-collar background. Member of the RCP(B) from 1920. An official in the apparatus of the CC of the AUCP(B) from 1925 and in that of the Moscow committee of the party from 1930. From 1934 to 1939 head of the Department of Leading Party Bodies of the CC of the AUCP(B). From 1939 secretary of the party CC (until 1953) and head of the Cadres Administration of the CC. From 1941 to 1945 member of the State Defense Committee. From February 1941 candidate member, and from 1946 member, of the Politburo of the CC of the AUCP(B). From 1946 to 1953 deputy chairman of the USSR Council of Ministers. From 1953 to 1955 chairman of the USSR Council of Ministers. From 1955 to 1957 minister of electricity stations. Member of the party CC from 1939 to 1957. For participating in the so-called antiparty group inside the CC of the CPSU removed in 1957 from his previous posts and appointed director of the Ust-Kamenogorsk hydroelectric station, then of the Ekibastuz thermoelectric station (both in Kazakhstan). Expelled from the CPSU in 1961.

**Malinin, M. S.** (1899–1960). Joined Red Army in 1919. At start of war, colonel. During the first year of war, chief of staff of the Seventh Motorized Corps on the Western Front, then chief of staff of the Sixteenth Army. Thereafter chief of staff successively of the Bryansk, Don, Central, Belorussian, and First Belorussian Fronts. After war engaged in staff work in the army. Hero of the Soviet Union.

**Malinovsky, R. Ya.** (1898–1967). Noncommissioned officer in the tsarist army. Joined Red Army in 1919. Before assuming senior command posts was a military adviser in the Spanish civil war and an instructor at the Frunze Military Academy. During the war commanded the Southern Front, the Don Operational Group (1942), the Second Guards Army in the counteroffensive at Stalingrad (1942–43), various Fronts engaged in offensive operations in Ukraine, Romania, Hungary, Austria, and Czechoslovakia (1943–45), and the Transbaikal Front in the war with Japan (1945). Commander in chief of Soviet forces in the Far East (1947–53). Commander of the Far Eastern Military District (1953–56). First deputy minister of defense and commander in chief of ground forces (1956–57). Minister of defense (1957–67).

**Malyshev, V. A.** (1902–57). Son of a teacher. Worker. Member of the AUCP(B) from 1926. From 1934 worked as a design engineer. From 1939 people's commissar of heavy machine building. From 1940 to 1944 deputy chairman of the Council of People's Commissars. From 1941 to 1956 people's commissar of tank industry, minister of transportation machine building, minister of shipbuilding, minister of transportation and heavy machine building, and minister of medium machine building. From 1947 to 1956 deputy chairman of the Council of Ministers. Member of the party CC from 1939. Hero of Socialist Labor from 1944. Colonel general of the engineering service from 1945. From 1952 to 1953 member of the Presidium of the CC of the CPSU.

**Mamonov, F. A.** First secretary of the Astrakhan province committee of the CPSU from 1950 to 1954.

**Mannerheim, K. G. E.** (1867–1951). Finnish. Lieutenant general of the Russian (tsarist) army in 1917. Marshal of Finland from 1933. Between 1927 and 1939 created the "Mannerheim line"—a strong system of military fortifications on the Karelian Isthmus along the Finnish-Soviet border. Commander in chief of the Finnish army from 1939 to 1944. From 1944 to 1946 President of Finland. Thereafter in retirement.

**Manuilsky, D. Z.** (1883–1959). From a peasant background. Member of the RSDLP from 1903. Participated actively in the social democratic movement. From 1917 occupied leading Soviet posts. From 1918 people's commissar of agriculture of the Ukrainian SSR. From 1922 an official in the Communist International. From 1928 to 1943 secretary of the executive committee of the Communist International. From 1944 deputy chairman of the Council of People's Commissars and people's commissar of foreign affairs of the Ukrainian SSR. Head of the delegation of the Ukrainian SSR at all the early sessions of the United Nations General Assembly. Member of the CC of the AUCP(B) from 1923 to 1952. Member of the CEC of the USSR. From 1953 on pension.

**Margolin, N. V.** Member of the RSDLP from 1914. After 1917 a prominent party official. Secretary of the Dnepropetrovsk province committee of the AUCP(B). Fate unclear, probably shot, posthumously rehabilitated.

**Matsuoka, Y.** (1880–1946). Japanese. Minister of foreign affairs of Japan from 1940 to 1941.

**Medved, F. D.** Member of the RSDLP from 1907. After 1917 occupied a number of posts in the All-Russian Cheka and the OGPU. An organizer of the labor camps for building the White Sea–Baltic Canal. Headed the Leningrad Province Administration of the OGPU.

**Mekhlis, L. Z.** (1889–1953). White-collar worker. Member of the RCP(B) from 1918. Occupied leading party and Soviet posts, including work in Stalin's secretariat. From 1930 head of the Press Department of the CC of the AUCP(B) and concurrently of the newspaper *Pravda*. From 1937 to 1941 (with an interval) head of the Main Political Administration of the Workers' and Peasants' Red Army. From 1941 to 1942 deputy people's commissar of defense. From 1940 deputy chairman of the Council of People's Commissars. From 1942 to 1945 member of the Military Councils of a number of fronts (with the rank of colonel general). Member of the Military Council of the Fourth Ukrainian Front from August 1944 to July 1945. From 1940 to 1950 people's commissar (minister) of state control. From 1937 member of the presidium of the USSR Supreme Soviet and from 1938 of the Orgburo of the CC of the AUCP(B). Member of the CC of the AUCP(B) from 1939.

**Meretskov, K. A.** (1897–1968). From a peasant background. Worker. Member of the RSDLP from 1917. Red Guard. Served in the Red Army from 1918. Fought in the Civil War. Occupied leading staff, political, and command posts. Took part in the civil war in Spain from 1936. In 1939 commanded the Seventh Army on the Karelian Isthmus, which broke through the "Mannerheim line." Thereafter commander of the Leningrad Military District. From August 1940 to January 1941 chief of the General Staff, then deputy people's commissar of defense. From 1941 to 1945 commanded armies and also the Volkhov, Karelian, and First Far Eastern Fronts. From the end of June to the end of August 1941 under investigation. Until 1955 commander of a number of military districts, then assistant minister of defense for higher military training institutions. Member of the Central Inspection Commission from 1956 to 1961. From 1964 general inspector of the Group of General Inspectors of the General Staff of the Ministry of Defense. Marshal of the Soviet Union from 1944.

**Mezhlauk, V. I.** (1893–1938). Son of a teacher. Participant in the revolutionary movement from 1907. Member of the RSDLP from 1917. After 1917 occupied various Soviet, party, and military posts. From 1924 deputy chairman of the Supreme Council of National Economy. From 1931 first deputy chairman of the State Planning Commission. From 1934 deputy chairman of the Council of People's Commissars and chairman of the State Planning Commission. Member of the CC of the AUCP(B) from 1934. Member of the CEC. People's commissar of heavy industry. Arrested and executed, posthumously rehabilitated. Khrushchev was well acquainted with his brother I. I. Mezhlauk (1891–1938), who in the early 1920s headed Yugostal (South Steel), and who was also subsequently a victim of Stalin's repression.

**Mikolajczyk, Stanislaw.** (1901–66). Polish. Politician and leader of the Polish Peasant Party. After the German conquest of Poland, became vice premier (in 1941) and premier (in 1943) of the Polish government-in-exile in London. In 1944 sought to reach agreement with the USSR about the Polish-Russian border and with the Polish Committee of National Liberation in Lublin about the future Polish government. After the Yalta Conference of February 1945, joined the new Polish government as vice premier and minister of agriculture. In 1947 emigrated to the United States.

**Mikoyan, A. I.** (1895–1978). From a working-class background. Member of the RSDLP from 1915. During Civil War took part in the struggle for Soviet power in the Transcaucasus. From 1920 occupied leading party posts. From 1926 to 1949 people's commissar (minister) successively of foreign and domestic trade, supply, food industry, and trade. From 1937 deputy chairman of the Council of People's Commissars. During Second World War member of the State Defense Committee. From 1946 deputy chairman (from 1955 first deputy chairman) of the Council of Ministers. From 1964 to 1965 chairman (from 1965 member) of the presidium of the USSR Supreme Soviet. Member of the party CC from 1923 to 1975. Member of the Politburo (Presidium) of the party CC from 1935 to 1966. From 1974 on pension.

**Mitrokhin, T. B.** Member of the AUCP(B) from 1925. Chemist. From 1941 to 1948 people's commissar (minister) of chemical industry.

**Moiseyenko, K. V.** Ukrainian. Member of the RSDLP from 1917. One of the leading party officials in Ukraine.

**Molotov, V. M.** (Skryabin) (1890–1986). Member of the RSDLP from 1906. Participated in the revolutionary movement. From 1909 to 1911 in exile in Totma, Solvychegodsk, and Vologda. From 1919 chairman of the Nizhny

Novgorod province executive committee. Secretary of the Donetsk province committee of the RCP(B). From 1921 to 1930 secretary of the party CC. From 1930 to 1941 chairman of the Council of People's Commissars. From 1942 to 1957 first deputy chairman of the Council of People's Commissars (Council of Ministers). From 1941 to 1945 deputy chairman of the State Defense Committee. From 1939 to 1949 and from 1953 to 1956 people's commissar of foreign affairs. From 1957 Soviet ambassador to Mongolia. From 1960 to 1962 permanent representative of the USSR at the International Atomic Energy Agency. At various times member of the CC, of the Orgburo and the Politburo of the CC, and of the All-Russian CEC and the CEC of the USSR. Deputy to the USSR Supreme Soviet from 1937 to 1958. In June 1957 removed from party posts for factional activity.

**Montgomery of Alamein, Viscount.** (Sir B. L. Montgomery) (1887–1976). British. Field marshal of British forces. From 1942 commander of the Eighth Army in North Africa, which defeated German and Italian forces on the approaches to El-Alamein. From 1944 to 1945 commander of a group of armies in France, Belgium, and Germany. After war commander in chief of British occupation forces in Germany. Until 1948 chief of the British General Staff. From 1951 to 1958 deputy commander in chief of the armed forces of NATO in Europe. Awarded the Order of Victory and the Order of Suvorov First Class by the USSR.

**Moskalenko, K. S.** (1902–85). Colonel general of artillery. Commanded the First Tank Army in July and August 1942. From August 1942 commanded the First Guards Army. From October 1942 to October 1943 commanded the 40th Army. From October 1943 to May 1945 commanded the 38th Army. After war occupied various command posts. Marshal of the Soviet Union from 1956. Hero of the Soviet Union.

**Muradeli, Vano Ilyich.** (1908–70). Georgian. Composer, conductor, and actor. Born in Gori, Georgia. In 1931 graduated from the Tbilisi Conservatory. From 1934 to 1938 worked at the Moscow Conservatory. From 1942 to 1944 principal and artistic director of the Central Ensemble of the Soviet Navy. Joined party in 1942. In 1948 his opera *The Great Friendship* was censured in a resolution of the party Central Committee. After Stalin's death restored to favor. People's Artiste of the USSR 1968.

**Nikolayev, L. V.** (1904–34). Member of the RCP(B) from 1924. Official of the Leningrad province committee of the party and lecturer at the Leningrad Institute of the History of the AUCP(B). Allegedly linked to the Trotskyist opposition. Dismissed in April 1934, remained without work, executed in December 1934 for the assassination of Kirov.

**Nikolayeva, K. I.** (1893–1944). Russian. Worker. Member of the RSDLP from 1909. From 1917 one of the leading activists of the Soviet women's movement. From 1924 to 1926 head of the Department for Women Workers in the CC of the AUCP(B), then a leading party official in the Caucasus, Moscow, Siberia, and Ivanovo. From 1936 secretary of the All-Russian Central Council of Trade Unions. From 1924 candidate member and member of the CC of the AUCP(B). From 1937 member of the presidium of the USSR Supreme Soviet.

**Novikov, A. A.** (1900–1976). In Red Army from 1919. From 1940 commanded air forces of the Leningrad Military District. In June 1941 air force major general. During war commanded air forces of the Northern, and from August 1941 of the Leningrad, Fronts. From April 1942 to end of war commanded air forces of the Red Army and in 1942–43 concurrently deputy people's commissar of defense for air forces. As representative of the Stavka coordinated the air forces of several fronts in the battles of Stalingrad and Kursk, in the operations to liberate the Northern Caucasus, Ukraine, Belorussia, and the Baltic, in the storming of Königsberg, in the Berlin operation, and in the crushing of the Japanese Kwantung Army. Organized the air blockade of encircled enemy forces at Stalingrad and the defeat of enemy air forces in aerial combat over the Kuban. Participated in the reorganization of air forces into bomber, fighter, and attack formations and into air armies and air corps. After war in command posts in the air forces. From March 1946 to June 1953 imprisoned. Rehabilitated and appointed commander of Strategic Air Forces. Hero of the Soviet Union. Air force chief marshal.

**Novotny, Antonin.** (1904–75). Czech. Member of the Communist Party of Czechoslovakia from 1921 and a member of its CC from 1946. First secretary of the CC of the Communist Party of Czechoslovakia from 1953 to 1968. President of Czechoslovakia from 1957 to 1968.

**Ordzhonikidze, G. K.** (1886–1937). From a gentry background. Member of the RSDLP from 1903. Participated in the revolutions of 1905, February 1917, and October 1917 and in the Iranian revolution (1909–11). After 1917 occupied a number of leading military, state, and political party posts. From 1922 to 1926 first secretary of the Transcaucasus and Northern Caucasus territory committees of the party. From 1926 to 1930 chairman of the Central Control Commission of the AUCP(B). People's commissar of workers' and peasants' inspection and deputy chairman of the Council of People's Commissars and of the Council of Labor and Defense. From 1930 chairman of the Supreme Council of National Economy. From 1932 people's commissar of heavy industry. In 1920 and then (after a gap) from 1921 member of the party CC. From 1930 member of the Politburo of the CC of the AUCP(B). Committed suicide.

**Paasikivi, Juho Kusti.** (1870–1956). Finnish. Prime minister of Finland in 1918 and from 1944 to 1946. President of Finland from 1946 to 1956. Known for his policy of maintaining good relations with the USSR on the basis of neutrality.

**Panch, P. I.** (Panchenko) (1891–1978). Son of a government official. Writer. Member of the AUCP(B) from 1940. From 1941 to 1945 head of programming at the radio station Radianska Ukraina (Soviet Ukraine).

**Patolichev, N. S.** (1908–90). From a peasant background. Member of the AUCP(B) from 1928. Thereafter engaged in important party work. From 1939 to 1946 first secretary of the Yaroslavl and Chelyabinsk province and city committees of the AUCP(B), then secretary of the CC of the AUCP(B) and of the CC of the CP(B)U and first secretary of the Rostov province and city committees of the party. From 1950 to 1956 first secretary of the CC of the Communist Party of Belorussia. From 1958 to 1985 minister of foreign trade. Member of the party CC from 1941 to 1986. Candidate member of the Presidium of the CC CPSU from 1952 to 1953. From 1985 on pension.

**Paton, Ye. O.** (1870–1953). Scientist. Specialist in welding. Member of the AUCP(B) from 1944. From 1905 professor at the Kiev Polytechnical Institute. From 1921 to 1931 head of the Kiev Bridge Testing Station. From 1934 director of the Scientific Research Institute of Electric Welding. Full member of the Academy of Sciences of the Ukrainian SSR from 1929. Vice-President of the Academy of Sciences of the Ukrainian SSR from 1945 to 1952. Author of numerous works on the theory and practice of welding and bridge construction.

**Patorzhinsky, I. S.** (1896–1960). Singer and educator. Member of the AUCP(B) from 1946. Soloist from 1925 at the Kharkov operatic theater. From 1935 sang in Kiev. From 1946 professor at the Kiev Conservatory. People's Artiste of the USSR from 1944.

**Paulus, Friedrich.** (1890–1957). German. General. Commanded the Sixth Army at Stalingrad in 1942. Shortly after promotion to field marshal in January 1943, surrendered with his army. Took part in the pro-Soviet National Committee *Freies Deutschland* (Free Germany). After war lived in East Germany.

**Pavlov, D. G.** (1897–1941). Prominent military commander. Member of the RCP(B) from 1919. Took part in the civil war in Spain from 1936. Army general from 1941. On the eve of the German invasion of the USSR commanded the Western Special Military District. Executed in 1941 for the defeats of the forces under his command at the beginning of the war.

**Pétain, Henri Philippe.** (1856–1951). French. Marshal of France from 1918. Commander in chief of the French army from 1917. From June 16, 1940, to April 1942, prime minister of France and simultaneously from July 1940 to August 1944 President of the pro-Nazi collaborationist regime in Vichy. From 1945 imprisoned as a traitor.

**Peters, Ya. Kh.** (1886–1938). From a peasant background. Worker. Member of the RSDLP from 1904 and member of the British Labour Party from 1909. After 1917 occupied leading posts in the All-Russian Cheka in Petrograd, Moscow, Kiev, Tula, and Turkestan. From 1923 member of the Collegium of the OGPU. Member of the Central Control Commission from 1923 to 1934, then a member of the Party Control Commission attached to the CC of the AUCP(B). From 1930 to 1934 headed the Party Control Commission of Moscow province. Arrested and executed, posthumously rehabilitated.

**Petlyura, S. V.** (1879–1926). Ukrainian. Son of a drayman. Active figure in the Ukrainian national movement. Publicist. From 1915 headed the Main Control Commission of the All-Russian Union of Zemstva (bodies of local self-government) for the Western Front. In 1917 chairman of the All-Ukrainian Army Committee and minister of the Central Rada (parliament of the Ukrainian People's Republic) for military affairs. In 1918 headed the All-Ukrainian Union of Zemstva. Became Chief Ataman (traditional title for Cossack military leader) of the armed forces of the Ukrainian People's Republic. In 1919 chairman of the Directorate (another independent Ukrainian government). In 1920 concluded the Warsaw Agreement with Poland for joint struggle against Soviet power, then emigrated.

**Petrov, G. G.** (died 1962). Before war, one of the most popular government photographers.

**Petrov, I. Ye.** (1896–1958). Joined Red Army in 1918. At start of war major general in command of the Second Cavalry Division, promoted in 1944 to army general. In June 1941 appointed commander of the 25th Infantry Division in the Maritime Army and in October 1941 commander of the Maritime Army. In August 1942 placed in command of the 44th Army, then in October 1942 of the Black Sea Grouping of the Transcaucasus Front. One of the leaders of the defense of Odessa and Sevastopol. In March 1943 became chief of staff, and in May 1943 commander, of the Northern Caucasus Front. In winter 1943–44 returned to the Maritime Army. In spring 1944 appointed commander of the 33rd Army and then of the Second Belorussian Front. In August 1944 placed in command of the Fourth Ukrainian Front. From April 1945 until the end of war, chief of staff of the First Ukrainian Front. Took part in the Kerch paratroop landing, in the liberation of the Black Sea coast, Transcarpathia, and Czechoslovakia, and in the assault on Berlin. After war occupied command posts in the army. Hero of the Soviet Union.

**Petrovsky, G. I.** (1878–1958). Craftsman. Participant in the revolutionary movement from 1897. Member of the RSDLP from 1898. Deputy to the fourth State Duma. From 1917 people's commissar of internal affairs of Soviet Russia. In 1919 chairman of the All-Ukrainian Revolutionary Committee. From 1919 to 1938 chairman of the All-Ukrainian CEC. From 1922 one of the chairmen of the CEC of the USSR. From 1921 to 1939 member of the party CC and from 1926 to 1939 candidate member of the Politburo of the party CC. From 1937 to 1946 deputy to the Supreme Soviet. From 1940 deputy director of the Museum of the Revolution. Later, on pension.

**Petrovsky, L. G.** (1902–41). Lieutenant general from 1941. Member of the RSDLP from 1916. Participated in the armed uprising of October 1917 in Petrograd. Red Guard. From 1918 in Red Army. Imprisoned from 1938 to 1940. Perished at the battlefront at the beginning of the war.

**Pilsudski, Józef.** (1867–1935). Polish. Prominent figure in the Polish Socialist Party from the beginning of the twentieth century. First head of state of the new Polish republic established in November 1918. Remained head of state until 1922. Prime minister of Poland from 1926 to 1928 and in 1930.

**Podlas, K. P.** (1893–1942). Member of the RCP(B) from 1918. Military man. Fought in Civil War. Commander of subunits, units, and formations. Deputy commander of the Kiev Special Military District. In 1941 lieutenant general, perished in battle near Kharkov.

**Poluboyarov, P. P.** (1901–84). Joined Red Army in 1919. At start of war, colonel, promoted to marshal of armored forces. During the first year of war, chief of the Administration for Armored Forces of the Northwestern Front, then deputy commander for armored forces of the Kaliningrad Front. In August 1942 placed in command of the Seventeenth Tank Corps, which fought in the Voronezh, Southwestern, and First Ukrainian Fronts and was renamed in January 1943 the 45th Guards Tank Corps. After war held important posts in the armored forces. Hero of the Soviet Union.

**Ponomarenko, P. K.** (1902–84). Between 1938 and 1947 first secretary of the CC of the CP(B) of Belorussia. During the first three years of war was a member of the Military Council of the Third Assault Army in the Kaliningrad Front, then a member of the Military Councils of the Western, Central, Bryansk, and First Belorussian Fronts. From 1942, as chief of the central staff of the partisan movement, was a leading organizer of resistance to the German occupation. In 1943 was given the rank of lieutenant general. Between 1944 and 1948 represented the Council of People's Commissars (Council of Ministers) of Belorussia. Thereafter engaged in other state and party work. Wrote many works about the partisan movement.

**Poplavsky, S. G.** (1902–73). Joined Red Army in 1923. At start of war, major in command of an infantry regiment. In the first three years of war was chief of staff of the 363rd Infantry Division, then commander of a number of infantry divisions, and finally of the 45th Infantry Corps in the Western, Kaliningrad, and First and Third Belorussian Fronts. In September 1944 placed in command of the Second Army, and in December 1944 of the First Army, of the Polish Forces. Between 1945 and 1956 commanded military districts and the ground forces, was also deputy minister of national defense of the Polish People's Republic. Thereafter engaged in important work in the Ministry of Defense. Hero of the Soviet Union.

**Popov, G. M.** (1906–68). From a white-collar background. Member of the AUCP(B) from 1926. From 1928 to 1938 a researcher at the Moscow Central Institute of Labor, then an official in the apparatus of the CC of the AUCP(B). From 1938 to 1945 second secretary of the Moscow city committee of the AUCP(B). From 1944 to 1950 chairman of the executive committee of the Moscow Soviet. From 1945 to 1949 first secretary of the Moscow committee and of the Moscow city committee of the AUCP(B). Secretary of the CC of the AUCP(B). From 1951 minister of city planning, then of agricultural machine building, thereafter director of a number of factories. From 1953 to 1954 Soviet ambassador to Poland. From 1965 on pension.

**Popov, M. M.** (1902–69). Joined Red Army in 1920. At start of war, lieutenant general. During the first year of war commanded the Northern and Leningrad Fronts and then the 61st and 40th Armies. In October 1942 appointed deputy commander of the Stalingrad and Southwestern Fronts and commander of the Fifth Assault Army and Fifth Tank Army. In April 1943 placed in command of the Reserve Front and the Steppe Military District, in June 1943 of the Bryansk Front, then in October 1943 of the Baltic and Second Baltic Fronts. Between April 1944 and the end of war, chief of staff of the Leningrad Front, the Second Baltic Front, and again the Leningrad Front. Took part in planning and conducting military operations in the battles of Leningrad, Moscow, Stalingrad, and Kursk and in Karelia and the Baltic. After war occupied command posts in the army.

**Popov, V. S.** (1894–1967). In Red Army from 1919. In June 1941 major general. During the war, commander of the 28th Infantry Corps in the Western Front, then from September 1941 deputy commander of the 50th Army, from February 1942 to April 1944 commander of the Tenth Army, then deputy commander of the First Belorussian Front, and from May 1944 commander of the 70th Army. After war occupied command posts in the army. Hero of the Soviet Union.

**Postyshev, P. P.** (1887–1939). Worker. Member of the RSDLP from 1904. Participated in the revolutions of 1905, February 1917, and October 1917. From 1917 to 1922 occupied a number of military, party, and state posts in the Far East, and from 1923 in Ukraine. Secretary of the CC and member of the Politburo of the CC of the CP(B) of Ukraine from 1926 to 1930. Secretary of the CC of the AUCP(B) from 1930 to 1933, then second secretary of the CC of the CP(B)U. From 1937 secretary of the Kuibyshev province committee of the AUCP(B). From 1934 to 1938 candidate member of the Politburo of the CC of the AUCP(B), member of the CC of the AUCP(B). Unjustly repressed, shot 1939, rehabilitated posthumously.

**Pramnek, E. K.** (Pramnieks) (1899–1938). Worker. Member of the RSDLP from 1917. Fought in Civil War. From 1924 engaged in party work in Nizhny Novgorod and Vyatka. From 1930 second secretary, and from 1934 first secretary, of the Gorky territory and province committees of the AUCP(B). From 1937 secretary of the Donetsk province committee of the CP(B)U. Member of the All-Russian CEC and of the CEC of the USSR. Arrested, fate unclear, probably shot, posthumously rehabilitated.

**Purkayev, M. A.** (1894–1953). Army general 1944. Commanded various armies, then the Kalinin, Far Eastern, and Second Far Eastern Fronts. From 1947 to 1952 chief of staff of troops in the Far East.

**Pyatakov, G. L.** (1890–1937). From a lower-middle-class background. Member of the RSDLP from 1910. In 1917 led the struggle for Soviet power in Kiev. In 1918 chairman of the Provisional Workers' and Peasants' Government of

Ukraine, then a member of the Revolutionary Military Councils of a number of armies. From 1920 deputy chairman of the State Planning Commission of the RSFSR, deputy chairman of the Supreme Council for National Economy, trade representative in France, and chairman of the board of the State Bank. From 1932 deputy (from 1934 first deputy) people's commissar of heavy industry. Member of the party CC from 1923. From 1927 subject to party persecution as a Trotskyist. Expelled from the party in 1936. Shot 1937, rehabilitated posthumously.

**Pyatnitsky, I. A.** (1882–1938). Son of a joiner. Member of the RSDLP from 1888. One of the most active Leninist party officials. A leader of the armed uprising of 1917 in Moscow, then engaged in trade-union and Soviet work. In 1920 secretary of the Moscow committee of the RCP(B). From 1921 occupied high posts in the Communist International. From 1935 an official in the apparatus of the CC of the AUCP(B). Member of the Central Control Commission from 1924 to 1927. Member of the CC of the AUCP(B) from 1927. Shot 1938, rehabilitated posthumously.

**Radchenko, A. F.** (1887–1938). Peasant. Member of the RSDLP from 1912. After 1917 worked as a Soviet and trade union official. From 1924 to 1925 secretary of the Stalino province committee of the CP(B)U. From 1925 to 1928 chairman of the All-Ukrainian Council of Trade Unions and member of the Politburo of the CC of the CP(B)U. From 1929 occupied various party posts. Arrested, fate unclear, probably shot, posthumously rehabilitated.

**Redens, S. F.** (1892–1940). Member of the RSDLP from 1914. Prominent official of the OGPU and the NKVD. From 1935 commissar of state security of the first rank. Fate unclear, probably shot, posthumously rehabilitated.

**Ribbentrop.** See **von Ribbentrop**.

**Rodimtsev, A. I.** (1905–77). In Red Army from 1927. In June 1941 colonel. Commanded the Fifth Paratroop Brigade, then the 87th (from January 1942 renamed the Thirteenth Guards) Infantry Division. From May 1943 until end of war commanded the 32nd Guards Infantry Corps. Took part in the defense of Kiev and Kharkov, then in the battles of Stalingrad and Kursk, in the liberation of Ukraine, and in the Lower Silesian, Berlin, and Prague military operations. After war, occupied command posts and engaged in diplomatic work. Twice Hero of the Soviet Union.

**Rogachev, D. D.** (1895–1963). In the navy from 1919. At start of war, rear admiral in command of the Pinsk Naval Flotilla. In February 1942 appointed commander of the Volga Naval Flotilla, then in July 1943 of a detachment of naval vessels on the Volga. Between 1944 and 1946 commander of the Kiev Naval Base of the Dnieper Flotilla. After war, occupied command posts in the navy.

**Rokossovsky, K. K.** (1896–1968). Son of a locomotive driver. Building worker. Member of RCP(B) from 1919. Red Guard in 1917. Fought in Civil War. Until 1936 in various command posts. Arrested in 1937. Released and reinstated in 1940. Commander of the Sixteenth Army in the battle for Moscow in 1941–42. Commander of the Don Front in the battle for Stalingrad from September 1942 to February 1943, then of the Central Front in the battle for Kursk. From February to November 1944 commander of the First Belorussian Front, then of the Second Belorussian Front. Commander in chief of Soviet forces in Poland from 1945. Minister of defense of Poland from 1949. Deputy minister of defense of the USSR from 1956. Inspector General of the Ministry of Defense from 1962. Marshal of the Soviet Union. Twice Hero of the Soviet Union.

**Rotert, P. P.** Chief of construction of the Moscow Metro. Author of many engineering designs and technical building specifications.

**Rotmistrov, P. A.** (1901–82). Joined Red Army in 1919. At start of war, colonel, chief of staff of the Third Mechanized Corps. In September 1941 placed in command of the Eighth Tank Brigade (renamed in January 1942 the Third Guards Tank Brigade), in April 1942 of the Seventh Tank Corps (later renamed the Third Guards Tank Corps), and then in February 1943 of the Fifth Guards Tank Army. In August 1944 became deputy commander of Red Army armored and mechanized forces, promoted to chief marshal of armored forces. Fought in the Western, Northwestern, Kaliningrad, Stalingrad, Voronezh, Steppe, Southwestern, Second Ukrainian, and Third Belorussian Fronts. After war, occupied command posts in the army.

**Rozengolts, A. P.** (1889–1938). From a merchant background. Member of the RSDLP from 1905. One of the leaders of the armed uprising of October 1917 in Moscow. From 1918 to 1927 occupied a number of leading military and state posts. From 1928 deputy people's commissar of workers' and peasants' inspection. From 1930 to 1937 people's commissar of foreign trade. At time of arrest head of the Administration of State Reserves at the Council of People's Commissars. Candidate member of the CC of the AUCP(B) from 1934. Shot 1938, posthumously rehabilitated.

**Ruben, R. G.** Member of the RSDLP from 1917. Occupied various Soviet, politicomilitary, and party posts.

**Rudenko, R. A.** (1907–81). From a peasant background. Member of the AUCP(B) from 1936. Worked from 1929 in the Prosecutor's Office. From 1944 to 1953 prosecutor of the Ukrainian SSR. From 1945 to 1946 main prosecutor for the USSR at the Nuremberg trial of Nazi war criminals. From 1953 to 1981 prosecutor general of the USSR. Member of the CC of the CPSU from 1961.

**Rudzutak, Ya. E.** (1887–1938). From a peasant background. Worker. Member of the RSDLP from 1905. Participated in the revolutions of 1905, February 1917, and October 1917. From 1917 chairman of the Moscow Council of National Economy, of the Central Administration of Textile Industry, of the CC of the Trade Union of Transportation Workers, of the Turkestan Commission of the All-Russian CEC and of the Turkestan (Central Asian) Bureau of the CC of the AUCP(B). From 1923 secretary of the party CC. From 1924 people's commissar of communications. From 1926 to 1937 deputy chairman of the Council of People's Commissars and of the Council of Labor and Defense. From 1931 people's commissar of workers' and peasants' inspection. From 1920 member of the party CC. From 1926 to 1932 member, and from 1923 to 1926 and from 1934 candidate member, of the Politburo of the CC of the AUCP(B). Member of the CEC. Shot 1938, posthumously rehabilitated.

**Rukhimovich, M. L.** (1889–1938). Worker. Member of the RSDLP from 1913. Played an active role in the Civil War and the struggle for Soviet power in Ukraine. From 1921 to 1922 chairman of the Yuzovka province executive committee. From 1923 to 1925 manager of the trust Donugol (Don Coal), then chairman of the Supreme Soviet of National Economy of the Ukrainian SSR and deputy chairman of the Supreme Soviet of National Economy of the USSR. From 1930 to 1934 people's commissar of communications of the RSFSR. Manager of the trust Kuzbassugol (Kuzbas Coal). At time of arrest was people's commissar of defense industry. Shot 1938, posthumously rehabilitated.

**Ryabyshev, D. I.** (1894–1985). Joined Red Army in 1918. Lieutenant general. At outbreak of war in command of the Eighth Mechanized Corps in the Southwestern Front. In July 1941 placed in command of the 38th Army, then in August 1941 of the Southern Front, in October 1941 of the 57th Army, and in May 1942 of the 28th Army. Between July 1942 and March 1943 carried out assignments of the Stavka. In May 1943 appointed commander of the Third Reserve Army, then deputy commander of the Third Guards Army. From April 1944 commanded the Third Guards Infantry Corps, then the 114th Infantry Corps. Took part in the liberation of Ukraine and in the assaults on East Prussia and Berlin. After war held command posts in the army.

**Ryazanov, V. G.** (1901–51). Joined Red Army in 1920. At start of war, colonel, promoted in 1943 to air force lieutenant general. During the first year of war deputy commander of air forces of the Fifth Army, then commander of the 76th Air Division, of the air maneuver grouping of the Southwestern Front, and of the Second Fighter Air Army. In September 1942 appointed commander of the First Guards Storm Air Corps and remained in this post until the end of war, fighting in the Southwestern, Southern, Kaliningrad, Northwestern, Voronezh, Steppe, and Second and First Ukrainian Fronts. Made his most important contributions in the forcing of the rivers Dnieper and Vistula. After war, occupied command posts in the air force. Twice Hero of the Soviet Union.

**Rybalko, P. S.** (1894–1948). At start of war, major general, promoted in 1945 to marshal of armored forces. In May 1942 appointed deputy commander of the Fifth Tank Army. In July 1942 placed in command of the Fifth Tank Army, in October 1942 of the Third Tank Army, and in May 1943 of the Third Guards Tank Army. Took part in the battle of Kursk, in the liberation of Ukraine, Poland, and Czechoslovakia, and in the assault on Berlin. After war occupied command posts in the army. Twice Hero of the Soviet Union.

**Rykov, A. I.** (1881–1938). Member of the RSDLP from 1898. Active participant in the revolutionary movement. People's commissar of internal affairs of the RSFSR from November 1917. Chairman of the Supreme Council of National Economy from 1918 to 1921 and from 1923 to 1924. Deputy chairman of the Council of People's Commissars and of the Council of Labor and Defense from 1921. Chairman of the Council of People's Commissars from 1924 to 1930 and chairman of the Council of Labor and Defense from 1926 to 1930. People's commissar of posts and telegraphs (people's commissar of communications) from 1931 to 1936. For many years was a member of the party CC, of the Politburo and Orgburo of the CC, of the All-Russian CEC, and of the CEC of the USSR. Defendant in the third major Moscow trial (1938); executed, posthumously rehabilitated.

**Rykov, Ye. P.** (1906–41). In Red Army from 1928. In June 1941 divisional commissar. Member of the Military Council of the Southwestern Front. Perished during the Kiev defensive operation.

**Rylsky, M. F.** (1895–1964). Poet, translator, and publicist. Teacher by profession. Member of the AUCP(B) from 1943. Full member of the Academy of Sciences of the Ukrainian SSR from 1943 and of the USSR Academy of Sciences from 1958. Chairman of the Writers' Union of the Ukrainian SSR from 1943 to 1946. Director of the Institute of Art Study, Folklore, and Ethnography of the Academy of Sciences of the Ukrainian SSR from 1944 to 1964. An active public figure.

**Ryndin, K. V.** (1893–1938). Son of a tailor. Worker. Member of the RSDLP from 1915. After 1917 occupied leading Soviet, party, and military posts. From 1924 to 1926 secretary of the Nizhny Tagil, and then of the Perm, province committees of the AUCP(B). In 1927 secretary of the Urals province committee of the AUCP(B). From 1928 worked in the apparatus of the CC of the AUCP(B). From 1929 to 1932 chairman of the Moscow Control Commission of the AUCP(B), head of the Moscow province Workers' and Peasants' Inspection, and second secretary of the Moscow committee and Moscow city committee of the AUCP(B). From 1934 secretary of the Chelyabinsk province committee of the AUCP(B). Member of the CC of the AUCP(B) from 1930. Fate unclear, probably shot, posthumously rehabilitated.

**Ryzhov, A. I.** (1895–1950). Joined Red Army in 1918. At start of war, major general and commandant of a fortified area, promoted in 1944 to lieutenant general. During the first year of war commander of the 296th Infantry Division, deputy commander and then commander of the Third Guards Infantry Corps in the Southern and the Northern Caucasus Fronts. In July 1942 placed in command of the 56th Army, in January 1943 of the Eighteenth Army, in February 1943 of the 46th Army, and in March 1943 of the 47th Army. From July 1943 deputy commander of the 37th and the Fourth Guards Army. In March 1944 appointed commander of the 70th Army, and in July 1944 of the 28th Guards Infantry Corps. After war occupied command posts in the army. Hero of the Soviet Union.

**Sarkisyan, S. A.** (1898–1937). Member of the RSDLP from 1917. Engaged in party and economic work. From 1933 to 1937 first secretary of the Donetsk province committee of the CP(B)U. From 1933 member of the Politburo of the CC of the CP(B)U. Fate unclear, probably shot, posthumously rehabilitated.

**Sato, E.** (1901–1975). Japanese. Premier of Japan from November 9, 1964, to June 17, 1972.

**Sedelnikov, A. I.** (1894–1937). Member of the RCP(B) from 1918. Secretary of the Tula province committee of the AUCP(B). From 1930 member of the bureau of the Moscow committee of the AUCP(B). Manager of a trust in Kuibyshev province. Fate unclear, probably shot, posthumously rehabilitated.

**Serdyuk, Z. T.** (1903–82). Second secretary from 1939 to 1941 and from 1943 to 1947, and first secretary from 1947 to 1949, of the Kiev province committee of the CP(B)U. From 1941 to 1943 engaged in political work in Red Army.

From 1949 to 1951 secretary of the CC of the CP(B)U. From 1952 to 1953 first secretary of the Lvov province committee of the CP(B)U. From 1954 to 1961 first secretary of the CC of the Communist Party of Moldavia, then first deputy chairman of the Party Control Commission attached to the CC of the CPSU.

**Sergeyev, K. M.** Member of the RSDLP from 1917. Thereafter occupied a number of party posts.

**Sergiyenko, V. T.** People's commissar of internal affairs of the Ukrainian SSR from June 1941 to 1943.

**Serov, I. A.** (1905–90). Member of the party from 1926. From 1935 to 1938 attended the Frunze Military Academy of the Workers' and Peasants' Red Army. From 1939 worked in the NKVD. From September 1939 people's commissar of internal affairs of the Ukrainian SSR. From 1941 first deputy people's commissar of state security, then deputy people's commissar of internal affairs. From 1945 to 1947 deputy head of the Soviet military administration in Eastern Germany. Until 1954 first deputy minister of internal affairs of the USSR. Until 1958 chairman of the KGB. Until 1963 head of the Main Intelligence Administration of the Ministry of Defense, then served until 1965 in the Turkestan and Volga Military Districts. Thereafter on pension.

**Shaposhnikov, B. M.** (1882–1945). Colonel of the tsarist army. Served in Red Army from 1918. Member of the AUCP(B) from 1930. During 1920s commanded a number of military districts. From 1928 chief of staff of the Workers' and Peasants' Red Army. From 1932 head of the Frunze Military Academy. From 1937 to 1943 (with a gap from August 1940) chief of the General Staff and deputy people's commissar of defense. Thereafter head of the Military Academy of the General Staff. Marshal of the Soviet Union from 1940. Author of works on military theory.

**Shatunovskaya, O. G.** (1901–91). Member of the RSDLP from 1916. Active during 1920s in the Young Communist League and the party. In 1930s before being arrested worked in the apparatus of the Moscow committee of the AUCP(B) and was secretary of the united party committee (for Moscow city and Moscow province).

**Shcherbakov, A. S.** (1901–45). Worker. Member of the RSDLP from 1918. From 1918 engaged in Communist youth, then in party work. From 1932 an official in the apparatus of the CC of the AUCP(B). From 1934 first secretary of the Writers' Union. From 1936 secretary of the Leningrad, Irkutsk, and Donetsk province committees of the party. From 1938 to 1945 first secretary of the Moscow committee and Moscow city committee of the AUCP(B). From 1941 secretary of the CC of the AUCP(B). From June 1942 head of the Main Political Administration of the Workers' and Peasants' Red Army, head of the Soviet Information Bureau, and deputy people's commissar of defense (with the rank of lieutenant general). Candidate member of the Politburo of the CC of the AUCP(B). Member of the CC of the AUCP(B) from 1939.

**Shchusev, A. V.** (1873–1949). Architect. Participant in the Plan for the Reconstruction of Moscow of 1918–25 and in the General Plan for the Reconstruction of Moscow. Director of the Tretyakov Gallery from 1926 to 1929 and of the Moscow Museum of Architecture from 1946 to 1949. Honored Architect of the USSR from 1930. Academician from 1943. Author of many building and city-planning designs and scholarly works.

**Sheboldayev, B. P.** (1895–1937). Son of a physician. Member of the RSDLP from 1914. After 1917 engaged in military work and from 1920 in party work. From 1923 head of a department of the CC of the CP(B) of Turkmenistan. Secretary of the Tsaritsyn province committee of the RCP(B). Official in the apparatus of the CC of the AUCP(B). From 1928 to 1937 secretary of the Lower Volga, Northern Caucasus, and Azov–Black Sea territory committees and of the Kursk province committee of the AUCP(B). Member of the CC of the AUCP(B) from 1930. Arrested, shot 1937, posthumously rehabilitated.

**Sheinis, L. P.** (1906–67). Member of the AUCP(B) from 1929. Official of the Criminal Investigation Department, then official of the NKVD. Writer and playwright.

**Shepilov, D. T.** (1905–92). Member of the AUCP(B) from 1926. From 1935 engaged in party and scholarly work. From 1945 major general. From 1946 a lecturer. From 1952 to 1956 editor in chief of the newspaper *Pravda*. From 1955 to 1957 secretary of the CC of the CPSU. From 1956 to 1957 minister of foreign affairs. For taking part in the so-called antiparty group inside the CC of the CPSU in 1957, transferred to work at a lower level. Member of the CC of the CPSU from 1952 to 1961.

**Shirin, A. P.** Member of the RCP(B) from 1919. Occupied a number of party posts.

**Shkiryatov, M. F.** (1883–1954). Worker. Member of the RSDLP from 1906. After 1917 engaged in Soviet and trade union work. From 1921 an official in the apparatus of the party CC and in the People's Commissariat of Workers' and Peasants' Inspection. From 1934 member of the Party Control Commission attached to the CC of the AUCP(B). From 1939 to 1952 deputy chairman, and from 1952 chairman, of the Party Control Commission. Member of the CC of the AUCP(B) from 1934. From 1952 to 1953 member of the Presidium of the CC CPSU.

**Shlikhter, A. G.** (1868–1940). Worker. Participated in the revolutionary movement from 1891. Member of the RSDLP from 1898. Took part in the revolutions of 1905, February 1917, and October 1917. From 1917 occupied leading state posts and from 1921 high diplomatic posts. From 1927 to 1929 people's commissar of agriculture of the Ukrainian SSR. From 1931 to 1938 vice president of the Academy of Sciences of the Ukrainian SSR. Candidate member of the Politburo of the CC of the CP(B)U from 1926 to 1937.

**Sholokhov, M. A.** (1905–84). Writer and public figure. Full member of the USSR Academy of Sciences from 1939. Twice Hero of Socialist Labor. Author of *Don Tales* (1926), the novels *The Quiet Don* (1928–40) and *Virgin Soil Upturned* (1932–60), the unfinished composition *They Fought for the Mother-land*, and many other works.

**Shtemenko, S. M.** (1901–76). Colonel general. Graduated from Military Academy of Armored Forces. From 1939 officer of the General Staff. Head of an Area Command Department in the Operational Administration of the General Staff from 1940. Deputy chief of operations from 1943, then chief of operations and deputy chief of the General Staff. Chief of the General Staff and deputy minister of defense from 1949. Temporarily demoted after Stalin's death. From 1959 deputy commander of the Volga Military District. From 1961 first deputy commander of the Transcaucasus Military District. From 1962 chief of staff of Ground Forces. From 1965 deputy chief of the General Staff. From 1968 chief of staff of Warsaw Pact Forces.

**Shumilov, M. S.** (1895–1975). Major general, then lieutenant general, from 1943 colonel general. Commanded the 64th Army from August 1942 until its transformation in April 1943 into the Seventh Guards Army. Commanded the Seventh Guards Army until May 1945. Hero of the Soviet Union.

**Shurov, V. Ya.** Member of the RSDLP from 1917. Political party official.

**Shvernik, N. M.** (1888–1970). Worker. Member of the RSDLP from 1905. Participated in the revolutions of 1905, February 1917, and October 1917. During Civil War, commissar and extraordinary plenipotentiary on the front lines, then in trade-union work. From 1923 people's commissar of workers' and peasants' inspection of the RSFSR. From 1925 secretary of the Leningrad province committee of the AUCP(B). From 1926 secretary of the CC of the AUCP(B). From 1927 secretary of the Urals province committee of the AUCP(B). From 1929 chairman of the CC of the metalworkers' trade union. From 1930 to 1944 first secretary (from 1953 to 1956 chairman) of the All-Union Central Council of Trade Unions. From 1944 first deputy chairman, and from 1946 to 1953 chairman, of the presidium of the USSR Supreme Soviet. From 1956 to 1962 chairman of the Party Commission attached to the CC of the CPSU. Member of the party CC from 1925. Candidate member of the Politburo of the CC of the AUCP(B) from 1939 to 1952. Member of the Presidium of the CPSU CC from 1957 to 1966.

**Simonov, Konstantin M.** (1915–79). Prominent writer, poet, and playwright. Member of the AUCP(B) from 1942. War correspondent and author of popular soldiers' lyrics. Well known for his novel about the battle of Stalingrad—*Days and Nights* (1943–44). After war, editor of the literary journal *Novy Mir* (New World) from 1946 to 1950 and again from 1954 to 1958.

**Skladkowski.** See **Slawoj-Skladkowski.**

**Skripko, N. S.** (1902–87). Joined Red Army in 1919. At start of war colonel, promoted in 1944 to air force marshal. During the first months of war commander of the Third Long-Range Bomber Air Corps, commander of the air forces of the Fifth Army, and then deputy commander of the air forces of the Southwestern Front. In March 1942 appointed deputy commander of Long-Range Air Forces, and in December 1944 first deputy commander of the Eighteenth Air Army. Helped organize the combat use of air forces in the battles of Leningrad, Stalingrad, and Kursk, in the liberation of the Northern Caucasus, the Crimea, Belorussia, and the Baltic, and in the assault on East Prussia. After war occupied command posts in the air force.

**Skrypnik, N. A.** (1872–1933). White-collar worker. Participated in the revolutionary movement from 1897. Member of the RSDLP from 1898. From 1917 to 1933 occupied a number of leading state posts in Ukraine. At the time of his death deputy chairman of the Council of People's Commissars of the Ukrainian SSR. Member of the CC of the AUCP(B) from 1927. Committed suicide in 1933 to avoid arrest.

**Slawoj-Skladkowski, General Felicjan.** (1885–1962). Polish. Prime minister of Poland from May 1936 to September 1939. Interned in Romania, where he remained until 1949.

**Smetona, Antanas.** (1874–1944). Lithuanian. Statesman and journalist. President of Lithuania from 1919 to 1920 and again from 1926 to 1940.

**Snegov, A. V.** (1891–1988). Member of the RSDLP from 1917. Later a well-known party official and active party publicist. From 1931 member of the bureau of the Transcaucasus territory committee of the AUCP(B), then engaged in party and Soviet work in Siberia, Ukraine, Kuibyshev, and Murmansk. Arrested. Rehabilitated in 1954. Thereafter in charge of rehabilitations of the unjustly imprisoned and executed at the Ministry of Internal Affairs.

**Soifer, Ya. G.** Member of the RSDLP from 1907. After 1917 occupied various administrative and party posts.

**Sokolovsky, V. D.** (1897–1968). Joined Red Army in 1918. At start of war lieutenant general, promoted in 1946 to Marshal of the Soviet Union. During the first part of war chief of staff of the Western Front and (at times simultaneously) also of the Western Area. Helped plan and carry out the counteroffensive in the battle for Moscow. From February 1943, as commander of the Western Front, took part in several offensive operations between Moscow and Smolensk. In April 1944 became chief of staff of the First Ukrainian Front, then in April 1945 deputy commander of the First Belorussian Front, participating in the liberation of Western Ukraine and Poland and in the assault on Berlin. After war occupied command posts in the army. Hero of the Soviet Union.

**Stakhanov, A. G.** (1906–77). Member of the AUCP(B) from 1936. Faceworker at the coal mine Tsentralnaya-Irmino in the town of Kadiyevka. On August 1, 1935, set a record for the extraction of coal, marking the beginning of the Stakhanovite movement. From 1941 engaged in administrative and engineering work in the coal industry.

**Stroganov, V. A.** (1888–1938). Peasant. Member of the RSDLP from 1905. From 1917 occupied leading Soviet and party posts. Secretary of the Stalino, then of the Kharkov, province committees of the CP(B)U from 1927 to 1930. Until 1932 second secretary of the CC of the CP(B)U. Secretary of the Dnepropetrovsk province committee of the CP(B)U. Member of the Politburo of the CC of the CP(B)U from 1930 to 1933. Arrested, fate unclear, probably shot, posthumously rehabilitated.

**Strokach, T. A.** (1903–63). Joined party in 1927. From March 1941 deputy people's commissar of internal affairs of the Ukrainian SSR. At the beginning of war, major general, promoted in 1944 to lieutenant general. Took part in the defense of Kiev and Moscow and formed partisan units in Ukraine. In May 1942 appointed chief of the Ukrainian Staff of the Partisan Movement. In October 1942 became a member of the underground CC of the CP(B)U. Planned and coordinated partisan attacks on the rear and communications of the enemy in Ukraine, assisting the Red Army during the winter offensive of 1942–43, at the battle of Kursk and the battle for the Dnieper, and during the liberation of western Ukraine in 1944. After war engaged in state work.

**Studinsky, K. I.** (1868–1941). Literary critic. Full member of the Academy of Sciences of the Ukrainian SSR from 1929. Lecturer, then professor, at Lvov University from 1900.

**Svanidze, A. S.** (1886–1941). Stalin's brother-in-law. Member of the RSDLP from 1903. Occupied a number of state posts in the People's Commissariats of Enlightenment, Foreign Affairs, and Finance. Wrote works on the history of the Far East. Arrested, shot, posthumously rehabilitated.

**Svoboda, L.** (1895–1979). Czech. In June 1939 escaped from German-occupied Czechoslovakia to Poland, where he formed the first Czechoslovak resistance group abroad. After the occupation of Poland in September 1939 transferred his group to the USSR. In February 1942 organized and commanded the First Czechoslovak Detached Infantry Battalion, which went into battle against the occupation forces in March 1943 in the Kharkov region. In summer 1943 placed in command (with the rank of colonel, promoted in December 1943 to general) of the First Czechoslovak Detached Brigade, then in September 1944 of the First Czechoslovak Army Corps, which fought in the First Ukrainian Front in the Kiev region and in Transcarpathia. Later the corps fought as part of the Fourth Ukrainian Front in the liberation of Slovakia and Moravia. After war engaged in state work, serving as president of Czechoslovakia between 1968 and 1975. Hero of the Soviet Union.

**Syrtsov, S. I.** (1893–1937). White-collar worker. Member of the RSDLP from 1913. Fought in the Civil War in Russia. Prominent party figure in the Donbas. From 1921 official in the apparatus of the CC of the AUCP(B). From 1924 editor of the newspaper *Kommunisticheskaia revoliutsiia* (Communist revolution). From 1926 secretary of the Siberian territory committee of the AUCP(B). From 1929 chairman of the RSFSR Council of People's Commissars. After 1931 in various leading administrative and party posts. Candidate member of the Politburo from 1929 to 1930. Fate unclear; never confessed or came to trial, but probably did not survive; posthumously rehabilitated.

**Tevosyan, I. F.** (1902–58). Son of a tailor. Member of the AUCP(B) from 1918. Fought in Civil War in Russia and Azerbaijan. Engineer. Thereafter occupied leading engineering and administrative posts. From 1936 first deputy people's commissar of defense industry. From 1939 to 1940 people's commissar of shipbuilding. From 1940 to 1953 people's commissar (minister) of ferrous metallurgy. From 1949 deputy chairman of the Council of Ministers.

From 1956 Soviet ambassador to Japan. Member of the CC of the AUCP(B) from 1939.

**Thorez, Maurice.** (1900–1964). French. Member of the French Communist Party from 1920, member of its CC from 1924 and of its Politburo from 1925. General secretary of the French Communist Party from 1930 to 1964. Member of the executive committee of the Communist International from 1928 to 1943 and of its presidium from 1935 to 1943.

**Timoshenko, S. K.** (1895–1970). From a peasant background. Soldier. Member of the RCP(B) from 1919. During Civil War commander of a cavalry brigade and a cavalry division. Thereafter occupied various command posts. From 1933 deputy commander of the Belorussian, then of the Kiev, Military District. In 1937 commander of the Northern Caucasus and Kharkov Military Districts. From 1938 commander of the Kiev Special Military District. In 1939 commander of the Ukrainian Front that liberated Western Ukraine and of the Northwestern Front in the campaign against Finland. From 1940 people's commissar of defense. From 1941 to 1945 representative and member of the Stavka and commander in chief of a number of fronts. From 1945 commander of the Baranovichi, South Urals, and Belorussian Military Districts. From 1960 general inspector of the Group of General Inspectors of the General Staff of the Ministry of Defense. From 1961 chairman of the Soviet Committee of War Veterans. From 1939 to 1952 member of the CC of the AUCP(B). Marshal of the Soviet Union from 1940.

**Togliatti, Palmiro.** (1893–1964). Italian. Member of the Communist Party of Italy from its founding in 1921, member of its CC from 1922 and of its leadership from 1923. General secretary of the Communist Party of Italy from 1926 to 1964. Member of the executive committee of the Communist International from 1924, of its presidium from 1928, and of its secretariat from 1935.

**Tolbukhin, F. I.** (1894–1949). In Red Army from 1918. In June 1941 major general. In 1941–42 chief of staff of the Transcaucasus, Caucasus, and Crimean Fronts. From May to July 1942 deputy commander of the Stalingrad Military District. Commander from July 1942 of the 57th Army, from February 1943 of the 68th Army, from March 1943 of the Southern Front, from October 1943 of the Fourth Ukrainian Front, and from May 1944 to June 1945 of the Third Ukrainian Front. Took part in the battle of Stalingrad, and in the Rostov, Donbas, Melitopol, Nikopol-Krivoi Rog, Crimean, Bereznegov-Snigirevsk, Odessa, Budapest, Balaton, and Vienna military operations. From September 1944 representative of the Allied Control Commission in Bulgaria. After the war, occupied command posts in the army. Marshal of the Soviet Union. Hero of the Soviet Union.

**Treivas, B. Ye.** Member of the RCP(B) from 1918. Party official engaged in political work.

**Trofimenko, S. G.** (1899–1953). Joined Red Army in 1919. At start of war major general, promoted in 1944 to colonel general. In the first months of war commanded the Medvezhegorsk operational grouping of the Karelian Front. In March 1942 placed in command of the 32nd Army, then in July 1942 of the Seventh Army, and in January 1943 of the 27th Army. After war, held command posts in the army. Hero of the Soviet Union.

**Trotsky, L. D.** (Bronshtein) (1879–1940). Participant in the social democratic movement from 1897. In 1903 joined the Mensheviks. In 1905 chairman of the Saint Petersburg Soviet. From 1917 to 1927 member of the Communist Party. In 1917 chairman of the Petrograd Soviet and one of the leaders of the October armed uprising, then people's commissar of foreign affairs of the RSFSR. From 1918 to 1925 people's commissar of military and naval affairs and chairman of the Revolutionary Military Council of the Republic. From 1920 people's commissar of communications. Member of the party CC from 1917 to 1927. Member of the Politburo of the CC in October 1917 and from 1919 to 1926. Member of the presidium of the Supreme Council of National Economy from 1925 to 1926. Member of the All-Russian CEC and of the CEC of the USSR. One of the organizers of the opposition. In 1929 exiled abroad. In 1932 deprived of Soviet citizenship. In 1938 created the Fourth International. Assassinated by an NKVD agent in Mexico.

**Trufanov, N. I.** (1900–1982). Joined Red Army in 1919. At start of war, brigade commander. In August 1941 appointed chief of staff (and in December 1941 also deputy commander) of the 47th Army in the Transcaucasus. In April 1942 placed in command of the First Detached Infantry Corps, then in October 1942 of the 51st Army. In June 1943 appointed deputy commander of the 69th Army. From March 1945 commander of the 25th Infantry Corps in the Second Ukrainian and First Belorussian Fronts. After war occupied important army posts.

**Tsikhon, A. M.** (1887–1939). Member of the RSDLP from 1906. Participant in the revolutionary movement. State and party figure. From 1928 to 1930 chairman of the CC of the Builders' Union. From 1930 to 1933 people's commissar of labor. Member of the Central Revision Commission from 1925 to 1927 and of the party CC from 1930 to 1934. Member of the All-Russian CEC and of the CEC of the USSR. Unjustly repressed, fate unclear, probably shot, posthumously rehabilitated.

**Tsvetayev, V. D.** (1893–1950). Joined Red Army in 1918. At start of war, lieutenant general, promoted in 1943 to colonel general. First wartime posts were as commander of the operational grouping of the Seventh Army, deputy commander of the Fourth Army, then commander of the Tenth Reserve Army. In December 1942 placed in command of the Fifth Assault Army. In May 1944 appointed deputy commander of the First Belorussian Front, then in September 1944 commander of the Sixth Army, and in October 1944 commander of the 33rd Army. After war held command posts in the army. Hero of the Soviet Union.

**Tsyganov, V. V.** (1896–1944). Joined Red Army in 1918. In June 1941 major general. During the war, deputy chief of staff for the rear of the Southwestern Area. Commanded the 38th Army from September 1941, then the 56th Army from December 1941. From July 1942 assistant, then deputy, commander of the Moscow Military District. Lieutenant general from 1943.

**Tukhachevsky, M. N.** (1893–1937). From a gentry background. Before 1917 an officer of the tsarist army. From 1918 in Red Army and member of the RCP(B). Until 1921 commanded the First, Eighth, Fifth, and Seventh Armies and troops on the eastern, Caucasus, and western battlefronts. Subsequently head of the Frunze Military Academy, commander of the Western Military District, assistant chief and chief of staff of the Workers' and Peasants' Red Army, commander of the Leningrad Military District, deputy chairman of the Revolutionary Military Council, chief of armaments of the Workers' and Peasants' Red Army, deputy and first deputy people's commissar of defense, and head of the Administration of Combat Training of the Workers' and Peasants' Red Army. Marshal of the Soviet Union from 1935. At time of arrest, commander of the Volga Military District. Shot 1937, posthumously rehabilitated.

**Tupikov, V. I.** (1901–41). Major general. In Red Army from 1922. From 1940 Soviet military attaché in Germany. Served in the army from 1940. Chief of staff of the Southwestern Front from July 1941. Fell on the southwestern battlefront on September 20, 1941, near Poltava (Ukraine).

**Turyanitsa, I. I.** (1901–55). Member of the AUCP(B) from 1925. Participant in the Hungarian revolution of 1919. From 1928 to 1930 secretary of the Mukachevo, then of the Uzhgorod city committee of the party. Studied at the Kharkov Communist Institute of Journalism, then continued to take part in the revolutionary movement of Transcarpathia. From 1944 to 1946 chairman of the People's Council of Transcarpathian Ukraine (by 1945 secretary of the CC of the Communist Party of Transcarpathian Ukraine). Until 1948 first secretary of the Transcarpathian province committee of the CP(B)U and chairman of the province executive committee. From 1949 member of the CC of the Communist Party of Ukraine.

**Tyagnibeda, Ya. F.** (1895–1942). Member of the RCP(B) from 1920. Deputy chairman of the Council of People's Commissars of the Ukrainian SSR from October 1937. Repressed in 1938; fate unclear, probably shot.

**Ugarov, A. I.** (1900–1939). Member of the RCP(B) from 1918. Engaged in Soviet and party work. From 1934 to 1938 second secretary of the Leningrad city committee of the AUCP(B). In 1938 first secretary of the Moscow committee and Moscow city committee of the AUCP(B). Shot 1939, posthumously rehabilitated.

**Uglanov, N. A.** (1886–1937). Member of the RSDLP from 1907. Active participant in the revolutionary movement and Civil War. Secretary of the Petrograd province committee of the party from 1921 to 1922 and of the Nizhny Novgorod province committee of the party from 1922 to 1924. Secretary of the party CC from 1924 to 1929. Secretary of the Moscow city and province committees of the party from 1924 to 1928. People's commissar of labor from 1928 to 1930. Member of the party CC from 1923 to 1930. Candidate member of the Politburo of the CC from 1926 to 1929. Member of the Orgburo of the CC from 1924 to 1929. Member of the All-Russian CEC and of the CEC of the USSR. Arrested and executed, posthumously rehabilitated.

**Ukhanov, K. V.** (1891–1937). Worker. Member of the RSDLP from 1917. Occupied various Soviet administrative posts in Moscow. From 1921 director of the Dinamo Factory. From 1922 manager of an electrical trust. From 1926 chairman of the Moscow city executive committee and from 1929 of the Moscow province executive committee. From 1932 deputy people's commissar of supply of the USSR. From 1934 people's commissar of local industry, then of light industry, of the RSFSR. Member of the party CC from 1923. Member of the presidium of the All-Russian CEC and of the CEC of the USSR. Arrested, apparently shot, posthumously rehabilitated.

**Ulbricht, Walter.** (1893–1973). German. Founding member of the Communist Party of Germany from 1918. Fled to Moscow in 1933. Member of the Politburo of the CC of the Communist Party of Germany from 1935. Candidate member of the executive committee of the Communist International.

During the war one of the leaders of the pro-Soviet National Committee *Freies Deutschland* (Free Germany). Leader of German Democratic Republic and general secretary of Socialist Unity Party of Germany from 1950 to 1971.

**Uspensky, A. I.** People's commissar of internal affairs of the Ukrainian SSR from 1938 to 1939.

**Vareikis, I. M.** (1894–1939). Worker. Member of the RSDLP from 1913. After 1917 occupied leading Soviet and party posts. From 1923 secretary of the Kiev province committee of the CP(B)U and of the Central Asian Bureau of the CC of the AUCP(B). Head of the Press Department of the party CC. First secretary of the Saratov, Central Black Earth, and Voronezh province committees, and of the Stalingrad and Far Eastern territory committees, of the AUCP(B). From 1930 member of the CC of the AUCP(B). Member of the All-Russian CEC and of the CEC of the USSR. Arrested and executed, posthumously rehabilitated.

**Vasilevsky, A. M.** (1895–1977). Son of a priest. Member of the AUCP(B) from 1931. Attended theological seminary. Tsarist officer during First World War. Joined Red Army in 1919 and fought in Civil War. During 1920s occupied various command posts. Officer of the General Staff from 1931. Graduated from Academy of the General Staff in 1938. Deputy head (from May 1940), then head (from August 1941) of the Operational Administration of the General Staff. Deputy chief, then chief of the General Staff from June 1942. Representative of the Stavka on the front lines. From February 1945 commander of the Third Belorussian Front, which conquered East Prussia. Commander in chief of the forces in the Far East that routed Japanese forces in Manchuria and Korea in August 1945. Again chief of the General Staff from 1946, simultaneously first deputy minister of defense, then from 1949 minister of defense. First deputy minister of defense from 1953. From 1957 in retirement. Marshal of the Soviet Union. Twice Hero of the Soviet Union.

**Vatutin, N. F.** (1901–44). Joined Red Army in 1920. Chief of staff of the Kiev Special Military District from November 1938 to September 1939. Before war, headed the Operational Administration of the General Staff. At start of war, lieutenant general and chief of staff of the Northwestern Front. From May 1942 deputy chief of the General Staff and simultaneously representative of the Stavka in the Bryansk Front. From July 1942 commanded in turn the Voronezh, the Southwestern, again the Voronezh, and finally (from October 1943) the First Ukrainian Front. Promoted to army general in 1943. Took part in planning the Stalingrad offensive, in the battles of Stalingrad and Kursk, and in the liberation of eastern and central Ukraine. Badly wounded on February 29, 1944, died on April 15. Posthumously made Hero of the Soviet Union.

**Veklichev, G. I.** (1898–1938). Worker. Member of the RCP(B) from 1918. Prominent politicomilitary official. Army commissar of the second rank. From 1934 member of the Military Council attached to the people's commissar of defense. Fate unclear, probably shot, posthumously rehabilitated. (Of eighty-five members of the Military Council, seventy-six were arrested and imprisoned, including sixty-eight executed.)

**Vinnichenko, V. K.** (1880–1951). Ukrainian. Writer. Ideologist of the Ukrainian national movement. From 1918 to 1919 chairman of the Ukrainian Directorate (the government that succeeded the Ukrainian People's Republic). In 1920 deputy chairman of the Council of People's Commissars of the Ukrainian SSR. Subsequently an émigré.

**Vlasik, N. S.** (1896–1967). Lieutenant general. Until 1952 headed the department for guarding the government in the Main Administration of State Security of the NKVD. Responsible for Stalin's personal guard.

**Vlasov, A. A.** (1901–46). Lieutenant general. In 1942 commander of the Second Assault Army of the Volkhov Front. After the Lyubansk operation to relieve the blockade of Leningrad was unable to extract the Second Assault Army from fascist encirclement and voluntarily surrendered to the enemy. Thereafter organized the Russian Liberation Army to take part in battle against the Red Army, though received official permission to fight from Berlin only in 1944. Sentenced to death in the Soviet Union as a traitor in 1946.

**Volsky, V. T.** (1897–1946). Joined Red Army in 1919. During war, major general, then colonel general of tank troops. Assistant for armored forces to the commander of the 21st Army, then to the commander of the Southwestern Front. In 1942 deputy inspector general of the Main Administration for Armored Forces and deputy commander for tank troops of Crimean and Northern Caucasus Fronts. From October 1942 to June 1943 commanded the Fourth Armored Corps (later renamed the Third Guards Armored Corps) in the battle of Stalingrad, then appointed deputy commander of Red Army armored and mechanized forces. Between August 1944 and March 1945 also in command of the Fifth Guards Tank Army.

**von Brauchitsch, V.** (1881–1948). German. General Field Marshal. Commander in chief of Germany's land forces from 1938. Retired in December 1941.

**von Ribbentrop, Joachim.** (1893–1946). German. Minister of foreign affairs of Germany from 1938 to 1945. Sentenced to death by the International Military Tribunal in Nuremberg.

**von Schulenburg, Count F. V.** (1875–1944). German. Ambassador to the USSR from 1934 to 1941. Executed by the Nazis for participating in the plot against Hitler.

**Vorobyov, V. N.** Member of the RSDLP from 1917. Participant in and organizer of the Young Communist movement and the general youth movement.

**Voronov, N. N.** (1899–1968). In Red Army from 1918. In June 1941 colonel general of artillery. From start of war, head of Main Administration of Anti-Air Defense. From July 1941 chief of artillery of the Red Army and deputy people's commissar of defense. From March 1943 commander of artillery of the Red Army. Several times representative of the Stavka to various Fronts. Took part in planning and conduct of large-scale operations. Provided general leadership in destruction of the encircled enemy forces at Stalingrad. Contributed to working out problems of the artillery offensive and antitank combat. Promoted the creation of large artillery formations and development of the artillery reserve of the supreme commander in chief. After war occupied leading posts in the army. Chief marshal of artillery.

**Voroshilov, K. Ye.** (1881–1969). Worker. Member of the RSDLP from 1903. Participated in the revolutions of 1905, February 1917, and October 1917 and in the Civil War. From 1921 commanded the Northern Caucasus, then the Moscow, Military Districts. From 1925 people's commissar of military and naval affairs (from 1934 people's commissar of defense). From 1940 deputy chairman of the Council of People's Commissars. During Second World War occupied a number of leading posts. From 1946 deputy chairman of the Council of Ministers. From 1953 chairman of the presidium of the Supreme Soviet. From 1935 Marshal of the Soviet Union. From 1926 to 1960 member of the Politburo (Presidium) of the CC of the CPSU. From 1960 member of the presidium of the Supreme Soviet.

**Vyshinsky, A. Ya.** (1883–1954). From a gentry background. Member of the RSDLP (Mensheviks) from 1903. Member of the RCP(B) from 1920. Jurist. After 1917 engaged in social, administrative, lecturing, and judicial work. From 1925 to 1928 rector of the First Moscow University, then member of the collegium of the People's Commissariat of Enlightenment of the RSFSR. From 1931 an official of the judiciary. From 1935 public prosecutor. Chief prosecutor in the Moscow trials of 1936–38. From 1939 to 1944 deputy chairman of the Council of People's Commissars. From 1940 to 1949 deputy minister, and from 1949 to 1953 minister, of foreign affairs, thereafter permanent representative of the USSR at the United Nations. Member of the CC of the AUCP(B) from 1939. Author of works on judicial subjects.

**Wasilewska, Wanda.** (1905–64). Polish. Writer. During war a regimental commissar, then colonel. Worked as an agitator for the Main Political Administration of the Workers' and Peasants' Red Army. Editor of the newspaper *Za Radiansku Ukrainu* (For Soviet Ukraine). From 1943 to 1945 editor in chief of the newspaper *Wolna Polska* (Free Poland). Chair of the Union of Polish Patriots in the USSR.

**Wasilewski, L.** Polish. Minister of foreign affairs of Poland from 1918 to 1919.

**Witos, Wincenty.** Polish. Prime minister of Poland in 1920–21 and again in 1923 and 1926.

**Yagoda, G. G.** (1891–1938). Member of the RSDLP from 1907. After 1917 worked as a military inspector and in the collegium of the People's Commissariat of Foreign Trade. From 1920 in the All-Russian Cheka. From 1924 deputy chairman of the OGPU. From 1934 to 1936 people's commissar of internal affairs. From 1934 to 1937 people's commissar of communications. From 1935 general commissar of state security of the first rank. Member of the CC of the AUCP(B) from 1934. Executed after an open trial.

**Yakir, I. E.** (1896–1937). Worker. Member of the RSDLP from 1917. Participated in the revolutions of February and October 1917. During Civil War occupied politicomilitary posts and commanded troop groupings and divisions. From 1921 commander of the Crimean and Kiev Military Sub-Districts, then of the Kiev Military District. Head of the Main Administration of Military Training Institutions of the Workers' and Peasants' Red Army. Commander until 1937 of the Ukrainian and Kiev Military Districts and in 1937 of the Leningrad Military District. Student at the Supreme Military Academy of the German General Staff (in 1927–28). From 1930 member of the Revolutionary Military Council, then member of the Military Council of the People's Commissariat of Defense. From 1934 member of the CC of the AUCP(B). Member of the CEC of the USSR. Army commander of the first rank from 1935. Shot 1937, posthumously rehabilitated.

**Yakovlev, N. D.** (1898–1972). Chief of artillery of the Kiev Special Military District. From June 1941 lieutenant general. From 1944 marshal of artillery.

**Yakovlev, Ya. A.** (1896–1938). Son of a teacher. Member of the RSDLP from 1913. Fought in Civil War in Ukraine. From 1921 a leading party official in Moscow. From 1926 deputy people's commissar of workers' and peasants' inspection. From 1929 to 1934 people's commissar of agriculture and chairman of the All-Russian Union of Agricultural Collectives. Subsequently worked in the apparatus of the CC of the AUCP(B). Member of the party CC from 1930. Imprisoned and executed, posthumously rehabilitated.

**Yaroslavsky, Ye. M.** (1878–1943). Son of an exiled settler. Member of the RSDLP from 1898. Participated in the revolutions of 1905, February 1917, and October 1917. A leader of the armed uprising of October 1917 in Moscow, then in leading party posts. Was on the editorial boards and was editor in chief of many sociopolitical publications. From 1931 headed the All-Union Society of Old Bolsheviks. From 1939 lecturer, publicist, and full member of the USSR Academy of Sciences. Author of works on the history of the Communist Party and other subjects. At various times member and secretary of the party CC, member of the Central Control Commission of the party, and member of the CEC of the USSR.

**Yegorov, A. I.** (1883–1939). From a lower-middle-class background. Tsarist officer. Joined the Left Socialist Revolutionary Party in 1917 and the RCP(B) in 1918. Served in Red Army. In Civil War commanded the Ninth and Tenth Armies and the southern and southwestern battlefronts. From 1921 commander of the Kiev and Petrograd Military Districts, of the Army of the Caucasus, and of troops in Ukraine and the Crimea. From 1925 to 1926 military attaché in China. From 1928 commander of the Belorussian Military District. From 1931 chief of staff of the Workers' and Peasants' Red Army. From 1937 first deputy people's commissar of defense. Marshal of the Soviet Union from 1935. Arrested and executed, posthumously rehabilitated.

**Yenukidze, A. S.** (1877–1937). From a peasant background. Member of the RSDLP from 1898. Active participant in the workers' movement and in the revolution of October 1917, then in leading posts in the All-Russian CEC. From 1922 to 1935 secretary of the presidium of the CEC of the USSR. From 1924 to 1930 member of the Central Control Commission. From 1934 member of the CC of the AUCP(B). Executed, posthumously rehabilitated.

**Yepishev, A. A.** (1908–85). Worker. During 1920s worked in the Young Communist movement. Member of the AUCP(B) from 1929. From 1930 in the armed forces. Specialist in the mechanization and motorization of the army. From 1938, remaining a military man, simultaneously party organizer of the CC of the AUCP(B) at the Comintern Kharkov Factory and secretary of the Comintern district committee of the party. From 1940 first secretary of the Kharkov province and city committees of the CP(B)U. From 1941 commissar of the Kharkov People's Militia Corps, leading organizer of the CC of the AUCP(B), plenipotentiary to the Stalingrad Front, deputy minister of medium machine building, and member of the Military Council of the 40th and 38th Armies. From 1946 secretary of the CC of the CP(B)U. From 1950 to 1955 first secretary of the Odessa province committee of the party (and from 1951 to 1953 deputy minister of state security). Soviet ambassador to Romania from 1955 and to Yugoslavia from 1961. From 1962 head of the Main Political Administration of the Soviet Army and Naval Fleet of the USSR. Member of the CC of the CPSU from 1964.

**Yeremenko, A. I.** (1892–1970). In Red Army from 1918. In June 1941 lieutenant general. Commanded the Western Front from July 1941, the Bryansk Front from August to October 1941, the Fourth Assault Army from December 1941, the Southeastern (from September 28 the Stalingrad) Front from August to December 1942, the Southern Front in January and February 1943, the Kalinin Front from April to October 1943, the First Baltic Front in October and November 1943, the Detached Maritime Army from February to April 1944, the Second Baltic Front from April 1944, and the Fourth Ukrainian Front from March 1945. Took part in the battles of Moscow and of Stalingrad, and in the Toropetsk-Kholmsk, Rostov, Smolensk, Crimean, Riga, Moravska-Ostrava, Prague, and other military operations. After war in command posts. Marshal of the Soviet Union. Hero of the Soviet Union.

**Yezhov, N. I.** (1895–1940). Worker. Member of the RSDLP from 1917. During Civil War a military commissar. From 1922 secretary of the Semipalatinsk (now renamed Semei) province committee and of the Kazakh territory committee of the party. From 1927 an official in the apparatus of the CC of the AUCP(B). From 1929 to 1930 deputy people's commissar of agriculture. From 1930 to 1934 head of the Personnel and of the Personnel Assignment Departments, and from 1934 of the Industrial Department, of the CC of the AUCP(B). From 1934 member of the CC of the AUCP(B). From 1935 member of the executive committee of the Communist International. From 1936 secretary of the CC of the AUCP(B), chairman of the Party Control Commission attached to the party CC, and deputy chairman of the Reserves Committee of the Council of Labor and Defense. From 1936 to 1938 people's commissar of internal affairs. From 1937 general commissar of state security of the first rank. From 1938 people's commissar of water transportation. Arrested in 1939 and executed for criminal activity.

**Zadionchenko, S. B.** (1898 or 1900–1972). Born in Rzhivshchev, Kiev gubernia. Originally named Tsadik Barukhovich Zaionchik, also known as Zadionchik. Graduated from Kremenchuk Handicrafts College in 1914, then worked in a tobacco factory. In 1916 and 1917 in tsarist army. From 1918 to 1925 in Red Army, where on promotion from private his Jewish or Polish-sounding name was changed to the more Ukrainian Semyon Borisovich Zadionchenko. Member of the RCP(B) from 1919. From 1925 to 1929 in a middle-level position in the Horse Farming Department of the agricultural cooperatives in Moscow province. From 1929 to 1936 occupied Soviet and party positions in Krasnodar territory, Kazakhstan, and Moscow, then in 1936 and 1937 secretary of the Bauman district party committee in Moscow (at the time Khrushchev was also in Moscow). In 1937 and 1938 deputy prime minister of the RSFSR. From 1938 to 1941 acting first secretary of the Dnepropetrovsk province party committee. (At this time he was accused of concealing his original name.) On outbreak of war in July 1941 member of the Military Council of the Southern Front and simultaneously first secretary of the Stalino province party committee. From November 1941 to January 1942 worked on agricultural matters in the party CC, became member of the party CC. From January 1942 to February 1943 first secretary of the Bashkir province party committee, then first secretary of the Kemerovo province party committee until May 1946. From 1946 to 1948 inspector of the party CC, then briefly deputy head of the Heavy Industry Department of the party CC. From 1948 to 1951 first deputy minister of agricultural procurements, then again inspector of the party CC. From 1952 sector head in the Personnel Department of the party CC. Retired in 1958.

**Zakharov, G. F.** (1897–1957). In Red Army from 1919. In June 1941 major general. From August 1941 chief of staff, and from October 1941 commander, of the Bryansk Front. From December 1941 deputy commander of the Western Front. Chief of staff of the Northern Caucasus Area, then from May 1942 of the Northern Caucasus Front, and from August 1942 of the Southeastern Front (on September 28 renamed the Stalingrad Front). From October 1942 deputy commander of the Stalingrad and Southern Fronts. From February 1943 commanded the 51st Army and from July 1943 the Second Guards Army, which broke through strong enemy defenses and distinguished itself in April 1944 in the liberation of Sevastopol. From June to November 1944 commanded the Second Belorussian Front and then the Fourth Guards Army, which took part in the encirclement of the Budapest grouping of the enemy. From April 1945 deputy commander of the Fourth Ukrainian Front. After war occupied command posts in the army.

**Zakharov, M. V.** (1898–1972). In Red Army from 1918. In June 1941 major general. During war, chief of staff of the Ninth Army, from July 1941 chief of staff of the Supreme Command of the Northwestern Area. From August 1941 deputy head of the Red Army's Main Administration of the Rear. Chief of staff from January 1942 of the Kalinin Front, from April 1943 of the Reserve and Steppe Fronts, from October 1943 of the Second Ukrainian

Front, and from July to September 1945 of the Transbaikal Front. Took part in the battle for Moscow and in the planning, preparation, and conduct of the Belgorod-Kharkov, Korsun-Shevchenkovsk, Uman-Botoshansk, Yassk-Kishinev, Budapest, Vienna, Prague, and Khingan-Mukden offensive operations. After war in command posts in the army, chief of the General Staff, first deputy minister of defense. Twice Hero of the Soviet Union. Marshal of the Soviet Union.

**Zasyadko, A. F.** (1910–63). Worker. Member of the AUCP(B) from 1931. From 1943 to 1947 deputy people's commissar of coal industry, then deputy people's commissar of the construction of fuel enterprises, minister of coal industry of the western regions of the USSR, and deputy chairman of the State Planning Commission. From 1956 deputy chairman of the Council of Ministers. From 1960 chairman of the State Scholarly Economic Council of the Council of Ministers. Member of the CC of the CPSU from 1952 to 1956 and from 1961.

**Zavenyagin, A. P.** (1901–56). Member of the RCP(B) from 1917. Director of the Magnitogorsk Metallurgical Combine. From 1933 first deputy people's commissar for heavy industry. From 1938 head of construction and director of the Norilsk Mining and Smelting Combine. From 1941 to 1950 deputy people's commissar (minister) of internal affairs. From 1953 deputy minister, and from 1955 minister, of medium machine building, and concurrently deputy chairman of the Council of Ministers.

**Zawadzki, A.** (1889–1964). Polish. Member of the Communist Party of Poland from 1923. From 1944 to 1945 deputy commander in chief of the Polish Army. From 1944 member of the Politburo of the CC of the Polish Workers' Party. From 1948 secretary of the CC of the Polish United Workers' Party. From 1949 to 1952 deputy chairman of the Council of Ministers of Poland. From 1952 chairman of the State Council of the Polish People's Republic.

**Zdobnov, A. Z.** Member of the RCP(B) from 1918. Thereafter occupied various party posts.

**Zemlyachka, Roza S.** (1876–1947). From a lower-middle-class background. Participant in the revolutionary movement from 1896. Member of the RSDLP from 1898. An active figure in the Bolshevik Party. An organizer of the armed uprising of October 1917 in Moscow, then engaged in politicomilitary work. In 1920 secretary of the Crimean province committee of the RCP(B). In 1924 member of the Southeastern Bureau of the CC of the RCP(B). From 1926 to 1933 member of the collegia of the People's Commissariat of Workers' and Peasants' Inspection and of the People's Commissariat of Communications.

From 1934 member, deputy chair, and chair of the Soviet Control Commission. From 1939 to 1943 deputy chair of the Council of People's Commissars, then deputy chair of the Party Control Commission attached to the CC of the AUCP(B). Member of the party CC from 1939.

**Zhadov, A. S.** (1901–77). Major general. Joined Red Army in 1919. At start of the war commanded the Fourth Paratroop Corps in the Western Front and was then chief of staff of the Third Army in the Central and Bryansk Fronts. In October 1942, after a brief period in command of the Eighth Cavalry Corps in the Bryansk Front, was appointed commander of the 66th Army (later renamed the Fifth Guards Army), and remained in that post until end of war. After war occupied positions of command in the army. Hero of the Soviet Union.

**Zhdanov, A. A.** (1896–1948). Son of a white-collar worker. Member of the RSDLP from 1915. After 1917 a political official. From 1922 chairman of the Tver province executive committee. From 1924 secretary of the Nizhny Novgorod province committee and of the Gorky territory committee of the AUCP(B). From 1934 to 1944 secretary of the Leningrad province and city committees of the party. From 1944 colonel general and secretary of the CC of the AUCP(B). Member of the party CC from 1930. Member of the Politburo of the CC of the AUCP(B) from 1939. Member of the All-Russian CEC and of the CEC of the USSR.

**Zhemchuzhina, P. S.** (Karpovich) (1897–1970). From 1936 to 1937 head of the Main Administration of Perfume, Cosmetics, Soap, and Synthetic Materials Industry of the People's Commissariat of Food Industry, then deputy people's commissar of food industry and people's commissar of fisheries. From 1939 head of the Main Administration of Textiles Industry. In 1949 sentenced to exile. In 1953 rehabilitated.

**Zhmachenko, F. F.** (1895–1966). Joined Red Army in 1918. At start of war a brigade commander. Later appointed commander of the 67th Infantry Corps, then deputy commander of the 61st Army, and finally commander in turn of the Third, 47th, and 40th Armies. At end of war colonel general. After war occupied positions of command in the army. Hero of the Soviet Union.

**Zhukov, G. K.** (1896–1974). Son of a shoemaker. Apprenticed to a furrier. Member of the RCP(B) from 1919. In tsarist army during First World War. Joined Red Army in 1918. From 1920 occupied various command posts in cavalry units. From 1938 deputy commander of the Belorussian Military District. Commander of the forces in the Far East that routed Japanese forces at Khalkin-Gol in Mongolia in August 1939. From June 1940 commander of the Kiev Special Military District. From January to July 1941 chief of the General Staff, then commander of the Reserve Front in the battle for Smolensk. Organized the defense of Leningrad (September 1941) and of Moscow (October 1941 to January 1942), then commander of the Western Front. From August 1942 first deputy supreme commander in chief. From March to May 1944 commander of the First Ukrainian Front. From November 1944 to June 1945 commander of the First Belorussian Front in the final offensive against Germany. From 1945 commander in chief of the Soviet occupation forces in Germany. From 1946 commander in chief of ground forces. From 1947 commander of the Odessa, then of the Urals Military District. First deputy minister of defense from 1953, then minister of defense from 1955. Candidate member (from February 1956), member (from June 1957), of the Presidium of the CC of the CPSU. Removed from all posts and retired in October 1957. Marshal of the Soviet Union. Four times Hero of the Soviet Union.

**Zhuravlev, Ye. P.** (1896–1983). Joined Red Army in 1918. At start of war major general, later promoted to lieutenant general. During 1941 appointed to the positions of deputy commander and then commander of the Fifth Motorized Corps, deputy commander of the 30th Army, and after that assistant and chief of staff to the commander of the Kaliningrad Front. From September 1942 was placed in command successively of the 29th, 53rd, 68th, 21st, and Eighteenth Armies. After war held important army positions.

**Zinoviev, G. Ye.** (Radomyslsky) (1883–1936). Member of the RSDLP from 1901. Active participant in the revolutionary movement. From December 1917 chairman of the Petrograd Soviet. From 1919 to 1926 chairman of the executive committee of the Communist International. Member of the party CC from 1907 to 1927. Member of the Politburo of the CC from 1921 to 1926. Member of the All-Russian CEC and of the CEC of the USSR. Unjustly arrested and executed after the first big Moscow trial (1936). Posthumously rehabilitated under Gorbachev.

**Zverev, A. G.** (1900–1969). From a peasant background. Member of the RCP(B) from 1919. Engaged in military, administrative, and financial work. From 1938 to 1960 people's commissar and then minister (in 1948 deputy minister) of finance. Member of the party CC from 1939 to 1961. Candidate member of the Presidium of the CC of the CPSU from 1952 to 1953.

**Zygin, A. I.** (1896–1943). Joined Red Army in 1918. At start of war major general and commander of the 174th Infantry Division of the 22nd Army in the Western Front. In summer 1942 appointed commander of the 58th, and then of the 39th, Army. In September 1943 placed in command of the Fourth Guards Army with the rank of lieutenant general. Perished later in the same month in the battle for the Dnieper.

# Index

Krylov, N. L., 413–14, 441 n. 18
Krymsk, 356 n. 4
Kryuchenkin, V. D., 505
Kryuchkov, Kuzma (cartoon character in World War I), 680–81
Kryuchkov, V. A., 793
Kuban region, 659, 677 n. 35. *See also* Krasnodar
Kucherenko, N. A., 269, 282, 294 n. 15, 295 n. 25
Kucherenko, V. A., 282, 295 n. 25
Kuibyshev, evacuations to, battle of Stalingrad, 409, 440 n. 8
Kuibyshev, V. V., 32–33, 94, 131, 182, 183, 207 n. 20
kulaks: collectivization and elimination, 62, 83 n. 1; impact of NEP, 14, 20 n. 1
Kuleshov, A. D., 317, 319–20
Kulik, G. I., 177, 208–9, 226 n. 5; defense of Rostov, 399, 404 n. 55; Dnieper River offensive, 552–53; execution, 320–21, 410–11, 441 n. 11, 671; Gordov's execution, 410; Soviet-Finnish conflict, 249–50, 261 n. 39; wartime inadequacies, 284–86, 295 n. 30, 330, 671–72
Kulkov, M. M., 105, 108, 183, 191
Kuomintang, 404 n. 59
Kupyansk, Soviet defense, 352, 358 n. 59
Kurdyumov, V. N., 261 n. 43
Kurile Islands, territorial dispute, 683, 688, 690–92, 696 n. 16, 697 nn. 29–30, 33
Kurochkin, P. A. (Col. General), Soviet advance on Germany, 631, 633, 636 n. 41
Kursk: battle of (Kursk salient), 378, 504–5, 510–19, 537–38, 668; Bukharin's activities, 17; German advances, 341, 357 n. 34, 395; recapture of Dnieper River, 534–58
Kutais, Khrushchev's recollection, 172, 206 n. 2
Kutuzov, Mikhail (general, 1745–1813), 99
Kuusinen, O. V., 249, 254

labor problems, during Moscow reconstruction, 77–78
Lake Baikal, Japanese threats to, in World War II, 219–20, 227 nn. 18–19
Lake Khasan military operations, 210–11, 218–19, 226 n. 8, 369
Lake Ladoga, 250–51, 261 n. 39
Lake Tsatsa, seige of Stalingrad, 433, 442 n. 45
Lakoba, N. A., 188–89
Laptev, K. A., 543, 558 n. 8
Larin, I. I. (General), 460–62, 471, 473
"Last Romantic, The," 83 n. 24
Latsis, V. T., 248
Latvia: Khrushchev's memories, 57–58; Soviet incorporation, 233, 247–48, 261 n. 33
Left Socialist Revolutionary Party, xv
"Left-Wing Opposition" group, 42 n. 4

Lena goldfield massacre, Khrushchev's involvement, 707
Lenin, Vladimir Ilyich: Communist traditions, 82; distrust of Stalin, 91–92, 94–95, 97–98, 156, 655, 658, 662; fondness for hunting, 224–25; foreign publication of writings, 738; Khrushchev's assessment, 84, 294; Krupskaya's memoirs, 93–94; New Economic Policy, 14; show trials of supporters, 156–58; as Sovnarkom chairman, xv; "Testament," 634, 637 n. 49; and Tukhachevsky, 656–57
Leningrad: siege of, 675 n. 4; wartime disruption of industry, 640, 675 n. 4
*Leningrad* magazine, 104, 137 n. 11
Lenin Institute, 64–65
Lensky. *See* Leszczinski
Leonidovna, Yuliya. *See* Petrov, Yuliya Khrushchev
Leonov, D. S., 334, 357 n. 34
Leselidze, K. N., 606, 613 n. 47
Leszczinski, J., 245, 261 n. 30
*Let History Judge,* 804
Levochkin, A. (party secretary), 34, 37
Library of Congress, Russian transliteration system, viii–x
Likhachev, Ivan Alekseyevich, 81–82
Likhachev auto plant, wartime production at, 218
Lipitsky, Vasily, 821–22
Lisichkin, Volodya, 764–65
Lithuania, Soviet incorporation, 233, 247–48, 261 n. 33
Little, Brown and Co., publication of Khrushchev's memoirs, 743, 787–88, 797–98, 810
Litvinenko-Volgemut, M. I., 141, 171 n. 11
Litvinov, M. M., 50, 59 n. 24
Liu Shaoqi, 101 n. 19
Livny: German occupation, 359–60, 402 n. 2; Soviet liberation, 362
Livshits, Ya. A., 152–53
Lodz, Soviet reconstruction plans, 624–25
Lominadze, V. V., 23, 33–34, 43 n. 7, 132–33, 156
*London Evening Standard,* 735
Lopan River, Soviet defense, 350–51, 358 n. 56
Lopatin, A. I., 399–400, 404 nn. 57, 66
Louis, Victor (Vitaly Yevgenyevich), 735–44, 754–55, 775, 777–78, 794
Lublin, Soviet liberation, 616–18, 635 n. 9
Luchkov, Vyacheslav, xxv
Lugansk, 25–26, 28 n. 5
Lukashov, P. V., 178–80
*Lutzoff* (German war cruiser), 258, 261 n. 46
Lvov region, 29, 30 n. 5; Khrushchev's recollections, 238–40, 246–47; liberation of Ukraine and reorganization, 603–7, 613 n. 39; nationalism, 233–34; Red Army protection, 228–29, 418;

collectivization of agriculture, 62–63; defense against German invasion, 304–23, 339–56, 363–64; liberation of Rostov (1943), 468–69, 492 n. 1; equipment shortages and weaknesses, 663–75; Finnish-Soviet conflict, 249–53, 261 n. 43; in Georgia, 173, 206 n. 3; German capture of divisions, 331; Khrushchev's recollections, 324–25; Kiev abandoned, 349–56, 358 n. 54; Kursk salient, 516–20; liberation of Kiev, 578–79; liberation of Ukraine, 605–12; losses in defense of Ukraine, 382–83, 403 n. 30; Manchurian offensive, 678–79, 696 n. 3; offensive against White Army, 324–25; preparations for World War II, 216–26, 297, 653–62; protection of Ukrainian front, 228–29, 260 n. 4, 366–67; purge in 1930s, 99–100, 108–36, 278–79, 285, 653–75; battle of Stalingrad, 408–68; summer-fall 1941, 327–56; Tukhachevsky and build-up, 93; in Ukraine, 138 n. 39; weakness during Finnish-Soviet war, 266, 276–87; weakness during World War II, 638–39, 654–75; weapons buildup, 74–75; "wreckers," 207. *See also* White Army

Red Army Song and Dance Ensemble, 103, 137 n. 8

Redens, Stanislav, 46, 50, 58 n. 12; arrest of, 180–81; as NKVD head, 78

Red October plant (Stalingrad), 394, 404 n. 40

Reichl, Joachim, 403 n. 34

rhomboids (military insignia), 62, 83 n. 12, 135, 138 n. 64

Ribbentrop, Joachim von, 223–25, 227 n. 30, 229–33; and Stalin-Hitler pact, 270—71

Right-Left Bloc, 23, 33–34, 43 n. 7

Right opposition (in Soviet Communist Party): at Industrial Academy, 32–39, 42 n. 4, 60, 210, 219; opposition to collectivization, 61–62; purge, 129–30; Stalin's criticism, 75–76, 156–58

"Rights." *See* Right opposition

Rimsky, Lev Abramovich, 17–19

Rodimtsev, A. I., 419, 441 n. 27

Rogachev, D. D., 424, 441 n. 37

Rokossovsky, K. K.: battle of Kursk, 511, 517–18, 532; battle of Stalingrad, 422, 441 n. 35, 454–55, 467, 470; Belorussian Front command, 614–16, 635 n. 1; Dnieper River offensive, 534–35, 545, 552; German advances on Soviet Union, 323 n. 25; liberation of Kiev, 567; Soviet expeditionary force in Germany, 652–53

Rola-Zymierski, Michal (Polish general), 617–18, 625, 635 n. 16

Romania: in battle of Stalingrad, 433, 443–50, 467 n. 2, 538; and Bessarabia, 261–64; German strategic aims, 264–65; Odessa taken, 596–97; Soviet border with, 221; Soviet Union rela-

tions, 143–44, 171 n. 20; Transcarpathian ethnic groups, 611

Rome-Berlin-Tokyo Axis, formation, 220

Roosevelt, Franklin Delano: American planes in Polish airfields, 620; death, 679, 696 n. 6; Stalin's relations with, 637, 650–52, 679–80; Teheran Conference, 650–51, 676 nn. 19–20; Yalta Conference, 593

Roosevelt, Theodore, 696 n. 1

Rosenberg, Julius and Ethel, 743, 825 n. 25

Rosengolts, A. P., 56, 83

Rosenthal, Felix, 803, 809

Rostov: German advances (1942), 398–99, 404 n. 56, 537; German prisoners, 361; Khrushchev's role (1941), 353–56; Soviet liberation (1943), 465–66, 468–92, 537; strategic importance, 337, 353, 355–56, 359, 384

Rotert, Pavel Pavlovich, 65, 68–72, 83 n. 17

Rotmistrov, P. A., 458, 468 n. 9, 474–76, 492 n. 8, 525, 531, 534 n. 54; battle of Kursk, 458, 468 n. 9, 474–76, 492 n. 8, 525, 531, 534 n. 54; liberation of Stalingrad, 458, 468 n. 9; recapture of Dnieper River, 536–37

Rovno: German advances, 308, 323 n. 24; Soviet liberation of Poland, 620–21, 635 n. 24, 636 n. 27

Rozov (party official [1931]), 49

Ruben, R. G., 135, 138 n. 63

Rudenko, R. A., 119–20, 155, 171 n. 41, 181–82, 207 n. 18

Rudzutak, Ya. E., 94, 113

Ruhr region (Germany), 282, 295 n. 23

Rukhimovich, M. L., 27, 28 n. 8

"Rushnichok" (song), xxxiii

Russian Bureau proposal, 103, 137 n. 6

Russian Center for the Preservation and Study of Documentation, 822, 826 n. 55

*Russian Fascism: Traditions, Tendencies, and Movements,* xxviii

Russian Federation, German occupation of, 358–59, 639

Russian Liberation Army, 582 n. 5

Russian names, spelling style, viii–x

Russian Social Democratic Labor Party (RSDLP): history, xvi–xvii; congresses and conferences, xix–xxii; in Fourth Duma, 8, 10 n. 13

Russian Socialist Federated Soviet Republic (RSFSR): political structure, 103, 136 n. 4; territorial-administrative structure, xi

Russo-Japanese War (1904–5), 227 n. 24; tsarist Russian holdings lost, 678, 683, 696 nn. 1, 16

Rutchenkovo mines, 26, 665

Ruthenia and Ruthenian (Rusyn) ethnic group, 608–10, 613 n. 54

Ryabyshev, D. I., 307–11, 323 n. 20, 332, 341, 357 n. 21, 513–14